A

abandon, v. **1.** leave, forsake, desert, relinquish, evacuate, drop, discard, cast off, quit, vacate. **2.** resign, retire, quit, abjure, forswear, withdraw, forgo. **3.** abdicate, waive, give up, yield, surrender, resign, cede, renounce, repudiate. —**Ant.** keep, maintain; pursue.

abandoned, adj. **1.** forsaken, left, deserted, relinquished, dropped, discarded, cast off, cast aside, cast out, rejected, demitted, sent down. **2.** unrestrained. **3.** wicked, depraved, unprincipled, sinful, corrupt, licentious, amoral, profligate, vicious, dissolute, shameless; shameful, immoral, incorrigible, impenitent, graceless, irreclaimable, reprobate, demoralized, vice-ridden. —**Ant.** virtuous, honest, good, righteous.

abase, v. lower, reduce, humble, degrade, downgrade, demote; disgrace, dishonor, debase, take down, humiliate. —**Ant.** elevate, exalt, honor.

abash, v. shame, embarrass, mortify, disconcert, discompose, confound, confuse; cow, humble, humiliate, discountenance, affront.

abate, v. **1.** lessen, diminish, reduce, discount, decrease, lower, slow. **2.** deduct, subtract, remit, rebate, allow, discount. **3.** omit, eliminate, disallow. **4.** (law) suppress; suspend, extinguish; annul; remove, disallow, nullify, repress. **5.** diminish, lessen, decrease, lower, slow, subside, decline, sink, wane, ebb, slack off, slacken, fade, fade out, fade away. —**Ant.** increase, intensify.

abatement, n. **1.** alleviation, mitigation, lessening, let-up, diminution, decrease, slackening. **2.** suppression, termination, ending, end, cessation. **3.** subsidence, decline, sinking, way, ebb, slack, fade-out, fading. —**Ant.** intensification, increase.

abbreviate, v. shorten, abridge, reduce, curtail, cut, contract, compress; crop, dock, pare down, prune, truncate; condense, digest, epitomize, abstract. —**Ant.** lengthen, expand. —**Syn. Study.** See SHORTEN.

abbreviation, n. shortening, abridgment, compendium, reduction, curtailment, cut, contraction, compression; truncation; condensation, digest, epitome, brief, essence, heart, core, soul. —**Ant.** lengthening, expansion.

ABC's, n. **1.** alphabet, letters of alphabet. **2.** essentials, rudiments, basics, fundamentals, principles, grammar, elements.

abdicate, v. renounce, disclaim, disavow, disown, repudiate; resign, retire, quit, relinquish, abandon, surrender, cede, give up, waive. —**Ant.** commit.

abdication, n. renunciation, disclaimer, disavowal, repudiation, resignation, retirement, quittance; abandonment, surrender, cession, waiver. —**Ant.** commitment.

abdomen, n. **1.** stomach, belly, visceral cavity, viscera, paunch. **2.** (slang) pot, guts, gut, potbelly, corporation, alderman, beer-barrel.

abduct, v. kidnap, carry off, bear off, capture, carry away, ravish, steal away, run away or off with, seize, rape.

abduction, n. kidnapping, capture, ravishment, deprehension, seizure, rape.

abductor, n. kidnapper, captor, ravisher, seizer, rapist.

aberrant, adj. **1.** straying, stray, deviating, deviate, wandering, errant, erring, devious, erratic, rambling, diverging, divergent. **2.** abnormal, irregular, unusual, odd, eccentric, peculiar, exceptional, weird, queer, curious, singular, strange; unconforming, nonconforming, anomalous. —**Ant.** direct.

aberration, n. **1.** wandering, straying, deviation, rambling, divergence, departure. **2.** strangeness, abnormality, abnormity, oddness, anomaly, irregularity, eccentricity; peculiarity, curiosity, oddity. **3.** unsoundness, illusion, hallucination, delusion, lapsus mentis.

abet, v. aid, assist, help, support, back, succor, sustain; countenance, sanction, uphold, second, condone, approve, favor; encourage, promote, conduce, advocate, advance, further, subsidize. —**Ant.** hinder.

abeyance, n. suspension, suspense, inactivity, hiatus, recess, deferral, intermission, interregnum, dormancy, quiescence. —**Ant.** operation, action.

abhor, v. hate, detest, loathe, abominate, despise, regard with repugnance, execrate, view with horror, shrink from, shudder at, bear malice or spleen. —**Ant.** love. —**Syn. Study.** See HATE.

abhorrence, n. hate, hatred, loathing, execration, odium, abomination, aversion, repugnance, revulsion, disgust, horror, antipathy, detestation, animosity, enmity. —**Ant.** love.

abhorrent, adj. **1.** hating, loathing, loathsome, execrating, execratory, antipathetic, detesting, detestable. **2.** horrible, horrifying, shocking, disgusting, revolting, sickening, nauseating, repugnant, repulsive, odious; hateful, detestable, abominable, invidious. **3.** remote, far, distant, removed. —**Ant.** amiable, lovable.

abide, v. **1.** remain, stay, wait, wait for, tarry, sojourn. **2.** dwell, reside, live, inhabit, tenant, stay. **3.** remain, continue, endure, last, persist, persevere, remain steadfast or faithful or constant, go on, keep on. **4.** stand by, support, second; await or accept the consequences of. **5.** await, attend, wait for. **6.** stand one's ground against, await or sustain defiantly. **7.** put up with, stand, suffer, brook, allow, tolerate, bear, endure.

ability, n. power, proficiency, expertness, dexterity, capacity, ableness, capability, knack, facility, competency, competence, enablement; puissance, prepotency. **2.** faculty, talent, aptitude, skill, skillfulness, aptness, ingenuity. —**Ant.** inability. —**Syn. Study.** ABILITY, FACULTY, TALENT denote power or capacity to do something. ABILITY is the general word for a natural or acquired capacity to do things; it usually implies doing them well: a leader of great ability; ability in mathematics. FACULTY denotes a natural or acquired ability for a particular kind of action: a faculty for putting people at ease. TALENT usually denotes an exceptional natural ability or aptitude in a particular field: a talent for music.

abject, adj. **1.** humiliating, disheartening, debasing, degrading. **2.** contemptible, despicable, scurvy, hateful; base, mean, low, vile, groveling, corrupt; faithless, treacherous, perfidious, dishonorable, inglorious, dishonest, false, fraudulent; disgraceful, ignominious, discreditable. —**Ant.** superciliously; exalted.

able, adj. **1.** qualified, fit, fitted, competent, capable, apt. **2.** talented, accomplished, gifted, endowed; skilled, clever, adroit, expert, ingenious, skillful, proficient, versed. —**Ant.** unable, incompetent, inept.

able-bodied, adj. well-knit, brawny, burly, sturdy, strapping, powerful, vigorous, red-blooded, robust, vital, lusty.

abnormal, adj. nonconforming, nonconformant, irregular, erratic, anomalous, unusual, unnatural, queer, odd, peculiar, aberrant, eccentric, weird, curious, strange, singular, idiosyncratic. —**Ant.** normal, regular.

abnormality, n. abnormity, irregularity, unconformity, anomaly, peculiarity, aberrance, idiosyncrasy, singularity, curiosity; malformation, monstrosity. —**Ant.** regularity, normality.

abolish, v. suppress, put an end to, cease, void, annul, invalidate, nullify, cancel, revoke, rescind, repeal, eradicate, stamp out, annihilate, extirpate, destroy, do away with, abrogate, obliterate, erase, extinguish, put out, eliminate. —**Ant.** establish.

abolition, n. destruction, annihilation, extirpation, abrogation, obliteration, eradication, elimination, extinction; annulment, nullification, invalidation, cancellation, revocation, repeal. —**Ant.** establishment.

abominable, adj. detestable, hateful, loathsome, abhorrent, odious, contemptible, despicable, scurvy; horrible, horrifying, disgusting, nauseating, sickening, revolting, repugnant, obnoxious, foul, noxious. —**Ant.** likable, admirable, delightful.

abominate, v. abhor, regard with aversion, detest, hate, loathe, execrate, contemn, despise, regard with repugnance, view with horror, shrink from, shudder at, bear malice or spleen. —**Ant.** like, love, enjoy.

abomination, n. **1.** hatred, loathing, abhorrence, detestation, revulsion, loathsomeness, odiousness, odium; aversion. **2.** vice, sin, impurity, corruption, wickedness, evil, viciousness, depravity, immorality, amorality, profligacy, defilement, pollution, filth.

abortive, adj. **1.** failing, unsuccessful, miscarrying, immature, premature. **2.** undeveloped, underdeveloped, rudimentary, primitive. **3.** (medicine) abortifacient. **4.** (pathology) short, mild, without symptoms. —**Ant.** consummate.

abound, v. prevail, teem, swarm, be very prevalent, pour, stream, shower. —**Ant.** want, need, lack.

about, prep. **1.** of, concerning, in regard to, respecting, with regard or respect or reference to, relating or relative to. **2.** connected with, in connection with, relating or relative to. **3.** near, around, round, not far from, close to. **4.** near, close to, approximately, almost. **5.** around, circling, encircling, inclosing, enclosing, surrounding. **6.** on one's person, having in one's possession. **7.** on the point of, ready, prepared. **8.** here and there, in, on, hither and yon, to and fro, back and forth, hither and thither. —adv. **9.** near, approximately, nearly, almost, well-nigh. **10.** nearby, close, not far, around. **11.** on every side, in every direction, all around, everywhere, every place, all over. **12.** half round, reversed, backwards, opposite direction. **13.** to and fro, back and forth, hither and thither, hither and yon, here and there. **14.** in succession, alternately, in rotation.

about-face, n. 180° turn, reversal, turnabout, reverse, changeabout, reversion, volte-face.

above, adv. **1.** overhead, aloft, on high, atop, on top of. **2.** higher, beyond, over, superior, surpassing. **3.** before, prior, earlier, sooner, previous, first. **4.** in heaven, on high, in excelsis. —prep. **5.** over, in a higher place than, higher than, superior to. **6.** more, greater than, more than, exceeding. **7.** superior to, beyond, surpassing. —adj. **8.** supra, said, written, mentioned previously, foregoing, preceding.

aboveboard, adv. **1.** in open sight, without tricks, without disguise, openly, overtly, candidly, honestly, frankly, sincerely, guilelessly, unequivocally, unequivocatingly. —adj. **2.** open, candid, overt, honest, frank, sincere, guileless, unequivocal, unequivocating. —**Ant.** underhand, treacherous, seditious.

abrade, v. wear off, wear down, scrape off; erode, wear away, rub off.

abrasion, n. **1.** sore, scrape, cut, scratch. **2.** friction, abrading, rubbing, erosion, wearing down, rubbing off.

abreast, adv., adj. side by side, alongside, equal, aligned, in alignment.

abridge, v. **1.** condense, digest, scale down, reduce, epitomize, abstract. **2.** curtail, reduce, lessen, diminish, contract. **3.** deprive, cut off, dispossess, divest. —**Ant.** expand, extend. —**Syn. Study.** See SHORTEN.

abridgment, n. **1.** condensation, shortening, digest, epitome, curtailment, reduction, abbreviation, contraction, retrenchment, compression; compendium, synopsis, abstract, abstraction, summary, syllabus, brief, outline, précis. **2.** dispossession, limitation. —**Ant.** expansion, extension, enlargement.

abroad, adv. **1.** overseas, beyond the sea, away. **2.** out-of-doors, outside, out of the house. **3.** astir, in circulation, bruited about. **4.** broadly, widely, expansively, at large, everywhere, ubiquitously, in all directions. **5.** untrue, wide of the truth. —**Ant.** here, domestically.

abrogate, v. abolish, cancel, annul, repeal, disannul, revoke, rescind, nullify, void, invalidate. —**Ant.** ratify, establish.

abrogation, n. abolition, cancellation, annulment, repeal, disannulment, revocation, rescission, nullification, invalidation. —**Ant.** establishment.

abrupt, adj. **1.** sudden, unceremonious, short, precipitous, hasty, blunt, curt, brusque, uncomplaisant; rude, rough, discourteous, inconsiderate, boorish. **2.** discontinuous, spasmodic, uneven. **3.** steep, precipitous, acclivitous, craggy. —**Ant.** gradual, slow, deliberate.

abscond, v. depart suddenly, depart secretly, steal away, sneak off or out, decamp, run away, run off, escape, flee, fly, bolt. —**Ant.** remain.

absence, n. **1.** want, lack, need, deficiency, defect. **2.** non-appearance. —**Ant.** presence.

absent, adj. **1.** away, out, not in, not present, off. **2.** lacking, missing, not present, away. —v. **3.** stay away, keep away. —**Ant.** present.

absent-minded, adj. forgetful, preoccupied, abstracted, oblivious, inattentive, wandering, withdrawn; musing, in a brown study, dreaming, daydreaming. —**Ant.** attentive.

absolute, adj. **1.** complete, whole, entire, perfect, free from imperfection, ideal. **2.** pure, unmixed, unadulterated, sheer, unqualified. **3.** unqualified, utter, total, entire, unconditional, unrestricted, unlimited, unbound, unbounded. **4.** arbitrary, despotic, autocratic, dictatorial, tyrannous, tyrannical, imperious, Nazi, Fascist, Fascistic. **5.** uncompared, categorical, certain, unquestionable, unequivocal. **6.** positive, affirmative, unquestionable, unquestionable, indubitable, certain, sure, unequivocal, unequivocating, firm, definite. —**Ant.** mixed; relative.

absolutely, adv. **1.** completely, wholly, entirely, unqualifiedly, definitely, unconditionally. **2.** positively, affirmatively, unquestionably, definitely, unequivocally, indubitably, really, without doubt, beyond doubt.

absolve, v. **1.** acquit, exonerate, free from blame, exculpate, excuse, forgive, pardon, clear, release, liberate, set free, free, disentangle, discharge, loose, rid. **2.** set free, loose, release, liberate, exempt. **3.** pardon, excuse, forgive. —**Ant.** blame, censure. —**Syn. Study.** ABSOLVE, ACQUIT, EXONERATE all mean to free from blame. ABSOLVE is a general word for this idea. To ACQUIT is to release from a specific and usu. formal accusation: The court must acquit the accused if there is insufficient evidence of guilt. To EXONERATE is to consider a person clear of blame or consequences for an act (even when the act is admitted), or to justify the person for having done it: to be exonerated for a crime committed in self-defense.

absorb, v. **1.** swallow, consume, assimilate, amalgamate, devour, engulf, ingurgitate; destroy. **2.** engross, occupy.

abstemious, adj. temperate, continent, sober, abstinent, self-denying, ascetic, sparing, austere, stinting, frugal. —**Ant.** greedy, gluttonous, grasping.

abstinence, n. **1.** abstemiousness, sobriety, soberness, teetotalism, moderation, temperance. **2.** self-restraint, forbearance, avoidance, self-denial, nonindulgence. —**Ant.** indulgence.

abstract, adj. **1.** apart, special, unrelated, separate, isolated. **2.** theoretical, unpractical. **3.** abstruse, difficult, deep, complex, complicated. **4.** (art) nonrepresentational, unrealistic, unphotographic. —n. **5.** summary, digest, epitome, abridgment, synopsis, compendium, condensation, brief; syllabus, outline, précis; gist, substance. **6.** essence, distillation, condensation, substance; core, heart, idea. —v. **7.** draw away, take away, remove, distill; separate, fractionate. **8.** divert, disengage. **9.** steal, purloin, rob, pilfer, shoplift, hijack. **10.** separate, consider apart, isolate, dissociate; disjoin, disunite. **11.** summarize, epitomize, distill, abridge, abbreviate, outline, condense, edit, digest. —**Ant.** concrete; interpolate.

abstruse, adj. esoteric, recondite, profound, deep, difficult, knotty, complex, involved, secret, hermetic, orphic. —**Ant.** open, straightforward, obvious.

absurd, adj. ridiculous, preposterous, foolish, inane, asinine, stupid, unwise, false, unreasonable, irrational, incongruous, self-contradictory. —**Ant.** sensible, rational. —**Syn. Study.** ABSURD, RIDICULOUS, PREPOSTEROUS all mean inconsistent with reason or common sense. ABSURD means utterly opposed to truth or reason: an absurd claim. RIDICULOUS implies that something is fit only to be laughed at, perhaps contemptuously: a ridiculous suggestion. PREPOSTEROUS implies an extreme of foolishness: a preposterous proposal.

abundance, n. **1.** overflow, plenty, copiousness, fertility, profusion, plenteousness, prodigality, extravagance, oversupply, flood. **2.** fullness, generosity, large-heartedness. **3.** affluence, wealth. —**Ant.** lack, need, paucity.

abundant, adj. abounding, teeming, thick, plentiful, plenteous, flowing, copious, profuse, overflowing, rich, replete. —**Ant.** sparse, scarce, poor. —**Syn. Study.** See PLENTIFUL.

abuse, v. **1.** misuse, misapply, mistreat, misemploy, misappropriate; desecrate, profane, prostitute; deceive, betray, seduce, subvert. **2.** maltreat, ill-use, injure, harm, hurt. **3.** revile, malign, vilify, vituperate, berate, rate, rail at, upbraid, scold, carp at, inveigh against, reproach; traduce, slander, defame, denounce, asperse, calumniate, disparage; satirize, lampoon. —n. **4.** misuse, misapplication, mistreatment, misemployment, misappropriation; desecration, profanation, prostitution; deception, betrayal, seduction, subversion. **5.** censure, adverse criticism, blame, condemnation, hostile condemnation; denunciation, vilification, malignment, vituperation, invective, slander, defamation, aspersion, calumniation, curse, disparagement; contumely, scorn, reproach, opprobrium. **6.** offense, crime, corruption. —**Ant.** esteem; praise, acclaim. —**Syn. Study.** ABUSE, CENSURE, INVECTIVE all mean strongly expressed disapproval. ABUSE implies an outburst of harsh and scathing words, often against one who is defenseless: abuse directed against an opponent. CENSURE implies blame, adverse criticism, or condemnation: severe censure of her bad judgment. INVECTIVE applies to strong but formal denunciation in speech or print, often in the public interest: invective against graft.

abyss, n. chasm, gulf, bottomless pit, abysm, depths, pit, crater, crevasse, shaft, well, hollow, cavity.

academic, adj. **1.** college, collegiate, university. **2.** unscientific, literary, lettered, scholastic, unprofessional. **3.** theoretical, unpractical, impractical. **4.** conventional, formal. —**Ant.** illiterate.

accept, v. **1.** receive, take. **2.** admit, agree to, accede to, acquiesce in, assent to, approve, allow, concede, acknowledge. **3.** resign oneself to, accommodate oneself to, yield, consent. **4.** believe, acknowledge. **5.** understand, construe, interpret. **6.** receive, acknowledge. —**Ant.** reject.

access, n. **1.** fit, seizure, attack, spasm, throe, outburst, eruption, explosion. **2.** entry, entrance, doorway, ingress, entrée, passage, adit, right of entry, admittance, way, way in, route, approach. —v. **3.** reach, approach, contact, get, communicate with, go into, enter.

accessory, See Syn. study at ADDITION.

accident, n. **1.** mischance, misfortune, disaster, calamity, catastrophe, casualty, mishap, misadventure, contingency. **2.** fortuity, chance. —**Ant.** intent, calculation.

accidental, adj. **1.** casual, fortuitous, undesigned, unplanned, contingent. **2.** nonessential, incidental, subsidiary, secondary, dispensable, expendable, adventitious. —**Ant.** planned, designed, essential.

acclaimed, adj. notable, distinguished, great, major, famous, honored, famed, renowned, celebrated, prominent, world-renowned, world-famous, stellar, world-class, outstanding, preeminent, premiere.

accolade, n. honor, praise, tribute, award, distinction, decoration, laurels, kudos.

accommodate, v. **1.** oblige, serve; aid, assist, help, abet. **2.** provide, supply, furnish, minister to. **3.** furnish room for, board, entertain. **4.** make suitable, suit, fit, adapt. **5.** bring into harmony, adjust, reconcile, compose, harmonize. **6.** contain, hold. **7.** conform, agree, concur, assent. —**Ant.** inconvenience, incommode. —**Syn. Study.** See OBLIGE. See also CONTAIN.

accompany, v. **1.** go along, attend, join, escort, convoy, wait on. **2.** co-exist with, consort with. **3.** associate with, consider together with, couple with. —**Ant.** desert, abandon, forsake. —**Syn. Study.** ACCOMPANY, ATTEND, CONVOY, ESCORT mean to go along with. To ACCOMPANY is to go as an associate or companion, usu. on equal terms: My daughter accompanied me on the trip. ATTEND usu. implies going along as a subordinate, as to render service: to attend the queen. To CONVOY is to accompany ships or other vehicles with an armed guard: to convoy a fleet of merchant vessels. To ESCORT is to accompany in order to protect, honor, or show courtesy: to escort a visiting dignitary.

accomplice, n. associate, partner, confederate, accessory.

accomplish, v. **1.** fulfill, complete, achieve, execute, do, carry out, perform, finish, attain, consummate, culminate, dispatch, effect, effectuate, perfect, realize. **2.** succeed in, be successful with or in, triumph over, win over. **3.** equip, supply, furnish, provide. —**Ant.** foil.

accomplishment, *n.* **1.** fulfillment, completion, effecting, execution. **2.** achievement, success, consummation. **3.** attainment, acquirement, acquisition, proficiency. —**Ant.** failure.

accord, *v.* **1.** agree, assent, concur, correspond, be harmonious *or* in harmony, harmonize. **2.** adapt, accommodate, reconcile, suit, fit. **3.** grant, concede, yield, give up *or* in, allow, deign, vouchsafe. —**Ant.** conflict, disagree.

accordingly, *adv.* **1.** correspondingly, conformably, agreeably. **2.** in due course, consequently, hence, therefore, thus, so, wherefore.

account, *n.* **1.** narrative, narration, recital, report, history, chronicle, journal, anecdote, description, story, exposé, tale. **2.** explanation, elucidation, explication, clearing up, exposition. **3.** reason, consideration, motive, excuse, purpose. **4.** consequence, importance, value, consideration, worth, distinction, repute, reputation. **5.** estimation, judgment, consideration, regard. **6.** profit, advantage, benefit. **7.** statement, ledger, inventory, register, score, book, books. **8.** record, ledger; balance. —*v.* **9.** give an explanation for, explain, elucidate. **10.** make excuse for, give reasons for, answer, reply. **11.** explain, explicate. **12.** cause death *or* capture for. **13.** count, reckon, estimate, consider, regard, judge, deem, rate, assess, hold, see, view, look upon. **14.** assign to, impute to, blame, credit, accuse.

accurate, *adj.* correct, exact, precise, careful, true, unerring. —**Ant.** inaccurate. —**Syn. Study.** See CORRECT.

accuse, *v.* **1.** arraign, indict, charge, incriminate, impeach. **2.** blame, inculpate, charge, involve, point to. —**Ant.** exonerate.

accustomed, *adj.* **1.** customary, habitual, usual, characteristic, familiar, common. **2.** wont, used to, in the habit of. —**Ant.** unused, unaccustomed.

acerbic, *adj.* **1.** sour, acerb, tart, acid, acidy, acidulous, acetose. **2.** sarcastic, mordant, sardonic, ironic, wry, satiric, caustic, biting, scathing, sour, vinegary, vinegarish. —**Ant.** sweet, dulcet, generous, upbeat, Pollyannaish, goody-goody.

ache, *v.* **1.** suffer, hurt, suffer pain. —*n.* **2.** pain, continued *or* dull pain, agony.

achieve, *v.* **1.** carry through, accomplish, consummate, complete, effect, execute, do, perform, realize, reach. **2.** gain, obtain, acquire, procure, secure, get, attain, realize, win. **3.** effect, result. —**Ant.** fail.

achievement, *n.* **1.** exploit, feat, deed. **2.** accomplishment, realization, attainment, consummation. —**Ant.** failure.

acid, *adj.* **1.** vinegary. **2.** sour, tart, biting, ill-natured, ill-tempered, sarcastic, sardonic, scornful. —**Ant.** sweet, mild.

acknowledge, *v.* **1.** admit, confess, own, declare, grant, concede, give in, allow, agree. **2.** realize, recognize. **3.** accept, receive, allow. **4.** appreciate, be grateful for, express gratitude for. **5.** reply to, receive, indorse, admit *or* certify receipt of. —**Syn. Study.** ACKNOWLEDGE, ADMIT, CONFESS agree in the idea of declaring something to be true. ACKNOWLEDGE implies making a statement reluctantly, often about something previously doubted or denied: *to acknowledge one's mistakes.* ADMIT esp. implies acknowledging under pressure: *to admit a charge.* CONFESS usu. means stating somewhat formally an admission of wrongdoing or shortcoming: *to confess guilt; to confess an inability to understand.*

acquaintance, *n.* **1.** associate, companion, friend. **2.** personal knowledge, familiarity. —**Syn. Study.** ACQUAINTANCE, ASSOCIATE, COMPANION, FRIEND refer to a person with whom one is in contact. An ACQUAINTANCE is a person one knows, though not intimately: *a casual acquaintance at school.* An ASSOCIATE is a person who is often in one's company, usu. because of some work or pursuit in common: *a business associate.* A COMPANION is a person who shares one's activities or fortunes; the term usu. suggests a familiar relationship: *a traveling companion; a companion in despair.* A FRIEND is a person with whom one is on intimate terms and for whom one feels a warm affection: *a trusted friend.*

acquiesce, *v.* assent, accede, comply, agree, concur, consent, bow, submit, yield, resign *or* reconcile oneself, rest, be satisfied *or* content (with). —**Ant.** protest, object.

acquire, *v.* **1.** appropriate, gain, win, earn, attain; take over, take possession of, procure, secure, obtain, get. **2.** accomplish, achieve. —**Ant.** forfeit. —**Syn. Study.** See GET.

acquit, *v.* **1.** absolve, exonerate, exculpate, pardon, excuse, forgive. **2.** release *or* discharge, liberate, set free. **3.** settle, pay, fulfill. —**Ant.** convict, condemn. —**Syn. Study.** See ABSOLVE.

acrimonious, *adj.* harsh, bitter, biting, sharp, rancorous, angry, contentious, disputatious, antagonistic, hostile, vitriolic. —**Ant.** peaceful, pacific, irenic, tactful, diplomatic.

act, *n.* **1.** feat, exploit, achievement, transaction, accomplishment, performance. **2.** deed, performance. **3.** decree, edict, law, statute, judgment, resolve, award. **4.** record, deed, enactment, ordinance. **5.** turn, routine, performance, stint. —*v.* **6.** exert energy *or* force, operate, function, perform, do, work. **7.** function, be active, substitute (for). **8.** produce an effect, operate, be efficient *or* effective *or* efficacious. **9.** behave, perform, conduct *or* deport *or* comport oneself. **10.** pretend, sham, dissemble, feign, fake, do imitations, dissimulate, play. **11.** play parts, do imitations *or* impersonations. **12.** represent, impersonate, imitate, play the part of. **13.** feign, counterfeit, fake, imitate. **14.** behave as, play the part of.

action, *n.* **1.** movement, work, performance, moving, working, performing, operation. **2.** deed, act. **3.** (*plural*) conduct, behavior. **4.** energetic activity. **5.** exertion, energy, effort. **6.** gesture. **7.** mechanism, contrivance, apparatus. **8.** skirmish, brush, affair, encounter, meeting, engagement, conflict, combat, fight, battle. **9.** (*law*) proceeding, process, case, suit, lawsuit. —**Ant.** lethargy, inactivity.

active, *adj.* **1.** acting, moving, working, operative. **2.** busy, energetic, strenuous, vigorous, animated, enterprising, efficient, fervent, earnest, eager, diligent, industrious; engaged, occupied, consumed with. **3.** nimble, sprightly, agile, alert, smart, quick, spirited, brisk, supple, lively. **4.** practical, working, applicable, applied. **5.** (*commerce*) busy, profitable; interest-bearing. **6.** (*medicine*) effective, productive. —**Ant.** inactive, lazy.

actual, *adj.* **1.** true, genuine, real, veritable, palpable, tangible, certain, positive, absolute, sure, categorical, decided, definite, determinate, substantial. **2.** now existing, present, here and now. —**Ant.** unreal, untrue, fake.

acute, *adj.* **1.** pointed, cuspidate, aciform, acicular, acuminate, sharp, sharpened. **2.** intense, poignant, touching; severe, fierce, violent, distressing, crucial, sudden, piercing, penetrating. **3.** sharp, penetrating, perceptive, keen, astute, discerning, intelligent, perspicacious, sharp-witted, shrewd, clever, knowing, wise, sage, sagacious, sapient; smart, bright, ingenious. **4.** sensitive, keen. **5.** alt, high, intense. —**Ant.** blunt.

adapt, *v.* suit, adjust, modify, fit, reconcile, accommodate, prepare, conform, make conformable *or* suitable, qualify, compose. —**Syn. Study.** See ADJUST.

add, *v.* **1.** unite, annex, connect, affix, join; append, attach, supplement, increase, make an addition to, augment, adjoin, tack on. **2.** total, tot, sum, aggregate. —**Ant.** subtract, deduct.

addiction, *n.* dependency, compulsive need, obsession, fixation, habit, craving, appetite, itch, lust, passion, monkey.

addition, *n.* **1.** uniting, adding, joining. **2.** summing up. **3.** increase, increment, enlargement, aggrandizement, accession; supplement, appendix, accessory, adjunct, attachment, addendum, appendage. —**Ant.** deduction, subtraction. —**Syn. Study.** ADDITION, ACCESSORY, ADJUNCT, ATTACHMENT refer to something joined to or used with something else. ADDITION is the general word for anything joined to something previously existing; it carries no implication of size, importance, or kind: *to build an addition to the town library.* An ACCESSORY is a non-essential part or object that makes something more complete, convenient, or attractive: *clothing accessories; camera accessories.* An ADJUNCT is a subordinate addition that aids or assists but is usu. separate: *a second machine as an adjunct to the first.*

An ATTACHMENT is a supplementary part that may be easily connected and removed: *a sewing machine attachment for pleating.*

address, *n.* **1.** discourse, lecture, speech, oration. **2.** location, post office. **3.** residence, domicile, abode, habitation, lodging, dwelling, home quarters, house. **4.** manner, bearing. **5.** skillful management, skill, art, adroitness, cleverness, tact, ingenuity, technique, dexterity, ability. —*v.* **6.** direct (speech or writing to), speak to; accost. **7.** invoke, appeal to, apply to. —**Syn. Study.** See SPEECH.

adequate, *adj.* commensurate, equal, suitable, fit for; satisfactory, competent, sufficient, enough; capable. —**Ant.** inadequate, insufficient.

adhere, *v.* **1.** stick fast, cleave, cling to, stick, hold, cohere. **2.** be devoted, identify, be attached, be a follower, be faithful, be true. **3.** hold closely *or* firmly to. —**Ant.** separate. —**Syn. Study.** See STICK.

adherent, *n.* **1.** supporter, follower, partisan, disciple; devotee, fan, aficionado. —*adj.* **2.** clinging, adhering, sticking, cleaving. —**Ant.** recreant, deserter. —**Syn. Study.** See FOLLOWER.

adjacent, *adj.* near, close, contiguous, adjoining, juxtaposed, neighboring, nearby, touching. —**Ant.** distant. —**Syn. Study.** See ADJOINING.

adjoining, *adj.* bordering, contiguous, adjacent, near or close or next to, touching. —**Syn. Study.** ADJOINING, ADJACENT both mean near or close to something. ADJOINING implies touching at a common point or line: *adjoining rooms.* ADJACENT implies being nearby or next to something else, with nothing of the same sort intervening: *a motel adjacent to the highway; the adjacent houses.*

adjourn, *v.* **1.** suspend (for a day), postpone, interrupt, put off, defer, delay, prorogue. **2.** postpone, defer, transfer. —**Ant.** convene; begin.

adjunct, *n.* **1.** addition, appendix, supplement, attachment. **2.** aide, attaché, subordinate, accessory. —**Syn. Study.** See ADDITION.

adjust, *v.* **1.** fit, make correspondent *or* conformable to, adapt, accommodate, suit. **2.** regulate, set, repair, fix; change, alter. **3.** arrange, rectify, reconcile, settle. **4.** adapt oneself, make oneself suitable *or* suited for. —**Syn. Study.** ADJUST, ADAPT, ALTER imply making necessary or desirable changes, as in position, shape, or the like. To ADJUST is to make a minor change, as to move into proper position for use: *to adjust the eyepiece of a telescope.* To ADAPT is to make a change in character, or to make something useful in a new way: *to adapt a method to a new task.* To ALTER is to change the appearance but not the use: *to alter a suit.*

ad-lib, *v.* **1.** improvise, extemporize, make up, invent, throw away, wing it. —*n.* **2.** improvisation, extemporization, invention, throwaway. —*adj.* **3.** improvised, extemporized, extemporaneous, made up, extempore, impromptu, unrehearsed, unpremeditated, spontaneous, off-hand, off-the-cuff, spur-of-the-moment, ad hoc.

administer, *v.* **1.** manage, conduct, control, execute; rule, govern; direct, superintend, oversee, supervise. **2.** dispense, distribute, supply, job, furnish, contribute. **3.** give, dispense, apply, dose, deal out, dole out. **4.** tender, offer, proffer; impose. **5.** provide aid, contribute assistance. **6.** (*law*) act as executor; act as administrator.

admirable, *adj.* estimable, praiseworthy, fine, rare, excellent. —**Ant.** abhorrent.

admiration, *n.* wonder, awe, pleasure, approbation, delight, esteem; liking, affection, regard. —**Ant.** abhorrence, disgust, hatred.

admire, *v.* esteem; revere, venerate; like, delight in. —**Ant.** detest, hate.

admission, *n.* **1.** entrance, introduction, access, admittance, entrée, ticket, pass, Annie Oakley, key, shibboleth. **2.** confession, acknowledgment, allowance, concession. —**Ant.** rejection.

admit, *v.* **1.** allow to enter, grant *or* afford entrance to, let in, afford access to, receive. **2.** permit, allow, agree to, concede, bear. **3.** acknowledge, own, avow, confess. **4.** permit entrance, give access. **5.** grant permission, be capable of. —**Ant.** reject. —**Syn. Study.** See ACKNOWLEDGE.

admittance, *n.* **1.** entrance, admission, introduction. **2.** access, reception.

admonish, *v.* **1.** caution, advise, warn, counsel. **2.** rebuke, censure, reprove. **3.** recall to duty, remind, notify, make aware, apprise, acquaint, inform. —**Syn. Study.** See WARN. See also REPRIMAND.

ado, *n.* fuss, stir, flurry, dither, pother, commotion, disturbance, hubbub, upset, uproar, upheaval, turmoil, hurly-burly, ruckus, brouhaha, foofaraw. —**Ant.** calm, serenity, tranquillity.

adolescent, *adj.* **1.** immature, youthful, young. —*n.* **2.** youth, teenager, minor. —**Ant.** adult.

adore, *v.* idolize, worship, love; respect, honor, esteem, reverence, revere, venerate, idolize. —**Ant.** abhor, detest, abominate, hate.

adorn, *v.* **1.** embellish, add luster to. **2.** decorate, enhance, beautify, deck, bedeck, ornament, trim, bedizen, array. —**Ant.** disfigure, deface.

adroit, *adj.* expert, ingenious, skillful, dexterous, clever, resourceful, ready, quick, apt, adept. —**Ant.** clumsy, maladroit. —**Syn. Study.** See DEXTEROUS.

adult, *adj.* **1.** mature, grown up, full-grown, ripe, of age. —*n.* **2.** grown-up, man, woman. —**Ant.** immature, adolescent.

advance, *v.* **1.** move *or* set *or* push or bring forward, further, forward. **2.** propose, bring to view *or* notice, adduce, propound, offer, allege. **3.** improve, further, forward, promote, strengthen. **4.** promote, elevate, dignify, exalt. **5.** increase, raise the pride of, augment. **6.** update, accelerate, quicken, hasten, speed up, bring forward. **7.** furnish *or* supply on credit, lend, loan. **8.** move *or* go forward, proceed, move on. **9.** improve, progress, make progress, grow, increase, flourish, rise, thrive. **10.** rise, increase, appreciate. —*n.* **11.** moving forward, progress, procedure, way; march, procession. **12.** advancement, promotion, improvement, advance, rise. **13.** overture, proposal, proposition, tender, offer, proffer, offering. **14.** price rise, raise, rise, increase. —*adj.* **15.** going before, preceding, precedent. **16.** beyond, ahead, before; prepublication. —**Ant.** retreat.

advantage, *n.* **1.** favorable opportunity *or* state *or* circumstance *or* means *or* situation, vantage point, superiority, superior condition. **2.** benefit, avail, gain, profit, value; return, dividend; utility, usefulness, expediency, use, service. **3.** superiority, ascendancy, preeminence. **4.** behalf, vantage; privilege, prerogative, convenience, accommodation. —*v.* **5.** be of service to, serve, avail, benefit, profit, help, aid, yield profit *or* gain to. —**Ant.** disadvantage. —**Syn. Study.** ADVANTAGE, BENEFIT, PROFIT all mean something that is of use or value. ADVANTAGE is anything that places a person in a favorable or superior position, esp. in coping with competition or difficulties: *It is to your advantage to have traveled widely.* BENEFIT is anything that promotes the welfare or improves the state of a person or group: *The new factory will be a great benefit to our town.* PROFIT is any valuable or useful gain, usually financial, moral, or educational: *profit from trade; profit from experience.*

adventurous, *adj.* daring, bold, audacious, courageous, venturous, venturesome, enterprising, dashing, risk-taking, cutting-edge, daredevil, brash, rash, foolhardy. —**Ant.** timid, tame, docile, cautious, unadventurous.

adversary, *n.* **1.** antagonist, opponent, enemy, foe. **2.** contestant, litigant, opponent. **3.** Satan, the Devil, the Evil One, the Prince of Darkness, Beelzebub, the Tempter. —**Ant.** ally, compatriot, friend. —**Syn. Study.** ADVERSARY, ANTAGONIST refer to a person, group, or personified force contending against another. ADVERSARY suggests an enemy who fights determinedly, continuously, and relentlessly: *a formidable adversary.* ANTAGONIST suggests one who, in hostile spirit, opposes another, often in a particular contest or struggle: *a duel with an antagonist.*

adverse, *adj.* **1.** antagonistic, contrary, opposite, conflicting, opposed, hostile, against, con, contra, inimical, unfriendly. **2.** unfavorable, unlucky, unfortunate; calamitous, disastrous, catastrophic. **3.** opposite, confronting, opposed, facing, vis-à-vis, face-to-face. —**Ant.** favorable, beneficial.

adversity, *n.* calamity, distress, catastrophe, disaster; bad luck, misfortune, misery, trouble, affliction, wretchedness. —**Ant.** happiness, wealth. —**Syn. Study.** See MISFORTUNE.

advice, *n.* **1.** admonition, warning, caution, counsel, opinion, recommendation, guidance, suggestion, persuasion, urging, exhortation. **2.** communication, information, news, report, intelligence, tidings, word, notice, notification. —**Syn. Study.** ADVICE, COUNSEL refer to opinions offered as worthy bases for thought, conduct, or action. ADVICE is a practical recommendation, generally from a person with relevant knowledge or experience: *Get a lawyer's advice about the purchase.* COUNSEL is weighty and serious advice, given after careful deliberation and consultation: *to seek counsel during a personal crisis.*

advisable, *adj.* **1.** expedient, advantageous, politic, proper, fit, suitable, desirable, correct, prudent, sensible, common-sense, judicious. **2.** receptive, open to suggestion *or* advice.

advise, *v.* **1.** give counsel to, counsel, admonish, caution, warn, recommend to. **2.** suggest, recommend. **3.** inform, notify, apprise, acquaint. **4.** take counsel, confer, deliberate, discuss, consult. **5.** give advice, offer counsel.

advocate, *v.* **1.** plead in favor of, support, urge, argue for, speak for, recommend. —*n.* **2.** lawyer, attorney, counselor, counselor-at-law, counsel, barrister, solicitor; intercessor. **3.** defender, vindicator, espouser, upholder, supporter, maintainer, promoter, patron, friend. —**Ant.** oppose; opponent.

aesthete, *n.* dilettante, connoisseur, virtuoso, expert, discriminator, collector.

affable, *adj.* courteous, urbane, debonair, suave, civil, approachable, polite, friendly, cordial, pleasant, amiable, obliging, gracious; benign, mild, easy, casual, social. —**Ant.** discourteous, boorish, reserved.

affect, *v.* **1.** effect, exert influence on, accomplish, bring about, influence, sway, act on; modify, alter, transform, change. **2.** move, impress, touch, stir, overcome. **3.** pretend, feign, fake, assume, adopt. **4.** imitate, act, mimic. **5.** use, adopt, prefer, choose, select. **6.** profess, pretend. —**Syn. Study.** See PRETEND.

affectation, *n.* pretension, airs, mannerisms, pose, artificiality, pretense, affectedness, unnaturalness, insincerity. —**Ant.** sincerity.

affected, *adj.* assumed, pretended, feigned. —**Ant.** sincere, genuine.

affecting, *adj.* touching, pathetic, piteous, moving, impressive.

affection, *n.* **1.** attachment, liking, friendliness, amity, fondness, devotion, friendship, tenderness, endearment, heart, love. **2.** feeling, inclination, partiality, proclivity, disposition, predisposition, bent, bias. **3.** (*pathology*) disease, disorder, affliction, malady, ailment, illness, complaint. —**Ant.** abhorrence.

affectionate, *adj.* tender, loving, fond, attentive, attached, devoted, warm, kind, sympathetic. —**Ant.** apathetic.

affirm, *v.* **1.** state, assert, aver, maintain, declare, asseverate, depose, testify, say, pronounce. **2.** establish, confirm, ratify, approve, endorse. —**Ant.** deny. —**Syn. Study.** See DECLARE.

affliction, *n.* **1.** pain, distress, grief, adversity, misfortune, trial, mishap, trouble, tribulation, calamity, catastrophe, disaster. **2.** sickness, loss, calamity, persecution, suffering, misery, woe, depression, wretchedness, heartbreak; plague, scourge, epidemic. —**Ant.** relief. —**Syn. Study.** See MISFORTUNE.

affluent, *adj.* abounding, rich, wealthy, opulent. **2.** abundant, free-flowing, teeming. —*n.* **3.** tributary, feeder. —**Ant.** poor; scarce.

affront, *n.* **1.** offense, slight, disrespect, insult, impertinence, contumely, scorn, indignity, abuse, outrage, injury. **2.** shame, disgrace, degradation. —*v.* **3.** offend, insult, slight, abuse, outrage. **4.** shame, disgrace, discountenance, confuse, confound, disconcert, abash. **5.** confront, encounter, face, meet. —**Ant.** compliment, honor. —**Syn. Study.** See INSULT.

afraid, *adj.* scared, fearful, alarmed, frightened, terrified, disquieted, shocked, apprehensive, timid, cowardly, pusillanimous, timorous, shy, cautious, overcautious. —**Ant.** bold, sanguine, confident.

age, *n.* **1.** period, life, duration. **2.** maturity, years of discretion. **3.** old age, decline. **4.** era, epoch, time, date, period. —v. **5.** grow old, mature, ripen. —**Ant.** youth. —**Syn.** AGE, EPOCH, ERA, PERIOD all refer to an extent of time. AGE usu. implies a considerable extent of time, esp. one associated with a dominant personality, influence, characteristic, or institution: *the age of chivalry.* EPOCH and ERA are often used interchangeably to refer to an extent of time characterized by changed conditions and new undertakings: *an era (or epoch) of invention.* EPOCH sometimes refers esp. to the beginning of an era: *The steam engine marked a new epoch in technology.* A PERIOD usu. has a marked condition or feature: *a period of industrial expansion; the Victorian period.*

aged, *adj.* **1.** old, ancient, decrepit, elderly. **2.** old, of the age of. —**Ant.** young.

aggravate, *v.* worsen, make severe, intensify, heighten, increase, make serious or grave. —**Ant.** assuage, improve, better.

aggregate, *adj.* **1.** added, combined, total, complete. —*n.* **2.** sum, mass, assemblage, total, gross, body, amount. —*v.* **3.** bring together, assemble, collect, amass, accumulate, gather. **4.** amount to, add up to. **5.** combine into a mass, form a collection. —**Ant.** particular.

aggressive, *adj.* **1.** pugnacious, attacking, offensive, assaulting, militant, assailing, take-no-prisoners. **2.** energetic, vigorous, pushing, enterprising, assertive, determined, forward. —**Ant.** retiring, bashful, shy.

aghast, *adj.* dismayed, horrified, appalled, horror-struck, undone, stricken, stunned, shocked, agape, dumbfounded, thunderstruck, overwhelmed, jolted, jarred, shaken up, shook-up.

agile, *adj.* quick, light, nimble, sprightly, active, lively, brisk, ready, smart, alert, spry. —**Ant.** awkward.

agitate, *v.* **1.** shake or move briskly, disturb, toss, jar. **2.** move to and fro. **3.** disturb, ruffle, stir or work up, perturb, excite, fluster. **4.** discuss, debate, controvert, campaign or argue for, dispute. **5.** plan, devise; revolve or turn over in the mind, cogitate, consider, deliberate. **6.** arouse public interest, ferment, disturb, rouse. —**Ant.** tranquilize.

agitation, *n.* **1.** agitating, shaking, jarring, disturbing. **2.** disturbance, excitement, turmoil, tumult, storm, unrest, disquiet, struggle, conflict, perturbation, flurry, ado, to-do. **3.** urging, persistence, debate, discussion, dispute, argument, campaign. —**Ant.** serenity, calm, tranquillity.

agnostic, See Syn. study at ATHEIST.

agony, *n.* **1.** pain, distress, suffering, torment, torture, rack; throe, paroxysm, spasm, seizure, pang; ache. **2.** excitement, suspense, anguish, torment, torture. —**Ant.** comfort.

agree, *v.* **1.** assent, yield, consent, accede, concede, acquiesce, allow, comply. **2.** harmonize, concur, unite, accord, combine. **3.** come to an agreement or arrangement or understanding, compromise, arrive at a settlement. **4.** accord, correspond, compare favorably, coincide, conform, tally, match, stand up, suit. **5.** be applicable or appropriate or similar, resemble. **6.** make or write a contract or bargain, contract, stipulate, bargain. **7.** concede, grant, allow, let, permit. —**Ant.** disagree.

agreement, *n.* **1.** agreeing, being in concord. **2.** bargain, contract, compact, understanding, arrangement, deal. **3.** unanimity, harmony, accord, concord, settlement, treaty, pact, word, conformity, unity, uniformity. —**Ant.** disagreement. —**Syn. Study.** AGREEMENT, BARGAIN, COMPACT, CONTRACT all suggest an arrangement between two or more parties. AGREEMENT ranges in meaning from a mutual understanding to a binding obligation: *an agreement to meet next week; a tariff agreement.* BARGAIN applies particularly to agreements about buying and selling; it suggests haggling: *We made a bargain that I would do the work if they supplied the materials.* COMPACT applies to treaties or alliances between nations or to solemn personal pledges: *a compact to preserve the peace.* CONTRACT is used esp. in law and business for such agreements as are legally enforceable: *a contract to sell a house.*

aid, *v.* **1.** support, help, succor, assist, serve, abet, back, second; spell, relieve. **2.** promote, facilitate, ease, simplify. **3.** be of help, give help or assistance. —*n.* **4.** help, support, succor, assistance, service, furtherance; relief, charity. **5.** assistant, helper,

supporter, servant, aide, aide-de-camp. —**Ant.** hinder, obstruct; obstacle, obstruction. —**Syn. Study.** See HELP.

ailing, *adj.* sickly, sick, ill, unwell. —**Ant.** healthy, well.

ailment, *n.* disorder, infirmity, affliction, malady, disease, sickness, complaint, ill, debility, disability, handicap, defect.

aim, *v.* **1.** direct, point, give direction to. **2.** direct, point. **3.** strive, try, purpose. —*n.* **4.** direction, sighting. **5.** target, object, end. **6.** purpose, end, object, goal; intent, intention, reason; design, scheme. —**Syn. Study.** AIM, END, OBJECT all imply something that is the goal of one's efforts. AIM implies a direct effort toward a goal, without diversion from it: *Her aim is to be an astronaut.* END emphasizes the goal as separate from the effort: *unscrupulous means to achieve noble ends.* OBJECT emphasizes the goal of a specific effort: *the object of my research.*

air, *n.* **1.** atmosphere. **2.** breeze, breath, zephyr, wind. **3.** circulation, publication, publicity. **4.** character, complexion, appearance, impression, aspect, look, mien; manner, demeanor, attitude, conduct, carriage, behavior, deportment, bearing. **5.** affectation, haughtiness. —*v.* **6.** ventilate. **7.** expose, display. —**Syn. Study.** See WIND¹.

alarm, *n.* **1.** fear, apprehension, fright, consternation, terror, panic, dismay. **2.** alarum, tocsin, distress-signal, siren. —*v.* **3.** terrify, frighten, scare, startle; appall, shock; dismay, daunt. —**Ant.** calm, comfort.

alert, *adj.* **1.** attentive, vigilant, watchful, aware, wary, observant, circumspect, heedful, cautious, on the lookout, on the qui vive. **2.** nimble, brisk, lively, quick, active, agile, sprightly, spirited. —*n.* **3.** vigilance, caution, wariness. **4.** air-raid alarm. —*v.* **5.** prepare for action, warn. —**Ant.** asleep, listless.

alien, *n.* **1.** stranger, foreigner, immigrant. —*adj.* **2.** strange, foreign. **3.** adverse, hostile, opposed, unfriendly, differing, unallied, unconnected, separate. —**Ant.** native, friendly. —**Syn. Study.** See STRANGER.

alienate, See Syn. study at ESTRANGE.

alive, *adj.* **1.** existing, living, breathing, quick. **2.** unextinguished, operative, functioning. **3.** lively, active, alert. **4.** swarming, thronged, aswarm. —**Ant.** dead.

all-around, *adj.* all-round, adaptable, versatile, many-sided, many-talented, flexible, elastic, well-rounded. —**Ant.** narrow, restricted, limited.

allay, *v.* quiet, appease, moderate, soothe, soften, assuage, alleviate, lighten, lessen, mitigate, mollify, temper, relieve, ease. —**Ant.** aggravate.

allege, *v.* **1.** declare, affirm, attest, state, asseverate, assert, aver. **2.** plead, advance. —**Ant.** deny.

allegiance, *n.* duty, obligation, faithfulness, loyalty, fealty, fidelity; homage. —**Ant.** treason, treachery.

alleviate, *v.* ease, lessen, diminish, quell, abate, mitigate, lighten, relieve, assuage, allay, mollify. —**Ant.** aggravate, intensify.

alley, *n.* back street, lane, byway, street.

alliance, *n.* **1.** association, coalition, combination, bloc, partnership, affiliation, connection, federation, confederacy, confederation, league, union, treaty, pact, compact. **2.** marriage, intermarriage, relation, relationship. **3.** affinity. —**Syn. Study.** ALLIANCE, LEAGUE, CONFEDERATION, UNION refer to the joining of states for mutual benefit or for the joint exercise of functions. ALLIANCE refers to a combination of states for the promotion of common interests: *a trade alliance.* LEAGUE usu. suggests a closer, more formal combination or a more definite purpose: *The League of Nations was formed to promote world peace.* CONFEDERATION applies to a fairly permanent combination for the exercise in common of certain governmental functions: *a confederation of Canadian provinces.* UNION implies an alliance so close and permanent that the separate states become essentially one: *the union of England and Scotland to form Great Britain.*

allocate, See Syn. study at ASSIGN.

allot, *v.* **1.** divide, distribute, parcel out, apportion, assign, deal out, dole out, mete out, deal, dispense, measure out. **2.** appropriate, allocate, set apart, appoint. —**Syn. Study.** See ASSIGN.

allow, *v.* **1.** let, permit, grant. **2.**

grant, yield, cede, relinquish, give. **3.** admit, acknowledge, concede, own, confess. **4.** set apart, abate, deduct, remit. **5.** bear, suffer, tolerate, put up with. —**Ant.** forbid, prohibit; refuse. —**Syn. Study.** ALLOW, PERMIT, LET imply granting or conceding the right of someone to do something. ALLOW suggests passivity or even oversight; it points to the absence of an attempt or intent to hinder: *The baby-sitter allowed the children to run around the house.* PERMIT implies a more positive or willing consent; it is often used of a formal authorization: *Bicycle riding is not permitted in this park.* LET is a familiar, conversational term used in a similar sense: *My parents let me stay up late.*

allowance, *n.* **1.** allotment, stipend. **2.** deduction, discount, rebate, remit. **3.** acceptance, admission, concession, acknowledgment. **4.** sanction, tolerance, leave, permission, license, permit, authorization, authority, approval, approbation, imprimatur, sufferance.

ally, *v.* **1.** unite, unify, join, confederate, combine, connect, league, marry, wed. **2.** associate, relate. **3.** join, unite. —*n.* **4.** associate, partner, friend, confederate, aide, accomplice, accessory, assistant, abettor; colleague, coadjutor, auxiliary. —**Ant.** enemy, foe, adversary.

almost, *adv.* nearly, well-nigh, somewhat, toward, towards.

alone, *adj.* apart, lone, lonely, lonesome, single, solitary, desolate, isolated, enisled, unaccompanied, solo. —**Ant.** together, accompanied.

also, *adv.* in addition, too, further, likewise, besides, moreover, furthermore.

alter, *v.* **1.** modify, adjust, change, permute, vary. **2.** castrate, spay. **3.** differ, vary, change. —**Ant.** preserve, keep. —**Syn. Study.** See ADJUST, CHANGE.

alternate, *v.* **1.** reciprocate. **2.** act or follow reciprocally, interchange successively. —*adj.* **3.** reciprocal, successive, in turn, one after another. —*n.* **4.** substitute, stand-in.

alternative, *n.* **1.** choice, option, selection, course, other. —*adj.* **2.** mutually exclusive *(choice between two things).* —**Syn. Study.** See CHOICE.

although, *conj.* though, even though, notwithstanding, even if, albeit.

altitude, *n.* height, elevation. —**Syn. Study.** See HEIGHT.

always, *adv.* **1.** all the time, uninterruptedly, perpetually, everlastingly, eternally, forever, continually, ever, evermore, forevermore, unceasingly. **2.** every time. —**Ant.** never.

amateur, *n.* dilettante, tyro, novice, nonprofessional, neophyte, greenhorn. —**Ant.** professional, expert.

amaze, *v.* astound, dumfound, surprise, astonish, stagger; stupefy, bewilder, confuse, perplex, daze.

ambiguous, *adj.* **1.** equivocal, doubtful, dubious, unclear, uncertain, vague, indistinct, indeterminate, deceptive. **2.** difficult, obscure, unclassifiable, anomalous. **3.** puzzling, enigmatic, problematic. —**Ant.** explicit, clear. —**Syn. Study.** AMBIGUOUS, EQUIVOCAL both refer to words or expressions that are not clear in meaning. AMBIGUOUS describes that which is capable of two or more contradictory interpretations, usu. unintentionally so: *an ambiguous line in a poem; an ambiguous smile.* EQUIVOCAL also means susceptible of contradictory interpretations, but usu. by a deliberate intent to mislead or mystify: *an equivocal response to an embarrassing question.*

ambition, *n.* **1.** aspiration, enterprise, yearning, longing. **2.** energy. —**Ant.** satisfaction.

ambitious, *adj.* **1.** aspiring, enterprising. **2.** eager, desirous, emulous. **3.** showy, pretentious, ostentatious. —**Ant.** apathetic, humble. —**Syn. Study.** AMBITIOUS, ENTERPRISING describe a person who wishes to rise above his or her present position or condition. An AMBITIOUS person strives for worldly success; such efforts may be admired or frowned on by others: *an ambitious college graduate; an ambitious social climber.* An ENTERPRISING person is characterized by energy and daring in undertaking projects: *This company needs an enterprising new manager.*

ambivalent, *adj.* undecided, uncertain, equivocal, contradictory, unresolved, dubious, mutable, fence-sitting, vacillating, irresolute, hesitant.

ameliorate, *v.* improve, better, amend, raise, elevate, promote.

—**Ant.** aggravate. —**Syn. Study.** See IMPROVE.

amend, revise, alter, emend, change. —**Syn. Study.** AMEND, EMEND both mean to alter, improve, or correct something written. AMEND is the general term, used of any such correction or improvement in conduct; it may refer to adding, taking away, or changing a character, word, or phrase: *to amend spelling and punctuation in a report; to amend a contract.* EMEND applies specifically to the critical alteration of a text in the process of editing or preparing it for publication; it implies improvement in the direction of greater accuracy: *The scholar emended the text by restoring the original reading.*

amiable, *adj.* **1.** gracious, agreeable, kind-hearted. **2.** kind, friendly, amicable. —**Ant.** hostile.

amid, *prep.* among, amidst, amongst, surrounded by.

amnesty, See Syn. study at PARDON.

among, *prep.* amid, between, surrounded by.

amorous, *adj.* **1.** loving, amatory, tender. **2.** enamored, in love, fond of, ardent, tender, passionate, impassioned, erotic, filled with desire, lustful, libidinous. —**Ant.** indifferent, cold.

ample, *adj.* **1.** large, spacious, extensive, vast, great, capacious, roomy, broad, wide. **2.** liberal, generous, free, abundant, copious, abounding, unrestricted, rich, lavish, inexhaustible, plenteous, plentiful, overflowing, full, bountiful, exuberant. —**Ant.** insufficient, meager, scanty, sparse. —**Syn. Study.** See PLENTIFUL.

amplify, *v.* **1.** enlarge, extend, greaten, expand, widen, broaden, develop, augment, dilate, magnify. **2.** exaggerate, overstate, blow up. —**Ant.** abridge, abbreviate.

amuse, *v.* entertain, divert, please, charm, cheer, enliven. —**Ant.** bore. —**Syn. Study.** AMUSE, DIVERT, ENTERTAIN mean to occupy the attention with something pleasant. That which AMUSES is usu. playful or humorous and pleases the fancy. DIVERT implies turning the attention from serious thoughts or pursuits to something light, amusing, or lively. That which ENTERTAINS usu. does so because of a plan or program that engages the attention by being pleasing and sometimes instructive.

amusing, *adj.* **1.** entertaining, diverting, pleasing, charming, cheering, lively. **2.** comical, comic, droll, risible, laughable, delightful, mirth-provoking, funny, farcical, ludicrous, ridiculous. —**Ant.** boring, tedious. —**Syn. Study.** AMUSING, COMICAL, DROLL describe that which causes mirth. That which is AMUSING is quietly humorous or funny in a gentle, good-humored way: *The baby's attempts to talk were amusing.* That which is COMICAL causes laughter by being incongruous, witty, or ludicrous: *His huge shoes made the clown look comical.* DROLL adds to COMICAL the idea of strangeness or peculiarity, and sometimes that of sly or waggish humor: *a droll imitation.*

ancestral, *adj.* hereditary, inherited, patrimonial.

ancestry, *n.* **1.** pedigree, descent, stock, genealogy. **2.** family, house, race, line, lineage. —**Ant.** posterity, descendants.

ancient, *adj.* **1.** old, primitive. **2.** old, aged, antique, antiquated, old-fashioned, out-of-date; antediluvian, prehistoric, of yore. —**Ant.** new, modern. —**Syn. Study.** ANCIENT, ANTIQUATED, ANTIQUE refer to something dating from the past. ANCIENT implies existence or first occurrence in the distant past: *an ancient custom.* ANTIQUATED connotes something that is outdated or no longer useful: *antiquated methods; antiquated ideas.* ANTIQUE suggests a curious or pleasing quality in something old: *antique furniture.*

anger, *n.* **1.** displeasure, resentment, exasperation, wrath, ire, fury, indignation, rage, choler, bile, spleen. —*v.* **2.** displease, vex, irritate, arouse, nettle, exasperate, infuriate, enrage, incense, madden. —**Ant.** patience. —**Syn. Study.** ANGER, INDIGNATION, RAGE, FURY describe deep and strong feelings aroused by injury, injustice, etc. ANGER is the general term for sudden violent displeasure accompanied by an impulse to retaliate: *insults that provoked a burst of anger.* INDIGNATION, a more formal word, implies deep and justified anger, often directed at something unworthy: *The scandal aroused public indignation.* RAGE is vehement, uncontrolled anger: *rage at being fired from a job.*

FURY is rage so great that it resembles insanity: *He smashed his fist against the wall in a drunken fury.*

angry, *adj.* indignant, resentful, irate, incensed, enraged, wrathful, wroth, infuriated, furious, mad, passionate, inflamed; provoked, irritated, nettled, galled, chafed, piqued. —**Ant.** patient, calm.

anguish, *n.* **1.** pain, pang, suffering, distress, agony, torment, torture, rack. —*v.* **2.** agonize, distress, torture. —**Ant.** comfort.

angular, *adj.* **1.** with angles or corners. **2.** bony, gaunt, skinny, cadaverous. **3.** awkward, stiff, unbending. —**Ant.** curved; plump; graceful.

animal, *n.* **1.** creature. **2.** beast, brute, monster. —*adj.* **3.** living, sentient. **4.** carnal, fleshly, unspiritual, physical; beastly, brutal. —**Syn. Study.** See CARNAL.

animate, *v.* **1.** vivify, enliven, vitalize, quicken. **2.** invigorate, encourage, inspire, inspirit, hearten, energize, fortify, stimulate, arouse, waken. **3.** refresh, exhilarate, buoy up, excite, fire, heat, urge, provoke, incite, kindle, prompt. —*adj.* **4.** alive, lively, vigorous. —**Ant.** thwart; inanimate, sluggish.

animation, *n.* liveliness, vivacity, spirit, life, vigor, energy; enthusiasm, ardor, exhilaration, cheerfulness, sprightliness, buoyancy, airiness. —**Ant.** sluggishness.

announce, *v.* proclaim, publish, declare, report, set forth, promulgate, publicize. —**Ant.** suppress. —**Syn. Study.** ANNOUNCE, PROCLAIM, PUBLISH mean to communicate something in a formal or public way. TO ANNOUNCE is to give out news, often of something expected in the future: *to announce a lecture series.* TO PROCLAIM is to make a widespread and general announcement of something of public interest: *to proclaim a holiday.* TO PUBLISH is to make public in an official way, now esp. by printing: *to publish a book.*

annoy, *v.* molest, harry, hector, badger, tease, irk, pester, harass, bother, worry, trouble, irritate, chafe, fret, disturb, disquiet. —**Ant.** comfort, soothe. —**Syn. Study.** See BOTHER.

answer, *n.* **1.** reply, response, retort, rejoinder. **2.** solution. **3.** defense, plea. —*v.* **4.** reply, make reply or response, respond, rejoin. **5.** be responsible or liable or accountable. **6.** pass, serve, do, suit; suffice, be sufficient. **7.** conform, correspond, be correlated. **8.** reply to, respond to. **9.** serve, suit, satisfy, fulfill. **10.** discharge (a responsibility, debt, etc.). **11.** conform or correspond to, be similar or equivalent to. **12.** atone for, make amends for. —**Ant.** ask, question; differ. —**Syn. Study.** ANSWER, REPLY, RESPONSE, REJOINDER, RETORT all refer to words used to meet a question, proposal, charge, etc. An ANSWER is something said or written in return: *an answer giving the desired information.* A REPLY is usually somewhat more formal or detailed: *a courteous reply to a letter.* A RESPONSE is often a reaction to an appeal, suggestion, etc.: *an enthusiastic response to a plea for cooperation.* A REJOINDER is a quick, usually clever answer to another person's reply or comment: *a rejoinder that silenced the opposition.* A RETORT is a keen, prompt answer, usually to a charge or criticism: *The false accusation provoked a sharp retort.*

antagonist, *n.* opponent, adversary, rival, competitor, contestant, enemy, foe. —**Ant.** ally, friend. —**Syn. Study.** See ADVERSARY.

anticipate, *v.* **1.** foresee, expect, foretaste, forecast. **2.** expect, await, wait for. **3.** preclude, obviate, prevent. **4.** forestall, antedate. **5.** accelerate, precipitate. —**Ant.** close, terminate; slow.

antipathy, *n.* **1.** repugnance, dislike, aversion, disgust, abhorrence, hatred, detestation, hate, loathing, horror. **2.** contrariety, opposition. —**Ant.** attraction, sympathy, love.

antiquated, See Syn. study at ANCIENT.

antique, *adj.* **1.** ancient, old, archaic, bygone; antediluvian. **2.** early, old. **3.** antiquated, old-fashioned, out-of-date, obsolescent, obsolete, passé, demoded, démodé. —*n.* **4.** object d'art, bibelot, curio, rarity. —**Ant.** modern, new. —**Syn. Study.** See ANCIENT.

antisocial, *adj.* unfriendly, asocial, unsociable, standoffish, aloof, distant, unapproachable, solitary, reclusive, hermitlike, eremitic, eremitical, withdrawn, misanthropic, sociopathic. **—Ant.** social, sociable, friendly, gregarious.

anxiety, *n.* **1.** apprehension, fear, foreboding; worry. distress, uneasiness, disquietude, disquiet; trouble, pain. **2.** solicitous desire, eagerness. **—Ant.** security, certainty.

anxious, *adj.* concerned, worried, apprehensive, uneasy. **—Ant.** secure, certain, sure, confident.

any, See Syn. study at SOME.

apartment, *n.* compartment, suite or set of rooms, flat, tenement.

apathetic, *adj.* unfeeling, passionless, emotionless, indifferent, unconcerned, impassive, stoical, cool, cold, uninterested, phlegmatic, dull, lifeless, flaccid, obtuse, sluggish, torpid, callous, cold-blooded, insensible, soulless. **—Ant.** alert, emotional, sensitive.

ape, *v.* imitate, mimic, counterfeit, copy, affect.

apex, *n.* tip, point, vertex, summit, top, pinnacle, zenith; acme, climax.

apology, *n.* **1.** excuse, plea, explanation, reparation. **2.** defense, justification, vindication. **3.** poor substitute, makeshift.

appall, *v.* frighten, horrify, terrify, dismay; daunt, shock, petrify. **—Ant.** reassure, comfort; activate, innervate.

apparel, *n.* **1.** clothes, dress, garb, attire, raiment, costume, garments, habiliments, vesture, vestments, robes, rig, accouterments, trappings, outfit, equipment. **2.** aspect, guise. **—v. 3.** dress, clothe, garb, attire; equip, rig, outfit, accouter; adorn, ornament, array, deck out.

apparent, *adj.* **1.** plain, clear, open, evident, obvious, conspicuous, patent, unquestionable, unmistakable, manifest. **2.** seeming, ostensible, unreal, specious, quasi, superficial, external. **3.** visible, open, in sight, perceptible, detectable, discernible. **4.** entitled. **—Ant.** concealed, obscure; real. **—Syn. Study.** APPARENT, EVIDENT, OBVIOUS all refer to something easily perceived. APPARENT applies to that which can readily be seen or perceived: *an apparent effort.* EVIDENT applies to that which facts or circumstances make plain: *Your innocence was evident.* OBVIOUS applies to that which is unquestionable, because of being completely manifest or noticeable: *an obvious change of method.*

apparition, *n.* **1.** specter, vision, illusion, phantom, wraith, spirit, sprite, ghost, phantasm, shade, chimera. **2.** appearance, appearing, manifestation, phenomenon.

appeal, *n.* **1.** entreaty, request, petition, prayer, supplication, invocation. **2.** application, suit, solicitation. **3.** attraction. **—v. 4.** entreat, supplicate, petition, ask, request. **5.** resort.

appear, *v.* **1.** become visible, come into sight or view, emerge, crop up, arise, turn up, see the light. **2.** have an appearance, seem, look, show, have the appearance. **3.** be obvious or manifest or clear. **—Ant.** disappear. **—Syn. Study.** See SEEM.

appearance, *n.* **1.** form, being, apparition; arrival, coming, advent. **2.** aspect, mien, guise, air, expression, look; manner, demeanor, presence. **3.** show, seeming, semblance, face, pretense, pretext, colors. **—Syn. Study.** APPEARANCE, ASPECT, GUISE refer to the way in which something outwardly presents itself to view. APPEARANCE refers to the outward look: *the shabby appearance of the car.* ASPECT refers to the appearance at some particular time or in special circumstances; it often has emotional implications, either ascribed to the object itself or felt by the beholder: *In the dusk the forest had a terrifying aspect.* GUISE suggests a misleading appearance, assumed for an occasion or a purpose: *an enemy in friendly guise.*

appease, *v.* **1.** pacify, quiet, soothe, calm, placate, tranquilize, mollify, alleviate, mitigate, temper, allay, assuage, ease, abate, lessen; still, hush, lull; keep down, quell, subdue. **2.** satisfy, fulfill, propitiate. **3.** conciliate, propitiate, win over, make amends, accede to the demands of, make favorable. **—Ant.** aggravate, perturb; dissatisfy. **—Syn. Study.** APPEASE, CONCILIATE, PROPITIATE imply trying to overcome hostility or win favor. To APPEASE is to make anxious overtures and often undue concessions to satisfy someone's demands: *Chamberlain tried to appease Hitler at Munich.* To CONCILIATE is to win over an enemy or opponent by friendly gestures and a willingness to cooperate: *to conciliate an opposing*

faction. To PROPITIATE is to soften the anger of a powerful superior who has been offended: *Offerings were made to propitiate the gods.*

appendix, *n.* appendage, supplement, addendum, adjunct, appurtenance, addition, extra; enhancement, corrigendum, excursus.

appetite, *n.* **1.** hunger, desire, longing, craving, thirst. **2.** demand. **3.** propensity, liking, relish, gusto, zest, zeal. **—Ant.** renunciation, anorexia.

appetizing, See Syn. study at PALATABLE.

applause, *n.* hand-clapping, shouting; approval, acclamation, approbation, acclaim, plaudit, laurel. **—Ant.** disapproval, condemnation.

appliance, *n.* instrument, apparatus, device, tool, appurtenance; adjunct, expedient, means, way, resource. **2.** application, use, practice, exercise.

applicable, *adj.* fit, suitable, suited, relevant, apt, fitting, befitting, proper, apropos, germane, pertinent, pointed. **—Ant.** inept.

application, *n.* **1.** applying, appliance, utilization, use, practice. **2.** usability, utility, relevance, aptness, aptitude, suitability, pertinence. **3.** request, petition, solicitation, appeal. **4.** attention, persistent effort, assiduity, industry, persistence, perseverance. **—Ant.** inattention, laziness. **—Syn. Study.** See EFFORT.

apply, *v.* **1.** lay on, place on or upon. **2.** use, employ, put to use, effect, utilize. **3.** devote, prescribe, dedicate, assign, appropriate, allot. **4.** have a bearing, refer, be pertinent, hold true or good, be appropriate, impinge. **5.** ask, petition, sue, entreat, solicit, appeal. **—Ant.** neglect.

appoint, *v.* **1.** nominate, assign, name, elect, select, set apart, designate, point out, allot, destine. **2.** constitute, ordain, establish, prescribe, direct, require, command, order, decree, impose or insist on. **3.** fix, settle, determine, agree on or upon. **4.** equip, rig, outfit, accouter, furnish, supply; apparel; decorate. **—Ant.** dismiss; strip. **—Syn. Study.** See FURNISH.

appointment, *n.* **1.** appointing, designating, designation, place, installation. **2.** office, post, station, sinecure, position. **3.** engagement, agreement, arrangement, assignation, rendezvous, tryst.

apportion, *v.* divide, allot, distribute, assign, allocate, appoint, partition, measure, mete, dole out, deal, dispense, parcel out.

appreciate, *v.* **1.** esteem, prize, value, estimate or rate highly. **2.** be aware of or conscious of, detect. **3.** raise the value of. **4.** rise or increase in value. **—Ant.** disparage; scorn. **—Syn. Study.** APPRECIATE, ESTEEM, VALUE, PRIZE imply holding a person or thing in high regard. To APPRECIATE is to exercise wise judgment, delicate perception, and keen insight in realizing worth: *to appreciate fine workmanship.* To ESTEEM is to feel respect combined with a warm, kindly sensation: *to esteem one's former teacher.* To VALUE is to attach importance because of worth or usefulness: *I value your opinion.* To PRIZE is to value highly and cherish: *to prize a collection of rare books.*

apprehension, *n.* **1.** anticipation, anxiety, misgiving, dread, fear, alarm; worry, uneasiness, suspicion, distrust, mistrust. **2.** understanding, intelligence, reason. **3.** view, opinion, idea, belief, sentiment. **4.** arrest, seizure, capture. **—Ant.** confidence, composure; release.

apprise, *v.* inform, tell, advise, give notice to, acquaint, notify, disclose to.

appropriate, *adj.* **1.** fitting, suitable, suited, apt, befitting, meet, felicitous, proper, opportune, apropos, seemly, due, becoming, germane, pertinent, to the point. **2.** proper, individual, unique, sui generis. **—v. 3.** set apart, direct, assign, apportion, allocate; adopt, take as one's own. **—Ant.** inappropriate, inept.

approve, *v.* **1.** commend, praise, recommend, appreciate, value, esteem, prize. **2.** sanction, authorize, confirm, endorse, ratify, validate, uphold, support, sustain. **—Ant.** disapprove.

apt, *adj.* **1.** inclined, disposed, prone, liable. **2.** likely. **3.** clever, bright, intelligent, brilliant, ingenious; adroit, handy, dexterous, skillful, expert. **4.** appropriate, suited, pertinent, relevant, fit, fitting, apt, befitting, meet, germane, applicable, apropos, felicitous. **—Ant.** inapt, indisposed, malapropos. **—Syn. Study.** APT, RELE-

VANT, PERTINENT all refer to something suitable or fitting. APT means to the point and particularly appropriate: *an apt comment.* RELEVANT means pertaining to the matter in hand: *a relevant question.* PERTINENT means directly related to and important to the subject: *pertinent information.*

aptitude, *n.* **1.** tendency, propensity, predilection, proclivity, inclination, bent, gift, genius, talent, knack, faculty. **2.** readiness, intelligence, cleverness, talent; understanding, ability, aptness. **3.** fitness, suitability, applicability.

arbitrary, *adj.* **1.** discretionary. **2.** capricious, uncertain, unreasonable, willful, fanciful, whimsical. **3.** uncontrolled, unlimited, unrestrained; absolute, despotic, dictatorial, totalitarian, tyrannical, imperious, overbearing, peremptory, domineering; Fascistic, undemocratic. **—Ant.** relative.

archaic, *adj.* old, ancient, antiquated, antique, old-fashioned, out-of-date. **—Ant.** modern, up-to-date.

archetype, *n.* model, form, pattern, prototype, example, type, paragon, ideal.

ardent, *adj.* **1.** passionate, glowing, fervent, fervid, intense, eager, sanguine, enthusiastic, zealous; vehement, forceful, impassioned, strenuous. **2.** glowing, flashing, flushed. **3.** hot, burning, fiery. **—Ant.** cool, apathetic.

ardor, *n.* **1.** warmth, fervor, fervency, eagerness, zeal, passion, enthusiasm. **2.** fire, burning, heat, warmth, glow. **—Ant.** indifference.

arduous, *adj.* **1.** laborious, hard, difficult, toilsome, onerous, burdensome, wearisome, exhausting, herculean. **2.** energetic, strenuous, fatiguing. **3.** steep, high, acclivitous. **4.** severe, unendurable. **—Ant.** easy.

argue, *v.* **1.** debate, discuss, reason, plead, hold. **2.** contend, dispute. **3.** reason upon, contest, controvert, debate, discuss, dispute. **4.** maintain, support, contend. **5.** persuade, drive, convince. **6.** show, indicate, prove, imply, infer, betoken, evince, denote. **—Ant.** agree.

argument, *n.* **1.** controversy, dispute, debate, discussion. **2.** reasoning, reason, proof, ground, evidence. **3.** fact, statement; theme, thesis, topic, subject, matter. **4.** summary, abstract, epitome, outline, précis. **—Ant.** agreement. **—Syn. Study.** ARGUMENT, CONTROVERSY, DISPUTE imply the expression and discussion of differing opinions. An ARGUMENT usu. arises from a disagreement between two persons, each of whom advances facts supporting his or her point of view: *an argument over a debt.* A CONTROVERSY is usu. a public expression of contrary opinions; it may be dignified and of some duration: *a political controversy.* A DISPUTE is an oral contention, usu. brief, and often of an angry or undignified character: *a heated dispute between neighbors.*

arid, *adj.* **1.** dry, moistureless, desert, parched; barren, infertile. **2.** dull, lifeless, uninteresting, dry, empty, jejune. **—Ant.** wet, damp. **—Syn. Study.** See DRY.

aroma, *n.* **1.** perfume, odor, scent, fragrance, bouquet, redolence. **2.** subtle quality, spirit, essence, characteristic, air; suggestion, hint. **—Ant.** stench. **—Syn. Study.** See PERFUME.

arouse, *v.* **1.** animate, stir, rouse, awaken; inspirit, inspire, excite, incite, provoke, instigate, stimulate, warm, kindle, fire. **2.** awaken, get up, arise. **—Ant.** alleviate, calm, mitigate.

arrange, *v.* **1.** order, place, adjust, array, group, sort, dispose, classify, class, rank, distribute. **2.** settle, determine, establish, adjust. **3.** prepare, plan, contrive, devise, concoct, organize. **4.** *(music)* adapt, adjust. **5.** settle, agree, come to terms. **6.** prepare, adjust, adapt, make preparations or plans. **—Ant.** disarrange, disorder, disturb.

array, *v.* **1.** arrange, order, range, marshal, rank, place, dispose, draw up. **2.** clothe, apparel, dress, attire, equip, accouter, rig, outfit; deck, bedeck, ornament, trim, decorate, garnish, adorn. **—n. 3.** order, arrangement, disposition; allotment. **4.** display, show, exhibit, exhibition, showing, demonstration. **5.** attire, dress, clothes, raiment, apparel, garments; panoply. **—Ant.** disarray.

arrest, *v.* **1.** seize, apprehend, capture, catch, take, trap, take into custody, take prisoner. **2.** catch, fix, secure, rivet, engage, capture, occupy, attract. **3.** stop, check, bring to a standstill, stay, hinder, deter, ob-

struct, delay, interrupt, restrain, hold, withhold. **—n. 4.** detention, custody, imprisonment, apprehension, capture. **5.** seizure, capture, rape. **6.** stoppage, halt, stay, staying, check, hindrance, obstruction, deterrent, detention, restraint, delay, interruption. **—Ant.** release; activate, animate; continue. **—Syn. Study.** See STOP.

arrival, *n.* **1.** advent, coming. **2.** reaching, attainment. **3.** arriver, comer. **—Ant.** departure.

arrive, *v.* come, reach a point, attain, attain a position of success. **—Ant.** depart; fail.

arrogance, *n.* haughtiness, pride, insolence, disdain, effrontery, superciliousness, scorn, contumely, self-confidence, self-importance, conceit, egotism, hauteur. **—Ant.** humility.

arrogant, *adj.* presumptuous, haughty, imperious, supercilious, assuming, proud, insolent, scornful, contumelious, overbearing, overweening, conceited, egotistic, egotistical. **—Ant.** humble, self-effacing.

art, *n.* **1.** trade, craft; skill, adroitness, dexterity, aptitude, ingenuity, knack, cleverness. **2.** cunning, craft, guile, deceit, duplicity, wiliness, dishonesty, artfulness.

articulate, *adj.* fluent, expressive, eloquent. **—Syn. Study.** See ELOQUENT.

artifice, *n.* **1.** ruse, device, subterfuge, wile, machination, expedient, trick, stratagem. **2.** craft, trickery, guile, deception, deceit, art, cunning, artfulness, fraud, duplicity, double-dealing. **3.** skillful, apt or artful contrivance. **—Syn. Study.** See TRICK.

artificial, *adj.* **1.** unreal, inauthentic, fabricated, manmade, fashioned, mock, false, fake, imitation, spurious, ersatz, pretend, counterfeit, simulated, sham, bogus. **2.** affected, put-on, insincere, pretentious, assumed, feigned, deceitful, disingenuous. **—Ant.** real, genuine, authentic.

artisan, See Syn. study at ARTIST.

artist, *n.* **1.** artisan, painter, sculptor, sketcher. **2.** actor, actress, thespian, singer, artiste. **3.** designer, artificer, workman. **4.** trickster, designer, contriver. **—Syn. Study.** ARTIST, ARTISAN both refer to a person having superior skill or ability, or one capable of superior workmanship or performance. An ARTIST is a creative person who is skilled in one of the fine or performing arts: *The concert featured a famous pianist and other noted artists.* An ARTISAN is one who is skilled in a craft or applied art that requires manual dexterity: *carpentry done by skilled artisans.*

artless, *adj.* ingenuous, naive, unsophisticated, natural, simple, guileless, open, frank, plain, unaffected, candid, honest, sincere, true, truthful, trusting, trustful, unsuspicious, unsuspecting; unskillful, rude, crude. **—Ant.** cunning, sly, crafty.

ascend, *v.* **1.** mount, rise, climb or go upward, soar, climb, arise. **2.** tower. **3.** climb, mount, scale, go or get up. **—Ant.** descend; fall.

ascertain, *v.* determine, establish, define, pinpoint, fix, certify, settle, verify; learn, find out, discover, uncover, get at. **—Ant.** guess, assume. **—Syn. Study.** See LEARN.

ascribe, *v.* attribute, impute, refer, assign, charge. **—Syn. Study.** See ATTRIBUTE.

ashamed, *adj.* **1.** abashed, humiliated, mortified, shamefaced, embarrassed, confused. **2.** unwilling, restrained. **—Ant.** vain, arrogant; willing.

ask, *v.* **1.** put a question to, interrogate, question, inquire of. **2.** inquire, seek information. **3.** request, solicit, petition, sue, appeal, seek, beseech, implore, beg, supplicate, entreat. **4.** demand, expect, require, exact, call for. **5.** invite, call in. **6.** make inquiry, inquire, question. **7.** request, petition, sue, appeal, pray, beg. **—Ant.** answer; refuse, decline.

askance, *adv.* **1.** sideways, sidewise, obliquely, crookedly, at an angle. **2.** suspiciously, dubiously, doubtfully, skeptically, mistrustfully, critically.

aspect, *n.* **1.** appearance, look, attitude, situation, condition. **2.** countenance, expression, mien, visage; air. **3.** view, viewpoint, point of view, attitude, outlook, prospect, direction, bearing. **—Syn. Study.** See APPEARANCE.

aspire, *v.* desire, long, yearn.

assail, *v.* assault, set or fall upon, attack; abuse, impugn, maltreat, asperse, malign. **—Syn. Study.** See ATTACK.

assassinate, *v.* murder, kill, blight, destroy, slay, dispatch.

assault, *n.* **1.** assailing, attack, onslaught, onset, combat, invasion, aggression; threat. **—v. 2.** attack, assail, storm, charge, invade; threaten. **—Syn. Study.** See ATTACK.

assemble, *v.* **1.** bring together, gather, congregate, collect, convene, convoke, summon, call, call together. **2.** put together, manufacture, connect, set up. **3.** meet, convene, congregate, gather, gather together, come together. **—Ant.** disperse. **—Syn. Study.** See GATHER.

assembly, *n.* **1.** company, assemblage, throng, mob, gathering, convention, congress, convocation, meeting, meet. **2.** congress, legislature, parliament, lower house, conclave, synod, council, diet. **—Syn. Study.** See CONVENTION.

assent, *v.* **1.** acquiesce, accede, concur, agree, fall in, consent, admit, yield, allow. **—n. 2.** agreement, concurrence, acquiescence, consent, allowance, approval, concord, accord, approbation. **—Ant.** refuse, deny, dissent.

assert, *v.* **1.** declare, asseverate, affirm, maintain, aver, say, pronounce, allege, avow. **2.** maintain, defend, uphold, support, vindicate, claim, emphasize. **3.** press, make felt, emphasize. **—Ant.** controvert, contradict, deny. **—Syn. Study.** See DECLARE.

assertion, *n.* allegation, statement, asseveration, avowal, declaration, claim, affirmation, predication, vindication, defense, maintenance, emphasis, support. **—Ant.** denial, contradiction.

assiduous, *adj.* constant, unremitting, continuous, applied, industrious, untiring, tireless, persistent, persisting, devoted, zealous, studious, attentive, diligent, solicitous, sedulous. **—Ant.** random, casual, lazy.

assign, *v.* **1.** distribute, allot, apportion, allocate, measure, appropriate. **2.** appoint, designate, specify; fix, determine, pinpoint. **3.** ascribe, attribute, refer, adduce, allege, advance, show, offer, bring up or forward. **—Syn. Study.** ASSIGN, ALLOCATE, ALLOT mean to apportion or measure out. To ASSIGN is to distribute available things, designating them to be given to or reserved for specific persons or purposes: *to assign duties.* To ALLOCATE is to earmark or set aside parts of things available or expected in the future, each for a specific purpose: *to allocate income to various types of expenses.* To ALLOT implies making restrictions as to amount, size, purpose, etc., and then apportioning or assigning: *to allot spaces for parking.*

assignment, See Syn. study at TASK.

assist, *v.* help, support, aid, sustain, patronize, befriend, further, second, abet, back, speed, promote, serve, succor, relieve, spell. **—Ant.** impede, obstruct, hinder. **—Syn. Study.** See HELP.

associate, *v.* **1.** connect, link. **2.** join, affiliate, team up with. **3.** unite, combine, couple. **4.** unite, combine. **5.** fraternize, consort, keep company. **—n. 6.** acquaintance, consort, comrade, fellow, companion, friend, mate, peer, compeer, equal. **7.** confederate, accomplice, ally, partner, colleague, fellow. **—Ant.** dissociate, alienate; adversary, opponent. **—Syn. Study.** See ACQUAINTANCE.

association, *n.* **1.** organization, alliance, union, guild, society, club, fraternity, sorority, lodge; company, corporation, firm, partnership; set, coterie, clique, band. **2.** companionship, intimacy, fellowship, friendship. **3.** connection, combination.

assume, *v.* **1.** suppose, presuppose, take for granted, infer. **2.** undertake, take on, take upon oneself. **3.** pretend, feign, affect, simulate, counterfeit, put on. **4.** appropriate, arrogate, usurp. **—Syn. Study.** See PRETEND.

assumption, *n.* **1.** supposition, presupposition, assuming, presumption, taking for granted; hypothesis, conjecture, guess, postulate, theory. **2.** arrogance, presumption, effrontery, forwardness, insolence, hauteur, haughtiness, superciliousness, lordliness, stateliness, pride, conceit.

assurance, *n.* **1.** declaration, avowal, asseveration, averment, deposition. **2.** pledge, warranty, surety, guaranty, oath. **3.** confidence, firmness, trust, certainty. **4.** courage, bravery, self-reliance, self-confidence, intrepidity, sang-froid. **5.** boldness, impudence, presumption, arrogance, effrontery, rudeness, impertinence, nerve, cheek. **—Ant.** denial; distrust, uncertainty; cowardice, diffidence. —**Syn. Study.** See CONFIDENCE.

astonish, v. amaze, strike with wonder, surprise, astound, shock, startle; daze, stun, stupefy, confound, stagger, overwhelm.

astringent, adj. **1.** (medical) contracting, constrictive, styptic, binding. **2.** stern, severe, austere, sharp, harsh, rigorous, hard, unrelenting.

astute, adj. keen, shrewd, cunning, artful, crafty, sly, wily, penetrating, eagle-eyed, sharp, quick, perspicacious, ingenious, intelligent, sagacious, discerning. —**Ant.** ingenuous, naive, candid, unsophisticated, dull.

asylum, n. **1.** hospital, institute, retreat, sanitarium. **2.** refuge, haven, preserve, reserve, sanctuary, shelter, retreat.

atheist, n. agnostic, disbeliever, nonbeliever, infidel, skeptic, doubter, heathen, pagan, gentile. —**Ant.** theist. —**Syn. Study.** ATHEIST, AGNOSTIC, INFIDEL refer to persons not inclined toward religious belief or a particular religious faith. An ATHEIST denies the existence of a deity or of divine beings. An AGNOSTIC believes it is impossible to know whether there is a God without sufficient evidence. An INFIDEL is an unbeliever, esp. one who does not accept Christianity or Islam; the word is usu. applied pejoratively.

atom, n. iota, jot, dot, whit, tittle, scintilla, mote; indivisible particle.

atrocious, adj. **1.** wicked, cruel, heinous, flagitious, monstrous, felonious, flagrant, grievous, outrageous, diabolical, devilish, infernal, hellish. **2.** bad, tasteless, execrable, detestable, abominable. —**Ant.** kind, benevolent; good, praiseworthy.

attach, v. **1.** fasten to, affix, join, cement, connect, subjoin, append, add, tack on, annex. **2.** go with, accompany. **3.** associate, attribute, assign. **4.** attract, charm, endear, enamour, captivate, engage, bind. **5.** adhere, pertain, belong, obtain. —**Ant.** detach, separate; repel.

attachment, n. **1.** affection, friendship, regard, admiration, fondness, liking, love, devotion; assiduity, bent, predilection. **2.** tie, fastening, junction, connection. **3.** device, apparatus, adjunct. —**Ant.** detachment, separation. —**Syn. Study.** See ADDITION.

attack, v. **1.** assail, assault, molest, threaten, interfere with, storm, charge, oppugn, engage in battle, set upon. **2.** criticize, impugn, censure, blame, abuse. **3.** affect. **4.** begin hostilities. —n. **5.** onslaught, assault, offense, onset, encounter, aggression. —**Ant.** defend; defense. —**Syn. Study.** ATTACK, ASSAIL, ASSAULT all mean to set upon someone forcibly, with hostile or violent intent. ATTACK is a general word that applies to the beginning of any planned aggressive action, physical or verbal: to attack an enemy from ambush; to attack a candidate's record. ASSAIL implies a vehement, sudden, and usu. repeated attack that aims to weaken an opponent: assailed by gunfire; assailed by gossip. ASSAULT implies a violent physical attack involving direct contact; it may also refer to a sudden and violent verbal attack: an elderly couple assaulted by a mugger; a reputation assaulted by the press.

attain, v. **1.** reach, achieve, accomplish, effect, secure, gain, procure, acquire, get, obtain, win. **2.** arrive at, reach. —**Ant.** fail. —**Syn. Study.** See GAIN.

attempt, v. **1.** try, undertake, seek, make an effort, essay. **2.** attack, assault, assail. **3.** trial, essay, effort, endeavor, enterprise, undertaking. **4.** attack, assault. —**Ant.** accomplish, attain. —**Syn. Study.** See TRY.

attend, v. **1.** be present at, frequent. **2.** accompany, go with, escort. **3.** minister to, serve, wait on. **4.** tend, take charge of. **5.** heed, listen to, pay attention to, respect. **6.** be present. **7.** pay attention, pay respect, give heed, listen. **8.** apply oneself. **9.** take care or charge. **10.** depend, rely. **11.** wait on, serve, minister. —**Syn. Study.** See ACCOMPANY.

attendant, n. **1.** escort, companion, comrade, follower; servant, waiter, valet, footman, lackey, flunky, menial, slave. **2.** attender, frequenter. **3.** concomitant, accompaniment, consequence. —adj. **4.** present, in attendance, accompanying, concomitant, consequent.

attention, n. **1.** attending. **2.** care, consideration, observation, heed, regard, mindfulness, notice, watchfulness, alertness. **3.** civility, courtesy,

homage, deference, respect, politeness, regard. **4.** (plural) regard, court, courtship, suit, devotion, wooing. —**Ant.** inattention.

attentive, adj. **1.** observant, regardful, mindful, heedful, thoughtful, alive, alert, awake, on the qui vive; wary, circumspect, watchful, careful. **2.** polite, courteous, respectful, deferential, assiduous. —**Ant.** inattentive, unwary; discourteous.

attitude, n. **1.** position, disposition, manner, bearing, mien, pose. **2.** position, posture. —**Syn. Study.** See POSITION.

attract, v. **1.** draw, cause to approach, magnetize. **2.** draw, invite, allure, win, engage, captivate, endear, enamor, charm. —**Ant.** repel, repulse.

attribute, v. **1.** ascribe, impute. —n. **2.** quality, character, characteristic, property, mark; peculiarity, quirk. —**Syn. Study.** ATTRIBUTE, ASCRIBE, IMPUTE mean to assign something to a definite cause or source. Possibly because of an association with tribute, ATTRIBUTE often has a complimentary connotation: to attribute one's success to a friend's encouragement. ASCRIBE is used in a similar sense, but has a neutral implication: to ascribe an accident to carelessness. IMPUTE usu. means to attribute something dishonest or discreditable to a person; it implies blame or accusation: to impute an error to a new employee. See also QUALITY.

audacious, adj. **1.** bold, daring, spirited, adventurous, fearless, intrepid, brave, courageous, dauntless, venturesome, undaunted, valiant. **2.** reckless, bold, impudent, presumptuous, assuming, unabashed, unashamed, shameless, flagrant, insolent, impertinent, brazen, forward. —**Ant.** cowardly, contumelious, feckless.

augment, v. **1.** enlarge, extend, increase, swell, bloat. **2.** increase. —**Ant.** reduce, abate.

aura, n. atmosphere, mood, feeling, feel, air, ambiance, climate, character, quality, spirit, overtone, sense, undertone.

austere, adj. **1.** harsh, hard, stern, strict, forbidding, severe, formal, stiff, inflexible, rigorous, uncompromising, relentless, stringent, restrictive. **2.** grave, sober, serious. **3.** simple, severe, without ornament, plain. **4.** rough, harsh, sour, astringent, acerb, bitter. —**Ant.** soothing, flexible; kind; sweet.

austerity, n. severity, harshness, strictness, asceticism, rigor, rigidity, rigorousness, stiffness, inflexibility. —**Ant.** lenience, flexibility.

authentic, adj. **1.** reliable, trustworthy, veritable, true, accurate, authoritative. **2.** genuine, real, true, unadulterated, pure, uncorrupted. —**Ant.** unreliable, inaccurate; sham, fraudulent, corrupt.

authoritative, adj. **1.** official, conclusive, unquestioned, authentic. **2.** impressive, positive; peremptory, dogmatic, authoritarian, dictatorial, imperious, arrogant, autocratic. —**Ant.** unofficial; servile.

authority, n. **1.** control, influence, command, rule, sway, power, supremacy. **2.** expert, adjudicator, arbiter, judge, sovereign. **3.** statute, law, rule, ruling. **4.** warrant, justification, permit, permission, sanction, liberty, authorization. **5.** testimony, witness. —**Syn. Study.** AUTHORITY, CONTROL, INFLUENCE denote a power or right to direct the actions or thoughts of others. AUTHORITY is a power or right, usu. because of rank or office, to issue commands and to punish for violations: to have authority over subordinates. CONTROL is either power or influence applied to the complete and successful direction or manipulation of persons or things: to be in control of a project. INFLUENCE is a personal and unofficial power derived from deference of others to one's character, ability, or station; it may be exerted unconsciously or may operate through persuasion: to have influence over one's friends.

authorize, v. **1.** empower, commission, allow, permit, let. **2.** sanction, approve. **3.** establish, entrench. **4.** warrant, justify, legalize, support, back. —**Ant.** forbid, prohibit.

automatic, adj. **1.** self-moving, self-acting, mechanical. **2.** involuntary, uncontrollable. —**Ant.** manual; deliberate, intentional.

auxiliary, adj. **1.** supporting, helping, helpful, aiding, assisting, abetting. **2.** subsidiary, subordinate, secondary, ancillary, additional. —n. **3.** helper, aide, ally, assistant, confederate. —**Ant.** chief, main.

available, adj. **1.** accessible, ready, at hand, handy, usable, of use or service, serviceable; suitable, fit, appropriate, fitting, befitting. **2.** valid, efficacious, profitable, advantageous. —**Ant.** unavailable; unbecoming; invalid, unprofitable.

avaricious, adj. greedy, covetous, grasping, acquisitive, appetent, predatory, mercenary, rapacious, grabby. —**Syn. Study.** AVARICIOUS, COVETOUS, GREEDY suggest a desire to possess more of something than one needs or is entitled to. AVARICIOUS often implies a pathological, driven greediness for money or other valuables and usually suggests a concomitant miserliness: an avaricious usurer. COVETOUS implies a powerful and often illicit desire for the property or possessions of another: The book collector was covetous of my first edition. GREEDY, the most general of these terms, suggests an uncontrolled desire for almost anything: greedy for knowledge; greedy for power.

avenge, v. revenge, vindicate, take vengeance, exact satisfaction for. —**Ant.** forgive, pardon.

average, n. **1.** mean, mean proportion, median. **2.** mediocrity. —adj. **3.** mean, medial, normal, intermediate, middle; mediocre, middling, ordinary, passable, tolerable, satisfactory. —v. **4.** reduce to a mean, equate; proportion. **5.** show or produce a mean.

averse, adj. disinclined, reluctant, unwilling, loath, opposed. —**Ant.** inclined, disposed. —**Syn. Study.** See RELUCTANT.

aversion, n. repugnance, disgust, antipathy, loathing, detestation, hate, hatred, abhorrence; dislike, distaste, objection, disinclination, unwillingness, reluctance. —**Ant.** predilection, liking; favor.

avoid, v. keep away from or clear of, shun, evade, escape, elude, fight shy of, eschew. —**Ant.** confront, face.

await, v. wait for, look for, expect. **2.** attend, be in store for, be ready for. **3.** wait.

aware, adj. cognizant or conscious (of), informed, mindful, apprised. —**Ant.** unaware, oblivious. —**Syn. Study.** See CONSCIOUS.

awe, n. **1.** reverence, respect, veneration; dread, fear, terror. —v. **2.** solemnize; daunt, cow, frighten, intimidate. —**Ant.** contempt; irreverence; scorn.

awkward, adj. **1.** clumsy, bungling, unskillful, inexpert, gauche, inept, maladroit. **2.** ungraceful, ungainly, unwieldy, unmanageable, coarse, rude, crude, wooden, stiff, constrained, gawky, unrefined, unpolished, rough. **3.** hazardous, dangerous. **4.** trying, embarrassing. —**Ant.** deft, adroit, adept; graceful, refined, polished.

B

babble, v. **1.** gibber, blabber, gabble, jabber, bibble-babble, blather, prate, prattle. **2.** talk, chat, gossip, chatter, natter, palaver, gab, jaw, schmooze. —n. **3.** nonsense, gibberish, twaddle, prattle, mumbo jumbo, drivel, blather.

back, n. **1.** rear, posterior, end. —v. **2.** support, sustain, second, aid, abet, favor, assist; countenance, allow, side with, endorse, stand by. **3.** reverse, move or push backward. **4.** retire, retreat, withdraw, go backward. —adj. **5.** hind, posterior, rear; remote, frontier, unpopulated. —**Ant.** front, fore, face. —**Syn. Study.** BACK, HIND, POSTERIOR, REAR refer to something situated behind something else. BACK means the opposite of front: a back window. HIND, and the more formal word POSTERIOR, refer to the rearmost of two or more, often similar objects: hind wings; posterior lobe. REAR is used of buildings, conveyances, etc., and in military language it is the opposite of fore: the rear end of a truck; rear echelon.

backward, adv. **1.** rearward, back foremost, retrogressively, behind. —adj. **2.** reversed, returning. **3.** behind, late, slow, tardy, behindhand. **4.** reluctant, hesitant, bashful, wavering, disinclined, timid, retired. **5.** slow, retarded, undeveloped, underdeveloped, ignorant. —**Ant.** forward; precocious.

backwater, n. back country, hinterland, outback, back woods, bush, up-country, sticks, boondocks, boonies, middle of nowhere.

bad, adj. **1.** evil, wicked, ill, corrupt, base, depraved, unprincipled, im-

moral, disingenuous, rascally, mischievous, sinful, criminal, dishonest, villainous, baneful; deleterious, pernicious, harmful, hurtful, injurious, detrimental. **2.** defective, worthless, poor, inferior, imperfect; incompetent, ill-qualified, inadequate. **3.** incorrect, faulty. **4.** invalid, unsound. **5.** sick, ill. **6.** regretful, sorry, contrite, wretched, upset. **7.** unfavorable, unfortunate, adverse, unlucky, unhappy. **8.** offensive, disagreeable, painful, mean, abominable. **9.** vile, wretched, shabby, scurvy. **10.** severe, serious. **11.** rotten, decayed. —**Ant.** good.

bag, n. **1.** pouch, receptacle, sack, reticule, wallet. **2.** handbag, purse, moneybag. —v. **3.** catch, net, trap, entrap, kill.

bailiwick, n. domain, field, sphere, purview, territory, province, department, jurisdiction, realm, terrain, precinct.

balance, n. **1.** scales. **2.** equilibrium, equilibration, symmetry, equipoise, equality. **3.** poise, composure, self-control, equilibrium, equipoise, self-possession. **4.** counterpoise, equalizer, stabilizer. —v. **5.** weigh, compare, equilibrate, estimate, assay. **6.** counterpoise, counterbalance, offset, counteract, neutralize, countervail, compensate, allow for, make up for. **7.** proportion, equalize, square, adjust. —**Syn. Study.** See SYMMETRY.

ball, n. **1.** sphere, globe, orb. **2.** bullet, shot, missile, projectile. **3.** dance, assembly, dancing-party.

ban, v. **1.** prohibit, interdict, outlaw, forbid, proscribe, taboo. —n. **2.** prohibition, interdiction, interdict, taboo, proscription. **3.** anathema, curse, malediction, excommunication, denunciation. —**Ant.** permit, allow; permission, blessing.

band, n. **1.** company, party, troop, crew, gang, group; body; clique, coterie, set, society, association, sodality, horde, host, assembly. **2.** strip, fillet, belt, tag, strap, cincture, girdle; (heraldry) bend. **3.** cord, fetter, shackle, manacle, bond, chain. —v. **4.** unite, confederate. **5.** stripe; mark, tag, identify.

banish, v. **1.** exile, expel, expatriate, deport, ostracize, outlaw. **2.** send or drive or put away, exclude, expel, dismiss, dispel. —**Ant.** admit, receive.

bank, n. **1.** pile, heap, embankment, mount, knoll, hillock, hill, tumulus, dike. **2.** slope, shore, acclivity, shoal, ridge. **3.** row, ridge, tier, course. —v. **4.** embank, border, bound, rim, edge, dike.

bankrupt, v. **1.** impoverish, pauperize, ruin, deplete, exhaust, drain dry, bleed. —adj. **2.** impoverished, pauperized, insolvent, indigent, impecunious, destitute, broke, stone-broke, flat broke, in receivership. **3.** ruined, worn out, jejune, exhausted, spent, broken, wasted.

banter, n. **1.** badinage, joking, jesting, pleasantry, persiflage; mockery, ridicule, derision. —v. **2.** tease, twit, make fun of; ridicule, deride, mock, jeer, chaff.

bar, n. **1.** rod, pole. **2.** obstruction, hindrance, deterrent, stop, impediment, obstacle, barrier, barricade. **3.** ridge, shoal, reef, sand-bunk, bank, sand-bar, shallow. **4.** counter; saloon, pub, café, bistro, nightclub, cocktail lounge. **5.** lawyers, the legal fraternity; tribunal, judgment-seat, court. **6.** stripe, band. —v. **7.** hinder, obstruct, deter, stop, impede, barricade, prevent, prohibit, restrain. **8.** exclude, shut out, eliminate, block, except. —**Ant.** suffer, allow, permit.

barbarian, n. **1.** savage, philistine, alien, brute, boor, ruffian. —adj. **2.** rude, uncivilized, savage, primitive, barbaric, barbarous, rough, crude, coarse, untutored, ignorant, uncultivated, unlettered. **3.** cruel, ferocious, wild, feral, inhuman, brutal, harsh, harsh-sounding, raucous. —**Ant.** cosmopolite; refined, civilized, cultivated; kind.

bare, adj. **1.** naked, nude, uncovered, unclothed, undressed, exposed, unprotected, unsheltered, unshielded, open. **2.** unfurnished, undecorated, plain, stark, mean, poor, destitute, meager, unadorned, bald, empty. **3.** simple, sheer, mere, alone, sole, just. **4.** unconcealed, undisguised, unreserved, conspicuous, obvious, glaring, evident, palpable. **5.** disclose, denude, lay open, expose. —**Ant.** covered, dressed.

barely, See Syn. study at HARDLY.

bargain, n. **1.** compact, agreement, stipulation, arrangement, contract,

convention, concord, concordat, treaty, stipulation, transaction. **2.** good purchase, buy. —v. **3.** contract, agree, stipulate, covenant, transact. **4.** trade, sell, transfer. —**Syn. Study.** See AGREEMENT.

barren, adj. **1.** sterile, unprolific, childless, infecund, unfruitful, infertile, unproductive, poor, bare. **2.** uninteresting, dull, stupid; uninstructive, unsuggestive, ineffectual, ineffective. —**Ant.** fertile; interesting, effectual.

barricade, n. **1.** barrier, obstruction, bar. —v. **2.** obstruct, block, bar, shut in, stop up, fortify.

barrier, n. **1.** bar, obstruction, hindrance, barricade, stop, impediment, obstacle, restraint; fence, railing, stockade, palisade, wall; limit, boundary.

barter, v. trade, exchange, traffic, bargain; sell.

base, n. **1.** bottom, stand, rest, pedestal, understructure, substructure, foot, basis, foundation, ground, groundwork; principle. **2.** fundamental part, ingredient, element. **3.** station, goal, starting-point, point of departure. —adj. **4.** (morally) low, despicable, contemptible, mean-spirited, mean, degraded, degrading, selfish, cowardly. **5.** servile, lowly, slavish, menial, beggarly, abject, sordid, ignoble. **6.** poor, inferior, cheap, tawdry, worthless, debased, counterfeit, fake, spurious, shabby, coarse. **7.** unrefined, plebeian, vulgar, lowly, humble, unknown, baseborn; impure, corrupted, corrupt, vile, venal. **8.** scandalous, shameful, disreputable, disgraceful, discreditable, dishonorable, infamous, notorious. —v. **9.** found, rest, establish, ground. —**Ant.** top; peak; moral, virtuous; good, valuable; refined, pure; honorable. —**Syn. Study.** BASE, BASIS, FOUNDATION refer to anything upon which a structure is built and upon which it rests. BASE usu. refers to a physical supporting structure: the base of a statue. BASIS more often refers to a figurative support: the basis of a report. FOUNDATION implies a solid, secure understructure: the foundation of a skyscraper; the foundation of a theory.

bashful, adj. diffident, shy, abashed, timid, timorous, coy, sheepish, modest, self-effacing, embarrassed, shamefaced, ashamed. —**Ant.** arrogant, immodest.

basics, n. fundamentals, essentials, rudiments, principles, grammar, rules, guidelines, ABC's.

basis, n. bottom, base, foundation. —**Syn. Study.** See BASE.

batter, v. beat, pound, belabor, smite, pelt; bruise, wound; break, shatter, shiver, smash, destroy, demolish, ruin.

battle, n. **1.** action, skirmish, campaign, contest, conflict, engagement, military engagement or encounter. **2.** warfare, combat, war, fight. —v. **3.** strive, struggle, fight, combat, war, contest, conflict.

beach, n. **1.** coast, seashore, littoral, shore, strand, sands, margin, rim. —v. **2.** run ashore, strand, put aground.

beam, n. **1.** girder. **2.** ray, pencil, streak, gleam, suggestion, hint, glimmer. —v. **3.** shine, gleam, glisten, glitter, radiate. **4.** smile, grin.

bear, v. **1.** support, hold up, uphold, sustain. **2.** carry, transport, convey, waft; conduct, guide, take. **3.** thrust, drive, force, push, press. **4.** render, give, yield, afford, produce. **5.** transmit, utter, spread, broadcast, advertise, exhibit, show, demonstrate. **6.** sustain, endure, suffer, undergo, tolerate, brook, abide, put up with, stand, stand for, submit to; allow, admit, permit, admit of, hold up under, be capable of. **7.** maintain, keep up, carry on. **8.** entertain, harbor, cherish. **9.** give birth to, bring forth. **10.** confirm, prove. **11.** hold, remain firm. **12.** be patient. **13.** tend, relate, be pertinent, concern, affect, refer. **14.** act, operate, take effect, work, succeed. —**Syn. Study.** BEAR, STAND, ENDURE refer to supporting the burden of something distressing, irksome, or painful. BEAR is the general word and suggests merely being able to put up with something: She is bearing the disappointment quite well. STAND is an informal equivalent, but with an implication of stout spirit: I couldn't stand the pain. ENDURE implies continued resistance and patience over a long period of time: to endure torture.

bearing, n. **1.** carriage, posture, manner, mein, deportment, demeanor, behavior, conduct, air. **2.** relation, connection, dependency, reference, application. **3.** direction, course, aim.

beastly, *adj.* **1.** bestial, animalistic, animal, brutish, brutal, primitive, barbaric, base, inhuman. **2.** unkind, cruel, uncivil, mean, pitiless. **3.** inclement, stormy, severe, disagreeable, miserable.

beat, *v.* **1.** hit, pound, strike, thrash belabor, batter, knock, thump, drub, maul, baste, pommel, thwack, whack, punch, cudgel, cane, whip, flog, lash, buffet. **2.** break, forge, hammer. **3.** conquer, subdue, overcome, vanquish, overpower, defeat, checkmate. **4.** excel, outdo, surpass. **5.** throb, pulsate. **6.** win, conquer. —*n.* **7.** stroke, blow. **8.** pulsation, throb, tattoo, rhythm. —**Syn. Study.** BEAT, HIT, POUND, STRIKE, THRASH refer to the giving of a blow or blows. BEAT implies the giving of repeated blows: *to beat a rug.* To HIT is usu. to give a single blow, definitely directed: *to hit a ball.* To POUND is to give heavy and repeated blows, often with the fist: *to pound the table.* To STRIKE is to give one or more forceful blows suddenly or swiftly: *to strike a gong.* To THRASH implies inflicting repeated blows as punishment, to show superior strength, or the like: *to thrash an opponent.*

beautiful, *adj.* handsome, comely, seemly, attractive, lovely, pretty, fair, fine, elegant, beauteous, graceful, pulchritudinous, to die for. —**Ant.** ugly; inelegant, ungraceful. —**Syn. Study.** BEAUTIFUL, HANDSOME, LOVELY, PRETTY refer to a pleasing appearance. BEAUTIFUL is used of a person or thing that gives intense pleasure to the senses; it may refer to a woman but rarely to a man: *a beautiful landscape; a beautiful actress.* HANDSOME often implies stateliness or pleasing proportions and symmetry; it is used of a man and sometimes a woman: *a handsome sofa; a handsome man.* That which is LOVELY is beautiful in a warm and endearing way: *a lovely smile.* PRETTY usu. suggests a moderate beauty in persons or things that are small or feminine: *a pretty blouse; a pretty child.*

beautify, *v.* embellish, adorn, ornament, decorate, bedeck, deck, deck out, dress up, enhance, prettify, glamorize, titivate, cosmeticize. —**Ant.** uglify, despoil, mar, deface, vandalize.

beauty, *n.* **1.** loveliness, pulchritude, elegance, grace, gracefulness, comeliness, seemliness, fairness, attractiveness. **2.** belle. **3.** grace, charm, excellence, attraction. —**Ant.** ugliness; witch; gracelessness.

because, *conj.* as, since, for, inasmuch as, for the reason that.

becoming, *adj.* **1.** attractive, comely, neat, pretty, graceful. **2.** fit, proper, apt, suitable, appropriate, meet, right, correct, decorous, congruous, fitting, seemly. —**Ant.** unbecoming, ugly; unfit, inappropriate, indecorous.

bedevil, *v.* pester, annoy, plague, nag, harass, harry, worry, beleaguer, bother, beset, trouble, vex, torment, try, persecute, hassle.

bedlam, *n.* hubbub, din, confusion, racket, noise, clamor, chaos, pandemonium, babel, tumult, uproar, hullabaloo, ruckus, rumpus. —**Ant.** calmness, tranquillity, peace, serenity.

befitting, *adj.* fitting, proper, suitable, seemly, appropriate, becoming, fit, apt. —**Ant.** unbecoming, improper, unsuitable, inappropriate.

beg, *v.* ask for, entreat, pray, crave, implore, beseech, importune, petition, sue, request, supplicate, sue for, solicit.

begin, *v.* **1.** commence, start, initiate, inaugurate, institute, enter upon, set about. **2.** originate, create; arise. —**Ant.** end, conclude, die. —**Syn. Study.** BEGIN, COMMENCE, INITIATE, START (when followed by noun or gerund) refer to setting into motion or progress something that continues for some time. BEGIN is the common term: *to begin knitting a sweater.* COMMENCE is a more formal word, often suggesting a more prolonged or elaborate beginning: *to commence proceedings in court.* INITIATE implies an active and often ingenious first act in a new field: *to initiate a new procedure.* START means to make a first move or to set out on a course of action: *to start paving a street.*

beginning, *n.* **1.** initiation, inauguration, inception, start, commencement, outset, rise, onset, arising, emergence. **2.** source, birth, origin, rise, first cause.

begrudge, *v.* envy, grudge, covet.

beguile, *v.* **1.** mislead, delude, charm, cheat, deceive, befool. **2.** divert, charm, amuse, entertain, cheer, solace.

behave, *v.* conduct oneself, act, deport *or* comport oneself, demean oneself, acquit oneself. —**Ant.** misbehave.

behavior, *n.* demeanor, conduct, manners, deportment, bearing, carriage, mien, air. —**Ant.** misbehavior.

belief, *n.* **1.** opinion, view, tenet, doctrine, dogma, creed. **2.** certainty, conviction, assurance, confidence, persuasion, believing, trust, reliance. **3.** credence, credit, acceptance, assent. —**Syn. Study.** BELIEF, CONVICTION refer to acceptance of or confidence in an alleged fact or body of facts as true or right without positive knowledge or proof. BELIEF is such acceptance in general: *belief in astrology.* CONVICTION is a settled, profound, or earnest belief that something is right: *a conviction that a decision is just.*

belt, *n.* **1.** girth, girdle, cinch, cincture, zone. **2.** band, zone, strip, stripe, stretch. —*v.* **3.** gird, girdle, surround, encircle.

bend, *v.* **1.** curve, crook, bow, deflect, draw, flex. **2.** cause to yield, subdue, persuade, influence, mold, dispose, bias, incline, direct, turn. **3.** stoop, bow. **4.** yield, submit, bow, stoop, kneel, give way, acquiesce, agree. **5.** crook, deflect, deviate, swerve, diverge, incline. —*n.* **6.** curve, crook, bow, rib, elbow, turn, angle, curvature, turning.

beneficial, *adj.* salutary, wholesome, serviceable, useful, favorable, helpful, profitable, advantageous. —**Ant.** unwholesome, unfavorable, disadvantageous.

benefit, See Syn. study at ADVANTAGE

benevolent, *adj.* kind, kindly, well-disposed, kindhearted, humane, tender, tender-hearted, unselfish, generous, liberal, obliging, benign, benignant, charitable, philanthropic, altruistic. —**Ant.** cruel, selfish, egotistical.

bent, *adj.* **1.** curved, crooked, hooked, bowed, flexed, deflected. **2.** determined, set on, resolved, fixed on. —*n.* **3.** inclination, leaning, bias, tendency, propensity, proclivity, disposition, turn, penchant, predilection, partiality, liking, fondness, proneness. —**Ant.** straight; undecided; disinclination.

bequeath, *v.* leave, will, pass on, pass along, devise, legate, hand down, transmit.

beseech, *v.* **1.** implore, beg, entreat, pray, petition, obsecrate, obtest, supplicate, importune, adjure. **2.** solicit, ask, entreat, beg, implore, importune, crave.

beset, *v.* **1.** assail, harass, surround, encompass, encircle, enclose, besiege, beleaguer. **2.** set, bestud, stud, decorate, ornament, embellish, garnish.

besides, *adv.* **1.** moreover, in addition, furthermore, else, otherwise, too, also, yet, further. —*prep.* **2.** over and above, in addition to, except, other than, save, distinct from.

betray, *v.* **1.** deliver, expose, give up, uncover, reveal. **2.** be unfaithful to, be a traitor to, deceive, be disloyal to, disappoint. **3.** show, exhibit, display, manifest, indicate, imply, betoken, evince, expose, uncover, reveal. —**Ant.** protect, safeguard.

better, *adj.* **1.** more good; more useful, more valuable; more suitable, more appropriate, more fit, more applicable. **2.** larger, greater, bigger. —*v.* **3.** improve, amend, ameliorate, meliorate, emend; advance, promote, reform, correct, rectify. **4.** improve upon, surpass, exceed. —**Ant.** worse; worsen. —**Syn. Study.** See IMPROVE.

bewilder, *v.* confuse, perplex, puzzle, mystify; confound, nonplus, astonish, daze, stagger, befog, muddle.

bewitch, *v.* throw a spell over, charm, enchant, captivate, transport, enrapture, fascinate, hypnotize.

bias, *n.* **1.** prejudice, inclination, preconception, predilection, prepossession, proclivity, propensity, proneness, partiality, predisposition, bent, leaning, tendency. —*v.* **2.** prejudice, warp, predispose, bend, influence, incline, dispose. —**Syn. Study.** BIAS, PREJUDICE mean a strong inclination of the mind or a preconceived opinion about something or someone. A BIAS may be favorable or unfavorable: *bias in favor of or against an idea.* PREJUDICE implies a preformed judgment even more unreasoning

than BIAS, and usu. implies an unfavorable opinion: *prejudice against a race.*

bid, *v.* **1.** command, order, direct, charge, require, enjoin, summon. **2.** greet, wish, say. **3.** offer, propose, tender, proffer. —*n.* **4.** offer, proposal, proffer. —**Ant.** forbid, prohibit, enjoin.

big, *adj.* **1.** large, great, huge, bulky, massive, immense, tremendous, capacious, gigantic, extensive. **2.** pregnant, with child, enceinte. **3.** filled, teeming, overflowing, productive. **4.** important, consequential, haughty, proud, arrogant, pompous, swelling, swollen, inflated, tumid, self-important, conceited, self-sufficient, bombastic, boastful. **5.** generous, big-hearted, kindly. —**Ant.** small; trivial, nugatory.

bigoted, *adj.* intolerant, narrow-minded, closed-minded, narrow, small-minded, illiberal, hidebound, parochial, biased, prejudiced, know-nothing, mean-spirited. —**Ant.** tolerant, broad-minded, open-minded, generous.

bill, *n.* **1.** account, reckoning, score, charges, invoice, statement. **2.** bulletin, handbill, notice, advertisement, broadside, poster, placard, announcement, throwaway, circular. **3.** beak, nib, neb, mandible.

billow, *v.* swell, expand, distend, inflate, bloat, balloon, belly, fill out, puff up, mushroom. —**Ant.** contract, shrink.

bind, *v.* **1.** band, bond, tie, make fast, fasten, secure, gird, attach. **2.** encircle, border; confine, restrain, restrict. **3.** engage, obligate, oblige. **4.** indenture, apprentice. —**Ant.** untie, unbind.

birth, *n.* **1.** act of bearing, bringing forth, parturition. **2.** lineage, extraction, parentage, descent, ancestry, line, blood, family, race. **3.** origin, beginning, rise, nativity. —**Ant.** death, end.

bit, *n.* **1.** particle, speck, grain, mite, crumb, iota, jot, atom, scintilla, tittle, whit, fragment. **2.** bridle, curb, control, rein, check, checkrein, restrainer.

bite, *v.* **1.** gnaw, chew, champ; nip, rip, rend, tear. **2.** cut, pierce; sting, burn, cause to smart. **3.** corrode, erode, eat away. **4.** cheat, deceive, defraud, dupe, trick, gull, make a fool of, cozen, outwit, fool, bamboozle, inveigle, mislead, beguile. —*n.* **5.** nip, sting, cut. **6.** food, snack; morsel, mouthful.

bitter, *adj.* **1.** harsh, acrid, biting. **2.** grievous, distasteful, painful, distressing, intense, sore, poignant, sorrowful, calamitous. **3.** piercing, stinging, biting, nipping. **4.** harsh, sarcastic, caustic, cutting, acrimonious, acerbate, severe, stern, sardonic, scornful, sneering. **5.** fierce, cruel, savage, mean, merciless, ruthless, relentless, virulent, dire. —**Ant.** sweet.

bizarre, See Syn. study at FANTASTIC.

black, *adj.* **1.** dark, dusky, sooty, inky, ebon, sable, swart, swarthy. **2.** soiled, dirty, dingy, dusky, stained. **3.** gloomy, sad, dismal, sullen, hopeless, dark, depressing, doleful, funereal, somber, mournful, forbidding, disastrous, calamitous. **4.** amoral, evil, wicked, sinful, fiendish, inhuman, devilish, diabolic, infernal, monstrous, atrocious, horrible, outrageous, heinous, flagitious, nefarious, treacherous, traitorous, infamous, villainous. **5.** ruined, desolate, empty. —**Ant.** white; clean, pure, undefiled; happy; good, upright.

blackguard, *n.* churl, scoundrel, scamp, rascal, rapscallion, rogue, roué, devil, rake, wastrel, villain. —**Ant.** hero, protagonist.

blame, *v.* **1.** reproach, reprove, reprehend, censure, condemn, find fault, criticize, disapprove. —*n.* **2.** censure, reprehension, condemnation, finger-pointing, stricture, disapproval, disapprobation, reproach, reproof, animadversion. **3.** guilt, culpability, fault, wrong, misdeed, misdoing, shortcoming, sin, defect, reproach. —**Ant.** credit, honor.

blameless, *adj.* irreproachable, guiltless, unimpeachable, faultless, innocent, inculpable, not guilty, undefiled, unsullied, unspotted, spotless, unblemished. —**Ant.** guilty, culpable; sullied, besmirched.

blanch, *v.* whiten, bleach, etiolate, pale, fade. —**Ant.** darken, blacken.

bland, *adj.* **1.** gentle, agreeable, affable, friendly, kindly, mild, amiable; suave, urbane, mild-mannered; complaisant, self-satisfied. **2.** soft, mild, balmy, soothing, nonirritating.

—**Ant.** cruel, unfriendly; boorish, crude; irritable, irksome.

blank, *adj.* **1.** unmarked, void, empty, unadorned, undistinguished. **2.** amazed, astonished, nonplussed, astounded, confused, dumfounded, disconcerted. **3.** complete, utter, pure, simple, unadulterated, unmixed; perfect, entire, absolute, unmitigated, unabated, unqualified, mere. —*n.* **4.** space, line, area; form; void, vacancy, emptiness. —**Ant.** distinguished, marked; blasé; impure; significant.

blarney, *n.* **1.** flattery, blandishment, cajolery, honey, sweet talk, soft soap. **2.** nonsense, rubbish, blather, humbug, claptrap, flummery.

blasé, *adj.* **1.** worldly-wise, sophisticated, jaded, knowing, worldly, disillusioned, world-weary. **2.** unconcerned, indifferent, uninterested, unsurprised, nonchalant, cool.

blasphemy, *n.* profanity, cursing, swearing, impiousness, sacrilege. —**Ant.** reverence, piety.

blast, *n.* **1.** wind, squall, gust, gale, blow, storm. **2.** blare, peal, clang. **3.** explosion, outburst, burst, outbreak, discharge. —*v.* **4.** blow, toot, blare. **5.** wither, blight, kill, shrivel. **6.** ruin, destroy, annihilate. **7.** explode, burst, split. —**Syn. Study.** See WIND.

blaze, *n.* **1.** fire, flame, holocaust, inferno; glow, gleam, brightness; outburst. —*v.* **2.** burn, shine, flame, flare up, flicker.

bleach, *v.* **1.** whiten, blanch, etiolate, pale. —*n.* **2.** whitener. —**Ant.** blacken, darken.

blemish, *v.* **1.** stain, sully, spot, taint, injure, tarnish, mar, damage, deface, impair. —*n.* **2.** stain, defect, blot, spot, speck, disfigurement, flaw, taint, fault. —**Ant.** purify; purity, immaculateness. —**Syn. Study.** See DEFECT.

blend, *v.* **1.** mingle, combine, coalesce, mix, intermingle, commingle, amalgamate, unite, compound. —*n.* **2.** mixture, combination, amalgamation. —**Ant.** separate, precipitate. —**Syn. Study.** See MIX.

blind, *adj.* **1.** sightless, stone-blind, purblind. **2.** ignorant, undiscerning, unenlightened, benighted. **3.** irrational, uncritical, indiscriminate, headlong, rash, heedless, careless, thoughtless, unreasoning, inconsiderate. **4.** hidden, concealed, obscure, remote, dim, confused, dark. **5.** closed, dead-end, shut. —*n.* **6.** curtain, shade, blinker, blinder, screen, cover. **7.** hiding place, ambush. **8.** cover, decoy, ruse, stratagem, pretense, pretext. —**Ant.** discerning, enlightened; rational, discriminating; open.

blink, *v.* **1.** wink, nictitate. **2.** flicker, flutter, twinkle. **3.** ignore, overlook, disregard, evade, avoid, condone. —*n.* **4.** wink, twinkle; glance, glimpse, peep, sight.

bliss, *n.* blitheness, happiness, gladness, joy, transport, rapture, ecstasy. —**Ant.** misery, unhappiness, dejection.

blithe, *adj.* joyous, merry, gay, glad, cheerful, happy, mirthful, sprightly, lighthearted, buoyant, lively, animated, elated, vivacious, joyful, blithesome. —**Ant.** unhappy, miserable, cheerless.

block, *n.* **1.** mass. **2.** blockhead, dolt, idiot, imbecile, simpleton, fool, dunce. **3.** mold. **4.** blank. **5.** pulley, tackle, sheave. **6.** obstacle, hindrance, impediment, blocking, blockade, obstruction, stoppage, blockage, jam. —*v.* **7.** mold, shape, form. **8.** obstruct, close, hinder, deter, arrest, stop, blockade, impede, check. —**Ant.** genius; encourage, advance, continue.

bloody, *adj.* **1.** bloodstained, sanguinary, ensanguined, gory. **2.** murderous, cruel, bloodthirsty, savage, barbarous, ferocious, homicidal, inhuman, ruthless.

bloom, *n.* **1.** flower, blossom, efflorescence. **2.** freshness, glow, flush, vigor, prime. —*v.* **3.** flourish, effloresce; glow.

blot, *n.* **1.** spot, stain, inkstain, erasure, blotting, blotch, obliteration, blur. **2.** blemish, reproach, stain, taint, dishonor, disgrace, spot. —*v.* **3.** spot, stain, bespatter; sully, disfigure, deface. **4.** darken, dim, obscure, eclipse, hide, overshadow. **5.** destroy, annihilate, obliterate, efface, erase, expunge, rub out, cancel, strike out, eliminate.

blow, *v.* **1.** stroke, buffet, thump, thwack, rap, slap, cuff, box, beat, knock. **2.** shock, calamity, reverse, disaster, misfortune, affliction. **3.** attack. **4.** blast, wind, gale, gust. **5.** blossom, flower, bloom. —*v.* **6.** pant,

puff, wheeze. **7.** blossom, bloom, flower.

blue, *n.* **1.** azure, cerulean, sky-blue, sapphire. **2.** prude, censor, pedant. —*adj.* **3.** depressed, dismal, unhappy, morose, gloomy, doleful, melancholy, dispiriting, dispirited, dejected, sad, glum, downcast, crestfallen, despondent. **4.** prudish, moral, rigid, unbending, righteous, puritanical, self-righteous, severe, rigorous. **5.** obscene, lewd, lascivious, licentious, indecent, risqué, ribald, irreverent, scurrilous, suggestive, immoral, amoral. —**Ant.** happy, mirthful.

blueprint, *n.* plan, outline, scheme, design, schema, master plan, ground plan, diagram, program, model, paradigm, game plan, strategy.

bluff, *adj.* **1.** abrupt, unconventional, blunt, direct, frank, open, honest, hearty, rough, crude. **2.** steep, precipitous, abrupt. —*n.* **3.** cliff, headland, hill, bank. **4.** fraud, deceit, lie, dissembling. —*v.* **5.** mislead, defraud, deceive, lie, dissemble, fake. —**Ant.** suave, diplomatic, tactful; gradual; plain.

blunder, *n.* **1.** mistake, error, faux pas, gaffe, lapse, slip, misstep, slipup, miscue, misjudgment, impropriety, solecism, indiscretion, indecorum, bungle, misdoing, boner, howler, blooper, goof, boo-boo, (*Brit.*) clanger. *v.* **2.** bungle, botch, bobble, bumble, muff, flub, fluff, mess up, goof up, louse up, screw up. —**Syn. Study.** See MISTAKE.

blunt, *adj.* **1.** rounded, not sharp, dull. **2.** abrupt, bluff, brusque, curt, short, obtuse, difficult, gruff, uncourtly, uncivil, rough, harsh, uncourteous, discourteous, rude, impolite. **3.** slow, dull, dimwitted, dullwitted, stupid, thick, stolid. —*v.* **4.** dull, obtund. **5.** numb, paralyze, deaden, stupefy, make insensible. —**Ant.** sharp, acute; courteous, civil, polite; quick, alert. —**Syn. Study.** BLUNT, BRUSQUE, CURT characterize manners and speech. BLUNT suggests unnecessary frankness and a lack of regard for the feelings of others: *blunt and tactless remarks.* BRUSQUE connotes a sharpness and abruptness that borders on rudeness: *a brusque denial.* CURT applies esp. to disconcertingly concise language: *a curt reply.*

boast, *v.* **1.** exaggerate, brag, vaunt, swagger, crow. —*n.* **2.** bragging, rodomontade, swaggering, braggadocio. —**Ant.** depreciate, belittle. —**Syn. Study.** BOAST, BRAG imply vocal self-praise or claims to superiority over others. BOAST usu. refers to a particular ability, possession, etc., that may justify a good deal of pride: *He boasts of his ability as a singer.* BRAG, a more informal term, usu. suggests a more ostentatious and exaggerated boasting but less well-founded: *He brags loudly about his marksmanship.*

bodily, See Syn. study at PHYSICAL.

body, *n.* **1.** carcass, corpse, cadaver. **2.** trunk, torso, substance, matter, bulk, main part; fuselage, hull. **3.** collection, group; company, party, band, coterie, society, clique, set; association, corporation. **4.** consistency, density, substance, thickness. —**Ant.** spirit, soul. —**Syn. Study.** BODY, CARCASS, CORPSE, CADAVER all refer to a physical organism, usu. human or animal. BODY denotes the material substance of a human or animal, either living or dead: *the muscles in a horse's body; the body of an accident victim.* CARCASS means the dead body of an animal, unless applied humorously or contemptuously to the human body: *a sheep's carcass; Save your carcass.* CORPSE usu. refers to the dead body of a human being: *preparing a corpse for burial.* CADAVER refers to a dead body, usu. a human one used for scientific study: *dissection of cadavers in anatomy classes.*

bogus, *adj.* false, sham, counterfeit, inauthentic, bastard, mock, phony, spurious, brummagem, pinchbeck, pseudo. —**Ant.** genuine, real, true, authentic.

bohemian, *adj.* **1.** free-living, free-spirited, unconventional, unconstrained, unorthodox, free and easy, offbeat, eccentric, artistic, arty, recusant. —*n.* **2.** nonconformist, free spirit, maverick, eccentric. —**Ant.** conformist, conservative, straight arrow.

boil, *v.* **1.** seethe, foam, froth, churn, stew, simmer, rage. —*n.* **2.** ebullition. **3.** furuncle, pustule. —**Syn. Study.** BOIL, SEETHE, SIMMER, STEW are used figuratively to refer to agitated states of emotion. To BOIL suggests being very hot with anger or rage: *He was boiling when the guests arrived late.* To SEETHE is to be deeply stirred, violently agitated, or greatly excited: *a mind seething with conflicting ideas.* To SIMMER means to be at the point of bursting out or boiling over: *to simmer with curiosity; to simmer with anger.* To STEW is an informal term that means to worry, or to be in a restless state of anxiety and excitement: *to stew over one's troubles.*

boisterous, *adj.* rough, noisy, loud, clamorous, roaring, unrestrained, wild, tumultuous, turbulent, violent, impetuous, stormy, tempestuous, uproarious, obstreperous, roistering, vociferous. **—Ant.** calm, serene, pacific.

bold, *adj.* **1.** fearless, courageous, brave, intrepid, daring, dauntless, valorous, valiant, heroic, manly, doughty, undaunted, hardy, spirited, mettlesome, gallant, stout-hearted, resolute. **2.** forward, brazen, brassy, presumptuous, shameless, insolent, impudent, immodest, defiant, overconfident, saucy, pushing. **3.** conspicuous, prominent, obvious, evident. **4.** steep, abrupt, precipitous. **—Ant.** cowardly, timorous, timid; backward, shy; inconspicuous; gradual. **—Syn. Study.** BOLD, BRAZEN, FORWARD, PRESUMPTUOUS refer to behavior or manners that break the rules of propriety. BOLD suggests shamelessness and immodesty: *a bold stare.* BRAZEN suggests the same, together with a defiant manner: *a brazen liar.* FORWARD implies making oneself unduly prominent or bringing oneself to notice with too much assurance: *The forward young man challenged the speaker.* PRESUMPTUOUS implies overconfidence, or taking too much for granted: *It was presumptuous of her to think she could defeat the champion.*

bombastic, *adj.* flowery, pretentious, pompous, turgid, verbose, portentous, loud, brassy. **—Syn. Study.** BOMBASTIC, FLOWERY, PRETENTIOUS all describe a use of language more elaborate than is justified by or appropriate to the content being expressed. BOMBASTIC suggests language with a theatricality or staginess of style far too powerful or declamatory for the meaning or sentiment being expressed: *a bombastic sermon on the evils of gambling.* FLOWERY describes language filled with extravagant images and ornate expressions: *a flowery eulogy.* PRETENTIOUS refers specifically to language that is purposely inflated in an effort to impress: *a pretentious essay filled with obscure literary allusions.*

bond, *n.* **1.** binder, fastener, fastening, band, cord, ligature, ligament, link, rope. **2.** tie, connection, link, attraction, attachment, union. **3.** bondsman, security, ward, promise; promissory note; obligation, contract, compact. **4.** (*pl.*) chains, fetters, captivity, constraint, restriction, bondage; prison, imprisonment. **—v. 5.** mortgage. **6.** cement, glue.

bondage, *n.* slavery, indenture, servitude, serfdom, thraldom, captivity, imprisonment, confinement. **—Ant.** freedom. **—Syn. Study.** See SLAVERY.

bonus, *n.* bounty, premium, reward, honorarium, gift, subsidy; dividend, perquisite. **—Syn. Study.** BONUS, BOUNTY, PREMIUM refer to a gift or an additional payment. A BONUS is a gift to reward performance, paid either by an employer or by a government: *a bonus based on salary; a soldier's bonus.* A BOUNTY is a public reward offered to stimulate interest in a specific purpose or undertaking and to encourage performance: *a bounty for killing wolves.* A PREMIUM is usu. something additional given as an inducement to buy, produce, or the like: *a premium received with a magazine subscription.*

border, *n.* **1.** side, edge, margin; orphrey; periphery, circumference, lip, brim, verge, brink. **2.** frontier, limit, confine, boundary. **—v. 3.** bound, limit, confine; adjoin. **—Syn. Study.** See BOUNDARY.

bore, *v.* **1.** perforate, drill, pierce. **2.** weary, fatigue, tire, annoy. **—n. 3.** caliber, hole. **4.** tidal wave, eagre. **—Ant.** amuse.

bosom, *n.* **1.** breast, heart, affection. **—adj. 2.** intimate, close, confidential.

bother, *v.* **1.** annoy, pester, worry, trouble, plague, tease, harass, vex, harry; molest, disturb. **2.** bewilder, confuse. **—Ant.** solace, comfort. **—Syn. Study.** BOTHER, ANNOY, PLAGUE imply persistent interference with one's comfort or peace of mind. To BOTHER is to cause irritation or weari-

ness, esp. by repeated interruptions in the midst of pressing duties: *Don't bother me while I'm working.* To ANNOY is to cause mild irritation or mental disturbance, as by repetition of an action that displeases: *The dog's constant barking annoyed the neighbors.* To PLAGUE is to trouble or bother, but usu. connotes severe mental distress: *The family was plagued by lack of money.*

bottom, *n.* **1.** base, foot. **2.** underside. **3.** foundation, base, basis, groundwork. **4.** seat, buttocks. **—adj. 5.** fundamental, basic, elementary; undermost, lowest. **—Ant.** top; superficial, superfluous.

bough, *n.* branch, limb, arm, shoot.

bound, *v.* **1.** leap, jump, spring. **2.** rebound, ricochet. **—n. 3.** (*usually plural*) limit, confine, boundary, verge, border. **—adj. 4.** constrained; destined for, tending, going. **—Ant.** free.

boundary, *n.* border, frontier, line, line of demarcation, delimitation, circumference, perimeter, division, dividing line, edge. **—Syn. Study.** BOUNDARY, BORDER, FRONTIER refer to that which divides one territory or political unit from another. BOUNDARY most often designates a line on a map; it may be a physical feature, such as a river: *Boundaries are shown in red.* BORDER refers to a political or geographic dividing line; it may also refer to the region adjoining the actual line: *crossing the Mexican border.* FRONTIER refers specifically to a border between two countries or the region adjoining this border: *Soldiers guarded the frontier.*

bountiful, See Syn. study at PLENTIFUL.

bounty, *n.* **1.** generosity, munificence, charity, liberality, beneficence. **2.** gift, award, present, benefaction. **3.** reward, premium, bonus. **—Syn. Study.** See BONUS.

bow, *v.* **1.** stoop, bend, buckle, give way. **2.** yield, submit. **3.** subdue, crush, depress, cast down. **4.** curve, bend, inflect. **—n. 5.** front, forepart, prow.

brace, *n.* **1.** clasp, clamp, vise. **2.** stay, support, prop, strut. **3.** bitstock. **4.** couple, pair. **—v. 5.** fasten firmly, strengthen, support, back up, fortify, prop, steady. **6.** tighten, tauten, make tense. **7.** stimulate, strengthen, fortify.

brag, *v.*, *n.* boast, rodomontade, bluster. **—Ant.** depreciate. **—Syn. Study.** See BOAST.

brains, *n.* understanding, intelligence, mind, intellect, sense, reason; capacity. **—Ant.** stupidity.

branch, *n.* **1.** bough, limb, arm, shoot, offshoot. **2.** limb, offshoot, ramification, arm. **3.** section, subdivision, department; member, portion, part; article. **4.** tributary, feeder. **—v. 5.** divide, subdivide, diverge, ramify.

bravado, *n.* boasting, swaggering, braggadocio, pretense, brag, bluster, bombast. **—Ant.** shame, modesty.

brave, *adj.* **1.** courageous, fearless, gallant, confident, cool, chivalrous, impetuous, dashing, intrepid, daring, dauntless, doughty, bold, valiant, heroic, manly, hard, mettlesome, stout-hearted. **2.** fine, showy, effective, brilliant; gay; debonair. **—n. 3.** warrior (*esp. American Indian*). **—v. 4.** face, defy, challenge, dare. **—Ant.** cowardly, fearful; craven, pusillanimous. **—Syn. Study.** BRAVE, COURAGEOUS, VALIANT, FEARLESS refer to facing danger or difficulties with moral strength and endurance. BRAVE is a general term that suggests fortitude, daring, and resolve: *a brave pioneer.* COURAGEOUS implies a higher or nobler kind of bravery, esp. as resulting from an inborn quality of mind or spirit: *courageous leaders.* VALIANT implies an inner strength manifested by brave deeds, often in battle: *a valiant knight.* FEARLESS implies unflinching spirit and coolness in the face of danger: *a fearless firefighter.*

bravery, *n.* boldness, courage, intrepidity, daring, prowess, heroism, pluck, gallantry, spirit, audacity, nerve, mettle, fearlessness, spunk, valor. **—Ant.** cowardice.

brawl, *n.* **1.** quarrel, squabble, argument, spat, wrangle, feud, disagreement, dispute, fracas, disturbance, disorder, row, tumult, clamor, rumpus, fray, fight, affray, altercation, melee, riot. **—v. 2.** quarrel, squabble, argue, wrangle, feud, disagree, dispute, fight, bicker.

brazen, *adj.* **1.** brassy. **2.** bold, forward, shameless, impudent, insolent, immodest, defiant. **—Ant.** shy, diffident, modest. **—Syn. Study.** See BOLD.

breach, *n.* **1.** break, rupture, fracture, crack, gap, fissure, rift, rent, opening, chasm. **2.** infraction, violation, infringement. **3.** alienation, disaffection, falling out, misunderstanding; split, rift, schism, severance, separation; dissension, disagreement, difference, variance, quarrel, dispute. **—Ant.** observance. **—Syn. Study.** BREACH, INFRACTION, VIOLATION all denote an act of breaking or disregarding a legal or moral code. BREACH is most often used of a legal offense, but it may refer to the breaking of any code of conduct: *breach of contract; breach of etiquette.* INFRACTION most often refers to the breaking of clearly formulated rules or laws: *an infraction of regulations.* VIOLATION often suggests a willful, forceful refusal to obey: *done in violation of instructions.*

break, *v.* **1.** fracture, crush, shatter, splinter, shiver, smash, batter, demolish, destroy. **2.** contravene, transgress, disobey, violate, infringe, infract. **3.** dissolve, annul, negate, dismiss. **4.** lacerate, wound, cut, injure, harm, hurt. **5.** interrupt, suspend, disrupt, stop; abbreviate, curtail. **6.** end, overcome. **7.** exceed, outdo, surpass, beat. **8.** disclose, open, unfold, divulge. **9.** ruin, bankrupt, make bankrupt. **10.** impair, weaken, enfeeble, enervate; dispirit. **11.** tame, make obedient. **12.** discharge, degrade, cashier, demote. **13.** shatter, shiver; burst. **14.** dissolve, separate, split. **15.** escape, break loose. **16.** dawn, open, appear. **17.** decline, weaken. **—n. 18.** disruption, separation, rent, tear, rip, rift, schism, severance, split; breach, gap, fissure, crack, chasm, rupture, fracture. **19.** suspension, stoppage, stop, caesura, hiatus, interruption, lacuna, pause, discontinuity. **—Ant.** repair.

breaker, *n.* wave, comber, surge, whitecap, roller; bore, eagre.

breed, *v.* **1.** beget, bear, bring forth, conceive, give birth to, produce, engender, father, mother. **2.** propagate, procreate, originate, create, beget, occasion, generate. **3.** raise, rear, bring up, nurture; train, educate, discipline, instruct, teach, school. **4.** grow, develop, flourish, arise, rise. **—n. 5.** race, lineage, strain, family, pedigree, line, extraction, stock, progeny. **6.** sort, kind, species, class, denomination, order, rank, character, nature, description.

breeze, *n.* wind, air, blow, zephyr. **—Ant.** calm. **—Syn. Study.** See WIND.

brevity, *n.* **1.** shortness, briefness. **2.** conciseness, compactness, condensation, succinctness, pithiness; terseness, curtness. **—Ant.** lengthiness. **—Syn. Study.** BREVITY, CONCISENESS refer to the use of few words in speaking. BREVITY emphasizes the short duration of speech: *reduced to extreme brevity.* CONCISENESS emphasizes compactness of expression: *clear in spite of great conciseness.*

bridle, *n.* **1.** curb, restraint, check, control, governor. **—v. 2.** restrain, check, curb, control, govern. **3.** bristle, ruffle. **—Ant.** freedom; decontrol.

brief, *adj.* **1.** short, short-lived, fleeting, transitory, ephemeral, transient, temporary. **2.** concise, succinct, pithy, condensed, compact, laconic; curt, short, terse, abrupt. **—n. 3.** outline, précis, synopsis, summary, epitome, syllabus, abstract, abridgment, conspectus, compendium, breviary. **—v. 4.** abstract, summarize, outline, epitomize, abridge, abbreviate. **—Ant.** long, tedious, boring. **—Syn. Study.** See SHORT. See also SUMMARY.

bright, *adj.* **1.** radiant, radiating, refulgent, resplendent, effulgent, lucent, lustrous, glowing, beaming, lambent, splendid, brilliant, shining, irradiant, gleaming, luminous; scintillating, sparkling, twinkling, glistening, glistering, shimmering, coruscating, glittering, flashing, flaming, blazing; shiny, sheeny, glossy, burnished; vivid, light, sunny, fulgid, fulgent. **2.** clear, transparent, pellucid, translucent, lucid, limpid, unclouded, crystal, cloudless, lambent. **3.** illustrious, distinguished, glorious, famous, golden, silver. **4.** quickwitted, intelligent, keen, discerning, acute, ingenious, sharp, clever. **5.** lively, animated, cheerful, merry, happy, sprightly, lighthearted, gay, vivacious, genial, pleasant. **6.** favorable, auspicious, propitious, promising, encouraging, inspiriting, inspiring, enlivening, exhilarating. **—Ant.** dull; opaque, dense; undistinguished, ignominious; slow, stupid; laconic,

doleful, melancholy; unfavorable, discouraging.

brilliance, *n.* **1.** brightness, splendor, luster, refulgence, effulgence, radiance, brilliancy; sparkle, glitter, glister, gleam. **2.** excellence, distinction, eminence, renown, prominence, preeminence, singularity, fame, illustriousness. **—Ant.** dullness; notoriety, oblivion.

brim, *n.* rim, edge, border; orphrey; periphery, circumference, bound, brink, lip. **—Ant.** center. **—Syn. Study.** See RIM.

bring, *v.* **1.** take along, conduct, convey, lead, fetch, guide, convoy, accompany, transport, carry. **2.** lead, induce, prevail upon, draw. **—Ant.** remove, withdraw.

brisk, *adj.* **1.** active, lively, energetic, peart, quick, nimble, agile, alert, spry, on the qui vive, spirited, bright, vivacious. **2.** sharp, stimulating, acute. **3.** effervescent, bubbly, bubbling. **—Ant.** slow, lethargic; dull; flat.

brittle, *adj.* fragile, frail, breakable, frangible. **—Ant.** supple, flexible, elastic. **—Syn. Study.** See FRAIL.

broad, *adj.* **1.** wide. **2.** large, extensive, vast, spacious, ample. **3.** diffused, diffuse, open, full. **4.** liberal, large, big, tolerant, open-minded, hospitable. **5.** main, general, chief, important, obvious. **6.** plain, clear, bold, plain-spoken, open, unconfined, free, unrestrained. **7.** rough, coarse, countrified, unrefined, vulgar, indecent, indelicate, gross. **—Ant.** narrow; penurious, stingy; refined, cultivated, decent.

broad-minded, *adj.* tolerant, open, open-minded, liberal, large-minded, progressive, generous-hearted, charitable, forbearing, lenient, live-and-let-live, unbigoted, unparochial, ecumenical. **—Ant.** narrow-minded, bigoted, close-minded.

brood, *n.* **1.** offspring, litter, young, progeny, issue. **2.** breed, kind, sort, line, lineage, stock, family, strain, species, class, order. **—v. 3.** incubate, sit. **4.** dwell on, ponder, ruminate over, meditate on. **5.** sit, hatch, set. **6.** rest. **7.** meditate morbidly.

brook, *n.* **1.** stream, rivulet, run, runnel, runlet, streamlet, rill, burn, branch. **—v. 2.** bear, suffer, tolerate, allow, stand, endure, abide, put up with, submit to.

brother, *n.* fellow man, fellow countryman, kinsman, associate; sibling.

brownie, *n.* goblin, fairy, elf, pixie, leprechaun, nix, nixie, sprite, imp.

brush, *n.* **1.** encounter, brief encounter, meeting; engagement, affair, contest, collision, action, fight, battle, skirmish, struggle, conflict. **2.** bushes, scrub, thicket, copse, shrubs, bracken, brake.

brusque, *adj.* abrupt, blunt, rough, unceremonious, bluff, gruff, ungracious, uncivil, discourteous, impolite, rude, crude, curt. **—Ant.** courteous, courtly, polished, refined, gentle. **—Syn. Study.** See BLUNT.

brutal, *adj.* **1.** savage, cruel, inhuman, ruthless, pitiless, unfeeling, barbarous, barbarian, uncivilized, ferocious, brutish, barbaric, truculent. **2.** crude, coarse, gross, harsh, rude, rough, uncivil, ungracious, impolite, unmannerly, ungentlemanly, brusque. **3.** irrational, unreasoning, brute, unthinking. **4.** bestial, beastly, animal, carnal. **—Ant.** kind, sensitive; artistic; gracious, rational, sensible; human.

brute, *n.* **1.** beast, quadruped. **2.** barbarian. **—adj. 3.** animal, brutish, irrational, unreasoning. **4.** savage, cruel, brutal. **5.** sensual, carnal. **—Ant.** human; kind; spiritual.

bubbly, *adj.* **1.** frothy, foamy, effervescent, sparkling, spumescent, carbonated. **2.** high-spirited, vivacious, animated, lively, bouncy, effusive, energetic, sprightly, effervescent, sparky, perky, pert, peppy, frisky. **—Ant.** flat, colorless.

building, *n.* edifice, structure, construction, erection.

bulk, *n.* **1.** size, magnitude, mass, volume, dimensions. **2.** greater part, majority, most; body, mass. **—v. 3.** grow, swell, bulge, expand, enlarge, aggrandize.

bulky, *adj.* massive, ponderous, unwieldy, clumsy, cumbersome; great, big, large, huge, vast. **—Ant.** small, delicate.

bunch, *n.* **1.** cluster; group, lot, bundle, batch, collection. **2.** knob, lump, protuberance.

bundle, *n.* **1.** bunch. **2.** parcel, pack, package, packet.

burden, *n.* **1.** load, weight. **2.** encumbrance, impediment, grievance, trial. **3.** substance, core, point, es-

sence, epitome, central idea, tenor, drift. **4.** refrain, chorus. **—v. 5.** load, overload, oppress. **—Ant.** disburden.

burlesque, *n.* caricature, parody, travesty, satire, farce, imitation, comedy, spoof, lampoon, sendup, takeoff. **—Syn. Study.** BURLESQUE, CARICATURE, PARODY, TRAVESTY refer to literary or dramatic forms that imitate works or subjects to achieve a humorous or satiric purpose. The characteristic device of BURLESQUE is mockery of serious or trivial subjects through association with their opposites: *a burlesque of high and low life.* CARICATURE, usu. associated with visual arts or with visual effects in literary works, implies exaggeration of characteristic details: *The caricature emphasized his large nose.* PARODY achieves its humor through application of the style or technique of a well-known work or author to unaccustomed subjects: *a parody of Hemingway.* TRAVESTY takes a serious subject and uses a style or language that seems incongruous or absurd: *a travesty of a senator making a speech.*

burn, *v.* **1.** flame. **2.** tingle, be hot, glow. **3.** consume, scorch, sear, singe, char, toast, brown, tan, bronze. **—n. 4.** brook, rivulet, rill, run, runnel, streamlet, runlet.

burst, *v.* **1.** explode, crack, blow up, split. **2.** rend, tear, break. **—n. 3.** explosion. **4.** spurt, outpouring, gust. **—Ant.** implode.

bury, *v.* **1.** inter, entomb, inhume, inearth. **2.** sink. **3.** cover, hide, conceal, secrete, shroud, enshroud. **—Ant.** disinter; rise; uncover.

business, *n.* **1.** occupation, trade, craft, metier, profession, calling, employment, vocation, pursuit. **2.** company, concern, enterprise, corporation, firm, partnership. **3.** affair, matter, concern, transaction. **4.** commerce, trade, traffic. **5.** function, duty, office, position.

busy, *adj.* **1.** engaged, occupied, diligent, industrious, employed, working, assiduous, active, sedulous, hardworking. **2.** active, brisk, bustling, spry, agile, nimble. **3.** officious, meddlesome, prying. **—Ant.** indolent, unoccupied, lazy.

but, *conj.* **1.** however, nevertheless, yet, further, moreover, still. **2.** excepting, save, except. **—prep. 3.** excepting, except, save, excluding. **—adv. 4.** only, just, no more than.

butcher, *n.* **1.** meat dealer. **2.** slaughterer, meat dresser. **3.** murderer, slayer, killer, assassin, cutthroat, thug. **—v. 4.** kill, slaughter. **5.** slaughter, massacre, murder, kill, assassinate. **6.** bungle, botch, fail in. **—Syn. Study.** See SLAUGHTER.

buy, *v.* **1.** purchase. **2.** hire, bribe, corrupt. **—Ant.** sell.

byword, *n.* **1.** slogan, motto. **2.** proverb, maxim, apothegm, aphorism, saw, adage, saying. **3.** epithet.

C

cabal, See Syn. study at CONSPIRACY.

cabin, *n.* **1.** hut, shanty, shack, cot, cottage, shed, hovel. **—v. 2.** cramp, confine, enclose, restrict.

cadaver, See Syn. study at BODY

cadaverous, *adj.* **1.** deathly pale, deathly, ghastly, ghostly, ghostlike, spectral, corpselike, pallid, livid. **2.** gaunt, haggard, drawn, withered, shriveled, emaciated, skeletal, wasted, hollow-eyed, scrawny, peaked, wizened. **—Ant.** robust, hearty, healthy.

cagey, *adj.* cunning, clever, shrewd, wily, astute, smart, wise, artful, canny, crafty, foxy, ingenious, sharp, slick, nimble-witted, quick-thinking, quick-witted, sharp-witted, savvy, hip.

cajole, *v.* wheedle, coax, beguile, entice, inveigle, flatter, soft-soap, sweet-talk, blandish.

calamity, *n.* affliction, adversity, ill fortune, misery, bad luck, distress, trouble, evil, hardship, trial, reverse, mischance, mishap, blow, misfortune, disaster, catastrophe, cataclysm. **—Ant.** fortune, blessing, boon. **—Syn. Study.** See DISASTER.

calculate, *v.* **1.** count, figure, reckon, cast, estimate, weigh, deliberate, compute, rate. **2.** suit, adapt, fit, adjust. **—Ant.** assume, guess.

calculation, *n.* **1.** computation, figuring, reckoning, estimate, estimation. **2.** estimate, forecast, expectation, prospect, anticipation. **3.** forethought, planning, circumspection, caution, wariness, foresight, cautiousness, discretion, prudence, deliberation. —Ant. guess, assumption.

call, v. **1.** cry out. **2.** announce, proclaim. **3.** awaken, waken, rouse, wake up, arouse. **4.** summon, invite, send for. **5.** convoke, convene, call together, assemble, muster. **6.** telephone, ring up. **7.** name, give a name to, label, term, designate, style, dub, christen, entitle, nominate, denominate. **8.** reckon, consider, estimate, designate. **9.** shout, cry, voice. **10.** visit, stop. —n. **11.** shout, cry, outcry. **12.** summons, signal; invitation, bidding; appointment. **13.** need, occasion; demand, claim, requisition.

callous, adj. **1.** hard, hardened, inured, indurated. **2.** unfeeling, insensible, blunt, apathetic, unimpressible, indifferent, unsusceptible, obtuse; dull, sluggish, torpid, slow. —Ant. soft; sensitive; alert.

calm, adj. **1.** still, quiet, smooth, motionless, tranquil, unruffled, mild, peaceful. **2.** tranquil, peaceful, serene, self-possessed, cool, collected, unruffled, composed, undisturbed, sedate, aloof. —n. **3.** stillness, serenity, calmness, quiet, smoothness, tranquillity, peacefulness, aloofness, self-possession, composure, repose, equanimity. —v. **4.** still, quiet, tranquilize, pacify, smooth, appease, compose; allay, assuage, mollify, soothe, soften. —Ant. perturbed; tempestuous; excite, agitate. —Syn. Study. CALM, COLLECTED, COMPOSED, COOL imply the absence of agitation. CALM implies an unruffled state in the midst of disturbance all around: *He remained calm throughout the crisis.* COLLECTED implies complete command of one's thoughts, feelings, and behavior, usu. as a result of effort: *The witness was remarkably collected during questioning.* COMPOSED implies inner peace and dignified self-possession: *pale but composed.* COOL implies clarity of judgment and absence of strong feeling or excitement: *cool in the face of danger.*

can, v. **1.** know how to, be able to, have the ability or power or right or qualifications or means to. —n. **2.** tin, container.

cancel, v. **1.** cross out, delete, dele, erase, expunge, obliterate, blot out, efface, rub out. **2.** void, annul, countermand, revoke, rescind, counterbalance, compensate for, allow for. —Ant. ratify.

candid, adj. **1.** frank, open, outspoken, sincere, ingenuous, naive, artless, honest, plain, guileless, straightforward, aboveboard, free, honorable. **2.** impartial, honest, just, fair, unprejudiced, unbiased. **3.** white, clear, pure, unadulterated, lucid, transparent, pellucid, lucent. —Ant. concealed, hidden, wily, deceitful; biased, prejudiced; turgid, cloudy, dull, impure. —Syn. Study. See FRANK.

candor, n. frankness, honesty, forthrightness, directness, candidness, truthfulness, sincerity, openness, outspokenness, bluntness, brusqueness, plain speaking. —Ant. evasiveness, deceitfulness.

canon, n. **1.** rule, law, standard, formula. **2.** criterion, principle, standard.

cantankerous, adj. irritable, irascible, quarrelsome, fractious, cross, crotchety, captious, choleric, foul-tempered, mean-tempered, grumpy, ornery, testy, touchy, peevish, surly, vinegary, vinegarish, petulant, snappish, waspish. —Ant. sweet-natured, kindly, gracious.

capable, adj. **1.** able, competent, efficient, intelligent, clever, skillful, ingenious, sagacious, gifted, accomplished. **2.** fitted, adapted, suited, qualified. **3.** susceptible, open, admitting, allowing, permitting, permissive. —Ant. incapable.

capacious, adj. spacious, roomy, ample, large, broad, comprehensive, wide. —Ant. confining, narrow.

capacity, n. **1.** cubic contents, volume, magnitude, dimensions, amplitude. **2.** ability, power, aptitude, faculty, wit, genius, aptness, bent, forte, leaning, propensity, ableness, talent, discernment; caliber, cleverness, skill, skillfulness, competency, competence, readiness, capability. **3.** position, relation, function, sphere, area, province; office, post, charge, responsibility. —Ant. incapacity, incompetence.

caper, v. **1.** gambol, frolic, frisk, play, romp, cavort, rollick. —n. **2.** escapade, prank, frolic, lark, antic, adventure, dido, bit of mischief.

capital, n. **1.** metropolis, seat. **2.** wealth, principal, investment, worth, resources, assets, stock. —adj. **3.** principal, first, important, chief, prime, primary, major, leading, cardinal, essential, vital. **4.** excellent, first-rate, splendid, fine. **5.** large-size, upper case. **6.** fatal, serious. —Ant. trivial, unimportant. —Syn. Study. CAPITAL, CHIEF, MAJOR, PRINCIPAL apply to a main or leading representative of a kind. CAPITAL may suggest preeminence, importance, or excellence: *a capital idea.* CHIEF often means highest in office or power; it may mean most important: *the chief clerk; the chief problem.* MAJOR refers to someone or something that is greater in number, quantity, or importance: *a major resource; a major poet.* PRINCIPAL refers to the most distinguished, influential, or foremost person or thing: *a principal stockholder; the principal reason.*

capricious, adj. wayward, arbitrary, whimsical, whimsied, inconstant, changeable, fickle, temperamental, mercurial, volatile, unstable, erratic. —Ant. predictable, stable, steady. —Syn. Study. See FICKLE.

capsize, v. overturn, upset. —Ant. right.

captivate, v. charm, enthrall, enchant, fascinate, hypnotize, bewitch, enamor, win, catch. —Ant. repel, repulse.

captivity, n. bondage, servitude, slavery, thralldom, serfdom, subjection; imprisonment, confinement, incarceration. —Ant. freedom.

capture, v. **1.** seize, take prisoner, catch, arrest, snare, apprehend, grab, nab; imprison, incarcerate. —n. **2.** arrest, seizure, apprehension, catch. —Ant. release.

carcass, n. **1.** body, corpse, cadaver. **2.** framework, skeleton. —Syn. Study. See BODY.

care, n. **1.** worry, anxiety, concern, solicitude, trouble. **2.** heed, caution, pains, anxiety, regard, attention, vigilance, carefulness, solicitude, circumspection, alertness, watchfulness, wakefulness. **3.** burden, charge, responsibility. —v. **4.** have concern or regard, be solicitous or anxious, worry, be troubled. **5.** like, be inclined or disposed or interested.

careen, v. sway, lurch, lean, heel over, swing, roll, rock, wobble, reel, weave, waver.

careful, adj. **1.** cautious, circumspect, watchful, wakeful, vigilant, guarded, chary, discreet, wary, suspicious, prudent, tactful; trustworthy. **2.** painstaking, meticulous, discerning, exact, thorough, concerned, scrupulous, finical, conscientious, attentive, heedful, thoughtful. —Ant. careless. —Syn. Study. CAREFUL, CAUTIOUS, DISCREET, WARY imply a watchful guarding against something. CAREFUL implies guarding against mistakes, harm, or bad consequences by paying close attention to details and by being concerned or solicitous: *He was careful not to wake the baby.* CAUTIOUS implies a fear of some unfavorable situation and investigation before acting: *cautious about investments.* DISCREET implies being prudent in speech or action and being trustworthy: *discreet inquiries about his credit rating.* WARY implies a vigilant lookout for a danger suspected or feared: *wary of polite strangers.*

caregiver, n. protector, safekeeper, guardian, caretaker, attendant, custodian, warden, patron, nurse.

careless, adj. **1.** inattentive, incautious, unwary, unthoughtful, forgetful, remiss, negligent, neglectful, unmindful, heedless, reckless, indiscreet, thoughtless, unconcerned. **2.** negligent, inaccurate, inexact. **3.** unconsidered; inconsiderate. —Ant. careful.

careworn, adj. drawn, worn, pinched, worn-down, strained, haggard, hollow-eyed, ravaged, woebegone.

cargo, n. freight, load, burden, lading.

caricature, n. **1.** burlesque, exaggeration, travesty, take-off, parody, farce, satire, lampoon, cartoon. —v. **2.** burlesque, exaggerate, travesty, parody, take off, satirize, lampoon. —Syn. Study. See BURLESQUE.

carnal, adj. **1.** human, temporal, worldly, mundane, earthly, unregenerate, natural, unspiritual. **2.** sensual, fleshly, bodily, animal. **3.** lustful, impure, gross, lecherous, worldly, lascivious, salacious, libidinous, concupiscent, lewd, lubricious, wanton, lubricous. —Ant. spiritual, moral, intellectual. —Syn. Study. CARNAL, SENSUAL, ANIMAL all refer to the physical rather than the rational or spiritual nature of human beings. CARNAL, although it may refer to any bodily need or urge, most often refers to sexuality: *carnal knowledge; the carnal sin of gluttony.* SENSUAL most often describes the arousal or gratification of erotic urges: *sensual eyes; sensual delights.* ANIMAL may describe any physical appetite, but is sometimes used of sexual appetite: *animal greediness; animal lust.*

carriage, n. **1.** vehicle, cart, wagon, conveyance; dog-cart, brougham, hansom, victoria, calash, buckboard, carry-all, shay, sulky, surrey. **2.** bearing, manner, mien, deportment, behavior, conduct, demeanor.

carry, v. **1.** convey, bear, transport, transmit, transfer, take, bring. **2.** bear, support, sustain, stand, suffer. **3.** lead, impel, drive, conduct, urge. **4.** effect, accomplish, gain, secure, win, capture.

cascade, n. **1.** waterfall, falls, cataract, Niagara, downpour, shower, torrent, deluge. —v. **2.** spill, spill over, overflow, fall, flow over, brim over, overbrim, pour, pour down, plummet.

case, n. **1.** instance, example, illustration, occurrence. **2.** state, circumstance, situation, condition, contingency; plight, predicament. **3.** patient; action, suit, lawsuit, cause, process, trial. **4.** receptacle, box, container, chest, folder, envelope, sheath. **5.** frame, framework.

cast, v. **1.** throw, fling, hurl, deposit, propel, put, toss, pitch, shy, sling, pitch. **2.** throw off, shed, slough, put off, lay aside. **3.** direct, turn, cause to fall, throw, shed, impart. **4.** throw out, send forth, hurl, toss. **5.** throw down, defeat, overwhelm. **6.** part with, lose. **7.** set aside, throw aside, discard, reject, dismiss, disband. **8.** emit, eject, vomit, spew forth, puke. **9.** bestow, confer. **10.** arrange, plan out, allot, apportion, appoint, assign. **11.** mold, form, found. **12.** compute, calculate, reckon; forecast, foretell. **13.** ponder, consider, contrive, devise, plan. **14.** throw. **15.** calculate, add. **16.** consider; plan, scheme. —n. **17.** throw, fling, toss. **18.** fortune, lot. **19.** appearance, form, shape, mien, demeanor. **20.** sort, kind, style. **21.** tendency, inclination, turn, bent, trend, air. **22.** turn, twist; warp. **23.** tinge, tint, hue, shade, touch; dash, trace, hint, suggestion. **24.** computation, calculation, addition. **25.** forecast, conjecture, guess.

caste, n. rank, class, status, social level, social stratum, standing, place, station, position, estate, echelon, grade.

castle, n. **1.** fortress, citadel, stronghold. **2.** palace, chateau, mansion. **3.** (chess) rook.

casual, adj. **1.** unexpected, fortuitous, unforeseen, chance, accidental. **2.** unpremeditated, offhand, unintentional. **3.** careless, negligent, unconcerned. **4.** irregular, occasional, random. —Ant. premeditated, deliberate, calculated; careful; regular, routine.

cataclysm, n. **1.** disaster, calamity, catastrophe, debacle, crash, collapse, convulsion, meltdown. **2.** flood, deluge, inundation. —Syn. Study. See DISASTER.

catalog, See Syn. study at LIST.

catalogue, n. list, roll, roster, register, record, inventory.

catastrophe, n. disaster, mishap, cataclysm, calamity, misfortune, mischance; end, dénouement, finale; upshot, conclusion, windup, termination. —Ant. triumph. —Syn. Study. See DISASTER.

catch, v. **1.** capture, apprehend, arrest. **2.** ensnare, entrap, deceive, entangle. **3.** surprise, detect, take unawares. **4.** strike, hit. **5.** lay hold of, grasp, seize, snatch, grip, entangle, clutch. **6.** captivate, charm, enchant, fascinate, win, bewitch. —n. **7.** capture, apprehension, arrest, seizure. **8.** ratchet, bolt. **9.** take. —Ant. release.

catchword, n. slogan, catchphrase, byword, motto, watchword, maxim, household word, tag line, battle cry, rallying cry.

cause, n. **1.** occasion, reason, ground, grounds, basis; motive, determinant, incitement, inducement. **2.** purpose, object, aim, end. —v. **3.** bring about, effect, determine, make, produce, create, originate, occasion, give rise to. —Syn. Study. See REASON.

caustic, adj. corrosive, cutting, scathing, stinging, slashing, mordant, incisive, keen, acid, trenchant, sharp, ironic, satiric, sarcastic, sardonic, mordacious. —Ant. bland, harmless, innocuous.

caution, n. **1.** prudence, discretion, circumspectness, watchfulness, circumspection, heed, care, wariness, heedfulness, vigilance, forethought, providence. **2.** warning, admonition, advice, injunction, counsel. —v. **3.** warn, admonish, advise, enjoin, counsel, forewarn. —Ant. carelessness. —Syn. Study. See WARN.

cautious, adj. prudent, careful, heedful, watchful, discreet, wary, vigilant, alert, provident, chary, circumspect, guarded. —Ant. careless, heedless, indiscreet. —Syn. Study. See CAREFUL.

caveat, n. warning, caution, forewarning, notice, notification, admonition, recommendation, suggestion, monition, verbum sapienti or verbum sap or verbum sat or verb. sap., word to the wise, tip, tip-off.

cavity, n. hollow, hole, void.

cease, v. **1.** stop, desist, stay. **2.** terminate, end, culminate. **3.** discontinue, end. —Ant. start, begin; continue, persist.

cede, v. yield, resign, surrender, relinquish, abandon, give up; make over, grant, transfer, convey. —Ant. persist, maintain.

celebrate, v. **1.** commemorate, honor, observe. **2.** proclaim, announce. **3.** praise, extol, laud, glorify, honor, applaud, commend. **4.** solemnize, ritualize.

celebrated, adj. famous, renowned, well-known, distinguished, illustrious, eminent, famed. —Ant. obscure, unknown. —Syn. Study. See FAMOUS.

celebrity, n. **1.** fame, renown, celebrityhood, stardom, superstardom, name, acclaim, acclamation, recognition, eminence, distinction, illustriousness, reputation, repute, éclat, notoriety. **2.** notable, big name, personage, star, superstar, luminary, VIP, name, somebody, nabob, big shot, biggie, megastar, celeb. —Ant. nobody, nonentity, has-been, wannabe.

celerity, See Syn. study at SPEED.

celestial, adj. heavenly, ethereal, empyreal, empyrean, elysian, otherworldly, transcendental, unearthly, divine, paradisial, paradisaic, supernal. —Ant. earthly, mundane, terrestrial.

censure, n. **1.** condemnation, reproof, disapproval, disapprobation, blaming, criticism, blame, reproach, reprehension, rebuke, reprimand, stricture, animadversion. —v. **2.** criticize, disapprove, condemn, find fault with. **3.** reprove, rebuke, reprimand, reprehend, chide, blame, reproach. —Ant. praise, commend. —Syn. Study. See ABUSE. See also REPRIMAND.

center, n. **1.** middle, midst. **2.** pivot, hub, point, axis. —Ant. brim, edge.

ceremony, n. rite, ritual, formality, observance. —Ant. informality.

certain, adj. **1.** confident, sure, assured, convinced, satisfied, indubitable, indisputable, unquestionable, undeniable, incontestable, irrefutable, unquestioned, incontrovertible, absolute, positive, plain, patent, obvious, clear. **2.** sure, inevitable, infallible, unfailing. **3.** fixed, agreed upon, settled, prescribed, determined, determinate, constant, stated, given. **4.** definite, particular, special, especial. **5.** unfailing, reliable, trustworthy, dependable, trusty. —Ant. uncertain; unclear, unsure; unsettled; indefinite; fallible, unreliable.

certainty, n. **1.** unquestionableness, inevitability, certitude, assurance, confidence, conviction. **2.** fact, truth. —Ant. doubt, uncertainty.

chagrin, n. **1.** embarrassment, distress, disconcertion, discomfiture, discomposure, abashment, humiliation, shame, mortification. —v. **2.** abash, take aback, discomfit, distress, disconcert, embarrass, shame, humiliate, mortify. —Syn. Study. See SHAME.

champion, n. **1.** winner, victor, hero. **2.** defender, protector, vindicator. **3.** fighter, warrior. —v. **4.** defend, support, maintain, fight for, advocate. —Ant. loser; oppose.

chance, n. **1.** fortune, fate, luck, accident, fortuity. **2.** possibility, contingency, probability. **3.** opportunity, opening, occasion. **4.** risk, hazard, peril, danger, jeopardy. —v. **5.** happen, occur, befall, take place. —adj. **6.** casual, accidental, fortuitous. —Ant. necessity, inevitability; surety.

change, v. **1.** alter, make different, turn, transmute, transform, vary, modify. **2.** exchange, substitute, convert, shift, replace; barter, trade, commute. **3.** interchange. —n. **4.** variation, alteration, modification, deviation, transformation, transmutation, mutation, conversion, transition. **5.** substitution, exchange. **6.** variety, novelty, innovation, vicissitude. —Ant. endure; immutability. —Syn. Study. CHANGE, ALTER both mean to make a difference in the state or condition of a thing. To CHANGE is to make a material or radical difference or to substitute one thing for another of the same kind: *to change a lock; to change one's plans.* To ALTER is to make some partial change, as in appearance, but usu. to preserve the identity: *to alter a garment; to alter a contract.*

chaotic, adj. confused, upset, tumultuous, turbulent, disordered, unruly, disorderly, anarchic, scattered, disarrayed, higgledy-piggledy.

character, n. **1.** individuality, personality. **2.** feature, trait, characteristic. **3.** nature, quality, disposition, mien, constitution, cast. **4.** name, reputation, repute. **5.** status, capacity. **6.** symbol, mark, sign, letter, figure, emblem. —Syn. Study. CHARACTER, PERSONALITY refer to the sum of the characteristics possessed by a person. CHARACTER refers esp. to the moral qualities and ethical standards that make up the inner nature of a person: *a man of sterling character.* PERSONALITY refers particularly to outer characteristics, as wittiness or charm, that determine the impression that a person makes upon others: *a pleasing personality.* See also REPUTATION.

characteristic, adj. **1.** typical, distinctive, discrete, special, peculiar, singular. —n. **2.** feature, quality, trait, peculiarity, mark, attribute, property. —Syn. Study. See FEATURE.

charge, v. **1.** load, lade, burden, freight. **2.** command, enjoin, exhort, order, urge, bid, require. **3.** impute, ascribe. **4.** blame, accuse, indict, arraign, impeach, inculpate, incriminate, involve, inform against, betray. **5.** attack, assault, set on. —n. **6.** load, burden, cargo, freight. **7.** duty, responsibility, commission, office, trust, employment. **8.** care, custody, superintendence, ward, management. **9.** command, injunction, exhortation, order, direction, mandate, instruction, precept. **10.** accusation, indictment, imputation, allegation, crimination, incrimination. **11.** price, cost. **12.** tax, lien, cost, expense, encumbrance, outlay, expenditure, liability, debt. **13.** onset, attack, onslaught, assault, encounter.

charismatic, adj. alluring, attractive, fascinating, magnetic, captivating, spellbinding, beguiling, glamorous, entrancing, riveting, bewitching, prepossessing.

charitable, adj. **1.** generous, openhanded, liberal, beneficent, benign, kind, benignant, benevolent, bountiful, lavish. **2.** broad-minded, liberal, lenient, considerate, mild, kindly. —Ant. mean, stingy; narrow-minded, inconsiderate. —Syn. Study. See GENEROUS.

charm, n. **1.** attractiveness, allurement, fascination, enchantment, bewitchment, spell, witchery, magic, sorcery. **2.** trinket, bauble, jewelry; amulet. —v. **3.** enchant, fascinate, captivate, catch, entrance, enrapture, transport, delight, please; attract, allure, enamor, bewitch; ravish. —Ant. revulsion; disgust.

chart, n. map, plan.

charter, n. **1.** privilege, immunity, guaranty, warranty. —v. **2.** lease, hire, rent, let. —Syn. Study. See HIRE.

chary, adj. **1.** careful, wary, cautious, circumspect. **2.** shy, bashful, self-effacing. **3.** fastidious, choosy, particular. **4.** sparing, stingy, frugal. —Ant. careless.

chaste, adj. virtuous, pure, moral, decent, undefiled, modest, continent; clean, elevated, unsullied; unaffected, simple, subdued, neat, straight, honest; refined, classic, elegant. —Ant. sinful, impure, immodest; unrefined, coarse, inelegant.

chasten, v. discipline, punish, chastise, restrain, subdue, humble. —Ant. indulge, humor.

chattels, See Syn. study at PROPERTY.

cheap, adj. **1.** inexpensive, low-priced. **2.** paltry, common, mean, low, lowly, poor, inferior, base. —Ant. dear, expensive, costly; exceptional, extraordinary, elegant. —Syn. Study. CHEAP, INEXPENSIVE agree in their suggestion of low cost. CHEAP now often suggests shoddiness, inferiority, showy imitation, untowardness, and the like: *a cheap fabric.* INEXPENSIVE emphasizes lowness of price (although more expensive than

CHEAP) and suggests that the value is fully equal to the cost: *an inexpensive dress.* It is often used as an evasion for the more pejorative CHEAP.

cheat, *n.* **1.** fraud, swindle, deception, trick, imposture, wile, deceit, artifice, chicanery, stratagem, hoax, imposition, snare, trap, pitfall, catch. **2.** swindler, imposter, trickster, sharper, cheater, dodger, charlatan, fraud, fake, phony, mountebank, rogue, knave. —*v.* **3.** deceive, defraud, trick, victimize, mislead, dupe, gudgeon, cog, gull, cozen, outwit, bamboozle, delude, hoodwink, beguile, inveigle, swindle, con; entrap, hoax, ensnare, fool, cajole; dissemble. —**Syn. Study.** CHEAT, DECEIVE, TRICK, VICTIMIZE refer to the use of fraud or artifice to obtain an unfair advantage or gain. CHEAT usu. means to be dishonest in order to make a profit for oneself: *to cheat customers by shortchanging them.* DECEIVE suggests misleading someone by false words or actions: *He deceived his parents about his whereabouts.* TRICK means to mislead by a ruse or stratagem, often of a crafty or dishonorable kind: *I was tricked into signing the note.* VICTIMIZE means to make a victim of; it connotes a particularly contemptible act: *to victimize a blind person.*

check, *v.* **1.** stop, halt, delay, arrest. **2.** curb, restrain, control, repress, chain, bridle, hinder, hobble, obstruct, curtail. **3.** investigate, verify, assess, test, measure, examine, compare. **4.** agree, correspond. **5.** pause, stop. —*n.* **6.** restraint, curb, bridle, bit, hindrance, obstacle, obstruction, impediment, control, bar, barrier, restriction, damper, interference, deterrent, repression. **7.** rebuff, arrest, stoppage, cessation, repulse, halt. **8.** ticket, receipt, coupon, tag, counterfoil, stub. —**Ant.** continue, advance, foster, support. —**Syn. Study.** CHECK, CURB, RESTRAIN refer to putting a control on movement, progress, action, etc. CHECK implies arresting suddenly, halting or causing to halt by means of drastic action: *to check a movement toward reform.* CURB implies slowing or stopping forward motion: *to curb inflation; to curb a horse.* RESTRAIN implies the use of force to put under control or hold back: *to restrain one's enthusiasm; to restrain unruly spectators.* See also STOP.

cheer, *n.* **1.** encouragement, comfort, solace. **2.** gladness, gaiety, animation, joy, mirth, glee, merriment, cheerfulness. **3.** food, provisions, victuals, repast, viands. —*v.* **4.** gladden, enliven, inspirit, exhilarate, animate, encourage. **5.** shout, applaud, acclaim, salute. —**Ant.** derision; misery; discourage, deride; boo, hiss.

cheerful, *adj.* **1.** cheery, gay, blithe, happy, lively, spirited, sprightly, joyful, joyous, mirthful, buoyant, gleeful, sunny, jolly. **2.** pleasant, bright, gay, winsome, gladdening, cheery, cheering, inspiring, animating. **3.** hearty, robust, ungrudging, generous. —**Ant.** sad, unhappy, cheerless, miserable; unpleasant; stingy, mean.

cherish, *v.* **1.** foster, harbor, entertain, humor, encourage, indulge. **2.** nurse, nurture, nourish, support, sustain, comfort. **3.** treasure, cling to, hold dear. —**Ant.** abandon, scorn. —**Syn. Study.** CHERISH, FOSTER, HARBOR imply the giving of affection, care, or shelter. CHERISH suggests regarding or treating something or someone as an object of affection or value: *to cherish a friendship.* FOSTER implies sustaining and nourishing something with care, esp. in order to promote, increase, or strengthen it: *to foster a hope.* HARBOR usu. suggests sheltering someone or entertaining something undesirable: *to harbor a criminal; to harbor a grudge.*

chicanery, *n.* dishonesty, deception, trickery, subterfuge, double-dealing, underhandedness, fraud, fraudulence, rascality, roguery, knavery, dupery, hanky-panky, villainy, dissimulation.

chide, *v.* **1.** scold, fret, fume, chafe. **2.** reprove, rebuke, censure, criticize, scold, admonish, upbraid, reprimand, blame, reprehend. —**Ant.** praise, commend.

chief, *n.* **1.** head, leader, ruler, chieftain, commander. —*adj.* **2.** principal, most important, prime, first, supreme, leading, paramount, great, grand, cardinal, master; vital, essential. —**Ant.** follower, disciple; unimportant, trivial, trifling; secondary. —**Syn. Study.** See CAPITAL[1].

chiefly, *adv.* mostly, principally, mainly, especially, particularly, eminently. —**Ant.** last, lastly.

childish, *adj.* childlike, puerile, infantile, young, tender; weak, silly, simple, ingenuous, guileless, trusting, confident. —**Ant.** adult, sophisticated. —**Syn. Study.** CHILDISH, INFANTILE, CHILDLIKE refer to characteristics or qualities of childhood. CHILDISH refers to characteristics that are undesirable and unpleasant: *childish selfishness.* INFANTILE usu. carries an even stronger idea of disapproval or scorn: *infantile temper tantrums.* CHILDLIKE refers to those characteristics that are desirable or merely neutral: *childlike innocence.*

childlike, See Syn. study at CHILDISH.

chill, *n.* **1.** cold, coldness, frigidity. **2.** shivering, ague. **3.** depression, damp. —*adj.* **4.** chilly, cool, unfriendly, depressing, discouraging, bleak. —*v.* **5.** cool, freeze; depress, discourage, deject, dishearten. —**Ant.** warm.

chivalrous, *adj.* courteous, gallant, noble, courtly, gracious, helpful, thoughtful, considerate, unselfish, attentive, generous, giving, magnanimous, greathearted, benevolent, altruistic, kindhearted, kindly. —**Ant.** selfish, self-centered, ungenerous.

choice, *n.* **1.** selection, choosing, election, option, alternative, preference. —*adj.* **2.** worthy, excellent, superior, fine, select, rare, uncommon, valuable, precious. —**Syn. Study.** CHOICE, ALTERNATIVE, OPTION suggest the power of choosing between things. CHOICE implies the opportunity to choose freely: *Her choice for dessert was ice cream.* ALTERNATIVE suggests a chance to choose only one of a limited number of possibilities: *I had the alternative of going to the party or staying home alone.* OPTION emphasizes the right or privilege of choosing: *He had the option of taking the prize money or a gift.*

choose, *v.* select, elect, prefer, pick, cull.

chop, *v.* cut, mince.

chore, See Syn. study at TASK.

chronic, *adj.* **1.** inveterate, constant, habitual, confirmed, hardened. **2.** perpetual, continuous, continuing, unending, never-ending, everlasting. —**Ant.** fleeting, temporary.

chuckle, *v.,* *n.* laugh, giggle, titter. —**Ant.** cry, sob.

chutzpah, *n.* audacity, pluck, self-confidence, self-assertiveness, brashness, boldness, temerity, temerariousness, aggressiveness, hardihood, effrontery, presumption, presumptuousness, brazenness, impudence, impertinence, insolence, nerve, cheek, gall, face, crust, brass. —**Ant.** timidity, modesty, self-effacement.

circle, *n.* **1.** ring, periphery, circumference, perimeter. **2.** ring, circlet, crown. **3.** compass, area, sphere, province, field, region, bounds, circuit. **4.** cycle, period, series. **5.** coterie, set, clique, society, club, company, class, fraternity. **6.** sphere, orb, globe, ball. —*v.* **7.** surround, encircle, encompass, round, bound, include. **8.** orbit, circuit, revolve. —**Syn. Study.** CIRCLE, CLUB, COTERIE refer to restricted social groups. A CIRCLE is a little group; in the plural it often suggests a section of society interested in one mode of life, occupation, etc.: *a sewing circle; theatrical circles.* CLUB implies an organized association with fixed requirements for membership: *an athletic club.* COTERIE suggests a small and exclusive group intimately associated because of similar backgrounds and interests: *a literary coterie.*

circuit, *n.* **1.** course, tour, journey, revolution, orbit. **2.** circumference, perimeter, periphery, boundary, compass. **3.** space, area, region, compass, range, sphere, province, district, field.

circuitous, *adj.* indirect, roundabout, circular, wandering, meandering, crooked, devious, deviant, tortuous, serpentine, twisting, vagrant, oblique, errant, circumambulatory, circumlocutory. —**Ant.** straight, straightforward, blunt.

civil, *adj.* polite, courteous, courtly, gracious, complaisant, respectful, deferential, obliging; affable, urbane, debonair, chivalrous, gallant, suave; refined, well-mannered, well-bred, civilized. —**Ant.** uncivil, discourteous; rude; ill-mannered, unrefined. —**Syn. Study.** CIVIL, COURTEOUS, POLITE imply avoidance of rudeness toward others. CIVIL suggests only minimal observance of social amenities: *a civil reply.* COURTEOUS implies more positive, sincere, and thoughtful consideration for others: *a courteous thank-you note.* POLITE implies habitual courtesy, arising from a consciousness of one's training and

the demands of good manners: *a polite young man.*

claim, *v.* **1.** demand, require, ask, call for, challenge. **2.** assert, maintain, uphold. —*n.* **3.** demand, request, requirement, requisition, call. **4.** right, title, privilege, pretension.

clamor, *n.* **1.** shouting, uproar, outcry, noise, hullabaloo. **2.** vociferation. —*v.* **3.** vociferate, cry out, shout. **4.** importune, demand noisily. —**Ant.** quiet, serenity, taciturnity. —**Syn. Study.** See NOISE.

clandestine, *adj.* secret, private, concealed, hidden, sly, underhand. —**Ant.** open, candid, aboveboard.

clannish, *adj.* exclusive, exclusionary, exclusory, select, selective, restricted, restrictive, cliquish, cliquey, snobbish, snobby, elite, elect, ethnocentric. —**Ant.** open, unrestricted, all-embracing.

clash, *v.* **1.** clang, crash, clap, dash, clatter, clank. **2.** collide. **3.** conflict, struggle, disagree, interfere, content. —*n.* **4.** collision. **5.** conflict, opposition, disagreement, interference, struggle, contradiction. —**Ant.** harmony, agreement.

clasp, *n.* **1.** brooch, pin, clip, hook, fastening, catch, hasp. **2.** embrace, hug, grasp. —*v.* **3.** clip. **4.** grasp, grip, clutch. **5.** embrace, hug, clutch, grasp, fold.

clean, *adj.* **1.** unsoiled, unstained, clear, unblemished, pure, flawless, spotless, unsullied, neat, immaculate. **2.** pure, purified, unmixed, unadulterated, clarified. **3.** uncontaminated, not radioactive. **4.** clear, readable, legible. **5.** unsullied, undefiled, moral, innocent, upright, honorable, chaste. **6.** neat, trim, shapely, graceful, delicate, light. **7.** adroit, deft, dextrous. **8.** complete, perfect, entire, whole, unabated, unimpaired. —*adv.* **9.** cleanly, neatly. **10.** wholly, completely, perfectly, entirely, altogether, fully, thoroughly, in all respects, out and out. —*v.* **11.** scour, scrub, sweep, brush, wipe, mop, dust, wash, rinse, lave, cleanse, deterge, purify, clear; decontaminate. —**Ant.** dirty, contaminated; radioactive; impure, immoral; clumsy, awkward.

cleanse, *v.* clean. —**Ant.** soil.

clear, *adj.* **1.** unclouded, light, bright, pellucid, limpid, diaphanous, crystalline, transparent, luminous. **2.** bright, shining, lucent. **3.** perceptible, understood, distinct, intelligible, orotund, comprehensible, lucid, plain, perspicuous, conspicuous, obvious. **4.** distinct, evident, plain, obvious, apparent, manifest, palpable, patent, unmistakable, unequivocal, unambiguous, indisputable, undeniable, unquestionable. **5.** convinced, certain, positive, definite, assured, sure. **6.** innocent, pure, not guilty, unsullied, irreproachable, unblemished, clean, unspotted, unadulterated, moral, undefiled, virtuous, immaculate, spotless. **7.** serene, calm, untroubled, fair, cloudless, sunny. **8.** unobstructed, open, free, unimpeded, unhindered, unhampered, unencumbered, unentangled. **9.** smooth, clean, even, regular, unblemished. **10.** emptied, empty, free, rid. **11.** limitless, unlimited, unqualified, unequivocal, boundless, free, open. **12.** net. —*adv.* **13.** clearly. —*v.* **14.** clarify, purify, refine, clean, cleanse. **15.** acquit, absolve, exonerate, vindicate, excuse, justify. **16.** extricate, disentangle, disabuse, rid, disencumber, disengage. **17.** liberate, free, emancipate, set free, disenthrall, loose, unchain, unfetter, let go. —**Ant.** cloudy, dim, obscure; indistinct, unclear; equivocal, doubtful; guilty, culpable; troubled, disturbed, perturbed, obstructed; limited, confined.

clearly, *adv.* definitely, distinctly, evidently, plainly, understandably, obviously, certainly, surely, assuredly, entirely, completely, totally. —**Ant.** confusedly, indefinitely; partly.

cleft, *n.* split, fissure, crack, crevice, cleaving, cleavage, rift, breach, break, fracture, cranny, gap, chasm. —**Ant.** joint, link.

clemency, *n.* mildness, mercy, lenience, leniency, forbearance, compassion, tenderness, kindness, kindliness, gentleness, mercifulness. —**Ant.** severity, austerity, cruelty, mercilessness.

clever, *adj.* **1.** bright, quick, able, apt, smart, intelligent, expert, gifted, talented, ingenious, quick-witted. **2.** skillful, adroit, dextrous, nimble, agile, handy. —**Ant.** dull, slow, dimwitted; clumsy, awkward, maladroit.

climb, *v.* **1.** mount, ascend, scale, surmount. **2.** rise, arise. —*n.* **3.** ascent, climbing, scaling, rise. —**Ant.** descend; descent.

cloister, *n.* monastery, nunnery, convent, abbey, priory.

close, *v.* **1.** stop, obstruct, shut, block, bar, stop up, clog, choke. **2.** enclose, cover in, shut in. **3.** bring together, join, unite. **4.** end, terminate, finish, conclude, cease, complete. **5.** terminate, conclude, cease, end. **6.** come together, unite, coalesce, join. **7.** grapple, fight. —*adj.* **8.** shut, tight, closed, fast, confined. **9.** enclosed, shut in. **10.** heavy, unventilated, muggy, oppressive, uncomfortable, dense, thick. **11.** secretive, reticent, taciturn, close-mouthed, silent, uncommunicative, incommunicative, reserved, withdrawn. **12.** parsimonious, stingy, tight, closefisted, penurious, niggardly, miserly, mean. **13.** scarce, rare. **14.** compact, condensed, dense, thick, solid, compressed, firm. **15.** near, nearby, adjoining, adjacent, neighboring, immediate. **16.** intimate, confidential, attached, dear, devoted. **17.** strict, searching, minute, scrupulous, exact, exacting, accurate, precise, faithful, nice. **18.** intent, fixed, assiduous, intense, concentrated, earnest, constant, unremitting, relentless, unrelenting. —*n.* **19.** end, termination, conclusion. **20.** junction, union, coalescence, joining. —**Ant.** open.

clothes, *n.* clothing, attire, raiment, dress, garments, vesture, habit, costume, garb, vestments, habiliments, accouterments.

cloud, *n.* **1.** fog, haze, mist, vapor. **2.** host, crowd, throng, multitude, swarm, horde, army. —*v.* **3.** becloud, bedim, shadow, overshadow, obscure, shade. —**Ant.** clarify.

cloudy, *adj.* **1.** overcast, shadowy, clouded, murky, lowering, gloomy, cloudy, dismal, depressing, sullen. **2.** obscure, indistinct, dim, blurred, blurry, unclear, befogged, muddled, confused, dark, turbid, muddy, opaque. —**Ant.** clear; distinct.

club, *n.* **1.** stick, cudgel, bludgeon, blackjack, billy; bat. **2.** society, organization, association, circle, set, coterie, clique, fraternity, sorority. —**Syn. Study.** See CIRCLE.

clumsy, *adj.* **1.** awkward, unskillful, ungainly, lumbering, ungraceful, lubberly. **2.** unhandy, maladroit, unskillful, inexpert, bungling, ponderous, heavy, heavy-handed, inept. —**Ant.** adroit, clever, dexterous.

coarse, *adj.* **1.** impure, base, common, inferior, faulty, crude, rude, rough. **2.** indelicate, unpolished, uncivil, impolite, gruff, bluff, boorish, churlish. **3.** gross, broad, indecent, vulgar, crass, ribald, lewd, lascivious, amoral, immoral, dirty. —**Ant.** pure, refined; civil, civilized, cultivated; decent, decorous.

coast, *n.* shore, seashore, strand, beach, seaside, seacoast, littoral.

coax, *v.* wheedle, cajole, beguile, inveigle, persuade, flatter. —**Ant.** force, bully; deter.

cockeyed, *adj.* **1.** askew, skewed, out of kilter, awry, deviant, crooked, alop, askance, topsy-turvy, oblique, (*Brit.*) wonky. **2.** foolish, silly, whimsical, loony, wacky. **3.** drunk, intoxicated, inebriated, dazed with drink, loaded, plastered.

coeval, See Syn. study at CONTEMPORARY.

cognizant, See Syn. study at CONSCIOUS.

cohere, See Syn. study at STICK.

coherence, *n.* **1.** cohesion, union, connection. **2.** connection, congruity, consistency, correspondence, harmony, harmoniousness, agreement, unity, rationality. —**Ant.** incoherence.

coincident, See Syn. study at CONTEMPORARY.

cold, *adj.* **1.** chilly, chill, cool, frigid, gelid, frozen, freezing. **2.** dead. **3.** impassionate, unemotional, unenthusiastic, passionless, apathetic, unresponsive, unsympathetic, unaffected, stoical, phlegmatic, unfeeling, unsusceptible, unimpressible, unimpressed, cool, sluggish, torpid, indifferent, cold-blooded, unconcerned, heartless, unperturbed, imperturbable. **4.** polite, formal, reserved, unresponsive, unfriendly, inimical, hostile. **5.** calm, deliberate, depressing, dispiriting, disheartening, uninspiring, spiritless, unaffecting, dull. **6.** faint, weak. **7.** bleak, raw, cutting, nipping, arctic, polar, frosty, icy, wintry, chill, chilly. —*n.* **8.** chill, shivers, ague. —**Ant.** warm, hot.

collect, *v.* gather, assemble, amass, accumulate, aggregate, scrape together. —**Ant.** strew, broadcast, spread. —**Syn. Study.** See GATHER.

collected, See Syn. study at CALM.

collection, *n.* **1.** set, accumulation,

mass, heap, pile, hoard, store, aggregation. **2.** contribution, alms.

colloquial, *adj.* conversational, informal. —**Ant.** formal. —**Syn. Study.** COLLOQUIAL, CONVERSATIONAL, INFORMAL refer to types of speech or to usages that are not on a formal level. COLLOQUIAL is often mistakenly used with a connotation of disapproval, as if it meant "vulgar" or "bad" or "incorrect" usage, whereas it merely describes a casual or familiar style used in speaking and writing: *colloquial expressions.* CONVERSATIONAL refers to a style used in the oral exchange of ideas, opinions, etc.: *The newsletter was written in an easy conversational style.* INFORMAL means without formality, without strict attention to set forms, unceremonious; it describes the ordinary, everyday language of cultivated speakers: *informal English.*

colossal, See Syn. study at GIGANTIC.

column, *n.* pillar, shaft, stele, pilaster.

combat, *v.* **1.** fight, contend, battle, oppose, struggle, contest, war, resist, withstand. —*n.* **2.** fight, skirmish, contest, battle, struggle, conflict, war, brush, affair, encounter, engagement. —**Ant.** support, defend.

combination, *n.* **1.** conjunction, association, union, connection, coalescence, blending. **2.** composite, compound, mixture, amalgamation, amalgam. **3.** alliance, confederacy, federation, union, league, coalition, association, society, club; cartel, combine, monopoly; conspiracy, cabal.

combine, *v.* **1.** unite, join, conjoin, associate, coalesce, blend, mix, incorporate, involve, compound, amalgamate. —*n.* **2.** combination (def. 3). —**Ant.** dissociate, separate. —**Syn. Study.** See MIX.

comfort, *v.* **1.** soothe, console, relieve, ease, cheer, pacify, calm, solace, gladden, refresh. —*n.* **2.** relief, consolation, solace, encouragement. —**Ant.** agitate, discommode, incommode; discomfort, discouragement. —**Syn. Study.** COMFORT, CONSOLE, SOOTHE imply assuaging sorrow, worry, discomfort, or pain. COMFORT means to lessen someone's grief or distress by giving strength and hope and restoring a cheerful outlook: *to comfort a despairing friend.* CONSOLE, a more formal word, means to make grief or distress seem lighter by means of kindness and thoughtful attentions: *to console a bereaved parent.* SOOTHE means to pacify or calm: *to soothe a crying child.*

comical, *adj.* amusing, humorous, funny, comic, laugh-provoking, silly, droll, risible, playful, clownish, ludic; laughable, ridiculous, ludicrous, absurd, foolish. —**Syn. Study.** See AMUSING.

command, *v.* **1.** order, direct, bid, demand, charge, instruct, enjoin, require. **2.** govern, control, oversee, manage, rule, lead, preside over; dominate, overlook. **3.** exact, compel, secure, demand, require, claim. —*n.* **4.** order, direction, bidding, injunction, charge, mandate, behest, commandment, requisition, requirement, instruction, dictum. **5.** control, mastery, disposal, ascendancy, rule, sway, superintendence, power, management, domination. —**Ant.** obey. —**Syn. Study.** See DIRECT.

commence, *v.* begin, open, start, originate, inaugurate, enter upon or into. —**Ant.** end, finish, terminate. —**Syn. Study.** See BEGIN.

commend, *v.* **1.** recommend, laud, praise, extol, applaud, eulogize. **2.** entrust. —**Ant.** censure, blame; distrust.

commendation, *n.* **1.** recommendation, praise, approval, approbation, applause; medal. **2.** eulogy, encomium, panegyric, praise. —**Ant.** censure, blame.

comment, *n.* **1.** explanation, elucidation, expansion, criticism, critique, note, addendum, annotation, exposition, commentary. **2.** remark, observation, criticism. —*v.* **3.** remark, explain, annotate, criticize.

commerce, *n.* **1.** interchange, traffic, trade, dealing, exchange, business. **2.** intercourse, conversation, converse, intimacy.

commercial, *adj.* **1.** mercantile, trafficking. —*n.* **2.** advertisement.

common, *adj.* **1.** mutual. **2.** joint, united. **3.** public, communal. **4.** notorious. **5.** widespread, general, ordinary, familiar, usual, customary, frequent, habitual, everyday. **7.** hackneyed, trite, stale, commonplace. **8.** mean, low, mediocre, inferior. **9.**

coarse, vulgar, ordinary, undistinguished, ill-bred. —**Ant.** exceptional, singular, extraordinary, separate; unfamiliar, strange. —**Syn. Study.** COMMON, ORDINARY, VULGAR refer, often with derogatory connotations, to what is usual or most often experienced. COMMON applies to what is widespread or unexceptional; it often suggests inferiority or coarseness: *common servants; common cloth.* ORDINARY refers to what is to be expected in the usual order of things; it suggests being average or below average: *a high price for something of such ordinary quality.* VULGAR means belonging to the people or characteristic of common people; it suggests low taste, coarseness, or ill breeding: *vulgar manners; vulgar speech.* See also GENERAL.

commonplace, *adj.* **1.** ordinary, uninteresting. **2.** trite, hackneyed, common, banal, stereotyped. —*n.* **3.** cliché, bromide. —**Ant.** extraordinary, original. —**Syn. Study.** COMMONPLACE, BANAL, TRITE, HACKNEYED describe words, remarks, and styles of expression that are lifeless and uninteresting. COMMONPLACE characterizes expression that is so ordinary, self-evident, or generally accepted as to be boring or pointless: *a commonplace affirmation of the obvious.* BANAL often suggests an inane or insipid quality: *banal conversation.* TRITE suggests that an expression has lost its force because of excessive repetition: *trite poetic imagery.* HACKNEYED is a stronger word implying that the expression has become meaningless from overuse: *hackneyed metaphors.*

commotion, *n.* **1.** tumult, disturbance, perturbation, agitation, disorder, pother, bustle, ado, turmoil, turbulence, riot, violence. **2.** sedition, insurrection, uprising, revolution. —**Ant.** peace, calm, serenity.

communicate, *v.* **1.** impart, transmit; give, bestow. **2.** divulge, announce, declare, disclose, reveal, make known. —**Ant.** withhold, conceal.

community, *n.* **1.** hamlet, town, village, city. **2.** public, commonwealth, society. **3.** agreement, identity, similarity, likeness. —*adj.* **4.** common, joint, cooperative.

compact, *adj.* **1.** dense, solid, firm, tightly packed, condensed. **2.** concise, pithy, terse, laconic, short, sententious, succinct, brief, pointed, meaningful. —*v.* **3.** condense, consolidate, compress. **4.** stabilize, solidify. —*n.* **5.** covenant, pact, contract, treaty, agreement, bargain, entente, arrangement, convention, concordat. —**Ant.** diverse, dispersed. —**Syn. Study.** See AGREEMENT.

companion, *n.* **1.** associate, comrade, partner, fellow, mate. **2.** assistant; nurse, governess. —**Syn. Study.** See ACQUAINTANCE.

company, *n.* **1.** group, band, party, troop, assemblage, body, unit. **2.** companionship, fellowship, association, society. **3.** assembly, gathering, concourse, crowd, circle, set, congregation. **4.** firm, partnership, corporation, concern, house, syndicate, association.

compare, *v.* **1.** liken, contrast. **2.** vie, compete, equal, resemble.

compartment, *n.* division, section, apartment, cabin, roomette.

compass, See Syn. study at RANGE.

compassion, *n.* sorrow, pity, sympathy, feeling, ruth, mercy, commiseration, kindness, kindliness, tenderness, heart, tender-heartedness, clemency. —**Ant.** mercilessness, indifference. —**Syn. Study.** See SYMPATHY.

compassionate, *adj.* pitying, sympathetic, tender, kind, merciful, tender-hearted, kindly, clement, gracious, benignant, gentle. —**Ant.** merciless, pitiless, harsh, cruel, mean.

compel, *v.* **1.** force, drive, coerce, constrain, oblige, commit, impel, motivate, necessitate. **2.** subdue, subject, bend, bow, overpower. **3.** unite, drive together, herd. —**Ant.** coax. —**Syn. Study.** COMPEL, IMPEL agree in the idea of forcing someone to be or do something. COMPEL implies an external force; it may be a persuasive urging from another person or a constraining reason or circumstance: *Bad health compelled him to resign.* IMPEL suggests an internal motivation deriving either from a moral constraint or personal feeling: *Guilt impelled him to offer money.*

compensate, *v.* **1.** counterbalance, counterpoise, offset, countervail, make up for. **2.** remunerate, reward,

---

pay, recompense, reimburse. **3.** atone, make amends.

compensation, *n.* **1.** recompense, remuneration, payment, amends, reparation, indemnity, reward. **2.** atonement, requital, satisfaction, indemnification.

compete, *v.* contend, vie, contest, rival, emulate, oppose, dispute, strive, cope, struggle. —**Ant.** support. —**Syn. Study.** COMPETE, CONTEND, CONTEST mean to strive or struggle. COMPETE emphasizes a sense of rivalry and of striving to do one's best: *to compete for a prize.* CONTEND suggests striving in opposition or debate as well as competition: *to contend against obstacles; to contend about minor details.* CONTEST implies struggling to gain or hold something in a formal competition or battle: *to contest with the incumbent for the nomination.*

competent, *adj.* **1.** fitting, suitable, sufficient, convenient, adequate, qualified, fit, apt, capable, proficient. **2.** permissible, allowable. —**Ant.** incompetent, inapt.

competitor, *n.* opponent, contestant, rival, antagonist. —**Ant.** ally, friend.

complain, *v.* grumble, growl, murmur, whine, moan, bewail, lament, bemoan. —**Syn. Study.** COMPLAIN, GRUMBLE, WHINE are terms for expressing dissatisfaction or discomfort. To COMPLAIN is to protest against or lament a condition or wrong: *to complain about high prices.* To GRUMBLE is to utter surly, ill-natured complaints half to oneself: *to grumble about the service.* To WHINE is to complain in a meanspirited, objectionable way, using a nasal tone; it often suggests persistence: *to whine like a spoiled child.*

complement, *v.* **1.** complete, supplement, add to, round out. —*n.* **2.** supplement. —**Syn. Study.** COMPLEMENT, SUPPLEMENT both mean to make additions to something; a lack or deficiency is implied. To COMPLEMENT means to complete or perfect a whole; it often refers to putting together two things, each of which supplies what is lacking in the other: *Statements from different points of view may complement each other.* To SUPPLEMENT is to add something in order to enhance, extend, or improve a whole: *Some additional remarks supplemented the sales presentation.*

complete, *adj.* **1.** whole, entire, full, intact, unbroken, unimpaired, undivided, one, perfect, developed, unabated, undiminished, fulfilled. **2.** finished, ended, concluded, consummated, done, consummate, perfect, thorough; through-and-through, dyed-in-the-wool. —*v.* **3.** finish, end, conclude, consummate, perfect, accomplish, do, fulfill, achieve, effect, terminate, close. —**Ant.** incomplete; unfinished; begin, commence, initiate. —**Syn. Study.** COMPLETE, ENTIRE, INTACT suggest that there is no lack or defect, nor has any part been removed. COMPLETE implies that a unit has all its parts, fully developed or perfected; it may also mean that a process or purpose has been carried to fulfillment: *a complete explanation; a complete assignment.* ENTIRE describes something having all its elements in an unbroken unity: *an entire book.* INTACT implies that something has remained in its original condition, complete and unimpaired: *a package delivered intact.*

complex, *adj.* **1.** compound, composite, complicated, mixed, mingled. **2.** involved, complicated, intricate, perplexing, tangled. —*n.* **3.** complexus, net, network, complication, web, tangle. —**Ant.** simple; simplex.

compliment, *n.* **1.** praise, commendation, admiration, tribute, honor, eulogy, encomium, panegyric. **2.** regard, respect, civility; flattery. —*v.* **3.** commend, praise, honor, flatter. **4.** congratulate, felicitate. —**Ant.** insult, injury; decry, disparage.

comply, *v.* acquiesce, obey, yield, conform, consent, assent, agree, accede, concede. —**Ant.** refuse.

component, *adj.* **1.** composing, constituent. —*n.* **2.** element, ingredient, part. —**Ant.** complex.

composed, *adj.* calm, tranquil, serene, undisturbed, peaceful, cool, placid, pacific, unruffled, sedate, unperturbed, self-possessed, controlled, imperturbable, quiet. —**Ant.** upset, perturbed, disturbed, disquieted. —**Syn. Study.** See CALM.

composite, *adj.* **1.** compound, complex. —**Ant.** divers.

composure, *n.* serenity, calm, calm-

---

ness, tranquillity, equability, peacefulness, quiet, coolness, equanimity, self-possession. —**Ant.** agitation.

comprehend, *v.* **1.** understand, conceive, know, grasp, see, discern, imagine, perceive. **2.** include, comprise, embrace, take in, embody, contain. —**Syn. Study.** See KNOW, INCLUDE.

comprehensive, *adj.* comprehending, inclusive, broad, wide, large, extensive, sweeping. —**Ant.** limited.

compress, *v.* **1.** condense, squeeze, constrict, contract, press, crowd. —*n.* **2.** pad, bandage. —**Ant.** spread, stretch.

comprise, *v.* include, comprehend, contain, embrace, embody; consist or be composed of. —**Ant.** exclude. —**Syn. Study.** See INCLUDE.

compulsory, *adj.* **1.** compelling, coercive, constraining. **2.** compelled, forced, obligatory, arbitrary, binding, necessary, unavoidable, inescapable, ineluctable. —**Ant.** free, unrestrained, unrestricted.

compute, *v.* reckon, calculate, estimate, count, figure.

comrade, *n.* associate, companion, friend, fellow, partner, mate, yokefellow, colleague, confrere, cohort, compeer, crony, ally, sidekick, chum, buddy, pal.

conceal, *v.* **1.** hide, secrete, cover, put away, bury, screen. **2.** keep secret, hide, disguise, dissemble. —**Ant.** reveal. —**Syn. Study.** See HIDE[1].

conceit, *n.* **1.** self-esteem, vanity, amour-propre, egotism, complacency. **2.** fancy, imagination, whim, notion, vagary; thought, idea, belief, conception. —**Ant.** humility, modesty. —**Syn. Study.** See PRIDE.

conceited, *adj.* vain, proud, egotistical, self-important, self-satisfied, smug, complacent, self-sufficient. —**Ant.** humble, modest, shy, retiring.

conceive, *v.* **1.** imagine, create, ideate, think. **2.** understand, apprehend, comprehend.

concentrate, *v.* **1.** focus, condense. **2.** intensify, purify, clarify. —**Ant.** dissipate, disperse.

conception, See Syn. study at IDEA.

concern, *v.* **1.** affect, touch, interest, relate to, engage, involve, include. **2.** disquiet, trouble, disturb. —*n.* **3.** business, affair, interest, matter. **4.** solicitude, anxiety, care, worry, burden, responsibility. **5.** relation, bearing, appropriateness, consequence. **6.** firm, company, business, establishment, corporation, partnership, house. —**Ant.** exclude; calm; unconcern, indifference. —**Syn. Study.** CONCERN, CARE, WORRY connote an uneasy and burdened state of mind. CONCERN implies an anxious sense of interest in or responsibility for something: *concern over a friend's misfortune.* CARE suggests a heaviness of spirit caused by dread, or by the constant pressure of burdensome demands: *Poverty weighed them down with care.* WORRY is a state of agitated uneasiness and restless apprehension: *distracted by worry over investments.*

conciliate, *v.* **1.** placate, win over, soothe, propitiate, appease. **2.** reconcile, pacify. —**Ant.** alienate, antagonize. —**Syn. Study.** See APPEASE.

concise, *adj.* succinct, terse, compact, to the point, crisp, curt, laconic, short. —**Syn. Study.** CONCISE, SUCCINCT, TERSE refer to speech or writing that uses few words to say much. CONCISE implies that unnecessary details or verbiage have been eliminated: *a concise summary of a speech.* SUCCINCT suggests clarity of expression as well as brevity: *praised for her succinct statement of the problem.* TERSE suggests brevity combined with wit or polish to produce particularly effective expression; however, it may also suggest brusqueness: *a terse prose style; offended by a terse reply.*

conciseness, *n.* brevity, laconicism, summary, terseness, pithiness, sententiousness. —**Ant.** diversity. —**Syn. Study.** See BREVITY.

conclusion, *n.* **1.** end, close, termination, completion, ending, finale. **2.** summing up, summation. **3.** result, issue, outcome. **4.** settlement, arrangement, wind-up. **5.** decision, judgment, determination. **6.** deduction, inference. —**Ant.** beginning, commencement.

concur, *v.* **1.** agree, consent, coincide, harmonize. **2.** cooperate, combine, help, conspire, contribute. —**Ant.** disagree.

condemn, *v.* **1.** blame, censure, disapprove. **2.** doom, find guilty, sen-

---

tence, damn. —**Ant.** liberate, release, exonerate.

condense, *v.* compress, concentrate, consolidate, contract; abridge, epitomize, digest, shorten, abbreviate, reduce, diminish, curtail. —**Ant.** expand.

condescend, *v.* deign, stoop, descend, degrade oneself.

condition, *n.* **1.** state, case, situation, circumstance, conjuncture, circumstances. **2.** requisite, prerequisite, requirement, contingency, consideration, proviso, provision, stipulation, sine qua non. —*v.* **3.** determine, limit, restrict.

conduct, *n.* **1.** behavior, demeanor, action, actions, deportment, bearing, carriage, mien, manners. **2.** direction, management, execution, guidance, leadership, administration. **3.** guidance, escort, leadership, convoy, guard. —*v.* **4.** behave, deport, act, bear. **5.** direct, manage, carry on, supervise, regulate, administrate, administer, execute, guide, lead. **6.** lead, guide, escort, convoy.

confederation, *n.* alliance, confederacy, league, federation, union, coalition. —**Syn. Study.** See ALLIANCE.

confer, *v.* **1.** bestow, give, donate, grant, vouchsafe, allow, promise. **2.** compare. **3.** consult together, discuss, deliberate, discourse, parley, converse, advise, talk. —**Syn. Study.** See CONSULT. See also GIVE.

conference, *n.* meeting, interview, parley, colloquy, convention, consultation. —**Syn. Study.** See CONVENTION.

confess, *v.* acknowledge, avow, own, admit, grant, concede; declare, aver, confirm. —**Syn. Study.** See ACKNOWLEDGE.

confidence, *n.* **1.** trust, belief, faith, reliance, dependence. **2.** self-reliance, assurance, boldness, intrepidity, self-confidence, courage. —**Ant.** distrust, mistrust; modesty. —**Syn. Study.** CONFIDENCE, ASSURANCE both imply a faith in oneself. CONFIDENCE usually implies a firm belief in oneself without a display of arrogance or conceit: *His friends admired his confidence at the party.* ASSURANCE implies even more sureness of one's own abilities, often to the point of offensive boastfulness: *She spoke with assurance but lacked the qualifications for the job.*

confident, *adj.* sure, bold, believing, assured, self-assured, certain, positive, convinced; brave, intrepid. —**Ant.** shy, modest, diffident.

confidential, *adj.* **1.** secret, restricted, private. **2.** familiar, trusted, trusty, trustworthy, faithful, honorable, honest. —**Syn. Study.** See FAMILIAR.

confine, *v.* **1.** enclose, bound, circumscribe, circle, encircle, limit, bind, restrict. **2.** immure, imprison, incarcerate. —*n.* **3.** (*usually plural*) bounds, boundary, perimeter, periphery, limits; frontiers, borders.

confirm, *v.* **1.** make certain or sure, assure, corroborate, verify, substantiate, authenticate. **2.** make valid or binding, ratify, sanction, approve, validate, bind. **3.** make firm, strengthen, settle, establish, fix, assure.

conflict, *v.* **1.** collide, clash, oppose, vary with, interfere. **2.** contend, fight, combat, battle. —*n.* **3.** battle, struggle, encounter, contest, collision, fight; siege, strife; contention, controversy, opposition, variance. **4.** interference, discord, disunity, disharmony, inconsistency, antagonism. —**Ant.** harmony.

conform, *v.* **1.** comply, yield, agree, assent, harmonize. **2.** tally, agree, correspond, square. **3.** adapt, adjust, accommodate. —**Ant.** disagree, dissent.

confuse, *v.* **1.** jumble, disorder, disarrange, disturb, disarray. **2.** confound, mix, mix up, intermingle, mingle. **3.** perplex, mystify, nonplus, bewilder, astonish, surprise, disarm, shock, disconcert, embarrass. **4.** disturb, disconcert, abash, mortify, shame, confound. —**Ant.** enlighten.

confusion, *n.* **1.** perplexity, embarrassment, surprise, astonishment, shock, bewilderment, distraction. **2.** disorder, disarray, disarrangement, jumble, mess, turmoil, chaos, tumult, furor, commotion, ferment, agitation, stir. **3.** embarrassment, abashment, shamefacedness, shame, mortification. —**Ant.** enlightenment; clarity.

congenial, *adj.* sympathetic, kindred, similar, friendly, favorable, genial, agreeable, pleasing, pleasant, complaisant, suited, adapted, well-suited, suitable, apt, proper. —**Ant.**

---

unsympathetic, disagreeable; unsuitable.

congenital, See Syn. study at INNATE.

congress, *n.* meeting, assembly, conference, council, convention.

conjecture, *n.* **1.** hypothesis, theory, guess, surmise, opinion, supposition, inference, deduction. —*v.* **2.** conclude, suppose, assume, presume, suspect, surmise, hypothesize, theorize, guess. —**Ant.** determine, ascertain. —**Syn. Study.** See GUESS.

conjoin, *v.* associate, unite, join, combine, connect. —**Ant.** disjoin, dissociate.

connect, *v.* join, unite, link, conjoin, couple, associate, combine; cohere. —**Ant.** disconnect, disjoin. —**Syn. Study.** See JOIN.

connection, *n.* **1.** junction, conjunction, union, joining, association, alliance, dependence, interdependence. **2.** link, yoke, connective, bond, tie, coupling. **3.** association, relationship, affiliation, affinity. **4.** circle, set, coterie, acquaintanceship. **5.** relation, relative, kinsman; kin, kith. —**Ant.** disjunction, dissociation.

conquer, *v.* **1.** win, gain. **2.** overcome, subdue, vanquish, overpower, overthrow, subjugate, defeat, master, subject, beat, rout, crush, reduce. **3.** surmount, overcome, overwhelm. —**Ant.** surrender, submit, give up, yield. —**Syn. Study.** See DEFEAT.

conquest, *n.* **1.** captivation, seduction, enchantment. **2.** vanquishment, victory, triumph. **3.** subjugation, overthrow, defeat, mastery, subjection, rout. —**Ant.** surrender. —**Syn. Study.** See VICTORY.

conscientious, *adj.* just, upright, honest, straightforward, incorruptible, faithful, careful, particular, painstaking, scrupulous, exacting, demanding; devoted, dedicated. —**Ant.** dishonest, corrupt, unscrupulous. —**Syn. Study.** See PAINSTAKING.

conscious, *adj.* **1.** awake, aware, sentient, knowing, cognizant, percipient, intelligent. **2.** sensible, sensitive, felt; rational, reasoning. **3.** deliberate, intentional, purposeful. —**Ant.** unconscious. —**Syn. Study.** CONSCIOUS, AWARE, COGNIZANT refer to a realization or recognition of something about oneself or one's surroundings. CONSCIOUS usually implies sensing or feeling certain facts, truths, conditions, etc.: *to be conscious of an extreme weariness; to be conscious of one's own inadequacy.* AWARE implies being mentally awake to something on a sensory level or through observation: *aware of the odor of tobacco; aware of gossip.* COGNIZANT, a more formal term, usually implies having knowledge about some object or fact through reasoning or through outside sources of information: *to be cognizant of the drawbacks of a plan.*

consecrate, *v.* **1.** sanctify, hallow, venerate, elevate. **2.** devote, dedicate. —**Ant.** desecrate. —**Syn. Study.** See DEVOTE.

consecutive, *adj.* successive, continuous, regular, uninterrupted. —**Ant.** alternate, random.

consent, *v.* **1.** agree, assent, permit, allow, let, concur, yield, comply, accede, acquiesce. —*n.* **2.** assent, acquiescence, permission, compliance, concurrence, agreement. **3.** accord, concord, agreement, consensus. —**Ant.** refuse, disagree; dissent.

consequence, *n.* **1.** effect, result, outcome, issue, upshot, sequel, event, end. **2.** importance, significance, moment, weight, concern, interest. **3.** distinction, importance, singularity, weight. —**Syn. Study.** See EFFECT. See also IMPORTANCE.

consider, *v.* **1.** contemplate, meditate, reflect, ruminate, ponder, deliberate, weigh, revolve, study, think about. **2.** think, suppose, assume, presume. **3.** regard, respect, honor. —**Ant.** ignore. —**Syn. Study.** See STUDY.

considerate, *adj.* thoughtful, kind, charitable, patient, concerned, well-disposed. —**Ant.** inconsiderate.

consideration, *n.* **1.** considering, meditation, reflection, rumination, deliberation, contemplation, attention, advisement, regard. **2.** regard, account. **3.** recompense, payment, remuneration, fee, compensation, pay. **4.** thoughtfulness, sympathy, kindness, kindliness, patience, concern. **5.** importance, consequence, weight, significance, moment, interest. **6.** estimation, esteem, honor.

consistent, *adj.* **1.** agreeing, concordant, compatible, congruous, consonant, harmonious, suitable, apt, conformable, conforming. **2.** constant, faithful, assiduous, unwavering. **—Ant.** inconsistent.

consolation, *n.* comfort, solace, relief, encouragement. **—Ant.** discomfort, discouragement.

console, *v.* comfort, solace, cheer, encourage, soothe, relieve, calm. **—Ant.** aggravate, agitate, disturb. **—Syn. Study.** See COMFORT.

consonant, *n.* **1.** sonorant, fricative, stop, continuant. **—adj. 2.** in agreement, concordant, consistent, harmonious, compatible, congruous, conformant, suitable. **—Ant.** vowel; discordant, inconsistent.

conspicuous, *adj.* **1.** visible, manifest, noticeable, clear, marked, salient, discernible, perceptible, plain, open, apparent. **2.** prominent, outstanding, obvious, striking, noteworthy, attractive, eminent, distinguished, noted, celebrated, illustrious. **—Ant.** unclear, imperceptible; undistinguished, trifling.

conspiracy, *n.* plot, secret plan, intrigue, cabal, scheme, machination, treason, betrayal. **—Syn. Study.** CONSPIRACY, PLOT, INTRIGUE, CABAL refer to surreptitious or covert schemes to accomplish some end, most often an illegal or evil one. A CONSPIRACY usually describes a treacherous or illicit plan formulated in secret by a group of persons: *a conspiracy to control prices.* A PLOT is a carefully planned secret scheme formulated by one or more persons: *a plot to seize control of a company.* An INTRIGUE usually involves duplicity and deceit aimed at achieving personal advantage: *the petty intrigues of civil servants.* CABAL usually refers to a scheme formulated by a small group of highly placed persons to gain control of a government: *The regime was overthrown by a cabal of generals.*

conspire, *v.* **1.** complot, plot, intrigue, cabal, contrive, devise. **2.** combine, concur, cooperate.

constancy, *n.* firmness, fortitude, resolution, determination, inflexibility, decision, tenacity, steadfastness, faithfulness, fidelity, fealty, devotion, loyalty, regularity, stability, immutability, uniformity, permanence, sameness. **—Ant.** randomness, faithlessness, irregularity, instability.

constant, *adj.* **1.** invariable, uniform, stable, unchanging, fixed, immutable, invariable, unvarying, permanent. **2.** perpetual, unremitting, uninterrupted, continual, recurrent, assiduous, unwavering, unfailing, persistent, persevering, determined. **3.** steadfast, faithful, loyal, stanch, true, trusty, devoted, steady, resolute, firm, unshaking, unshakable, unwavering, unswerving, determined. **—Ant.** inconstant, variable, random, unstable, changeable; sporadic; unsteady, wavering. **—Syn. Study.** See FAITHFUL.

consternation, *n.* amazement, dread, dismay, bewilderment, awe, alarm, terror, fear, panic, fright, horror. **—Ant.** composure, equanimity.

constrain, *v.* **1.** force, compel, oblige, coerce. **2.** confine, check, bind, restrain, curb. **—Ant.** liberate, free.

constrict, *v.* compress, contract, shrink, cramp, squeeze, bind, tighten. **—Ant.** unbind, untie.

construct, *v.* build, frame, form, devise, erect, make, fabricate, raise. **—Ant.** raze.

consult, *v.* confer, deliberate. **—Syn. Study.** CONSULT, CONFER imply talking over a situation or a subject with someone. To CONSULT is to seek advice, opinions, or guidance from a presumably qualified person or source: *to consult with a financial analyst.* To CONFER is to exchange views, ideas, or information in a discussion: *The partners conferred about the decline in sales.*

consume, *v.* **1.** destroy, expend, use up, use, exhaust, spend, waste, dissipate, squander, eat up, devour. **2.** be absorbed *or* engrossed.

consummate, *v.* **1.** complete, perfect, fulfill, accomplish, achieve, finish, effect, execute, do. **—adj. 2.** complete, perfect, done, finished, effected, fulfilled, excellent, supreme. **—Ant.** imperfect, unfinished, base.

contagious, *adj.* **1.** communicable, infectious, catching. **2.** noxious, pestilential, poisonous, deadly, foul. **—Syn. Study.** CONTAGIOUS, INFECTIOUS are usu. distinguished in technical medical use. CONTAGIOUS, literally "communicable by contact," describes a very easily transmitted disease, as influenza or the common cold. INFECTIOUS refers to a disease involving a microorganism that can be transmitted from one person to an-

other only by a specific kind of contact; venereal diseases are usu. infectious. In nontechnical senses, CONTAGIOUS emphasizes the rapidity with which something spreads: *Contagious laughter ran through the hall.* INFECTIOUS suggests the pleasantly irresistible quality of something: *Her infectious good humor made her a popular guest.*

contain, *v.* hold, accommodate, include, embody, embrace. **—Syn. Study.** CONTAIN, HOLD, ACCOMMODATE express the idea that something is designed that something else can exist or be placed within it. CONTAIN refers to what is actually within a given container. HOLD emphasizes the idea of keeping within bounds; it refers also to the greatest amount or number that can be kept within a given container. ACCOMMODATE means to contain comfortably or conveniently, or to meet the needs of a certain number. A plane that ACCOMMODATES fifty passengers may be able to HOLD sixty, but at a given time may CONTAIN only thirty.

contaminate, *v.* defile, pollute, sully, stain, soil, tarnish, taint, corrupt, befoul, besmirch, infect, poison, vitiate.

contemplate, *v.* **1.** look at, view, observe, regard, survey. **2.** consider, reflect upon, meditate on, study, ponder, deliberate, think about, revolve. **3.** intend, mean, purpose, design, plan.

contemplative, *adj.* reflective, meditative, thoughtful, studious, musing. **—Ant.** inattentive.

contemporaneous, See Syn. study at CONTEMPORARY.

contemporary, *adj.* coexisting, coeval, contemporaneous, coincident. **—Ant.** antecedent; succeeding. **—Syn. Study.** CONTEMPORARY, CONTEMPORANEOUS, COEVAL, COINCIDENT mean happening or existing at the same time. CONTEMPORARY often refers to persons or their acts or achievements: *Hemingway and Fitzgerald, though contemporary, shared my values.* CONTEMPORANEOUS is applied chiefly to events: *the rise of industrialism, contemporaneous with the spread of steam power.* COEVAL refers either to very long periods of time, or to remote or distant times: *coeval stars, shining for millennia; coeval with the dawning of civilization.* COINCIDENT means occurring at the same time but without causal relationship: *World War II was coincident with the presidency of Franklin D. Roosevelt.*

contempt, *n.* **1.** scorn, disdain, derision, contumely. **2.** dishonor, disgrace, shame. **—Ant.** respect, reverence; honor. **—Syn. Study.** CONTEMPT, DISDAIN, SCORN imply strong feelings of disapproval and aversion toward what seems base, mean, or worthless. CONTEMPT is disapproval tinged with disgust: *to feel contempt for a weakling.* DISDAIN is a feeling that a person or thing is beneath one's dignity and unworthy of one's notice, respect, or concern: *a disdain for crooked dealing.* SCORN denotes open or undisguised contempt often combined with derision: *He showed only scorn for those who were not as ambitious as himself.*

contemptible, *adj.* despicable, mean, low, miserable, base, vile. **—Ant.** splendid, admirable.

contemptuous, *adj.* disdainful, scornful, sneering, insolent, arrogant, supercilious, haughty. **—Ant.** humble, respectful.

contend, *v.* **1.** struggle, strive, fight, battle, combat, vie, compete, rival. **2.** debate, dispute, argue, wrangle. **3.** assert, maintain, claim. **—Syn. Study.** See COMPETE.

content, *adj.* **1.** satisfied, contented, sanguine. **2.** assenting, acceding, resigned, willing, agreeable. **—v. 3.** appease, gratify, satisfy. **—Ant.** dissatisfy.

contention, *n.* **1.** struggling, struggle, strife, discord, dissension, quarrel, disagreement, squabble, feud, rupture, break, falling out; opposition, combat, conflict, competition, rivalry, contest. **2.** disagreement, dissension, debate, wrangle, altercation, dispute, argument, controversy. **—Ant.** agreement.

contentment, *n.* happiness, satisfaction, content, ease. **—Ant.** misery.

contest, *n.* **1.** struggle, conflict, battle, combat, fight, encounter. **2.** competition, contention, rivalry, match, tournament, tourney, game. **3.** strife, dispute, controversy, debate, argument, altercation, quarrel, contention. **—v. 4.** struggle, fight, compete, contend, vie, combat, battle. **5.** argue

against, dispute, controvert, litigate, debate, oppose, contend against. **6.** doubt, question, challenge, dispute. **7.** rival, strive, compete, vie, contend for. **—Syn. Study.** See COMPETE.

continual, *adj.* unceasing, incessant, ceaseless, uninterrupted, unremitting, constant, continuous, unbroken, successive, perpetual, unending, habitual, permanent, everlasting, eternal; recurrent, recurring, frequentative, repeated, repetitious, repetitive. **—Ant.** periodic, sporadic.

continue, *v.* **1.** keep on, go onward or forward, persist, persevere. **2.** last, endure, remain, persist. **3.** remain, abide, tarry, stay, rest. **4.** persist in, extend, perpetuate, prolong, carry on, maintain, retain; carry over, postpone, adjourn. **—Ant.** cease, interrupt. **—Syn. Study.** CONTINUE, ENDURE, PERSIST, LAST imply existing uninterruptedly for an appreciable length of time. CONTINUE implies duration or existence without break or interruption: *The rain continued for two days.* ENDURE, used of people or things, implies persistent continuance despite influences that tend to weaken, undermine, or destroy: *The temple has endured for centuries.* PERSIST implies steadfast and longer than expected existence in the face of opposition: *to persist in an unpopular belief.* LAST implies remaining in good condition or adequate supply: *I hope the cake lasts until the end of the party.*

contract, *n.* **1.** agreement, compact, bargain, covenant, arrangement, pact, convention, concordat, treaty, stipulation. **—v. 2.** draw together, compress, concentrate, condense, reduce, lessen, shorten, narrow, shrivel, shrink. **3.** elide, abbreviate, apocopate, abridge, epitomize. **—Ant.** disperse, spread. **—Syn. Study.** See AGREEMENT.

contradict, *v.* deny, gainsay, dispute, controvert, impugn, challenge, assail. **—Ant.** corroborate, support.

contradictory, *adj.* contrary, opposed, opposite, opposing, antagonistic, irreconcilable, paradoxical, inconsistent, contrary. **—Ant.** corroborative.

contrary, *adj.* **1.** opposite, opposed, contradictory, conflicting, discordant, counter, opposing. **2.** untoward, unfavorable, adverse, unfriendly, hostile, oppugnant, antagonistic, disagreeable, irreconcilable. **3.** perverse, self-willed, intractable, obstinate, refractory, headstrong, stubborn, pigheaded, contumacious. **—Ant.** obliging, compliant, tractable.

contrast, *v.* **1.** oppose, compare, differentiate, discriminate, distinguish, set off. **—n. 2.** opposition, comparison, differentiation, difference, discrimination, contrariety.

contrive, *v.* plan, devise, invent, design, hatch, brew, concoct, form, make; plot, complot, conspire, scheme; manage, effect.

control, *v.* **1.** dominate, command, manage, govern, rule, direct, reign over. **2.** check, curb, hinder, restrain, bridle, constrain. **3.** test, verify, prove. **—n. 4.** regulation, domination, command, management, direction, government, rule, reign, sovereignty, mastery, superintendence. **—Syn. Study.** See AUTHORITY.

controversy, *n.* dispute, contention, debate, disputation, disagreement, altercation; quarrel, wrangle, argument. **—Ant.** concord, agreement, accord. **—Syn. Study.** See ARGUMENT.

convene, *v.* assemble, meet, congregate, collect, gather. **2.** convoke, summon. **—Ant.** disperse, adjourn.

convenient, *adj.* suited, fit, appropriate, suitable, adapted, serviceable, well-suited, favorable, easy, comfortable, agreeable, helpful, advantageous, useful. **2.** at hand, accessible, handy. **—Ant.** inconvenient.

convention, *n.* **1.** assembly, conference, convocation, meeting. **2.** agreement, contract, compact, pact, treaty. **3.** agreement, consent. **4.** custom, precedent. **—Syn. Study.** CONVENTION, ASSEMBLY, CONFERENCE, CONVOCATION refer to meetings for particular purposes. CONVENTION usually suggests a formal meeting of members or delegates of a political, social, or professional group: *an annual medical convention.* ASSEMBLY usually implies a regular meeting for a customary purpose: *an assembly of legislators; a school assembly in the auditorium.* CONFERENCE suggests a meeting for consultation or discussion: *a sales conference.* CONVOCATION usually refers to an ecclesiastical or academic meeting whose participants

were summoned: *a convocation of economic experts.*

conventional, *adj.* **1.** formal, conforming, conformant. **2.** accepted, usual, habitual, customary, regular, common. **—Ant.** unconventional, unusual.

conversant, *adj.* **1.** familiar, versed, learned, skilled, practiced, well-informed, proficient. **2.** acquainted, associating. **—Ant.** unfamiliar, ignorant.

conversational, See Syn. study at COLLOQUIAL.

converse, *v.* **1.** talk, chat, speak, discuss, confabulate. **—n. 2.** discourse, talk, conversation, discussion, colloquy. **3.** opposite, reverse, transformation.

convert, *v.* **1.** change, transmute, transform, proselyte, proselytize. **—n. 2.** proselyte, neophyte, disciple. **—Ant.** renegade, recreant. **—Syn. Study.** See TRANSFORM.

convey, *v.* **1.** carry, transport, bear, bring, transmit, lead, conduct. **2.** communicate, impart.

conviction, See Syn. study at BELIEF.

convince, *v.* persuade, satisfy.

convocation, See Syn. study at CONVENTION.

convoy, *v.* **1.** accompany, escort, attend. **—n. 2.** escort, guard, attendance, protection. **—Ant.** desert. **—Syn. Study.** See ACCOMPANY.

convulsion, *n.* seizure, frenzy, paroxysm, fit, spasm, attack, outburst, outbreak, irruption, upheaval, eruption, storm, tumult, furor.

cool, *adj.* **1.** cold. **2.** calm, unexcited, unmoved, deliberate, composed, collected, self-possessed, unruffled, sedate, undisturbed, placid, quiet, dispassionate, unimpassioned. **3.** frigid, distant, superior, chilling, freezing, apathetic, repellent. **4.** indifferent, lukewarm, unconcerned, cold-blooded. **5.** audacious, impudent, shameless. **—v. 6.** allay, calm, moderate, quiet, temper, assuage, abate, dampen. **—Ant.** warm, tepid, lukewarm, hot. **—Syn. Study.** See CALM.

copious, *adj.* abundant, large, ample, plentiful, overflowing, profuse, rich, full, plenteous. **—Ant.** scarce, scanty, meager.

copy, *n.* **1.** transcript, reproduction, imitation, carbon, duplicate, facsimile. **2.** original, manuscript, pattern, model, archetype. **—v. 3.** imitate, duplicate, transcribe. **—Ant.** original.

corporal, *adj.* corporeal, bodily, physical, material. **—Ant.** spiritual. **—Syn. Study.** See PHYSICAL.

corporeal, See Syn. study at PHYSICAL.

corpse, *n.* body, remains, carcass. **—Syn. Study.** See BODY.

correct, *v.* **1.** set right, rectify, amend, emend, reform, remedy, cure. **2.** admonish, warn, rebuke, discipline, chasten, punish, castigate. **—adj. 3.** factual, truthful, accurate, proper, precise, exact, faultless, perfect, right, true. **—Ant.** ruin, spoil; incorrect, wrong. **—Syn. Study.** CORRECT, ACCURATE, PRECISE imply conformity to fact, standard, or truth. A CORRECT statement is one free from error, mistakes, or faults: *The student gave a correct answer in class.* An ACCURATE statement is one that, as a result of an active effort to comprehend and verify, shows careful conformity to fact, truth, or spirit: *The two witnesses said her account of the accident was accurate.* A PRECISE statement shows scrupulously strict and detailed conformity to fact: *The chemist gave a precise explanation of the experiment.*

correspond, *v.* **1.** conform, agree, harmonize, accord, match, tally, concur, coincide, fit, suit. **2.** communicate. **—Ant.** differ, diverge.

corrode, *v.* **1.** eat, gnaw, consume, erode, wear away. **2.** impair, deteriorate. **3.** canker, rust, crumble.

corrupt, *adj.* **1.** dishonest, venal, false, untrustworthy, bribable. **2.** debased, depraved, base, perverted, wicked, sinful, evil, dissolute, profligate, abandoned, reprobate. **3.** putrid, impure, putrescent, rotten, contaminated, adulterated, tainted, corrupted, spoiled, infected. **—v. 4.** bribe, lure, entice, demoralize, lead astray. **5.** pervert, deprave, debase, vitiate. **6.** infect, taint, pollute, contaminate, adulterate, spoil, defile, putrefy. **—Ant.** honest; honorable; pure, unspoiled, unadulterated; purify.

corruption, *n.* **1.** perversion, depravity, abandon, dissolution, sinfulness, evil, immorality, wickedness, profligacy. **2.** dishonesty, baseness, bribery. **3.** decay, rot, putrefaction, putrescence, foulness, pollution, de-

filement, contamination, adulteration. **—Ant.** righteousness; honesty; purity.

cosmetic, *n.* **1.** makeup, greasepaint, cover-up, paint, rouge, foundation, pancake, war paint. **—adj. 2.** beautifying, decorative, enhancing, improving, corrective. **3.** superficial, surface, shallow, cursory, passing, slap-dash, skin-deep.

cost, *n.* **1.** price, charge, expense, expenditure, outlay. **2.** sacrifice, loss, penalty, damage, detriment, suffering, pain.

costly, *adj.* valuable, dear, high-priced, sumptuous, expensive, precious, rich, splendid. **—Ant.** cheap.

coterie, *n.* society, association, set, circle, clique, club, brotherhood, fraternity. **—Syn. Study.** See CIRCLE.

cottage, *n.* cabin, lodge, hut, shack, cot, shanty. **—Ant.** palace, castle.

counsel, *n.* **1.** advice, opinion, instruction, suggestion, recommendation, caution, warning, admonition. **2.** consultation, deliberation, forethought. **3.** purpose, plan, design, scheme. **4.** lawyer, solicitor, barrister, advocate, counselor, adviser. **—Syn. Study.** See ADVICE.

countenance, *n.* **1.** aspect, appearance, look, expression, mien. **2.** face, visage, physiognomy. **3.** favor, encouragement, aid, assistance, support, patronage, sanction, approval, approbation. **—v. 4.** favor, encourage, support, aid, abet, patronize, sanction, approve. **—Ant.** condemn, prohibit. **—Syn. Study.** See FACE.

counteract, *v.* neutralize, counterbalance, annul, countervail, offset, contravene, thwart, oppose, resist, hinder, check, frustrate, defeat. **—Ant.** cooperate.

counterfeit, *adj.* **1.** spurious, false, fraudulent, forged. **2.** sham, pretended, feigned, simulated, fraudulent, false, mock, fake, unreal, ersatz. **—n. 3.** imitation, forgery, falsification, sham. **—v. 4.** imitate, forge, copy, fake, falsify. **5.** resemble. **6.** simulate, feign, sham, pretend. **7.** feign, dissemble. **—Ant.** genuine. **—Syn. Study.** See FALSE.

countryman, *n.* **1.** compatriot, fellow citizen. **2.** native, inhabitant. **3.** rustic, farmer, peasant, husbandman. **—Ant.** alien, foreigner.

couple, *n.* **1.** pair, duo, duet, yoke, brace, two, span. **—v. 2.** fasten, link, join, unite, associate, pair, conjoin, connect. **—Ant.** separate, disjoin.

courage, *n.* fearlessness, dauntlessness, intrepidity, fortitude, pluck, spirit, heroism, daring, audacity, bravery, mettle, valor, hardihood, bravado, gallantry, chivalry. **—Ant.** cowardice.

courageous, See Syn. study at BRAVE.

course, *n.* **1.** advance, direction, bearing. **2.** path, route, channel, way, road, track, passage. **3.** progress, passage, process. **4.** process, career, race. **5.** conduct, behavior, deportment. **6.** method, mode, procedure. **7.** sequence, succession, order, turn, regularity. **8.** range, row, series, layer, order. **—v. 9.** chase, pursue, follow, hunt. **10.** run, race.

courteous, *adj.* civil, polite, well-mannered, well-bred, urbane, debonair, affable, gracious, courtly, respectful, obliging. **—Ant.** discourteous, rude, curt, brusque. **—Syn. Study.** See CIVIL.

cover, *v.* **1.** overlay, overspread, envelop, enwrap, clothe, invest. **2.** shelter, protect, shield, guard, defend. **3.** hide, screen, cloak, disguise, secrete, veil, shroud, mask, enshroud. **4.** include, comprise, provide for, take in, embrace, contain, embody, comprehend. **5.** suffice, defray, offset, compensate for, counterbalance. **—n. 6.** lid, top, case, covering, tegument, integument. **7.** protection, shelter, asylum, refuge, concealment, guard, defense. **8.** woods, underbrush, covert, shrubbery, growth, thicket, copse. **9.** veil, screen, disguise, mask, cloak. **—Ant.** uncover; exposure.

covet, *v.* desire, envy, long for. **—Ant.** relinquish, renounce.

covetous, See Syn. study at AVARICIOUS.

coward, *n.* **1.** poltroon, cad, dastard, milksop. **—adj.** **2.** timid, cowardly.

cowardice, *n.* poltroonery, dastardliness, pusillanimity, timidity. **—Ant.** boldness, bravery, temerity.

cowardly, *adj.* craven, poltroon, dastardly, pusillanimous, recreant, timid, timorous, faint-hearted, white-livered, lily-livered, chicken-hearted, yellow, fearful, afraid, scared. **—Ant.** brave, bold, valiant.

coxcomb, *n.* dandy, fop, dude, exquisite, beau, popinjay, jackanapes.

coy, *adj.* retiring, diffident, shy, self-effacing, bashful, modest, shrinking, timid, demure. —**Ant.** bold, pert, brazen, arch.

cozy, *adj.* comfortable, snug, secure, safe, warm, easeful, comforting, intimate, close, homespun, homelike, homey, soft, comfy. —**Ant.** cold, unwelcoming.

crack, *v.* **1.** snap. **2.** break, snap, split; crackle, craze. —*n.* **3.** snap, report. **4.** break, flaw, split, fissure, cleft, chink, breach, crevice, cranny, interstice.

crackpot, *n.* **1.** eccentric, crank, character, oddity, odd duck, oddball, queer fish, crackbrain, screwball, nutcase. **2.** fanatic, zealot, faddist, believer, true believer. —*adj.* **3.** impractical, crazy, lunatic, visionary.

craft, *n.* **1.** skill, ingenuity, dexterity, talent, ability, aptitude, expertness. **2.** skill, art, artfulness, craftiness, subtlety, artifice, cunning, deceit, guile, shrewdness, deceitfulness, deception. **3.** handicraft, trade, art, vocation, metier, calling. **4.** boat, vessel, ship; aircraft, airplane, plane.

craftsman, *n.* artisan, artificer, mechanic, handicraftsman, workman. —**Ant.** bungler, shoemaker.

crafty, *adj.* skillful, sly, cunning, deceitful, artful, wily, insidious, tricky, designing, scheming, plotting, arch, shrewd. —**Ant.** gullible, naive.

cram, *v.* stuff, crowd, pack, compress, squeeze, overcrowd, gorge, glut, press.

cranky, *adj.* **1.** ill-tempered, cross, crotchety, cantankerous, perverse. **2.** eccentric, queer, odd, strange, peculiar, curious. **3.** shaky, unsteady, loose, disjointed, out of order, broken. **4.** bent, twisted, crooked. —**Ant.** amiable, good-natured; firm; solid.

crash, *v.* **1.** break, shatter, shiver, splinter, dash, smash. —*n.* **2.** falling, collapse, depression, failure, ruin.

crave, *v.* **1.** long for, desire, want, yearn *or* hunger for. **2.** require, need. **3.** beg for, beseech, entreat, implore, solicit, supplicate. —**Ant.** relinquish, renounce.

craven, *adj.* cowardly. —**Ant.** brave, bold, intrepid, fearless.

craving, See Syn. study at DESIRE.

crazy, *adj.* **1.** demented, insane, mad, deranged, crazed, lunatic, cracked. **2.** rickety, shaky, tottering, doddering, loose. **3.** weak, infirm, confused, impaired. —**Ant.** sane, well-balanced; firm; strong.

create, *v.* **1.** produce, originate, invent, cause, occasion. **2.** make, constitute.

credit, *n.* **1.** belief, trust, confidence, faith, reliance, credence. **2.** influence, authority, power. **3.** trustworthiness, credibility. **4.** repute, estimation, character; reputation, name, esteem, regard, standing, position, rank, condition; notoriety. **5.** commendation, honor, merit. **6.** acknowledgment, ascription. —*v.* **7.** believe, trust, confide in, have faith in, rely upon. —**Ant.** discredit.

creditable, *adj.* praiseworthy, meritorious, estimable, reputable, honorable, respectable. —**Ant.** disreputable, dishonorable.

credulous, *adj.* believing, trusting, trustful, unsuspecting, gullible. —**Ant.** incredulous, cautious, wary.

crime, *n.* offense, wrong, sin; infraction, violation, breach, misdemeanor, tort, felony; trespassing, breaking and entering, theft, robbery, assault, battery, statutory rape, rape, embezzlement, slander, libel, treason, manslaughter, murder. —**Syn. Study.** CRIME, OFFENSE, SIN agree in referring to a breaking of law. CRIME usu. refers to any serious violation of a public law: *the crime of treason.* OFFENSE is used of a less serious breaking of a public law, or of a violation of a social or moral rule: *a traffic offense; an offense against propriety.* SIN means a breaking of a moral or divine law: *the sin of envy.*

criminal, *adj.* **1.** felonious, unlawful, illegal, nefarious, flagitious, iniquitous, wicked, sinful, wrong. —*n.* **2.** convict, malefactor, evildoer, transgressor, sinner, culprit, delinquent, offender, felon; crook, hoodlum, gangster. —**Syn. Study.** See ILLEGAL.

cripple, *v.* disable, maim, weaken, impair, break down, ruin, destroy.

crisis, *n.* climax, juncture, exigency, strait, pinch, emergency.

criterion, *n.* standard, rule, principle, measure, parameter, touchstone, test, proof. —**Syn. Study.** See STANDARD.

critic, *n.* **1.** reviewer, censor, judge,

connoisseur. **2.** censurer, carper, faultfinder.

critical, *adj.* **1.** captious, carping, censorious, faultfinding, caviling, severe. **2.** discriminating, tasteful, judicial, fastidious, nice, exact, precise. **3.** decisive, climacteric, crucial, determining, momentous, important. **4.** dangerous, perilous, risky, suspenseful, hazardous, precarious, ticklish. —**Ant.** unimportant, superficial, trivial.

criticism, *n.* **1.** censure, faultfinding, stricture, animadversion, reflection. **2.** review, critique, comment.

crooked, *adj.* **1.** bent, curved, winding, devious, sinuous, flexuous, serpentine. **2.** deformed, misshapen, disfigured, twisted, awry, askew, crippled. **3.** dishonest, unscrupulous, knavish, tricky, fraudulent, dishonorable, unlawful, illegal, deceitful, insidious, crafty, treacherous. —**Ant.** straight; honest, upright.

crop, *n.* **1.** harvest, produce, yield. **2.** craw, stomach. —*v.* **3.** cut, cut short, clip, lop, mow.

cross, *n.* **1.** opposing, thwarting, opposition, frustration. **2.** trouble, misfortune, misery, burden. —*v.* **3.** intersect, traverse. **4.** oppose, thwart, frustrate, baffle, contradict, foil. **5.** interbreed, mongrelize. —*adj.* **6.** petulant, fractious, irascible, waspish, crabbed, cranky, curmudgeonly, churlish, sulky, cantankerous, ill-natured, peevish, sullen, ill-tempered, intemperate, impatient, complaining, snappish, irritable, fretful, moody, touchy, testy, unpleasant, unkind, mean, angry, spiteful, resentful, gloomy, glowering, morose, sour. —**Ant.** supporting; aid, support; complaisant, amenable, agreeable, sweet.

crowd, *n.* **1.** throng, multitude, swarm, company, host, horde, herd. **2.** masses, proletariat, plebians, rabble, mob, people, populace. —*v.* **3.** assemble, throng, swarm, flock together, herd. **4.** push, shove, cram, pack, press, squeeze, cramp, force. —**Syn. Study.** CROWD, MULTITUDE, SWARM, THRONG refer to large numbers of people. CROWD suggests a jostling, uncomfortable, and possibly disorderly company: *A crowd gathered to listen to the speech.* MULTITUDE emphasizes the great number of persons or things but suggests that there is space enough for all: *a multitude of people at the market.* SWARM as used of people is usu. contemptuous, suggesting a moving, restless, often noisy, crowd: *A swarm of dirty children played in the street.* THRONG suggests a company that presses together or forward, often with some common aim: *The throng pushed forward to see the cause of the excitement.*

crude, *adj.* **1.** unrefined, unfinished, unprepared, coarse, raw. **2.** unripe, immature, undeveloped. **3.** unpolished, unfinished, incomplete, coarse, boorish, uncouth, rough, rude, clumsy, awkward. **4.** undisguised, blunt, bare, rough, direct. —**Ant.** refined; aged, mature, ripe; complete, perfect; indirect, subtle.

cruel, *adj.* **1.** barbarous, bloodthirsty, sanguinary, ferocious, fell, merciless, unmerciful, relentless, implacable, pitiless, distressing, ruthless, truculent, brutal, savage, inhuman, brutish, barbarian, unmoved, unfeeling, unrelenting. **2.** severe, hard, bitter. —**Ant.** kind, benevolent, beneficial.

cruelty, *n.* harshness, brutality, ruthlessness, barbarity, inhumanity, atrocity. —**Ant.** kindness, benevolence.

crush, *v.* **1.** squeeze, press, bruise, crumple, rumple, wrinkle, compress. **2.** break, shatter, pulverize, granulate, powder, mash, smash, crumble, disintegrate. **3.** put down, quell, overpower, subdue, overwhelm, overcome, quash, conquer, oppress.

cry, *v.* **1.** lament, grieve, weep, bawl, sorrow, sob, shed tears, bewail, bemoan, squall, blubber, whimper, mewl, pule, wail. **2.** call, shout, yell, yowl, scream, exclaim, ejaculate, clamor, roar, bellow, vociferate. **3.** yelp, bark, bellow, hoot. —*n.* **4.** shout, scream, wail, shriek, screech, yell, yowl, roar, whoop, bellow. **5.** exclamation, outcry, clamor, ejaculation. **6.** entreaty, appeal. **7.** proclamation, announcement. **8.** weeping, lament, lamentation, tears. —**Ant.** laugh.

crying, *adj.* **1.** weeping, wailing. **2.** flagrant, notorious, demanding, urgent, important, great, enormous. —**Ant.** laughing; nugatory, trifling.

cunning, *n.* **1.** ability, skill, adroitness, expertness. **2.** craftiness, skill-

fulness, shrewdness, artfulness, wiliness, trickery, finesse, intrigue, artifice, guile, craft, deceit, deceitfulness, slyness, deception. —*adj.* **3.** ingenious, skillful. **4.** artful, wily, tricky, foxy, crafty. —**Ant.** stupidity, inability; dullness; naive, gullible, dull.

curb, *n.* **1.** restraint, check, control, bridle, rein, checkrein. —*v.* **2.** control, restrain, check, bridle, repress. —**Ant.** encourage, further, foster.

cure, *n.* **1.** remedy, restorative, specific, antidote. —*v.* **2.** remedy, restore, heal, make well *or* whole, mend, repair, correct.

cure-all, *n.* remedy, cure, relief, nostrum, elixir, panacea, sovereign remedy, universal remedy, theriac, catholicon.

curious, *adj.* **1.** inquisitive, inquiring, prying, spying, peeping, meddlesome, interested. **2.** strange, novel, unusual, singular, rare, foreign, exotic, queer, extraordinary, unique. —**Ant.** blasé; common, commonplace, usual, customary.

current, *adj.* **1.** present, prevailing, prevalent, general, common, circulating, widespread, popular, rife. **2.** accepted, stylish, in vogue, *à la mode,* fashionable, du jour. —*n.* **3.** stream, river, tide, course, progress, progression. —*adj.* outmoded, uncommon, unpopular.

curse, *n.* **1.** imprecation, execration, fulmination, malediction, oath, denunciation, anathema, ban. **2.** evil, misfortune, calamity, trouble, vexation, annoyance, affliction, torment, bane, thorn, plague, scourge. —*v.* **3.** blaspheme, swear, imprecate, execrate, fulminate, damn, denunciate, accurse, maledict, anathematize, condemn, profane, excommunicate. **4.** doom, destroy, plague, scourge, afflict, trouble, vex, annoy. —**Ant.** blessing, benediction.

cursed, *adj.* **1.** damned, accursed, banned, blighted. **2.** execrable, damnable, hateful, abominable, villainous. —**Ant.** blessed.

curt, *adj.* **1.** short, shortened, brief, abbreviated, concise, laconic, blunt, terse. **2.** rude, snappish, abrupt, dry. —**Ant.** long, drawn-out, lengthy; courteous, courtly. —**Syn. Study.** See BLUNT.

curtail, *v.* lessen, diminish, decrease, dock, shorten, abbreviate, blunt, abridge. —**Ant.** extend, expand.

curtain, *n.* drape, drapery, hanging, portière, lambrequin, valance, blind, shade, shutter, shutters. **2.** cover, concealment. —**Ant.** window.

cushion, *n.* **1.** pillow, bolster, pad; shock-absorber. —*v.* **2.** absorb, check, slow, alleviate, meliorate.

custody, *n.* **1.** keeping, guardianship, care, custodianship, charge, safekeeping, watch, preserving, protection, preservation; possession, ownership, mastery, holding. **2.** imprisonment, confinement.

custom, *n.* **1.** habit, practice, usage, procedure, rule. **2.** rule, convention, form, observance, formality. **3.** tax, duty, impost, tribute, toll. **4.** patronage, customers, patrons, clientele. —**Syn. Study.** CUSTOM, HABIT, PRACTICE mean an established way of doing things. CUSTOM, applied to a community or to an individual, implies a more or less permanent way of acting reinforced by tradition and social attitudes: *the custom of giving gifts at Christmas.* HABIT, applied particularly to an individual, implies such repetition of the same action as to develop a natural, spontaneous, or rooted tendency or inclination to perform it: *He has an annoying habit of interrupting the speaker.* PRACTICE applies to a regularly followed procedure or pattern in conducting activities: *It is his practice to verify all statements.*

customary, *adj.* usual, habitual, wonted, accustomed, conventional, common, regular. —**Ant.** unusual, rare, uncommon, irregular. —**Syn. Study.** See USUAL.

cut, *v.* **1.** gash, slash, slit, lance, pierce, penetrate, incise, wound. **2.** wound, hurt, move, touch, slight, insult. **3.** divide, sever, carve, cleave, sunder, bisect, chop, hack, hew, fell, saw. **4.** lop off, crop. **5.** reap, mow, harvest. **6.** clip, shear, pare, prune. **7.** cross, intersect, transect. **8.** abridge, edit, shorten, abbreviate, curtail. **9.** lower, lessen, reduce, diminish. **10.** dissolve, dilute, thin, water, water down. **11.** facet, make, fashion. **12.** hollow out, excavate, dig. —*n.* **13.** incision, wound, slash, gash, slit; channel, passage, strait. **14.** style, fashion, mode, kind, sort.

cutting, *n.* **1.** root, shoot, leaf, branch, limb. —*adj.* **2.** sharp, keen, incisive, trenchant, piercing. **3.** mordant, mordacious, caustic, biting, acid, wounding, sarcastic, sardonic, bitter, severe. —**Ant.** dull; kind.

cynical, *adj.* distrustful, pessimistic, sarcastic, satirical, unbelieving, disbelieving, sneering, contemptuous, derisive, cutting, scornful, ridiculing, censorious, captious, waspish, petulant, testy, fretful, touchy, cross, surly, ill-tempered, ill-natured, crusty, cantankerous. —**Ant.** optimistic, hopeful; good-natured, calm, pleasant.

D

dabbler, *adj.* **1.** nonprofessional, amateur, dilettante, putterer, trifler, dallier, sciolist, Sunday painter. **2.** beginner, tyro, starter, novice, neophyte, abecedarian, tenderfoot, greenhorn, raw recruit. —**Ant.** professional, expert, adept.

dainty, *adj.* **1.** delicate, beautiful, charming, exquisite, fine, elegant. **2.** toothsome, delicious, savory, palatable, tender, juicy, delectable, luscious. **3.** particular, fastidious, scrupulous. **4.** squeamish, finical, overnice. —*n.* **5.** delicacy, tidbit, sweetmeat. —**Ant.** clumsy, inelegant; disgusting, distasteful; sloppy. —**Syn. Study.** See DELICATE.

dally, *v.* **1.** sport, play, trifle, fondle, toy, caress. **2.** waste time, loiter, delay, dawdle. —**Ant.** hasten, hurry. —**Syn. Study.** See LOITER.

damage, *n.* **1.** injury, harm, hurt, detriment, mischief, impairment, loss. —*v.* **2.** injure, harm, hurt, impair, mar. —**Ant.** improvement; improve, better.

damp, *adj.* **1.** moist, humid, dank, steamy, wet. —*n.* **2.** moisture, humidity, dankness, wet, wetness, dampness, fog, vapor, steam. **3.** dejection, depression, dispiritedness, chill, discouragement, check. —*v.* **4.** dampen, moisten, wet, humidify. **5.** check, retard, slow, inhibit, restrain, moderate, abate, allay, slow, interfere with. **6.** stifle, suffocate, extinguish. —**Ant.** dry, arid.

danger, *n.* hazard, risk, peril, jeopardy, liability, exposure; injury, evil. —**Ant.** security, safety. —**Syn. Study.** DANGER, HAZARD, PERIL imply harm that one may encounter. DANGER is the general word for liability to injury or harm, either near at hand and certain, or remote and doubtful: *to be in danger of being killed.* HAZARD suggests a danger that one can often foresee but cannot avoid: *A mountain climber is exposed to many hazards.* PERIL usually denotes great and imminent danger: *The passengers on the disabled ship were in great peril.*

dappled, *adj.* multicolored, multihued, varicolored, mottled, motley, spotted, polka-dot, flecked, maculate, freckled, freckly, pied, shadowed, shadowy.

dare, *v.* venture, hazard, risk, brave, challenge, defy, endanger.

daredevil, *adj.* daring, rash, adventurous, risk-taking, reckless, heedless, foolhardy, wild, devil-may-care, venturesome, nervy, temerarious, gutsy.

daring, *n.* **1.** courage, adventurousness, boldness, bravery, audacity, intrepidity, heroism. —*adj.* **2.** courageous, venturesome, adventurous, bold, brave, audacious, dauntless, undaunted, intrepid, fearless, valiant, valorous, gallant, chivalrous, doughty, heroic. —**Ant.** cowardice; timid, cowardly, pusillanimous, fearful.

dark, *adj.* **1.** dim, gloomy, murky, umbrageous, shadowy, penumbral, dusky, unilluminated, unlit, sunless, shady, swarthy, black, pitchy, ebon, Cimmerian. **2.** gloomy, cheerless, dismal, sad, morose, morbid, disheartening, discouraging. **3.** sullen, frowning. **4.** unenlightened, ignorant, untaught, untutored, uneducated, unlettered, benighted, in the dark. **5.** obscure, recondite, abstruse, dim, incomprehensible, unintelligible, occult, cabalistic, mysterious, puzzling, enigmatic, enigmatical, mystic, mystical. **6.** hidden, secret, concealed. **7.** silent, reticent. **8.** infernal, wicked, sinful, nefarious, flagitious, foul, infamous, hellish, devilish, evil, bad, satanic. —**Ant.** light, fair; cheerful; pleasant; intelligent, educated; clear, intelligible; open, revealed; voluble; heavenly, godly.

dart, *n.* **1.** arrow, barb. —*v.* **2.**

spring, start, dash, bolt, rush, fly, shoot.

dash, *v.* **1.** strike, break; throw, thrust; splash, splatter. **2.** adulterate, mix, deteriorate, mingle. **3.** rush, dart, bolt, fly. —*n.* **4.** pinch, bit, suggestion, soupçon, hint, touch, tinge, smack, sprinkle, sprinkling. **5.** vigor, spirit, élan, flourish, éclat.

daub, **1.** dab, smear, bedaub, besmear, besmirch, smudge, spot, stain, soil. —*n.* **2.** spot, stain, mark, blot, blotch, smudge, smirch.

daunt, *v.* **1.** intimidate, overawe, subdue, dismay, frighten, appall. **2.** discourage, dispirit, dishearten, thwart, frustrate. —**Ant.** encourage, actuate.

dauntless, *adj.* fearless, bold, undaunted, intrepid, brave, courageous, daring, indomitable, unconquerable, valiant, valorous, heroic, chivalrous, doughty, undismayed. —**Ant.** fearful, cowardly, timid, timorous.

dawdle, *v.* idle, linger, loiter, tarry, lag, poke along, dally, dilly-dally, loll, laze, lallygag, take one's time, procrastinate, temporize, put off. —**Ant.** hasten, hurry. —**Syn. Study.** See LOITER.

dawn, *n.* **1.** daybreak, sunrise, dawning. —*v.* **2.** appear, open, begin, break. —**Ant.** sunset; disappear.

daydream, *v.* **1.** imagine, fantasize, dream, muse, pipe-dream, woolgather, build castles in the air. —*n.* **2.** reverie, dream, fantasy, imagining, woolgathering.

dazzle, *v.* **1.** bedazzle, blind, daze, bedaze. **2.** astonish, amaze, stun, stupefy, overwhelm, astound, confound, flabbergast.

dead, *adj.* **1.** deceased, lifeless, extinct, inanimate, defunct, departed. **2.** insensible, numb, unfeeling, indifferent, cool, cold, callous, obtuse, frigid, unsympathetic, apathetic, lukewarm. **3.** infertile, barren, sterile. **4.** still, motionless, inert, inoperative, useless, dull, inactive, unemployed. **5.** extinguished, out. **6.** complete, absolute, utter, entire, total. **7.** straight, direct, unerring, exact, precise, sure. —**Ant.** alive, live, animate; fervid, eager, warm, animated; fertile; partial; crooked, indirect, devious.

deadly, *adj.* **1.** fatal, lethal, mortal. **2.** implacable, sanguinary, murderous, bloodthirsty. —**Syn. Study.** See FATAL.

deal, *v.* **1.** act, behave. **2.** trade, do business, traffic. **3.** distribute, dole, mete, dispense, apportion, allot, give, assign. —*n.* **4.** bargain, arrangement, pact, contract. **5.** quantity, amount, extent, degree. **6.** dealing, distribution, share. —**Ant.** gather, collect.

dear, *adj.* **1.** beloved, loved, precious, darling, esteemed. **2.** expensive, high-priced, costly, high; exorbitant. —**Ant.** hateful; cheap.

death, *n.* **1.** decease, demise, passing, departure. **2.** stop, cessation, surcease, estoppage, end, finale. —**Ant.** life.

debar, *v.* **1.** exclude, shut out. **2.** prevent, prohibit, hinder, interdict, outlaw. —**Ant.** include, welcome; encourage, support.

debase, *v.* **1.** adulterate, corrupt, vitiate, contaminate, pollute, defile, foul, befoul. **2.** lower, depress, reduce, impair, deteriorate, degrade, abase, demean. —**Ant.** purify; elevate, raise, exalt.

debate, *n.* **1.** discussion, argument, controversy, disputation, dispute, contention. **2.** deliberation, consideration. —*v.* **3.** discuss, dispute, argue, contend, hold. **4.** deliberate, consider, discuss, argue. —**Ant.** agreement.

debt, *n.* liability, obligation, duty, due, debit.

debut, *n.* **1.** introduction, appearance, arrival, coming out, introduction, inauguration, induction, initiation, unveiling, launching, installation, premiere. —*v.* **2.** come out, appear, arrive, enter, launch, premiere, make a debut.

decadence, *n.* decline, degeneration, retrogression, decay, fall. —**Ant.** flourishing, progress.

decay, *n.* **1.** deteriorate, decline, retrogress, degenerate, fall, fall away, wither, perish. **2.** decompose, putrefy, rot, disintegrate. —*n.* **3.** decline, deterioration, degeneration, decadence, impairment, dilapidation. **4.** decomposition, putrefaction, rotting, rot. —**Ant.** flourish, grow; progress. —**Syn. Study.** DECAY, DECOMPOSE, DISINTEGRATE, ROT imply a deterioration or falling away from a sound condition. DECAY implies either entire or partial deterioration by progressive natural changes: *Teeth de-*

cay. DECOMPOSE suggests the reducing of a substance to its component elements: *Moisture makes some chemical compounds decompose.* DISINTEGRATE emphasizes the breaking up, going to pieces, or wearing away of anything, so that its original wholeness is impaired: *Rocks disintegrate.* ROT is applied esp. to decaying vegetable matter, which may or may not emit offensive odors: *Potatoes rot.*

deceit, *n.* **1.** deceiving, concealment, fraud, deception, cheating, guile, hypocrisy, craftiness, slyness, insincerity, disingenuousness. **2.** trick, stratagem, artifice, wile, trickery, chicane, chicanery, device, cozenage. **3.** falseness, duplicity, treachery, perfidy. —**Ant.** honesty, forthrightness. —**Syn. Study.** DECEIT, GUILE, DUPLICITY, FRAUD refer either to practices designed to mislead or to the qualities in a person that prompt such behavior. DECEIT is intentional concealment or misrepresentation of the truth: *Consumers are often victims of deceit.* GUILE is crafty or cunning deceit; it suggests subtle but treacherous tactics: *The agent used guile to gain access to the documents.* DUPLICITY is doing the opposite of what one says or pretends to do; it suggests hypocrisy or pretense: *the duplicity of a friend who does not keep a secret.* FRAUD refers to deceit or trickery by which one may derive benefit at another's expense; it often suggests illegal or dishonest practices: *an advertiser convicted of fraud.*

deceitful, *adj.* **1.** insincere, disingenuous, false, hollow, empty, deceiving, fraudulent, designing, tricky, wily, two-faced. **2.** misleading, fraudulent, deceptive, counterfeit, illusory, fallacious. —**Ant.** sincere, honest, forthright; genuine.

deceive, *v.* mislead, delude, cheat, cozen, dupe, gull, fool, bamboozle, hoodwink, trick, double-cross, defraud, outwit; entrap, ensnare, betray. —**Syn. Study.** See CHEAT.

decent, *adj.* **1.** fitting, appropriate, suited, suitable, apt, proper, fit, becoming. **2.** conformant, tasteful, modest, seemly, proper, decorous. —**Ant.** indecent, indecorous, improper, unfit, unsuitable.

deception, *n.* **1.** deceiving, gulling. **2.** artifice, sham, cheat, imposture, treachery, subterfuge, stratagem, ruse, hoax, fraud, trick, wile.

deceptive, *adj.* deceiving, misleading, delusive, fallacious, specious, false, deceitful. —**Ant.** genuine, authentic.

decide, *v.* determine, settle, resolve, purpose, conclude. —**Ant.** waver, hesitate, vacillate. —**Syn. Study.** DECIDE, RESOLVE, DETERMINE imply settling something in dispute or doubt. To DECIDE is to make up one's mind after consideration: *I decided to go to the party.* To RESOLVE is to settle conclusively with firmness of purpose: *She resolved to ask for a promotion.* To DETERMINE is to settle after investigation or observation: *It is difficult to determine the best course of action.*

decided, *adj.* **1.** unambiguous, unquestionable, definite, unmistakable, undeniable, indeniable, indisputable, indubitable, certain, sure, emphatic, pronounced, absolute, unequivocal, categorical, incontrovertible. **2.** resolute, determined, resolved, unwavering, unhesitating. —**Ant.** undecided, ambiguous, indefinite; irresolute, hesitant.

decipher, *v.* decode, decrypt, unravel, break, crack, solve, figure out, translate, unriddle, work out, dope out, puzzle out, explain, elucidate, analyze, interpret, resolve. —**Ant.** encode, encipher, obscure, hide.

decisive, *adj.* incontrovertible, firm, resolute, determined, conclusive, final. —**Ant.** indecisive, irresolute, vacillating, wavering.

deck, *v.* clothe, attire, bedeck, array, garnish, trim, dress, bedizen, adorn, embellish, decorate. —**Ant.** undress.

declaim, *v.* orate, perorate, hold forth, elocute, lecture, preach, sermonize, harangue, speechify, rant, rave, thunder, trumpet, shout, tubthump, mouth off. —**Ant.** mumble, mutter.

declare, *v.* **1.** announce, proclaim, pronounce. **2.** affirm, assert, aver, protest, make known, state, asseverate, utter. **3.** manifest, reveal, disclose, publish. —**Ant.** deny, controvert; suppress. —**Syn. Study.** DECLARE, AFFIRM, ASSERT imply making something known emphatically, openly, or formally. To DECLARE is to make known, sometimes in the face of actual or potential contradiction:

to declare someone the winner of a contest. To AFFIRM is to make a statement based on one's reputation for knowledge or veracity, or so related to a generally recognized truth that denial is not likely: *to affirm the necessity of high standards.* To ASSERT is to state boldly, usu. without other proof than personal authority or conviction: *to assert that the climate is changing.*

decline, *v.* **1.** refuse, avoid, reject, deny. **2.** descend, slope, incline or bend downward. **3.** stoop, condescend, lower oneself, abase, debase. **4.** fail, weaken, deteriorate, pale, diminish, degenerate, decay, languish. **5.** incline, declivity, slope, hill. **6.** failing, loss, enfeeblement, deterioration, degeneration, enervation, weakening, decay, diminution, lessening, retrogression. —**Ant.** agree; rise; improve, increase; strengthening. —**Syn. Study.** See REFUSE.

decompose, *v.* **1.** separate, distill, fractionate, analyze, disintegrate. **2.** rot, putrefy, decay, mould. —**Syn. Study.** See DECAY.

decorate, *v.* adorn, bedeck, beautify, ornament, embellish, deck, deck out, bedizen, dress, dress up, trim, spruce up, smarten, appoint, garnish, pretty up, titivate, accouter, furbish, dandify, prettify, doll up, gussy up. —**Ant.** simplify, streamline, strip.

decorous, *adj.* proper, decent, seemly, becoming, sedate, conventional, fitting, fit, suitable. —**Ant.** indecorous, indecent, unseemly, unbecoming, unfit.

decorum, *n.* etiquette, politeness, politesse, manners, manner, behavior, comportment, deportment, decency, propriety, dignity. —**Ant.** indecency, impropriety.

decrease, *v.* **1.** diminish, lessen, abate, fall off, decline, contract, dwindle, shrink, wane, ebb, subside. **2.** abatement, diminution, reduction, decline, wane, subsidence, falling-off, contraction, shrinking, dwindling, lessening, ebb, ebbing. —**Ant.** increase. —**Syn. Study.** DECREASE, DIMINISH, DWINDLE, SHRINK imply becoming smaller or less in amount. DECREASE commonly implies a sustained reduction in stages, esp. of bulk, size, volume, or quantity, often from some imperceptible cause or inherent process: *The swelling decreased daily.* DIMINISH usu. implies the action of some external cause that keeps taking away: *Disease caused the number of troops to diminish steadily.* DWINDLE implies an undesirable reduction by degrees, resulting in attenuation: *His followers dwindled to a mere handful.* SHRINK esp. implies contraction through an inherent property under specific conditions: *Many fabrics shrink in hot water.*

decree, *n.* **1.** order, directive, edict, command, commandment, dictum, injunction, mandate, proclamation, declaration, directive, instruction, prescription, prescript, ruling, fiat, ukase, pronunciamento. **2.** order, direct, command, dictate, rule, require, prescribe, direct, enjoin, bid, mandate, instruct, pronounce, ordain.

decrepit, *adj.* weak, feeble, enfeebled, infirm, aged, superannuated, effete, broken-down. —**Ant.** sturdy, strong.

decry, *v.* disparage, censure, belittle, discredit, depreciate, condemn. —**Ant.** praise, laud, commend. —**Syn. Study.** DECRY, DENIGRATE, DEPRECATE involve the expression of censure or disapproval. DECRY means to denounce or to express public disapproval of: *to decry all forms of discrimination.* DENIGRATE means to defame or to sully the reputation or character of: *to denigrate the memory of a ruler.* DEPRECATE means to express regretful disapproval of or to plead against: *to deprecate a new policy.*

dedicate, See Syn. study at DEVOTE.

deduce, *v.* conclude, infer, reason, gather, assume, presume, judge, make out, dope out, conjecture, speculate, guess, glean, reckon, suppose, surmise, think, understand.

deduct, *v.* subtract, remove, detract, withdraw. —**Ant.** add.

deed, *n.* act, performance, exploit, achievement, action, feat.

deem, *v.* judge, regard, think, consider, hold, believe, account, count, suppose.

deep, *adj.* **1.** recondite, abstruse, abstract, difficult, profound, mysterious, obscure, unfathomable. **2.** grave, serious, grievous. **3.** absorbing, absorbed, involved, intense, heartfelt, great, extreme. **4.** penetrat-

ing, intelligent, bright, cunning, sagacious, wise, discerning, astute, shrewd, artful. —*n.* **5.** ocean, sea, abyss. —**Ant.** shallow.

deface, *v.* mar, disfigure, deform, spoil, soil, injure, harm; blot out, efface, obliterate, erase, eliminate. —**Ant.** beautify.

defeat, *v.* **1.** overcome, conquer, overwhelm, vanquish, subdue, overthrow, subjugate, suppress, rout, check. **2.** frustrate, thwart, foil, baffle, disconcert, unnerve, balk. —*n.* **3.** overthrow, vanquishment, downfall, rout. **4.** frustration, bafflement. —**Ant.** yield, surrender, submit. —**Syn. Study.** DEFEAT, CONQUER, OVERCOME, SUBDUE imply gaining victory or control over an opponent. DEFEAT usu. means to beat or frustrate in a single contest or conflict: *Confederate forces were defeated at Gettysburg.* CONQUER means to finally gain control over by physical, moral, or mental force, usu. after long effort: *to conquer poverty; to conquer a nation.* OVERCOME emphasizes perseverance and the surmounting of difficulties: *to overcome opposition; to overcome a bad habit.* SUBDUE means to conquer so completely that resistance is broken: *to subdue a rebellious spirit.*

defect, *n.* **1.** blemish, flaw, fault, shortcoming, imperfection, mar, blotch, scar, blot, foible, weakness. **2.** deficiency, want, lack, destitution. —*v.* **3.** desert, abandon, revolt, rebel, betray. —**Ant.** sufficiency, perfection; support. —**Syn. Study.** DEFECT, BLEMISH, FLAW refer to faults, both literal and figurative, that detract from perfection. DEFECT is the general word for any kind of shortcoming, imperfection, or deficiency, whether hidden or visible: *a birth defect; a defect in a plan.* A BLEMISH is usu. a surface defect that mars the appearance; it is also used of a moral fault: *a skin blemish; a blemish on his reputation.* A FLAW is usu. a structural defect or weakness that mars the quality or effectiveness: *a flaw in a diamond; a flaw in Hamlet's character.*

defective, *adj.* imperfect, incomplete, faulty, deficient, insufficient, inadequate, (euphemism, applied to humans) challenged. —**Ant.** perfect, complete, adequate.

defend, *v.* **1.** guard, garrison, fortify, shield, shelter, screen, preserve, protect, keep, watch over, safeguard, secure. **2.** uphold, maintain, assert, justify, plead, espouse, vindicate. —**Ant.** attack.

defer, *v.* delay, postpone, put off, prevent, adjourn; procrastinate. —**Ant.** speed, expedite. —**Syn. Study.** DEFER, DELAY, POSTPONE imply keeping something from occurring until a future time. To DEFER is to decide to do something at a more convenient time in the future; it often suggests avoidance: *to defer making a payment.* DELAY is sometimes equivalent to DEFER, but it usu. suggests a hindrance, obstacle, or dilatory tactic: *Completion of the building was delayed by bad weather.* To POSTPONE is to put off to a particular time in the future, often to wait for new information or developments: *to postpone a trial.*

deference, *n.* **1.** homage, honor, veneration, reverence, obeisance, respect, esteem, appreciation, admiration. **2.** submission, subjection, submissiveness, compliance, acquiescence. —**Ant.** disrespect, insolence.

defiant, *adj.* antagonistic, insubordinate, contumacious, refractory, recalcitrant, rebellious, insolent, resistant, in-your-face; daring, courageous, brave, bold. —**Ant.** friendly, amiable; cowardly.

definite, *adj.* **1.** defined, determined, specific, particular, exact, fixed, precise, determinate. **2.** certain, clear, express, sure. —**Ant.** indefinite, undetermined, indeterminate; uncertain, unclear.

deform, *v.* misshape, deform, disfigure, deface, efface, mar, spoil, ruin; transform.

deformed, *adj.* malformed, misshapen, crippled, disfigured.

deft, See Syn. study at DEXTEROUS.

defy, *v.* challenge, resist, dare, brave, flout, scorn, despise. —**Ant.** encourage, support, help.

degradation, *n.* humiliation, disgrace, debasement, dishonor, degeneration, decline, decadence, degeneracy, perversity. —**Ant.** exaltation.

degrade, *v.* **1.** demote, depose, downgrade, lower, break, cashier. **2.** debase, deprave, lower, abase, vitiate, deteriorate. **3.** humiliate, dis-

honor, disgrace, discredit. —**Ant.** exalt. —**Syn. Study.** See HUMBLE.

dejected, *adj.* depressed, dispirited, disheartened, low-spirited, discouraged, despondent, downhearted, sad, unhappy, miserable. —**Ant.** happy, cheerful, lighthearted.

delay, *v.* **1.** put off, defer, postpone, procrastinate. **2.** impede, slow, retard, hinder, detain, stop, arrest. **3.** linger, loiter, tarry. —*n.* **4.** delaying, procrastination, loitering, tarrying, dawdling, stay, stop. **5.** deferment, postponement, respite, deferring. —**Ant.** expedite, hasten, speed. —**Syn. Study.** See DEFER.

delegate, *n.* **1.** representative, deputy, envoy, ambassador, legate. —*v.* **2.** depute, entrust, commission.

delete, *v.* cancel, strike or take out, dele, erase, expunge, eradicate, remove, efface, blot out.

deleterious, *adj.* injurious, hurtful, harmful, pernicious, destructive, deadly, lethal; noxious, poisonous. —**Ant.** salutary, beneficial, advantageous.

deliberate, *adj.* **1.** weighed, considered, studied, intentional, purposive, purposeful, premeditated, voluntary, willful. **2.** careful, slow, unhurried, leisurely, methodical, thoughtful, circumspect, cautious, wary. —*v.* **3.** weigh, consider, ponder over, reflect, think, ruminate, meditate. **4.** consult, confer. —**Ant.** haphazard, unintentional; careless, unwary, incautious. —**Syn. Study.** DELIBERATE, INTENTIONAL, VOLUNTARY refer to something not happening by chance. DELIBERATE is applied to what is done not hastily but with full realization of what one is doing: *a deliberate attempt to evade justice.* INTENTIONAL is applied to what is definitely intended or done on purpose: *an intentional omission.* VOLUNTARY is applied to what is done by a definite exercise of the will and not because of outside pressures: *a voluntary enlistment.* See also SLOW.

delicacy, *n.* **1.** tenderness, sensitivity, tact, diplomacy, feeling, sensibility, consideration, thoughtfulness, solicitude, solicitousness, refinement, finesse, dexterity, skill, deftness, facility, artistry, artfulness, adroitness, grace. **2.** frailty, unhealthiness, fragility, feebleness, weakness, debility, valetudinarianism. **3.** treat, rare treat, tidbit, morsel, choice morsel, dainty, goody.

delicate, *adj.* **1.** fine, dainty, exquisite, nice, fragile, graceful, elegant, choice. **2.** fine, slight, subtle. **3.** tender, fragile, frail, dainty, slight, weak, slender, sensitive, frangible. **4.** critical, precarious, sensitive. **5.** scrupulous, careful, painstaking, exact, exacting, precise, accurate. **6.** discriminating, fastidious, careful, demanding. —**Ant.** rude, crude; blunt; rough, insensitive, unbreakable; careless. —**Syn. Study.** DELICATE, DAINTY, EXQUISITE imply beauty or subtle refinement such as might belong in rich surroundings. DELICATE suggests something fragile, soft, light, or fine: *a delicate carving.* DAINTY suggests a smallness, gracefulness, and beauty that forbids rough handling: *a dainty handkerchief;* of persons, it refers to fastidious sensibilities: *a dainty eater.* EXQUISITE suggests an outstanding beauty and elegance that appeals to the most refined taste: *an exquisite tapestry.*

delicious, *adj.* pleasing, luscious, palatable, savory, dainty, delicate. —**Ant.** unpleasant, bitter, acrid, unpalatable.

delight, *n.* **1.** enjoyment, pleasure, transport, delectation, joy, rapture, ecstasy. —*v.* **2.** please, satisfy, transport, enrapture, enchant, charm, ravish. —**Ant.** disgust, revulsion, displeasure; displease.

delightful, *adj.* pleasing, pleasant, pleasurable, enjoyable, charming, enchanting, agreeable, delectable, rapturous. —**Ant.** unpleasant, disagreeable, revolting, repellent.

deliver, *v.* **1.** give up, surrender, hand over, transfer, give over, yield, resign, cede, grant, relinquish. **2.** give forth, emit, cast, direct, deal, discharge. **3.** utter, pronounce, announce, proclaim, declare, communicate, publish, impart, promulgate, advance. **4.** set free, liberate, release, free, emancipate. **5.** redeem, rescue, save, release, extricate, disentangle. —**Ant.** limit, confine.

delude, *v.* mislead, deceive, beguile, cozen, cheat, dupe, gull, defraud, trick. —**Ant.** enlighten.

deluge, *n.* inundation, flood, downpour, overflow, cataclysm, catastrophe.

delusion, *n.* illusion, deception,

trick, fancy, fallacy, error, mistake, hallucination.

demand, *v.* **1.** claim, require, exact, ask for, call for, challenge. **2.** ask, inquire. —*n.* **3.** claim, requisition, requirement. **4.** inquiry, question, asking, interrogation. —**Ant.** waive, relinquish.

demolish, *v.* ruin, destroy, put an end to, lay waste, raze, level. —**Ant.** construct, build, create. —**Syn. Study.** See DESTROY.

demonstrate, *v.* **1.** show, explain, explicate, expound, spell out, illustrate, make clear, make plain, show and tell. **2.** exhibit, manifest, display, evidence, evince, present, disclose, divulge. **3.** protest, object, march, rally, boycott, strike, picket.

demur, *v.* **1.** object, take exception, raise or make objection; refuse. —*n.* **2.** objection, hesitation, refusal. —**Ant.** agree, accede, consent.

demure, *adj.* **1.** prudish, prim, overmodest, priggish. **2.** sober, modest, serious, sedate, decorous, coy. —**Ant.** licentious, immodest; indecorous. —**Syn. Study.** See MODEST.

denigrate, See Syn. study at DECRY.

denounce, *v.* **1.** condemn, assail, censure, attack, stigmatize, blame, brand, label. **2.** inform against, accuse, denunciate, give away. —**Ant.** commend, exonerate.

deny, *v.* **1.** dispute, controvert, oppose, gainsay, contradict. **2.** reject, renounce, abjure, disavow. **3.** refuse, repudiate, disown. —**Ant.** concede, agree, concur; accept; receive.

depart, *v.* **1.** go away, start, set out, leave, quit, retire, withdraw, absent, go. **2.** turn aside, diverge, deviate, vary. **3.** die, pass on or away. —**Ant.** arrive; converge.

depict, *v.* **1.** represent, portray, paint, limn, delineate, sketch, reproduce, draw. **2.** describe.

deplore, *v.* grieve, regret, lament, bemoan, bewail, mourn. —**Ant.** boast.

deposit, *v.* **1.** place, put, lay down, lay. **2.** throw down, drop, precipitate. **3.** bank, save, store, hoard; secure. —*n.* **4.** sediment, deposition, precipitate; silt, mud, slime, sand, alluvium; snow, rain, sleet, hail. **5.** coating; lode, vein.

depot, *n.* station, terminal; storehouse, warehouse, depository.

depraved, *adj.* corrupt, perverted, corrupted, immoral, wicked, evil, sinful, iniquitous, profligate, debased, dissolute, reprobate, degenerate, licentious, lascivious, lewd. —**Ant.** upright, honest; honorable, decorous, modest.

deprecate, See Syn. study at DECRY.

depress, *v.* **1.** dispirit, deject, oppress, dishearten, discourage, dampen, chill, sadden. **2.** reduce, weaken, dull, lower. **3.** devalue, cheapen. **4.** humble, humiliate, abase, debase, degrade, abash. —**Ant.** inspirit, encourage; elevate; gladden.

depressed, *adj.* dejected, downcast, sad, unhappy, miserable, morose, saddened, blue, despondent, melancholy, gloomy, morbid. —**Ant.** happy, cheerful.

deprive, *v.* dispossess, bereave, strip, divest, disallow, deny. —**Ant.** endow.

dereliction, *n.* neglect, negligence, delinquency, fault, abandonment, desertion, renunciation.

deride, See Syn. study at RIDICULE.

derogatory, *adj.* disparaging, belittling, demeaning, derogative, depreciatory, deprecatory, depreciative, slighting, uncomplimentary, insulting, disdainful, scornful, contemptuous, spiteful, abusive, pejorative, defamatory, malicious, maligning. —**Ant.** flattering, complimentary.

descent, *n.* **1.** falling, fall, sinking, descending. **2.** inclination, declination, slope, declivity, grade, decline. **3.** extraction, lineage, derivation, parentage, genealogy. **4.** incursion, attack, assault, raid, foray. —**Ant.** ascent, rise.

describe, *v.* narrate, account, recount, tell, relate; delineate, portray, characterize, limn, represent, depict.

desert, *n.* **1.** waste, wilderness. —*adj.* **2.** desolate, barren, forsaken, wild, uninhabited. —*v.* **3.** abandon, forsake, leave behind, give up, relinquish, leave, quit, renounce.

design, *v.* **1.** plan, devise, project, contrive. **2.** intend, purpose, mean, propose. **3.** sketch, draw, delineate. —*n.* **4.** plan, scheme, proposal, proposition, project. **5.** sketch, plan, drawings, blueprint, outline, draught. **6.** end, intention, purpose, intent, aim, object. **7.** meaning, purport, drift. —**Ant.** achieve, execute, accomplish; execution; accident, fortuity, chance.

designing, *adj.* contriving, scheming, sly, artful, cunning, tricky, wily, crafty, deceitful, treacherous, arch, Machiavellian, astute, unscrupulous. —**Ant.** open, candid, frank, honest, guileless, artless, naive.

desire, *v.* **1.** wish *or* long for, crave, want, wish, covet, fancy. **2.** ask, request, solicit. —*n.* **3.** linging, craving, yearning, wish, need, hunger, appetite, thirst. **4.** request, wish, aspiration. **5.** lust. —**Ant.** abominate, loathe, abhor. —**Syn. Study.** DESIRE, CRAVING, LONGING, YEARNING suggest feelings that impel a person to the attainment or possession of something. DESIRE is a strong wish, worthy or unworthy, for something that is or seems to be within reach: *a desire for success.* CRAVING implies a deep and compelling wish for something, arising from a feeling of (literal or figurative) hunger: *a craving for food; a craving for companionship.* LONGING is an intense wish, generally repeated or enduring, for something that is at the moment beyond reach but may be attainable in the future: *a longing to visit Europe.* YEARNING suggests persistent, uneasy, and sometimes wistful or tender longing: *a yearning for one's native land.*

desolate, *adj.* **1.** barren, laid waste, devastated, ravaged, scorched, destroyed. **2.** deserted, uninhabited, desert, lonely, alone, lone, solitary, forsaken, lonesome. **3.** miserable, wretched, unhappy, sad, woeful, woebegone, disconsolate, inconsolable, forlorn, lost, cheerless. **4.** dreary, dismal, wild. —*v.* **5.** lay waste, devastate, ravage, ruin, sack, destroy, despoil. **6.** depopulate. **7.** sadden, depress. **8.** forsake, abandon, desert. —**Ant.** fertile; populous, crowded; happy, delighted; cultivated; build, create; cheer.

despair, *n.* hopelessness, desperation, despondency, discouragement, gloom, disheartenment. —**Ant.** encouragement, hope, optimism. —**Syn. Study.** DESPAIR, DESPERATION, DESPONDENCY refer to a state of mind caused by circumstances that seem too much to cope with. DESPAIR suggests total loss of hope, usu. accompanied by apathy and low spirits: *He sank into despair after the bankruptcy.* DESPERATION is a state in which loss of hope drives a person to struggle against circumstances, with utter disregard of consequences: *In desperation, they knocked down the door.* DESPONDENCY is a state of deep gloom due to loss of hope and a sense of futility and resignation: *despondency after a serious illness.*

desperate, *adj.* **1.** reckless, despairing, rash, headlong, frantic. **2.** hopeless, serious, grave, dangerous. **3.** wretched, forlorn, hopeless, desolate. **4.** extreme, excessive, great, heroic, prodigious, foolhardy. —**Ant.** careful; hopeful.

desperation, See Syn. study at DESPAIR.

despicable, *adj.* despisable, contemptible, vile, base, worthless, mean, abject, low, pitiful. —**Ant.** lovable, likable, worth.

despise, *v.* contemn, scorn, disdain, spurn. —**Ant.** love, like, admire.

despite, *prep.* notwithstanding, in spite of.

despondency, *n.* depression, dejection, discouragement, melancholy, gloom, desperation, despair, sadness, blues. —**Ant.** elation, joy, happiness. —**Syn. Study.** See DESPAIR.

despondent, *adj.* desponding, depressed, dejected, discouraged, disheartened, downhearted, melancholy, sad, blue, dispirited, hopeless, low-spirited. —**Ant.** elated, joyful, happy.

destiny, *n.* fate, karma, kismet, lot, fortune, future, doom, destination. —**Syn. Study.** See FATE.

destitute, *adj.* needy, poor, indigent, penniless, impoverished, poverty-stricken. —**Ant.** affluent, rich, opulent.

destroy, *v.* **1.** smash, dash, demolish, raze, spoil, consume, level, ruin, waste, ravage, devastate, desolate, lay waste. **2.** end, extinguish, extirpate, annihilate, eradicate, slay, kill, uproot. **3.** nullify, invalidate. —**Ant.** create; originate, start. —**Syn. Study.** DESTROY, DEMOLISH, RAZE imply completely ruining or doing away with something. To DESTROY is to reduce something to nothingness or to take away its powers and functions so that restoration is impossible: *Disease destroys tissues.* To DEMOLISH is to destroy something organized or structured by smashing it

to bits or tearing it down: *The evidence demolished the attorney's case.* To RAZE is to level a building or other structure to the ground: *to raze a fortress.*

destruction, *n.* **1.** extinction, extermination, desolation, devastation, ruin, eradication. **2.** demolition, annihilation, murder, slaughter, death, massacre, genocide. **3.** plague, shipwreck, holocaust. —**Ant.** birth, origin; creation.

destructive, *adj.* **1.** ruinous, baleful, pernicious, mischievous, deleterious, fatal, deadly, lethal. **2.** extirpative, eradicative. —**Ant.** salutary; creative.

detain, *v.* **1.** delay, arrest, retard, stop, slow, stay, check, keep. **2.** restrain, confine, arrest. **3.** keep back, withhold, retain. —**Ant.** promote, encourage; advance.

detect, *v.* discover, catch, expose, descry, find, find out, ascertain, learn, hear of, hear. —**Syn. Study.** See LEARN.

deter, *v.* discourage, restrain, dissuade, hinder, prevent, stop. —**Ant.** encourage, further, continue.

determine, *v.* **1.** settle, decide, conclude, adjust. **2.** conclude, ascertain, verify, check, certify. **3.** fix, decide, establish, condition, influence, resolve. **4.** impel, induce, lead, incline. —**Syn. Study.** See DECIDE.

determined, *adj.* staunch, resolute, unflinching, firm, inflexible, rigid, rigorous, unfaltering, unwavering. —**Ant.** irresolute, vacillating, wavering, faltering, flexible.

detest, *v.* abhor, hate, loathe, abominate, execrate, despise. —**Ant.** love, like. —**Syn. Study.** See HATE.

detestable, *adj.* abominable, hateful, execrable, loathsome, vile, odious, abhorred, abhorrent, despicable. —**Ant.** lovable, likable.

detraction, *n.* detracting, disparagement, belittling, defamation, vilification, calumny, abuse, slander, aspersion, depreciation. —**Ant.** praise, commendation.

detriment, *n.* loss, damage, injury, hurt, harm, impairment, disadvantage, prejudice. —**Ant.** advantage, profit.

devastate, *v.* ravage, lay waste, desolate, destroy, strip, pillage, plunder, sack, spoil, despoil. —**Ant.** build, erect, create.

development, *n.* **1.** expansion, growth, elaboration, progress, increase. **2.** opening, disclosure, developing, unfolding, maturing, maturation. **3.** community, project, housing project. —**Ant.** deterioration, decadence, degeneration.

deviate, *v.* **1.** depart, swerve, digress, diverge, part, wander, veer, err, stray. **2.** turn aside, avert. —**Ant.** converge. —**Syn. Study.** DEVIATE, DIGRESS, DIVERGE imply turning or going aside from a path. To DEVIATE is to stray from a usual or established standard, course of action, or route: *Fear caused him to deviate from the truth.* To DIGRESS is to wander from the main theme in speaking or writing: *The speaker digressed to relate an amusing anecdote.* To DIVERGE is to differ or to move in different directions from a common point or course: *Their interests gradually diverged.*

device, *n.* **1.** invention, contrivance, gadget. **2.** plan, scheme, project, design, expedient. **3.** wile, ruse, artifice, shift, trick, stratagem, evasion, maneuver. **4.** design, figure, emblem, trademark, badge, logotype, colophon, symbol, crest, seal. **5.** motto, slogan, legend. **6.** (*plural*) will, desire, inclination, bent, abilities, aptitudes.

devilish, *adj.* satanic, diabolic, diabolical, demonic, infernal, Mephistophelian, fiendish, hellish. —**Ant.** good, fine, upstanding, righteous, godly.

devise, *v.* order, arrange, plan, think out, contrive, invent, prepare, concoct, scheme, project, design. —**Ant.** disorder, disarrange.

devote, *v.* assign, apply, consign, give up, dedicate, consecrate. —**Ant.** resign, relinquish. —**Syn. Study.** DEVOTE, DEDICATE, CONSECRATE share the sense of assigning or committing someone or something to a particular activity, function, or end. DEVOTE is the most general of these terms, although it carries overtones of religious commitment: *He devoted his evenings to mastering the computer.* DEDICATE implies a more solemn or noble purpose and carries an ethical or moral tone: *We are dedicated to the achievement of equality for all.* CONSECRATE, even in nonreli-

gious contexts, implies an intense and sacred commitment: *consecrated to the service of humanity.*

devotee, See Syn. study at FANATIC.

devotion, *n.* **1.** dedication, consecration. **2.** attachment, affection, love. **3.** devotedness, zeal, ardor, eagerness, earnestness. **4.** (*theology*) religion, religiousness, piety, faith, devoutness, sanctity, saintliness, godliness.

devout, *adj.* **1.** pious, devoted, religious, worshipful, holy, saintly. **2.** earnest, sincere, hearty, serious, honest. —**Ant.** atheistic, agnostic; insincere, scornful. —**Syn. Study.** See RELIGIOUS.

dexterous, *adj.* skillful, adroit, deft, handy, nimble, clever, expert, apt, ready, quick, able. —**Ant.** clumsy, awkward, maladroit, unapt. —**Syn. Study.** DEXTEROUS, ADROIT, DEFT imply facility and ease in performance. DEXTEROUS most often refers to physical, esp. manual, ability but can also refer to mental ability: *a dexterous woodcarver; dexterous handling of a delicate situation.* ADROIT usu. implies mental cleverness and ingenuity but can refer to physical ability: *an adroit politician; an adroit juggler.* DEFT suggests a light and assured touch in physical or mental activity: *a deft magician; deft handling of the reporters after the tragedy.*

dialect, *n.* **1.** provincialism, idiom, localism, jargon, patois, variant. **2.** branch, subfamily, subgroup. **3.** language, tongue, speech. —**Syn. Study.** See LANGUAGE.

diction, *n.* phraseology, wording, style, usage, grammar, language; distinctness, enunciation, pronunciation.

die, *v.* **1.** decease, pass away *or* on, perish, expire, depart. **2.** cease, end, vanish, disappear. **3.** weaken, fail, subside, fade, sink, faint, decline, wither, decay. —*n.* **4.** cube, block. **5.** stamp. —**Syn. Study.** DIE, PERISH mean to relinquish life. To DIE is to cease to live from any cause or circumstance; it is used figuratively of anything that has displayed activity: *He died of cancer. Her anger died.* PERISH, a more literary term, implies death under harsh circumstances such as hunger or violence; figuratively, it connotes permanent disappearance: *Hardship caused many pioneers to perish. Ancient Egyptian civilization has perished.*

difference, *n.* **1.** discrepancy, disparity, dissimilarity, inconsistency, unlikeness, variation, diversity, imbalance, disagreement, inequality, dissimilitude, divergence, contrast, contrariety. **2.** discrimination, distinction. —**Ant.** similarity; agreement.

different, *adj.* **1.** differing, unlike, diverse, divergent, altered, changed, contrary, contrasted, deviant, deviating, variant. **2.** sundry, divers, miscellaneous, various, manifold. —**Ant.** similar, like; uniform, identical. —**Syn. Study.** See VARIOUS.

differentiate, *v.* **1.** set off, distinguish, alter, change. **2.** distinguish, discriminate, separate, contrast. —**Ant.** group together. —**Syn. Study.** See DISTINGUISH.

difficult, *adj.* **1.** hard, arduous. **2.** obscure, complex, intricate, perplexing. **3.** austere, rigid, reserved, forbidding, unaccommodating. **4.** fastidious, particular. —**Ant.** easy, simple; clear, plain; accommodating; careless, sloppy.

difficulty, *n.* **1.** dilemma, predicament, quandary, fix, exigency, emergency. **2.** trouble, problem. **3.** reluctance, unwillingness, obstinacy, stubbornness. **4.** demur, objection, obstacle. —**Ant.** ease; willingness.

diffident, *adj.* shy, self-conscious, self-effacing, bashful, abashed, embarrassed, timid, sheepish, modest. —**Ant.** forward, bold, unabashed.

digest, *v.* **1.** understand, assimilate, study, ponder, consider, contemplate, ruminate over, reflect upon. **2.** arrange, systematize, think over, classify, codify. —*n.* **3.** summary, epitome, abstract, synopsis, abridgment, brief, conspectus. —**Ant.** expand. —**Syn. Study.** See SUMMARY.

dignify, *v.* ennoble, exalt, uplift, glorify, honor, elevate, grace, build up, raise, promote, magnify. —**Ant.** mean, humble.

digress, *v.* deviate, diverge, wander. —**Syn. Study.** See DEVIATE.

dilate, *v.* expand, spread out, enlarge, engross, widen, extend, swell, distend. —**Ant.** shrink, constrict.

dilemma, *n.* predicament, problem,

question, quandary, difficulty, strait. —**Syn. Study.** See PREDICAMENT.

dilettante, *n.* **1.** amateur, dabble, nonprofessional, tyro, putterer. **2.** connoisseur, aesthete, expert, authority, specialist, collector, maven.

diligence, *n.* persistence, effort, application, industry, assiduity, perseverance, assiduousness. —**Ant.** carelessness, laziness.

diligent, *adj.* **1.** industrious, assiduous, sedulous, occupied, busy, constant, attentive, persistent. **2.** painstaking, persevering, indefatigable, untiring, tireless, unremitting, industrious. —**Ant.** lazy, careless; remiss.

dim, *adj.* **1.** obscure, dark, shadowy, dusky, nebulous, hazy, cloud, faint, indistinct. **2.** indistinct, unclear, ill-defined, blurred, vague, confused, indefinite. **3.** dull, tarnished, blurred, slow, stupid, dense, foggy. **4.** disparaging, adverse, uncomplimentary. —*v.* **5.** darken, cloud, obscure, dull. **6.** blur, dull, fade. —**Ant.** clear, bright, distinct; definite.

diminish, *v.* lessen, reduce, decrease, subside, ebb, dwindle, shrink, abate, contract, shrivel up. —**Ant.** increase. —**Syn. Study.** See DECREASE.

diminutive, *adj.* little, small, tiny, dwarf, dwarflike, dwarfish, minute, microscopic, submicroscopic. —**Ant.** large, immense.

din, See Syn. study at NOISE.

dip, *v.* **1.** plunge, immerse, dive, duck. **2.** sink, drop, incline, decline, slope downward. —**Ant.** rise. —**Syn. Study.** DIP, IMMERSE, PLUNGE refer to putting something into liquid. To DIP is to put down into a liquid quickly or partially and lift out again: *to dip a finger into water to test the temperature.* IMMERSE denotes a lowering into a liquid until covered by it: *to immerse meat in salt water.* PLUNGE adds a suggestion of force or suddenness to the action of dipping: *to plunge a lobster into boiling water.*

diplomatic, *adj.* politic, tactful, artful. —**Ant.** tactless, rude, naive. —**Syn. Study.** DIPLOMATIC, POLITIC, TACTFUL imply ability to avoid offending others, esp. in situations where this is important. DIPLOMATIC suggests a smoothness and skill in handling others, usually in such a way as to attain one's own ends and yet avoid any unpleasantness or opposition: *diplomatic inquiries about the stockbroker's finances.* POLITIC emphasizes expediency or prudence in looking out for one's own interests, thus knowing how to treat people of different types in delicate situations: *a truth which it is not politic to insist on.* TACTFUL suggests a nice touch in the handling of delicate matters or situations; it often involves a sincere desire not to hurt the feelings of others: *a tactful way of correcting someone.*

direct, *v.* **1.** guide, advise, regulate, conduct, manage, control, dispose, lead, govern, rule. **2.** order, command, instruct. **3.** point, aim. —*adj.* **4.** straight, undeviating. **5.** immediate, personal, unbroken, simple, evident. **6.** straightforward, downright, plain, categorical, unequivocal, unambiguous, express, open, sincere, outspoken, frank, earnest, ingenuous, obvious, naive. —**Ant.** divert, mislead; crooked; devious; ambiguous, sly. —**Syn. Study.** DIRECT, ORDER, COMMAND mean to issue instructions. DIRECT suggests also giving explanations or advice; the emphasis is on steps necessary to accomplish a purpose: *He directed me to organize the files.* ORDER connotes a more personal relationship and instructions that leave no room for refusal: *She ordered him out of the class.* COMMAND suggests greater formality and a more fixed authority: *The officer commanded the troops to advance.*

directly, See Syn. study at IMMEDIATELY.

dirty, *adj.* **1.** soiled, foul, unclean, filthy, squalid, defiled, grimy. **2.** dirtying, soiling, befouling, besmirching. **3.** vile, mean, base, vulgar, low, groveling, scurvy, shabby, contemptible, despicable. **4.** indecent, obscene, nasty, lascivious, lewd, lecherous, licentious, immoral, amoral. **5.** contaminated, radioactive. **6.** stormy, squally, rainy, foul, sloppy, disagreeable, nasty. **7.** dark-colored, dingy, dull, dark, sullied, clouded. —**Ant.** clean; elevated, exalted; decent, moral; fair; clear.

disability, *n.* incapacity, disqualification, inability, incompetence, impotence, incapability. —**Ant.** ability, capacity, capability.

disable, *v.* **1.** weaken, destroy, cripple, incapacitate, enfeeble, paralyze. **2.** disqualify, incapacitate, eliminate. —**Ant.** strengthen; qualify; include.

disadvantage, *n.* **1.** drawback, inconvenience, hindrance, deprivation. **2.** detriment, hurt, harm, damage, injury, loss, disservice. —**Ant.** advantage.

disaffect, See Syn. study at ESTRANGE.

disappear, *v.* vanish, fade, cease, pass away, end. —**Ant.** appear. —**Syn. Study.** DISAPPEAR, FADE, VANISH mean that something or someone passes from sight or existence. DISAPPEAR is used of whatever suddenly or gradually goes away: *We watched them turn down a side street and disappear.* FADE suggests a complete or partial disappearance that proceeds gradually and often by means of a blending into something else: *Dusk faded into darkness.* VANISH suggests complete, generally rapid disappearance: *The sun vanished behind clouds.*

disappointment, *n.* **1.** failure, defeat, frustration, unfulfillment. **2.** mortification, frustration, chagrin. —**Ant.** fulfillment, victory; consummation.

disaster, *n.* misfortune, calamity, mischance, mishap, accident, misadventure, blow, reverse, catastrophe, adversity, affliction. —**Ant.** luck, fortune. —**Syn. Study.** DISASTER, CALAMITY, CATASTROPHE, CATACLYSM refer to adverse happenings usu. occurring suddenly and unexpectedly. DISASTER may be caused by negligence, bad judgment, or the like, or by natural forces, as a hurricane or flood: *a railroad disaster that claimed many lives.* CALAMITY suggests great affliction, either personal or general; the emphasis is on the grief or sorrow caused: *the calamity of losing a child.* CATASTROPHE refers esp. to the tragic outcome of a personal or public situation; the emphasis is on the destruction or irreplaceable loss: *the catastrophe of a defeat in battle.* CATACLYSM, physically a sudden and violent change in the earth's surface, also refers to a personal or public upheaval of unparalleled violence: *a cataclysm that turned our lives in a new direction.*

disband, *v.* break up, disorganize, demobilize, dissolve, disperse, dismiss, scatter, separate. —**Ant.** organize, unite.

disburse, *v.* spend, pay, expend, lay out. —**Ant.** bank, save.

discern, *v.* **1.** perceive, see, recognize, notice, apprehend, discover, descry, espy, come upon, behold. **2.** discriminate, distinguish, differentiate, judge. —**Syn. Study.** See NOTICE.

discharge, *v.* **1.** unload, disburden, relieve, unburden. **2.** remove, send forth, get rid of, expel, eject, emit. **3.** fire, shoot, set off, detonate. **4.** relieve, release, absolve, exonerate, clear, acquit, liberate, set free, free. **5.** fulfill, perform, execute, observe. **6.** dismiss, cashier, fire, remove, expel, send down, break. **7.** pay, honor, disburse, make good on, liquidate, dissolve, settle. —*n.* **8.** emission, ejection, expulsion, removal, evacuation, voiding. **9.** detonation, firing, shooting. **10.** fulfillment, execution, performance, observance. —**Ant.** load, burden. —**Syn. Study.** See RELEASE.

disciple, *n.* follower, adherent, supporter; pupil, student, scholar. —**Ant.** leader; rebel.

discipline, *n.* **1.** training, drill, exercise, instruction, practice. **2.** punishment, chastisement, castigation, correction. **3.** subjection, order, control, regulation, subjugation, government. **4.** rules, regulations. —*v.* **5.** train, exercise, drill, practice, instruct, teach, educate. **6.** punish, correct, chastise, castigate.

disclose, *v.* **1.** reveal, make known, divulge, show, tell, unveil, communicate. **2.** uncover, lay open, expose, bring to light; muckrake. —**Ant.** conceal, hide; cover.

disconcert, *v.* disturb, confuse, perturb, ruffle, discompose, perplex, bewilder, frustrate, embarrass, abash; disarrange, disorder. —**Ant.** calm; order, arrange.

disconsolate, *adj.* inconsolable, unhappy, desolate, forlorn, heartbroken, sad, melancholy, dejected, gloomy, miserable, cheerless, sorrowful. —**Ant.** happy, cheerful, delighted.

discontent, *adj.* **1.** discontented, dissatisfied. —*n.* **2.** discontentment, dissatisfaction, uneasiness, inquietude, restlessness, displeasure.

—**Ant.** contentment; satisfaction, pleasure, ease, restfulness.

discontinue, v. put an end to, interrupt, stop, cease, quit; desist. —**Ant.** continue, further.

discourage, v. **1.** dishearten, dispirit, daunt, depress, deject, overawe, cow, awe, subdue, abash, embarrass, dismay, intimidate, frighten. **2.** dissuade, deter, hinder, prevent, obstruct. —**Ant.** encourage, hearten, embolden. —**Syn. Study.** DISCOURAGE, DISMAY, INTIMIDATE mean to dishearten or frighten a person so as to prevent some action. To DISCOURAGE is to dishearten by expressing disapproval or by suggesting that a contemplated action will probably fail: *He was discouraged from going into business.* To DISMAY is to dishearten, shock, or bewilder by sudden difficulties or danger: *a prosecutor dismayed by disclosures of new evidence.* To INTIMIDATE is to deter by making timid: *The prospect of making a speech intimidates me.*

discouragement, n. **1.** depression, dejection, hopelessness, despair. **2.** deterrent, damper, wet blanket, cold water, chilling effect, impediment, obstacle, obstruction. —**Ant.** encouragement.

discover, v. **1.** learn of, ascertain, unearth, determine, ferret out, dig up; find out, detect, espy, descry, discern, see, notice. **2.** originate, bring to light, invent. —**Ant.** conceal. —**Syn. Study.** See LEARN.

discreet, adj. wise, judicious, prudent, circumspect, cautious, careful, heedful, considerate, wary. —**Ant.** indiscreet, careless, imprudent; incautious, inconsiderate. —**Syn. Study.** See CAREFUL.

discrepancy, n. difference, inconsistency, incongruity, disagreement, discordance, contrariety, variance, variation. —**Ant.** similarity, congruity, consistency, concord, accord, agreement.

discriminate, v. **1.** distinguish, set apart, differentiate. —adj. **2.** critical, distinguishing, discriminative, discriminatory. —**Ant.** group, unite; indiscriminate, undistinguished. —**Syn. Study.** See DISTINGUISH.

discuss, v. examine, reason, deliberate, argue, debate, talk over, sift, consider.

disdain, v. **1.** contemn, despise, scorn, spurn. —n. **2.** contempt, scorn, contumely, contemptuousness, haughtiness, arrogance, superciliousness, hauteur. —**Ant.** accept, like, love; love, admiration, regard. —**Syn. Study.** See CONTEMPT.

disdainful, adj. contemptuous, scornful, haughty, arrogant, supercilious, contumelious. —**Ant.** friendly, amiable, considerate, attentive.

disease, n. morbidity, illness, sickness, ailment, complaint, affection, disorder, malady, abnormality, derangement, distemper, indisposition, infirmity. —**Ant.** health, salubriety.

disfigure, v. mar, deface, injure, deform, spoil, ruin, blemish. —**Ant.** beautify.

disgrace, n. **1.** ignominy, shame, dishonor, infamy, disfavor, disapproval, disapprobation, disparagement, stain, taint, notoriety, baseness. **2.** odium, obloquy, degradation, opprobrium, scandal. —v. **3.** shame, dishonor, defame, disfavor, humiliate, disapprove, discredit, degrade, debase, stain, sully, taint, tarnish, reproach. —**Syn. Study.** DISGRACE, DISHONOR, IGNOMINY, INFAMY imply a very low position in the opinion of others. DISGRACE implies being excluded and held in strong disfavor by others: *to bring disgrace to one's family by not paying debts.* DISHONOR suggests a loss of honor or honorable reputation; it usu. relates to one's own conduct: *He preferred death to dishonor.* IGNOMINY is disgrace that invites public contempt: *the ignominy of being caught cheating.* INFAMY is shameful notoriety, or baseness of action or character that is widely known and recognized: *The children never outlived their father's infamy.*

disgust, v. **1.** sicken, nauseate, turn one's stomach. **2.** offend, displease, repel, repulse, revolt, abhor, detest. —n. **3.** distaste, nausea, loathing, hatred, abhorrence, disrelish. **4.** dislike, detestation, repugnance, aversion, dissatisfaction, antipathy. —**Ant.** please, delight, attract; relish, liking, love; satisfaction.

disgusting, adj. offensive, offending, loathsome, sickening, nauseous, nauseating, repulsive, revolting, odious, hateful, repugnant, foul, abominable, abhorrent, distasteful, detesta-

ble. —**Ant.** delightful, delectable, attractive, beautiful.

dishonest, adj. unscrupulous, conniving, corrupt, knavish, thievish, deceitful, treacherous, perfidious; false, fraudulent, counterfeit. —**Ant.** honest.

dishonor, See Syn. study at DISGRACE.

dishonorable, adj. **1.** ignoble, base, disgraceful, shameful, shameless, false, fraudulent. **2.** infamous, notorious, unscrupulous, unprincipled, disreputable, disgraceful, scandalous, ignominious, discreditable. —**Ant.** honorable.

disintegrate, v. reduce to particles or fragments, break up, decay, rot, fall apart, separate. —**Ant.** integrate. —**Syn. Study.** See DECAY.

disinterested, adj. unbiased, unprejudiced, unselfish, impartial, fair, generous, liberal. —**Ant.** biased, prejudiced, illiberal, bigoted, selfish, partial. —**Syn. Study.** See FAIR.

dislike, v. **1.** have an aversion or be averse to, be disinclined or reluctant. —n. **2.** disrelish, disgust, distaste, repugnance, antipathy, loathing, aversion, antagonism. —**Ant.** like; relish, delight, delectation.

disloyal, adj. unfaithful, false, perfidious, treacherous, traitorous, treasonable, subversive, disaffected, untrue, unpatriotic. —**Ant.** loyal, faithful, true, honest.

disloyalty, n. unfaithfulness, perfidy, treachery, treason, betrayal, disaffection, faithlessness, subversion. —**Ant.** loyalty, fealty, allegiance.

dismay, v. **1.** discourage, dishearten, daunt, appall, terrify, horrify, frighten, scare, intimidate, disconcert, put out, alarm, paralyze. —n. **2.** consternation, terror, horror, panic, fear, alarm. —**Ant.** encourage, hearten, embolden; security, confidence. —**Syn. Study.** See DISCOURAGE.

dismiss, v. release, let go, discharge, discard, reject, set or put aside; fire. —**Ant.** hire, employ. —**Syn. Study.** See RELEASE.

disobedient, adj. insubordinate, contumacious, defiant, refractory, unruly, rebellious, obstinate, stubborn, unsubmissive, uncompliant. —**Ant.** obedient.

disobey, v. transgress, violate, disregard, defy, infringe. —**Ant.** obey.

disorder, n. **1.** disorderliness, disarray, jumble, mess, litter, clutter, disarrangement, confusion, irregularity, disorganization, derangement. **2.** disturbance, tumult, brawl, uproar, fight, unrest, quarrel, bustle, clamor, riot, turbulence. **3.** ailment, malady, derangement, illness, complaint, sickness, disease, indisposition. —v. **4.** disarrange, disarray, mess up, disorganize, unsettle, disturb, derange, discompose, upset, confuse, confound. —**Ant.** order.

disparity, n. dissimilarity, inequality, difference, distinction, dissimilitude. —**Ant.** similarity, equality, similitude.

dispel, See Syn. study at SCATTER.

dispense, v. deal, distribute, apportion, allot, dole.

disperse, v. **1.** scatter, dissipate, spread, diffuse, disseminate, broadcast, sow, scatter. **3.** dispel. **4.** vanish, disappear, evanesce. —**Ant.** unite, combine; appear. —**Syn. Study.** See SCATTER.

displace, v. **1.** misplace, move, dislocate. **2.** replace, remove, depose, oust, dismiss, cashier.

display, v. **1.** show, exhibit, demonstrate, make visible, evince, manifest. **2.** reveal, uncover, betray. **3.** unfold, open out, spread out. **4.** show, flourish, flaunt, parade, show off. —n. **5.** show, exhibition, manifestation. **6.** parade, ostentation, flourish, flaunting. —**Ant.** conceal, hide; cover. —**Syn. Study.** DISPLAY, EXHIBIT, MANIFEST mean to show or bring to the attention of another or others. To DISPLAY is literally to spread something out so that it may be most completely and favorably seen: *to display goods for sale.* To EXHIBIT is to display something to the public for inspection or appraisal: *to exhibit African violets at a flower show.* They may both refer to showing or revealing one's qualities or feelings: *to display wit; to exhibit surprise.* MANIFEST means to show feelings or qualities plainly or clearly: *He manifested his anger with a scowl.*

displeasure, n. dissatisfaction, annoyance, disapprobation, disapproval, distaste, dislike; anger, ire, wrath, indignation, vexation; offense. —**Ant.** pleasure, satisfaction, approval, delight; calm, peace.

disposition, n. **1.** temper, temperament, nature, character, humor. **2.** inclination, willingness, bent, tendency, proneness, bias, predisposition, proclivity. **3.** arrangement, order, grouping, location, placement. **4.** settlement, outcome, finale, result, dispensation. **5.** regulation, appointment, management, control, direction. **6.** bestowal, endowment. —**Ant.** indisposition, unwillingness.

dispute, v. **1.** argue, discuss, debate, agitate. **2.** wrangle, contest, quarrel, bicker, spat, squabble, spar, brawl. **3.** oppose, controvert, contradict, deny, impugn. —n. **4.** argumentation, argument, contention, debate, controversy, disputation, altercation, quarrel, wrangle, bickering, spat, squabble, tiff. —**Ant.** agree, concur; agreement, concurrence. —**Syn. Study.** See ARGUMENT.

disregard, v. **1.** ignore, neglect, overlook, disobey, pay no attention or heed or regard to, take no notice of. **2.** slight, insult. —n. **3.** neglect, inattention, inattentiveness, oversight. **4.** disrespect, slight, indifference. —**Ant.** regard, view, notice, note; attention; respect. —**Syn. Study.** See SLIGHT.

disrespectful, adj. discourteous, impolite, rude, crude, uncivil, impudent, impertinent, irreverent. —**Ant.** respectful, courteous, polite, civil, reverent.

dissatisfaction, n. discontent, displeasure, dislike, disappointment, disapproval, disapprobation, uneasiness. —**Ant.** satisfaction, approval, approbation.

dissension, See Syn. study at QUARREL.

dissent, v. **1.** differ, disagree. —n. **2.** difference, dissidence, disagreement, dissatisfaction, opposition, nonconformity, separation. —**Ant.** agree, concur; agreement, concurrence, satisfaction, unity.

dissipate, v. **1.** scatter, disperse, dispel, disintegrate. **2.** waste, squander. **3.** scatter, disappear, vanish, disintegrate. **4.** debauch. —**Ant.** integrate, unite; appear; join. —**Syn. Study.** See SCATTER.

dissolve, v. **1.** melt, liquefy. **2.** sever, loose, loosen, free, disunite, break up; dismiss, disperse, adjourn. **3.** destroy, dispel, ruin, disintegrate, break down, terminate, end; perish, crumble, die, expire. **4.** solidify; unite; meet; integrate; originate.

distaste, n. dislike, disinclination, aversion, repugnance, disgust, displeasure, dissatisfaction, disrelish. —**Ant.** taste, delectation, liking, love, satisfaction; relish.

distasteful, adj. **1.** disagreeable, displeasing, offensive, repugnant, repulsive, unpleasant. **2.** unpalatable, unsavory, nauseating, loathsome, disgusting, sickening. —**Ant.** tasteful, agreeable, pleasant, inoffensive; attractive, delightful.

distend, v. expand, swell, stretch, dilate, bloat, enlarge. —**Ant.** contract, shrink, reduce.

distinct, adj. **1.** distinguished, distinguishable, different, individual, separate, dividual, various, varied; dissimilar. **2.** definite, well-defined, clear, plain, unmistakable, unconfused. —**Ant.** indistinct, blurred, same; similar; indefinite, unclear, confused. —**Syn. Study.** See VARIOUS.

distinction, n. **1.** difference, differentiation, discrimination. **2.** honor, repute, name, fame, celebrity, renown, importance, note, account, eminence, superiority. —**Ant.** indifference; similarity; disrepute, dishonor.

distinguish, v. **1.** mark, characterize. **2.** discriminate, differentiate, separate, divide, classify, categorize. **3.** discern, recognize, perceive, know, tell. **4.** make prominent or conspicuous or eminent. —**Syn. Study.** DISTINGUISH, DIFFERENTIATE, DISCRIMINATE mean to note the difference between two or more similar things. To DISTINGUISH is to recognize differences based on characteristic features or qualities: *to distinguish a light cruiser from a heavy cruiser.* To DIFFERENTIATE is to find and point out the exact differences in detail: *The symptoms of both diseases are so similar that it is hard to differentiate one from the other.* To DISCRIMINATE is to note fine or subtle distinctions and to judge their significance: *to discriminate prejudiced from unprejudiced testimony.*

distinguished, adj. **1.** conspicuous, marked, extraordinary. **2.** noted, eminent, famed, famous, celebrated, renowned, illustrious. **3.** distingué, refined. —**Ant.** undistinguished.

common; infamous; unknown; unrefined, coarse.

distress, n. **1.** pain, anxiety, sorrow, grief, agony, anguish, misery, adversity, hardship, trial, tribulation, suffering, trouble, affliction. **2.** need, necessity, want, privation, deprivation, destitution, poverty, indigence. —v. **3.** trouble, worry, afflict, bother, grieve, pain, make miserable or unhappy. —**Ant.** comfort; fulfillment, opulence; console, mitigate, delight.

distribute, v. **1.** deal out, deal, allot, apportion, assign, mete, dole, dispense, give. **2.** disperse, spread, scatter. **3.** divide, separate, classify, categorize, dispose, sort, arrange. —**Ant.** collect, keep; unite.

distrust, v. **1.** doubt, suspect, mistrust. —n. **2.** doubt, suspicion, mistrust, misgiving. —**Ant.** trust, depend. —**Syn. Study.** See SUSPICION.

disturbance, n. **1.** perturbation, agitation, commotion, disorder, confusion, derangement. **2.** disorder, tumult, riot, uproar. —**Ant.** order, organization; calm, serenity.

diverge, v. **1.** branch off, separate, fork, bifurcate, divide. **2.** differ, deviate, disagree, vary. —**Ant.** converge, unite; agree, concur. —**Syn. Study.** See DEVIATE.

diverse, adj. **1.** unlike, dissimilar, separate, different, disagreeing. **2.** various, varied, multiform, manifold, variant, divergent. —**Ant.** similar, like. —**Syn. Study.** See VARIOUS.

divert, v. **1.** turn aside, deflect. **2.** draw aside or away, turn aside, distract. **3.** distract, entertain, amuse, delight, gratify, exhilarate. —**Ant.** fix; weary, bore, tire. —**Syn. Study.** See AMUSE.

divest, v. **1.** strip, unclothe, denude, disrobe, undress. **2.** strip, dispossess, deprive. —**Ant.** invest.

divide, v. **1.** separate, sunder, cut off, sever, shear, cleave, part. **2.** apportion, share, deal out, partition, distribute, portion. **3.** alienate, disunite, cause to disagree, estrange. **4.** distinguish, classify, sort, arrange, distribute. —**Ant.** unite; keep, retain; disarrange.

division, n. **1.** partition, dividing, separation, apportionment, allotment, distribution, sharing. **2.** mark, boundary, partition, demarcation. **3.** section, part, compartment, partition, segment. **4.** disagreement, dissension, difference, variance, rupture, disunion, discord, breach, rift, estrangement, alienation, feud. —**Ant.** agreement, union, accord.

divulge, v. disclose, reveal, make known, impart, tell, broadcast. —**Ant.** conceal.

do, v. **1.** perform, act. **2.** execute, finish, carry out, conclude, end, terminate, complete. **3.** accomplish, finish, achieve, attain, effect, bring about, execute, carry out. **4.** exert, put forth. **5.** cover, traverse. **6.** serve, suffice for. **7.** behave, proceed, act, fare, manage.

doctrine, n. tenet, dogma, theory, precept, belief, principle, teachings.

dodge, v. equivocate, quibble, evade, be evasive, elude.

dogged, See Syn. study at STUBBORN.

dominant, adj. **1.** ruling, governing, controlling, most influential, prevailing, prevalent, common, principal, predominant, paramount, preeminent, outstanding, important, first, ascendant. **2.** commanding, advantageous. —**Ant.** secondary, disadvantageous. —**Syn. Study.** DOMINANT, PREDOMINANT, PARAMOUNT describe something outstanding or supreme. DOMINANT applies to something that exerts control or influence: *the dominant powers at an international conference.* PREDOMINANT applies to something that is foremost at a specific time: *English is one of the world's predominant languages.* PARAMOUNT refers to something that is first in rank or order: *Safety is of paramount importance.*

donation, n. gift, contribution, offering, grant, benefaction, boon, largess, present, gratuity.

doom, n. **1.** fate, destiny, lot, fortune. **2.** ruin, death. **3.** judgment, decision, sentence, condemnation. —v. **4.** destine, predestine, foreordain, decree. **5.** condemn, sentence, ordain.

dormant, adj. **1.** asleep, inactive, torpid, quiescent. **2.** quiescent, inoperative, in abeyance, latent, potential, inert, suspended. —**Ant.** awake, active; operative; kinetic. —**Syn. Study.** See INACTIVE.

doubt, v. **1.** distrust, mistrust, suspect, question. **2.** hesitate, waver. —n. **3.** undecidedness, indecision, uncertainty, faltering, irresolution, hesitation, hesitancy, vacillation,

misgiving, suspense; mistrust, distrust, suspicion. —**Ant.** trust; decision, certainty, conviction.

doubtful, adj. **1.** uncertain, unsure, ambiguous, equivocal, indeterminate, undecided, fifty-fifty. **2.** undetermined, unsettled, indecisive, dubious, enigmatic, problematic, puzzled. **3.** hesitating, hesitant, wavering, irresolute, vacillating, dubious, skeptical, incredulous. —**Ant.** certain, sure, unambiguous, decided; settled; unhesitating, resolute. —**Syn. Study.** DOUBTFUL, DUBIOUS, INCREDULOUS, SKEPTICAL all involve a reluctance to be convinced. DOUBTFUL implies a strong feeling of uncertainty or indecision about something or someone: *to be doubtful about the outcome of a contest.* DUBIOUS usu. implies vacillation or hesitation caused by mistrust or suspicion: *dubious about the statements of a witness.* INCREDULOUS suggests an unwillingness or reluctance to believe: *incredulous at the good news.* SKEPTICAL implies a general disposition to doubt or question: *skeptical of human progress.*

dowdy, adj. ill-dressed, frumpy, shabby, old-maidish, old-fashioned. —**Ant.** fashionable, chic, modish, à la mode.

downhearted, adj. dejected, discouraged, depressed, downcast, despondent, disheartened, sad, sorrowful, unhappy, dispirited, crestfallen. —**Ant.** happy.

downright, adj. utter, absolute, complete, outright, positive, perfect, arrant, out-and-out, thoroughgoing, flat-out, unqualified, unmitigated.

drag, v. **1.** draw, pull, haul, trail, tug. **2.** trail, linger, loiter, slow. —**Ant.** drive, push; speed, expedite.

draw, v. **1.** drag, haul, pull, tug, tow, lead. **2.** attract, magnetize. **3.** delineate, sketch, draught, depict, trace. **4.** frame, formulate, compose, write, draw up, prepare, form. **5.** suck, inhale, drain. **6.** get, derive, deduce, infer, understand. **7.** produce, bring in, bear. **8.** draw or pull out, attenuate; extend, stretch, lengthen. **9.** extract. —**Ant.** drive, push.

dread, n. **1.** fear. —v. **2.** terror, fear, apprehension. **3.** awe, reverence, veneration. —adj. **4.** frightful, dire, terrible, dreadful, horrible. —**Ant.** intrepidity, bravery; pleasant, delightful.

dreary, adj. **1.** gloomy, dismal, drear, cheerless, chilling, chill, depressing, comfortless. **2.** monotonous, tedious, wearisome, dull, boring, uninteresting, tiresome. —**Ant.** cheerful, comforting; interesting, engaging.

drench, v. steep, wet, soak, ret, saturate. —**Ant.** dry.

dress, n. **1.** costume, frock, gown. **2.** clothing, raiment, garb, attire, apparel, vesture, garments, vestments, clothes, suit, habit, habiliment. **3.** regalia, array, panoply. —v. **4.** attire, robe, garb, clothe, array, accouter, apparel, rig, deck out. **5.** trim, ornament, adorn, decorate. **6.** straighten, align. **7.** prepare, fit. —**Ant.** undress.

drink, v. **1.** imbibe, sip, quaff, swallow. **2.** tipple, tope. —n. **3.** beverage, potion, liquid refreshment, draft. —**Syn.** DRINK, IMBIBE, SIP refer to taking liquids into the mouth. They are also used figuratively in the sense of taking in something through the mind or the senses. DRINK is the general word: *to drink coffee; to drink in the music.* IMBIBE is a more formal word, used most often in a figurative sense but also in reference to liquids, esp. alcohol: *to imbibe culture; to imbibe with discretion.* SIP implies drinking or absorbing little by little: *to sip a soda; to sip the words of Shakespeare.*

drive, v. **1.** push, force, impel, propel, send. **2.** overwork, overtask, overburden, overtax. **3.** urge, constrain, impel, compel, force. **4.** go, travel, ride. —n. **5.** vigor, pressure, effort, energy. —**Ant.** curb, restrain.

droll, adj. **1.** queer, odd, diverting, amusing, comical, waggish, witty, funny. —n. **2.** wag, buffoon, jester, comedian, clown, zany, punch, merry-andrew. **3.** joke, jest, clown. —**Ant.** common; serious. —**Syn. Study.** See AMUSING.

droop, v. sink, bend, hang down, flag, languish, fail, weaken, decline, faint, wilt, wither, fade. —**Ant.** rise.

drove, n. herd, flock, company, crowd, host, collection.

drudgery, n. work, labor. —**Syn. Study.** See WORK.

drunkard, n. toper, sot, tippler, drinker, inebriate, dipsomaniac, alcoholic. —**Ant.** teetotaler, dry.

drunken, *adj.* drunk, sotted, besotted, tipsy, inebriated, intoxicated, befuddled. —**Ant.** sober.

dry, *adj.* **1.** arid, parched. **2.** wiped *or* drained away, evaporated. **3.** thirsty. **4.** plain, bald, unadorned, unembellished. **5.** dull, uninteresting, dreary, tiresome, boring, tedious, jejune, barren, vapid. **6.** humorous, sarcastic, biting, sardonic, keen, sharp, pointed, sly. —**Ant.** wet, drenched; interesting, fascinating; dull. —**Syn. Study.** DRY, ARID both mean without moisture. DRY is the general word indicating absence of water or freedom from moisture, which may be favorable or unfavorable: *a dry well; a dry bath towel.* ARID suggests intense dryness in a region or climate, resulting in bareness or in barrenness: *arid tracts of desert.*

dubious, *adj.* **1.** doubtful, undecided, indeterminate, uncertain, dubitable, fluctuating, wavering. **2.** questionable, equivocal, ambiguous, obscure, unclear. —**Ant.** definite, incisive, certain; unquestionable, unequivocal, clear. —**Syn. Study.** See DOUBTFUL.

dull, *adj.* **1.** slow, obtuse, stupid, blunted, unimaginative, sluggish, unintelligent, stolid. **2.** insensible, unfeeling, insensate, apathetic, unimpassioned, lifeless, callous, dead. **3.** listless, spiritless, torpid, inactive, lifeless, inert, inanimate. **4.** boring, depressing, ennuyant, tedious, uninteresting, tiresome, drear, dreary, vapid, wearisome, dry, jejune. **5.** blunt, dulled. —*v.* **6.** blunt, deaden, stupefy, paralyze, obtund, benumb. **7.** depress, dishearten, discourage, dispirit, sadden, deject. —**Ant.** bright, imaginative, quick; sensitive; spirited, active, animated; interesting; sharp, clever; encourage, inspirit, hearten.

dumb, *adj.* **1.** mute, speechless, silent, voiceless. **2.** stupid. —**Ant.** voluble, talkative, loquacious.

duplicate, *adj.* **1.** double, twofold. —*n.* **2.** facsimile, copy, replica, reproduction, transcript. —*v.* **3.** copy, replicate, reproduce, repeat, double, imitate. —**Ant.** original.

duplicity, *n.* deceitfulness, deceit, double-dealing, deception, guile, hypocrisy, dissimulation, chicanery, artifice, fraud, dishonesty, perfidy, treachery. —**Ant.** naïveté, honesty, openness, simplicity. —**Syn. Study.** See DECEIT.

durable, *adj.* lasting, enduring, stable, constant, permanent. —**Ant.** unstable, temporary, temporal.

dusky, *adj.* **1.** swarthy, dark. **2.** dim, shadowy, murky, cloudy, shady, obscure, clouded, penumbral. —**Ant.** fair, blond, light; clear, unclouded.

dutiful, *adj.* respectful, docile, submissive, deferential, reverential, obedient. —**Ant.** disrespectful, disobedient, irreverent.

duty, *n.* **1.** obligation. **2.** office, function, responsibility, service, business. **3.** homage, respect, deference, reverence. **4.** levy, tax, impost, custom, toll, excise. —**Syn. Study.** DUTY, OBLIGATION refer to something a person feels bound to do. A DUTY often applies to what a person performs in fulfillment of the permanent dictates of conscience, piety, right, or law: *one's duty to tell the truth; a parent's duty to raise children properly.* An OBLIGATION is what is expected at a particular time in fulfillment of a specific and often personal promise, contract, or agreement: *social or financial obligations.*

dwarf, *n.* **1.** homunculus, manikin, pygmy, midget, Lilliputian. **2.** runt. —*adj.* **3.** diminutive, tiny, small, little, Lilliputian, stunted, dwarfed, undersized. —*v.* **4.** stunt. —**Ant.** giant, colossus; huge, gigantic, immense, colossal. —**Syn. Study.** DWARF, MIDGET, PYGMY are terms for a very small person. A DWARF is someone checked in growth or stunted, or in some way not normally formed. A MIDGET (not in technical use) is someone normally proportioned, but diminutive. A PYGMY is properly a member of one of certain small-sized peoples of Africa and Asia, but the word is often used imprecisely to mean dwarf or midget. DWARF is a term often used to describe very small plants. PYGMY is used to describe very small animals.

dwell, *v.* **1.** abide, reside, stay, live, inhabit. **2.** continue, perpetuate. **3.** linger, emphasize. —**Ant.** leave, depart; cease, end, terminate, stop.

dwelling, See Syn. study at HOUSE.

dwindle, *v.* diminish, lessen, decline, decrease, wane, shrink, waste away, degenerate, sink, decay.

—**Ant.** increase, grow, wax. —**Syn. Study.** See DECREASE.

E

eager, *adj.* avid, ardent, enthusiastic, zealous, breathless, impatient, anxious, atingle, champing at the bit, raring to go. —**Ant.** reluctant, disinclined, hesitant.

earn, *v.* **1.** gain, acquire, win, get, obtain, secure, procure. **2.** merit, deserve. —**Syn. Study.** See GAIN.

earnest, *adj.* **1.** sincere, zealous, ardent, eager, fervent, resolute, serious, fervid, determined, purposeful. **2.** deep, firm, stable, intent, steady, faithful, true. —**Ant.** insincere, faithless, unfaithful, wavering. —**Syn. Study.** EARNEST, RESOLUTE, SERIOUS, SINCERE imply having qualities of steady purposefulness. EARNEST implies having a purpose and being steadily and soberly eager in pursuing it: *an earnest student.* RESOLUTE adds a quality of determination: *resolute in defending the rights of others.* SERIOUS implies having depth and a soberness of attitude that contrasts with gaiety and frivolity; it may include the qualities of both earnestness and resolution: *serious and thoughtful.* SINCERE suggests genuineness, trustworthiness, and absence of superficiality: *a sincere interest in a person's welfare.*

earth, *n.* **1.** globe, world. **2.** ground, soil, turf, sod, dirt, terra firma. —**Ant.** heaven; sky.

earthly, *adj.* **1.** terrestrial, worldly, mundane, earthy. **2.** possible, conceivable, imaginable. —**Ant.** spiritual; impossible, inconceivable. —**Syn. Study.** EARTHLY, TERRESTRIAL, WORLDLY, MUNDANE refer to that which is concerned with the earth literally or figuratively. EARTHLY now almost always implies a contrast to that which is heavenly: *earthly pleasures; our earthly home.* TERRESTRIAL applies to the earth as a planet or to land as opposed to water: *the terrestrial globe; terrestrial areas.* WORLDLY is commonly used in the sense of being devoted to the vanities, cares, advantages, or gains of physical existence to the exclusion of spiritual interests or the afterlife: *worldly success; worldly standards.* MUNDANE is a formal equivalent of WORLDLY and suggests that which is bound to the earth, is not exalted, and therefore is commonplace: *mundane pursuits.*

earthy, *adj.* **1.** plain, simple, unadorned, down-to-earth, unpretentious, matter-of-fact, unsophisticated, uncomplicated, direct, practical, pragmatic, clear-eyed. **2.** unrefined, impolite, rude, crude, vulgar, scatological, obscene, blue, gross. —**Ant.** refined, elevated, delicate.

ease, *n.* **1.** comfort, relaxation, rest, repose, well-being, effortlessness, contentment, happiness. **2.** tranquility, serenity, calmness, quiet, quietude, peace. **3.** informality, unaffectedness, naturalness, lightness, flexibility, freedom. —*v.* **4.** comfort, relieve, disburden. **5.** tranquilize, soothe, allay, alleviate, mitigate, abate, assuage, lighten, lessen, reduce. **6.** facilitate. —**Ant.** discomfort, effort; disturbance, perturbation; affectation; burden; increase.

easy, *adj.* **1.** facile, light, gentle, moderate. **2.** tranquil, untroubled, comfortable, contented, satisfied, quiet, at rest. **3.** easygoing, compliant, submissive, complying, accommodating, agreeable, yielding. **4.** lenient. **5.** informal, unrestrained, unconstrained, brash, unembarrassed, smooth. —**Ant.** difficult, hard, immoderate; troubled, disturbed, uncomfortable, disagreeable, unyielding; restrained, embarrassed.

easygoing, *adj.* relaxed, placid, calm, serene, tranquil, even-tempered, composed, collected, easy, unruffled, posed, self-possessed, imperturbable, nonchalant, insouciant, laid-back, cool. —**Ant.** tense, rigid, demanding.

ebb, *n.* **1.** reflux, regression, regress, retrogression. **2.** decline, decay, deterioration, degeneration, wane. —*v.* **3.** subside, abate, recede, retire. **4.** decline, sink, wane, decrease, decay, waste *or* fade away. —**Ant.** flow, neap; wax; increase, swell, well; rise.

eccentric, *adj.* **1.** off-center, uncentered, off-balance, unbalanced. **2.** odd, unusual, peculiar, unconventional, strange, curious, bizarre, aberrant, weird, freakish, offbeat, off-the-wall, oddball, bizzarro. —*n.* **3.** character, oddity, original, strange one, crank, freak, oddball, odd duck.

eccentricity, *n.* idiosyncrasy, quirk, peculiarity, foible, odd characteristic, uncommon behavior, quirkiness. —**Syn. Study.** ECCENTRICITY, PECULIARITY, QUIRK, IDIOSYNCRASY all refer to some noticeable deviation in behavior, style, or manner from what is normal or expected. ECCENTRICITY suggests a mildly amusing but harmless characteristic or style: *a whimsical eccentricity of dress.* PECULIARITY is the most general of these words, referring to almost any perceptible oddity or departure from any norm: *a peculiarity of the language.* QUIRK often refers to a minor, unimportant kind of oddity: *Her one quirk was a habit of writing long, rambling letters.* Sometimes QUIRK has overtones of strangeness: *sexual quirks.* IDIOSYNCRASY refers to a variation in behavior or manner exclusive to or characteristic of a single individual: *idiosyncrasies of style that irritated editors but often delighted readers.*

economical, *adj.* saving, provident, sparing, thrifty, frugal; stingy, tight, penurious. —**Ant.** lavish, spendthrift. —**Syn. Study.** ECONOMICAL, THRIFTY, FRUGAL imply careful and efficient use of resources. ECONOMICAL implies prudent planning in the disposition of resources so as to avoid unnecessary waste or expense: *It is economical to buy in large quantities.* THRIFTY adds the idea of industry and successful management: *a thrifty shopper looking for bargains.* FRUGAL suggests saving by denying oneself luxuries: *so frugal that he never takes taxis.*

economy, *n.* **1.** frugality, thriftiness, thrift, saving. **2.** management, system, method. —**Ant.** lavishness.

ecstasy, *n.* rapture, transport, exultation, apotheosis, jubilation, happiness, elation, delight, happiness, joy, bliss. —**Syn. Study.** ECSTASY, RAPTURE, TRANSPORT, EXULTATION share a sense of being taken out of oneself or one's normal state and entering a state of heightened feeling. ECSTASY suggests an emotion so overpowering and engrossing as to produce a trancelike state: *religious ecstasy; an ecstasy of grief.* RAPTURE most often refers to an elevated sensation of bliss or delight, either carnal or spiritual: *the rapture of first love.* TRANSPORT suggests a strength of feeling that often results in expression of some kind: *They jumped up and down in a transport of delight.* EXULTATION refers to a heady sense of personal well-being so powerful that one is lifted above normal emotional levels: *wild exultation at having finally broken the record.*

ecstatic, *adj.* overjoyed, joyful, elated, bursting, rapturous, delirious, exultant, jubilant, transported, on cloud nine, in seventh heaven, beside oneself, happy as a lark. —**Ant.** glum, dispirited, downhearted.

edge, *n.* **1.** border, rim, lip, margin, boundary, verge, brink. —*v.* **2.** inch, sidle. —**Ant.** center.

edifice, *n.* structure, building, construction, erection, pile.

edify, *v.* enlighten, educate, illuminate, improve, better, transform, uplift, raise, boost, lift, elevate.

educate, *v.* teach, instruct, school, drill, indoctrinate, train, discipline. —**Syn. Study.** See TEACH.

education, *n.* **1.** instruction, schooling, tuition, training. **2.** learning, knowledge, enlightenment, culture. —**Ant.** illiteracy.

eerie, *adj.* fearful, awesome, weird, uncanny, strange. —**Ant.** common, ordinary. —**Syn. Study.** See WEIRD.

effect, *n.* **1.** result, consequence, end, outcome, issue. **2.** power, efficacy, force, validity, weight. **3.** operation, execution; accomplishment, fulfillment. **4.** purport, intent, tenor, significance, signification, meaning, import. —*v.* **5.** bring about, accomplish, make happen, achieve, do, perform, complete, consummate, bring about, realize. —**Ant.** cause. —**Syn. Study.** EFFECT, CONSEQUENCE, RESULT refer to something produced by an action or a cause. An EFFECT is that which is produced, usu. more or less immediately and directly: *The drug had the effect of producing sleep.* A CONSEQUENCE, something that follows naturally or logically, as in a train of events or sequence of time, is less intimately connected with its cause than is an effect: *One consequence of a recession is a rise in unemployment.* A RESULT may be near or remote, and often is the sum of effects or consequences as making an end or final outcome: *The English language is the result of the fusion of many different elements.*

effective, *adj.* **1.** capable, competent, efficient, efficacious, effectual. **2.** operative, in force, active. —**Ant.** ineffective, incompetent, inefficient, ineffectual; inactive, inoperative. —**Syn. Study.** EFFECTIVE, EFFECTUAL, EFFICACIOUS, EFFICIENT refer to that which produces or is able to produce an effect. EFFECTIVE is applied to something that produces a desired or expected effect, often a lasting one: *an effective speech.* EFFECTUAL usually refers to something that produces a decisive outcome or result: *an effectual settlement.* EFFICACIOUS refers to something capable of achieving a certain end or purpose: *an efficacious remedy.* EFFICIENT, usually used of a person, implies skillful accomplishment of a purpose with little waste of effort: *an efficient manager.*

effects, See Syn. study at PROPERTY.

effectual, *adj.* effective. —**Ant.** ineffective. —**Syn. Study.** See EFFECTIVE.

effeminate, See Syn. study at FEMALE.

efficacious, *adj.* effective. —**Ant.** ineffective. —**Syn. Study.** See EFFECTIVE.

efficient, *adj.* effective. —**Ant.** inefficient, ineffective. —**Syn. Study.** See EFFECTIVE.

effort, *n.* application, endeavor, exertion, nisus, attempt, struggle, striving. —**Ant.** ease. —**Syn. Study.** EFFORT, APPLICATION, ENDEAVOR, EXERTION imply energetic activity and expenditure of energy. EFFORT is an expenditure of physical or mental energy to accomplish some objective: *He made an effort to control himself.* APPLICATION is continuous effort plus careful attention and diligence: *application to one's studies.* ENDEAVOR means a continued and sustained series of efforts to achieve some end, often worthy and difficult: *an endeavor to rescue survivors.* EXERTION is vigorous action or effort, frequently without an end in view: *out of breath from exertion.*

effusive, *adj.* demonstrative, extravagant, gushing, profuse, unrestrained, unrepressed, expansive, unreticent, talkative. —**Ant.** taciturn, laconic.

egocentric, *adj.* self-centered, self-referencing, conceited, egotistic, egotistical, egomaniacal, selfish, spoiled, narcissistic, self-loving, self-absorbed, vain, vainglorious, stuck-up, stuck on oneself. —**Ant.** modest, self-effacing, humble.

egoism, *n.* self-love, egotism, selfishness, self-conceit. —**Ant.** altruism. —**Syn. Study.** See EGOTISM.

egotism, *n.* self-centeredness, egoism, boastfulness, conceit. —**Ant.** altruism, modesty. —**Syn. Study.** EGOTISM, EGOISM refer to preoccupation with one's ego or self. EGOTISM is the common word for a tendency to speak or write about oneself too much; it suggests selfishness and an inordinate sense of one's own importance: *His egotism alienated most of his colleagues.* EGOISM, a less common word, emphasizes the moral justification of a concern for one's own welfare and interests, but carries less of an implication of boastful self-importance: *a healthy egoism that stood him well in times of trial.*

elaborate, *adj.* **1.** perfected, painstaking, labored, studied; detailed, ornate, intricate, complicated, complex. —*v.* **2.** produce, develop, work out, refine, improve. —**Ant.** simple; simplify.

elate, *v.* cheer, cheer up, excite, exhilarate, inspirit, exalt, lift, uplift. —**Ant.** depress, discourage.

elect, *v.* **1.** select, choose, prefer, pick out. —*adj.* **2.** select, chosen, choice. —**Ant.** refuse, reject; spurned.

elegant, *adj.* tasteful, fine, luxurious; refined, polished, cultivated, genteel, courtly, graceful; choice, nice, superior; excellent. —**Ant.** inelegant, distasteful; unrefined, disgraceful; inferior.

element, *n.* **1.** component, constituent, ingredient, unit, part, essential. **2.** rudiments, principle, basis, basics. **3.** habitat, environment, medium, milieu. —**Ant.** whole, nonessential; compound. —**Syn. Study.** ELEMENT, COMPONENT, CONSTITUENT, INGREDIENT refer to units that are parts of whole or complete substances, systems, compounds, or mixtures. ELEMENT denotes a fundamental, ultimate part: *the elements of matter; the elements of a problem.* COMPONENT refers to one of a number of separate parts: *Iron and carbon are components of steel.* CONSTITUENT refers to an active and necessary part: *The constituents of a molecule of water are two atoms of hydrogen and one of oxygen.* INGREDIENT is most frequently used in nonscientific contexts to denote any part that is combined into a mixture: *the ingredients of a cake; the ingredients of a successful marriage.*

elementary, *adj.* primary, rudimentary, basic, fundamental, rudimental; uncompounded, simple, uncomplicated. —**Ant.** advanced, secondary; complex, complicated.

elevate, *v.* raise, lift up, exalt, heighten, increase, intensify, promote, advance, improve, enhance, dignify, refine; animate, cheer. —**Ant.** lower, debase, decrease; depress. —**Syn. Study.** ELEVATE, ENHANCE, EXALT, HEIGHTEN mean to raise or make higher in some respect. To ELEVATE is to raise up to a higher level, position, or state: *to elevate the living standards of a group.* To ENHANCE is to add to the attractions or desirability of something: *Landscaping enhances the beauty of the grounds.* To EXALT is to raise very high in rank, character, estimation, mood, etc.: *A king is exalted above his subjects.* To HEIGHTEN is to increase the strength or intensity: *to heighten one's powers of concentration.*

elevation, *n.* **1.** eminence, height, hill; altitude. **2.** loftiness, grandeur, dignity, nobility, nobleness, refinement, exaltation. —**Ant.** valley; depths. —**Syn. Study.** See HEIGHT.

elf, See Syn. study at FAIRY.

eligible, *adj.* suitable, qualified, acceptable, fitted, fit, worthy, admissible, desirable. —**Ant.** unsuitable, ineligible.

eliminate, *v.* get rid of, expel, remove, exclude, reject, omit, ignore. —**Ant.** include, accept.

elocution, *n.* oratory, declamation, rhetoric.

eloquent, *adj.* articulate, communicative, fluent, facile, persuasive, powerful, silver-tongued, stirring. —**Syn. Study.** ELOQUENT, ARTICULATE both refer to effective language or an effective user of language. ELOQUENT implies vivid, moving, and convincing expression: *an eloquent plea for disarmament.* ARTICULATE suggests fluent, clear, and coherent expression: *an articulate speaker.*

elucidate, *v.* explain, explicate, clarify, make plain *or* clear. —**Ant.** becloud, bedim, confuse. —**Syn. Study.** See EXPLAIN.

elude, *v.* **1.** avoid, escape, evade, slip away from, shun, dodge. **2.** baffle, confound, foil, thwart, confuse, frustrate, disconcert. —**Ant.** pursue, follow. —**Syn. Study.** See ESCAPE.

emanate, *v.* emerge, issue, proceed, come forth, originate, arise, spring, flow. —**Syn. Study.** See EMERGE.

embarrass, *v.* **1.** disconcert, abash, make uncomfortable, confuse, discomfit, discompose, chagrin. **2.** complicate, make difficult, perplex, mystify. **3.** impede, hamper, hinder, annoy, vex, trouble, harass, distress. —**Ant.** comfort, console; simplify.

embarrassment, *n.* **1.** disconcertment, abashment, perplexity, confusion, discompose, discomfort, mortification, chagrin. **2.** trouble, annoyance, vexation, distress, harassment, hindrance, deterrent. —**Ant.** comfort, composure; encouragement. —**Syn. Study.** See SHAME.

embellish, *v.* **1.** beautify, ornament, adorn, decorate, garnish, bedeck, embroider. **2.** enhance, embroider, exaggerate about. —**Ant.** mar, disfigure, deface.

emblem, *n.* token, sign, symbol, figure, image, badge, device, mark.

embrace, *v.* **1.** clasp, hug. **2.** accept, adopt, espouse, welcome, seize. **3.** encircle, surround, enclose, contain. **4.** include, contain, comprise, comprehend, cover, embody. —**Ant.** exclude.

emend, See Syn. study at AMEND.

emerge, *v.* come forth, emanate, issue, spread, stream. —**Ant.** enter. —**Syn. Study.** EMERGE, EMANATE, ISSUE mean to come forth from a place or source. EMERGE is used of coming forth from concealment, obscurity, or something that envelops: *The sun emerged from behind the clouds.* EMANATE is used of intangible or immaterial things, as light or ideas, spreading from a source: *Rumors often emanate from irresponsible persons.* ISSUE is most often used of a number of persons, a mass of matter, or a volume of smoke, sound, or the like, coming forth through any outlet or outlets: *The crowd issued from the building.*

emergency, *n.* crisis, straits, urgency, turning-point, exigency, necessity, extremity, pinch, dilemma, quandary.

emigrate, See Syn. study at MIGRATE.

eminence, *n.* **1.** repute, distinction, prominence, celebrity, renown, conspicuousness, note, fame, rank, position. **2.** elevation, hill, prominence. —**Ant.** disrepute.

eminent, *adj.* **1.** distinguished, signal, notable, noteworthy, noted, reputable, prominent, celebrated, renowned, outstanding, illustrious, conspicuous, exalted. **2.** lofty, high, prominent, projecting, protruding, protuberant. —**Ant.** disreputable, commonplace, ordinary; low, debased; inconspicuous.

emit, *v.* **1.** send *or* give forth, discharge, eject, vent, exhale, exude, expel. **2.** issue, circulate, publish. —**Ant.** inspire, inhale, accept; hide.

emotion, *n.* feeling; sympathy, empathy. —**Ant.** apathy. —**Syn. Study.** See FEELING.

empathy, *n.* compassion, understanding, responsiveness, concern, caring, sensitivity, identification, involvement, sharing, fellow feeling, perceptiveness, perceptivity, sympathy. —**Ant.** callousness, indifference. —**Syn. Study.** See SYMPATHY.

emphasize, *v.* stress, accent, accentuate, italicize, bring out, underline, underscore, play up, highlight, feature, mark, spotlight, single out, punctuate. —**Ant.** de-emphasize, play down, underplay.

emphatic, *adj.* significant, marked, striking, positive, energetic, forcible, forceful, pronounced, strong, decided, unequivocal, definite. —**Ant.** insignificant, uncertain, unsure.

enhance, See Syn. study at ELEVATE.

enigma, *n.* puzzle, riddle, problem, question.

employ, *v.* **1.** use, engage, hire, retain, occupy. **2.** use, apply, make use of. —*n.* **3.** service, employment.

employee, *n.* worker, servant, agent, clerk, wage earner. —**Ant.** employer, boss.

empower, *v.* **1.** enable, enfranchise, inspire, actualize, self-actualize. **2.** authorize, sanction, entitle, warrant, license. —**Ant.** disenfranchise, marginalize.

empty, *adj.* **1.** void, vacant, blank, unoccupied, uninhabited. **2.** unsatisfactory, meaningless, superficial, hollow, delusive, vain, ineffectual, ineffective, unsatisfying. **3.** frivolous, foolish. —*v.* **4.** unload, unburden, pour out, evacuate, drain, discharge. —**Ant.** full, replete, occupied, inhabited; satisfactory, effectual; serious.

emulation, *n.* competition, rivalry, contention, strife, envy.

enamor, *v.* inflame, captivate, bewitch, charm, fascinate, enchant.

enchant, *v.* fascinate, captivate, charm, enrapture, transport, bewitch, delight. —**Ant.** bore.

encircle, *v.* surround, encompass, environ, gird, enfold, enclose.

enclose, *v.* surround, encircle, encompass, circumscribe. —**Ant.** exclude.

encounter, *v.* **1.** meet, confront, face. **2.** contend against, engage with, attack, cope with, compete with. —*n.* **3.** meeting. **4.** battle, combat, conflict.

encourage, *v.* **1.** inspirit, embolden, hearten, stimulate, incite; reassure, assure, console, comfort. **2.** urge, abet, second, support, favor, countenance, advance, foster, promote, aid, help, foment. —**Ant.** discourage, dispirit.

encroach, *v.* trespass, intrude, invade, infringe. —**Syn. Study.** See TRESPASS.

encumber, *v.* **1.** impede, hamper, retard, embarrass, obstruct, complicate, involve, entangle. **2.** load, oppress, overload, burden. —**Ant.** disencumber; unload, unburden.

end, *n.* **1.** extremity, extreme. **2.** limit, bound, boundary, termination, tip, terminus. **3.** close, termination, conclusion, finish, outcome, issue, consequence, result, completion, attainment. **4.** finale, conclusion, peroration. **5.** purpose, aim, object, objective, intention, design, intent, drift. —*v.* **6.** terminate, conclude, wind up, finish, complete, close. **7.** stop, cease, discontinue, conclude. —**Ant.** beginning, start; begin, commence, open; continue. —**Syn. Study.** See AIM.

endeavor, *v.* **1.** attempt, essay, try, make an effort, strive, struggle, la-

bor; seek, aim. —*n.* **2.** exertion, struggle, essay, attempt, trial. —**Syn. Study.** See TRY. See also EFFORT.

endless, *adj.* limitless, unlimited, vast, illimitable, immeasurable, unending, boundless, infinite, interminable, incessant, unceasing, eternal, continuous, perpetual, everlasting. —**Ant.** limited, finite. —**Syn. Study.** See ETERNAL.

endow, *v.* equip, invest, clothe, endue, enrich; confer, bestow, give. —**Ant.** divest.

endowment, *n.* gift, grant, bequest, largess, bounty, present; capacity, talent, faculties, quality, power, ability, aptitude, capability, genius. —**Ant.** incapacity.

endure, *v.* **1.** sustain, hold out against, undergo, bear, support, suffer, experience. **2.** experience, stand, tolerate, bear, brook, allow, permit, submit. **3.** continue, last, persist, remain. —**Ant.** fail, subside; refuse, die, perish, fail. —**Syn. Study.** See BEAR. See also CONTINUE.

enemy, *n.* foe, adversary, opponent, antagonist. —**Ant.** friend, ally.

energetic, *adj.* **1.** forcible, vigorous, active. **2.** powerful, effective, effectual, strong, efficacious, potent. —**Ant.** lazy, inactive; ineffective, impotent, weak.

energy, *n.* **1.** activity, exertion, power, force, operation, dynamism, vigor, potency, zeal, push, spirit, animation, life. **2.** force, power, might, efficacy, strength, intensity. —**Ant.** inertia, inactivity; weakness.

engender, *v.* **1.** produce, cause, give rise to, beget, create, occasion, excite, stir up, incite, generate, breed. **2.** procreate, beget, create, generate, breed. —**Ant.** terminate; kill.

enjoin, *v.* **1.** charge, order, direct, prescribe, bid, command, require. **2.** prohibit, proscribe, interdict, ban, preclude. —**Ant.** encourage, allow.

enjoyment, *n.* delight, delectation, pleasure, gratification, happiness. —**Ant.** detestation, abhorrence, displeasure.

enlarge, *v.* extend, augment, amplify, dilate, increase, aggrandize, magnify, expand, greaten. —**Ant.** limit, decrease, lessen, abate.

enlighten, *v.* illumine, edify, teach, inform, instruct, educate. —**Ant.** confuse.

enliven, *v.* **1.** invigorate, animate, inspirit, vivify, stimulate, quicken. **2.** exhilarate, gladden, cheer, brighten, inspire, delight. —**Ant.** dispirit, slow; depress.

enormous, *adj.* **1.** huge, immense, vast, colossal, mammoth, gigantic, prodigious, elephantine, monstrous. **2.** outrageous, atrocious, flagitious, depraved, wicked, flagrant, scandalous, egregious. —**Ant.** small, diminutive, tiny; honorable. —**Syn. Study.** See HUGE.

enrage, *v.* infuriate, anger, incense, inflame, provoke, madden, exasperate, aggravate. —**Ant.** tranquilize, calm, assuage. —**Syn. Study.** ENRAGE, INCENSE, INFURIATE imply stirring to violent anger. To ENRAGE or INFURIATE is to provoke wrath: *They enrage (infuriate) her by their deliberate and continual harassment.* To INCENSE is to inflame with indignation or anger: *to incense a person by making insulting remarks.*

ensue, *v.* follow, succeed; issue, arise, result, flow. —**Ant.** lead; precede. —**Syn. Study.** See FOLLOW.

entangle, *v.* **1.** complicate, ensnare, enmesh, tangle, knot, mat. **2.** embarrass, confuse, perplex, bewilder, involve, ensnare. —**Ant.** simplify.

enterprise, *n.* **1.** project, plan, undertaking, venture. **2.** boldness, readiness, spirit, energy.

enterprising, *adj.* ambitious, ready, resourceful, adventurous, venturesome, dashing, bold, energetic, spirited, eager, zealous. —**Ant.** smug, phlegmatic. —**Syn. Study.** See AMBITIOUS.

entertain, *v.* **1.** divert, amuse, please. **2.** receive, consider, admit. **3.** harbor, cherish, hold. —**Ant.** bore; refuse, reject, expel. —**Syn. Study.** See AMUSE.

enthusiasm, *n.* eagerness, earnestness, sincerity, interest, warmth, fervor, zeal, ardor, passion, devotion. —**Ant.** coolness.

enthusiast, *n.* zealot, devotee, fan. **2.** zealot, bigot, fanatic.

enthusiastic, *adj.* ardent, zealous, eager, fervent, passionate, vehement, fervid, burning, impassioned.

—**Ant.** blasé, dispassionate, cool, unenthusiastic.

entice, *v.* allure, inveigle, excite, lure, attract, decoy, tempt, seduce, coax, cajole, wheedle, persuade. —**Ant.** discourage, deter, dissuade.

entire, *adj.* **1.** whole, complete, unbroken, perfect, unimpaired, intact, undiminished, undivided, continuous. **2.** full, complete, thorough, unqualified, unrestricted, unmitigated. —*n.* **3.** entirety. —**Ant.** partial, imperfect, divided; restricted, incomplete. —**Syn. Study.** See COMPLETE.

entitle, *v.* **1.** empower, qualify. **2.** name, designate, call, title, dub. —**Ant.** disqualify.

entrance, *n.* **1.** entry, ingress, access, entree. **2.** entry, door, portal, gate, doorway, stoa, passage, inlet. **3.** admission, entry, admittance. —*v.* **4.** enrapture, enchant, charm, delight, transport. —**Ant.** exit; disenchant.

entreat, *v.* appeal, implore, beg, beseech, obsecrate, obtest, supplicate, crave, solicit, pray, importune, petition, sue.

entreaty, *n.* supplication, appeal, suit, plea, solicitation, petition.

enumerate, *v.* count, name, recount, recapitulate, rehearse, cite.

envelop, *v.* **1.** wrap, cover, enfold, hide, conceal. **2.** surround, enclose, encompass, cover, enfold.

environment, *n.* surroundings, atmosphere, environs, setting, milieu, ambience, medium, situation, position, site. —**Syn. Study.** ENVIRONMENT, MILIEU, AMBIANCE, SETTING refer to the objects, conditions, or circumstances that influence the life of an individual or community. ENVIRONMENT may refer to physical or to social and cultural surroundings: *an environment of grinding poverty.* MILIEU, encountered most often in literary writing, refers to intangible surroundings: *a milieu of artistic innovation.* AMBIANCE applies to the mood or tone of the surroundings: *an ambiance of ease and elegance.* SETTING tends to highlight the person or thing surrounded by or set against a background: *a lovely setting for a wedding.*

envy, *n.* **1.** jealousy, enviousness, grudge, covetousness. —*v.* **2.** covet, begrudge, resent. —**Ant.** generosity. —**Syn. Study.** ENVY and JEALOUSY are very close in meaning. ENVY denotes a longing to possess something awarded to or achieved by another: *to feel envy when a friend inherits a fortune.* JEALOUSY, on the other hand, denotes a feeling of resentment that another has gained something that one more rightfully deserves: *to feel jealousy when a coworker receives a promotion.* JEALOUSY also refers to anguish caused by fear of losing someone or something to a rival: *a husband's jealousy of other men.*

ephemeral, *adj.* short-lived, transitory, temporary, fleeting, momentary, brief, evanescent. —*n.* **2.** will o' the wisp, St. Elmo's fire, corposant, ephemeron. —**Ant.** concrete, permanent.

epicure, *n.* gastronome, gourmet, epicurean, voluptuary, sensualist, glutton, gourmand.

episode, *n.* occurrence, event, incident, happening. —**Syn. Study.** See EVENT.

epoch, *n.* age, era, period, date. —**Syn. Study.** See AGE.

equable, *adj.* even, uniform, tranquil, steady, regular, even-tempered, temperate. —**Ant.** uneven, irregular, turbulent, intemperate.

equal, *adj.* **1.** proportionate, commensurate, balanced, coordinate, correspondent, equivalent, tantamount, like, alike. **2.** uniform, even, regular, unvarying, invariant. **3.** adequate, sufficient, competent, suitable, fit. —*n.* **4.** peer, compeer, match, mate, fellow. —*v.* **5.** match, be commensurate with. —**Ant.** unequal, disproportionate, incommensurate, dissimilar; uneven, irregular, variable; inadequate, insufficient, unsuitable.

equip, *v.* furnish, provide, fit out, outfit, rig, array, accouter. —**Syn. Study.** See FURNISH.

equipment, *n.* apparatus, paraphernalia, gear, accouterment.

equivocal, *adj.* **1.** ambiguous, uncertain. **2.** doubtful, uncertain, questionable, dubious, indeterminate. —**Ant.** unequivocal, certain; definite, unquestionable. See AMBIGUOUS.

era, *n.* See Syn. study at AGE.

eradicate, *v.* remove, destroy, extirpate, abolish, obliterate, uproot, exterminate, annihilate. —**Ant.** insert, add; originate, create.

erase, *v.* efface, expunge, cancel, obliterate. —**Ant.** create.

erect, *v.* **1.** upright, standing, vertical. —*v.* **2.** build, raise, construct, upraise. **3.** set up, found, establish, institute. —**Ant.** horizontal; raze, destroy; dissolve, liquidate.

erroneous, *adj.* mistaken, incorrect, inaccurate, false, wrong, untrue. —**Ant.** correct, accurate, true.

error, *n.* **1.** mistake, blunder, slip, oversight. **2.** offense, wrongdoing, fault, sin, transgression, trespass, misdeed, iniquity. —**Syn. Study.** See MISTAKE.

erudition, See Syn. study at LEARNING.

escape, *v.* **1.** flee, abscond, decamp, fly, steal away, run away. **2.** shun, fly, elude, evade, avoid. —*n.* **3.** flight; release. —**Syn. Study.** ESCAPE, ELUDE, EVADE mean to keep free of something. To ESCAPE is to succeed in keeping away from danger, pursuit, observation, etc.: *to escape punishment.* To ELUDE is to slip through an apparently tight net, thus avoiding, often by a narrow margin, whatever threatens; it implies using adroitness or slyness to baffle or foil: *The fox eluded the hounds.* To EVADE is to turn aside from or go out of reach of a person or thing, usually by directing attention elsewhere: *to evade the police.*

escort, *n.* **1.** convoy, guard, guide, protection, safeguard, guidance. —*v.* **2.** conduct, usher, guard, guide, convoy, accompany, attend. —**Syn. Study.** See ACCOMPANY.

especially, *adv.* particularly, chiefly, principally, unusually, significantly, prominently, signally, specially, markedly.

espouse, *v.* adopt, embrace, take up, ratify, endorse, accept. —**Ant.** renounce, apostatize, abjure.

espy, *v.* catch sight of, descry, discover, perceive, make out. —**Ant.** overlook.

essential, *adj.* **1.** indispensable, necessary, vital, fundamental, rudimentary, elementary, basic, inherent, intrinsic, important. —*n.* **2.** necessity, basic, element. —**Ant.** dispensable, unnecessary, unimportant. —**Syn. Study.** ESSENTIAL, INHERENT, INTRINSIC refer to that which is in the natural composition of a thing. ESSENTIAL suggests that which is in the very essence or constitution of a thing: *Quiet is essential in a public library.* INHERENT means inborn or fixed from the beginning as a permanent quality or constituent of a thing: *properties inherent in iron.* INTRINSIC implies belonging to the nature of a thing itself and comprised within it, without regard to external considerations or accidentally added properties: *the intrinsic value of diamonds.* See also NECESSARY.

establish, *v.* **1.** set up, found, institute, form, organize, fix, settle, install. **2.** verify, substantiate, prove. **3.** appoint, ordain, fix, enact, decree. —**Ant.** liquidate, dissolve; disprove.

estate, See Syn. study at PROPERTY.

esteem, *v.* **1.** prize, value, honor, revere, respect, appreciate, estimate, regard. —*n.* **2.** respect, regard, favor, admiration, honor, reverence, veneration. **3.** estimation, valuation, estimate, appreciation. —**Ant.** disregard; disrespect, disfavor; depreciation. —**Syn. Study.** See APPRECIATE. See also RESPECT.

estimable, *adj.* respectable, reputable, worthy, deserving, meritorious, good, excellent. —**Ant.** disreputable, unworthy, bad, inferior.

estimate, *v.* **1.** judge, compute, reckon, gauge, count, assess, value, evaluate, appraise. —*n.* **2.** judgment, calculation, valuation, estimation, opinion, computation.

estimation, *n.* judgment, opinion, appreciation, regard, honor, veneration, esteem, respect, reverence.

estrange, *v.* alienate, disaffect, antagonize, drive apart, make hostile, make unfriendly. —**Syn. Study.** ESTRANGE, ALIENATE, DISAFFECT share the sense of turning away from a state of affection, comradeship, or allegiance. ESTRANGE refers to the replacement of affection by apathy or hostility; it often involves physical separation: *lovers estranged by a misunderstanding.* ALIENATE often emphasizes the cause of antagonism: *His inconsiderate behavior alienated his friends.* DISAFFECT usu. refers to relationships involving allegiance or loyalty rather than love or affection: *disaffected workers ready to strike.*

eternal, *adj.* **1.** endless, everlasting, infinite, unending, never-ending, interminable, unceasing, perpetual,

ceaseless, permanent. **2.** timeless, immortal, deathless, undying, imperishable, indestructible. —**Ant.** transitory, ephemeral; perishable, mortal. —**Syn. Study.** ETERNAL, ENDLESS, EVERLASTING, PERPETUAL imply lasting or going on without ceasing. That which is ETERNAL is, by its nature, without beginning or end: *God, the eternal Father.* That which is ENDLESS never stops but goes on continuously as if in a circle: *an endless succession of years.* That which is EVERLASTING will endure through all future time: *a promise of everlasting life.* PERPETUAL implies continuous renewal far into the future: *perpetual strife between nations.*

ethical, *adj.* moral, virtuous, principled, high-principled, honest, upright, decent, honorable, conscientious, righteous, right-minded, right-thinking, upstanding, just, scrupulous. —**Ant.** unethical, immoral.

etiquette, *n.* decorum, propriety, code of behavior, convention, dignity. —**Ant.** impropriety, indignity.

eulogize, *v.* praise, extol, laud, commend, panegyrize, applaud. —**Ant.** criticize, condemn.

evade, *v.* **1.** escape, elude, escape from, avoid, shun, sidestep, dodge. **2.** baffle, foil, elude. **3.** prevaricate, equivocate, quibble, fence. —**Ant.** face, confront. —**Syn. Study.** See ESCAPE.

evaporate, *v.* **1.** vaporize, dehydrate, dry. **2.** disappear, fade, vanish, evanesce. —**Ant.** condense, sublimate.

evasion, *n.* **1.** avoidance, dodging, escape. **2.** prevarication, equivocation, quibbling, subterfuge, sophistry.

even, *adj.* **1.** level, flat, smooth, plane. **2.** parallel, level. **3.** regular, equable, uniform, steady, well-balanced, in equilibrium, conforming, standard. **4.** commensurate, equal; square, balanced. **5.** calm, placid, tranquil, even-tempered, temperate, composed, peaceful. **6.** fair, just, equitable, impartial. —*adv.* **7.** still, yet; just; fully, quite, completely; indeed. —*v.* **8.** level, smooth; balance, equilibrate, counterpoise. —**Ant.** uneven, irregular; unsteady; unequal, incommensurate; agitated, intemperate; unfair, unjust, prejudiced, biased.

evening, *n.* eventide, dusk, twilight, gloaming, nightfall, eve, even, sundown. —**Ant.** dawn, sunrise.

event, *n.* **1.** occurrence, happening, affair, case, circumstance, episode, incident. **2.** result, issue, consequence, outcome. —**Syn. Study.** EVENT, EPISODE, INCIDENT refer to a happening. An EVENT is usu. an important happening, esp. one that comes out of and is connected with previous happenings: *historical events.* An EPISODE is one of a series of happenings, frequently distinct from the main course of events but arising from them and having an interest of its own: *an episode in her life.* An INCIDENT is usu. a minor happening that is connected with an event or series of events of greater importance: *an amusing incident in a play.*

ever, *adv.* **1.** continuously, eternally, perpetually, constantly, always. **2.** by any chance, at all, at any time. —**Ant.** never.

everlasting, *adj.* eternal. —**Ant.** ephemeral, transitory. —**Syn. Study.** See ETERNAL.

evidence, *n.* **1.** ground, grounds, proof, testimony. **2.** indication, sign, signal. **3.** information, deposition, affidavit, exhibit, testimony, proof. —*v.* **4.** make clear, show, manifest, demonstrate.

evident, *adj.* plain, clear, obvious, manifest, palpable, patent, unmistakable, apparent. —**Ant.** concealed, hidden. —**Syn. Study.** See APPARENT.

evil, *adj.* **1.** wicked, bad, immoral, amoral, sinful, iniquitous, flagitious, depraved, vicious, corrupt, perverse, wrong, base, vile, nefarious, malicious, malignant, malevolent. **2.** harmful, injurious, wrong, bad, pernicious, destructive, mischievous. **3.** unfortunate, disastrous, miserable. —*n.* **4.** wickedness, depravity, iniquity, unrighteousness, sin, corruption, baseness, badness. **5.** harm, mischief, misfortune, disaster, calamity, misery, pain, woe, suffering, sorrow. —**Ant.** good.

exact, *adj.* **1.** accurate, correct, precise, literal, faithful, close. **2.** strict, rigorous, rigid, unbending, exacting, demanding, severe, scrupulous. **3.** methodical, careful, punctilious, accurate, critical, nice, regular, precise, orderly. —v. 4. call for, demand, require, force, compel. 5. extort, wrest, wring, extract. —**Ant.** inexact, inaccurate, imprecise, unfaithful, free; disorderly.

exalt, v. 1. elevate, promote, dignify, raise, ennoble. 2. praise, extol, glorify, bless. 3. elate, make proud, please. 4. stimulate. 5. intensify. —**Ant.** lower, debase; damn, condemn; displease. —**Syn. Study.** See ELEVATE.

examination, n. 1. inspection, inquiry, observation, investigation, scrutiny, scanning, inquisition. 2. test, trial. —**Syn. Study.** EXAMINATION, INSPECTION, SCRUTINY refer to a looking at something. An EXAMINATION is an orderly attempt to test or to obtain information about something, often something presented for observation: an examination of merchandise for sale. An INSPECTION is usu. a formal and official examination: An inspection of the plumbing revealed a defective pipe. SCRUTINY implies a critical and minutely detailed examination: His testimony was given close scrutiny.

examine, v. 1. inspect, scrutinize, search, probe, explore, study, investigate, test. 2. catechize.

example, n. sample, specimen, representative, illustration, case, pattern, model.

exasperate, v. irritate, annoy, vex, infuriate, exacerbate, anger, incense, provoke, nettle, needle, enrage, inflame. —**Ant.** calm, assuage, tranquilize.

exceed, v. overstep, transcend, surpass, cap, top, outdo, excel, outstrip, beat.

excel, v. surpass, outdo, exceed, transcend, outstrip, eclipse, beat, win over, cap, top.

excellence, n. superiority, eminence, preeminence, transcendence, distinction; merit, virtue, purity, goodness, uprightness. —**Ant.** baseness; inferiority.

excellent, adj. good, choice, worthy, fine, first-rate, estimable, superior, better, admirable, prime, (slang) def. —**Ant.** bad, inferior, base.

except, prep. 1. but, save, excepting, excluding. —v. 2. exclude, leave out, omit, bar, reject. —**Ant.** including, include, admit.

exceptional, adj. unusual, extraordinary, irregular, peculiar, rare, strange, unnatural, anomalous, abnormal, aberrant. —**Ant.** customary, common, usual, normal, regular, natural.

excess, n. 1. superfluity, superabundance, nimiety, redundancy. 2. surplus, remainder. 3. immoderation, intemperance, over-indulgence, dissipation. —**Ant.** lack, need, want.

excessive, adj. immoderate, extravagant, extreme, exorbitant, inordinate, outrageous, unreasonable, disproportionate. —**Ant.** reasonable, proportionate.

exchange, v. 1. barter, trade, interchange, commute, swap, reciprocate. —n. 2. interchange, trade, traffic, business, commerce, reciprocity, barter. 3. market, bourse. —**Ant.** embargo.

exchangeable, adj. interchangeable, replaceable, returnable.

excitable, adj. emotional, passionate, fiery, quick-tempered, hot-tempered, hasty, irascible, irritable, choleric. —**Ant.** unemotional, cool, calm, serene, tranquil.

excite, v. 1. stir, arouse, rouse, awaken, stimulate, animate, kindle, inflame, incite. 2. stir up, provoke, disturb, agitate, irritate, discompose. —**Ant.** pacify, calm, soothe.

excited, adj. ruffled, discomposed, stormy, perturbed, impassioned, stimulated, brisk, agitated, stirred up, agog, eager, enthusiastic. —**Ant.** calm, unruffled, composed, pacific.

excitement, n. agitation, commotion, ado, to do, perturbation, disturbance. —**Ant.** serenity, peace.

exclamation, n. outcry, ejaculation, interjection, cry, complaint, protest, vociferation, shout, clamor.

exclude, v. 1. bar, restrain, keep out, shut out. 2. debar, eliminate, expel, eject, reject, prohibit, withhold, except, omit, preclude; proscribe, prevent. —**Ant.** include; accept.

exclusive, adj. 1. incompatible, excluding, barring. 2. restrictive, cliquish, snobbish, fastidious. 3. single, sole, only, special. 4. select, narrow, clannish, snobbish, selfish, illiberal, narrow, narrow-minded, uncharitable. 5. fashionable, chic, aristocratic, choice. —**Ant.** inclusive, including; general; liberal; poor.

excursion, n. 1. journey, tour, trip,

jaunt, junket, outing, cruise. 2. deviation, digression, episode.

excuse, v. 1. forgive, pardon, overlook, acquit, absolve, exonerate, exculpate. 2. apologize for, exonerate, exculpate, clear, vindicate. 3. extenuate, palliate, justify. 4. release, disoblige, free, liberate, disencumber. —n. 5. plea, apology, absolution, justification. 6. pretext, pretense, subterfuge, evasion, makeshift. —**Ant.** condemn; oblige, shackle. —**Syn. Study.** EXCUSE, FORGIVE, PARDON imply being lenient or giving up the wish to punish. EXCUSE means to overlook some (usu.) slight offense, because of circumstance, realization that it was unintentional, or the like: to excuse rudeness. FORGIVE is applied to excusing more serious offenses; the person wronged not only overlooks the offense but harbors no ill feeling against the offender: to forgive and forget. PARDON often applies to an act of leniency or mercy by an official or superior; it usu. involves a serious offense or crime: The governor was asked to pardon the condemned criminal.

execute, v. 1. carry out, accomplish, do, perform, achieve, effect, consummate, finish, complete. 2. kill, put to death, hang. 3. enforce, effectuate, administer; sign, seal, and deliver.

exemption, n. immunity, impunity, privilege, freedom, exception. —**Ant.** culpability. —**Syn. Study.** EXEMPTION, IMMUNITY, IMPUNITY imply special privilege or freedom from requirements imposed on others. EXEMPTION implies release or privileged freedom from sharing with others some duty or legal requirement: exemption from military service. IMMUNITY implies freedom from a penalty or from some natural or common liability, esp. one that is disagreeable or threatening: immunity from prosecution; immunity from disease. IMPUNITY (limited mainly to the expression with impunity) suggests freedom from punishment: The police force was so inadequate that crimes could be committed with impunity.

exercise, n. 1. exertion, labor, toil, work, action, activity. 2. drill, practice, training, schooling, discipline. 3. practice, use, application, employment, performance, operation. 4. ceremony, ritual, procedure, observance, service. —v. 5. discipline, drill, train, school. 6. practice, use, apply, employ, effect, exert. 7. discharge, perform. 8. worry, annoy, make uneasy, try, burden, trouble, pain, afflict. —**Ant.** laziness.

exertion, n. effort, action, activity, endeavor, struggle, attempt, strain, trial. —**Syn. Study.** See EFFORT.

exhaust, v. 1. empty, drain, void. 2. use up, expend, consume, waste, squander, dissipate, spend, fritter away. 3. enervate, tire, prostrate, wear out, fatigue, weaken, cripple, debilitate. —n. 4. fumes, smoke, vapor, effluvium. —**Ant.** fill; use; innervate, invigorate, strengthen.

exhaustion, n. weariness, lassitude, weakness, fatigue. —**Ant.** energy, exhilaration, strength.

exhibit, v. 1. expose, present, display, show, demonstrate, offer. 2. manifest, display, show, betray, reveal, express, disclose, indicate, evince. —n. 3. exhibition, showing, show, display, demonstration, offering, exposition, manifestation. 4. evidence, testimony. —**Ant.** conceal, hide. —**Syn. Study.** See DISPLAY.

exhilarate, v. make cheerful or merry, cheer, gladden, enliven, inspirit, animate, inspire, elate. —**Ant.** depress, sadden, deject.

exonerate, v. 1. absolve, exculpate, clear, acquit, vindicate, justify. 2. relieve, release, discharge, except, exempt, free. —**Ant.** blame, condemn; imprison. —**Syn. Study.** See ABSOLVE.

exorbitant, adj. exceeding, excessive, inordinate, extravagant, unreasonable, unconscionable, enormous. —**Ant.** reasonable, inexpensive.

expand, v. 1. increase, extend, swell, enlarge, dilate, distend, inflate, bloat, aggrandize, spread or stretch out, unfold, develop. —**Ant.** contract, shrink. —**Syn. Study.** See INCREASE.

expect, v. look forward to, anticipate, await, hope for, wait for, count on, rely on.

expectation, n. expectancy, anticipation, hope, trust, prospect.

expedient, adj. 1. advantageous, fit, suitable, profitable, advisable, proper, appropriate, desirable. —n. 2. device, contrivance, means, resource, shift, resort. —**Ant.** unsuitable, inapt, undesirable.

expedite, v. speed up, hasten, quicken, speed, push, accelerate, hurry, precipitate; dispatch. —**Ant.** slow.

expedition, n. 1. excursion, journey, voyage, trip, junket, safari. 2. promptness, speed, haste, quickness, dispatch, alacrity. —**Ant.** sloth. —**Syn. Study.** See TRIP.

expel, v. drive or force away, drive or force out, discharge, eject; dismiss, oust, banish, exile, expatriate, (British) send down. —**Ant.** accept, invite.

expend, v. 1. use, employ, consume, spend, exhaust, use up. 2. pay, disburse, spend, lay out. —**Ant.** save, husband, conserve.

expense, n. 1. cost, charge, price, outlay, expenditure. 2. loss, injury, harm, debit, detriment.

expensive, adj. costly, dear, high-priced. —**Ant.** inexpensive, cheap, tawdry.

experience, n. 1. undergoing, feeling, encountering. 2. knowledge, wisdom, sagacity. —v. 3. meet with, undergo, feel, encounter, live through, know, observe; endure; suffer. —**Ant.** inexperience, naiveté.

experienced, adj. skilled, expert, veteran, practiced, accomplished, versed, qualified, adroit, adept. —**Ant.** inexperienced, inexpert, naive, artless, unqualified.

experiment, n. 1. test, trial, examination, proof, assay, procedure. 2. experimentation, research, investigation. —v. 3. try, test, examine, prove, assay.

expert, n. 1. specialist, authority, connoisseur, master. —adj. 2. trained, skilled, skillful, experienced, proficient, dexterous, adroit, clever, apt, quick. —**Ant.** butcher, shoemaker, dolt; untrained, inexperienced, maladroit. —**Syn. Study.** See SKILLFUL.

explain, v. 1. elucidate, expound, explicate, interpret, clarify, throw light on, make plain or manifest. 2. account for, justify. —**Ant.** confuse. —**Syn. Study.** EXPLAIN, ELUCIDATE, EXPOUND, INTERPRET imply making the meaning of something clear or understandable. To EXPLAIN is to make plain, clear, or intelligible something that is not known or understood: to explain a theory. To ELUCIDATE is to throw light on what before was dark and obscure, usu. by illustration and commentary and sometimes by elaborate explanation: They asked her to elucidate her statement. To EXPOUND is to give a methodical, detailed, scholarly explanation of something, usu. Scriptures, doctrines, or philosophy: to expound the doctrine of free will. To INTERPRET is to give the meaning of something by paraphrase, by translation, or by an explanation based on personal opinion: to interpret a poem.

explanation, n. 1. explaining, elucidation, explication, exposition, definition, interpretation, description. 2. meaning, interpretation, solution, key, answer, definition, account, justification.

explicit, adj. 1. clear, unequivocal, express, unambiguous, precise, definite, exact, categorical, determinate. 2. open, outspoken, definite, unashamed, unabashed. —**Ant.** unclear, equivocal, ambiguous, indefinite; clandestine, concealed.

exploit, n. 1. deed, feat, accomplishment, achievement. —v. 2. use, utilize, take advantage of.

expose, v. 1. lay open, subject, endanger, imperil, jeopardize. 2. bare, uncover; exhibit, display. 3. make known, betray, uncover, unveil, disclose, reveal, unmask, bring to light; muckrake. —**Ant.** conceal, hide.

exposition, n. 1. exhibit, exhibition, show, demonstration, display. 2. explanation, elucidation, commentary, treatise, critique, interpretation, exegesis, explication.

exposure, n. 1. exposing; disclosure, unmasking, presentation, display, divulgement, revelation, exposé. 2. aspect, orientation. —**Ant.** hiding, concealment.

expound, See Syn. study at EXPLAIN.

express, v. 1. utter, declare, state, word, speak, assert, asseverate. 2. show, manifest, reveal, expose, indicate, exhibit, represent. 3. indicate, signify, designate, denote. 4. press or squeeze out. —adj. 5. clear, distinct, definite, explicit, plain, obvious, positive, unambiguous, categorical; unsubtle. 6. special, particular, singular, signal. 7. faithful, exact, accurate, precise, true, close. 8. swift, direct, fast, rapid, nonstop.

—n. 9. courier, special messenger. —**Ant.** conceal.

expression, n. 1. utterance, declaration, assertion, statement. 2. phrase, term, idiom. 3. language, diction, phraseology, wording, phrasing, presentation. 4. manifestation, sign. 5. look, countenance, aspect, air, mien, intonation, tone. —**Ant.** silence.

expressive, adj. 1. meaning, significant, suggestive, meaningful, indicative. 2. lively, vivid, strong, emphatic. —**Ant.** expressionless, meaningless.

exquisite, adj. 1. dainty, beautiful, elegant, rare, delicate, appealing, charming. 2. fine, admirable, consummate, perfect, matchless, complete, valuable, precious. 3. intense, acute, keen, poignant. 4. sensitive, responsive. 5. rare, select, choice, excellent, precious, valuable, priceless; vintage. 6. refined, elegant, delicate, discriminating, polished, debonair. —**Ant.** ugly, hideous; imperfect, valueless, worthless; dull, vacuous, vapid; common, ordinary; poor, inferior; boorish. —**Syn. Study.** See DELICATE.

extemporaneous, adj. extemporary, extempore, impromptu, improvised, unpremeditated, offhand, off the cuff. —**Ant.** prepared, premeditated. —**Syn. Study.** EXTEMPORANEOUS, IMPROMPTU are used of expression that is not planned. EXTEMPORANEOUS may refer to a speech given without any advance preparation: extemporaneous remarks. IMPROMPTU is also used of a speech, but often refers to a poem, song, etc., delivered without preparation and at a moment's notice: She entertained the guests with some impromptu rhymes.

extend, v. 1. stretch or draw out, attenuate. 2. lengthen, prolong, protract, continue. 3. expand, spread out, dilate, enlarge, widen, diffuse, fill out. 4. hold forth, offer, bestow, grant, give, impart, yield. —**Ant.** shorten, abbreviate; discontinue; shrink, curtail. —**Syn. Study.** See LENGTHEN.

extension, n. 1. stretching, expansion, enlargement, dilation, dilatation, increase. 2. prolongation, lengthening, protraction, continuation; delay. 3. extent, limit. —**Ant.** shrinking, decrease; curtailment.

extensive, adj. 1. wide, broad, large, extended, spacious, ample, vast. 2. far-reaching, comprehensive, thorough; inclusive.

extent, n. space, degree, magnitude, measure, amount, scope, compass, range, expanse, stretch, reach, size; length, area, volume.

exterior, adj. 1. outer, outside, outward, external, outer, superficial. 2. outlying, extraneous, foreign, extrinsic. —n. 3. outside, face. 4. appearance, mien, aspect, face. —**Ant.** interior, inner; important; interior, inside.

exterminate, v. extirpate, annihilate, destroy, eradicate, abolish, eliminate. —**Ant.** create, generate, originate.

extinct, adj. 1. extinguished, quenched, out, put out. 2. obsolete, archaic. 3. ended, terminated, over, dead, gone, vanished. —**Ant.** extant; modern; begun, initiated.

extol, v. praise, laud, eulogize, commend, glorify, exalt, celebrate, applaud, panegyrize. —**Ant.** condemn, damn.

extort, v. extract, exact, wrest, wring, blackmail, bleed.

extract, v. 1. draw forth or out, get, pull or pry out. 2. deduce, divine, understand. 3. extort, exact, evoke, educe, draw out, elicit, wrest, wring, bleed. 4. derive, withdraw, distill. —n. 5. excerpt, quotation, citation, selection. 6. decoction, distillate, solution.

extraneous, adj. external, extrinsic, foreign, alien, adventitious; inappropriate, not germane, not pertinent, nonessential, superfluous. —**Ant.** internal, intrinsic; appropriate, pertinent, essential, vital.

extraordinary, adj. exceptional, special, inordinate, uncommon, singular, signal, rare, phenomenal, remarkable, unusual, egregious, unheard-of, drop-dead. —**Ant.** ordinary, common, usual, customary.

extravagant, adj. 1. imprudent, wasteful, lavish, spendthrift, prodigal, immoderate, excessive, inordinate, exorbitant. 2. unreasonable, fantastic, wild, foolish, absurd. —**Ant.** prudent, thrifty; moderate; reasonable, thoughtful, sensible.

extreme, adj. 1. utmost, greatest, rarest, highest; superlative. 2. outer-

most, endmost, ultimate, last, uttermost, remotest. 3. extravagant, immoderate, excessive, fanatical, uncompromising, radical, outré, unreasonable. 4. last, final, ultimate. —n. 5. farthest, furthest, remotest. 6. acme, limit, end; extremity. —**Ant.** reasonable.

extremity, n. 1. terminal, limit, end, termination, extreme, verge, border, boundary, bounds. 2. utmost, extreme.

exuberance, n. exuberancy, superabundance, excess, copiousness, profusion, luxuriance, lavishness, superfluity, redundancy, overflow. —**Ant.** paucity, lack, need, want.

exultation, See Syn. study at ECSTASY.

F

fable, n. 1. legend, tale, apologue, parable, allegory, myth, story. 2. lie, untruth, falsehood, fib, fiction, invention, fabrication, forgery. —v. 3. lie, fib, fabricate, invent. —**Ant.** truth, gospel. —**Syn. Study.** See LEGEND.

fabricate, v. 1. construct, build, frame, erect, make, manufacture. 2. assemble, put together, erect. 3. devise, invent, coin, feign; forge, fake. —**Ant.** destroy, raze.

fabulous, adj. 1. unbelievable, incredible, amazing, astonishing, astounding. 2. untrue, unreal, unrealistic, invented, fabled, fictional, fictitious, fabricated, coined, made up, imaginary. —**Ant.** commonplace; real, natural.

face, n. 1. countenance, visage, front, features, look, expression, appearance, aspect, mien; sight, presence. 2. show, pretense, pretext, exterior. 3. name, prestige, reputation. —v. 4. meet face to face, confront, encounter, meet, meet with. 5. oppose. 6. cover, veneer. —**Ant.** back; absence; interior. —**Syn. Study.** FACE, COUNTENANCE, VISAGE refer to the front of the (usu. human) head. FACE is used when referring to physical features: a pretty face with high cheekbones. COUNTENANCE, a more formal word, denotes the face as it is affected by or reveals a person's state of mind; hence, it often signifies the look or expression on the face: a thoughtful countenance. VISAGE, still more formal, refers to the face as seen in a certain aspect, esp. as revealing a person's character: a stern visage.

facet, n. aspect, side, angle, position, posture, phase, view, viewpoint, feature, light, slant, particular, detail.

facetious, adj. amusing, humorous, comical, funny, witty, droll, jocular. —**Ant.** sad.

facile, adj. 1. effortless, easy, adroit, deft, dexterous, fluent, flowing, smooth, graceful, elegant. 2. superficial, glib, slick, surface, shallow, slight. —**Ant.** labored, laborious, profound.

faction, n. side, bloc, camp, group, party, sect, interest, division, wing, denomination, order, school, society, body.

factory, n. manufactory, mill, workshop, plant.

factual, adj. actual, real, true, demonstrable, provable, evidential, evidentiary, verifiable, de facto, genuine, certain, undoubted, unquestioned, valid. —**Ant.** imaginary, groundless, illusory.

faculty, n. ability, capacity, aptitude, capability, knack, turn, talent. —**Ant.** inability, incapacity. —**Syn. Study.** See ABILITY.

fade, v. 1. wither, droop, languish, decline, decay. 2. blanch, bleach, pale. 3. disappear, vanish, die out, pass away, evanesce. —**Ant.** flourish; flush; appear. —**Syn. Study.** See DISAPPEAR.

fail, v. 1. come short, fall short, disappoint. 2. fall off, dwindle, pass or die away, decline, fade, weaken, sink, wane, give out, cease, disappear. 3. desert, forsake, disappoint. —**Ant.** succeed.

failing, n. shortcoming, weakness, foible, deficiency, defect, frailty, imperfection, fault, flaw. —**Ant.** success, sufficiency; strength. —**Syn. Study.** See FAULT.

failure, n. 1. unsuccessfulness, miscarriage, abortion, failing. 2. neglect, omission, dereliction, nonperformance. 3. deficiency, insufficiency, defectiveness. 4. decline, decay, deterioration, loss. 5. bankruptcy, insolvency, failing; bust; dud.

—**Ant.** success; adequacy, sufficiency, effectiveness.

faint, *adj.* **1.** indistinct, ill-defined, dim, faded, dull. **2.** feeble, half-hearted, faltering, irresolute, weak, languid, drooping. **3.** feeble, languid, swooning. **4.** cowardly, timorous, pusillanimous, fearful, timid, dastardly, faint-hearted. —*v.* **5.** swoon, pass out, black out. —*n.* **6.** swoon, unconsciousness. —**Ant.** strong; distinct; brave, bold.

fair, *adj.* **1.** unbiased, equitable, just, honest, impartial, disinterested, unprejudiced. **2.** reasonable, passable, tolerable, average, middling. **3.** likely, favorable, promising, hopeful. **4.** bright, sunny, cloudless; fine. **5.** unobstructed, open, clear, distinct, unencumbered, plain. **6.** clean, spotless, pure, untarnished, unsullied, unspotted, unblemished, unstained. **7.** clear, legible, distinct. **8.** light, blond, white, pale. **9.** beautiful, lovely, comely, pretty, attractive, pleasing, handsome. **10.** courteous, civil, polite, gracious. —*adv.* **11.** straight, directly. **12.** favorably, auspiciously. —*n.* **13.** exhibit, exhibition, festival, kermis. —**Ant.** unfair. —**Syn. Study.** FAIR, IMPARTIAL, DISINTERESTED refer to lack of bias in opinions, judgments, etc. FAIR implies the treating of all sides alike, justly and equitably: *a fair compromise.* IMPARTIAL also implies showing no more favor to one side than another, but suggests particularly a judicial consideration of a case: *an impartial judge.* DISINTERESTED implies a fairness arising from lack of desire to obtain a selfish advantage: *a disinterested concern that the best person win.*

fairy, *n.* fay, pixy, leprechaun, nix, nixie, brownie, elf, sprite.

faith, *n.* **1.** confidence, trust, reliance, credit, credence, assurance. **2.** belief, doctrine, tenet, creed, dogma, religion, persuasion. —**Ant.** discredit, distrust.

faithful, *adj.* **1.** strict, thorough, true, devoted. **2.** true, reliable, trustworthy, trusty. **3.** stable, dependable, steadfast, stanch, loyal, constant. **4.** credible, creditable, believable, trustworthy, reliable. **5.** strict, rigid, accurate, precise, exact, conscientious, close. —*n.* **6.** believers. —**Ant.** unfaithful, faithless. —**Syn. Study.** FAITHFUL, CONSTANT, LOYAL imply qualities of stability, dependability, and devotion. FAITHFUL implies enduring fidelity to what one is bound to by a pledge, duty, or obligation: *a faithful friend.* CONSTANT suggests lack of change in affections or loyalties: *a constant companion through thick and thin.* LOYAL implies firm support and defense of a person, cause, institution, or idea considered to be worthy: *a loyal citizen.*

faithless, *adj.* **1.** disloyal, false, inconstant, fickle, perfidious, treacherous. **2.** unreliable, untrustworthy, untrue. **3.** untrusting, unbelieving, doubting. **4.** atheistic, agnostic, heathen, infidel. —**Ant.** faithful.

fake, *adj.* **1.** fraudulent, false, unreal, forged, fabricated, counterfeit, bogus, phony, sham, spurious, pretend, pinchbeck. —*n.* **2.** fraud, hoax, imposture, deception, counterfeit, sham, phony. —*v.* **3.** pretend, feign, affect, counterfeit, sham, simulate, act.

false, *adj.* **1.** erroneous, incorrect, mistaken, wrong, untrue, improper. **2.** untruthful, lying, mendacious, untrue. **3.** deceitful, treacherous, faithless, insincere, hypocritical, disingenuous, disloyal, unfaithful, two-faced, inconstant, recreant, perfidious, traitorous. **4.** deceptive, deceiving, misleading, fallacious. **5.** spurious, artificial, bogus, phony, forged, sham, counterfeit. **6.** substitute, ersatz, supplementary, stand-in. —**Ant.** true; genuine. —**Syn. Study.** FALSE, SHAM, COUNTERFEIT agree in referring to something that is not genuine. FALSE is used mainly of imitations of concrete objects; it sometimes implies an intent to deceive: *false teeth; false hair.* SHAM is rarely used of concrete objects and usu. has the suggestion of intent to deceive: *sham title; sham tears.* COUNTERFEIT always has the implication of cheating; it is used particularly of spurious imitation of coins and paper money.

falsehood, *n.* lie, fib, untruth, distortion, fabrication, fiction. —**Ant.** truth.

falsify, *v.* See Syn. study at MISREPRESENT.

falter, *v.* **1.** hesitate, vacillate, waver, tremble. **2.** stammer, stutter.

fame, *n.* reputation, estimation, opinion, consensus, repute, renown,

eminence, celebrity, honor, glory; notoriety. —**Ant.** infamy, disrepute.

familiar, *adj.* **1.** common, well-known, frequent. **2.** well-acquainted, conversant, well-versed. **3.** easy, informal, unceremonious, unconstrained, free. **4.** intimate, close, friendly, amicable. **5.** presuming, presumptive, unreserved, disrespectful. **6.** tame, domesticated. —*n.* **7.** friend, associate, companion. —**Ant.** unfamiliar, unknown. —**Syn. Study.** FAMILIAR, CONFIDENTIAL, INTIMATE suggest a friendly relationship between persons, based on frequent association, common interests, etc. FAMILIAR suggests an easygoing and unconstrained relationship between persons who are well-acquainted: *on familiar terms with one's neighbors.* CONFIDENTIAL implies a sense of mutual trust that extends to the sharing of confidences and secrets: *a confidential adviser.* INTIMATE connotes a very close and warm relationship characterized by empathy and sharing of private thoughts: *intimate letters to a friend.*

familiarity, *n.* **1.** acquaintance, knowledge, understanding. **2.** intimacy, liberty, freedom, license, disrespect. **3.** informality, unconstraint, freedom. —**Ant.** unfamiliarity.

famous, *adj.* celebrated, renowned, well-known, famed, notable, eminent, distinguished, illustrious, honored. —**Ant.** unknown, undistinguished. —**Syn. Study.** FAMOUS, CELEBRATED, RENOWNED, NOTORIOUS refer to someone or something widely known. FAMOUS is the general word for a person or thing that receives wide public notice, usu. favorable: *a famous lighthouse.* CELEBRATED refers to a famous person or thing that enjoys wide public praise or honor for merit, services, etc.: *a celebrated poet.* RENOWNED usu. implies wider, greater, and more enduring fame and glory: *a renowned hospital.* NOTORIOUS means widely known and discussed because of some bad or evil quality or action: *a notorious criminal.*

fanatic, *n.* zealot, devotee, extremist, maniac, hothead, *(slang)* freak, nut. —**Syn. Study.** FANATIC, ZEALOT, DEVOTEE refer to persons showing more than ordinary enthusiasm or support for a cause, belief, or activity. FANATIC and ZEALOT both suggest extreme or excessive devotion. FANATIC further implies unbalanced or obsessive behavior: *a wild-eyed fanatic.* ZEALOT, slightly less unfavorable in implication, implies single-minded partisanship: *a tireless zealot for tax reform.* DEVOTEE is a milder term, suggesting enthusiasm but not to the exclusion of other interests or possible points of view: *a devotee of baseball.*

fanatical, *adj.* zealous, enthusiastic, visionary, frenzied, rabid. —**Ant.** apathetic.

fancy, *n.* **1.** imagination, fantasy. **2.** image, conception, idea, thought, notion, impression; hallucination. **3.** caprice, whim, vagary, quirk, humor, crotchet. **4.** preference, liking, inclination, fondness. **5.** judgment, taste, sensitivity, sensitiveness. —*adj.* **6.** fine, elegant, choice. **7.** ornamental, decorated, ornate. **8.** fanciful, capricious, whimsical, irregular, extravagant. —*v.* **9.** picture, envision, conceive, imagine. **10.** like, be pleased with, take a fancy to. —**Ant.** plain; regular, ordinary; dislike, abhor.

fantastic, *adj.* bizarre, grotesque, eccentric, outlandish, outre, odd, queer, absurd, unbelievable, strange, outlandish, singular, unnatural, weird. —**Syn. Study.** FANTASTIC, BIZARRE, GROTESQUE share a sense of deviation from what is normal or expected. FANTASTIC suggests a wild lack of restraint and a fancifulness so extreme as to lose touch with reality: *a fantastic new space vehicle.* BIZARRE implies striking or odd elements that surprise and captivate the observer: *bizarre costumes for Mardi Gras.* GROTESQUE implies shocking distortion or incongruity, sometimes ludicrous, but more often pitiful or tragic: *the grotesque gestures of a mime.*

fascinate, *v.* bewitch, charm, enchant, entrance, enrapture, captivate, allure, infatuate, enamor. —**Ant.** repel, disgust.

fashion, *n.* **1.** custom, style, vogue, mode, fad, rage, craze. **2.** custom, style, conventionality, conformity. **3.** haut monde, beau monde, four hundred, society. **4.** manner, way, mode, method, approach. **5.** make, form, figure, shape, stamp, mold, pattern, model, cast. **6.** kind, sort. —*v.* **7.** make, shape, frame, construct, mold,

form. **8.** accommodate, adapt, suit, fit, adjust.

fashionable, *adj.* stylish, chic, in vogue, in fashion, in style, smart, trendy, du jour, voguish, exclusive, inside, swank, tony, au courant, à la mode, soigné, soignée, all the rage, hip, with-it. —**Ant.** unfashionable, dowdy.

fast, *adj.* **1.** quick, swift, rapid, fleet. **2.** energetic, active, alert, quick. **3.** dissolute, dissipated, profligate, unmoral, wild, reckless, extravagant, prodigal. **4.** strong, resistant, impregnable. **5.** immovable, fixed, secure, steadfast, stanch, firm. **6.** inescapable, inextricable. **7.** tied, knotted, fastened, fixed, tight, close. **8.** permanent, lasting, enduring, eternal. **9.** loyal, faithful, steadfast. **10.** deep, sound, profound. **11.** deceptive, insincere, inconstant, unreliable. —*adv.* **12.** tightly, fixedly, firmly, securely, tenaciously. **13.** quickly, swiftly, rapidly, speedily. **14.** energetically, recklessly, extravagantly, wildly, prodigally. —**Ant.** slow, lethargic; upright, moral; weak, defenseless; feeble; temporary; disloyal, faithless; shallow; sincere, constant, reliable. —**Syn. Study.** See QUICK.

fasten, *v.* make fast, fix, secure, attach, pin, rivet, bind, tie, connect, link, hook, clasp, clinch, clamp, tether. —**Ant.** loosen, loose, untie.

fat, *adj.* **1.** fleshy, plump, corpulent, obese, adipose, stout, portly, chubby, pudgy. **2.** oily, fatty, unctuous, greasy, pinguid. **3.** rich, profitable, remunerative, lucrative. **4.** fertile, rich, fruitful, productive. **5.** thick, broad, extended, wide. **6.** plentiful, copious, abundant. **7.** dull, stupid, sluggish, coarse. —**Ant.** thin, skinny, cadaverous; poor; scarce, scanty; barren; clever.

fatal, *adj.* **1.** deadly, mortal, lethal, destructive, ruinous, pernicious, calamitous, catastrophic. **2.** fateful, inevitable, doomed, predestined, foreordained, damned. —**Ant.** lifegiving, constructive; indeterminate. —**Syn. Study.** FATAL, DEADLY, LETHAL, MORTAL apply to something that has caused or is capable of causing death or dire misfortune. FATAL may refer to the future or the past; in either case, it emphasizes inevitability or inescapable consequences: *a fatal illness; fatal errors.* DEADLY refers to the future, and suggests something that causes death by its very nature, or has death as its purpose: *a deadly disease; a deadly poison.* LETHAL is usu. used in technical contexts: *Carbon monoxide is a lethal gas.* MORTAL usu. refers to death that has actually occurred: *He received a mortal blow.*

fate, *n.* **1.** fortune, luck, lot, chance, destiny, karma, kismet, doom. **2.** death, destruction, ruin. —*v.* **3.** predetermine, destine, predestine, foreordain, preordain. —**Syn. Study.** FATE, DESTINY refer to a predetermined and usu. inescapable course or outcome of events. The two words are frequently interchangeable. FATE stresses the irrationality and impersonal character of events: *It was Napoleon's fate to be exiled.* The word is often used lightly: *It was my fate to meet her that very afternoon.* DESTINY is often used of a favorable or exalted lot in life: *It was her destiny to save her people.*

fateful, See Syn. study at OMINOUS.

fatherly, *adj.* paternal, protecting, protective; kind, tender, benign.

fatuous, *adj.* stupid, dense, dull, dimwitted, foolish, silly, idiotic. —**Ant.** clever, bright, intelligent. —**Syn. Study.** See FOOLISH.

fault, *n.* **1.** defect, imperfection, blemish, flaw, failing, frailty, foible, weakness, shortcoming, vice. **2.** error, mistake, slip. **3.** misdeed, sin, transgression, trespass, misdemeanor, offense, wrong, delinquency, indiscretion, culpability. —**Ant.** strength. —**Syn. Study.** FAULT, FOIBLE, WEAKNESS, FAILING, VICE refer to human shortcomings or imperfections. FAULT refers to any ordinary shortcoming; condemnation is not necessarily implied: *Of his many faults the greatest is vanity.* FOIBLE suggests a weak point that is slight and often amusing, manifesting itself in eccentricity rather than in wrongdoing: *the foibles of an artist.* WEAKNESS suggests that a person is unable to control a particular impulse or response, and gives way to it: *a weakness for ice cream.* FAILING is particularly applied to humanity at large, suggesting common, often venial, shortcomings: *Procrastination is a common failing.* VICE is the strongest term and designates a habit that is

detrimental, immoral, or evil: *to succumb to the vice of compulsive gambling.*

faulty, *adj.* **1.** defective, imperfect, incomplete, bad. **2.** blameworthy, culpable, reprehensible, censurable. —**Ant.** perfect, complete, consummate; exonerated, blameless.

favor, *n.* **1.** kindness, good will, benefit, good deed. **2.** partiality, bias, patronage, prejudice. **3.** gift, present. —*v.* **4.** prefer, encourage, patronize, approve, countenance, allow. **5.** facilitate, ease; propitiate, conciliate, appease. **6.** aid, help, support, assist. —**Ant.** cruelty; disfavor; disapprove, disallow, discourage.

favorite, *adj.* **1.** preferred, chosen, pet, best-liked, best-loved, fair-haired, popular, beloved, loved, prized, treasured, dearest, precious, adored, esteemed, dearly beloved. —*n.* **2.** preference, pet, darling, chosen one, apple of one's eye, fair-haired one.

fear, *n.* **1.** apprehension, consternation, dismay, alarm, trepidation, dread, terror, fright, horror, panic. **2.** anxiety, solicitude, concern. **3.** awe, reverence, veneration. —*v.* **4.** be afraid of, apprehend, dread. **5.** revere, venerate, reverence. —**Ant.** boldness, bravery, intrepidity; security, confidence.

fearless, *adj.* brave, intrepid, bold, courageous, heroic. —**Ant.** cowardly. —**Syn. Study.** See BRAVE.

feasible, *adj.* **1.** practicable, workable, possible. **2.** suitable, suited, usable, practical, practicable. **3.** likely, probable. —**Ant.** unfeasible, impractical, impossible; unsuitable, unsuited; unlikely, improbable. —**Syn. Study.** See POSSIBLE.

feast, *n.* **1.** celebration, anniversary, commemoration, ceremony, banquet, fête, entertainment, carousal. **2.** repast, sumptuous repast. —*v.* **3.** eat, gourmandize, glut *or* stuff *or* gorge oneself. **4.** gratify, delight.

feat, *n.* achievement, accomplishment, deed, action, act, exploit.

feature, *n.* characteristic, peculiarity, trait, property, mark. —**Syn. Study.** FEATURE, CHARACTERISTIC, PECULIARITY refer to a distinctive trait of an individual or of a class. FEATURE suggests an outstanding or marked property that attracts attention: *A large art exhibit was a feature of the convention.* CHARACTERISTIC means a distinguishing mark or quality always associated in one's mind with a particular person or thing: *A fine sense of humor is one of his characteristics.* PECULIARITY means a distinctive and often unusual property exclusive to one individual, group, or thing: *A blue-black tongue is a peculiarity of the chow chow.*

feeble, *adj.* **1.** weak, feckless, ineffective, ineffectual. **2.** infirm, sickly, debilitated, enervated, declining, frail. **3.** faint, dim, weak. —**Ant.** strong, effective, effectual; healthy; clear.

feed, *v.* **1.** nourish, sustain, purvey. **2.** satisfy, minister to, gratify, please. **3.** eat. **4.** subsist. —*n.* **5.** fodder, forage, provender, food. —**Ant.** starve. —**Syn. Study.** FEED, FODDER, FORAGE, PROVENDER mean food for animals. FEED is the general word; however, it most often applies to grain: *chicken feed.* FODDER is applied to coarse feed that is fed to livestock: *Cornstalks are good fodder.* FORAGE is feed that an animal obtains (usu. grass, leaves, etc.) by grazing or searching about for it: *Lost cattle can usually live on forage.* PROVENDER denotes dry feed for livestock, such as hay, oats, or corn: *a supply of provender in the haymow.*

feeling, *n.* **1.** consciousness, impression; emotion, passion, sentiment, sensibility; sympathy, empathy. **2.** tenderness, sensitivity, sentiment, sentimentality, susceptibility, pity. **3.** sentiment, opinion, tenor. —*adj.* **4.** sentient, emotional, sensitive, tender; sympathetic. **5.** emotional, impassioned, passionate. —**Ant.** apathy, coolness; unemotional, insensitive, unsympathetic; cool. —**Syn. Study.** FEELING, EMOTION, PASSION, SENTIMENT refer to pleasurable or painful sensations experienced when one is stirred to sympathy, anger, fear, love, grief, etc. FEELING is a general term for a subjective point of view as well as for specific sensations: *to be guided by feeling rather than by facts; a feeling of pride, of dismay.* EMOTION is applied to an intensified feeling: *agitated by emotion.* PASSION is strong or violent emotion, often so overpowering that it masters the mind or judgment: *stirred to a passion of anger.* SENTIMENT is a mixture of thought and

feeling, esp. refined or tender feeling: *Recollections are often colored by sentiment.*

feign, *v.* **1.** invent, concoct, devise, fabricate, forge, counterfeit. **2.** simulate, pretend, counterfeit, affect; emulate, imitate, mimic. **3.** make believe, pretend, imagine. —**Syn. Study.** See PRETEND.

felicitous, *adj.* **1.** apt, suitable, appropriate, cogent, germane, relevant, fitting, fit, applicable, proper, meet, just, happy. **2.** enjoyable, pleasant, delightful, pleasing, pleasurable, happy, felicific.

female, *n.* **1.** woman, girl. —*adj.* **2.** feminine, delicate, womanly, soft, gentle, maternal, nurturing. —**Ant.** male; masculine, manly. —**Syn. Study.** FEMALE, FEMININE, EFFEMINATE describe women and girls or whatever is culturally attributed to them. FEMALE classifies individuals on the basis of their genetic makeup or their ability to produce offspring in sexual reproduction. It contrasts with MALE in all uses: *her oldest female relative; the female parts of the flower.* FEMININE refers to qualities and behavior deemed especially appropriate to or ideally associated with women and girls. In American and Western European culture, these have traditionally included such features as charm, gentleness, and patience: *to dance with feminine grace; a feminine sensitivity to moods.* FEMININE is sometimes used of physical features too: *small, feminine hands.* EFFEMINATE is most often applied derogatorily to men or boys, suggesting that they have traits culturally regarded as appropriate to women and girls rather than to men: *an effeminate speaking style.* See also WOMAN, WOMANLY.

feminine, See Syn. study at FEMALE.

ferocious, *adj.* fierce, savage, wild, cruel, violent, ravenous, rapacious. —**Ant.** mild, tame, calm. —**Syn. Study.** See FIERCE.

fertile, *adj.* productive, prolific, fecund, fruitful, rich, teeming. —**Ant.** sterile, barren. —**Syn. Study.** See PRODUCTIVE.

fervent, *adj.* fervid, ardent, earnest, warm, heated, hot, burning, glowing, fiery, inflamed, eager, zealous, vehement, impassioned, passionate, enthusiastic. —**Ant.** cool, apathetic.

fervor, *n.* ardor, intensity, earnestness, eagerness, enthusiasm, passion, fire, heat, vehemence. —**Ant.** coolness, apathy.

feud, *n.* hostility, quarrel, argument, difference, falling-out.

fickle, *adj.* inconstant, disloyal, faithless, changeable, shifting, unstable, capricious, unpredictable, irresolute, inconsistent, volatile. —**Syn. Study.** FICKLE, INCONSTANT, CAPRICIOUS describe persons or things that are not firm or steady in affection, behavior, opinion, or loyalty. FICKLE implies an underlying perversity as a cause for the lack of stability: *once lionized, now rejected by a fickle public.* INCONSTANT suggests an innate disposition to change: *an inconstant lover, flitting from affair to affair.* CAPRICIOUS implies unpredictable changeability arising from sudden whim: *a capricious reversal of policy.*

fiction, *n.* **1.** novel, fantasy. **2.** fabrication, figment, unreality, falsity. —**Ant.** nonfiction, fact; reality.

fictitious, *adj.* **1.** imaginary, illusory, fanciful, fancied, invented, created, concocted, made-up, dreamed-up, unreal, visionary, chimerical, mythical. **2.** artificial, bogus, fake, mock, ungenuine, deceptive, counterfeit, factitious, synthetic. —**Ant.** real, genuine.

fidelity, *n.* **1.** loyalty, faithfulness, devotion, fealty. **2.** accuracy, precision, faithfulness, exactness, closeness. —**Ant.** disloyalty, unfaithfulness; inaccuracy.

fierce, *adj.* **1.** ferocious, wild, vehement, violent, savage, cruel, fell, brutal, bloodthirsty, murderous, homicidal. **2.** truculent, barbarous, untamed, furious, passionate, turbulent, impetuous. —**Ant.** tame, domesticated; calm; civilized; cool, temperate. —**Syn. Study.** FIERCE, FEROCIOUS, TRUCULENT suggest vehement hostility and unrestrained violence. FIERCE implies an aggressive, savage, or wild temperament and appearance: *the fiercest of foes; a fierce tiger.* FEROCIOUS implies merciless cruelty or brutality, esp. of a bloodthirsty kind: *a ferocious tiger.* TRUCULENT implies an intimidating or menacing fierceness: *a truculent bully.*

fiery, *adj.* **1.** hot, flaming, heated, fervent, fervid, burning, afire, glowing. **2.** fervent, fervid, vehement, inflamed, impassioned, spirited, ardent, impetuous, passionate, fierce. —**Ant.** cool, cold; dispassionate.

fight, n. **1.** battle, war, combat, encounter, conflict, contest, scrimmage, engagement, fray, affray, action, skirmish, affair, struggle. **2.** melee, struggle, scuffle, tussle, riot, row, fray. —v. **3.** contend, strive, battle, combat, conflict, contest, engage, struggle.

figment, n. invention, fiction, fabrication, fable. —**Ant.** fact, reality.

filthy, adj. **1.** dirty, foul, unclean, defiled, squalid. **2.** obscene, vile, dirty, pornographic, licentious, lascivious. —**Ant.** clean, spotless, immaculate.

final, adj. **1.** last, latest, ultimate, drop-dead. **2.** conclusive, decisive. —**Ant.** prime, primary.

financial, adj. monetary, fiscal, pecuniary. —**Syn. Study.** FINANCIAL, FISCAL, MONETARY, PECUNIARY refer to matters concerned with money. FINANCIAL usu. refers to money matters or transactions of some size or importance: a lucrative financial deal. FISCAL is used esp. in connection with government funds, or funds of any organization: the end of the fiscal year. MONETARY relates esp. to money as such: The dollar is a monetary unit. PECUNIARY refers to money as used in making ordinary payments: a pecuniary obligation; pecuniary rewards.

fine, adj. **1.** superior, high-grade, choice, excellent, admirable, elegant, exquisite, finished, consummate, perfect, refined, select, delicate. **2.** powdered, pulverized, minute, small, little. **3.** keen, sharp, acute. **4.** skilled, accomplished, brilliant. **5.** affected, ornate, ornamented, fancy. —**Ant.** inferior, poor, bad, unfinished; dull; unskilled, maladroit; plain.

finery, n. regalia, dress-up, frills, frillery, frippery, trappings, toggery, fancy dress, Sunday best. —**Ant.** rags, tatters.

finish, v. **1.** bring to an end, end, terminate, conclude, close. **2.** use up, complete, consume. **3.** complete, perfect, consummate, polish. **4.** accomplish, achieve, execute, complete, perform, do. —n. **5.** end, conclusion, termination, close. **6.** polish, elegance, refinement. —**Ant.** begin, start, commence; originate, create; beginning.

finished, adj. **1.** ended, completed, consummated, over, done, done with; complete, consummate, perfect. **2.** polished, refined, elegant, perfected; trained, experienced, practiced, qualified, accomplished, proficient, skilled, gifted, talented. —**Ant.** begun; incomplete, imperfect; unrefined, inelegant; inexperienced, unqualified, unskilled, maladroit.

firm, adj. **1.** hard, solid, stiff, rigid, inelastic, compact, condensed, compressed, dense. **2.** steady, unshakable, rooted, fast, fixed, stable, secure, immovable. **3.** fixed, settled, unalterable, established, confirmed. **4.** steadfast, unwavering, determined, immovable, resolute, stanch, constant, steady, reliable. —n. **5.** company, partnership, association, business, concern, house, corporation. —**Ant.** flabby, flaccid, elastic, soft; unsteady, unstable; wavering, irresolute, inconstant, unreliable.

fiscal, See Syn. study at FINANCIAL.

fitness, n. **1.** condition, physical condition, conditioning, tone, shape, fettle, health, healthfulness, trim, repair, order, salubrity, salubriousness. **2.** appropriateness, suitability, applicability, aptness, cogency, propriety.

fix, v. **1.** make, fast, fasten, pin, attach, tie, secure, stabilize, establish, set, plant, implant. **2.** settle, determine, establish, define, limit. **3.** assign, refer. **4.** repair, mend, correct, emend. —n. **5.** predicament, dilemma, plight, spot. —**Ant.** loosen, loose, detach; unsettle; break.

flagrant, adj. glaring, overdone, excessive, gross, shameless, bodacious, brazen, blatant, scandalous, shocking, disgraceful, outrageous, heinous, monstrous. —**Syn. Study.** FLAGRANT, GLARING, GROSS suggest something offensive that cannot be overlooked. FLAGRANT implies a conspicuous offense so far beyond the limits of decency as to be insupportable: a flagrant violation of the law. GLARING emphasizes conspicuousness but lacks the imputation of evil or immorality: a glaring error by a bank teller. GROSS suggests a mistake or impropriety of major proportions: a gross miscarriage of justice.

flame, n. **1.** blaze, conflagration, holocaust, inferno, fire. **2.** heat, ar-

dor, zeal, passion, fervor, warmth, enthusiasm. —v. **3.** burn, blaze. **4.** glow, burn, warm; shine, flash. **5.** inflame, fire.

flash, n. **1.** flame, outburst, flare, gleam, glare. **2.** instant, split second, moment, twinkling, wink. **3.** ostentation, display. —v. **4.** glance, glint, glitter, scintillate, gleam. —adj. **5.** showy, ostentatious, flashy, gaudy, tawdry, flaunting, pretentious, superficial. **6.** counterfeit, sham, fake, false, fraudulent.

flat, adj. **1.** horizontal, level, even, equal, plane, smooth. **2.** low, supine, prone, prostrate. **3.** collapsed, deflated. **4.** unqualified, downright, positive, outright, peremptory, absolute. **5.** uninteresting, dull, tedious, lifeless, boring, spiritless, prosaic, unanimated. **6.** insipid, vapid, tasteless, stale, dead, unsavory. **7.** pointless. —adv. **8.** horizontally, levelly. **9.** positively, absolutely, definitely. —n. **10.** apartment, suite. —**Ant.** vertical, upright, perpendicular; doubtful, dubious; spirited, animated; tasteful, savory; pointed.

flatter, v. apple-polish, fawn, toady, kowtow, truckle, blandish, cajole, wheedle, coax, beguile, entice, inveigle, flatter, soft-soap, honey, sweettalk, butter up, bootlick, suck up to. —**Ant.** insult, affront, offend.

flavor, n. **1.** taste, savor. **2.** seasoning, extract, flavoring. **3.** characteristic, essence, quality, spirit, soul. **4.** smell, odor, aroma, perfume, fragrance.

flaw, n. defect, imperfection, blot, blemish, spot, fault, crack, crevice, breach, break, cleft, fissure, rift, fracture. —**Syn. Study.** See DEFECT.

fleet, adj. swift, fast, quick, rapid, speedy, expeditious, fleet-footed, nimble-footed, hasty, express, snappy. —**Ant.** slow, sluggish.

flexible, adj. **1.** pliable, pliant, flexile, limber, plastic, elastic, supple. **2.** adaptable, tractable, compliant, yielding, gentle. —**Ant.** inflexible, rigid, solid, firm; intractable, unyielding.

flit, v. fly, dart, skim along; flutter.

flock, n. bevy, covey, flight, gaggle, brood, hatch, litter; shoal, school; swarm; pride; drove, herd, pack; group, company, crowd.

flood, n. **1.** deluge, inundation, overflow, flash flood, freshet. —v. **2.** overflow, inundate, deluge, flow.

flourish, v. **1.** thrive, prosper, be successful, grow, increase, succeed. **2.** luxuriate. **3.** brandish, wave. **4.** parade, flaunt, display, show off, be ostentatious, boast, brag, vaunt. **5.** embellish, adorn, ornament, decorate. —n. **6.** parade, ostentation, show, display, dash. **7.** decoration, ornament, adornment, embellishment. —**Ant.** decline, die, fail; disfigure, mar. —**Syn. Study.** See SUCCEED.

flow, v. **1.** gush, spout, stream, spurt, jet, discharge. **2.** proceed, run, pour, roll on. **3.** overflow, abound, teem, pour. —n. **4.** current, flood, stream. **5.** stream, river, rivulet, rill, streamlet. **6.** outpouring, discharge, overflowing.

flowery, See Syn. study at BOMBASTIC.

fluctuate, v. waver, vacillate, change, vary; wave, undulate, oscillate.

fluent, adj. flowing, glib, voluble, copious, smooth. —**Syn. Study.** FLUENT, GLIB, VOLUBLE may refer to an easy flow of words or to a person able to communicate with ease. FLUENT suggests the easy and ready flow of an accomplished speaker or writer; it is usually a term of commendation: a fluent orator. GLIB implies an excessive fluency and lack of sincerity or profundity; it suggests talking smoothly and hurriedly to cover up or deceive: a glib salesperson. VOLUBLE implies the copious and often rapid flow of words characteristic of a person who loves to talk and will spare the audience no details: a voluble gossip.

fluid, n. **1.** liquid; gas, vapor. —adj. **2.** liquid, gaseous. —**Ant.** solid. —**Syn. Study.** See LIQUID.

fly, v. **1.** take wing, soar, hover, flutter, flit, wing, flap. **2.** elapse, pass, glide, slip.

fodder, See Syn. study at FEED.

foe, n. enemy, opponent, adversary, antagonist. —**Ant.** friend, ally, associate.

fog, n. **1.** cloud, mist, haze; smog. **2.** cloud, confusion, obfuscation, dimming, blurring, darkening. —v. **3.** befog, becloud, obfuscate, dim, blur, darken. **4.** daze, bewilder, befuddle,

muddle. —**Ant.** clarity; clear, brighten; clarify.

foible, n. weakness, fault, failing, frailty, defect, imperfection, infirmity. —**Ant.** strength, perfection. —**Syn. Study.** See FAULT.

follow, v. **1.** succeed, ensue. **2.** conform, obey, heed, comply, observe. **3.** accompany, attend. **4.** pursue, chase, trail, track, trace. **5.** ensue, succeed, result, come next, arise, proceed. —**Ant.** lead; order. —**Syn. Study.** FOLLOW, ENSUE, RESULT, SUCCEED imply coming after something else, in a natural sequence. FOLLOW is the general word: We must wait to see what follows. A detailed account follows. ENSUE implies a logical sequence, what might be expected normally to come after a given act, cause, etc.: When the power lines were cut, a paralysis of transportation ensued. RESULT emphasizes the connection between a cause or event and its effect, consequence, or outcome: The accident resulted in injuries to those involved. SUCCEED implies coming after in time, particularly coming into a title, office, etc.: Formerly the oldest son succeeded to his father's title.

follower, n. **1.** adherent, partisan, disciple, pupil. **2.** attendant, servant; supporter, retainer, companion, associate. —**Ant.** leader, teacher; enemy, foe. —**Syn. Study.** FOLLOWER, ADHERENT, PARTISAN refer to someone who demonstrates allegiance to a person, doctrine, cause, or the like. FOLLOWER often has an implication of personal relationship or of deep devotion to authority or to a leader: a follower of Gandhi. ADHERENT, a more formal word, suggests active championship of a person or point of view: an adherent of monetarism. PARTISAN suggests firm loyalty, as to a party, cause, or person, that is based on emotions rather than on reasoning: a partisan of the conservatives.

food, n. provisions, rations, nutrition, nutriment, aliment, bread, sustenance, victuals; meat, viands; diet, regimen, fare, menu.

fool, n. **1.** simpleton, dolt, dunce, blockhead, nincompoop, ninny, numskull, ignoramus, booby, sap, dunderhead, dunderpate, idiot. **2.** jester, buffoon, drool, harlequin, zany, clown, merry-andrew. **3.** imbecile, moron, idiot. —v. **4.** impose on, trick, deceive, delude, hoodwink, cozen, cheat, gull, gudgeon, hoax, dupe. **5.** joke, jest, play, toy, trifle, dally, idle, dawdle, loiter, tarry. —**Ant.** genius.

foolish, adj. **1.** silly, senseless, fatuous, stupid, inane, dull, vacant, vapid, slow, asinine, simple, witless. **2.** ill-considered, unwise, thoughtless, irrational, imprudent, unreasonable, absurd, ridiculous, nonsensical, preposterous, foolhardy. —**Ant.** bright, brilliant, clever, intelligent; wise, sage, sagacious. —**Syn. Study.** FOOLISH, FATUOUS, INANE imply weakness of intellect and lack of judgment. FOOLISH implies lack of common sense or good judgment or, sometimes, weakness of mind: a foolish decision; a foolish child. FATUOUS implies being not only foolish, dull, and vacant in mind, but complacent and highly self-satisfied as well: a fatuous grin. INANE suggests a lack of content, meaning, or purpose: inane conversation about the weather.

forage, See Syn. study at FEED.

forbid, v. inhibit, prohibit, taboo, interdict, prevent, preclude, stop, obviate, deter, discourage. —**Ant.** allow, permit, encourage.

forbidding, adj. unappealing, dismaying, grim, disagreeable, rebarbative, off-putting, menacing, threatening, minatory. —**Ant.** attractive, appealing.

force, n. **1.** strength, power, impetus, intensity, might, vigor, energy. **2.** coercion, violence, compulsion, constraint, enforcement. **3.** efficacy, effectiveness, effect, efficiency, validity, potency, potential. **4.** effect, operation. —v. **5.** compel, constrain, oblige, coerce, necessitate. **6.** drive, propel, impel. **7.** overcome, overpower, violate, ravish, rape. —**Ant.** weakness, frailty; ineffectiveness, inefficiency.

forecast, v. **1.** predict, augur, foretell, foresee, anticipate. **2.** prearrange, plan, contrive, project. **3.** conjecture, guess, estimate. —n. **4.** prediction, augury, conjecture, guess, estimate, foresight, prevision, prescience. —**Syn. Study.** See PREDICT.

foreigner, n. alien, stranger, nonnative, outsider, outlander. —**Ant.** native. —**Syn. Study.** See STRANGER.

foresee, See Syn. study at PREDICT.

foresight, n. **1.** prudence, forethought, prevision, anticipation, precaution; forecast. **2.** prescience, prevision, foreknowledge, prospect.

forest, n. grove, wood, woods, woodland. —**Ant.** plain.

foreword, See Syn. study at INTRODUCTION.

forgive, v. pardon, excuse; absolve, acquit. —**Ant.** blame, condemn, censure. —**Syn. Study.** See EXCUSE.

forlorn, adj. **1.** abandoned, deserted, forsaken, desolate, alone, lost, solitary. **2.** desolate, dreary, unhappy, miserable, wretched, pitiable, pitiful, helpless, woebegone, disconsolate, comfortless, destitute. —**Ant.** accompanied; happy, cheerful.

form, n. **1.** shape, figure, outline, mold, appearance, cast, cut, configuration. **2.** mold, model, pattern. **3.** manner, style, arrangement, sort, kind, order, type. **4.** assemblage, group. **5.** ceremony, ritual, formula, formality, conformity, rule, convention. **6.** document, paper, application, business form, blank. **7.** method, procedure, system, mode, practice, formula, approach. —v. **8.** construct, frame, shape, model, mold, fashion, outline, cast. **9.** make, produce, create, originate. **10.** compose, make up, serve for, constitute. **11.** order, arrange, organize, systematize, dispose, combine. **12.** instruct, teach, educate, discipline, train. **13.** frame, invent, contrive, devise.

formal, adj. **1.** academic, conventional, conformal, conforming, conformist. **2.** ceremonial, ceremonious, ritual, conventional. **3.** ceremonious, stiff, prim, precise, punctilious, starched. **4.** perfunctory, external. **5.** official, express, explicit, strict, rigid, rigorous, stodgy. **6.** rigorous, methodical, regular, set, fixed, rigid, stiff.

formidable, adj. dread, dreadful, appalling, threatening, menacing, fearful, terrible, frightful, horrible. —**Ant.** pleasant, friendly, amiable.

forsake, v. **1.** quit, leave, desert, abandon. **2.** give up, renounce, forswear, relinquish, recant, drop, forgo.

fortification, n. **1.** fortifying, strengthening, bolstering, arming. **2.** fort, castle, fortress, citadel, stronghold, bulwark, fastness.

fortuitous, adj. accidental, chance, casual, incidental. —**Ant.** purposeful, intentional.

fortunate, adj. lucky, happy, propitious, favorable, advantageous, auspicious; successful, prosperous. —**Ant.** unlucky, unfortunate. —**Syn. Study.** FORTUNATE, HAPPY, LUCKY refer to persons who enjoy, or events that produce, good fortune. FORTUNATE implies that the success is obtained by the operation of favorable circumstances more than by direct effort: fortunate in one's choice of a wife; a fortunate investment. HAPPY emphasizes a pleasant ending or something that happens at just the right moment: By a happy accident I received the package on time. LUCKY, a more colloquial word, is applied to situations that turn out well by chance: lucky at cards; my lucky day.

forward, adv. **1.** onward, ahead, up ahead, in advance, frontward. **2.** out, forth. —adj. **3.** well-advanced, up front, ahead. **4.** ready, prompt, eager, willing, sincere, earnest, zealous. **5.** pert, bold, presumptuous, assuming, confident, impertinent, impudent, brazen, flippant. **6.** radical, extreme, unconventional, progressive. **7.** early, premature, future, preliminary. —**Ant.** backward.

foster, v. **1.** promote, encourage, further, favor, patronize, forward, advance. **2.** bring up, rear, breed, nurse, nourish, sustain, support. **3.** care for, cherish. —**Ant.** discourage. —**Syn. Study.** See CHERISH.

foul, adj. **1.** offensive, gross, disgusting, loathsome, repulsive, repellent, noisome, fetid, putrid, stinking. **2.** filthy, dirty, unclean, squalid, polluted, sullied, soiled, tarnished, stained, tainted, impure. **3.** stormy, unfavorable, rainy, tempestuous. **4.** abominable, wicked, vile, base, shameful, infamous, sinful, scandalous. **5.** scurrilous, obscene, smutty, profane, vulgar, low, coarse. **6.** unfair, dishonorable, underhanded, cheating. **7.** entangled, caught, jammed, tangled. —adv. **8.** unfairly, foully. —v. **9.** soil, defile, sully, stain, dirty, besmirch, smut, taint, pollute, poison. **10.** entangle, clog, tangle, catch. **11.** defile, dishonor, disgrace, shame. —**Ant.** delightful, attractive, pleasant; pure; saintly, angelic; fair;

honorable; clean, purify; clear; honor.

foundation, n. **1.** base, basis, ground, footing. **2.** establishment, settlement; endowment. —**Ant.** superstructure. —**Syn. Study.** See BASE.

fractious, adj. cross, fretful, peevish, testy, captious, petulant, touchy, splenetic, pettish, waspish, snappish, irritable; unruly, refractory, stubborn. —**Ant.** temperate, kind, even-tempered; amenable, tractable, obedient.

fragile, See Syn. study at FRAIL.

fragrance, See Syn. study at PERFUME.

fragrant, adj. perfumed, odorous, redolent, sweet-smelling, sweetscented, aromatic, odoriferous. —**Ant.** noxious.

frail, adj. brittle, fragile, breakable, frangible, delicate, weak, feeble. —**Ant.** strong, pliant, elastic, unbreakable. —**Syn. Study.** FRAIL, BRITTLE, FRAGILE imply a delicacy or weakness of substance or construction. FRAIL applies particularly to health and immaterial things: a frail constitution; frail hopes. BRITTLE implies a hard material that snaps or breaks to pieces easily: brittle as glass. FRAGILE implies that the object must be handled carefully to avoid breakage or damage: fragile bric-a-brac.

frank, adj. **1.** open, unreserved, unrestrained, unrestricted, nonrestrictive, unsuspicious, outspoken, sincere, free, bold, truthful, uninhibited. **2.** artless, ingenuous, undisguised, avowed, downright, outright, direct. —n. **3.** signature, mark, sign, seal; franchise. —**Ant.** secretive, restrained, restricted; sly, artful, dissembling. —**Syn. Study.** FRANK, CANDID, OPEN, OUTSPOKEN imply a freedom and boldness in speaking. FRANK implies a straightforward, almost tactless expression of one's real opinions or sentiments: He was frank in his rejection of the proposal. CANDID suggests sincerity, truthfulness, and impartiality: a candid appraisal of her work. OPEN implies a lack of reserve or of concealment: open antagonism. OUTSPOKEN suggests free and bold expression, even when inappropriate: an outspoken and unnecessary show of disapproval.

fraud, n. deceit, trickery, duplicity, treachery, sharp practice, breach of confidence, trick, deception, guile, artifice, ruse, stratagem, wile, hoax, humbug. —**Ant.** honesty. —**Syn. Study.** See DECEIT.

free, adj. **1.** unfettered, independent, at liberty, unrestrained, unrestricted. **2.** unregulated, unrestricted, unimpeded, open, unobstructed. **3.** clear, immune, exempt, uncontrolled, decontrolled. **4.** easy, firm, swift, unimpeded, unencumbered. **5.** loose, unattached, lax. **6.** frank, open, unconstrained, unceremonious, familiar, informal, easy. **7.** loose, licentious, ribald, lewd, immoral, libertine. **8.** liberal, lavish, generous, bountiful, unstinted, munificent, charitable, open-handed. —v. **9.** liberate, set free, release, unfetter, emancipate, manumit, deliver, disenthrall. **10.** exempt, deliver. **11.** rid, relieve, disengage, clear. —**Ant.** dependent, restrained, restricted; close, obstructed; difficult; unfamiliar; moral, upright; stingy, niggardly; confine, enthrall. —**Syn. Study.** See RELEASE.

freedom, n. **1.** liberty, independence. **2.** immunity, franchise, privilege. **3.** ease, facility. **4.** frankness, openness, ingenuousness. **5.** familiarity, license, looseness, laxity. —**Ant.** dependence; restriction; difficulty; secrecy; unfamiliarity; restraint.

freight, n. **1.** cargo, shipment, load. **2.** freightage, transportation, expressage. —v. **3.** load, lade, burden, charge.

frenzy, n. agitation, excitement, paroxysm, enthusiasm; rage, fury, raving, mania, insanity, delirium, derangement, aberration, lunacy, madness. —**Ant.** calm, coolness; sanity, judgment.

frequently, adv. often, many times, repeatedly. —**Ant.** seldom. —**Syn. Study.** See OFTEN.

fresh, adj. **1.** new, recent, novel. **2.** youthful, healthy, robust, vigorous, well, hearty, hardy, strong. **3.** refreshing, pure, cool, unadulterated, sweet, invigorating. **4.** inexperienced, artless, untrained, raw, green, uncultivated, unskilled. —**Ant.** stale, old; impure, contaminated; experienced, skilled. —**Syn. Study.** See NEW.

fret, v. **1.** worry, fume, rage. **2.** torment, worry, harass, annoy, irritate, vex, taunt, goad, tease, nettle, needle. **3.** wear away, erode, gnaw, corrode, rust. —*n.* **4.** annoyance, vexation, harassment, agitation, worry, irritation. **5.** erosion, corrosion, eating away, gnawing. **6.** fretwork, ornament.

fretful, *adj.* irritable, peevish, petulant, querulous, touchy, testy, waspish, pettish, splenetic, captious, snappish, short-tempered, ill-tempered. —**Ant.** calm, even-tempered, temperate, easy-going.

friction, *n.* discord, disaccord, disharmony, conflict, dissension, antagonism, strain, incompatibility, contentiousness, enmity. —**Ant.** friendliness, amity, cooperation.

friend, *n.* **1.** companion, crony, chum, acquaintance, intimate, confidant. **2.** well-wisher, patron, supporter, backer, encourager, advocate, defender. **3.** ally, associate, confrère. —**Ant.** enemy, foe, adversary. —**Syn. Study.** See ACQUAINTANCE.

friendly, *adj.* **1.** kind, kindly, amicable, fraternal, amiable, cordial, genial, well-disposed, benevolent, affectionate, kind-hearted. **2.** helpful, favorable, advantageous, propitious. —**Ant.** unfriendly, inimical; unfavorable.

fright, *n.* dismay, consternation, terror, fear, alarm, panic. —**Ant.** bravery, boldness.

frighten, *v.* scare, terrify, alarm, appall, shock, dismay, intimidate.

frightful, *adj.* dreadful, terrible, alarming, terrific, fearful, awful, shocking, dread, dire, horrid, horrible, hideous, ghastly, gruesome. —**Ant.** delightful, attractive, beautiful.

frivolous, *adj.* **1.** unimportant, trifling, petty, paltry, trivial, flimsy. **2.** idle, silly, foolish, childish, puerile. —**Ant.** important, vital; mature, adult, sensible.

frontier, See Syn. study at BOUNDARY.

froward, *adj.* perverse, contrary, refractory, obstinate, willful, disobedient, uncooperative, fractious, contumacious, wayward, unmanageable, difficult, defiant, fresh, impudent. —**Ant.** tractable, lenient, cooperative, easy.

frugal, *adj.* economical, thrifty, chary, provident, saving, sparing, careful; parsimonious, stingy, penurious. —**Ant.** lavish, wasteful. —**Syn. Study.** See ECONOMICAL.

fruitful, *adj.* prolific, fertile, fecund, productive, profitable; plentiful, abundant, rich, copious. —**Ant.** barren, scarce, scanty, unprofitable, fruitless. —**Syn. Study.** See PRODUCTIVE.

fruitless, *adj.* **1.** useless, inutile, unavailing, profitless, ineffectual, unprofitable, vain, idle, futile, abortive. **2.** barren, sterile, unfruitful, unproductive, infecund, unprolific. —**Ant.** fruitful, useful, profitable, effectual; abundant, fertile.

frustrate, *v.* defeat, nullify, baffle, disconcert, foil, disappoint, balk, check, thwart. —**Ant.** encourage, foster.

fulfill, *v.* **1.** carry out, consummate, execute, discharge, accomplish, achieve, complete, effect, realize, perfect. **2.** perform, do, obey, observe, discharge. **3.** satisfy, meet, answer, fill, comply with. **4.** complete, end, terminate, bring to an end, finish, conclude. —**Ant.** fail; dissatisfy; create, originate.

fume, *n.* **1.** smoke, vapor, exhalation, steam. **2.** rage, fury, agitation, storm. —*v.* **3.** smoke, vaporize. **4.** chafe, fret, rage, rave, flare up, bluster, storm.

fun, *n.* merriment, enjoyment, pleasure, amusement, divertissement, sport, diversion, joking, jesting, playfulness, gaiety, frolic. —**Ant.** misery, melancholy.

fundamental, *adj.* basic, underlying, principal, main, central, chief, essential, primary, elementary, necessary, indispensable. **2.** original, first. —*n.* **3.** principle, rule, basic law, essence, essential. —**Ant.** superficial, superfluous, dispensable; last, common; nonessential.

funny, *adj.* amusing, diverting, comical, farcical, absurd, ridiculous, droll, witty, facetious, humorous, laughable, ludicrous, incongruous, foolish. —**Ant.** sad, melancholy, humorless.

furnish, *v.* **1.** provide, supply; purvey, cater. **2.** appoint, equip, fit up, rig, deck out, decorate, outfit, fit out. —**Syn. Study.** FURNISH, APPOINT, EQUIP refer to providing something necessary or useful. FURNISH often refers to providing necessary or customary objects or services that in-

crease living comfort: *to furnish a bedroom with a bed, desk, and chair.* APPOINT, a more formal word, now usu. used in the past participle, means to supply completely with all requisites or accessories, often in an elegant style: *a well-appointed hotel; a fully appointed suite.* EQUIP means to supply with necessary materials or apparatus for a particular action, service, or undertaking; it emphasizes preparation: *to equip a vessel; to equip a soldier.*

fury, *n.* **1.** passion, furor, frenzy, rage, ire, anger, wrath. **2.** violence, turbulence, fierceness, impetuousness, impetuosity, vehemence. **3.** shrew, virago, termagant, vixen, nag, hag, maenad, bacchante. —**Ant.** calm, serenity. —**Syn. Study.** See ANGER.

fuse, *v.* **1.** melt, liquefy, dissolve, smelt; combine, blend, intermingle, coalesce, intermix, commingle, amalgamate, homogenize, merge. —*v.* **2.** match, fusee, fuze. —**Ant.** solidify, separate.

fuss, *n.* **1.** activity, ado, bustle, pother, to-do, stir, commotion. —*v.* **2.** bother, annoy, pester. —**Ant.** inactivity.

futile, *adj.* **1.** ineffectual, useless, unsuccessful, vain, unavailing, idle, profitless, unprofitable, bootless, worthless, valueless, fruitless, unproductive. **2.** trivial, frivolous, minor, nugatory, unimportant, trifling. —**Ant.** effective, effectual, successful; profitable, worthy; basic, important, principal, major. —**Syn. Study.** See USELESS.

G

gadget, *n.* device, tool, appliance, implement, instrument, utensil, mechanism, contrivance, contraption, invention, creation, doohickey, dingus, thingamabob, gizmo, thingamajig, doodad, widget, whatchamacallit.

gaiety, *n.* **1.** merriment, mirth, glee, jollity, joyousness, liveliness, sportiveness, hilarity, vivacity, life, cheerfulness, joviality, animation, spirit. **2.** showiness, finery, gaudiness, brilliance, glitter, flashiness, flash. —**Ant.** sadness, melancholy, misery.

gain, *v.* **1.** obtain, secure, procure, get, acquire, attain, earn, win. **2.** reach, get to, arrive at, attain. **3.** improve, better, progress, advance, forward; near, approach. —*n.* **4.** profit, increase, advantage, advance; profits, winnings. —**Ant.** lose; worsen; retreat; losses. —**Syn. Study.** GAIN, ATTAIN, EARN, WIN imply obtaining a reward or something advantageous. GAIN suggests the expenditure of effort to get or reach something desired: *After battling the blizzard, we finally gained our destination.* ATTAIN suggests a sense of personal satisfaction in having reached a lofty goal: *to attain stardom.* EARN emphasizes a deserved reward for labor or services: *to earn a promotion.* WIN stresses attainment in spite of competition or opposition: *to win support in a campaign.*

gall, *v.* **1.** irritate, annoy, irk, vex, nettle, peeve, provoke, aggravate, exasperate, get one's goat. —*n.* **2.** effrontery, brazenness, brashness, impudence, insolence, nerve, cheek, gall, face, crust, brass.

gallant, *adj.* brave, high-spirited, valorous, valiant, chivalrous, courageous, bold, intrepid, fearless, daring. **2.** gay, showy, magnificent, splendid, fine. **3.** polite, courtly, chivalrous, noble, courteous. —*n.* **4.** suitor, wooer, lover, paramour. —**Ant.** cowardly, fearful; tawdry; impolite, discourteous.

gambol, *v., n.* frolic, spring, caper, romp, dance.

game, *n.* **1.** amusement, pastime, diversion, divertissement, play, sport, contest, competition. **2.** scheme, artifice, strategy, stratagem, plan, plot, undertaking, venture, adventure. **3.** fun, sport, joke, diversion. **4.** prey, quarry. —*adj.* **5.** plucky, brave, bold, resolute, intrepid, dauntless, valorous, fearless, heroic, gallant.

gang, *n.* **1.** band, group, crew, crowd, company, party, set, clique, coterie; horde. **2.** squad, shift, team.

gape, *v.* **1.** yawn. **2.** stare, wonder, gaze. **3.** split, open, dehisce, separate.

garb, *n.* **1.** fashion, mode, style, cut. **2.** clothes, clothing, dress, costume, attire, apparel, habiliments, habit, garments, raiment, vesture. —*v.* **3.** dress, clothe, attire, array, apparel.

garish, *adj.* **1.** glaring, loud, showy, tawdry, gaudy, flashy. **2.** ornate, ornamented, decorated. —**Ant.** elegant; plain, simple.

garnish, *v.* **1.** adorn, decorate, ornament, embellish, grace, enhance, beautify, trim, bedeck, bedizen, set off. —*n.* **2.** decoration, ornamentation, ornament, adornment, garniture, garnishment. —**Ant.** strip.

garrulous, *adj.* talkative, loquacious, prating, prattling, wordy, diffuse, babbling, verbose, prolix. —**Ant.** taciturn, silent, reticent. —**Syn. Study.** See TALKATIVE.

gasp, *v.* pant, puff, blow.

gather, *v.* **1.** get together, collect, aggregate, assemble, muster, marshal, bring or draw together. **2.** learn, infer, understand, deduce, assume, conclude. **3.** accumulate, amass, garner, hoard. **4.** pluck, garner, reap, harvest, glean, cull, crop. **5.** select, cull, sort, sort out. **6.** grow, increase, accrete, collect, thicken, condense. —*n.* **7.** contraction, drawing together, tuck, pucker, fold, pleat, plait. —**Ant.** disperse; decrease. —**Syn. Study.** GATHER, ASSEMBLE, COLLECT, MUSTER, MARSHAL imply bringing or drawing together. GATHER expresses the general idea usu. with no implication of arrangement: *to gather seashells.* ASSEMBLE is used of persons, objects, or facts brought together in a specific place or for a specific purpose: *to assemble data for a report.* COLLECT implies purposeful accumulation to form an ordered whole: *to collect evidence.* MUSTER, primarily a military term, suggests thoroughness in the process of collection: *to muster all one's resources.* MARSHAL, another chiefly military term, suggests rigorously ordered, purposeful arrangement: *to marshal facts for effective presentation.*

gathering, *n.* **1.** assembly, meeting, assemblage, crowd, convocation, congregation, concourse, company, throng, muster. **2.** swelling, boil, abscess, carbuncle, pimple, sore, pustule, tumor.

gaudy, *adj.* showy, tawdry, garish, brilliant, loud, flashy, conspicuous, obvious, vulgar, unsubtle. —**Ant.** elegant, refined, subtle.

gaunt, *adj.* **1.** thin, emaciated, haggard, lean, spare, skinny, scrawny, lank, angular, raw-boned, meager, attenuated, slender. **2.** bleak, desolate, grim, dreary. —**Ant.** obese, fat; populous.

gay, *adj.* **1.** joyous, gleeful, jovial, glad, happy, lighthearted, lively, convivial, vivacious, animated, frolicsome, sportive, hilarious, jolly, joyful, merry, good-humored, expansive, cheerful, sprightly, blithe, airy. **2.** bright, showy, fine, brilliant. **3.** homosexual; lesbian. —**Ant.** unhappy, miserable; dull; straight.

gaze, *v., n.* stare, gape, wonder.

genealogy, See Syn. study at PEDIGREE.

general, *adj.* **1.** impartial, unparticular, catholic, universal. **2.** common, usual, prevalent, customary, regular, ordinary, popular, nonexclusive, widespread, prevailing. **3.** miscellaneous, unrestricted, unspecialized, nonspecific. **4.** vague, lax, indefinite, ill-defined, inexact, imprecise. —**Ant.** special, partial; uncommon, unusual, extraordinary; specific; definite, exact, precise. —**Syn. Study.** GENERAL, COMMON, POPULAR, UNIVERSAL agree in the idea of being nonexclusive and widespread. GENERAL means pertaining to or true of all or most of a particular class or body, irrespective of individuals: *a general belief.* COMMON means shared or experienced frequently or by a majority of group members: *a common problem.* POPULAR means belonging to or favored by the people or the public generally, rather than a particular class: *a popular misconception.* UNIVERSAL means found everywhere with no exception: *a universal need.*

generally, *adv.* usually, commonly, ordinarily, often, in general. —**Ant.** especially, particularly, unusually. —**Syn. Study.** See OFTEN.

generosity, *n.* **1.** readiness, liberality, munificence, charity, bounteousness. **2.** nobleness, disinterestedness, magnanimity. —**Ant.** stinginess, niggardliness, parsimony.

generous, *adj.* **1.** munificent, bountiful, unselfish, unstinting, liberal, charitable, open-handed, beneficent. **2.** noble, high-minded, magnanimous; large, big. **3.** ample, plentiful, abundant, flowing, overflowing, copious. —**Ant.** stingy, tightfisted, selfish, niggardly; small, parsimonious; scarce, scanty, barren. —**Syn. Study.** GENEROUS, CHARITABLE, LIBERAL,

MUNIFICENT all describe giving or sharing something of value. GENEROUS stresses the warm and sympathetic nature of the giver: *a retired executive, generous with her time.* CHARITABLE stresses the goodness and kindness of the giver and the indigence or need of the receiver: *a charitable contribution to a nursing home.* LIBERAL emphasizes the large size of the gift and the openhandedness of the giver: *a liberal bequest to the university.* MUNIFICENT refers to a gift or award so strikingly large as to evoke amazement or admiration: *a lifetime income, a truly munificent reward for his loyalty.*

genial, *adj.* **1.** cheerful, sympathetic, cordial, friendly, pleasant, agreeable, kindly, well-disposed, hearty, encouraging. **2.** enlivening, lively, warm, mild. —**Ant.** unsympathetic, unpleasant, discouraging; cool.

genius, *n.* **1.** capacity, ability, talent, gift, aptitude, faculty, bent. **2.** spirit, guardian angel, genie, jinn. —**Ant.** inability, incapacity.

gentle, *adj.* **1.** soft, bland, peaceful, clement, moderate, pacific, soothing, kind, tender, humane, lenient, merciful, meek, mild, kindly, amiable, submissive, gentle-hearted, kind-hearted. **2.** gradual, moderate, temperate, tempered, light, mild. **3.** well-born, noble, highborn. **4.** honorable, respectable, refined, cultivated, polished, well-bred, polite, elegant, courteous, courtly. **5.** manageable, tractable, tame, docile, trained, peaceable, quiet. —**Ant.** immoderate, turbulent, unkind, cruel, heartless; sudden, abrupt; unrefined, unpolished, impolite; intractable, wild, noisy.

gentleman, See Syn. study at MAN.

genuine, *adj.* authentic, real, true, bona fide, verifiable, factual, provable, honest-to-God, the real McCoy. —**Ant.** false, counterfeit.

get, *v.* **1.** obtain, acquire, procure, secure, gain. **2.** earn, win, gain. **3.** learn, apprehend, grasp. **4.** capture, seize upon. **5.** prepare, get ready. **6.** prevail on or upon, persuade, induce, influence, dispose. **7.** beget, engender, generate, breed, procreate. **8.** come to, reach, arrive. **9.** become, grow. —**Ant.** lose. —**Syn. Study.** GET, OBTAIN, ACQUIRE, PROCURE, SECURE imply gaining possession of something. GET suggests gaining possession in any manner, either voluntarily or without effort: *to get a copy of a book.* OBTAIN suggests putting forth effort to gain possession of something wanted: *to obtain information.* ACQUIRE often suggests possessing something after a prolonged effort: *to acquire a fortune in the oil business.* PROCURE stresses the use of special means or measures to get something: *to procure a rare etching from an art dealer.* SECURE suggests obtaining something and making possession safe and sure: *to secure benefits for striking workers.*

ghastly, *adj.* **1.** dreadful, horrible, frightful, hideous, grisly, dismal, terrible, shocking. **2.** pale, deathly, white, wan, cadaverous. —**Ant.** lovely, attractive, beautiful; ruddy, robust, healthy.

ghost, *n.* **1.** apparition, phantom, spirit, phantasm, wraith, revenant, shade, spook, specter, supernatural being. **2.** shadow, hint, suggestion.

giant, *adj.* **1.** oversize, outsize, huge, enormous, great, grand, king-size, gigantic, mammoth, jumbo, colossal, gargantuan, immense, massive, monstrous, monster, vast, Brobdingnagian. **2.** colossus, titan, Atlas, Goliath, amazon, behemoth, monster. —**Ant.** Lilliputian, tiny.

giddy, *adj.* **1.** light-headed, light, dizzy, vertiginous, swimmy, reeling, spacey, seeing double, groggy, confused. **2.** silly, frivolous, lighthearted, merry, playful, whimsical, pixilated, foolish, goofy, wacky. **3.** empty-headed, flighty, featherbrained, witless. **4.** high, tipsy, tiddly, pixilated. —**Ant.** sober.

gift, *n.* **1.** donation, present, contribution, offering, boon, alms, gratuity, tip, benefaction, grant, largess, subsidy, allowance, endowment, bequest, legacy, dowry, inheritance, bounty. **2.** talent, endowment, power, faculty, ability, capacity, forte, capability, genius, bent.

gigantic, *adj.* huge, enormous, tremendous, colossal, mammoth, monstrous, elephantine, immense, prodigious, herculean, titanic, cyclopean, vast, extensive, infinite. —**Ant.** small, tiny, infinitesimal, microscopic. —**Syn. Study.** GIGANTIC, COLOSSAL, MAMMOTH are used of whatever is physically or metaphorically

of great magnitude. GIGANTIC refers to the size of a giant, or to anything that is of unusually large size: *a gigantic country.* COLOSSAL refers to the awesome effect and extraordinary size or power of a colossus or of something of similar size, scope, or effect: *a colossal mistake.* MAMMOTH refers to the size of the animal of that name and is used esp. of anything large and heavy: *a mammoth battleship.*

gingerly, *adj.* **1.** cautious, careful, circumspect, mindful, heedful, prudent, discreet, guarded, politic. —*adv.* **2.** cautiously, carefully, heedfully.

give, *v.* **1.** deliver, bestow, hand over, offer, vouchsafe, impart, accord, furnish, provide, supply, donate, contribute, afford, spare, accommodate with, confer, grant, cede, relinquish, yield, turn over, assign, present. **2.** enable, assign, award. **3.** set forth, issue, show, present, offer. **4.** assume, suppose, assign. **5.** afford, yield, produce. **6.** perform, make do. **7.** issue, put forth, emit, publish, utter, give out (with), pronounce, render. **8.** communicate, impart, divulge. **9.** draw back, recede, retire, relax, cede, yield, give over, give away, sink, give up. **10.** break down, fail. —**Ant.** receive. —**Syn. Study.** GIVE, CONFER, GRANT, PRESENT mean that something concrete or abstract is bestowed on one person by another. GIVE is the general word: *to give someone a book.* CONFER usu. means to give as an honor or as a favor; it implies courteous and gracious giving: *to confer a medal.* GRANT is usu. limited to the idea of acceding to a request or fulfilling an expressed wish; it often involves a formal act or legal procedure: *to grant a prayer; to grant immunity.* PRESENT, a more formal word than GIVE, usu. implies a certain ceremony in the giving: *to present an award.*

glad, *adj.* **1.** delighted, pleased, elated, happy, gratified, contented. **2.** cheerful, joyous, joyful, happy, merry, cheery, animated, light. —**Ant.** miserable, unhappy, sad.

glamour, *n.* **1.** allure, allurement, attraction, seductiveness, appeal, charm, charisma, fascination, magnetism, exoticism, star quality. —**Ant.** ordinariness.

glance, *v.* **1.** glitter, flash, glimpse, gleam, glisten, scintillate, shine. **2.** cast, reflect. —*n.* **3.** glitter, gleam; glimpse, look.

glare, *n.* **1.** dazzle, flare, glitter, luster, brilliance, sparkle, flash. **2.** showiness. **3.** scowl, glower. —*v.* **4.** shine, dazzle, gleam. **5.** glower, gloat, scowl.

glaring, See Syn. study at FLAGRANT.

gleam, *n.* **1.** ray, flash, beam, glimmer, glimmering. —*v.* **2.** shine, glimmer, flash, glitter, sparkle, beam.

glee, *n.* joy, exultation, merriment, jollity, hilarity, mirth, joviality, gaiety, liveliness, verve, life. —**Ant.** misery, sadness, melancholy.

glib, *adj.* **1.** fluent, voluble, talkative, ready. **2.** slippery, smooth, facile, artful. —**Ant.** taciturn, silent, quiet; artless, guileless. —**Syn. Study.** See FLUENT.

glide, *v., n.* slide, slip, flow. —**Ant.** stick.

glisten, *v.* glimmer, shimmer, sparkle, shine, gleam, glitter.

gloom, *n.* **1.** darkness, dimness, shadow, shade, obscurity, gloominess. **2.** melancholy, sadness, depression, dejection, despondency. —**Ant.** brightness, effulgence; joy, glee, happiness.

gloomy, *adj.* **1.** dark, shaded, obscure, shadowy, dim, dusky; dismal, lowering. **2.** depressed, dejected, sad, melancholy, despondent, downcast, crestfallen, downhearted, glum, dispirited, disheartened. —**Ant.** bright, effulgent, dazzling; happy, delighted, gleeful.

glorious, *adj.* **1.** admirable, delightful. **2.** famous, renowned, noted, celebrated, famed, eminent, distinguished, illustrious. —**Ant.** horrible; unknown; notorious.

glory, *n.* **1.** praise, honor, distinction, renown, fame, eminence, celebrity. **2.** resplendence, splendor, magnificence, grandeur, pomp, brilliance, effulgence. —*v.* **3.** exult, rejoice, triumph. —**Ant.** infamy, dishonor; gloom.

gloss, *n.* **1.** luster, sheen, polish, glaze, shine. **2.** front, mien, appearance, pretext, pretense. **3.** explanation, exegesis, critique, comment, note, interpretation, analysis, annotation, commentary. —*v.* **4.** polish, shine, glaze, varnish. **5.** annotate, explain, interpret, analyze. —**Syn. Study.** See POLISH.

glossy, adj. 1. lustrous, shiny, shining, glazed, smooth, sleek. 2. specious, plausible.

glum, adj. morose, depressed, gloomy, sad, dejected; moody, sullen, sulky, sour, dour —**Syn. Study.** GLUM, MOROSE, SULLEN describe a gloomy, unsociable attitude. GLUM suggests a depressed, spiritless disposition or manner, usu. temporary: *The runner had a glum expression after losing the race.* MOROSE, which adds a sense of bitterness and peevishness, implies a habitual and pervasive gloominess: *His chronic illness put him in a morose mood.* SULLEN usu. implies a reluctance or refusal to speak, accompanied by a glowering look expressing anger or a sense of injury: *The child had a sullen look after being scolded.*

gluttonous, adj. greedy, devouring, voracious, ravenous, grasping, insatiable, ravening, hoggish, piggish, piggy, avid, rapacious, edacious. —**Ant.** abstinent, abstemious, restrained.

gnome, n. goblin, troll, sylph, gremlin. —**Syn. Study.** See GOBLIN.

gobble, v. gulp, bolt, devour, swallow.

goblin, n. gnome, gremlin, troll, elf, bogeyman, ogre, demon —**Syn. Study.** GOBLIN, GNOME, GREMLIN refer to supernatural beings thought to be malevolent to people. GOBLINS are demons of any size, usu. in human or animal form, that are supposed to assail, afflict, and even torture human beings. GNOMES are small ugly creatures that live in the earth, guarding mines, treasures, etc. They are mysteriously malevolent and terrify human beings by causing dreadful mishaps to occur. GREMLINS are thought to disrupt machinery and are active in modern folklore.

godly, adj. pious, saintly, devout, religious, holy, righteous, good. —**Ant.** ungodly.

good, adj. 1. moral, righteous, religious, pious, pure, virtuous, conscientious, meritorious, worthy, exemplary, upright. 2. commendable, adroit, efficient, proficient, able, skillful, expert, ready, dexterous, clever, capable, qualified, fit, suited, suitable, convenient. 3. satisfactory, excellent, exceptional, valuable, precious, capital, admirable, commendable. 4. well-behaved, obedient, heedful. 5. kind, beneficent, friendly, kindly, benevolent, humane, favorable, well-disposed, gracious, obliging. 6. honorable, worthy, deserving, fair, unsullied, immaculate, unblemished, unimpeached. 7. reliable, safe, trustworthy, honest, competent. 8. genuine, sound, valid. 9. agreeable, pleasant, genial, cheering. 10. satisfactory, advantageous, favorable, auspicious, propitious, fortunate, profitable, useful, serviceable, beneficial. 11. ample, sufficient. 12. full, adequate, all of. 13. great, considerable, large. —n. 14. profit, worth, advantage, benefit, usefulness, utility, gain. 15. excellence, merit, righteousness, kindness, virtue. 16. (*plural*) property, belongings, effects, chattel, furniture. 17. (*plural*) wares, merchandise, stock, commodities. —**Ant.** bad. —**Syn. Study.** See PROPERTY.

goodness, n. 1. virtue, morality, integrity, honesty, uprightness, probity, righteousness, good. 2. kindness, benevolence, generosity, kindliness, benignity, humanity. 3. excellence, worth, value, quality. 4. essence, strength. —**Ant.** evil. —**Syn. Study.** GOODNESS, MORALITY, VIRTUE refer to qualities of character or conduct that entitle the possessor to approval and esteem. GOODNESS is the simple word for a general quality recognized as an inherent part of one's character: *Many could tell of her goodness and honesty.* MORALITY implies conformity to the recognized standards of right conduct: *a citizen of the highest morality.* VIRTUE is a rather formal word, and usually suggests GOODNESS that is consciously or steadily maintained, often in spite of temptations or evil influences: *a man of unassailable virtue.*

goodwill, 1. friendliness, benevolence, favor, kindness. 2. acquiescence, heartiness, ardor, zeal, earnestness.

gorge, n. 1. defile, pass, cleft, fissure, ravine, notch. 2. disgust, repulsion, revulsion. —v. 3. stuff, glut, cram, fill. 4. bolt, gulp, gobble, devour, gormandize.

gorgeous, adj. sumptuous, magnificent, splendid, rich, grand, resplend-

ent, brilliant, glittering, dazzling, superb, to die for. —**Ant.** poor; ugly.

gossip, n. 1. scandal, small talk, hearsay, palaver, idle talk, newsmongering. 2. chatterer, babbler, gabber, nosy Parker. —v. 3. chatter, prattle, prate, palaver, tattle.

govern, v. 1. rule, reign, hold sway, control, command, sway, influence, have control. 2. direct, guide, restrain, check, conduct, manage, supervise, superintend. —**Ant.** obey; follow.

gown, n. dress, robe, frock, evening gown or dress.

grace, n. 1. attractiveness, charm, gracefulness, comeliness, ease, elegance, symmetry, beauty; polish, refinement. 2. favor, kindness, kindliness, love, good will, benignity, condescension. 3. mercy, clemency, pardon, leniency, lenity, forgiveness. 4. love, sanctity, holiness, devoutness, devotion, piety. —v. 5. adorn, embellish, beautify, enhance, deck, decorate, ornament; honor, dignify. —**Ant.** ugliness; disfavor; condemnation; hate, abhorrence; dishonor, disgrace.

gracious, adj. 1. kind, kindly, benevolent, benign, courteous, polite, courtly, friendly, well-disposed, favorable. 2. compassionate, tender, merciful, lenient, clement, mild, gentle. 3. indulgent, beneficent, condescending, patronizing. —**Ant.** ungracious, unkind, impolite, unfavorable; dispassionate, cool, cruel, inclement.

gradual, adj. slow, by degrees, little by little, step by step, moderate, gentle. —**Ant.** sudden, precipitous, abrupt, immoderate. —**Syn. Study.** See SLOW.

grand, adj. 1. imposing, stately, august, majestic, dignified, exalted, elevated, eminent, princely, regal, kingly, royal, great, illustrious. 2. lofty, magnificent, great, large, palatial, splendid, brilliant, superb, glorious, sublime, noble, fine. 3. main, principal, chief. 4. important, distinctive, pretentious. 5. complete, comprehensive, inclusive, all-inclusive. —**Ant.** base, undignified; ignoble; secondary; unimportant; incomplete.

grandeur, n. magnificence, splendor, grandness, resplendence, magnitude, sweep, amplitude, scope, loftiness, nobility, stateliness, majesty. —**Ant.** insignificance, nullity.

grandiloquent, adj. lofty, pompous, bombastic, turgid, inflated, declamatory, rhetorical, oratorical, high-flown, pretentious, haughty, highfalutin. —**Ant.** base, servile, lowly.

grandiose, adj. ostentatious, pretentious, pompous, overblown, inflated, highfalutin, in poor taste, brassy; awesome, dramatic, formidable. —**Syn. Study.** GRANDIOSE, OSTENTATIOUS, PRETENTIOUS, POMPOUS refer to a conspicuous outward display designed to attract attention. GRANDIOSE may suggest impressiveness that is not objectionable; however, it most often implies exaggeration or affectation to the point of absurdity: *the grandiose sweep of an arch; a grandiose idea to take a limousine to work.* OSTENTATIOUS has the negative connotation of trying to impress or outdo others: *ostentatious furnishings.* PRETENTIOUS is always derogatory, suggesting falseness or exaggeration in claims made or implied: *pretentious language that masked the absence of real content.* POMPOUS implies a display of exaggerated dignity or importance: *a pompous bureaucrat.*

grant, v. 1. bestow, confer, award, bequeath, give. 2. agree or accede to, admit, allow, concede, accept, cede, yield. 3. transmit, convey, transfer. —n. 4. cession, concession, bequest, conveyance. —**Ant.** receive. —**Syn. Study.** See GIVE.

graphic, adj. 1. lifelike, vivid, picturesque, striking, telling. 2. diagrammatic, well-delineated, detailed. —**Syn. Study.** See FLAGRANT.

grasp, v. 1. seize, hold, clasp, grip, clutch, grab, catch. 2. lay hold of, seize upon, fasten on; concentrate on, comprehend, understand. —n. 3. grip, hold, clutches. 4. hold, possession, mastery. 5. reach, comprehension, compass, scope. —**Ant.** loose, loosen; misunderstand.

grateful, adj. 1. appreciative, thankful, obliged, indebted. 2. pleasing, agreeable, welcome, refreshing, pleasant, gratifying, satisfying, satisfactory. —**Ant.** ungrateful; unpleasant, disagreeable, unsatisfactory.

gratify, v. please, indulge, humor, satisfy. —**Ant.** displease, dissatisfy.

grave, n. 1. place of interment, tomb, sepulchre, pit, excavation.

—adj. 2. sober, solemn, serious, dignified, sedate, earnest, staid, thoughtful. 3. weighty, momentous, important, serious, consequential, critical. —**Ant.** undignified, thoughtless; unimportant, trivial, trifling. —**Syn. Study.** GRAVE, SOBER, SOLEMN refer to the condition of being serious in demeanor or appearance. GRAVE indicates a dignified seriousness due to heavy responsibilities or cares: *The jury looked grave while pondering the evidence.* SOBER implies a determined but sedate and restrained manner: *a wise and sober judge.* SOLEMN suggests an impressive and earnest seriousness marked by the absence of gaiety or mirth: *The minister's voice was solemn as he announced the text.*

great, adj. 1. immense, enormous, huge, gigantic, vast, ample, grand, large, big. 2. numerous, countless. 3. unusual, considerable, important, momentous, serious, weighty. 4. notable, remarkable, noteworthy. 5. distinguished, famous, famed, eminent, noted, prominent, celebrated, illustrious, grand, renowned. 6. consequential, important, vital, critical. 7. chief, principal, main, grand, leading. 8. noble, lofty, grand, exalted, elevated, dignified, majestic, august. 9. admirable, notable. —**Ant.** small; insignificant; paltry; infamous, notorious; trivial; secondary.

greed, n. desire, avidity, avarice, cupidity, covetousness, greediness, voracity, ravenousness, rapacity. —**Ant.** generosity.

greedy, adj. 1. grasping, rapacious, selfish, avaricious. 2. gluttonous, voracious, ravenous, starved, insatiable. 3. desirous, covetous, eager, anxious. —**Ant.** generous, unselfish. —**Syn. Study.** See AVARICIOUS.

greet, v. address, welcome, hail, accost, salute.

gremlin, See Syn. study at GOBLIN.

grief, n. suffering, distress, sorrow, regret, anguish, heartache, woe, misery, sadness, melancholy, moroseness. —**Ant.** joy, happiness, glee, delight.

grieve, v. 1. lament, weep, mourn, sorrow, suffer, bewail, bemoan. 2. distress, sadden, depress, agonize, break one's heart, pain. —**Ant.** delight in.

grievous, adj. 1. distressing, sad, sorrowful, painful, lamentable, regrettable. 2. deplorable, lamentable, calamitous, heinous, outrageous, flagrant, atrocious, flagitious, dreadful, gross, shameful, iniquitous. —**Ant.** delighted, happy, joyful; delightful, pleasant, favorable.

grim, adj. 1. stern, unrelenting, merciless, uncompromising, harsh, unyielding. 2. sinister, ghastly, repellent, frightful, horrible, dire, appalling, horrid, grisly, gruesome, hideous, dreadful. 3. severe, stern, harsh, hard, fierce, forbidding, ferocious, cruel, savage, ruthless. —**Ant.** merciful, lenient, sympathetic; wonderful, delightful, pleasant; amenable, genial, congenial, amiable.

grind, v. 1. smooth, sharpen. 2. bray, triturate, pulverize, powder, crush, comminute, pound. 3. oppress, torment, harass, persecute, plague, afflict, trouble. 4. grate, rub, abrade.

grit, n. 1. sand, gravel. 2. spirit, pluck, fortitude, courage, resolution.

groggy, adj. confused, muddled, dazed, muzzy, dopey, woozy, punchy, slap-happy. —**Ant.** clearheaded, alert.

gross, adj. 1. whole, entire, total, aggregate. 2. glaring, flagrant, outrageous, shameful, heinous, grievous. 3. coarse, indelicate, indecent, low, animal, sensual, vulgar, broad, lewd. 4. large, big, bulky, massive, great. 5. thick, dense, heavy. —n. 6. body, bulk, mass. —**Ant.** partial, incomplete; delicate, decent; small, dainty. —**Syn. Study.** See FLAGRANT.

grotesque, See Syn. study at FANTASTIC.

grouchy, adj. cantankerous, irritable, irascible, fractious, cross, crotchety, choleric, foul-tempered, mean-tempered, grumpy, ornery, testy, touchy, peevish, surly, vinegary. —**Ant.** even-tempered, gracious.

ground, n. 1. land, earth, soil, mold, loam, dirt. 2. (*often plural*) foundation, basis, base, premise, motive, reason, cause, consideration, factor, account. 3. (*plural*) lees, dregs, sediment, silt, deposit. —v. 4. found, fix, settle, establish, base, set. 5. instruct, train. —**Ant.** sky, heaven; embellishment.

grow, v. 1. increase, swell, enlarge,

dilate, greaten, expand, extend. 2. sprout, germinate; arise, originate. 3. swell, wax, extend, advance, improve. 4. raise, cultivate, produce. —**Ant.** decrease, shrink; wane, deteriorate.

growl, v. 1. snarl. 2. grumble, complain, mumble.

growth, n. 1. development, increase, augmentation, expansion. 2. product, outgrowth, result; produce. 3. (*pathology*) tumor, excrescence. 4. source, production. —**Ant.** failure, stagnation.

grudge, n. 1. malice, ill will, spite, resentment, bitterness, rancor, malevolence, enmity, hatred. —v. 2. suffer, yield, submit to. 3. begrudge, envy. —**Ant.** good will, amiability.

grudging, adj. reluctant, unenthusiastic, unwilling, begrudging, apathetic, indifferent, perfunctory, lukewarm, tepid, ungenerous, mean-spirited. —**Ant.** enthusiastic, generous.

grumble, See Syn. study at COMPLAIN.

guarantee, n. 1. guaranty, warrant, pledge, assurance, promise, surety, security. —v. 2. guaranty, secure, ensure, insure, warrant.

guard, v. 1. protect, keep safe, preserve, save, watch over, shield, defend, shelter. 2. hold, check, watch, be careful. —n. 3. protector, guardian, sentry, watchman, defender, sentinel. 4. convoy, escort. 5. defense, protection, shield, bulwark, security, aegis, safety. —**Ant.** attack, assault; ignore; danger.

guardian, n. 1. guard, protector, defender. 2. trustee, warden, keeper. —**Ant.** assailant.

guess, v. 1. conjecture, hazard, suppose, fancy, believe, imagine, think. 2. estimate, solve, answer, penetrate. —n. 3. notion, judgment, conclusion, conjecture, surmise, supposition. —**Ant.** know. —**Syn. Study.** GUESS, CONJECTURE, SURMISE imply attempting to form an opinion as to the probable. To GUESS is to risk an opinion regarding something one does not know about, or, wholly or partly by chance, to arrive at the correct answer to a question: *to guess the outcome of a game.* To CONJECTURE is to make inferences in the absence of sufficient evidence to establish certainty: *to conjecture the circumstances of the crime.* SURMISE implies making an intuitive conjecture that may or may not be correct: *to surmise the motives that led to the crime.*

guest, n. visitor, company. —**Ant.** host.

guide, v. 1. lead, pilot, steer, conduct, direct, show or point the way, escort, instruct, induce, influence, regulate, manage, govern, rule. —n. 2. pilot, steersman, helmsman, director, conductor. 3. mark, sign, signal, indication, key, clue. —**Ant.** follow.

guile, n. cunning, treachery, deceit, artifice, duplicity, deception, trickery, fraud, craft, artfulness. —**Ant.** ingenuousness. —**Syn. Study.** See DECEIT.

guileless, adj. artless, honest, sincere, open, candid, frank, truthful, ingenuous, naive, unsophisticated, simple-minded. —**Ant.** cunning, sly, deceitful, artful, treacherous.

guilt, n. guiltiness, culpability, criminality. —**Ant.** exoneration.

guiltless, adj. innocent, spotless, blameless, immaculate, pure, unsullied, unpolluted, untarnished. —**Ant.** culpable, guilty, sullied, tarnished.

guise, n. appearance, aspect, semblance, form, shape, fashion, mode, manner. —**Syn. Study.** See APPEARANCE.

guru, n. teacher, guide, instructor, tutor, coach, trainer, handler, preceptor, master, docent, expert. —**Ant.** student, acolyte, follower.

gush, v. pour, stream, spurt, flow, spout, flood.

gust, See Syn. study at WIND.

H

habit, n. 1. disposition, tendency, bent, wont. 2. custom, practice, way, usage, wont, manner. 3. garb, dress, rig, habiliment. —v. 4. dress, clothe, garb, array, attire, deck out, rig, equip. —**Syn. Study.** See CUSTOM.

habitat, n. home, locality, haunt, environment, turf, locale, site, neighborhood, precincts, range, territory, surroundings, environs, vicinity, stamping ground, home ground, milieu.

habitual, adj. confirmed, inveterate,

accustomed, customary, usual, common, regular, familiar, ordinary. —**Ant.** rare, unaccustomed, unusual, uncommon, irregular. —**Syn. Study.** See USUAL.

habituate, v. accustom, familiarize, acclimate, acclimatize, train, inure, harden, make used (to).

hack, v. 1. cut, notch, chop, hew, mangle. 2. let, hire, lease, rent. 3. hackney. —n. 4. cut, notch, gash. 5. jade, nag. —adj. 6. hired, hackney, mercenary. 7. hackneyed, trite, clichéd, overdone, old, used, worn out, commonplace, stale, stereotyped; old hat. —**Ant.** novel, new.

hackneyed, adj. trite, clichéd, stale, timeworn, overused, tired, well-worn, unoriginal, bromidic, platitudinous, commonplace, pedestrian, worn-out, banal, cornball, bathetic, stock, set, old-hat, warmed-over, moth-eaten, threadbare, corny. —**Ant.** original, inventive. —**Syn. Study.** See COMMONPLACE.

haggard, adj. wild-looking, careworn, gaunt, emaciated, drawn, hollow-eyed, meager, spare, worn, wasted. —**Ant.** hale, hearty, robust.

haggle, v. 1. bargain, chaffer, higgle, palter, negotiate. 2. wrangle, dispute, cavil, argue. 3. harass, annoy, vex, tease, worry, badger, bait, fret. 4. hack, mangle, chop, cut. —n. 5. haggling, wrangle, dispute, argument, disagreement.

hale, adj. 1. robust, healthy, vigorous, sound, strong, hearty. —v. 2. drag, haul, pull, tug, draw. —**Ant.** haggard, weak, feeble.

half-hearted, adj. unenthusiastic, indifferent, uninterested, cold, cool, perfunctory, curt, abrupt, discouraging. —**Ant.** enthusiastic, eager, encouraging.

hallowed, adj. sacred, consecrated, holy, blessed; honored, revered. —**Ant.** execrative, blasphemous. —**Syn. Study.** See HOLY.

hallucination, n. illusion, delusion, aberration, phantasm, vision. —**Ant.** reality.

halt, v. 1. hold, stop, cease, desist. 2. waver, hesitate. —**Ant.** continue, persist. —**Syn. Study.** See STOP.

hamlet, n. village, community, town, dorp.

hamper, v. 1. impede, hinder, hold back, encumber, prevent, obstruct, restrain, clog. —n. 2. basket; crate. —**Ant.** further, encourage. —**Syn. Study.** See PREVENT.

handsome, adj. 1. comely, fine, admirable, good-looking. 2. liberal, considerable, ample, large, generous, magnanimous. 3. gracious, generous. —**Ant.** ugly, unattractive; stingy, penurious, parsimonious. —**Syn. Study.** See BEAUTIFUL.

handy, adj. 1. convenient, useful, practical, functional, serviceable. 2. near, nearby, at hand, close, adjacent, convenient, close-by, near-at-hand, close-at-hand. 3. adept, dexterous, skilled, skillful, artful, adroit, deft, clever, proficient.

hang, v. 1. suspend, dangle. 2. execute, lynch. 3. drape, decorate, adorn, furnish. 4. depend, rely, rest; hold fast, cling, adhere. 5. be doubtful or undecided, waver, hesitate, demur, halt. 6. loiter, linger, hover, flot. 7. impend, be imminent.

hanker, See Syn. study at YEARN.

happen, v. come to pass, take place, occur, chance; befall, betide.

happiness, n. good fortune, pleasure, contentment, gladness, bliss, content, contentedness, beatitude, blessedness, delight, joy, enjoyment, gratification, satisfaction. —**Ant.** misery, dissatisfaction.

happy, adj. 1. joyous, joyful, glad, blithe, merry, cheerful, contented, gay, blissful, delighted, satisfied, pleased, gladdened. 2. favored, lucky, fortunate, propitious, advantageous, successful, prosperous. 3. appropriate, fitting, apt, felicitous, opportune, befitting, pertinent. —**Ant.** unhappy, sad, cheerless, melancholy; unlucky, luckless, unfortunate; inappropriate, inapt.

harangue, n. 1. address, speech, bombast. —v. 2. declaim, address. —**Syn. Study.** See SPEECH.

harass, v. trouble, harry, raid, molest, disturb, distress; plague, vex, worry, badger, pester, annoy, torment, torture.

harbinger, n. 1. forerunner, herald, precursor, announcer, messenger, outrider, evangel, evangelist, stormy petrel. —v. 2. announce, herald, presage, forerun, foreshow, preindicate, augur, foretell.

harbor, n. 1. haven, port. 2. shelter, refuge, asylum, protection, cover, sanctuary, retreat. —v. 3. shelter, protect, lodge. **4.** conceal, hide, secrete. **5.** entertain, indulge, foster, cherish. **—Syn. Study.** HARBOR, PORT, HAVEN refer to a shelter for ships. A HARBOR is a natural or an artificially constructed shelter and anchorage for ships: *a fine harbor on the eastern coast.* A PORT is a harbor viewed esp. with reference to its commercial activities and facilities: *a thriving port.* HAVEN is a literary word meaning refuge, although occasionally referring to a natural harbor that can be utilized by ships as a place of safety: *to seek a haven in a storm.* See also CHERISH.

hard, *adj.* **1.** solid, firm, inflexible, rigid, unyielding, resistant, resisting, adamantine, flinty, impenetrable, compact. **2.** difficult, toilsome, burdensome, wearisome, exhausting, laborious, arduous, onerous, fatiguing, wearying. **3.** difficult, complex, intricate, complicated, perplexing, tough, puzzling. **4.** vigorous, severe, violent, stormy, tempestuous; inclement. **5.** oppressive, harsh, rough, cruel, severe, unmerciful, grinding, unsparing, unrelenting. **6.** severe, harsh, stern, austere, strict, exacting, callous, unfeeling, unsympathetic, impassionate, insensible, unimpressible, insensitive, indifferent, unpitying, inflexible, relentless, unyielding, cruel, obdurate, adamant, hardhearted. **7.** undeniable, irrefutable, incontrovertible. **8.** unfriendly, unkind; harsh, unpleasant. **9.** unsympathetic, unsentimental, shrewd, hardheaded, callous. **10.** strong, spirituous, intoxicating. **—***adv.* **11.** energetically, vigorously, violently. **12.** earnestly, intently, incessantly. **13.** harshly, severely, gallingly, with difficulty. **14.** solidly, firmly. **—Ant.** soft; easy; fair; merciful; sympathetic; kind.

harden, *v.* **1.** solidify, indurate, ossify, petrify. **2.** strengthen, confirm, fortify, steel, brace, nerve, toughen, inure; habituate, accustom, season, train, discipline.

hardly, *adv.* **1.** barely, scarcely, nearly. **2.** harshly, severely, roughly, cruelly, unkindly, rigorously. **—Syn. Study.** HARDLY, BARELY, SCARCELY imply a narrow margin of sufficiency. HARDLY usu. emphasizes the difficulty or sacrifice involved: *We could hardly endure the winter.* BARELY implies no more than the minimum, as in performance or quantity: *We barely succeeded.* SCARCELY implies an even narrower margin, usu. below a satisfactory level: *He can scarcely read.*

hardship, *n.* trial, oppression, privation, need, austerity, trouble, affliction, burden, suffering, misfortune, grievance.

hardy, *adj.* **1.** vigorous, hearty, sturdy, hale, robust, stout, strong, sound, healthy. **2.** bold, daring, courageous, brave. **—Ant.** weak, feeble, unsound, unhealthy; cowardly, pusillanimous.

harm, *n.* **1.** injury, damage, hurt, mischief, detriment. **2.** wrong, evil, wickedness, sinfulness. **—***n.* **3.** injure, hurt, damage; maltreat, molest, abuse. **—Ant.** good.

harmful, *adj.* injurious, detrimental, hurtful, deleterious, pernicious, mischievous. **—Ant.** beneficial.

harmonious, *adj.* **1.** amicable, congenial, sympathetic. **2.** consonant, congruous, concordant, consistent, correspondent, symmetrical. **3.** melodious, tuneful, agreeable, concordant. **—Ant.** unsympathetic; discordant, incongruous, asymmetrical; cacophonous, noisy.

harmony, *n.* **1.** agreement, concord, unity, peace, amity, friendship, accord, unison. **2.** congruity, consonance, conformity, correspondence, consistency, congruence, fitness, suitability. **3.** melody, melodiousness, concord, euphony. **—Ant.** discord, disagreement; nonconformity, unfitness; cacophony, noise. **—Syn. Study.** See SYMMETRY.

harrowing, *adj.* trying, stressful, distressing, painful, agonizing, torturous, frightening, excruciating, harsh, hairy. **—Ant.** pleasant, relaxing.

harry, *v.* **1.** harass, torment, worry, molest, plague, trouble, vex, gall, fret, disturb, harrow, chafe, annoy, pester. **2.** ravage, devastate, plunder, strip, rob, pillage. **—Ant.** please, delight, enrapture.

harsh, *adj.* **1.** rough; ungentle, unpleasant, severe, austere, brusque, rough, hard, unfeeling, unkind, brutal, cruel, stern, acrimonious, bad-tempered, ill-natured, crabbed, morose. **2.** jarring, unaesthetic, inartistic, discordant, dissonant, unharmonious. **—Ant.** gentle,

---

pleasant, kind, good-natured; artistic, aesthetic, harmonious. **—Syn. Study.** See STERN.

haste, *n.* **1.** swiftness, celerity, alacrity, quickness, rapidity, dispatch, speed, expedition, promptitude. **2.** need, hurry, flurry, bustle, ado, precipitancy, precipitation. **—Ant.** sloth.

hasten, *v.* hurry, accelerate, urge, press, expedite, quicken, speed, precipitate, dispatch.

hasty, *adj.* **1.** speedy, quick, hurried, swift, rapid, fast, fleet, brisk. **2.** precipitate, rash, foolhardy, reckless, indiscreet, thoughtless, headlong, unthinking. **3.** quick-tempered, testy, touchy, irascible, petulant, waspish, fretful, fiery, pettish, excitable, irritable, peevish. **—Ant.** slow, deliberate; discreet, thoughtful; even-tempered, amiable.

hatch, *v.* **1.** incubate, breed, brood. **2.** contrive, devise, plan, plot, concoct, design, scheme, project. **3.** shade, line. **—***n.* **4.** brood. **5.** door, cover, deck, hatchway.

hate, *v.* **1.** dislike; detest, abhor, loathe, despise, execrate, abominate. **—***n.* **2.** hatred. **—Ant.** like, love. **—Syn. Study.** HATE, ABHOR, DETEST imply feeling intense dislike or aversion toward something. HATE, the simple and general word, suggests passionate dislike and a feeling of enmity: *to hate autocracy.* ABHOR expresses a deep-rooted horror and a sense of repugnance or complete rejection: *to abhor cruelty.* DETEST implies intense, even vehement, dislike and antipathy, besides a sense of disdain: *to detest a combination of ignorance and arrogance.*

hateful, *adj.* detestable, odious, abominable, execrable, loathsome, abhorrent, repugnant, invidious, obnoxious, offensive, disgusting, nauseating, revolting, vile, repulsive. **—Ant.** lovable, appealing, attractive, likable. **—Syn. Study.** HATEFUL, ODIOUS, OFFENSIVE, OBNOXIOUS refer to something that provokes strong dislike or aversion. HATEFUL implies causing dislike along with hostility and ill will: *a hateful task.* ODIOUS emphasizes a disgusting or repugnant quality: *odious crimes.* OFFENSIVE is a general term that stresses the resentment or displeasure aroused by something that is insulting or unpleasant: *an offensive remark; an offensive odor.* OBNOXIOUS implies causing annoyance or discomfort by objectionable qualities: *His constant bragging is obnoxious.*

hatred, *n.* aversion, animosity, hate, detestation, loathing, abomination, odium, horror, repugnance. **—Ant.** attraction, love, favor.

haughty, *adj.* disdainful, proud, arrogant, supercilious, snobbish, lordly, contemptuous. **—Ant.** humble, shy, self-effacing.

have, *v.* **1.** hold, occupy, possess, own, contain. **2.** get, receive, take, obtain, acquire, gain, secure, procure. **3.** experience, enjoy, suffer, undergo. **4.** permit, allow. **5.** assert, maintain, hold, aver, state, asseverate, testify.

haven, *n.* See Syn. study at HARBOR.

havoc, *n.* devastation, ruin, destruction, desolation, waste, damage.

hazard, *n.* **1.** danger, peril, jeopardy, risk. **2.** chance, hap, accident, luck, fortuity, fortuitousness. **3.** uncertainty, doubt. **—***v.* **4.** venture, offer. **5.** imperil, risk, endanger. **—Ant.** safety, security; certainty, surety. **—Syn. Study.** See DANGER.

haze, *n.* **1.** vapor, dust, mist, cloud, fog, smog. **2.** obscurity, dimness, cloud, vagueness. **—***v.* **3.** torment, torture, abuse, trick. **—Ant.** clearness, clarity.

head, *n.* **1.** command, authority. **2.** commander, director, chief, chieftain, leader, principal, commander in chief, master. **3.** top, summit, acme. **4.** culmination, crisis, conclusion. **5.** cape, headland, promontory, ness. **6.** source, origin, rise, beginning, headwaters. **7.** froth, foam. **—***adj.* **8.** front, leading, topmost, chief, principal, main, cardinal, foremost, first. **—***v.* **9.** lead, precede, direct, command, rule, govern. **10.** outdo, excel, surpass, beat.

headlong, *adj.* rushed, precipitate, precipitous, hasty, abrupt, hurried, impetuous, sudden, impulsive, reckless.

headstrong, *adj.* willful, stubborn, obstinate, intractable, self-willed, dogged, pigheaded, froward. **—Ant.** amenable, tractable, genial, agreeable. **—Syn. Study.** See WILLFUL.

heal, *v.* **1.** cure, remedy, restore. **2.** amend, settle, harmonize, compose,

---

soothe. **3.** cleanse, purify, purge, disinfect. **—Ant.** discompose; soil, pollute, infect.

healthful, See Syn. study at HEALTHY.

healthy, *adj.* **1.** healthful, hale, sound, hearty, well, robust, vigorous, strong. **2.** nutritious, nourishing, salubrious, salutary, hygienic, invigorating, bracing, wholesome. **—Ant.** unhealthy, ill, sick, weak; unwholesome, enervating. **—Syn. Study.** HEALTHY, HEALTHFUL, WHOLESOME refer to physical, mental, or moral health and well-being. HEALTHY most often applies to what possesses health, but may apply to what promotes health: *a healthy child; a healthy climate.* HEALTHFUL is usu. applied to something conducive to physical health: *a healthful diet.* WHOLESOME, connoting freshness and purity, applies to something that is physically or morally beneficial: *wholesome food; wholesome entertainment.*

heap, *n.* **1.** mass, stack, pile, accumulation, collection. **—***v.* **2.** pile or heap up, amass, accumulate. **3.** bestow, confer, cast.

hear, *v.* **1.** listen, perceive, attend. **2.** regard, heed, attend.

heat, *n.* **1.** warmth, caloricity, caloric, hotness. **2.** warmth, intensity, ardor, fervor, zeal. **3.** ardor, flush, fever, excitement, impetuosity, vehemence, violence. **—***v.* **4.** stimulate, warm, stir, animate, arouse, excite, rouse. **—Ant.** coolness; phlegm; cool, discourage.

heathen, *n.* **1.** gentile, pagan. **—***adj.* **2.** gentile, pagan, heathenish, irreligious, unenlightened, barbarous. **—Ant.** Christian. **—Syn. Study.** HEATHEN, PAGAN are both applied to peoples who are not Christian, Jewish, or Muslim; these terms may also refer to irreligious peoples. HEATHEN is often used of those whose religion is unfamiliar and therefore regarded as primitive, unenlightened, or uncivilized: *heathen idols; heathen rites.* PAGAN is most frequently used of the ancient Greeks and Romans who worshiped many deities: *a pagan civilization.*

heave, *v.* **1.** raise, lift, hoist, elevate. **2.** pant, exhale, breathe. **3.** vomit, retch. **4.** rise, swell, dilate, bulge, expand.

heavenly, *adj.* **1.** blissful, beautiful, divine, seraphic, cherubic, angelic, saintly, sainted, holy, beatific, blessed, beatified, glorified. **2.** celestial. **—Ant.** hellish, satanic, diabolical, devilish.

heavy, *adj.* **1.** weighty, ponderous, massive. **2.** burdensome, harsh, oppressive, depressing, onerous, distressing, severe, grievous, cumbersome. **3.** broad, thick, coarse, blunt. **4.** serious, intense, momentous, weighty, important, pithy, concentrated. **5.** trying, difficult. **6.** depressed, serious, grave, sorrowful, gloomy, mournful, melancholy, morose, morbid, dejected, sad, disconsolate, crushed, despondent, heavy-hearted, downcast, crestfallen, down-hearted. **7.** overcast, cloudy, lowering, oppressive, gloomy. **8.** clumsy, slow. **9.** ponderous, dull, tedious, tiresome, wearisome, burdensome, boring, lifeless. **10.** thick, unleavened, dense, concentrated. **—Ant.** light.

hectic, *adj.* **1.** frantic, rushed, overactive, bustling, furious, frenzied, frenetic, perfervid, hysterical, hyper. **2.** feverish, fevered, febrile, hot, heated, burning, flushed. **—Ant.** calm, cool.

heed, *v.* **1.** pay or give attention to, consider, regard, notice, mark, observe, obey. **—***n.* **2.** attention, notice, observation, consideration, care, caution, heedfulness, watchfulness, vigilance. **—Ant.** disregard, ignore.

height, *n.* **1.** altitude, stature, elevation, tallness. **2.** hill, prominence, mountain. **3.** top, peak, pinnacle, apex, eminence, acme, summit, zenith, culmination. **—Ant.** depth, abyss. **—Syn. Study.** HEIGHT, ALTITUDE, ELEVATION refer to distance above a level. HEIGHT denotes extent upward (as from foot to head) as well as any measurable distance above a given level: *The tree grew to a height of ten feet. They looked down from a great height.* ALTITUDE usually refers to the distance above level, commonly mean sea level: *The airplane flew at an altitude of 30,000 feet.* ELEVATION implies a distance to which something has been raised or uplifted above a level: *a hill's elevation above the surrounding country.*

heighten, See Syn. study at ELEVATE.

heinous, *adj.* hateful, odious, repre-

---

hensible, grave, wicked, infamous, flagrant, flagitious, atrocious, villainous, nefarious. **—Ant.** good, beneficial.

hell, *n.* Gehenna, Tartarus, inferno, Abaddon, Avernus, Hades, Erebus, pandemonium, abyss, limbo. **—Ant.** heaven.

help, *v.* **1.** cooperate, aid, assist, encourage, befriend, support, second, uphold, back, abet, succor, save. **2.** further, facilitate, promote, ease, foster. **3.** relieve, ameliorate, alleviate, remedy, cure, heal, restore, improve, better. **4.** refrain from, avoid, forbear. **—***n.* **5.** support, backing, aid, assistance, relief, succor. **6.** helper, handyman, assistant. **—Ant.** discourage, attack. **—Syn. Study.** HELP, AID, ASSIST, SUCCOR agree in the idea of furnishing someone with something that is needed. HELP implies furnishing anything that furthers one's efforts or satisfies one's needs: *I helped her plan the party.* AID and ASSIST, somewhat more formal, imply a furthering or seconding of another's efforts. AID suggests an active helping; ASSIST suggests less need and less help: *to aid the poor; to assist a teacher in the classroom.* To succor, still more formal and literary, is to give timely help and relief to someone in difficulty or distress: *Succor him in his hour of need.*

helper, *n.* aid, assistant, supporter, auxiliary, ally, colleague, partner.

helpful, *adj.* useful, convenient, beneficial, advantageous, profitable. **—Ant.** useless, inconvenient, disadvantageous, uncooperative.

herd, *n.* **1.** drove, flock, clutch, crowd. **—***v.* **2.** flock, assemble, associate, keep company.

hereditary, See Syn. study at INNATE.

heritage, *n.* inheritance, estate, patrimony.

heroic, *adj.* intrepid, dauntless, gallant, valorous, brave, courageous, bold, daring, fearless; epic. **—Ant.** cowardly, fearful.

heroism, *n.* intrepidity, valor, prowess, gallantry, bravery, courage, daring, fortitude, boldness. **—Ant.** cowardice.

hesitate, *v.* **1.** waver, vacillate, falter. **2.** demur, delay, pause, wait. **—Ant.** resolve, decide.

hesitation, *n.* **1.** hesitancy, indecision, vacillation, irresolution, delay, uncertainty, doubt. **2.** halting, stammering, faltering. **—Ant.** resolution, certainty.

heterogeneous, *adj.* mixed, assorted, miscellaneous, motley, varied, multifarious, jumbled, scrambled. **—Ant.** uniform, homogeneous.

hew, *v.* **1.** cut, chop, hack. **2.** make, shape, fashion, form. **3.** sever, cut down, fell.

hide, *v.* **1.** conceal, secrete, screen, mask, cloak, veil, shroud, cover, disguise, withhold, suppress. **—***n.* **2.** skin, pelt, rawhide. **—Ant.** open, reveal. **—Syn. Study.** HIDE, CONCEAL, SECRETE mean to keep something from being seen or discovered. HIDE is the general word: *A rock hid them from view.* CONCEAL, somewhat more formal, usually means to intentionally cover up something: *He concealed the evidence of the crime.* SECRETE means to put away carefully, in order to keep secret: *The spy secreted the important papers.*

hideous, *adj.* horrible, frightful, ugly, grisly, grim, revolting, repellent, repulsive, detestable, odious, monstrous, dreadful, appalling, terrifying, terrible, ghastly, macabre, shocking. **—Ant.** beautiful, lovely, attractive.

high, *adj.* **1.** lofty, tall, elevated, towering, skyscraping. **2.** intensified, energetic, intense, strong. **3.** expensive, costly, dear, high-priced. **4.** exalted, elevated, eminent, prominent, preeminent, distinguished. **5.** shrill, sharp, acute, high-pitched, strident. **6.** chief, main, principal, head. **7.** consequential, important, grave, serious, capital, extreme. **8.** lofty, haughty, arrogant, snobbish, proud, lordly, supercilious. **9.** elated, merry, hilarious, happy. **10.** remote, primeval, early, antediluvian, prehistoric; northerly, arctic, southerly, polar. **—Ant.** low.

highminded, See Syn. study at NOBLE.

hilarity, *n.* glee, mirth, merriment, levity, jollity, hilariousness, hysterics, joy, jocularity.

hill, *n.* elevation, prominence, eminence, mound, monticule, knoll, hillock, foothill. **—Ant.** valley, dale, glen, hollow, depth.

---

hind, See Syn. study at BACK.

hinder, *v.* **1.** interrupt, check, retard, impede, encumber, delay, hamper, obstruct, trammel. **2.** block, thwart, prevent, obstruct. **—Ant.** encourage, disencumber. **—Syn. Study.** See PREVENT.

hindrance, *n.* **1.** impeding, stopping, stoppage, estoppage, preventing. **2.** impediment, deterrent, hitch, encumbrance, obstruction, check, restraint, hobble, obstacle. **—Ant.** help, aid, support. **—Syn. Study.** See OBSTACLE.

hint, *n.* **1.** suggestion, implication, intimation, allusion, insinuation, innuendo, memorandum, reminder, inkling. **—***v.* **2.** imply, intimate, insinuate, suggest, mention. **—Syn. Study.** HINT, INTIMATE, INSINUATE, SUGGEST denote the conveying of an idea to the mind indirectly or without full or explicit statement. To HINT is to convey an idea covertly or indirectly, but in a way that can be understood: *She hinted that she would like a bicycle for her birthday.* To INTIMATE is to give a barely perceptible hint, often with the purpose of influencing action: *He intimated that a conciliation was possible.* To INSINUATE is to hint artfully, often at what one would not dare to say directly: *Someone insinuated that the defendant was guilty.* SUGGEST denotes recalling something to the mind or starting a new train of thought by means of association of ideas: *Her restlessness suggested that she wanted to leave.*

hire, *v.* **1.** engage, employ; let, lease, rent, charter. **2.** bribe, reward. **—***n.* **3.** rent, rental; pay, stipend, salary, wages, remuneration. **—Syn. Study.** HIRE, CHARTER, RENT refer to paying money for the use of something. HIRE is most commonly applied to paying money for a person's services, but is also used in reference to paying for the temporary use of something: *to hire a gardener; to hire a convention hall.* CHARTER is applied to hiring a vehicle for the exclusive use of a group or individual: *to charter a boat.* RENT, although used in the above senses, is most often applied to paying a set sum at regular intervals for the use of a dwelling or other property: *to rent an apartment.*

history, *n.* record, chronicle, account, annals, story, relation, narrative.

hit, *v.* **1.** strike. **2.** reach, attain, gain, win, accomplish, achieve. **3.** touch, suit, fit, befit, affect. **4.** find, come upon, meet with, discover, happen upon. **5.** collide, strike, clash. **6.** assail. **—***n.* **7.** blow, stroke; success. **—Syn. Study.** See BEAT.

hitch, *v.* **1.** make fast, fasten, connect, hook, tether, attach, tie, unite, harness, yoke. **—***n.* **2.** halt, obstruction, hindrance, catch, impediment. **—Ant.** loose, loosen, untie.

hoarse, *adj.* husky, throaty, guttural, gruff, harsh, grating, raucous, rough.

hobble, *v.* **1.** restrain, hamper, hinder, shackle, fetter, encumber, entrammel, trammel, handicap. **2.** limp, halt, totter, stagger. **—Ant.** enable, empower.

hoist, *v.* **1.** raise, elevate, lift, heave. **—***n.* **2.** derrick, crane, elevator, lift. **—Ant.** lower.

hold, *v.* **1.** have, keep, retain, possess, occupy. **2.** bear, sustain, hold up, support, maintain, keep (up), continue, carry on. **3.** engage in, observe, celebrate, preside over, carry on, pursue. **4.** hinder, restrain, keep back, deactivate, confine, detain. **5.** occupy, possess, own. **6.** contain, admit. **7.** think, believe, embrace, espouse, entertain, have, regard, consider, esteem, judge, deem. **8.** continue, persist, last, endure, remain. **9.** adhere, cling, remain, stick. **—***n.* **10.** grasp, grip. **11.** control, influence. **12.** prison, keep, tower, cell, dungeon, deep. **—Syn. Study.** See CONTAIN.

hole, *n.* **1.** aperture, opening, cavity, excavation, pit, hollow, concavity. **2.** burrow, lair, den, retreat, cave. **3.** hovel, den, cot.

holy, *adj.* **1.** blessed, sacred, consecrated, hallowed, dedicated. **2.** saintly, godly, divine, pious, devout, spiritual, pure. **—Ant.** unholy, desecrated, impious, piacular, sinful, impure, corrupt. **—Syn. Study.** HOLY, SACRED, HALLOWED refer to something that is the object of worship or veneration. HOLY refers to the divine, that which has its sanctity directly from God or is connected with Him: *Remember the Sabbath day to keep it holy.* Something that is SACRED is usually dedicated to a religious purpose by human authority: *a sacred shrine.* Something that is HALLOWED has been made holy by being worshiped or venerated: *The church graveyard is hallowed ground.*

homage, *n.* **1.** respect, reverence, deference, obeisance, honor, tribute. **2.** fealty, allegiance, faithfulness, fidelity, loyalty, devotion. **3.** devotion, worship, adoration. —**Ant.** disrespect, irreverence, dishonor; faithlessness, disloyalty.

home, *n.* **1.** house, apartment, residence, household, abode, dwelling, domicile, habitation. **2.** refuge, retreat, institution, asylum. **3.** hearth, fireside, family; rightful place. —**Syn. Study.** See HOUSE.

homely, *adj.* plain, simple, unpretentious, unattractive, coarse, inelegant, uncomely, ugly. —**Ant.** beautiful.

homograph, See Syn. study at HOMONYM.

homonym, *n.* homophone, homograph —**Syn. Study.** HOMONYM, HOMOPHONE, and HOMOGRAPH designate words that are identical to other words in spelling or pronunciation, or both, while differing from them in meaning and usu. in origin. HOMOPHONES are words that sound alike, whether or not they are spelled differently. The words *pear* "fruit," *pare* "cut off," and *pair* "two of a kind" are HOMOPHONES that are different in spelling; *bear* "carry; support" and *bear* "animal" are HOMOPHONES that are spelled alike. HOMOGRAPHS are words that are spelled identically but may or may not share a pronunciation. *Spruce* "tree" and *spruce* "neat" are HOMOGRAPHS, but so are *row* (rō) "line" and *row* (rou) "fight" as well as *sewer* (sōō′ər) "conduit for waste" and *sewer* (sō′ər) "person who sews." HOMONYMS are, in the strictest sense, both HOMOPHONES and HOMOGRAPHS, alike in spelling *and* pronunciation, as the two forms *bear*. HOMONYM, however, is used more frequently than HOMOPHONE, a technical term, when referring to words with the same pronunciation without regard to spelling. HOMONYM is also used as a synonym of HOMOGRAPH. Thus, it has taken on a broader scope than either of the other two terms and is often the term of choice in a nontechnical context.

homophone, See Syn. study at HOMONYM.

honest, *adj.* **1.** honorable, upright, fair, just, incorruptible, trusty, trustworthy, truthful, virtuous, moral. **2.** open, sincere, candid, straightforward, frank, unreserved, ingenuous. **3.** genuine, pure, unadulterated. **4.** chaste, virtuous, pure, virginal, decent. —**Ant.** dishonest; corrupt, disingenuous, untrustworthy, secretive; false, counterfeit; impure, venal, indecent.

honesty, *n.* **1.** uprightness, probity, integrity, justice, fairness, rectitude, equity, honor. **2.** truthfulness, sincerity, candor, frankness, truth, veracity. —**Ant.** dishonesty, inequity; deceit, insincerity. —**Syn. Study.** See HONOR.

honor, *n.* **1.** esteem, fame, glory, repute, reputation, credit. **2.** credit, distinction, dignity. **3.** respect, deference, homage, reverence, veneration, consideration, distinction. **4.** privilege, favor. **5.** character, principle, probity, uprightness, honesty, integrity, nobleness. **6.** purity, chastity, virginity. —*v.* **7.** revere, esteem, venerate, respect, reverence; adore, worship, hallow. —**Ant.** dishonor, disrepute, discredit; indignity; disfavor; indecency; execrate, abominate. —**Syn. Study.** HONOR, HONESTY, INTEGRITY, SINCERITY refer to the highest moral principles. HONOR denotes a fine sense of, and a strict conformity to, what is considered morally right or due: *The soldier conducted himself with honor.* HONESTY denotes moral virtue and particularly the absence of deceit or fraud: *known for her honesty in business dealings.* INTEGRITY indicates a soundness of moral principle that no power or influence can impair: *a judge of unquestioned integrity.* SINCERITY particularly implies the absence of deceit and a strong adherence to the truth: *Your sincerity was evident in every word.*

honorable, *adj.* **1.** upright, honest, noble, highminded, just, fair, trusty, trustworthy, true, virtuous. **2.** dignified, distinguished, noble, illustrious, great. **3.** creditable, reputable, estimable, right, proper, equitable. —**Ant.** ignoble, untrustworthy, corrupt; undignified; disreputable.

hope, *n.* **1.** expectation, expectancy, longing, desire. **2.** confidence, trust, reliance, faith. —*v.* **3.** trust, expect. —**Ant.** hopelessness.

hopeful, *adj.* expectant, sanguine, optimistic, confident. —**Ant.** hopeless.

hopeless, *adj.* **1.** desperate, despairing, despondent, forlorn, disconsolate. **2.** irremediable, remediless, incurable. —**Ant.** hopeful.

horrendous, *adj.* terrible, overwhelming, frightful, fearful, horrific, dreadful, ghastly, terrifying, stupefying, dire, atrocious.

horrible, *adj.* **1.** horrendous, terrible, horrid, dreadful, awful, appalling, frightful, hideous, grim, ghastly, shocking, revolting, repulsive, repellent, dire, formidable, horrifying, harrowing. **2.** unpleasant, deplorable, shocking, abominable, odious. —**Ant.** attractive, delightful, beautiful; pleasant.

horror, *n.* **1.** fear, abhorrence, terror, dread, dismay, consternation, panic, alarm. **2.** aversion, repugnance, loathing, antipathy, detestation, hatred, abomination. —**Ant.** calm, serenity; attraction, delight, love.

hospital, *n.* retreat, sanatorium, asylum, sanitarium, clinic.

hostile, *adj.* opposed, adverse, averse, unfriendly, inimical, antagonistic, contrary, warlike, oppugnant, repugnant. —**Ant.** friendly, amiable, amicable.

hostility, *n.* **1.** enmity, antagonism, animosity, animus, ill will, unfriendliness, opposition, hatred. **2.** (*plural*) war, warfare, fighting, conflict. —**Ant.** friendliness, good will, love; peace, truce.

hot, *adj.* **1.** heated, torrid, sultry, burning, fiery. **2.** pungent, piquant, sharp, acrid, spicy, peppery, biting, blistering. **3.** ardent, fervent, fervid, angry, furious, vehement, intense, excited, excitable, irascible, animated, violent, passionate, impetuous. —**Ant.** cold.

hotel, *n.* hostelry, hostel, inn, house, guest house, motel, tavern.

hotheaded, *adj.* reckless, rash, incautious, headstrong, impetuous, emotional, hot-tempered, passionate, fiery. —**Ant.** cool, serene, phlegmatic.

house, *n.* **1.** domicile, dwelling, residence, home, household. **2.** firm, company, partnership, business, establishment. —*v.* **3.** lodge, harbor, shelter, reside, dwell. —**Syn. Study.** HOUSE, HOME, RESIDENCE, DWELLING are terms applied to a place in which people live. HOUSE is generally applied to a structure built for one or two families or social units: *a ranch house in the suburbs.* HOME may be used of an apartment or a private house; it retains connotations of domestic comfort and family ties: *Their home is full of charm and character.* RESIDENCE is characteristic of formal usage and often implies spaciousness and elegance: *the private residence of the prime minister.* DWELLING is a general and neutral word (*a houseboat is a floating dwelling*) and therefore commonly used in legal, scientific, and other technical contexts, as in a lease or in the phrases *multiple dwelling, single-family dwelling.*

household, *n.* **1.** family, ménage, people, brood, folks, occupants, dwellers, home, homestead, hearth, fireside, hearth and home. —*adj.* **2.** domestic, family, home, domiciliary, residential. **3.** simple, ordinary, common, commonplace, plain, prosaic, everyday, garden-variety, homespun, plain-Jane. **4.** familiar, well-known, public, famous, unmistakable, notorious.

hubbub, *n.* noise, tumult, uproar, clamor, din, racket, disorder, confusion, disturbance, riot. —**Ant.** serenity, calm. —**Syn. Study.** See NOISE.

huge, *adj.* large, extensive, mammoth, vast, gigantic, colossal, stupendous, bulky, enormous, immense, tremendous, Cyclopean. —**Ant.** tiny, small, infinitesimal, microscopic. —**Syn. Study.** HUGE, ENORMOUS, TREMENDOUS, IMMENSE imply great magnitude. HUGE, when used of concrete objects, usually adds the idea of massiveness, bulkiness, or even lack of shape: *a huge mass of rock.* ENORMOUS applies to what exceeds a norm or standard in extent, magnitude, or degree: *an enormous iceberg.* TREMENDOUS suggests something so large as to be astonishing or to inspire awe: *a tremendous amount of equipment.* IMMENSE, literally not measurable, is particularly applicable to what is exceedingly large, without reference to a standard: *immense buildings.* All of these terms are used figuratively: *a huge success; enor-*

mous curiosity; tremendous effort; immense joy.

humane, *adj.* **1.** merciful, kind, kindly, kindhearted, tender, human, benevolent, sympathetic, compassionate, gentle, accommodating, benignant, charitable. **2.** refining, polite, cultivating, elevating, humanizing, spiritual. —**Ant.** inhumane, cruel, ruthless, merciless; boorish, degrading.

humble, *adj.* **1.** low, lowly, unassuming, plain, common, poor, meek, modest, submissive, unpretending, unpretentious. **2.** respectful, polite, courteous, courtly. —*v.* **3.** lower, abase, debase, degrade, humiliate, reduce, mortify, shame, subdue, abash, crush, break. —**Ant.** haughty, immodest, snobbish, conceited, pretentious; impolite, discourteous; raise, elevate. —**Syn. Study.** HUMBLE, DEGRADE, HUMILIATE suggest a lowering in self-respect or in the estimation of others. HUMBLE most often refers to a lowering of pride or arrogance, but may refer to a lessening of power or importance: *humbled by failure; to humble an enemy.* DEGRADE literally means to demote in rank or standing, but commonly refers to a bringing into dishonor or contempt: *You degrade yourself by cheating.* To HUMILIATE is to make another feel inadequate or unworthy, esp. in a public setting: *humiliated by criticism.*

humbug, *n.* **1.** trick, hoax, fraud, imposture, deception, imposition. **2.** falseness, deception, sham, pretense, hypocrisy, charlatanism. **3.** cheat, impostor, swindler, charlatan, pretender, confidence man, deceiver, quack. —*v.* **4.** impose upon, delude, deceive, cheat, swindle, trick, fool, dupe.

humid, *adj.* damp, dank, wet, moist. —**Ant.** dry.

humiliate, *v.* mortify, degrade, debase, dishonor, disgrace, abash, shame, humble. —**Ant.** honor, elevate, exalt. —**Syn. Study.** See HUMBLE.

humiliation, *n.* mortification, shame, abasement, degradation, humbling, dishonoring. —**Ant.** honor, elevation. —**Syn. Study.** See SHAME.

humility, *n.* lowliness, meekness, humbleness, submissiveness. —**Ant.** haughtiness.

humongous, *adj.* **1.** huge, bulky, giant, jumbo, king-size. **2.** remarkable, amazing, outstanding, awesome.

humor, *n.* **1.** wit, fun, facetiousness, pleasantry. **2.** disposition, tendency, temperament, mood; whim, caprice, fancy, vagary. —*v.* **3.** indulge, gratify. —**Syn. Study.** HUMOR, WIT refer to an ability to perceive and express a sense of the clever or amusing. HUMOR consists principally in the recognition and expression of incongruities or peculiarities present in a situation or character. It is frequently used to illustrate some fundamental absurdity in human nature or conduct, and is generally thought of as a kindly trait: *a genial and mellow type of humor.* WIT is a purely intellectual, often spontaneous, manifestation of cleverness and quickness in discovering analogies between things really unlike, and expressing them in brief, diverting, and often sharp observations or remarks: *biting wit.* See also SPOIL.

humorous, *adj.* amusing, funny, jocose, jocular, droll, comic, comical, witty, facetious, waggish, sportive, ludicrous, laughable. —**Ant.** serious, sad, melancholy.

hunch, *n.* feeling, impression, presentiment, suspicion, premonition, intimation, gut sense, instinct, foreboding, funny feeling.

hungry, *adj.* ravenous, famishing, famished, starved, starving. —**Ant.** sated.

hunt, *v.* **1.** chase, pursue, track. **2.** search for, seek, scour. —*n.* **3.** chase, pursuit, hunting; search.

hurly-burly, *n.* commotion, activity, busyness, excitement, whirl, hurry, hurry-scurry, ferment, tumult, turmoil, uproar, agitation, frenzy. —**Ant.** calm, torpor.

hurry, *v.* **1.** rush, haste, hasten, be quick, move swiftly *or* quickly. **2.** hasten, urge, forward, accelerate, quicken, expedite, hustle, dispatch. —*n.* **3.** bustle, haste, dispatch, celerity, speed, quickness, alacrity, promptitude, expedition. **4.** bustle, ado, precipitation, flurry, flutter, confusion, perturbation. —**Ant.** delay, slow.

hurt, *v.* **1.** injure, harm, damage, mar, impair. **2.** pain, ache, grieve, afflict, wound. —*n.* **3.** injury, harm,

damage, detriment, disadvantage; bruise, wound.

hut, *n.* cottage, cot, cabin, shed, hovel.

hybrid, *n.* half-breed, mongrel, mutt.

hypocrite, *n.* deceiver, pretender, dissembler, pharisee.

hypocritical, *adj.* sanctimonious, pharisaical, Pecksniffian; insincere, deceiving, dissembling, pretending, false, hollow, empty, deceptive, misleading, deceitful. —**Ant.** honest, direct, forthright, sincere.

hypothesis, See Syn. study at THEORY.

I

icon, *n.* picture, image, symbol, idol, representation, sign.

iconoclast, *n.* unbeliever, disbeliever, doubter, questioner, challenger, heretic, nonconformist. —**Ant.** believer, supporter.

idea, *n.* **1.** thought, conception, notion; impression, apprehension, fancy. **2.** opinion, view, belief, sentiment, judgment, supposition. **3.** intention, plan, object, objective, aim. —**Syn. Study.** IDEA, THOUGHT, CONCEPTION, NOTION refer to a product of mental activity. IDEA refers to a mental representation that is the product of understanding or creative imagination: *She had an excellent idea for the party.* THOUGHT emphasizes the intellectual processes of reasoning, contemplating, reflecting, or recollecting: *I welcomed his thoughts on the subject.* CONCEPTION suggests imaginative, creative, and somewhat intricate mental activity: *The architect's conception of the building was a glass skyscraper.* NOTION suggests a fleeting, vague, or imperfect thought: *I had only a bare notion of how to proceed.*

ideal, *n.* **1.** example, model, conception, epitome, standard. **2.** aim, object, intention, objective. —*adj.* **3.** perfect, consummate, complete. **4.** unreal, unpractical, impractical, imaginary, visionary, fanciful, fantastic, illusory, chimerical.

identical, *adj.* same, alike, twin, indistinguishable, exact, equal, selfsame, undifferentiated, duplicated, reduplicated, clonal, cloned, one and the same, same-old same-old. —**Ant.** unique, nonpareil.

ideology, *n.* philosophy, belief, belief system, credo, creed, ethos, ethic, view, outlook, faith, religion, school, cult, weltanschauung. —**Ant.** nihilism.

idiosyncrasy, *n.* mannerism, quirk, tic, trait, habit, trick, peculiarity, characteristic, attribute, property, mark, hallmark, token, singularity, trademark, affectation. —**Syn. Study.** See ECCENTRICITY.

idiotic, *adj.* foolish, senseless, halfwitted, stupid, fatuous, imbecilic. —**Ant.** intelligent, sensible.

idle, *adj.* **1.** unemployed, unoccupied, inactive. **2.** indolent, slothful, lazy, sluggish. **3.** worthless, unimportant, trivial, trifling, insignificant, useless, fruitless, vain, ineffective, unavailing, ineffectual, abortive, baseless, groundless. **4.** frivolous, vain, wasteful. —*v.* **5.** waste, fritter away, idle away, loiter. —**Ant.** employed, occupied; active, energetic; worthy, important; thrifty. —**Syn. Study.** IDLE, INDOLENT, LAZY, SLOTHFUL apply to a person who is not active. IDLE means to be inactive or not working at a job; it is not necessarily derogatory: *pleasantly idle on a vacation.* INDOLENT means naturally disposed to avoid exertion: *an indolent and contented fisherman.* LAZY means averse to exertion or work, and esp. to continued application; the word is usually derogatory: *too lazy to earn a living.* SLOTHFUL denotes a reprehensible unwillingness to do one's share; it describes a person who is slow-moving and lacking in energy: *The heat made the workers slothful.* See also LOITER.

idol, *n.* **1.** image, icon, symbol, statue, false god, pagan deity. **2.** favorite, fair-haired boy, darling, pet. **3.** figment, delusion, illusion.

if, *conj.* **1.** in case, provided, providing, granting, supposing, even though, though; whether, whether or not. —*n.* **2.** condition, supposition.

iffy, *adj.* uncertain, unsure, doubtful, problematic, chancy, unsettled, ambiguous, conjectural, speculative, unpredictable, incalculable, unforeseeable, dicey. —**Ant.** certain, sure.

ignite, *v.* kindle, fire, set fire to, set

on fire. —**Ant.** quench. —**Syn. Study.** See KINDLE.

ignoble, *adj.* **1.** mean, base, ignominious, degraded, dishonorable, contemptible, vulgar, low, peasant. **2.** inferior, base, mean, insignificant. **3.** lowly, humble, obscure, plebeian, contemptible. —**Ant.** noble, honorable; superior, significant; haughty.

ignominious, *adj.* discreditable, humiliating, degrading, disgraceful, dishonorable, shameful, infamous, disreputable, opprobrious, despicable, scandalous, contemptible. —**Ant.** creditable, honorable, reputable.

ignominy, *n.* disgrace, dishonor, disrepute, contempt, discredit, shame, infamy, obloquy, opprobrium, scandal, odium, abasement. —**Ant.** credit, honor, repute, fame, distinction. —**Syn. Study.** See DISGRACE.

ignorant, *adj.* illiterate, unlettered, uneducated, unlearned, uninstructed, untutored, untaught, unenlightened, nescient. —**Ant.** literate, lettered, educated. —**Syn. Study.** IGNORANT, ILLITERATE, UNEDUCATED mean lacking in knowledge or training. IGNORANT may mean knowing little or nothing, or it may mean uninformed about a particular subject: *An ignorant person can be dangerous. I confess I'm ignorant of higher mathematics.* ILLITERATE most often means unable to read or write; however, it sometimes means not well-read or not well versed in literature: *classes for illiterate soldiers; an illiterate mathematician.* UNEDUCATED particularly refers to lack of schooling: *an intelligent but uneducated clerk.*

ignore, *v.* overlook, slight, disregard, neglect. —**Ant.** notice, note, regard, mark.

ill, *adj.* **1.** unwell, sick, indisposed, unhealthy, ailing, diseased, afflicted. **2.** evil, wicked, bad, wrong, iniquitous, naughty. **3.** objectionable, unsatisfactory, poor, faulty. **4.** hostile, unkindly, unkind, unfavorable, adverse. —*n.* **5.** evil, wickedness, depravity, badness. **6.** harm, injury, hurt, pain, affliction, misery, trouble, misfortune, calamity. **7.** disease, ailment, illness, affliction. —*adv.* **8.** illy, wickedly, badly. **9.** poorly, unsatisfactorily. **10.** unfavorably, unfortunately. **11.** faultily, improperly. —**Ant.** well, hale, healthy; good; satisfactory; favorably, properly. —**Syn. Study.** ILL, SICK being in bad health, not being well. ILL is the more formal word. In the U.S. the two words are used practically interchangeably except that SICK is always used when the word modifies the following noun: *He looks sick* (*ill*); *a sick person.* In England, SICK is not interchangeable with ILL, but usu. has the connotation of nauseous: *She got sick and threw up.* SICK, however, is used before nouns just as in the U.S.: *a sick man.*

illegal, *adj.* unauthorized, unlawful, illegitimate, illicit, unlicensed. —**Ant.** legal, licit, authorized. —**Syn. Study.** ILLEGAL, UNLAWFUL, ILLICIT, CRIMINAL describe actions not in accord with law. ILLEGAL refers to violation of statutes or, in games, codified rules: *an illegal seizure of property; an illegal block in football.* UNLAWFUL is a broader term that may refer to lack of conformity with any set of laws or precepts, whether natural, moral, or traditional: *an unlawful transaction.* ILLICIT most often applies to matters regulated by law, with emphasis on the way things are carried out: *the illicit sale of narcotics.* CRIMINAL refers to violation of a public law that is punishable by a fine or imprisonment: *Robbery is a criminal act.*

illicit, See Syn. study at ILLEGAL.

illiterate, See Syn. study at IGNORANT.

ill-mannered, *adj.* impolite, uncivil, discourteous, uncourtly, rude, coarse, uncouth, unpolished, crude, rough, ill-bred.

illusion, *n.* delusion, hallucination, deception, fantasy, chimera. —**Ant.** fact, reality.

illusory, *adj.* deceptive, misleading, unreal, fancied, fanciful, visionary, imaginary, misleading, delusional, chimerical. —**Ant.** real, concrete.

illustration, *n.* comparison, example, case, elucidation, explanation, explication.

image, *n.* **1.** icon, idol, representation, statue. **2.** reflection, likeness, effigy, figure, representation. **3.** idea, conception, notion, mental picture. **4.** form, appearance, semblance. **5.** counterpart, facsimile, copy. —*v.* **6.** imagine, conceive. —**Ant.** original.

imagery, *n.* picture, pictures, pictorialization, illustration, visualization, iconography, representation, portrayal, depiction, rendering, rendition.

imaginary, adj. fanciful, unreal, visionary, baseless, chimerical, shadowy, fancied, illusory, imagined. —**Ant.** real.

imagine, v. conceive, image, picture, conceive of, realize, think, believe, fancy, assume, suppose, guess, conjecture, hypothesize.

imbibe, v. drink, absorb, swallow, take in, receive. —**Syn. Study.** See DRINK.

imbue, v. fill, infuse, steep, suffuse, permeate, pervade, inform, perfuse.

imitate, v. follow, mimic, ape, mock, impersonate, copy, duplicate, reproduce, simulate, counterfeit.

immediate, adj. **1.** instant, without delay, present, instantaneous. **2.** present, next, near, close, proximate. **3.** direct, unmediated. —**Ant.** later.

immediately, adv. **1.** instantly, at once, without delay, presently, directly, instanter, instantaneously, forthwith; *esp. in business contexts* ASAP. **2.** directly, closely, without intervention. —**Ant.** later, anon. —**Syn. Study.** IMMEDIATELY, INSTANTLY, DIRECTLY, PRESENTLY were once close synonyms, all denoting complete absence of delay or any lapse of time. IMMEDIATELY and INSTANTLY still almost always have that sense and usu. mean at once: *He got up immediately.* She responded instantly to the request. DIRECTLY is usu. equivalent to soon, in a little while rather than at once: *You go ahead, we'll join you directly.* PRESENTLY changes sense according to the tense of the verb with which it is used. With a present tense verb it usu. means now, at the present time: *The author presently lives in San Francisco. She is presently working on a new novel.* In some contexts, esp. those involving a contrast between the present and the near future, PRESENTLY can mean soon or in a little while: *She is at the office now but will be home presently.*

immense, adj. huge, great, vast, extensive. —**Ant.** small, tiny, submicroscopic. —**Syn. Study.** See HUGE.

immerse, v. **1.** plunge, dip, sink, immerge, duck, douse. **2.** embed, bury; involve, absorb, engage. —**Ant.** withdraw; disinter. —**Syn. Study.** See DIP[1].

immigrate, See Syn. study at MIGRATE.

imminent, adj. **1.** impending, threatening, near, at hand. **2.** overhanging, leaning forward. —**Ant.** delayed, far off.

immoderate, adj. excessive, extreme, exorbitant, unreasonable, inordinate, extravagant, intemperate. —**Ant.** moderate, reasonable, temperate.

immoral, adj. abandoned, depraved, self-indulgent, dissipated, licentious, dissolute, profligate, unprincipled, vicious, sinful, corrupt, amoral, wicked, bad, wrong, evil. —**Ant.** moral, pious, good.

immortal, adj. undying, eternal, everlasting, deathless, enduring, imperishable, indestructible, endless, unending, perpetual, perdurable, permanent, never-ending. —**Ant.** passing, ephemeral.

immunity, n. **1.** insusceptibility. **2.** exemption, franchise, privilege, license, charter, right, liberty, prerogative. —**Ant.** susceptibility; proneness. —**Syn. Study.** See EXEMPTION.

impair, v. injure, worsen, diminish, deteriorate, lessen. —**Ant.** repair. —**Syn. Study.** See INJURE.

impart, v. **1.** communicate, disclose, divulge, reveal, make known, tell, relate. **2.** give, bestow, grant, cede, confer. —**Ant.** conceal, hide.

impartial, adj. unbiased, just, fair, unprejudiced, disinterested, equitable. —**Ant.** partial. —**Syn. Study.** See FAIR[1].

impatient, adj. **1.** uneasy, restless, unquiet. **2.** hasty, impetuous, vehement, precipitate, sudden, curt, brusque, abrupt. **3.** irritable, testy, fretful, violent, hot. —**Ant.** patient, restful, quiet; gradual, slow; calm, unperturbed.

impeach, v. censure, accuse, blame, reproach, charge, indict, arraign.

impecunious, adj. penniless, poor, destitute, poverty-stricken. —**Ant.** wealthy, rich. —**Syn. Study.** See POOR.

impede, v. retard, slow, delay, hinder, hamper, prevent, obstruct, check, stop, block, thwart, interrupt, restrain. —**Ant.** aid, encourage. —**Syn. Study.** See PREVENT.

impediment, n. bar, hindrance, obstacle, obstruction, encumbrance, check. —**Ant.** help, support, encouragement. —**Syn. Study.** See OBSTACLE.

impel, v. compel, drive, urge, press on, incite, constrain, force, actuate. —**Ant.** restrain. —**Syn. Study.** See COMPEL.

imperfect, adj. **1.** defective, faulty, incomplete. **2.** rudimentary, undeveloped, underdeveloped, incomplete; immature.

imperious, adj. **1.** domineering, overbearing, dictatorial, tyrannical, despotic, arrogant. **2.** urgent, imperative, necessary. —**Ant.** submissive; unnecessary.

impersonate, v. act, personate, mimic, ape, mime, parrot, enact, act out, personify, represent, portray, illustrate.

impertinent, adj. **1.** intrusive, presumptuous, impudent, insolent, rude, fresh, bold, arrogant, insulting, officious, saucy, pert, brazen. **2.** irrelevant, inappropriate, incongruous, inapplicable. **3.** trivial, silly, absurd, ridiculous, inane. —**Ant.** polite, courteous; appropriate; important, serious. —**Syn. Study.** IMPERTINENT, IMPUDENT, INSOLENT refer to bold and rude persons or behavior. IMPERTINENT, from its primary meaning of not pertinent and hence inappropriate or out of place, has come to imply an unseemly intrusion into the affairs of others; it may also refer to a presumptuous rudeness toward persons entitled to respect: *impertinent questions; an impertinent interruption.* IMPUDENT suggests a bold and shameless rudeness: *an impudent young rascal.* INSOLENT suggests the insulting or contemptuous behavior of an arrogant person: *The boss fired the insolent employee.*

impetuous, adj. impulsive, rash, precipitate, spontaneous, violent, hasty, furious, hot. —**Ant.** planned, careful. —**Syn. Study.** IMPETUOUS, IMPULSIVE both refer to persons who are hasty and precipitate in action, or to actions not preceded by thought. IMPETUOUS suggests great energy, overeagerness, and impatience: *an impetuous lover; impetuous words.* IMPULSIVE emphasizes spontaneity and lack of reflection: *an impulsive act of generosity.*

implacable, adj. unappeased, unpacified, inexorable, inflexible, unbending, relentless, unappeasable, rancorous, merciless. —**Ant.** flexible, merciful.

implement, See Syn. study at TOOL.

implicate, v. involve, concern, entangle. —**Ant.** disentangle.

implore, v. call upon, supplicate, beseech, entreat, crave, beg, solicit.

impolite, adj. uncivil, rude, discourteous, disrespectful, insolent, unpolished, unrefined, boorish, ill-mannered, rough, savage. —**Ant.** polite.

importance, n. consequence, weight, moment, significance, import, momentousness, weightiness. —**Ant.** unimportance, insignificance. —**Syn. Study.** IMPORTANCE, CONSEQUENCE, SIGNIFICANCE, MOMENT refer to something valuable, influential, or worthy of note. IMPORTANCE is the most general of these terms, assigning exceptional value or influence to a person or thing: *the importance of Einstein's discoveries.* CONSEQUENCE may suggest personal distinction, or may suggest importance based on results to be produced: *a woman of consequence in world affairs; an event of great consequence for our future.* SIGNIFICANCE carries the implication of importance not readily or immediately recognized: *The significance of the discovery became clear many years later.* MOMENT, on the other hand, usu. refers to immediately apparent, self-evident importance: *an international treaty of great moment.*

impostor, n. pretender, deceiver, cheat, confidence man, con man, intruder, trickster, knave, hypocrite, charlatan, mountebank.

impotent, adj. powerless, helpless, enfeebled, forceless, weak, ineffectual, ineffective, uninfluential, lightweight, wimpish, wimpy, nebbishy. —**Ant.** powerful, strong.

impoverished, See Syn. study at POOR.

impregnable, adj. unassailable, invincible, invulnerable. —**Ant.** pregnable, vulnerable. —**Syn. Study.** See INVINCIBLE.

impromptu, See Syn. study at EXTEMPORANEOUS.

improper, adj. **1.** inapplicable, unsuited, unfit, inappropriate, unsuitable. **2.** indecent, unbecoming, unseemly, indecorous, unfitting. **3.** abnormal, irregular. —**Ant.** proper. —**Syn. Study.** IMPROPER, INDECENT, UNBECOMING, UNSEEMLY are applied to that which is inappropriate or not in accordance with propriety. IMPROPER has a wide range, being applied to whatever is not suitable or fitting, and often specifically to what does not conform to the standards of conventional morality: *an improper diet; improper clothes; improper behavior in church.* INDECENT, a strong word, is applied to what is offensively contrary to standards of propriety and esp. of modesty: *indecent photographs.* UNBECOMING is applied to what is especially unfitting in the person concerned: *conduct unbecoming a minister.* UNSEEMLY is applied to whatever is unfitting or improper under the circumstances: *unseemly mirth.*

impropriety, n. **1.** misbehavior, misconduct, indecorousness, indecorum, unseemliness, naughtiness, vulgarity, disorderliness. **2.** error, indiscretion, faux pas, solecism, gaffe, vulgarism, indecency.

improve, v. **1.** ameliorate, better, amend, emend, correct, right, rectify. **2.** mend, gain, get better. —**Ant.** worsen, impair; fail, sink. —**Syn. Study.** IMPROVE, AMELIORATE, BETTER imply bringing to a more desirable state. IMPROVE usu. implies remedying a lack or a felt need: *to improve a process.* AMELIORATE, a formal word, implies improving oppressive, unjust, or difficult conditions: *to ameliorate working conditions.* BETTER implies improving conditions that are adequate but could be more satisfactory: *to better a previous attempt; to better oneself by study.*

improvident, adj. incautious, unwary, thoughtless, careless, imprudent, heedless, without or lacking foresight. **2.** thriftless, shiftless, neglectful, wasteful, prodigal. —**Ant.** provident, cautious; thrifty.

improvised, adj. extemporaneous, impromptu, unpremeditated, unrehearsed, spontaneous. —**Ant.** premeditated.

impudence, n. impertinence, effrontery, insolence, rudeness, brass, brazenness, face, lip, boldness, presumption, presumptiveness, sauciness, pertness, flippancy; (colloquial) nerve. —**Ant.** politeness, courtesy.

impudent, adj. bold, brazen, brassy, presumptuous, insolent, impertinent, insulting, rude, presumptive, saucy, pert, flippant, fresh. —**Ant.** polite, courteous, well-behaved. —**Syn. Study.** See IMPERTINENT.

impulsive, adj. emotional, impetuous, rash, quick, hasty, unpremeditated. —**Ant.** cool, cold, unemotional, premeditated. —**Syn. Study.** See IMPETUOUS.

impunity, n. exemption, license, permission. —**Ant.** responsibility, blame, culpability. —**Syn. Study.** See EXEMPTION.

impute, v. attribute, charge, ascribe, refer. —**Syn. Study.** See ATTRIBUTE.

inability, n. incapability, incapacity, disqualification, impotence, incompetence. —**Ant.** ability.

inaccuracy, n. **1.** incorrectness, erroneousness, inexactness, inexactitude. **2.** error, blunder, mistake, slip. —**Ant.** accuracy.

inaccurate, adj. inexact, loose, general, unspecific; incorrect, wrong, erroneous, faulty, improper. —**Ant.** accurate.

inactive, adj. inert, dormant, unmoving, immobile, inoperative; indolent, lazy, sluggish, torpid, passive, idle, slothful, dilatory. —**Ant.** active. —**Syn. Study.** INACTIVE, DORMANT, INERT, TORPID suggest lack of activity. INACTIVE describes a person or thing that is not acting, moving, functioning, or operating: *an inactive board member; inactive laws.* DORMANT suggests the quiescence or inactivity of that which sleeps or seems to sleep, but may be roused to action: *a dormant geyser.* INERT suggests something with no inherent power of motion or action; it may also refer to a person disinclined to move or act: *the inert body of an accident victim.* TORPID suggests a state of suspended activity, esp. of animals that hibernate: *Snakes are torpid in cold weather.*

inadequate, adj. inapt, incompetent, insufficient, incommensurate, defective, imperfect, incomplete. —**Ant.** adequate.

inadvertent, adj. heedless, inattentive, unintentional, thoughtless, careless, negligent. —**Ant.** intentional, purposive, purposeful.

inane, See Syn. study at FOOLISH.

inanimate, adj. **1.** lifeless, inorganic, vegetable, mineral, mechanical. **2.** spiritless, lifeless, sluggish, inert, spiritless; dead, defunct. —**Ant.** animate, alive; spirited.

inborn, adj. innate, inbred, native, natural, congenital, inherent, instinctive, inherited. —**Ant.** acquired, learned, conditioned, environmental. —**Syn. Study.** See INNATE.

incapable, adj. unable, incompetent, inefficient, impotent, unqualified; incapacious. —**Ant.** capable, competent, efficient, potent, qualified. —**Syn. Study.** INCAPABLE, INCOMPETENT are applied to a person or thing lacking in ability, preparation, or power for whatever is to be done. INCAPABLE usu. means inherently lacking in ability or power to meet and fill ordinary requirements: *a bridge incapable of carrying heavy loads; a worker described as clumsy and incapable.* INCOMPETENT, generally used only of persons, means unfit or unqualified for a particular task: *incompetent as an administrator.*

incarcerate, v. imprison, commit, confine, jail; constrict, enclose, restrict. —**Ant.** liberate, free.

incense, n. **1.** perfume, aroma, scent, fragrance. —v. **2.** inflame, enrage, exasperate, provoke, irritate, goad, vex, excite. —**Syn. Study.** See ENRAGE.

incentive, n. motive, inducement, incitement, enticement, stimulus, spur, impulse, goad, encouragement, prod. —**Ant.** discouragement. —**Syn. Study.** See MOTIVE.

incessant, adj. uninterrupted, unceasing, ceaseless, continual, continuous, constant, unending, never-ending, relentless, unrelenting, unremitting, perpetual, eternal, everlasting. —**Ant.** interrupted, spasmodic, sporadic; temporary.

incident, n. event, occurrence, happening, circumstance. —**Syn. Study.** See EVENT.

incidental, adj. fortuitous, chance, accidental, casual, contingent. —**Ant.** fundamental.

incisive, adj. **1.** penetrating, trenchant, biting, acute, sarcastic, sardonic, satirical, acid, severe, cruel. **2.** sharp, keen, acute. —**Ant.** superficial; dull.

incite, v. urge on, stimulate, encourage, back, prod, push, spur, goad, instigate, provoke, arouse, fire; induce. —**Ant.** discourage. —**Syn. Study.** INCITE, ROUSE, PROVOKE mean to goad or inspire an individual or group to take some action or express some feeling. INCITE means to induce activity of any kind, although it often refers to violent or uncontrolled behavior: *incited to greater effort; incited to rebellion.* ROUSE is used in a similar way, but has an underlying sense of awakening from sleep or inactivity: *to rouse an apathetic team.* PROVOKE means to stir to sudden, strong feeling or vigorous action: *Kicking the animal provoked it to attack.*

inclination, n. **1.** bent, leaning, tendency, set, propensity, liking, preference, predilection, predisposition, proclivity, bias, proneness, prejudice, penchant. **2.** slope, slant, leaning, inclining; verging, tending, tendency. —**Ant.** dislike, antipathy.

include, v. contain, embrace, comprise, comprehend, embody. —**Ant.** exclude, preclude. —**Syn. Study.** INCLUDE, COMPREHEND, COMPRISE, EMBRACE imply containing parts of a whole. INCLUDE means to contain as a part or member of a larger whole; it may indicate one, several, or all parts: *This anthology includes works by Sartre and Camus. The price includes appetizer, main course, and dessert.* COMPREHEND means to have within the limits or scope of a larger whole: *The plan comprehends several projects.* COMPRISE means to consist of; it usu. indicates all of the various parts serving to make up the whole: *This group comprises 50 species.* EMBRACE emphasizes the extent or assortment of that which is included: *The report embraces a great variety of subjects.*

income, n. return, returns, receipts, revenue, profits, salary, wages, pay, stipend, interest, annuity, gain, earnings. —**Ant.** expense, expenditure.

incompatible, adj. **1.** inconsistent, incongruous, unsuitable, unsuited, contradictory, irreconcilable. **2.** discordant, contrary, opposed, difficult, contradictory, inharmonious. —**Ant.** compatible, consistent, appropriate; harmonious.

incompetent, adj. unqualified, unable, incapable, inadequate, unfit, insufficient. —**Ant.** competent, efficient, able, capable, adequate, fit. —**Syn. Study.** See INCAPABLE.

incongruous, adj. **1.** unbecoming, inappropriate, incompatible, out of keeping, discrepant, absurd. **2.** inconsonant, inharmonious, discordant. **3.** inconsistent, incoherent, illogical, unfitting, contrary, contradictory. —**Ant.** congruous, becoming, appropriate, proper; harmonious; logical, consistent, coherent, sensible.

inconsistent, adj. incompatible, inharmonious, incongruous, unsuitable, irreconcilable, incoherent, discrepant, out of keeping, inappropriate. —**Ant.** consistent, coherent, harmonious, suitable.

inconstant, adj. changeable, fickle, inconsistent, variable, moody, capricious, vacillating, wavering, mercurial, volatile, unsettled, unstable, mutable, uncertain. —**Ant.** constant, steady, invariant, settled, staid. —**Syn. Study.** See FICKLE.

incontrovertible, adj. undeniable, indisputable, incontestable, unquestionable. —**Ant.** deniable, controvertible, disputable, questionable.

inconvenient, adj. awkward, inopportune, disadvantageous, troublesome, annoying, vexatious, untimely, incommodious, discommodious. —**Ant.** convenient, opportune, advantageous.

incorrect, adj. **1.** wrong, not valid, untrue, false, erroneous, inexact, inaccurate. **2.** improper, faulty; indecent. —**Ant.** correct.

increase, v. **1.** augment, add to, enlarge, greaten; extend, prolong. **2.** grow, dilate, expand, enlarge, multiply. —n. **3.** growth, augmentation, enlargement, expansion, addition, extension. —**Ant.** decrease.

incredulous, adj. unbelieving, skeptical, doubtful, dubious. —**Ant.** credulous. —**Syn. Study.** See DOUBTFUL.

indecent, adj. offensive, distasteful, improper, unbecoming, unseemly, outrageous, vulgar, indelicate, coarse, rude, gross, immodest, unrefined, indecorous, obscene, filthy, lewd, licentious, lascivious, pornographic. —**Ant.** decent. —**Syn. Study.** See IMPROPER.

indefinite, adj. **1.** unlimited, unconfined, unrestrained, undefined, undetermined, indistinct, confused. **2.** vague, obscure, confusing, equivocal, dim, unspecific, doubtful, unsettled, uncertain. —**Ant.** definite.

independence, n. freedom, liberty. —**Ant.** dependence, reliance.

indifference, n. **1.** unconcern, listlessness, apathy, insensibility, coolness, insensitiveness, inattention. **2.** unimportance, triviality, insignificance. **3.** mediocrity, inferiority. —**Ant.** concern, warmth, sensibility; importance, significance, superiority.

indignation, n. consternation, resentment, exasperation, wrath, anger, ire, fury, rage, choler. —**Ant.** calm, serenity, composure. —**Syn. Study.** See ANGER.

indignity, n. injury, slight, contempt, humiliation, affront, insult, outrage, scorn, obloquy, contumely, reproach, abuse, opprobrium, dishonor, disrespect. —**Ant.** dignity; honor, respect. —**Syn. Study.** See INSULT.

indiscriminate, adj. **1.** miscellaneous, undiscriminating, undistinguishing. **2.** confused, undistinguishable, mixed, promiscuous. —**Ant.** discriminating; distinguishing.

indispensable, adj. necessary, requisite, essential, needed. —**Ant.** dispensable, disposable, unnecessary, nonessential. —**Syn. Study.** See NECESSARY.

indisposed, adj. **1.** sick, ill, unwell, ailing. **2.** disinclined, unwilling, reluctant, averse, loath. —**Ant.** well, healthy, hardy, hale; eager, willing.

indisputable, adj. incontrovertible, incontestable, unquestionable, undeniable, indubitable; evident, apparent, obvious, certain, sure. —**Ant.** questionable, dubitable, dubious; uncertain.

indolent, adj. idle, lazy, slothful, slow, inactive, sluggish, torpid, listless, inert. —**Ant.** energetic, active, industrious. —**Syn. Study.** See IDLE.

indomitable, adj. invincible, unconquerable, unyielding. —**Ant.** yielding, weak, feeble. —**Syn. Study.** See INVINCIBLE.

induce, v. **1.** persuade, influence, move, actuate, prompt, instigate, incite, urge, impel, spur, prevail upon. **2.** bring about, produce, cause, effect, bring on. —**Ant**. dissuade. —**Syn**. **Study**. See PERSUADE.

inducement, n. incentive, motive, cause, stimulus, spur, incitement. —**Ant**. discouragement. —**Syn**. **Study**. See MOTIVE.

indulge, v. yield to, satisfy, gratify, humor, pamper, give way to, favor; suffer, foster, permit, allow. —**Ant**. dissatisfy; disallow, forbid. —**Syn**. **Study**. See SPOIL.

industrious, adj. busy, hard-working, diligent, assiduous, operose, sedulous, persistent, persevering. —**Ant**. lazy, indolent.

inebriate, v. 1. intoxicate, make drunk; exhilarate. —n. 2. drunkard.

ineffectual, adj. 1. useless, unavailing, futile, nugatory, ineffective, fruitless, pointless, abortive, purposeless. 2. powerless, impotent, feeble, weak. —**Ant**. effectual, efficacious, efficient.

inefficient, adj. incapable, ineffective, feeble, weak. —**Ant**. efficient, effectual, efficacious.

inept, adj. 1. inapt, unfitted, unfitting, unsuitable, unsuited, inappropriate, out of place, anomalous. 2. absurd, foolish, stupid, pointless, inane, ridiculous. —**Ant**. fit, suitable, apt, appropriate.

inert, adj. inactive, immobile, unmoving, lifeless, passive, motionless. —**Ant**. active, kinetic. —**Syn**. **Study**. See INACTIVE.

inexorable, adj. unyielding, unalterable, inflexible, unbending, firm, solid, steadfast, severe; relentless, unrelenting, implacable, merciless, cruel, pitiless. —**Ant**. flexible, yielding; merciful, relenting.

inexpensive, adj. cheap, low-priced, low. —**Ant**. expensive. —**Syn**. **Study**. See CHEAP.

inexperienced, adj. untrained, unskilled, raw, green, unknowledgeable, unpracticed, unschooled, untutored, uninformed, naive, uninitiated. —**Ant**. experienced, skilled, practiced.

infallible, adj. trustworthy, sure, certain, reliable, unfailing. —**Ant**. fallible, unreliable, uncertain.

infamous, adj. 1. disreputable, ill-famed, notorious. 2. disgraceful, scandalous, detestable, dishonorable, shameful, bad, nefarious, odious, wicked, outrageous, shocking, vile, base, ignominious, dark, heinous, villainous. —**Ant**. reputable, famed; honorable, good.

infamy, n. notoriety, disgrace, dishonor, discredit, shame, disrepute, obloquy, odium, opprobrium, scandal, debasement, abasement, ignominy. —**Ant**. honor, credit, repute. —**Syn**. **Study**. See DISGRACE.

infantile, adj. babyish, childish, puerile, immature, weak. —**Ant**. mature, adult. —**Syn**. **Study**. See CHILDISH.

infectious, adj. contagious, catching, communicable. —**Syn**. **Study**. See CONTAGIOUS.

infidel, See Syn. study at ATHEIST.

inflame, v. kindle, excite, rouse, arouse, incite, fire, stimulate. —**Ant**. discourage. —**Syn**. **Study**. See KINDLE.

inflate, v. distend, swell, swell out, dilate, expand, puff up or out, bloat, blow up. —**Ant**. deflate.

inflexible, adj. rigid, unbending, undeviating, unyielding, rigorous, implacable, stern, relentless, unrelenting, inexorable, unremitting, immovable, resolute, steadfast, firm, stony, solid, persevering, stubborn, dogged, pigheaded, obstinate, refractory, willful, headstrong, intractable, obdurate, adamant. —**Ant**. flexible.

influence, n. 1. sway, rule, authority, power, control, predominance, direction. —v. 2. modify, affect, sway, impress, bias, direct, control. 3. move, impel, actuate, activate, incite, rouse, arouse, instigate, induce, persuade. —**Syn**. **Study**. See AUTHORITY.

inform, v. 1. apprise, make known, advise, notify, tell, acquaint. 2. animate, inspire, quicken, enliven, inspirit. —**Ant**. conceal, hide.

informal, adj. 1. irregular, unusual, anomalous, unconventional, natural, easy, unceremonious. 2. colloquial, flexible. —**Ant**. formal, regular, customary, conventional; inflexible. —**Syn**. **Study**. See COLLOQUIAL.

information, n. knowledge, news, data, facts, circumstances, situation, intelligence, advice. —**Ant**. secret.

infraction, See Syn. study at BREACH.

infringe, v. 1. violate, transgress, breach, break, disobey. 2. trespass, encroach; poach. —**Ant**. obey. —**Syn**. **Study**. See TRESPASS.

infuriate, v. enrage, anger, incense.

—**Ant**. calm, pacify. —**Syn**. **Study**. See ENRAGE.

ingenious, adj. clever, skillful, adroit, bright, gifted, able, resourceful, inventive. —**Ant**. unskillful, maladroit.

ingenuous, adj. unreserved, unrestrained, frank, candid, free, open, guileless, artless, innocent, naive, straightforward, sincere, open-hearted. —**Ant**. reserved, restrained, secretive, sly, insincere.

ingredient, n. constituent, element, component. —**Ant**. whole.

inherent, adj. innate, inherited, native, natural, inborn, inbred, essential. —**Ant**. acquired. —**Syn**. **Study**. See ESSENTIAL.

inheritance, n. heritage, patrimony.

inhibit, v. 1. restrain, hinder, arrest, check, repress, obstruct, stop; discourage. 2. prohibit, forbid, interdict, prevent. —**Ant**. encourage, support, abet.

inimical, adj. 1. adverse, unfavorable, harmful, noxious. 2. unfriendly, hostile, antagonistic, contrary. —**Ant**. friendly, favorable.

initiate, v. 1. begin, originate, set going, start, commence, introduce, inaugurate, open. 2. teach, instruct, indoctrinate, train. —adj. 3. initiated, begun, started. —n. 4. new member, pledge, tyro, beginner, learner, amateur, freshman. —**Ant**. terminate, conclude, finish. —**Syn**. **Study**. See BEGIN.

injure, v. 1. damage, impair, harm, hurt, spoil, ruin, break, mar. 2. wrong, maltreat, mistreat, abuse. —**Syn**. **Study**. INJURE, IMPAIR mean to harm or damage something. INJURE is a general term referring to any kind or degree of damage: to injure one's spine; to injure one's reputation. To IMPAIR is to make imperfect in any way, often with a suggestion of progressive deterioration: One's health can be impaired by overwork.

injurious, adj. 1. harmful, hurtful, damaging, ruinous, detrimental, pernicious, deleterious, baneful, destructive, mischievous. 2. unjust, wrongful, prejudicial, biased, inequitable, iniquitous. 3. offensive, insulting, abusive, derogatory, defamatory, slanderous, libelous, contumelious, scornful, deprecatory. —**Ant**. beneficial; just, right; complimentary.

injury, n. 1. harm, damage, ruin, detriment, wound, impairment, mischief. 2. wrong, injustice.

inn, n. hotel, hostelry, hostel, tavern.

innate, adj. inborn, congenital, hereditary, inbred, native, genetic, familial. —**Syn**. **Study**. INNATE, INBORN, CONGENITAL, HEREDITARY describe qualities, characteristics, or possessions acquired before or at the time of birth. INNATE, of Latin origin, and INBORN, a native English word, share the literal basic sense "existing at the time of birth," and they are interchangeable in most contexts: innate (or inborn) stodginess, strength, abilities. CONGENITAL refers most often to characteristics acquired during fetal development, esp. defects or undesirable conditions: a congenital deformity; congenital blindness. HEREDITARY describes qualities or things passed on from ancestors, either through the genes or by social or legal means: Hemophilia is a hereditary condition; a hereditary title.

innocent, adj. 1. pure, untainted, sinless, virtuous, virginal, blameless, faultless, impeccable, spotless, immaculate. 2. guiltless, blameless. 3. upright, honest, forthright. 4. naive, simple, unsophisticated, artless, guileless, ingenuous. —**Ant**. impure, tainted, sinful, piacular; guilty, culpable; dishonest; disingenuous, sophisticated, artful.

innocuous, adj. 1. harmless, inoffensive, innocent, unhurtful, benign. 2. well-meaning, unthreatening, insipid, neutral, dull.

innumerable, adj. countless, numberless, many, numerous; infinite. —**Syn**. **Study**. See MANY.

inquire, v. ask, question, query, investigate, examine. —**Ant**. answer, reply.

inquiry, n. 1. investigation, examination, study, scrutiny, exploration, research. 2. inquiring, questioning, interrogation; query, question. —**Ant**. anwer, reply.

inquisitive, adj. inquiring, prying, curious, scrutinizing, questioning.

insane, adj. deranged, demented, lunatic, crazed, crazy, maniacal, non compos mentis, of unsound mind, mad; paranoiac, schizophrenic, delirious; foolish, senseless, stupid, thoughtless. —**Ant**. sane.

insanity, n. derangement, dementia,

lunacy, madness, craziness, mania, aberration; dementia praecox, schizophrenia, paranoia. —**Ant**. sanity, probity.

inscrutable, adj. impenetrable, unpenetrable, mysterious, hidden, incomprehensible, undiscoverable, inexplicable, unexplainable, unfathomable. —**Ant**. penetrable, comprehensible, understandable. —**Syn**. **Study**. See MYSTERIOUS.

insecure, adj. 1. unsafe, exposed, unprotected. 2. uncertain, unsure, risky. —**Ant**. secure, safe; certain, sure.

insensibility, n. 1. unconsciousness. 2. indifference, apathy, insusceptibility. —**Ant**. consciousness; concern, sensibility.

inside, prep. 1. within, inside of, in. —n. 2. interior. 3. (plural) innards, organs. —**Ant**. outside.

insidious, adj. 1. corrupting, entrapping, beguiling, guileful. 2. treacherous, stealthy, deceitful, artful, cunning, sly, wily, intriguing, subtle, crafty, tricky, arch, crooked, foxy. —**Ant**. upright, forthright; artless, ingenuous.

insinuate, v. 1. hint, suggest, intimate. 2. instill, infuse, introduce, inject, inculcate. —**Syn**. **Study**. See HINT.

insolent, adj. bold, rude, disrespectful, impertinent, brazen, brassy, abusive, overbearing, contemptuous, insulting. —**Ant**. polite, courteous, retiring; complimentary. —**Syn**. **Study**. See IMPERTINENT.

inspection, n. examination, investigation, scrutiny. —**Syn**. **Study**. See EXAMINATION.

instance, n. case, example, illustration, exemplification.

instant, n. moment, minute, second, twinkling, flash, jiffy, trice. —**Syn**. **Study**. See MINUTE[1].

instantly, adv. immediately, at once, instanter, instantaneously, forthwith, in a flash or trice or jiffy. —**Ant**. later. —**Syn**. **Study**. See IMMEDIATELY.

instruct, v. 1. direct, command, order, prescribe. 2. teach, train, educate, tutor, coach, drill, discipline, indoctrinate, school, inform, enlighten, apprise. —**Ant**. learn, study. —**Syn**. **Study**. See TEACH.

instruction, n. 1. education, tutoring, coaching, training, drill, exercise, indoctrination, schooling, teaching. 2. order, direction, mandate, command.

instructor, n. teacher, tutor, pedagogue, schoolmaster, preceptor. —**Ant**. student, pupil.

instrument, n. tool, implement, utensil. —**Syn**. **Study**. See TOOL.

insult, v. 1. affront, offend, scorn, injure, slander, abuse. —n. 2. affront, indignity, offense, contumely, scorn, outrage. —**Ant**. compliment, dignify; dignity. —**Syn**. **Study**. INSULT, INDIGNITY, AFFRONT, SLIGHT refer to acts or words that offend or demean. INSULT refers to a deliberately discourteous or rude remark or act that humiliates, wounds the feelings, and arouses anger: an insult about her foreign accent. INDIGNITY refers to an injury to one's dignity or self-respect: The prisoners suffered many indignities. AFFRONT implies open offense or disrespect, esp. to one's face: Criticism of my book was a personal affront. SLIGHT implies inadvertent indifference or disregard, but may also indicate ill-concealed contempt: Not inviting me was an unforgivable slight.

insurrection, n. revolt, uprising, rebellion, mutiny, insurgency.

intact, adj. uninjured, unaltered, sound, whole, unimpaired, complete, undiminished, unbroken, entire. —**Ant**. impaired, unsound, incomplete. —**Syn**. **Study**. See COMPLETE.

integrity, n. 1. uprightness, honesty, honor, rectitude, right, righteousness, probity, principle, virtue, goodness. 2. wholeness, entirety, completeness. —**Ant**. dishonesty, disrepute; part. —**Syn**. **Study**. See HONOR.

intellect, n. mind, understanding, reason, sense, common sense, brains. —**Ant**. inanity. —**Syn**. **Study**. See MIND.

intellectual, adj. 1. mental; intelligent; high-brow. —n. 2. (colloquial) high-brow, egghead, professor, brain, mental giant, longhair. —**Ant**. sensual, low-brow; dunderpate, fool.

intelligence, n. 1. mind, understanding, discernment, reason, acumen, aptitude, penetration. 2. knowledge, news, information, advice. —**Ant**. stupidity.

intelligent, adj. 1. understanding,

intellectual, quick, bright. 2. astute, clever, quick, alert, bright, apt, discerning, shrewd, smart. —**Ant**. stupid, unintelligent; slow; dull. —**Syn**. **Study**. See SHARP.

intend, v. have in mind, mean, design, propose, contemplate, expect, meditate, project, aim for or at, purpose.

intensify, v. aggravate, deepen, quicken, strengthen; concentrate. —**Ant**. alleviate, lessen, weaken, dilute.

intent, n. 1. intention, design, purpose, meaning, plan, plot, aim, end, object, mark. —adj. 2. fixed, steadfast, bent, resolute, set, concentrated, unshakable, eager. —**Ant**. phlegmatic, undetermined, irresolute, apathetic.

intention, n. intent.

intentional, adj. deliberate, purposeful, premeditated, designed, planned, intended. —**Ant**. unintentional, purposeless, unpremeditated; involuntary. —**Syn**. **Study**. See DELIBERATE.

interesting, adj. pleasing, attractive, gratifying, engaging, absorbing, exciting, fulfilling, entertaining. —**Ant**. uninteresting, dull, prosaic.

interpret, v. 1. explain, explicate, elucidate, shed or cast light on, define, translate, decipher, decode. 2. explain, construe, understand. —**Syn**. **Study**. See EXPLAIN.

interrupt, v. 1. discontinue, suspend, intermit. 2. stop, cease, break off, disturb, hinder, interfere with. —**Ant**. continue.

intimate, adj. 1. close, closely associated, familiar, dear, confidential. 2. private, personal, privy, secret. 3. detailed, deep, cogent, exacting, exact, precise. 4. inmost, deep within; intrinsic, inner, deep-rooted, deep-seated. —n. 5. friend, associate, confidant, crony, familiar. —v. 6. hint, suggest, insinuate, allude to. —**Ant**. open, public, known, blatant; enemy, foe; announce, proclaim. —**Syn**. **Study**. See FAMILIAR.

intimidate, v. overawe, cow, subdue, dismay, frighten, alarm; discourage, dissuade. —**Ant**. encourage, calm. —**Syn**. **Study**. See DISCOURAGE.

intolerable, adj. unbearable, unendurable, insufferable, insupportable. —**Ant**. tolerable, bearable, endurable.

intolerant, adj. bigoted, illiberal, narrow, proscriptive, prejudiced, biased, dictatorial, fascistic, totalitarian, fanatical. —**Ant**. tolerant, liberal, unprejudiced.

intractable, adj. stubborn, obstinate, unmanageable, perverse, fractious, refractory, headstrong, pigheaded, dogged, unbending, inflexible, obdurate, adamant, stony, willful, unyielding, contumacious, froward. —**Ant**. tractable, amiable, amenable, easygoing, flexible. —**Syn**. **Study**. See UNRULY.

intrigue, See Syn. study at CONSPIRACY.

intrinsic, adj. essential, native, innate, inborn, inbred, natural, true, real, genuine. —**Ant**. extrinsic. —**Syn**. **Study**. See ESSENTIAL.

introduce, v. present, acquaint; lead, bring, conduct. —**Syn**. **Study**. INTRODUCE, PRESENT mean to bring persons into personal acquaintance with each other, as by announcement of names. INTRODUCE is the ordinary term, referring to making persons acquainted who are ostensibly equals: to introduce a friend to one's sister. PRESENT, a more formal term, suggests a degree of ceremony in the process, and implies (if only as a matter of compliment) superior dignity, rank, or importance in the person to whom another is presented: to present a visitor to the president.

introduction, n. foreword, preface, front matter; preamble. —**Syn**. **Study**. INTRODUCTION, FOREWORD, PREFACE refer to material in the front of a book that introduces and explains it to the reader. An INTRODUCTION is a formal preliminary statement, often extensive, that serves as a guide to the book. It is written by the author and usu. printed as part of the text: The introduction outlined the subjects covered in the book. A FOREWORD is a short introductory statement that precedes the text proper. It is usu. written by someone other than the author, often an authority on the subject of the book: The writer of the foreword praised the book and its author. A PREFACE, also separate from the text proper, is the author's informal statement about the purpose, preparation, etc., of the book; it usu.

includes acknowledgments: The author thanked his family in the preface. A PREFACE usu. follows a FOREWORD, if there is one.

introductory, See Syn. study at PRELIMINARY.

intrude, v. trespass, obtrude, encroach, violate, infringe. —**Syn**. **Study**. See TRESPASS.

inundate, v. flood, deluge, overflow, overspread, overwhelm, glut.

invaluable, adj. priceless, precious, valuable, inestimable. —**Ant**. worthless.

invariable, adj. unalterable, unchanging, uniform, constant, invariant, changeless, unvarying, unchangeable, immutable. —**Ant**. variable, changing, varying, mutable.

invective, n. 1. denunciation, censure, reproach, abuse, contumely, scorn. 2. accusation, vituperation, railing. —adj. 3. abusive, censorious, denunciatory, vituperative, captious. —**Ant**. praise; honor; commendation. —**Syn**. **Study**. See ABUSE.

invent, v. 1. devise, contrive, originate, discover. 2. produce, create, imagine, fancy, conceive, fabricate, concoct.

inventory, n. roll, list, roster, listing, record, account, catalogue, register. —**Syn**. **Study**. See LIST[1].

invert, v. reverse, turn around or upside down.

investigation, n. examination, inspection, inquiry, scrutiny, research, exploration.

invigorate, v. animate, innerve, enliven, strengthen, fortify, energize, quicken, vitalize. —**Ant**. enervate, enfeeble, weaken, devitalize.

invincible, adj. unconquerable, unvanquishable, insuperable, insurmountable, impregnable, impenetrable, indomitable, persistent, unyielding, irrepressible. —**Ant**. conquerable, pregnable, penetrable. —**Syn**. **Study**. INVINCIBLE, IMPREGNABLE suggest that which cannot be overcome or mastered. INVINCIBLE is applied to that which cannot be conquered in combat or war, or overcome or subdued in any manner: an invincible army; invincible courage. IMPREGNABLE is applied to a place or position that cannot be taken by assault or siege, and hence to whatever is proof against attack: an impregnable fortress; impregnable virtue. INDOMITABLE implies having an unyielding spirit, or stubborn persistence in the face of opposition or difficulty: indomitable will.

invite, v. 1. call, request, ask, bid, summon, solicit. 2. attract, allure, lure, tempt, entice, draw.

involuntary, adj. 1. unintentional, reluctant, accidental. 2. automatic, reflex, unwilled, instinctive, uncontrolled. —**Ant**. voluntary, intentional.

involve, v. 1. include, embrace, contain, comprehend, comprise, entail, imply. 2. entangle, implicate, connect, tie, bind. —**Ant**. exclude, preclude.

iota, n. tittle, jot, bit, whit, particle, atom, grain, mite, scrap, scintilla, trace, glimmer, shadow, spark.

irascible, adj. testy, short-tempered, hot-tempered, quick-tempered, touchy, temperamental, irritable, waspish, snappish, petulant, peppery, choleric. —**Ant**. calm, even-tempered, temperate. —**Syn**. **Study**. See IRRITABLE.

irate, adj. angry, enraged, furious, piqued, provoked, irritated. —**Ant**. pleased, calm.

irony, n. sarcasm, satire, mockery, derision. —**Syn**. **Study**. IRONY, SATIRE, SARCASM indicate mockery of a person or thing. IRONY is exhibited in the organization or structure of either language or literary material. It indirectly presents a contradiction between an action or expression and the context in which it occurs. One thing is said and its opposite implied, as in "Beautiful weather, isn't it?" said when it is raining. Ironic literature exploits the contrast between an ideal and an actual condition, as when events turn out contrary to expectations. SATIRE, also a literary and rhetorical form, is the use of ridicule in exposing human vice and folly. Jonathan Swift wrote social and political satires. SARCASM is a harsh and cutting type of humor. Its distinctive quality is present in the spoken word; it is manifested chiefly by vocal inflection. Sarcastic language may have the form of irony, as in "What a fine musician you turned out to be!", or it may be a direct statement, as in "You couldn't play one piece correctly if you had two assistants!"

irregular, *adj.* **1.** unsymmetrical, uneven. **2.** unmethodical, unsystematic, disorderly, capricious, erratic, eccentric, lawless, aberrant, devious, unconforming, nonconformist, unusual, abnormal, anomalous. —**Ant.** regular.

irrepressible, *adj.* unrestrained, unconstrained, enthusiastic, effervescent, vivacious, uninhibited, exuberant, high-spirited. —**Ant.** gloomy, depressive.

irritable, *adj.* testy, irascible, touchy, cranky, snappish, petulant, argumentative, cantankerous, fractious —**Syn. Study.** IRRITABLE, TESTY, IRASCIBLE, TOUCHY mean easily excited, provoked, or disturbed. IRRITABLE means easily annoyed or bothered; it implies cross and snappish behavior, often of short duration: *The irritable clerk had no patience for my questions.* TESTY describes the same kind of response, particularly to minor annoyances: *Too little sleep put her in a testy mood.* IRASCIBLE is a stronger term that means habitually angry or easily angered: *an irascible boss, roaring at employees for the slightest error.* TOUCHY stresses oversensitivity and readiness to take offense, even though none is intended: *touchy about any reference to shyness.*

irritate, *v.* vex, annoy, chafe, fret, gall, nettle, ruffle, pique, incense, anger, ire, enrage, infuriate, exasperate, provoke. —**Ant.** please, delight.

isolation, *n.* solitude, loneliness; separation, disconnection, segregation, detachment.

issue, *n.* **1.** delivery, emission, sending, promulgation. **2.** copy, number, edition, printing. **3.** point, crux; problem, question. **4.** product, effect, result, consequence, event, outcome, upshot, denouement, conclusion, end, consummation. **5.** egress, outlet, vent. **6.** offspring, progeny, children. —*v.* **7.** put out, deliver, circulate, publish, distribute. **8.** send out, discharge, emit. **9.** come forth, emerge, flow out. **10.** come, proceed, emanate, flow, arise, spring, originate, ensue. —**Syn. Study.** See EMERGE.

itinerant, *adj.* wandering, nomadic, unsettled, roving, roaming, traveling, journeying, itinerating. —**Ant.** stationary, fixed, settled.

J

jabber, *v.* prattle, chatter, babble, prate, run on, natter, palaver, gabble, blather, tittle-tattle. —**Ant.** discourse, orate.

jaded, *adj.* **1.** world-weary, bored, blasé, spoiled, sated, satiated, glutted, burned-out. **2.** tired, weary, spent, exhausted, worn-out, fatigued. —**Ant.** fresh, bright-eyed, eager.

jam, *v.* **1.** wedge, pack, crowd, ram, force, squeeze, bruise, crush. —*n.* **2.** preserve, conserve, marmalade.

jargon, *n.* **1.** idiom, vocabulary, phraseology, language, vernacular, argot, patois, patter, lingo, cant, slang. **2.** mumbo-jumbo, nonsense, double-talk, gibberish. —**Syn. Study.** See LANGUAGE.

jaunty, *adj.* **1.** sprightly, cheerful, lighthearted, upbeat, buoyant, perky, carefree, debonair, breezy. **2.** dashing, smart, natty, spruce, dapper. —**Ant.** dull, drab, subfusc.

jealous, *adj.* **1.** envious, resentful, suspicious. **2.** solicitous, watchful, vigilant. —**Ant.** generous, open, trusting.

jealousy, See Syn. study at ENVY.

jeer, *v.* **1.** deride, scoff, gibe, mock, taunt, sneer at, ridicule, flout. —*n.* **2.** sneer, scoff, gibe, derision, ridicule, flout. —**Syn. Study.** See SCOFF.

jeopardy, *n.* hazard, risk, danger, peril. —**Ant.** security.

jest, *n.* **1.** witticism, joke, pleasantry, mot, quip. **2.** raillery, banter; sport, fun, jape, gibe. —*v.* **3.** joke, trifle (with). **4.** deride, jeer, scoff, gibe.

job, *n.* position, situation, post, employment. —**Ant.** unemployment. —**Syn. Study.** See TASK.

jocose, *adj.* joking, jesting, jovial, humorous, playful, facetious, waggish, witty, funny, comical, droll, sportive, jocular, merry. —**Ant.** serious, morose, melancholy.

jocular, *adj.* jocose. —**Syn. Study.** See JOVIAL.

join, *v.* **1.** link, couple, fasten, attach, conjoin, combine, confederate, associate, consolidate, amalgamate, connect, unite, bring together. **2.** adjoin, abut, touch, be adjacent to. —**Ant.**

separate, divide. —**Syn. Study.** JOIN, CONNECT, UNITE imply bringing two or more things together more or less closely. JOIN may refer to a connection or association of any degree of closeness, but often implies direct contact: *to join pieces of wood to form a corner.* CONNECT implies a joining as by a tie, link, or wire: *to connect two batteries.* UNITE implies a close joining of two or more things, so as to form one: *to unite layers of veneer sheets to form plywood.*

joke, *n.* witticism, jape, quip, jest, sally, trick, raillery, prank.

jolly, *adj.* gay, glad, happy, spirited, jovial, merry, sportive, playful, cheerful, convivial, festive, joyous, mirthful, jocund, frolicsome. —**Ant.** serious, morose, mirthless. —**Syn. Study.** See JOVIAL.

journey, *n.* **1.** excursion, trip, tour, expedition, pilgrimage, travel. —*v.* **2.** travel, tour, peregrinate, roam, rove; go, proceed, fare. —**Syn. Study.** See TRIP.

jovial, *adj.* merry, jolly, convivial, gay, jocose, jocular, jocund, joyous, joyful, blithe, happy, glad, mirthful. —**Ant.** serious, mirthless, cheerless, unhappy. —**Syn. Study.** JOVIAL, JOCULAR, JOLLY refer to someone who is in good spirits. JOVIAL suggests a sociable and friendly person, full of hearty good humor: *The jovial professor enlivened the party.* JOCULAR refers to an amusing person, given to joking or jesting in a playful way: *His jocular sister teased him about his haircut.* JOLLY suggests a cheerful person, full of fun and laughter: *a jolly Santa Claus.*

joy, *n.* **1.** satisfaction, exultation, gladness, delight, rapture. **2.** happiness, felicity, bliss, pleasure, ecstasy, transport. —**Ant.** dissatisfaction, misery; unhappiness.

joyful, *adj.* glad, delighted, joyous, happy, blithe, buoyant, elated, jubilant, gay, merry, jocund, blithesome, jolly, jovial. —**Ant.** sad, unhappy, melancholy, depressed.

joyless, *adj.* sad, cheerless, unhappy, gloomy, dismal, miserable. —**Ant.** joyous.

judge, *n.* **1.** justice, magistrate; arbiter, arbitrator, umpire, referee. —*v.* **2.** try, pass sentence upon. **3.** estimate, consider, regard, esteem, appreciate, reckon, deem. **4.** decide, determine, conclude, form an opinion, pass judgment. —**Syn. Study.** JUDGE, REFEREE, UMPIRE indicate a person who is entrusted with decisions affecting others. JUDGE, in its legal and other uses, implies that the person has qualifications and authority for rendering decisions in matters at issue: *a judge appointed to the Supreme Court; a judge in a baking contest.* REFEREE refers to an officer who examines and reports on the merits of a case as an aid to a court; it is also used of a person who settles disputes, esp. in a game or sport: *a referee in bankruptcy; a basketball referee.* UMPIRE refers to a person who gives the final ruling when arbitrators of a case disagree; it is also used of a person who enforces the rules in a game: *an umpire to settle the labor dispute; a baseball umpire.*

judgment, *n.* **1.** verdict, decree, decision, determination, conclusion, opinion, estimate. **2.** understanding, discrimination, discernment, perspicacity, sagacity, wisdom, intelligence, prudence, brains, taste, penetration, discretion, common sense.

judicial, *adj.* critical, discriminating, judicious, juridical, forensic.

judicious, *adj.* **1.** practical, expedient, discreet, prudent, politic. **2.** wise, sensible, well-advised, rational, reasonable, sober, sound, enlightened, sagacious, considered, common-sense. —**Ant.** impractical, indiscreet, imprudent; silly, nonsensical, unsound, unreasonable. —**Syn. Study.** See PRACTICAL.

jumble, *v.* **1.** mix, confuse, mix up. —*n.* **2.** medley, mixture, hodgepodge, hotchpotch, muddle, mess, farrago, chaos, disorder, confusion, gallimaufry, potpourri. —**Ant.** separate, isolate; order.

jump, *v.* **1.** spring, bound, skip, hop, leap, vault. —*n.* **2.** leap, bound, spring, caper, vault, hop, skip.

junction, *n.* combination, union, joining, connection, linking, coupling; juncture; seam, welt, joint. —**Syn. Study.** JUNCTION, JUNCTURE refer to a place, line, or point at which two or more things join. A JUNCTION is also a place where things come together: *the junction of two rivers.* A JUNCTURE is a line or point at which two bodies are joined, or a point of exigency or crisis in time: *the junc-*

ture of the head and neck; a critical juncture in a struggle.

juncture, See Syn. study at JUNCTION.

junket, *n.* excursion.

just, *adj.* **1.** upright, equitable, fair, impartial, evenhanded, right, lawful. **2.** true, correct, accurate, exact, proper, regular, normal. **3.** rightful, legitimate, lawful, legal; deserved, merited, appropriate, condign, suited, suitable, apt, due. **4.** righteous, blameless, honest, upright, pure, conscientious, good, uncorrupt, virtuous, honorable, straightforward. —**Ant.** unjust.

justify, *v.* vindicate, exonerate, exculpate, absolve, acquit, defend, warrant, excuse. —**Ant.** inculpate, convict, indict, accuse, condemn.

K

keen, *adj.* **1.** sharp, acute, honed, razor-sharp. **2.** sharp, cutting, biting, severe, bitter, poignant, caustic, acrimonious. **3.** piercing, penetrating, discerning, astute, sagacious, sharp-witted, quick, shrewd, clever, keen-eyed, keen-sighted, clear-sighted, clear-headed. **4.** ardent, eager, zealous, earnest, fervid. —**Ant.** dull. —**Syn. Study.** See SHARP.

keep, *v.* **1.** maintain, reserve, preserve, retain, hold, withhold, have, continue. —*n.* **2.** subsistence, board and room. **3.** tower, dungeon, stronghold. —**Ant.** lose. —**Syn. Study.** KEEP, RETAIN, RESERVE, WITHHOLD refer to having or holding in one's possession, care, or control. KEEP means to continue to have or hold, as opposed to losing, parting with, or giving up: *to keep a book for a week.* RETAIN, a more formal word, often stresses keeping something in spite of resistance or opposition: *The dictator managed to retain power.* To RESERVE is to keep for some future use, occasion, or recipient, or to hold back for a time: *to reserve a seat; to reserve judgment.* To WITHHOLD is generally to hold back altogether: *to withhold evidence.*

keeper, *n.* guard, warden, custodian, jailer, guardian.

keeping, *n.* **1.** congruity, harmony, conformity, consistency, agreement. **2.** custody, protection, care, charge, guardianship, trust. —**Ant.** incongruity, nonconformity, inconsistency.

kibitz, *v.* **1.** meddle, interfere, second-guess, Monday-morning quarterback, pry, snoop. **2.** advise, counsel, coach, direct.

kill, *v.* **1.** slaughter, slay, assassinate, massacre, butcher, execute; murder; hang, electrocute, behead, guillotine, strangle, garrote. **2.** extinguish, destroy, do away with. —**Ant.** create, originate.

killjoy, *n.* doomsayer, Cassandra, pessimist, damper, crepehanger, worrywart, spoilsport, wet blanket, grouch, sourpuss, grinch, drag, party pooper, gloomy Gus, dog in the manger. —**Ant.** optimist, positivist, enthusiast.

kind, *adj.* **1.** gracious, kindhearted, kindly, good, mild, benign, bland; benevolent, benignant, beneficent, friendly, humane, generous, bounteous, accommodating; gentle, affectionate, living, tender, compassionate, sympathetic, tender-hearted, soft-hearted, good-natured. —*n.* **2.** sort, nature, character, race, genus, species, breed, set, class. —**Ant.** unkind.

kindhearted, *adj.* kind. —**Ant.** hardhearted, cruel.

kindle, *v.* **1.** set fire to, ignite, inflame, fire, light. **2.** rouse, arouse, awaken, bestir, inflame, provoke, incite, stimulate, animate, foment. —**Ant.** extinguish, quench. —**Syn. Study.** KINDLE, IGNITE, INFLAME literally mean to set something on fire. To KINDLE is to cause something gradually to begin burning; it is often used figuratively: *to kindle logs; to kindle someone's interest.* To IGNITE is to set something on fire with a sudden burst of flame; it also has figurative senses: *to ignite straw; to ignite dangerous hatreds.* INFLAME is most often used figuratively, meaning to intensify, excite, or rouse: *to inflame passions.*

kindly, *adj.* **1.** benevolent, kind, good-natured, sympathetic, compassionate. **2.** gentle, mild, benign. **3.** pleasant, genial, benign. —*adv.* **4.** cordially, politely, heartily; favorably. —**Ant.** unkindly, malevolent, unsympathetic; cruel, harsh; unpleasant; unfavorable.

kindness, *n.* **1.** service, favor, good

turn. **2.** benevolence, beneficence, humanity, benignity, generosity, philanthropy, charity, sympathy, compassion, tenderness, amiability. —**Ant.** unkindness, malevolence.

kingdom, *n.* monarchy, realm, sovereignty, dominion, empire, domain.

kingly, *adj.* kinglike, princely, regal, royal, imperial, sovereign, majestic, august, magnificent, grand, grandiose. —**Ant.** serflike, slavish, low, lowly.

kinship, *n.* relationship, affinity, connection, bearing.

knack, *n.* **1.** aptitude, aptness, facility, dexterity, skill, adroitness, dexterousness, skillfulness, expertness. **2.** habit, practice.

knave, *n.* rascal, rogue, scoundrel, blackguard, villain, scamp, scapegrace, swindler. —**Ant.** hero. —**Syn. Study.** KNAVE, RASCAL, ROGUE, SCOUNDREL are disparaging terms applied to persons considered base, dishonest, or unprincipled. KNAVE, which formerly meant a male servant, in modern use emphasizes baseness of nature and intention: *a swindling knave.* RASCAL suggests a certain shrewdness and trickery: *The rascal ran off with my money.* ROGUE often refers to a worthless person who preys on the community: *pictures of criminals in a rogues' gallery.* SCOUNDREL, a stronger term, suggests a base, immoral, even wicked person: *Those scoundrels finally went to jail.* RASCAL and ROGUE are often used affectionately or humorously to describe a mischievous person: *I'll bet that rascal hid my slippers. The little rogues ate all the cookies.*

knot, *n.* **1.** group, company, cluster, clique, hand, crew, gang, squad, crowd. **2.** lump, knob. **3.** difficulty, perplexity, puzzle, conundrum, rebus.

knotty, *adj.* complicated, complex, involved, intricate, difficult, hard, tough, thorny, perplexing. —**Ant.** easy, straightforward, uncomplicated.

know, *v.* **1.** perceive, understand, apprehend, comprehend, discern. **2.** recognize. **3.** distinguish, discriminate. —**Syn. Study.** KNOW, COMPREHEND, UNDERSTAND refer to perceiving or grasping facts and ideas. To KNOW is to be aware of, sure of, or familiar with something through observation, study, or experience: *I know that he agrees with me.* To COMPREHEND is to grasp something mentally and to perceive its relationships to certain other facts or ideas: *to comprehend a difficult text.* To UNDERSTAND is to be fully aware not only of the meaning or nature of something but also of its implications: *I could comprehend everything you said, but did not understand that you were joking.*

knowledge, *n.* **1.** enlightenment, erudition, wisdom, science, information, learning, scholarship, lore. **2.** understanding, discernment, perception, apprehension, comprehension, judgment.

kvetch, *v.* **1.** complain, whine, find fault, grouse, gripe, bellyache. —*n.* **2.** complainer, whiner, faultfinder, nitpicker, smellfungus.

L

labor, *n.* **1.** toil, work, exertion, drudgery. **2.** travail, childbirth, parturition, delivery. **3.** workingmen, working class; bourgeoisie. —*v.* **4.** work, toil, strive, drudge. **5.** be burdened or troubled or distressed, suffer. **6.** overdo, elaborate. —**Ant.** idleness, indolence, sloth. —**Syn. Study.** See WORK.

labored, *adj.* overdone, overworked, overwrought, ornate, unnatural.

laborious, *adj.* **1.** toilsome, arduous, onerous, burdensome, difficult, tiresome, wearisome, fatiguing. **2.** diligent, hard-working, assiduous, industrious, sedulous, painstaking. —**Ant.** easy, simple.

lacerate, *v.* **1.** tear, mangle, maim, rend, claw. **2.** hurt, injure, harm, wound, damage.

lachrymose, *adj.* **1.** tearful, weeping, teary, weepy, crying, sobbing, blubbering, blubbery. **2.** mournful, disconsolate, sorrowful, griefstricken, woeful, anguished. —**Ant.** cheerful, happy, sunny.

lack, *n.* **1.** deficiency, need, want, dearth, scarcity, paucity, shortcoming, deficit, scantiness, insufficiency, defectiveness. —*v.* **2.** want, need. —**Ant.** sufficiency, copiousness, abundance. —**Syn. Study.** LACK, WANT, NEED, REQUIRE indicate the ab-

sence of something desirable, important, or necessary. LACK means to be without or to have less than a desirable quantity of something: *to lack courage; to lack sufficient money.* WANT stresses the urgency of fulfilling a desire or providing what is lacking: *The room wants some final touch to make it homey.* NEED suggests even more urgency, stressing the necessity of supplying something essential: *to need an operation.* REQUIRE has a similar sense, although it is used in formal or serious contexts: *The report requires some editing.*

lackadaisical, *adj.* listless, indolent, enervated, blasé, indifferent, languid, languorous, lazy, unconcerned, uninvolved, apathetic, nonchalant, lethargic, sluggish, limp, bovine, numb. —**Ant.** effervescent, peppy, alert.

lackluster, *adj.* dull, ordinary, plain, pedestrian, routine, unexceptional, banal, colorless, prosaic, commonplace, everyday, mediocre, so-so, wishy-washy, drab, lifeless, flat, leaden. —**Ant.** brilliant.

laconic, *adj.* brief, concise, succinct, sententious, pithy, concentrated, terse, compact. —**Ant.** voluble.

lady, See Syn. study at WOMAN.

lag, *v.* **1.** fall behind or back, loiter, linger. —*n.* **2.** retardation, slowing, slowdown. —**Ant.** speed, quicken, expedite; expedition.

laggard, *n.* **1.** lingerer, dawdler, slowpoke, plodder, foot-dragger, procrastinator, delayer, dillydallier. —*adj.* **2.** slow, lingering, poky, delaying, dilatory, foot-dragging, procrastinating, lagging, indolent, slothful. —**Ant.** go-getting, industrious.

laid-back, *adj.* relaxed, easygoing, at ease, casual, off-hand, free-and-easy, dégagé, undemanding, loose, lax, nonchalant, blasé, flexible. —**Ant.** rigid, strict, severe.

lament, *v.* **1.** bewail, bemoan, deplore, grieve, weep, mourn or sorrow over or for. —*n.* **2.** lamentation, moan, wail, wailing, moaning. **3.** dirge, elegy, monody, threnody. —**Ant.** rejoice.

lane, *n.* path, way, passage, track, channel, course, alley.

language, *n.* **1.** speech, communication, tongue. **2.** dialect, jargon, terminology, vernacular; lingo, lingua franca. **3.** speech, phraseology, jargon, style, expression, diction. —**Syn. Study.** LANGUAGE, DIALECT, JARGON, VERNACULAR refer to patterns of vocabulary, syntax, and usage characteristic of communities of various sizes and types. LANGUAGE is applied to the general pattern of a people or nation: *the English language.* DIALECT is applied to regionally or socially distinct forms or varieties of a language, often forms used by provincial communities that differ from the standard variety: *the Scottish dialect.* JARGON is applied to the specialized language, esp. the vocabulary, used by a particular (usu. occupational) group within a community or to language considered unintelligible or obscure: *technical jargon.* The VERNACULAR is the natural, everyday pattern of speech, usu. on an informal level, used by people indigenous to a community.

languid, *adj.* **1.** faint, weak, feeble, weary, exhausted, debilitated. **2.** indifferent, spiritless, listless, inactive, inert, sluggish, torpid, dull. —**Ant.** strong, distinct, sharp, tireless; active, energetic.

large, *adj.* **1.** big, huge, enormous, immense, gigantic, colossal, massive, vast, great, extensive, broad, sizeable, grand, spacious; pompous. **2.** multitudinous; abundant, copious, ample, liberal, plentiful. —**Ant.** small, tiny; scanty, sparse, scarce, rare.

lascivious, *adj.* lustful, lecherous, salacious, lewd, libidinous, lubricious, lickerish, goatish, horny, randy, obscene, prurient. —**Ant.** chaste.

last, *adj.* **1.** final, ultimate, latest, concluding, conclusive, utmost, extreme, terminal, hindmost. —*v.* **2.** go on, continue, endure, perpetuate, remain. —**Ant.** first; fail, die. —**Syn. Study.** See CONTINUE.

late, *adj.* **1.** tardy, slow, dilatory, delayed, belated. **2.** continued, lasting, protracted. **3.** recent, modern, advanced. **4.** former, recently deceased. —**Ant.** early, fast.

latent, *adj.* hidden, concealed, veiled; potential. —**Ant.** kinetic, open.

latitude, *n.* range, scope, extent, liberty, freedom, indulgence. —**Syn. Study.** See RANGE.

laud, *v.* praise, extol, applaud, celebrate, esteem, honor. —Ant. censure, condemn, criticize.

laugh, v. 1. chortle, cackle, cachinnate, hawhaw, guffaw, roar; giggle, snicker, snigger, titter. —n. 2. chuckle, grin, smile; laughter, cachinnation. —Ant. cry, mourn, wail.

laughable, adj. funny, amusing, humorous, droll, comical, ludicrous, farcical, ridiculous, risible. —Ant. sad, melancholy.

lavish, adj. 1. unstinted, extravagant, excessive, prodigal, profuse, generous, openhanded; wasteful, improvident. —v. 2. expend, bestow, endow; waste, dissipate, squander. —Ant. stingy, niggardly; provident; save. —Syn. Study. LAVISH, PRODIGAL, PROFUSE refer to that which exists in abundance and is poured out in great amounts. LAVISH suggests an unlimited, sometimes excessive generosity and openhandedness: lavish hospitality. PRODIGAL suggests wastefulness, improvidence, and reckless impatience: He has lost his inheritance because of his prodigal ways. PROFUSE emphasizes abundance, but may suggest exaggeration, emotionalism, or the like: profuse thanks; profuse apologies.

lawful, adj. 1. legal, legitimate, valid. 2. licit, sanctioned, allowed. —Ant. illegal, illicit, illegitimate; forbidden.

lax, adj. 1. loose, relaxed, slack, drooping, droopy. 2. negligent, careless, remiss, neglectful, unrigorous, heedless, slipshod, slovenly. —Ant. rigorous, responsible.

lay, v. 1. place, put, deposit, set, locate. 2. allay, appease, calm, still, quiet, suppress. 3. wager, bet, stake, risk. 4. impute, ascribe, attribute, charge. 5. burden, penalize, assess, impose. —n. 6. position, lie, site. 7. song, lyric, musical poem, poem, ode. —adj. 8. unclerical, laic, laical. 9. unprofessional, amateur.

lazy, adj. 1. idle, indolent, slothful, slow-moving, sluggish, inert, inactive, torpid. —Ant. industrious, quick. —Syn. Study. See IDLE.

lead, v. 1. conduct, go before, precede, guide, direct, escort. 2. guide, influence, induce, persuade, convince, draw, entice, lure, allure, seduce, lead on. 3. excel, outstrip, surpass. —n. 4. precedence, advance, vanguard, head. 5. weight, plumb. —Ant. follow.

leading, n. 1. guidance, direction, lead. 2. lead, spacing, space. —adj. 3. chief, principal, most important, foremost, capital, ruling, governing. —Ant. deputy; secondary; following.

league, n. 1. covenant, compact, alliance, confederation, combination, coalition, confederacy, union. —v. 2. unite, combine, confederate. —Syn. Study. See ALLIANCE.

lean, v. 1. incline, tend toward, bend, slope. 2. repose, rest, rely, depend, trust, confide. —adj. 3. skinny, thin, gaunt, emaciated, lank, meager. 4. sparse, barren, unfruitful, inadequate, deficient, jejune. —n. 5. meat, essence. —Ant. fat, obese; fertile, fruitful, adequate; superfluity, excess.

leap, v., n. jump, bound, spring, vault, hop.

learn, v. ascertain, detect, discover, memorize, acquire, hear. —Syn. Study. LEARN, DISCOVER, ASCERTAIN, DETECT imply adding to one's store of knowledge or information. To LEARN is to come to know by chance, or by study or other application: to learn of a friend's death; to learn to ski. To DISCOVER is to find out something previously unseen or unknown; it suggests that the new information is surprising to the learner: I discovered that they were selling their house. To ASCERTAIN is to find out and verify information through inquiry or analysis: to ascertain the truth about the incident. To DETECT is to become aware of something obscure, secret, or concealed: to detect a flaw in reasoning.

learning, n. erudition, lore, knowledge, scholarship, store of information. —Syn. Study. LEARNING, ERUDITION, SCHOLARSHIP refer to facts or ideas acquired through systematic study. LEARNING usu. refers to knowledge gained from extensive reading and formal instruction: Her vast learning is reflected in her many books. ERUDITION suggests a thorough and profound knowledge of a difficult subject: His erudition in languages is legendary. SCHOLARSHIP suggests a high degree of mastery in a specialized field, along with an analytical or innovative ability suited to the academic world: The author is re-

nowned for several works of classical scholarship.

leave, v. 1. quit, vacate, abandon, forsake, desert, depart from, retire from, withdraw or escape from, relinquish, renounce. 2. desist from, stop, forbear, cease, abandon, let alone. 3. omit, forget, exclude. 4. bequeath, will, devise, transmit. —n. 5. permission, allowance, freedom, liberty, license. —Ant. arrive, gain.

legend, n. fable, myth, story, fiction. —Ant. fact, history. —Syn. Study. LEGEND, MYTH, FABLE refer to stories handed down from earlier times, often by word of mouth. A LEGEND is a story associated with a people or a nation; it is usu. concerned with a real person, place, or event and is popularly believed to have some basis in fact: the legend of King Arthur. A MYTH is one of a class of purportedly historical stories that attempt to explain some belief, practice, or natural phenomenon: the characters are usu. gods or heroes: the Greek myth about Demeter. A FABLE is a fictitious story intended to teach a moral lesson; the characters are usu. animals: the fable about the fox and the grapes.

legitimate, adj. 1. legal, lawful, licit, sanctioned. 2. normal, regular. 3. reasonable, logical, sensible, common-sense, valid, warranted, called-for, correct, proper. —v. 4. authorize, justify, legalize. —Ant. illegitimate; unreasonable, incorrect, improper.

leisurely, adj. deliberate, slow, premeditated, unhurried, easily. —Ant. unpremeditated, quick, hurried, hasty. —Syn. Study. See SLOW.

lengthen, v. extend, stretch, prolong, protract, attenuate, elongate, draw out, continue, increase. —Ant. shorten, abbreviate. —Syn. Study. LENGTHEN, EXTEND, PROLONG, PROTRACT agree in the idea of making longer. To LENGTHEN is to make longer, either in a material or immaterial sense: to lengthen a dress; to lengthen human life. To EXTEND is to lengthen beyond some original point or so as to reach a certain point: to extend a railway line another fifty miles. Both PROLONG and PROTRACT mean esp. to lengthen in time. To PROLONG is to continue beyond the desired, estimated, or allotted time: to prolong an interview. To PROTRACT is to draw out to undue length or to be slow in coming to a conclusion: to protract a discussion.

lenient, adj. mild, clement, merciful, easy, gentle, soothing, tender, forbearing, long-suffering. —Ant. harsh, cruel, brutal, merciless.

lessen, v. 1. diminish, decrease, abate, dwindle, fade, shrink. 2. diminish, decrease, depreciate, disparage, reduce, micrify, lower, degrade. 3. decrease, diminish, abate, abridge, reduce. —Ant. increase; raise; lengthen, enlarge.

let, v. 1. allow, permit, suffer, grant. 2. disappoint, fail. 3. lease, rent, sublet, hire. —Ant. prevent, disallow. —Syn. Study. See ALLOW.

lethal, See Syn. study at FATAL.

level, adj. 1. even, flat, smooth, uniform, plain, flush. 2. horizontal. 3. equal, on a par, equivalent. 4. even, equable, uniform. —v. 5. even, equalize, smooth, flatten. 6. raze, demolish, destroy. 7. aim, direct, point. —Ant. uneven; vertical; unequal.

liable, adj. 1. subject, exposed, likely, open. 2. obliged, responsible, answerable, accountable. —Ant. protected, secure.

liberal, adj. 1. progressive, reform. 2. tolerant, unbigoted, broad-minded, unprejudiced, magnanimous, generous, honorable. 3. generous, bountiful, beneficent, free, charitable, openhanded, munificent; abundant, ample, bounteous, unstinting, lavish, plentiful. —Ant. illiberal; intolerant, prejudiced; stingy, parsimonious, niggardly.

liberate, v. set free, release, emancipate, free, disengage, unfetter, disenthrall, deliver, set loose, loose, let out, discharge. —Ant. imprison, incarcerate; enthrall, enslave. —Syn. Study. See RELEASE.

libertine, n. rake, roué, debauchee, lecher, sensualist, profligate. —adj. 2. amoral, licentious, lascivious, lewd, dissolute, depraved, corrupt, perverted, immoral, sensual. —Ant. prude.

liberty, n. freedom, liberation, independence; franchise, permission, leave, license, privilege, immunity.

licentious, adj. sensual, libertine, lewd, lascivious, libidinous, lustful, lecherous, lawless, immoral, wanton, concupiscent, loose, amoral, un-

chaste, impure. —Ant. prudish, moral; chaste, pure.

lie, n. 1. falsehood, prevarication, mendacity, untruth, falsification, fib. 2. place, position, location, lay, site. —v. 3. falsify, prevaricate, fib. 4. recline. —Ant. truth.

life, n. 1. animation, vigor, vivacity, vitality, sprightliness, verve, effervescence, sparkle, spirit, activity, energy. 2. biography, memoir. 3. existence, being.

lifeless, adj. 1. inanimate, inorganic, mineral. 2. dead, defunct, extinct. 3. dull, inactive, inert, passive, sluggish, torpid, spiritless. —Ant. alive, animate, live, organic; alive, extant; active, animated, spirited.

lift, v. raise, elevate, hold up, exalt, uplift. —Ant. lower.

light, n. 1. illumination, radiance, daylight; dawn, sunrise, daybreak. 2. aspect, viewpoint, point of view, angle, approach. —adj. 3. pale, whitish, blanched. 4. buoyant, lightsome, easy. 5. shallow, humorous, slight, trivial, trifling, inconsiderable, unsubstantial, flimsy, insubstantial, gossamer, airy, flighty. 6. airy, nimble, agile, alert. 7. carefree, gay, cheery, cheerful, happy, light-hearted. 8. frivolous, lightsome, light-headed, volatile. 9. wanton. 10. dizzy, delirious, light-headed, giddy. —v. 11. alight, get or come down, descend, land, disembark. 12. kindle, set fire to, ignite, set afire, fire. —Ant. darkness, sunset; swarthy; difficult; deep, considerable, substantial; cheerless, sad; serious; board, embark, mount; quench.

lighten, v. 1. illuminate, brighten, shine, gleam, illume. 2. mitigate, disburden, unburden, ease. 3. cheer, gladden. —Ant. darken, adumbrate; intensify, aggravate; sadden.

light-hearted, adj. carefree, cheerful, lightsome, gay, cheery, joyous, joyful, blithe, glad, happy, merry, jovial, jocund. —Ant. heavy-hearted, cheerless, morose, sad, gloomy, melancholy.

likely, adj. apt, liable, probable, possible, suitable, appropriate. —Ant. unlikely.

liking, n. preference, inclination, favor, disposition, bent, bias, leaning, propensity, capacity, proclivity, proneness, predilection, predisposition, tendency; partiality, fondness, affection. —Ant. dislike, disfavor, disinclination.

limb, n. 1. part, member, extremity; leg, arm, wing. 2. branch, bough, offshoot.

limber, adj. pliant, flexible, supple, pliable, lithe. —Ant. rigid, unbending, unyielding.

limelight, n. public eye, public notice, cynosure, publicness, fame, notoriety, exposure, publicity, réclame. —Ant. reclusiveness, seclusion.

limit, n. 1. bound, extent, boundary, confine, frontier, termination. 2. restraint, restriction, constraint, check, hindrance. —v. 3. restrain, restrict, confine, check, hinder, bound, circumscribe, define.

limpid, adj. clear, transparent, pellucid, lucid, crystal-clear. —Ant. cloudy, dim, dull.

linger, v. remain, stay on, tarry, delay, dawdle, loiter.

link, n. 1. bond, tie, connection, connective, copula, vinculum. —v. 2. bond, join, unite, connect, league, conjoin, fasten, pin, bind, tie. —Ant. separation; separate, split, rive.

liquid, n., adj. fluid, liquor. —n. solid, gas. —Syn. Study. LIQUID, FLUID agree in referring to matter that is not solid. LIQUID commonly refers to substances, as water, oil, alcohol, and the like, that are neither solids nor gases: Water ceases to be a liquid when it is frozen or turned to steam. FLUID is applied to anything that flows, whether liquid or gaseous: Pipes can carry fluids from place to place.

lissome, adj. lithesome, lithe, limber, supple, agile, active, energetic. —Ant. inflexible, rigid, clumsy, awkward.

list, n. 1. catalogue, inventory, roll, schedule, series, register. 2. border, strip, selvage, band, edge. 3. leaning, tilt, tilting, careening. —v. 4. register, catalogue, enlist, enroll. 5. border, edge. 6. careen, incline, lean. —Syn. Study. LIST, CATALOG, INVENTORY, ROLL imply a meaningful arrangement of items. LIST denotes a series of names, figures, or other items arranged in a row or rows: a grocery list. CATALOG adds the idea of an alphabetical or other orderly arranged list of goods or services, usu.

with descriptive details: a mail-order catalog. INVENTORY refers to a detailed, descriptive list of goods or property, made for legal or business purposes: The company's inventory consists of 2,000 items. A ROLL is a list of names of members of a group, often used to check attendance: The teacher called the roll.

listen, v. hearken, hear, hark, attend, give ear, lend an ear.

listlessness, n. indifference, inattention, inattentiveness, heedlessness, thoughtlessness, carelessness. —Ant. concern, care, attention, attentiveness.

literature, n. belles-lettres, letters, humanities, writings.

litter, n. 1. rubbish, shreds, fragments. 2. untidiness, disorder, confusion. 3. brood. 4. stretcher. 5. straw or hay bedding. —v. 6. strew, scatter, derange, mess up, disarrange, disorder.

little, adj. 1. small, diminutive, minute, tiny, infinitesimal, wee. 2. short, brief. 3. weak, feeble, slight, inconsiderable, trivial, paltry, insignificant, unimportant, petty, scanty. 4. mean, narrow, illiberal, paltry, stingy, selfish, small, niggardly. —adv. 5. slightly, barely, just. —Ant. large, immense, huge; important; liberal, generous.

livelihood, n. maintenance, living, sustenance, support, subsistence.

lively, adj. 1. energetic, active, vigorous, brisk, peart, vivacious, alert, spry, nimble, agile, quick. 2. animated, spirited, vivacious, sprightly, gay, blithe, blithesome, buoyant, gleeful. 3. eventful, stirring, moving. 4. strong, keen, distinct, vigorous, forceful, clear, piquant. 5. striking, telling, effective. 6. vivid, bright, brilliant, fresh, clear, glowing. 7. sparkling, fresh. —Ant. inactive, torpid; leaden; uneventful; weak, dull, unclear; ineffective; dim; stale.

living, adj. 1. alive, live, quick, existing; extant, surviving. 2. active, lively, strong, vigorous, quickening. —n. 3. livelihood, maintenance, sustenance, subsistence, support. —Ant. dead.

load, n. 1. burden, onus, weight, encumbrance, incubus, pressure. —v. 2. lade, weight, weigh down, burden, encumber, freight, oppress. —Ant. disburden, unload, lighten.

loath, adj. reluctant, averse, unwilling, disinclined, backward. —Ant. eager, anxious, willing. —Syn. Study. See RELUCTANT.

loathe, v. abominate, detest, hate, abhor. —Ant. adore, love.

loathing, n. disgust, dislike, aversion, abhorrence, hatred, hate, antipathy; animus, animosity, hostility. —Ant. liking; love; friendship, regard.

loathsome, adj. disgusting, nauseating, sickening, repulsive, offensive, repellent, revolting, detestable, abhorrent, hateful, odious, abominable, execrable. —Ant. attractive, delightful, lovable.

locale, n. place, location, site, spot, locality.

lodge, n. 1. shelter, habitation, cabin, hut, cottage, cot. 2. club, association, society. —v. 3. shelter, harbor, house, quarter. 4. place, put, set, plant, infix, deposit, lay, settle.

lofty, adj. 1. high, elevated, towering, tall. 2. exalted, elevated, sublime. 3. haughty, proud, arrogant, prideful. —Ant. lowly; debased; humble.

loiter, v. linger, dally, dawdle, idle, loaf, delay, tarry, lag. —Syn. Study. LOITER, DALLY, DAWDLE, IDLE imply moving or acting slowly, stopping for unimportant reasons, and in general wasting time. To LOITER is to linger aimlessly: to loiter outside a building. To DALLY is to loiter indecisively or to delay as if free from care or responsibility: to dally on the way home. To DAWDLE is to saunter, stopping often, and taking a great deal of time, or to fritter away time working in a halfhearted way: to dawdle over a task. To IDLE is to move slowly and aimlessly, or to spend a great deal of time doing nothing: to idle away the hours.

lone, adj. 1. alone, unaccompanied, solitary, lonely, secluded, apart, separate, separated; deserted, uninhabited, unoccupied, unpopulated, empty. 2. isolated, solitary, sole, unique, lonely. —Ant. accompanied, together; inhabited, occupied.

lonely, adj. lone, solitary, lonesome, sequestered, remote, dreary. —Ant. crowded, populous.

lonesome, adj. lonely, alone, secluded; desolate, isolated.

long, adj. 1. lengthy, extensive, drawn out, attenuated, protracted, stretched, prolonged, extended. 2. overlong, long-winded, tedious, boring, wordy, prolix. —v. 3. crave, desire, yearn for, pine for, hanker for or after. —Ant. short, abbreviated; interesting; forgo. —Syn. Study. See YEARN.

longing, n. craving, desire, hankering, yearning, aspiration. —Ant. disinterest, antipathy, apathy.

look, v. 1. gaze, glance, watch. 2. appear, seem. 3. await, wait for, expect, anticipate. 4. face, front. 5. seek, search for. —n. 6. gaze, glance. 7. search, examination. 8. appearance, aspect, mien, manner, air. —Syn. Study. See SEEM.

loose, adj. 1. free, unfettered, unbound, untied, unrestrained, unrestricted, released, unattached, unfastened, unconfined. 2. uncombined. 3. lax, slack, careless, negligent, heedless. 4. wanton, libertine, unchaste, immoral, dissolute, licentious. 5. general, vague, indefinite, inexact, imprecise, ill-defined, indeterminate, indistinct. —v. 6. loosen, free, set free, unfasten, undo, unlock, unbind, untie, unloose, release, liberate. 7. relax, slacken, ease, loosen. —Ant. bound, fettered; combined; tight, taut; moral, chaste; definite, specific; bind, commit; tighten.

loot, n. 1. spoils, plunder, booty. —v. 2. plunder, rob, sack, rifle, despoil, ransack, pillage, rape.

loquacious, adj. talkative, garrulous, wordy, verbose, voluble. —Ant. taciturn, close-mouthed. —Syn. Study. See TALKATIVE.

lordly, adj. 1. grand, magnificent, majestic, royal, regal, kingly, aristocratic, dignified, noble, lofty. 2. haughty, arrogant, lofty, imperious, domineering, insolent, overbearing, despotic, dictatorial, tyrannical. —Ant. menial, servile; humble, obedient.

lore, n. 1. learning, kowledge, erudition. 2. wisdom, counsel, advice, teaching, doctrine, lesson.

loss, n. 1. detriment, disadvantage, damage, injury, destruction. 2. privation, deprivation. —Ant. gain.

lost, adj. 1. forfeited, gone, missing, missed. 2. bewildered, confused, perplexed, puzzled. 3. wasted, misspent, squandered, dissipated. 4. defeated, vanquished. 5. destroyed, ruined. 6. depraved, abandoned, dissolute, corrupt, reprobate, profligate, licentious, shameless, hardened, irredeemable, irreclaimable. —Ant. found; pure, honorable, chaste.

loud, adj. 1. noisy, clamorous, resounding, deafening, stentorian, boisterous, tumultuous. 2. gaudy, flashy, showy, obtrusive, vulgar, obvious, blatant, coarse, rude, crude, cheap. —Ant. soft, quiet; sedate, tasteful, artistic.

loutish, adj. boorish, unrefined, uncouth, ill-bred, rough, cloddish, clumsy, crass, churlish, coarse, crude, brutish, beastly. —Ant. refined, gracious, graceful.

love, n. 1. affection, predilection, liking, inclination, regard, friendliness, kindness, tenderness, fondness, devotion, warmth, attachment, passion, adoration. —v. 2. like, be fond of, have affection for, be enamored of, be in love with, adore, adulate, worship. —Ant. hatred, dislike; detest, abhor, abominate, hate.

lovely, adj. beautiful, charming, exquisite, enchanting, winning. —Ant. ugly, unattractive, homely. —Syn. Study. See BEAUTIFUL.

low, adj. 1. prostrate, dead, prone, supine. 2. profound, deep. 3. feeble, weak, exhausted, sinking, dying, expiring. 4. depressed, dejected, dispirited, unhappy, sad, miserable. 5. undignified, infra dig, lowly, dishonorable, disreputable, unbecoming, disgraceful. 6. groveling, abject, sordid, mean, base, lowly, degraded, menial, servile, ignoble, vile. 7. humble, lowly, meek, lowborn, poor, plain, plebeian, vulgar, base. 8. coarse, vulgar, rude, crude. 9. soft, subdued, gentle, quiet. —adv. 10. cheaply, inexpensively. —v. 11. moo, bellow. —Ant. high, upright. —Syn. Study. See MEAN.

lower, v. 1. reduce, decrease, diminish, lessen. 2. soften, turn down, quiet down. 3. degrade, humble, abase, humiliate, disgrace, debase. 4. let down, drop, depress, take down, sink. 5. darken, threaten, glower; frown, scowl. —Ant. raise, increase; elevate, honor; brighten.

loyal, adj. faithful, true, patriotic, devoted, constant. —Ant. faithless, disloyal, treacherous. **—Syn. Study.** See FAITHFUL.

loyalty, *n.* faithfulness, allegiance, fealty, devotion, constancy, patriotism, fidelity. **—Ant.** faithlessness, disloyalty.

antique, *adj.* **1.** ancient, old, archaic, bygone; antediluvian. **2.** early, old. **3.** antiquated, old-fashioned, out-of-date, obsolescent, obsolete, passé, demoded, démodé. *—n.* **4.** object d'art, bibelot, curio, rarity. **—Ant.** modern, new. **—Syn. Study.** See ANCIENT.

lucid, *adj.* **1.** shining, bright, lucent, radiant, brilliant, resplendent, luminous. **2.** clear, transparent, pellucid, limpid, crystalline; luculent, intelligible, plain, unmistakable, obvious, distinct, evident, understandable; rational, sane, sober, sound, reasonable. **—Ant.** dull; unclear, dull; unreasonable.

lucky, *adj.* fortunate, fortuitous, happy, favored, blessed; propitious, favorable, prosperous. **—Ant.** unfortunate, unlucky.

ludicrous, *adj.* laughable, ridiculous, amusing, comical, funny, droll, absurd, farcical. **—Ant.** miserable, serious, tragic.

lugubrious, *adj.* doleful, mournful, dismal, sorrowful, melancholy, gloomy, depressing. **—Ant.** cheerful, happy.

lukewarm, *adj.* **1.** tepid, warmish, moderately warm, room-temperature. **2.** halfhearted, unenthusiastic, so-so, unimpassioned, unmoved, indifferent, unsympathetic, Laodicean. **—Ant.** dedicated, enthusiastic.

luminous, *adj.* **1.** bright, shining, lucid, lucent, radiant, brilliant, resplendent. **2.** lighted, lit, illuminated. **3.** brilliant, bright, intelligent, smart, clever, enlightening. **4.** clear, intelligible, understandable, perspicacious, perspicuous, plain, lucid. **—Ant.** dull; dark; stupid; unclear, unintelligible.

lunacy, *n.* **1.** madness, craziness, insanity, psychosis, daftness, mania, dementia, dementedness. **2.** folly, foolishness, foolhardiness, absurdity, fatuity, silliness. **—Ant.** sanity, normalcy, sobriety.

lure, *n.* **1.** enticement, decoy, attraction, allurement, temptation, bait; fly, minnow. *—v.* **2.** allure, decoy, entice, draw, attract, tempt, seduce.

lurid, *adj.* **1.** vivid, glaring, sensational; shining, fiery, red, intense, fierce, terrible, unrestrained, passionate. **2.** wan, pale, pallid, ghastly, gloomy, murky, dismal, lowering. **—Ant.** mild, controlled; cheery.

lurk, *v.* skulk, sneak, prowl, slink, steal; lie in wait, lie in ambush, lie hidden *or* concealed. **—Syn. Study.** LURK, SKULK, SNEAK, PROWL suggest avoiding observation, often because of a sinister purpose. To LURK is to lie in wait for someone or to move stealthily: *The thief lurked in the shadows.* SKULK has a similar sense, but usu. suggests cowardice or fear: *The dog skulked about the house.* SNEAK emphasizes the attempt to avoid being seen or discovered; it suggests a sinister intent or the desire to avoid punishment: *The children sneaked out the back way.* PROWL usu. implies seeking prey or loot; it suggests quiet and watchful roaming: *The cat prowled around in search of mice.*

luscious, *adj.* **1.** delicious, juicy, delectable, palatable, savory. **2.** sweet, cloying, saccharine, honeyed. **—Ant.** unpalatable, disgusting, nauseating; bitter, acrid, acid.

lush, *adj.* **1.** tender, juicy, succulent, luxuriant, fresh. *—n.* **2.** *(slang)* drunk, toper, tippler, dipsomaniac, alcoholic, heavy drinker. **—Ant.** stale, moldy.

lust, *n.* **1.** desire, passion, appetite, craving, eagerness, cupidity. **2.** lechery, concupiscence, carnality, lubricity, salaciousness, licentiousness, wantonness, lasciviousness, libertinism, license. *—v.* **3.** crave, desire, need, want, demand, hunger for.

luster, *n.* **1.** glitter, glisten, sheen, gloss. **2.** brilliance, brightness, radiance, luminosity, resplendence. **3.** excellence, merit, distinction, glory, honor, repute, renown, eminence, celebrity, dash, élan, éclat. **4.** chandelier, sconce, candelabrum. **—Ant.** dullness, tarnish; disrepute, dishonor.

lusty, *adj.* hearty, vigorous, strong, healthy, robust, sturdy, stout. **—Ant.** weak, frail, unhealthy.

luxurious, *adj.* **1.** splendid, rich, sumptuous, ornate, delicate, opulent, well-appointed. **2.** voluptuous, sen-

sual, self-indulgent, epicurean. **—Ant.** poor, squalid.

lyrical, *adj.* lilting, airy, songful, graceful, lighthearted, lightsome, buoyant, sunny, exuberant, rhapsodic. **—Ant.** sorrowful, elegiac.

M

macabre, *adj.* gruesome, horrible, grim, ghastly, morbid, weird. **—Ant.** beautiful, lovely, attractive, delightful.

Machiavellian, *adj.* crafty, deceitful, cunning, wily, astute, unscrupulous, clever, artful, designing, insidious, sly, shrewd, subtle, arch, crooked, tricky, intriguing, double-dealing, equivocal. **—Ant.** naive, ingenuous, honest.

machination, *n.* manipulation, maneuver, stratagem, ploy, artifice, tactic, wile, device, trick, plot, cabal, intrigue, scheme, conspiracy.

machismo, *n.* manliness, supermanliness, virility, potency, boldness, courageousness, dominance, prepotency, primacy, arrogance.

mad, *adj.* **1.** insane, lunatic, deranged, raving, distracted, crazed, maniacal, crazy. **2.** furious, exasperated, angry, enraged, raging, incensed, provoked, wrathful, irate. **3.** violent, furious, stormy. **4.** excited, frantic, frenzied, wild, rabid. **5.** senseless, foolish, imprudent, impractical, ill-advised, excessive, reckless, unsound, unsafe, harmful, dangerous, perilous. **6.** infatuated, wild about, desirous. **—Ant.** sane; calm; serene; sensible, wise.

madden, *v.* infuriate, irritate, provoke, vex, annoy, enrage, anger, inflame, exasperate. **—Ant.** calm, mollify.

maelstrom, *n.* **1.** whirlpool, vortex, eddy, whirl, Charybdis, sea puss. **2.** turmoil, agitation, bustle, turbulence, ferment, hubbub, commotion, confusion, storm. **—Ant.** tranquillity, smoothness.

magic, *n.* enchantment, sorcery, necromancy, witchcraft, legerdemain, conjuring, sleight of hand.

magician, *n.* sorcerer, necromancer, witch doctor, enchanter, conjuror.

magisterial, *adj.* dictatorial, dominating, dogmatic, doctrinaire, imperious, authoritarian, lordly. **2.** masterful, masterly, authoritative, commanding, expert.

magnanimous, *adj.* **1.** big, large, generous, forgiving, unselfish, liberal, disinterested. **2.** noble, lofty, honorable, elevated, high-minded, exalted. **—Ant.** small, niggardly; base, vile. **—Syn. Study.** See NOBLE.

magnificence, *n.* splendor, grandeur, impressiveness, sumptuousness, pomp, state, majesty, luxury, luxuriousness, éclat. **—Ant.** squalor, poverty.

magnificent, *adj.* **1.** splendid, fine, superb, august, stately, majestic, imposing, sumptuous, rich, lavish, luxurious, grand, gorgeous, beautiful, princely, impressive, dazzling, brilliant, radiant, excellent, exquisite, elegant, superior, extraordinary; showy, ostentatious. **2.** noble, sublime, dignified, great. **—Ant.** squalid, poor; base.

magnify, *v.* **1.** enlarge, augment, increase, add to, amplify. **2.** exaggerate, overstate. **—Ant.** decrease, minify; understate.

maid, *n.* **1.** girl, maiden, demoiselle, lass, lassie, virgin. **2.** maidservant.

maim, *v.* mutilate, cripple, lacerate, mangle, injure, disable, wound, deface, mar, impair.

main, *adj.* **1.** chief, cardinal, prime, paramount, primary, principal, leading, capital. **2.** pure, sheer, utmost, direct. *—n.* **3.** pipe, duct, conduit, channel. **4.** force, power, strength, might, effort. **5.** point, idea, crux. **6.** ocean, sea, high seas. **—Ant.** secondary, unimportant; least; weakness.

mainstay, *n.* support, backbone, spine, sine qua non, supporter, upholder, sustainer, pillar, brace, standby, prop, crutch.

maintain, *v.* **1.** keep, continue, preserve, retain, keep up, uphold, support. **2.** affirm, assert, aver, asseverate, state, hold, allege, declare. **3.** contend, hold, claim, defend, vindicate, justify. **4.** provide for, support, sustain, keep up. **—Ant.** discontinue.

maintenance, *n.* subsistence, support, livelihood, living, bread, victuals, food, provisions. **—Ant.** desuetude.

majestic, *adj.* regal, royal, princely,

kingly, imperial, noble, lofty, stately, grand, august, dignified, imposing, pompous, splendid, magnificent, sublime. **—Ant.** base, squalid.

major, *adj.* greater, larger, capital. **—Ant.** minor. **—Syn. Study.** See CAPITAL.

make, *v.* **1.** form, build, produce, fabricate, create, construct, manufacture, fashion, mold, shape. **2.** cause, render, constitute. **3.** transform, convert, change, turn, compose. **4.** give rise to, prompt, occasion. **5.** get, gain, acquire, obtain, secure, procure, earn, win. **6.** do, effect, bring about, perform, execute, accomplish, practice, act. **7.** estimate, reckon, judge, gauge. **8.** cause, induce, compel, force. *—n.* **9.** style, form, build, shape, brand, trade name, construction, structure, constitution. **10.** disposition, character, nature. **11.** quantity made, output, produce, production, product. **—Ant.** destroy.

makeshift, *adj.* **1.** improvised, stopgap, provisional, expedient, temporary, substitute, reserve, spare, make-do, jerry-built. *—n.* **2.** improvisation, expedient, substitute, reserve, stopgap, resort, make-do.

maladroit, *adj.* unskillful, awkward, clumsy, bungling, inept. **2.** tactless, gauche. **—Ant.** adroit; tactful, subtle.

malady, *n.* disease, illness, sickness, affliction, disorder, complaint, ailment, indisposition.

malcontent, *adj.* **1.** dissatisfied, discontented, unsatisfied, unfulfilled. **—Ant.** satisfied, contented, content

male, *adj.* masculine, manly, virile, paternal. **—Ant.** female. **—Syn. Study.** MALE, MASCULINE, VIRILE describe men and boys or whatever is culturally attributed to them. MALE classifies individuals on the basis of their genetic makeup or their ability to fertilize an ovum in bisexual reproduction. It contrasts with FEMALE in all uses: *his oldest male relative; the male parts of the flower.* MASCULINE refers to qualities or behavior deemed especially appropriate to or ideally associated with men or boys. In American and W European culture, this has traditionally included such traits as strength, aggressiveness, and courage: *a firm, masculine handshake; masculine impatience at indecision.* VIRILE implies the muscularity, vigor, and sexual potency of mature manhood: *a swaggering, virile walk.* See also MANLY, MAN.

malediction, *n.* curse, imprecation, denunciation, cursing, damning, damnation, execration; slander. **—Ant.** benediction, blessing.

malefactor, *n.* evildoer, culprit, criminal, felon, outlaw, offender. **—Ant.** benefactor.

malevolence, *n.* ill will, rancor, malignity, resentment, malice, maliciousness, spite, spitefulness, grudge, hate, hatred, venom. **—Ant.** benevolence, good will.

malevolent, *adj.* malicious, malignant, resentful, spiteful, begrudging, hateful, venomous, vicious, hostile, ill-natured, evil-minded, rancorous, mischievous, envious. **—Ant.** benevolent, friendly, amiable.

malfeasance, *n.* misbehavior, misconduct, misdemeanor, misdeed, badness, wrongdoing, malpractice, delinquency, criminality, illegality, wickedness. **—Ant.** lawfulness, honesty.

malice, *n.* ill will, spite, spitefulness, animosity, animus, enmity, malevolence, grudge, venom, hate, hatred, bitterness, rancor. **—Ant.** good will, benevolence.

malicious, *adj.* malevolent. **—Ant.** benevolent.

malign, *v.* **1.** slander, libel, revile, abuse, calumniate, defame, disparage, vilify. *—adj.* **2.** evil, pernicious, baleful, injurious, unfavorable, baneful. **3.** malevolent. **—Ant.** compliment, praise; good, favorable, benevolent.

malignant, *adj.* **1.** malicious, spiteful, malevolent, rancorous, bitter. **2.** dangerous, perilous, harmful, hurtful, virulent, pernicious, lethal, deadly. **—Ant.** benevolent; benign.

malignity, *n.* malevolence. **—Ant.** benignity.

malinger, *v.* shirk, slack, slack off, dodge, duck duty, get out of, goldbrick.

malleable, *adj.* adaptable, plastic, shapable, bendable, ductile, moldable, pliant, pliable, supple, flexible, elastic, compliant. **—Ant.** rigid, refractory.

maltreat, *v.* mistreat, abuse, injure, ill-treat. **—Ant.** amuse, entertain.

mammoth, *adj.* huge, gigantic, immense, colossal. **—Ant.** tiny, microscopic. **—Syn. Study.** See GIGANTIC.

man, *n.* **1.** male, gentleman, adult male **2.** humanity, humankind, mankind; human being, human **—Syn. Study.** MAN, MALE, GENTLEMAN refer to adult humans of the sex that produces sperm for procreation. MAN, the most commonly used of the three, can be neutral: *a man of deep faith.* It can also signify possession of typical or desirable masculine qualities: *to take one's punishment like a man.* MALE emphasizes physical or sexual characteristics and can also apply to an animal or a plant: *two males and three females in the pack.* GENTLEMAN, once used only of men of high social rank, now also specifies a man of courtesy and consideration: *to behave like a gentleman.* It is used too as a polite term of reference (*This gentleman is next*) or, only in the plural, of address (*Are we ready, gentlemen?*). See also MANLY, MALE.

manage, *v.* **1.** bring about, succeed, accomplish, arrange, contrive. **2.** conduct, handle, direct, govern, control, guide, regulate, engineer, rule, administer, supervise, superintend. **3.** handle, wield, manipulate, control. **4.** dominate, influence; train, educate, handle. **—Ant.** mismanage, bungle.

management, *n.* handling, direction, control, regulation, conduct, charge, administration, superintendence, care, guidance, disposal, treatment, oversight, surveillance. **—Ant.** mismanagement.

manager, *n.* administrator, executive, superintendent, supervisor, boss, director, overseer, governor. **—Ant.** employee.

mandate, *n.* command, order, fiat, decree, ukase, injunction, edict, ruling, commission, requirement, precept, requisite, prerequisite.

maneuver, *n.* **1.** procedure, move; scheme, plot, plan, design, stratagem, ruse, artifice, trick. *—v.* **2.** manipulate, handle, intrigue, trick, scheme, plot, plan, design, finesse.

manful, *adj.* manly. **—Ant.** feminine, cowardly. **—Syn. Study.** See MANLY.

mangle, *v.* cut, lacerate, crush, slash, disfigure, maim, ruin, spoil, mar, deface, mutilate, destroy.

mania, *n.* **1.** excitement, enthusiasm, craze, fad. **2.** insanity, madness, aberration, derangement, dementia, frenzy, lunacy. **—Ant.** phobia; rationality.

manifest, *adj.* **1.** evident, obvious, apparent, plain, clear, distinct, patent, open, palpable, visible, unmistakable, conspicuous. *—v.* **2.** show, display, reveal, disclose, open, exhibit, evince, evidence, demonstrate, declare, express, make known. **—Ant.** latent, hidden, inconspicuous; conceal. **—Syn. Study.** See DISPLAY.

manifold, *adj.* **1.** various, many, numerous, multitudinous. **2.** varied, various, divers, multifarious, multifaceted. **—Ant.** simple, singular. **—Syn. Study.** See MANY.

manly, *adj.* **1.** manful, mannish, masculine, male, virile. **2.** strong, brave, honorable, courageous, bold, valiant, intrepid, undaunted. **—Ant.** feminine; weak, cowardly. **—Syn. Study.** MANLY, MANFUL, MANNISH mean having traits or qualities considered typical of or appropriate to adult males. MANLY, a term of approval, suggests such admirable traits as maturity and steadiness: *a manly acceptance of responsibility.* MANFUL, also an approving term, stresses such qualities as courage and strength: *a manful effort to overcome great odds.* MANNISH is most often used, esp. derogatorily, in referring to the qualities or accouterments of a woman considered more appropriate to a man: *the mannish abruptness of her speech; She wore a severely mannish suit.* See also MALE.

manner, *n.* **1.** mode, fashion, style, way, habit, custom, method, form. **2.** demeanor, deportment, air, bearing, behavior, carriage, mien, aspect, look, appearance. **3.** kind, sort. **4.** nature, guise, character.

mannish, *adj.* manly. **—Ant.** feminine; cowardly, pusillanimous. **—Syn. Study.** See MANLY.

manufacture, *v.* assemble, fabricate, make, construct, build, compose. **—Ant.** destroy.

many, *adj.* numerous, multifarious, abundant, myriad, innumerable, manifold, divers, sundry, various,

varied. **—Ant.** few. **—Syn. Study.** MANY, NUMEROUS, INNUMERABLE, MANIFOLD imply the presence of a large number of units. MANY is a general word that refers to a large but indefinite number of units or individuals: *many years ago; many friends and supporters.* NUMEROUS, a more formal word, stresses the individual and separate quality of the units: *to receive numerous letters.* INNUMERABLE denotes a number that is too large to be counted or, more loosely, that is very difficult to count: *the innumerable stars.* MANIFOLD implies that the number is large, but also varied or complex: *manifold responsibilities.*

map, *n.* chart, graph, plan, outline, diagram.

mar, *v.* damage, impair, ruin, spoil, injure, blot, deface, disfigure, deform, distort, maim.

maraud, *v.* raid, plunder, pillage, ravage, ransack.

margin, *n.* border, edge, rim, limit, confine, bound, marge, verge, brink. **—Ant.** center.

mariner, *n.* sailor, seaman, tar, seafarer, seafaring man. **—Ant.** landlubber. **—Syn. Study.** See SAILOR.

mark, *n.* **1.** trace, impression, line, cut, dent, stain, bruise. **2.** badge, brand, sign. **3.** symbol, sign, token, inscription, indication. **4.** note, importance, distinction, eminence, consequence. **5.** trait, characteristic, stamp, print. **6.** aim, target, end, purpose, object, objective. *—v.* **7.** label, tag, mark up, mark down. **8.** indicate, designate, point out, brand, identify, imprint, impress, characterize. **9.** destine, single out. **10.** note, pay attention to, heed, notice, observe, regard, eye, spot.

marriage, *n.* **1.** wedding, nuptials; wedlock, matrimony. **2.** union, alliance, association, confederation. **—Ant.** divorce; separation.

marshal, *v.* arrange, array, order, rank, dispose; gather, convoke. **—Ant.** disorder; scatter. **—Syn. Study.** See GATHER.

marvelous, *adj.* **1.** wonderful, wondrous, extraordinary, amazing, astonishing, astounding, miraculous. **2.** improbable, incredible, unbelievable, surprising. **—Ant.** terrible, ordinary, commonplace; believable.

masculine, See Syn. study at MALE.

mask, *n.* **1.** face-covering, veil, false face. **2.** disguise, concealment, pretense, pretext, ruse, trick, subterfuge, evasion. **3.** masquerade, revel, *bal masqué, ballo in maschera,* mummery. *—v.* **4.** disguise, conceal, hide, veil, screen, cloak, shroud, cover.

mass, *n.* **1.** aggregate, aggregation, assemblage, heap, congeries, combination. **2.** collection, accumulation, conglomeration, pile, assemblage, quantity. **3.** main body, bulk, majority. **4.** size, bulk, massiveness, magnitude, dimension. **5.** *(plural)* proletariat, working class, common people, plebeians. *—v.* **6.** assemble; collect, gather, marshal, amass, convoke; heap *or* pile up, aggregate.

massacre, *n.* **1.** killing, slaughter, carnage, extermination, annihilation, butchery, murder, genocide. *—v.* **2.** kill, butcher, slaughter, murder, slay. **—Syn. Study.** See SLAUGHTER.

massive, *adj.* **1.** bulky, heavy, large, immense, huge, tremendous. **2.** solid, substantial, great, imposing, massy, ponderous, predominant. **6.** diminutive; flimsy.

master, *n.* **1.** adept, expert. **2.** employer, boss. **3.** commander, chief, head, commander in chief, captain. *—adj.* **4.** chief, principal, head, leading, cardinal, primary, prime, main. **5.** dominating, predominant. **6.** skilled, adept, expert, skillful. *—v.* **7.** conquer, subdue, subject, subjugate, overcome, overpower. **8.** rule, direct, govern, manage, superintend, oversee.

matchless, *adj.* peerless, unrivaled, unequaled, inimitable, unparalleled, incomparable, unmatched, consummate, exquisite. **—Ant.** unimportant, unimpressive.

material, *n.* **1.** substance, matter, stuff. **2.** element, constituent. *—adj.* **3.** physical, corporeal. **4.** important, essential, vital, consequent, momentous. **—Ant.** spiritual; immaterial. **—Syn. Study.** See MATTER.

matter, *n.* **1.** substance, material, stuff. **2.** thing, affair, business, question, subject, topic. **3.** consequence, importance, essence, import, significance, moment. **4.** trouble, difficulty. **5.** ground, reason, cause. *—v.* **6.** signify, be of importance, count. **—Ant.** insignificance; ease. **—Syn.** MATTER, MATERIAL, STUFF, SUBSTANCE refer to that of which physical objects are composed. MATTER applies to anything occupying space and perceptible to the senses; it may denote a particular kind: *solid matter; vegetable matter*. MATERIAL refers to a definite kind of matter, esp. that used to manufacture or construct something: *woolen material; building materials*. STUFF is an informal term that applies to the basic material of which something is made; it may also denote an unspecified kind of material: *Do you have the stuff to make the rug?* SUBSTANCE is usu. a definite kind of matter thought of in relation to its characteristic properties: *a sticky substance*. These terms are also used abstractly, esp. with reference to thought or expression: *controversial matter; material for a novel; the stuff of dreams; the substance of a speech*.

mature, *adj.* **1.** ripe, aged, complete, grown, adult, full-grown, fully-developed, maturated. **2.** completed, perfected, elaborated, ready, prepared. —*v.* **3.** ripen, age, develop. **4.** perfect, complete. —**Ant.** immature, childish, adolescent.

maxim, *n.* proverb, aphorism, saying, adage, apothegm. —**Syn. Study.** See PROVERB.

meager, *adj.* scanty, deficient, sparse, mean, insignificant; thin, lean, emaciated, spare, gaunt, skinny, lank. —**Ant.** abundant. —**Syn. Study.** See SCANTY.

mealy-mouthed, *adj.* devious, hypocritical, false, duplicitous, two-faced, insincere, smarmy. —**Ant.** straightforward, candid.

mean, *v.* **1.** intend, purpose, contemplate, destine, foreordain, predestinate, design. **2.** signify, indicate, denote, imply, express. —*adj.* **3.** inferior. **4.** common, humble, low, undignified, ignoble, plebeian, coarse, rude, vulgar. **5.** unimportant, unessential, nonessential, inconsequent, dispensable, insignificant, petty, paltry, little, poor, wretched, despicable, contemptible, low, base, vile, foul, disgusting, repulsive, repellent, depraved, immoral; small-minded. **6.** unimposing, shabby, sordid, unclean, unscrupulous, squalid, poor. **7.** penurious, parsimonious, illiberal, stingy, miserly, tight, niggardly, scotch, selfish, narrow, mercenary. **8.** intermediate, middle, medium, average, moderate. —*n.* (*plural*) **9.** agency, instrumentality, method, approach, mode, way. **10.** resources, backing, support. **11.** revenue, income, substance, wherewithal, property, wealth. **12.** (*sing.*) average, median, middle, midpoint, center. —**Ant.** exalted, dignified; important, essential; imposing, splendid, rich, generous; superior. —**Syn. Study.** MEAN, LOW, BASE refer to characteristics worthy of dislike, contempt, or disgust. MEAN suggests a petty selfishness or lack of generosity, and may describe spiteful, unkind, or even vicious behavior: *mean rumors; a mean bully*. LOW means dishonorable in purpose or character; it describes that which is morally reprehensible or vulgar: *low deeds; low company*. BASE suggests moral depravity, greed, and cowardice; it describes dishonorable or exploitative behavior: *base motives*.

meander, *v.* **1.** wander, stroll; wind, turn. —*n.* **2.** labyrinth, maze, intricacy.

meaning, *n.* **1.** tenor, gist, trend, idea, purport, significance, signification, sense, import, denotation, connotation, interpretation. **2.** intent, intention, aim, object, purpose, design. —*adj.* **3.** expressive, significant, poignant, pointed, knowing, meaningful. —**Ant.** insignificant, meaningless. —**Syn. Study.** MEANING, SENSE, SIGNIFICANCE, PURPORT denote that which is expressed or indicated by language or action. MEANING is a general word describing that which is intended to be, or actually is, expressed: *the meaning of a statement*. SENSE often refers to a particular meaning of a word or phrase: *The word "run" has many senses*. SENSE may also be used of meaning that is intelligible or reasonable: *There's no sense in what you say*. SIGNIFICANCE refers to a meaning that is implied rather than expressed: *the significance of a glance*. It may also refer to a meaning the importance of which is not immediately perceived: *We did not grasp the significance of the event until years later*. PURPORT usu. refers to the gist or essential meaning of something fairly complicated: *the purport of a theory*.

measureless, *adj.* limitless, boundless, immeasurable, immense, vast,

endless, infinite, unending. —**Ant.** limited, finite.

mechanic, *n.* repairman, workman, machinist; craftsman, artificer, artisan.

meddlesome, *adj.* prying, curious, interfering, intrusive, officious.

mediate, *v.* intercede, interpose, arbitrate, reconcile, settle.

medicine, *n.* medication, medicament, remedy, drug, physic.

mediocre, *adj.* indifferent, ordinary, common, commonplace, medium, average, middling, passable, mean. —**Ant.** superior.

meditate, *v.* **1.** contemplate, plan, reflect on, devise, scheme, plot, concoct, contrive, think over, dwell on. **2.** reflect, ruminate, contemplate, ponder, muse, cogitate, think, study.

meditative, *adj.* pensive, thoughtful, reflecting, contemplative; studious. —**Ant.** impetuous. —**Syn. Study.** See PENSIVE.

medium, *n.* **1.** mean, average, mean proportion, mean average. **2.** means, agency, instrumentality, instrument. **3.** environment, atmosphere, ether, air, temper, conditions, influences. —*adj.* **4.** average, mean, middling; mediocre.

meek, *adj.* humble, patient, submissive, spiritless, tame, yielding, forbearing, docile, unassuming, mild, peaceful, pacific, calm, soft, gentle, modest. —**Ant.** forward, unyielding, immodest.

meet, *v.* **1.** join, connect, intersect, cross, converge, come together, unite. **2.** encounter, come upon, confront, face. **3.** encounter, oppose, conflict. **4.** settle, discharge, fulfill, satisfy, gratify, answer, comply with. **5.** gather, assemble, congregate, convene, collect, muster. **6.** concur, agree, see eye to eye, unite, conjoin. —*n.* **7.** meeting, contest, competition, match. —*adj.* **8.** suited, suitable, apt, fitting, proper, appropriate, fit, befitting, adapted. —**Ant.** diverge; dissatisfy; scatter; disagree, diverge; unsuited, unapt.

melancholy, *n.* **1.** gloom, depression, sadness, dejection, despondency, gloominess, blues, hypochondria. **2.** pensiveness, thoughtfulness, sobriety, seriousness. —*adj.* **3.** sad, depressed, dejected, gloomy, despondent, blue, dispirited, sorrowful, unhappy, disconsolate, inconsolable, miserable, dismal, doleful, lugubrious, moody, glum, down-in-the-mouth, downhearted, downcast, low-spirited. **4.** sober, serious, thoughtful, pensive. —**Ant.** cheer, happiness; cheerful, happy.

mellifluous, *adj.* flowing, smooth, honeyed, melodious, musical, euphonious, pleasant-sounding, lyrical, dulcet, sweet, sweet-sounding, sonorous, silvery, golden-tongued. —**Ant.** harsh, discordant.

mellow, *adj.* **1.** ripe, full-flavored, soft, mature, well-matured. **2.** softened, toned down, improved. **3.** soft, rich, delicate, mellifluous, dulcet, melodious, tuneful, sweet, smooth. **4.** genial, jovial, good-humored, good-natured. —*v.* **5.** soften, ripen, develop, mature, improve, perfect. —**Ant.** immature.

melody, *n.* tune, song, air, descant, theme.

melt, *v.* **1.** liquefy, fuse, dissolve, thaw. **2.** pass, dwindle, fade, fade out, blend. **3.** soften, gentle, mollify, relax. —**Ant.** freeze.

member, *n.* **1.** limb, leg, arm, wing, head, branch. **2.** constituent, element, part, portion.

memento, *n.* keepsake, remembrance, souvenir, token, reminder, relic, memorial, trophy, monument, favor, commemoration, testimonial, memento mori.

memorable, *adj.* notable, noteworthy, newsworthy, impressive, significant, remarkable, marked, signal, unforgettable, outstanding, standout, extraordinary, exceptional, indelible, haunting. —**Ant.** forgettable, unimpressive, fleeting.

menace, *n.* **1.** threat, minaciousness, minacity, threatening. —*v.* **2.** threaten, intimidate.

mend, *v.* **1.** darn, patch, repair, renew, fix, restore, retouch. **2.** correct, rectify, make better, amend, emend, ameliorate, meliorate, improve, set right. **3.** heal, recover, amend, improve, become better. —*n.* **4.** repair, improvement, amelioration, emendation, correction, restoration, rectification, amendment, renewal. —**Ant.** ruin, destroy; die, languish.

mendacious, *adj.* lying, untrue, false, untruthful, deceitful. —**Ant.** truthful, honest.

menial, *adj.* **1.** servile, mean, base, low. —*n.* **2.** servant, domestic, attend-

ant, footman, butler, valet, maid, maidservant, waiter; flunky, slave, underling, hireling, serf, minion, lackey. —**Ant.** noble, dignified; master.

mental, *adj.* **1.** intellectual, cerebral, intellective, rational, reasoning, cognitive, psychological, psychic. **2.** neurotic, delusional, irrational, crazy, insane, psychotic, daft, batty.

mention, *v.* **1.** refer to, allude to, name, specify, speak of, make known, impart, disclose, divulge, communicate, declare, state, tell, aver. —*n.* **2.** reference, indirect reference, allusion.

mercenary, *adj.* venal, grasping, sordid, acquisitive, avaricious, covetous, penurious, parsimonious, stingy, tight, miserly, mean, niggardly, selfish. —**Ant.** generous, unselfish.

merciful, *adj.* compassionate, kind, clement, lenient, forgiving, gracious, benignant, beneficent, generous, big, large; tender, humane, kindhearted, tender-hearted, soft-hearted, sympathetic. —**Ant.** merciless.

merciless, *adj.* pitiless, cruel, hard, hard-hearted, severe, relentless, unrelenting, fell, unsympathetic, uncompassionate, unfeeling, inexorable. —**Ant.** merciful.

mercurial, *adj.* **1.** sprightly, volatile, active, spirited, lively, nimble, energetic. **2.** flighty, fickle, changeable, volatile, inconstant, undecided. —**Ant.** inactive, dispirited, phlegmatic; constant, steady.

mercy, *n.* **1.** compassion, pity, benevolence, consideration, forgiveness, indulgence, clemency, leniency, forbearance, lenity, kindness, tenderness, mildness, gentleness. **2.** disposal, discretion, disposition. —**Ant.** cruelty, pitilessness, harshness.

mere, *adj.* bare, scant, simple, pure, sheer, unmixed, entire. —**Ant.** considerable.

meretricious, *adj.* tawdry, showy, gaudy, ornate, spurious, sham, false. —**Ant.** genuine, sincere.

merit, *n.* **1.** worth, excellence, value, desert, entitlement, due, credit. —*v.* **2.** deserve, be worthy of, earn, be entitled to.

merriment, *n.* gaiety, mirth, hilarity, laughter, jollity, joviality, jocularity. —**Ant.** misery, melancholy.

merry, *adj.* jolly, gay, happy, jovial, joyful, joyous, mirthful, hilarious, gleeful, blithe, blithesome, frolicsome, cheery, cheerful, glad. —**Ant.** sad, unhappy.

mess, *n.* **1.** dirtiness, untidiness. **2.** confusion, muddle, medley, farrago, hodgepodge, hotchpotch, jumble, litter, mixture, miscellany, mélange, salmagundi. **3.** unpleasantness, difficulty, predicament, plight, muddle, pickle. —*v.* **4.** muddle, confuse, mix, mix up. —**Ant.** tidiness; order, system; arrange.

metamorphosis, *n.* change, transformation, transmutation, mutation. —**Ant.** stasis.

mete, *v.* **1.** distribute, apportion, parcel out, dole, allot, deal, measure. —*n.* **2.** limit, bound, boundary, term.

method, *n.* **1.** mode, procedure, way, means, manner, fashion, technique, process, course. **2.** order, system, arrangement, disposition, rule. —**Syn. Study.** METHOD, MODE, WAY refer to the manner in which something is done. METHOD implies a fixed procedure, usu. following a logical and systematic plan: *the open-hearth method of making steel*. MODE, a more formal word, implies a customary or characteristic manner: *Kangaroos have an unusual mode of carrying their young*. WAY is a general word that may often be substituted for more specific words: *the best way to solve a problem; an attractive way of wearing the hair*.

methodical, See Syn. study at ORDERLY.

meticulous, *adj.* careful, finical, finicky, solicitous, exact, precise, demanding. —**Ant.** careless, inexact, imprecise. —**Syn. Study.** See PAINSTAKING.

mettle, *n.* **1.** disposition, temper, character, spirit. **2.** spirit, courage, valor, pluck, vigor, ardor, fire, nerve, fiber. —**Ant.** cowardice, pusillanimity.

middle, *adj.* **1.** central, equidistant, halfway, medial. **2.** intermediate, intervening. —*n.* **3.** center, midpoint, midst. —**Ant.** end, final, initial.

midget, See Syn. study at DWARF.

midst, *n.* middle, center stage, arena, center, thick, heart, core. —**Ant.** rim, edge.

miffed, *adj.* offended, insulted, resentful, angry, annoyed, irritated, peeved, nettled, vexed, aggravated,

put-out, teed off, bugged. —**Ant.** pleased.

might, *n.* power, ability, force, main, puissance, strength, efficacy. —**Ant.** weakness, inability.

mighty, *adj.* **1.** powerful, strong, vigorous, robust, sturdy, puissant, potent. **2.** sizable, huge, immense, enormous, vast, tremendous. —**Ant.** feeble, weak, impotent; small, negligible.

migrate, *v.* immigrate, emigrate, move, resettle. —**Ant.** remain, stay.

mild, *adj.* **1.** amiable, gentle, temperate, kind, compassionate, indulgent, clement, soft, pleasant. **2.** placid, peaceful, tranquil, pacific, calm. **3.** bland, emollient, mollifying, assuasive, soothing. —**Ant.** intemperate, unkind, unpleasant; stormy, turbulent; piquant, biting, bitter.

milieu, *n.* environment, medium, background, class, sphere, surroundings, element. —**Syn. Study.** See ENVIRONMENT.

mind, *n.* **1.** intellect, intelligence, understanding, reason, sense. **2.** brain, brains. **3.** sanity, reason, mental balance. **4.** disposition, temper, inclination, bent, intention, leaning, proclivity, bias. **5.** opinion, sentiments, belief, contemplation, judgment, consideration. **6.** purpose, intention, intent, will, wish, liking, desire, wont. **7.** remembrance, recollection, recall, memory. —*v.* **8.** pay attention, heed, obey, attend, attend to, mark, regard, notice, note. **9.** tend, take care of, watch, look after. **10.** be careful *or* cautious *or* wary. **11.** care, object. —**Syn. Study.** MIND, INTELLECT, BRAIN refer to that part of a conscious being that thinks, feels, wills, perceives, or judges. MIND is a philosophical, psychological, and general term for the center of all mental activity, as contrasted with the body and the spirit: *His mind grasped the complex issue*. INTELLECT refers to reasoning power, as distinguished from the faculties of feeling: *a book that appeals to the intellect, rather than the emotions*. BRAIN is a physiological term for the organic structure that makes mental activity possible, but is often applied to mental ability or capacity: *a fertile brain*. These words may also refer to a person of great mental ability or capacity: *a great mind of our age; a fine scholar and intellect; the brain in the family*.

mindless, *adj.* **1.** inane, simple, unthinking, undemanding, silly, purposeless, unpurposeful, aimless, pointless, uninvolved, uninvolving, stupid, no-brain. **2.** heedless, careless, unmindful, thoughtless. —**Ant.** aware, dutiful.

mingle, *v.* **1.** mix, blend, unite, commingle, intermix, join, conjoin, combine, intermingle, concoct, compound. **2.** participate, associate. —**Syn. Study.** See MIX.

minor, *adj.* **1.** lesser, smaller, inferior, secondary, subordinate, petty, inconsiderable, unimportant, small. —*n.* **2.** child, adolescent. —**Ant.** major.

minute, *n.* **1.** moment, instant; jiffy, second. **2.** (*plural*) note, memorandum, record, proceedings. —*adj.* **3.** small, tiny, little, infinitesimal, minuscule, diminutive. **4.** detailed, exact, precise, critical. —**Ant.** tremendous, huge, large; general, inexact, rough.

miraculous, *adj.* **1.** marvelous, wonderful, wondrous, extraordinary, incredible. **2.** supernatural, preternatural. —**Ant.** prosaic, commonplace; natural. —**Syn. Study.** MIRACULOUS, PRETERNATURAL, SUPERNATURAL refer to that which seems to transcend the laws of nature. MIRACULOUS refers to something that apparently contravenes known laws governing the universe: *a miraculous recovery*. PRETERNATURAL suggests the possession of supernormal qualities: *Dogs have a preternatural sense of smell*. It may also mean supernatural: *Elves are preternatural beings*. SUPERNATURAL suggests divine or superhuman properties: *supernatural aid in battle*.

mirth, *n.* rejoicing, joy, joyousness, gaiety, jollity, glee, merriment, joviality, laughter, hilarity. —**Ant.** sadness, misery.

misadventure, *n.* mischance, mishap, ill fortune, ill luck, misfortune, accident, disaster, calamity, catastrophe. —**Ant.** luck, fortune.

miscellaneous, *adj.* indiscriminate, promiscuous, mixed, heterogeneous, divers, diversified, varied, various, mingled, confused. —**Ant.** specific, special, discerning.

mischief, *n.* **1.** harm, trouble, injury, damage, hurt, detriment, disadvantage. **2.** evil, malice, malicious

mischief, vandalism; misfortune, trouble. —**Ant.** good, advantage.

misconstrue, *v.* misinterpret, misread, misunderstand, misapprehend, misjudge, mistake. —**Ant.** construe, understand.

misdemeanor, *n.* misbehavior, misdeed, transgression, fault, misconduct; offense, trespass.

miser, *n.* niggard, skinflint, tightwad, pinchpenny. —**Ant.** Maecenas.

miserable, *adj.* **1.** wretched, unhappy, uneasy, uncomfortable, distressed, disconsolate, doleful, forlorn, broken-hearted, heartbroken. **2.** poverty-stricken, poor, needy, destitute, penniless. **3.** contemptible, bad, wretched, mean, despicable, low, abject, worthless. **4.** deplorable, pitiable, lamentable, unfortunate, unlucky, ill-starred, star-crossed, luckless; calamitous, catastrophic. —**Ant.** happy; wealthy; good; fortunate, lucky.

miserly, *adj.* penurious, niggardly, cheap, stingy, parsimonious, tight-fisted, penny-pinching, close, mean. —**Ant.** generous, unselfish. —**Syn. Study.** See STINGY[1].

misery, *n.* **1.** wretchedness, distress, tribulation, woe, trial, suffering, agony, anguish, torture. **2.** grief, anguish, woe, unhappiness, sorrow, torment, desolation. —**Ant.** happiness, joy; delight.

misfortune, *n.* **1.** ill luck, bad luck, ill fortune. **2.** accident, disaster, calamity, catastrophe, reverse, affliction, mishap, mischance, adversity, distress, hardship, trouble, blow. —**Ant.** luck, fortune.

misgiving, *n.* apprehension, doubt, distrust, suspicion, mistrust, hesitation. —**Ant.** trust.

mislead, *v.* misguide, lead astray, misconduct, delude, deceive, misdirect. —**Ant.** lead, conduct.

misplace, *v.* displace, mislay, lose. **2.** misapply, misbestow. —**Ant.** find; apply, place.

misprint, *n.* typographical error, erratum, typo.

misshapen, *adj.* distorted, deformed, malformed, contorted, warped, misproportioned, disproportionate, ill-formed, crooked, twisted, unshapely, irregular. —**Ant.** shapely, well-formed.

mist, *n.* **1.** cloud, fog, fogbank, haze, smog; soup. **2.** bewilderment, haze, perplexity, obscurity. —*v.* **3.** fog, cloud over, drizzle, foggle. —**Ant.** clarity.

mistake, *n.* **1.** error, blunder, slip, inaccuracy, erratum, typo, misprint, fault, oversight. **2.** misapprehension, misconception, misunderstanding. —*v.* **3.** misapprehend, misconceive, misunderstand, misjudge, err. —**Ant.** accuracy; understanding.

mistaken, *adj.* erroneous, wrong, incorrect, misconceived, inaccurate. —**Ant.** correct, accurate.

misunderstanding, *n.* **1.** mistake, misapprehension, error, misconception. **2.** disagreement, dissension, discord, difference, difficulty, quarrel. —**Ant.** understanding; agreement, concord.

mix, *v.* **1.** blend, combine, mingle, commingle, confuse, jumble, unite, compound, amalgamate, homogenize. **2.** consort, mingle, associate, join. —*n.* **3.** mixture, concoction. —**Ant.** separate; dissociate. —**Syn. Study.** MIX, BLEND, COMBINE, MINGLE concern the bringing of two or more things into more or less intimate association. MIX means to join elements or ingredients into one mass, generally with a loss of distinction between them: *to mix fruit juices*. BLEND suggests a smooth and harmonious joining, often a joining of different varieties to obtain a product of a desired quality: *to blend whiskeys*. COMBINE means to bring similar or related things into close union, usu. for a particular purpose: *to combine forces*. MINGLE usu. suggests a joining in which the identity of the separate elements is retained: *voices mingling at a party*.

mixed, *adj.* mingled, commingled, joined; coeducational, coed. —**Ant.** separated.

mixture, *n.* **1.** blend, combination, compound. **2.** hodgepodge, hotchpotch, gallimaufry, conglomeration, jumble, medley, melange, olio, potpourri, miscellany, farrago, salmagundi; variety, diversity. —**Ant.** element, constituent.

moan, *n.* **1.** groan, wail, lament, lamentation; dirge, elegy, threnody, monody. —*v.* **2.** bemoan, bewail, grieve, lament, mourn, deplore.

mock, *v.* **1.** ridicule, deride, taunt,

flout, gibe, tantalize, tease, jeer, chaff, scoff, banter, make sport of; mimic, ape, satirize, imitate. **2.** defy. **3.** deceive, delude, disappoint, cheat, dupe, fool, defeat, mislead. —*n.* **4.** mockery, derision, ridicule, banter, sport, sneer. —*adj.* **5.** feigned, pretended, counterfeit, sham, false, spurious, fake. —**Ant.** praise, honor. —**Syn. Study.** See RIDICULE.

mockery, *n.* **1.** ridicule, derision, scorn, contumely. **2.** imitation, show, mimicry. **3.** travesty, pretense, pretext, sham, satire.

mode, *n.* **1.** method, way, manner, style, fashion. **2.** form, variety, degree, modification, graduation. —**Syn. Study.** See METHOD.

model, *n.* **1.** standard, paragon, prototype, ideal, pattern, example, archetype, mold, original. **2.** representation, facsimile, copy, image, imitation. —*v.* **3.** form, plan, pattern, mold, shape, fashion, design. —**Syn. Study.** See IDEAL.

moderate, *adj.* **1.** reasonable, temperate, judicious, just, fair, deliberate, mild, cool, steady, calm, peaceful. **2.** medium, average, usual. **3.** mediocre, fair. **4.** middle-of-the-road, conservative, temperate. —*n.* **5.** mugwump, middle-of-the-roader, conservative. —*v.* **6.** allay, meliorate, pacify, calm, assuage, sober, mitigate, soften, mollify, temper, qualify, appease, abate, lessen, diminish, reduce. **7.** preside, chair, arbitrate, referee, regulate, umpire. —**Ant.** immoderate; unusual; radical; disturb, increase, intensify.

modern, *adj.* recent, up-to-date, late, present, new, novel, fresh, neoteric. —**Ant.** old, archaic, ancient, obsolete. —**Syn. Study.** MODERN, RECENT, LATE apply to that which is near to or characteristic of the present as contrasted with any other time. MODERN, which is applied to those things that exist in the present age, sometimes has the connotation of up-to-date and, thus, good: *modern ideas.* That which is RECENT is separated from the present or the time of action by only a short interval; it is new, fresh, and novel: *recent developments.* LATE may mean nearest to the present moment: *the late reports on the battle.*

modest, *adj.* **1.** moderate, humble, unpretentious, decent, becoming, proper. **2.** inextravagant, unostentatious, retiring, unassuming, unobtrusive. **3.** decent, demure, prudish, chaste, pure, virtuous. —**Ant.** immodest, immoderate, improper; extravagant.

modesty, *n.* **1.** unobtrusiveness. **2.** moderation, decency, propriety, simplicity, purity, chastity, prudery, prudishness. —**Ant.** indecency, licentiousness.

modify, *v.* **1.** change, alter, vary, qualify, temper, adjust, restrict, limit, shape, reform. **2.** reduce, qualify, moderate.

moil, *v.* **1.** work hard, toil, drudge, labor. —*n.* **2.** toil, drudgery, labor. **3.** confusion, turmoil, trouble. —**Ant.** indolence, laziness.

moist, *adj.* damp, humid, dank, wet. —**Ant.** dry, arid.

molest, *v.* attack, assail; harass, harry, disturb, trouble, annoy, vex, plague, tease, pester, torment, torture, irritate, fret, hector, inconvenience, discommode, worry, bother.

moment, *n.* **1.** minute, instant, second, jiffy, trice, flash, twinkling. **2.** importance, consequence, significance, weight, gravity, import, consideration. **3.** momentum, force, power, impetus, drive. —**Ant.** insignificance, inertia. —**Syn. Study.** See IMPORTANCE.

momentous, *adj.* important, consequent, vital, weighty, serious. —**Ant.** unimportant, trivial, trifling.

monarchy, *n.* kingdom, realm, empire.

monetary, *adj.* pecuniary, financial; nummary, nummular. —**Syn. Study.** See FINANCIAL.

money, *n.* **1.** coin, cash, currency, specie, change; coin of the realm. **2.** funds, capital, assets, property, wealth, riches. **3.** (*slang*) mazuma, long green, lettuce, dough, (*small amt.*) chump change.

mongrel, *n.* **1.** cross, hybrid, mutt, half-breed. —*adj.* **2.** hybrid. —**Ant.** purebred, thoroughbred.

monk, *n.* friar, brother; cenobite, eremite.

monopolize, *v.* consume, possess, corner, control, appropriate, co-opt, engross, usurp, arrogate, preempt, take over, gobble up, grab, hog. —**Ant.** share.

monotonous, *adj.* tedious, humdrum, tiresome, uniform, boring,

dull, unvaried, unvarying. —**Ant.** interesting, amusing, diverting.

monster, *n.* **1.** brute, griffin, gargoyle, sphinx, centaur, hippogriff. **2.** mooncalf, monstrosity. **3.** fiend, brute, miscreant, wretch, villain, demon, devil. —*adj.* **4.** huge, enormous, monstrous.

monstrous, *adj.* **1.** huge, great, large, tremendous, gigantic, monster, prodigious, enormous, immense, vast, stupendous, colossal. **2.** frightful, hideous, revolting, shocking, repulsive, horrible, atrocious, terrible, dreadful, horrendous. —**Ant.** small, tiny; delightful, attractive.

mood, *n.* disposition, frame of mind, humor, temper, vein. **2.** mode.

moody, *adj.* gloomy, sullen, ill-humored, perverse, sulky, waspish, snappish, pettish, testy, short-tempered, irritable, irascible, captious, peevish, fretful, spleeny, splenetic, spiteful, morose, intractable, stubborn. —**Ant.** amiable, temperate, tractable.

moonstruck, *adj.* **1.** romantic, starry-eyed, moony, sentimental, mushy. **2.** unbalanced, mental, touched, daft. —**Ant.** down-to-earth.

moot, *adj.* **1.** doubtful, debatable, disputable, disputed, unsettled. —*v.* **2.** argue, debate, dispute, discuss. —**Ant.** indubitable, indisputable; agree, concur.

moral, *adj.* **1.** ethical, upright, honest, straightforward, righteous, open, just, good, virtuous, honorable. —*n.* **2.** (*plural*) ethics, integrity, standards, morality. —**Ant.** immoral, amoral.

morality, See Syn. study at GOODNESS.

morbid, *adj.* **1.** gloomy, sensitive, extreme. **2.** unwholesome, diseased, unhealthy, sick, sickly, tainted, corrupted, vitiated. —**Ant.** cheerful, wholesome, salubrious.

moreover, *adv.* besides, further, furthermore, and, also, too, likewise.

morning, *n.* morn, daybreak, sunrise, dawn. —**Ant.** evening.

morose, *adj.* sullen, gloomy, moody, sour, sulky, churlish, splenetic, surly, ill-humored, ill-natured, perverse. —**Ant.** cheerful, happy, good-natured. —**Syn. Study.** See GLUM.

mortal, *adj.* **1.** human. **2.** fatal, final, lethal, deadly. —*n.* **3.** human being, man. —**Ant.** immortal. —**Syn. Study.** See FATAL.

mortify, *v.* **1.** shame, humiliate, humble, abash, abase, subdue, restrain. **2.** gangrene, necrose. —**Ant.** honor.

mostly, *adv.* in the main, generally, chiefly, especially, particularly, for the most part, customarily. —**Ant.** seldom.

motion, *n.* **1.** movement, move, action. **2.** gait, deportment, bearing, air. **3.** gesture, movement, move. —*v.* **4.** move, gesture. —**Ant.** stasis.

motionless, *adj.* stable, fixed, unmoving, still, transfixed, quiescent, stationary. —**Ant.** mobile.

motive, *n.* motivation, inducement, incentive, incitement, stimulus, spur, influence, occasion, reason, ground, cause, purpose. —**Syn. Study.** MOTIVE, INDUCEMENT, INCENTIVE apply to something that moves or prompts a person to action. MOTIVE is usu. applied to an inner urge that moves a person; it may also apply to a contemplated goal, the desire for which moves the person: *Her motive was a wish to be helpful. Money was the motive for the crime.* INDUCEMENT is used mainly of opportunities offered by another person or by situational factors: *The salary they offered me was a great inducement.* INCENTIVE is usu. applied to something offered as a reward or to stimulate competitive activity: *Profit sharing is a good incentive for employees.*

mount, *v.* **1.** go up, ascend, climb, scale, get up on. **2.** raise, put into position, fix on. **3.** prepare, produce, make ready, ready. —*n.* **4.** horse, steed, charger, palfrey. **5.** mountain, hill. —**Ant.** descend.

mountebank, *n.* quack, pitchman, charlatan, pretender, phony.

mourn, *v.* grieve, lament, bewail, bemoan, sorrow for. **2.** deplore. —**Ant.** laugh, rejoice.

move, *v.* **1.** stir, advance, budge, progress, make progress, proceed, move on, remove. **2.** turn, revolve, spin, gyrate, rotate, operate. **3.** act, bestir oneself, take action. **4.** stir, shake, agitate, excite, arouse, rouse; shift, transfer, propel. **5.** prompt, actuate, induce, influence, impel, activate, incite, rouse, instigate. **6.** af-

fect, touch. **7.** propose, recommend, suggest, bring up *or* forward. —*n.* **8.** motion, movement, action.

movement, *n.* **1.** move, motion, change. **2.** motion, progress, activity, eventfulness. **3.** (*music*) part, section, division; motion, rhythm, time, tempo. —**Ant.** inertia, stasis.

multifarious, *adj.* numerous, various, many, abundant, multitudinous, manifold, diverse, sundry, multifold, multivarious, legion, myriad, various and sundry. —**Ant.** singular, unique.

multitude, *n.* host, crowd, throng, mass, army, swarm, collection. —**Syn. Study.** See CROWD.

mumble, *v.* murmur, mutter, muffle. —**Ant.** articulate, enunciate, pronounce.

mundane, *adj.* worldly, earthly, terrestrial, terraqueous, secular, temporal. —**Ant.** unearthly, clerical. —**Syn. Study.** See EARTHLY.

munificent, *adj.* liberal, generous, bountiful, beneficent, bounteous. —**Ant.** stingy, penurious, mean, niggardly. —**Syn. Study.** See GENEROUS.

murder, *n.* **1.** killing, assassination, homicide, manslaughter. —*v.* **2.** kill, slay, assassinate, destroy, put an end to. **3.** spoil, mar, ruin, abuse.

murky, *adj.* dark, gloomy, cheerless, obscure, dim, cloudy, dusky, lowering, overcast, misty, hazy. —**Ant.** bright, light, clear.

murmur, *n.* **1.** grumble, susurration, susurrus, mumble, complaint, plaint, whimper, mutter. —*v.* **2.** mumble, mutter, whisper. **3.** complain, grumble, grouse.

muscular, *adj.* brawny, sinewy, well-muscled, well-built, well-knit, beefy, sturdy, burly, husky, strong, powerful, mighty, Bunyanesque, (*slang*) hunky, buff. —**Ant.** weak, feeble, underdeveloped.

muse, *v.* reflect, meditate, ponder, contemplate, think of *or* about, cogitate, deliberate, ruminate, think, brood; dream.

muster, *v.* **1.** assemble, gather, summon, convoke, collect, marshal, convene, congregate. —*n.* **2.** gathering, assembly, assemblage, collection, convention, congregation. —**Ant.** scatter, separate.

mutable, *adj.* **1.** changeable, alterable, variable. **2.** fickle, changing, inconstant, unstable, vacillating, unsettled, wavering, unsteady, flickering, varying, variable. —**Ant.** immutable, invariable; stable, settled, motionless.

mute, *adj.* silent, dumb, speechless, still. —**Ant.** loquacious, voluble, talkative.

mutilate, *v.* injure, disfigure, maim, damage, mar, cripple, mangle.

mutinous, *adj.* **1.** seditious, insurrectionary, revolutionary, insurgent. **2.** rebellious, refractory, insubordinate, unruly, contumacious, turbulent, riotous. —**Ant.** patriotic; obedient.

mutiny, *n.* **1.** revolt, rebellion, insurrection, revolution, uprising, sedition. —*v.* **2.** revolt, rebel, rise up. —**Ant.** obedience.

mutter, *v.* murmur.

mutual, *adj.* reciprocal, balanced, correlative, common, interchangeable. —**Ant.** single, singular.

mysterious, *adj.* secret, esoteric, occult, cryptic, inscrutable, mystical, obscure, puzzling, inexplicable, unexplainable, unintelligible, incomprehensible, enigmatic, impenetrable, recondite, hidden, concealed, dark, abstruse, cabalistic, unfathomable. —**Ant.** open. —**Syn. Study.** MYSTERIOUS, INSCRUTABLE, MYSTICAL, OBSCURE refer to that which is not easily comprehended or explained. That which is MYSTERIOUS, by being unknown or puzzling, excites curiosity, amazement, or awe: *a mysterious disease.* INSCRUTABLE applies to that which is impenetrable, so enigmatic that one cannot interpret its significance: *an inscrutable smile.* That which is MYSTICAL has a secret significance, such as that attaching to certain rites or signs: *mystical symbols.* That which is OBSCURE is discovered or comprehended dimly or with difficulty: *obscure motives.*

mystical, See Syn. study at MYSTERIOUS.

myth, *n.* legend, story, fiction, fable, tradition, epic. —**Syn. Study.** See LEGEND.

N

nag, *v.* **1.** torment, pester, harass, harry, hector, importune, irritate, an-

noy, vex. —*n.* **2.** shrew, virago, pest, termagant, maenad. **3.** horse, pony.

naive, *adj.* unsophisticated, ingenuous, simple, unaffected, natural, unsuspecting, artless, guileless, candid, open, plain. —**Ant.** sophisticated, disingenuous, artful, sly.

naked, *adj.* **1.** nude, bare, uncovered, undressed, unclothed. **2.** bare, stripped, destitute, desert, denuded. **3.** unsheathed, exposed, bare. **4.** unfurnished, bare. **5.** defenseless, unprotected, unguarded, exposed, unarmed, open. **6.** simple, plain, manifest, evident, undisguised, unadorned, mere, bare, sheer. **7.** plainspoken, blunt, direct, outspoken, unvarnished, uncolored, unexaggerated, plain. —**Ant.** covered, dressed; protected; ornate; exaggerated, embellished.

name, *n.* **1.** appellation, title, label, tag, designation, epithet. **2.** reputation, repute, character, credit. **3.** fame, repute, note, distinction, renown, eminence, honor, praise. —*v.* **4.** call, title, entitle, dub, denominate. **5.** specify, mention, indicate, designate, identify, nominate.

nameless, *adj.* **1.** anonymous, unknown, obscure, undistinguished, unremarked, unnamed, untitled, unspecified, incognito. **2.** ineffable, unnamable, indescribable, inexpressible, unutterable, unspeakable.

narrate, *v.* recount, relate, tell, retail, describe, detail, recite.

narrative, *n.* story, account, recital, history, chronicle, tale, description.

narrow-minded, *adj.* prejudiced, biased, bigoted, intolerant, illiberal, partial. —**Ant.** liberal, broadminded, tolerant, unprejudiced.

nasty, *adj.* **1.** filthy, dirty, disgusting, unclean, foul, impure, loathsome, polluted, defiled. **2.** nauseous, nauseating, disgusting, sickening, offensive, repulsive, repellent, objectionable. **3.** obscene, smutty, pornographic, lewd, licentious, lascivious, indecent, ribald, gross, indelicate. **4.** vicious, spiteful, ugly, bad-tempered, disagreeable. **5.** unpleasant, inclement, stormy. —**Ant.** clean, pure, unpolluted; delightful; decent, honorable; amiable, agreeable; pleasant, fair.

nation, *n.* **1.** race, stock, ethnic group, population, people, tribe. **2.** state, country, commonwealth, kingdom, realm.

native, *adj.* **1.** inborn, inherent, inherited, natural, innate, inbred, congenital. **2.** indigenous, autochthonous, aboriginal, natural. **3.** unadorned, natural, real, genuine, original. —*n.* **4.** inhabitant, aborigine. —**Ant.** acquired; imported; decorated; foreigner, alien.

nature, *n.* **1.** character, quality, attributes, qualification. **2.** kind, sort, character, type, species, quality. **3.** universe, world, earth. **4.** reality, matter.

naughty, *adj.* **1.** ill-behaved, misbehaved, bad, disobedient. **2.** risqué, improper, off-color, ribald, profane, dirty.

nauseate, *v.* **1.** sicken, revolt, disgust. **2.** loathe, abhor, abominate, detest, reject. —**Ant.** delight, enchant, attract; like, love, adore.

nauseous, *adj.* **1.** sickening, revolting, nasty, repellent, disgusting, loathsome, abhorrent, detestable, despicable, nauseating, offensive. **2.** ill, sick to one's stomach. —**Ant.** attractive, lovable; well.

near, *adj.* **1.** close, nigh, at, within, at hand, nearby, adjacent, contiguous, touching, adjoining, bordering, abutting. **2.** imminent, impending, approaching, forthcoming, at hand. **3.** related, connected, intimate, familiar, allied, attached. **4.** faithful, close, accurate, literal. **5.** narrow, close, niggardly, parsimonious, stingy, miserly, tight, tightfisted. —**Ant.** far; generous.

nearly, *adv.* **1.** almost, approximately, well-nigh. **2.** intimately, closely. **3.** parsimoniously, penuriously.

neat, *adj.* **1.** orderly, ordered, trim, tidy, spruce, smart, nice. **2.** clever, effective, adroit, finished, well-planned, dexterous, apt. **3.** unadulterated, undiluted, straight, unmixed, pure. —**Ant.** disorderly, sloppy; maladroit, ineffective; adulterated; impure.

nebulous, *adj.* **1.** hazy, vague, confused, indistinct. **2.** cloudy, cloudlike, nebular. —**Ant.** clear, fair, distinct.

necessary, *adj.* **1.** essential, indispensable, required, requisite, needed, needful, vital, unavoidable. **2.** involuntary. —*n.* **3.** requisite, prerequi-

site, requirement, necessity, *sine qua non*, essential. —**Ant.** unnecessary, dispensable; voluntary; nonessential. —**Syn. Study.** NECESSARY, REQUISITE, INDISPENSABLE, ESSENTIAL indicate something that cannot be done without. NECESSARY refers to something needed for existence, for proper functioning, or for a particular purpose: *Food is necessary for life. Sugar is a necessary ingredient in this recipe.* REQUISITE refers to something required for a particular purpose or by particular circumstances: *She has the requisite qualifications for the job.* INDISPENSABLE means absolutely necessary to achieve a particular purpose or to complete or perfect a unit: *He made himself indispensable in the laboratory.* ESSENTIAL refers to something that is part of the basic nature or character of a thing and is vital to its existence or functioning: *Water is essential to life.*

necessity, *n.* **1.** needfulness, indispensability, need, indispensableness. **2.** requirement, requisite, demand, necessary, *sine qua non*, essential, prerequisite. **3.** compulsion, fate, destiny, kismet, karma, inevitability, inevitableness, unavoidability, unavoidableness, irresistibility. **4.** poverty, neediness, indigence, necessitousness, need, want. —**Ant.** dispensability; wealth.

necromancy, *n.* magic, enchantment, conjuration, sorcery, divination.

need, *n.* **1.** requirement, want, necessity, exigency, emergency, urgency. **2.** want, necessity, lack, demand. **3.** destitution, poverty, neediness, want, deprivation, necessity, indigence, penury, distress, privation. —*v.* **4.** require, want, lack. —**Ant.** wealth, opulence. —**Syn. Study.** See LACK.

nefarious, *adj.* wicked, depraved, iniquitous, evil, abominable, detestable, atrocious, execrable, flagitious, heinous, vile, horrible, dreadful, horrendous, infamous, villainous, base. —**Ant.** good, honest, honorable, exalted.

neglect, *v.* **1.** disregard, ignore, slight, overlook, omit, be remiss. —*n.* **2.** disregard, dereliction, negligence, remissness, carelessness, failure, omission, default, inattention, heedlessness. —**Ant.** regard, attend; regard, attention, care.

neglectful, *adj.* disregardful, remiss, careless, negligent, inattentive, indifferent, heedless, thoughtless. —**Ant.** regardful, careful, thoughtful.

negligence, *n.* neglect. —**Ant.** regard.

negligent, *adj.* neglectful. —**Ant.** regardful.

negligible, *adj.* remote, insignificant, slight, marginal, small, slender, slim, minuscule, outside, off. —**Ant.** significant, important.

negotiate, *v.* **1.** arrange, arrange for, settle. **2.** circulate; sell, transfer, deliver, assign.

neophyte, *n.* **1.** convert, proselyte. **2.** beginner, tyro, amateur, greenhorn, novice, novitiate, pupil, student. —**Ant.** old hand, expert.

nerve, *n.* **1.** strength, vigor, energy, power, force, might. **2.** courage, firmness, steadfastness, intrepidity, fortitude, resolution, resoluteness, endurance. —*v.* **3.** strengthen, fortify, innervate, invigorate, steel, brace. —**Ant.** weakness, frailty, cowardice; weaken, enervate.

nerveless, *adj.* feeble, weak, enervated, flaccid, spiritless, flabby, cowardly, pusillanimous. —**Ant.** strong, brave, bold, fearless.

nervous, *adj.* excitable, uneasy, apprehensive, fearful, timid, timorous. —**Ant.** confident, bold, intrepid.

new, *adj.* **1.** recent, modern, up to date, late, neoteric, novel, fresh. **2.** further, additional, fresh. **3.** unaccustomed, unused, fresh. —*adv.* **4.** recently, lately; freshly, anew, newly, afresh. —**Ant.** old, stale. —**Syn. Study.** NEW, FRESH, NOVEL describe things that have not existed or have not been known or seen before. NEW refers to something recently made, grown, or built, or recently found, invented, or discovered: *a new car; new techniques.* FRESH refers to something that has retained its original properties, or has not been affected by use or the passage of time: *fresh strawberries; fresh ideas.* NOVEL refers to something new that has an unexpected, strange, or striking quality, generally pleasing: *a novel experience.*

nice, *adj.* **1.** pleasing, pleasant, agreeable, delightful, good. **2.** kind, amiable, pleasant, friendly. **3.** accurate, precise, skilled, delicate, fastidious, exact, exacting, critical, rigorous, strict, demanding, scrupulous. **4.** tactful, careful, delicate, discriminating, discerning, particular. **5.** minute, fine, subtle, refined. **6.** refined, well-mannered, well-spoken. **7.** suitable, proper, polite. **8.** neat, trim, fastidious, finical, finicky, dainty, squeamish, fussy. —**Ant.** unpleasant; unkind; inaccurate; tactless, careless; unrefined; improper, impolite; sloppy.

nickname, *n.* sobriquet.

niggardly, *adj.* stingy, parsimonious, penurious, miserly, mean, tight-fisted, close-fisted, small, avaricious, mercenary; illiberal, niggard, close, tight; scanty, poor, saving, chary, sparing. —**Ant.** generous, liberal.

nimble, *adj.* agile, quick, lively, active, brisk, spry, ready, alert, swift, light, awake, on the qui vive. —**Ant.** slow, clumsy, awkward.

noble, *n.* **1.** high-born, aristocratic. **2.** high-minded, magnanimous, superior, elevated, exalted, worthy, lofty, honorable, great, large, generous. **3.** admirable, dignified, imposing, stately, magnificent, impressive, grand, lordly, splendid. —*n.* **4.** nobleman, peer, aristocrat, lord, lady. —**Ant.** lowborn; base; undignified; serf, slave. —**Syn. Study.** NOBLE, HIGH-MINDED, MAGNANIMOUS suggest moral excellence and high ideals. NOBLE implies superior moral qualities and an exalted mind, character, or spirit that scorns the petty, base, or dishonorable: *a noble sacrifice*. HIGH-MINDED suggests exalted moral principles, thoughts, or sentiments: *a high-minded speech on social reform.* MAGNANIMOUS adds the idea of generosity, shown by a willingness to forgive injuries or overlook insults: *The magnanimous ruler granted amnesty to the rebels.*

noise, *n.* **1.** clamor, din, hubbub, racket, clatter, rattle, blare, uproar, outcry, tumult, ado. —*v.* **2.** spread, rumor, bruit about. —**Ant.** quiet, peace. —**Syn. Study.** NOISE, CLAMOR, HUBBUB, DIN, RACKET refer to nonmusical or confused sounds. NOISE is a general word that usu. refers to loud, harsh, or discordant sounds: *noise from the street.* CLAMOR refers to loud noise, as from shouting or cries, that expresses feelings, desires, or complaints: *the clamor of an angry crowd.* HUBBUB refers to a confused mingling of sounds, usu. voices; it may also mean tumult or confused activity: *the hubbub on the floor of the stock exchange.* DIN is a very loud, continuous noise that greatly disturbs or distresses: *the din of a factory.* RACKET refers to a rattling sound or clatter: *to make a racket when doing the dishes.*

noiseless, *adj.* silent, quiet, still, inaudible, soundless. —**Ant.** noisy, clamorous, tumultuous.

noisome, *adj.* **1.** offensive, disgusting, fetid, putrid, foul, rotten. **2.** harmful, injurious, poisonous, noxious, nocuous, lethal, deadly, mephitic, miasmatic, miasmal, miasmic, pestilential, hurtful, pernicious, unhealthy, detrimental, deleterious, unwholesome, baneful, destructive. —**Ant.** delightful; pleasant, wholesome, healthful.

noisy, *adj.* loud, stentorian, clamorous, boisterous, tumultuous, riotous, vociferous, obstreperous, blustering, blatant, uproarious. —**Ant.** quiet, silent, peaceful.

nominal, *adj.* titular, so-called, formal.

nonchalant, *adj.* unconcerned, indifferent, cool, apathetic, unexcited, calm, casual. —**Ant.** concerned, excitable.

nondescript, *adj.* odd, peculiar, strange, unclassifiable, amorphous, indescribable. —**Ant.** regular, natural, ordinary.

nonesuch, *n.* paragon, ideal, model, pattern, nonpareil.

nonpareil, *adj.* **1.** peerless, unequaled, unparalleled. —*n.* **2.** nonesuch. —**Ant.** average, common, ordinary.

nonplus, *v.* puzzle, confound, confuse, perplex, disconcert.

nonsense, *n.* twaddle, balderdash, senselessness, moonshine, absurdity, folly, trash.

notable, *adj.* **1.** noteworthy, noted, noticeable, remarkable, signal, distinguished, unusual, uncommon, extraordinary, great, conspicuous, memorable. **2.** prominent, important, eminent, distinguished, famed, famous, well-known, conspicuous, notorious. **3.** capable, thrifty, industrious, diligent, sedulous, assiduous,

careful, clever, smart, alert, watchful. —*n.* **4.** celebrity. —**Ant.** common, ordinary; unimportant, undistinguished; careless.

note, *n.* **1.** memorandum, record, minute. **2.** comment, remark, commentary, criticism, critique, assessment, annotation, footnote. **3.** IOU. **4.** eminence, distinction, repute, celebrity, fame, renown, reputation, name. **5.** notice, heed, observation, consideration, regard. —*v.* **6.** mark down, jot down, record, make a note of, register. **7.** mention, designate, refer to, indicate, denote. **8.** notice, see, perceive, spot, remark, observe, regard, look at.

noted, *adj.* famous, celebrated, distinguished, famed, notable, renowned, eminent, illustrious, well-known. —**Ant.** unknown, undistinguished; notorious, infamous.

noteworthy, *adj.* notable, significant, remarkable, newsworthy, impressive, signal, outstanding, standout, extraordinary, exceptional, great, major. —**Ant.** insignificant.

notice, *n.* **1.** information, intelligence, advice, news, notification, mention, announcement. **2.** intimation, warning, premonition. **3.** sign, placard, poster, billboard, advertisement. **4.** observation, perception, attention, heed, note, cognizance. **5.** comment, mention, account, criticism, critique, review. —*v.* **6.** discern, perceive, see, become aware of, pay attention to, distinguish, discriminate, recognize, understand, regard, heed, note, observe, mark, remark. —**Syn. Study.** NOTICE, PERCEIVE, DISCERN imply becoming aware of something through the senses or the intellect. NOTICE means to pay attention to something one sees, hears, or senses: *to notice a newspaper ad; to notice someone's absence; to notice one's lack of enthusiasm.* PERCEIVE is a more formal word meaning to detect by means of the senses; with reference to the mind, it implies realization, understanding, and insight: *to perceive the sound of hoofbeats; to perceive the significance of an event.* DISCERN means to detect something that is obscure or concealed; it implies keen senses or insight: *to discern the outlines of a distant ship; to discern the truth.*

notify, *v.* give notice to, inform, apprise, acquaint, make known to.

notion, *n.* **1.** conception, idea, concept. **2.** opinion, view, belief, sentiment, impression, judgment. **3.** whim, caprice, fancy, crotchet. —**Syn. Study.** See IDEA.

notorious, *adj.* See Syn. study at FAMOUS.

notwithstanding, *prep.* **1.** despite, in spite of. —*adv.* **2.** nevertheless, yet, however. —*conj.* **3.** although, though, however, yet, nevertheless. —**Ant.** on account of, because of.

nourish, *v.* **1.** nurture, nurse, sustain, support, tend, attend. **2.** foster, promote, promulgate, foment, succor, aid, help, encourage. —**Ant.** discourage; neglect.

novel, *n.* **1.** romance, fiction, tale, story. —*adj.* **2.** new, different. —**Syn. Study.** See NEW.

novelty, *n.* **1.** originality, newness, innovation, uniqueness, freshness, inventiveness. **2.** fad, rage, wrinkle, craze. **3.** knickknack, curio, trinket, trifle, bibelot, whatnot, gewgaw, gimcrack, tchotchke.

noxious, *adj.* **1.** harmful, hurtful, unhealthy, unwholesome, injurious, mephitic, miasmatic, nocuous, noisome, detrimental, baneful, deleterious, pestilential, poisonous, destructive, deadly. **2.** corrupting, immoral, pernicious. —**Ant.** harmless, wholesome, beneficial; moral.

nucleus, *n.* center, kernel, core, heart.

nude, *adj.* uncovered, undressed, unclothed, undraped, naked, bare, exposed, denuded, stark naked, *au naturel*, in the altogether. —**Ant.** covered, dressed.

nugatory, *adj.* **1.** trifling, worthless, futile, vain, trivial. **2.** useless, ineffectual, inoperative. —**Ant.** important, vital; useful, effectual.

nullify, *v.* invalidate, negate, annul, abrogate, quash, undo, cancel out, vitiate. —**Ant.** confirm, establish.

number, *n.* **1.** sum, total, count, aggregate, collection. **2.** numeral, digit, figure. **3.** issue, copy, edition. **4.** quantity, collection, company, multitude, horde, many. **5.** beat, rhythm. —*v.* **6.** count, enumerate, calculate, compute, reckon, numerate, tell; account; include, consist of.

numberless, *adj.* innumerable, numerous, myriad, countless, uncounted, untold, infinite. —**Ant.** finite.

numerous, *adj.* many, numberless. —**Ant.** few. —**Syn. Study.** See MANY.

nurse, *v.* **1.** tend, take care of, attend. **2.** foster, cherish, succor, promote, foment, encourage, aid, abet, help. **3.** nourish, nurture, feed, rear, raise. **4.** suckle, feed, give suck to. —**Ant.** neglect.

nurture, *v.* nurse.

nutrition, *n.* food, nutriment, aliment, nourishment, sustenance, subsistence.

nymph, *n.* sylph, naiad, nereid, oceanid, oread, dryad, hamadryad.

O

oaf, *n.* **1.** simpleton, blockhead, dunce, dolt, fool, nincompoop, ninny. **2.** idiot, imbecile, moron. **3.** changeling. —**Ant.** genius.

oath, *n.* **1.** promise, vow, pledge, affirmation. **2.** profanity, curse, blasphemy, malediction, imprecation.

obdurate, *adj.* **1.** hard-hearted, hardened, hard, firm, obstinate, callous, stubborn, pigheaded, unyielding, unbending, inflexible, inexorable. **2.** penitent, lost, unregenerate, reprobate, irreclaimable, shameless, graceless. —**Ant.** soft-hearted, soft, malleable; abashed, humble.

obedient, *adj.* submissive, compliant, docile, tractable, yielding, deferential, respectful, dutiful, subservient. —**Ant.** disobedient, recalcitrant, refractory.

obeisance, *n.* **1.** deference, honor, homage, reverence, fealty, allegiance, respect, submission. **2.** bow, curtsy, salaam, genuflection, kowtow, bob, prostration. —**Ant.** disrespect, impertinence.

obese, *adj.* fat, stout, plump, pudgy, corpulent, portly, gross. —**Ant.** thin, skinny, slender, slim.

obfuscate, *v.* **1.** confuse, stupefy, muddle, bewilder, perplex. **2.** darken, obscure, adumbrate, cloud. —**Ant.** clarify; brighten.

object, *n.* **1.** thing, reality, fact, manifestation, phenomenon. **2.** target, objective, goal, end, destination, aim. **3.** purpose, reason, basis, base, target, goal, end, motive, intent, intention. —*v.* **4.** protest, disapprove, be averse, refuse. —**Ant.** approve. —**Syn. Study.** See AIM.

objective, *n.* **1.** end, termination, object, destination, aim, target, butt. —*adj.* **2.** unprejudiced, unbiased, impartial, fair, impersonal. —**Ant.** subjective, biased, personal.

obligation, *n.* **1.** requirement, duty, responsibility, accountableness. **2.** agreement, contract, covenant, bond, stipulation. —**Syn. Study.** See DUTY.

oblige, *v.* **1.** require, constrain, compel, force, necessitate, bind, coerce. **2.** obligate, bind. **3.** favor, accommodate, serve, please, benefit. —**Ant.** disoblige, liberate, free; unfetter. —**Syn. Study.** OBLIGE, ACCOMMODATE imply making a gracious and welcome gesture of some kind. OBLIGE emphasizes the idea of doing a favor (and often of taking some trouble to do it): *to oblige someone with a loan.* ACCOMMODATE emphasizes providing a service or convenience: *to accommodate someone with lodgings and meals.*

obliging, *adj.* helpful, accommodating, amiable, friendly, outgoing, considerate, courteous, thoughtful, solicitous. —**Ant.** unhelpful, selfish.

obliterate, *v.* destroy, erase, efface, do away with, expunge, rub out, cancel, dele, delete, blot out. —**Ant.** construct, create, originate; restore.

oblivious, *adj.* heedless, disregardful, neglectful, careless, negligent. —**Ant.** heedful, regardful, careful.

obloquy, *n.* **1.** discredit, disgrace. **2.** censure, blame, reproach, odium, calumny, contumely, scorn, defamation, aspersion, revilement. —**Ant.** credit; exoneration, favor.

obnoxious, *adj.* **1.** objectionable, offensive, odious, hateful. **2.** exposed, liable, subject, answerable. —**Ant.** delightful, favorable; franchised, licensed, irresponsible. —**Syn. Study.** See HATEFUL.

obscene, *adj.* immodest, indecent, lewd, pornographic, coarse, ribald, smutty, offensive, filthy, immoral, indelicate, impure, unchaste, gross, disgusting, lubricious. —**Ant.** modest, decent, moral, pure, chaste.

obscure, *adj.* **1.** unclear, uncertain, doubtful, dubious, ambiguous, mysterious. **2.** inconspicuous, unnoticeable, unnoticed, unknown, undistinguished, undistinguishable, unnoted. **3.** remote, retired, secluded. **4.** indistinct, blurred, blurry, imperfect, dim, veiled. **5.** dark, murky, dim, clouded, cloudy, gloomy, dusky, somber, shadowy, lurid, unilluminated. —**Ant.** clear, certain, unambiguous, conspicuous, noted; distinct; bright. —**Syn. Study.** See MYSTERIOUS.

obsequious, *adj.* servile, compliant, deferential, cringing, slavish, mean, submissive. **2.** deferential, fawning, sycophantic, flattering. —**Ant.** haughty, overbearing, domineering. —**Syn. Study.** See SERVILE.

observant, *adj.* **1.** attentive, watchful, heedful, mindful, aware. **2.** perceptive, quick, alert. **3.** careful, obedient. —**Ant.** inattentive, careless; dull; disobedient.

observation, *n.* **1.** noticing, perceiving, watching, regarding, attending. **2.** notice, observance, attention. **3.** information, record, memorandum. **4.** remark, comment, aside, utterance.

observe, *v.* **1.** perceive, notice, see, discover, detect. **2.** regard, witness, mark, watch, note, view. **3.** remark, comment, mention; utter, say. **4.** obey, comply, conform, follow, fulfill. **5.** solemnize, celebrate, keep. —**Ant.** ignore.

obsession, *n.* preoccupation, domination.

obsolete, *adj.* antiquated, old-fashioned, ancient, old, archaic. —**Ant.** modern, new, up-to-date.

obstacle, *n.* obstruction, hindrance, impediment, interference, check, block, barrier. —**Ant.** aid, support; license, franchise, permission. —**Syn. Study.** OBSTACLE, OBSTRUCTION, HINDRANCE, IMPEDIMENT refer to something that interferes with or prevents action or progress and must be removed, overcome, or bypassed. An OBSTACLE is something, material or nonmaterial, that stands in the way of progress: *an obstacle in a steeplechase; an obstacle to success.* An OBSTRUCTION is something that more or less completely blocks passage: *an obstruction in a drainpipe.* A HINDRANCE interferes and causes delay or difficulty: *Interruptions are a hindrance to my work.* An IMPEDIMENT slows down proper functioning or interferes with free movement: *Heavy rain was an impediment to our departure.*

obstinate, *adj.* **1.** mulish, obdurate, unyielding, recusant, stubborn, perverse, unbending, contumacious, inflexible, willful, headstrong, refractory, firm, intractable, resolute, pertinacious, persistent, dogged. **2.** uncontrollable, wild. —**Ant.** submissive, flexible, tractable, irresolute; controlled, tame. —**Syn. Study.** See STUBBORN.

obstreperous, *adj.* unruly, uncontrolled, boisterous, noisy, clamorous, tumultuous, riotous, uproarious. —**Ant.** obedient, calm.

obstruct, *v.* block, stop, close, occlude, oppilate, choke, clog, bar, hinder, barricade, dam up, impede, prevent; retard, slow, check, arrest, interrupt. —**Ant.** encourage, help, support, further.

obstruction, *n.* **1.** obstacle, hindrance, barrier, occlusion, impediment, bar. **2.** stopping, estoppage. —**Ant.** encouragement, furtherance; continuation. —**Syn. Study.** See OBSTACLE.

obtain, *v.* get, acquire, procure, secure, gain, achieve, earn, win, attain. —**Ant.** lose, forgo. —**Syn. Study.** See GET.

obtrusive, *adj.* **1.** meddlesome, intrusive, interfering, impertinent, invasive, interruptive, disruptive, presumptuous, officious, busybody, forward, prying, pushy, nosy. **2.** protruding, prominent, pronounced, noticeable, conspicuous. —**Ant.** reticent, circumspect.

obviate, *v.* preclude, prevent, avert, anticipate. —**Ant.** include, foster.

obvious, *adj.* plain, manifest, evident, clear, open, apparent, patent, palpable, perceptible, distinct, unmistakable. —**Ant.** concealed, hidden, indistinct, imperceptible. —**Syn. Study.** See APPARENT.

occasion, *n.* **1.** occurrence, event, time, incident. **2.** opportunity, chance, convenience, opening. **3.** ground, reason, cause, motive, inducement, influence. —*v.* **4.** bring about, cause, motivate, originate, create, move, give rise to, produce. —**Ant.** cease, stop.

occult, *adj.* **1.** mysterious, hidden, concealed, secret, undisclosed, unrevealed, unknown, mystical, recondite, cabalistic, veiled, shrouded. **2.** supernatural, metaphysical. —**Ant.** open, manifest, obvious; natural.

occupation, *n.* calling, trade, business, profession, metier, vocation, employment, pursuit, craft. **2.** possession, tenure, use, occupancy. **3.** seizure, invasion, capture.

occupy, *v.* **1.** take up, use, engage, employ, busy. **2.** possess, capture, seize, keep, take hold of.

occur, *v.* **1.** come to pass, take place, happen, befall. **2.** appear, be met with, be found, arise, offer, meet the eye.

occurrence, *n.* event, incident, circumstance, affair, proceeding, transaction.

odd, *adj.* **1.** different, extraordinary, unusual, strange, weird, peculiar, singular, unique, queer, quaint, eccentric, uncommon, rare, fantastic, bizarre, whimsical. **2.** out-of-the-way, secluded, retired. **3.** occasional, casual. —*n.* **4.** (*plural*) bits, scraps, remnants, oddments. —**Ant.** ordinary, common, unexceptional, usual.

odious, *adj.* **1.** hateful, despicable, detestable, execrable, abominable, invidious. **2.** obnoxious, offensive, disgusting, loathsome, repellent, repulsive, forbidding. —**Ant.** attractive, lovable; inviting. —**Syn. Study.** See HATEFUL.

odium, *n.* **1.** hatred, detestation, abhorrence, dislike, antipathy. **2.** reproach, discredit, opprobrium, obloquy. —**Ant.** love.

odor, *n.* smell, aroma, fragrance, redolence, scent, perfume. —**Syn. Study.** ODOR, SMELL, SCENT, STENCH all refer to a sensation perceived by means of the olfactory nerves. ODOR refers to a relatively strong sensation that may be agreeable or disagreeable, actually or figuratively: *the odor of freshly roasted coffee; the odor of duplicity.* SMELL is used in similar contexts, although it is a more general word: *cooking smells; the sweet smell of success.* SCENT may refer to a distinctive smell, usu. delicate and pleasing, or to a smell left in passing: *the scent of lilacs; the scent of an antelope.* STENCH refers to a foul, sickening, or repulsive smell: *the stench of rotting flesh.*

odoriferous, *adj.* odorous, fragrant, aromatic, perfumed, redolent. —**Ant.** noisome, noxious.

offbeat, *adj.* unusual, unconventional, uncommon, unexpected, out-of-the-ordinary, out-of-the-way, rare, special, eccentric, unique, way-out, far-out. —**Ant.** commonplace, conventional.

offend, *v.* **1.** irritate, annoy, vex, chafe, provoke, nettle, mortify, gall, fret, displease, affront, insult. **2.** sin, transgress, err, stumble. —**Ant.** please, delight, compliment.

offense, *n.* **1.** transgression, wrong, sin, trespass, misdemeanor, crime, fault, felony. **2.** displeasure, unpleasantness, umbrage, resentment, wrath, indignation, anger, ire. **3.** attack, assault, onset, aggression. **4.** besiegers, enemy, foe, attackers. —**Ant.** delight, pleasure; defense; allies, friends. —**Syn. Study.** See CRIME.

offensive, *adj.* **1.** displeasing, irritating, annoying, vexing, vexatious, unpleasant, impertinent, rude, insolent, hateful, detestable, opprobrious, insulting, abusive. **2.** disagreeable, distasteful, disgusting, repulsive, obnoxious, unpalatable, unpleasant, revolting, repellent, nauseating, nauseous, sickening, loathsome. **3.** repugnant, insulting, execrable, abominable, shocking, revolting. **4.** aggressive, assailant, invading, attacking. —**Ant.** pleasing, pleasant, polite, courteous; agreeable, tasteful, attractive; delightful; defensive. —**Syn. Study.** See HATEFUL.

offer, *v.* **1.** present, proffer, tender. **2.** propose, give, move, put forward, tender. **3.** volunteer, sacrifice, immolate, present. —*n.* **4.** proposal, proposition, overture; bid. —**Ant.** refuse; refusal, denial. —**Syn. Study.** OFFER, PROFFER, TENDER mean to put something forward for acceptance or rejection. OFFER is the general word for presenting anything for acceptance, sale, consideration, or the like: *to offer help; to offer a cold drink.* PROFFER, chiefly a literary word, implies presenting something freely and unselfishly: *to proffer one's services.* TENDER is used in formal, legal, business, and polite social contexts: *to tender one's resignation; to tender payment.*

offhand, *adj.* **1.** casual, nonchalant, informal, unceremonious, relaxed, easygoing, unstudied, laid-back. **2.** unpremeditated, spontaneous, impromptu, improvisatory, extemporaneous, impulsive, ad-lib, spur-of-the-moment, off-the-cuff. —**Ant.** studied, formal.

office, *n.* **1.** staff, organization. **2.** position, post, station, berth, situation. **3.** duty, function, responsibility, charge, appointment, trust. **4.** service, task, work, duty.

officious, *adj.* forward, obtrusive, forceful, direct, interfering, meddlesome. —**Ant.** retiring, shy, backward.

often, *adv.* frequently, generally, usually, repeatedly, customarily. —**Ant.** seldom. —**Syn. Study.** OFTEN, FREQUENTLY, GENERALLY, USUALLY refer to experiences that are habitual or customary. OFTEN and FREQUENTLY are used interchangeably in most cases, but OFTEN implies numerous repetitions: *We often go there;* whereas FREQUENTLY suggests repetition at comparatively short intervals: *It happens frequently.* GENERALLY emphasizes a broad or nearly universal quality: *It is generally understood. He is generally liked.* USUALLY emphasizes time, and means in numerous instances: *We usually have hot summers.*

ointment, *n.* unguent, nard, salve, balm.

old, *adj.* **1.** aged, elderly. **2.** familiar, known. **3.** former, past, ancient, primeval, olden, primitive, antediluvian, antiquated, passé, antique, old-fashioned. **4.** deteriorated, dilapidated, worn, decayed. **5.** experienced, practiced, skilled, adroit. **6.** sedate, sensible, wise, intelligent, thoughtful. —**Ant.** new, modern; inexperienced, green; wild, senseless.

old-fashioned, *adj.* outmoded, obsolete, antique, passé, antiquated, old, ancient, archaic. —**Ant.** modern.

omen, *n.* sign, augury, foreboding, portent. —**Syn. Study.** See SIGN.

ominous, *adj.* **1.** portentous, inauspicious, threatening, unpropitious. **2.** significant, foreboding. —**Ant.** favorable, propitious; insignificant, meaningless. —**Syn. Study.** OMINOUS, PORTENTOUS, FATEFUL, THREATENING describe something that foretells a serious and significant outcome or consequence. OMINOUS suggests an evil or harmful consequence: *ominous storm clouds.* PORTENTOUS, although it may point to evil or disaster, more often describes something momentous or important: *a portentous change in foreign policy.* FATEFUL also stresses the great or decisive importance of what it describes: *a fateful encounter between two influential leaders.* THREATENING may point to calamity or mere unpleasantness, but usu. suggests that the outcome is imminent: *a threatening rumble from a volcano.*

omnipresent, *adj.* ubiquitous, present. —**Ant.** nowhere.

only, *adv.* **1.** alone, solely, exclusively. **2.** merely, but, just, no more than. **3.** singly, uniquely. —*adj.* **4.** sole, single, unique, solitary, lone. **5.** distinct, exclusive, alone. —*conj.* **6.** but, excepting *or* except that, however.

onus, *n.* burden, responsibility, load. —**Ant.** relief.

onward, *adv.* **1.** forward, ahead. —*adj.* **2.** forward, advanced, improved; advancing. —**Ant.** backward; retreating, retrograde.

ooze, *v.* **1.** percolate, exude, seep, drip, drop. —*n.* **2.** mire, slime, mud. —**Ant.** pour, flood.

opalescent, *adj.* iridescent, nacreous, polychromatic.

open, *adj.* **1.** unclosed, uncovered, unenclosed. **2.** accessible, available, public, unrestricted, free. **3.** unfilled, unoccupied. **4.** undecided, unsettled, undetermined, debatable, disputable. **5.** liable, subject to, unprotected, bare, undefended, exposed. **6.** mild, moderate. **7.** unreserved, candid, frank, ingenuous, artless, guileless, unconcealed, undisguised; sincere, honest, fair, aboveboard. **8.** perforated, porous, reticulated. **9.** expanded, patulous, extended, spread out, unclosed. **10.** generous, liberal, free, bounteous, bountiful, munificent, magnanimous, open-handed. **11.** obvious, evident, clear, apparent, plain. —*v.* **12.** unclose. **13.** recall, revoke. **14.** uncover, lay bare, bare, expose, reveal, divulge, disclose. **15.** expand, extend, spread out. **16.** begin, start, commence, initiate. —**Ant.** closed; close. —**Syn. Study.** See FRANK.

opening, *n.* **1.** gap, hole, aperture, orifice, perforation; slit, slot, breach, rift, chasm, cleft, fissure, rent. **2.** beginning, start, commencement, initiation, dawn. **3.** vacancy, chance, opportunity. —**Ant.** closing.

operate, *v.* **1.** work, run, use, act. **2.** manage, carry on, perform. **3.** bring about, effect, produce, occasion, cause. —**Ant.** fail.

operation, *n.* **1.** action, process, procedure, manipulation, performance, proceeding. **2.** efficacy, influence, virtue, effect, force, action. **3.** course, transaction, business, affair, maneuver. —**Ant.** failure.

operative, *n.* **1.** worker, workman, artisan, hand, laborer. **2.** detective, investigator, private eye, agent. —*adj.* **3.** operating, exerting, influencing, influential. **4.** effective, efficacious, efficient, effectual, serviceable. —**Ant.** inoperative; ineffectual, inefficient.

opiate, *n.* narcotic, drug, anodyne, sedative, sedation, soporific. —**Ant.** stimulant.

opinion, *n.* sentiment, view, conclusion, persuasion, belief, judgment, notion, conception, idea, impression, estimation. —**Syn. Study.** OPINION, SENTIMENT, VIEW are terms for one's conclusion about something. An OPINION is a belief or judgment that falls short of absolute conviction, certainty, or positive knowledge: *an opinion about modern art.* SENTIMENT refers to a rather fixed opinion, usu. based on feeling or emotion rather than reasoning: *sentiments on the subject of divorce.* A VIEW is an intellectual or critical judgment based on one's particular circumstances or standpoint; it often concerns a public issue: *views on government spending.*

opinionated, *adj.* obstinate, stubborn, conceited, dogmatic, prejudiced, biased, bigoted. —**Ant.** liberal, open-minded, unprejudiced.

opponent, *n.* adversary, antagonist, competitor, rival, contestant; enemy, foe. —**Ant.** ally, friend, associate.

opportune, *adj.* appropriate, favorable, suitable, apt, suited, fit, fitting, fitted, fortunate, propitious. **2.** convenient, timely, well-timed, lucky, felicitous, seasonable, timely. —**Ant.** inopportune, inappropriate; inconvenient.

opportunity, *n.* chance, occasion, time, opportune moment.

oppose, *v.* **1.** resist, combat, withstand, thwart, confront, contravene, interfere, oppugn. **2.** hinder, obstruct, prevent, check. **3.** offset, contrast. **4.** contradict, gainsay, deny, refuse. —**Ant.** support, aid, help. —**Syn. Study.** OPPOSE, RESIST, WITHSTAND imply holding out or acting against something. OPPOSE implies offensive action against the opposite side in a conflict or contest; it may also refer to attempts to thwart displeasing ideas, methods, or the like: *to oppose an enemy; to oppose the passage of a bill.* RESIST suggests defensive action against a threatening force or possibility; it may also refer to an inner struggle in which the will is divided: *to resist an enemy onslaught; hard to resist chocolate.* WITHSTAND generally implies successful resistance; it stresses the determination and endurance necessary to emerge unharmed: *to withstand public criticism; to withstand a siege.*

opposite, *adj.* **1.** facing, fronting. **2.** contrary, reverse, incompatible, irreconcilable, inconsistent, unlike, differing, different. **3.** opposed, adverse, refractory, hostile, antagonistic, inimical. —**Ant.** compatible, consistent, like, same; friendly, amiable.

opposition, *n.* **1.** opposing, resisting, combating. **2.** antagonism, hostility, resistance, counteraction. **3.** competition, enemy, foe, adversary, antagonist. **4.** offset, antithesis, contrast. **5.** contrariety, inconsistency, incompatibility, difference. —**Ant.** help, support, furtherance; consistency, compatibility.

oppress, *v.* **1.** depress, weigh down, burden, load. **2.** maltreat, persecute, wrong. **3.** overwhelm, crush, overpower, subdue, suppress. —**Ant.** unburden, liberate, disencumber.

oppression, *n.* **1.** cruelty, injustice, tyranny, despotism, persecution, severity. **2.** hardship, misery, suffering, calamity. **3.** depression, sadness, misery. —**Ant.** kindness, justice; happiness, joy.

opprobrious, *adj.* **1.** reproachful, infamous, abusive, scurrilous, vituperative, contemptuous, insolent, offensive, insulting, scandalous. **2.** disgraceful, shameful, infamous, dishonorable, disreputable, ignominious, hateful. —**Ant.** complimentary.

praising, laudatory; honorable, reputable.

optimistic, *adj.* hopeful, upbeat, sanguine, full of hope, expectant, confident, sunny, rosy, cheerful, Pollyanna, Pollyannaish, Panglossian. —**Ant.** pessimistic, discouraged, doubtful.

option, *n.* choice, election, selection, preference. —**Syn. Study.** See CHOICE.

opulent, *adj.* **1.** wealthy, rich, affluent, moneyed, sumptuous, luxurious. **2.** abundant, copious, plentiful. —**Ant.** poor, squalid; scarce.

oracular, *adj.* **1.** prophetic, portentous, auspicious. **2.** authoritative, inspired, inspirational, dogmatic, sententious. **3.** ambiguous, obscure, equivocal, two-faced.

oral, *adj.* verbal, spoken, mouthed, uttered, said, vocal. —**Ant.** tacit, silent, taciturn.

oration, *n.* speech, address, lecture, discourse, declamation, harangue. —**Syn. Study.** See SPEECH.

orb, *n.* sphere, globe, ball.

orbit, *n.* **1.** path, course. —*v.* **2.** circle, circumvent.

ordain, *v.* **1.** appoint, call, nominate, elect, select, destine. **2.** decree, order, enact, prescribe, determine. **3.** predestine, predetermine, destine, fate.

ordeal, *n.* trial, test, proof, assay.

order, *n.* **1.** direction, injunction, mandate, law, ukase, command, instruction, rule, canon, prescription. **2.** succession, sequence. **3.** method, arrangement, harmony, regularity, symmetry. **4.** disposition, array, arrangement. **5.** class, kind, sort, genus, subclass; tribe, family. **6.** rank, status, grade, class, degree. **7.** fraternity, society, brotherhood, community. **8.** peace, calm, serenity. **9.** custom, usage. **10.** direction, commission. —*v.* **11.** direct, command, instruct, bid, require; ordain. **12.** regulate, conduct, manage, run, operate, adjust, arrange, systematize. —**Syn. Study.** See DIRECT.

orderly, *adj.* **1.** regular, systematic, methodical. **2.** well-regulated, neat, trim, organized, well-organized. **3.** well-disciplined, well-trained, well-behaved. —**Ant.** irregular, unsystematic; sloppy, unregulated; undisciplined. —**Syn. Study.** ORDERLY, SYSTEMATIC, METHODICAL characterize that which is efficient, thorough, and carefully planned. ORDERLY emphasizes neatness, harmony, and logical sequence or arrangement: *an orderly library.* SYSTEMATIC emphasizes an extensive, detailed plan and a relatively complex procedure designed to achieve some purpose: *a systematic search.* METHODICAL is similar in meaning, but stresses a carefully developed plan and rigid adherence to a fixed procedure: *methodical examination of the evidence.*

ordinary, *adj.* **1.** common, usual, customary, regular, normal, accustomed, habitual, frequent. **2.** inferior, second-rate, mean, mediocre, indifferent. **3.** plain, homely, commonlooking, commonplace. —**Ant.** uncommon, extraordinary, unusual; superior, beautiful. —**Syn. Study.** See COMMON.

organic, *adj.* **1.** systematic, systematized, organized. **2.** constitutional, structural, inherent, fundamental, essential, vital, radical. —**Ant.** inorganic.

organize, *v.* **1.** coordinate, harmonize, unite, construct, form, dispose, constitute, make, shape, frame. **2.** systematize, order. **3.** combine, unionize. —**Ant.** destroy, ruin; disorder.

origin, *n.* **1.** source, rise, fountainhead, derivation, beginning, root, cradle, foundation, birthplace. **2.** parentage, birth, extraction, lineage, heritage, descent. —**Ant.** end; posterity.

original, *adj.* **1.** primary, primordial, primeval, primitive, aboriginal. **2.** new, fresh, novel, inventive, creative. —*n.* **3.** archetype, pattern, prototype, model. —**Ant.** secondary; old, old-fashioned.

originate, *v.* **1.** arise, spring, rise, begin, emanate, flow, proceed. **2.** initiate, invent, discover, create, author. —**Ant.** terminate; follow.

ornament, *n.* **1.** accessory, detail, embellishment, adornment, decoration, ornamentation, design. —*v.* **2.** decorate, adorn, embellish, beautify, trim, garnish, grace, bedeck. —**Ant.** essential, necessity.

ornate, *adj.* elaborate, adorned, embellished, showy, splendid, sumptuous, elegant, decorated, florid; flowery. —**Ant.** simple, plain.

orthodox, *adj.* conventional, regular, customary, expected, accepted, recognized, approved, sanctioned, canonical, received, traditional, standard, conformable, conformist, conforming, correct, regular, kosher, conservative, reactionary, die-hard, hidebound, pedantic. —**Ant.** freethinking, unconventional, rebellious.

oscillate, *v.* vibrate, vacillate, swing, fluctuate, vary.

ostensible, *adj.* apparent, professed, pretended, ostensive, specious, plausible. —**Ant.** concealed, hidden, implausible.

ostentation, *n.* pretension, pretentiousness, semblance, show, showiness, pretense, pretext, display, pageantry, pomp, pompousness, flourish.

ostentatious, See Syn. study at GRANDIOSE.

ostracize, *v.* banish, exile, expatriate, disenfranchise, excommunicate. —**Ant.** accept.

outcome, *n.* end, result, consequence, issue.

outdo, *v.* surpass, excel, exceed, beat, outstrip, outdistance.

outgoing, *adj.* friendly, sociable, approachable, open, gregarious, communicative, talkative, extroverted, demonstrative, expansive, effusive. —**Ant.** restrained, shy.

outgrowth, *n.* **1.** development, product, result. **2.** offshoot, excrescence.

outlaw, *n.* **1.** criminal, highwayman, holdup man, robber, thief, bandit, brigand. —*v.* **2.** proscribe, prohibit.

outline, *n.* **1.** contour, silhouette. **2.** plan, draft, drawing, rough, sketch, cartoon. —*v.* **3.** delineate, draft, draw.

outlive, *v.* survive, outlast. —**Syn. Study.** See SURVIVE.

outrage, *n.* **1.** violence, violation. **2.** affront, insult, offense, abuse, indignity. —*v.* **3.** shock, abuse, maltreat, injure, offend. **4.** ravish, rape.

outspoken, *adj.* frank, open, unreserved, candid, free. —**Ant.** reserved, taciturn. —**Syn. Study.** See FRANK[1].

outstanding, *adj.* **1.** prominent, eminent, conspicuous, striking. **2.** unsettled, unpaid, owing, due. —**Ant.** inconspicuous; paid, settled.

overbearing, *adj.* domineering, dictatorial, haughty, arrogant, imperious, supercilious. —**Ant.** humble, servile.

overcome, *v.* **1.** conquer, defeat, subdue, vanquish, rout, crush. **2.** surmount. **3.** overpower, overwhelm, discomfit. —**Syn. Study.** See DEFEAT.

overlook, *v.* **1.** slight, disregard, miss, neglect, ignore. **2.** excuse, forgive, pardon. **3.** oversee, superintend, supervise. **4.** bewitch. —**Syn. Study.** See SLIGHT.

overpower, *v.* overcome, overwhelm, vanquish, subjugate, subdue, conquer, overmaster, rout, defeat, beat.

overrule, *v.* disallow, rescind, revoke, repeal, recall, repudiate, set aside, nullify, cancel, annul; prevail over, influence. —**Ant.** allow, permit, approve.

oversee, *v.* supervise, direct, manage, superintend, survey, watch, overlook.

oversight, *n.* **1.** mistake, blunder, slip, error, erratum, omission, lapse, neglect, fault, inattention. **2.** management, direction, control, superintendence, supervision, charge, surveillance, care. —**Ant.** attention.

overt, *adj.* open, plain, manifest, showing, apparent, public. —**Ant.** private, concealed, clandestine, secret.

overthrow, *v.* **1.** cast down, overcome, defeat, vanquish, overwhelm, conquer, master, overpower, subjugate, crush. **2.** upset, overturn. **3.** knock down, demolish, destroy, raze, level. **4.** subvert, ruin, destroy. —*n.* **5.** deposition, fall, displacement. **6.** defeat, destruction, ruin, rout, dispersion, demolition. —**Ant.** support.

overture, *n.* **1.** opening, proposal, proposition, offer. **2.** prelude, introduction; prologue. —**Ant.** finale, termination, close, end, epilogue.

overturn, *v.* **1.** overthrow, destroy, vanquish, conquer, upset. **2.** upset, capsize, founder.

overwhelm, *v.* **1.** overpower, crush, overcome, subdue, defeat, vanquish.

2. overload, overburden, cover, bury, sink, drown, inundate.

own, *v.* **1.** have, hold, possess. **2.** acknowledge, admit, allow, confess, concede, avow; recognize.

P

pace, *n.* **1.** step, rate; gait. **2.** step, walk, trot, jog, singlefoot, amble, rack, canter, gallop, run. **3.** dais, platform. —*v.* **4.** step, plod, trudge, walk, move, go. —**Syn. Study.** PACE, PLOD, TRUDGE refer to a steady and monotonous kind of walking. PACE suggests steady, measured steps, as of someone lost in thought or impelled by some distraction: *to pace up and down the hall.* PLOD implies a slow, heavy, laborious walk: *The mail carriers plod their weary way.* TRUDGE implies a spiritless but usu. steady and doggedly persistent walk: *The farmer trudged to the village to buy supplies.*

pacific, *adj.* **1.** conciliatory, appeasing. **2.** peaceable, peaceful, calm, tranquil, at peace, quiet, unruffled, gentle. —**Ant.** hostile; agitated, perturbed.

pacify, *v.* **1.** quiet, calm, tranquilize, assuage, still, smooth, moderate, soften, ameliorate, mollify, meliorate, better, soothe. **2.** appease, conciliate. —**Ant.** agitate, perturb, aggravate, worsen; estrange.

pack, *n.* **1.** package, bundle, parcel, packet; knapsack. **2.** set, gang, group, band, company, crew, squad. —*v.* **3.** stow, compress, cram. **4.** load, burden, lade.

package, *n.* **1.** bundle, parcel, packet, pack, bale. **2.** case, crate, carton, box.

pact, *n.* agreement, compact, contract, deal, arrangement, treaty, bond, covenant, league, union, concordat, alliance, bargain.

paean, *n.* hymn, anthem, hosanna, hallelujah, laudation, laud, praise, encomium, tribute, homage, accolade.

pagan, *n.* **1.** heathen, idolater, gentile. —*adj.* **2.** heathen, heathenish, gentile, irreligious, idolatrous. —**Ant.** Christian, believer; pious, religious. —**Syn. Study.** See HEATHEN.

pageant, *n.* **1.** spectacle, extravaganza, show, masque. **2.** display, show, procession, parade.

pain, *n.* **1.** suffering, distress, torture, misery, anguish, agony, torment, throe, pang, ache, twinge, stitch. **2.** (*plural*) care, efforts, labor. —*v.* **3.** afflict, torture, torment, distress, hurt, harm, injure, trouble, grieve, aggrieve, disquiet, discommode, incommode, inconvenience, displease, worry, tease, irritate, vex, annoy. —**Ant.** joy, delight, pleasure; ease; please.

painful, *adj.* **1.** distressing, torturous, agonizing, tormenting, excruciating. **2.** laborious, difficult, arduous, severe. —**Ant.** pleasant, soothing; easy, simple.

painstaking, *adj.* careful, assiduous, diligent, sedulous, strenuous. —**Ant.** careless, frivolous. —**Syn. Study.** PAINSTAKING, METICULOUS, CONSCIENTIOUS mean extremely careful or precise about details. PAINSTAKING stresses laborious effort and diligent attention to detail in achieving a desired objective: *the painstaking editing of a manuscript.* METICULOUS suggests a more extreme attention to minute details: *to be meticulous about matching shoes and clothing.* CONSCIENTIOUS stresses scrupulous effort to obey one's sense of moral obligation to perform tasks well: *a conscientious description of the facts.*

pair, *n.* **1.** brace, couple, span, yoke, two, team. —*v.* **2.** match, mate, couple, marry, join.

palatable, *adj.* agreeable, savory, sapid, tasty, gustatory, luscious, delicious, delectable, flavorsome. —**Ant.** unpalatable, distasteful, tasteless, flavorless. —**Syn. Study.** PALATABLE, APPETIZING, TASTY, SAVORY refer to tastes or aromas pleasing to the palate, and sometimes to the senses of sight and smell. PALATABLE usu. refers to food that is merely acceptable: *a barely palatable plate of vegetables.* APPETIZING suggests stimulation of the appetite by the smell, taste, or sight of food: *an appetizing display of meats and cheeses.* TASTY refers to food that has an appealing taste: *a tasty sausage.* SAVORY refers most often to well or highly seasoned food that is pleasing to the taste or smell: *a savory stew.*

palatial, *adj.* magnificent, grand,

grandiose, imposing, noble, stately, majestic, splendid, splendiferous, sumptuous, luxurious, extravagant, swank, posh, ritzy. —**Ant.** humble, simple.

pale, *adj.* **1.** pallid, wan, white, ashy, ashen, colorless. **2.** dim, faint, feeble, obscure. —*v.* **3.** blanch, etiolate, whiten. —*n.* **4.** picket, stake. **5.** enclosure, fence, barrier, paling, limits, bounds, confines. —**Ant.** ruddy, hale, hearty; robust; blacken, soil. —**Syn. Study.** PALE, PALLID, WAN imply an absence of color, esp. from the human countenance. PALE implies a faintness or absence of color, which may be natural when applied to things (*the pale blue of a violet*), but when used to refer to the human face usu. means an unnatural and often temporary absence of color, as arising from sickness or sudden emotion: *pale cheeks.* PALLID, limited mainly to the human countenance, implies an excessive paleness induced by intense emotion, disease, or death: *the pallid lips of the dying man.* WAN implies a sickly paleness, as after a long illness: *wan and thin;* or it may suggest weakness: *a wan smile.*

pall, *n.* **1.** shroud, blanket, cover, covering, veil. —*v.* **2.** glut, satiate, fill, cloy, sate, surfeit, overstuff, gorge. **3.** weary, tire, fatigue, wear on, jade.

palliate, *v.* **1.** moderate, abate, relieve, alleviate, ease, modify, reduce, diminish, lessen, mitigate, soften, cushion. **2.** qualify, hedge, temper, season, excuse, sugarcoat, gloss over, prettify, whitewash, varnish, camouflage. —**Ant.** intensify, worsen.

pallid, *adj.* **1.** pale, faded, washed-out, colorless, white, whitish, ashen, sallow, wan, pasty, ghastly, whey-faced. **2.** dull, colorless, insipid, anemic, unexciting, flat, lifeless. —**Ant.** robust. —**Syn. Study.** See PALE.

palpable, *adj.* **1.** obvious, evident, manifest, plain, unmistakable. **2.** tangible, material, real, corporeal. —**Ant.** obscure, unclear; intangible, spiritual.

palpitate, *v.* pulsate, throb, flutter, beat.

paltry, *adj.* trifling, petty, minor, trashy, mean, worthless, contemptible, insignificant, unimportant, trivial, inconsiderable, slight. —**Ant.** important, major, significant, considerable, essential. —**Syn. Study.** See PETTY.

pamper, *v.* indulge, gratify, humor, coddle, baby, cater to, spoil. —**Ant.** discipline.

pan, *v.* criticize, faultfind, deprecate, disparage, censure, put down, fault, disparage, denigrate, disdain, despise, excoriate, reject, ridicule, knock, rap, flame. —**Ant.** praise, extol.

panacea, *n.* cure, cure-all, remedy, relief, nostrum, catholicon, theriac.

panache, *n.* showiness, dash, flair, style, flamboyance, dazzle, showmanship, élan, verve, bravura, brilliance, virtuosity.

pandemic, *adj.* general, prevalent, universal, epidemic. —**Ant.** isolated, unique, singular.

panegyric, *n.* eulogy, encomium, tribute, commendation, praise. —**Ant.** condemnation, invective.

pang, *n.* **1.** pain, stab, stitch, twinge, prick, throe. **2.** qualm, scruple, compunction, scrupulousness.

panic, *n.* **1.** terror, fright, alarm. —*v.* **2.** terrorize, frighten. —**Ant.** security; soothe, calm.

pant, *v.* **1.** gasp, breathe heavily, puff, blow. **2.** long, yearn, thirst, hunger, desire. **3.** throb, pulsate, palpitate. —*n.* **4.** puff, gasp, heave; throb.

paradigm, *n.* model, ideal, guide, archetype, example, exemplar, standard, pattern, blueprint, criterion, classic example, locus classicus.

paragon, *n.* model, ideal, pattern, nonesuch, masterpiece.

parallel, *adj.* **1.** corresponding, similar, analogous, like, resembling, correspondent. **2.** tonic, harmonic. —*n.* **3.** match, counterpart. **4.** correspondence, analogy, similarity, resemblance, likeness. —*v.* **5.** match, resemble. **6.** equal, be equivalent to. —**Ant.** unique, unlike, singular, unusual; dissimilitude; differ.

paralyze, *v.* stun, shock, benumb, unnerve, deaden.

paramount, *adj.* superior, preeminent, chief, principal. —**Ant.** base, inferior, unimportant. —**Syn. Study.** See DOMINANT.

paraphernalia, *n.* belongings, ef-

fects; equipment, apparatus, appointments, appurtenances, accouterments, trappings, rig, equipage.

paraphrase, *n.* **1.** rendering, version, translation. —*v.* **2.** restate, render, translate; explain, explicate, interpret.

parasite, *n.* yes-man, sycophant, leech, hanger-on, bloodsucker, toady, flatterer, flunky.

parcel, *n.* **1.** package, bundle, pack, packet. **2.** quantity, lot, group, batch, collection. **3.** lot, plot, tract, acreage, portion, land. —*v.* **4.** divide, distribute, mete out, apportion, deal out, allot.

pardon, *n.* **1.** indulgence, allowance, excuse, forgiveness; remission, amnesty, absolution. —*v.* **2.** forgive, absolve, remit, condone, excuse, overlook; acquit, clear, release. —**Ant.** censure, blame. —**Syn. Study.** PARDON, AMNESTY, REPRIEVE refer to the remission or delay of a penalty or punishment for an offense; these terms do not imply absolution from guilt. A PARDON is often granted by a government official; it releases the individual from any punishment due: *The governor granted a pardon to the prisoner.* AMNESTY is usu. a general pardon granted to a group of persons for offenses against a government; it often includes an assurance of no further prosecution: *to grant amnesty to the rebels.* A REPRIEVE is a delay of impending punishment, usu. for a specific period of time or until a decision can be made as to the possibility of pardon or reduction of sentence: *a last-minute reprieve, allowing the prisoner to file an appeal.* See also EXCUSE.

pare, *v.* **1.** peel; clip, cut, shave. **2.** diminish, lessen, clip, reduce. —**Ant.** increase.

parentage, *n.* birth, descent, lineage, ancestry, origin, extraction, pedigree, family, stock.

pariah, *n.* outcast, undesirable, untouchable, castaway, castoff, Ishmael, persona non grata.

parity, *n.* equality; equivalence, correspondence, similarity, analogy, parallelism, likeness; sameness. —**Ant.** inequality, dissimilarity, difference.

parlance, *n.* phraseology, language, idiom, diction, wording, words, phrasing, usage, grammar, wordage, locution, expression, formulation, tongue, lingo.

parley, *n.* **1.** conference, discussion, talk, conversation, discourse. —*v.* **2.** confer, discuss, speak, converse, talk, discourse.

parody, *n.* travesty, burlesque, imitation, caricature. —**Syn. Study.** See BURLESQUE.

paroxysm, *n.* fit, spasm, attack, access, seizure, throe, convulsion, outburst, eruption, irruption, explosion, storm.

parry, *v.* ward off, avert, avoid, evade, elude; prevent, obviate, preclude. —*n.* **2.** prevention; avoidance, evasion. —**Ant.** encourage, further.

parsimonious, *adj.* sparing, frugal, stingy, tight, tight-fisted, close, niggardly, miserly, illiberal, mean, close-fisted, grasping, avaricious, penurious, covetous. —**Ant.** generous, open-handed, unsparing. —**Syn. Study.** See STINGY.

parsimony, *n.* economy, frugality, niggardliness, stinginess, miserliness, sparingness, closeness, illiberality, close-fistedness, tight-fistedness, cupidity, meanness. —**Ant.** generosity, liberality.

part, *n.* **1.** portion, division, piece, fragment, fraction, section, constituent, component, ingredient, element, member, organ. **2.** allotment, share, apportionment, portion, lot, dividend, concern, participation, interest, stock. **3.** (*usually plural*) region, quarter, district, section. **4.** duty, function, role, office, responsibility, charge. —*v.* **5.** divide, break, cleave, separate, sever, sunder, disunite, dissociate, dissever, disconnect, disjoin, detach. **6.** share, allot, portion, parcel out, apportion, distribute, deal out, mete out. **7.** depart, leave, go, quit; pass on or away, die. —**Ant.** all, none, everything.

partake, *v.* participate, share.

partial, *adj.* **1.** incomplete, unfinished, imperfect, limited. **2.** constituent, component. **3.** biased, prejudiced, one-sided, unfair, unjust, influenced. —**Ant.** complete, perfect; unbiased, unprejudiced, liberal, just, fair.

partiality, *n.* **1.** bias, favor, prejudice, one-sidedness, injustice, unfairness, favoritism. **2.** fondness, liking, preference, bent, leaning, tendency,

predilection, inclination. —**Ant.** justice, fairness; dislike, disfavor.

participate, *v.* share, partake.

particle, *n.* **1.** mite, whit, jot, iota, tittle, bit, mote, grain, ace, scrap, speck. **2.** molecule, atom, meson, deuteron, electron, positron, neutron, neutrino.

particular, *adj.* **1.** special, specific, especial. **2.** one, individual, single, separate, distinct, discrete. **3.** noteworthy, marked, unusual, notable, extraordinary; peculiar, singular, strange, odd, uncommon. **4.** exceptional, especial, characteristic, distinctive. **5.** certain, personal, special. **6.** detailed, descriptive, minute, circumstantial, critical, scrupulous, strict, careful, exact, precise. **7.** critical, finical, finicky, discriminating, dainty, nice, fastidious, scrupulous. —*n.* **8.** point, detail, circumstance, item, feature, particularity. —**Ant.** general, overall; common, ordinary; inexact, imprecise; undiscriminating, indiscriminate.

particularly, *adv.* **1.** exceptionally, especially, specially. **2.** specially, especially, individually, characteristically, uniquely, separately, discretely, unusually, specifically, singly. **3.** in detail, minutely, exactly, precisely, strictly. —**Ant.** generally; commonly, usually, customarily.

partisan, *n.* **1.** adherent, supporter, follower, disciple. —*adj.* **2.** biased, partial. —**Ant.** leader; unbiased, impartial. —**Syn. Study.** See FOLLOWER.

partition, *n.* **1.** division, distribution, portion, share, allotment, apportionment. **2.** separation, division. **3.** part, section, division, segment, piece. **4.** barrier, wall, dividing wall, screen. —*v.* **5.** divide, separate, apportion, portion, parcel out, deal out, mete out, share. —**Ant.** unity; unite, blend.

partner, *n.* **1.** sharer, partaker, associate, accessory, accomplice, participant, colleague. **2.** husband, wife, spouse.

party, *n.* **1.** group, gathering, assembly, assemblage, company. **2.** body, faction, circle, coterie, clique, set, combination, ring, league, alliance. **3.** attachment, devotion, partisanship.

parvenu, *n.* upstart, snob, Johnny-come-lately, climber.

pass, *v.* **1.** go, move, proceed. **2.** disregard, pass over, skim over, skim, ignore. **3.** transcend, exceed, surpass, excel. **4.** spend; circulate. **5.** convey, transfer, transmit, send, deliver. **6.** sanction, approve, okay, enact. **7.** express, pronounce, utter, deliver. **8.** leave, go away, depart. **9.** end, terminate, expire, cease. **10.** go on, happen, take place, occur. **11.** vanish, fade, die, disappear. —*n.* **12.** notch, defile, ravine, gorge, gulch, canyon, channel. **13.** permission, license, ticket, passport, visa. **14.** thrust, lunge. **15.** stage, state, juncture, situation, condition. —**Ant.** attend, regard, note, notice; disapprove; arrive, come; initiate, begin, start; appear.

passage, *n.* **1.** paragraph, verse, line, section, clause, text, passus. **2.** way, route, avenue, channel, road, path, byway, lane, street, thoroughfare. **3.** movement, transit, transition, passing. **4.** voyage, trip, tour, excursion, journey. **5.** progress, course. **6.** passing, enactment. **7.** exchange, altercation, dispute, encounter, combat, skirmish, conflict, affair. **8.** transference, transmission. —*v.* **9.** cross, pass, voyage.

passion, *n.* **1.** feeling, emotion, zeal, ardor, fervor, transport, rapture, excitement, impulse; hope, fear, joy, grief, anger, love, desire. **2.** love, desire, attachment, affection, fondness, warmth. **3.** anger, ire, resentment, fury, wrath, rage, vehemence, indignation. —**Ant.** coolness, apathy. —**Syn. Study.** See FEELING.

passionate, *adj.* **1.** impassioned, emotional, ardent, vehement, excited, excitable, impulsive, fervent, fervid, zealous, warm, enthusiastic, earnest, glowing, burning, fiery. **2.** quick-tempered, irascible, short-tempered, testy, touchy, choleric, hasty, hot-headed, fiery. —**Ant.** dispassionate, cool, cold; calm, collected.

passive, *adj.* **1.** inactive, quiescent, inert, receptive, prone. **2.** suffering, receiving, submitting, submissive, patient, unresisting. —**Ant.** active, energetic; hostile, resisting.

password, *n.* watchword, shibboleth, countersign.

pastime, *n.* diversion, amusement, sport, entertainment, recreation.

patch, *v.* mend, repair, restore, fix, correct, emend; settle, smooth. —**Ant.** break, crack, ruin, spoil.

patent, *n.* **1.** invention. —*adj.* **2.** patented, trademarked, copyrighted. **3.** open, manifest, evident, plain, clear, apparent, obvious, palpable, unmistakable, conspicuous, unconcealed. —**Ant.** concealed, hidden, unclear, dim.

path, *n.* way, walk, lane, trail, footpath, pathway, route, course, track, passage, road, avenue.

pathetic, *adj.* **1.** pitiable, touching, moving, affecting, tender, plaintive. **2.** emotional, pathetical. —**Ant.** cruel, ruthless; unemotional, apathetical.

patience, *n.* **1.** calmness, composure, endurance, fortitude, stoicism, stability, courage, self-possession, inner strength, submissiveness, submission, sufferance, resignation. **2.** perseverance, diligence, assiduity, sedulousness, indefatigability, indefatigableness, persistence. —**Ant.** hostility; weakness, frailty; fatigue.

patient, *n.* **1.** invalid. —*adj.* **2.** persevering, diligent, persistent, sedulous, assiduous, indefatigable, untiring. **3.** long-suffering, submissive, resigned, passive, unrepining, calm. **4.** quiet, calm, serene, unruffled, unexcited, self-possessed, stoical, composed. **5.** susceptible. —**Ant.** hostile, agitated; excited, perturbed; unsusceptible, impervious.

patron, *n.* **1.** customer, client. **2.** protector, supporter, advocate, defender. —**Ant.** critic.

pattern, *n.* **1.** decoration, design, figure. **2.** style, type, kind, sort. **3.** original, model, paragon, example, exemplar, guide, archetype, prototype. **4.** sample, example, specimen, illustration. —*v.* **5.** model, imitate, copy, follow.

paucity, *n.* smallness, fewness, sparseness, scarcity, poverty. —**Ant.** abundance.

pause, *n.* **1.** rest, wait, hesitation, suspension, lacuna, hiatus, interruption, delay, intermission, break; stop, halt, cessation, stoppage. —*v.* **2.** hesitate, waver, deliberate, wait, rest, interrupt, tarry, delay. **3.** cease, stop, arrest, halt, desist, forbear. —**Ant.** continuity, continuousness.

pay, *v.* **1.** settle, liquidate, discharge. **2.** satisfy, compensate, reimburse, remunerate, recompense; reward; indemnify. **3.** yield, be profitable to, repay, requite. **4.** punish, repay, retaliate, requite, revenge. **5.** make amends, suffer, be punished, make compensation. —*n.* **6.** payment, wages, salary, income, stipend, remuneration, emolument, fee, allowance. **7.** requital, reward, punishment, just deserts. —*adj.* **8.** profitable, interest-bearing, gold-bearing, precious, valuable. —**Ant.** dissatisfy; unprofitable.

payment, *n.* pay.

peace, *n.* **1.** agreement, treaty, armistice, truce, pact, accord, entente, entente cordiale, amity, harmony, concord. **2.** order, security. **3.** calm, quiet, tranquillity, peacefulness, calmness. —**Ant.** insecurity; agitation, disturbance.

peaceable, *adj.* pacific, peaceful, amicable, friendly, amiable, mild, gentle; calm, tranquil, serene, quiet. —**Ant.** hostile, unfriendly; noisy.

peaceful, *adj.* tranquil, placid, serene, unruffled, calm, complacent; composed, dignified, gracious, mellow; unexcited, unagitated, pacific. —**Ant.** perturbed, disturbed. —**Syn. Study.** PEACEFUL, PLACID, SERENE, TRANQUIL refer to what is characterized by lack of strife or agitation. PEACEFUL is rarely applied to persons; it refers to situations, scenes, and activities free of disturbances or, occasionally, of warfare: *a peaceful afternoon; a peaceful protest.* PLACID, SERENE, TRANQUIL are used mainly of persons; when used of things (usu. elements of nature) there is a touch of personification. PLACID suggests an unruffled calm that verges on complacency: *a placid disposition; a placid stream.* SERENE is a somewhat nobler word; when used of persons it suggests dignity, composure, and graciousness; when applied to nature there is a suggestion of mellowness: *a serene summer landscape.* TRANQUIL implies a command of emotions that keeps one unagitated even in the midst of excitement or danger: *She remained tranquil despite the chaos around her.*

peak, *n.* point, top, crest, summit, arete, acme, pinnacle. —**Ant.** base, bottom, abyss.

peaked, *adj.* pale, sickly, wan,

drawn, haggard, pinched, emaciated, unhealthy, infirm, wasted, hollow-eyed. —**Ant.** hale, hearty, robust.

pearly, *adj.* opalescent, opaline, nacreous, iridescent, mother-of-pearl, pale, whitish, light, snowy, dove-gray, pearl-gray.

peccadillo, *n.* petty sin or offense, slight crime, trifling fault; shortcoming, weakness.

peculiar, *adj.* **1.** strange, odd, queer, eccentric, bizarre, uncommon, unusual, extraordinary, singular, exceptional. **2.** distinguished, distinctive. **3.** characteristic, appropriate, proper, individual, particular, select, especial, special, specific, unique, exclusive. —**Ant.** usual, common, ordinary; general, unspecific.

peculiarity, *n.* **1.** idiosyncrasy, characteristic, odd trait. **2.** singularity, oddity, rarity, eccentricity. **3.** distinction, feature, characteristic. —**Syn. Study.** See ECCENTRICITY. See also FEATURE.

pecuniary, *adj.* monetary, financial, nummular. —**Syn. Study.** See FINANCIAL.

pedestrian, *n.* **1.** walker, stroller. —*adj.* **2.** on foot, walking, afoot. **3.** commonplace, prosaic, dull. —**Ant.** interesting, fascinating, engaging.

pedigree, *n.* genealogy, descent, family tree, family, heritage, ancestry, lineage, line, race, derivation; patrimony. —**Syn. Study.** PEDIGREE, GENEALOGY refer to an account of ancestry. A PEDIGREE is a table or chart recording a line of ancestors, either of persons or (more commonly) of animals, as horses, cattle, and dogs; in the case of animals, such a table is used as proof of superior qualities: *a detailed pedigree.* A GENEALOGY is an account of the descent of a person or family traced through a series of generations, usu. from the first known ancestor: *a genealogy that includes a king.*

peek, *v.* peep, peer, pry.

peel, *v.* **1.** strip, skin, decorticate, pare, flay. —*n.* **2.** skin, rind, bark. —**Ant.** cover, plate.

peer, *n.* **1.** equal, compeer, match. **2.** nobleman, lord; duke, count, marquis, earl, viscount, baron.

peerless, *adj.* matchless, unequaled, unsurpassed, unique, superlative, unmatched.

peevish, *adj.* cross, querulous, fretful, vexatious, vexed, captious, discontented, petulant, testy, irritable, crusty, snappish, waspish, acrimonious, splenetic, short-tempered, ill-tempered, ill-natured, unpleasant, disagreeable, nasty. —**Ant.** good-natured, friendly, pleasant, amiable, agreeable.

pejorative, *adj.* depreciative, deprecatory, disparaging, opprobrious. —**Ant.** favorable, complimentary.

pell-mell, *adv.* headlong, hurriedly, recklessly, agitatedly, frantically, frenziedly, wildly, higgledy-piggledy.

pellucid, *adj.* translucent; limpid, clear, crystalline, crystal-clear, transparent. —**Ant.** dull, opaque.

pelt, *v.* **1.** strike (*with missiles*), beat, belabor, batter. —*n.* **2.** blow, stroke. **3.** skin, hide, peltry.

penchant, *n.* liking, leaning, inclination, taste, fondness, bent, propensity, proclivity, affinity, preference, predilection, disposition, predisposition, prejudice, bias, partiality, soft spot.

pendulous, *adj.* **1.** hanging, suspended, overhanging, pendent, dangling, swinging. **2.** hesitant, vacillating, wavering, tentative, uncertain, indecisive, irresolute, waffling. —**Ant.** resolute, certain.

penetrate, *v.* **1.** pierce, bore, probe, enter; permeate, sink in. **2.** affect or impress deeply, touch. **3.** understand, discern, comprehend, fathom. —**Syn. Study.** See PIERCE.

penetrating, *adj.* **1.** piercing, sharp, acute, subtle. **2.** acute, discerning, critical, keen, shrewd, sharp, sharp-witted, intelligent, wise, sagacious. —**Ant.** blunt; uncritical, silly, stupid, undiscriminating.

penitent, *adj.* sorry, contrite, repentant, atoning, amending, remorseful.

penniless, *adj.* poor, indigent, poverty-stricken, destitute, needy, necessitous, impecunious. —**Ant.** rich, wealthy. —**Syn. Study.** See POOR.

pensive, *adj.* serious, sober, thoughtful, meditative, reflective, dreamy, wistful, contemplative, thinking. —**Ant.** frivolous, silly, unthinking, thoughtless, vapid. —**Syn. Study.** PENSIVE, MEDITATIVE, REFLECTIVE suggest quiet modes of apparent or real thought. PENSIVE suggests dreaminess or wistfulness, and may involve little or no thought to any purpose: *a pensive, faraway look.* MEDITATIVE involves thinking of certain facts or phenomena, perhaps in the religious sense of "contemplation," without necessarily having a goal of complete understanding or of action: *a slow, meditative reply.* REFLECTIVE has a strong implication of orderly, perhaps analytic, processes of thought, usu. with a definite goal of understanding: *a reflective critic.*

pent-up, *adj.* confined, restrained, frustrated.

penurious, *adj.* mean, parsimonious, stingy, tight, tightfisted, closefisted, close, miserly, niggardly, mercenary. —**Ant.** generous.

penury, *n.* poverty, destitution, indigence, need, want. —**Ant.** wealth, opulence, abundance.

people, *n.* **1.** community, tribe, race, nation, clan, family. **2.** persons, human beings, humans, men, man; folks. **3.** populace, commonalty, public. —*v.* **4.** populate; stock.

peppery, *adj.* **1.** pungent, hot, spicy. **2.** sharp, stinging, biting. **3.** irascible, irritable, hottempered, short-tempered, hotheaded, touchy, testy, petulant, snarling, snappish, waspish, churlish, choleric. —**Ant.** mild, tasteless; insipid; calm, amiable, friendly, good-natured.

perceive, *v.* **1.** see, discern, notice, note, discover, observe, descry, espy, distinguish. **2.** apprehend, understand, see, discern, appreciate. —**Ant.** ignore. —**Syn. Study.** See NOTICE.

perceptible, *adj.* cognizable, appreciable, understandable, discernible, apparent, perceivable. —**Ant.** undiscernible, concealed.

perception, *n.* **1.** cognition, recognition, perceiving, apprehension, understanding, discernment. **2.** percept. —**Ant.** misapprehension, misunderstanding.

perceptive, *adj.* astute, discerning, sensitive, responsive, keen, sharp, insightful, perspicacious, understanding, appreciative, sagacious, judicious. —**Ant.** obtuse, insensitive.

perdition, *n.* ruin, damnation, destruction, downfall, hell. —**Ant.** blessedness, sanctity.

peremptory, *adj.* **1.** imperative, undeniable, irrefutable; categorical, positive, absolute. **2.** dictatorial, imperious, dogmatic, arbitrary, authoritative. —**Ant.** refutable, indefinite, uncertain, unsure; obedient; lenient.

perennial, *adj.* lasting, enduring, perpetual, perdurable, everlasting, permanent, imperishable, undying, deathless, eternal, immortal; constant, incessant, continual, uninterrupted, unceasing. —**Ant.** evanescent, temporary, flimsy, mortal; inconstant; sporadic.

perfect, *adj.* **1.** complete, finished, completed, full, consummate. **2.** faultless, spotless, unblemished, excellent, exquisite. **3.** skilled, adept, adroit, expert, accomplished. **4.** typical, exact; thorough, sound, unqualified, pure, unmixed, unadulterated. —*v.* **5.** complete, finish, bring to perfection, consummate, accomplish. —**Ant.** incomplete, unfinished; imperfect; maladroit; mixed, impure.

perfidious, *adj.* faithless, treacherous, false, disloyal, dishonest; unfaithful, traitorous, deceitful, venal, untrustworthy. —**Ant.** faithful, honest, loyal, trustworthy.

perfidy, *n.* treachery, faithlessness, traitorousness, treason, disloyalty. —**Ant.** allegiance, faithfulness, faith, loyalty.

perform, *v.* **1.** carry out, execute, do, discharge, transact. **2.** fulfill, accomplish, achieve, effect. —**Ant.** fail.

perfume, *n.* **1.** essence, attar, scent, toilet water; incense. **2.** redolence, scent, odor, smell, aroma, fragrance. —**Ant.** stench, stink, noxiousness. —**Syn.** PERFUME, FRAGRANCE, AROMA all refer to agreeable odors. PERFUME often indicates a strong, rich smell: *the perfume of flowers.* FRAGRANCE is usu. applied to a sweet, delicate, and fresh smell, esp. from growing things: *the fragrance of new-mown hay.* AROMA is usu. restricted to a distinctive, pervasive, somewhat spicy smell: *the aroma of coffee.*

perfunctory, *adj.* mechanical, indifferent, careless, superficial, negligent, slovenly, heedless, reckless, uninterested, thoughtless. —**Ant.** careful, diligent, thoughtful.

peril, *n.* **1.** risk, jeopardy, danger, hazard. —*v.* **2.** imperil, endanger, risk. —**Ant.** safety, security. —**Syn. Study.** See DANGER.

period, *n.* **1.** interval, age, era, ep-

och, term, time. **2.** course, cycle. —**Ant.** See AGE.

periphery, *n.* **1.** boundary, circumference, perimeter. **2.** surface, outside. —**Ant.** center; meat.

perish, *v.* **1.** die, pass away, pass on, expire, decease. **2.** decay, wither, shrivel, rot, molder, disappear, vanish. —**Ant.** appear. —**Syn. Study.** See DIE.

perky, *adj.* jaunty, pert, brisk. —**Ant.** flaccid, retiring.

permanent, *adj.* lasting, unchanging, unchanged, unaltered, stable, immutable, invariant, invariable, constant; enduring, durable, abiding, perpetual, everlasting, remaining, perdurable. —**Ant.** unstable, temporary, variable, inconstant; temporal.

permeate, *v.* pass through, penetrate, pervade, diffuse through, osmose, saturate, sink in.

permission, *n.* liberty, license, enfranchisement, franchise, leave, permit, liberty, freedom, allowance, consent. —**Ant.** refusal.

permit, *v.* **1.** allow, let, tolerate, agree to, endure, suffer. —*n.* **2.** license, franchise, permission. —**Ant.** refuse, disallow. —**Syn. Study.** See ALLOW.

permutation, *n.* change, variation, modification, transformation, mutation, transmutation, transmogrification, metamorphosis, vicissitude, rearrangement, interchange, transposition, replacement, commutation. —**Ant.** sameness, regularity.

pernicious, *adj.* **1.** ruinous, harmful, hurtful, detrimental, deleterious, injurious, destructive, damaging, baneful, noxious. **2.** deadly, fatal, lethal. **3.** evil, wicked, malevolent, malicious, bad. —**Ant.** beneficial, salubrious, healthful; good.

perpendicular, *adj.* vertical, upright, standing. —**Ant.** horizontal, parallel.

perpetrate, *v.* do, cause, effect, effectuate, commit, bring about, bring off, perform, carry out, pull off, accomplish, execute.

perpetual, *adj.* everlasting, permanent, continuing, continuous, enduring, constant, eternal, ceaseless, unceasing, incessant, unending, endless, uninterrupted, interminable, infinite. —**Ant.** temporary, finite, impermanent; discontinuous. —**Syn. Study.** See ETERNAL.

perplex, *v.* **1.** confuse, puzzle, bewilder, mystify, confound. **2.** complicate, confuse, tangle, snarl, entangle, involve, encumber. **3.** hamper, discourage, vex, annoy, bother, trouble, harass, disturb. —**Ant.** clarify; disencumber; encourage, calm.

persecute, *v.* **1.** oppress, harass, badger, molest, vex, afflict. **2.** punish, discriminate against; torture, torment. **3.** importune, annoy, tease, bother, pester, harass, harry.

perseverance, *n.* persistence, tenacity, pertinacity, resolution, doggedness, determination, steadfastness, indefatigability. —**Ant.** irresolution. —**Syn. Study.** PERSEVERANCE, PERSISTENCE, TENACITY imply determined continuance in a state or in a course of action. PERSEVERANCE suggests effort maintained in spite of difficulties or long-continued application; it is used in a favorable sense: *The scientist's perseverance finally paid off in a coveted prize.* PERSISTENCE, which may be used in a favorable or unfavorable sense, implies steadfast, unremitting continuance in spite of opposition or protest: *an annoying persistence in a belief.* TENACITY is a dogged and determined holding on: *the stubborn tenacity of a salesman.*

persevere, *v.* persist, continue, keep on, last, stick it out, hold on. —**Ant.** fail, cease, desist.

persist, *v.* **1.** persevere, continue, last, endure, remain. **2.** insist. —**Ant.** stop, discontinue. —**Syn. Study.** See CONTINUE.

persistence, See Syn study at PERSEVERANCE.

persistent, *adj.* **1.** persisting, persevering, enduring, indefatigable, pertinacious, tenacious, stubborn, pigheaded, immovable, steadfast. **2.** continued, continual, continuous, repeated, constant, steady. —**Ant.** amenable, obedient; inconstant, sporadic. —**Syn. Study.** See STUBBORN.

person, *n.* **1.** human being, human, man, somebody, individual, personage, one. **2.** character, part, role.

personality, *n.* character; personal identity. —**Syn. Study.** See CHARACTER.

perspicacious, *adj.* keen, perceptive, discerning, acute, penetrating,

sharp-witted, clear-sighted. —**Ant.** dull, stupid, dim-witted.

perspicacity, *n.* perception, discernment, penetration, shrewdness, acuity, astuteness, insight, sharpness, acumen. —**Ant.** dullness, stupidity.

perspicuity, *n.* clearness, clarity, lucidity, transparency, plainness, distinctness, explicitness, intelligibility. —**Ant.** dimness, opacity.

perspicuous, *adj.* clear, lucid, intelligible, plain, distinct, explicit, transparent, unequivocal. —**Ant.** opaque, unintelligible, indistinct, unclear, confused, clouded.

perspiration, *n.* sweat, diaphoresis, water. —**Syn. Study.** PERSPIRATION, SWEAT refer to moisture exuded by animals and people from the pores of the skin. PERSPIRATION is the more polite word, and is often used overfastidiously by those who consider SWEAT coarse: *a deodorant that retards perspiration.* However, SWEAT is a strong word and in some cases is more appropriate: *the sweat of one's brow.* SWEAT is always used when referring to animals: *Sweat dripped from the horse's flanks.* It may also be used metaphorically of objects: *Sweat forms on apples after they are gathered.*

persuade, *v.* **1.** prevail on, induce, urge, influence, actuate, move, entice, impel. **2.** win over, convince, satisfy. —**Ant.** dissuade, discourage. —**Syn. Study.** PERSUADE, INDUCE imply influencing someone's thoughts or actions. They are used mainly in the sense of winning over a person to a certain course of action: *I persuaded her to call a doctor. I induced her to join the club.* They differ in that PERSUADE suggests appealing more to the reason and understanding: *I persuaded him to go back to work;* INDUCE emphasizes only the idea of successful influence, whether achieved by argument or promise of reward: *What can I say that will induce you to stay at your job?* Owing to this idea of compensation, INDUCE may be used in reference to the influence of factors as well as of persons: *The prospect of a raise in salary induced me to stay.*

pert, *adj.* bold, forward, impertinent, saucy, presumptuous, impudent, flippant. —**Ant.** retiring, shy, bashful; polite, courteous.

pertinacious, *adj.* tenacious, persevering, persistent, dogged. —**Ant.** relenting, flexible.

pertinent, *adj.* pertaining, relating, relevant, apt, appropriate, apposite, fit, fitting, fitted, suited, suitable, applicable, proper. —**Ant.** irrelevant, inappropriate, unsuited, unsuitable, improper. —**Syn. Study.** See APT.

perturb, *v.* **1.** disturb, disquiet, agitate, stir up, trouble. **2.** disturb, derange, disorder, confuse, addle, muddle. —**Ant.** pacify, calm, tranquilize; clarify.

peruse, *v.* study, read, scrutinize, examine, survey, pore over, inspect, review, vet. —**Ant.** skim.

pervade, *v.* permeate, diffuse, fill; penetrate, pass through.

perverse, *adj.* **1.** contrary, contumacious, disobedient, wayward, cantankerous. **2.** willful, persistent, obstinate, stubborn, headstrong, pigheaded, dogged, intractable, unyielding. **3.** wicked, evil, bad, sinful, piacular, perverted, distorted. —**Ant.** amiable, obedient; amenable, tractable; good. —**Syn. Study.** See WILLFUL.

perverted, *adj.* wicked, misguided, misapplied, distorted. —**Ant.** straight, good, sensible.

pessimistic, *adj.* cynical, gloomy, dark, foreboding. —**Ant.** optimistic, rosy, bright.

pest, *n.* **1.** nuisance, annoyance. **2.** pestilence, plague, scourge, bane; epidemic, pandemic.

pester, *v.* harass, annoy, vex, torment, torture, molest, harry, hector, tease, trouble, plague, nettle, disturb, provoke, bother, worry, gall, badger, irritate, chafe. —**Ant.** please, delight, entertain, divert.

pet, *n.* **1.** favorite, darling; lap-dog. **2.** peevishness, cantankerousness, moodiness. —*v.* **3.** fondle, indulge, baby, caress. **4.** sulk, be peevish.

petition, *n.* **1.** request, supplication, suit, prayer, entreaty, solicitation, appeal, application. —*v.* **2.** entreat, supplicate, beg, pray, appeal, solicit, sue.

petty, *adj.* **1.** unimportant, trifling, paltry, nugatory, trivial, lesser, little, small, insignificant, negligible, inconsiderable, slight, diminutive. **2.** narrow, narrow-minded, small. **3.** mean, ungenerous, stingy, miserly. —**Ant.**

important, considerable, significant; broad-minded; generous. —**Syn. Study.** PETTY, PALTRY, TRIVIAL, TRIFLING apply to something that is so insignificant as to be almost unworthy of notice. PETTY implies lack of significance or worth: *petty quarrels.* PALTRY applies to something that is contemptibly small or worthless: *I was paid a paltry sum.* TRIVIAL applies to something that is slight or insignificant, often being in contrast to something that is important: *a trivial task.* TRIFLING is often interchangeable with TRIVIAL; however, TRIFLING implies an even lesser, almost negligible, importance or worth: *to ignore a trifling error.*

petulance, *n.* petulancy, irritability, peevishness, fretfulness, pettishness, testiness, waspishness. —**Ant.** calm, tranquillity.

petulant, *adj.* irritable, peevish, fretful, vexatious, waspish, snappish, testy, short-tempered, hotheaded, hot-tempered, peppery, pettish, touchy, irascible, cross, snarling, captious, acrimonious. —**Ant.** even-tempered, temperate, pleasant.

phantasm, *n.* apparition, specter, phantom, vision, illusion, ghost. —**Ant.** reality.

phantom, *n.* **1.** phantasm. —*adj.* **2.** unreal, illusive, spectral, illusory, phantasmal; imaginary, hallucinatory. —**Ant.** real, flesh-and-blood, material.

phenomenon, *n.* **1.** fact, occurrence, event, incident, circumstance. **2.** prodigy, marvel, wonder, miracle.

philander, *v.* flirt, coquet, trifle, dally.

phlegm, *n.* **1.** mucus. **2.** sluggishness, stoicism, apathy, indifference. **3.** coolness, calm, self-possession, coldness, impassivity, impassiveness. —**Ant.** concern; interest, warmth.

phobia, *n.* dread, fear, aversion, hatred. —**Ant.** like, attraction, love.

phony, *adj.* **1.** false, sham, counterfeit, inauthentic, bastard, mock, phony, spurious, brummagem, pinchbeck, pseudo. —*n.* **2.** impostor, faker, mountebank, charlatan, pretender, fraud, humbug, bluffer, four-flusher. **3.** imposture, counterfeit, sham, pretense. —**Ant.** genuine, authentic.

phraseology, *n.* diction, expression, style, language.

physical, *adj.* **1.** bodily, corporeal, corporal, mortal; tangible, sensible. **2.** material, real, natural. —**Ant.** mental, spiritual; unnatural, unreal. —**Syn. Study.** PHYSICAL, BODILY, CORPOREAL, CORPORAL agree in pertaining to the body. PHYSICAL means connected with or pertaining to the animal or human body as a material organism: *physical strength.* BODILY means belonging to or concerned with the human body as distinct from the mind or spirit: *bodily sensations.* CORPOREAL, a more poetic and philosophical word, refers esp. to the mortal substance of which the body is composed, as opposed to spirit: *our corporeal existence.* CORPORAL is usu. reserved for reference to suffering inflicted on the human body: *corporal punishment.*

pick, *v.* **1.** choose, select, cull. **2.** criticize, find fault with. **3.** steal, rob, pilfer. **4.** pierce, indent, dig into, break up, peck. **5.** pluck, gather, reap, collect, get, acquire. —*n.* **6.** pickax. **7.** choice, selection, choicest part, best. **8.** plectrum.

picture, *n.* **1.** painting, drawing, photograph, representation. **2.** image, representation, similitude, semblance, likeness. **3.** description, account, representation. **4.** motion picture, movie, screen play, photoplay, film. —*v.* **5.** imagine; depict, describe, delineate, paint, draw, represent.

picturesque, *adj.* **1.** striking, interesting, colorful, scenic, beautiful. **2.** graphic, vivid, impressive; intense, lively. —**Ant.** uninteresting, dull.

piece, *n.* **1.** portion, quantity, segment, section, scrap, shred, fragment, part. **2.** thing, example, instance, specimen. **3.** short story, story, article, essay, composition, paper, theme, novella; poem, ode, sonnet; play. —*v.* **4.** mend, patch. **5.** complete, enlarge, extend, augment; join. —**Ant.** all, everything; none, nothing.

piecemeal, *adv.* **1.** gradually, bit by bit, inchmeal, inchwise, by degrees. **2.** separately, fractionally, disjointedly, spasmodically.

pierce, *v.* **1.** penetrate, enter, run through or into, perforate, stab, puncture, bore, drill. **2.** affect, touch, move, rouse, strike, thrill, excite.

—**Syn. Study.** PIERCE, PENETRATE suggest the action of one object passing through another or making a way through and into another. These terms are used both concretely and figuratively. To PIERCE is to perforate quickly, as by stabbing; it suggests the use of a sharp, pointed instrument impelled by force: *to pierce the flesh with a knife; a scream that pierced my ears.* PENETRATE suggests a slow or difficult movement: *No ordinary bullet can penetrate an elephant's hide; to penetrate the depths of one's ignorance.*

piety, *n.* **1.** reverence, regard, respect. **2.** godliness, devoutness, devotion, sanctity, grace, holiness. —**Ant.** irreverence, disrespect.

pile, *n.* **1.** assemblage, collection, mass, heap, accumulation. **2.** pyre, burning ghat. **3.** building, edifice, structure. **4.** pier, post. **5.** hair, down; wool, fur, pelage; nap. —*v.* **6.** heap up, accumulate, assemble, amass, collect.

pilfer, *v.* steal, rob, thieve, appropriate, take, purloin, pinch, filch, lift, nick, pocket, swipe, rifle, shoplift, rip off.

pilgrim, *n.* palmer, crusader. **2.** wayfarer, sojourner, traveler, wanderer.

pilgrimage, *n.* journey, trip, excursion, tour, expedition. —**Syn. Study.** See TRIP.

pillage, *v.* **1.** rob, plunder, rape, despoil, sack, spoil. —*n.* **2.** booty, plunder, spoils. **3.** rapine, depredation, devastation, spoliation.

pillar, *n.* shaft, column, stele, Lally column, support, pier, prop.

pillory, *v.* mock, ridicule, deride, scorn, revile, sneer at, vilify, slur, stigmatize, brand, besmirch, smear, tarnish, blacken, skewer, crucify. —**Ant.** praise, esteem.

pillow, *n.* cushion, pad, bolster.

pin, *n.* **1.** peg, fastening, bolt. **2.** brooch. —*v.* **3.** fasten, fix.

pine, *v.* yearn, long, ache, hunger, thirst, crave, itch, sigh. **2.** languish, fade, dwindle, wilt, droop, pine away. —**Syn. Study.** See YEARN.

pinnacle, *n.* peak, eminence, culmination, tower, summit, apex, acme, zenith. —**Ant.** base.

pioneer, *v.* **1.** lead, precede, blaze a trail, guide, forerun. **2.** initiate, introduce, invent, create, dream up. —*n.* **3.** forerunner, precursor, pathfinder, trailblazer, vanguard, bellwether, point man, point woman, point person. —*adj.* **4.** first, earliest, advance, original, maiden, initial, avant-garde, trail-blazing, cutting-edge.

pious, *adj.* **1.** devout, reverent, godly, religious, holy. **2.** sacred. —**Ant.** impious, irreligious, unholy; unsacred, defiled. —**Syn. Study.** See RELIGIOUS.

piquant, *adj.* **1.** pungent, sharp, flavorsome, tart, spicy. **2.** stimulating, interesting, attractive, sparkling. **3.** smart, racy, sharp, clever. —**Ant.** insipid; uninteresting, unattractive; dull.

pique, *v.* **1.** offend, nettle, sting, irritate, chafe, vex; affront, wound, displease. **2.** interest, stimulate, excite, incite, stir, spur, prick, goad. —**Ant.** please, delight; compliment.

pirate, *n.* plunderer, filibuster, freebooter, picaroon, buccaneer, corsair.

pit, *n.* **1.** hole, cavity, burrow, hollow. **2.** excavation, well, pitfall, trap. **3.** hollow, depression, dent, indentation. **4.** stone, pip, seed, core.

piteous, *adj.* pathetic, pitiable, deplorable, wretched, miserable; affecting, distressing, moving, pitiful, lamentable, woeful, sorrowful, sad, mournful, morose, doleful. —**Ant.** good, fine, pleasant, delightful. —**Syn. Study.** See PITIFUL.

pithy, *adj.* terse, concise, brief, short, compact, epigrammatic, succint, compendious, laconic, summary, to the point, short and sweet. —**Ant.** expansive, prolix, verbose.

pitiable, See Syn study at PITIFUL.

pitiful, *adj.* **1.** pitiable, pathetic, piteous. **2.** contemptible, deplorable, mean, low, base, vile, despicable. —**Ant.** superior, delightful, lovable. —**Syn. Study.** PITIFUL, PITIABLE, PITEOUS apply to that which arouses pity (with compassion or with contempt). That which is PITIFUL is touching and excites pity or is mean and contemptible: *a pitiful leper; a pitiful exhibition of cowardice.* PITIABLE may mean lamentable, or wretched and paltry: *a pitiable hovel.* PITEOUS refers only to that which exhibits suffering and misery, and is therefore heartrending: *piteous poverty.*

pitiless, *adj.* merciless, cruel, mean, unmerciful, ruthless, implacable, relentless, inexorable, hard-hearted. —**Ant.** merciful, soft-hearted, kind, kindly.

pity, n. **1.** sympathy, compassion, commiseration, condolence, mercy. —v. **2.** commiserate, be or feel sorry for, sympathize with, feel for. —**Ant.** apathy, cruelty, ruthlessness. —**Syn. Study.** See SYMPATHY.

placate, v. appease, satisfy, conciliate. —**Ant.** dissatisfy, displease.

place, n. **1.** space, plot, spot, location, locale, locality, site. **2.** position, situation, circumstances. **3.** job, post, office, function, duty, charge, responsibility, employment, rank. **4.** region, area, section, sector. **5.** residence, dwelling, house, home, domicile, abode. **6.** stead, lien. **7.** opportunity, occasion, reason, ground, cause. —v. **8.** position, range, order, dispose, arrange, situate, put, set, locate, station, deposit, lay, seat, fix, establish. **9.** appoint, hire, induct. **10.** identify, connect. —**Ant.** misplace, displace; forget.

placid, adj. calm, peaceful, unruffled, tranquil, serene, quiet, undisturbed. —**Ant.** turbulent, tumultuous, perturbed. —**Syn. Study.** See PEACEFUL.

plague, n. **1.** epidemic, pestilence, disease, Black Death, Great Plague, Oriental Plague. **2.** affliction, calamity, evil, curse. **3.** trouble, vexation, annoyance, nuisance, torment. —v. **4.** trouble, torment, torture, molest, bother, incommode. discommode. **5.** vex, harry, hector, harass, fret, worry, pester, badger, annoy, tease, irritate, disturb. —**Syn. Study.** See BOTHER.

plain, adj. **1.** clear, distinct, lucid, unambiguous, unequivocal, intelligible, understandable, perspicuous, evident, manifest, obvious, unmistakable, patent, apparent. **2.** downright, sheer, direct, transparent. **3.** unambiguous, candid, outspoken, blunt, direct, frank, guileless, artless, ingenuous, open, unreserved, honest, sincere, open-hearted. **4.** homely, unpretentious, homey, simple, unadorned, frugal. **5.** ugly, homely, unattractive. **6.** ordinary, common, commonplace, unostentatious. **7.** flat, level, plane, smooth, even. —n. **8.** mesa, plateau, savanna, prairie, pampas. —**Ant.** unclear, ambiguous, unintelligible; artful, sly, cunning, deceptive, insincere; beautiful, attractive; uncommon, extraordinary.

plaint, n. **1.** protest, complaint, accusation, reproach. **2.** lament, cry, grieving, lamentation, wail, keening.

plaintive, adj. sorrowful, melancholy, mournful, sad, wistful, discontented. —**Ant.** happy, pleasant.

plan, n. **1.** scheme, plot, complot, procedure, project, formula, method, system, design, contrivance. **2.** drawing, sketch, floorplan, draft, map, chart, diagram, representation. —v. **3.** arrange, scheme, plot, design, devise, contrive, invent, concoct, hatch.

platform, n. **1.** stage, dais, rostrum, pulpit; landing. **2.** principles, beliefs, tenets.

platitude, n. cliché, commonplace, banality, bromide, truism, generalization, prosaicism, old saw, chestnut. —**Ant.** witticism, mot.

plausible, adj. **1.** specious, deceptive, deceiving, deceitful, hypocritical. **2.** fair-spoken, glib, convincing. —**Ant.** implausible.

play, n. **1.** drama, piece, show; comedy, tragedy, melodrama, farce. **2.** amusement, recreation, game, sport, diversion, pastime. **3.** fun, jest, trifling, frolic. **4.** action, activity, movement, exercise, operation, motion. **5.** freedom, liberty, scope, elbow-room. —v. **6.** act, perform, enact, characterize, impersonate, personate. **7.** compete, contend with or against, engage. **8.** use, employ. **9.** stake, bet, wager. **10.** represent, imitate, emulate, mimic. **11.** do, perform, bring about, execute. **12.** toy, trifle, sport, dally, caper, romp, disport, frolic, gambol, skip, revel, frisk. —**Ant.** work.

playful, adj. frisky, coltish, antic, frolicsome, sportive, sprightly, prankish, puckish, impish, puppyish, kittenish, whimsical, larky. —**Ant.** somber, sober.

plead, v. **1.** entreat, appeal, beg, supplicate. **2.** argue, persuade, reason. **3.** allege, cite, make a plea, apologize, answer, make excuse.

pleasant, adj. **1.** pleasing, agreeable, enjoyable, pleasurable, acceptable, welcome, gratifying. **2.** delightful, congenial, polite, courteous, friendly, personable, amiable. **3.** fair, sunny. **4.** gay, sprightly, merry, cheery, cheerful, lively, sportive, vivacious.

5. jocular, facetious, playful, humorous, witty, amusing, clever, jocose. —**Ant.** unpleasant, displeasing.

pleasing, adj. agreeable, pleasant, acceptable, pleasurable, charming, delightful, interesting, engaging. —**Ant.** disagreeable, unpleasant, unacceptable.

pleasure, n. **1.** happiness, gladness, delectation, enjoyment, delight, joy, well-being, satisfaction, gratification. **2.** luxury, sensuality, voluptuousness. **3.** will, desire, choice, preference, purpose, wish, mind, inclination, predilection. —**Ant.** displeasure, unhappiness; disinclination.

plentiful, adj. bountiful, ample, plenteous, copious, abundant, full, rich, fertile, fruitful, bounteous, productive, exuberant, luxuriant. —**Ant.** sparse, scanty, barren, fruitless. —**Syn. Study.** PLENTIFUL, AMPLE, ABUNDANT, BOUNTIFUL describe a more than adequate supply of something. PLENTIFUL suggests a large or full quantity: a plentiful supply of fuel. AMPLE suggests a quantity that is sufficient for a particular need or purpose: an auditorium with ample seating for students. ABUNDANT and BOUNTIFUL both imply a greater degree of plenty: an abundant rainfall; a bountiful harvest.

plenty, n. **1.** fullness, abundance, copiousness, plenteousness, plentifulness, profusion, luxuriance, exuberance, affluence, overflow, extravagance, prodigality; superabundance, overfullness, plethora. —**Ant.** paucity, scarcity.

pliant, adj. pliable, supple, flexible, flexile, lithe, limber; compliant, easily influenced, yielding, adaptable, manageable, tractable, ductile, facile, docile. —**Ant.** inflexible; unyielding, rigid, intractable.

plight, n. **1.** condition, state, situation, predicament, category, case, dilemma. —v. **2.** propose, pledge, hypothecate. —**Syn. Study.** See PREDICAMENT.

plod, v. **1.** walk heavily, pace, trudge. **2.** toil, moil, labor, drudge, sweat. —**Syn. Study.** See PACE.

plot, n. **1.** plan, scheme, complot, intrigue, conspiracy, cabal, stratagem, machination. **2.** story, theme, thread, story line. —v. **3.** devise, contrive, concoct, brew, hatch, frame. **4.** conspire, scheme, contrive.

ploy, n. stratagem, strategy, tactic, trick, maneuver, artifice, tactic, scheme, gimmick, dodge, wile, device, feint, gambit, ruse.

pluck, v. **1.** pull, jerk, yank, snatch, tug, tear, rip. —n. **2.** courage, resolution, spirit, bravery, boldness, determination, mettle, nerve.

plump, adj. **1.** fleshy, fat, chubby, stout, portly, corpulent, obese, round. **2.** direct, downright, blunt, unqualified, unreserved, complete, full. —v. **3.** gain weight; fatten. **4.** drop, sink, fall. —n. **5.** fall, drop. —adv. **6.** directly, bluntly, suddenly, abruptly. —**Ant.** thin, slender, skinny; subtle.

plunder, v. **1.** rob, despoil, fleece, pillage, ravage, rape, sack, devastate, strip, lay waste. —n. **2.** pillage, rapine, spoliation, robbery, theft, plundering. **3.** loot, booty, spoils.

plunge, v. **1.** immerse, submerge, dip. **2.** dive; rush, hasten; descend, drop, hurtle over. —n. **3.** leap, dive, rush, dash, dip. —**Syn. Study.** See DIP.

poetry, n. verse, meter, rhythm, poesy, numbers.

poignant, adj. **1.** distressing, heartfelt, serious, intense, severe, bitter, sincere. **2.** keen, strong, biting, mordant, caustic, acid, pointed. **3.** pungent, piquant, sharp, biting, acrid, stinging. —**Ant.** superfluous, trivial; mild.

pointed, adj. **1.** sharp, piercing, penetrating, epigrammatic, stinging, piquant, biting, mordant, sarcastic, caustic, severe, keen. **2.** directed, aimed, explicit, marked, personal. **3.** marked, emphasized, accented, accentuated. —**Ant.** blunt, dull, mild.

poise, n. **1.** balance, equilibrium, equipoise, counterpoise. **2.** composure, self-possession, steadiness, stability, self-control, control. **3.** suspense, indecision. **4.** carriage, mien, demeanor, savoir-faire, breeding, behavior. —v. **5.** balance, equilibrate. —**Ant.** instability, unsteadiness; decision.

poison, n. **1.** toxin, venom, virus. —v. **2.** envenom, infect. **3.** corrupt, ruin, vitiate, contaminate, pollute, taint, canker. —**Syn. Study.** POISON, TOXIN, VENOM are terms for any substance that injures the health or destroys life when absorbed into the

system. POISON is the general word: a poison for insects. A TOXIN is a poison produced by an organism; it is esp. used in medicine in reference to disease-causing bacterial secretions: A toxin produces diphtheria. VENOM is esp. used of the poisons injected by bite, sting, etc.: snake venom; bee venom.

policy, n. **1.** course (of action), expediency, tactic, approach, procedure, rule, management, administration, handling. **2.** prudence, wisdom, sagacity, shrewdness, acumen, astuteness, discretion, skill, art, cunning, stratagem. —**Ant.** ingenuousness, naiveté.

polish, v. **1.** brighten, smooth, burnish, shine. **2.** finish, refine, civilize, make elegant. —n. **3.** smoothness, gloss, shine, sheen, luster, brightness, brilliance. **4.** refinement, elegance, poise, grace. —**Ant.** dull. —**Syn. Study.** POLISH, GLOSS, LUSTER, SHEEN refer to a smooth, shining, or bright surface from which light is reflected. POLISH suggests the smooth, bright reflection often produced by friction: a lamp rubbed to a high polish. GLOSS suggests a superficial, hard smoothness characteristic of lacquered, varnished, or enameled surfaces: a gloss on oilcloth. LUSTER denotes the characteristic quality of the light reflected from the surfaces of certain materials, as pearls or freshly cut metals: a pearly luster. SHEEN sometimes suggests a glistening brightness such as that reflected from the surface of silk: the sheen of a satin gown.

polished, adj. **1.** smooth, glossy, burnished, shining, shiny, shined, lustrous, brilliant. **2.** refined, cultured, finished, elegant, polite, poised. **3.** flawless, excellent, perfect. —**Ant.** dull, dim; unrefined, impolite; inelegant; imperfect.

polite, adj. **1.** well-mannered, courteous, civil, well-bred, gracious, genteel, urbane, polished, poised, courtly, cultivated, refined, finished, elegant. —**Ant.** impolite, rude, discourteous, uncivil. —**Syn. Study.** See CIVIL.

politic, adj. **1.** sagacious, prudent, wise, tactful, diplomatic, discreet, judicious, provident, astute, wary, prudential. **2.** shrewd, artful, sly, cunning, underhanded, tricky, foxy, clever, subtle, Machiavellian, wily, intriguing, scheming, crafty, unscrupulous, strategic. **3.** expedient, judicious, political. —**Ant.** imprudent, indiscreet, improvident; artless, ingenuous, direct, open, honest. —**Syn. Study.** See DIPLOMATIC.

politician, n. statesman, political leader, national leader; politico, Slang pol —**Syn. Study.** POLITICIAN, STATESMAN refer to one skilled in politics. POLITICIAN is more often derogatory, and STATESMAN laudatory. POLITICIAN suggests the schemes of a person who engages in politics for party ends or personal advantage: a dishonest politician. STATESMAN suggests the eminent ability, foresight, and patriotic devotion of a person dealing with important affairs of state: a distinguished statesman.

pollute, v. **1.** befoul, dirty, defile, soil, taint, tarnish, stain, contaminate, vitiate, corrupt, debase, deprave. **2.** desecrate, profane, blaspheme, violate, dishonor, defile. —**Ant.** purify; honor, revere, respect.

pompous, See Syn. study at GRANDIOSE.

ponder, v. consider, meditate, reflect, cogitate, deliberate, ruminate, muse, think, study; weigh, contemplate, examine. —**Ant.** forget, ignore.

ponderous, adj. **1.** heavy, massive, weighty, bulky. **2.** important, momentous, weighty. —**Ant.** light, weightless; unimportant.

poor, adj. **1.** needy, indigent, necessitous, straitened, destitute, penniless, poverty-stricken, impecunious, impoverished, reduced, hard up, distressed. **2.** deficient, insufficient, meager, lacking, incomplete. **3.** faulty, inferior, unsatisfactory, substandard, shabby, jerry-built, seedy, worthless, valueless. **4.** sterile, barren, unfertile, fruitless, unproductive. **5.** lean, emaciated, thin, skinny, meager, hungry, underfed, lank, gaunt, shrunk. **6.** cowardly, abject, mean, base. **7.** scanty, paltry, meager, insufficient, inadequate. **8.** humble, unpretentious. **9.** unfortunate, hapless, unlucky, star-crossed, doomed, luckless, miserable, unhappy, pitiable, piteous. —**Ant.** rich, wealthy; sufficient, adequate, complete; superior; fertile; well-fed;

bold, brave; bold, pretentious; fortunate, lucky. —**Syn. Study.** POOR, IMPECUNIOUS, IMPOVERISHED, PENNILESS refer to those lacking money. POOR is the simple word for the condition of lacking the means to obtain the comforts of life: a very poor family. IMPECUNIOUS often suggests that the poverty is a consequence of unwise habits: an impecunious actor. IMPOVERISHED often implies a former state of greater plenty: the impoverished aristocracy. PENNILESS refers to extreme poverty; it means entirely without money: The widow was left penniless.

popular, adj. **1.** favorite, approved, accepted, received, liked. **2.** common, prevailing, current, general, prevalent, in vogue, faddish. —**Ant.** unpopular; uncommon, rare, unusual. —**Syn. Study.** See GENERAL.

populous, adj. crowded, filled, overcrowded, packed, jam-packed, crammed, teeming, swarming, bristling, crawling, alive.

port, n. harbor, haven, refuge, anchorage. —**Syn. Study.** See HARBOR.

portent, n. indication, omen, augury, sign, warning, presage. —**Syn. Study.** See SIGN.

portentous, See Syn. study at OMINOUS.

portion, n. **1.** part, section, segment, piece, bit, scrap, morsel, fragment. **2.** share, allotment, quota, dole, dividend, division, apportionment, lot. **3.** serving. **4.** dowry, dot. —v. **5.** divide, distribute, allot, apportion, deal or parcel out. **6.** endow. —**Ant.** all, everything; none, nothing.

portray, v. picture, delineate, limn, depict, paint, represent, sketch.

pose, v. **1.** sit, model; attitudinize. **2.** state, assert, propound. —n. **3.** attitude, posture, position; affectation.

position, n. **1.** station, place, locality, spot, location, site, locale, situation, post. **2.** situation, condition, state, circumstances. **3.** status, standing, rank, place. **4.** post, job, situation, place, employment. **5.** placement, disposition, array, arrangement. **6.** posture, attitude, pose. **7.** proposition, thesis, contention, principle, dictum, predication, assertion, doctrine. —v. **8.** put, place, situate. **9.** locate, fix, discover. —**Syn. Study.** POSITION, POSTURE, ATTITUDE, POSE refer to an arrangement or disposal of the body or its parts. POSITION is the general word for the arrangement of the body: in a reclining position. POSTURE is usu. an assumed arrangement of the body, esp. when standing: a relaxed posture. ATTITUDE is often a posture assumed for imitative effect or the like, but may be one adopted for a purpose (as that of a fencer or a tightrope walker): an attitude of prayer. A POSE is an attitude assumed, in most cases, for artistic effect: an attractive pose.

positive, adj. **1.** explicit, express, sure, certain, definite, precise, clear, unequivocal, categorical, unmistakable, direct. **2.** arbitrary, enacted, decided, determined, decisive, unconditional. **3.** incontrovertible, substantial, indisputable, indubitable. **4.** stated, expressed, emphatic. **5.** confident, self-confident, self-assured, assured, convinced, unquestioning, over-confident, stubborn, peremptory, obstinate, dogmatic, overbearing. **6.** absolute. **7.** practical. —**Ant.** unsure, indefinite, unclear, equivocal; conditional; doubtful; tacit; tractable, self-effacing; relative; impractical, unpractical.

possess, v. **1.** have, hold, own. **2.** occupy, hold, have, control. **3.** impart, inform, familiarize, acquaint, make known. —**Ant.** lose.

possession, n. **1.** custody, occupation, tenure. **2.** ownership. —**Ant.** loss.

possible, adj. feasible, practicable, likely, potential. —**Ant.** impossible, impractical, unlikely. —**Syn. Study.** POSSIBLE, FEASIBLE, PRACTICABLE refer to that which may come about or take place without prevention by serious obstacles. That which is POSSIBLE is naturally able or even likely to happen, other circumstances being equal: He offered a possible compromise. FEASIBLE refers to the ease with which something can be done and implies a high degree of desirability for doing it: Which plan is the most feasible? PRACTICABLE applies to that which can be done with the means at hand and with conditions as they are: We ascended the slope as far as was practicable.

post, n. **1.** column, pillar, pole, support, upright. **2.** position, office, assignment, appointment. **3.** station,

round, beat, position. —v. **4.** announce, advertise, publicize. **5.** station, place, set.

posterior, See Syn. study at BACK.

postpone, v. **1.** put off, defer, delay, procrastinate, adjourn. **2.** subordinate. —**Syn. Study.** See DEFER.

posture, n. **1.** position, pose, attitude. **2.** position, condition, state. —**Syn. Study.** See POSITION.

potent, adj. **1.** powerful, mighty, strong, puissant. **2.** cogent, influential, efficacious. —**Ant.** weak, impotent, powerless, feeble, frail; ineffectual.

potential, adj. **1.** possible. **2.** capable, able, latent. —n. **3.** possibility, potentiality. —**Ant.** kinetic, impossible; incapable, unable; impossibility.

pound, v. **1.** strike, beat, thrash. **2.** crush, bray, pulverize, powder, triturate, comminute. **3.** impound, imprison, pen, jail, shut up, confine, coop up. —n. **4.** pound avoirdupois, pound troy, pound sterling, pound Scots. **5.** enclosure, pen, confine, trap. —**Syn. Study.** See BEAT.

poverty, n. **1.** destitution, need, lack, want, privation, necessitousness, necessity, neediness, indigence, penury, distress. **2.** deficiency, sterility, barrenness, unfruitfulness. **3.** scantiness, jejuneness, sparingness, meagerness. —**Ant.** wealth; abundance, fertility, fruitfulness.

power, n. **1.** ability, capability, capacity, faculty, competence, competency, might, strength, puissance. **2.** strength, might, force, energy. **3.** control, command, dominion, authority, sway, rule, ascendancy, influence, sovereignty, suzerainty, prerogative. —**Ant.** inability, incapacity, incompetence.

powerful, adj. **1.** mighty, potent, forceful, strong. **2.** cogent, influential, forcible, convincing, effective, efficacious, effectual. —**Ant.** weak, frail, feeble; ineffective, ineffectual.

practicable, adj. possible, feasible, workable, performable, doable, achievable, attainable. —**Ant.** impracticable, impossible, unattainable. —**Syn. Study.** See POSSIBLE.

practical, adj. **1.** sensible, businesslike, pragmatic, efficient. **2.** judicious, discreet, sensible, discriminating, balanced, reasoned, sound, shrewd. —**Ant.** impractical, inefficient; indiscreet, unsound. —**Syn. Study.** PRACTICAL, JUDICIOUS, SENSIBLE refer to good judgment in action, conduct, and the handling of everyday matters. PRACTICAL suggests the ability to adopt means to an end or to turn what is at hand to account: to adopt practical measures for settling problems. JUDICIOUS implies the possession and use of discreet judgment, discrimination, and balance: a judicious use of one's time. SENSIBLE implies the possession and use of reason and shrewd common sense: a sensible suggestion.

practice, n. **1.** custom, habit, wont. **2.** exercise, drill, experience, application, study. **3.** performance, operation, action, process. **4.** plotting, intriguing, trickery, chicanery; plot, intrigue, stratagem, ruse, maneuver. —v. **5.** carry out, perform, do, drill, exercise. **6.** follow, observe. —**Ant.** inexperience. —**Syn. Study.** See CUSTOM.

praise, n. **1.** praising, commendation, acclamation, plaudit, compliment, laudation, approval, approbation, applause, kudos. **2.** encomium, eulogy, panegyric. —v. **3.** laud, approve, commend, admire, extol, celebrate, eulogize, panegyrize. **4.** glorify, magnify, exalt, worship, bless, adore, honor. —**Ant.** condemnation, disapprobation, disapproval, criticism.

pray, v. importune, entreat, supplicate, beg, beseech, implore, sue, petition, invoke.

precarious, adj. **1.** uncertain, unstable, unsure, insecure, dependent, unsteady. **2.** doubtful, dubious, unreliable, undependable, risky, perilous, hazardous, dangerous. **3.** groundless, unfounded, baseless. —**Ant.** certain, stable, sure, secure, independent, reliable, dependable; well-founded.

precaution, n. foresight, prudence, providence, wariness, forethought.

precious, adj. **1.** valuable, costly, dear, invaluable, priceless. **2.** dear, beloved, darling, cherished. **3.** choice, fine, delicate, select, pretty. **4.** arrant, gross, egregious. —**Ant.** inexpensive, cheap; worthless; ugly, unattractive.

precipitate, v. **1.** hasten, accelerate, hurry, speed up, expedite, speed, rush, quicken, advance, dispatch. **2.** cast down, hurl or fling down, plunge. —*adj.* **3.** headlong, hasty, rash, reckless, indiscreet. **4.** sudden, abrupt, violent. —**Ant.** slow, retard; considered.

precipitous, *adj.* steep, abrupt, sheer, perpendicular. —**Ant.** gradual, sloping.

precise, *adj.* **1.** definite, exact, defined, fixed, correct, strict, explicit, accurate. **2.** rigid, particular, puritanical, demanding, crucial. —**Ant.** indefinite, incorrect, inexact, lenient; flexible, tractable. —**Syn. Study.** See CORRECT.

predatory, *adj.* predacious, plundering, ravaging, pillaging, rapacious, voracious.

predicament, *n.* dilemma, plight, quandary; situation, state, condition, position, case. —**Syn. Study.** PREDICAMENT, PLIGHT, DILEMMA, QUANDARY refer to unpleasant or puzzling situations. PREDICAMENT and PLIGHT stress more the unpleasant nature, DILEMMA and QUANDARY the puzzling nature, of a situation. PREDICAMENT, though often used lightly, may also refer to a crucial situation: *Stranded in a strange city without money, he was in a predicament.* PLIGHT, however, is usually used to refer to an unfortunate or distressing situation: *the plight of the homeless.* DILEMMA means a position of doubt or perplexity in which a person is faced by two equally undesirable alternatives: *the dilemma of a person who must support one of two friends in an election.* QUANDARY is the state of mental perplexity of one faced with a difficult situation: *We were in a quandry about plans for a vacation.*

predict, *v.* foretell, prophesy, foresee, forecast, presage, augur, prognosticate, foretoken, portend, divine. —**Syn. Study.** PREDICT, PROPHESY, FORESEE, FORECAST mean to know or tell beforehand what will happen. To PREDICT is usu. to foretell with precision of calculation, knowledge, or shrewd inference from facts or experience: *Astronomers can predict an eclipse;* it may, however, be used without the implication of knowledge or expertise: *I predict it will be a successful party.* To PROPHESY is usu. to predict future events by the aid of divine or supernatural inspiration: *Merlin prophesied that two knights would meet in conflict;* this verb, too, may be used in a less specific sense: *I prophesy she'll be back in the old job.* FORESEE refers specifically not to the uttering of predictions but to the mental act of seeing ahead; there is often a practical implication of preparing for what will happen: *He was able to foresee their objections.* FORECAST means to predict by observation or study; however, it is most often used of phenomena that cannot be accurately predicted: *Rain is forecast for tonight.*

prediction, *n.* prophecy, forecast, augury, prognostication, foretoken, portent, divination, soothsaying, presage.

predilection, *n.* prepossession, favoring, partiality, predisposition, position, inclination, bent, preference, leaning, bias, prejudice. —**Ant.** disfavor, disinclination, dislike.

predominant, *adj.* ascendant, prevailing, prevalent, dominant, in sway, sovereign. —**Ant.** rare, retrograde. —**Syn. Study.** See DOMINANT.

predominate, *v.* preponderate, prevail, outweigh, overrule, surpass, dominate.

preeminent, *adj.* eminent, surpassing, dominant, superior, over, above, distinguished, excellent, peerless, unequalled, paramount, consummate, predominant, supreme. —**Ant.** undistinguished, inferior.

preface, *n.* introduction, foreword, preamble, prologue, proem, prelude, preliminary, prolegomena. —**Ant.** appendix, epilogue. —**Syn. Study.** See INTRODUCTION.

prefer, *v.* **1.** like better, favor, choose, elect, select, pick out, pick, single out, fix upon, fancy. **2.** put forward, advance, present, offer, proffer, tender, promote. —**Ant.** exclude, dislike; retract, withdraw.

preference, *n.* choice, selection, pick, predilection. —**Ant.** exclusion.

prejudice, *n.* **1.** preconception, bias, partiality, prejudgment, predilection, predisposition, disposition. —*v.* **2.** bias, influence, warp, twist. —**Ant.** judgment, decision. —**Syn. Study.** See BIAS.

preliminary, *adj.* **1.** preceding, introductory, preparatory, prefatory, precursive, prior. —*n.* **2.** introduc-

tion, prelude, preface, prolegomena, preparation. —**Ant.** resulting, concluding; conclusion, end, appendix, epilogue. —**Syn. Study.** PRELIMINARY, INTRODUCTORY both refer to that which comes before the principal subject of consideration. That which is PRELIMINARY is in the nature of preparation or of clearing away details that would encumber the main subject or problem; it often deals with arrangements and the like that have to do only incidentally with the principal subject: *preliminary negotiations.* That which is INTRODUCTORY leads with natural, logical, or close connection directly into the main subject of consideration: *introductory steps.*

premeditate, *v.* consider, plan, deliberate, precontrive, predetermine, prearrange, predesign.

premium, *n.* **1.** prize, door prize, bounty. **2.** bonus, gift, reward, recompense. —**Ant.** punishment. —**Syn. Study.** See BONUS.

preoccupied, *adj.* absorbed, engrossed, meditating, meditative, pondering, musing, concentrating, inattentive, in a brown study. —**Ant.** unthinking, thoughtless, frivolous.

prepare, *v.* **1.** contrive, devise, plan, plan for, anticipate, get or make ready, provide, arrange, order. **2.** manufacture, make, compound, fix, compose. —**Ant.** destroy, ruin.

preposterous, *adj.* absurd, senseless, foolish, inane, asinine, unreasonable, ridiculous, excessive, extravagant, irrational. —**Ant.** rational, reasonable, sensible. —**Syn. Study.** See ABSURD.

prerogative, *n.* right, privilege, precedence, license, franchise, immunity, freedom, liberty. —**Syn. Study.** See PRIVILEGE.

presage, *n.* **1.** presentiment, foreboding, foreshadowing, indication, premonition, foreknowledge. **2.** portent, omen, sign, token, augury, warning, signal, prognostic. **3.** forecast, prediction. —*v.* **4.** portend, foreshadow, forecast, predict.

prescribe, *v.* lay down, determine, appoint, ordain, enjoin, direct, dictate, decree, establish, hand down, institute.

presence, *n.* **1.** attendance, company. **2.** nearness, vicinity, neighborhood, proximity, vicinage, closeness. **3.** personality; bearing, carriage, mien, aspect, impression, appearance. —**Ant.** absence.

present, *adj.* **1.** current, existing, extant; here, at hand, near, nearby. —*n.* **2.** now. **3.** gift, donation, bonus, benefaction, largess, grant, gratuity, boon, tip. —*v.* **4.** give, endow, bestow, grant, confer, donate. **5.** afford, furnish, yield, offer, proffer. **6.** show, exhibit, introduce. **7.** represent, personate, act, enact, imitate, impersonate. **8.** point, level, aim, direct. —**Ant.** absent; then; receive. —**Syn. Study.** See GIVE. See also INTRODUCE.

presently, *adv.* anon, at once, immediately, directly, right away, without delay, shortly, forthwith, soon. —**Ant.** later. —**Syn. Study.** See IMMEDIATELY.

preserve, *v.* **1.** keep, conserve. **2.** guard, safeguard, shelter, shield, protect, defend, save. **3.** keep up, maintain, continue, uphold, sustain. **4.** retain, keep. —**Ant.** forgo; lose.

prestige, *n.* reputation, influence, weight, importance, distinction. —**Ant.** disrepute, notoriety.

presume, *v.* **1.** assume, presuppose, suppose, take for granted, believe. **2.** venture, undertake.

presumptuous, *adj.* bold, impertinent, forward, arrogant, insolent, audacious, rude, fresh. —**Ant.** modest, polite. —**Syn. Study.** See BOLD.

pretend, *v.* **1.** feign, affect, put on, assume, falsify, simulate, fake, sham, counterfeit. **2.** allege, profess; lie. **3.** make believe. —**Syn. Study.** PRETEND, AFFECT, ASSUME, FEIGN imply an attempt to create a false appearance. To PRETEND is to create an imaginary characteristic or to play a part: *to pretend sorrow.* To AFFECT is to make a consciously artificial show of having qualities that one thinks would look well and impress others: *to affect shyness.* To ASSUME is to take on or put on a specific outward appearance, often with intent to deceive: *to assume an air of indifference.* To FEIGN implies using ingenuity in pretense, and some degree of imitation of appearance or characteristics: *to feign surprise.*

pretense, *n.* **1.** pretending, feigning, shamming, make-believe; subterfuge, fabrication, pretext, excuse. **2.** show,

cover, cover-up, semblance, dissembling, mask, cloak, veil; pretension.

pretentious, *adj.* vain, vainglorious, affected, ostentatious, showy, la-di-da, posy, highfalutin, mannered, precious. —**Ant.** earthy, plain. —**Syn. Study.** See BOMBASTIC. See also GRANDIOSE.

preternatural, *adj.* abnormal, unusual, peculiar, odd, strange, extraordinary, irregular, unnatural, anomalous; supernatural. —**Ant.** usual, common, regular, natural. —**Syn. Study.** See MIRACULOUS.

pretty, *adj.* **1.** fair, attractive, comely, pleasing, beautiful. **2.** fine, pleasant, excellent, splendid. —*adv.* **3.** moderately, fairly, somewhat, to some extent. **4.** very, quite. —**Ant.** ugly; unpleasant; completely. —**Syn. Study.** See BEAUTIFUL.

prevail, *v.* **1.** predominate, preponderate. **2.** win, succeed. —**Ant.** lose.

prevailing, *adj.* prevalent, predominant, preponderating, dominant, preponderant. **2.** current, general, common. **3.** superior, influential, effectual, effective, efficacious, successful. —**Ant.** rare, uncommon; inferior, ineffectual, ineffective, unsuccessful.

prevalent, *adj.* widespread, current, common, prevailing, extensive, predominant, predominating, accepted, used, general. —**Ant.** rare, unusual, uncommon.

prevaricate, *v.* equivocate, quibble, cavil, shift; fib, lie.

prevent, *v.* hinder, stop, obstruct, hamper, impede, forestall, thwart, intercept, preclude, obviate, interrupt. —**Ant.** encourage, aid, help, abet, support, continue. —**Syn. Study.** PREVENT, HAMPER, HINDER, IMPEDE refer to different degrees of stoppage of action or progress. To PREVENT is to stop something effectually by forestalling action and rendering it impossible: *to prevent the sending of a message.* To HAMPER is to clog or entangle or put an embarrassing restraint upon: *to hamper preparations for a trip.* To HINDER is to keep back by delaying or stopping progress or action: *to hinder the progress of an expedition.* To IMPEDE is to make difficult the movement or progress of anything by interfering with its proper functioning: *to impede a discussion by demanding repeated explanations.*

previous, *adj.* prior, earlier, former, preceding, foregoing. —**Ant.** later, following.

price, *n.* charge, cost, expense, outlay, expenditure.

pride, *n.* **1.** conceit, self-esteem, vanity, arrogance, vainglory, self-importance. **2.** insolence, haughtiness, snobbishness, superciliousness, hauteur, presumption. —**Ant.** modesty; humility. —**Syn. Study.** PRIDE, CONCEIT, EGOTISM, VANITY imply a favorable view of one's own appearance, advantage, achievements, etc., and often apply to offensive characteristics. PRIDE is a lofty and often arrogant assumption of superiority in some respect: *Pride must have a fall.* CONCEIT implies an exaggerated estimate of one's own abilities or attainments, together with pride: *blinded by conceit.* EGOTISM implies an excessive preoccupation with oneself or with one's own concerns, usu. but not always accompanied by pride or conceit: *Her egotism blinded her to others' difficulties.* VANITY implies self-admiration and an excessive desire to be admired by others: *His vanity was easily flattered.*

prim, *adj.* stiff, starched, formal, straitlaced, precise, proper, puritanical, rigid, blue, priggish; prunes and prisms. —**Ant.** flexible, informal; lewd, licentious, profligate.

primary, *adj.* **1.** first, highest, chief, principal, main. **2.** first, earliest, primitive, original, primeval, aboriginal. **3.** elementary, beginning, opening, fundamental, basic, ordinate. **4.** direct, immediate. —**Ant.** last, final, ultimate; secondary; indirect.

prime. See PRIMARY.

primeval, *adj.* prime, primary, primordial, primitive, original, primigenial, pristine.

primitive, *adj.* **1.** prehistoric, primal, primeval, prime, primary, primordial, original, aboriginal, pristine, prehistoric, first, antediluvian. **2.** uncivilized, uncultured, simple, unsophisticated, quaint. —**Ant.** secondary; civilized, sophisticated, cultured.

principal, *adj.* **1.** first, highest, prime, paramount, capital, chief, foremost, main, leading, cardinal, preeminent. —*n.* **2.** chief, head, leader, chieftain. **3.** headmaster,

dean, master. —**Ant.** ancillary, secondary. —**Syn. Study.** See CAPITAL.

principally, *adv.* especially, chiefly, mainly, primarily, firstly, particularly. —**Ant.** lastly.

principle, *n.* **1.** canon, rule, standard, test, parameter. **2.** theorem, axiom, postulate, maxim, law, proposition. **3.** doctrine, tenet, belief, opinion. **4.** integrity, honesty, probity, righteousness, uprightness, rectitude, virtue, incorruptibility, goodness, trustworthiness, honor.

private, *adj.* individual, personal, singular, especial, special, particular, peculiar. **2.** confidential, secret, top secret, "eyes only." **3.** alone, secluded, cloistered, sequestered, solitary, retired. —**Ant.** public, general; known; open.

privation, *n.* hardship, deprivation, loss; destitution, want, need, necessity, distress, lack. —**Ant.** ease, wealth.

privilege, *n.* right, immunity, leave, prerogative, advantage, license, freedom, liberty, permission, franchise. —**Syn. Study.** PRIVILEGE, PREROGATIVE refer to a special advantage or right possessed by an individual or group. A PRIVILEGE is a right or advantage gained by birth, social position, effort, or concession. It can have either legal or personal sanction: *the privilege of paying half fare; the privilege of calling whenever one wishes.* PREROGATIVE refers to an exclusive right claimed and granted, often officially or legally, on the basis of social status, heritage, sex, etc.: *the prerogatives of a king; the prerogatives of management.*

prize, *n.* **1.** reward, premium. —*v.* **2.** value, esteem, appraise. —**Syn. Study.** See APPRECIATE. See also REWARD.

probe, *v.* examine, explore, question, investigate, scrutinize, search, sift, prove, test. —**Ant.** overlook, ignore.

probity, *n.* honesty, uprightness, rectitude, integrity. —**Ant.** dishonesty.

problem, *n.* question, doubt, uncertainty, puzzle, riddle, enigma. —**Ant.** certainty, certitude, surety.

procedure, *n.* proceeding, conduct, management, operation, course, process. **2.** act, deed, transaction, maneuver, goings-on.

proceed, *v.* **1.** advance, go on, progress, move on, continue, pass on. **2.** go or come forth, issue, emanate, spring, arise, result, ensue, originate. —**Ant.** retreat.

process, *n.* course, procedure, operation, proceeding.

proclaim, *v.* announce, declare, advertise, promulgate, publish. —**Syn. Study.** See ANNOUNCE.

proclivity, *n.* inclination, tendency, bent, leaning, propensity, predisposition, disposition, proneness, favor, bias, prejudice. —**Ant.** dislike, aversion.

procrastinate, *v.* delay, postpone, put off, defer, adjourn, prolong. —**Ant.** speed, expedite.

procure, *v.* **1.** acquire, gain, get, secure, win, obtain. **2.** bring about, effect, cause, contrive. **3.** pander, bawd, pimp. —**Ant.** lose. —**Syn. Study.** See GET.

prod, *v.* poke, jab; goad, rouse, incite.

prodigal, *adj.* **1.** reckless, profligate, extravagant, lavish, wasteful, profuse. **2.** abundant, profuse, plenteous, copious, plentiful, bounteous, bountiful. —*n.* **3.** spendthrift, waster, wastrel, squanderer, carouser, playboy. —**Ant.** cautious, provident, thrifty; scarce, scanty. —**Syn. Study.** See LAVISH.

prodigious, *adj.* **1.** enormous, immense, huge, gigantic, tremendous, monstrous. **2.** wonderful, marvelous, amazing, stupendous, astonishing, astounding, extraordinary, miraculous, wondrous, uncommon, unusual, strange. **3.** abnormal, monstrous, anomalous. —**Ant.** small, tiny, infinitesimal; negligible, common; normal, usual.

produce, *v.* **1.** give rise to, cause, generate, occasion, originate, create, effect, make, manufacture, bring about. **2.** bear, bring forth, yield, furnish, supply, afford, give. **3.** exhibit, show, demonstrate, bring forward. —*n.* **4.** yield, product, crops, fruits, production. —**Ant.** destroy, ruin; subdue, squelch; hide, conceal.

productive, *adj.* generative, creative; prolific, fertile, fruitful. —**Ant.** barren, sterile, unproductive. —**Syn. Study.** PRODUCTIVE, FERTILE, FRUITFUL, PROLIFIC apply to the generative aspect of something. PRODUCTIVE

refers to a generative source of continuing activity: *productive soil; a productive influence.* FERTILE applies to that in which seeds, literal or figurative, take root: *fertile soil; a fertile imagination.* FRUITFUL refers to that which has already produced and is capable of further production: *fruitful species; fruitful discussions.* PROLIFIC means highly productive: *a prolific farm; a prolific writer.*

profane, *adj.* **1.** irreverent, irreligious, blasphemous, sacrilegious, piacular, wicked, impious, ungodly, godless, unredeemed, unredeemable. **2.** unconsecrated, secular, temporal. **3.** unholy, heathen, pagan, unhallowed, impure, polluted. **4.** common, low, mean, base, vulgar. —*v.* **5.** debase, misuse, defile, desecrate, violate, pollute. —**Ant.** sacred, repentant; spiritual; pure, hallowed, holy; elevated, exalted.

profession, *n.* **1.** vocation, calling, occupation, business, employment. **2.** professing, avowal, declaration, asseveration, assertion.

proffer, *v.* offer, tender, volunteer, propose, suggest, hint. —**Ant.** refuse. —**Syn. Study.** See OFFER.

proficient, *adj.* skilled, adept, skillful, competent, practiced, experienced, qualified, trained, conversant, accomplished, finished, able, apt. —**Ant.** unskilled, maladroit, awkward, clumsy, untrained, unable, inept.

profit, *n.* **1.** gain, return. **2.** returns, proceeds, revenue, dividend. **3.** advantage, benefit, gain, good, welfare, improvement, advancement. —*v.* **4.** gain, improve, advance, better. —**Ant.** loss; lose. —**Syn. Study.** See ADVANTAGE.

profound, *adj.* deep, intense, extreme, penetrating, sagacious; abstruse. —**Ant.** shallow, superficial.

profuse, *adj.* extravagant, abundant, lavish, prodigal, wasteful, profligate, improvident. —**Ant.** scarce, scanty, thrifty. —**Syn. Study.** See LAVISH.

profusion, *n.* abundance, plenty, copiousness, bounty, prodigality, profligacy, excess, waste. —**Ant.** scarcity, need, want; penury, niggardliness.

progress, *n.* **1.** proceeding, advancement, advance, progression. **2.** growth, development, improvement, increase, betterment. —*v.* **3.** advance, proceed; develop, improve, grow, increase. —**Ant.** retrogression; recession; recede, decrease, diminish.

prohibit, *v.* **1.** forbid, interdict, disallow. **2.** prevent, hinder, preclude, obstruct. —**Ant.** allow, permit; encourage, foster, further.

prohibition, *n.* interdiction, prevention, embargo, ban, restriction. —**Ant.** permission.

project, *n.* **1.** plan, scheme, design, proposal. **2.** activity, lesson, homework. —*v.* **3.** propose, contemplate, plan, contrive, scheme, plot, devise, concoct, brew, frame. **4.** throw, cast, toss. **5.** extend, protrude, obtrude, bulge, jut out, stick out.

prolific, *adj.* **1.** fruitful, fertile, productive, teeming. **2.** abundant. —**Ant.** fruitless, unfruitful, barren, sterile; scarce. —**Syn. Study.** See PRODUCTIVE.

prolix, See Syn. study at WORDY.

prolong, *v.* lengthen, extend, protract. —**Ant.** abbreviate, shorten, curtail. —**Syn. Study.** See LENGTHEN.

prominent, *adj.* **1.** conspicuous, noticeable, outstanding, manifest, principal, chief, important, main. **2.** projecting, jutting out, protuberant, embossed. **3.** important, leading, well-known, eminent, celebrated, famed, famous, distinguished. —**Ant.** inconspicuous, unimportant; recessed; negligible, unknown.

promiscuous, *adj.* miscellaneous, hodgepodge, hotchpotch, indiscriminate, confused, mixed, intermixed, intermingled, mingled, jumbled, garbled. **2.** nonselective, indiscriminate, careless. —**Ant.** special, discriminate, pure, unmixed; selective, careful, select.

promise, *n.* **1.** word, pledge, assurance. —*v.* **2.** pledge, covenant, agree, engage.

promote, *v.* **1.** further, advance, encourage, forward, assist, aid, help, support. **2.** elevate, raise, exalt. —**Ant.** discourage, obstruct; lower, debase.

prone, *adj.* **1.** inclined, disposed, liable, tending, bent. **2.** prostrate, recumbent. —**Ant.** averse; upright.

proof, *n.* **1.** evidence, testimony, certification, confirmation, demonstration. **2.** test, trial, examination, essay. **3.** impression. —*adj.* **4.**

impenetrable, impervious, invulnerable, steadfast, firm.

propensity, *n.* inclination, bent, leaning, tendency, disposition, bias. —**Ant.** disinclination, aversion, distaste.

proper, *adj.* **1.** appropriate, fit, suitable, suited, adapted, convenient, fitting, befitting, correct, right, becoming, meet. **2.** correct, decorous, decent, respectable, polite, well-mannered. **3.** special, specific, individual, peculiar. **4.** strict, accurate, precise, exact, just, formal, correct. —**Ant.** improper.

property, *n.* **1.** possession, possessions, goods, effects, chattels, estate, belongings. **2.** land, real estate, acreage. **3.** ownership, right. **4.** attribute, quality, characteristic, feature. —**Syn. Study.** PROPERTY, CHATTELS, EFFECTS, ESTATE, GOODS refer to what is owned. PROPERTY is the general word: *She owns a great deal of property. He said that the umbrella was his property.* CHATTELS is a term for pieces of personal property or movable possessions; it may be applied to livestock, automobiles, etc.: *a mortgage on chattels.* EFFECTS is a term for any form of personal property, including even things of the least value: *All my effects were insured against fire.* ESTATE refers to property of any kind that has been, or is capable of being, handed down to descendants or otherwise disposed of in a will: *He left most of his estate to his niece.* It may consist of personal estate (money, valuables, securities, chattels, etc.) or real estate (land and buildings). GOODS refers to household possessions or other movable property, esp. the stock in trade of a business: *The store arranged its goods on shelves.* See also QUALITY.

prophesy, *v.* foretell, predict, augur, prognosticate, divine. —**Syn. Study.** See PREDICT.

propitiate, *v.* appease, conciliate, pacify. —**Ant.** anger, arouse. —**Syn. Study.** See APPEASE.

proportion, *n.* **1.** relation, arrangement; comparison, analogy. **2.** size, extent, dimensions. **3.** portion, part, piece, share. **4.** symmetry, harmony, agreement, balance, distribution, arrangement. —*v.* **5.** adjust, regulate, redistribute, arrange, balance, harmonize. —**Ant.** disproportion. —**Syn. Study.** See SYMMETRY.

proposal, *n.* plan, scheme, offer, recommendation, suggestion, design, overture, approach, proposition.

propose, *v.* **1.** offer, proffer, tender, suggest, recommend, present. **2.** nominate, name. **3.** plan, intend, design, mean, purpose. **4.** state, present, propound, pose, posit. —**Ant.** refuse.

proposition. See PROPOSAL.

propriety, *n.* **1.** decorum, etiquette, protocol, good behavior, decency, modesty. **2.** suitability, appropriateness, aptness, fitness, suitableness, seemliness. **3.** rightness, justness, correctness, accuracy. —**Ant.** impropriety, immodesty, indecency; unseemliness, ineptitude; inaccuracy.

prosaic, *adj.* prosy, commonplace, dull, matter-of-fact, unimaginative, vapid, humdrum, tedious, tiresome, wearisome, uninteresting. —**Ant.** interesting, fascinating, beguiling.

prospect, *n.* **1.** anticipation, expectation, expectance, contemplation. **2.** view, scene, outlook, survey, vista, perspective. —*v.* **3.** search, explore. —**Syn. Study.** See VIEW.

prosper, *v.* succeed, thrive, flourish. —**Ant.** fail, die. —**Syn. Study.** See SUCCEED.

prosperous, *adj.* **1.** fortunate, successful, flourishing, thriving. **2.** wealthy, rich, well-to-do, well-off. **3.** favorable, propitious, fortunate, lucky, auspicious, golden, bright. —**Ant.** unfortunate, unsuccessful; poor, impoverished; unfavorable.

prostitute, *n.* **1.** harlot, whore, strumpet, call girl, trollop, quean, street walker, courtesan. —*v.* **2.** misapply, misuse, abuse.

protect, *v.* defend, guard, shield, cover, screen, shelter, save, harbor, house, secure. —**Ant.** attack, assail.

protection, *n.* **1.** preservation, guard, defense, shelter, screen, cover, security, refuge, safety. **2.** shield, aegis, bulwark. **3.** treaty, safe-conduct, passport, visa, pass, permit. **4.** aegis, patronage, sponsorship. —**Ant.** attack.

protest, *n.* **1.** objection, disapproval, protestation. —*v.* **2.** remonstrate, complain, object. **3.** declare, affirm, assert, asseverate, avow, aver, testify, attest. —**Ant.** approval; approve.

prototype, *n.* model, pattern, example, exemplar, original, archetype.

protract, *v.* draw out, lengthen, extend, prolong, continue. —**Ant.** curtail, abbreviate, discontinue. —**Syn. Study.** See LENGTHEN.

proud, *adj.* **1.** contented, self-satisfied, egotistical, vain, conceited. **2.** arrogant, overweening, haughty, overbearing, self-important, overconfident, disdainful, supercilious, snooty, imperious, presumptuous. **3.** honorable, creditable. **4.** stately, majestic, magnificent, noble, imposing, splendid. —**Ant.** discontented, dissatisfied; humble, self-effacing; dishonorable; ignoble, base.

prove, *v.* **1.** demonstrate, show, confirm, manifest, establish, evince, evidence, substantiate, verify, justify, ascertain, determine. **2.** try, test, examine, assay. —**Ant.** disprove.

provender. See Syn. study at FEED.

proverb, *n.* maxim, saying, adage, epigram, precept, truth, saw, aphorism, by-word, apothegm. —**Syn. Study.** PROVERB, MAXIM are terms for short, pithy sayings. A PROVERB is such a saying popularly known and repeated, usu. expressing simply and concretely, though often metaphorically, a truth based on common sense or practical human experience: *A stitch in time saves nine.* A MAXIM is a brief statement of a general and practical truth, esp. one that serves as a rule of conduct: *It is wise to risk no more than one can afford to lose.*

provide, *v.* **1.** furnish, supply, afford, yield, produce, contribute, give. **2.** prepare, get ready, procure, provide for, make provision for. —**Ant.** deprive.

provided, *conj.* on the condition *or* supposition that, if, in case, granted. —**Ant.** lest.

provision, *n.* **1.** stipulation, condition, if, proviso. **2.** catering, purveying, supplying. **3.** (*plural*) food, supplies, stores, provender, stock.

provoke, *v.* **1.** anger, enrage, exasperate, irk, vex, irritate, incense, annoy, chafe, aggravate, exacerbate, infuriate, ire, nettle, affront. **2.** stir up, arouse, call forth, incite, stimulate, excite, fire, rouse, inflame, animate, inspirit, instigate. **3.** give rise to, induce, bring about. —**Ant.** assuage, calm, propitiate. —**Syn. Study.** See INCITE.

prowl, *v.* lurk, rove, roam, wander; prey, plunder, pillage, steal. —**Syn. Study.** See LURK.

prudence, *n.* **1.** calculation, foresight, forethought, judgment, discretion, common sense, circumspection, caution, wisdom. **2.** providence, care, economy, frugality, carefulness. —**Ant.** carelessness, imprudence, incaution.

prudent, *adj.* **1.** wise, judicious, cautious, discreet, tactful, sensible, sagacious, circumspect, careful, wary, provident. **2.** provident, frugal, sparing, economical, thrifty, saving, careful. —**Ant.** imprudent, indiscreet, tactless, careless; improvident, prodigal.

prudish, *adj.* modest, proper, demure, pure, coy, reserved. —**Ant.** immodest, indecent. —**Syn. Study.** See MODEST.

prying, *adj.* curious, inquisitive, peeping, peering, peeking; nosy. —**Ant.** blasé, unconcerned, uninterested.

pseudo, *adj.* sham, counterfeit, false, spurious, pretended, fake. —**Ant.** genuine, real.

publish, *v.* **1.** issue, distribute. **2.** announce, proclaim, promulgate, declare, disclose, divulge, reveal, impart, advertise, publicize. —**Ant.** conceal, hide. —**Syn. Study.** See ANNOUNCE.

puerile, *adj.* **1.** boyish, juvenile, childish, youthful. **2.** childish, immature, foolish, irrational, trivial, nugatory, silly, ridiculous, idle. —**Ant.** manly; mature, rational.

pulsate, *v.* beat, palpitate, pulse, throb; vibrate, quiver.

punctilious, *adj.* strict, exact, precise, demanding, scrupulous, nice, careful, conscientious. —**Ant.** inexact, careless. —**Syn. Study.** See SCRUPULOUS.

pungent, *adj.* **1.** biting, acrid, hot, peppery, piquant, sharp. **2.** poignant, distressing, painful. **3.** caustic, biting, sarcastic, sardonic, mordant, penetrating, piercing, trenchant, cutting, severe, acrimonious, bitter, waspish. **4.** stimulating, acute, keen, sharp. —**Ant.** mild, bland; painless; dull.

punish, *v.* **1.** correct, discipline, penalize, reprove. **2.** castigate, scold, berate, chastise, chasten, flog, whip.

---

pupil, *v.* disciple, scholar, student, learner, tyro, greenhorn, neophyte, novice, beginner. —**Ant.** teacher, expert.

purblind, *adj.* blind, sightless, dim-sighted, myopic, short-sighted, near-sighted. —**Ant.** sighted, clearsighted, presbyopic.

purchase, *v.* **1.** buy, acquire, get, obtain, procure. **2.** haul, draw, raise. —*n.* **3.** buying, acquisition. **4.** bargain. **5.** tackle, lever, winch, capstan. —**Ant.** sell, lose; lower; sale.

pure, *adj.* **1.** unmixed, unadulterated, uncontaminated, unalloyed, clean, unsullied, untainted, unstained, undefiled, spotless, untarnished, immaculate, unpolluted, uncorrupted. **2.** unmodified, simple, homogeneous, genuine, faultless, perfect. **3.** thoroughbred, purebred, pedigreed. **4.** utter, sheer, unqualified, absolute. **5.** innocent, chaste, undefiled, unsullied, modest, virtuous. **6.** guiltless, innocent, true, guileless, honest, upright. —**Ant.** impure.

purge, *v.* purify, cleanse, clear, clean, clarify. —**Ant.** pollute.

purport, *v.* **1.** profess, claim, mean, intend, signify. **2.** express, imply. —*n.* **3.** tenor, import, meaning, intention, claim, design, significance, signification, implication, drift, suggestion, gist, spirit. —**Ant.** understand, see; infer; insignificance, meaninglessness. —**Syn. Study.** See MEANING.

purpose, *n.* **1.** object, intent, intention, determination, aim, end, design, view. **2.** result, effect, advantage, consequence. —*v.* **3.** propose, design, intend, mean, contemplate, plan. —**Ant.** purposelessness.

push, *v.* **1.** shove, shoulder, thrust, drive, move, slide. **2.** press, urge, persuade, drive, impel. —*n.* **3.** attack, effort, onset.

put, *v.* **1.** place, lay, set, deposit. **2.** set, levy, impose, inflict. **3.** render, translate. **4.** express, state, utter.

puzzle, *n.* **1.** riddle, enigma, problem, poser, maze, question. —*v.* **2.** bewilder, perplex, confound, mystify, confuse.

pygmy, *n.* dwarf, midget, Lilliputian, runt. —**Ant.** giant, colossus. —**Syn. Study.** See DWARF.

Q

quagmire, *n.* **1.** swamp, marsh, fen, bog, mire, morass, slough. **2.** predicament, difficulty, dilemma, pickle, tight spot, fix, jam, corner, box.

quail, See Syn. study at WINCE.

quaint, *adj.* **1.** strange, odd, curious, unusual, extraordinary, unique, uncommon. **2.** picturesque, charming, old-fashioned, antiquated, antique, archaic. —**Ant.** common, usual, ordinary; modern, new-fangled.

quake, *v.* **1.** shake, shudder, tremble, shiver, quaver, quiver. —*n.* **2.** temblor, earthquake.

qualify, *v.* **1.** fit, suit, adapt, prepare, equip. **2.** characterize, call, name, designate, label, signify. **3.** modify, limit, mitigate, restrain, narrow, restrict. **4.** moderate, mitigate, meliorate, soften, mollify, soothe, ease, assuage, temper, reduce, diminish.

quality, *n.* **1.** characteristic, attribute, property, character, feature, trait. **2.** nature, grade, kind, sort, description, status, rank, condition. **3.** excellence, superiority, standing. **4.** accomplishment, deed, feat, attainment. **5.** distinction, class. —*n.* inferiority, baseness; failure. —**Syn. Study.** QUALITY, ATTRIBUTE, PROPERTY refer to a distinguishing feature or characteristic of a person, thing, or group. A QUALITY is an innate or acquired characteristic that, in some particular, determines the nature and behavior of a person or thing: *the qualities of patience and perseverance.* An ATTRIBUTE is a quality that we assign or ascribe to a person or to something personified; it may also mean a fundamental or innate characteristic: *an attribute of God; attributes of a logical mind.* PROPERTY is applied only to a thing; it refers to a principal characteristic that is part of the constitution of a thing and serves to define or describe it: *the physical properties of limestone.*

qualm, *n.* uneasiness, compunction, scruple, twinge, remorse, misgiving. —**Ant.** ease, confort, security.

quandary, *n.* dilemma, predicament, strait, uncertainty, doubt.

—**Ant.** certainty, assurance. —**Syn. Study.** See PREDICAMENT.

quarrel, *n.* **1.** dispute, altercation, disagreement, argument, contention, controversy, dissension, feud, breach, break, rupture, difference, spat, tiff, fight, misunderstanding, wrangle, brawl, tumult. —*v.* **2.** squabble, fall out, disagree with, differ, disagree, bicker, dispute, argue, wrangle, spar, brawl, clash, jar, fight. —**Syn. Study.** QUARREL, DISSENSION refer to disagreement and conflict. QUARREL applies chiefly to a verbal disagreement between individuals or groups and is used with reference to a large variety of situations, from a slight and petty difference of opinion to a violent altercation: *There was little more than a domestic quarrel. Their quarrel led to an actual fight.* DISSENSION usu. implies a profound disagreement and bitter conflict. It also applies chiefly to conflict within a group or between members of the same group: *dissension within the union; dissension among the Democrats.*

quarrelsome, *adj.* argumentative, disputatious, cantankerous, combative, belligerent, bellicose, truculent, pugnacious, antagonistic. —**Ant.** peaceable, amicable.

queasy, *adj.* **1.** squeamish, fastidious, overfastidious, delicate, finicky, finical, picky, particular. **2.** nauseated, nauseous, qualmish, sickish, seasick, airsick, carsick, queer, queerish, puky, barfy.

queer, *adj.* strange, unconventional, odd, singular, curious, fantastic, uncommon, weird, peculiar, extraordinary, eccentric, freakish. —**Ant.** conventional, ordinary, common.

quell, *v.* **1.** suppress, stifle, extinguish, put an end to, crush, quash, subdue, overpower, overcome. **2.** vanquish, put down, defeat, conquer. **3.** quiet, allay, calm, pacify, compose, lull, hush. —**Ant.** encourage, foster; defend, lose; agitate, disturb, perturb.

querulous, *adj.* complaining, petulant, peevish, snappish, abrupt, waspish, testy; caviling, carping, discontented, fault-finding. —**Ant.** calm, equable; pleased, contented.

question, *n.* **1.** inquiry, query, interrogation. **2.** dispute, controversy. —*v.* **3.** interrogate; ask, inquire, query, examine. **4.** doubt. **5.** dispute, challenge. —**Ant.** answer, reply; agree, concur.

questionable, *adj.* doubtful, uncertain, dubitable, dubious, debatable, disputable, controvertible. —**Ant.** certain, sure, positive.

quibble, *n.* **1.** evasion, prevarication, equivocation, sophism, shift, subterfuge, cavil. —*v.* **2.** evade, prevaricate, equivocate, cavil, shuffle, trifle.

quick, *adj.* **1.** prompt, immediate, rapid, fast, swift, speedy, instantaneous, fleet, hasty, hurried, expeditious. **2.** impatient, hasty, abrupt, curt, short, precipitate, sharp, unceremonious; testy, waspish, snappish, irritable, peppery, irascible, petulant, touchy. **3.** lively, keen, acute, sensitive, alert, sharp, shrewd, intelligent, discerning. **4.** vigorous, energetic, active, nimble, animated, agile, lively, alert, brisk. —**Ant.** slow; patient, deliberate; calm; dull, stupid; lethargic, lazy. —**Syn. Study.** QUICK, FAST, SWIFT, RAPID describe a speedy rate of motion or progress. QUICK applies particularly to an action or reaction that is almost instantaneous, or of brief duration: *to take a quick look around.* FAST refers to a person or thing that acts or moves speedily; when used of communication or transportation, it suggests a definite goal and continuous movement: *a fast swimmer; a fast train.* SWIFT, a more formal word, suggests great speed as well as graceful movement: *The panther is a swift animal.* RAPID applies to one or a series of actions or movements; it stresses the rate of speed: *to perform rapid calculations.* See also SHARP.

quiet, *n.* **1.** tranquillity, rest, repose, calm, stillness, quietude, serenity, peace, calmness, silence. **2.** peace. —*adj.* **3.** peaceable, peaceful, pacific, calm, tranquil, serene, silent. **4.** motionless, still, unmoving, unmoved. **5.** inconspicuous, subdued, unobtrusive. —*v.* **6.** still, hush, silence. **7.** tranquilize, pacify, calm, compose, lull, soothe. —**Ant.** disturbance, perturbation; war; warlike, noisy, clamorous; conspicuous, obvious, blatant; disturb, perturb.

quip, *v.* **1.** joke, banter, jest, gibe, wisecrack, josh, crack wise. —*n.* **2.**

---

witticism, joke, jape, gibe, wisecrack, gag, bon mot, sally.

quirk, See Syn. study at ECCENTRICITY.

quit, *v.* **1.** stop, cease, discontinue, desist. **2.** depart from, leave, go, withdraw *or* retire from. **3.** give up, let go, relinquish, release, resign, surrender. —*adj.* **4.** released, free, clear, liberated, rid, absolved, acquitted, discharged. —**Ant.** start; initiate, originate; continue; arrive, enter; chained, confined.

quiver, *v.* **1.** shake, tremble, vibrate, quake, shudder, shiver. —*n.* **2.** tremble, tremor, shudder, shiver, trembling, shake. **3.** arrow-case.

quixotic, *adj.* visionary, impractical, romantic, imaginary, wild. —**Ant.** realistic, practicable, practical.

quizzical, *adj.* **1.** questioning, curious, inquisitive, inquiring, interrogatory. **2.** skeptical, suspicious, dubious, doubting, wary, distrustful, incredulous, unbelieving.

R

rabid, *adj.* **1.** overwrought, frantic, frenzied, frenetic, furious, raging, wild, mad, maniacal. **2.** extreme, extremist, radical, fanatic, fanatical, fervent, perfervid, overzealous, irrational, wild-eyed, over-the-top. —**Ant.** calm, composed, reasonable.

race, *n.* **1.** competition, contest. **2.** course, stream. **3.** nation, people, clan, family, tribe, generation, stock, line, lineage, breed, kin, kindred, progeny, descendants, offspring, children. **4.** man, mankind. —*v.* **5.** run, speed, hurry, hasten, hie.

rack, *n.* **1.** frame, framework, crib. **2.** torment, anguish, torture, pain, agony. —*v.* **3.** torture, distress, torment, agonize, excruciate. **4.** strain, force, wrest, stretch.

racket, *n.* **1.** din, uproar, noise, clamor, fuss, tumult, hubbub, outcry, disturbance. **2.** excitement, gaiety, dissipation. —**Ant.** quiet, tranquillity, peace. —**Syn. Study.** See NOISE.

racy, *adj.* **1.** vigorous, lively, animated, spirited. **2.** sprightly, piquant, pungent, strong, flavorful. **3.** suggestive, risqué. —**Ant.** dispirited, dejected; mild, bland.

radiant, *adj.* shining, bright, brilliant, beaming, effulgent, resplendent, sparkling, splendid, glittering. —**Ant.** dull.

radiate, *v.* **1.** shine, beam, glow, gleam, burn, luminesce, incandesce, twinkle, glimmer, sparkle, flash, glare, dazzle. **2.** diffuse, disperse, emit, spread, propagate, scatter, emanate, throw off, give off.

radical, *adj.* **1.** fundamental, basic, original, constitutional, essential, innate, ingrained. **2.** thoroughgoing, extreme, complete, unqualified, thorough, fanatical, excessive, immoderate, extravagant, violent. —*n.* **3.** extremist. —**Ant.** superfluous; incomplete, moderate.

radioactive, *adj.* hot, dirty. —**Ant.** clean.

rage, *n.* **1.** anger, ire, fury, frenzy, passion, vehemence, wrath, madness, raving. **2.** fury, violence, turbulence, tumultuousness, storm. **3.** ardor, fervor, enthusiasm, eagerness, desire, vehemence. **4.** mode, fashion, fad, craze, vogue. —*v.* **5.** rave, fume, storm, chafe, fret. —**Ant.** calm, equanimity. —**Syn. Study.** See ANGER.

ragged, *adj.* **1.** tattered, torn, shredded, rent. **2.** shabby, poor, mean. —**Ant.** neat, whole.

raid, *n.* **1.** onset, attack, seizure. **2.** invasion, inroad, incursion. —**Ant.** defense.

raillery, *n.* banter, kidding, kidding around, teasing, joshing, ribbing, ragging, twitting, fooling around, badinage, persiflage, give-and-take, back-and-forth.

raiment, *n.* clothes, clothing, garments, apparel, attire, dress, habiliment, things, costume, habit, togs, toggery, gear, duds, getup, threads.

raise, *v.* **1.** lift, lift up, elevate, heave, hoist, loft. **2.** rouse, arouse, awake, awaken, call forth, evoke, stir up, excite. **3.** build, erect, construct, rear, set up. **4.** cause, promote, cultivate, grow, propagate. **5.** originate, engender, give rise to, bring up *or* about, produce, effect, cause. **6.** invigorate, animate, inspirit, heighten, intensify. **7.** advance, elevate, promote, exalt. **8.** gather, collect, assemble, bring together. **9.** increase, intensify, heighten, aggravate, amplify, augment, enhance, enlarge. —**10.** increase, rise. —**Ant.** lower; pacify;

destroy, raze; kill; weaken, dispirit; debase, dishonor; scatter, disperse, broadcast; decrease.

ramble, v. **1.** stroll, amble, walk, wander, saunter, stray, roam, rove, range, straggle. —n. **2.** walk, stroll, amble, excursion, tour.

rambling adj. wandering, aimless, irregular, straggling, straying, discursive. —**Ant.** direct, pointed.

rambunctious, adj. boisterous, high-spirited, exuberant, roisterous, rollicking, unrestrained, uninhibited, irrepressible, untamed, knockabout, uproarious, wild, rowdy. —**Ant.** docile.

rampage, n. **1.** spree, tear, binge, outburst, orgy, riot, furor, furore, convulsion. —v. **2.** rage, storm, rave, rant, tear, tear around, riot.

rampart, n. fortification, breastwork, bulwark, barricade, stronghold, security, guard, defense.

ramshackle, adj. shaky, rickety, flimsy, dilapidated. —**Ant.** luxurious, sumptuous.

rancor, n. resentment, bitterness, ill will, hatred, malice, spite, venom, malevolence, animosity, enmity. —**Ant.** amiability, good will, benevolence.

random, adj. haphazard, chance, fortuitous, casual, stray, aimless. —**Ant.** specific, particular.

range, n. **1.** extent, limits, scope, sweep, latitude, reach, compass. **2.** rank, class, order, kind, sort. **3.** row, line, series, tier, file. **4.** area, trace, region. —v. **5.** align, rank, classify, class, order, arrange, array, dispose. **6.** vary, course. **7.** extend, stretch out, run, go, lie. **8.** roam, rove, wander, stroll, straggle. **9.** extend, be found, occupy, lie, run. —**Syn. Study.** RANGE, COMPASS, LATITUDE, SCOPE refer to extent or breadth. RANGE emphasizes extent and diversity: *the range of one's interests.* COMPASS suggests definite limits: *within the compass of one's mind.* LATITUDE emphasizes the idea of freedom from narrow confines, thus breadth or extent: *granted latitude of action.* SCOPE suggests great freedom but a proper limit: *the scope of one's obligations.*

rank, n. **1.** position, standing, station, order, class, level, division. **2.** row, line, tier, series, range. **3.** distinction, eminence, dignity. **4.** membership, body, rank and file. **5.** order, arrangement, array, alignment. —v. **6.** arrange, line up, align, array, range. **7.** classify, dispose, sort, class, arrange. —adj. **8.** tall, vigorous, luxuriant, abundant, overabundant, exuberant. **9.** strong, gamy, pungent, offensive, noxious, fetid, rancid, putrid. **10.** utter, absolute, complete, entire, sheer, gross, extravagant, excessive. **11.** offensive, disgusting, repulsive, repellent, miasmatic, mephitic. **12.** coarse, indecent, foul, gross.

rankle, v. irritate, annoy, vex, distress, plague, nettle, fester, gall, inflame, incense, embitter, rile, aggravate. —**Ant.** placate, please.

ransom, n. **1.** redemption, deliverance, liberation, release. —v. **2.** redeem, release, restore, deliver, deliver up.

rapacious, adj. greedy, predatory, extortionate, ravenous, voracious, avaricious, grasping; predacious, raptorial, preying. —**Ant.** generous, yielding; parasitic.

rapid, adj. speedy, fast, quick, swift, fleet. —**Ant.** slow. —**Syn. Study.** See QUICK.

rapidity, n. swiftness, speed, fleetness, quickness, haste, velocity, alacrity, celerity. —**Ant.** sloth, lethargy.

rapport, n. relationship, interrelationship, affinity, attraction, sympathy, empathy, closeness, understanding, like-mindedness, accord, concord, harmony, compatibility, goodwill, fellow feeling, fellowship, kinship, oneness, unity. —**Ant.** enmity, discordance.

rapt, adj. **1.** engrossed, preoccupied, occupied, absorbed, abstracted, thoughtful, bemused, faraway, single-minded, concentrated, fixed, fixated. **2.** enraptured, rapturous, transported, ecstatic, transfigured, enthralled, fascinated, enchanted, gripped, held, riveted. —**Ant.** distracted, distrait.

rapture, n. ecstasy, joy, delight, transport, bliss, beatitude, exultation. —**Ant.** misery, disgust, revulsion. —**Syn. Study.** See ECSTASY.

rare, adj. **1.** scarce, uncommon, exceptional, unusual, sparse, infrequent, extraordinary, singular. **2.** excellent, admirable, fine, choice, exquisite, incomparable, inimitable. **3.** underdone. —**Ant.** common.

usual, frequent, ordinary; base, inferior; medium, well done.

rarefied, adj. **1.** thin, attenuated, tenuous, ethereal, vaporous, insubstantial, airy, gaseous, diffuse, diluted, dilute, adulterated, weak, watered-down, porous. **2.** refined, esoteric, special, secret, recondite, inside, privileged.

rascal, n. **1.** rapscallion, knave, rogue, scamp, villain, scoundrel, miscreant, scapegrace. —adj. **2.** knavish, roguish, miscreant, dishonest, base, paltry, mean, low, rascally. —**Syn. Study.** See KNAVE.

rash, adj. **1.** hasty, impetuous, reckless, headlong, precipitate, impulsive, thoughtless, heedless, indiscreet, incautious, unwary, foolhardy, audacious. —n. **2.** eruption, efflorescence, eczema, dermatitis, breaking out, exanthema. —**Ant.** thoughtful, considered, discreet, cautious.

ratify, v. confirm, corroborate, consent to, agree to, approve, sanction, substantiate, validate, establish. —**Ant.** refute, veto, disapprove.

ration, n. **1.** allowance, portion, food. —v. **2.** apportion, distribute, mete, dole, deal, parcel out. **3.** put on rations, restrict to rations.

rational, adj. **1.** reasonable, sensible. **2.** intelligent, wise; judicious, discreet, sagacious, enlightened. **3.** sane, lucid, sound, sober. —**Ant.** irrational, unreasonable; unintelligent, stupid, unwise, indiscreet; unsound, dim.

rationalize, v. **1.** explain, clarify, elucidate, explicate, illuminate. **2.** justify, excuse, alibi, exculpate, palter, extenuate, explain away, whitewash, gloss over.

raucous, adj. **1.** noisy, discordant, strident, harsh, dissonant, rackety, cacophonous, stridulant, shrill, grating, piercing, jarring, screechy, shrieky, squawky. **2.** obstreperous, riotous, disorderly, boisterous, unruly, rowdy. —**Ant.** melodious, sweet-sounding.

ravage, n. **1.** devastation, destruction, ruin, waste, desolation, damage, havoc, despoilment, plunder, pillage. —v. **2.** damage, mar, ruin, devastate, destroy, lay waste, despoil, plunder, pillage, sack. —**Ant.** construction, creation; build; repair.

ravening. See RAVENOUS.

ravenous, adj. ravening, voracious, greedy, starved, hungry, famished, insatiable, gluttonous, devouring; rapacious, raptorial, predacious, predatory. —**Ant.** sated, satisfied.

raw, adj. **1.** unprepared, unfinished, unrefined, unmade, crude, rude, rough, makeshift. **2.** uncooked. **3.** ignorant, inexperienced, untrained, undisciplined, green, unskilled, untried, unpracticed. **4.** frank, candid, bold, exposed. **5.** damp, chilly, cold, wet, windy. —**Ant.** prepared, finished, refined, done, polished; cooked, done; intelligent, disciplined, skilled, secretive, dry, warm, arid. —**Syn. Study.** RAW, CRUDE, RUDE refer to something not in a finished or highly refined state. RAW applies particularly to material not yet changed by a process, by manufacture, or by preparation for consumption: *raw leather.* CRUDE refers to that which still needs refining: *crude petroleum.* RUDE refers to what is still in a condition of rough simplicity or in a roughly made form: *rude agricultural implements.*

raze, See Syn. study at DESTROY.

reach, v. **1.** get to, attain, arrive at, come to. **2.** touch, seize. **3.** stretch, extend. —n. **4.** extent, distance, range, compass, area, sphere, influence, stretch, scope, grasp. —**Ant.** fail.

reactionary, n., adj. conservative. —**Ant.** radical.

readily, adv. promptly, quickly, easily; willingly, cheerfully. —**Ant.** slowly, lethargically; reluctantly.

ready, adj. **1.** prepared, set, fitted, fit. **2.** equipped, geared, completed, adjusted, arranged. **3.** willing, agreeable, cheerful, disposed, inclined. **4.** prompt, quick, alert, acute, sharp, keen, adroit, facile, clever, skillful, nimble. —v. **5.** make ready, prepare. —**Ant.** unprepared, unfit; unwilling, indisposed, disinclined; slow, deliberate, unskillful.

real, adj. true, actual, faithful, factual, authentic, genuine; sincere, unfeigned. —**Ant.** false, fake, counterfeit, fraudulent; insincere.

realistic, adj. practical, hardheaded, clear-eyed, clear-sighted, clearheaded, sober, blunt, factual, pragmatic, tough-minded, undeceived, ungullible, unsentimental, unromantic. —**Ant.** impractical, flighty.

realize, v. **1.** grasp, understand, comprehend, conceive. **2.** imagine. **3.** accomplish, effect, effectuate, perform. —**Ant.** misunderstand; begin.

realm, n. **1.** kingdom. **2.** sovereignty, sphere, domain, province, department.

rear, n. **1.** back, background. —v. **2.** bring up, nurture, raise, nurse. **3.** raise, elevate, lift, loft, lift up, hold up. **4.** build, put up, erect, construct. **5.** rise; buck. —**Ant.** front; face.

reason, n. **1.** ground, cause, motive, purpose, end, design, *raison d'être*, objective, aim, object. **2.** justification, explanation, excuse, rationale, ratiocination, rationalization. **3.** judgment, common sense, understanding, intellect, intelligence, mind. **4.** sanity. —v. **5.** argue, ratiocinate, justify; rationalize. **6.** conclude, infer. **7.** bring, persuade, convince, influence. —**Syn. Study.** REASON, CAUSE, MOTIVE are terms for a circumstance (or circumstances) that brings about or explains certain results. A REASON is an explanation of a situation or circumstance that made certain results seem possible or appropriate: *The reason for the robbery was the victim's careless display of money.* The CAUSE is the way in which the circumstances produce the effect; that is, make a specific action seem necessary or desirable: *The cause was the robber's immediate need of money.* A MOTIVE is the hope, desire, or other force that starts the action (or an action) in an attempt to produce specific results: *The motive was to use the stolen money to gamble.*

reasonable, adj. **1.** rational, logical, sensible, intelligent, wise, judicious, right, fair, equitable. **2.** moderate, tolerable. **3.** sane, rational, sober, sound. —**Ant.** unreasonable, illogical, irrational; immoderate, intolerable; unsound, insane.

reassure, v. encourage, hearten, embolden, bolster, comfort, inspirit. —**Ant.** disconcert, unnerve, dishearten, discourage.

rebel, n. **1.** insurgent, insurrectionist, mutineer, traitor. —adj. **2.** insurgent, mutinous, rebellious, insubordinate. —v. **3.** revolt. —**Ant.** patriot; loyal, obedient.

rebellion, n. resistance, defiance, insurrection, mutiny, sedition, revolution, revolt; insubordination, disobedience, contumacy.

rebellious, adj. defiant, insubordinate, mutinous, rebel, seditious, insurgent, refractory, disobedient, contumacious. —**Ant.** subordinate, obedient, patriotic.

rebuff, v. **1.** reject, snub, slight, spurn, cut, dismiss, drop, repulse, repel, brush off, high-hat, kiss off. —n. **2.** rejection, snub, dismissal, repulsion, brush-off, kiss-off. —**Ant.** welcome, embrace.

rebuke, v. **1.** reprove, reprimand, censure, upbraid, chide, reproach, reprehend, admonish, scold, remonstrate with. —n. **2.** reproof, reprimand, censure, reproach, reprehension, chiding, scolding, remonstration, expostulation. —**Ant.** praise.

recalcitrant, adj. resistant, resistive, disobedient, uncompliant, refractory, rebellious, contumacious, opposing. —**Ant.** obedient, compliant. —**Syn. Study.** See UNRULY.

recall, v. **1.** recollect, remember. **2.** call back, revoke, rescind, retract, withdraw, recant, repeal, annul, countermand, nullify. —n. **3.** memory, recollection. **4.** revocation, retraction, repeal, withdrawal, recantation, nullification; impeachment. —**Ant.** forget; enforce; ratify; sanction.

recapitulate, v. review, summarize, repeat, reiterate. —**Syn. Study.** See REPEAT.

recent, adj. late, modern, up-to-date, fresh, new, novel. —**Ant.** early, old, ancient. —**Syn.** See MODERN.

receptive, adj. responsive, open, open-minded, hospitable, welcoming, sympathetic, impressionable, susceptible, amenable, reachable, teachable, educable, influenceable, swayable, persuadable, suggestible. —**Ant.** resistant, recalcitrant.

recherché, adj. **1.** unusual, exotic, rare, novel, uncommon, unfamiliar, strange, foreign, unheard-of, mysterious. **2.** quaint, choice, exquisite, precious, special, superior, select, peerless, superlative. **3.** affected, overrefined, unnatural, artificial, put-on, stagy, theatrical. —**Ant.** down-to-earth, everyday.

reciprocal, adj. **1.** mutual, correlative, interchangeable. —n. **2.** equiva-

lent, counterpart, complement. —**Ant.** unequal.

recital, n. account, narrative, description, relation, history, story.

recite, v. **1.** repeat, relate, narrate, recount, describe. **2.** enumerate, count, number, detail, recapitulate. —**Syn. Study.** See RELATE.

reckless, adj. careless, rash, heedless, incautious, negligent, thoughtless, imprudent, improvident, remiss, inattentive, indifferent, regardless, unconcerned. —**Ant.** careful, heedful, cautious, thoughtful, provident.

reckon, v. **1.** count, compute, calculate, enumerate. **2.** esteem, consider, regard, account, deem, estimate, judge, evaluate.

reclaim, v. recover, bring or get back, regain, restore.

recoil, v. **1.** draw or shrink back, falter, flinch, quail. **2.** rebound, spring or fly back, react, reverberate. —**Ant.** advance. —**Syn. Study.** See WINCE.

recollect, v. recall, remember. —**Ant.** forget.

recommend, v. **1.** commend, approve, condone. **2.** advise, counsel. —**Ant.** condemn, disapprove.

recompense, v. **1.** repay, remunerate, reward, requite, compensate for. —n. **2.** compensation, payment, reward, requital, remuneration, repayment, amends, indemnification, satisfaction, retribution.

reconcile, v. **1.** content, win over, convince, persuade. **2.** pacify, conciliate, placate, propitiate, appease. **3.** compose, settle, adjust, make up, harmonize, make compatible or consistent. —**Ant.** dissuade; anger, arouse; disturb.

recondite, adj. **1.** abstruse, profound, deep. **2.** obscure, dim, mysterious, hidden, occult, dark, secret, concealed. —**Ant.** clear, obvious, patent.

record, v. **1.** set down, enter, register, enroll. —n. **2.** account, chronicle, history, note, register, memorandum.

recount, v. **1.** relate, narrate, tell, recite, describe, enumerate. —**Syn. Study.** See RELATE.

recourse, n. resource, resort, refuge, hope, expedient, means, device, help, strength, last resort, pis aller.

recover, v. **1.** regain, get again, reclaim, retrieve, restore. **2.** heal, mend, recuperate, rally.

recreant, adj. **1.** cowardly, craven, dastardly, base, pusillanimous, fainthearted, yellow. **2.** unfaithful, disloyal, false, faithless, untrue, treacherous, apostate. —n. **3.** coward, craven, dastard. **4.** apostate, traitor, renegade. —**Ant.** bold, brave; faithful, loyal, true; hero; patriot.

rectify, v. **1.** set right, correct, remedy, mend, emend, amend, improve, better, ameliorate. **2.** adjust, regulate, put right, straighten. —**Ant.** worsen, ruin.

redeem, v. **1.** buy or pay off, ransom, recover, buy back, repurchase. **2.** ransom, free, liberate, rescue, save. **3.** discharge, fulfill, perform.

redress, n. **1.** reparation, restitution, amends, indemnification, compensation, satisfaction, indemnity, restoration, remedy, relief, atonement, *Wiedergutmachung*. —v. **2.** remedy, repair, correct, amend, mend, emend, right, rectify, adjust, relieve, ease. —**Ant.** blame, punishment; damage. —**Syn. Study.** REDRESS, REPARATION, RESTITUTION suggest making amends or giving compensation for a wrong. REDRESS may refer either to the act of setting right an unjust situation or to satisfaction sought or gained for a wrong suffered: *the redress of grievances.* REPARATION refers to compensation or satisfaction for a wrong or loss inflicted. The word may have the moral idea of amends, but more frequently it refers to financial compensation: *to make reparation for one's neglect; the reparations demanded by the aggressor nations.* RESTITUTION means literally the giving back of what has been taken from the lawful owner, but may refer to restoring the equivalent of what has been taken: *The servant convicted of robbery made restitution to his employer.*

reduce, v. **1.** diminish, decrease, shorten, abridge, curtail, retrench, abate, lessen, attenuate, contract. **2.** subdue, suppress, subject, subjugate, conquer, vanquish, overcome, overpower, overthrow, depose. **3.** debase, depress, lower, degrade. **4.** control, adjust, correct. —**Ant.** increase; defend; honor, exalt, elevate.

redundant, See Syn. study at WORDY.

reel, See Syn. study at STAGGER.

refer, v. **1.** direct, commit, deliver, consign. **2.** assign, attribute, ascribe, impute. **3.** relate, apply, obtain, pertain, belong, respect. **4.** advert, allude, hint at.

referee, n. **1.** arbitrator, umpire, judge, arbiter. **2.** judge, arbitrate, umpire. —**Syn. Study.** See JUDGE.

reference, n. **1.** direction, allusion, referral, mention, citation. **2.** witness. **3.** testimonial, endorsement. **4.** relation, regard, respect, conern.

refined, adj. **1.** cultivated, polished, genteel, elegant, polite, courteous, courtly, civilized, well-bred. **2.** purified, clarified, distilled, strained. **3.** subtle. **4.** minute, precise, exact, exquisite. —**Ant.** unrefined, inelegant, impolite, discourteous; polluted, contaminated; obvious, direct, candid; general, inexact.

reflect, v. **1.** mirror, cast or throw back, rebound. **2.** reproduce, show, manifest, espouse. **3.** meditate, think, ponder, ruminate, cogitate, muse, deliberate, study, contemplate, consider. —**Syn. Study.** See STUDY.

reflection, n. **1.** image, representation, counterpart. **2.** consideration, deliberation, cogitation, rumination, meditation, study, comtemplation, thinking, musing. **3.** imputation, aspersion, reproach, censure. —**Ant.** original; thoughtlessness; praise.

reflective, adj. pensive, meditative, contemplative, thoughtful, pondering, deliberating, reflecting, reasoning, cogitating. —**Ant.** thoughtless, inconsiderate, unthinking. —**Syn. Study.** See PENSIVE.

reform, n. **1.** improvement, amendment, correction, reformation, betterment, amelioration. —v. **2.** better, rectify, correct, amend, emend, ameliorate, mend, improve, repair, restore. —**Ant.** deterioration; worsen, deteriorate.

reformation, n. improvement, betterment, correction, reform, amendment.

refractory, adj. stubborn, unmanageable, obstinate, perverse, mulish, headstrong, pigheaded, contumacious, intractable, disobedient, recalcitrant, cantankerous, ungovernable, unruly. —**Ant.** obedient, tractable. —**Syn. Study.** See UNRULY.

refrain, v. **1.** restrain, cease, abstain, desist, curb oneself, hold oneself back, withhold. —n. **2.** chorus, verse, theme, burden. —**Ant.** continue, persist.

refresh, v. **1.** reinvigorate, revive, stimulate, freshen, cheer, enliven, reanimate. **2.** restore, repair, renovate, renew, retouch. —**Ant.** dispirit, discourage.

refuge, n. **1.** shelter, protection, security, safety. **2.** asylum, retreat, sanctuary, hiding place, haven, harbor, stronghold, cloister.

refurbish, v. renovate, refurnish, redecorate, brighten.

refuse, v. **1.** decline, reject, spurn, turn down, deny, rebuff, repudiate. —n. **2.** rubbish, trash, waste, garbage; slag, lees, dregs, scum, sediment, marc, scoria, dross. —**Ant.** allow, permit, sanction, approve. —**Syn. Study.** REFUSE, REJECT, SPURN, DECLINE imply nonacceptance of something. REFUSE is direct and emphatic in expressing a determination not to accept what is offered or proposed: *to refuse an offer of help.* REJECT is even more forceful and definite: *to reject an author's manuscript.* To SPURN is to reject with scorn: *to spurn a bribe.* DECLINE is a milder and more courteous term: *to decline an invitation.*

refute, v. disprove, rebut, confute. —**Ant.** agree, concur.

regain, v. recover, recapture, repossess, retrieve, get back. —**Ant.** lose, miss.

regal, adj. royal, kingly, stately, princely, splendid. —**Ant.** servile.

regale, v. amuse, divert, entertain, beguile, refresh, please, delight, gladden, titillate, tickle.

regard, v. **1.** look upon, think of, consider, esteem, account, judge, deem, hold, suppose, estimate. **2.** respect, esteem, honor, revere, reverence, value. **3.** look at, observe, notice, see, remark, mark. **4.** relate to, concern, refer to, respect. —n. **5.** reference, relation. **6.** point, particular, detail, matter, consideration. **7.** thought, concern, attention. **8.** look, gaze, view. **9.** respect, deference, concern, esteem, estimation, consideration, reverence. **10.** liking, affection, interest, love. —**Ant.** disregard; disrespect, dishonor; inattention; dislike.

regardless, *adj.* inattentive, negligent, neglectful, indifferent, heedless, disregarding, ignoring, unmindful, unconcerned. —**Ant.** attentive, mindful.

region, *n.* part, area, division, district, section, portion, quarter, territory, locale, site, sphere, vicinity, vicinage, space, tract.

register, *n.* **1.** record, catalogue, account book, ledger, archive. **2.** roll, roster, catalogue, list, record, chronicle, schedule, annals. **3.** registry, entry, registration, enrollment. —*v.* **4.** enroll, list, record, catalogue, chronicle, enter. **5.** demonstrate, show, evince.

regret, *v.* **1.** deplore, lament, feel sorry about, grieve at, bemoan, bewail, rue, mourn for, repent. —*n.* **2.** sorrow, lamentation, grief. **3.** remorse, penitence, contrition, repentance, compunction. —**Ant.** rejoice; joy; unregeneracy. —**Syn. Study.** REGRET, REMORSE imply a sense of sorrow about events in the past, usu. wrongs committed or errors made. REGRET is a feeling of sorrow or disappointment for what has been done or not been done: *I remembered our bitter quarrel with regret.* REMORSE is a deep sense of guilt and mental anguish for having done wrong: *The killer seemed to have no remorse.*

regular, *adj.* **1.** usual, normal, customary. **2.** conforming, symmetrical, uniform, even, systematic, formal, fixed, orderly, invariant, unvarying, methodical, constant. **3.** recurrent, periodic, habitual, established, fixed. **4.** (*colloquial*) out-and-out, thorough, complete, unregenerate, perfect. —**Ant.** irregular.

regulate, *v.* control, direct, manage, rule, order, adjust, arrange, set, systematize, dispose, conduct, guide.

regulation, *n.* **1.** rule, order, direction, law, precept. **2.** direction, control, management, arrangement, ordering, disposition, disposal, adjustment. —**Ant.** misdirection, mismanagement.

rehearse, *v.* **1.** recite, act, practice, drill, train, repeat. **2.** relate, enumerate, recount, delineate, describe, portray, narrate, recapitulate. —**Ant.** extemporize.

reign, *n.* **1.** rule, sway, dominion, sovereignty, suzerainty, power, influence. —*v.* **2.** rule, govern, prevail, predominate, hold sway, influence. —**Ant.** obey.

reiterate, See Syn. study at REPEAT.

reject, *v.* **1.** refuse, repudiate, decline, deny, rebuff, repel, renounce. **2.** discard, throw away, exclude, eliminate; jettison. —*n.* **3.** second. —**Ant.** accept. —**Syn. Study.** See REFUSE.

rejoinder, *n.* answer, reply, riposte, response, replication, surrejoinder. —**Syn. Study.** See ANSWER.

relate, *v.* **1.** tell, recite, narrate, recount, rehearse, report, describe, delineate, detail, repeat. **2.** associate, connect, ally. —**Ant.** dissociate, disconnect, separate, alienate. —**Syn. Study.** RELATE, RECITE, RECOUNT mean to tell, report, or describe in some detail an occurrence or circumstance. To RELATE is to give an account of happenings, events, circumstances, etc.: *to relate one's adventures.* To RECITE may mean to give details consecutively, but more often applies to the repetition from memory of something learned with verbal exactness: *to recite a poem.* To RECOUNT is usu. to set forth consecutively the details of an occurrence, argument, experience, etc., to give an account in detail: *to recount an unpleasant experience.*

relation, *n.* **1.** connection, relationship, association, alliance, dependence. **2.** reference, regard, respect. **3.** narration, recitation, recital, description, rehearsal, relating, telling. **4.** narrative, account, recital, report, story, chronicle, tale, history. —**Ant.** independence.

relationship, *n.* **1.** relation, connection, association. **2.** kinship, affinity, family tie, consanguinity. —**Ant.** dissociation.

relax, *v.* **1.** loosen, slacken. **2.** diminish, mitigate, weaken, lessen, reduce, remit, abate, debilitate, enfeeble, enervate. **3.** ease, unbend, relent, soften. —**Ant.** tighten; intensify, increase; harden.

release, *v.* **1.** free, liberate, set free, loose, unloose, unfasten, set at liberty, discharge, deliver, dismiss. **2.** disengage, loose, extricate. **3.** proclaim, publish, announce. —*n.* **4.** liberation, deliverance, emancipation, discharge, freedom. —**Ant.** fasten, fetter, imprison; engage, involve; hide, conceal; incarceration, impris-

onment. —**Syn. Study.** RELEASE, FREE, DISMISS, DISCHARGE, LIBERATE all mean to let loose or let go. RELEASE and FREE both suggest a helpful action; they may be used of delivering a person from confinement or obligation: *to release prisoners; to free a student from certain course requirements.* DISMISS usually means to force to go unwillingly; however, it may also refer to giving permission to go: *to dismiss an employee; to dismiss a class.* DISCHARGE usually means to relieve of an obligation, office, etc.; it may also mean to permit to go: *The soldier was discharged. The hospital discharged the patient.* LIBERATE suggests particularly the deliverance from unjust punishment, oppression, or the like, and often means to set free through forcible or military action: *to liberate occupied territories.*

relentless, *adj.* unrelenting, inflexible, rigid, stern, severe, unbending, unforgiving, unappeasable, implacable, merciless, ruthless, unmerciful, pitiless, unpitying, hard, obdurate, adamant, unyielding, remorseless, inexorable. —**Ant.** relenting, flexible, soft, pliant, merciful, remorseful.

relevant, *adj.* pertinent, applicable, germane, apposite, appropriate, suitable, fitting, apt, proper, suited. —**Ant.** irrelevant. —**Syn. Study.** See APT.

reliable, *adj.* trustworthy, trusty, dependable, infallible, unfailing. —**Ant.** unreliable, untrustworthy, undependable.

relief, *n.* **1.** deliverance, alleviation, ease, assuagement, mitigation, comfort. **2.** help, assistance, aid, succor, redress, remedy. **3.** release, replacement. —**Ant.** intensity, intensification.

relieve, *v.* **1.** ease, alleviate, assuage, mitigate, allay, lighten, comfort, soothe, lessen, abate, diminish. **2.** unburden, disburden, ease. **3.** aid, help, assist, succor, remedy, support, sustain. —**Ant.** intensify, increase; burden.

religious, *adj.* **1.** pious, holy, devout, faithful, reverent, godly. **2.** conscientious, scrupulous, exacting, punctilious, strict, rigid, demanding. —*n.* **3.** monk, friar, nun. —**Ant.** irreligious, impious, unfaithful, irreverent; flexible, lenient. —**Syn. Study.** RELIGIOUS, DEVOUT, PIOUS indicate a spirit of reverence toward God. RELIGIOUS is a general word, indicating adherence to a particular set of beliefs and practices: *a religious family.* DEVOUT indicates a fervent spirit, usu. genuine and often independent of outward observance: *a deeply devout though unorthodox church member.* PIOUS implies constant attention to, and extreme conformity with, outward observances; it can also suggest sham or hypocrisy: *a pious hypocrite.*

relinquish, *v.* renounce, surrender, give up, resign, yield, cede, waive, forswear, forgo, abdicate, leave, forsake, desert, renounce, quit, abandon, let go, resign. —**Ant.** demand, require.

relish, *n.* **1.** liking, taste, enjoyment, appreciation, gusto, zest, inclination, bent, partiality, predilection, preference. **2.** condiment, appetizer. **3.** taste, flavor, savor. —*v.* **4.** like, enjoy, appreciate, prefer. —**Ant.** distaste, disfavor.

reluctant, *adj.* unwilling, disinclined, hesitant, loath, averse, indisposed. —**Ant.** willing, agreeable, amenable, unhesitating. —**Syn. Study.** RELUCTANT, LOATH, AVERSE describe disinclination toward something. RELUCTANT implies some sort of mental struggle, as between disinclination and sense of duty: *reluctant to expel students.* LOATH describes extreme disinclination: *loath to part from a friend.* AVERSE describes a long-held dislike or unwillingness, though not a particularly strong feeling: *averse to an idea; averse to getting up early.*

remain, *v.* **1.** continue, stay, last, abide, endure. **2.** wait, tarry, delay, stay, rest. —*n.* **3.** remnant, scrap, remainder, refuse, leavings, crumbs, orts, residue, relics. **4.** corpse, dead body, cadaver. —**Ant.** leave, depart.

remainder, *n.* residuum, remnant, excess, residue, rest, balance, surplus. —**Ant.** insufficiency, inadequacy.

remark, *v.* **1.** say, observe, note, perceive, heed, regard, notice. **2.** comment, say, state. —*n.* **3.** notice, regard, observation, heed, attention, consideration. **4.** comment, utterance, note, observation, declaration, assertion, asseveration, statement.

—**Ant.** disregard, ignore; inattention.

remarkable, *adj.* notable, conspicuous, unusual, extraordinary, noteworthy, striking, wonderful, uncommon, strange, rare, distinguished, prominent, singular. —**Ant.** common, usual, ordinary.

remedy, *n.* **1.** cure, relief, medicine, treatment, restorative, specific, medicament, medication, ointment, nard, balm. **2.** antidote, corrective, antitoxin, counteraction. —*v.* **3.** cure, heal, put or set right, restore, recondition, repair, redress. **4.** counteract, remove, correct, right. —**Ant.** sicken, worsen.

remember, *v.* **1.** recall, recollect. **2.** retain, memorize, keep or bear in mind. —**Ant.** forget.

remembrance, *n.* **1.** recollection, reminiscence; memory. **2.** keepsake, memento, souvenir, remembrancer, trophy, token, memorial.

remiss, *adj.* **1.** negligent, careless, thoughtless, lax, neglectful; inattentive, heedless. **2.** languid, sluggish, dilatory; slothful, slow, tardy, lax. —**Ant.** careful, thoughtful, attentive; energetic, quick.

remission, *n.* **1.** pardon, forgiveness, absolution, indulgence, exoneration, discharge. **2.** abatement, diminution, lessening, relaxation, moderation, mitigation. **3.** release, relinquishment. **4.** decrease, subsidence, respite, stoppage, pause, interruption, relief, hiatus, suspense, suspension, abatement. —**Ant.** blame, censure, conviction; increase, intensification; increase.

remit, *v.* **1.** transmit, send, forward. **2.** pardon, release, forgive, excuse, overlook, absolve. **3.** slacken, abate, diminish, relax. **4.** return, give back, restore, replace. **5.** put off, postpone. —**Ant.** retain, keep, hold; condemn; increase.

remnant, *n.* **1.** remainder, remains, residue, residuum, rest. **2.** trace, vestige.

remorse, *n.* regret, compunction, penitence, contrition. —**Ant.** conviction, assertion, assertiveness. —**Syn. Study.** See REGRET.

remorseful, *adj.* regretful, penitent, contrite, repentant. —**Ant.** impenitent.

remorseless, *adj.* relentless, pitiless, uncompassionate, unrelenting, merciless, unmerciful, ruthless, cruel, savage, implacable, inexorable. —**Ant.** merciful, relenting.

remote, *adj.* **1.** distant, far apart, far off, removed, alien, foreign, unrelated, unconnected. **2.** slight, faint, inconsiderable. **3.** separated, abstracted. —**Ant.** close, near, connected, related; considerable, substantial.

remove, *v.* **1.** replace, displace, dislodge, transfer, transport, carry. **2.** take, withdraw, separate, extract, eliminate. **3.** kill, assassinate, do away with, destroy, murder.

rend, *v.* tear apart, split, divide, rip, rive, sunder, sever, cleave, chop, fracture, tear, dissever, crack, snap, lacerate, rupture.

render, *v.* **1.** make, cause to be, cause to become. **2.** do, perform. **3.** furnish, supply, give, contribute, afford. **4.** exhibit, show, demonstrate. **5.** present, give, assign. **6.** deliver. **7.** translate, interpret. **8.** give back, restore, return. **9.** give up, surrender, cede, yield.

renew, *v.* **1.** restore, replenish, restock. **2.** re-create, rejuvenate, regenerate, restore, reinstate, renovate, repair, mend. **3.** revive, reestablish. —**Syn. Study.** RENEW, RENOVATE, REPAIR, RESTORE suggest making something the way it formerly was. RENEW means to bring back to an original condition of freshness and vigor: *to renew one's faith.* RENOVATE means to bring back to a good condition, or to make as good as new: *to renovate an old house.* To REPAIR is to put into good or sound condition after damage, wear and tear, etc.: *to repair the roof of a house.* To RESTORE is to bring back to a former, original, or normal condition or position: *to restore a painting.*

renounce, *v.* **1.** give up, put aside, forsake, forgo, relinquish, abandon, forswear, leave, quit, resign, abdicate. **2.** repudiate, disown, disclaim, reject, disavow, deny, recant. —**Ant.** claim, accept, desire.

renovate, See Syn. study at RENEW.

renown, *n.* repute, fame, celebrity, glory, distinction, note, eminence, reputation, name, honor. —**Ant.** disrepute, infamy.

renowned, See Syn. study at FAMOUS.

rent, *n.* **1.** rental, return, payment. **2.** tear, split, fissure, slit, crack, crevice, cleft, rift, gap, opening, rip, rupture, breach, break, fracture, laceration. **3.** schism, separation, disunion, breach. —*v.* **4.** lease, let, hire. —**Syn. Study.** See HIRE.

repair, *v.* **1.** restore, mend, remodel, renew, renovate, patch, amend, fix. **2.** make good, make up for, remedy, retrieve. **3.** make amends for, atone for, redress. —**Ant.** break, destroy, ruin. —**Syn. Study.** See RENEW.

reparation, *n.* **1.** (usually plural) amends, indemnification, atonement, restitution, satisfaction, compensation, Wiedergutmachung. **2.** restoration, repair, renewal, renovation. —**Ant.** destruction. —**Syn. Study.** See REDRESS.

repay, *v.* payback, return, reimburse, indemnify, refund.

repeat, *v.* **1.** reiterate, recapitulate, iterate, recite, rehearse, relate. **2.** reproduce, echo, reecho, redo. —*n.* **3.** repetition, iteration. —**Syn. Study.** REPEAT, RECAPITULATE, REITERATE refer to saying or doing a thing more than once. To REPEAT is to say or do something over again: *to repeat an order.* To RECAPITULATE is to restate in brief form often by repeating the principal points in a discourse: *to recapitulate a news broadcast.* To REITERATE is to say (or, sometimes, to do) something over and over again, often for emphasis: *to reiterate a refusal.*

repel, *v.* **1.** repulse, parry, ward off. **2.** resist, withstand, rebuff, oppose, confront. **3.** reject, decline, refuse, discourage. —**Ant.** attract; approve, accept.

repent, *v.* regret, atone.

repentance, *n.* compunction, contrition; contriteness, penitence, remorse, sorrow, regret. —**Ant.** impenitence.

replace, *v.* **1.** supersede, supplant, substitute, succeed. **2.** restore, return, make good, refund, repay; replenish. —**Syn. Study.** REPLACE, SUPERSEDE, SUPPLANT refer to putting one thing or person in place of another. To REPLACE is to take the place of, to succeed: *Ms. Jones will replace Mr. Smith as president.* SUPERSEDE implies that that which is replacing another is an improvement: *The computer has superseded the typewriter.* SUPPLANT implies that that which takes the other's place has ousted the former holder and usurped the position or function, esp. by art or fraud: *to supplant a former favorite.*

reply, *v.* **1.** answer, respond, echo, rejoin. —*n.* **2.** answer, rejoinder, riposte, replication, surrejoinder, response. —**Syn. Study.** See ANSWER.

represent, *v.* **1.** designate, stand for, denote, symbolize, exemplify, image, depict, express, portray, personate, delineate, figure, present. **2.** set forth, describe, state.

repress, *v.* **1.** check, suppress, subdue, put down, quell, quash, reduce, crush. **2.** check, restrain, curb, bridle, control. —**Ant.** foster, support, help, aid.

reprieve, See Syn. study at PARDON.

reprimand, *v.* **1.** upbraid, admonish, censure, berate, rebuke, chide, scold, dress down; *Informal* bawl out, chew out —**Syn. Study.** REPRIMAND, UPBRAID, ADMONISH, CENSURE mean to criticize or find fault with someone for behavior deemed reprehensible. REPRIMAND implies a formal criticism, as by an official or person in authority: *The lawyer was reprimanded by the judge.* UPBRAID suggests relatively severe criticism, but of a less formal kind: *The minister upbraided the parishioners for their poor church attendance.* ADMONISH refers to a more gentle warning or expression of disapproval, often including suggestions for improvement: *I admonished the children to make less noise.* CENSURE suggests harsh, vehement criticism, often from an authoritative source: *The legislators voted to censure their fellow senator.*

reprisal, *n.* **1.** retaliation, revenge, vengeance, redress, vendetta. —**Syn. Study.** See REVENGE.

reproach, *v.* **1.** chide, abuse, reprimand, condemn, criticize, rebuke, scold, reprove, call to account, censure, blame, find fault with, shame, abash, discredit, reprehend, upbraid. —*n.* **2.** blame, censure, upbraiding, reproof, abuse, vilification, discredit, reprehension, rebuke, criticism, remonstrance, condemnation, expostulation, disapproval, disapprobation. **3.** disgrace, dishonor, shame, disrepute, odium, scandal, obloquy, opprobrium, ignominy, indignity, in-

famy, insult, scorn, offense. —**Ant.** praise, honor.

reproduce, *v.* **1.** copy, duplicate, repeat, imitate, represent. **2.** generate, propagate, beget. —**Ant.** initiate, originate.

reprove, *v.* rebuke, blame, censure, reproach, reprimand, upbraid, chide, lecture, reprehend, admonish. Remonstrate or expostulate with. —**Ant.** praise; exonerate.

repudiate, *v.* **1.** reject, disclaim, disavow, disown, discard, renounce. **2.** condemn, disapprove. —**Ant.** accept; approve, commend.

repugnance, *n.* **1.** objection, distaste, aversion, dislike, reluctance, hatred, hostility, antipathy. **2.** contradictoriness, inconsistency, contrariety, unsuitableness, irreconcilableness, incompatibility. —**Ant.** attractiveness, attraction, liking, sympathy; consistency, compatibility.

repugnant, *adj.* **1.** distasteful, objectionable, offensive. **2.** opposing, objecting, protesting, averse, unfavorable, antagonistic, inimical, adverse, contrary, hostile, opposed. —**Ant.** attractive, tasteful; favorable, amiable.

reputation, *n.* **1.** estimation, regard, repute, standing, position, name, character. **2.** credit, esteem, honor, fame, celebrity, distinction, renown. —**Ant.** disrepute; dishonor, infamy. —**Syn. Study.** REPUTATION and CHARACTER are often confused. REPUTATION, however, is the word which refers to the position one occupies or the standing that one has in the opinion of others, in respect to attainments, integrity, and the like: *a fine reputation; a reputation for honesty.* CHARACTER is the combination of moral and other traits which make one the kind of person one actually is (as contrasted with what others think of one): *Honesty is an outstanding trait of her character.*

repute, *n.* **1.** estimation, reputation. **2.** name, distinction, credit, honor. —*v.* **3.** consider, esteem, account, regard, hold, deem, reckon. —**Ant.** disrepute; dishonor; condemn, scorn.

request, *n.* **1.** solicitation, petition, suit, entreaty, supplication, prayer. **2.** demand. —*v.* **3.** ask for, sue, petition, entreat, beg, supplicate, solicit, beseech, require.

require, *v.* **1.** need, demand, request, order, enjoin, direct, ask. **2.** obligate, necessitate, want, need, call for. —**Ant.** forgo. —**Syn. Study.** See LACK.

requirement, *n.* **1.** requisite, need, claim, requisition, prerequisite, demand. **2.** mandate, order, command, directive, injunction, ukase, charge, claim, precept. —**Syn. Study.** REQUIREMENT, REQUISITE refer to that which is necessary. A REQUIREMENT is some quality or performance demanded of a person in accordance with certain fixed regulations: *requirements for admission to college.* A REQUISITE is not imposed from outside; it is a factor that is judged necessary according to the nature of things, or to the circumstances of the case: *Efficiency is a requisite for success in business.* REQUISITE may also refer to a concrete object judged necessary: *the requisites for perfect grooming.*

requisite, *adj.* **1.** required, necessary, essential, indispensable, needed, needful. —*n.* **2.** necessity, requirement. —**Ant.** dispensable, unnecessary; luxury, superfluity. —**Syn. Study.** See NECESSARY. See also REQUIREMENT.

requite, *v.* **1.** repay, remunerate, reimburse, recompense, pay, satisfy, compensate. **2.** retaliate, avenge, revenge, punish. —**Ant.** dissatisfy; forgive.

rescue, *v.* **1.** save, deliver, liberate, set free, release, redeem, ransom, extricate; recover, preserve. —*n.* **2.** liberation, release, redemption, ransom, recovery, deliverance. —**Ant.** incarceration, imprisonment.

research, *n.* **1.** inquiry, investigation, examination, scrutiny, study. —*v.* **2.** investigate, study, inquire, examine, scrutinize.

resemblance, *n.* **1.** similarity, likeness, analogy, semblance, similitude. **2.** appearance, representation, semblance, image. —**Ant.** dissimilarity; misrepresentation.

reserve, *v.* **1.** keep back, save, retain, husband, keep, hold, store up. **2.** set apart, set aside, bank. —*n.* **3.** reservation, qualification, exception. **4.** store, stock, supply. **5.** self-restraint, restraint, reticence, silence, taciturnity, constraint, coldness, coolness, retention. —**Ant.** splurge, squander, waste; prodigality; warmth, enthusiasm. —**Syn. Study.** See KEEP.

reside, v. **1.** dwell, abide, live, sojourn, stay, lodge, inhabit, remain. **2.** abide, lie, be present, habituate, inhere, exist.

residence, n. **1.** dwelling, house, home, habitation, domicile, mansion, manse. **2.** habitancy, stay, abode, sojourn, inhabitancy. —**Syn. Study.** See HOUSE.

residue, n. remainder, rest, remains, residuum; surplus.

resign, v. **1.** give up, submit, yield, cede, surrender, abdicate, relinquish, forgo, abandon, forsake, quit, leave. **2.** renounce, withdraw.

resignation, n. **1.** abdication, abandonment, surrender, relinquishment. **2.** submission, meekness, patience, acquiescence, endurance, compliance, forbearance, sufferance. —**Ant.** application; boldness, recalcitrance.

resilient, adj. rebounding, elastic, recoiling; buoyant, cheerful. —**Ant.** rigid, inflexible, inelastic.

resist, v. **1.** withstand, strive against, oppose, impugn, confront, assail, attack, counteract, rebuff. **2.** refrain or abstain from. —**Ant.** defend; continue. —**Syn. Study.** See OPPOSE.

resolute, adj. resolved, firm, steadfast, determined, set, opinionated, purposeful, earnest, sincere, fixed, unflinching, unwavering, inflexible, hardy, unshaken, bold, undaunted, pertinacious. —**Ant.** weak, feeble, frail, flexible, lenient. —**Syn. Study.** See EARNEST.

resolve, v. **1.** fix or settle on, determine, decide, confirm, establish. **2.** break up, disintegrate, separate, analyze, reduce. **3.** convert, transform, reduce, change. **4.** explain, explicate, solve. **5.** clear, dispel, scatter, disperse. —n. **6.** resolution, determination, decision, purpose, intention. —**Ant.** unite, amalgamate; consolidate; indecision. —**Syn. Study.** See DECIDE.

respect, n. **1.** particular, detail, point, regard, feature, matter. **2.** relation, reference, connection, regard. **3.** esteem, deference, regard, estimation, veneration, reverence, homage, honor, admiration, approbation, approval, affection, feeling. **4.** discrimination, bias, partiality, prejudice, preference, inclination. —v. **5.** honor, revere, reverence, esteem, venerate, regard, consider, defer to, admire, adulate, adore, love. **6.** regard, heed, attend, notice, consider. **7.** regard, relate to, refer to. —**Ant.** disregard. —**Syn. Study.** RESPECT, ESTEEM, VENERATION imply recognition of a person's worth, or of a personal quality, trait, or ability. RESPECT is commonly the result of admiration and approbation, together with deference: to feel respect for a great scholar. ESTEEM is deference combined with admiration and often with affection: to hold a friend in great esteem. VENERATION is an almost religious attitude of reverence and love, such as one feels for persons or things of outstanding superiority, endeared by long association: veneration for noble traditions.

respectable, adj. **1.** estimable, worthy, honorable. **2.** proper, decent, honest, respected, reputable. **3.** fair, fairly good, moderate, middling, passable, tolerable. **4.** considerable, large, moderate. —**Ant.** unworthy, dishonorable; improper; poor, intolerable; small, insignificant.

respectful, adj. courteous, polite, well-mannered, well-bred, courtly, decorous, civil, deferential. —**Ant.** disrespectful, discourteous, impolite.

respite, n. **1.** relief, delay, hiatus, cessation, postponement, interval, rest, recess. **2.** stay, reprieve, suspension. —v. **3.** relieve, delay, alleviate, postpone, put off, suspend. —**Ant.** intensity, perseverance.

response, n. answer, reply, rejoinder, replication. —**Syn. Study.** See ANSWER.

responsible, adj. **1.** accountable, answerable, liable. **2.** chargeable, blamable, censurable. **3.** capable, able, reliable, solvent, trustworthy, trusty, dutiful, honest. —**Ant.** irresponsible; innocent; incapable, unable, unreliable.

restful, adj. calm, tranquil, peaceful, undisturbed, serene, pacific. —**Ant.** perturbed, disturbed, agitated.

restitution, n. reparation, redress, indemnification, restoration, recompense, amends, compensation, remuneration, requital, satisfaction, repayment, Wiedergutmachung. —**Syn. Study.** See REDRESS.

restive, adj. **1.** uneasy, restless,

nervous, impatient, ill at ease, recalcitrant, unquiet. **2.** refractory, disobedient, obstinate, mulish, stubborn, pigheaded. —**Ant.** restful, patient, quiet, serene; obedient.

restore, v. **1.** reestablish, replace, reinstate, renew. **2.** renew, renovate, repair, mend. **3.** return, give back. **4.** reproduce, reconstruct, rebuild. —**Ant.** disestablish, destroy; break, ruin; accept, receive; raze. —**Syn. Study.** See RENEW.

restrain, v. **1.** check, keep down, repress, curb, bridle, suppress, hold, keep, constrain. **2.** restrict, circumscribe, confine, hinder, abridge, narrow. —**Ant.** unbridle; broaden, widen. —**Syn. Study.** See CHECK.

restrict, v. confine, limit, restrain, abridge, curb, circumscribe, bound. —**Ant.** free, broaden, disencumber.

result, n. **1.** outcome, consequence, effect, conclusion, issue, event, end, termination, product, fruit. —v. **2.** spring, arise, proceed, follow, flow, come, issue, ensue, rise, originate. **3.** terminate, end, resolve, eventuate. —**Ant.** cause. —**Syn. Study.** See FOLLOW. See also EFFECT.

retain, v. **1.** keep, hold, withhold, preserve, detain, reserve. **2.** remember, recall. **3.** hire, engage, employ. —**Ant.** loose, lose; forget; disengage, fire. —**Syn. Study.** See KEEP.

retaliate, v. avenge, requite, return, repay, revenge. —**Ant.** forgive, pardon.

retard, v. slow, delay, hinder, impede, decelerate, clog, obstruct, check. —**Ant.** speed, expedite, accelerate.

reticent, adj. taciturn, silent, reserved, quiet, uncommunicative. —**Ant.** voluble, communicative.

retire, v. withdraw, leave, depart, go away, retreat, retrograde, retrocede, fall back, recede; retract. —**Ant.** advance, attack.

retired, adj. withdrawn, secluded, sequestered, cloistered, isolated, enisled, removed, apart, solitary, abstracted. —**Ant.** advanced.

retort, v. **1.** reply, respond, return, answer, retaliate, rejoin. —n. **2.** reply, response, answer, riposte, rejoinder, surrejoinder, replication; repartee. —**Syn. Study.** See ANSWER.

retreat, n. **1.** departure, withdrawal, retirement, seclusion, privacy, solitude. **2.** shelter, refuge, asylum. —v. **3.** retire, retrocede, retrograde, withdraw, leave, depart, draw back. **4.** recede, slope backward. —**Ant.** advance.

retribution, n. requital, revenge, vengeance, retaliation, repayment, reward, recompense, compensation. —**Ant.** forgiveness, pardon. —**Syn. Study.** See REVENGE.

retrieve, v. **1.** recover, regain, restore. **2.** make good, repair, make amends for. **3.** rescue, save.

reveal, v. make known, communicate, disclose, divulge, unveil, uncover, discover, publish, impart, tell, announce, proclaim. —**Ant.** conceal, hide, veil, cover.

revenge, n. **1.** vengeance, retaliation, requital, reprisal, retribution. **2.** vindictiveness, revengefulness, vengefulness. —v. **3.** avenge, retaliate, requite, vindicate. —**Ant.** forgiveness, pardon. —**Syn. Study.** REVENGE, REPRISAL, RETRIBUTION, VENGEANCE suggest a punishment or injury inflicted in return for one received. REVENGE is the carrying out of a bitter desire to injure another for a wrong done to oneself or to those who are close to oneself: to plot revenge for a friend's betrayal. REPRISAL is used specifically in the context of warfare; it means retaliation against an enemy: The guerrillas expected reprisals for the raid. RETRIBUTION usu. suggests deserved punishment for some evil done: a just retribution for wickedness. VENGEANCE is usu. vindictive, furious revenge: He swore vengeance against his enemies.

revengeful, adj. vindictive, spiteful, malevolent, resentful, malicious, malignant, implacable. —**Ant.** forgiving, benevolent.

reverence, n. **1.** worship, veneration, respect, homage, awe. **2.** bow, curtsy, obeisance. —v. **3.** venerate, revere, honor, adore, adulate. —**Ant.** disrespect; despise.

reverse, adj. **1.** opposite, contrary, converse. —n. **2.** opposite, contrary, converse, counterpart. **3.** back, rear, hind. **4.** check, misfortune, defeat, mishap, misadventure, affliction. —v. **5.** transpose, invert. **6.** alter, change. **7.** revoke, annul, repeal, veto, rescind, overthrow, countermand. —**Ant.** same.

review, n. **1.** critique, criticism,

judgment, survey. **2.** rereading, study, reconsideration, reexamination. **3.** inspection, examination, investigation. —v. **4.** survey, inspect, criticize.

revive, v. **1.** reactivate, revitalize, reanimate, resuscitate, revivify, reinvigorate, reinspirit. **2.** bring back, quicken, renew, refresh, rouse. **3.** recover, recall, reawake. —**Ant.** kill; languish, die.

revoke, v. take back, withdraw, annul, cancel, reverse, rescind, repeal, retract.

revolt, v. **1.** rebel, mutiny, rise. **2.** disgust, repel, shock, nauseate, sicken. —n. **3.** insurrection, rebellion, mutiny, revolution, uprising, overthrow, sedition. **4.** aversion, disgust, loathing. —**Ant.** attract, delight.

revolution, n. **1.** overthrow, change, revolt, rebellion, mutiny. **2.** cycle, rotation, circuit, turn, round.

revolve, v. **1.** rotate, spin, circulate, turn, roll. **2.** orbit, circle. **3.** consider, think about, ruminate upon, ponder, reflect upon, brood over, study. —**Syn. Study.** See TURN.

reward, n. **1.** recompense, prize, desert, compensation, pay, remuneration, requital, merit. **2.** bounty, premium, bonus. —v. **3.** recompense, requite, compensate, pay, remunerate.

ribald, adj. scurrilous, offensive, coarse, mocking, abusive, wanton, irreverent, loose, indecent, low, base, mean, vile, obscene, gross, filthy, dirty, vulgar. —**Ant.** pure, inoffensive, refined, polished, elegant.

rich, adj. **1.** well-to-do, wealthy, moneyed, opulent, affluent. **2.** abounding, abundant, bounteous, bountiful, fertile, plenteous, plentiful, copious, ample, luxuriant, productive, fruitful, prolific. **3.** valuable, valued, precious, costly, estimable, sumptuous. **4.** dear, expensive, high-priced, elegant. **5.** deep, strong, vivid, bright, gay. **6.** full, mellow, pear-shaped, harmonious, sweet. **7.** fragrant, aromatic. —**Ant.** poor, impoverished; scarce, barren, sterile; cheap; weak; dull; flat; noisome.

riddle, n. **1.** conundrum, puzzle, enigma, poser, question, problem. **2.** sieve, colander, strainer. —v. **3.** perforate, pierce, puncture.

ridicule, n. **1.** derision, mockery, gibes, jeers, taunts, raillery, satire, burlesque, sarcasm, sneer, banter, wit, irony. —v. **2.** deride, banter, rally, chaff, twit, mock, taunt, make fun of, sneer at, burlesque, satirize, rail at, lampoon, jeer or scoff at. —**Ant.** praise, honor; respect. —**Syn. Study.** RIDICULE, DERIDE, MOCK, TAUNT mean to make fun of a person. To RIDICULE is to make fun of, either playfully or with the intention of humiliating: to ridicule a pretentious person. To DERIDE is to laugh at scornfully: a student derided for acting silly. To MOCK is to make fun of by imitating the appearance or actions of another: She mocked the seriousness of his expression. To TAUNT is to call attention to something annoying or humiliating, usu. maliciously and in the presence of others: The bully taunted the smaller boy.

ridiculous, adj. absurd, preposterous, laughable, nonsensical, funny, ludicrous, droll, comical, farcical. —**Ant.** sensible. —**Syn. Study.** See ABSURD.

rife, adj. **1.** common, prevalent, widespread, prevailing. **2.** current. **3.** abundant, plentiful, numerous, plenteous, abounding, multitudinous. —**Ant.** rare, unusual; scarce, scanty.

right, adj. **1.** just, good, equitable, fair, upright, honest, lawful. **2.** correct, proper, suitable, fit, appropriate, convenient, becoming, de rigueur, befitting, seemly, comme il faut. **3.** correct, true, accurate. **4.** sound, sane, normal. **5.** healthy. **6.** principal, front, upper, obverse. **7.** genuine, legitimate, rightful. **8.** straight, true, direct. —n. **9.** claim, title, due, ownership. **10.** virtue, justice, fairness, integrity, equity, equitableness, uprightness, rectitude, goodness, lawfulness. —adv. **11.** straight, directly. **12.** quite, completely. **13.** immediately. **14.** precisely, exactly, just, truly, actually. **15.** uprightly, righteously, rightfully, lawfully, rightly, justly, fairly, equitably. **16.** properly, fittingly, appropriately, fitly, suitably. **17.** advantageously, favorably, well. —**Ant.** wrong.

righteous, adj. moral, upright, justifiable, virtuous, good, honest, fair, right, equitable. —**Ant.** immoral, bad, dishonest, unfair.

rigid, adj. **1.** stiff, unyielding, un-

bending, firm, hard, inflexible. **2.** unmoving, immovable, static, stationary. **3.** inflexible, strict, severe, stern, rigorous, austere, unbending, harsh, stringent, inelastic. —**Ant.** flexible, soft; compliant, elastic, lenient. —**Syn. Study.** See STRICT.

rigorous, adj. **1.** rigid, severe, harsh, stern, austere, strict, hard, inflexible, stiff, unyielding, stringent. **2.** exact, demanding, finical, accurate. **3.** inclement, bitter, severe, sharp. —**Ant.** flexible, soft; inaccurate; fair, mild, bland. —**Syn. Study.** See STRICT.

rim, n. **1.** edge, border, lip, margin, brim, boundary, verge, skirt, confine. —v. **2.** edge, border, bound, margin, confine. —**Ant.** center, inside. —**Syn.** RIM, BRIM refer to the boundary of a circular or curved area. A RIM is a line or surface bounding such an area; an edge or border: the rim of a glass. BRIM usu. means the inside of the rim, at the top of a hollow object (except of a hat), and is used particularly when the object contains something: The cup was filled to the brim.

ring, n. **1.** circlet, loop, hoop; annulus. **2.** arena, rink, circle. **3.** competition, contest. **4.** clique, coterie, set, combination, confederacy, league; gang, mob, syndicate. —v. **5.** surround, encircle, circle. **6.** peal, resonate, vibrate, reverberate, resound, reecho; tinkle, jingle, jangle. **7.** announce, proclaim, usher in or out, summon, call, signal.

riot, n. **1.** outbreak, disorder, brawl, uproar, tumult, disturbance, commotion, fray, melee, altercation. **2.** disorder, confusion. **3.** revelry, festivity. —v. **4.** create disorder, disturb the peace, create a disturbance, brawl, fight. **5.** carouse, revel.

rip, v. **1.** cut, tear, tear apart, slash, slit, rend. —n. **2.** rent, tear, laceration, cut.

ripe, adj. **1.** mature, mellow, grown, aged. **2.** ruddy, full, complete, consummate, perfect, finished. **3.** developed, ready, prepared, set. —**Ant.** immature; imperfect, unfinished; undeveloped, unprepared.

ripen, v. mature, age, grow, develop, mellow, grow up, maturate, evolve, blossom, flower, come into season.

ripple, n. **1.** wave, undulate, ruffle, purl. **2.** agitate, curl, dimple. —n. **3.** wavelet, wave, ruffling, undulation.

rise, v. **1.** get up, arise, stand, stand up. **2.** revolt, rebel, oppose, resist. **3.** spring up, grow. **4.** come into existence, appear, come forth. **5.** occur, happen. **6.** originate, issue, arise, come up, be derived, proceed. **7.** move upward, ascend, mount, arise. **8.** succeed, be promoted, advance. **9.** swell, puff up, enlarge, increase. **10.** adjourn, close. —n. **11.** rising, ascent, mounting. **12.** advance, elevation, promotion. **13.** increase, augmentation, enlargement, swelling. **14.** source, origin, beginning. —**Ant.** sink; support; die; fail; decrease, deflate; open; end.

risible, adj. funny, amusing, comic, comical, laugh-provoking, laughable, droll, humorous, hilarious, rich, ludicrous, absurd, ridiculous, farcical, priceless, hysterical. —**Ant.** sober, solemn.

risk, n. **1.** hazard, chance, dangerous chance, venture, peril, jeopardy, exposure. —v. **2.** hazard, take a chance, endanger, imperil; jeopardize. **3.** venture upon, dare.

rite, n. ceremony, procedure, practice, observance, form, usage.

ritual, n. **1.** ceremony, rite. —adj. **2.** ceremonial, formal, sacramental. —**Ant.** unceremonious, informal.

rival, n. **1.** competitor, contestant, emulator, antagonist, opponent. —adj. **2.** competing, competitive, opposed, emulating, opposing. —v. **3.** compete or contend with, oppose. **4.** match, equal, emulate. —**Ant.** ally, friend; associate with.

roam, v. walk, go, travel, ramble, wander, peregrinate, rove, stray, stroll, range; prowl.

roar, v. **1.** cry, bellow, bawl, shout, yell, vociferate. **2.** laugh. **3.** resound, boom, thunder, peal.

rob, v. **1.** rifle, sack, steal, deprive, plunder, pillage, pilfer, pinch, despoil. **2.** defraud, cheat, deprive, rook.

robber, n. thief, highwayman, footpad, second-story man, kleptomaniac, shoplifter, pilferer, brigand, bandit, marauder, freebooter, pirate, picaroon. —**Syn. Study.** See THIEF.

robust, adj. **1.** sturdy, healthy, strong, hardy, vigorous, stalwart, hale, dusty, powerful, firm, sound, athletic, brawny, muscular, sinewy. **2.** rough, rude, coarse, boisterous,

rambunctious, wild. —**Ant.** weak, feeble, unhealthy; refined, cultivated.

rogue, n. rascal, scamp, rapscallion, knave, mischief-maker, villain, scoundrel, scapegrace, trickster, swindler, cheat, mountebank, quack, sharper. —**Syn. Study.** See KNAVE.

roil, v. **1.** muddy, foul, dirty, pollute, befoul, contaminate. **2.** disturb, agitate, perturbate, stir, stir up, churn, whip, whip up. **3.** rile, anger, irritate, irk, vex, peeve, provoke, gripe. —**Ant.** clarify, calm.

roll, v. **1.** turn, revolve, rotate, wheel, gyrate, spin, whirl, bowl. **2.** wave, undulate. **3.** sway, rock, swing, list, tilt. **4.** wrap, enfold, envelop, cover. —n. **5.** scroll, document. **6.** register, list, inventory, catalogue, roster. **7.** cylinder, roller, spindle. —**Syn. Study.** See LIST.

roly-poly, adj. fat, plump, rotund, five-by-five, pudgy. —**Ant.** scrawny, gaunt, skinny.

romance, n. **1.** novel, roman, tale, story, fiction, (slang) bodice ripper. **2.** fancy, extravagance, exaggeration; falsehood, fable, fiction, lie. **3.** love affair, amour.

romantic, adj. **1.** fanciful, unpractical, quixotic, extravagant, exaggerated, wild, imaginative, unrealistic, fantastic. **2.** improbable, imaginary, fantastic, chimerical, fictitious, fabulous, unreal. **3.** picturesque. —**Ant.** practical, realistic; probable.

romp, v. **1.** play, frolic, gambol, frisk, cavort, caper, rollick, revel, roister, lark about, kick up one's heels. —n. **2.** gambol, frolic, caper, revel, escapade. **3.** triumph, easy victory, walkover, walkaway, runaway, pushover.

rook, n. **1.** crow, raven. **2.** castle. **3.** sharper, cardsharp, cheat, swindler. —v. **4.** cheat, swindle, rob, fleece, defraud.

rosy, adj. **1.** pink, reddish, roseate. **2.** red, rubicund, flushed, blooming, ruddy, healthy. **3.** bright, promising, cheerful, optimistic. —**Ant.** dark, dim, cheerless, pessimistic.

rot, v. **1.** decompose, decay, mold, molder, putrefy, spoil, corrupt. **2.** corrupt, degenerate. —n. **3.** decay, putrefaction, decomposition, corruption, mold. —**Ant.** purify. —**Syn. Study.** See DECAY.

rotate, v. turn, spin, revolve, wheel, whirl. —**Syn. Study.** See TURN.

rotten, adj. **1.** decomposed, decayed, putrefied, putrescent, putrid, tainted, foul, miasmatic, noxious, ill-smelling, fetid, rank. **2.** corrupt, offensive, amoral, immoral. **3.** contemptible, disgusting, unwholesome, treacherous, dishonest, deceitful, corrupt. **4.** soft, yielding, friable; unsound, defective. —**Ant.** pure; moral; wholesome, honest; hard, inflexible; sound.

roué, n. debauchee, rake, profligate.

rough, adj. **1.** uneven, bumpy, irregular, rugged, jagged, scabrous, craggy. **2.** shaggy, coarse, hairy, bristly, hirsute. **3.** violent, disorderly, wild, boisterous, turbulent, riotous; sharp, severe, harsh. **4.** disturbed, stormy, agitated, tempestuous, inclement. **5.** harsh, grating, jarring, noisy, cacophonous, inharmonious, discordant, flat, raucous. **6.** uncultured, indelicate, unrefined, impolite, uncivil, unpolished, rude, inconvenient, uncomfortable, crude, coarse. **7.** plain, imperfect, unpolished, uncorrected, unfinished. **8.** vague, inexact, incomplete. **9.** crude, unwrought, undressed, unpolished, unprepared, unset, uncut. —**Ant.** even, regular; bald, hairless, smooth; orderly; fair; harmonious; cultured, refined; finished, polished; precise, exact; dressed, polished.

round, adj. **1.** circular, disklike. **2.** ring-shaped, hooplike, annular. **3.** curved, arched. **4.** cylindrical. **5.** spherical, globular, rotund, orbed. **6.** full, complete, entire, whole, unbroken. **7.** full, sonorous. **8.** vigorous, brisk, smart, quick. **9.** plain, honest, straightforward, candid, outspoken, frank, open, upright, fair. **10.** unmodified, positive, unqualified. —n. **11.** circle, ring, curve. **12.** cylinder, rung. **13.** course, cycle, revolution, period, series, succession. —**Ant.** angular, square, rectangular, polygonal.

rouse, v. **1.** stir, excite, animate, kindle, fire, inflame, stimulate, awaken, provoke. **2.** anger, provoke, incite, ire. —**Ant.** calm; pacify. —**Syn. Study.** See INCITE.

rove, v. roam, wander, range, ramble, stroll, amble, stray.

row, n. **1.** argument, disagreement, quarrel, dispute, altercation, squabble, fight, set-to, donnybrook, scrap, knock-down-drag-out. —v. **2.** argue, quarrel, squabble, fight.

rowdy, *adj.* **1.** boisterous, noisy, raucous, rackety, rambunctious, disorderly, unruly, brawling, roistering, obstreperous, rip-roaring, riotous, ruffian, ruffianly, rough-and-tumble. —*n.* **2.** mischief-maker, ruffian, hooligan, brawler, street fighter, tough, street-tough, hood, hoodlum, hooligan, thug, bullyboy, (*Brit.*) teddy boy, yob, yobbo.

royal, *adj.* regal, majestic, kingly, imperial, princely. —**Ant.** servile.

ruckus, *n.* commotion, disturbance, fuss, row, to-do, hubbub, ruction, rumpus, uproar, racket, turmoil, brouhaha, foofaraw.

ruddy, *adj.* **1.** red, reddish, rose-colored, rosy, rufous, rubicund. **2.** rosy-cheeked, rosy, glowing, florid, flushed, high-colored, blushing.

rude, *adj.* **1.** discourteous, unmannerly, ill-mannered, impolite, unrefined, uncivil, coarse, curt, brusque, saucy, pert, impertinent, impudent, fresh. **2.** unlearned, untutored, uneducated, untaught, ignorant, uncultured, unrefined, untrained, uncivilized, coarse, uncouth, vulgar, boorish. **3.** rough, harsh, ungentle, coarse, rugged, crude. **4.** unwrought, raw, crude, rough, shapeless, amorphous. **5.** inartistic, inelegant, primitive, rustic, artless, simple, unadorned, unpolished, undecorated. **6.** violent, tempestuous, stormy, fierce, tumultuous, turbulent. **7.** robust, sturdy, vigorous. —**Ant.** courteous, mannerly; learned; gentle; artistic, elegant; calm. —**Syn. Study.** See RAW.

rudimentary, *adj.* **1.** rudimental, elementary, fundamental, primary, initial. **2.** undeveloped, embryonic, elementary, imperfect. **3.** vestigial, abortive. —**Ant.** advanced; mature, perfect; complete.

ruffle, *v.* **1.** disarrange, rearrange, disorder, rumple, wrinkle, damage, derange. **2.** disturb, discompose, irritate, vex, annoy, upset, agitate, trouble, torment, plague, harry, harass, worry, molest. —*n.* **3.** disturbance, perturbation, annoyance, vexation, confusion, commotion, flurry, tumult, bustle, agitation. **4.** frill, trimming; ruff. **5.** drumbeat. —**Ant.** arrange, order; compose, composure, peace.

rugged, *adj.* **1.** broken, uneven, rocky, hilly, craggy, irregular. **2.** wrinkled, furrowed. **3.** rough, harsh, stern, severe, hard, stormy, austere. **4.** severe, hard, trying, difficult. **5.** tempestuous, stormy, rough. **6.** harsh, grating, inharmonious, cacophonous, scabrous. **7.** rude, uncultivated, unrefined, unpolished, crude. **8.** homely, plain, ugly. —**Ant.** even, smooth, regular; easy, flexible; fair; harmonious; cultivated; refined; pretty, lovely, beautiful.

ruin, *n.* **1.** decay, dilapidation, ruination, perdition, destruction, havoc, damage, disintegration, devastation, spoliation. **2.** downfall, destruction, decay, fall, overthrow, defeat, undoing, subversion, wreck. —*v.* **3.** spoil, demolish, destroy, damage, reduce to ruin. —**Ant.** construction; creation; create, build.

rule, *n.* **1.** principle, regulation, standard, law, canon, ruling, guide, precept, order, ukase. **2.** control, government, dominion, command, domination, mastery, sway, authority, direction. —*v.* **3.** administer, command, govern, manage, control, handle, lead, direct, guide, conduct. **4.** decree, decide, deem, judge, settle, establish, order, demand.

ruminate, *v.* **1.** chew cud. **2.** ponder, muse, think, meditate, reflect.

rumor, *n.* story, talk, gossip, hearsay, bruit, news, report.

run, *v.* **1.** race, hasten, hie, scud, speed, scamper. **2.** flow, pour, stream; go, move, proceed. **3.** melt, fuse, liquefy. **4.** leak, overflow, flood, spread. **5.** creep, trail, climb. **6.** operate, continue. **7.** extend, stretch, reach, spread. **8.** contend, compete, challenge. **9.** pursue, hunt, chase. **10.** convey, transport, ferry, carry. **11.** pierce, stab, thrust, force, drive. **12.** operate, carry on, conduct, manage. **13.** melt, fuse, smelt, liquefy. —*n.* **14.** period, spell, interval. **15.** series, set, course, passage, motion, extent, progress. **16.** stream, rivulet, rill, runnel, brook, channel, burn. **17.** ordinary, standard, average, regular. **18.** way, track. **19.** herd, school, pack, bevy, covey, brood, flock, gaggle, pride; group, company, crowd.

rupture, *n.* **1.** breaking, bursting, breach, fracture, break, split, burst, disruption. **2.** hernia. —*v.* **3.** break, fracture, split, burst, disrupt, separate. —**Ant.** seam, union; unite, organize.

rural, *adj.* rustic, unsophisticated, rugged, rough; crude, boorish. —**Ant.** urban. —**Syn. Study.** RURAL and RUSTIC are terms that refer to the country. RURAL is the neutral term: *rural education.* It is also used subjectively, usu. in a favorable sense: *the charm of rural life.* RUSTIC, however, may have either favorable or unfavorable connotations. In a derogatory sense, it means provincial, boorish, or crude; in a favorable sense, it may suggest a homelike simplicity and lack of sophistication: *rustic manners.*

ruse. See Syn. study at TRICK.

rush, *v.* **1.** dash, hasten, run. **2.** attack, overcome. —*v.* **3.** busyness, haste, hurry. **4.** straw, reeds, fiber. —**Ant.** sloth, lethargy.

rustic. See RURAL.

ruthless, *adj.* pitiless, merciless, unpitying, unmerciful, cruel, hard, harsh, severe, hard-hearted, uncompassionate, unrelenting, adamant, relentless, inexorable, fell, truculent, inhuman, ferocious, savage, barbarous. —**Ant.** merciful, compassionate, humane.

S

Sabbath, *n.* Lord's day, Sunday, day of rest. —**Syn. Study.** See SUNDAY.

sabotage, *n.* **1.** subversion, subversiveness, damage, injury, undermining, weakening. —*v.* **2.** undermine, subvert, damage, hurt, disable, weaken, incapacitate, wreck.

saccharine, *adj.* **1.** oversweet, sickly-sweet, cloying, treacly, sugary. **2.** mawkish, oversentimental, maudlin, bathetic, sticky, treacly, cloying, mushy, soppy, sappy, icky. **3.** ingratiating, fawning, obsequious, insinuating, silken, silky, suave, sycophantic. —**Ant.** astringent, bracing.

sack, *n.* **1.** bag, pouch. **2.** pillaging, looting, plundering, pillage, destruction, devastation, desolation, spoliation, ruin, ruination, waste, ravage, rapine. —*v.* **3.** pillage, loot, rob, spoil, despoil, ruin, lay waste, plunder, devastate, demolish, destroy, ravage, rape.

sacred, *adj.* **1.** consecrated, holy, sainted, venerable, hallowed, divine, worshipful. **2.** dedicated, consecrated, revered. **3.** secure, protected, sacrosanct, immune, inviolate, inviolable. —**Ant.** blasphemous. —**Syn. Study.** See HOLY.

sacrilege, *n.* blasphemy, impiety, irreverence, profanity, desecration, profanation, heresy, sin, offense, abomination, violation, crime, infamy, disgrace, scandal.

sacrosanct, *adj.* sacred, holy, sanctified, hallowed, blessed, venerable, inviolate, inviolable, untouchable, taboo, tabu.

sad, *adj.* **1.** sorrowful, mournful, unhappy, despondent, disconsolate, depressed, dejected, melancholy, discouraged, gloomy, downcast, downhearted. **2.** somber, dark, dull. **3.** grievous, deplorable, disastrous, dire, calamitous. —**Ant.** happy.

safe, *adj.* **1.** secure, protected, sound, guarded. **2.** dependable, trustworthy, sure, reliable. **3.** cautious, wary, careful. —*n.* **4.** repository, strongbox, coffer, chest, safe deposit box. —**Ant.** unsafe.

safeguard, *n.* **1.** defense, guard, protection, precaution, palladium, bulwark, shield, aegis, armor, armament, cushion, security, insurance. —*v.* **2.** defend, guard, protect, shield, secure, bulwark, preserve.

saga, *n.* edda, epic, tale, tradition, legend, history.

sagacious, *adj.* wise, sage, shrewd, discerning, clever, intelligent, judicious, rational, acute, sharp, keen, perspicacious, sharp-witted. —**Ant.** unwise, irrational.

sage, *n.* **1.** wise man, philosopher. —*adj.* **2.** prudent, sagacious. —**Ant.** dolt; imprudent.

sailor, *n.* mariner, salt, tar, seaman, seafarer, seafaring man. —**Ant.** landlubber. —**Syn. Study.** SAILOR, SEAMAN, MARINER, SALT are terms for a person who leads a seafaring life. A SAILOR or SEAMAN is one whose occupation is on board a ship at sea, esp. a member of a ship's crew below the rank of petty officer: *a sailor before the mast; an able-bodied seaman.* MARINER is a term found in certain technical expressions: *mariner's compass* (ordinary compass as used on ships); the word now seems elevated or quaint: *The Rime of the Ancient Mariner.* SALT is an informal term for an experienced sailor: *an old salt.*

sake, *n.* **1.** cause, account, interest, score, regard, consideration, respect, reason. **2.** purpose, end, reason.

salacious, *adj.* lustry, lecherous, rakish, lewd, carnal, wanton, lascivious, libidinous, concupiscent; obscene, pornographic, prurient. —**Ant.** modest, prudish.

salient, *adj.* prominent, conspicuous, important, remarkable, striking. —**Ant.** inconspicuous; unimportant.

sallow, *adj.* pallid, washed-out, wan, waxen, sickly, bloodless, anemic, pasty, pasty-faced, whey-faced, greenish, green around the gills, yellowish, jaundiced.

salt. See Syn. study at SAILOR.

salutary, *adj.* healthy, health-giving, salubrious, wholesome. —**Ant.** unwholesome.

salvage, *v.* rescue, redeem, deliver, save, recover, regain, retrieve, recoup, ransom, recycle. —**Ant.** discard.

same, *adj.* **1.** identical; similar, like, corresponding, interchangeable, equal. **2.** agreeing; unchanging. —**Ant.** different; disagreeing.

sameness, *n.* identity, uniformity, monotony. —**Ant.** difference.

sample, *n.* specimen, example, illustration, pattern, model.

sanctify, *v.* bless, consecrate, dedicate, hallow, purify, beatify, enshrine. —**Ant.** desecrate.

sanctimonious, *adj.* hypocritical, unctuous, pious, canting, pietistic, pharisaical, holier-than-thou, smug, Tartuffian, Pecksniffian, simon-pure, self-righteous, goody-goody, goody-two-shoes. —**Ant.** sincere.

sanction, *n.* **1.** authority, permission, countenance, support, ratification, solemnification, authorization. —*v.* **2.** authorize, countenance, approve, confirm, ratify, support, allow, bind. —**Ant.** disapproval; disallow, disapprove.

sanctuary, *n.* church, temple, shrine, altar, sanctum, adytum.

sane, *adj.* rational, reasoning, reasonable, lucid, clear-headed, clear-thinking, lucid, sound, normal, all there, compos mentis, wise, judicious, sapient, sagacious, sage, prudent, sensible. —**Ant.** insane, foolish.

sanguinary, *adj.* bloody, murderous, bloodthirsty, cruel, savage, fell, ruthless, truculent, pitiless, unmerciful, merciless. —**Ant.** merciful, kind.

sanguine, *adj.* cheerful, hopeful, confident, enthusiastic, buoyant, animated, lively, spirited. —**Ant.** morose, dispirited.

sanitary, *adj.* hygienic, unpolluted, clean, germfree; healthy, salutary. —**Ant.** polluted; unhealthy, unwholesome.

sapient, *adj.* wise, sage, sagacious. —**Ant.** stupid, dull, unwise.

sarcasm, *n.* irony, derision, bitterness, ridicule; taunt, gibe, jeer. —**Syn. Study.** See IRONY.

sarcastic, *adj.* cynical, biting, cutting, mordant, bitter, derisive, ironical, sardonic, satirical. —**Syn. Study.** See CYNICAL.

sardonic, *adj.* sarcastic, bitter, ironical, sneering, malignant, malicious.

satanic, *adj.* evil, wicked, diabolical, devilish, infernal, hellish, malicious, fiendish. —**Ant.** godly, angelic, benevolent.

satiate, *v.* cloy, glut, stuff, gorge, sate, surfeit; gall, disgust, weary.

satire, *n.* irony, sarcasm, ridicule, lampoon, pasquinade, burlesque, exposure, denunciation. —**Syn. Study.** See IRONY.

satirical, *adj.* cynical, sarcastic, sardonic, ironical, taunting, biting, keen, sharp, cutting, severe, mordant, mordacious, bitter, acid.

satisfaction, *n.* **1.** gratification, enjoyment, pleasure, contentment, ease, comfort. **2.** reparation, restitution, amends, expiation, atonement, compensation, indemnification, remuneration, recompense, requital, *Wiedergutmachung.* **3.** payment, discharge, repayment. —**Ant.** dissatisfaction, displeasure, discomfort.

satisfy, *v.* **1.** gratify, meet, appease, pacify, content, please. **2.** fulfill, fill, satiate, sate, suffice, surfeit. **3.** assure, convince, persuade. —**Ant.** dissatisfy, displease.

saturate, *v.* soak, impregnate, imbue, wet, ret, drench. —**Ant.** ted, dry.

saucy, *adj.* impudent, pert, cheeky, flippant, irrepressible, forward, impertinent, cocky, sassy, fresh, flip.

saunter, *v.* stroll, walk, ramble, amble.

savage, *adj.* **1.** wild, rugged, uncultivated, sylvan, rough. **2.** barbarous, uncivilized, rude, unpolished, wild. **3.** fierce, ferocious, wild, untamed, feral, ravenous. **4.** enraged, furious, angry, irate, infuriated. **5.** cruel, brutal, beastly; inhuman, fell, merciless, unmerciful, pitiless, ruthless, bloodthirsty, truculent, sanguinary. —**Ant.** cultivated, cultured; tame; calm; merciful.

savant, *n.* scholar, sage, intellectual, polymath, expert, authority, pundit, egghead, wonk, brain, rocket scientist, maven, (*Brit.*) boffin.

save, *v.* **1.** rescue, salvage, preserve. **2.** safeguard, keep. **3.** set apart, reserve, lay by, economize, hoard, store up, husband. —*prep., conj.* **4.** except, but.

savior, *n.* rescuer, deliverer, saver, lifesaver, safekeeper, preserver, liberator, redeemer, emancipator.

savor, *n.* **1.** taste, flavor, relish; odor, scent, fragrance. —*v.* **2.** flavor, season, spice.

savory. See Syn. study at PALATABLE.

say, *v.* **1.** utter, pronounce, speak, remark, affirm, allege. **2.** express, state, word, declare, tell, argue. **3.** recite, repeat, iterate, reiterate, rehearse. **4.** report, allege, maintain, hold.

scale, *n.* **1.** plate, lamina, flake, peel. **2.** coating, crust, incrustation. **3.** pan, dish. **4.** (*plural*) balance. **5.** steps, degrees, series, gradation, progression. —*v.* **6.** skip, play at ducks and drakes. **7.** weigh, balance. **8.** climb, ascend, mount. **9.** progress, gradate.

scamp, *n.* rascal, imp, mischief-maker, rapscallion, cutup, rogue, little devil, scalawag, scapegrace. —**Ant.** goody two-shoes.

scandal, *n.* **1.** disgrace, damage, discredit, dishonor, offense, shame, disrepute, opprobrium, odium, ignominy. **2.** defamation, gossip, slander, character assassination, aspersion, detraction, calumny, obloquy. —**Ant.** honor, repute; praise, kudos.

scanty, *adj.* meager, sparse, insufficient, inadequate, deficient, thin, spare, small, paltry, poor, stinted, gaunt, lean. —**Ant.** abundant, adequate. —**Syn. Study.** SCANTY, MEAGER, SPARSE refer to insufficiency or deficiency in quantity, number, etc. SCANTY denotes smallness or insufficiency of quantity, number, supply, etc.: *a scanty supply of food.* MEAGER indicates that something is poor, stinted, or inadequate: *meager fare; a meager income.* SPARSE applies particularly to that which grows thinly or is thinly distributed: *The crowd jeered at the pitcher.* To SNEER is to show by facial expression or tone of voice ill-natured contempt or disparagement: *He sneered unpleasantly in referring to his opponent's misfortunes.*

scold, *v.* **1.** chide, reprove, reproach, rate, berate, censure, rail at, reprimand, blame, rebuke. —*v.* **2.** nag, shrew, virago, termagant, maenad, bacchante. —**Ant.** praise, honor.

scope, *n.* range, extent, space, opportunity, margin, room, latitude, liberty; tract, area, length. —**Syn. Study.** See RANGE.

scorch, *v.* **1.** burn, singe, char, blister, parch, shrivel. **2.** criticize, excoriate, condemn. —**Ant.** praise, laud.

score, *n.* **1.** record, account, reckoning. **2.** notch, scratch, stroke, line, mark. **3.** twenty. **4.** account, reason, ground, consideration, motive, purpose. —*v.* **5.** record, reckon, tabulate, count. **6.** notch, mark, scratch, cut. **7.** gain, win.

scorn, *n.* **1.** contempt, disdain, contumely. **2.** mockery, derision, scoff, sneer. —*v.* **3.** disdain, contemn, despise, detest. —**Ant.** affection, pleasure. —**Syn. Study.** See CONTEMPT.

scoundrel, *n.* villain, knave, rogue, poltroon, scamp, cad, rascal, rapscallion, miscreant, trickster, sharper, cheat, mountebank, wretch. —**Ant.** hero, protagonist. —**Syn. Study.** See KNAVE.

scourge, *n.* **1.** whip, lash, strap, thong. **2.** flogging, punishment. **3.** affliction, calamity, plague, band, pest, nuisance. —*v.* **4.** lash, whip. **5.** punish, chastise, chasten, correct, castigate, afflict, torment.

scramble, *v.* **1.** hasten, rush, scurry, scamper, scuttle, bustle, hustle. **2.** clamber, creep, scrabble, claw, crawl, go on all fours. **3.** vie, compete, contend, jostle, struggle, strive. **4.** mix, intermix, blend, mix up, mingle, jumble. **5.** confuse, mix up, muddle, garble. —*n.* **6.** bustle, rush, hurry, flurry, flutter, commotion. **7.** clutter, jumble, mix, mishmash.

scrap, *n.* **1.** fragment, piece, portion; morsel, crumb, bit, bite. —*adj.* **2.** fragmentary, piecemeal; waste. —*v.* **3.** break up, demolish. **4.** throw away, discard. —**Ant.** whole.

scrappy, *adj.* contentious, disputatious, argumentative, spirited, mettlesome, hot-tempered, hotheaded, feisty, spunky, pugnacious, combative.

scream, *v.* **1.** shriek, screech, cry, screak. —*n.* **2.** outcry, cry, shriek, screech, screak.

screen, *n.* **1.** partition, shelter, cover, protection, guard, shield, defense. **2.** sieve, riddle, grating. —*v.* **3.** shelter, protect, veil, defend, shield, conceal, hide, cover, cloak, mask, shroud. **4.** sift.

screwball, *adj.* **1.** eccentric, offcenter, whimsical, capricious, zany, kooky, oddball, madcap, nutty, goofy, wacky. —*n.* **2.** oddity, character, oddball, zany, kook, nut, nutcase.

scrumptious, *adj.* delicious, tasty, savory, palatable, sapid, flavorful, flavorsome, succulent, luscious, ambrosial, delectable, toothsome,

---

or quaint: *The Rime of the Ancient Mariner.* SALT is an informal term for an experienced sailor: *an old salt.*

ruthless... (continued in middle column)

scheme, *n.* **1.** plan, design, program, project, system. **2.** plot, intrigue, stratagem, cabal, conspiracy, contrivance, machination. **3.** system, pattern, diagram, schema, arrangement. —*v.* **4.** plan, plot, contrive, project, devise, design.

schmaltz, *n.* **1.** sentimentality, sentimentalism, emotionalism, schwarmerei, mawkishness, bathos, mush, mushiness. —**Ant.** realism, hardheadedness.

scholar, *n.* **1.** savant, wise man, sage. **2.** student, pupil, disciple, learner. —**Ant.** teacher.

scholarship, *n.* learning, knowledge, erudition, wisdom. —**Ant.** stupidity. —**Syn. Study.** See LEARNING.

schooling, *n.* education, training, instruction, tuition, tutelage, learning.

scion, *n.* offspring, child, descendant, fruit, heir, heiress.

scoff, *n.*, *v.* mock, scorn, jeer, gibe, sneer, taunt, ridicule. —**Ant.** envy, praise, exalt. —**Syn. Study.** SCOFF, JEER, SNEER imply behaving with scornful disapproval toward someone or about something. To SCOFF is to express insolent doubt or derision, openly and emphatically: *to scoff at a new invention.* To JEER suggests expressing disapproval and scorn more loudly, coarsely, and unintelligently than in scoffing: *The crowd jeered at the pitcher.* To SNEER is to show by facial expression or tone of voice ill-natured contempt or disparagement: *He sneered unpleasantly in referring to his opponent's misfortunes.*

scamper... (see scramble)

mouth-watering, yummy. —Ant. tasteless, insipid.

scruple, n. 1. hesitation, reluctance, conscience, restraint, compunction, qualm. —v. 2. hesitate, waver, doubt.

scrupulous, adj. 1. conscientious, reluctant, hesitant, cautious, wary, careful, circumspect. 2. punctilious, minute, careful, exacting, exact, precise, demanding, rigorous. —Ant. unscrupulous; careless. —Syn. Study. SCRUPULOUS, PUNCTILIOUS imply being very careful to do the right or proper thing. SCRUPULOUS implies conscientious care in attending to details: The scientist described his observations with scrupulous accuracy. PUNCTILIOUS suggests strictness and rigidity, esp. in observance of social conventions: punctilious adherence to the rules of etiquette.

scrutinize, v. examine, investigate, dissect, study, sift. —Ant. neglect, overlook.

scrutiny, n. examination, investigation, dissection, study, inquiry, inspection, inquisition, search. —Syn. Study. See EXAMINATION.

scurrilous, adj. 1. gross, indecent, abusive, opprobrious, vituperative, reproachful, insolent, insulting, offensive, ribald. 2. coarse, jocular, derisive, vulgar, obscene. —Ant. decent, polite; proper.

scurvy, adj. low, mean, base, contemptible, vile, despicable, worthless. —Ant. honorable, dignified, noble.

scuttlebutt, n. rumor, gossip, hearsay, report, item, whisper, talk, ondit, bruit, buzz, dish, talk of the town.

seaman. See Syn. study at SAILOR.

sear, v. 1. burn, char, singe, scorch. 2. brand, cauterize. 3. dry up, wither. 4. harden, callus.

search, v. 1. look for, seek, explore, investigate, examine, scrutinize, inspect. 2. probe; pierce, penetrate. —n. 3. exploration, examination, investigation, inspection, scrutiny, searching, inquiry, inquisition, pursuit, quest.

seasonable, adj. suitable, timely, opportune, fit, convenient, appropriate. —Ant. unseasonable, unsuitable, untimely, inopportune.

seasoning, n. 1. flavoring, flavor, seasoner, condiment, spice, herb. 2. experience, practice, maturation, development, mellowing, tempering, hardening, strengthening, toughening.

seat, n. 1. chair, bench, banquette, easy chair, throne, stool. 2. bottom, base, fundament. 3. site, situation, location, locality, locale.

secede, v. abdicate, withdraw, retire, separate, resign. —Ant. join.

secluded, adj. withdrawn, isolated, retired, sequestered, private. —Ant. public.

secret, adj. 1. clandestine, hidden, concealed, covert, private, privy, unrevealed, mysterious, unknown, cabalistic, cryptic. 2. reticent, closemouthed, secretive. 3. retired, secluded, private. 4. occult, obscure, mysterious, latent, abstruse, recondite. —n. 5. mystery. —Ant. open, manifest, obvious, apparent.

secrete, v. hide, conceal, cover, shroud, disguise. —Ant. open, manifest. —Syn. Study. See HIDE.

secular, adj. worldly, temporal, mundane, earthly, earthy, lay, nonclerical, material, unspiritual, profane. —Ant. religious, spiritual, ecclesiastical.

secure, adj. 1. safe, protected. 2. fixed, stable, fast, fastened. 3. sure, certain, confident, assured. —v. 4. obtain, procure, get, acquire, gain. 5. protect, guard, safeguard. 6. make certain, ensure, assure, guarantee. 7. make firm, fasten. —Ant. insecure; unstable; unsure; lose; unloose, loosen. —Syn. Study. See GET.

sedate, adj. calm, quiet, composed, sober, undisturbed, unexcited, staid, cool, collected, serene, placid, tranquil, unruffled, unperturbed, imperturbable, serious, settled, demure, grave, thoughtful, contemplative. —Ant. disturbed, perturbed, excited, nervous.

sedative, adj. soporific, tranquilizer, opiate, drug, narcotic, calmative, barbiturate, antispasmodic, hypnotic, quieter, quietener, soother, pacifier, anodyne. —adj. 2. soothing, sleep-inducing, tranquilizing, narcotic, calmative, somniferous, soporific, palliative. —Ant. stimulant.

sediment, n. lees, dregs, grounds, precipitate.

sedition, n. treason, mutiny, rebellion, revolt, revolution, riot, insurrection, uprising. —Ant. allegiance, patriotism. —Syn. Study. See TREASON.

seduce, v. tempt, lead astray, corrupt, entice, beguile, inveigle, decoy, allure, lure, deceive. —Ant. repel, disgust. —Syn. Study. See TEMPT.

seductive, adj. tempting, captivating, alluring, enticing, attractive, beguiling; deceptive. —Ant. repulsive, repellent, abhorrent.

sedulous, adj. diligent, industrious, assiduous, busy, hardworking, zealous, tireless, painstaking, meticulous, thoroughgoing, persevering, steadfast. —Syn. Study. See MEANING.

see, v. 1. perceive, look at, spy, espy, notice, discern, observe, distinguish, behold, regard. 2. view, visit, watch. 3. perceive, discern, penetrate, understand, comprehend, remark. 4. learn, ascertain, find out, determine. 5. experience, live through, know, feel, meet with, suffer, undergo. 6. receive, entertain, visit with. 7. attend, escort, accompany. 8. consider, think, deliberate. —n. 9. diocese, bishopric. —Syn. Study. See WATCH.

seedy, adj. 1. shabby, run-down, dilapidated, ramshackle, ragged, shoddy, shopworn, scruffy, tatty, ratty, down-at-heel, fly-blown, motheaten. 2. unwell, ailing, ill, sick, sickish, under the weather, rundown, exhausted, beat. —Ant. spruce, trim, smart.

seek, v. 1. search for, look for. 2. pursue, follow, solicit, go after. 3. ask for, request, inquire after.

seem, v. appear, look; pretend, assume. —Syn. Study. SEEM, APPEAR, LOOK refer to an outward aspect that may or may not be contrary to reality. SEEM is applied to something that has an aspect of truth and probability: It seems warmer today. APPEAR suggests the giving of an impression that may be superficial or illusory: The house appears to be deserted. LOOK more vividly suggests the use of the eye (literally or figuratively) or the aspect as perceived by the eye: She looked frightened.

seemly, adj. fitting, becoming, suited, well-suited, suitable, appropriate, proper, befitting, meet; decent, decorous, right. —Ant. unseemly.

seep, v. ooze, osmose. —Ant. pour.

seethe, v. 1. soak, steep, ret, saturate. 2. boil; surge, foam, froth. —Syn. Study. See BOIL.

segregate, v. isolate, separate, set apart, dissociate. —Ant. unite, associate, blend; desegregate.

seize, v. 1. grasp, grab, clutch. 2. capture, take into custody, arrest, apprehend, catch, take. —Ant. loose.

seldom, adv. rarely, infrequently, not often. —Ant. often, frequently.

select, v. 1. choose, prefer, pick, pick out. —adj. 2. selected, chosen, preferred, choice, special, picked, valuable, excellent. 3. careful, fastidious, exclusive, selective.

selective, adj. discriminating, choosy, scrupulous, particular, discerning, eclectic, fastidious, picky, fussy, finicky. —Ant. undiscriminating.

self-evident, adj. evident, obvious, axiomatic, self-explanatory, clear. —Ant. mysterious.

self-governed, adj. self-governing, autonomous, independent. —Ant. dependent.

selfish, adj. self-interested, self-seeking, egoistic, illiberal, parsimonious, stingy, mean. —Ant. unselfish.

self-satisfied, adj. self-complacent, complacent, smug, satisfied. —Ant. dissatisfied.

sell, v. trade, barter, vend, exchange, deal in. —Ant. buy.

semblance, n. 1. appearance, aspect, form, show, exterior, mien, bearing, air. 2. likeness, similarity, resemblance. —Ant. dissimilarity, difference.

seminal, adj. original, progenitive, creative, primary, primal, basic, fundamental, basal, founding, germinal, germinative, generative. —Ant. derivative, imitative.

send, v. 1. transmit, dispatch, forward, convey. 2. impel, throw, cast, hurl, toss, propel, fling, project. —Ant. receive.

senile, adj. senescent, decrepit, feeble, geriatric, doddering, doddery, rickety, fogyish, old-fogyish, forgetful, absentminded, oblivious, simpleminded, childish. —Ant. youthful, alert.

sensation, n. 1. sense, feeling, perception. 2. excitement, stimulation, animation; agitation, commotion, perturbation.

sensational, adj. startling, thrilling, exciting, stimulating. —Ant. prosaic, dull.

sense, n. 1. feeling, perception, sensation. 2. awareness, recognition, realization, apprehension, appreciation, understanding, consciousness. 3. perception, estimation, appreciation, discernment. 4. meaning, signification, signficance, import, interpretation, denotation, connotation. 5. opinion, judgment, feeling, idea, notion, sentiment. —v. 6. perceive, become aware of, discern, appreciate, recognize. —Syn. Study. See MEANING.

senseless, adj. 1. insensate, unconscious, insensible, inert, knocked out, cold. 2. unperceiving, undiscerning, unappreciative, unfeeling, apathetic, uninterested. 3. stupid, foolish, silly, idiotic, inane, simple, weak-minded, witless; nonsensical, meaningless, asinine. —Ant. sensitive; intelligent.

sensibility, n. 1. responsiveness, alertness, awareness, susceptibility, impressibility. 2. quickness, keenness, acuteness, sensitivity, sensitiveness. 3. consciousness, appreciation, understanding, rapport. 4. delicacy, sensitiveness, perceptiveness. —Ant. insensibility; dullness; boorishness.

sensible, adj. 1. judicious, intelligent, sagacious, sage, wise, rational, sound, sober, reasonable. 2. cognizant, aware, conscious, understanding, observant. 3. appreciable, considerable. 4. perceptible, discernible, identifiable. —Ant. insensible, irrational, unsound; unaware; trifling. —Syn. Study. See PRACTICAL.

sensitive, adj. 1. impressionable, susceptible, easily affected. 2. sensate. 3. delicate. —Ant. insensitive; hard, obdurate, indelicate.

sensitivity, n. See sensibility.

sensual, adj. 1. voluptuous, sensuous, luxurious. 2. lewd, unchaste, gross, licentious, lascivious, dissolute. —Ant. modest, prudish. —Syn. Study. SENSUAL, SENSUOUS both refer to experience through the senses. SENSUAL refers to the enjoyments derived from the senses, esp. to the gratification or indulgence of physical appetites: sensual pleasures. SENSUOUS refers to that which is aesthetically pleasing to the senses: sensuous poetry. See also CARNAL.

sensuous, adj. sentient, feeling, sensible. —Ant. insensible. —Syn. Study. See SENSUAL.

sententious, adj. 1. pithy, concise, laconic, epigrammatic, terse, succinct, didactic. 2. judicial, magisterial. —Ant. prosaic, prosy, longdrawn.

sentient, adj. aware, alive, conscious, awake, cognizant, sensitive, sensible, witting, susceptible, susceptive, feeling, perceptive, responsive, receptive, impressionable, sensate, reactive, discriminative, discriminatory. —Ant. dulled, insensible.

sentiment, n. 1. attitude, disposition, opinion, feeling, judgment, thought. 2. emotion, sentimentality, sensitiveness, sensibility, tenderness. —Ant. coolness. —Syn. Study. See FEELING. See also OPINION.

sentimentality, n. sentiment.

separate, v. 1. keep apart, divide, part, put apart, disjoin, disconnect, dissever, sever, disunite, sunder, disengage, dissociate, split, break up. 2. withdraw, cleave. —adj. 3. separated, disjoined, disunited, unattached, apart, divided, severed, detached, distinct, discrete, dissociate, apart, withdrawn, sequestered, alone, isolated. 4. independent, individual, particular. —Ant. unite, connect; together, indistinct, conglomerate; dependent, general.

sepulcher, n. 1. tomb, grave, burial vault, ossuary. —v. 2. bury, entomb, inter. —Ant. cradle, womb; unearth, disinter.

sequence, n. 1. following, succession, order, arrangement, series. 2. outcome, sequel, consequence, result. —Syn. Study. See SERIES.

seraglio, n. harem.

serendipity, n. luck, chance, happenstance, fortuity, fortuitousness, adventitiousness, randomness, fortune, fluke, flukiness, dumb luck.

serene, adj. 1. calm, peaceful, tranquil, unruffled, undisturbed, imperturbable, unperturbed, placid, composed, sedate, staid, collected, cool. 2. fair, clear, unclouded, bright. —Ant. active, disturbed, upset; clouded, inclement. —Syn. Study. See PEACEFUL.

serenity, n. calmness, composure, tranquillity, peacefulness, calm, sereneness, peace. —Ant. perturbation, disturbance.

serf, n. slave, esne, ryot, bondman, villein, thrall. —Ant. master.

series, n. sequence, succession, set, line; order, arrangement. —Syn. Study. SERIES, SEQUENCE, SUCCESSION are terms for an orderly following of things one after another. SERIES is applied to a number of things of the same kind, usu. related to each other, arranged or happening in order: a series of baseball games. SEQUENCE stresses the continuity in time, thought, cause and effect, etc.: The scenes came in a definite sequence. SUCCESSION implies that one thing is followed by another or others in turn, usu. though not necessarily with a relation or connection between them: a succession of calamities.

serious, adj. 1. thoughtful, grave, solemn, sober, sedate, staid, earnest. 2. weighty, important, momentous, grave, critical. —Ant. jocular; trivial. —Syn. Study. See EARNEST.

servant, n. domestic, maidservant, servant-girl, employee, maid, menial, servitor, attendant, retainer, butler, footman. —Ant. master.

serve, v. 1. wait on, attend. 2. assist, help, aid, succor. 3. function, answer, do, suffice. 4. promote, contribute, forward, advance, assist. 5. provide, cater, satisfy, purvey.

serviceable, adj. helpful, useful, handy, utile, aidful, employable, utilitarian, convenient, available, effective, valuable. 2. adequate, tolerable, passable, fair, fairish, unexceptional, middling, so-so, decent, respectable, acceptable, satisfactory.

servile, adj. submissive, obsequious, menial, slavish, cringing, low, fawning, abject, mean, base, sycophantic, groveling. —Ant. aggressive, overbearing, dignified. —Syn. Study. SERVILE, OBSEQUIOUS, SLAVISH describe the submissive or compliant behavior of a slave or an inferior. SERVILE suggests cringing, fawning, and abject submission: servile responses to questions. OBSEQUIOUS implies the ostentatious subordination of oneself to the wishes of another, either from fear or from hope of gain: an obsequious waiter. SLAVISH stresses the dependence and laborious toil of one who follows or obeys without question: slavish attentiveness to orders.

servitude, n. slavery, bondage, serfdom, thralldom. —Syn. Study. See SLAVERY.

set, v. 1. put, place, position, pose, locate, situate, post, appoint, station, plant. 2. value, price, rate, prize, evaluate, estimate. 3. fix, appoint, ordain, settle, establish, determine. 4. prescribe, assign, predetermine. 5. adjust, arrange, order, dispose, place, regulate. 6. frame, mount. 7. calibrate, regulate. 8. decline, sink, wane, go down. 9. solidify, congeal, harden. —n. 10. assortment, outfit, collection, series. 11. group, clique, coterie, company, circle, class, sect. 12. direction, bent, inclination, disposition, attitude. 13. bearing, carriage, mien, posture, appearance, aspect. 14. stage, scene, scenery, decoration, setting. —adj. 15. fixed, prefixed, predetermined. 16. prescribed, foreordained. 17. customary, usual. 18. fixed, rigid, immovable. 19. resolved, determined, habitual, stubborn, fixed, obstinate, stiff, unyielding.

setting. See syn. study at ENVIRONMENT.

settle, v. 1. fix, agree upon, establish. 2. pay, discharge, repay, liquidate. 3. locate in, people, colonize. 4. quiet, tranquilize, calm, compose, still, pacify. 5. stabilize, establish, confirm. 6. decide, arrange, agree, adjust. 7. calm down, rest. 8. sink down, decline, subside, sink, fall.

sever, v. separate, divide, put or cut apart, part, cut, cleave, sunder, break off, disunite, disjoin, detach, disconnect. —Ant. unite.

severe, adj. 1. harsh, extreme, trenchant, biting, acerb, bitter, caustic, satirical, keen, stinging, mordant, mordacious, sharp, cutting. 2. serious, grave, stern, austere, rigid, rigorous, strict, strait-laced, relentless, hard, unrelenting, inexorable, abrupt, peremptory, curt, short. 3. rigid, restrained, plain, simple, unadorned, unornamented, chaste. 4. uncomfortable, distressing, unpleasant, acute, afflictive, violent, intense. 5. rigid, exact, critical, demanding, accurate, methodical, systematic, exacting. —Ant. mild; gradual; flexible; comfortable; inaccurate. —Syn. Study. See STERN.

shabby, adj. 1. threadbare, worn, ragged, bedraggled, shopworn, motheaten, tattered, scruffy, tatty, out-at-the-elbows. 2. shoddy, ramshackle, run-down, neglected, decrepit, seedy, squalid, sordid, slummy, wretched. 3. mean, mean-spirited, base, contemptible, deplorable, egregious, scurvy. 4. disreputable, discreditable, dishonorable, shameful, ignominious, shady. 5. unfair, inequitable, unjust, unsporting, unsportsmanlike, discriminatory.

shack, n. shanty, hut, shed, hutch, hovel, cabin, crib, outbuilding, outhouse, lean-to, dump.

shackle, n. 1. fetter, chain, anklet, handcuff, manacle, gyve, hobble. 2. impediment, obstacle, obstruction, encumbrance. —v. 3. confine, restrain, restrict, fetter, chain, handcuff, hobble. 4. restrict, trammel, impede, slow, stultify, dull. —Ant. liberate, free.

shade, n. 1. darkness, shadow, obscurity, gloom, gloominess, dusk, umbrage. 2. specter, ghost, apparition, spirit, phantom. 3. variation, amount, degree, hair, trace, hint, suggestion. 4. veil, curtain, screen. —v. 5. obscure, dim, darken, cloud, blur, obfuscate. 6. screen, hide, protect, conceal, cover, shelter. —Ant. light.

shake, v. 1. sway, vibrate, oscillate, quiver, waver, tremble, agitate, shudder, shiver, totter. 2. brandish, flourish. 3. agitate, disturb, move, intimidate, frighten, daunt. 4. unsettle, weaken, enfeeble. —n. 5. tremor, blow, disturbance, shock.

shaky, adj. 1. unsteady, unstable, rickety, unbalanced, teetery, teetering, tottery, tottering, wobbly, doddering, fragile, spindly. 2. tremulous, trembly, shivery, quivering, quivery, tremulant, jittery, jumpy, skittish. 3. uncertain, unsure, doubtful, dubious, precarious, problematic, risky, ticklish, dicey, iffy, (Brit.) dodgy. —Ant. steady, solid.

sham, n. 1. imitation, pretense. 2. pretended, counterfeit, false, spurious, mock. —v. 3. pretend; imitate, deceive, feign, defraud, impose. —Ant. genuine. —Syn. Study. See FALSE.

shamble, v. shuffle, scuff, scuffle, plod, trudge, tramp, plug, lumber, stumble, stump, clump, slog, schlep, drag one's feet. —Ant. swagger, strut.

shambles, n. 1. destruction, ruin, wreckage, ruination, devastation, holocaust, carnage, slaughter. 2. mess, disorder, confusion, chaos, turmoil, jumble.

shame, n. 1. humiliation, mortification, abashment, chagrin. 2. disgrace, derision, ignominy, dishonor, reproach, obloquy, opprobrium, odium, infamy, contempt. 3. scandal. —v. 4. abash, humiliate, mortify, humble, confuse, disconcert. 5. disgrace, reproach, dishonor, scandalize, debase, tarnish, stain, taint, sully, soil. —Ant. honor. —Syn. Study. SHAME, EMBARRASSMENT, HUMILIATION, CHAGRIN designate different kinds or degrees of painful feeling caused by injury to one's pride or self-respect. SHAME is a painful feeling caused by the consciousness or exposure of unworthy or indecent conduct or circumstances: One feels shame at being caught in a lie. It is similar to guilt in the nature and origin of the feeling. EMBARRASSMENT usu. refers to a less painful feeling, one associated with less serious situations, often of a social nature: embarrassment over breaking a vase at a party. HUMILIATION is a feeling of embarrassment at being humbled in the estimation of others: Being ignored gave him a sense of humiliation. CHAGRIN is humiliation mingled with vexation or anger: She felt chagrin at her failure to do well on the test.

shameful, adj. disgraceful, scandalous, mortifying, humiliating, dishonorable, ignominious, disreputable, outrageous, infamous, vile, base, low. —Ant. honorable.

shameless, adj. 1. immodest, audacious, unblushing, brazen, impudent, bold, insolent, indelicate, unabashed, unashamed. 2. corrupt, sinful, unprincipled, depraved, profligate, piacular, dissolute, reprobate, vicious, hard, hardened, stony, obdurate, adamant, incorrigible, lost. —Ant. modest, proper, principled, flexible.

shanty, n. cottage, shack, cot, hut, hovel, cabin, house. —Ant. castle, palace.

shape, n. 1. outline, silhouette, form, figure, appearance, aspect. 2. phantom, specter, manifestation. 3. guise, disguise. 4. arrangement, order, pattern. **5.** condition, situation, order. **6.** mold, cast, pattern, form. —*v.* **7.** form, fashion, mold, model. **8.** word, express, term. adjust, adapt, regulate, frame.

share, *n.* **1.** portion, part, allotment, contribution, quota, lot, proportion. **2.** dividend, stock. —*v.* **3.** divide, apportion, allot, portion, parcel out, deal out, dole, mete out. **4.** partake, participate.

sharp, *adj.* **1.** keen, acute, trenchant. **2.** pointed, peaked. **3.** abrupt, sudden. **4.** distinct, marked, clear. **5.** pungent, biting, acrid, spicy, burning, hot, mordacious, bitter, piquant, sour. **6.** shrill, piercing, loud, high. **7.** cold, piercing, freezing, nipping, biting. **8.** painful, distressing, intense, severe, sore, excruciating, agonizing. **9.** harsh, merciless, unmerciful, severe, acute, cutting, caustic, acid, sarcastic, sardonic, acrimonious, pointed, biting, poignant. **10.** fierce, violent, intense. **11.** keen, eager, hungry. **12.** quick, brisk. **13.** vigilant, alert, awake, on the qui vive, attentive. **14.** acute, shrewd, astute, clever, penetrating, discerning, perspicacious, ingenious, discriminating, ready, smart, cunning, intelligent, bright, quick, sensitive, alert, observant, incisive, vigorous, understanding, active, reasoning. **15.** dishonest, shady, unlawful, deceitful, cheating. —**Ant.** dull; blunt; unclear; mild; soft; warm; merciful. —**Syn. Study.** SHARP, KEEN, INTELLIGENT, QUICK may all be applied to mental qualities and abilities. SHARP means mentally alert or acute; it implies a clever and astute quality: *a sharp mind.* KEEN suggests an incisive, observant, or penetrating nature: *a keen observer.* INTELLIGENT means not only acute, alert, and active, but also able to reason and understand: *an intelligent reader.* QUICK suggests lively and rapid comprehension, prompt response to instruction, and the like: *quick at figures.*

shatter, *v.* break, crush, shiver, split, crack; explode.

sheen. See Syn. study at POLISH.

sheer, *adj.* **1.** transparent, diaphanous, thin, clear. **2.** unmixed, mere, simple, pure, downright, unadulterated, unqualified, utter. **3.** steep, precipitous, abrupt, perpendicular. —*adv.* **4.** clear, quite, completely, totally, entirely. —*n.* **5.** chiffon, voile. —*v.* **6.** swerve, deviate, turn aside. —**Ant.** opaque; gradual.

shelter, *n.* **1.** protection, refuge, retreat, asylum, cover, screen, sanctuary, shield, haven, harbor. —*v.* **2.** protect, guard, cover, safeguard, shield, hide, shroud, house, harbor, defend. —**Ant.** open.

shiftless, *adj.* **1.** lazy, indolent, slothful, unambitious, slack, dilatory, time-wasting, clock-watching, goldbricking, good-for-nothing. **2.** improvident, inefficient, unresourceful. —**Ant.** vigorous, practical.

shimmer, *v.*, *n.* glisten, shine, gleam, glimmer.

shine, *v.* **1.** beam, glare, gleam, glisten, glimmer, shimmer, sparkle, glow, radiate. —*n.* **2.** radiance, light. **3.** polish, luster, gloss.

shining, *adj.* **1.** radiant, gleaming, bright, brilliant, resplendent, glistening, effulgent, lustrous. **2.** conspicuous, fine, outstanding, distinguished, eminent, prime, splendid, choice, excellent, select.

shipment, *n.* freight, consignment, cargo, lading.

shirk, *v.* evade, avoid, dodge, shun, duck, elude, escape, sidestep, burke, malinger, goldbrick, slack off, goof off.

shiver, *v.*, *n.* tremble, quake, shudder, shake.

shock, *n.* **1.** blow, impact, collision, encounter, concussion, clash. **2.** disturbance, commotion, agitation. —*v.* **3.** startle, stagger, surprise, stun, astound, paralyze, stupefy, bewilder, dumfound. **4.** horrify, disgust, outrage, nauseate, offend, sicken, revolt. **5.** collide, strike, meet.

shore, *n.* **1.** beach, coast, bank, seashore, riverbank, margin, strand. **2.** support, prop, brace, buttress, stay, post, beam, strut.

short, *adj.* **1.** brief; low. **2.** concise, brief, terse, succinct, laconic, condensed, curt, sententious. **3.** abrupt, curt, sharp, petulant, short-tempered, testy, uncivil, rude. **4.** scanty, poor, insufficient, deficient, inadequate, wanting, lacking. **5.** substandard, inferior, unacceptable, below. **6.** friable, brittle, crumbly. **7.** brachycephalic. —*adv.* **8.** suddenly, abruptly, without notice or warning. **9.** briefly, curtly. —**Ant.** long. —**Syn. Study.**

SHORT, BRIEF are opposed to LONG, and indicate slight extent or duration. SHORT may imply duration but is also applied to physical distance and certain purely spatial relations: *a short journey.* BRIEF refers esp. to duration of time: *brief intervals.*

shorten, *v.* **1.** curtail, abbreviate, abridge, condense, lessen, limit, restrict, reduce. **2.** take in, reduce, diminish, lessen, contract. —**Ant.** lengthen. —**Syn. Study.** SHORTEN, ABBREVIATE, ABRIDGE, CURTAIL mean to make shorter or briefer. SHORTEN is a general word meaning to make less in extent or duration: *to shorten a dress; to shorten a prison sentence.* The other three terms suggest methods of shortening. ABBREVIATE usu. means to shorten a word or group of words, as by omission of letters: *to abbreviate a name.* To ABRIDGE is to reduce in length or size by condensing, summarizing, and the like: *to abridge a document.* CURTAIL suggests a lack of completeness due to the omission of some part: *to curtail an explanation.*

short-sighted, *adj.* **1.** myopic, nearsighted. **2.** indiscreet, unthinking, thoughtless, imprudent, inconsiderate, tactless. —**Ant.** presbyopic, farsighted; discreet, thoughtful, prudent.

shout, *v.* cry out, hoot, exclaim, vociferate. —**Ant.** whisper.

shove, *v.* **1.** push, propel. **2.** jostle.

show, *v.* **1.** exhibit, display, demonstrate. **2.** point out, indicate. **3.** guide, accompany, lead, usher, conduct. **4.** interpret, make clear *or* known, clarify, elucidate, explain, discover, reveal, disclose, divulge, publish, proclaim. **5.** prove, demonstrate, evidence. **6.** allege, assert, asseverate; plead. **7.** accord, grant, bestow, confer. **8.** look, appear, seem. —*n.* **9.** display, ostentation, pomp, exhibition, flourish, dash, pageantry, ceremony. **10.** showing, spectacle, appearance. **11.** deception, pretense, pretext, simulation, illusion. **12.** trace, indication. **13.** sight, spectacle, exhibition. —**Ant.** hide, conceal.

showy, *adj.* ostentatious, gaudy, flashy, garish, loud. —**Ant.** humble, quiet.

shrew, *n.* termagant, virago, hussy, nag, scold, bacchante, maenad.

shrewd, *adj.* astute, sharp, acute, quick, discerning, discriminating, perceptive, perspicuous, perspicacious, keen, intelligent, penetrating, ingenious, sagacious. —**Ant.** dull, stupid.

shriek, *n.*, *v.* cry, scream, screech, yell.

shrink, *v.* **1.** retreat, withdraw, avoid, recoil, flinch, retire. **2.** contract, wither, shrivel, lessen, diminish, decrease, dwindle, wane, peter out. —**Ant.** advance; inflate, dilate, increase. —**Syn. Study.** See DECREASE. See also WINCE.

shrivel, *v.* wither, wrinkle, decrease, contract, shrink. —**Ant.** blossom.

shroud, *v.* cover, veil, cloak, shield, curtain, hide, conceal, obscure, cloud, becloud. —**Ant.** reveal.

shudder, *v.*, *n.* tremble, shiver, quiver, shake.

shun, *v.* elude, avoid, evade, eschew. —**Ant.** seek.

shut, *v.* **1.** close; slam. **2.** confine, enclose, jail, imprison. **3.** bar, exclude, prohibit, preclude. —*adj.* **4.** closed, fastened. —**Ant.** open.

shy, *adj.* **1.** bashful, diffident, retiring, timid, coy. **2.** suspicious, distrustful, wary, heedful, cautious, careful, chary, reluctant. **3.** short. —*v.* **4.** recoil, draw back, shrink. **5.** throw, toss, hurl, pitch, cast, fling. —**Ant.** forward; trusting; incautious, careless; advance.

sick, *adj.* **1.** ill, unwell, ailing, infirm, indisposed. **2.** (*British*) nauseous, vomiting, nauseated. **3.** pale, wan, white, sickly. **4.** impaired, unsound, out of order. —**Ant.** well, hale, healthy. —**Syn. Study.** See ILL.

sickly, *adj.* **1.** unhealthy, ailing, sick, unwell, puny, weak, frail, feeble, infirm, weakly. **2.** weak, mawkish, sentimental, faint. —**Ant.** strong, healthy.

sidekick, *n.* partner, associate, confederate, cohort, henchman, subordinate, assistant, right hand, man Friday, girl Friday, gal Friday.

siege, *n.* blockade, besieging, attack.

sign, *n.* **1.** token, indication, trace, vestige, hint, suggestion. **2.** mark, symbol; abbreviation. **3.** omen, presage, portent, augury, foreboding. —*v.* **4.** signify, betoken, indicate, mean, signal. **5.** affix a signature to. —**Syn. Study.** SIGN, OMEN, PORTENT refer to something that gives evidence of a future event. SIGN is a

general word for a visible trace or indication of an event, either past, present, or future: *Dark clouds are a sign of rain.* An OMEN is a happening or phenomenon that serves as a warning of things to come; it may foreshadow good or evil: *She believed it was a bad omen if a black cat crossed her path.* PORTENT also refers to an indication of future events, usu. ones that are momentous or of ominous significance: *the portents of war.*

significance, *n.* **1.** importance, consequence, moment, weight. **2.** import, meaning, sense, purport. **3.** meaningfulness, expressiveness. —**Ant.** triviality. —**Syn. Study.** See IMPORTANCE. See also MEANING.

significant, *adj.* **1.** important, consequential, momentous, weighty, critical, crucial, vital. **2.** meaningful, expressive, signifying, indicative *or* suggestive of. —**Ant.** insignificant.

signify, *v.* **1.** signal, make known, express, indicate, communicate. **2.** mean, portend, represent, denote, indicate, betoken, purport, imply.

silent, *adj.* **1.** quiet, still, noiseless, soundless. **2.** speechless, dumb, mute; close-mouthed, taciturn, tacit. **3.** inactive, dormant, quiescent. —**Ant.** noisy, clamorous; voluble, talkative; active, kinetic.

silhouette, *n.* outline, profile, contour, delineation, lineation, lineaments, shape, configuration, shadow, gestalt. —*v.* **2.** outline, profile, delineate, contour, limn.

silly, *adj.* **1.** foolish, stupid, dull-witted, dim-witted, witless, senseless. **2.** absurd, ridiculous, inane, asinine, frivolous, nonsensical, preposterous, idiotic. —**Ant.** sensible.

similar, *adj.* like, resembling. —**Ant.** unlike, dissimilar, different.

similarity, *n.* likeness, resemblance, similitude, correspondence, parallelism. —**Ant.** difference.

simmer, *v.* seethe, bubble, boil. —**Syn. Study.** See BOIL.

simple, *adj.* **1.** clear, intelligible, understandable, unmistakable, lucid. **2.** plain, unadorned, natural, unaffected, unembellished, neat. **3.** unaffected, unassuming, homely, unpretentious. **4.** mere, bare, elementary, simplex, uncomplicated. **5.** sincere, innocent, artless, naive, guileless, ingenuous, unsophisticated. **6.** humble, lowly. **7.** unimportant, insignificant, trifling, trivial, nonessential, unnecessary, immaterial, inconsequential. **8.** common, ordinary, usual, customary. **9.** unlearned, ignorant, uneducated, untutored, stupid, dense, silly, foolish, credulous, shallow. —**Ant.** complicated, complex.

simulate, *v.* imitate, mimic, pretend, feign, parrot, assume, affect, counterfeit, act, fake, sham, play-act, put on.

sin, *n.* **1.** transgression, trespass, violation, crime, offense, wrong, wickedness. —*v.* **2.** transgress, trespass, do wrong, offend. —**Syn. Study.** See CRIME.

since, *adv.* **1.** subsequently. **2.** ago, before now. —*conj.* **3.** because, inasmuch as.

sincere, *adj.* candid, honest, open, earnest, guileless, artless, plain, simple; genuine, true, unaffected, real, unfeigned. —**Ant.** insincere. —**Syn. Study.** See EARNEST.

sincerity, *n.* honesty, candor, frankness, probity, genuineness, artlessness, ingenuousness, guilelessness. —**Ant.** insincerity. —**Syn. Study.** See HONOR.

sinful, *adj.* wicked, iniquitous, depraved, evil, immoral, amoral, bad, mischievous, piacular.

singe, *v.* char, burn, scorch.

single, *adj.* **1.** separate, only, individual, sole, distinct, particular. **2.** alone, solitary, isolated. **3.** unmarried, unwed, spinsterish, old-maid. **4.** sincere, honest, whole-hearted, concentrated, unbiased. **5.** simple, unmixed, pure, uncompounded, unadulterated. —*v.* **6.** pick, choose, select, single out. —*n.* **7.** one, individual, singleton. —**Ant.** conglomerate; married, wed; insincere, biased; adulterated, mixed.

single-minded, *adj.* resolute, resolved, determined, dedicated, uncompromising, unswerving, unfaltering, persistent, relentless, purposeful, committed, obstinate, dogged, tenacious. —**Ant.** uncertain, distracted.

singular, *adj.* **1.** extraordinary, remarkable, unusual, uncommon, rare, strange, peculiar. **2.** strange, odd, bizarre, fantastic, peculiar, unusual, eccentric, queer, curious, unaccountable, exceptional, unparalleled, unprecedented. **3.** unique. **4.** separate,

individual, single. —**Ant.** plural; common.

sinister, *adj.* **1.** threatening, portending, portentous, ominous, inauspicious, unlucky, unfavorable, unfortunate, disastrous. **2.** bad, evil, base, wicked, sinful, piacular, depraved, corrupt, perverse, dishonest, crooked. —**Ant.** benign, favorable, fortunate; good, honest.

sinuous, *adj.* **1.** winding, sinuate, curved, crooked, serpentine. **2.** indirect, devious, roundabout. —**Ant.** straight; direct.

sip, *v.* **1.** drink; absorb; extract. **2.** savor, taste. —*n.* **3.** drink. **4.** taste, savor, sapor. —**Syn.** See DRINK.

siren, *n.* seductress, temptress, Circe, vampire, vamp, mermaid.

sirocco, *n.* simoom, cyclone, windstorm, dust storm. See WIND.

sit, *v.* **1.** be seated, roost, perch. **2.** be situated, dwell, settle, lie, rest, remain, abide, repose, stay. **3.** meet, convene. —**Ant.** stand, lie.

situation, *n.* **1.** location, position, site, place, locality, locale, spot. **2.** condition, case, plight, state, circumstances, predicament. **3.** position, post, job.

size, *n.* **1.** dimensions, proportions, magnitude, extent; volume, bulk, mass. **2.** amount, extent, range. **3.** glue, glaze, coating. —*v.* **4.** sort, catalogue; measure.

skeptic, *n.* disbeliever, agnostic, atheist, doubter, cynic, infidel, heathen, nullifidian. —*adj.* **2.** skeptical, cynical. —**Ant.** believer, theist.

skeptical, *adj.* skeptic, doubtful, dubious, incredulous, unbelieving. —**Ant.** confident. —**Syn. Study.** See DOUBTFUL.

sketch, *n.* **1.** drawing, outline, draft, design, delineation. **2.** skit, play, act, routine, stint. —*v.* **3.** depict, draw, outline, design, rough out, delineate, portray, represent.

sketchy, *adj.* hasty, imperfect, slight, superficial. —**Ant.** careful, perfect.

skew, *v.* **1.** angle, slant, twist, turn, veer, sideslip, sheer, slew, slue, diverge, divagate. **2.** distort, twist, alter, change, unbalance, upset. —**Ant.** straighten, align.

skilled, *adj.* skillful. —**Ant.** unskilled. —**Syn. Study.** See SKILLFUL.

skillful, *adj.* skilled, expert, ready, adroit, deft, adept, proficient, dexterous, competent, qualified, practiced, accomplished, apt, clever, ingenious, intelligent, learned, knowledgeable. —**Ant.** unskillful, inexpert, maladroit, unqualified. —**Syn. Study.** SKILLFUL, SKILLED, EXPERT refer to ability or competence in an occupation, craft, or art. SKILLFUL suggests adroitness and dexterity: *a skillful watchmaker.* SKILLED implies having had long experience and thus having acquired a high degree of proficiency: *not an amateur but a skilled worker.* EXPERT means having the highest degree of proficiency; it may mean much the same as SKILLFUL or SKILLED, or both: *expert workmanship.*

skin, *n.* **1.** hide, pelt, fur. **2.** integument, covering, peel, rind, hull, shell, husk, crust, coating, outside, film, membrane. —*v.* **3.** flay, peel, pare, strip, husk, excoriate.

skip, *v.* **1.** spring, jump, gambol, leap, bound, caper, hop. **2.** disregard, skip over, skim over. **3.** ricochet, rebound, bounce. —*n.* **4.** leap, jump, spring, bound, caper, hop.

skirmish, *n.* encounter, battle, fight, conflict, combat, brush.

skittish, *adj.* **1.** sensitive, nervous, anxious, skittery, jumpy, quivery, flighty, fidgety, edgy, fluttery, excitable, high-strung. **2.** shy, timid, bashful, timorous, coy. **3.** frisky, lively, giddy, frivolous, whimsical, capricious. **4.** unpredictable, uncertain, fluctuant, unstable. **5.** cautious, wary, chary, hesitant. —**Ant.** down-to-earth, stolid.

skulk, *v.* lurk, slink, sneak, hide, lie in wait. **2.** shirk, malinger. —**Syn. Study.** See LURK.

slack, *adj.* **1.** loose, relaxed. **2.** indolent, negligent, lazy, remiss, weak. **3.** slow, sluggish, dilatory, tardy, late, lingering. **4.** dull, inactive, blunted, idle, quiet. —*n.* **5.** decrease, slowing, loosening, relaxation, indolence, negligence, laziness, remissness, weakness. —*v.* **6.** shirk, neglect, skulk, malinger. **7.** relax, abate, reduce, slacken, moderate, mitigate. —**Ant.** tight, tense, taut.

slacken, *v.* **1.** deactivate, relax, slack, abate. **2.** loosen, relax, relieve, abate, mitigate, remit, lessen, diminish. **3.** fail, neglect, defer. **4.** restrain, check, curb, bridle, repress, subdue, control. —**Ant.** tighten; increase.

slang, *n.* argot, jargon, patois, dialect, cant, colloquialism.

slant, *v.* **1.** slope, lean, incline. —*n.* **2.** incline, inclination, pitch, slope, obliquity, obliqueness. **3.** bent, leaning, prejudice, bias, inclination.

slapdash, *adj.* careless, slipshod, sloppy, haphazard, any which way, hit-or-miss, hit-and-miss, hasty, superficial, cursory, lick-and-a-promise, quick-and-dirty, once-over-lightly. —**Ant.** careful, meticulous.

slash, *v.* **1.** cut, lash, slit, slice. **2.** cut, reduce, alter, abridge, abbreviate. —*n.* **3.** stroke, cut, wound, gash, slit.

slaughter, *n.* **1.** killing, butchering. **2.** massacre, carnage, homicide, murder, butchery, slaying, killing, bloodshed, genocide. —*v.* **3.** butcher, massacre, murder, slay, kill, wipe out, devastate, decimate. —**Syn. Study.** SLAUGHTER, BUTCHER, MASSACRE all imply violent and bloody methods of killing when applied to human beings. SLAUGHTER and BUTCHER emphasize brutal or indiscriminate killing: *to slaughter enemy soldiers in battle; to butcher tribal peoples.* MASSACRE indicates a wholesale destruction of helpless or unresisting victims: *to massacre an entire village.*

slave, *n.* bond servant, esne, thrall, ryot, villein, serf, drudge, vassal, bondman. —**Ant.** master.

slavery, *n.* **1.** bondage, servitude, subjection, thralldom, captivity, enthrallment. **2.** toil, drudgery, moil, labor. —**Syn. Study.** SLAVERY, BONDAGE, SERVITUDE refer to involuntary subjection to another or others. SLAVERY emphasizes the idea of complete ownership and control by a master: *to be sold into slavery.* BONDAGE indicates a state of subjugation or captivity often involving burdensome and degrading labor: *in bondage to a cruel master.* SERVITUDE is compulsory service, often such as is required by a legal penalty: *penal servitude.*

slavish, *adj.* **1.** submissive, abject, servile, groveling, menial, drudging. **2.** base, mean, ignoble, low, obsequious, fawning, sycophantic, sneaking, cringing. **3.** imitative, emulative. —**Ant.** independent; elevated, exalted. —**Syn. Study.** See SERVILE.

slay, *v.* **1.** murder, kill, slaughter, massacre, butcher, assassinate. **2.** destroy, extinguish, annihilate, ruin.

sleek, *adj.* smooth, glossy, polished, groomed, slick, elegant, trim, clean, streamlined, svelte. —**Ant.** lumpish.

sleep, *v.* **1.** rest, repose, slumber, nap, drowse, doze. —*n.* **2.** dormancy, inactivity, slumber, rest, repose, nap.

slender, *adj.* **1.** slight, slim, thin, spare, narrow. **2.** small, trivial, few, meager, trifling, insignificant, inadequate, insufficient. **3.** thin, weak, fragile, feeble, fine, delicate, flimsy, frangible, breakable. —**Ant.** large, fat, obese, corpulent. —**Syn. Study.** SLENDER, SLIGHT, SLIM imply a tendency toward thinness. As applied to the human body, SLENDER implies a generally attractive and pleasing thinness: *slender hands.* SLIGHT often adds the idea of frailness to that of thinness: *a slight, almost fragile, figure.* SLIM implies a lithe or delicate thinness: *a slim and athletic figure.*

slide, *v.* slip, slither, glide.

slight, *adj.* **1.** small, insignificant, superficial, shallow, trivial, nugatory, paltry, unimportant. **2.** slender, slim. **3.** frail, flimsy, weak, feeble, delicate, fragile. **4.** unsubstantial, inconsiderable. —*v.* **5.** ignore, disregard, disrespect, neglect, disdain, overlook, scorn, (*slang*) dis. —*n.* **6.** neglect, disregard, disdain, indifference, scorn, contumely, contempt, inattention. **7.** affront, insult, disrespect. —**Ant.** considerable; compliment. —**Syn. Study.** SLIGHT, DISREGARD, NEGLECT, OVERLOOK mean to pay no attention or too little attention to someone or something. To SLIGHT is to ignore or treat as unimportant: *to slight one's neighbors.* To DISREGARD is to ignore or treat without due respect: *to disregard the rules.* To NEGLECT is to fail in one's duty toward a person or thing: *to neglect one's correspondence.* To OVERLOOK is to fail to notice or consider someone or something, possibly because of carelessness: *to overlook a bill that is due.* See INSULT. See also SLENDER.

slim, *adj.* **1.** slender, thin, slight. **2.** small, poor, insignificant, trifling, trivial, nugatory, unimportant, paltry, inconsiderable, scanty, weak, unsubstantial. —**Ant.** fat; important. —**Syn. Study.** See SLENDER.

slip, *v.* **1.** slide, slither, glide. **2.** be mistaken, err, blunder, mistake. —*n.* **3.** mistake, error, blunder, fault, oversight; faux pas, indiscretion, backsliding. **4.** scion, cutting, strip. —**Syn. Study.** See MISTAKE.

slippery, *adj.* **1.** slick, smooth, lubricious, slithery, oily, lubricated, greased. **2.** risky, precarious, hazardous, unsafe, ticklish. **3.** changeable, mutable, unstable, shifting, uncertain. **4.** untrustworthy, shifty, tricky, deceitful, devious, evasive, wily, cagey, (*Brit.*) dodgy.

slope, *v.*, *n.* slant, incline.

slothful, *adj.* idle, sluggardly, indolent, lazy, sluggish, inactive, inert, torpid, slack, supine. —**Ant.** industrious, active, energetic. —**Syn. Study.** See IDLE.

slovenly, *adj.* untidy, careless, loose, disorderly, slipshod. —**Ant.** careful, tidy, neat.

slow, *adj.* **1.** deliberate, gradual, moderate, leisurely, unhurried. **2.** sluggish, sluggardly, dilatory, indolent, lazy, slothful. **3.** dull, dense, stupid. **4.** slack. **5.** dragging, late, tardy, behindhand. **6.** tedious, humdrum, dull, boring. —*v.* **7.** retard, hinder, impede, obstruct. —**Ant.** fast; advance. —**Syn. Study.** SLOW, DELIBERATE, GRADUAL, LEISURELY mean unhurried or not happening rapidly. SLOW means acting or moving without haste: *a slow procession of cars.* DELIBERATE implies the slowness that marks careful consideration: *a deliberate and calculating manner.* GRADUAL suggests the slowness of something that advances one step at a time: *a gradual improvement.* LEISURELY means moving with the slowness allowed by ample time or the absence of pressure: *a leisurely stroll.*

sluggish, *adj.* inactive, slow, lazy, slothful, indolent, dull, inert, dronish, phlegmatic. —**Ant.** quick, active, energetic.

slumber. See SLEEP.

slur, *v.* **1.** slight, disregard, pass over, ignore, overlook. **2.** calumniate, disparage, slander, depreciate, asperse. —*n.* **3.** slight, innuendo, insult, affront. **4.** blot, stain, stigma, brand, mark, disgrace. —**Ant.** compliment.

sly, *adj.* **1.** cunning, wily, artful, subtle, foxy, crafty. **2.** stealthy, surreptitious, furtive, insidious, secret, underhanded, clandestine. **3.** mischievous, roguish, shrewd, astute, cautious. —**Ant.** direct, obvious.

small, *adj.* **1.** little, tiny, diminutive. **2.** slender, thin, slight, narrow. **3.** unimportant, trivial, minor, secondary, trifling, nugatory, inconsequential, petty, paltry, insignificant. **4.** humble, modest, unpretentious. **5.** mean-spirited, mean, stingy, ungenerous, parsimonious, niggardly, selfish, tight, illiberal, narrow. **6.** ashamed, mortified, abashed. **7.** weak, feeble, faint, diluted. **8.** gentle, soft, low. —**Ant.** large.

small-minded, *adj.* **1.** narrow-minded, narrow, small, illiberal, mean, petty, close-minded, bigoted, intolerant. **2.** provincial, parochial, insular, limited, confined. —**Ant.** liberal, eclectic.

smarmy, *adj.* **1.** insincere, false, disingenuous, hypocritical, mealy-mouthed, sanctimonious. **2.** suave, sleek, smug, insinuating, unctuous, fulsome, oily, buttery. **3.** obsequious, flattering, sycophantic, ingratiating.

smart, *v.* **1.** pain, hurt, sting. **2.** wound, insult, affront. —*adj.* **3.** sharp, keen, stinging, poignant, penetrating, painful, severe. **4.** brisk, vigorous, active, energetic, effective, lively, quick. **5.** quick, prompt, nimble, agile, alert, active. **6.** intelligent, bright, sharp, clever, expert, adroit. **7.** shrewd, cunning, adept, quick. **8.** neat, trim, dashing, spruce, pretentious, showy. **9.** elegant, chic, fashionable, voguish, à la mode. —**Ant.** pleasure; dull, stupid.

smash, *v.* **1.** break, shatter, crush, crash. **2.** defeat, overthrow, destroy. **3.** ruin, bankrupt. —*n.* **4.** smashing, shattering, crash. **5.** collision, destruction, ruin; collapse.

smell. See Syn. study at ODOR.

smirch, *v.* **1.** besmirch, discolor, soil, smear, smudge, smut, smutch, dirty. **2.** sully, tarnish, disgrace, taint, blot, smear. —*n.* **3.** smear, mark, smudge, smut, smutch, dirt. **4.** stain, blot, taint. —**Ant.** clean; honor.

smitten, *adj.* enamored, captivated, charmed, infatuated, bewitched, beguiled, lovestruck, moonstruck, besotted, doting, gaga. —**Ant.** repelled, antipathetic.

smooth, *adj.* **1.** level, even, plain, flat. **2.** bald, hairless, glossy, polished, sleek. **3.** flat, unruffled, calm, undisturbed. **4.** regular, even, easy, fluent. **5.** unruffled, undistorted,

calm, peaceful, tranquil, equable, pacific, peaceable. **6.** elegant, polished, flowing, glib, voluble, soft-spoken, suave, unctuous, oily, bland. **7.** pleasant, agreeable, polite, courtly, courteous. —*v.* **8.** plane, stroke, scrape, level, press, flatten, iron, roll. **9.** polish, refine. **10.** tranquilize, calm, soothe, assuage, mollify, better. **11.** gloss over, palliate, soften, soothe. —**Ant.** rough, uneven, irregular.

smug, *adj.* **1.** complacent, self-satisfied, self-complacent, satisfied, conceited, self-sufficient, self-confident, self-important, egoistic, self-opinionated, self-reliant. **2.** trim, spruce, neat, smooth, sleek. —**Ant.** dissatisfied.

snare, *n.* **1.** trap, noose, net, seine. —*v.* **2.** trap, entrap, entangle, catch.

snarl, *v.* **1.** growl, grumble, complain, murmur. **2.** entangle, tangle, mat, complicate, confuse, ravel, involve, knot. —*n.* **3.** growl, grumble. **4.** tangle, entanglement, complication, knot, confusion, involvement, intricacy, difficulty.

sneak, *v.* **1.** slink, lurk, skulk, steal. —*n.* **2.** sneaker, lurker. —**Syn. Study.** See LURK.

sneer, *v.* **1.** scorn, jeer, gibe, scoff, disdain, deride, ridicule, criticize, contemn. —*n.* **2.** scoff, gibe, jeer, derision, disdain. —**Syn. Study.** See SCOFF.

sneeze, *v.* sternutate.

snide, *adj.* derogatory, nasty, insinuating, vicious, slanderous, libelous. —**Ant.** complimentary, favorable.

snub, *v.* **1.** disdain, contemn, mortify, humiliate, abash, humble, slight, discomfit. **2.** check, rebuke, stop, reprove, reprimand. —*n.* **3.** rebuke, slight, affront, insult. —**Ant.** accept.

soak, *v.* **1.** steep, drench, wet, sop, saturate. **2.** permeate, osmose, penetrate. —**Ant.** dry.

soar, *v.* **1.** fly, glide. **2.** tower, rise, ascend, mount.

sober, *adj.* **1.** unintoxicated; temperate, abstinent, abstemious. **2.** serious, grave, solemn, quiet, sedate, subdued, staid. **3.** calm, serene, tranquil, peaceful, cool, moderate, composed, unexcited, unimpassioned, unruffled, collected, dispassionate, unconcerned, reasonable, rational, controlled, sane, sound. **4.** somber, dull, neutral, dark. —**Ant.** drunk; wild; immoderate. —**Syn. Study.** See GRAVE.

sociable, *adj.* social. —**Ant.** unfriendly.

social, *adj.* friendly, sociable, amiable, companionable, genial, affable, familiar. —**Ant.** unfriendly.

society, *n.* **1.** organization, association, circle, fellowship, club, fraternity, brotherhood, company, partnership, corporation. **2.** community. **3.** companionship, company, fellowship, sodality.

soft, *adj.* **1.** yielding, pliable, plastic, moldable, malleable, impressible. **2.** smooth, agreeable, delicate. **3.** gentle, low, subdued, melodious, mellifluous, dulcet, sweet, pleasing, pleasant, flowing. **4.** gentle, mild, balmy, genial. **5.** gentle, mild, lenient, compassionate, tender, bland, sympathetic. **6.** smooth, soothing, ingratiating, mollifying. **7.** impressionable, yielding, affected, compliant, flexible, irresolute, submissive, undecided, weak, delicate, sensitive. **8.** sentimental, weak, feeble, poor, wishy-washy. —**Ant.** hard, inflexible, unyielding.

soften, *v.* **1.** melt, tenderize. **2.** appease, assuage, mollify, moderate, mitigate, modify, soothe, alleviate, calm, quell, still, quiet, ease, allay, abate, qualify, temper, blunt, dull. —**Ant.** harden.

solace, *n.* **1.** comfort, alleviation, cheer, consolation, relief. —*v.* **2.** comfort, console, cheer, soothe. **3.** relieve, alleviate, soothe, mitigate, assuage, allay, soften.

sole, *adj.* only, single, solitary, alone, individual, unattended, unique.

solemn, *adj.* **1.** grave, sober, mirthless, unsmiling, serious. **2.** impressive, awe-inspiring, august, imposing, venerable, grand, majestic, stately. **3.** earnest, serious. **4.** formal, dignified, serious, ceremonious, ritual, ceremonial. **5.** religious, reverential, devotional, sacred, ritual. —**Ant.** obstreperous; jovial; unimpressive; insincere; informal. —**Syn. Study.** See GRAVE².

solicit, *v.* **1.** seek, entreat, ask for, request, apply for, beseech, pray, beg, importune, urge, implore, crave, supplicate, sue, petition, appeal to. **2.** influence, incite, activate, urge,

impel, excite, arouse, awaken, stimulate.

solicitous, *adj.* **1.** anxious, concerned, apprehensive, uneasy, troubled, disturbed, restless, restive, worried. **2.** desirous, anxious to please. **3.** eager. **4.** careful, particular. —**Ant.** unconcerned, undisturbed; careless.

solid, *adj.* **1.** three-dimensional, cubic. **2.** dense, compact, firm, hard. **3.** unbroken, continuous, undivided, whole, entire, uniform. **4.** firm, cohesive, compact. **5.** dense, thick, heavy, substantial, sound, stable, stout. **6.** real, genuine, complete, sound, good. **7.** sober-minded, sober, sensible. **8.** thorough, vigorous, strong, solid, big, great, stout. **9.** united, consolidated, unanimous. **10.** successful, solvent, wealthy, rich, reliable, honorable, established, well-established, sound, trustworthy, honest, safe. —**Ant.** flat, two-dimensional; loose; divided; sparse; counterfeit; weak; separate; unsuccessful.

solitary, *adj.* **1.** unattended, alone, lone, lonely. **2.** isolated, retired, lonely, deserted, unfrequented, remote, secluded. —*n.* **3.** hermit, eremite, recluse.

solitude, *n.* **1.** seclusion, isolation, remoteness, loneliness, retirement, privacy. **2.** desert, waste, wilderness.

somber, *adj.* **1.** gloomy, dark, shadowy, dim, unlighted, dusky, murky, cloudy, dull, sunless, dismal. **2.** depressing, dismal, lugubrious, mournful, doleful, funereal, melancholy. —**Ant.** cheerful.

some, *adj.* **1.** any, one, anyone, unspecified. **2.** certain, specific, special, particular. —**Ant.** none.

soothe, *v.* **1.** tranquilize, calm, relieve, comfort, refresh. **2.** allay, mitigate, assuage, alleviate, appease, mollify, soften, lull, balm. —**Ant.** upset, disturb. —**Syn. Study.** See COMFORT.

sophisticated, *adj.* **1.** artificial, changed, mundane, worldly. **2.** deceptive, misleading. —**Ant.** unsophisticated.

sorcery, *n.* magic, witchery, enchantment, witchcraft, spell, necromancy, divination, charm.

sordid, *adj.* **1.** dirty, filthy, soiled, unclean, foul, squalid. **2.** mean, ignoble, amoral, degraded, depraved, low, base. **3.** selfish, self-seeking, mercenary, avaricious, stingy, tight, close, close-fisted, parsimonious, penurious, miserly, niggardly. —**Ant.** clean; honorable; generous.

sore, *adj.* **1.** painful, sensitive, tender, irritated. **2.** grieved, distressed, aggrieved, sorrowful, hurt, pained, depressed, vexed. **3.** grievous, distressing, painful, depressing, severe, sharp, afflictive. —*n.* **4.** infection, abscess, wound, ulcer, pustule, boil, cancer, canker. —**Ant.** tough.

sorrow, *n.* **1.** distress, anxiety, anguish, grief, sadness, woe, suffering, misery, wretchedness, regret. **2.** affliction, adversity, trouble, misfortune. —*v.* **3.** grieve, mourn, bemoan, bewail, lament. —**Ant.** joy, gladness, delight.

sorrowful, *adj.* **1.** grieved, sad, unhappy, melancholy, depressed, dejected, aggrieved, afflicted, mournful, plaintive, grievous, lamentable. **2.** distressing, dismal, dreary, doleful, sorry, lugubrious, piteous. —**Ant.** happy.

sorry, *adj.* **1.** regretful, sorrowing, sympathetic, pitying. **2.** pitiable, miserable, deplorable. **3.** sorrowful, grieved, sad, unhappy, melancholy, depressed. **4.** grievous, melancholy, dismal, mournful, painful. **5.** wretched, poor, mean, pitiful, base, low, vile, abject, contemptible, bad, despicable, paltry, worthless, shabby. —**Ant.** happy. —**Syn. Study.** See MISERABLE.

sort, *n.* **1.** kind, species, phylum, genera, variety, class, group, family, description, order, race, rank, character, nature, type. **2.** character, quality, nature. **3.** example, pattern, sample, exemplar. **4.** manner, fashion, way, method, means, style. —*v.* **5.** arrange, order, classify, class, separate, divide, assort, distribute. **6.** assign, join, unite.

sound, *n.* **1.** noise, tone. **2.** strait, channel. —*v.* **3.** resound, echo. **4.** utter, pronounce, express. **5.** plumb, probe; dive, plunge. **6.** examine, inspect, investigate, fathom, ascertain, determine. —*adj.* **7.** uninjured, unharmed, unbroken, whole, entire, complete, unimpaired, healthy, hale, hearty, robust, hardy, vigorous. **8.** solvent, secure, well-established. **9.** reliable, trustworthy, honest, honora-

ble. **10.** true, truthful, just, fair, judicious, reasonable, rational, sane, sensible, wholesome. **11.** enduring, substantial. **12.** correct, orthodox, right, proper. **13.** upright, honest, good, honorable, loyal, true, virtuous. **14.** unbroken, deep, profound, fast, undisturbed. **15.** vigorous, hearty, thorough, complete. —**Ant.** unsound.

soupçon, *n.* hint, trace, suggestion, suspicion, flavor, taste, sip. —**Ant.** plethora.

sour, *adj.* **1.** acid, tart. **2.** fermented. **3.** distasteful, disagreeable, unpleasant, bitter. **4.** harsh, ill-tempered, bad-tempered, austere, severe, morose, peevish, testy, short-tempered, hot-tempered, touchy, acrimonious, cross, petulant, crabbed, snappish, waspish, uncivil, rude, crude, rough. —**Ant.** sweet.

sovereign, *n.* **1.** monarch, king, queen, emperor, empress, prince, lord, ruler, potentate. **2.** senate, government. —*adj.* **3.** regal, royal, majestic, princely, imperial, monarchical, kingly. **4.** supreme, chief, paramount, principal, predominant. **5.** utmost, extreme, greatest. **6.** potent, effective, efficacious, effectual.

spacious, *adj.* ample, large, capacious, roomy, wide. **2.** extensive, vast, huge, extended, tremendous, trackless. —**Ant.** small, cramped, crowded.

span, *n.* **1.** distance, amount, piece, length, extent; nine inches. **2.** extension, reach, extent, stretch. **3.** period, spell. **4.** pair, team, yoke, couple, brace. —*v.* **5.** measure; extend over, reach, pass over, stretch across, cross, compass.

spare, *v.* **1.** forbear, omit, refrain from, withhold, keep from. **2.** save, lay away or aside, reserve, set aside or apart. —*adj.* **3.** reserved, extra, reserve. **4.** restricted, meager, frugal, sparing, scanty, parsimonious. **5.** lean, thin, slender, slight, gaunt, lank, skinny, raw-boned, emaciated. **6.** economical, temperate, careful.

sparkle, *v.* **1.** glisten, glitter, shine, twinkle, gleam, coruscate, scintillate. **2.** effervesce, bubble. —*n.* **3.** luster, spark, scintillation, glister, glitter, twinkle, twinkling, coruscation. **4.** brilliance, liveliness, vivacity, spirit, glow, piquancy.

sparse, *adj.* **1.** thin, scattered, here and there. **2.** scanty, meager, spare, restricted. —**Ant.** abundant. —**Syn. Study.** See SCANTY.

speak, *v.* utter, talk, voice, converse, communicate, disclose, reveal, pronounce, say, articulate, significate.

special, *adj.* **1.** distinct, distinguished, different, particular, especial, peculiar, singular, specific, plain, unambiguous, certain, individual, single, unusual, uncommon. **2.** extraordinary, exceptional. —**Ant.** unparticular, common; ordinary.

specific. See SPECIAL.

specimen, *n.* type, example, sample, model, pattern.

specious, *adj.* plausible, ostensible, feasible; deceptive, false, misleading. —**Ant.** implausible; genuine.

specter, *n.* ghost, phantom, spirit, apparition, shade, shadow. —**Ant.** reality.

speculation, *n.* **1.** contemplation, consideration. **2.** conclusion, supposition, conjecture, surmise, view, hypothesis, theory.

speech, *n.* **1.** utterance, remark, observation, declaration, assertion, asseveration, averral, comment, mention, talk. **2.** talk, oration, address, discourse, harangue. **3.** language, words, lingo, tongue, dialect, patois. **4.** parlance, conversation, parley, communication. —**Syn. Study.** SPEECH, ADDRESS, ORATION, HARANGUE are terms for a communication to an audience. SPEECH is the general word, with no implication of kind or length, or whether planned or not. An ADDRESS is a rather formal, planned speech, appropriate to a particular subject or occasion. An ORATION is a polished, rhetorical address, given usu. on a notable occasion, that employs eloquence and studied methods of delivery. A HARANGUE is an impassioned, vehement speech intended to arouse strong feeling and sometimes to lead to mob action.

speechless, *adj.* **1.** dumb, dumbfounded, shocked, mute. **2.** silent, dumb, mute. —**Ant.** loquacious, voluble, talkative.

speed, *n.* **1.** rapidity, alacrity, celerity, quickness, fleetness, velocity, swiftness, dispatch, expedition, haste, hurry. —*v.* **2.** promote, advance, further, forward, expedite, favor. **3.** direct, guide. **4.** accelerate.

—**Ant.** sloth. —**Syn. Study.** SPEED, VELOCITY, CELERITY refer to swift or energetic movement or operation. SPEED may apply to human or nonhuman activity; it emphasizes the rate in time at which something travels or operates: *the speed of an automobile; the speed of thought.* VELOCITY, a more technical term, is commonly used to refer to high rates of speed: *the velocity of a projectile.* CELERITY, a somewhat literary term, usu. refers to human movement or operation, and emphasizes dispatch or economy in an activity: *the celerity of his response.*

spellbound, *adj.* rapt, held, gripped, enthralled, fascinated, intrigued, mesmerized, hypnotized, caught, stunned, transfixed. —**Ant.** uninterested, detached.

spend, *v.* **1.** disburse, expend, pay out, dispose of, squander, throw out, waste, lavish, dissipate. **2.** exhaust, use up, consume. **3.** employ, use, apply, devote. —**Ant.** earn.

sphere, *n.* **1.** ball, orb, globe. **2.** shell, ball. **3.** planet, star. **4.** environment, orbit, area, place, province, circle, compass, coterie, set, realm, domain, quarter. **5.** stratum, walk of life, rank.

spin, *v.* **1.** draw out, twist, wind. **2.** twirl, whirl, turn, rotate, gyrate. **3.** produce, fabricate, evolve, develop. **4.** tell, narrate, relate. **5.** draw out, extend, protract, prolong, lengthen. —*n.* **6.** run, ride, drive. —**Syn. Study.** See TURN.

spindly, *adj.* **1.** gaunt, bony, thin, lean, spare, skeletal, scrawny, skinny, lanky, gangly, gangling. **2.** unsteady, shaky, rickety, teetery, teetering, tottery, tottering, wobbly, doddering, fragile. —**Ant.** robust, sturdy.

spineless, *adj.* limp, weak, feeble, irresolute, undetermined, thewless. —**Ant.** strong.

spirit, *n.* **1.** animation, vitality, soul, essence, life, mind, consciousness. **2.** goblin, sprite, elf, fairy, hobgoblin; angel, genius, demon, *prāna.* **3.** ghost, specter, apparition, phantom, shade, shadow. **4.** God, The Holy Ghost, The Holy Spirit, The Comforter, The Spirit of God. **5.** mettle, vigor, liveliness, enthusiasm, energy, zeal, zealousness, ardor, fire, vivacity, enterprise, resourcefulness. **6.** temper, disposition, attitude, mood, humor, sorts, frame of mind. **7.** character, nature, drift, tenor, gist, sense, complexion, quintessence, essence. **8.** meaning, intent, intention, significance, purport. —*v.* **9.** inspirit, vitalize, animate, instill, encourage, excite.

spirited, *adj.* excited, animated, vivacious, ardent, active, agog, energetic, lively, vigorous, courageous, mettlesome, bold. —**Ant.** dispirited, inactive, indolent.

spite, *n.* **1.** ill will, malevolence, maliciousness, malice, rancor, gall, malignity, venom, spleen. **2.** grudge, hate, pique, hatred. —*v.* **3.** annoy, thwart, injure, hurt, harm.

spiteful, *adj.* malicious, venomous, malevolent, revengeful, vindictive, mean, cruel, hateful, rancorous. —**Ant.** benevolent, friendly.

splendid, *adj.* **1.** gorgeous, magnificent, sumptuous, luxurious, superb, dazzling, imposing. **2.** grand, beautiful, impressive. **3.** glorious, renowned, famed, famous, illustrious, eminent, conspicuous, distinguished, remarkable, celebrated, brilliant, noble. **4.** fine, striking, admirable. —**Ant.** sordid, squalid; ignoble.

splendor, *n.* **1.** magnificence, brilliance, grandeur, pomp, show, display, dash, élan, éclat. **2.** distinction, glory, brilliance, fame, eminence, renown, celebrity. **3.** brightness, brilliance, light, luster, dazzle, refulgence. —**Ant.** squalor.

splenetic, *adj.* spleenish, spleeny, irritable, peevish, spiteful, vexatious, irascible, testy, fretful, touchy, edgy, petulant, snappish, waspish, cross, choleric. —**Ant.** moderate, temperate.

spoil, *v.* **1.** damage, impair, ruin, wreck, disfigure, destroy, demolish, mar, harm. **2.** corrupt, vitiate. **3.** plunder, pillage, rob, rape, despoil, ravage, waste. —*n.* **4.** (*often plural*) booty, plunder, loot, pillage. —**Syn. Study.** SPOIL, HUMOR, INDULGE imply attempting to satisfy the wishes or whims of oneself or others. SPOIL implies being so lenient or permissive as to cause harm to a person's character: *to spoil a grandchild.* To HUMOR is to comply with a mood, fancy, or caprice, as in order to satisfy, soothe, or manage: *to humor an invalid.* INDULGE suggests a yielding, though temporary or infrequent, to wishes that perhaps should not be satisfied: *to indulge an irresponsible son.*

spontaneous, *adj.* unpremeditated, natural, unconstrained, voluntary, gratuitous, free, unselfish. —**Ant.** premeditated.

sporadic, *adj.* scattered, occasional, isolated, unconnected, separate. —**Ant.** continuous.

sport, *n.* **1.** pastime, game, athletics, amusement, diversion, fun, entertainment, frolic, recreation, play. **2.** derision, jesting, ridicule, mockery. **3.** laughingstock. **4.** toy, plaything. —*v.* **5.** play, frolic, gambol, romp, caper, skip. **6.** trifle, deal lightly, discount. **7.** ridicule, make fun.

sportive, *adj.* **1.** playful, frolicsome, jesting, jocose, merry, jocular, gay, sprightly, frisky. **2.** joking, prankish, facetious. —**Ant.** sober, serious.

spot, *n.* **1.** mark, stain, blot, speck. **2.** blemish, flaw, stain, taint, stigma. **3.** place, locality, locale, site, situation. —*v.* **4.** stain, mark, blot, speckle. **5.** sully, blemish, stain, taint, stigmatize, soil, tarnish.

spout, *v.* **1.** spurt, squirt, flow, stream, pour. —*n.* **2.** pipe, tube, nozzle, nose.

sprain, *v.* strain, overstrain, wrench, injure, twist.

spread, *v.* **1.** unroll, unfold, open, expand, stretch out, draw out. **2.** extend, stretch, expand, dilate. **3.** display, set forth. **4.** dispose, distribute, scatter, disperse, ted. **5.** overlay, cover, coat. **6.** emit, scatter, diffuse, radiate. **7.** shed, scatter, diffuse, disseminate, broadcast, publish, circulate, divulge, promulgate, propagate, disperse. —*n.* **8.** expansion, extension, diffusion. **9.** extent, reach, compass; stretch, expanse. **10.** bedspread, cloth, cover, tablecloth. **11.** preserve, jam, jelly, peanut butter.

spring, *v.* **1.** leap, jump, bound, hop, vault. **2.** recoil, fly back, rebound. **3.** shoot, dart, fly. **4.** arise, start, originate, rise, issue, emanate, flow. **5.** grow, develop, increase, wax, thrive. **6.** emerge, emanate, issue, flow, proceed. **7.** bend, warp. **8.** explode. **9.** split, crack. —*n.* **10.** leap, jump, hop, bound, vault. **11.** elasticity, springiness, resiliency, buoyancy, vigor. **12.** split, crack, fissure; bend, warp. **13.** source, origin, mouth, fountainhead, head. —*adj.* **14.** vernal, springtime.

sprinkle, *v.* **1.** scatter, strew, spread, disperse, fling, distribute, rain. **2.** diversify, intersperse.

spry, *adj.* active, nimble, agile, brisk, lively, energetic, animated, quick, smart, alert, ready, prompt. —**Ant.** inactive.

spur, *n.* **1.** goad, prick, rowel. **2.** whip, goad, incitement, stimulus, incentive, inducement, provocation, impulse, instigation. —*v.* **3.** urge, goad, prick, whip, incite, provoke, stimulate, induce, instigate. —**Ant.** discourage.

spurious, *adj.* **1.** counterfeit, sham, false, pretended, unauthentic, bogus, phony, mock, feigned; meretricious, deceitful, fictitious. **2.** illegitimate, bastard. —**Ant.** genuine.

spurn, *v.* reject, disdain, scorn, despise, refuse, contemn. —**Ant.** accept. —**Syn. Study.** See REFUSE.

spurt, *v.* **1.** gush, spout, flow, issue, stream, jet, well, spring. —*n.* **2.** outburst, jet, spout. —**Ant.** drip, ooze.

squalid, *adj.* foul, repulsive, unclean, dirty, filthy, nasty. **2.** wretched, miserable, degraded. —**Ant.** splendid.

squalor, *n.* squalidness, filth, misery, foulness. —**Ant.** splendor.

squander, *v.* spend, waste, dissipate, throw away, lavish, misuse, expend. —**Ant.** save.

squeamish, *adj.* **1.** modest, prudish; blue. **2.** moral, particular, scrupulous, fastidious, finical, finicky, dainty, delicate, hypercritical, nice. —**Ant.** bold.

stab, *v.* **1.** pierce, wound, gore, spear, penetrate, pin, transfix. **2.** thrust, plunge. —*n.* **3.** thrust, blow, wound.

stability, *n.* firmness, continuance, permanence, constancy, steadiness, steadfastness, strength, immovability, fixedness. —**Ant.** instability.

stable, *n.* **1.** barn, mews. —*adj.* **2.** firm, steady, rigid, fixed, strong, sturdy, established, immovable, permanent, invariable, unvarying, steadfast, unchangeable, unchanging. **3.** enduring, permanent, constant, perdurable, lasting, abiding, secure, fast, perpetual, eternal, everlasting. **4.** unwavering, steadfast, staunch, constant, reliable, steady, solid. —**Ant.** unstable.

stagger, *v.* **1.** sway, reel, totter,

waver, falter, vacillate. **2.** hesitate, doubt. **3.** shock, astound, astonish, confound, amaze, nonplus, dumbfound, surprise. **4.** alternate, zigzag, rearrange, reorder, overlap.

staid, *adj.* sedate, settled, sober, serious, proper, decorous, correct, quiet, composed, serene, calm, solemn, grave. —**Ant.** wild, indecorous.

stain, *n.* **1.** discoloration, spot, blemish, mark, imperfection, blot. **2.** stigma, disgrace, dishonor, taint, blot, tarnish. **3.** dye, reagent, tint. —*v.* **4.** discolor, taint, spot, streak, soil, dirty, blemish, blot. **5.** blemish, sully, spot, taint, soil, tarnish, disgrace, dishonor, stigmatize, corrupt, debase, defile, contaminate, pollute. **6.** tint, dye, tinge, color.

stake, *n.* **1.** stick, post, pale, picket, pike. **2.** wager, bet. **3.** (*often plural*) prize, winnings, purse. **4.** risk, jeopardy, hazard. —*v.* **5.** risk, hazard, jeopardize, wager, venture, bet, imperil.

stale, *adj.* **1.** vapid, flat, dry, hardened, hard, tasteless, sour, insipid. **2.** uninteresting, hackneyed, trite, stereotyped, old hat, old, common, commonplace. —**Ant.** fresh, modern.

stalemate, *n.* impasse, deadlock, standstill.

stalwart, *adj.* **1.** strong, stout, well-developed, robust, sturdy, brawny, sinewy, muscular, athletic, strapping, vigorous. **2.** strong, brave, valiant, bold, valorous, intrepid, daring, fearless, firm, resolute, indomitable, gallant. **3.** firm, steadfast, resolute, uncompromising, redoubtable, formidable. —**Ant.** weak, feeble; fearful; infirm, unsteady.

stamina, *n.* strength, vigor, resistance, power, health, robustness. —**Ant.** weakness.

stammer, *v.* stutter, pause, hesitate, falter.

stamp, *v.* **1.** strike, beat, trample, crush, pound. **2.** eliminate, abolish, squash, quash, eradicate. **3.** impress, mark, label, brand, imprint. **4.** characterize, distinguish, reveal. —*n.* **5.** die, block, cut, engraving, brand, branding iron. **6.** impression, design, pattern, brand, mark, print, seal. **7.** character, kind, type, sort, description, cut, style, cast, mold, fashion, form, make.

stand, *v.* **1.** halt, stop, pause. **2.** remain, continue, persist, stay, abide, be firm or resolute or steadfast or steady. **3.** set, erect, place, put, fix. **4.** face, meet, encounter, resist, oppose. **5.** endure, undergo, submit to, bear, sustain, weather, outlast. **6.** tolerate, abide, stomach, endure, suffer, bear, admit, allow. —*n.* **7.** halt, stop, rest, stay. **8.** position, effort, determination, attitude. **9.** station, post, place, position, spot. **10.** platform, dais, grandstand. **11.** stall, booth, table, case, counter. **12.** copse, grove, forest, wood; growth, crop. —**Syn. Study.** See BEAR.

standard, *n.* **1.** criterion, measure, gauge, test, model, example, exemplar, sample, basis, pattern, guide, rule. **2.** grade, level. **3.** emblem, flag, symbol, ensign, banner, pennant, pennon, streamer. **4.** upright, support; bar, rod, timber. —*adj.* **5.** basic, exemplary, guiding, sample, typical. —**Syn. Study.** STANDARD, CRITERION refer to the basis for making a judgment. A STANDARD is an authoritative principle or rule that usu. implies a model or pattern for guidance, by comparison with which the quantity, excellence, correctness, etc., of other things may be determined: *She could serve as the standard of good breeding.* A CRITERION is a rule or principle used to judge the value, suitability, probability, etc., of something, without necessarily implying any comparison: *Wealth is no criterion of a person's worth.*

standing, *n.* **1.** position, status, rank, credit, reputation, condition. **2.** existence, continuation, duration, residence, membership, experience. **3.** station, booth. —*adj.* **4.** still, stationary, stagnant, unmoving, motionless. **5.** continuing, continuous, unceasing, constant, permanent, unchanging, steady, lasting, durable. **6.** idle, out of use, unused. **7.** operative, in force, effective, in effect, established, settled.

stanza, *n.* quatrain, stave, poem, staff.

stare, *v.*, *n.* gaze.

stark, *adj.* **1.** sheer, utter, downright, arrant, simple, mere, pure, absolute, entire, unmistakable. **2.** stiff, rigid. **3.** harsh, grim, desolate, dreary, drear. —*adv.* **4.** utterly, absolutely, completely; quite, irrevocable. —**Ant.** vague.

start, *v.* **1.** begin, set out or forth, commence, depart. **2.** issue, come up, come, arise. **3.** jump, jerk, twitch, spring. **4.** set up, begin, establish, found, institute, initiate. —*n.* **5.** beginning, outset, initiation, commencement, onset. **6.** impulse, signal, go-ahead, starting gun. **7.** jerk, spasm, fit, twitch, jump. **8.** headstart, lead. **9.** chance, opportunity. —**Ant.** end, terminate. —**Syn. Study.** See BEGIN.

startle, *v.* **1.** disturb, shock, agitate, surprise, alarm, amaze, astound, astonish, scare, frighten. —*n.* **2.** shock, surprise, alarm. —**Ant.** calm.

state, *n.* **1.** condition, case, circumstances, predicament, pass, plight, situation, status, surroundings, environment, rank, position, standing, stage. **2.** constitution, structure, form, phase. **3.** estate, station, rank, position, standing. **4.** dignity, pomp, display, grandeur, glory, magnificence. **5.** sovereign government, government, federation, commonwealth, community, territory. —*adj.* **6.** public, national, government, federal. **7.** ceremonial, ceremonious, pompous, stately, imposing, sumptuous, dignified. —*v.* **8.** declare, aver, assert, asseverate, set forth, express, affirm, specify. **9.** say. **10.** fix, settle, determine, authorize.

stately, *adj.* imposing, grand, dignified, majestic, elegant, magnificent, state. —**Ant.** base, mean, vile.

statement, *n.* declaration, communication, report, announcement, proclamation.

statesman. See Syn. study at POLITICIAN.

station, *n.* **1.** position, post, place, situation, location. **2.** depot, terminal, way-station, whistle-stop. **3.** standing, rank, dignity. **4.** position, office, rank, calling, occupation, metier, trade, business, employment, office, appointment. —*v.* **5.** assign, place, post, position, locate, establish, set, fix.

status, *n.* **1.** condition, state. **2.** condition, position, standing, rank.

staunch, *adj.* firm, steadfast, stable, steady, constant, resolute, true, faithful, principled, loyal, substantial, strong, sound, stout. —*v.* unsteady, disloyal. —**Syn. Study.** See STEADFAST.

stay, *v.* **1.** remain, dwell, reside, abide, sojourn, tarry, rest, lodge. **2.** continue, remain. **3.** stop, halt. **4.** pause, wait, delay, linger. **5.** hold back, detain, restrain, obstruct, arrest, check, hinder, delay, hold, curb, prevent. **6.** suspend, delay, adjourn. **7.** suppress, quell. **8.** appease, satisfy, curb, allay. **9.** wait out. **10.** support, prop, brace, buttress. **11.** rest, rely or depend on, confide or trust in, lean on. **12.** sustain, bolster, strengthen, uphold. —*n.* **13.** stop, halt, pause, delay, standstill; interruption, break, hiatus, lacuna. **14.** sojourn, rest, repose. **15.** prop, brace, support; crutch. **16.** rope, guy, guy wire. —**Ant.** leave.

steadfast, *adj.* **1.** fixed, directed, fast, firm, established, stable. **2.** stanch, steady, sure, dependable, reliable, resolute, constant, strong, firm, loyal, regular, purposeful, faithful, unwavering. —**Ant.** unsteady; weak; sporadic, unfaithful. —**Syn. Study.** STEADFAST, STAUNCH, STEADY imply a sureness and continuousness that may be depended upon. STEADFAST literally means fixed in place, but is chiefly used figuratively to indicate undeviating constancy or resolution: *steadfast in one's faith.* STAUNCH literally means watertight, as of a vessel, and therefore strong and firm; figuratively, it is used of loyal support that will endure strain: *a staunch advocate of free trade.* Literally, STEADY is applied to that which is relatively firm in position or continuous in movement or duration: *a steady flow;* figuratively, it implies sober regularity or persistence: *a steady worker.*

steady, *adj.* **1.** firm, fixed, steadfast, stable, balanced, even, regular. **2.** undeviating, invariable, unvarying, regular, constant, unchanging, uninterrupted, uniform, unremitting, continuous. **3.** habitual, regular, constant, unchangeable. **4.** firm, unwavering, steadfast. **5.** settled, staid, sedate, sober. —*v.* **6.** stabilize. —**Ant.** unsteady. —**Syn. Study.** See STEADFAST.

steal, *v.* **1.** take, pilfer, purloin, filch, embezzle, peculate, swindle. **2.** win, gain, draw, lure, allure. —**Ant.** provide.

stealthy, *adj.* furtive, surreptitious,

secret, clandestine, sly. —**Ant.** obvious, open, manifest.

stem, *n.* **1.** axis, stalk, trunk, petiole, peduncle, pedicel. **2.** stock, family, descent, pedigree, ancestry, lineage, race. —*v.* **3.** rise, arise, originate. **4.** stop, check, dam up, obstruct, hinder, stay. **5.** tamp, plug, tighten. **6.** progress against, oppose, breast, make headway against, withstand.

stench. See Syn. study at ODOR.

stereotyped, *adj.* fixed, settled, conventional, hackneyed, overused, commonplace, trite, banal, dull, ordinary, lifeless, uninteresting, stale, boring, worn, pointless, insipid, inane. —**Ant.** rare, uncommon, unusual; interesting, fresh, sensible.

sterile, *adj.* **1.** uncontaminated, unpolluted, uncorrupted, antiseptic. **2.** barren, unproductive, fruitless, infecund. —**Ant.** fertile.

stern, *adj.* **1.** firm, strict, adamant, unrelenting, uncompromising, severe, harsh, hard, inflexible, forbidding, unsympathetic, rough, cruel, unfeeling. **2.** rigorous, austere, steadfast, rigid. —**Ant.** lenient, flexible. —**Syn. Study.** STERN, SEVERE, HARSH mean strict or firm and can be applied to methods, aspects, manners, or facial expressions. STERN implies uncompromising, inflexible firmness, and sometimes a forbidding aspect or nature: *a stern parent.* SEVERE implies strictness, lack of sympathy, and a tendency to discipline others: *a severe judge.* HARSH suggests a great severity and roughness, and cruel, unfeeling treatment of others: *a harsh critic.*

stew, *v.* **1.** simmer, boil, seethe. —*n.* **2.** ragout. —**Syn. Study.** See BOIL.

stick, *n.* **1.** branch, shoot, switch. **2.** rod, wand, baton. **3.** club, cudgel; bat. **4.** thrust, stab. **5.** interrruption. —*v.* **6.** pierce, puncture, stab, penetrate, spear, transfix, pin, gore. **7.** impale. **8.** fasten, attach, glue, cement, paste. **9.** adhere, cohere, cling, cleave, hold. **10.** remain, stay, persist, abide. **11.** hesitate, scruple, stickle, waver, doubt. —**Syn. Study.** STICK, ADHERE, COHERE mean to be fastened or attached to something. STICK is the general term; it means to be fastened with glue, pins, nails, etc.: *A gummed label will stick to a package.* Used figuratively, STICK means to hold faithfully or keep steadily to something: *to stick to a promise.* ADHERE is a more formal term meaning to cling or to stay firmly attached: *Wallpaper will not adhere to a rough surface.* Used figuratively, ADHERE means to be attached as a follower: *to adhere to religious beliefs.* COHERE means to hold fast to something similar to itself: *The particles of sealing wax cohered into a ball.* Used figuratively, COHERE means to be logically connected or attached: *The pieces of evidence did not cohere.*

stiff, *adj.* **1.** rigid, firm, solid, unflexible, unbendable, unbending, unyielding. **2.** violent, strong, steady, unremitting, fresh. **3.** firm, purposive, unrelenting, unyielding, resolved, obstinate, stubborn, pertinacious. **4.** graceless, awkward, clumsy, inelegant, crude, harsh, abrupt. **5.** formal, ceremonious, punctilious, constrained, starched, prim, priggish. **6.** laborious, difficult. **7.** severe, rigorous, straitlaced, austere, strict, dogmatic, uncompromising, positive, absolute, inexorable. **8.** great, high. **9.** taut, tight, tense. **10.** dense, compact, tenacious. —*n.* **11.** prude, prig. —**Ant.** flexible.

stifle, *v.* **1.** smother, suffocate, strangle, garrote, choke. **2.** keep back, repress, check, stop, suppress. **3.** crush, stop, obviate, prevent, preclude, put down, destroy, suppress. —**Ant.** encourage, further, foster.

stigma, *n.* **1.** mark, stain, reproach, taint, blot, spot, tarnish, disgrace, infamy, disrepute. **2.** brand.

still, *adj.* **1.** in place, at rest, motionless, stationary, unmoving, inert, quiescent. **2.** soundless, quiet, hushed, noiseless, silent, mute. **3.** tranquil, calm, peaceful, peaceable, pacific, placid, serene. —*conj.* **4.** but, nevertheless, and yet. —*v.* **5.** silence, hush, quiet, mute, stifle, muffle, smother. **6.** calm, appease, allay, soothe, compose, pacify, smooth, tranquilize. —*n.* **7.** stillness, quiet, hush, calm. **8.** distillery. —**Ant.** mobile, moving; noisy, clamorous; noise. —**Syn. Study.** See BUT.

stimulate, *v.* **1.** rouse, arouse, activate, incite, animate, excite, urge, provoke, instigate, goad, spur, prod, prick, inflame, fire. **2.** invigorate. —**Ant.** discourage.

stimulus, *n.* incentive, incitement, enticement, stimulation, motive,

provocation; stimulant. —**Ant.** discouragement; wet blanket; soporific.

stingy, *adj.* niggardly, penurious, parsimonious, miserly, mean, close, tight, avaricious. —**Ant.** generous. —**Syn. Study.** STINGY, PARSIMONIOUS, MISERLY mean reluctant to part with money, possessions, or other things. STINGY means unwilling to give, share, or spend anything of value: *a stingy employer; an expert stingy with advice.* PARSIMONIOUS describes a stinginess arising from excessive frugality or unwillingness to spend money: *a parsimonious family.* MISERLY implies a pathological pleasure in acquiring and hoarding money: *a miserly recluse.*

stint, *v.* **1.** limit, restrict, confine, restrain; pinch, straiten. —*n.* **2.** limit, limitation, restriction, restraint, constraint. **3.** share, rate, allotment, portion. —**Ant.** liberate, free.

stir, *v.* **1.** move, agitate, disturb. **2.** shake. **3.** incite, instigate, prompt, rouse, foment, arouse, provoke, stimulate, animate, urge, goad, spur. **4.** affect, excite, move. —*n.* **5.** movement, bustle, ado, agitation, commotion, disorder, uproar, tumult. **6.** impulse, sensation, feeling, emotion.

stock, *n.* **1.** store, goods, inventory, supplies, supply, provision, reserve, hoard. **2.** livestock, cattle, horses, sheep. **3.** trunk, stem. **4.** race, lineage, family, descent, pedigree, ancestry, line, parentage, house, tribe. **5.** handle, haft. **6.** pillory. —*adj.* **7.** staple, standard, standing, customary, permanent. **8.** common, commonplace, ordinary, usual. —*v.* **9.** supply, store, fill.

stoical, *adj.* stoic, impassive, calm, austere, apathetic, imperturbable, cool, indifferent. —**Ant.** sympathetic, warm.

stony, *adj.* **1.** rocky, pebbly, gritty. **2.** unfeeling, merciless, obdurate, adamant, inflexible, stiff, hard, flinty, pitiless, unbending. **3.** motionless, rigid, stock-still.

stoop, *v.* **1.** bend, lean, bow, crouch. **2.** descend, condescend, deign, lower oneself. **3.** stoop down, descend. —*n.* **4.** descent, indignity, condescension, humiliation.

stop, *v.* **1.** cease, leave off, discontinue, desist or refrain from. **2.** interrupt, arrest, check, halt, restrain, intermit, terminate, end. **3.** cut off, intercept, withhold, thwart, interrupt, obstruct, impede, hinder, prevent, preclude, delay, restrain, repress, suppress. **4.** block, obstruct, close, seal off, blockade. **5.** cease, pause, quit. —*n.* **6.** halt, cessation, arrest, end, termination, check. **7.** stay, sojourn, stopover. **8.** station, depot, terminal. **9.** block, obstruction, obstacle, hindrance, impediment; plug, stopper, cork. **10.** check, control, governor. —**Ant.** start. —**Syn. Study.** STOP, ARREST, CHECK, HALT imply causing a cessation of movement or progress (literal or figurative). STOP is the general term for the idea: *to stop a clock.* ARREST usu. refers to stopping by imposing a sudden and complete restraint: *to arrest development.* CHECK implies bringing about an abrupt, partial, or temporary stop: *to check a trotting horse.* To HALT means to make a temporary stop, esp. one resulting from a command: *to halt a company of soldiers.*

storm, *n.* **1.** gale, hurricane, tempest, tornado, cyclone, sirocco, simoom, dust storm, squall, northeaster, wind, rainstorm, bise, whirlwind, hailstorm, snowstorm, blizzard, thunderstorm. **2.** assault, siege, attack. **3.** violence, commotion, disturbance, strife. **4.** outburst, outbreak. —*v.* **5.** blow; rain, snow, hail, thunder and lightning. **6.** rage, rant, fume, complain. **7.** rush, attack, assault, besiege.

story, *n.* **1.** narrative, tale, legend, fable, romance, anecdote, record, history, chronicle. **2.** plot, theme, incident. **3.** narration, recital, rehearsal, relation. **4.** report, account, description, statement, allegation. **5.** floor, level.

stout, *adj.* **1.** bulky, thick-set, fat, corpulent, plump, portly, fleshy. **2.** bold, hardy, dauntless, brave, valiant, gallant, intrepid, fearless, indomitable, courageous. **3.** firm, stubborn, obstinate, contumacious, resolute. **4.** strong, stalwart, sturdy, sinewy, athletic, brawny, vigorous, able-bodied. **5.** thick, heavy. —**Ant.** slim, slender, thin; fearful; weak; light.

straight, *adj.* **1.** direct, right. **2.** candid, frank, open, honest, direct. **3.** honorable, honest, virtuous, upright, erect, just, fair, equitable, straightforward. **4.** right, correct. **5.** unmodified, unaltered, unchanged. —**Ant.** devious, crooked.

straightforward, *adj.* **1.** direct, straight, undeviating, unwavering, unswerving. **2.** honest, truthful, honorable, just, fair. —**Ant.** devious; dishonest.

strain, *v.* **1.** stretch, tighten, tauten. **2.** exert. **3.** sprain, impair, injure, weaken, wrench, twist, tear, overexert. **4.** filter, sift, sieve, filtrate, purify, percolate, seep through. **5.** clasp, hug, embrace, press. **6.** filter, percolate, ooze, seep. —*n.* **7.** force, pressure, effort, exertion. **8.** sprain, injury, wrench. **9.** family, stock, descent, race, pedigree, lineage, ancestry, extraction. **10.** character, tendency, trait. **11.** streak, trace, hint, suggestion.

strait, *n.* difficulty, distress, need, emergency, exigency, crisis, pinch, dilemma, predicament, plight. —**Ant.** ease.

straitlaced, *adj.* prim, stuffy, hidebound, prudish, moralistic, rigid, priggish, puritanical, bluenosed, prissy, Victorian. —**Ant.** free and easy, relaxed, licentious.

strange, *adj.* **1.** unusual, extraordinary, curious, bizarre, odd, queer, singular, peculiar, unfamiliar, inexplicable, unexplained, irregular, unconventional, rare, mysterious, mystifying, eccentric, abnormal, anomalous, exceptional. **2.** alien, foreign, exotic, outlandish, unfamiliar. **3.** unacquainted, unaccustomed, unused, unfamiliar, unknown, unexperienced. **4.** distant, reserved, aloof, supercilious, superior. —**Ant.** usual, commonplace.

stranger, *n.* alien, foreigner, outsider. —**Ant.** friend, relative, ally. —**Syn. Study.** STRANGER, ALIEN, FOREIGNER all refer to someone regarded as outside of or distinct from a particular group. STRANGER may apply to one who does not belong to some group—social, professional, national, etc.—or may apply to a person with whom one is not acquainted. ALIEN emphasizes a difference in political allegiance and citizenship from that of the country in which one is living. FOREIGNER emphasizes a difference in language, customs, and background.

strangle, *v.* garrote; choke, stifle, suffocate, smother, throttle.

stratagem, *n.* plan, scheme, trick, ruse, deception, artifice, wile, intrigue, device, maneuver, contrivance, machination. —**Syn. Study.** See TRICK.

strategy, *n.* tactics, generalship; skillful management.

stream, *n.* **1.** current, rivulet, rill, streamlet, run, runnel, river. **2.** flow, course, tide. **3.** flow, succession, torrent, rush. —*v.* **4.** pour, flow, run, issue, emit.

street, *n.* way, road, roadway, avenue, boulevard, concourse, highway; path, footpath, alley, alleyway.

strength, *n.* **1.** power, force, vigor, health, might, potency, energy, capacity. **2.** firmness, courage, fortitude, resolution. **3.** effectiveness, efficacy, potency, cogency, soundness, validity. **4.** intensity, brightness, loudness, vividness, pungency. **5.** support, stay, prop, brace. —**Ant.** weakness.

strenuous, *adj.* vigorous, energetic, active, animated, spirited, eager, zealous, ardent, resolute, determined, forceful, earnest. —**Ant.** easy.

stress, *v.* **1.** emphasize, accent. **2.** strain. —*n.* **3.** importance, significance, emphasis, weight, accent, force. —**Ant.** unstress, deemphasize, ease, underplay.

stretch, *v.* **1.** draw out, extend, lengthen, elongate. **2.** hold out, reach forth, reach, extend, stretch forth. **3.** spread. **4.** tighten, tauten, strain. **5.** lengthen, widen, distend, dilate, enlarge, broaden. **6.** strain, exaggerate. **7.** recline, lie down. —*n.* **8.** length, distance, tract, expanse, extent, extension, range, reach, compass. —**Ant.** curtail, abbreviate.

strew, *v.* scatter, sprinkle, overspread, broadcast. —**Ant.** gather, reap.

strict, *adj.* **1.** rigid, rigorous, stringent, inflexible, stiff, severe, unbending, unyielding, exacting, demanding, stern, narrow, illiberal, uncompromising, harsh, austere, straitlaced. **2.** exact, precise, accurate, scrupulous, particular. **3.** close, careful, minute, critical. **4.** absolute, perfect, complete. —**Ant.** flexible. —**Syn. Study.** STRICT, RIGID, RIGOROUS, STRINGENT imply inflexibility, severity, and an exacting quality. STRICT suggests close conformity to rules, require-

ments, obligations, or principles: *to maintain strict discipline.* RIGID suggests an inflexible, uncompromising, or unyielding nature or character: *a rigid parent.* RIGOROUS suggests that which is harsh or severe, esp. in action or application: *rigorous self-denial.* STRINGENT refers to something that is vigorously exacting, or absolutely binding: *stringent measures to suppress disorder.*

strife, *n.* **1.** conflict, discord, variance, difference, disagreement, contrariety, opposition. **2.** quarrel, struggle, clash, fight, conflict. —**Ant.** peace.

strike, *v.* **1.** thrust, hit, smite, knock, beat, pound, slap, cuff, buffet. **2.** catch, arrest, impress. **3.** come across, meet with, meet, encounter. **4.** affect, overwhelm, impress. —**Syn. Study.** See BEAT.

stringent, *adj.* **1.** strict. **2.** narrow, binding, restrictive. **3.** urgent, compelling, constraining. **4.** convincing, forceful, powerful, effective, forcible, persuasive. —**Ant.** flexible, mollifying, emollient; ineffective. —**Syn. Study.** See STRICT.

strip, *v.* **1.** uncover, peel, decorticate, denude. **2.** remove. **3.** withhold, deprive, divest, dispossess, dismantle. **4.** rob, plunder, despoil, pillage, sack, devastate, spoil, desolate, lay waste. —*n.* **5.** band, ribbon. —*v.* **6.** cover.

strive, *v.* **1.** endeavor, try, exert oneself, essay, struggle, toil. **2.** contend, compete, fight, struggle. —**Syn. Study.** See TRY.

stroke, *n.* **1.** striking, blow, hitting, beating, beat, knock, rap, tap, pat, thump. **2.** throb, pulsation, beat; rhythm. **3.** apoplexy, paralysis, shock, attack. **4.** feat, achievement, accomplishment. —*v.* **5.** caress, rub gently, massage.

stroll, *v.* **1.** ramble, saunter, meander. **2.** wander, roam, rove, stray. —*n.* **3.** ramble, saunter, promenade, walk.

strong, *adj.* **1.** powerful, vigorous, hale, hearty, healthy, robust, mighty, sturdy, brawny, athletic, sinewy, hardy, muscular, stout, stalwart, Herculean. **2.** powerful, able, competent, potent, capable, puissant, efficient. **3.** firm, courageous, valiant, brave, valorous, bold, intrepid, fearless. **4.** influential, resourceful, persuasive, cogent, impressive. **5.** clear, firm, loud. **6.** well-supplied, rich, substantial. **7.** cogent, forceful, forcible, effective, efficacious, conclusive, potent, powerful. **8.** resistive, resistant, solid, firm, secure, compact, impregnable, impenetrable. **9.** firm, unfaltering, tenacious, unwavering, resolute, solid, tough, staunch, stout. **10.** intoxicating, alcoholic, potent. **11.** intense, brilliant, glaring, vivid, dazzling. **12.** distinct, marked, sharp, stark, contrasty. **13.** strenuous, energetic, forceful, vigorous, zealous, eager, earnest, ardent. **14.** hearty, fervent, fervid, thoroughgoing, vehement, stubborn. **15.** pungent, racy, olent, aromatic, odoriferous; sharp, piquant, spicy, hot, biting. **16.** smelly, rank. —**Ant.** weak.

structure, *n.* **1.** construction, organization, system, arrangement, form, configuration, shape. **2.** building, edifice, bridge, dam, framework. **3.** composition, arrangement.

struggle, *v.* **1.** contend, strive, oppose, contest, fight, conflict. —*n.* **2.** brush, clash, encounter, skirmish, fight, battle, conflict, strife. **3.** effort, strive, endeavor, exertion, labor, pains.

strut, *v.* **1.** swagger, parade. —*n.* **2.** brace, support, prop, stretcher. —**Syn. Study.** STRUT and SWAGGER refer esp. to carriage in walking. STRUT implies swelling pride or pompousness; it means to walk with a stiff, seemingly affected or self-conscious gait: *A turkey struts about the barnyard.* SWAGGER implies a domineering, sometimes jaunty, superiority or challenge and a self-important manner: *to swagger down the street.*

stubborn, *adj.* **1.** obstinate, perverse, contrary, dogged, persistent, intractable, refractory, inflexible, unyielding, unbending, rigid, stiff, contumacious, headstrong, pigheaded, obdurate. **2.** fixed, set, opinionated, resolute, persevering. **3.** hard, tough, stiff, strong, stony. —**Ant.** tractable, flexible; irresolute. —**Syn. Study.** STUBBORN, OBSTINATE, DOGGED, PERSISTENT imply fixity of purpose or condition and resistance to change. STUBBORN and OBSTINATE both imply resistance to advice, entreaty, protest, or force; but STUBBORN implies an innate characteristic and is the term usu. used when referring to inani-

mate things: *a stubborn child; a stubborn lock; an obstinate customer.* DOGGED implies willfulness and tenacity, esp. in the face of obstacles: *dogged determination.* PERSISTENT implies having staying or lasting qualities, resoluteness, and perseverance: *persistent questioning.*

student, *n.* pupil, scholar; observer. —**Ant.** teacher.

studied, *adj.* deliberate, premeditated, predetermined, willful, considered, elaborate. —**Ant.** unpremeditated.

study, *n.* **1.** attention, application, investigation, inquiry, research, reading, reflection, meditation, cogitation, thought, consideration, contemplation. **2.** field, area, subject. **3.** zealousness, endeavor, effort, assiduity, sedulousness, assiduousness. **4.** thought, reverie, abstraction. **5.** library, den. —*v.* **6.** read, investigate, practice. **7.** think, reflect, consider, ponder, weigh, estimate, examine, contemplate, scrutinize, turn over. —**Syn. Study.** STUDY, CONSIDER, REFLECT, WEIGH imply fixing the mind upon something, generally doing so with a view to some decision or action. STUDY implies an attempt to obtain a grasp of something by methodical or exhaustive thought: *to study a problem.* CONSIDER implies fixing the mind on something and giving it close attention before making a decision or taking action: *to consider the alternatives.* REFLECT implies looking back quietly over past experience and giving it consideration: *to reflect on similar cases in the past.* WEIGH implies a deliberate and judicial estimate, as by a balance: *to weigh a decision.*

stuff, *n.* **1.** material, substance, matter. **2.** character, qualities, capabilities. **3.** rubbish, trash, waste, nonsense, twaddle, balderdash, inanity, absurdity. —*v.* **4.** fill, cram, pack, crowd, press, stow. **5.** stop up, choke, plug, obstruct. —**Syn. Study.** See MATTER.

stun, *v.* **1.** knock out, shock, dizzy. **2.** astound, stupefy, daze, astonish, amaze, overcome, bewilder, overwhelm, confound.

stupid, *adj.* **1.** dull, vapid, pointless, prosaic, tedious, uninteresting, boring, insipid, flat, humdrum, tiresome, heavy. **2.** foolish, inane, asinine, senseless, simple, half-witted, witless, obtuse, stolid, dumb. —**Ant.** bright, intelligent, clever, shrewd.

sturdy, *adj.* **1.** well-built, strong, robust, stalwart, hardy, muscular, brawny, sinewy, stout, powerful. **2.** firm, stout, indomitable, unbeatable, unconquerable, persevering, resolute, vigorous, determined. —**Ant.** weak.

style, *n.* **1.** kind, sort, type, form, appearance, character. **2.** mode, manner, method, approach, system. **3.** fashion, elegance, smartness, chic, élan, éclat. **4.** touch, characteristic, mark. **5.** stylus. **6.** etching, point *or* needle, graver. **7.** gnomon. —*v.* **8.** call, denominate, name, designate, address, entitle, title, christen, dub, characterize, term.

suave, *adj.* smooth, agreeable, polite, bland, urbane, sophisticated, worldly, mundane. —**Ant.** boorish.

subdue, *v.* **1.** conquer, defeat, suppress, subjugate, vanquish, overcome, overpower, subject. **2.** repress, reduce, overcome. **3.** tame, break, discipline, domesticate. **4.** tone down, soften, mollify. —**Syn. Study.** See DEFEAT.

subject, *n.* **1.** theme, topic, conception, point, thesis, object, subject matter. **2.** ground, motive, reason, rationale, cause. **3.** minion, dependent, subordinate. —*adj.* **4.** subordinate, subjacent, subservient, subjected, inferior. **5.** obedient, submissive. **6.** open, exposed, prone, liable. **7.** dependent, conditional, contingent. —*v.* **8.** dominate, control, influence. **9.** make liable, lay open, expose. —**Syn. Study.** SUBJECT, TOPIC, THEME refer to the central idea or matter considered in speech or writing. SUBJECT refers to the broad or general matter treated in a discussion, literary work, etc.: *The subject of the novel was a poor Southern family.* TOPIC often applies to one specific part of a general subject; it may also apply to a limited and well-defined subject: *We covered many topics at the meeting. The topic of the news story was an escaped prisoner.* THEME usu. refers to the underlying idea of a discourse or composition, perhaps not clearly stated but easily recognizable: *The theme of social reform runs throughout her work.*

subjective, *adj.* **1.** mental, unreal, imaginary, illusory, fancied, imag-

ined. **2.** personal, individual. **3.** introspective, contemplative, introversive. **4.** substantial, essential, inherent. —**Ant.** objective.

submerge, *v.* submerse, dip, sink, plunge, immerse.

submissive, *adj.* **1.** unresisting, humble, obedient, tractable, compliant, pliant, yielding, amenable, agreeable. **2.** passive, resigned, patient, docile, tame, long-suffering, subdued.

submit, *v.* yield, surrender, bow, comply, obey, agree, resign. —**Ant.** fight. —**Syn. Study.** See YIELD.

subordinate, *adj.* **1.** lower, inferior. **2.** secondary, unimportant, ancillary. **3.** subservient; dependent. —*n.* **4.** inferior, subject. —*v.* **5.** lower, subject, reduce. —**Ant.** superior; primary.

subside, *v.* **1.** sink, lower, decline, precipitate, descend, settle. **2.** quiet, abate, decrease, diminish, lessen, wane, ebb. —**Ant.** rise; increase.

subsidiary, *adj.* supplementary, auxiliary, tributary, subordinate, secondary, ancillary. —**Ant.** primary, principal.

subsidy, *n.* aid, grant, subvention, support, tribute.

substance, *n.* **1.** matter, material, stuff. **2.** essence, subject matter, theme, subject. **3.** meaning, gist, significance, import, pith, essence. —**Syn. Study.** See MATTER.

substantial, *adj.* **1.** real, actual, material, corporeal. **2.** ample, considerable, sizable. **3.** solid, stout, firm, strong, resolute, stable, sound. **4.** wealthy, influential, responsible. **5.** worthy, valuable. **6.** material, essential, important. —**Ant.** insubstantial, immaterial; trivial; unstable, unsound; poor; unworthy; unimportant.

subtract, *v.* withdraw, take away, deduct, diminish, detract, lessen, lower. —**Ant.** add.

subvention, *n.* See SUBSIDY.

succeed, *v.* **1.** flourish, prosper, thrive, go well, make a hit, go swimmingly, prevail. **2.** follow, replace. —**Ant.** fail; precede. —**Syn. Study.** SUCCEED, FLOURISH, PROSPER, THRIVE mean to do well. To SUCCEED is to turn out well or do well; it may also mean to attain a goal: *The strategy succeeded. She succeeded in school.* To FLOURISH is to grow well or fare well: *The plants flourished in the sun. The business flourished under new management.* To PROSPER is to do well, esp. materially or financially: *They worked hard and prospered.* To THRIVE is to do well, esp. to achieve wealth; it may also mean to grow or develop vigorously: *The shopping center thrived. The dog thrived on the new diet.* See also FOLLOW.

succession, *n.* **1.** order, sequence, course, series. **2.** descent, transmission, lineage, race. —**Syn. Study.** See SERIES.

successive, *adj.* consecutive, following, sequential, ordered.

succinct, See Syn. study at CONCISE.

succor, *n.* **1.** help, relief, aid, support, assistance. —*v.* **2.** aid, assist, relieve, help, support. —**Syn. Study.** See HELP.

sudden, *adj.* unexpected, abrupt, unlooked for, unforeseen, quick, unanticipated. —**Ant.** deliberate, premeditated, foreseen.

suffer, *v.* undergo, experience, sustain, bear, tolerate, allow, permit, stomach, stand, meet with, feel.

sufficient, *adj.* enough, adequate, ample, satisfactory, competent. —**Ant.** insufficient.

suggest, *v.* propose, recommend, indicate, hint, insinuate, intimate, prompt, advise. —**Syn. Study.** See HINT.

suggestive, *adj.* See EXPRESSIVE.

sulky, *adj.* sullen, ill-humored, resentful, aloof, moody, surly, morose, cross, splenetic, churlish. —**Ant.** temperate, good-natured.

sullen, *adj.* **1.** silent, reserved, sulky, morose, moody. **2.** ill-humored, sour, vexatious, splenetic, bad-tempered. **3.** gloomy, dismal, cheerless, clouded, overcast, somber, mournful, dark. **4.** slow, sluggish, dull, stagnant. —**Ant.** cheerful. —**Syn. Study.** See GLUM.

sully, *v.* **1.** soil, stain, tarnish, taint, blemish, disgrace, dishonor. **2.** dirty, contaminate, corrupt, pollute. —**Ant.** honor.

summary, *n.* **1.** digest, extract, abstract, brief, synopsis, compendium, epitome, essence, outline, précis, abridgment. —*adj.* **2.** brief, comprehensive, concise, short, condensed, compact, succinct, pithy. **3.** curt, terse, peremptory, laconic. —**Syn. Study.** SUMMARY, BRIEF, DIGEST, SYNOPSIS are terms for a short version of a

longer work. A SUMMARY is a brief statement or restatement of main points, esp. as a conclusion to a work: *a summary of a chapter.* A BRIEF is a concise statement, usu. of the main points of a legal case: *The attorney filed a brief.* A DIGEST is a condensed and systematically arranged collection of literary, legal, or scientific matter: *a digest of Roman law.* A SYNOPSIS is a condensed statement giving a general overview of a subject or a brief summary of a plot: *a synopsis of a play.*

summit, *n.* top, peak, apex, pinnacle, acme, vertex, culmination, zenith. —**Ant.** base, bottom.

summon, *v.* **1.** call, invite, bid; convene, convoke. **2.** call forth, rouse, arouse, activate, incite.

superannuated, *adj.* old, aged, decrepit, obsolete, antiquated, antique, anile, senile, passé. —**Ant.** young, youthful, new, voguish.

superb, *adj.* stately, majestic, grand, magnificent, admirable, fine, excellent, exquisite, elegant, splendid, sumptuous, rich, luxurious, gorgeous. —**Ant.** inferior.

supercilious, *adj.* haughty, disdainful, contemptuous, arrogant, scornful, contumelious. —**Ant.** humble.

superficial, *adj.* shallow, external, outward, exterior, slight. —**Ant.** basic, profound.

superfluous, *adj.* unnecessary, extra, needless, *de trop,* redundant, excessive, superabundant. —**Ant.** essential.

superintend, *v.* oversee, supervise, manage, direct, control, conduct, run.

supernatural, *adj.* **1.** unnatural, superhuman, miraculous, preternatural. **2.** extraordinary, abnormal. —**Syn. Study.** See MIRACULOUS.

supersede, *v.* **1.** replace, displace, supplant, succeed, remove. **2.** void, overrule, annul, neutralize, revoke, rescind. —**Syn. Study.** See REPLACE.

supplant, *v.* displace, supersede, replace, succeed, remove. —**Syn. Study.** See REPLACE.

supple, *adj.* **1.** flexible, pliant, pliable, lithe, limber, lissome, elastic. **2.** compliant, yielding, agreeable, submissive. **3.** obsequious, servile, sycophantic, groveling, slavish, cringing, fawning. —**Ant.** rigid, inflexible.

supplement, *n.* **1.** reinforcement, extension, addition, complement, addendum, appendix, epilogue, postscript. —*v.* **2.** complete, add to, complement. —**Syn. Study.** See COMPLEMENT.

supplicate, *v.* pray, entreat, petition, appeal to, beg, implore, crave, importune, sue, solicit, beseech. —**Ant.** order, command.

supply, *v.* **1.** furnish, provide, replenish, stock, fill. **2.** make up, make up for, satisfy, fulfill. **3.** fill, substitute for, occupy. —*n.* **4.** stock, store, inventory, hoard, reserve.

support, *v.* **1.** bear, hold up, sustain, uphold. **2.** undergo, endure, suffer, submit to, tolerate, bear, stand, stomach, go through, put up with. **3.** sustain, keep up, maintain, provide for, nourish, nurture. **4.** back, uphold, second, further, advocate, endorse, forward, defend. **5.** aid, countenance, maintain, help, assist, advocate, succor, abet, relieve, patronize. **6.** corroborate, confirm. —*n.* **7.** maintenance, sustenance, living, livelihood, subsistence, keep. **8.** help, aid, succor, assistance, relief. **9.** prop, brace, stay. —**Ant.** fail.

suppose, *v.* **1.** assume, presume, infer, presuppose, take for granted. **2.** believe, think, consider, judge, deem, conclude.

sure, *adj.* **1.** undoubted, indubitable, indisputable. **2.** confident, certain, positive, assured, convinced. **3.** reliable, certain, trusty, trustworthy, honest, infallible, unfailing. **4.** firm, stable, solid, safe, secure, steady. **5.** unerring, accurate, precise, certain, infallible. **6.** inevitable, unavoidable, destined. —**Ant.** uncertain, unsure.

surfeit, *n.* **1.** excess, superabundance, superfluity. **2.** disgust, satiety, nausea. —*v.* **3.** supply, satiate, fill, stuff, gorge, overfeed. —**Ant.** insufficiency.

surmise, *v.* **1.** think, infer, conjecture, guess, imagine, suppose, suspect. —*n.* **2.** conjecture, idea, thought, possibility, likelihood. —**Syn. Study.** See GUESS.

surpass, *v.* exceed, excel, transcend, outdo, beat, outstrip.

surplus, *n.* remainder, excess, surfeit, superabundance, residue. —**Ant.** insufficiency, inadequacy.

surprise, *v.* **1.** astonish, amaze, astound, take unawares, startle, discon-

cert, bewilder, confuse. —n. **2.** assault, attack. **3.** amazement, astonishment, wonder.

surrender, v. **1.** yield, give or deliver up, cede. **2.** give up, abandon, relinquish, renounce, resign, waive, forgo. **3.** submit, yield, capitulate, give up. —n. **4.** resignation, capitulation, relinquishment. —**Syn. Study.** See YIELD.

surreptitious, adj. secret, unauthorized, stealthy, clandestine, subreptitious. —**Ant.** open.

surrogate, n. **1.** substitute, replacement, stand-in, fill-in, alternate, backup, locum tenens, deputy, agent, relief, proxy, pinch hitter, understudy. —adj. **2.** substitute, alternate, alternative, backup. —**Ant.** original, prototype.

surveillance, n. watch, care, control, management, supervision, superintendence.

survey, v. **1.** view, scan, observe, watch, inspect, examine, scrutinize. —n. **2.** examination, inspection. **3.** poll.

survive, v. continue, persist, live, remain, succeed, outlive. —**Ant.** languish, die, fail. —**Syn. Study.** SURVIVE, OUTLIVE refer to remaining alive longer than someone else or after some event. SURVIVE usu. means to succeed in staying alive against odds, to live after some event that has threatened one: to survive an automobile accident. It also means to live longer than another person (usu. a relative), but, today, it is used mainly in the passive, as in the fixed expression: The deceased is survived by his wife and children. OUTLIVE stresses capacity for endurance, the time element, and sometimes a sense of competition: She outlived all her enemies. It is also used, however, of a person or thing that has lived or lasted beyond a certain point: The machine has outlived its usefulness.

susceptibility, n. sensibility, sensitivity, sensitiveness, susceptiveness, susceptibleness, impressibility. —**Ant.** insusceptibility.

suspect, v. **1.** distrust, mistrust, doubt. **2.** imagine, believe, surmise, consider, suppose, guess, conjecture. —n. **3.** defendant. —adj. **4.** suspected, suspicious. —**Ant.** trust.

suspend, v. **1.** hang, attach. **2.** defer, postpone, delay, withhold. **3.** stop, cease, desist, hold up, hold off, discontinue, intermit, interrupt, arrest, debar.

suspense, n. **1.** uncertainty, doubt, unsureness, incertitude, indetermination. **2.** indecision, vacillation, hesitation, hesitancy, wavering, irresolution, scruple, misgiving. **3.** suspension, intermission, pause, interruption, cessation, stop, remission, surcease, relief, respite, stay, rest, quiescence. —**Ant.** certainty; decision.

suspicion, n. **1.** doubt, mistrust, misgiving, distrust. **2.** imagination, notion, idea, supposition, conjecture, guess. **3.** trace, hint, suggestion. —**Ant.** trust. —**Syn. Study.** SUSPICION, DISTRUST are terms for a feeling that appearances are not reliable. SUSPICION is the positive tendency to doubt the trustworthiness of appearances and therefore to believe that one has detected possibilities of something unreliable, unfavorable, menacing, or the like: to feel suspicion about the honesty of a prominent man. DISTRUST may be a passive want of trust, faith, or reliance in a person or thing: to feel distrust of one's own ability.

sustain, v. **1.** hold or bear up, bear, carry, support, uphold. **2.** undergo, support, suffer, endure, bear. **3.** maintain, support, subsist, nourish, nurture. **4.** purvey, supply, cater, furnish, support, aid, countenance, help. **5.** uphold, confirm, establish, approve. **6.** confirm, ratify, corroborate, justify. —**Ant.** fail; disapprove.

swagger, v. **1.** strut, parade. **2.** boast, brag, bluster, blow. —n. **3.** boasting, bragging, arrogance, affectation, braggadocio. —**Syn. Study.** See STRUT.

swallow, v. **1.** eat, gorge, gulp, engorge, imbibe, drink. **2.** consume, assimilate, absorb, engulf, devour. **3.** accept, receive. —n. **4.** mouthful, gulp, draught, drink.

swap, v., n. trade, barter, exchange.

swarm, n. **1.** horde, bevy, crowd, multitude, throng, mass, host, flock, shoal. —v. **2.** crowd, throng. **3.** abound, teem. —**Syn. Study.** See CROWD.

swarthy, adj. dark, dusky, brown, dark-skinned, tawny, swart. —**Ant.** pale.

sway, v. **1.** swing, wave, brandish. **2.** incline, lean, bend, tend. **3.** fluctuate, vacillate. **4.** rule, reign, govern, prevail. **5.** direct, dominate, control, influence. —n. **6.** rule, dominion, control, power, sovereignty, government, authority, mastery, predominance, ascendency. **7.** influence, power, authority, bias.

swear, v. **1.** declare, affirm, avow, depose, state, vow, testify. **2.** promise. **3.** curse, imprecate, blaspheme.

sweat, v. **1.** perspire. —n. **2.** perspiration. —**Syn. Study.** See PERSPIRATION.

sweeping, adj. **1.** broad, wide, extensive, comprehensive, wholesale, vast. **2.** exaggerated, overstated, extravagant, unqualified, hasty. —**Ant.** narrow; qualified.

sweet, adj. **1.** sugary, honeyed, syrupy, saccharine. **2.** fresh, pure, clean, new. **3.** musical, melodious, mellifluous, harmonious, tuneful, in tune, dulcet, tuneful, mellow. **4.** fragrant, redolent, aromatic, perfumed, scented. **5.** pleasing, pleasant, agreeable, pleasurable, enjoyable, delightful, charming, lovable, kind, amiable, gracious, engaging, winning, winsome, attractive, gentle. **6.** dear, beloved, precious. **7.** manageable, tractable, easygoing. —**Ant.** sour, bitter.

swell, v. **1.** inflate, dilate, distend, grow, expand, blow up. **2.** bulge, protrude. **3.** grow, increase, augment, enlarge. **4.** arise, grow, well up, glow, warm, thrill, heave, expand. **5.** bloat, strut, swagger. —n. **6.** bulkiness, distention, inflation, swelling. **7.** bulge, protuberance, augmentation, growth. **8.** wave, sea, billow. **9.** (slang) fop, dandy, coxcomb, popinjay, blade, buck. —adj. **10.** stylish, elegant, fashionable, grand. **11.** grand, fine, first-rate. —**Ant.** decrease, diminish.

swerve, v. deviate, diverge, depart.

swift, adj. **1.** speedy, quick, fleet, rapid, fast, expeditious. **2.** quick, prompt, ready, eager, alert, zealous. —n. **3.** swallow. —**Ant.** slow, slothful. —**Syn. Study.** See QUICK.

swindle, v. **1.** cheat, cozen, defraud, dupe, trick, gull, victimize, deceive, con. —n. **2.** fraud, trickery, confidence game, thimblerig, shell game, deception, knavery.

swindler, n. confidence man, cheat, deceiver, charlatan, mountebank, rogue, rascal, knave, sharper, trickster, impostor.

swing, v. **1.** sway, oscillate, rock, wave, vibrate. **2.** suspend, hang. —n. **3.** sway, vibration, oscillation. **4.** freedom, margin, range, scope, play, sweep. **5.** jazz, ragtime.

sybarite, n. voluptuary, epicurean, sensualist.

sycophant, n. flatterer, toady, fawner, parasite, boot-licker, yes-man.

sylph, n. salamander, undine, nymph, gnome.

symbiotic, adj. mutual, reciprocal, commensal, cooperative, cooperating, synergistic, interacting, interactive, interrelating. —**Ant.** independent, isolated.

symmetry, n. balance, proportion, symmetricalness, equilibrium, order, regularity, harmony. —**Syn. Study.** SYMMETRY, BALANCE, PROPORTION, HARMONY all denote qualities based on a correspondence or agreement, usu. pleasing, among the parts of a whole. SYMMETRY implies a regularity in form and arrangement of corresponding parts: the perfect symmetry of pairs of matched columns. BALANCE implies equilibrium of dissimilar parts, often as a means of emphasis: a balance of humor and seriousness. PROPORTION implies a proper relation among parts: His long arms were not in proportion to his body. HARMONY suggests a consistent, pleasing, or orderly combination of parts: harmony of color.

sympathetic, adj. **1.** sympathizing, compassionate, commiserating, kind, tender, affectionate. **2.** congenial, attached, affected or touched by. —**Ant.** unsympathetic.

sympathy, n. compassion, pity, empathy, understanding, compassionateness, fellow feeling, concern, support. —**Syn. Study.** SYMPATHY, COMPASSION, PITY, EMPATHY denote the tendency or capacity to share the feelings of others. SYMPATHY signifies a general kinship with another's feelings, no matter of what kind: sympathy with their yearning for freedom; sympathy for the bereaved. COMPASSION implies a deep sympathy for the sorrows or troubles of another, and a powerful urge to alleviate distress: compassion for homeless refugees. PITY suggests a kindly, but sometimes condescending, sorrow aroused by the suffering or misfortune of others: Mere pity for the flood victims is no help. EMPATHY refers to a vicarious participation in the emotions of another, or to the ability to imagine oneself in someone else's predicament: to feel empathy with a character in a play.

synopsis, n. compendium, condensation, summary, brief, digest, epitome, abstract, abridgment, précis, outline, syllabus. —**Syn. Study.** See SUMMARY.

system, n. **1.** assemblage, combination, complex, correlation. **2.** plan, scheme, procedure, arrangement, classification. **3.** world, universe, cosmos. **4.** taxonomy, order.

systematic, See Syn. study at ORDERLY.

T

taboo, adj. **1.** forbidden, interdicted, prohibited, banned, sacred, unclean. —n. **2.** prohibition, interdiction, exclusion, ostracism. —**Ant.** allowed, sanctioned, approved; permission, approval.

tacit, adj. silent, unexpressed, unspoken, unsaid, implied, implicit, understood, inferred. —**Ant.** expressed.

taciturn, adj. silent, reserved, uncommunicative, reticent, quiet. —**Ant.** voluble, talkative.

tacky, adj. **1.** inferior, tinny, junky, second-hand, shoddy, broken-down, shabby, run-down, ramshackle, seedy, tatty, threadbare. **2.** unfashionable, unstylish, dowdy, frumpy, frumpish, frowzy, drab, stale, old-fashioned, outmoded, stodgy, colorless. **3.** tasteless, gaudy, vulgar, chintzy, cheap, tawdry, cheesy, glitzy, sleazy, loud, garish, low-class, low-rent. —**Ant.** elegant, classy.

tactful, adj. diplomatic, adroit, skillful, clever, perceptive, sensitive. —**Ant.** tactless, maladroit. —**Syn. Study.** See DIPLOMATIC.

tactics, n. strategy, generalship, maneuvering; maneuvers, procedure.

taint, n. **1.** fault, defect, blemish, spot, stain, blot, flaw. **2.** infection, contamination, corruption, defilement. **3.** dishonor, discredit, disgrace. —v. **4.** infect, contaminate, defile, poison, corrupt, pollute. **5.** sully, tarnish, blemish, stain, blot.

take, v. **1.** get, acquire, procure, obtain, secure. **2.** seize, catch, capture, grasp. **3.** grasp, grip, embrace. **4.** receive, accept. **5.** pick, select, choose, elect. **6.** subtract, deduct. **7.** carry, convey, transfer. **8.** conduct, escort, lead. **9.** obtain, exact, demand. **10.** occupy, use up, consume. **11.** attract, hold, draw. **12.** captivate, charm, delight, attract, interest, engage, bewitch, fascinate, allure, enchant. **13.** assume, adopt, accept. **14.** ascertain, determine, fix. **15.** experience, feel, perceive. **16.** regard, consider, suppose, assume, presume, hold. **17.** perform, discharge, assume, adopt, appropriate. **18.** grasp, apprehend, comprehend, understand. **19.** do, perform, execute. **20.** suffer, undergo, experience, bear, stand, tolerate, submit to, endure. **21.** employ, use, make use of. **22.** require, need, demand. **23.** deceive, cheat, trick, defraud. **24.** catch, engage, fix. —**Ant.** give.

tale, n. **1.** story, narrative, fairy tale, account, fiction. **2.** lie, fib, falsehood, fable.

talent, n. ability, aptitude, capacity, capability, gift, genius, faculty, forte. —**Ant.** inability, incapability, weakness. —**Syn. Study.** See ABILITY.

talisman, n. fetish, charm, amulet, mascot, lucky-piece, good-luck charm, periapt, phylactery, juju, rabbit's foot, four-leaf clover.

talk, v. **1.** speak, converse. **2.** consult, confer, discuss; gossip. **3.** chatter, prattle, prate. **4.** communicate. **5.** utter, speak, mention. —n. **6.** speech, talking, conversation, colloquy, discourse, dialogue, chat, communication, parley, conference, confabulation. **7.** report, rumor, gossip, bruit. **8.** prattle, empty words, words. **9.** language, dialect, lingo.

talkative, adj. garrulous, loquacious, wordy, verbose, prolix, long-drawn. —**Ant.** taciturn, silent. —**Syn.** TALKATIVE, GARRULOUS, LOQUACIOUS characterize a person who talks a great deal. TALKATIVE is a neutral or mildly unfavorable word for a person who is much inclined to talk, some-

times without significance: a talkative child. The GARRULOUS person talks with wearisome persistence, usu. about trivial things: a garrulous cab driver. A LOQUACIOUS person, intending to be sociable, talks continuously and at length: a loquacious host.

tall, adj. high, elevated, towering, lofty. —**Ant.** short.

tame, adj. **1.** domesticated, mild, docile, gentle. **2.** gentle, fearless. **3.** tractable, docile, submissive, meek, subdued, crushed, suppressed. **4.** dull, insipid, unanimated, spiritless, flat, empty, vapid, vacuous, jejune, prosaic, boring, uninteresting, tedious. **5.** spiritless, cowardly, pusillanimous, dastardly. **6.** cultivated. —v. **7.** domesticate, break, subdued, make tractable. **8.** soften, tone down, calm, repress, subjugate, enslave. —**Ant.** wild.

tamper, v. **1.** meddle, interfere, damage, misuse, alter. **2.** bribe, suborn, seduce, lead astray, corrupt. —**Ant.** neglect, ignore.

tangible, adj. **1.** touchable, discernible, material, substantial, palpable, corporeal. **2.** real, actual, genuine, certain, open, plain, positive, obvious, evident, in evidence, perceptible. **3.** definite, specific, ineluctable. —**Ant.** intangible; unreal, imperceptible.

tantalize, v. torment, tease, torture, irritate, vex, provoke.

tantamount, adj. equal, equivalent. —**Ant.** unequal.

tar, n. **1.** pitch, creosote, asphalt. **2.** sailor, seaman, seafaring man, gob, mariner, swabby, seafarer.

tardy, adj. **1.** late, behindhand, slack, dilatory, slow, backward. **2.** slow, sluggish; reluctant. —**Ant.** early, punctual.

tarnish, v. **1.** dull, discolor. **2.** sully, stain, taint, blemish, soil. —n. **3.** stain, blot, blemish, taint. —**Ant.** brighten.

tarry, v. **1.** remain, stay, sojourn, rest, lodge, stop, abide. **2.** delay, linger, loiter; wait. —**Ant.** leave, depart.

tart, adj. **1.** sour, sourish, acidic, acerbic, sharp, piquant, bitter. **2.** caustic, sarcastic, mordent, acrimonious, cutting, biting, stinging. —**Ant.** sweet, mellow.

task, n. duty, job, chore, assignment, work, labor, drudgery, toil. —**Syn. Study.** TASK, CHORE, ASSIGNMENT, JOB refer to a specific instance or act of work. TASK refers to a clearly defined piece of work, usu. of short or limited duration, assigned to or expected of a person: the task of collecting dues. A CHORE is a minor, usu. routine task, often more tedious than difficult: the chore of taking out the garbage. ASSIGNMENT usu. refers to a specific task assigned by someone in authority: a homework assignment. JOB is the most general of these terms, referring to almost any work or duty, including one's livelihood: the job of washing the windows; a well-paid job in advertising.

taste, v. **1.** try, sip, savor. **2.** undergo, experience, feel. **3.** smack, savor. —n. **4.** sensation, flavor, savor, scent. **5.** morsel, bit, sip. **6.** relish, liking, fondness, predilection, disposition, partiality, preference, predisposition. **7.** discernment, perception, sense, judgment. **8.** manner, style, character.

tasteless, adj. **1.** flavorless, insipid, bland, dull, savorless, flat, watery, uninteresting, wishy-washy, vapid, blah. **2.** inconsiderate, thoughtless, careless, unthinking, unfeeling, hurtful. **3.** inappropriate, unseemly, unsuitable, inapt, improper, ill-chosen, infelicitous. **4.** indelicate, offensive, objectionable, coarse, crass, crude, tacky, vulgar. —**Ant.** tasteful.

tasty, See Syn. study at PALATABLE.

taunt, v. **1.** reproach, insult, censure, upbraid, sneer at, flout, revile. **2.** ridicule, mock, jeer, scoff at, make fun of, twit, provoke. —n. **3.** gibe, jeer, sarcasm, scorn, contumely, reproach, challenge, scoff, derision, insult, reproach, censure, ridicule. —**Syn. Study.** See RIDICULE.

taut, adj. tense, stretched, rigid, unrelaxed, inelastic, tight, drawn, stiff, high-strung, strained. —**Ant.** loose, relaxed.

tavern, n. **1.** bar, cafe; pub. **2.** inn, hotel, public house, hostelry.

tawdry, adj. cheap, gaudy, showy, ostentatious, flashy, meretricious. —**Ant.** expensive, elegant.

teach, v. instruct, educate, inform, enlighten, discipline, train, drill, tutor, school, indoctrinate. —**Ant.** learn. —**Syn. Study.** TEACH, INSTRUCT, TUTOR, TRAIN, EDUCATE share

the meaning of imparting information, understanding, or skill. TEACH is the most general of these terms, referring to any practice that furnishes a person with skill or knowledge: to teach children to write. INSTRUCT usu. implies a systematic, structured method of teaching: to instruct paramedics in first aid. TUTOR means to give private instruction, focusing on an individual's difficulties in a specific subject: to tutor him in geometry every Thursday afternoon. TRAIN stresses the development of a desired proficiency or behavior through practice, discipline, and instruction: to train military recruits. EDUCATE stresses the development of reasoning and judgment; it often involves preparing a person for an occupation or for mature life: to educate the young.

teacher, n. instructor, tutor, lecturer, professor, don. —**Ant.** student, pupil.

tear, n. **1.** (plural) grief, sorrow, regret, affliction, misery. **2.** rip, rent, fissure. **3.** rage, passion, flurry, outburst. —v. **4.** pull apart, rend, rip, sunder, sever. **5.** distress, shatter, afflict, affect. **6.** rend, split, divide. **7.** cut, lacerate, wound, injure, mangle.

tease, adj. **1.** worry, irritate, bother, trouble, provoke, disturb, annoy, rail at, vex, plague, molest, harry, harass, chafe, hector. **2.** separate, comb, card, shred. **3.** raise a nap, teasel, dress. —**Ant.** calm, assuage, mollify; unite; smooth.

technique, n. method, system, apparatus, procedure, practice, mechanism, routine, modus operandi, way, manner, fashion, style, mode.

tedious, adj. long, tiresome, irksome, wearisome, prolix, labored, wearing, exhausting, tiring, fatiguing, monotonous, dull, boring. —**Ant.** interesting.

teem, v. **1.** abound, swarm, be prolific or fertile. **2.** empty, pour out, discharge.

tell, v. **1.** narrate, relate, give an account of, recount, describe, report. **2.** communicate, make known, apprise, acquaint, inform, teach, impart, explain. **3.** announce, proclaim, publish, publicize. **4.** utter, express, word, mouth, mention, speak. **5.** reveal, divulge, disclose, betray, declare; acknowledge, own, confess. **6.** say, make plain. **7.** discern, identify, describe, distinguish, discover, make out. **8.** bid, order, command, urge. **9.** mention, enumerate, count, reckon, number, compute, calculate. **10.** operate, have force or effect.

temper, n. **1.** temperament, constitution, make-up, nature. **2.** disposition, mood, humor. **3.** passion, irritation, anger, resentment. **4.** calmness, aloofness, moderation, coolness, equanimity, tranquillity, composure. **5.** hardness, elasticity. —v. **6.** moderate, mitigate, assuage, mollify, tone down, soften, soothe, calm, pacify, tranquilize, restrain. **7.** suit, adapt, fit, accommodate, adjust. **8.** moisten, mix, blend, work, knead. **9.** modify, qualify.

temperament, n. disposition, make-up, temper, constitution, nature.

temperamental, adj. moody, irritable, sensitive, hypersensitive, touchy, testy, hot-tempered, bad-tempered, short-tempered. —**Ant.** serene, composed.

temperate, adj. moderate, self-restrained, continent, sober, calm, cool, detached, dispassionate. —**Ant.** intemperate, immoderate. —**Syn. Study.** See MODERATE.

tempestuous, adj. turbulent, tumultuous, violent, stormy, impetuous. —**Ant.** peaceful, pacific, serene, calm.

temporary, adj. transient, transitory, impermanent, discontinuous, fleeting, passing, evanescent, short-lived, ephemeral. —**Ant.** permanent, infinite. —**Syn. Study.** TEMPORARY, TRANSIENT, TRANSITORY agree in referring to that which is not lasting or permanent. TEMPORARY implies an arrangement established with no thought of continuance but with the idea of being changed soon: a temporary structure. TRANSIENT describes that which is in the process of passing by, and which will therefore last or stay only a short time: a transient condition. TRANSITORY describes an innate characteristic by which a thing, by its very nature, lasts only a short time: Life is transitory.

tempt, v. **1.** induce, persuade, entice, allure, seduce, attract, lead astray, invite, inveigle, decoy, lure. **2.** provoke, test, try, prove. —**Syn. Study.** TEMPT, SEDUCE both mean to allure or entice someone into an unwise, wrong, or wicked action. To TEMPT is to attract by holding out the probability of gratification or advantage, often in regard to what is wrong or unwise: *to tempt a high official with a bribe.* To SEDUCE is to lead astray, as from duty or principles, but more often from moral rectitude, chastity, etc.: *to seduce a soldier from loyalty.*

tempting, *adj.* enticing, inviting, seductive, attractive, alluring. —Ant. repulsive, repellent.

tenable, *adj.* defensible, defendable, supportable, admissible, viable, reasonable, believable, plausible, credible. —Ant. indefensible, unbelievable.

tenacious, *adj.* 1. retentive. 2. pertinacious, persistent, stubborn, obstinate, opinionated, sure, positive, certain. 3. adhesive, sticky, viscous, glutinous. 4. cohesive, clinging, tough. —Ant. unsure, uncertain.

tenacity, *n.* perseverance, persistency, pertinacity, obstinacy. —Ant. transitoriness. —Syn. Study. See PERSEVERANCE.

tendency, *n.* direction, trend, disposition, predisposition, proneness, proclivity, inclination, leaning, bias, prejudice, drift, bent; movement. —Ant. failure, disinclination.

tender, *adj.* 1. soft, delicate. 2. weak, delicate, feeble. 3. young, immature, youthful. 4. gentle, delicate, soft, lenient, mild. 5. soft-hearted, sympathetic, tender-hearted, compassionate, pitiful, kind, merciful, affectionate. 6. affectionate, loving, sentimental, amatory. 7. considerate, careful, chary, reluctant. 8. acute, painful, sore, sensitive. 9. fragile, breakable, frangible, friable. 10. ticklish, delicate, sensitive. —*v.* 11. offer, proffer, present. —*n.* 12. offer, offering, proposal, proffer. 13. dinghy, skiff, rowboat, lifeboat, motorboat, boat, pinnace, gig. 14. coal car, coaler. —Ant. coarse, rough; strong; mature, adult; merciless, ruthless; apathetic; inconsiderate; tough; accept. —Syn. Study. See OFFER.

tenet, *n.* belief, principle, doctrine, dogma, opinion, notion, position, creed.

tense, *adj.* 1. tight, taut, stretched, rigid, strained. 2. nervous, neurotic, excited, strained. —Ant. lax; relaxed.

tentative, *adj.* experimental, trial, probationary, indefinite. —Ant. definite, confirmed.

tenuous, *adj.* 1. thin, slender, small, attenuated, minute. 2. rare, thin, rarefied. 3. unimportant, insignificant, trivial, trifling, nugatory, unsubstantial. —Ant. thick; substantial, significant.

termagant, *n.* shrew, maenad, bacchante, virago, nag, beldam, Xantippe, vixen.

terminate, *v.* 1. end, finish, conclude, close, complete. 2. bound, limit. 3. issue, result, turn out, eventuate, prove. —Ant. begin, open.

terminology, *n.* language, nomenclature, vocabulary, vernacular, lexicon, verbiage, speech, jargon, dialect, lingo.

terrain, *n.* 1. land, topography, geography, territory, region. 2. arena, area, field, bailiwick, sphere, province, domain, specialty.

terrestrial, *adj.* earthly, mundane, worldly, terrene. —Ant. celestial. —Syn. Study. See EARTHLY.

terrible, *adj.* 1. dreadful, awful, fearful, frightful, appalling, dire, horrible, horrifying, terrifying, terrific, horrendous, horrid, gruesome, hideous, monstrous. 2. distressing, severe, extreme, excessive. —Ant. delightful, pleasant; moderate.

terror, *n.* horror, fear, panic, fright, alarm, dismay, consternation. —Ant. security, calm.

terrorize, *v.* dominate, coerce, intimidate. —Ant. ameliorate, mollify.

terse, *adj.* brief, concise, pithy, neat, compact, succinct, curt, sententious, concentrated. —Ant. attenuated. —Syn. Study. See CONCISE.

test, *n.* 1. trial, proof, assay. 2. examination, quiz, exam. —*v.* 3. try, essay, prove, examine; refine, assay.

testimony, *n.* evidence, deposition, attestation, declaration, affirmation, corroboration.

testy, *adj.* irritable, impatient, touchy, tetchy, petulant, edgy, short-tempered, peevish, vexatious, choleric, snappish, waspish, splenetic, cross, cranky, irascible, fretful. —Ant. composed, calm. —Syn. See IRRITABLE.

thankful, *adj.* grateful, indebted, beholden, obliged. —Ant. thankless, ungrateful.

thaw, *v.* melt, liquefy, dissolve; warm. —Ant. freeze, solidify, sublimate, cool.

theatrical, *adj.* dramatic, histrionic, melodramatic, stagy, operatic, exaggerated, ostentatious, sensational, artificial, mannered, actorish, actressy. —Ant. modest, low-key.

theme, *n.* 1. subject, topic, thesis, point, text. 2. composition, essay, paper. 3. motif, thread, tenor, ideas; trend. —Syn. Study. See SUBJECT.

theory, *n.* 1. assumption, hypothesis, rationale, explanation, system, conjecture, guess, plan, scheme, proposal. 2. view, contemplation, conception. —Syn. Study. THEORY, HYPOTHESIS are used in non-technical contexts to mean an untested idea or opinion. A THEORY in technical use is a more or less verified or established explanation accounting for known facts or phenomena: *Einstein's theory of relativity.* A HYPOTHESIS is a conjecture put forth as a possible explanation of phenomena or relations, which serves as a basis of argument or experimentation to reach the truth: *This idea is only a hypothesis.*

therapeutic, *adj.* healing, curative, remedial, corrective, restorative, theriacal, adjuvant, alleviative, palliative, helpful, beneficial, salutary. —Ant. harmful, toxic.

therefore, *adv.* hence, whence, wherefore, accordingly, consequently, so, then.

thesaurus, *n.* storehouse, repository, treasury; dictionary, encyclopedia.

thick-skinned, *adj.* pachydermatous, insensitive, dull, obtuse, callous. —Ant. thin-skinned, sensitive.

thief, *n.* 1. robber; pickpocket, mugger. 2. burglar, cracksman, second-story man, housebreaker, safecracker. —Syn. Study. THIEF, ROBBER refer to one who steals. A THIEF takes the goods or property of another by stealth without the latter's knowledge: *like a thief in the night.* A ROBBER trespasses upon the house, property, or person of another, and makes away with things of value, even at the cost of violence: *An armed robber held up the store owner.*

thin, *adj.* 1. slim, slender, lean, skinny, poor, lank, gaunt, scrawny, emaciated. 2. sparse, scanty, meager. 3. fluid, rare, rarefied, tenuous. 4. unsubstantial, slight, flimsy. 5. transparent, weak. 6. faint, slight, poor, feeble. —*v.* 7. rarefy, dilute, reduce, diminish. —Ant. thick, fat, obese; abundant; substantial; opaque; strong; increase.

think, *v.* 1. conceive, imagine, picture. 2. mediate, ponder, consider, regard, suppose, look upon, judge, deem, esteem, count, account. 3. bear in mind, recollect, recall, remember. 4. intend, mean, design, purpose. 5. believe, suppose. 6. anticipate, expect. 7. cogitate, meditate, reflect, muse, ponder, ruminate, contemplate.

thirst, *n.* desire, craving, eagerness, hankering, yearning, hunger, appetite. —Ant. distaste, apathy.

thorough, *adj.* complete, entire, thoroughgoing, unqualified, perfect, done, finished, completed, total. —Ant. incomplete, unfinished.

thought, *n.* 1. concept, conception, opinion, judgment, belief, idea, notion, tenet, conviction, speculation, consideration, contemplation. 2. meditation, reflection, musing, cogitation, thinking. 3. intention, design, purpose, intent. 4. anticipation, expectation. 5. consideration, attention, care, regard. 6. trifle, mote. —Syn. Study. See IDEA.

thoughtful, *adj.* 1. contemplative, meditative, reflective, pensive, deliberative. 2. careful, heedful, mindful, regardful, considerate, attentive, discreet, prudent, wary, circumspect. —Ant. thoughtless.

thoughtless, *adj.* unthinking, careless, heedless, inattentive, inconsiderate, negligent, neglectful, remiss, unmindful, unobservant, unwatchful, reckless, flighty, scatter-brained, light-headed, giddy. —Ant. thoughtful.

thrash, *v.* beat, defeat, punish, flog, wallop, maul, drub. —Syn. Study. See BEAT.

threaten, *v.* menace, endanger, indicate, presage, impend, portend, augur, forebode, foreshadow, prognosticate. —Ant. protect, defend.

threatening, See Syn. study at OMINOUS.

thrifty, *adj.* 1. frugal, provident, economical, sparing, saving. 2. thriving, prosperous, successful. 3. growing, flourishing, vigorous. —Ant. wasteful, prodigal, improvident; poor, unsuccessful; stunted. —Syn. Study. See ECONOMICAL.

thrive, *v.* prosper, succeed, flourish, increase, advance, luxuriate. —Ant. languish, die. —Syn. Study. See SUCCEED.

throb, *v.* pulse, beat, drum, pulsate, palpitate, thump, pound, thrum, resonate, vibrate, flutter, quake.

throe, *n.* 1. seizure, attack, fit, pang, pain, spasm, paroxysm, access, turn, spell. 2. struggle, distress, stress, strife, difficulty.

throng, *n.* 1. multitude, crowd, assemblage, swarm, horde, host. —*v.* 2. swarm, assemble, crowd, press, jostle; herd. —Syn. Study. See CROWD.

throw, *v.* 1. project, propel, cast, hurl, pitch, toss, fling, launch, send, let fly. 2. cast, fling. 3. venture, chance. 4. scarf, boa, stole. 5. blanket, afghan, robe.

thrust, *v.* 1. push, force, shove, drive. 2. stab, pierce, puncture, penetrate. —*n.* 3. lunge, stab, push, drive, tilt, shove.

thwart, *v.* 1. frustrate, baffle, oppose, prevent, hinder, obstruct, defeat. —*n.* 2. seat. —*adj.* 3. cross, transverse. 4. adverse, unfavorable. —Ant. favor, encourage, support, help.

tidy, *adj.* neat, trim, orderly. —Ant. messy, sloppy, untidy.

tie, *v.* 1. bind, fasten. 2. knot. 3. fasten, join, unite, connect, link, knit, yoke, lock. 4. confine, restrict, limit, obligate, constrain. 5. equal. —*n.* 6. cord, string, rope, band, ligature. 7. necktie, cravat. 8. knot; link, connection, bond. —Ant. loose, loosen, release.

tiff, *n.* quarrel, dispute, disagreement, altercation, spat, argument, bickering, falling out, scrap, dustup, run-in.

time, *n.* 1. duration. 2. period, interval, term, spell, span, space. 3. epoch, era, period, season, age, date. 4. tempo, rhythm, measure. —*v.* 5. regulate, gauge.

timely, *adj.* seasonable, opportune, well-timed, prompt, punctual. —Ant. untimely, inappropriate, inopportune.

timid, *adj.* fearful, shy, diffident, bashful, retiring, coy, blushing, shrinking, timorous, fainthearted, tremulous, cowardly, dastardly, pusillanimous. —Ant. bold, fearless, intrepid.

tinny, *adj.* 1. unresonant, reedy, thin, hollow, weak, feeble. 2. inferior, cheap, low-grade, insubstantial, flimsy, cheapjack. —Ant. hearty, sturdy.

tint, *n.* 1. color, hue, tinge, dye, stain, tincture; rinse; pastel. —*v.* 2. color, tinge, stain.

tirade, *n.* denunciation, outburst, harangue, declamation.

tire, *v.* 1. exhaust, weary, fatigue, jade. 2. exasperate, bore, weary, irk.

tired, *adj.* exhausted, fatigued, weary, wearied, enervated. —Ant. energetic, fiery, tireless.

tireless, *adj.* untiring, indefatigable, energetic, active. —Ant. tired, tiresome.

tiresome, *adj.* 1. wearisome, tedious, dull, fatiguing, humdrum. 2. annoying, vexatious. —Ant. interesting, enchanting.

title, *n.* 1. name, designation, epithet, appellation, denomination, cognomen. 2. championship. 3. right, claim. —*v.* 4. designate, entitle, denominate, term, call, style.

toady, *n.* sycophant, fawner, flatterer, yes-man.

toil, *n.* 1. work, labor, effort, drudgery, exertion, travail, pains. —*v.* 2. labor, work, strive, moil, exert. —Ant. indolence, sloth. —Syn. Study. See WORK.

tolerance, *n.* 1. toleration, patience, sufferance, forbearance, endurance. 2. liberality, catholicity, impartiality, magnanimity, open-mindedness. 3. allowance, variation. —Ant. intolerance.

tool, *n.* instrument, implement, utensil, contrivance, device. —Syn. Study. TOOL, IMPLEMENT, INSTRUMENT, UTENSIL refer to contrivances for doing work. A TOOL is a contrivance held in and worked by the hand and used for cutting, digging, etc.: *a carpenter's tools.* An IMPLEMENT is any tool or contrivance designed or used for a particular purpose: *agricultural implements.* An INSTRUMENT is anything used in doing certain work or

producing a certain result, esp. such as requires delicacy, accuracy, or precision: *surgical or musical instruments.* A UTENSIL is usu. an article for domestic use: *kitchen utensils.* When used figuratively of human agency, TOOL is generally used in a contemptuous sense; INSTRUMENT, in a neutral or good sense: *a tool of unscrupulous men; an instrument of Providence.*

top, *n.* 1. apex, zenith, acme, peak, summit, pinnacle, vertex, culmination. 2. best, chief. —*adj.* 3. highest, uppermost, upper, greatest. 4. foremost, chief, principal. —*v.* 5. surpass, excel, outdo. 6. crop, prune, lop. —Ant. bottom, foot; worst; lowest; least.

topic, *n.* subject, theme, thesis, subject matter. —Syn. Study. See SUBJECT.

top-notch, *adj.* excellent, fine, superlative, capital, superior, peerless, splendid, matchless, A1, first-rate, first-class, top-shelf, top-drawer, blue-chip, gilt-edge, sterling, five-star, world-class. —Ant. third-rate, third-string, inferior.

torment, *v.* 1. afflict, pain, rack, torture, harass, harry, hector, vex, annoy, irritate, agonize, distress, excruciate. 2. plague, worry, annoy, pester, tease, provoke, needle, nettle, trouble, tantalize, fret. —*n.* 3. agony, torture, misery, distress, anguish. —Ant. please.

torpid, *adj.* 1. inactive, sluggish, slow, dull, apathetic, lethargic, motionless, inert, indolent. 2. dormant, hibernating, estivating. —Ant. active, energetic. —Syn. Study. See INACTIVE.

torrent, *n.* stream, flow, downpour. —Ant. drop, drip, dribble.

torrid, *adj.* 1. hot, tropical, burning, scorching, fiery, parching. 2. ardent, passionate. —Ant. arctic, frigid, cold; dispassionate, cool.

tortuous, *adj.* 1. twisted, crooked, winding, curved, twisting, bent, sinuous, serpentine, sinuate. 2. evasive, roundabout, circuitous, indirect, deceitful, ambiguous, crooked, dishonest. —Ant. straight.

torture, *n.*, *v.* See TORMENT.

toss, *v.*, *n.* See THROW.

total, *adj.* 1. whole, entire, complete, finished, final, full, absolute, utter, unqualified. —*n.* 2. sum, whole, entirety, totality, aggregate, gross. —*v.* 3. add up, amount to.

totality, *n.* total, all, sum total, grand total, everything, entirety, all and sundry, kit and caboodle, whole nine yards, whole bit, whole schmear, whole shebang, whole shooting match, whole ball of wax, the works, the lot.

totter, *v.* 1. stagger, falter, reel. 2. sway, rock, waver. 3. shake, tremble, oscillate, quiver.

touch, *v.* 1. handle, feel. 2. tap, pat, strike, hit. 3. come up to, attain, reach, arrive at. 4. modify, improve. 5. play, perform. 6. treat, affect, impress, move, strike, stir, melt, soften. 7. deal with, treat. 8. pertain or relate to, concern, regard, affect. —*n.* 9. contact; contiguity. 10. stroke, pat, tap, blow. 11. hint, trace, suggestion. 12. characteristic, trait, style. 13. quality, kind.

touchy, *adj.* 1. sensitive, hypersensitive, thin-skinned, temperamental, volatile. 2. irritable, irascible, cranky, cross, cantankerous, testy, tetchy. 3. delicate, ticklish, difficult, tricky, sticky, precarious, slippery. —Syn. Study. See IRRITABLE.

tough, *adj.* 1. firm, strong, hard, hardy. 2. sturdy, hardy, durable. 3. hardened, incorrigible, troublesome, inflexible, rigid. 4. vigorous, severe, violent. —Ant. weak, feeble, sickly; flexible, soft; slight.

tour, *v.* 1. travel, visit. —*n.* 2. excursion, trip, journey, expedition.

towering, *adj.* tall, lofty, high, great, elevated. —Ant. short, low.

town, *n.* city, metropolis, borough, community, village, burgh, dorp, thorp, hamlet. —Ant. country.

toxic, *adj.* harmful, injurious, damaging, deleterious, poisonous, venomous, virulent, malignant, mephitic, deadly, lethal. —Ant. beneficial, healthful.

toxin, *n.* poison, venom, virus. —Ant. serum, antitoxin. —Syn. Study. See POISON.

trace, *n.* 1. vestige, mark, sign, track, spoor, footprint, trail, record. 2. mark, indication, evidence. 3. hint, suggestion, touch, taste, soupçon. —*v.* 4. track, follow, trail. 5. ascertain, find out, discover. 6. draw, delineate, outline, diagram. 7. copy. —Ant. abundance, plethora. —Syn. Study. TRACE, VESTIGE agree

in denoting marks or signs of something, usu. of the past. TRACE, the broader term, denotes any mark or slight indication of something past or present: *a trace of ammonia in water.* VESTIGE is more limited and refers to some slight, though actual, remains of something that no longer exists: *vestiges of one's former wealth.*

tract, *n.* 1. stretch, extent, district, territory, region. 2. space, period. 3. treatise, pamphlet, essay, sermon, homily, dissertation, disquisition.

tractable, *adj.* docile, malleable, manageable, willing, governable. —Ant. intractable.

trade, *n.* 1. commrce, traffic, business, dealing, exchange, barter. 2. purchase, sale, exchange, swap. 3. occupation, vocation, metier, livelihood, living, employment, pursuit, business, profession, craft, calling, avocation. —*v.* 4. barter, traffic or deal in, exchange. 5. barter, interchange, bargain, deal.

traduce, *v.* slander, calumniate, malign, defame, vilify, abuse, revile, asperse, depreciate, blemish, decry, disparage. —Ant. praise, honor.

traffic, *n.*, *v.* trade.

tragic, *adj.* mournful, melancholy, pathetic, distressing, pitiful, calamitous, sorrowful, disastrous, fatal, dreadful. —Ant. comic.

trail, *v.* 1. drag, draw. 2. track, trace, hunt down. —*n.* 3. path, track; scent, spoor.

train, See Syn. study at TEACH.

trance, *n.* daze, daydream, reverie, brown study, stupor, coma, swoon, rapture, ecstasy, fugue.

tranquil, See Syn. study at PEACEFUL.

transact, *v.* carry on, enact, conclude, settle, perform, manage, negotiate, conduct.

transform, *v.* change, alter, metamorphose, convert, transfigure, transmute. —Ant. retain. —Syn. Study. TRANSFORM, CONVERT mean to change one thing into another. TRANSFORM means to radically change the outward form or inner character: *a frog transformed into a prince; delinquents transformed into responsible citizens.* CONVERT usually means to modify or adapt so as to serve a new or different use or function: *to convert a barn into a house.*

transgress, *v.* 1. violate, break, contravene, disobey, infringe. 2. offend, sin, err, trespass. —Ant. obey.

transient, *adj.* transitory, temporary, fleeting, passing, flitting, flying, brief, fugitive. —Ant. permanent. —Syn. Study. See TEMPORARY.

transitory, See TRANSIENT. See also TEMPORARY.

translation, *n.* paraphrase, version, interpretation, rendering, treatment.

translucent, *adj.* semitransparent, translucid; transparent. —Ant. opaque, dense, solid. —Syn. Study. See TRANSPARENT.

transmit, *v.* send, forward, dispatch, convey, transport, carry, transfer, bear, remit.

transparent, *adj.* 1. transpicuous, diaphanous, clear, pellucid, lucid, limpid, crystalline; translucent. 2. open, frank, candid. 3. manifest, obvious. —Ant. opaque; clandestine, secretive; concealed. —Syn. Study. TRANSPARENT, TRANSLUCENT agree in describing material that light rays can pass through. That which is TRANSPARENT allows objects to be seen clearly through it: *Clear water is transparent.* That which is TRANSLUCENT allows light to pass through, diffusing it, however, so that objects beyond are not distinctly seen: *Ground glass is translucent.*

transport, *v.* 1. carry, convey. 2. banish, exile. —*n.* 3. conveyance, transportation. 4. freighter, troopship, tanker, oiler. 5. joy, bliss, rapture, ecstasy, happiness. —Syn. Study. See ECSTASY.

trap, *n.* 1. pitfall, snare, springe. 2. ambush, pitfall, artifice, stratagem. —*v.* 3. ensnare, entrap, spring. 4. ambush.

traumatic, *adj.* injurious, harmful, acute, upsetting, wrenching, painful, shocking, stunning, devastating, excruciating.

traverse, *v.* 1. go counter to, obstruct, thwart, frustrate, contravene. 2. contradict, deny. 3. pass or go across, cross, cross over. —*n.* 4. obstruction, bar, obstacle. 5. crosspiece, crossbar, barrier, railing, lattice, screen. —*adj.* 6. transverse, cross.

travesty, *n.*, *v.* burlesque, parody, lampoon, caricature, take-off. —Syn. Study. See BURLESQUE.

treacherous, *adj.* 1. traitorous, unfaithful, faithless, untrustworthy, treasonable, treasonous, perfidious, disloyal. **2.** deceptive, unreliable, insidious, recreant, deceitful. **3.** unstable, insecure. **—Ant.** faithful, trustworthy, loyal; reliable; stable, secure.

treachery, *n.* betrayal, treason, disloyalty, faithlessness, perfidy. **—Ant.** loyalty, fealty.

treason, *n.* sedition, treachery, disaffection, lese majesty. **—Ant.** loyalty, allegiance. **—Syn. Study.** TREASON, SEDITION mean disloyalty or treachery to one's country or its government. TREASON is any attempt to overthrow the government or impair the well-being of a state to which one owes allegiance. According to the U.S. Constitution, it is the crime of levying war against the U.S. or giving aid and comfort to its enemies. SEDITION is any act, writing, speech, etc., directed unlawfully against state authority, the government, or the constitution, or calculated to bring it into contempt or to incite others to hostility or disaffection; it does not amount to treason and therefore is not a capital offense.

treasure, *n.* **1.** wealth, riches, hoard, funds; valuables, jewels. **—v. 2.** lay away, store, stock, husband, save, garner. **3.** prize, cherish.

treat, *v.* **1.** act *or* behave toward. **2.** look upon, consider, regard, deal with. **3.** discuss, deal with, handle. **4.** entertain, regale, feast. **5.** negotiate, settle, bargain, come to terms. **—n. 6.** feast, fête, entertainment, banquet.

tremble, *v.* **1.** shake, quiver, quaver, quake, shiver, shudder. **2.** vibrate, oscillate, totter. **—n. 3.** trembling, shaking, quivering.

tremendous, *adj.* **1.** huge, gigantic, colossal. **2.** dreadful, awful, horrid, horrendous, terrible, terrific, terrifying, horrifying, appalling. **—Ant.** small, tiny, microscopic. **—Syn. Study.** See HUGE.

tremor, *n.* **1.** trembling, shaking, vibration, oscillation, shivering, quivering, quaking. **2.** quake, earthquake, temblor.

tremulous, *adj.* **1.** fearful, timorous, timid, frightened, afraid. **2.** vibratory, vibrating, quivering, shaking, trembling, shivering. **—Ant.** fearless, intrepid; solid, firm.

trenchant, *adj.* **1.** incisive, keen, sharp, cutting, biting, sarcastic, sardonic, acute, pointed, caustic, piquant. **2.** thoroughgoing, vigorous, effective. **—Ant.** weak, mollifying; ineffective.

trend, *n.* **1.** course, drift, tendency, direction, inclination. **—v. 2.** tend, extend, stretch, run, incline.

trespass, *n.* **1.** invasion, encroachment, intrusion, infringement. **2.** offense, sin, wrong, transgression, crime, misdemeanor, misdeed, error, fault. **—v. 3.** encroach, infringe, intrude, invade. **4.** transgress, offend, sin. **—Syn. Study.** TRESPASS, ENCROACH, INFRINGE imply overstepping boundaries or violating the rights of others. To TRESPASS is to invade the property or rights of another, esp. to pass unlawfully within the boundaries of private land: *The hunters trespassed on the farmer's fields.* To ENCROACH is to intrude, gradually and often stealthily, on the territory, rights, or privileges of another, so that a footing is imperceptibly established: *The sea slowly encroached on the land.* To INFRINGE is to break in upon or invade another's rights, customs, or the like, by violating or disregarding them: *to infringe on a patent.*

trial, *n.* **1.** test, proof, experiment, examination, testing. **2.** attempt, effort, endeavor, struggle, essay. **3.** test, assay, criterion, proof, touchstone, standard. **4.** probation. **5.** affliction, suffering, tribulation, distress, sorrow, grief, trouble, misery, woe, hardship.

trick, *n.* **1.** device, expedient, artifice, wile, stratagem, ruse, deception, fraud, trickery, cheating, deceit, duplicity. **2.** semblance, appearance. **3.** prank, joke, practical joke. **4.** shift, dodge, swindle, maneuver, hoax, confidence game. **5.** jugglery, sleight-of-hand, legerdemain, prestidigitation. **—v. 6.** cheat, swindle, beguile, dupe, fool, deceive, defraud, delude, cozen. **7.** dress, array, deck. **—Syn. Study.** TRICK, ARTIFICE, RUSE, STRATAGEM are terms for crafty or cunning devices intended to deceive. TRICK, the general term, refers usu. to an underhanded act designed to cheat someone, but it sometimes refers merely to a pleasurable deceiving of the senses: *to win by a trick.* Like TRICK, but to a greater degree, ARTI-

FICE emphasizes the cleverness or cunning with which the proceeding is devised: *an artifice of diabolical ingenuity.* RUSE and STRATAGEM emphasize the purpose for which the trick is designed; RUSE is the more general term, and STRATAGEM sometimes implies a more elaborate procedure or a military application: *We gained entrance by a ruse. His stratagem gave the army command of the hill.* See also CHEAT.

trickery, *n.* artifice, trick, stratagem, fraud, deception, deceit, chicanery, knavery. **—Ant.** honesty.

trifling, *adj.* **1.** trivial, insignificant, unimportant, petty, paltry, negligible, nugatory, slight, worthless, piddling, immaterial. **2.** frivolous, shallow, light, empty. **—Ant.** important, significant, worthy; profound. **—Syn. Study.** See PETTY.

trim, *v.* **1.** reduce, pare, clip, prune, shave, shear, cut, lop, curtail. **2.** modify, adjust, prepare, arrange. **3.** dress, array, deck, bedeck, ornament, decorate, adorn, embellish, garnish, trick out. **—n. 4.** condition, order, case, plight, situation, state. **5.** dress, array, equipment, gear, trappings, trimmings. **6.** trimming embellishment, decoration; cutting, clipping, priming, reduction. **—adj. 7.** neat, smart, compact, tidy, well-ordered, ordered. **8.** prepared, well-equipped. **—Ant.** augment, increase.

trip, *n.* **1.** journey, voyage, excursion, pilgrimage, travel, tour, jaunt, junket. **2.** stumble, misstep. **3.** slip, mistake, error, blunder, erratum, lapse, oversight, miss. **—v. 4.** stumble. **5.** bungle, blunder, err, slip, miss, overlook. **6.** hop, skip, dance. **7.** tip, tilt. **—Syn. Study.** TRIP, EXPEDITION, JOURNEY, PILGRIMAGE, VOYAGE are terms for a course of travel made to a particular place, usu. for some specific purpose. TRIP is the general word, indicating going any distance and returning, for either business or pleasure, and in either a hurried or a leisurely manner: *a trip to Europe; a bus trip.* An EXPEDITION, made often by an organized group, is designed for a specific purpose: *an archaeological expedition.* JOURNEY indicates a trip of considerable length, mainly by land, and is usu. applied to travel that is more fatiguing than a trip: *an arduous journey to Tibet.* A PILGRIMAGE is made as to a shrine, from motives of piety or veneration: *a pilgrimage to Lourdes.* A VOYAGE usu. indicates leisurely travel by water to a distant place: *a voyage around the world.*

trite, *adj.* commonplace, ordinary, common, hackneyed, stereotyped, stale. **—Ant.** original, uncommon, unusual, extraordinary. **—Syn. Study.** See COMMONPLACE.

triumph, *n.* **1.** victory, conquest, success. **2.** joy, exultation, ecstasy, jubilation, celebration. **—v. 3.** win, succeed, prevail. **4.** rejoice, exult, celebrate. **5.** glory, be elated *or* glad, rejoice. **—Ant.** defeat, loss. **—Syn. Study.** See VICTORY.

trivial, *adj.* trifling, petty, unimportant, insignificant, nugatory, paltry, slight, immaterial, frivolous, small. **—Ant.** important, significant, material. **—Syn. Study.** See PETTY.

troop, *n.* **1.** assemblage, crowd, band, squad, party, body, unit, company, group, troupe. **2.** herd, flock, swarm, throng. **—v. 3.** gather, flock together, swarm, throng, collect. **4.** associate, consort. **5.** assemble, group, convene.

trophy, *n.* **1.** token, remembrance, memento, souvenir, keepsake, commemoration, memorial. **2.** prize, reward, laurel, laurels, garland, award.

trouble, *v.* **1.** disturb, distress, worry, concern, agitate, upset, disorder, disarrange, confuse, derange. **2.** inconvenience, put out, discommode, incommode. **3.** annoy, vex, bother, irritate, irk, pester, plague, fret, torment, torture, harry, hector, harass, badger, disquiet, molest, perturb. **—n. 4.** molestation, harassment, annoyance, difficulty, embarrassment. **5.** misery, distress, affliction, concern, worry, grief, agitation, care, suffering, calamity, dolor, adversity, tribulation, trial, misfortune, woe, pain, sorrow. **6.** disturbance, disorder. **7.** inconvenience, exertion, pains, effort. **—Ant.** calm, mollify; convenience, encourage, accommodate; happiness, fortune.

troublesome, *adj.* **1.** annoying, vexatious, perplexing, galling, harassing. **2.** laborious, difficult, arduous, hard, burdensome, wearisome. **—Ant.** simple, easy; trouble-free.

troupe, *n.* See TROOP.

truculent, *adj.* fierce, brutal, savage,

harsh, threatening, bullying, overbearing, ferocious, cruel, malevolent. **—Ant.** affable, amiable. **—Syn. Study.** See FIERCE.

trudge, *v.* walk, pace, tramp, plod. **—Syn. Study.** See PACE.

true, *adj.* **1.** factual, actual, real, authentic, genuine, veracious, truthful, veritable. **2.** sincere, honest, honorable, just, faithful, equitable, fair. **3.** loyal, faithful, trusty, trustworthy, staunch, constant, steady, steadfast, unwavering, unfaltering. **4.** accurate, exact, faithful, correct, precise; agreeing. **5.** right, proper. **6.** legitimate, rightful. **7.** reliable, sure, unfailing, persevering. **—adv. 8.** truly, truthfully. **9.** exactly, accurately, precisely. **—v. 10.** shape, adjust, place. **—Ant.** untrue.

trust, *n.* **1.** reliance, confidence, assurance, security, certainty, belief, faith. **2.** expectation, hope, faith. **3.** credit. **4.** obligation, responsibility, charge. **5.** commitment, office, duty, charge. **—v. 6.** rely on, confide in, have confidence in, depend upon. **7.** believe, credit. **8.** expect, hope. **9.** entrust, commit, consign. **—Ant.** mistrust, distrust.

trustworthy, *adj.* reliable, true, honest, honorable, faithful, staunch, loyal, steadfast, steady, straightforward.

truth, *n.* **1.** fact, reality, verity, veracity. **2.** genuineness, reality, actuality. **3.** honesty, uprightness, integrity, sincerity, candor, frankness, openness, ingenuousness, probity, fidelity, virtue. **4.** accuracy, precision, exactness, nicety. **—Ant.** lie, fiction, fabrication, untruth; fraudulence; dishonesty; inaccuracy.

try, *v.* **1.** attempt, essay, endeavor, strive, put forth effort. **2.** test, prove, examine, investigate. **3.** melt, render; extract, refine, distill. **—Syn. Study.** TRY, ATTEMPT, ENDEAVOR, STRIVE all mean to put forth an effort toward a specific end. TRY is the most often used and most general term: *to try to decipher a message; to try hard to succeed.* ATTEMPT, often interchangeable with TRY, sometimes suggests the possibility of failure and is often used in reference to more serious or important matters: *to attempt to formulate a new theory of motion.* ENDEAVOR emphasizes serious and continued exertion of effort, sometimes aimed at dutiful or socially appropriate behavior: *to endeavor to fulfill one's obligations.* STRIVE stresses persistent, vigorous, even strenuous effort, often in the face of obstacles: *to strive to overcome a handicap.*

tryst, *n.* appointment, meeting, rendezvous, assignation.

tumid, *adj.* **1.** swollen, distended, dilated, enlarged, turgid. **2.** pompous, turgid, bombastic, inflated, grandiloquent, grandiose, rhetorical, declamatory. **—Ant.** deflated, self-effacing.

tumult, *n.* **1.** commotion, disturbance, disorder, turbulence, uproar, hubbub, fracas, agitation, affray, melee; riot, outbreak, uprising, revolt, revolution, mutiny. **2.** agitation, perturbation, excitement, ferment. **—Ant.** peace, order; calm, serenity.

tumultuous, *adj.* **1.** uproarious, turbulent, riotous, violent. **2.** noisy, disorderly, irregular, boisterous, obstreperous. **3.** disturbed, agitated, unquiet, restive, restless, nervous, uneasy. **—Ant.** calm, peaceful, pacific; regular, orderly; quiet, restful.

tuneful, *adj.* musical, melodious, harmonious, dulcet, sweet. **—Ant.** discordant, sour, flat.

turbid, *adj.* muddy, foul, polluted, murky, mucky, cloudy, clouded, beclouded, dark, smoky, roiled, roily, thick, opaque. **—Ant.** clear, pellucid.

turgid, *adj.* **1.** swollen, distended, tumid. **2.** pompous, bombastic. **—Ant.** humble.

turmoil, *n.* commotion, disturbance, tumult, agitation, disquiet, turbulence, confusion, disorder, bustle, trouble, uproar. **—Ant.** quiet, serenity, order, peace.

turn, *v.* **1.** rotate, spin, revolve. **2.** change, reverse, divert, deflect, transfer. **3.** change, alter, metamorphose, transmute, transform, convert. **4.** direct, aim. **5.** shape, form, fashion, mold. **6.** send, drive. **7.** curve, bend, twist. **8.** disturb, derange, infuriate, infatuate, distract. **9.** sour, ferment. **—n. 10.** rotation, spin, gyration, revolution. **11.** change, reversal. **12.** direction, drift, trend. **13.** change, deviation, twist, bend, turning, vicissitude, variation. **14.** shape, form, mold, cast, fashion, manner. **15.** inclination, bent, tendency, aptitude, talent, proclivity, propensity. **16.** need, exigency, requirement, ne-

cessity. **—Syn. Study.** TURN, REVOLVE, ROTATE, SPIN indicate moving in a more or less rotary, circular fashion. TURN is the general and popular word for motion on an axis or around a center, but it is used also of motion that is less than a complete circle: *A gate turns on its hinges.* REVOLVE refers esp. to movement in an orbit around a center, but is sometimes exchangeable with ROTATE, which refers only to the motion of a body around its own center or axis: *The moon revolves about the earth. The earth rotates on its axis.* To SPIN is to rotate very rapidly: *A top spins.*

tussle, *v.* **1.** struggle, fight, wrestle, scuffle, conflict. **—n. 2.** struggle, fight, scuffle, conflict.

tutor, See Syn. study at TEACH.

twilight, *n.* **1.** evening, dusk, eventide, gloaming, sunset, sundown, nightfall, crepuscule, (*Brit. dial.*) cockshut. **2.** decline, diminution, close, end, ending, finish, conclusion.

twist, *v.* **1.** intertwine, braid, plait. **2.** combine, associate. **3.** contort, distort. **4.** change, alter, pervert. **5.** wind, coil, curve, bend, roll. **6.** writhe, squirm, wriggle. **7.** turn, spin, rotate, revolve. **—n. 8.** curve, bend, turn. **9.** turning, turn, rotation, rotating, spin. **10.** spiral, helix, coil. **11.** turn, bent, bias, proclivity, propensity. **12.** torsion, torque.

twit, *v.* **1.** taunt, gibe at, banter, tease. **2.** deride, reproach, upbraid.

tycoon, *n.* magnate, leader, top executive, baron, personage, mogul, panjandrum, nabob, VIP, worthy, big shot, wheel, big wheel, bigwig, brass hat, big-time operator. **—Ant.** nobody, nonentity, cipher.

type, *n.* **1.** kind, sort, class, classification, group, family, genus, phylum, form, stamp. **2.** sample, specimen, example, representative, prototype, pattern, model, exemplar, original, archetype. **3.** form, character, stamp. **4.** image, figure, device, sign, symbol.

tyrannical, *adj.* arbitrary, despotic, dictatorial, cruel, harsh, severe, oppressive, unjust, imperious, domineering, inhuman. **—Ant.** judicious, unbiased, just, humane.

tyrant, *n.* despot, autocrat, dictator, oppressor. **—Ant.** slave, serf.

tyro, *n.* beginner, neophyte, novice, greenhorn; learner, student. **—Ant.** expert.

U

ubiquitous, *adj.* omnipresent, being, everywhere, present. **—Ant.** absent, missing.

ugly, *adj.* **1.** repulsive, offensive, displeasing, ill-favored, hard-featured, unlovely, unsightly, homely. **2.** revolting, terrible, base, vile, monstrous, corrupt, heinous, amoral. **3.** disagreeable, unpleasant, objectionable. **4.** troublesome, disadvantageous, threatening, dangerous, ominous. **5.** rough, stormy, tempestuous. **6.** surly, spiteful, ill-natured, quarrelsome, vicious, bad-tempered. **—Ant.** beautiful.

ulterior, *adj.* **1.** unacknowledged, unavowed, unexpressed, hidden, concealed, covert, secret, latent, obscure, ambiguous, cryptic, enigmatic. **2.** further, farther, distant, thither, yon, yonder, remoter. **—Ant.** open, explicit; close, present.

ultimate, *adj.* final, decisive, last, extreme, furthest, farthest, remotest. **—Ant.** prime, primary.

ultimatum, *n.* warning, notice, threat, demand, insistence, final offer.

umbrage, *n.* offense, pique, resentment, displeasure, grudge. **—Ant.** pleasure.

umpire, *n.* **1.** referee, arbitrator, arbiter, judge. **—v. 2.** arbitrate, referee, judge; decide, settle. **—Syn. Study.** See JUDGE.

unabashed, *adj.* **1.** bold, brazen, undaunted, fearless, doughty, confident, sure. **2.** shameless, brazenfaced, forward, immodest, unblushing. **—Ant.** timid, retiring; modest, prim.

unaccountable, *adj.* **1.** unanswerable, irresponsible. **2.** inexplicable, inscrutable, strange, unexplainable, incomprehensible, unintelligible. **—Ant.** accountable.

unaccustomed, *adj.* **1.** unusual, unfamiliar, new. **2.** unused. **—Ant.** accustomed.

unaffected, *adj.* **1.** sincere, genuine, honest, real, unfeigned, natural, plain, naive, simple, guileless, art-

less. **2.** unmoved, untouched, unimpressed, unstirred. **—Ant.** affected.

unanimity, *n.* accord, agreement, unanimousness, harmony, unity, unison, concert. **—Ant.** discord, disagreement.

unapt, *adj.* **1.** unfitted, unsuited, unsuitable, unfit, inappropriate, inapplicable, irrelevant. **2.** unlikely, indisposed. **3.** slow, inapt, unskillful, inept, incompetent, unqualified. **—Ant.** apt.

unassuming, *adj.* modest, unpretending, unpretentious, humble, unostentatious. **—Ant.** immodest, pretentious.

unbearable, *adj.* unendurable, intolerable, insufferable, insupportable. **—Ant.** bearable.

unbecoming, *adj.* **1.** inappropriate, unsuited, unapt, unsuitable, unfitted, unfit. **2.** unseemly, improper, indecent. **—Ant.** becoming, appropriate; seemly, proper. **—Syn. Study.** See IMPROPER.

unbiased, *adj.* fair, equitable, impartial, tolerant, unprejudiced, neutral, disinterested. **—Ant.** biased, prejudiced.

unbounded, *adj.* **1.** unlimited, boundless, limitless, immense, vast, infinite, immeasurable, endless, interminable, illimitable. **2.** unrestrained, unconfined, unfettered, unchained, uncontrolled, unbridled, immoderate. **—Ant.** bounded, limited; restrained.

unbroken, *adj.* **1.** whole, intact, complete, entire. **2.** uninterrupted, continuous, deep, sound, fast, profound, undisturbed. **3.** undisturbed, unimpaired. **—Ant.** broken, incomplete; interrupted, discontinuous; impaired.

unburden, *v.* **1.** disburden, unload, relieve. **2.** disclose, reveal; confess. **—Ant.** burden.

uncalled-for, *adj.* unnecessary, improper, unwarranted. **—Ant.** necessary, essential, proper.

uncanny, *adj.* strange, preternatural, supernatural, weird, odd. **—Ant.** common, usual, natural. **—Syn. Study.** See WEIRD.

uncertain, *adj.* **1.** insecure, precarious, unsure, doubtful, unpredictable, problematical, unstable, unreliable, unsafe, fallible, perilous, dangerous. **2.** unassured, undecided, indeterminate, undetermined, unfixed, unsettled, indefinite, ambiguous, questionable, dubious. **3.** doubtful, vague, indistinct. **4.** undependable, changeable, variable, capricious, unsteady, irregular, fitful, desultory, chance. **—Ant.** certain.

uncivil, *adj.* **1.** ill-mannered, unmannerly, rude, impolite, discourteous, disrespectful, uncouth, boorish, brusque, curt, impudent. **2.** uncivilized. **—Ant.** civil.

unclean, *adj.* **1.** dirty, soiled, filthy, nasty, foul. **2.** evil, vile, base, impure, unvirtuous, unchaste, sinful, corrupt, polluted. **—Ant.** clean.

uncomfortable, *adj.* **1.** disquieting, discomforting. **2.** uneasy, ill at ease, unhappy, miserable, cheerless. **—Ant.** comfortable.

uncommon, *adj.* unusual, rare, scarce, infrequent, odd, singular, strange, peculiar, remarkable, queer, extraordinary, exceptional. **—Ant.** common.

uncommunicative, *adj.* reserved, taciturn, close-mouthed, reticent. **—Ant.** communicative, talkative, voluble.

uncompromising, *adj.* unyielding, inflexible, rigid, firm, steadfast, obstinate. **—Ant.** compromising, yielding, flexible.

unconcern, *n.* indifference, nonchalance, insouciance. **—Ant.** concern.

unconditional, *adj.* unrestricted, absolute, complete, unqualified, unconditioned, unreserved, categorical. **—Ant.** conditional, restricted, qualified.

unconscionable, *adj.* **1.** unscrupulous, shady, dishonest, unlawful. **2.** unreasonable, excessive, extravagant, exorbitant. **—Ant.** scrupulous; reasonable.

uncouth, *adj.* **1.** awkward, clumsy, unmannerly, discourteous, rude, ill-mannered, uncivil. **2.** unusual, strange, odd, unknown, unfamiliar. **—Ant.** courteous; natural, usual.

uncover, *v.* lay bare, disclose, reveal, expose, open, strip. **—Ant.** cover, conceal.

unctuous, *adj.* **1.** fatty, oily, greasy, oleaginous, unguent, lardaceous. **2.** insinuating, smarmy, obsequious, flattering, sycophantic, ingratiating, Pecksniffian. **—Ant.** affected.

undaunted, *adj.* undiscouraged,

fearless, brave, intrepid, undismayed. —**Ant.** daunted, discouraged.

undeniable, *adj.* **1.** irrefutable, indisputable, indubitable, incontrovertible, incontestable, unquestionable; obvious, evident, clear, certain, sure, unimpeachable, unassailable. —**Ant.** good, unexceptionable. —**Ant.** doubtful, dubitable, questionable; poor.

undergo, *v.* experience, suffer, bear, tolerate, sustain, endure. —**Ant.** avoid.

underground, *adj.* **1.** subterranean, subterrestrial, subsurface, belowground, underearth, buried. **2.** secret, clandestine, hidden, undercover, cabalistic, surreptitious. **3.** avant-garde, experimental, antiestablishment, revolutionary, radical, subversive.

underhand, *adj.* secret, stealthy, sly, crafty, dishonorable, clandestine, surreptitious. —**Ant.** open, candid.

understand, *v.* **1.** perceive, grasp, realize, comprehend, interpret, conceive, know, see, apprehend, discern. **2.** learn, hear. **3.** accept, believe. —**Ant.** misunderstand. —**Syn. Study.** See KNOW.

undertow, *n.* underset, undercurrent, riptide, cross-current.

undying, *adj.* immortal, deathless, unending, eternal, everlasting, permanent. —**Ant.** dying, mortal, temporary.

unearthly, *adj.* weird, ultramundane, supernatural, preternatural, ghostly, spectral, unnatural, strange. —**Ant.** earthly, terrestrial.

uneducated, *adj.* untutored, unschooled, unenlightened, uninstructed, uncultivated, untaught, uninformed, unlettered, illiterate, ignorant. —**Ant.** cultivated, cultured, literate. —**Syn.** See IGNORANT.

unemployed, *adj.* unoccupied, idle, at liberty, jobless, between engagements. —**Ant.** employed, occupied.

unequaled, *adj.* unparalleled, matchless, unmatched, unrivaled, peerless, inimitable, incomparable. —**Ant.** parallel, rival, comparable.

unequivocal, *adj.* clear, plain, simple, direct, unambiguous, certain, obvious, evident, incontestable, absolute, explicit, unmistakable. —**Ant.** equivocal, ambiguous.

unerring, *adj.* unfailing, right, correct, exact, precise, sure, infallible, certain, accurate, definite. —**Ant.** errant, failing, fallible.

unessential, *adj.* nonessential, unimportant, dispensable, immaterial, unnecessary. —**Ant.** essential.

unexpected, *adj.* unforeseen, unanticipated, sudden, abrupt; surprising. —**Ant.** expected, foreseen, anticipated, gradual.

unfair, *adj.* biased, partial, prejudiced, unjust, inequitable. —**Ant.** fair.

unfaithful, *adj.* **1.** false, disloyal, perfidious, faithless, treacherous, traitorous, deceitful, recreant, untrustworthy. **2.** dishonest, crooked, unlawful. **3.** inaccurate, inexact, imprecise. **4.** fickle, untrue, inconstant; adulterous. —**Ant.** faithful.

unfavorable, *adj.* disadvantageous, unpropitious, adverse, inimical. —**Ant.** favorable.

unfeeling, *adj.* insensible, insensate, numb, callous, unsympathetic, hard, hard-hearted. —**Ant.** feeling, sympathetic.

unfit, *adj.* **1.** unfitted, unsuited, unsuitable, inappropriate, inapt, unapt. **2.** unqualified, incompetent, incapable. —*v.* **3.** disqualify. —**Ant.** fit.

unfortunate, *adj.* unlucky, unhappy, luckless, unsuccessful, hapless, star-crossed, ill-starred. —**Ant.** fortunate.

unfriendly, *adj.* inimical, unkindly, hostile, unkind. —**Ant.** friendly.

unfruitful, *adj.* unproductive, barren, sterile, fruitless. —**Ant.** fruitful.

ungainly, *adj.* awkward, clumsy, ungraceful, uncouth. —**Ant.** graceful.

ungodly, *adj.* irreligious, impious, sinful, piacular, profane, wicked, depraved, polluted, corrupted, base, vile, evil. —**Ant.** godly.

unguarded, *adj.* **1.** unprotected, undefended, open, naked, defenseless. **2.** incautious, imprudent, thoughtless, careless. —**Ant.** guarded, protected; cautious, careful.

unhappy, *adj.* **1.** sad, miserable, wretched, sorrowful, downcast, cheerless, disconsolate, inconsolable, distressed, afflicted. **2.** unlucky, unfortunate, hapless. **3.** unfavorable, inauspicious, unpropitious. **4.** infelicitous, inappropriate, inapt, unapt. —**Ant.** happy.

unhealthful, *adj.* **1.** insalubrious, unwholesome, unhealthy, noxious, poisonous, harmful. **2.** ill, unhealthy, sick. —**Ant.** healthy, healthful, hale, hearty.

unhealthy, *adj.* **1.** sickly, delicate, frail, weak, feeble, enfeebled, ill, diseased, afflicted. **2.** unwholesome, unhealthful, unsanitary, unhygienic, insalubrious, deleterious, poisonous, noxious. —**Ant.** healthy.

uniform, *adj.* **1.** invariable, unchanging, unwavering, unvarying, unvaried, unchanged, constant, regular. **2.** undiversified, unvariegated, dun, solid, plain. **3.** regular, even. **4.** consistent, regular, constant. **5.** agreeing, alike, similar. —*n.* **6.** livery. —**Ant.** irregular, wavering; diversified; uneven; inconsistent.

unimpeachable, *adj.* irreproachable, unassailable, blameless, unexceptionable. —**Ant.** reproachable, censurable.

unimportant, *adj.* trivial, trifling, paltry, nugatory, secondary, insignificant, petty, slight. —**Ant.** important.

uninterested, *adj.* indifferent, unconcerned. —**Ant.** interested.

union, *n.* **1.** junction, combination, unity, coalition. **2.** society, association, league, confederacy, alliance. **3.** marriage, matrimony, wedlock. **4.** brotherhood. —**Ant.** separation, fissure. —**Syn. Study.** See ALLIANCE.

unique, *adj.* **1.** sole, only, single. **2.** unequaled, alone, peerless. **3.** rare, unusual, singular, odd, peculiar, strange, uncommon. —**Ant.** common, usual.

unite, *v.* **1.** join, combine, incorporate, connect, conjoin, couple, link, yoke, associate. **2.** combine, amalgamate, compound, blend, coalesce, fuse, weld, consolidate. **3.** marry, wed. —**Ant.** separate, sever. —**Syn. Study.** See JOIN.

unity, *n.* **1.** oneness, union, singleness, singularity, individuality. **2.** concord, harmony, agreement, unison, concert, unanimity, uniformity. —**Ant.** disunity; disharmony.

universal, *adj.* general, whole, total, entire; ecumenical. —*n.* **2.** concept. —**Ant.** local; special. —**Syn. Study.** See GENERAL.

unjust, *adj.* **1.** inequitable, partial, unfair, prejudiced, biased. **2.** undeserved, unjustified, unjustifiable, unmerited. —**Ant.** just.

unkind, *adj.* harsh, cruel, unmerciful, unfeeling, distressing. —**Ant.** kind.

unlawful, *adj.* illegal, illicit, illegitimate; bastard, spurious, natural. —**Ant.** lawful, legal. —**Syn. Study.** See ILLEGAL.

unlike, *adj.* different, dissimilar, diverse, variant, heterogeneous. —**Ant.** like.

unlimited, *adj.* unrestricted, unconstrained, unrestrained, boundless, unfettered, limitless, unbounded, vast, extensive, infinite. —**Ant.** limited.

unlucky, *adj.* unfortunate, hapless, ill-fated, unsuccessful, ill-omened. —**Ant.** lucky.

unmeasured, *adj.* **1.** unlimited, measureless, immense, vast, infinite. **2.** unrestrained, intemperate, unconstrained; unstinting, lavish. —**Ant.** measured, finite; temperate, constrained.

unmerciful, *adj.* merciless, pitiless, unpitying, relentless, cruel, unsparing; unconscionable. —**Ant.** merciful.

unmindful, *adj.* heedless, regardless, careless, inattentive, neglectful, negligent, unobservant, forgetful. —**Ant.** mindful, aware.

unmistakable, *adj.* clear, plain, evident, obvious, palpable, patent. —**Ant.** unclear, dim.

unmitigated, *adj.* unqualified, absolute, complete, consummate. —**Ant.** mitigated.

unmixed, *adj.* pure, unalloyed, unmingled, unadulterated. —**Ant.** mixed, impure, mongrel.

unnatural, *adj.* **1.** affected, forced, strained, out of character. **2.** unusual, strange, abnormal, irregular, anomalous, aberrant. **3.** cruel, evil, inhuman, heartless, hard-hearted, brutal. —**Ant.** natural; humane.

unnecessary, *adj.* needless, superfluous, de trop. —**Ant.** necessary.

unnerve, *v.* discourage, disarm, shake, fluster, disconcert, upset. —**Ant.** steel, encourage.

unparalleled, *adj.* matchless, unmatched, unequaled, unrivaled, peerless. —**Ant.** equaled.

unpleasant, *adj.* unpleasing, disagreeable, unpalatable, unappetizing, offensive, obnoxious, noisome, repulsive, repellent; noxious. —**Ant.** pleasant.

unpractical, *adj.* impractical, visionary, speculative, theoretical. —**Ant.** practical.

unprejudiced, *adj.* unbiased, impartial, fair. —**Ant.** prejudiced, biased.

unpretentious, *adj.* modest, unassuming, shy, abashed, bashful, self-effacing, unpretending, retiring, unobtrusive. —**Ant.** pretentious.

unprincipled, *adj.* unscrupulous, tricky, shrewd, dishonest, cagey, wicked, bad, evil, amoral. —**Ant.** principled; scrupulous. —**Syn. Study.** See UNSCRUPULOUS.

unqualified, *adj.* **1.** unfit, incompetent. **2.** absolute, unmitigated, out-and-out, thorough, complete, direct, unrestricted, downright. —**Ant.** qualified.

unquestionable, *adj.* indisputable, indubitable, incontrovertible, undeniable, irrefutable, incontestable; unexceptionable. —**Ant.** questionable.

unquiet, *adj.* restless, restive, turbulent, tumultuous, disturbed, agitated, upset, uneasy, nervous, perturbed, fidgety. —**Ant.** quiet.

unreal, *adj.* imaginary, artificial, unpractical, visionary, sham, spurious, fictitious, illusive, illusory, vague, theoretical, impractical. —**Ant.** real.

unreasonable, *adj.* **1.** irrational, senseless, foolish, silly, preposterous, absurd, stupid, nonsensical, idiotic. **2.** immoderate, exorbitant, excessive, unjust, unfair, extravagant. —**Ant.** reasonable.

unreconstructed, *adj.* unapologetic, impenitent, unrepenting, stubborn, defiant, obdurate, die-hard, standpat.

unrefined, *adj.* **1.** unpurified, coarse, harsh, crude. **2.** unpolished, uncultured, ill-bred, rude, boorish, vulgar, gross. —**Ant.** refined.

unrelenting, *adj.* unabating, relentless, unremitting, implacable, inexorable, merciless, unmerciful, ruthless, pitiless, unpitying, uncompassionate, cruel, hard, bitter, harsh, stern, remorseless, austere. —**Ant.** relenting.

unreserved, *adj.* **1.** full, entire, complete, unlimited. **2.** frank, open, ingenuous, candid, naive, artless, guileless, undesigning, sincere. —**Ant.** reserved, incomplete; artful.

unruffled, *adj.* smooth, calm, unperturbed, tranquil, serene, collected, imperturbable, cool, composed, peaceful, controlled, undisturbed. —**Ant.** ruffled.

unruly, *adj.* ungovernable, disobedient, insubordinate, unmanageable, uncontrollable, refractory, stubborn, lawless; turbulent, tumultuous, disorderly, riotous. —**Ant.** obedient, subordinate. —**Syn. Study.** UNRULY, INTRACTABLE, RECALCITRANT, REFRACTORY describe persons or things that resist management or control. UNRULY suggests constant disorderly behavior or character: *an unruly child; unruly hair.* INTRACTABLE suggests in persons a determined resistance to all attempts to guide or direct them, and in things a resistance to attempts to shape, improve, or modify them: *an intractable social rebel; an intractable problem.* RECALCITRANT suggests stubborn rebellion against authority or direction: *a recalcitrant prisoner.* REFRACTORY also implies a mulish disobedience, but leaves open the possibility of eventual compliance: *The refractory youth needs more understanding.*

unsatisfactory, *adj.* disappointing, inadequate, insufficient. —**Ant.** satisfactory.

unsavory, *adj.* tasteless, insipid; unpleasant, offensive, distasteful. —**Ant.** savory, tasteful.

unscrupulous, *adj.* unrestrained, unrestricted, conscienceless, unprincipled, unethical. —**Ant.** scrupulous, restrained. —**Syn. Study.** UNSCRUPULOUS, UNPRINCIPLED refer to a lack of moral or ethical standards. UNSCRUPULOUS means not controlled by one's conscience and contemptuous of what one knows to be right or honorable: *an unscrupulous landlord.* UNPRINCIPLED means lacking or not aware of moral standards that should restrain one's actions: *an unprincipled rogue.*

unseasonable, *adj.* inopportune, ill-timed, untimely, inappropriate. —**Ant.** seasonable, opportune.

unseat, *v.* displace, depose; throw. —**Ant.** place.

unseemly, *adj.* unfitting, unbecoming, improper, indecorous, indecent, unbefitting, inappropriate. —**Ant.** seemly, fitting, becoming. —**Syn. Study.** See IMPROPER.

unsettled, *adj.* unstable, unsteady, shaky, undependable, unsure, unfixed, undetermined, indeterminate, changeable, wavering, vacillating, infirm, fickle, faltering, irresolute. —**Ant.** settled, stable, steady.

unsightly, *adj.* unpleasant, unattractive, ugly, disagreeable, hideous. —**Ant.** beautiful.

unskillful, *adj.* untrained, inexpert, awkward, bungling, clumsy, inapt, maladroit. —**Ant.** skillful.

unsophisticated, *adj.* **1.** simple, artless, ingenuous, guileless, naive. **2.** unadulterated, pure, genuine. —**Ant.** sophisticated.

unsound, *adj.* **1.** diseased, defective, impaired, decayed, rotten, sickly, sick, ill, infirm, unhealthy, unwholesome. **2.** fallacious, unfounded, invalid, false, erroneous, untenable, faulty. **3.** fragile, breakable, frangible. **4.** unreliable, unsubstantial. —**Ant.** sound.

unsparing, *adj.* liberal, profuse, generous, lavish, bountiful; unmerciful, merciless, ruthless, pitiless, unsympathetic, severe, unforgiving, harsh, inexorable, unrelenting, relentless, uncompromising. —**Ant.** illiberal, sparing, penurious.

unspeakable, *adj.* unutterable, inexpressible, ineffable, indescribable.

unstable, *adj.* **1.** infirm, unsteady, precarious. **2.** unsteadfast, inconstant, wavering, vacillating, undecided, unsettled. —**Ant.** stable.

unsteady, *adj.* **1.** unfixed, infirm, faltering. **2.** fluctuating, wavering, unsettled, vacillating, fickle, changeable, unstable. **3.** irregular, unreliable. —**Ant.** steady.

unsuitable, *adj.* inappropriate, unfitting, unbefitting, unbecoming. —**Ant.** suitable.

untangle, *v.* unravel, unsnarl, disentangle. —**Ant.** tangle, snarl, entangle.

unthinkable, *adj.* inconceivable. —**Ant.** conceivable.

untidy, *adj.* slovenly, disordered; sloppy. —**Ant.** tidy.

untie, *v.* unfasten, loose, unknot, undo, unbind. —**Ant.** tie.

untimely, *adj.* unpropitious, unseasonable, inappropriate. —**Ant.** timely.

untruth, *n.* falsehood, fib, lie, fiction, story, tale, tall tale, fabrication, fable, forgery, invention. —**Ant.** truth.

unusual, *adj.* uncommon, extraordinary, exceptional, rare, strange, remarkable, singular, curious, queer, odd. —**Ant.** usual.

unvarnished, *adj.* plain, unembellished, unexaggerated. —**Ant.** embellished, exaggerated.

unwary, *adj.* incautious, unguarded, imprudent, indiscreet, hasty, careless, rash, heedless, precipitous, headlong. —**Ant.** wary.

unwholesome, *adj.* unhealthy, insalubrious, unhealthful, deleterious, noxious, noisome, poisonous, baneful, pernicious; corrupt. —**Ant.** wholesome.

unwieldy, *adj.* bulky, unmanageable, clumsy, ponderous, heavy. —**Ant.** manageable, light.

unwise, *adj.* foolish, imprudent, injudicious, ill-advised, indiscreet. —**Ant.** wise.

unwitting, *adj.* unaware, unknowing, unconscious, inadvertent, unintentional, ignorant. —**Ant.** intentional, aware.

unworthy, *adj.* inadequate, undeserving; worthless, base. —**Ant.** worthy.

unyielding, *adj.* **1.** inflexible, firm, stanch, steadfast, adamant, resolute, indomitable, pertinacious, determined. **2.** stubborn, obstinate, stiff, intractable, perverse, headstrong, willful. —**Ant.** flexible.

upbraid, *v.* reproach, chide, reprove, blame, censure, condemn. —**Ant.** praise, laud. —**Syn. Study.** See REPRIMAND.

uphold, *v.* **1.** support, sustain, maintain, countenance. **2.** raise, elevate. —**Ant.** attack.

uplifting, *adj.* edifying, improving, bettering, educational, informative, informational, instructive, enlightening. —**Ant.** debasing, corruptive.

uppermost, *adj.* highest, topmost, predominant, supreme. —**Ant.** lowermost, lowest.

uppity, *adj.* arrogant, haughty, disdainful, scornful, presumptuous, cocky, supercilious, snobbish, snobby, stuck-up, snooty, (*Brit.*) toffee-nosed. —**Ant.** modest, unassuming, down-to-earth.

upright, *adj.* **1.** erect, vertical, perpendicular, plumb. **2.** honest, just,

righteous, honorable, straightforward, virtuous, true, good, pure, conscientious. —*n.* **3.** pole, prop, support, pile, pier, column, Lally column. —**Ant.** horizontal, prone.

uprising, *n.* insurrection, revolt, revolution, rebellion.

uproar, *n.* disturbance, tumult, disorder, turbulence, commotion, hubbub, furor, din, clamor, noise; fracas, melee, riot. —**Ant.** peace.

upset, *v.* **1.** overturn, capsize. **2.** overthrow, defeat, depose, displace. **3.** disturb, derange, unnerve, disconcert, agitate, perturb, fluster. —*n.* **4.** overturn, overthrow, defeat. **5.** nervousness, perturbation, disturbance. **6.** disorder, mess. —*adj.* **7.** overturned, capsized. **8.** disordered, messy; sloppy. **9.** worried, concerned, disconcerted, agitated, disturbed, perturbed, irritated. —**Ant.** steady, stabilize.

urbane, *adj.* courteous, polite, refined, elegant, polished, smooth, suave. —**Ant.** discourteous, impolite.

urge, *v.* **1.** push, force, impel, drive. **2.** press, push, hasten. **3.** impel, constrain, move, activate, animate, incite, instigate, goad, stimulate, spur. **4.** induce, persuade, solicit, beg, beseech, importune, entreat, implore. **5.** insist upon, allege, assert, aver, declare, asseverate. **6.** recommend, advocate, advise. —*n.* **7.** impulse, influence, force, drive, push. **8.** reflex. —**Ant.** deter, discourage.

urgent, *adj.* **1.** pressing, compelling, forcing, driving, imperative, requiring, immediate. **2.** insistent, importunate, earnest, eager. —**Ant.** unimportant.

use, *v.* **1.** employ, utilize, make use of, apply, avail oneself of. **2.** expend, consume, use up, waste, exhaust. **3.** practice, put to use, exercise. **4.** act or behave toward, treat, deal with. **5.** accustom, habituate, familiarize, inure. —*n.* **6.** employment, utilization, application, exercise. **7.** utility, usefulness, service, advantage, profit, benefit, avail. **8.** help, profit, good. **9.** custom, practice, usage, habit. **10.** occasion, need. **11.** treatment, handling. —**Ant.** disuse. —**Syn. Study.** USE, UTILIZE mean to put something into action or service. USE is a general word referring to the application of something to a given purpose: *to use a telephone.* USE may also imply that the thing is consumed or diminished in the process: *I used all the butter.* When applied to persons, USE implies a selfish or sinister purpose: *He used his friend to advance himself.* UTILIZE, a more formal word, implies practical, profitable, or creative use: *to utilize solar energy to run a machine.*

useful, *adj.* **1.** serviceable, advantageous, profitable, helpful, effectual, effective, efficacious, beneficial, salutary. **2.** practical, practicable, workable. —**Ant.** useless.

useless, *adj.* **1.** unavailing, futile, inutile, fruitless, vain, ineffectual, profitless, bootless, valueless, worthless, hopeless. **2.** unserviceable, unusable. —**Ant.** useful. —**Syn. Study.** USELESS, FUTILE, VAIN refer to something that is of no use, value, profit, or advantage. USELESS refers to something of no avail because of the circumstances or because of some inherent defect: *It is useless to reason with him.* FUTILE suggests wasted or ill-advised effort and complete failure to achieve a desired end: *Their attempts to save the business were futile.* VAIN describes something that is fruitless or unsuccessful in spite of all possible effort: *It is vain to keep on hoping.*

usual, *adj.* habitual, accustomed, customary; common, ordinary, familiar, prevailing, prevalent, everyday, general, frequent, regular, expected, predictable, settled, constant, fixed. —**Ant.** unusual. —**Syn. Study.** USUAL, CUSTOMARY, HABITUAL refer to something that is familiar because it is commonly met with or observed. USUAL indicates something that is to be expected by reason of previous experience, which shows it to occur more often than not: *There were the usual crowds at the monument.* CUSTOMARY refers to something that accords with prevailing usage or individual practice: *customary courtesies; a customary afternoon nap.* HABITUAL refers to a practice that has become fixed by regular repetition: *a clerk's habitual sales pitch.*

usually. See Syn. study at OFTEN.

utensil. See Syn. study at TOOL.

utilitarian, *adj.* useful, practical, serviceable, helpful, functional, pragmatical, workaday, handy, utile, aidful, convenient, effective, valuable. —**Ant.** impractical, useless.

utilize, v. See Syn. study at USE.

utter, v. **1.** express, speak, pronounce, say, voice. **2.** publish, proclaim, announce, promulgate. **3.** circulate. —adj. **4.** complete, total, absolute, unconditional, unqualified, entire. —**Ant.** partial, incomplete, relative.

V

vacant, adj. **1.** empty, void. **2.** devoid or destitute of, lacking, wanting. **3.** untenanted, unoccupied, empty. **4.** free, unoccupied, unemployed, leisure, unencumbered. **5.** unthinking, thoughtless. **6.** vacuous, blank, inane. —**Ant.** full; occupied; encumbered; thoughtful.

vacate, v. quit, abandon, leave, evacuate, desert, forsake, withdraw from, relinquish, clear, move. —**Ant.** occupy.

vacillate, v. **1.** sway, waver, reel, stagger. **2.** fluctuate, waver, hesitate. —**Syn. Study.** See WAVER.

vacuous, adj. vacant, empty, hollow, void, bland, blank, insipid, fatuous, inane, empty-headed, airheaded, vapid, bubbleheaded, bubblebrained, out to lunch, nobody home, foolish, silly, asinine —**Ant.** serious, lofty.

vagabond, adj. **1.** wandering, nomadic, homeless, vagrant. **2.** good-for-nothing, worthless. —n. **3.** tramp, vagrant, hobo, gypsy, outcast, loafer. **4.** scamp, rascal, knave, idler, vagrant.

vagary, n. whim, whimsy, fancy, twist, turn, conceit, caprice, crotchet, quirk, kink, megrim, peculiarity, oddity, notion, inspiration, brainstorm.

vagrant. See VAGABOND.

vague, adj. **1.** indefinite, unspecific, imprecise, obscure, dim, uncertain, unsure, indistinct, undetermined, indeterminate, unsettled. **2.** unclear, unknown, unfixed, lax, loose. —**Ant.** definite, specific.

vain, adj. **1.** useless, hollow, idle, worthless, unimportant, nugatory, trifling, trivial, inefficient, unavailing, unfruitful, futile, vapid. **2.** conceited, egotistical, self-complacent, proud, vainglorious, arrogant, overweening, inflated. —**Ant.** useful; humble. —**Syn. Study.** See USELESS.

vainglory, n. **1.** egotism, vanity, conceit. **2.** pomp, show, ostentation. —**Ant.** humility.

valiant, adj. brave, bold, courageous, stout, stouthearted, intrepid. —**Ant.** cowardly. —**Syn. Study.** See BRAVE.

valid, adj. just, well-founded, sound, substantial, logical, good, cogent, authoritative, effectual, efficient, efficacious, effective, binding, legal. —**Ant.** invalid, unjust.

valor, n. courage, boldness, firmness, bravery, intrepidity, spirit. —**Ant.** cowardice.

valuable, adj. **1.** costly, expensive, rare, precious, dear. **2.** useful, serviceable, important, estimable, worthy. —**Ant.** worthless.

value, n. **1.** worth, merit, desirability, usefulness, utility, importance. **2.** cost, price. **3.** valuation, evaluation, estimation. **4.** force, import, significance. —v. **5.** estimate, rate, price, appraise. **6.** regard, esteem, appreciate, prize. —**Syn. Study.** VALUE, WORTH both imply excellence and merit. VALUE is excellence based on desirability, usefulness, or importance; it may be measured in terms of its equivalent in money, goods, or services: *the value of sunlight; the value of a painting.* WORTH usu. implies inherent excellence based on spiritual and moral qualities that command esteem: *Few knew her true worth.* See also APPRECIATE.

vanish, v. **1.** disappear, evanesce. **2.** end, cease, fade. —**Ant.** appear; begin. —**Syn. Study.** See DISAPPEAR.

vanity, n. **1.** pride, conceit, self-esteem, egotism, self-complacency, self-admiration. **2.** hollowness, emptiness, sham, unreality, folly, triviality, futility. —**Ant.** humility. —**Syn. Study.** See PRIDE.

vanquish, v. conquer, defeat, overcome, overpower, subjugate, suppress, subdue, crush, quell, rout. —**Ant.** lose.

vapid, adj. **1.** lifeless, dull, flavorless, insipid, flat. **2.** spiritless, unanimated, dull, uninteresting, tedious, tiresome, prosaic. —**Ant.** spirited, animated.

variable, adj. **1.** changeable, alterable. **2.** inconstant, fickle, vacillating,

wavering, fluctuating, unsteady. —**Ant.** invariable; constant.

variance, n. **1.** divergence, discrepancy, difference. **2.** disagreement, dispute, quarrel, controversy, dissension, discord, strife. —**Ant.** invariance, similitude, sameness.

variation, n. **1.** change, mutation, vicissitude, alteration, modification. **2.** deviation, divergence, difference, discrepancy; diversity. —**Ant.** sameness.

variety, n. **1.** diversity, difference, discrepancy, divergence. **2.** diversity, multiplicity. **3.** assortment, collection, group. **4.** kind, sort, class, species. —**Ant.** sameness.

various, adj. differing, different, divers, distinct, several, many, diverse, sundry, diversified, variegated, varied. —**Ant.** same, similar. —**Syn. Study.** VARIOUS, DIVERSE, DIFFERENT, DISTINCT describe things that are not identical. VARIOUS stresses the multiplicity and variety of sorts or instances of a thing or class of things: *various kinds of seaweed.* DIVERSE suggests an even wider variety or disparity: *diverse opinions.* DIFFERENT points to a separate identity, or a dissimilarity in quality or character: *two different versions of the same story.* DISTINCT implies a uniqueness and lack of connection between things that may possibly be alike: *plans similar in objective but distinct in method.*

vary, v. **1.** change, alter, diversify, modify. **2.** transform, metamorphose, transmute, change. **3.** differ, deviate. **4.** alternate.

vast, adj. extensive, immense, huge, enormous, gigantic, colossal, measureless, boundless, unlimited, prodigious, stupendous. —**Ant.** limited, small.

vault, n. **1.** arch, ceiling, roof. **2.** cellar, catacomb, crypt, tomb. **3.** safe, safety deposit box. —v. **4.** arch. **5.** leap, spring, jump.

vaunt, v. boast, brag, crow, trumpet, gloat, exult, flaunt, parade, gasconade, show off, grandstand, hotdog.

vehemence, n. eagerness, impetuosity, verve, fire, ardor, violence, fervor, zeal, passion, enthusiasm, fervency, fury. —**Ant.** coolness, apathy, antipathy.

vehement, adj. eager, impetuous, impassioned, passionate, violent, ardent, zealous, earnest, fervent, fervid, burning, fiery, afire, ablaze. —**Ant.** cool, dispassionate.

velocity, n. rapidity, swiftness, quickness, speed, alacrity, celerity. —**Syn. Study.** See SPEED.

venal, adj. corrupt, bribable, unscrupulous, mercenary, purchasable, sordid. —**Ant.** pure, scrupulous.

veneration, n. respect, reverence, awe. —**Ant.** disrespect, irreverence. —**Syn. Study.** See RESPECT.

vengeance, n. avenging, revenge, retribution, requital, retaliation. —**Ant.** forgiveness, pardon. —**Syn. Study.** See REVENGE.

venial, adj. excusable, forgivable, pardonable. —**Ant.** inexcusable, unforgivable, mortal.

venom, n. **1.** poison, virus. **2.** spite, malice, malignity, maliciousness, spitefulness, acrimony, bitterness, acerbity, malevolence, gall, spleen, hate, contempt. —**Syn. Study.** See POISON.

ventilate, v. **1.** air, air out, cross-ventilate, freshen, refresh, aerate. **2.** tell, relate, disclose, reveal, divulge, lay open, express, air, vent, make known, make public, discuss. —**Ant.** seal; repress, suppress, clam up, keep mum.

venture, n. **1.** hazard, danger, jeopardy, risk, peril. **2.** speculation. —v. **3.** endanger, imperil, risk, jeopardize, hazard. **4.** dare, presume, make bold.

verbal, adj. oral, nuncupative, spoken, worded. —**Ant.** mental, physical.

verbose, See Syn. study at WORDY.

verge, n. **1.** edge, rim, margin, brim, lip. **2.** brink, limit. **3.** belt, strip, border. **4.** room, area, scope. **5.** rod, wand, mace, staff. —v. **6.** border, tend, lean, incline.

vernacular, adj. **1.** ordinary, colloquial, informal, conversational, spoken, nonliterary, vulgate, vulgar, demotic, general, popular, everyday, commonplace, household, down-to-earth. **2.** local, localized, regional, areal, parochial, provincial, limited, confined. —n. **3.** terminology, language, nomenclature, vocabulary, lexicon, verbiage, tongue, speech, jargon, dialect, lingo. —**Syn. Study.** See LANGUAGE.

verse, n. **1.** stich. **2.** poetry, meter,

poesy, versification, numbers. **3.** stanza, strophe, stave, section.

versed, adj. experienced, practiced, skilled. —**Ant.** inexperienced, unskilled.

version, n. **1.** translation, rendering, interpretation. **2.** variant, form, rendition.

vertical, adj. upright, plumb, zenithal, erect, perpendicular. —**Ant.** horizontal.

verve, n. spirit, spiritedness, buoyancy, dash, stylishness, animation, joie de vivre, brio, élan, gusto, panache, fire, esprit, vivacity, zest, oomph, zing.

vestige, n. trace, hint, suggestion, mark, evidence, token. —**Syn. Study.** See TRACE.

vex, v. **1.** irritate, annoy, pester, provoke, anger, irk, fret, nettle. **2.** torment, plague, worry, hector, harry, harass, torture, persecute. **3.** agitate, discuss, debate. —**Ant.** delight.

vexatious, adj. disturbing, annoying, vexing, troublesome, irritating. —**Ant.** delightful, pleasant.

vexed, adj. **1.** disturbed, troubled, annoyed. **2.** disputed, discussed. —**Ant.** delighted.

viable, adj. workable, doable, achievable, tenable, supportable, operable, manageable, feasible, practicable. —**Ant.** impractical, unworkable, unachievable.

vibrant, adj. **1.** vibrating, shaking, oscillating; resonant. **2.** pulsating, energetic, powerful, vigorous; exciting, thrilling.

vibrate, v. **1.** oscillate; shake, tremble, quiver, shiver. **2.** resound, echo.

vicarious, adj. substituted; delegated, deputed. —**Ant.** real, actual.

vice, n. **1.** fault, sin, depravity, iniquity, wickedness, corruption. **2.** blemish, blot, imperfection, defect. —**Ant.** virtue. —**Syn. Study.** See FAULT.

vicinity, n. **1.** area, neighborhood, environs, precincts, purlieus, vicinage, district, surroundings, environment, milieu. **2.** proximity, nearness, closeness, propinquity.

vicious, adj. **1.** immoral, depraved, profligate, sinful, corrupt, bad, abandoned, iniquitous. **2.** reprehensible, blameworthy, censurable, wrong, improper. **3.** spiteful, malignant, malicious, malevolent. **4.** faulty, defective. **5.** ill-tempered, bad-tempered, refractory. —**Ant.** moral; commendatory; benevolent; temperate.

victimize, v. dupe, swindle, cheat, deceive, trick, defraud, cozen, fool, hoodwink, beguile. —**Syn. Study.** See CHEAT.

victory, n. conquest, triumph, success. —**Ant.** defeat. —**Syn. Study.** VICTORY, CONQUEST, TRIUMPH refer to a successful outcome of a struggle. VICTORY suggests the decisive defeat of an opponent in a contest of any kind: *victory in battle; a football victory.* CONQUEST implies the taking over of control by the victor, and the obedience of the conquered: *a war of conquest; the conquest of Peru.* TRIUMPH implies a particularly outstanding victory: *the triumph of a righteous cause; the triumph of justice.*

vie, v. compete, rival, contend, strive.

view, n. **1.** sight, vision. **2.** prospect, scene, vista. **3.** aspect, appearance. **4.** contemplation, examination, survey, inspection. **5.** aim, intention, purpose, reason, end, design, intent, object. **6.** consideration, regard. **7.** account, description. **8.** conception, idea, notion, opinion, theory, belief, judgment, estimation, assessment, impression, valuation. —v. **9.** see, behold, witness, contemplate, regard, look at, survey, inspect, examine. —**Syn. Study.** VIEW, PROSPECT, SCENE, VISTA refer to whatever lies open to sight. VIEW is the general word: *a fine view of the surrounding countryside.* PROSPECT suggests a sweeping and often distant view, as from a vantage point: *The prospect from the mountaintop was breathtaking.* SCENE suggests an organic unity in the details, as is found in a picture: *a woodland scene.* VISTA suggests a long, narrow view, as along an avenue between rows of trees: *a pleasant vista.* See also OPINION.

vigilant, adj. attentive, wary, alert, awake, sleepless, watchful. —**Ant.** inattentive, unwary.

vigorous, adj. strong, active, robust, sturdy, sound, healthy, hale, energetic, forcible, powerful, effective, forceful. —**Ant.** weak, inactive.

vile, adj. **1.** wretched, bad; base, low, vicious, evil, depraved, iniquitous. **2.** offensive, obnoxious, objectionable, repulsive, disgusting, despi-

cable, revolting, repellent, nauseous, nauseating. **3.** foul, vulgar, obscene. **4.** poor, wretched, mean, menial, low, degraded, ignominious, contemptible. **5.** valueless, paltry, trivial, trifling, niggling, nugatory. —**Ant.** good, elevated.

vilify, v. defame, traduce, depreciate, slander, disparage, malign, calumniate, revile, abuse, blacken, asperse, slur, decry. —**Ant.** commend, honor, praise.

village, n. town, hamlet, municipality, community.

villain, n. scoundrel, cad, bounder, knave, rascal, rapscallion, scamp, rogue, scapegrace, miscreant, reprobate. —**Ant.** hero, protagonist.

vindicate, v. **1.** clear, exonerate. **2.** uphold, justify, maintain, defend, assert, support. —**Ant.** convict, blame.

vindictive, adj. revengeful, vengeful, spiteful, unforgiving, rancorous, unrelenting. —**Ant.** forgiving.

violation, n. **1.** breach, infringement, transgression. **2.** desecration, defilement. **3.** ravishment, rape, defloration, debauchment. —**Ant.** obedience. —**Syn. Study.** See BREACH.

violence, n. **1.** injury, wrong, outrage, injustice. **2.** vehemence, impetuosity, fury, intensity, severity, acuteness. **3.** energy, force.

virgin, n. **1.** maiden, maid, ingenue. —adj. **2.** pure, unsullied, undefiled, chaste, unpolluted. **3.** unmixed, unalloyed, pure, unadulterated. **4.** untouched, untried, unused, fresh, new, maiden. —**Ant.** defiled, polluted, impure, unchaste; adulterated.

virile, adj. masculine, manly, vigorous, male. —**Ant.** effeminate. —**Syn. Study.** See MALE.

virtue, n. **1.** goodness, uprightness, morality, probity, rectitude, integrity. **2.** chastity, virginity, purity. **3.** justice, prudence, temperance, fortitude; faith, hope, charity. **4.** excellence, merit, quality, asset. **5.** effectiveness, efficacy, force, power, potency. —**Ant.** vice. —**Syn. Study.** See GOODNESS.

virtuous, adj. right, upright, moral, righteous, good, chaste, pure. —**Ant.** vicious.

virulent, adj. **1.** poisonous, malignant, deadly, venomous. **2.** hostile, bitter, acrimonious, acerb, spiteful, vicious. —**Ant.** harmless.

virus, n. poison, venom, toxin.

visage, n. **1.** face, countenance, physiognomy. **2.** aspect, appearance. —**Syn. Study.** See FACE.

viscous, adj. sticky, adhesive, glutinous, ropy, thick.

visible, adj. **1.** perceptible, discernible, open. **2.** understandable, discernible. **3.** apparent, manifest, obvious, evident, open, clear, patent, palpable, conspicuous, observable, unmistakable. —**Ant.** invisible.

vision, n. **1.** sight. **2.** perception, discernment. **3.** view, image, conception, idea, anticipation. **4.** apparition, specter, ghost, phantom, phantasm, illusion, chimera.

visionary, adj. **1.** fanciful, unpractical, impractical, impracticable, fancied, unreal, ideal, imaginary, speculative, illusory, chimerical, romantic. —n. **2.** romantic, dreamer, idealist, theorist, enthusiast. —**Ant.** practical, practicable.

visitor, n. caller, guest, visitant. —**Ant.** host, hostess.

vista. See Syn. study at VIEW.

vital, adj. indispensable, essential, necessary, important, critical. —**Ant.** dispensable, secondary, unimportant.

vitriolic, adj. acid, bitter, caustic, scathing. —**Ant.** bland, mild, sweet.

vituperate, v. abuse, revile, objurgate, censure, vilify, reproach, upbraid, berate, scold. —**Ant.** praise, commend.

vivacious, adj. lively, animated, sprightly, spirited, brisk, sportive. —**Ant.** inanimate, dull, inactive.

vivid, adj. **1.** bright, brilliant, intense, clear, lucid. **2.** animated, spirited, vivacious, lively, intense. **3.** vigorous, energetic. **4.** picturesque, lifelike, realistic. **5.** perceptible, clear, discernible, apparent. **6.** strong, distinct, striking. —**Ant.** dull.

vocation, n. business, occupation, profession, calling, trade, métier, employment, pursuit.

vociferous, adj. clamorous, noisy, loud, obstreperous, uproarious. —**Ant.** quiet, pacific, peaceful.

vogue, n. fashion, style, mode; currency, acceptance, favor, usage, custom, practice.

void, adj. **1.** useless, ineffectual,

vain, ineffective, nugatory. **2.** empty, devoid, destitute, vacant. **3.** unoccupied, vacated, unfilled. —n. **4.** space, vacuum; gap, opening. —v. **5.** invalidate, nullify, annul. **6.** empty, discharge, evacuate, vacate, emit. —**Ant.** useful; full; occupied; validate; fill.

volition, n. will, will-power, determination, preference, discretion, choice, option.

voluble, adj. fluent, glib, talkative, loquacious. —**Ant.** taciturn, quiet, silent. —**Syn. Study.** See FLUENT.

volume, n. **1.** book, tome; scroll, manuscript, codex, papyrus. **2.** size, measure, amount, magnitude. **3.** mass, quantity, amount. **4.** loudness, softness.

voluntary, adj. **1.** deliberate, considered, purposeful, willful, intentional, intended, designed, planned. **2.** spontaneous, impulsive, free, unforced, natural, unconstrained. —**Ant.** involuntary. —**Syn. Study.** See DELIBERATE.

voluptuous, adj. sensual, luxurious, epicurean. —**Ant.** intellectual.

voracious, adj. ravenous, greedy, hungry, rapacious. —**Ant.** apathetic.

vouchsafe, v. give, grant, bestow, confer, accord, award, concede, allow, permit, condescend, stoop, deign. —**Ant.** deny, refuse.

vow, n., v. pledge, promise.

voyage, n. trip, flight, cruise, sailing. —**Syn. Study.** See TRIP.

vulgar, adj. **1.** coarse, inelegant, ribald. **2.** underbred, unrefined, boorish, common, mean, ignoble, plebeian, crude, rude. **3.** vernacular, colloquial. —**Ant.** elegant; refined; standard. —**Syn. Study.** See COMMON.

vulnerable, adj. **1.** defenseless, exposed, unprotected, unguarded, helpless, penetrable, woundable, damageable, assailable, attackable, vincible. **2.** liable, open, susceptible, prone, at risk. —**Ant.** invulnerable, impregnable, invincible, impervious.

vying, adj. competing, competitive.

W

wacky, adj. eccentric, irrational, whimsical, knockabout, zany, madcap, foolish, silly, crazy, screwball, goofy, oddball. —**Ant.** serious, sobersided.

waffle, v. **1.** vacillate, dither, equivocate, hesitate, tergiversate, waver, seesaw, fluctuate, hem and haw, back and fill, yo-yo, (Brit.) haver. **2.** blather, babble, prattle, gabble, prate.

wage, n. **1.** (usually plural) hire, pay, salary, stipend, earnings, emolument, compensation, remuneration, allowance. **2.** recompense, return, reward. —v. **3.** carry on, undertake, engage in.

wager, n. **1.** stake, hazard, bet, risk, venture, pledge. —v. **2.** stake, bet, hazard, risk, lay a wager.

waggish, adj. roguish, jocular, humorous, mischievous, tricky, sportive, merry, jocose, droll, comical, funny.

wagon, n. cart, van, truck, dray; lorry, wain; buckboard, dogcart.

wait, v. **1.** stay, rest, expect, await, remain, be inactive or quiescent, linger, abide, tarry, pause, delay. —n. **2.** delay, halt, waiting, tarrying, lingering, pause, stop. **3.** ambushment, ambush. —**Ant.** proceed.

waive, v. **1.** relinquish, forgo, resign, demit, surrender, renounce, give up, remit. **2.** defer, put off or aside. —**Ant.** require, demand.

wake, v. **1.** awake, rise, arise, get up. **2.** rouse, waken, arouse, awaken. **3.** stimulate, activate, animate, kindle, provoke, motivate. —n. **4.** vigil, deathwatch. **5.** track, path, course, trail. —**Ant.** sleep.

wakeful, adj. **1.** sleepless, awake, insomnious, restless. **2.** watchful, vigilant, wary, alert, observant, on the qui vive. —**Ant.** sleepy.

waken, v. See WAKE.

walk, v. **1.** step, stride, stroll, saunter, ambulate, perambulate, promenade, pace, march, tramp, hike, tread. —n. **2.** stroll, promenade, march, tramp, hike, constitutional. **3.** gait, pace, step, carriage. **4.** beat, sphere, area, field, course, career; conduct, behavior. **5.** sidewalk, path, lane, passage, footpath, alley, avenue.

wall, n. **1.** battlement, breastwork, bulwark, barrier, bunker, rampart, bastion. **2.** barrier, obstruction.

embankment, dike. —v. **4.** enclose, shut off, divide, protect; immure.

wallow, v. welter, flounder, roll.

wan, adj. pale, pallid, sickly, ashen. —**Ant.** ruddy, robust. —**Syn. Study.** See PALE.

wander, v. **1.** ramble, rove, roam, stray, range, stroll, meander, saunter. **2.** move, pass, extend. **3.** deviate, err, go astray, digress, swerve, veer. **4.** rave, be delirious.

wane, v. **1.** decrease, decline, diminish, fail, sink. —n. **2.** decrease, decline, diminution; failure, decay. —**Ant.** wax.

wangle, v. manipulate, maneuver, finagle, connive, machinate, scheme, plot, intrigue, connive, con, talk into, angle, (Brit.) nobble.

wannabe, n. aspirant, aspirer, emulator, hopeful, seeker, wisher, wanter, imitator, candidate, postulant, applicant, solicitant.

want, v. **1.** need, desire, wish, require, lack. —n. **2.** necessity, need, requirement, desideratum. **3.** lack, dearth, scarcity, scarceness, inadequacy, insufficiency, scantiness, paucity, meagerness, deficiency, defectiveness. **4.** destitution, poverty, privation, penury, indigence, straits. —**Ant.** relinquish. —**Syn. Study.** See LACK.

wanton, adj. **1.** reckless, malicious, unjustifiable, careless, heedless, willful, inconsiderate, groundless. **2.** deliberate, calculated, uncalled-for. **3.** unruly, wild, reckless. **4.** lawless, unbridled, loose, lascivious, lewd, licentious, dissolute, lustful, prurient, lecherous, salacious, incontinent, concupiscent, libidinous. **5.** luxurious, magnificent, elegant, lavish. —v. **6.** squander, waste. —**Ant.** justifiable, careful; lawful; prudish; inelegant; save.

warble, v. sing, trill, vocalize, carol, lilt, give voice, descant, croon, chant, intone, pipe, belt.

warden, n. warder, guardian, guard, custodian, keeper, caretaker, superintendent.

wardrobe, n. furnishings, apparel, wear, clothing, clothes, garb, attire, garments, habiliment, dress, haberdashery, raiment, gear, duds, togs, threads.

warlike, adj. martial, military; bellicose, belligerent, hostile, inimical, unfriendly. —**Ant.** peaceful.

warm, adj. **1.** lukewarm, tepid, heated. **2.** hearty, enthusiastic, emotional, zealous, fervent, fervid, ardent, excited, eager. **3.** cordial, hearty, glowing. **4.** attached, friendly, amiable, amicable, close, intimate. **5.** heated, irritated, annoyed, vexed, angry, irate, furious. **6.** animated, lively, brisk, vigorous, vehement. **7.** strong, fresh. —v. **8.** warm up, heat up, heat, make warm. **9.** animate, excite, waken, stir, stir up, rouse, arouse. —**Ant.** cool.

warn, v. **1.** caution, admonish, forewarn. **2.** notify, apprise, inform. —**Syn. Study.** WARN, CAUTION, ADMONISH imply attempting to prevent someone from running into danger or unpleasant circumstances. To WARN is to inform plainly and strongly of possible or imminent trouble, or to advise that doing or not doing something will have dangerous consequences: The scout warned the fort of the attack. I warned them not to travel to that country. To CAUTION is to advise to be careful and to take necessary precautions: Tourists were cautioned to watch their belongings. To ADMONISH is to advise of negligence or a fault in an earnest, authoritative, but friendly way, so that corrective action can be taken: to admonish a student for constant lateness.

warning, n. caution, admonition, advice; omen, sign, augury, presage, portent.

warp, v. **1.** bend, twist, turn, contort, distort, spring. **2.** swerve, deviate. **3.** distort, bias, pervert. —**Ant.** straighten.

warrant, n. **1.** authorization, sanction, justification, commission. **2.** pledge, guarantee, assurance, security, surety, warranty. **3.** certificate, license, receipt, commission, permit, voucher, writ, order, chit. —v. **4.** authorize, sanction, approve, justify, guarantee, vouch for. **5.** assure, promise, guarantee, assure, affirm, vouch for, attest.

wary, adj. alert, cautious, vigilant, careful, circumspect, watchful, scrupulous, discreet. —**Ant.** unwary. —**Syn. Study.** See CAREFUL.

wash, v. **1.** cleanse, clean, lave, launder, scrub, mob, swab, rub. **2.** wet, bedew, moisten. **3.** bathe. —n.

4. washing, ablution, cleansing, bathing. **5.** fen, marsh, bog, swamp, morass, slough.

washout, n. failure, loss, flop, fiasco, botch, fizzle, clinker, nonstarter, loser, dud, bust, turkey, also-ran. —**Ant.** success, win, triumph.

waspish, adj. **1.** resentful, snappish. **2.** irascible, petulant, testy.

waste, v. **1.** consume, spend, throw out, expend, squander, misspend, dissipate. **2.** destroy, consume, wear away, erode, eat away, reduce, wear down, emaciate, enfeeble. **3.** lay waste, devastate, ruin, ravage, pillage, plunder, desolate, sack, spoil, despoil. **4.** diminish, dwindle, perish, wane, decay. —n. **5.** consumption, expenditure, dissipation, diminution, decline, emaciation, loss, destruction, decay, impairment. **6.** ruin, devastation, spoliation, desolation, plunder, pillage. **7.** desert, wilderness, wild. **8.** refuse, rubbish, trash, garbage. —adj. **9.** unused, useless, superfluous, extra, de trop. **10.** uninhabited, desert, deserted, wild, desolate, barren. **11.** decayed, ghost; devastated, laid waste, ruined, ravaged, sacked, destroyed. **12.** rejected, refuse. —**Ant.** save.

watch, v. **1.** look, see, observe. **2.** contemplate, regard, mark, view, look upon. **3.** wait for, await, expect. **4.** guard, protect, tend. —n. **5.** observation, inspection, attention. **6.** lookout, sentinel, sentry, watchman, guard; vigil, watchfulness, alertness. **7.** timepiece.

watchful, adj. vigilant, alert, observant, attentive, heedful, careful, circumspect, cautious, wary, wakeful, awake. —**Ant.** unwary, inattentive, incautious.

watchword, n. **1.** password, countersign, shibboleth. **2.** slogan, motto.

watery, adj. **1.** wet, fluid, liquid, flowing, runny, liquidy, aqueous, serous, hydrous, hydrated, teary. **2.** dilute, diluted, watered, watered-down, weak, thin, feeble, wishy-washy, tasteless, bland. —**Ant.** dry, sere, parched, arid; strong, potent, fullstrength.

wave, n. **1.** ridge, swell, undulation, ripple, breaker, surf, sea. —v. **2.** undulate, fluctuate, oscillate; flutter, float, sway, rock. —**Ant.** hollow.

waver, v. **1.** sway, flutter. **2.** thicker, quiver. **3.** shake, tremble, quiver, shiver. **4.** vacillate, fluctuate, alternate, hesitate. —**Syn. Study.** WAVER, VACILLATE refer to an inability to decide or to stick to a decision. WAVER usu. implies a state of doubt, uncertainty, or fear that prevents one from pursuing a chosen course: He made plans to move, but wavered at the last minute. VACILLATE means to go back and forth between choices without reaching a decision, or to make up one's mind and change it again suddenly: Stop vacillating and set a day.

wax, v. **1.** increase, extend, grow, lengthen, enlarge, dilate. **2.** grow, become, come or get to be. —**Ant.** wane.

way, n. **1.** manner, mode, fashion, method. **2.** habit, custom, usage, practice, wont. **3.** means, course, plan, method, scheme, device. **4.** respect, particular, detail, part. **5.** direction. **6.** passage, progress, extent. **7.** distance, space, interval. **8.** path, course, passage, channel, road, route, track, avenue, highroad, highway, freeway, throughway. —**Syn. Study.** See METHOD.

wayward, adj. **1.** contrary, headstrong, stubborn, capricious, captious, obstinate, disobedient, unruly, refractory, intractable, willful, perverse. **2.** irregular, unsteady, inconstant, changeable. —**Ant.** agreeable, obedient, tractable; regular, constant. —**Syn. Study.** See WILLFUL.

weak, adj. **1.** fragile, frail, breakable, delicate. **2.** feeble, senile, anile, old, infirm, decrepit, weakly, sickly, unhealthy, unwell, debilitated, invalid. **3.** impotent, ineffectual, ineffective, inefficient, inadequate, inefficacious. **4.** unconvincing, inconclusive, lame, illogical, unsatisfactory, vague. **5.** unintelligent, simple, foolish, stupid, senseless, silly. **6.** irresolute, vacillating, unstable, unsteady, wavering, weak-kneed, fluctuating, undecided. **7.** faint, slight, slender, slim, inconsiderable, flimsy, poor, trifling, trivial. **8.** deficient, wanting, short, lacking, insufficient. —**Ant.** strong.

weaken, v. enfeeble, debilitate, enervate, undermine, sap, exhaust, deplete, diminish, lessen, lower, reduce, impair, minimize, invalidate. —**Ant.** strengthen.

weakling, n. coward, craven, recreant, dastard, poltroon, caitiff, milk-

sop, baby, doormat, yes-man, Milquetoast, mollycoddle, jellyfish, weak sister, empty suit, invertebrate, wuss, wimp, crybaby, mama's boy, pantywaist, sissy, nebbish, gutless wonder, chicken, quitter.

weakly, adj. weak, feeble, sickly. —**Ant.** strong.

weakness, n. **1.** feebleness, fragility. **2.** flaw, defect, fault. **3.** tenderness, liking, inclination. —**Ant.** strength. —**Syn. Study.** See FAULT.

wealth, n. **1.** property, riches. **2.** abundance, profusion. **3.** assets, possessions, goods, property. **4.** affluence, opulence, fortune, treasure, funds, cash, pelf. —**Ant.** poverty.

wealthy, adj. **1.** rich, affluent, opulent, prosperous, well-to-do, moneyed. **2.** abundant, ample, copious. —**Ant.** poor, poverty-stricken; scanty, scarce.

wearisome, adj. **1.** fatiguing, tiring. **2.** tiresome, boring, tedious, irksome, monotonous, humdrum, dull, prosy, prosaic, vexatious, trying. —**Ant.** energetic; interesting.

weary, adj. **1.** exhausted, tired, wearied, fatigued, spent. **2.** impatient, dissatisfied. **3.** tiresome, tedious, irksome, wearisome. —v. **4.** fatigue, tire, exhaust, tire or wear out, jade. **5.** harass, harry, irk. —**Ant.** energetic; patient; interesting; interest, captivate.

weather-beaten, adj. **1.** weathered, weather-scarred, roughened, storm-tossed, battered, run-down, worn-down, faded, worn, washed-out, bleached, damaged, eroded, etiolated. **2.** tanned, bronzed, darkened, toughened, roughened.

weave, v. **1.** interlace, intertwine, braid, plait. **2.** contrive, fabricate, construct, compose. **3.** introduce, insert, intermix, intermingle.

weep, v. shed tears, cry, sob, lament, bewail, bemoan. —**Ant.** laugh, rejoice.

weigh, v. consider, balance, ponder, contemplate, study. —**Syn. Study.** See STUDY.

weight, n. influence, importance, power, moment, efficacy, import, consequence, significance.

weighty, adj. **1.** heavy, ponderous. **2.** burdensome, onerous. **3.** important, momentous, significant, serious, grave, consequential. —**Ant.** light; unimportant, insignificant.

weird, adj. eerie, ghostly, unearthly, ultramundane, uncanny, mysterious, unnatural, supernatural, preternatural. —**Ant.** natural. —**Syn. Study.** WEIRD, EERIE, UNCANNY refer to that which is mysterious and apparently outside natural law. WEIRD suggests the intervention of supernatural influences in human affairs: weird doings in the haunted house; a weird coincidence. EERIE refers to something ghostly that makes one's flesh creep: eerie moans from a deserted house. UNCANNY refers to an extraordinary or remarkable thing that seems to defy the laws established by experience: an uncanny ability to recall numbers.

welfare, n. well-being, prosperity, success, happiness, weal, benefit, profit, advantage.

well, adv. **1.** satisfactorily, favorable, advantageously, fortunately, happily. **2.** commendably, meritoriously, excellently. **3.** properly, correctly, skillfully, adeptly, efficiently, accurately. **4.** judiciously, reasonably, suitably, properly. **5.** adequately, sufficiently, satisfactorily. **6.** thoroughly, soundly, abundantly, amply, fully. **7.** considerably, rather, quite, fairly. **8.** personally, intimately. —adj. **9.** sound, healthy, healthful, hale, hearty. **10.** satisfactory, good, fine. **11.** proper, fitting, suitable, befitting, appropriate. **12.** fortunate, successful, well-off, happy. —**Ant.** poorly, badly; ill, sick.

well-built, adj. **1.** able-bodied, well-knit, well-proportioned, muscular, well-muscled, athletic, brawny, burly, thickset, stacked, hunky. **2.** sturdy, strong, durable, solid, rugged, well-constructed, well-made, well-finished. —**Ant.** scrawny, fragile.

wet, adj. **1.** soaked, drenched, dampened, moistened. **2.** damp, moist, dank, humid. **3.** humid, misty, drizzling, rainy. —n. **4.** moisture, wetness, rain, humidity, drizzle, dampness, dankness. —v. **5.** drench, saturate, soak, ret. —**Ant.** dry.

wherewithal, n. means, resources, resorts, recourses, money, cash, funds, capital, bankroll, finances, purse, assets.

whim, n. fancy, notion, caprice, whimsy, humor, vagary, quirk, crotchet, chimera. —**Ant.** consideration.

whimsical, adj. capricious, notional, changeable, crotchety, freakish, fanciful, odd, peculiar, curious, singular, queer, quaint.

whine, v. complain, grumble; moan, cry. —**Syn. Study.** See COMPLAIN.

whip, v. **1.** lash, beat; flog, thrash, scourge, beat, switch, punish, flagellate, chastise; castigate. **2.** pull, jerk, snatch, seize, whisk. —n. **3.** switch, leash, scourge.

whirl, v. **1.** gyrate, pirouette, spin, rotate, revolve, twirl, wheel. —n. **2.** rotation, gyration, spin, revolution.

whiten, v. blanch, bleach, etiolate. —**Ant.** blacken, darken.

whitewash, v. **1.** gloss over, cover up, hide, conceal, disguise, camouflage, paper over, mask. **2.** justify, excuse, alibi, exculpate, palter, extenuate, explain away, vindicate.

whole, adj. **1.** entire, full, total, undiminished, undivided, integral, complete, unbroken, unimpaired, perfect, uninjured, faultless, undamaged, sound, intact. —n. **2.** totality, total, sum, entirety, aggregate, sum total. —**Ant.** partial; part.

wholesome, adj. **1.** salutary, beneficial, helpful, good. **2.** healthful, salubrious, nourishing, nutritious, healthy, salutary, invigorating. —**Ant.** unwholesome. —**Syn. Study.** See HEALTHY.

wicked, adj. evil, bad, immoral, amoral, unprincipled, sinful, piacular, unrighteous, ungodly, godless, impious, profane, blasphemous; profligate, corrupt, depraved, dissolute, heinous, vicious, vile, iniquitous, abandoned, flagitious, nefarious, treacherous, villainous, atrocious. —**Ant.** good.

wide, adj. **1.** broad. **2.** extensive, vast, spacious, ample, comprehensive, large, expanded, distended. —**Ant.** narrow.

wild, adj. **1.** untamed, undomesticated, feral, ferine, savage, unbroken, ferocious. **2.** uncultivated, uninhabited. **3.** uncivilized, barbarous, barbarian. **4.** violent, furious, boisterous, tempestuous, stormy, disorderly, frenzied, turbulent, impetuous. **5.** frantic, mad, distracted, crazy, insane. **6.** enthusiastic, eager, anxious. **7.** excited. **8.** undisciplined, unruly, lawless, turbulent, self-willed, ungoverned, unrestrained, riotous, wayward, outrageous. **9.** unrestrained, unbridled, uncontrolled, untrammeled. **10.** reckless, rash, fantastic, extravagant, impracticable. **11.** queer, grotesque, bizarre, strange, imaginary, fanciful, visionary. **12.** disorderly, disheveled, unkempt. —n. **13.** waste, wilderness, desert. —**Ant.** tame, domesticated.

wilderness, n. wild.

wild-eyed, adj. **1.** wild, manic, maniacal, rabid, frantic, frenzied, raving, amok, mad, crazy, berserk. **2.** visionary, quixotic, unrealistic, extreme, fanatical, fanatic, far-out, off-the-wall, harebrained. —**Ant.** calm, composed; sensible, practical.

wile, n. **1.** trick, artifice, stratagem, ruse, deception, contrivance, maneuver, device. **2.** deceit, cunning, trickery, chicanery, fraud, cheating, defrauding, imposture, imposition.

will, n. **1.** determination, resolution, resoluteness, decision, forcefulness. **2.** volition, choice. **3.** wish, desire, pleasure, disposition, inclination. **4.** purpose, determination. **5.** order, direction, command, behest, bidding. —v. **6.** decide, decree, determine, direct, command, bid. **7.** bequeath, devise, leave.

willful, adj. **1.** willed, voluntary, intentional, volitional. **2.** self-willed, headstrong, perverse, obstinate, intractable, wayward, stubborn, intransigent, persistent, contrary, contumacious, refractory, disagreeable, pigheaded, cantankerous, unruly, inflexible, obdurate, adamant. —n. **3.** unintentional, involuntary; tractable. —**Syn. Study.** WILLFUL, HEADSTRONG, PERVERSE, WAYWARD refer to a person who stubbornly persists in doing as

he or she pleases. WILLFUL implies opposition to those whose wishes, suggestions, or commands ought to be respected or obeyed: a willful son who ignored his parents' advice. HEADSTRONG is used in a similar way, but implies foolish and sometimes reckless behavior: headstrong teens who could not be restrained. PERVERSE implies stubborn persistence in opposing what is right or acceptable, often with the express intention of being contrary or disagreeable: taking a perverse delight in arguing with others. WAYWARD suggests stubborn disobedience that gets one into trouble: a reform school for wayward youths.

wily, adj. crafty, cunning, artful, sly, foxy, tricky, intriguing, arch, designing, deceitful, treacherous, crooked, seditious. —**Ant.** dull, stupid.

win, v. **1.** succeed, advance, win out. **2.** obtain, gain, procure, secure, earn, acquire, achieve, attain, reach. **3.** win over, persuade, convince. —**Ant.** lose. —**Syn. Study.** See GAIN.

wince, v. recoil, shrink, quail, cringe, flinch, draw back. —**Syn. Study.** WINCE, RECOIL, SHRINK, QUAIL all mean to draw back from what is dangerous, fearsome, difficult, or unpleasant. WINCE suggests an involuntary contraction of the facial features triggered by pain, embarrassment, or revulsion: to wince as a needle pierces the skin; to wince at coarse language. RECOIL denotes a physical movement away from something disgusting or shocking, or a similar psychological shutting out or avoidance: to recoil at the sight of a dead body; to recoil from the idea of retiring. SHRINK may imply a fastidious and scrupulous avoidance of the distasteful, or a cowardly withdrawal from what is feared: to shrink from mentioning a shameful act; to shrink from asking for a raise. QUAIL often suggests trembling or other physical manifestations of fear: to quail before an angry mob.

wind, n. **1.** air, blast, breeze, gust, zephyr, draught. **2.** hint, intimation, suggestion. **3.** vanity, conceitedness, flatulence, emptiness. **4.** winding, bend, turn, curve, twist, twisting. —v. **5.** bend, turn, meander, curve, be devious. **6.** coil, twine, twist, encircle, wreathe. —**Syn. Study.** WIND, BREEZE, ZEPHYR, GUST, BLAST refer to a current of air set in motion naturally. WIND applies to air in motion, blowing with any degree of gentleness or violence: a strong wind; a westerly wind. A BREEZE is usu. a cool, light wind; technically, it is a wind of 4–31 mph: a refreshing breeze. ZEPHYR, a literary word, refers to a soft, mild breeze: a zephyr whispering through palm trees. A GUST is a sudden, brief rush of air: A gust of wind scattered the leaves. A BLAST is a brief but more violent rush of air, usu. a cold one: a wintry blast.

wink, v. **1.** blink, nictitate. **2.** twinkle, sparkle.

winning, adj. taking, engaging, charming, captivating, attractive, winsome. —**Ant.** losing, repulsive.

wisdom, n. **1.** discretion, judgment, discernment, sense, common sense, sagacity, insight, understanding, prudence. **2.** knowledge, information, learning, sapience, erudition, enlightenment. —**Ant.** stupidity.

wise, adj. **1.** discerning, judicious, sage, sensible, penetrating, sagacious, intelligent, perspicacious, profound, rational, prudent, reasonable. **2.** learned, erudite, schooled. —n. **3.** manner, fashion; respect, degree. —**Ant.** unwise.

wish, v. **1.** want, crave, desire, long for; need, lack. **2.** bid, direct, command, order. —n. **3.** desire, will, want, inclination.

wit, n. **1.** drollery, facetiousness, repartee, humor. **2.** understanding, intelligence, sagacity, wisdom, intellect, mind, sense. —**Syn. Study.** See HUMOR.

withdraw, v. **1.** draw back or away, take back, subtract, remove; retract, recall, disavow, recant, revoke, rescind. **2.** depart, retire, retreat, secede. —**Ant.** advance.

wither, v. **1.** shrivel, fade, decay, wrinkle, shrink, dry, decline, wilt, languish, droop, waste, waste away. —**Ant.** flourish, thrive.

withhold, v. hold back, restrain, check, keep back, suppress, repress. —**Ant.** promote, advance. —**Syn. Study.** See KEEP.

withstand, v. resist, oppose, confront, face, face up to, hold out against. —**Ant.** fail. —**Syn. Study.** See OPPOSE.

witness, *v.* **1.** see, perceive, observe, watch, look at, mark, notice, note. **2.** testify, bear witness. —*n.* **3.** beholder, spectator, eyewitness. **4.** testimony, evidence.

witty, *adj.* facetious, droll, humorous, funny, clever, original, sparkling, brilliant, jocose, jocular. —**Ant.** silly, stupid.

wizard, *n.* enchanter, magician, sorcerer, necromancer, conjurer, charmer, diviner, seer, soothsayer.

woe, *n.* distress, affliction, trouble, sorrow, grief, misery, anguish, tribulation, trial, agony, wretchedness, disconsolateness, depression, melancholy. —**Ant.** joy, happiness.

woman, *n.* female, lady. —**Ant.** man. —**Syn. Study.** WOMAN, FEMALE, LADY are nouns referring to adult human beings who are biologically female, that is, capable of bearing offspring. WOMAN is the general, neutral term: *a wealthy woman.* In scientific, statistical, and other objective use FEMALE is the neutral contrastive term to MALE: *104 females to every 100 males.* FEMALE is sometimes used disparagingly: *a gossipy female.* LADY in the sense "polite, refined woman" is a term of approval: *We know you will always behave like a lady.*

womanish, See Syn. study at WOMANLY.

womanlike, See Syn. study at WOMANLY.

womanly, *adj.* womanlike, womanish; feminine, female; attractive, mature, motherly, fully developed, ripe —**Syn. Study.** WOMANLY, WOMANLIKE, WOMANISH mean having traits or qualities considered typical of or appropriate to adult human females. WOMANLY, a term of approval, suggests such admirable traits as self-possession, modesty, and motherliness: *a womanly consideration for others.* WOMANLIKE may be a neutral synonym for WOMANLY, or it may convey mild disapproval: *womanlike tears and reproaches.* WOMANISH is usually disparaging. Applied to women, it suggests traits not socially approved: *a womanish petulance*; applied to men, it suggests traits not culturally acceptable for men but (in what is regarded as a sexist notion) typical of women: *a womanish shrillness in his speech.* See also FEMALE.

wonder, *v.* **1.** think, speculate, conjecture, mediate, ponder, question. **2.** marvel, be astonished *or* astounded. —*n.* **3.** surprise, astonishment, amazement, awe, bewilderment, puzzlement; admiration.

wonderful, *adj.* marvelous, extraordinary, remarkable, awesome, startling, wondrous, miraculous, prodigious, astonishing, amazing, astounding, phenomenal, unique, curious, strange, odd, peculiar, (*slang*) phat. —**Ant.** usual, ordinary, common.

wont, *adj.* accustomed, used, habituated, wonted. —*n.* **2.** custom, habit, practice, use. —**Ant.** unaccustomed.

word, *n.* **1.** expression, utterance; assertion, affirmation, declaration, statement, asseveration. **2.** warrant, assurance, promise, pledge. **3.** intelligence, tidings, news, report, account, advice, information. **4.** signal, catchword, password, watchword, shibboleth, countersign. **5.** order, command, bidding. —*v.* **6.** express, style, phrase.

wording, *n.* diction, phrasing, expressing.

wordy, *adj.* prolix, redundant, verbose, pleonastic, tedious, superfluous —**Syn. Study.** WORDY, PROLIX, REDUNDANT, VERBOSE all mean using more words than necessary to convey the desired meaning. WORDY, the broadest of these terms, may merely refer to the use of many words but usu. implies that the speech or writing is wearisome or ineffectual: *a wordy review that obscured the main point.* PROLIX refers to speech or writing extended to tedious length by the inclusion of inconsequential details: *a prolix style that robs the story of all its excitement.* REDUNDANT refers to unnecessary repetition by using different words or expressions to convey the same idea: *The editor cut four redundant paragraphs from the article.* VERBOSE adds the idea of pompous or bombastic speech or writing that has little substance: *a verbose speech that put everyone to sleep.*

work, *n.* **1.** exertion, labor, toil, drudgery, moil. **2.** undertaking, task, enterprise, project, responsibility. **3.** employment, industry, occupation, business, profession, trade, calling, vocation, metier. **4.** deed, performance, fruit, fruition, feat, achievement. —*v.* **5.** labor, toil, moil, drudge. **6.** act, operate. **7.** operate, use, manipulate, manage, handle. **8.** bring about, perform, produce, cause, do, execute, finish, effect, originate, accomplish, achieve. **9.** make, fashion, execute, finish. **10.** move, persuade, influence. —**Ant.** leisure, indolence, idleness, sloth. —**Syn. Study.** WORK, DRUDGERY, LABOR, TOIL refer to exertion of body or mind in performing or accomplishing something. WORK is a general word that refers to exertion that is either easy or hard: *pleasurable work; backbreaking work.* DRUDGERY suggests continuous, dreary, and dispiriting work, esp. of a menial or servile kind: *Cleaning these blinds is sheer drudgery.* LABOR denotes hard manual work, esp. for wages: *Repairing the bridge will require months of labor.* TOIL suggests wearying or exhausting labor: *The farmer's health was failing from constant toil.*

worked, *adj.* wrought, formed, fashioned, forged, crafted, devised —**Syn. Study.** WORKED, WROUGHT both apply to something on which effort has been applied. WORKED implies expended effort of almost any kind: *a worked silver mine.* WROUGHT implies fashioning, molding, or making, esp. of metals: *wrought iron.*

worldly, *adj.* **1.** secular, earthly, mundane, temporal, terrestrial, common. **2.** mundane, urbane, cosmopolitan, suave. —**Ant.** spiritual; naive. —**Syn. Study.** See EARTHLY.

world-weary, *adj.* apathetic, depressed, anomic, jaded, indifferent, uncaring, blasé, impassive, detached, listless, burned-out, downbeat, pessimistic, cynical. —**Ant.** optimistic, cheerful, hopeful.

worry, *v.* **1.** fret, torment oneself, chafe, be troubled *or* vexed, fidget. **2.** trouble, torment, annoy, plague, pester, bother, vex, tease, harry, hector, harass, molest, persecute, badger, irritate, disquiet, disturb. —*n.* **3.** uneasiness, anxiety, apprehension, solicitude, concern, disquiet, fear, misgiving, care. —**Syn. Study.** See CONCERN.

worship, *n.* **1.** reverence, homage, adoration, honor. **2.** regard, idolizing, idolatry, deification. —*v.* **3.** revere, respect, venerate, reverence, honor, glorify, adore. **4.** adore, adulate, idolize, deify, love, like. —**Ant.** detest.

worth, *adj.* **1.** deserving, meriting, justifying. —*n.* **2.** usefulness, value, importance, merit, worthiness, credit, excellence. —**Ant.** uselessness. —**Syn. Study.** See VALUE.

worthy, *adj.* commendable, meritorious, worthwhile, deserving, estimable, excellent, exemplary, righteous, upright, honest. —**Ant.** unworthy.

wound, *n.* **1.** injury, hurt, cut, stab, laceration, lesion, damage. **2.** harm, insult, pain, grief, anguish. —*v.* **3.** injure, hurt, harm, damage, cut, stab, lacerate.

wrath, *n.* anger, ire, rage, resentment, indignation, dudgeon, irritation, fury, choler, exasperation, passion. —**Ant.** equanimity, pleasure, delight.

wrathful, *adj.* angry, ireful, irate, furious, enraged, raging, incensed, resentful, indignant. —**Ant.** equable, pleased.

wreck, *n.* **1.** ruin, destruction, devastation, desolation. **2.** shipwreck. —*v.* **3.** shipwreck, spoil, destroy, devastate, ruin, shatter. —**Ant.** create.

wrest, *v.* extract, take. —**Ant.** give, yield.

wretched, *adj.* **1.** miserable, pitiable, dejected, distressed, woeful, afflicted, woebegone, forlorn, unhappy, depressed. **2.** sorry, miserable, despicable, mean, base, vile, bad, contemptible, poor, pitiful, worthless. —**Ant.** happy. —**Syn. Study.** See MISERABLE.

wrong, *adj.* **1.** bad, evil, wicked, sinful, immoral, piacular, iniquitous, reprehensible, unjust, crooked, dishonest. **2.** erroneous, inaccurate, incorrect, false, untrue, mistaken. **3.** improper, inappropriate, unfit, unsuitable. **4.** awry, amiss, out of order. —*n.* **5.** evil, wickedness, misdoing, misdeed, sin, vice, immorality, iniquity. —*v.* **6.** injure, harm, maltreat, abuse, oppress, cheat, defraud, dishonor. —**Ant.** right.

wrongheaded, *adj.* perverse, stubborn, contrary, ornery, balky, wayward, obstinate, unreasonable, froward, difficult, mulish. —**Ant.** reasonable, compliant.

wrought, See Syn. study at WORKED.

wry, *adj.* **1.** bent, twisted, crooked, distorted, awry, askew. **2.** devious, misdirected, perverted. —**Ant.** straight; pointed.

X

xenophobic, *adj.* restrictive, exclusive, exclusionary, prohibitionary, closed-door, selective, restricted, restrictive, chauvinist, chauvinistic, jingoistic, insular, separatist, segregationist, discriminatory, intolerant, biased, bigoted, racist, ethnocentric. —**Ant.** inclusive, welcoming.

X-rated, *adj.* erotic, sexy, sexual, adult, salacious, lewd, bawdy, ribald, obscene, pornographic. —**Ant.** clean, wholesome, innocuous.

x-ray, *v.* **1.** roentgenize. —*n.* **2.** roentgenogram.

Y

yahoo, *n.* **1.** boor, vulgarian, churl, lout, barbarian, know-nothing, ignoramus, redneck, ruffian, Neanderthal, slob. **2.** rube, yokel, hayseed, hick, groundling. **3.** dullard, dope, dunce, buffoon, clown, dimwit, bozo.

yawn, *v.* **1.** gape. —*n.* **2.** opening, space, chasm.

yearn, *v.* long, hanker, pine, yen, crave, hunger, covet. —**Syn. Study.** YEARN, LONG, HANKER, PINE all mean to feel a strong desire for something. YEARN stresses the depth and power of the desire: *to yearn to begin a new life.* LONG implies a wholehearted desire for something that is or seems unattainable: *to long to relive one's childhood.* HANKER suggests a restless or incessant craving: *to hanker after fame and fortune.* PINE adds the notion of physical or emotional suffering due to the real or apparent hopelessness of one's desire: *to pine for a lost love.*

yearning, *n.* longing, craving, desire. —**Syn. Study.** See DESIRE.

yes-man, *n.* flatterer, sycophant, toady, apple-polisher, stooge, bootlicker, flunky, lackey, rubber stamp, minion, myrmidon.

yield, *v.* **1.** give forth, produce, furnish, supply, render, bear, impart, afford, bestow. **2.** give up, cede, surrender, submit, give way, concede, relinquish, abandon, abdicate, resign, waive, forgo. **3.** relax, bend, bow. —*n.* **4.** produce, harvest, fruit, crop. —**Syn. Study.** YIELD, SUBMIT, SURRENDER mean to give way or give up to a person or thing. To YIELD is to relinquish or concede under some degree of pressure, either from a position of weakness or from one of advantage: *to yield ground to an enemy; to yield the right of way.* To SUBMIT is to give up more completely to authority or superior force and to cease opposition, usu. with reluctance: *The mutineers finally submitted to the captain's orders.* To SURRENDER is to give up complete possession of and claim to, usu. after resistance: *to surrender a fortress; to surrender one's rights.*

young, *adj.* **1.** youthful, juvenile, immature. —*n.* **2.** offspring. —**Ant.** old, ancient; progenitors, parents.

youngster, *n.* youth, lad, stripling, child, boy. —**Ant.** oldster.

youth, *n.* **1.** youngness, minority, adolescence, teens, immaturity. **2.** young man, youngster, teen-ager, adolescent, stripling, lad, boy, juvenile. —**Ant.** maturity; man, adult.

youthful, *adj.* young. —**Ant.** old.

yo-yo, *v.* vacillate, fluctuate, vary, shift, dither, equivocate, waffle, hesitate, tergiversate, waver, seesaw, fluctuate, hem and haw, come and go, (*Brit.*) haver. —**Ant.** stabilize.

Yule, *n.* Christmas, Christmastide.

Z

zaftig, *adj.* rounded, Rubenesque, full, plump, pleasingly plump, curvaceous, curvy, buxom, voluptuous, pneumatic, built for comfort. —**Ant.** gaunt, skinny, emaciated, shapeless.

zany, *adj.* **1.** comic, comical, farcical, funny, droll, whimsical, waggish, prankish, lunatic, ludicrous, hilarious, crazy, off-the-wall, loopy. —*n.* **2.** comic, clown, comedian, joker, jokester, cutup, prankster, merryandrew, madcap, buffoon, kook, nut, weirdo.

zap, *v.* eliminate, annihilate, terminate, take out, waste, nuke, cancel, stop, undo, do in, finish, finish off, knock out, abort, scrub, censor, censor out, edit out, delete, erase.

zeal, *n.* ardor, enthusiasm, diligence, eagerness, fervor, desire, endeavor, fervency, warmth, earnestness, intensity, intenseness, passion, spirit. —**Ant.** apathy, coolness.

zealot, *n.* bigot, fanatic, maniac. —**Syn. Study.** See FANATIC.

zealous, *adj.* ardent, enthusiastic, eager, earnest, fervid, fervent, warm, intense, passionate, spirited. —**Ant.** apathetic, uninterested, dispassionate, cool.

zephyr, *n.* See Syn. study at WIND.

zest, *n.* piquancy, interest, charm; relish, gusto, heartiness, enjoyment, spice, tang. —**Ant.** dullness.

zilch, *n.* nothing, zero, nil, naught, aught, zip, nada, nix, goose egg, diddly, diddly-squat, squat.

zone, *n.* **1.** belt, tract, area, region, district, section, girth. **2.** region, climate, clime. —*v.* **3.** encircle, gird, girdle, band.

How to Use the Index

The Index is particularly useful when you have not been able to find a word you are looking for in the A–Z section of the book. Here, in a single alphabetical list, is every word that appears as a synonym under one or more main-entry terms. It is therefore quite likely that a word you want to find (in order to replace it!) will be in the Index. That word will in turn lead you to an entry in the Thesaurus that contains a list of effective substitute terms.

Here is an example of how you can use the index to expand your search for a word. Suppose you are writing a story and want to replace the word *adventure* with another word. Perhaps you have already used *adventure* twice and do not want to sound repetitious. You want to hold your readers' attention by adding some variety to your vocabulary. Unfortunately, *adventure* itself is not a main entry in the Thesaurus. However, it is listed in the Index, where you can see that it appears as a synonym under two Thesaurus entries: **caper** and **game.**

Now you can turn to **caper,** in the body of the book, where you will find, under the list of nouns, *escapade, prank, frolic, lark, antic, adventure, dido,* and *bit of mischief.* Perhaps *escapade* is the word you want, or *prank.* If none of these suits you, you can look under **game.** There you will find another list of terms, with a rather different slant on the meaning of *adventure:* That list includes *scheme, plan,* and *plot,* words that can lend an interesting, more threatening tone to your story. One of these may be exactly the word you want.

You can, in fact, use the lists in both the A–Z portion of the book and the Index to go from group to group of words until you find one that strikes you as just right. The Index and the Thesaurus together give you an easy, useful way to enlarge your vocabulary and make your writing more effective.

A1: top-notch
Abaddon: hell
abandon: abdicate; cede; corruption; defect; desert; desolate; forsake; leave; relinquish; renounce; resign; surrender; vacate; yield
abandoned: corrupt; forlorn; immoral; lost; vicious; wicked
abandonment: abdication; dereliction; resignation
abase: debase; decline; degrade; depress; humble; lower; mortify
abasement: humiliation; ignominy; infamy
abash: affront; chagrin; confuse; depress; disconcert; discourage; embarrass; humble; humiliate; mortify; reproach; shame; snub
abashed: ashamed; bashful; diffident; small; unpretentious
abashment: chagrin; confusion; embarrassment; shame
abate: alleviate; allow; appease; cool; damp; decrease; diminish; ease; ebb; lessen; moderate; palliate; reduce; relax; relieve; remit; slack; slacken; slacken; soften; subside
abatement: decrease; remission
abbey: cloister
abbreviate: abstract; break; brief; condense; contract; curtail; cut; shorten; slash
abbreviated: curt
abbreviation: abridgment; sign
ABC's: basics
abdicate: abandon; relinquish; renounce; resign; secede; yield
abdication: resignation
abecedarian: dabbler
aberrance: abnormality
aberrant: abnormal; eccentric; exceptional; irregular; unnatural
aberration: frenzy; hallucination; insanity; mania
abet: accommodate; aid; assist; back; countenance; encourage; help; nurse; support
abetting: auxiliary
abettor: ally
abhor: abominate; detest; disgust; hate; loathe; nauseate
abhorred: detestable
abhorrence: abomination; antipathy; aversion; disgust; horror; loathing; odium
abhorrent: abominable; detestable; disgusting; hateful; loathsome; nauseous
abide: bear; brook; continue; dwell; remain; reside; sit; stand; stay; stick; tarry; wait
abiding: permanent; stable
abilities: device
ability: address; aptitude; capacity; craft; cunning; endowment; faculty; genius; gift; might; power; talent
abject: base; despicable; low; miserable; poor; servile; slavish; sorry
abjure: abandon; deny
ablaze: vehement
able-bodied: stout; well-built
able: capable; clever; dexterous; good; ingenious; potential; proficient; responsible; strong
ableness: ability; capacity
ablution: wash

abnormal: aberrant; exceptional; improper; irregular; preternatural; prodigious; strange; supernatural; unnatural
abnormality: aberration; disease
abnormity: aberration; abnormality
abode: address; home; place; residence
abolish: abrogate; eradicate; exterminate; stamp
abolition: abrogation
abominable: abhorrent; atrocious; bad; cursed; detestable; disgusting; foul; hateful; horrible; loathsome; nefarious; odious; offensive
abominate: abhor; detest; hate; loathe; nauseate
abomination: abhorrence; hatred; horror; sacrilege
aboriginal: native; original; primary; primitive
aborigine: native
abort: zap
abortifacient: abortive
abortion: failure
abortive: fruitless; idle; ineffectual; rudimentary
abound: flow; swarm; teem
abounding: abundant; affluent; ample; rich; rife
above: preeminent
aboveboard: candid; open
abrade: grind
abrading: abrasion
abridge: abbreviate; abstract; brief; condense; contract; curtail; cut; lessen; reduce; restrain; restrict; shorten; slash
abridgment: abbreviation; abstract; brief; digest; summary; synopsis
abrogate: abolish; nullify
abrogation: abolition
abrupt: bluff; blunt; bold; brief; brusque; curt; half-hearted; headlong; impatient; precipitate; precipitous; querulous; quick; severe; sharp; sheer; short; stiff; sudden; unexpected
abruptly: plump; short
abscess: gathering; sore
abscond: escape
absent: depart
absentminded: senile
absolute: actual; arbitrary; blank; certain; dead; decided; downright; flat; peremptory; positive; pure; rank; stark; stiff; strict; total; unconditional; unequivocal; unmitigated; unqualified; utter
absolutely: flat; stark
absolution: excuse; pardon; remission
absolve: acquit; clear; discharge; excuse; exonerate; forgive; justify; pardon; remit
absolved: quit
absorb: cushion; imbibe; immerse; sip; swallow
absorbed: deep; preoccupied; rapt
absorbing: deep; interesting
abstain: refrain
abstemious: sober
abstemiousness: abstinence
abstinent: abstemious; sober
abstract: abbreviate; abridge; abridgment; argument; brief; brief; deep; digest; summary; synopsis

abstracted: absent-minded; rapt; remote; retired
abstraction: abridgment; study
abstruse: abstract; dark; deep; mysterious; profound; recondite; secret
absurd: comical; extravagant; fantastic; foolish; funny; impertinent; incongruous; inept; ludicrous; preposterous; ridiculous; risible; silly; unreasonable
absurdity: lunacy; nonsense; stuff
abudant: fruitful; generous
abundance: plenty; profusion; wealth
abundant: affluent; ample; copious; fat; large; liberal; many; multifarious; opulent; plentiful; prodigal; profuse; prolific; rank; rich; rife; wealthy
abundantly: well
abuse: affront; assail; attack; detraction; harm; haze; indignity; injure; insult; invective; malign; maltreat; murder; outrage; outrage; prostitute; reproach; reproach; traduce; vilify; vituperate; wrong
abusive: derogatory; injurious; insolent; invective; offensive; opprobrious; ribald; scurrilous
abut: join
abutting: near
abysm: abyss
abyss: deep; hell
academic: formal
accede to the demands of: appease
accede to: accept
accede: acquiesce; agree; assent; comply; consent
acceding: content
accelerate: advance; anticipate; expedite; hasten; hurry; precipitate; speed
accent: emphasize; stress
accented: pointed
accentuate: emphasize
accentuated: pointed
accept: acknowledge; embrace; espouse; grant; swallow; take; understand
acceptable: eligible; pleasant; pleasing; serviceable
acceptance: allowance; belief; vogue
accepted: conventional; current; orthodox; popular; prevalent
access: admission; admittance; entrance; paroxysm; throe
accessible: available; convenient; open
accession: addition
accessory: accomplice; addition; adjunct; ally; ornament; partner
accident: chance; disaster; hazard; misadventure; misfortune
accidental: casual; chance; fortuitous; incidental; involuntary
acclaim: applause; celebrity; cheer
acclamation: applause; celebrity; praise
acclimate: habituate
acclimatize: habituate
acclivitous: abrupt; arduous
acclivity: bank
accolade: paean
accommodate oneself to: accept
accommodate with: give
accommodate: accord; adapt; adjust; conform; contain; fashion; oblige; temper

accommodating: easy; humane; kind; obliging
accommodation: advantage
accompaniment: attendant
accompany: attach; attend; bring; convoy; escort; follow; see; show
accompanying: attendant
accomplice: ally; associate; partner
accomplish: achieve; acquire; affect; attain; carry; complete; consummate; do; effect; execute; finish; fulfill; hit; make; manage; perfect; perform; perpetrate; realize; work
accomplished: able; capable; experienced; fine; finished; perfect; proficient; skillful
accomplishment: achievement; act; effect; exploit; feat; quality; stroke
accord: agree; agreement; assent; consent; correspond; give; harmony; peace; rapport; show; unanimity; vouchsafe
accordingly: therefore
accost: address; greet
account book: register
account for: explain
account: bill; consideration; deem; describe; distinction; explanation; ground; history; inventory; narrative; notice; number; picture; recital; reckon; record; regard; relation; repute; sake; score; story; tale; think; view; word
accountable: liable; responsible
accountableness: obligation
accouter: apparel; appoint; array; decorate; dress; equip
accouterment: equipment
accoutrements: apparel; clothes; paraphernalia
accrete: gather
accumulate: aggregate; collect; gather; heap; pile
accumulation: collection; heap; mass; pile
accuracy: fidelity; propriety; truth
accurate: authentic; close; correct; delicate; exact; express; faithful; just; near; nice; precise; proper; right; rigorous; severe; strict; sure; true; unerring
accurately: true; well
accurse: curse
accursed: cursed
accusation: charge; invective; plaint
accuse: account; charge; denounce; impeach
accustom: habituate; harden; use
accustomed: customary; addition; ordinary; usual; wont
ace: particle
acerb: acerbic; austere; severe; virulent
acerbate: bitter
acerbic: tart
acerbity: venom
acetose: acerbic
ache: agony; hurt; pain; pine
achievable: practicable; viable
achieve: accomplish; acquire; attain; complete; consummate; do; effect; execute; finish; fulfill; hit; obtain; perform; win; work
achievement: accomplishment; act; deed; exploit; feat; stroke; work
acicular: acute

acid: acerbic; caustic; cutting; incisive; poignant; satirical; sharp; sour; vitriolic
acidic: tart
acidulous: acerbic
acidy: acerbic
aciform: acute
acknowledge: accept; accept; accept; admit; allow; confess; own; tell
acknowledgment: admission; allowance; credit
acme: apex; extreme; head; height; peak; pinnacle; summit; top
acquaint: admonish; advise; apprise; inform; introduce; notify; possess; tell
acquaintance: associate; familiarity; friend
acquaintanceship: connection
acquainted: conversant
acquiesce in: accept
acquiesce: agree; assent; bend; comply; consent
acquiescence: assent; consent; deference; goodwill; resignation
acquire: achieve; attain; earn; gain; get; have; learn; make; obtain; pick; procure; purchase; secure; take; win
acquirement: accomplishment
acquisition: accomplishment; purchase
acquisitive: avaricious; mercenary
acquit oneself: behave
acquit: absolve; clear; discharge; excuse; exonerate; forgive; justify; pardon
acquitted: quit
acreage: parcel; property
acrid: bitter; hot; poignant; pungent; sharp
acrimonious: bitter; harsh; keen; peevish; petulant; pungent; sharp; sour; tart; virulent
acrimony: venom
act or behave toward: treat; use
act or follow reciprocally: alternate
act as administrator: administer
act as executor: administer
act of bearing: birth
act on: affect
act out: impersonate
act: action; affect; bear; behave; conduct; deal; deed; do; fake; feat; impersonate; make; move; operate; play; present; procedure; rehearse; simulate; sketch; work
acting: active
action: battle; brush; case; conduct; deed; exercise; exertion; feat; fight; motion; move; operation; operation; play; practice
actions: conduct
activate: influence; move; solicit; stimulate; summon; urge; wake
active: agile; alert; alive; brisk; busy; effective; energetic; fast; lissome; lively; living; mercurial; nimble; quick; sharp; smart; spirited; spry; strenuous; tireless; vigorous
activity: energy; exercise; exertion; fuss; hurly-burly; life; movement; play; project
actor: artist
actorish: theatrical
actress: artist
actressy: theatrical

actual: factual; real; substantial; tangible; true
actuality: truth
actualize: empower
actually: right
actuate: impel; induce; influence; move; persuade
acuity: perspicacity
acumen: intelligence; perspicacity; policy
acuminate: acute
acute: bright; brisk; exquisite; fine; high; incisive; incisive; keen; penetrating; penetrating; perspicacious; pungent; quick; ready; sagacious; severe; sharp; shrewd; tender; traumatic; trenchant
acuteness: sensibility; violence
ad hoc: ad-lib
ad-lib: offhand
adage: byword; maxim; proverb
adamant: hard; inflexible; intractable; relentless; ruthless; shameless; stern; stony; unyielding; willful
adamantine: hard
adapt oneself: adjust
adapt: accommodate; accord; adjust; arrange; calculate; conform; fashion; qualify; shape; temper
adaptable: all-around; flexible; malleable; pliant
adapted: capable; congenial; convenient; meet; proper
add luster to: adorn
add to: complement; increase; magnify; piece; supplement
add up to: aggregate
add up: total
add: attach; cast
added: aggregate
addendum: addition; appendix; comment; supplement
adding: addition
addition: adjunct; appendix; cast; increase; supplement
additional: auxiliary; new
addle: perturb
address: greet; harangue; harangue; oration; speech; style
adduce: advance; assign
adept: adroit; experienced; handy; master; perfect; proficient; skillful; smart
adeptly: well
adequate: competent; equal; good; serviceable; sufficient
adequately: well
adhere: attach; hang; hold; stick
adherent: disciple; follower; partisan
adhering: adherent
adhesive: tenacious; viscous
adipose: fat
adit: access
adjacent: adjoining; close; handy; near
adjoin: add; border; join
adjoining: adjacent; close; near
adjourn: continue; defer; dissolve; postpone; procrastinate; rise; stay
adjudicator: authority
adjunct: addition; appendix; appliance; attachment
adjure: beseech
adjust: accommodate; adapt; alter; arrange; balance; calculate; conform; determine; fashion; modify; order; proportion; reconcile; rectify; redress; reduce; regulate; set; settle; shape; temper; trim; true
adjusted: ready
adjustment: regulation
adjuvant: therapeutic
administer: conduct; execute; manage; rule
administrate: conduct
administration: conduct; management; policy
administrator: manager
admirable: excellent; exquisite; fine; glorious; good; great; handsome; noble; rare; splendid; superb
admiration: attachment; compliment; deference; esteem; respect; wonder
admire: praise; respect
admissible: eligible; tenable
admission: admittance; allowance; entrance
admit or certify receipt of: acknowledge
admit of: bear
admit: accept; acknowledge; allow; assent; bear; confess;

entertain; grant; hold; own; stand
admittance: access; admission; entrance
admitting: capable
admonish: advise; caution; chide; correct; rebuke; reprimand; reprove; warn
admonition: advice; caution; caveat; counsel; warning
ado: agitation; commotion; excitement; fuss; haste; hurry; noise; stir
adolescence: youth
adolescent: minor; youth
adopt: affect; appropriate; embrace; espouse; take
adoration: homage; love; worship
adore: honor; love; praise; respect; reverence; worship
adored: favorite
adorn: apparel; array; beautify; deck; decorate; dress; embellish; flourish; garnish; grace; hang; ornament; trim
adorned: ornate
adornment: flourish; garnish; ornament
adroit: able; apt; clean; clever; dexterous; experienced; expert; facile; good; handy; ingenious; neat; old; perfect; ready; skillful; smart; tactful
adroitness: address; art; cunning; delicacy; knack
adulate: love; respect; reverence; worship
adult male: man
adult: mature; X-rated
adulterate: corrupt; dash; debase
adulterated: corrupt; rarefied
adulteration: corruption
adulterous: unfaithful
adumbrate: obfuscate
advance: abet; advance; allege; assign; better; course; deliver; elevate; encourage; foster; gain; grow; lead; move; pioneer; precipitate; prefer; proceed; profit; progress; promote; raise; rise; serve; speed; thrive; win
advanced: late; onward
advancement: advance; profit; progress
advancing: onward
advantage: account; gain; good; privilege; profit; purpose; use; welfare
advantageous: advisable; available; beneficial; convenient; dominant; expedient; fortunate; friendly; good; happy; helpful; useful
advantageously: right; well
advent: appearance; arrival
adventitious: accidental; extraneous
adventitiousness: serendipity
adventure: caper; game
adventurous: audacious; daredevil; daring; enterprising
adventurousness: daring
adversary: antagonist; enemy; foe; opponent; opposition
adverse criticism: abuse
adverse: alien; bad; contrary; dim; hostile; ill; inimical; opposite; repugnant; thwart; unfavorable
adversity: affliction; calamity; disaster; distress; misfortune; sorrow; trouble
advert: refer
advertise: bear; post; proclaim; publish
advertisement: bill; commercial; notice
advice: caution; counsel; information; lore; notice; warning; word
advisable: expedient
advise: admonish; apprise; caution; confer; direct; inform; kibitz; recommend; suggest; urge
advisement: consideration
adviser: counsel
advocate: abet; champion; counsel; friend; patron; support; urge
adytum: sanctuary
aegis: guard; protection; safeguard
aerate: ventilate
aesthete: dilettante
affable: bland; civil; courteous; social
affair: action; brush; business; combat; concern; event; fight; matter; occurrence; operation; passage
affect or impress deeply: penetrate
affect: ape; assume; attack; bear; concern; fake; feign; hit; influ-

ence; move; pierce; pretend; simulate; stir; strike; tear; touch
affectation: air; idiosyncrasy; pose; swagger
affected or touched by: sympathetic
affected: artificial; fine; pretentious; recherch.; soft; unnatural
affectedness: affectation
affecting: pathetic; piteous
affection: admiration; attachment; bosom; devotion; disease; liking; love; passion; regard; respect
affectionate: friendly; kind; sympathetic; tender
affidavit: evidence
affiliate: associate
affiliation: alliance; connection
affinity: alliance; connection; kinship; penchant; rapport; relationship
affirm: allege; assert; declare; maintain; protest; say; state; swear; warrant
affirmation: assertion; oath; testimony; word
affirmative: absolute
affirmatively: absolutely
affix a signature to: sign
affix: add; attach
afflict: curse; distress; exercise; grind; hurt; pain; persecute; scourge; tear; torment
afflicted: ill; sorrowful; unhappy; unhealthy; wretched
affliction: adversity; affection; ailment; blow; calamity; curse; disaster; distress; hardship; ill; malady; misfortune; plague; reverse; scourge; sorrow; tear; trial; trouble; woe
afflictive: severe; sore
affluence: abundance; plenty; wealth
affluent: opulent; rich; wealthy
afford access to: admit
afford: bear; give; present; produce; provide; render; yield
affray: brawl; fight; tumult
affront: abash; indignity; insult; offend; outrage; pique; provoke; slight; slur; smart; snub
afghan: throw
aficionado: adherent
afire: fiery; vehement
afoot: pedestrian
afraid: cowardly; tremulous
afresh: new
against: adverse
agape: aghast
age: epoch; mature; period; ripen; time
aged: ancient; decrepit; mature; old; ripe; superannuated
agency: mean; medium
agent: employee; operative; surrogate
aggrandize: bulk; enlarge; expand
aggrandizement: addition
aggravate: enrage; gall; intensify; provoke; raise; rankle
aggravated: miffed
aggregate: add; collect; gather; gross; mass; number; total; whole
aggregation: collection; mass
aggression: assault; attack; offense
aggressive: offensive
aggressiveness: chutzpah
aggrieve: pain
aggrieved: sore; sorrowful
agile: active; alert; brisk; busy; clever; light; lissome; lively; nimble; quick; smart; spry
agitate: dispute; excite; move; perturb; ripple; roil; ruffle; shake; shake; startle; stir; trouble; upset; vex
agitated: excited; rough; tumultuous; unquiet; upset
agitatedly: pell-mell
agitating: agitation
agitation: commotion; confusion; disturbance; excitement; frenzy; fret; fume; hurly-burly; maelstrom; ruffle; sensation; shock; stir; trouble; tumult; turmoil
agnostic: atheist; faithless; skeptic
ago: since
agog: excited; spirited
agonize: anguish; grieve; rack; torment
agonizing: harrowing; painful; sharp
agony: ache; anguish; distress; misery; pain; rack; torment; woe
agree or accede to: grant
agree on or upon: appoint
agree to: accept; admit; permit; ratify

agree upon: settle
agree: accommodate; accord; acknowledge; acquiesce; arrange; assent; bargain; bend; check; comply; concur; conform; consent; correspond; meet; promise; settle; submit
agreeable: amiable; bland; congenial; content; convenient; delightful; easy; genial; good; grateful; harmonious; nice; palatable; pleasant; pleasing; ready; smooth; soft; suave; submissive; supple; sweet
agreeably: accordingly
agreed upon: certain
agreeing: agreement; consistent; same; true; uniform
agreement: appointment; assent; bargain; coherence; community; compact; consent; contract; convention; harmony; keeping; obligation; pact; peace; proportion; unanimity; unity
ague: chill; cold
ahead: advance; forward; onward
aid: abet; accommodate; advantage; assist; back; countenance; countenance; encourage; favor; help; helper; nourish; nurse; promote; relief; relieve; serve; subsidy; succor; support; sustain
aide-de-camp: aid
aide: adjunct; aid; ally; auxiliary
aidful: serviceable; utilitarian
aiding: auxiliary
ailing: ill; indisposed; seedy; sick; sickly
ailment: affection; disease; disorder; ill; malady
aim for or at: intend
aim: bearing; cause; design; direct; end; endeavor; idea; ideal; intent; level; mark; meaning; object; objective; present; purpose; reason; turn; view
aimed: pointed
aimless: mindless; rambling; random
air out: ventilate
air-raid alarm: alert
air: appearance; aroma; aspect; aura; bearing; behavior; breeze; cast; expression; look; manner; medium; melody; motion; semblance; ventilate; wind
aircraft: craft
airheaded: vacuous
airiness: animation
airplane: craft
airs: affectation
airsick: queasy
airy: gay; light; light; lyrical; rarefied
alacrity: expedition; haste; hurry; rapidity; speed; velocity
... la mode: fashionable; smart
... la mode: current
alarm: apprehension; consternation; dismay; fear; fright; frighten; horror; intimidate; panic; scare; startle; terror
alarmed: afraid
alarming: frightful
alarum: alarm
albeit: although
alcoholic: drunkard; lush; strong
alderman: abdomen
alert: active; agile; alive; attentive; brisk; cautious; fast; intelligent; light; lively; nimble; notable; observant; quick; ready; sharp; smart; spry; swift; vigilant; wakeful; wary; watchful
alertness: attention; care; sensibility; watch
alibi: rationalize; whitewash
alien: barbarian; extraneous; foreigner; remote; strange; stranger
alienate: divide; estrange,
alienation: breach; division
alight: light
align: dress; range; rank
aligned: abreast
alignment: rank
alike: equal; identical; uniform
aliment: food; nutrition
alive: animate; attentive; living; populous; sentient
all and sundry: totality
all around: about
all of: good
all over: about
all the rage: fashionable
all the time: always
all there: sane
all-inclusive: grand
all-round: all-around
all: totality

allay: alleviate; appease; calm; cool; damp; ease; lay; moderate; quell; relieve; soften; solace; soothe; stay; still
allegation: assertion; charge; story
allege: advance; assert; assign; maintain; plead; pretend; say; show; urge
allegiance: homage; loyalty; obeisance
allegory: fable
alleviate: allay; appease; cushion; ease; help; palliate; relieve; respite; soften; solace; soothe
alleviation: abatement; relief; solace
alleviative: therapeutic
alley: lane; street; walk
alleyway: street
alliance: association; combination; confederation; connection; league; marriage; pact; party; relation; union
allied: near
allocate: allot; apportion; appropriate; assign
allot: apply; appoint; apportion; assign; cast; deal; dispense; distribute; mete; parcel; part; portion; share
allotment: allowance; array; division; part; partition; portion; share; stint
allow for: balance; cancel
allow to enter: admit
allow: abate; abide; accept; accord; acknowledge; admit; agree; assent; authorize; back; bear; brook; confer; consent; endure; favor; grant; have; indulge; let; own; permit; sanction; stand; suffer; vouchsafe
allowable: competent
allowance: admission; assent; gift; leave; pardon; pay; permission; ration; tolerance; wage
allowed: lawful
allowing: capable
allude to: intimate; mention
allude: refer
allure: attract; charm; entice; fascinate; glamour; invite; lead; lure; seduce; steal; take; tempt
allurement: charm; glamour; lure
alluring: charismatic; seductive; tempting
allusion: hint; mention; reference
alluvium: deposit
ally: associate; auxiliary; comrade; friend; helper; relate
almost: about; nearly
alms: collection; gift
aloft: above
alone: bare; desolate; forlorn; lone; lonesome; only; private; separate; single; sole; solitary; unique
alongside: abreast
aloof: antisocial; calm; strange; sulky
aloofness: calm; temper
alop: cockeyed
alphabet: ABC's
also-ran: washout
also: besides; moreover
alt: acute
altar: sanctuary
alter: adjust; affect; amend; change; differentiate; modify; reverse; skew; slash; tamper; transform; turn; twist; vary
alterable: mutable; variable
alteration: change; variation
altercation: brawl; contention; contest; controversy; dispute; passage; quarrel; riot; row; tiff
altered: different
alternate: stagger; surrogate; surrogate; vary; waver
alternately: about
alternative: choice; surrogate
although: notwithstanding
altitude: elevation; height
altogether: clean
altruistic: benevolent; chivalrous
always: ever
amalgam: combination
amalgamate: absorb; blend; combine; fuse; join; mix; unite
amalgamation: blend; combination
amass: aggregate; collect; gather; heap; mass; pile
amateur: dabbler; dilettante; initiate; lay; neophyte
amatory: amorous; tender
amaze: astonish; dazzle; stagger; startle; stun; surprise
amazed: blank
amazement: consternation; surprise; wonder

amazing: fabulous; humongous; marvelous; prodigious; wonderful

amazon: giant

ambassador: delegate

ambiance: aura

ambience: environment,

ambiguous: doubtful; dubious; equivocal; iffy; obscure; oracular; tortuous; ulterior; uncertain

ambitious: enterprising

amble: pace; ramble; rove; saunter

ambrosial: scrumptious

ambulate: walk

ambush: blind; trap; wait

ambushment: wait

ameliorate: better; help; improve; mend; pacify; rectify; reform

amelioration: mend; reform

amenable: receptive; submissive

amend: ameliorate; better; correct; heal; improve; mend; rectify; redress; reform; repair

amending: penitent

amendment: mend; reform; reformation

amends: compensation; recompense; redress; reparation; restitution; satisfaction

American Indian: brave

amiability: kindness

amiable: affable; bland; friendly; gentle; mild; nice; obliging; peaceable; pleasant; social; sweet; warm

amicable: amiable; familiar; friendly; harmonious; peaceable; warm

amid: among

amidst: amid

amiss: wrong

amity: affection; harmony; peace

amnesty: pardon

amok: wild-eyed

among: amid

amongst: amid

amoral: abandoned; black; blue; coarse; dirty; evil; immoral; libertine; licentious; rotten; sinful; sordid; ugly; unprincipled; wicked

amorality: abomination

amorphous: nondescript; rude

amount to: aggregate; total

amount: aggregate; deal; extent; shade; size; span; volume

amour: romance

amour-propre: conceit

ample: broad; capacious; copious; extensive; generous; good; great; handsome; large; liberal; plentiful; rich; spacious; substantial; sufficient; wealthy; wide

amplify: enlarge; magnify; raise

amplitude: capacity; grandeur

amply: well

amulet: charm; talisman

amuse: beguile; divert; entertain; regale

amusement: fun; game; pastime; play; sport

amusing: comical; droll; facetious; funny; humorous; laughable; ludicrous; pleasant; risible

analogous: parallel

analogy: parallel; parity; proportion; resemblance

analysis: gloss

analyze: decipher; decompose; gloss; resolve

anarchic: chaotic

anathema: ban; curse

anathematize: curse

ancestry: birth; parentage; pedigree; stem; stock; strain

anchorage: port

ancient: aged; antique; archaic; antique; obsolete; old; old-fashioned

ancillary: auxiliary; subordinate; subsidiary

and deliver: execute

and yet: still

and: moreover

anecdote: account; story

anemic: pallid; sallow

anew: new

angel: spirit

angelic: heavenly

anger: displeasure; enrage; exasperate; fury; indignation; infuriate; irritate; madden; offense; passion; provoke; rage; roil; rouse; temper; vex; wrath

angle: bend; facet; light; skew; wangle

angry: acrimonious; cross; hot; irate; mad; miffed; savage; warm; wrathful

anguish: agony; distress; grief; misery; misery; pain; rack; sorrow; torment; woe; wound

anguished: lachrymose

angular: gaunt

anile: superannuated; weak

animadversion: blame; censure; criticism

animal: beastly; brutal; brute; carnal; gross

animalistic: beastly

animate: arouse; cheer; elevate; enliven; excite; exhilarate; heat; inform; invigorate; kindle; provoke; raise; rouse; spirit; stimulate; stir; urge; wake; warm

animated: active; blithe; bright; bubbly; gay; glad; hot; lively; passionate; quick; racy; sanguine; spirited; spry; strenuous; vivacious; vivid; warm

animating: cheerful

animation: cheer; energy; gaiety; life; sensation; spirit; verve

animosity: abhorrence; hatred; hostility; loathing; malice; rancor

animus: hostility; loathing; malice

anklet: shackle

annals: history; register

annex: add; attach

Annie Oakley: admission

annihilate: abolish; blast; blot; destroy; eradicate; exterminate; slay; zap

annihilation: abolition; destruction; massacre

anniversary: feast

annotate: comment; gloss

annotation: comment; gloss; note

announce: call; celebrate; communicate; declare; deliver; harbinger; post; proclaim; publish; release; reveal; ring; tell; utter

announcement: bill; cry; notice; statement

announcer: harbinger

annoy: bedevil; bore; bother; curse; embarrass; exasperate; exercise; fret; fuss; gall; haggle; harass; harry; irritate; madden; molest; nag; offend; pain; perplex; persecute; pester; plague; provoke; rankle; ruffle; spite; tease; torment; trouble; vex; worry

annoyance: curse; displeasure; embarrassment; fret; pest; plague; ruffle; trouble

annoyed: miffed; vexed; warm

annoying: inconvenient; offensive; tiresome; troublesome; vexatious

annuity: income

annul: abate; abolish; abrogate; break; cancel; counteract; nullify; overrule; recall; reverse; revoke; supersede; void

annular: round

annulment: abolition; abrogation

annulus: ring

anodyne: opiate; sedative

anomalous: aberrant; abnormal; ambiguous; exceptional; inept; informal; irregular; preternatural; prodigious; strange; unnatural

anomaly: aberration; abnormality

anomic: world-weary

anon: presently

anonymous: nameless

answer: account; explanation; guess; meet; plead; rejoinder; reply; response; retort; serve

answerable: liable; obnoxious; responsible

antagonism: conflict; dislike; friction; hostility; opposition

antagonist: adversary; competitor; enemy; foe; opponent; opposition; rival

antagonistic: acrimonious; adverse; contradictory; contrary; defiant; hostile; inimical; opposite; quarrelsome; repugnant

antagonize: estrange,

antedate: anticipate

antediluvian: ancient; antique; high; antique; old; primitive

anthem: paean

antic: caper; playful

anticipate: expect; forecast; look; obviate; prepare; think

anticipation: apprehension; calculation; expectation; forecast; foresight; prospect; thought; vision

antidote: cure; remedy

antiestablishment: underground

antipathetic: abhorrent

antipathy: abhorrence; aversion; disgust; dislike; horror; loathing; odium; repugnance

antiquated: ancient; antique; archaic; antique; obsolete; old; old-fashioned; quaint; superannuated

antique: ancient; archaic; old; old-fashioned; quaint; superannuated

antiseptic: sterile

antispasmodic: sedative

antithesis: opposition

antitoxin: remedy

anwer: fulfill

anxiety: apprehension; care; concern; distress; fear; sorrow; worry

anxious to please: solicitous

anxious: eager; greedy; skittish; solicitous; wild

any which way: slapdash

any: some

anyone: some

apart: abstract; alone; lone; retired; separate

apartment: compartment; flat; home

apathetic: callous; cold; cool; dead; dull; grudging; lackadaisical; nonchalant; senseless; stoical; torpid; world-weary

apathy: indifference; insensibility; phlegm

ape: imitate; impersonate; mock

aperture: hole; opening

apex: height; pinnacle; summit; top

aphorism: byword; maxim; proverb

apocopate: contract

apologize for: excuse

apologize: plead

apologue: fable

apology: excuse

apoplexy: stroke

apostate: recreant

apothegm: byword; maxim; proverb

apotheosis: ecstasy,

appall: alarm; daunt; dismay; frighten

appalled: aghast

appalling: formidable; grim; hideous; horrible; terrible; tremendous

apparatus: action; appliance; attachment; equipment; paraphernalia; technique

apparel: appoint; array; dress; garb; raiment; wardrobe

apparent: clear; conspicuous; evident; indisputable; manifest; obvious; open; ostensible; overt; patent; perceptible; plain; visible; vivid

apparition: appearance; ghost; phantasm; shade; specter; spirit; vision

appeal to: address; solicit; supplicate

appeal: application; apply; ask; cry; entreat; entreaty; glamour; petition; plead

appealing: exquisite

appear: break; dawn; debut; look; occur; rise; seem; show

appearance: air; apparition; aspect; cast; countenance; debut; exterior; face; form; gloss; guise; image; look; manner; presence; resemblance; semblance; set; shape; show; style; trick; view; visage

appearing: apparition

appease: allay; calm; conciliate; content; favor; lay; moderate; pacify; placate; propitiate; reconcile; satisfy; soften; soothe; stay; still

appeasing: pacific

appellation: name; title

append: add; attach

appendage: addition; appendix

appendix: addition; adjunct; supplement

appetent: avaricious,

appetite: addiction; desire; lust; thirst

appetizer: relish

applaud: celebrate; cheer; commend; eulogize; extol; laud

applause: commendation; praise

apple of one's eye: favorite

apple-polish: flatter

apple-polisher: yes-man

appliance: application; gadget

applicability: aptitude; fitness

applicable: active; apt; felicitous; pertinent; relevant

applicant: wannabe

application: appeal; appliance; bearing; diligence; effort; exercise; form; petition; practice; study; use

applied: active; assiduous

apply for: solicit

apply oneself: attend

apply to: address

apply: administer; devote; employ; exercise; refer; spend; use

applying: application

appoint: allot; apportion; assign; cast; decorate; establish; furnish; ordain; place; prescribe; set; set

appointing: appointment

appointment: call; disposition; office; post; station; tryst

appointments: paraphernalia

apportion: allot; apportion; assign; cast; deal; dispense; distribute; divide; mete; parcel; part; partition; portion; ration; share

apportionment: division; part; partition; portion

apposite: pertinent; relevant

appraise: estimate; prize; value

appreciable: perceptible; sensible

appreciate: acknowledge; advance; approve; esteem; judge; perceive; relish; sense; value

appreciation: deference; esteem; estimation; relish; sense; sensibility

appreciative: grateful; perceptive

apprehend: arrest; capture; catch; conceive; discern; fear; get; know; perceive; seize; take; understand

apprehension: alarm; anxiety; arrest; capture; catch; dread; fear; idea; knowledge; misgiving; perception; sense; worry

apprehensive: afraid; anxious; nervous; solicitous

apprentice: bind

apprise: admonish; advise; inform; instruct; notify; tell; warn

apprised: aware

approach: access; access; fashion; form; gain; light; mean; policy; proposal; style

approachable: affable; outgoing

approaching: near

approbation: admiration; allowance; applause; assent; commendation; countenance; praise; respect

appropriate: acquire; allot; apply; apt; assign; assume; available; becoming; befitting; convenient; decent; expedient; felicitous; happy; just; likely; meet; monopolize; opportune; peculiar; pertinent; pilfer; proper; relevant; right; seasonable; seemly; take; well

appropriately: right

appropriateness: concern; fitness; propriety

approval: allowance; applause; assent; commendation; countenance; praise; respect

approve: abet; accept; affirm; authorize; confirm; countenance; favor; pass; praise; ratify; recommend; sanction; sustain; warrant

approved: orthodox; popular

approximately: about; about; nearly

appurtenance: appendix; appliance

appurtenances: paraphernalia

apropos: applicable; appropriate; apt

apt or artful contrivance: artifice

apt: able; adroit; applicable; appropriate; apt; becoming; befitting; clever; competent; congenial; consistent; decent; dexterous; expert; felicitous; happy; intelligent; just; likely; meet; neat; opportune; pertinent; proficient; relevant; skillful

aptitude: ability; application; art; capacity; craft; endowment; faculty; genius; intelligence; knack; talent; turn

aptitudes: device

aptness: ability; application; aptitude; capacity; fitness; knack; propriety

aqueous: watery

arbitary: tyrannical

arbiter: authority; judge; referee; umpire

arbitrary: absolute; capricious; compulsory; peremptory; positive

arbitrate: mediate; moderate; referee; umpire

arbitrator: judge; referee; umpire

arch: crafty; designing; insidious; Machiavellian; vault; vault; wily

archaic: antique; extinct; antique; obsolete; old-fashioned; quaint

arched: round

archetype: copy; model; original; paradigm; pattern; prototype; type

archive: register

arctic: cold; high

ardent: amorous; eager; earnest; enthusiastic; fervent; fiery; hot; keen; passionate; spirited; strenuous; strong; torrid; vehement; warm; zealous

ardor: animation; devotion; enthusiasm; fervor; flame; goodwill; heat; mettle; passion; rage; spirit; vehemence; zeal

arduous: difficult; hard; laborious; painful; troublesome

area: blank; capacity; circle; circuit; extent; place; range; reach; region; scope; sphere; study; terrain; verge; vicinity; walk; zone

areal: vernacular

arena: midst; ring; scene; terrain

arete: peak

argot: jargon; slang

argue against: contest

argue for: advocate

argue: brawl; contend; debate; debate; discuss; dispute; haggle; moot; plead; quarrel; reason; row; say

argument: agitation; brawl; contention; contest; controversy; debate; dispute; feud; haggle; quarrel; row; tiff

argumentation: dispute

argumentative: irritable; quarrelsome; scrappy

arid: dry

arise: appear; arouse; ascend; begin; breed; climb; emanate; ensue; follow; grow; issue; occur; originate; proceed; result; rise; spring; start; stem; swell; wake

arising: beginning

aristocrat: noble

aristocratic: exclusive; lordly; noble

arm: bough; branch; limb; member

armament: safeguard

arming: fortification

armistice: peace

armor: safeguard

army: cloud; multitude

aroma: flavor; incense; odor; perfume; scent

aromatic: fragrant; odoriferous; rich; strong; sweet

around: about

arouse public interest: agitate

arouse: anger; animate; call; excite; heat; incite; inflame; influence; kindle; move; provoke; raise; solicit; stimulate; stir; summon; wake; warm

arraign: accuse; charge; impeach

arrange for: negotiate

arrange: adjust; array; cast; devise; digest; distribute; divide; form; manage; marshal; negotiate; order; place; plan; prepare; proportion; range; rank; regulate; set; settle; sort; trim

arranged: ready

arrangement: agreement; appointment; array; bargain; compact; conclusion; contract; deal; disposition; form; method; order; pact; position; proportion; rank; regulation; scheme; sequence; series; shape; structure; system

arrant: downright; precious; stark

array: adorn; apparel; arrange; deck; dress; equip; garb; habit; marshal; order; position; range; rank; trick; trim

arrest: apprehension; block; capture; catch; check; delay; detain; inhibit; obstruct; pause; seize; stay; stop; strike; suspend

arrival: appearance; debut

arrive at a settlement: agree

arrive at: attain; gain; reach; touch

arrive: debut; get

arriver: arrival

arrogance: assumption; assurance; disdain; machismo; pride; swagger

arrogant: authoritative; big; contemptuous; disdainful; haughty; high; imperious; impertinent; lofty; lordly; overbearing; pre-

sumptuous; proud; supercilious; uppity; vain
arrogate: assume; monopolize
arrow-case: quiver
arrow: dart
art: address; artifice; craft; craft; policy
artful: astute; cagey; crafty; cunning; deep; designing; diplomatic; glib; handy; insidious; Machiavellian; politic; sly; wily
artfulness: art; artifice; craft; cunning; delicacy; guile
article: branch; piece
articulate: eloquent; speak
artifice: cheat; craft; cunning; deceit; deception; device; duplicity; fraud; game; guile; machination; maneuver; ploy; stratagem; trap; trick; trickery; wile
artificer: artist; craftsman; mechanic
artificial: false; fictitious; recherch,; sophisticated; theatrical; unreal
artificiality: affectation
artisan: artist; craftsman; mechanic; operative
artiste: artist
artistic: bohemian
artistry: delicacy
artless: candid; frank; fresh; guileless; ingenuous; innocent; naive; open; plain; rude; simple; sincere; unaffected; unreserved; unsophisticated
artlessness: sincerity
arty: bohemian
as: because
ascend: climb; mount; rise; scale; soar
ascendancy: advantage; command; power
ascendant: dominant; predominant
ascendency: sway
ascent: climb; rise
ascertain: detect; determine; discover; learn; prove; see; sound; take; trace
ascetic: abstemious
asceticism: austerity
ascribe: assign; attribute; charge; impute; lay; refer
ascription: credit
ashamed: bashful; small
ashen: pale; pallid; wan
ashy: pale
aside: observation
asinine : vacuous
asinine: absurd; foolish; preposterous; senseless; silly; stupid
ask for: beg; demand; request; seek; solicit
ask: appeal; apply; beseech; claim; demand; desire; inquire; invite; question; require
askance: cockeyed
askew: cockeyed; crooked; wry
asking: demand
asleep: dormant
asocial: antisocial
aspect: air; apparel; appearance; countenance; exposure; expression; exterior; face; facet; guise; light; look; manner; presence; semblance; set; shape; view; visage
asperse: abuse; assail; slur; traduce; vilify
aspersion: abuse; detraction; obloquy; reflection; scandal
asphalt: tar
aspirant: wannabe
aspiration: ambition; desire; longing
aspirer: wannabe
aspiring: ambitious
assail: assault; attack; attempt; beset; contradict; denounce; hit; molest; resist
assailable: vulnerable
assailant: offensive
assailing: aggressive; assault
assassin: butcher
assassinate: butcher; kill; murder; remove; slay
assassination: murder
assault: assail; attack; attempt; charge; crime; descent; offense; storm; surprise
assaulting: aggressive
assay: balance; experiment; ordeal; prove; test; trial
assemblage: aggregate; assembly; company; form; gathering; mass; muster; party; pile; system; throng; troop
assemble: aggregate; call; collect; convene; crowd; fabricate; gath-

er; herd; manufacture; mass; meet; muster; pile; raise; throng; troop
assembly: ball; band; company; congress; convention; gathering; muster; party
assent to: accept
assent: accommodate; accord; acquiesce; agree; belief; comply; conform; consent
assenting: content
assert: affirm; allege; claim; contend; declare; defend; express; have; maintain; pose; protest; show; state; urge; vindicate
assertion: expression; position; profession; remark; speech; word
assertive: aggressive
assess: account; check; estimate; lay
assessment: note; view
asset: virtue
assets: capital; money; wealth; wherewithal
asseverate: affirm; allege; assert; declare; express; have; maintain; protest; show; state; urge
asseveration: assertion; assurance; profession; remark; speech; word
assiduity: application; attachment; diligence; patience; study
assiduous: attentive; busy; close; consistent; constant; diligent; industrious; laborious; notable; painstaking; patient; sedulous
assiduousness: diligence; study
assign to: account
assign: allot; apply; appoint; apportion; appropriate; ascribe; attach; cast; deal; devote; distribute; fix; give; negotiate; refer; render; set; sort; station
assignation: appointment; tryst
assignment: post; task
assimilate: absorb; digest; swallow
assist: abet; accommodate; aid; back; favor; help; promote; relieve; serve; succor; support
assistance: aid; countenance; help; relief; succor; support
assistant: aid; ally; auxiliary; companion; help; helper; sidekick
assisting: auxiliary
associate with: accompany
associate: accomplice; acquaintance; ally; attach; brother; combine; companion; comrade; conjoin; connect; couple; familiar; follower; friend; herd; intimate; join; mingle; mix; partner; relate; sidekick; troop; twist; unite
associating: conversant
association: alliance; band; body; club; combination; company; connection; coterie; firm; lodge; marriage; relation; relationship; society; union
assort: sort
assorted: heterogeneous
assortment: set; variety
assuage: allay; alleviate; appease; calm; cool; ease; moderate; pacify; qualify; relieve; smooth; soften; solace; soothe; temper
assuagement: relief
assuasive: mild
assume: affect; conjecture; consider; deduce; gather; give; imagine; presume; pretend; seem; simulate; suppose; take
assumed: affected; artificial
assuming: arrogant; assumption; audacious; forward
assumption: theory
assurance: belief; certainty; confidence; faith; guarantee; promise; trust; warrant; word
assure: confirm; encourage; satisfy; secure; warrant
assured: certain; clear; confident; positive; secure; sure
assuredly: clearly
astir: abroad
astonish: amaze; bewilder; confuse; dazzle; stagger; startle; stun; surprise
astonished: blank
astonishing: fabulous; marvelous; prodigious; wonderful
astonishment: confusion; surprise; wonder
astound: amaze; astonish; dazzle; shock; stagger; startle; stun; surprise
astounded: blank
astounding: fabulous; marvelous; prodigious; wonderful
astringent: austere

astute: acute; cagey; deep; designing; intelligent; keen; Machiavellian; perceptive; politic; sharp; shrewd; sly
astuteness: perspicacity; policy
aswarm: alive
asylum: cover; harbor; home; hospital; refuge; retreat; shelter
at all: ever
at an angle: askance
at any time: ever
at ease: laid-back
at hand: available; convenient; handy; imminent; near; present
at large: abroad
at liberty: free; unemployed
at once: immediately; instantly; presently
at peace: pacific
at rest: easy; still
at risk: vulnerable
at: near
atheist: skeptic
atheistic: faithless
athletic: robust; stalwart; stout; strong; well-built
athletics: sport
atingle: eager
Atlas: giant
atmosphere: air; aura; environment; medium
atom: bit; iota; particle
atone for: answer; repair
atone: compensate; repent
atonement: compensation; redress; reparation; satisfaction
atoning: penitent
atop: above
atrocious: black; enormous; grievous; heinous; horrendous; monstrous; nefarious; wicked
atrocity: cruelty
attach,: adjunct
attach: add; bind; fasten; fix; hitch; join; stick; suspend
attached: affectionate; close; near; sympathetic; warm
attachment: addition; adjunct; affection; bond; devotion; love; party; passion
attack: access; assail; assault; attempt; blow; charge; convulsion; denounce; descent; encounter; molest; offense; paroxysm; push; raid; resist; rush; siege; storm; stroke; surprise; throe
attackable: vulnerable
attackers: offense
attacking: aggressive; offensive
attain a position of success: arrive
attain: accomplish; achieve; acquire; arrive; do; gain; hit; obtain; reach; touch; win
attainable: practicable
attainment: accomplishment; achievement; arrival; end; quality
attar: perfume
attempt: effort; endeavor; exertion; trial; try
attend to: mind
attend: abide; accompany; await; convoy; escort; follow; hear; hear; listen; mind; nourish; nurse; respect; see; serve
attendance: convoy; presence
attendant: caregiver; follower; menial; servant
attender: attendant
attending: attention; observation
attention: application; care; consideration; heed; notice; observation; regard; remark; study; thought; watch
attentive: affectionate; alert; assiduous; careful; chivalrous; diligent; observant; sharp; thoughtful; vigilant; watchful
attenuate: draw; extend; lengthen; reduce
attenuated: gaunt; long; rarefied; tenuous
attest: allege; protest; warrant
attestation: testimony
attire: apparel; array; clothes; deck; dress; garb; habit; raiment; wardrobe
attitude: air; aspect; pose; position; posture; sentiment; set; spirit; stand
attitudinize: pose
attorney: advocate
attract: arrest; attach; charm; draw; entice; invite; lure; take; tempt
attraction: appeal; beauty; bond; glamour; lure; rapport

attractive: beautiful; becoming; charismatic; conspicuous; fair; interesting; piquant; pretty; seductive; sweet; tempting; winning; womanly
attractiveness: beauty; charm; grace
attribute: ascribe; assign; attach; characteristic; idiosyncrasy; impute; lay; property; quality; refer
attributes: nature
au courant: fashionable
audacious: adventurous; cool; daring; presumptuous; rash; shameless
audacity: bravery; chutzpah; courage; daring
aught: zilch
augment: add; advance; amplify; enlarge; increase; magnify; piece; raise; swell
augmentation: growth; increase; rise; swell
augur: forecast; harbinger; predict; prophesy; threaten
augury: forecast; omen; portent; prediction; presage; sign; warning
august: grand; great; kingly; magnificent; majestic; solemn
au naturel: nude
auspicious: bright; fortunate; good; lucky; oracular; prosperous
auspiciously: fair
austere: abstemious; astringent; difficult; hard; harsh; rigid; rigorous; rugged; severe; sour; stern; stiff; stoical; strict; unrelenting
austerity: hardship
authentic: authoritative; genuine; real; true
authenticate: confirm
author: originate
authoritarian: authoritative; magisterial
authoritative: authentic; magisterial; oracular; peremptory; valid
authority: allowance; credit; dilettante; empire; expert; head; influence; power; rule; sanction; savant; sway; sway
authorization: allowance; authority; sanction; warrant
authorize: approve; empower; legitimate; sanction; state; warrant
autochthonous: native
autocrat: tyrant
autocratic: absolute; authoritative
automatic: involuntary
autonomous: self-governed
auxiliary: aid; helper; subsidiary
avail oneself of: use
avail: advantage; use
available: open; serviceable
avant-garde: pioneer; underground
avarice: greed
avaricious: greedy; mercenary; niggardly; parsimonious; rapacious; sordid; stingy
avenge: requite; retaliate; revenge
avenging: vengeance
avenue: passage; path; street; walk; way
aver: affirm; allege; assert; confess; declare; have; maintain; mention; protest; state; urge
average: fair; mean; mediocre; medium; moderate; run
averment: assurance
Avernus: hell
averral: speech
averse: hostile; indisposed; loath; reluctant; repugnant
aversion: abhorrence; abomination; antipathy; disgust; dislike; distaste; hatred; horror; loathing; phobia; repugnance; revolt
avert: deviate; obviate; parry
avid: eager; gluttonous
avidity: greed
avocation: trade
avoid: blink; decline; elude; escape; evade; help; parry; shirk; shrink; shun
avoidance: abstinence; evasion; parry
avow: admit; assert; confess; own; protest; swear
avowal: assertion; assurance; profession
avowed: frank
await or accept the consequences of: abide
await or sustain defiantly: abide
await: abide; anticipate; expect; look; wait; watch

awake: attentive; conscious; nimble; raise; sentient; sharp; vigilant; wake; wakeful; watchful
awaken: arouse; call; excite; kindle; raise; rouse; solicit; wake
award: accolade; act; bounty; give; grant; trophy; vouchsafe
aware: alert; conscious; observant; sensible; sentient
awareness: sense; sensibility
away: abroad; absent
awe-inspiring: solemn
awe: admiration; consternation; discourage; dread; fear; reverence; veneration; wonder
awesome: eerie; grandiose; humongous; wonderful
awful: frightful; horrible; terrible; tremendous
awkward: angular; clumsy; crude; inconvenient; maladroit; stiff; uncouth; ungainly; unskillful
awry: cockeyed; crooked; wrong; wry
axiom: principle
axiomatic: self-evident
axis: center; stem
azure: blue
babble: jabber; waffle
babbler: gossip
babbling: garrulous
babel: bedlam
baby: pamper; pet; weakling
babyish: infantile
bacchante: fury; scold; shrew; termagant
back and fill: waffle
back and forth: about
back country: backwater
back foremost: backward
back street: alley
back up: brace
back woods: backwater
back-and-forth: raillery
back: abet; aid; assist; authorize; help; incite; rear; reverse; support
backbone: mainstay
backer: friend
background: milieu; rear
backing: help; mean
backsliding: slip
backup: surrogate
backward: loath; tardy
backwards: about
bad luck: adversity; calamity; misfortune
bad-tempered: harsh; nasty; sour; sullen; temperamental; ugly; vicious
bad: atrocious; dark; evil; evil; faulty; ill; immoral; infamous; miserable; naughty; pernicious; perverse; sinful; sinister; sorry; unprincipled; vicious; vile; wicked; wretched; wrong
badge: device; emblem; mark
badger: annoy; haggle; harass; persecute; pester; plague; trouble; worry
badinage: banter; raillery
badly: ill
badness: evil; ill; malfeasance
baffle: cross; defeat; elude; evade; frustrate; thwart
bafflement: defeat
bag: sack
bailiwick: terrain
bait: haggle; lure
balance: account; even; poise; proportion; remainder; scale; symmetry; weigh
balanced: equal; even; mutual; practical; steady
bald: bare; dry; smooth
balderdash: nonsense; stuff
bale: package
baleful: destructive; malign
balk: defeat; frustrate
balky: wrongheaded
ball: circle; orb; sphere; sphere
ballo in maschera: mask
balloon: billow
balm: ointment; remedy; soothe
bal masqu.: mask
balmy: bland; soft
bamboozle: bite; cheat; deceive
ban: curse; enjoin; prohibition
banal: commonplace; hackneyed; lackluster; stereotyped
banality: platitude
band: association; bar; belt; bind; body; bond; company; gang; list; pack; scourge; strip; tie; troop; zone
bandage: compress
bandit: outlaw; robber
bane: curse; pest

baneful: bad; injurious; malign; noisome; noxious; pernicious; unwholesome

banish: expel; ostracize; transport

bank: bar; bluff; deposit; reserve; shore

bankroll: wherewithal

bankrupt: break; smash

bankruptcy: failure

banned: cursed; taboo

banner: standard

banquet: feast; treat

banquette: seat

banter: jest; mock; mock; quip; raillery; ridicule; ridicule; twit

bar: barricade; barricade; barrier; check; close; except; exclude; impediment; obstruct; obstruction; shut; standard; tavern; traverse

barb: dart

barbarian: brutal; brute; cruel; wild; yahoo

barbaric: barbarian; beastly; brutal

barbarity: cruelty

barbarous: barbarian; bloody; brutal; cruel; fierce; heathen; ruthless; savage; wild

barbiturate: sedative

bare: barren; crude; expose; mere; naked; nude; open; simple

barely: hardly; little; scarcely

barfy: queasy

bargain: agree; agreement; barter; compact; contract; deal; haggle; pact; purchase; trade; treat

bark: cry; peel

barn: stable

baron: peer; tycoon

barren: arid; bare; dead; desert; desolate; dry; fruitless; lean; poor; sterile; unfruitful; waste

barrenness: poverty

barricade: bar; barrier; obstruct; rampart

barrier: bar; barricade; check; obstacle; obstruction; pale; partition; traverse; wall

barring: exclusive

barrister: advocate; counsel

barter: change; exchange; exchange; sell; swap; trade; trade; trade

basal: seminal

base: abject; bad; basis; beastly; bottom; cheap; coarse; contemptible; corrupt; despicable; dirty; dishonorable; evil; foul; foundation; ground; ignoble; infamous; low; mean; menial; nefarious; object; pitiful; poor; profane; rascal; recreant; ribald; scurvy; seat; servile; shabby; shameful; sinister; slavish; sordid; sorry; ugly; unclean; ungodly; unworthy; vile; wretched

baseborn: base

baseless: idle; imaginary; precarious

baseness: corruption; disgrace; evil

bashful: backward; chary; coy; diffident; shy; skittish; timid; unpretentious

basic law: fundamental

basic: bottom; elementary; essential; essential; fundamental; primary; radical; seminal; standard

basics: ABC's; element

basis: base; bottom; cause; element; foundation; ground; object; standard

basket: hamper

bastard: bogus; phony; spurious; unlawful

baste: beat

bastion: wall

bat: club; stick

batch: bunch; parcel

bathe: wash

bathetic: hackneyed; saccharine

bathing: wash

bathos: schmaltz

baton: stick

batter: beat; break; pelt

battered: weather-beaten

battery: crime

battle cry: catchword

battle: action; brush; combat; conflict; contend; contest; encounter; fight; skirmish; struggle

battlement: wall

batty: mental

bauble: charm

bawd: procure

bawdy: X-rated

bawl: cry; roar

be or feel sorry for: pity

---

be a follower: adhere

be a traitor to: betray

be able to: can

be absorbed or engrossed: consume

be active: act

be adjacent to: join

be afraid of: fear

be applicable or appropriate or similar: agree

be appropriate: apply

be astonished or astounded: wonder

be attached: adhere

be averse: object

be aware or conscious of: appreciate

be burdened or troubled or distressed: labor

be capable of: admit; bear

be careful or cautious or wary: mind

be careful: guard

be commensurate with: equal

be correlated: answer

be delirious: wander

be derived: rise

be devious: wind

be devoted: adhere

be disinclined or reluctant: dislike

be disloyal to: betray

be doubtful or undecided: hang

be efficient or effective or efficacious: act

be elated or glad: triumph

be enamored of: love

be entitled to: merit

be equivalent to: parallel

be evasive: dodge

be faithful: adhere

be firm or resolute or steadfast or steady: stand

be fond of: love

be found: occur; range

be grateful for: acknowledge

be harmonious or in harmony: accord

be hot: burn

be imminent: hang

be in love with: love

be in store for: await

be inactive or quiescent: wait

be inclined or disposed or interested: care

be met with: occur

be mistaken: slip

be obvious or manifest or clear: appear

be of help: aid

be of importance: matter

be of service to: advantage

be ostentatious: flourish

be patient: bear

be peevish: pet

be pertinent: apply; bear

be pleased with: fancy

be present at: attend

be present: attend; reside

be profitable to: pay

be prolific or fertile: teem

be promoted: rise

be punished: pay

be quick: hurry

be ready for: await

be remiss: neglect

be responsible or liable or accountable: answer

be satisfied or content (with): acquiesce

be seated: sit

be similar or equivalent to: answer

be situated: sit

be solicitous or anxious: care

be successful with or in: accomplish

be successful: flourish

be sufficient: answer

be troubled or vexed: worry

be troubled: care

be true: adhere

be unfaithful to: betray

be very prevalent: abound

be worthy of: merit

beach: coast; shore

beak: bill

beam: gleam; radiate; shine; shore

beaming: bright; radiant

bear in mind: think

bear malice or spleen: abhor; abominate

bear off: abduct

bear witness: witness

bear: abide; admit; allow; breed; brook; carry; conduct; convey; draw; endure; hold; produce; stand; suffer; support; sustain; take; transmit; undergo; yield

---

bearing: address; air; aspect; attitude; behavior; carriage; concern; conduct; course; kinship; manner; motion; presence; semblance; set

beast: animal; brute

beastly: animal; brutal; loutish; savage

beat: batter; blow; break; conquer; exceed; excel; head; number; outdo; overpower; palpitate; pelt; post; pound; pulsate; seedy; stamp; strike; stroke; surpass; thrash; throb; walk; whip

beatific: heavenly

beatified: heavenly

beatify: sanctify

beating: stroke

beatitude: happiness; rapture

beau monde: fashion

beau: coxcomb

beauteous: beautiful

beautiful: dainty; exquisite; fair; heavenly; lovely; magnificent; picturesque; pretty; splendid

beautify: adorn; decorate; embellish; garnish; grace; ornament

beautifying: cosmetic

beauty: grace

because: since

becloud: cloud; fog; shroud

beclouded: turbid

become aware of: notice; sense

become better: mend

become visible: appear

become: get; wax

becoming: appropriate; befitting; decent; decorous; modest; proper; right; seemly

bedaub: daub

bedaze: dazzle

bedazzle: dazzle

bedeck: adorn; array; beautify; deck; decorate; embellish; garnish; ornament; trim

bedew: wash

bedim: cloud

bedizen: adorn; deck; decorate; garnish

bedraggled: shabby

bedspread: spread

beefy: muscular

Beelzebub: adversary

beer-barrel: abdomen

befall: chance; happen; occur

befit: hit

befitting: applicable; appropriate; apt; available; happy; meet; proper; right; seemly; well

befog: bewilder; fog

befogged: cloudy

befool: beguile

before now: since

before: above; advance

befoul: contaminate; debase; pollute; roil

befouling: dirty

befriend: assist; help

befuddle: fog

befuddled: drunken

beg for: crave

beg: ask; beseech; entreat; implore; mooch; petition; plead; pray; request; solicit; supplicate; urge

beget: breed; breed; engender; get; reproduce

beggarly: base

begin hostilities: attack

begin: commence; dawn; initiate; open; originate; start

beginner: dabbler; initiate; neophyte; pupil; tyro

beginning: birth; head; opening; origin; primary; rise; start

begrudge: envy; grudge

begrudging: grudging; malevolent

beguile: bite; cajole; cheat; coax; delude; flatter; regale; seduce; trick; victimize

beguiled: smitten

beguiling: charismatic; insidious; seductive

begun: initiate

behalf: advantage

behave as: act

behave: act; conduct; deal; do

behavior: action; air; bearing; carriage; conduct; course; decorum; manner; poise; walk

behead: kill

behemoth: giant

behest: command; will

behind: backward; backward

behindhand: backward; slow; tardy

behold: discern; see; view

beholden: thankful

beholder: witness

being in concord: agreement

being: appearance; life; ubiquitous

---

belabor: batter; beat; pelt

belated: late

beldam: termagant

beleaguer: bedevil; beset

belief system: ideology

belief: apprehension; conceit; confidence; credit; doctrine; faith; idea; ideology; mind; notion; opinion; principle; tenet; thought; trust; view

beliefs: platform

believable: faithful; tenable

believe: accept; credit; deem; guess; hold; imagine; presume; suppose; suspect; think; trust; understand

believer: crackpot

believers: faithful

believing: belief; confident; credulous

belittle: decry

belittling: derogatory; detraction

belle: beauty

belles-lettres: literature

bellicose: quarrelsome; warlike

belligerent: quarrelsome; warlike

bellow: cry; low; roar

bellwether: pioneer

belly: abdomen; billow

bellyache: kvetch

belong: attach; refer

belongings: good; paraphernalia; property

beloved: dear; favorite; precious; sweet

below: short

belowground: underground

belt: band; verge; warble; zone

bemoan: complain; cry; deplore; grieve; lament; moan; mourn; regret; sorrow; weep

bemused: rapt

bench: seat

bend: bias; bow; compel; droop; lean; spring; stoop; sway; turn; twist; warp; wind; yield

bend (heraldry): band

bendable: malleable

benefaction: bounty; donation; gift; present

beneficence: bounty; kindness

beneficent: charitable; generous; good; gracious; kind; liberal; merciful; munificent

beneficial: good; helpful; therapeutic; useful; wholesome

benefit: account; advantage; advantage; favor; good; oblige; profit; use; welfare

benevolence: goodness; goodwill; kindness; mercy

benevolent: charitable; chivalrous; friendly; good; gracious; humane; kind; kindly

benighted: blind; dark

benign: affable; benevolent; charitable; fatherly; gracious; innocuous; kind; kindly

benignant: benevolent; charitable; compassionate; humane; kind; merciful

benignity: goodness; grace; kindness

bent: affection; aptitude; attachment; bias; capacity; cast; cranky; crooked; device; disposition; genius; gift; habit; inclination; intent; liking; mind; partiality; penchant; predilection; proclivity; prone; propensity; relish; set; slant; tendency; tortuous; turn; twist; wry

benumb: dull; paralyze

bequeath: grant; leave; will

bequest: endowment; gift; grant

berate: abuse; punish; reprimand; scold; vituperate

bereave: deprive

berserk: wild-eyed

berth: office

beseech: ask; beg; crave; entreat; implore; pray; request; solicit; supplicate; urge

beset: bedevil

beside oneself: ecstatic

besides: also; moreover

besiege: beset; storm

besiegers: offense

besieging: siege

besmear: daub

besmirch: contaminate; daub; foul; pillory; smirch

besmirching: dirty

besotted: drunken; smitten

bespatter: blot

best-liked: favorite

best-loved: favorite

best: pick; top

bestial: beastly; brutal

bestir oneself: move

---

bestir: kindle

bestow: cast; communicate; confer; endow; extend; give; grant; heap; impart; lavish; present; show; vouchsafe; yield

bestowal: disposition

bestud: beset

bet: lay; play; stake; wager

betide: happen

betoken: argue; betray; sign; signify

betray: abuse; charge; deceive; defect; display; exhibit; expose; tell

betrayal: abuse; conspiracy; disloyalty; treachery

better: ameliorate; edify; excellent; gain; help; improve; pacify; profit; rectify; reform; smooth

bettering: uplifting

betterment: progress; reform; reformation

between engagements: unemployed

between: among

beverage: drink

bevy: flock; run; swarm

bewail: complain; cry; deplore; grieve; lament; moan; mourn; regret; sorrow; weep

bewilder: amaze; bother; confuse; disconcert; entangle; fog; obfuscate; perplex; puzzle; shock; stun; surprise

bewildered: lost

bewilderment: confusion; consternation; mist; wonder

bewitch: captivate; catch; charm; enamor; enchant; fascinate; overlook; take

bewitched: smitten

bewitching: charismatic

bewitchment: charm

beyond doubt: absolutely

beyond the sea: abroad

beyond: above; above; advance

bias: affection; bend; bent; disposition; favor; inclination; influence; liking; mind; partiality; penchant; predilection; prejudice; proclivity; propensity; respect; slant; sway; tendency; twist; warp

biased: bigoted; injurious; intolerant; narrow-minded; opinionated; partial; partisan; unfair; unjust; xenophobic

bibble-babble: babble

bibelot: antique; novelty

bicker: brawl; dispute; quarrel

bickering: dispute; tiff

bid: charge; command; decree; enjoin; invite; offer; order; summon; tell; will; wish

bidding: call; command; will; word

bifurcate: diverge

big name: celebrity

big shot: celebrity; tycoon

big wheel: tycoon

big-hearted: big

big-time operator: tycoon

big: broad; bulky; generous; great; gross; large; magnanimous; merciful; solid

bigger: better

biggie: celebrity

bigot: enthusiast; zealot

bigoted: intolerant; narrow-minded; opinionated; small-minded; xenophobic

bigwig: tycoon

bile: anger

billboard: notice

billow: swell

billy: club

bind: attach; confine; confirm; constrain; constrict; fasten; involve; link; oblige; sanction; tie

binder: bond

binding: astringent; compulsory; stringent; valid

binge: rampage

biography: life

birth: beginning; origin; parentage

birthplace: origin

bise: storm

bisect: cut

bishopric: see

bistro: bar

bit by bit: piecemeal

bit of mischief: caper

bit: check; dash; iota; particle; portion; scrap; taste

bite: scrap

biting: acerbic; acid; acrimonious; bitter; cutting; dry; hot; incisive; keen; peppery; poignant; pointed; pungent; sarcastic; satirical; severe; sharp; strong; tart

bits: odd
bitstock: brace
bitter: acrimonious; austere; cruel; cutting; keen; malignant; poignant; pungent; rigorous; sarcastic; sardonic; satirical; severe; sharp; sour; tart; unrelenting; virulent; vitriolic
bitterness: grudge; malice; rancor; sarcasm; venom
bitting: trenchant
bizarre: eccentric; fantastic; odd; peculiar; singular; strange; wild
bizzarro: eccentric
blabber: babble
Black Death: plague
black out: faint
black: dark
blacken: pillory; vilify
blackguard: knave
blackjack: club
blackmail: extort
blade: swell
blah: tasteless
blamable: responsible
blame: abuse; account; accuse; attack; censure; charge; chide; condemn; denounce; impeach; obloquy; reproach; reprove; scold; upbraid
blameless: guiltless; innocent; just; unimpeachable
blameworthy: faulty; vicious
blaming: censure
blanch: bleach; fade; pale; whiten
blanched: light
bland: gentle; kind; mild; smooth; soft; suave; tasteless; vacuous; watery
blandish: cajole; flatter
blandishment: blarney
blank: block; empty; form; vacant; vacuous
blanket: pall; throw
blare: blast; noise
blasé: jaded; lackadaisical; laid-back; world-weary
blaspheme: curse; pollute; swear
blasphemous: profane; wicked
blasphemy: oath; sacrilege
blast: blow; wind
blatant: flagrant; loud; noisy
blather: babble; blarney; jabber; waffle
blaze a trail: pioneer
blaze: flame; flame
blazing: bright
bleach: blanch; fade; whiten
bleached: weather-beaten
bleak: chill; cold; gaunt
bleed: bankrupt; extort; extract
blemish: blot; defect; disfigure; fault; flaw; spot; stain; sully; taint; tarnish; traduce; vice
blend: combine; fuse; melt; mingle; mix; mixture; scramble; temper; unite
blending: combination
bless: exalt; praise; sanctify
blessed: hallowed; heavenly; holy; lucky; sacrosanct
blessedness: happiness
blight: assassinate; blast
blighted: cursed
blind: curtain; dazzle; purblind
blinder: blind
blink: wink
blinker: blind
bliss: ecstasy; happiness; joy; rapture; transport
blissful: happy; heavenly
blister: scorch
blistering: hot
blithe: cheerful; gay; happy; jovial; joyful; light-hearted; lively; merry
blitheness: bliss
blithesome: blithe; joyful; lively; merry
blizzard: storm
bloat: augment; billow; distend; expand; inflate; swell
bloc: alliance; faction
block: bar; barricade; close; die; hinder; impede; obstacle; obstruct; stamp; stop
blockade: block; siege; stop
blockage: block
blockhead: block; fool; oaf
blocking: block
blond: fair
blood: birth
bloodless: sallow
bloodshed: slaughter
bloodstained: bloody
bloodsucker: parasite
bloodthirsty: bloody; cruel; deadly; fierce; sanguinary; savage
bloody: sanguinary
bloom: blow

blooming: rosy
blooper: blunder
blossom: bloom; blow; ripen
blot out: cancel; deface; delete; obliterate
blot: blemish; daub; defect; flaw; mar; slur; smirch; spot; stain; stigma; taint; tarnish; vice
blotch: blot; daub; defect
blotting: blot
blow up: amplify; burst; inflate; swell
blow: beat; blast; breeze; calamity; disaster; gasp; hit; misfortune; pant; pelt; shake; shock; stab; storm; stroke; swagger; touch
blubber: cry
blubbering: lachrymose
blubbery: lachrymose
bludgeon: club
blue-chip: top-notch
blue: depressed; despondent; earthy; melancholy; prim; squeamish
bluenosed: straitlaced
blueprint: design; paradigm
blues: despondency; melancholy
bluff: blunt; brusque; coarse
bluffer: phony
blunder: error; inaccuracy; mistake; oversight; slip; slip; trip; trip
blunt: abrupt; bluff; brusque; callous; crude; curt; curtail; dull; heavy; naked; plain; plump; realistic; soften
blunted: dull; slack
bluntly: plump
bluntness: candor
blur: blot; dim; fog; shade
blurred: cloudy; dim; obscure
blurring: fog
blurry: cloudy; obscure
blushing: ruddy; timid
bluster: brag; bravado; fume; swagger
blustering: noisy
boa: throw
board and room: keep
board: accommodate
boast: brag; flourish; swagger; vaunt
boastful: big
boastfulness: egotism
boasting: bravado; swagger
boat: craft; tender
bob: obeisance
bobble: blunder
bodacious: flagrant,
bodice ripper: romance
bodily: carnal; corporal; physical
body: aggregate; band; bulk; carcass; company; corpse; faction; gross; party; rank; troop
boffin: savant
bog: quagmire; wash
bogeyman: goblin,
bogus: artificial; fake; false; fictitious; spurious
boil: gathering; seethe; simmer; sore; stew
boisterous: loud; noisy; obstreperous; rambunctious; raucous; robust; rough; tumultuous; wild
bold: adventurous; audacious; brave; brazen; broad; confident; daring; dauntless; defiant; enterprising; fearless; forward; frank; gallant; game; hardy; heroic; impertinent; impudent; insolent; manly; pert; presumptuous; raw; resolute; shameless; spirited; stalwart; stout; strong; unabashed; valiant
boldness: assurance; bravery; chutzpah; confidence; daring; enterprise; heroism; impudence; machismo; pluck; valor
bolster: cushion; pillow; reassure; stay
bolstering: fortification
bolt: abscond; catch; dart; dash; gobble; gorge; pin
bombast: bravado; harangue
bombastic: big; grandiloquent; tumid; turgid
bon mot: quip
bona fide: genuine
bond servant: slave
bond: band; bind; connection; link; obligation; pact; tie
bondage: bond; captivity; servitude; slavery
bondman: serf; slave
bondsman: bond
boner: blunder
bonus: bounty; premium; present; reward
bony: angular; spindly
boo-boo: blunder

booby: fool
book: account; volume
books: account
boom: roar
boon: donation; gift; present
boondocks: backwater
boonies: backwater
boor: barbarian; yahoo
boorish: abrupt; coarse; crude; impolite; loutish; rude; rural; uncivil; unrefined; vulgar
boost: edify
boot-licker: sycophant; yes-man
booth: stand; standing
bootless: futile; useless
bootlick: flatter
booty: loot; pillage; plunder; spoil
border: bank; bind; bound; boundary; brim; edge; extremity; list; margin; rim; verge
bordering: adjoining; near
borders: confine
bore: breaker; penetrate; pierce; tire
bored: jaded
boring: dreary; dry; dull; flat; heavy; long; monotonous; slow; stereotyped; stupid; tame; tedious; wearisome
borough: town
boss: manager; master
botch: blunder; butcher; washout
bother: annoy; bedevil; distress; fuss; molest; perplex; persecute; pester; plague; tease; trouble; worry
bottom: base; basis; seat
bottomless pit: abyss
bough: branch; limb
boulevard: street
bounce: skip
bouncy: bubbly
bound: bank; border; brim; circle; confine; end; jump; leap; limit; margin; mete; restrict; rim; skip; spring; terminate
boundary: barrier; border; bound; circuit; confine; division; edge; end; extremity; limit; mete; periphery; rim
bounder: villain
boundless: clear; endless; measureless; unbounded; unlimited; vast
bounds: circle; confine; extremity; pale
bounteous: kind; liberal; munificent; open; plentiful; prodigal; rich
bounteousness: generosity
bountiful: ample; charitable; free; generous; liberal; munificent; open; plentiful; prodigal; rich; unsparing
bounty: bonus; endowment; gift; premium; profusion; reward
bouquet: aroma
bourgeoisie: labor
bourse: exchange
bovine: lackadaisical
bow: acquiesce; bend; compel; obeisance; reverence; stoop; submit; yield
bowed: bent
bowl: roll
box: blow; case; package; quagmire
boy: youngster; youth
boycott: demonstrate
boyish: puerile
bozo: yahoo
brace: couple; harden; mainstay; nerve; pair; shore; span; stay; strength; strut; support
brachycephalic: short
bracing: healthy
bracken: brush
brag: boast; bravado; flourish; swagger; vaunt
braggadocio: boast; bravado; swagger
bragging: boast; swagger
braid: twist; weave
brain: intellectual; mind; savant
brains: intellect; judgment; mind
brainstorm: vagary
brake: brush
branch off: diverge
branch: bough; brook; cutting; dialect; limb; member; stick
brand: denounce; make; pillory; sear; slur; stamp; stigma
branding iron: stamp
brandish: flourish; shake; sway
brash: adventurous; easy
brashness: chutzpah; gall
brass hat: tycoon
brass: chutzpah; gall; impudence
brassy: bold; bombastic; brazen; grandiose; impudent; insolent
bravado: courage

brave: audacious; bold; confident; dare; daring; dauntless; defiant; defy; fearless; gallant; game; hardy; heroic; manly; stalwart; stout; strong; undaunted; valiant
bravery: assurance; courage; daring; heroism; pluck; valor
bravura: panache
brawl: disorder; dispute; quarrel; riot
brawler: rowdy
brawling: rowdy
brawny: able-bodied; muscular; robust; stalwart; stout; strong; sturdy; well-built
bray: grind; pound
brazen-faced: unabashed
brazen: audacious; bold; flagrant; forward; impertinent; impudent; insolent; shameless; unabashed
brazenness: chutzpah; gall; impudence
breach of confidence: fraud
breach: break; cleft; crack; crime; division; flaw; infringe; opening; quarrel; rent; rupture; violation
bread: food; maintenance
break down: cripple; dissolve; give
break loose: break
break off: interrupt; sever
break one's heart: grieve
break up: disband; disintegrate; dissolve; pick; resolve; scrap; separate
break: batter; beat; breach; burst; cleft; contention; crack; crush; dash; dawn; decipher; degrade; discharge; flaw; humble; infringe; injure; part; pause; quarrel; rent; rupture; shatter; smash; stay; subdue; tame; transgress
breakable: brittle; frail; slender; tender; unsound; weak
breaker: wave
breaking and entering: crime
breaking out: rash
breaking: rupture
breast: bosom; stem
breastwork: rampart; wall
breath: air
breathe heavily: pant
breathe: heave
breathing: alive
breathless: eager
breed: brood; engender; foster; get; hatch; kind; race
breeding: poise
breeze: air; wind; zephyr
breezy: jaunty
breviary: brief
brevity: conciseness
brew: contrive; plot; project
bribable: corrupt; venal
bribe: buy; corrupt; hire; tamper
bribery: corruption
bridge: structure
bridle: bit; check; control; curb; repress; restrain; slacken
brief encounter: brush
brief: abbreviation; abridgment; abstract; compact; curt; digest; ephemeral; laconic; little; pithy; short; summary; synopsis; terse; transient
briefly: short
briefness: brevity
brigand: outlaw; robber
bright: acute; apt; brisk; cheerful; clear; clever; deep; fair; gay; ingenious; intelligent; lively; lucid; luminous; prosperous; radiant; rich; rosy; serene; sharp; shining; smart; vivid
brighten: enliven; lighten; polish; refurbish
brightness: blaze; brilliance; luster; polish; splendor; strength
brillance: luster; splendor
brilliance: gaiety; glare; glory; panache; polish; sparkle; splendor
brilliancy: brilliance
brilliant: apt; brave; bright; fine; gaudy; gay; gorgeous; grand; lively; lucid; luminous; magnificent; polished; radiant; shining; splendid; strong; vivid; witty
brim over: cascade
brim: border; rim; verge
bring or draw together: gather
bring or get back: reclaim
bring about: affect; cause; do; effect; induce; make; manage; occasion; operate; perpetrate; play; procure; produce; provoke; work
bring back: revive
bring forth: bear; breed; produce

bring forward: advance; produce
bring in: draw
bring into harmony: accommodate
bring off: perpetrate
bring on: induce
bring out: emphasize
bring to a standstill: arrest
bring to an end: finish; fulfill
bring to light: disclose; discover; expose
bring to perfection: perfect
bring to view or notice: advance
bring together: aggregate; assemble; close; join; raise
bring up or about: raise
bring up or forward: assign; move
bring up: breed; foster; rear
bring: carry; convey; introduce; reason
bringing forth: birth
brink: border; brim; edge; margin; verge
brio: verve
brisk: active; agile; alert; busy; excited; hasty; lively; nimble; perky; quick; round; sharp; smart; spry; vivacious; warm
bristle: bridle
bristling: populous
bristly: rough
brittle: frail; short
broad-minded: charitable; liberal
broad: ample; capacious; coarse; comprehensive; extensive; fat; gross; heavy; large; sweeping; wide
broadcast: bear; disperse; divulge; scatter; spread; strew
broaden: amplify; stretch
broadly: abroad
broadside: bill
Brobdingnagian: giant
broke: bankrupt
broken-down: decrepit; tacky
broken-hearted: miserable
broken: bankrupt; cranky; rugged
bromide: commonplace; platitude
bromidic: hackneyed
bronze: burn
bronzed: weather-beaten
brooch: clasp; pin
brood over: revolve
brood: flock; hatch; household; litter; muse; run
brook: abide; bear; burn; endure; run
brother: monk
brotherhood: coterie; order; society; union
brougham: carriage
brouhaha: ado; ruckus
brown study: trance
brown: burn; swarthy
brownie: fairy
bruise: batter; crush; hurt; jam; mark
bruit about: noise
bruit: rumor; scuttlebutt; talk
bruited about: abroad
brummagem: bogus; phony
brush off: rebuff
brush-off: rebuff
brush: action; clean; combat; skirmish; struggle
brusque: abrupt; blunt; brutal; harsh; impatient; rude; uncivil
brusqueness: candor
brutal: animal; barbarian; beastly; brute; cruel; fierce; harsh; savage; truculent; unnatural
brutality: cruelty
brute: animal; barbarian; brutal; monster
brutish: beastly; brutal; brute; cruel; loutish
bubble: simmer; sparkle
bubblebrained: vacuous
bubbleheaded: vacuous
bubbling: brisk
bubbly: brisk
buccaneer: pirate
buck: rear; swell
buckboard: carriage; wagon
buckle: bow
buddy: comrade
budge: move
buff: muscular
buffet: beat; blow; strike
buffoon: droll; fool; yahoo; zany
bugged: miffed
build castles in the air: daydream
build up: dignify
build: construct; erect; fabricate; make; manufacture; raise; rear
building: edifice; pile; structure
built for comfort: zaftig
bulge: bulk; heave; project; swell
bulk: body; gross; mass; size

bulkiness: swell
bulky: big; gross; huge; humongous; massive; ponderous; stout; unwieldy
bullet: ball
bulletin: bill
bullyboy: rowdy
bullying: truculent
bulwark: fortification; guard; protection; rampart; safeguard; wall
bum: mooch
bumble: blunder
bumpy: rough
bunch: bundle
bundle: bunch; pack; package; parcel
bungle: blunder; butcher; trip
bungling: awkward; clumsy; maladroit; unskillful
bunker: wall
Bunyanesque: muscular
buoy up: animate
buoyancy: animation; spring; verve
buoyant: blithe; cheerful; jaunty; joyful; light; lively; lyrical; resilient; sanguine
burden: care; cargo; charge; concern; cross; encumber; exercise; freight; hardship; lay; load; onus; oppress; pack; refrain
burdensome: arduous; hard; heavy; heavy; laborious; troublesome; weighty
burgh: town
burglar: thief
burial vault: sepulcher
buried: underground
burke: shirk
burlesque: caricature; parody; ridicule; satire; travesty
burly: able-bodied; muscular; well-built
burn: bite; blaze; brook; flame; radiate; run; scorch; sear; singe
burned-out: jaded; world-weary
burning ghat: pile
burning: ardent; ardor; enthusiastic; fervent; fiery; hectic; hot; passionate; sharp; torrid; vehement
burnish: polish
burnished: bright; polished
burrow: hole; pit
burst: blast; break; rupture
bursting: ecstatic; rupture
bury: conceal; immerse; overwhelm; sepulcher
bush: backwater
bushes: brush
business form: form
business: commerce; concern; duty; exchange; firm; house; matter; occupation; operation; profession; station; trade; vocation; work
businesslike: practical
bust: failure; washout
bustle: commotion; disorder; fuss; haste; hurry; maelstrom; ruffle; scramble; stir; turmoil
bustling: busy; hectic
busy: active; diligent; industrious; occupy; sedulous
busybody: obtrusive
busyness: hurly-burly; rush
but: except; only; save; still
butcher: kill; massacre; slaughter; slay
butchering: slaughter
butchery: massacre; slaughter
butler: menial; servant
butt: objective
butter up: flatter
buttery: smarmy
buttocks: bottom
buttress: shore; stay
buxom: zaftig
buy or pay off: redeem
buy back: redeem
buy: bargain; purchase
buying: purchase
buzz: scuttlebutt
by any chance: ever
by degrees: gradual; piecemeal
by-word: proverb
bygone: antique
byway: alley; passage
byword: catchword
cabal: combination; conspiracy; conspire; machination; plot; scheme
cabalistic: dark; mysterious; occult; secret; underground
cabin: compartment; cottage; hut; lodge; shack; shanty
cachinnate: laugh
cachinnation: laugh
cackle: laugh

cacophonous: raucous; rough; rugged
cad: coward; scoundrel; villain
cadaver: body; carcass; remain
cadaverous: angular; ghastly
cadge: mooch
caesura: break
caf.: bar
cafe: tavern
cagey: slippery; unprincipled
caitiff: weakling
cajole: cheat; coax; entice; flatter
cajolery: blarney
calamitous: adverse; bitter; black; fatal; grievous; miserable; sad; tragic
calamity: accident; adversity; affliction; blow; cataclysm; catastrophe; curse; disaster; evil; ill; misadventure; misfortune; oppression; plague; scourge; trouble
calash: carriage
calculate: cast; compute; number; reckon; tell
calculated: wanton
calculation: cast; estimate; prudence
caliber: bore; capacity
calibrate: set
call back: recall
call for: ask; claim; demand; exact; require
call forth: provoke; raise; summon
call girl: prostitute
call in: ask
call to account: reproach
call together: assemble; call
call upon: implore
call: assemble; claim; cry; entitle; invite; name; ordain; qualify; ring; style; summon; title
called-for: legitimate
caller: visitor
calling: business; craft; occupation; profession; station; trade; vocation; work
callous: apathetic; dead; dull; hard; hard; obdurate; thick-skinned; unfeeling
callus: sear
calm down: settle
calm: appease; clear; cold; comfort; composed; composure; console; cool; easygoing; even; lay; meek; mild; moderate; nonchalant; order; pacific; pacify; patient; peace; peaceable; phlegm; placid; quell; quiet; restful; sedate; serene; serenity; settle; smooth; sober; soften; soothe; staid; still; stoical; tame; temper; temperate; unruffled
calmative: sedative; sedative
calmness: calm; composure; ease; patience; peace; quiet; serenity; temper
caloric: heat
caloricity: heat
calumniate: abuse; malign; slur; traduce; vilify
calumniation: abuse
calumny: detraction; obloquy; scandal
camouflage: palliate; whitewash
camp: faction
campaign or argue for: agitate
campaign: agitation; battle
cancel out: nullify
cancel: abolish; abrogate; blot; delete; erase; obliterate; overrule; revoke; zap
cancellation: abolition; abrogation
cancer: sore
candelabrum: luster
candid: aboveboard; artless; frank; guileless; honest; ingenuous; naive; open; outspoken; plain; raw; round; sincere; straight; transparent; unreserved
candidate: wannabe
candidly: aboveboard
candidness: candor
candor: honesty; sincerity; truth
cane: beat
canker: corrode; poison; sore
canny: cagey
canon: order; principle; rule
canonical: orthodox
cant: jargon; slang
cantankerous: cranky; cross; cynical; grouchy; irritable; perverse; quarrelsome; refractory; touchy; willful
cantankerousness: pet
canter: pace
canting: sanctimonious
canyon: pass
cap: exceed; excel
capabilities: stuff

capability: ability; capacity; endowment; faculty; gift; power; talent
capable: able; adequate; competent; effective; good; notable; potential; responsible; strong
capacious: ample; big; spacious
capacity: ability; brains; character; endowment; faculty; genius; gift; liking; power; strength; talent
cape: head
caper: gambol; jump; play; romp; skip; sport
capital: good; high; leading; main; major; money; principal; top-notch; wherewithal
capitulate: surrender
capitulation: surrender
caprice: fancy; humor; notion; vagary; whim
capricious: arbitrary; fancy; fickle; inconstant; irregular; screwball; skittish; uncertain; wayward; whimsical
capsize: overturn; upset
capsized: upset
capstan: purchase
captain: master
captious: cantankerous; critical; cynical; fractious; fretful; invective; moody; peevish; petulant; wayward
captivate: attach; attract; bewitch; catch; charm; enamor; enchant; fascinate; take
captivated: smitten
captivating: charismatic; seductive; winning
captivation: conquest
captivity: bond; bondage; slavery
captor: abductor
capture: abduct; abduction; apprehension; arrest; carry; get; occupation; occupy; seize; take
carbon: copy
carbonated: bubbly
carbuncle: gathering
carcass: body; corpse
card: tease
cardinal: capital; chief; head; main; master; principal
cardsharp: rook
care for: foster
care: attention; caution; charge; concern; custody; heed; keeping; management; mind; oversight; pain; prudence; surveillance; thought; trouble; worry
careen: list
careening: list
career: course; walk
carefree: jaunty; light; light-hearted
careful: accurate; attentive; cautious; chary; conscientious; deliberate; delicate; discreet; exact; frugal; gingerly; meticulous; nice; notable; observant; painstaking; particular; prudent; punctilious; safe; scrupulous; select; shy; solicitous; spare; strict; tender; thoughtful; wary; watchful
carefully: gingerly
carefulness: care; prudence
careless: blind; casual; improvident; inadvertent; lax; loose; mindless; neglectful; oblivious; perfunctory; promiscuous; reckless; remiss; slapdash; slovenly; tasteless; thoughtless; unguarded; unmindful; unwary; wanton
carelessness: listlessness; neglect
caress: dally; pet; stroke
caretaker: caregiver; warden
careworn: haggard
cargo: charge; freight; shipment
caricature: burlesque; parody; travesty
caring: empathy
carnage: massacre; shambles; slaughter
carnal: animal; brutal; brute; salacious
carnality: lust
carol: warble
carousal: feast
carouse: riot
carouser: prodigal
carp at: abuse
carper: critic
carping: critical; querulous
carriage: air; bearing; behavior; conduct; manner; poise; presence; set; walk
carry away: abduct
carry off: abduct
carry on: bear; conduct; continue; hold; operate; run; transact; wage

carry out: accomplish; do; execute; fulfill; perform; perpetrate; practice
carry over: continue
carry through: achieve
carry-all: carriage
carry: bear; bring; convey; remove; run; sustain; take; transmit; transport
carsick: queasy
cart: carriage; wagon
cartel: combination
carton: package
cartoon: caricature; outline
carve: cut
case: action; condition; cover; event; example; illustration; instance; package; plight; predicament; situation; stand; state; trim
cash: money; wealth; wherewithal
cashier: break; degrade; discharge; displace
Cassandra: killjoy
cast or throw back: reflect
cast aside: abandoned
cast down: bow; overthrow; precipitate
cast off: abandon; abandoned
cast out: abandoned
cast: calculate; character; deliver; fashion; form; glance; heap; project; send; shape; shy; stamp; throw; turn
castaway: pariah
castigate: correct; discipline; punish; scourge; whip
castigation: discipline
castle: fortification; rook
castoff: pariah
castrate: alter
casual: accidental; affable; chance; fortuitous; incidental; laid-back; nonchalant; odd; offhand; random
casualty: accident
cataclysm: calamity; catastrophe; deluge
catacomb: vault
catalogue: inventory; list; register; roll; schedule; size
cataract: cascade
catastrophe: accident; adversity; affliction; calamity; cataclysm; deluge; disaster; misadventure; misfortune
catastrophic: adverse; fatal; miserable
catch sight of: espy
catch: arrest; bag; captivate; capture; charm; cheat; clasp; detect; foul; grasp; hitch; seize; snare; strike; take
catching: contagious; infectious
catchphrase: catchword
catchword: word
catechize: examine
categorical: absolute; actual; decided; direct; explicit; express; peremptory; positive; unconditional
categorize: distinguish; distribute
category: plight
cater to: pamper
cater: furnish; serve; sustain
catering: provision
catholic: general
catholicity: tolerance
catholicon: cure-all; panacea
cattle: stock
caught: foul; spellbound
cause death or capture for: account
cause to approach: attract
cause to be: render
cause to become: render
cause to disagree: divide
cause to fall: cast
cause to smart: bite
cause to yield: bend
cause: case; create; engender; ground; induce; inducement; make; matter; motive; occasion; operate; perpetrate; place; procure; produce; raise; reason; sake; subject; work
caustic: acerbic; bitter; cutting; keen; poignant; pointed; pungent; severe; sharp; tart; trenchant; vitriolic
cauterize: sear
caution: admonish; advice; alert; calculation; care; caveat; counsel; heed; prudence; warn; warning
cautious: afraid; alert; careful; chary; deliberate; discreet; gingerly; prudent; safe; scrupulous; shy; skittish; sly; wary; watchful
cautiously: gingerly

cautiousness: calculation
cave: hole
cavil: haggle; prevaricate; quibble; quibble
caviling: critical; querulous
cavity: abyss; hole; pit
cavort: caper; romp
cease: abolish; close; die; disappear; discontinue; end; fail; halt; interrupt; leave; pass; pause; quit; refrain; stop; suspend; vanish
ceaseless: continual; eternal; incessant; perpetual
cede: abandon; abdicate; allow; deliver; give; grant; impart; relinquish; render; resign; surrender; yield
ceiling: vault
celeb: celebrity
celebrate: extol; hold; laud; observe; praise; triumph
celebrated: acclaimed; conspicuous; distinguished; eminent; famous; glorious; great; noted; prominent; splendid
celebration: feast; triumph
celebrity: distinction; eminence; fame; glory; luster; notable; note; renown; reputation; splendor
celebrityhood: celebrity
celerity: haste; hurry; rapidity; speed; velocity
celestial: heavenly
cell: hold
cellar: vault
cement: attach; bond; stick
cenobite: monk
censor out: zap
censor: blue; critic; zap
censorious: critical; cynical; invective
censurable: faulty; responsible; vicious
censure: abuse; admonish; attack; blame; chide; condemn; criticism; decry; denounce; impeach; invective; obloquy; pan; rebuke; reflection; reprimand; reproach; reprove; scold; taunt; upbraid; vituperate
censurer: critic
centaur: monster
center stage: midst
center: mean; middle; midst; nucleus
central idea: burden
central: fundamental; middle
cerebral: mental
ceremonial: formal; ritual; solemn; state
ceremonious: formal; solemn; state; stiff
ceremony: exercise; feast; form; rite; ritual; show
certain: absolute; actual; clear; confident; decided; definite; factual; indisputable; infallible; particular; positive; secure; some; special; sure; tangible; tenacious; undeniable; unequivocal; unerring
certainly: clearly
certainty: assurance; belief; trust
certificate: warrant
certification: proof
certify: ascertain; determine
certitude: certainty
cerulean: blue
cessation: abatement; check; death; pause; respite; stop; suspense
cession: abdication; grant
chafe: annoy; chide; fume; harry; irritate; offend; pester; pique; provoke; rage; tease; worry
chafed: angry
chaff: banter; mock; ridicule
chaffer: haggle
chagrin: disappointment; embarrass; embarrassment; shame
chain: band; check; shackle
chains: bond
chair: moderate; seat
challenge: brave; claim; contest; contradict; dare; defy; demand; question; run; taunt
challenged: defective
challenger: iconoclast
champ: bite
champing at the bit: eager
championship: title
chance: accident; casual; fate; fortuitous; happen; hazard; incidental; occasion; opening; opportunity; random; serendipity; start; throw; uncertain
chancy: iffy
chandelier: luster

change: adjust; affect; alter; amend; convert; differentiate; fluctuate; make; metamorphosis; modify; money; movement; permutation; resolve; reverse; revolution; skew; transform; turn; twist; variation; vary

changeable: capricious; inconstant; mercurial; mutable; slippery; uncertain; unsettled; unsteady; variable; wayward; whimsical

changeabout: about-face

changed: different; sophisticated

changeless: invariable

changeling: oaf

changing: mutable

channel: course; cut; lane; main; pass; passage; run; sound; way

chant: warble

chaos: bedlam; confusion; jumble; shambles

char: burn; scorch; sear; singe

character assassination: scandal

character: air; attribute; aura; breed; crackpot; credit; disposition; eccentric; honor; kind; make; manner; mettle; name; nature; person; personality; quality; reputation; screwball; sort; spirit; stamp; strain; stuff; style; taste; type

characteristic: accustomed; aroma; attribute; character; feature; flavor; idiosyncrasy; mark; particular; peculiar; peculiarity; property; quality; style; touch

characteristically: particularly

characterize: describe; distinguish; mark; play; qualify; stamp; style

charge: accuse; ascribe; assault; attack; bid; capacity; care; command; cost; custody; enjoin; expense; freight; impeach; impute; keeping; lay; management; office; oversight; part; place; price; requirement; trust

chargeable: responsible

charger: mount

charges: bill

charisma: glamour

charitable: benevolent; broadminded; considerate; free; generous; humane; liberal

charity: aid; bounty; generosity; kindness; virtue

charlatan: cheat; humbug; impostor; mountebank; phony; swindler

charlatanism: humbug

charm: amuse; attach; attract; beauty; beguile; bewitch; captivate; catch; delight; enamor; enchant; entrance; fascinate; glamour; grace; sorcery; take; talisman; zest

charmed: smitten

charmer: wizard

charming: amusing; dainty; delightful; exquisite; lovely; pleasing; quaint; sweet; winning

chart: map; plan

charter: hire; immunity

chary: careful; cautious; frugal; niggardly; shy; skittish; tender

Charybdis: maelstrom

chase: course; follow; hunt; run

chasm: abyss; breach; break; cleft; opening; yawn

chaste: clean; honest; modest; pure; severe; virgin; virtuous

chasten: correct; punish; scourge

chastise: chasten; discipline; punish; scourge; whip

chastisement: discipline

chastity: honor; modesty; virtue

chat: babble; converse; talk

chateau: castle

chattel: good

chattels: property

chatter: babble; gossip; jabber; talk

chatterer: gossip

chauvinist: xenophobic

chauvinistic: xenophobic

cheap: base; inexpensive; loud; miserly; tacky; tawdry; tinny

cheapen: depress

cheapjack: tinny

cheaply: low

cheat: beguile; bite; deceive; deception; delude; fool; humbug; impostor; mock; rob; rogue; rook; scoundrel; swindle; take; trick; victimize; wrong

cheater: cheat

cheating: deceit; foul; sharp; trick; wile

check: arrest; bit; block; bridle; constrain; control; counteract; curb; cushion; damp; defeat; detain; determine; frustrate; govern; guard; hinder; hindrance; impede; impediment; inhibit; limit; obstacle; obstruct; oppose; repress; restrain; retard; reverse; slacken; snub; stay; stem; stifle; stop; withhold

checkmate: beat

checkrein: bit; curb

cheek: assurance; chutzpah; gall

cheeky: saucy

cheer up: elate

cheer: amuse; beguile; comfort; console; elate; elevate; enliven; exhilarate; lighten; refresh; solace

cheerful: blithe; bright; gay; genial; glad; happy; jaunty; jolly; light; light-hearted; merry; optimistic; pleasant; ready; resilient; rosy; sanguine

cheerfully: readily

cheerfulness: animation; cheer; gaiety

cheering: amusing; cheerful; good

cheerless: dark; desolate; disconsolate; dreary; joyless; murky; sullen; uncomfortable; unhappy

cheery: cheerful; glad; light; light-hearted; merry; pleasant

cheesy: tacky

cherish: bear; entertain; foster; harbor; nurse; treasure

cherished: precious

cherubic: heavenly

chest: case; safe

chestnut: platitude

chew cud: ruminate

chew out : reprimand,

chew: bite

chic: exclusive; fashionable; smart; style

chicane: deceit

chicanery: cheat; deceit; duplicity; practice; trickery; wile

chicken-hearted: cowardly

chicken: weakling

chide: censure; rebuke; reprimand; reproach; reprove; scold; upbraid

chiding: rebuke

chief: broad; capital; fundamental; grand; great; head; high; leading; main; master; paramount; primary; principal; prominent; sovereign; top

chiefly: especially; mostly; principally

chieftain: chief; head; principal

chiffon: sheer

child: minor; scion; youngster

childbirth: labor

childish: frivolous; infantile; puerile; senile

childless: barren

childlike: childish

children: issue; race

chill: cold; cold; cold; damp; depress; dreary

chilling effect: discouragement

chilling: cool; dreary

chilly: chill; cold; raw

chimera: apparition; illusion; vision; whim

chimerical: fictitious; ideal; illusory; imaginary; romantic; visionary

chink: crack

chintzy: tacky

chit: warrant

chivalrous: brave; civil; daring; dauntless; gallant

chivalry: courage

choice morsel: delicacy

choice: alternative; delicate; elect; elegant; excellent; exclusive; exquisite; fancy; fine; option; pick; pleasure; precious; preference; rare; recherch.; select; shining; volition; will

choicest part: cream

choke: close; obstruct; stifle; strangle; stuff

choler: anger; indignation; wrath

choleric: cantankerous; excitable; grouchy; irascible; passionate; peppery; splenetic; testy

choose: affect; elect; pick; prefer; select; single; take

choosing: choice

choosy: chary; selective

chop: cut; hack; haggle; hew; rend

chore: task

chortle: laugh

chorus: burden; refrain

chosen one: favorite

chosen: elect; favorite; select

christen: call; style

Christmas: Yule

Christmastide: Yule

chronicle: account; history; narrative; record; register; relation; story

chubby: fat; plump

chuckle: laugh

chum: comrade; friend

chump change: money

church: sanctuary

churl: blackguard; yahoo

churlish: coarse; cross; loutish; morose; peppery; sulky

churn: boil; roil

Cimmerian: dark

cinch: belt

cincture: band

cinture: belt

Circe: siren

circle: club; company; confine; connection; coterie; orbit; party; revolve; ring; round; set; society; sphere

circlet: circle; ring

circling: about

circuit: circle; revolution

circuitous: tortuous

circular: bill; circuitous; round

circulate: emit; issue; negotiate; pass; revolve; spread; utter

circulating: current

circulation: air

circumambulatory: circuitous

circumference: border; boundary; brim; circle; circuit; periphery

circumlocutory: circuitous

circumscribe: confine; enclose; limit; restrain; restrict

circumspect: alert; attentive; careful; cautious; chary; deliberate; discreet; gingerly; prudent; scrupulous; thoughtful; wary; watchful

circumspection: calculation; care; caution; prudence

circumspectness: caution

circumstance: case; condition; event; incident; occurrence; particular; phenomenon

circumstances: condition; information; place; position; situation; state

circumstantial: particular

circumvent: orbit

citadel: castle; fortification

citation: extract; reference

cite: enumerate; plead

city: community; town

civil: affable; courteous; fair; polite; respectful

civility: attention; compliment

civilize: polish

civilized: civil; refined

claim: assert; assertion; call; command; contend; demand; maintain; purport; requirement; right; title

clamber: scramble

clamor: bedlam; brawl; cry; disorder; exclamation; hubbub; noise; racket; uproar

clamorous: boisterous; loud; noisy; obstreperous; vociferous

clamp: brace; fasten

clan: people; race

clandestine: secret; sly; stealthy; surreptitious; underground; underhand

clang: blast; clash

clanger: blunder

clank: clash

clannish: exclusive

clap: clash

claptrap: blarney

clarified: clean; refined

clarify: clear; concentrate; elucidate; explain; purge; rationalize; show

clarity: perspicuity

clash: conflict; hit; quarrel; shock; strife; struggle

clasp: brace; embrace; fasten; grasp; strain

class: arrange; breed; brood; caste; circle; kind; milieu; order; quality; range; rank; set; sort; type; variety

classic example: paradigm

classic: chaste

classification: system; type

classify: arrange; digest; distinguish; distribute; divide; range; rank; schedule; sort

clatter: clash; noise

clause: passage

claw: lacerate; scramble

clean: chaste; cleanse; clear; fair; pure; purge; sanitary; sleek; sweet; wash

cleanly: clean

cleanse: clean; heal; purge; wash

cleansing: wash

clear-eyed: earthy; realistic

clear-headed: keen; realistic; sane

clear-sighted: keen; perspicacious; realistic

clear-thinking: sane

clear: absolve; apparent; bright; broad; candid; certain; clean; conspicuous; definite; discharge; distinct; evident; excuse; exonerate; explicit; express; fair; free; limpid; lively; lucid; luminous; manifest; obvious; open; pardon; patent; pellucid; perspicuous; plain; positive; purge; quit; resolve; self-evident; serene; sharp; sheer; simple; strong; transparent; undeniable; unequivocal; unmistakable; vacate; vindicate; visible; vivid

clearing up: account

clearly: clear

clearness: perspicuity

cleavage: cleft

cleave: adhere; cut; divide; part; rend; separate; sever; stick

cleaving: adherent; cleft

cleft: crack; flaw; gorge; opening; rent

clemency: compassion; grace; mercy

clement: compassionate; gentle; gracious; lenient; merciful; mild

clerk: employee

clever: able; acute; adroit; apt; bright; cagey; capable; dexterous; expert; good; handy; ingenious; intelligent; keen; luminous; Machiavellian; neat; notable; piquant; pleasant; politic; ready; sagacious; sharp; skillful; smart; tactful; witty

cleverness: address; aptitude; art; capacity

clich,: commonplace; platitude

clichéd: hack; hackneyed

client: patron

clientele: custom

cliff: bluff

climacteric: critical

climate: aura; zone

climax: apex; crisis

climb or go upward: ascend

climb: ascend; ascend; mount; run; scale

climber: parvenu

climbing: climb

clime: zone

clinch: fasten

cling to: adhere; cherish

cling: hang; hold; stick

clinging: adherent; tenacious

clinic: hospital

clinker: washout

clip: clasp; crop; cut; pare; trim

clipping: trim

clique: association; band; body; circle; club; coterie; gang; knot; party; ring; set

cliquey: clannish

cliquish: clannish; exclusive

cloak: cover; hide; mask; pretense; screen; shroud

clock-watching: shiftless

cloddish: loutish

clog: close; foul; hamper; obstruct; retard

cloister: refuge

cloistered: private; retired

clonal: identical

cloned: identical

close to: about; about

close-at-hand: handy

close-by: handy

close-fisted: niggardly; parsimonious; penurious; sordid

close-fistedness: parsimony

close-minded: small-minded

close-mouthed: close; secret; silent; uncommunicative

close: about; adjacent; block; bosom; complete; conclusion; cozy; end; exact; express; faithful; familiar; fast; finish; handy; immediate; intimate; miserly; near; niggardly; obstruct; parsimonious; penurious; rise; shut; sordid; stingy; stop; strict; terminate; twilight; warm

closed-door: xenophobic

closed-minded: bigoted

closed: blind; close; shut

closefisted: close

closely associated: intimate

closely: immediately; nearly

closeness: fidelity; parsimony; presence; rapport; vicinity

cloth: spread

clothe: apparel; array; cover; deck; dress; endow; garb; habit

clothes: apparel; array; dress; garb; raiment; wardrobe

clothing: clothes; dress; garb; raiment; wardrobe

cloud over: mist

cloud: dim; dim; fog; fog; haze; haze; mist; obfuscate; shade; shroud

clouded: cloudy; dirty; dusky; obscure; sullen; turbid

cloudless: bright; clear; fair

cloudlike: nebulous

cloudy: cloudy; dusky; heavy; murky; nebulous; obscure; somber; turbid

clown: droll; fool; yahoo; zany

clownish: comical

cloy: pall; satiate

cloying: luscious; saccharine; saccharine

club: association; circle; combination; coterie; lodge; society; stick

clue: guide

clump: shamble

clumsy: awkward; bulky; crude; heavy; loutish; maladroit; stiff; uncouth; ungainly; unskillful; unwieldy

cluster: bunch; knot

clutch: catch; clasp; grasp; herd; seize

clutches: grasp

clutter: disorder; scramble

co-opt: monopolize

coach: guru; instruct; kibitz

coaching: instruction

coadjutor: ally

coal car: tender

coaler: tender

coalesce: blend; close; combine; fuse; unite

coalescence: close; combination

coalition: alliance; combination; confederation; league; union

coarse: awkward; barbarian; base; broad; brutal; common; crude; fat; foul; gross; heavy; homely; ill-mannered; indecent; loud; loutish; low; mean; obscene; rank; ribald; robust; rough; rude; scurrilous; tasteless; unrefined; vulgar

coast: beach; shore

coat: spread

coating: deposit; scale; size; skin

coax: cajole; entice; flatter

cockshut: twilight

cocktail lounge: bar

cocky: saucy; uppity

coddle: pamper

code of behavior: etiquette

codex: volume

codify: digest

coed: mixed

coeducational: mixed

coerce: compel; constrain; force; oblige; terrorize

coercion: force

coercive: compulsory

coeval: contemporary

coexist with: accompany

coexisting: contemporary

coffer: safe

cog: cheat

cogency: fitness; strength

cogent: felicitous; intimate; potent; powerful; strong; valid

cogitate: agitate; meditate; muse; ponder; reflect; think

cogitating: reflective

cogitation: reflection; study; thought

cognition: perception

cognitive: mental

cognizable: perceptible

cognizance: notice

cognizant or conscious (of): aware

cognizant: conscious; sensible; sentient

cognomen: title

cohere: adhere; connect; stick

cohesion: coherence

cohesive: solid; tenacious

cohort: comrade; sidekick

coil: twist; wind

coin of the realm: money

coin: fabricate; money

coincide: agree; concur; correspond

coincident: contemporary

coined: fabulous

colander: riddle

cold water: discouragement

cold-blooded: apathetic; cold; cool

cold: apathetic; chill; cool; dead; half-hearted; raw; senseless; sharp

coldness: chill; phlegm; reserve
collapse: cataclysm; crash; smash
collapsed: flat
colleague: ally; associate; comrade; helper; partner
collect: aggregate; assemble; convene; gather; mass; meet; muster; pick; pile; raise; troop
collected: calm; cool; easygoing; sedate; serene; sober; unruffled
collection: body; bunch; drove; heap; mass; multitude; muster; number; parcel; pile; set; variety
collector: aesthete; dilettante
college: academic
collegiate: academic
collide: clash; conflict; hit; shock
collision: brush; clash; conflict; shock; smash
colloquial: informal; vernacular; vulgar
colloquialism: slang
colloquy: conference; converse; talk
colonize: settle
colophon: device
color: stain; tint; tint
colorful: picturesque
colorless: lackluster; pale; pallid; pallid; tacky
colors: appearance
colossal: enormous; giant; gigantic; huge; large; mammoth; monstrous; tremendous; vast
colossus: giant
coltish: playful
column: pillar; post; upright
coma: trance
comb: tease
combat: action; assault; battle; conflict; contend; contention; contest; encounter; fight; oppose; passage; skirmish
combating: opposition
combative: quarrelsome; scrappy
comber: breaker
combination (def: combine
combination: alliance; association; blend; junction; league; mass; mixture; party; ring; system; union
combine into a mass: aggregate
combine: agree; ally; associate; associate; blend; combination; concur; conjoin; connect; conspire; form; fuse; join; league; mingle; mix; organize; twist; unite; unite
combined: aggregate
come or get to be: wax
come across: strike
come and go: yo-yo
come forth: emanate; emerge; issue; rise
come into existence: rise
come into season: ripen
come into sight or view: appear
come next: follow
come out: debut
come short: fail
come to an agreement or arrangement or understanding: agree
come to pass: happen; occur
come to terms: arrange; treat
come to: get; reach
come together: assemble; close; meet
come up to: touch
come up: rise; start
come upon: discern; hit; meet
come: arrive; issue; result; start
comedian: droll; zany
comedy: burlesque; play
comeliness: beauty; grace
comely: beautiful; becoming; fair; handsome; pretty
comer: arrival
comfort: cheer; cherish; consolation; console; ease; ease; encourage; reassure; relief; relieve; satisfaction; solace; solace; soothe
comfortable: convenient; cozy; easy
comforting: cozy
comfortless: dreary; forlorn
comfy: cozy
comic: amusing; comical; humorous; risible; zany
comical: amusing; droll; facetious; funny; humorous; jocose; laughable; ludicrous; ridiculous; risible; waggish; zany
coming out: debut
coming: appearance; arrival
command: appoint; authority; bid; charge; control; decree; direct; empire; enjoin; govern; head; instruct; instruction; mandate;

order; power; requirement; rule; tell; will; wish; word
commander in chief: head; master
commander: chief; head; master
commanding: dominant; magisterial
commandment: command; decree
comme il faut: right
commemorate: celebrate
commemoration: feast; memento; trophy
commence: begin; initiate; open; start
commencement: beginning; opening; start
commend: approve; celebrate; compliment; eulogize; extol; praise; recommend
commendable: good; worthy
commendably: well
commendation: compliment; credit; panegyric; praise
commensal: symbiotic
commensurate: adequate; equal; even
comment: criticism; gloss; note; notice; observation; observe; remark; remark; speech
commentary: comment; exposition; gloss; note
commerce: business; exchange
commingle: blend; fuse; mingle; mix
commingled: mixed
comminute: grind; pound
commiserate: pity
commiserating: sympathetic
commiseration: compassion; pity
commission: authorize; charge; delegate; mandate; order; warrant
commit: compel; incarcerate; perpetrate; refer; trust
commitment: trust
committed: single-minded
commodities: good
common people: mass
common sense: intellect; judgment; prudence; reason; wisdom
common-looking: ordinary
common-sense: advisable; judicious; legitimate
common: accustomed; cheap; coarse; commonplace; community; conventional; current; customary; dominant; familiar; general; habitual; household; humble; mean; mediocre; mutual; ordinary; plain; popular; prevailing; prevalent; profane; rife; simple; stale; stock; trite; usual; vulgar; worldly
commonalty: people
commonly: generally
commonplace: common; hack; hackneyed; household; lackluster; mediocre; ordinary; pedestrian; plain; platitude; prosaic; stale; stereotyped; stock; trite; vernacular
commonwealth: community; nation; state
commotion: ado; confusion; disturbance; excitement; fuss; hurly-burly; maelstrom; riot; ruckus; ruffle; scramble; sensation; shock; stir; storm; tumult; turmoil; uproar
commrce: trade
communal: common
communicable: contagious; infectious
communicate with: access
communicate: convey; correspond; deliver; disclose; give; impart; mention; reveal; signify; speak; talk; tell
communication: advice; language; speech; statement; talk
communicative: eloquent; outgoing
community: development; hamlet; order; people; society; state; town; village
commutation: permutation
commute: change; exchange
compact: agreement; alliance; bargain; bond; brief; close; concise; contract; convention; firm; hard; laconic; league; pact; pithy; solid; solid; stiff; strong; summary; terse; trim
compactness: brevity
companion: acquaintance; associate; attendant; comrade; familiar; follower; friend
companionable: social
companionship: association; company; society

company: assembly; association; band; body; business; circle; concern; crowd; drove; firm; flock; gang; gathering; guest; house; knot; number; pack; party; presence; run; set; society; society; troop
compare favorably: agree
compare: balance; check; confer; contrast
comparison: contrast; illustration; proportion
compartment: apartment; division
compass: circle; extent; grasp; range; reach; span; sphere; spread; stretch
compassion: clemency; empathy; kindness; mercy; pity; sympathy;
compassionate: gracious; humane; kind; kindly; merciful; mild; soft; sympathetic; tender
compassionateness: sympathy,
compatibility: rapport
compatible: consistent; consonant
compatriot: countryman
compeer: associate; comrade; equal; peer
compel: command; constrain; drive; exact; force; impel; make; oblige
compelled: compulsory
compelling: compulsory; stringent; urgent
compendious: pithy
compendium: abbreviation; abridgment; abstract; brief; summary; synopsis
compensate for: cancel; cover; recompense
compensate: balance; pay; requite; reward
compensation: consideration; recompense; redress; reparation; restitution; retribution; reward; satisfaction; wage
compete or contend with: rival
compete with: encounter
compete: compare; contend; contest; contest; play; run; scramble; strive; vie
competence: ability; capacity; power
competency: ability; capacity; power
competent: able; adequate; capable; effective; equal; good; proficient; skillful; strong; sufficient
competing: rival; vying
competition: contention; contest; emulation; game; meet; opposition; race; ring
competitive: rival; vying
competitor: antagonist; opponent; rival
complacency: conceit
complacent: conceited; peaceful; self-satisfied; smug
complain: growl; kvetch; murmur; protest; snarl; storm; whine
complainer: kvetch
complaining: cross; querulous
complaint: affection; ailment; disease; disorder; exclamation; malady; murmur; plaint
complaisant: bland; civil; congenial
complement: reciprocal; supplement; supplement
complete: absolute; accomplish; achieve; aggregate; blank; clean; close; complement; consummate; dead; do; downright; effect; end; entire; execute; exquisite; finish; finished; fulfill; grand; ideal; intact; mature; perfect; piece; plump; radical; rank; regular; ripe; round; solid; sound; strict; supplement; terminate; thorough; total; unbroken; unconditional; unmitigated; unqualified; unreserved; utter; whole
completed: finished; mature; perfect; ready; thorough
completely: absolutely; clean; clearly; even; right; sheer; stark
completeness: integrity
completion: accomplishment; conclusion; end
complex: abstract; abstruse; composite; difficult; elaborate; hard; knotty; system
complexion: air; spirit
complexus: complex
compliance: consent; deference; resignation
compliant: easy; flexible; malleable; obedient; obsequious; pliant; soft; submissive; supple
complicate: embarrass; encumber; entangle; perplex; snarl

complicated: abstract; complex; complex; elaborate; hard; knotty
complication: complex; snarl
compliment: praise
complot: conspire; contrive; plan; plot
comply with: fulfill; meet
comply: acquiesce; agree; conform; consent; follow; observe; submit
complying: easy
component: element; ingredient; part; partial
comportment: decorum
compos mentis: sane
compose: accommodate; adapt; calm; draw; form; heal; make; manufacture; prepare; quell; quiet; reconcile; settle; still; weave
composed: calm; cool; easygoing; even; patient; peaceful; sedate; serene; sober; staid; unruffled
composing: component
composite: combination; complex
composition: piece; structure; theme
composure: balance; calm; patience; poise; serenity; temper
compound: blend; combination; combine; complex; composite; mingle; mix; mixture; prepare; unite
comprehend: comprise; conceive; cover; embrace; grasp; include; involve; know; penetrate; realize; see; take; understand
comprehending: comprehensive
comprehensible: clear
comprehension: grasp; knowledge
comprehensive: capacious; extensive; grand; summary; sweeping; wide
compress: abbreviate; compact; condense; constrict; contract; cram; crush; pack
compressed: close; firm
compression: abbreviation; abridgment
comprise: comprehend; cover; embrace; include; involve
compromise: agree
compulsion: force; necessity
compulsive need: addiction
compunction: pang; qualm; regret; remorse; repentance; scruple
computation: calculation; cast; estimate
compute: calculate; cast; estimate; number; reckon; tell
comrade: associate; attendant; companion
comtemplate: reflect
comtemplation: reflection
con man: impostor
con: adverse; cheat; swindle; wangle
concavity: hole
conceal: bury; envelop; harbor; hide; mask; screen; secrete; shade; shroud; whitewash
concealed: blind; clandestine; dark; latent; mysterious; occult; recondite; secret; ulterior
concealment: cover; curtain; deceit; mask
concede: accept; accord; acknowledge; admit; agree; allow; comply; confess; grant; own; vouchsafe; yield
conceit: arrogance; assumption; egotism; pride; vagary; vainglory; vanity
conceited: arrogant; big; egocentric; opinionated; proud; smug; vain
conceitedness: wind
conceivable: earthly
conceive of: imagine
conceive: breed; comprehend; fancy; image; imagine; invent; realize; think; understand
concentrate on: grasp
concentrate: condense; contract; intensify
concentrated: close; heavy; intent; laconic; rapt; single; terse
concentrating: preoccupied
concept: notion; thought; universal
conception: conceit; fancy; idea; ideal; image; notion; opinion; subject; theory; thought; view; vision
concern: bear; business; care; company; consequence; consideration; empathy; fear; firm; implicate; part; regard; sympathy; touch; trouble; worry

concerned: anxious; careful; considerate; solicitous; upset
concerning: about
concert: unanimity; unity
concession: admission; allowance; grant
conciliate: appease; favor; pacify; placate; propitiate; reconcile
conciliatory: pacific
concise: brief; compact; curt; laconic; pithy; sententious; short; summary; terse
conciseness: brevity
conclave: assembly
conclude: close; complete; conjecture; decide; deduce; determine; do; end; finish; fulfill; gather; judge; reason; suppose; terminate; transact
concluded: complete
concluding: last
conclusion: catastrophe; close; end; finish; guess; head; issue; judgment; opinion; result; speculation; twilight
conclusive: authoritative; decisive; final; last; strong
concoct: arrange; contrive; devise; feign; hatch; invent; meditate; mingle; plan; plot; project
concocted: fictitious
concoction: mix
concomitant: attendant
concord: agreement; assent; bargain; consent; harmony; peace; rapport; unity
concordant: consistent; consonant; harmonious
concordat: bargain; compact; contract; pact
concourse: company; gathering; street
concupiscence: lust
concupiscent: carnal; licentious; salacious; wanton
concur: accommodate; accord; acquiesce; agree; assent; consent; conspire; correspond; meet
concurrence: assent; consent
concussion: shock
condemn: blame; censure; curse; decry; denounce; doom; reproach; repudiate; scorch; upbraid
condemnation: abuse; blame; censure; doom; reproach
condensation: abbreviation; abridgment; abstract; brevity; synopsis
condense: abbreviate; abridge; abstract; compact; compress; concentrate; contract; gather; shorten
condensed: brief; close; compact; firm; short; summary
condescend: decline; stoop; vouchsafe
condescending: gracious
condescension: grace; stoop
condign: just
condiment: relish; seasoning
condition: aspect; case; credit; determine; fitness; if; pass; plight; position; posture; predicament; provision; quality; shape; situation; standing; state; status; status; trim
conditional: subject
conditioning: fitness
conditions: medium
condolence: pity
condone: abet; blink; pardon; recommend
conduce: abet
conduct or deport or comport oneself: act
conduct oneself: behave
conduct: action; administer; air; bear; bearing; behavior; bring; carriage; carry; convey; course; direct; escort; govern; guide; introduce; lead; manage; management; order; procedure; regulate; rule; run; show; superintend; take; transact; walk
conductor: guide
conduit: main
conern: reference
confabulate: converse
confabulation: talk
confederacy: alliance; combination; confederation; league; ring; union
confederate: accomplice; ally; associate; auxiliary; band; join; league; sidekick
confederation: alliance; league; marriage
confer: advise; cast; consult; deliberate; endow; give; grant; heap;

impart; parley; present; show; talk; vouchsafe

conference: congress; convention; parley; talk

confess: acknowledge; admit; allow; own; tell; unburden

confession: admission

confidant: friend; intimate

confide or trust in: stay

confide in: credit; trust

confide: lean

confidence game: swindle; trick

confidence man: humbug; impostor; swindler

confidence: assurance; belief; certainty; credit; faith; hope; trust

confident: brave; certain; childish; forward; hopeful; optimistic; positive; sanguine; secure; sure; unabashed

confidential: bosom; close; intimate; private

configuration: form; silhouette; structure

confine: bind; border; bound; cabin; constrain; detain; hold; incarcerate; limit; margin; pound; restrain; restrict; rim; shackle; shut; stint; tie

confined: close; pent-up; small-minded; vernacular

confinement: bondage; captivity; custody

confines: pale

confirm: affirm; approve; bear; confess; harden; prove; ratify; resolve; sanction; settle; support; sustain; sustain

confirmation: proof

confirmed: chronic; firm; habitual

conflagration: flame

conflict: action; agitation; battle; brush; clash; combat; contention; contest; encounter; fight; friction; hostility; meet; passage; skirmish; strife; struggle; tussle

conflicting: adverse; contrary

conform or correspond to: answer

conform: accommodate; adapt; agree; answer; comply; correspond; follow; observe

conformable: consistent; orthodox

conformably: accordingly

conformal: formal

conformant: consonant; conventional; decent

conforming: consistent; conventional; even; formal; orthodox; regular

conformist: formal; orthodox

conformity: agreement; fashion; form; harmony; keeping

confound: abash; affront; astonish; bewilder; confuse; dazzle; disorder; elude; nonplus; perplex; puzzle; stagger; stun

confrere: comrade

confront: affront; encounter; face; meet; oppose; repel; resist; withstand

confronting: adverse

confuse: abash; affront; amaze; bewilder; bother; disconcert; disorder; elude; embarrass; entangle; jumble; mess; mix; nonplus; obfuscate; perplex; perplex; perturb; puzzle; scramble; shame; snarl; surprise; trouble

confused: ashamed; blank; blind; chaotic; cloudy; crazy; dim; giddy; groggy; indefinite; indiscriminate; lost; miscellaneous; nebulous; promiscuous

confusing: indefinite

confusion: bedlam; disorder; disturbance; embarrassment; fog; hubbub; hurry; jumble; litter; maelstrom; mess; moil; riot; ruffle; shambles; snarl; turmoil

confute: refute

congeal: set

congenial: harmonious; pleasant; sympathetic

congenital: inborn; innate; native

congeries: mass

conglomeration: mass; mixture

congratulate: compliment

congregate: assemble; convene; meet; muster

congregation: company; gathering; muster

congress: assembly

congruence: harmony

congruity: coherence; harmony; keeping

congruous: becoming; consistent; consonant; harmonious

conjectural: iffy

conjecture: assumption; cast; deduce; forecast; guess; imagine; speculation; surmise; suspect; suspicion; theory; wonder

conjoin: combine; connect; couple; join; link; meet; mingle; unite

conjunction: combination; connection

conjuncture: condition

conjuration: necromancy

conjurer: wizard

conjuring: magic

conjuror: magician

connect: add; ally; assemble; associate; attach; conjoin; couple; fasten; hitch; involve; join; link; meet; place; relate; tie; unite

connected with: about

connected: near

connection: alliance; association; attachment; bearing; bond; coherence; combination; junction; kinship; link; relation; relationship; respect; tie

connective: connection; link

connive: wangle; wangle

conniving: dishonest

connoisseur: aesthete; critic; dilettante; expert

connotation: meaning; sense

conquer: beat; crush; defeat; master; overcome; overpower; overthrow; overturn; quell; reduce; subdue; vanquish

conquest: triumph; victory

consanguinity: relationship

conscience: scruple

conscienceless: unscrupulous

conscientious: careful; ethical; faithful; good; just; punctilious; religious; scrupulous; upright

conscious: sensible; sentient

consciousness: feeling; sense; sensibility; spirit

consecrate: devote; sanctify

consecrated: hallowed; holy; sacred; sacred

consecration: devotion

consecutive: successive

consensus: consent; fame

consent to: ratify

consent: accept; acquiesce; agree; assent; comply; concur; convention; permission

consequence: account; attendant; concern; consideration; effect; end; event; importance; issue; mark; matter; moment; outcome; purpose; result; sequence; significance; weight

consequent: attendant; material; momentous

consequential: big; grave; great; high; significant; weighty

consequently: accordingly; therefore

conservative: moderate; orthodox; reactionary

conserve: jam; preserve

consider apart: abstract

consider together with: accompany

consider: account; agitate; call; cast; contemplate; debate; deem; deliberate; digest; discuss; entertain; heed; hold; judge; ponder; premeditate; reckon; reflect; regard; repute; respect; revolve; see; study; suppose; suspect; take; think; treat; weigh

considerable: good; great; handsome; respectable; sensible; substantial

considerably: well

considerate: charitable; chivalrous; discreet; obliging; tender; thoughtful

consideration: account; attention; condition; debate; delicacy; ground; heed; honor; mercy; mind; moment; note; reflection; regard; remark; sake; score; speculation; study; thought; view

considered: deliberate; judicious; studied; voluntary

considering: consideration

consign: devote; refer; trust

consignment: shipment

consist or be composed of: comprise

consist of: number

consistency: body; coherence; harmony; keeping

consistent: consonant; harmonious; uniform

consolation: comfort; solace

console: comfort; encourage; solace

consolidate: compact; condense; join; unite

consolidated: solid

consonance: harmony

consonant: consistent; harmonious

consort with: accompany

consort: associate; mix; troop

conspectus: brief; digest

conspicuous: apparent; bare; bold; clear; distinguished; eminent; gaudy; manifest; notable; notable; obtrusive; outstanding; patent; prominent; remarkable; salient; shining; splendid; visible

conspicuousness: eminence

conspiracy: combination; machination; plot; scheme

conspire: concur; contrive; plot

constancy: loyalty; stability

constant: assiduous; certain; chronic; close; consistent; continual; diligent; durable; faithful; firm; incessant; invariable; loyal; perennial; permanent; perpetual; persistent; regular; stable; standing; staunch; steadfast; steady; true; uniform; usual

constantly: ever

consternation: alarm; dismay; fear; fright; horror; indignation; terror

constituent: component; element; ingredient; material; member; part; partial

constitute: appoint; create; form; make; organize

constitution: character; make; state; temper; temperament

constitutional: organic; radical; walk

constrain: compel; control; drive; force; impel; oblige; restrain; tie; urge

constrained: awkward; bound; stiff

constraining: compulsory; stringent

constraint: bond; force; limit; reserve; stint

constrict: compress; incarcerate

constrictive: astringent

construct: erect; fabricate; fashion; form; make; manufacture; organize; raise; rear; weave

construction: building; edifice; make; structure

construe: accept; interpret

consult together: confer

consult: advise; deliberate; talk

consultation: conference; counsel

consume: absorb; burn; corrode; destroy; exhaust; expend; finish; monopolize; spend; swallow; take; use; waste

consumed with: active

consummate: accomplish; achieve; complete; effect; execute; exquisite; fine; finish; finished; fulfill; ideal; matchless; perfect; preeminent; ripe; unmitigated

consummated: complete; finished

consummation: accomplishment; achievement; issue

consumption: waste

contact: access; touch

contagious: infectious

contain: accommodate; comprehend; comprise; cover; embrace; embrace; have; hold; include; involve

container: can; case

contaminate: corrupt; debase; poison; pollute; roil; stain; sully; taint

contaminated: corrupt; dirty

contamination: corruption; taint

contemn: abominate; despise; disdain; scorn; sneer; snub; spurn

contemplate: consider; digest; intend; mean; meditate; muse; ponder; project; purpose; study; think; view; watch; weigh

contemplation: consideration; mind; prospect; speculation; study; theory; thought; view

contemplative: meditative; pensive; reflective; sedate; subjective; thoughtful

contemporaneous: contemporary

contempt: disdain; ignominy; indignity; scorn; shame; slight; venom

contemptible: abject; abominable; base; despicable; dirty; ignoble; ignominious; mean; miserable; paltry; pitiful; rotten; scurvy; shabby; sorry; vile; wretched

contemptuous: cynical; derogatory; disdainful; haughty; insolent; opprobrious; supercilious

contemptuousness: disdain

contend against: contest; encounter

contend for: contest

contend with or against: play

contend: argue; argue; combat; compete; conflict; contest; debate; fight; maintain; run; scramble; strive; struggle; vie

content: clash; contentment; happiness; reconcile; satisfy

contented: content; easy; glad; happy; proud

contentedness: happiness

contention: conflict; contest; contest; controversy; debate; dispute; emulation; position; quarrel

contentious: acrimonious; scrappy

contentiousness: friction

contentment: ease; happiness; satisfaction

contest: argue; battle; brush; combat; compete; conflict; contention; dispute; fight; game; meet; race; ring; struggle

contestant: adversary; antagonist; competitor; opponent; rival

contiguity: touch

contiguous: adjacent; adjoining; near

continent: abstemious; chaste; temperate

contingency: accident; case; chance; condition

contingent: accidental; incidental; subject

continual: constant; incessant; perennial; persistent

continually: always

continuance: stability

continuant: consonant

continuation: extension; standing

continue: abide; dwell; endure; extend; hold; keep; last; lengthen; maintain; persevere; persist; preserve; proceed; protract; remain; run; stand; stay; survive

continued or dull pain: ache

continued: late; persistent

continuing: chronic; perpetual; standing

continuous: assiduous; chronic; consecutive; continual; endless; entire; incessant; perpetual; persistent; solid; standing; steady; unbroken

continuously: ever

contort: twist; warp

contorted: misshapen

contour: outline; silhouette; silhouette

contra: adverse

contract: abbreviate; abridge; agree; agreement; bargain; bond; compact; compress; condense; constrict; convention; deal; decrease; diminish; obligation; pact; reduce; shorten; shrink; shrivel

contracting: astringent

contraction: abbreviation; abridgment; decrease; gather

contradict: cross; deny; dispute; oppose; traverse

contradiction: clash

contradictoriness: repugnance

contradictory: ambivalent; contrary; incompatible; incompatible; incongruous

contraption: gadget

contrariety: antipathy; contrast; difference; discrepancy; opposition; repugnance; strife

contrary: adverse; contradictory; different; froward; hostile; incompatible; incongruous; inimical; opposite; perverse; repugnant; reverse; reverse; stubborn; wayward; willful; wrongheaded

contrast: compare; difference; differentiate; oppose; opposition

contrasted: different

contrasty: strong

contravene: break; counteract; oppose; transgress; traverse

contribute assistance: administer

contribute: administer; concur; give; provide; render; serve

contribution: collection; donation; gift; share

contrite: bad; penitent; remorseful

contriteness: repentance

contrition: regret; remorse; repentance

contrivance: action; device; expedient; gadget; plan; scheme; stratagem; tool; wile

contrive: arrange; cast; conspire; design; devise; forecast; form; hatch; invent; manage; meditate; plan; plot; prepare; procure; project; scheme; weave

contriver: artist

contriving: designing

control: administer; authority; bit; bridle; check; command; curb; direct; discipline; disposition; empire; govern; hold; influence; manage; management; monopolize; oversight; poise; possess; power; reduce; regulate; regulation; repress; rule; slacken; stop; subject; superintend; surveillance; sway

controlled: composed; sober; unruffled

controlling: dominant

controversy: argument; conflict; contention; contest; debate; dispute; quarrel; question; variance

controvert: agitate; argue; contest; contradict; deny; dispute

controvertible: questionable

contumacious: contrary; defiant; disobedient; froward; intractable; mutinous; obstinate; perverse; rebellious; recalcitrant; refractory; stout; stubborn; willful

contumacy: rebellion

contumelious: arrogant; disdainful; injurious; supercilious

contumely: abuse; affront; arrogance; contempt; disdain; indignity; insult; invective; mockery; obloquy; scorn; slight; taunt

conundrum: knot; riddle

convene: assemble; assemble; call; meet; muster; sit; summon; troop

convenience: advantage; occasion

convenient: competent; good; handy; helpful; opportune; proper; right; seasonable; serviceable; utilitarian

convent: cloister

convention: assembly; bargain; compact; conference; congress; contract; custom; etiquette; form; muster

conventional: academic; customary; decorous; formal; formal; orthodox; stereotyped

conventionality: fashion

converge: meet

conversant: familiar; proficient

conversation: commerce; converse; parley; speech; talk

conversational: colloquial; vernacular

converse: commerce; confer; parley; reverse; speak; talk

conversion: change

convert: change; make; neophyte; resolve; transform; turn

convey: bear; bring; carry; cede; grant; pass; run; send; take; transmit; transport

conveyance: carriage; grant; transport

convict: criminal

conviction: belief; certainty; thought

convince: argue; lead; persuade; reason; reconcile; satisfy; win

convinced: certain; clear; confident; positive; sure

convincing: plausible; powerful; stringent

convivial: gay; jolly; jovial

convocation: assembly; convention; gathering

convoke: assemble; call; convene; marshal; mass; muster; summon

convoy: accompany; bring; conduct; escort; guard

convulsion: cataclysm; paroxysm; rampage

cool: apathetic; blasé; brave; calm; chill; cold; composed; dead; easygoing; fresh; half-hearted; moderate; nonchalant; sedate; serene; sober; stoical; temperate; unruffled

coolness: composure; indifference; phlegm; reserve; temper

coop up: pound

cooperate: concur; conspire; help

cooperating: symbiotic

cooperative: community; symbiotic

coordinate: equal; organize

cope with: encounter

cope: compete

copious: abundant; ample; fat; fluent; fruitful; generous; large; opulent; plentiful; prodigal; rich; wealthy

copiousness: abundance; exuberance; plenty; profusion
copse: brush; cover; stand
copula: link
copy: ape; counterfeit; duplicate; image; imitate; issue; model; number; pattern; reproduce; trace
copyrighted: patent
coquet: philander
cord: band; bond; tie
cordial: affable; friendly; genial; warm
cordially: kindly
core: abbreviation; abstract; burden; midst; nucleus; pit
cork: stop
cornball: hackneyed
corner: monopolize; quagmire
corny: hackneyed
corporal: physical
corporation: abdomen; association; body; business; company; concern; firm; society
corporeal: corporal; material; palpable; physical; substantial; tangible
corposant: ephemeral
corpse: body; carcass; remain
corpselike: cadaverous
corpulent: fat; obese; plump; stout
correct: accurate; advisable; becoming; better; cure; discipline; exact; fix; improve; just; legitimate; mend; orthodox; patch; precise; proper; punish; rectify; redress; reduce; reform; remedy; right; scourge; sound; staid; straight; true; unerring
correction: discipline; mend; reform; reformation
corrective: cosmetic; remedy; therapeutic
correctly: well
correctness: propriety
correlation: system
correlative: mutual; reciprocal
correspond: accord; agree; answer; check; conform
correspondence: coherence; harmony; parallel; parity; similarity
correspondent: equal; harmonious; parallel
corresponding: parallel; same
correspondingly: accordingly
corrigendum: appendix
corroborate: confirm; ratify; support; sustain
corroboration: testimony
corrode: bite; fret
corrosion: fret
corrosive: caustic
corrupt: abandoned; abject; bad; base; buy; contaminate; debase; depraved; dishonest; evil; immoral; libertine; lost; poison; pollute; rot; rotten; seduce; shameless; sinister; spoil; stain; sully; taint; tamper; ugly; unclean; unwholesome; venal; vicious; wicked
corrupted: base; corrupt; depraved; morbid; ungodly
corrupting: insidious; noxious
corruption: abomination; abuse; evil; rot; taint; vice
corsair: pirate
coruscate: sparkle
coruscating: bright
coruscation: sparkle
cosmeticize: beautify
cosmopolitan: worldly
cosmos: system
cost: charge; expense; price; value
costly: dear; expensive; high; precious; rich; valuable
costume: apparel; clothes; dress; garb; raiment
cot: cabin; cottage; hole; hut; lodge; shanty
coterie: association; band; body; circle; club; connection; gang; party; ring; set; sphere
cottage: cabin; hut; lodge; shanty
council: assembly; congress
counsel: admonish; advice; advise; advocate; caution; kibitz; lore; recommend
counselor-at-law: advocate
counselor: advocate; counsel
count on: expect
count: account; calculate; compute; deem; enumerate; estimate; matter; number; peer; recite; reckon; score; tell; think
countenance: abet; aspect; back; encourage; expression; face; favor; sanction; support; sustain; uphold; visage
counter: bar; contrary; stand

counteract: balance; remedy; resist
counteraction: opposition; remedy
counterbalance: balance; cancel; compensate; counteract; cover
counterfeit: act; ape; artificial; assume; base; bogus; deceitful; dishonest; fake; false; feign; fictitious; flash; imitate; mock; phony; pretend; pseudo; sham; simulate; spurious
counterfoil: check
countermand: cancel; recall; reverse
counterpart: image; parallel; reciprocal; reflection; reverse
counterpoise: balance; balance; compensate; even; poise
countersign: password; watchword; word
countervail: balance; compensate; counteract
countless: great; innumerable; numberless
countrified: broad
country: nation
couple with: accompany
couple: associate; brace; connect; join; pair; span; unite
coupling: connection; junction
coupon: check
courage: assurance; bravery; confidence; daring; grit; heroism; mettle; nerve; patience; pluck; strength; valor
courageous: adventurous; audacious; bold; brave; daring; dauntless; defiant; fearless; gallant; hardy; heroic; manly; spirited; stout; strong; valiant
courageousness: machismo
courier: express
course (of action): policy
course: alternative; bank; bearing; circuit; current; lane; method; operation; orbit; passage; path; period; procedure; process; race; range; round; run; stream; succession; trend; wake; walk; way
court: attention; bar
courteous: affable; attentive; chivalrous; civil; fair; gallant; gentle; gracious; humble; obliging; pleasant; polite; refined; respectful; smooth; urbane
courtesan: prostitute
courtesy: attention
courtly: chivalrous; civil; courteous; elegant; gallant; gentle; gracious; humble; polite; refined; respectful; smooth
courtship: attention
covenant: bargain; compact; contract; league; obligation; pact; promise
cover in: close
cover up: whitewash
cover-up: cosmetic; pretense
cover: blind; bury; conceal; curtain; do; embrace; envelop; face; harbor; hatch; hide; mask; overwhelm; pall; pretense; protect; protection; roil; reen; screen; secrete; shade; shelter; shroud; spread
covering: cover; pall; skin
covert: cover; secret; ulterior
covet: begrudge; desire; envy; yearn
covetous: avaricious; greedy; mercenary; parsimonious
covetousness: envy; greed
covey: flock; run
cow: abash; awe; discourage; intimidate
coward: recreant; weakling
cowardly: afraid; base; coward; craven; faint; nerveless; poor; recreant; tame; timid
coxcomb: swell
coy: bashful; demure; prudish; shy; skittish; timid
cozen: bite; cheat; deceive; delude; fool; swindle; trick; victimize
cozenage: deceit
crabbed: cross; harsh; sour
crack wise: quip
crack: breach; break; burst; cleft; decipher; flaw; rend; rent; shatter; spring
crackbrain: crackpot
cracked: crazy
crackle: crack
cracksman: thief
cradle: origin
craft: art; art; artifice; business; cunning; guile; occupation; trade
crafted: worked,
craftiness: craft; cunning; deceit
craftsman: mechanic

crafty: astute; cagey; crooked; cunning; designing; insidious; Machiavellian; politic; sly; underhand; wily
craggy: abrupt; rough; rugged
cram: crowd; gorge; pack; stuff
crammed: populous
cramp: cabin; constrict; crowd
crane: hoist
crank: crackpot; eccentric
cranky: cross; irritable; testy; touchy
cranny: cleft; crack
crash: cataclysm; clash; smash; smash
crass: coarse; loutish; tasteless
crate: hamper; package
crater: abyss
cravat: tie
crave: beg; beseech; desire; entreat; implore; long; lust; pine; solicit; supplicate; wish; yearn,
craven: cowardly; recreant; recreant; weakling
craving: addiction; appetite; desire; longing; lust; thirst; yearning
craw: crop
crawl: scramble
crawling: populous
craze: crack; fashion; mania; novelty; rage
crazed: crazy; insane; mad
craziness: insanity; lunacy
crazy: crackpot; insane; mad; mental; wacky; wild; wild-eyed; zany
create a disturbance: riot
create disorder: riot
create: begin; breed; cause; conceive; engender; form; invent; make; occasion; originate; pioneer; produce
created: fictitious
creation: gadget
creative: original; productive; seminal
creature: animal
credence: belief; credit; faith
credibility: credit
credible: faithful; tenable
credit: account; belief; faith; honor; merit; name; reputation; repute; standing; trust; worth
creditable: faithful; honorable; proud
credo: ideology
credulous: simple
creed: belief; faith; ideology; tenet
creep: run; scramble
creosote: tar
crepehanger: killjoy
crepuscule: twilight
crest: device; peak
crestfallen: blue; downhearted; gloomy; heavy
crevasse: abyss
crevice: cleft; crack; flaw; rent
crew: band; gang; knot; pack
crib: rack; shack
crime: abuse; offense; sacrilege; sin; trespass
criminal: bad; malefactor; outlaw
criminality: guilt; malfeasance
crimination: charge
cringe: wince
cringing: obsequious; servile; slavish; supple
cripple: disable; exhaust; maim; mutilate
crippled: crooked; deformed
crisis: emergency; head; strait
crisp: concise,
criterion: canon; paradigm; standard; trial
critical: delicate; discriminate; exact; grave; great; judicial; minute; nice; particular; penetrating; serious; severe; significant; strict; vital
critically: askance
criticism: censure; comment; note; notice; reproach; review
criticize: attack; blame; censure; chide; comment; pan; pick; reproach; review; scorch; sneer
critique: comment; criticism; exposition; gloss; note; notice; review
crony: comrade; friend; intimate
crook: bend; criminal
crooked: bent; circuitous; cockeyed; cranky; insidious; Machiavellian; misshapen; sinister; sinuous; tortuous; unfaithful; wily; wrong; wry
crookedly: askance
croon: warble
crop up: appear

crop: abbreviate; cut; gather; stand; top; yield
crops: produce
cross out: cancel
cross over: traverse
cross-current: undertow
cross-ventilate: ventilate
cross: cantankerous; cranky; cut; cynical; fractious; grouchy; meet; mongrel; passage; peevish; petulant; sour; span; splenetic; sulky; testy; thwart; touchy; traverse; traverse
crossbar: traverse
crosspiece: traverse
crotchet: fancy; notion; vagary; whim
crotchety: cantankerous; cranky; grouchy; whimsical
crouch: stoop
crow: boast; rook; vaunt
crowd: cloud; company; compress; cram; drove; flock; gang; gathering; herd; jam; knot; multitude; run; stuff; swarm; swarm; throng; throng; troop
crowded: populous
crown: circle
crucial: acute; critical; precise; significant
crucify: pillory
crude: artless; awkward; barbarian; bluff; brusque; brutal; coarse; disrespectful; earthy; ill-mannered; loud; loutish; low; raw; rough; rude; rugged; rural; sour; stiff; tasteless; unrefined; vulgar
cruel: atrocious; barbarian; beastly; bitter; bloody; brutal; brute; ferocious; fierce; grim; hard; harsh; incisive; inexorable; merciless; pitiless; remorseless; ruthless; sanguinary; savage; spiteful; stern; truculent; tyrannical; unkind; unmerciful; unnatural; unrelenting
cruelly: hardly
cruelty: oppression
cruise: excursion; voyage
crumb: bit; scrap
crumble: corrode; crush; dissolve
crumbly: short
crumbs: remain
crumple: crush
crusader: pilgrim
crush: bow; break; conquer; grind; humble; jam; mangle; oppress; overcome; overpower; overthrow; overwhelm; pound; quell; repress; shatter; smash; stamp; stifle; vanquish
crushed: heavy; tame
crust: chutzpah; gall; scale; skin
crusty: cynical; peevish
crutch: mainstay; stay
crux: issue; main
cry out: call; clamor; shout
cry: call; call; exclamation; plaint; roar; scream; shriek; weep; whine
crybaby: weakling
crying: lachrymose
crypt: vault
cryptic: mysterious; secret; ulterior
crystal-clear: limpid; pellucid
crystal: bright
crystalline: clear; lucid; pellucid; transparent
cube: die
cubic contents: capacity
cubic: solid
cudgel: beat; club; stick
cuff: blow; strike
cull: choose; gather; pick
culminate: accomplish; cease
culmination: head; height; pinnacle; summit; top
culpability: blame; fault; guilt
culpable: faulty
culprit: criminal; malefactor
cult: ideology
cultivate: grow; raise
cultivated: elegant; gentle; polite; refined; tame
cultivating: humane
culture: education
cultured: polished
cumbersome: bulky; heavy
cunning: art; artifice; astute; cagey; craft; crafty; deep; designing; guile; insidious; Machiavellian; policy; politic; sharp; sly; smart; wile; wily
cupidity: greed; lust; parsimony
curative: therapeutic
curb oneself: refrain
curb: bit; bridle; check; constrain; control; repress;

restrain; restrict; slacken; stay
cure-all: panacea
cure: correct; cure-all; heal; help; panacea; remedy
curio: antique; antique; novelty
curiosity: aberration; abnormality
curious: aberrant; abnormal; cranky; eccentric; inquisitive; meddlesome; prying; quaint; queer; quizzical; singular; strange; unusual; whimsical; wonderful
curl: ripple
curmudgeonly: cross
currency: money; vogue
current: flow; popular; present; prevailing; prevalent; rife; stream
curse: abuse; ban; malediction; oath; plague; swear
cursing: blasphemy; malediction
cursory: cosmetic; slapdash
curt: abrupt; blunt; brief; brusque; concise; half-hearted; impatient; quick; rude; severe; short; short; summary; terse; uncivil
curtail: abbreviate; abridge; break; check; condense; cut; reduce; shorten; trim
curtailment: abbreviation; abridgment
curtain: blind; shade; shroud
curtly: short
curtness: brevity
curtsy: obeisance; reverence
curvaceous: zaftig
curvature: bend
curve: bend; bend; bow; round; turn; twist; wind
curved: bent; crooked; round; sinuous; tortuous
curvy: zaftig
cushion: palliate; pillow; safeguard
cuspidate: acute
custodian: caregiver; keeper; warden
custodianship: custody
custody: arrest; charge; keeping; possession
custom: convention; duty; fashion; fashion; habit; manner; order; practice; use; vogue; way; wont
customarily: mostly; often
customary: accustomed; common; conventional; general; habitual; ordinary; orthodox; regular; set; simple; stock; usual
customer: patron
customers: custom
cut down: hew
cut off: abridge; divide; stop
cut short: crop
cut: abbreviate; abbreviation; abrasion; bite; break; chop; crop; form; garb; hack; haggle; hew; mangle; mark; pare; rebuff; rip; score; sever; slash; stamp; tear; trim; wound
cutthroat: butcher
cutting-edge: adventurous; pioneer
cutting: bitter; caustic; cold; cynical; keen; pungent; sarcastic; satirical; severe; sharp; slip; tart; trenchant; trim
cutup: scamp; zany
cycle: circle; period; revolution; round
cyclone: sirocco; storm
cyclopean: gigantic
Cyclopean: huge
cylinder: roll; round

d,gag,: laid-back
d,nouement: catastrophe
dab: daub
dabble: dilettante
daft: mental; moonstruck
daftness: lunacy
dainty: delicacy; delicate; delicious; exquisite; nice; particular; squeamish
dais: pace; platform; stand
dallier: dabbler
dally: dawdle; fool; loiter; philander; play
dam up: obstruct; stem
dam: structure
damage: blemish; cost; detriment; disadvantage; harm; havoc; hurt; injure; injury; lacerate; loss; mar; mischief; mutilate; ravage; ruffle; ruin; sabotage; scandal; spoil; tamper; wound
damageable: vulnerable
damaged: weather-beaten
damaging: injurious; pernicious; toxic
damn: condemn; curse
damnable: cursed

damnation: malediction; perdition
damned: cursed; fatal
damning: malediction
damp: chill; humid; moist; raw; wet
dampen: cool; damp; depress
dampened: wet
damper: check; discouragement; killjoy
dampness: damp; wet
dance: ball; gambol; trip
dancing-party: ball
dandify: decorate
dandy: coxcomb; swell
danger: chance; hazard; jeopardy; peril; venture
dangerous chance: risk
dangerous: awkward; critical; desperate; mad; malignant; precarious; ugly; uncertain
dangle: hang
dangling: pendulous
dank: damp; humid; moist; wet
dankness: damp; wet
dapper: jaunty
dare: brave; defy; risk; venture
daredevil: adventurous
daring: adventurous; audacious; bold; brave; bravery; courage; daredevil; dauntless; defiant; gallant; hardy; heroic; heroism; stalwart
dark-colored: dirty
dark-skinned: swarthy
dark: black; blind; cloudy; dim; dirty; dusky; gloomy; infamous; murky; mysterious; obscure; pessimistic; recondite; sad; sober; somber; sullen; swarthy; turbid
darken: blot; dim; fog; lower; obfuscate; shade
darkened: weather-beaten
darkening: fog
darkness: gloom; shade
darling: dear; favorite; idol; pet; precious
darn: mend
dart: dash; flit; spring
dash: cast; clash; crash; dart; destroy; flourish; luster; panache; plunge; rush; show; splendor; verve
dashing: adventurous; brave; enterprising; jaunty; smart
dastard: coward; recreant; weakling
dastardliness: cowardice
dastardly: cowardly; faint; recreant; tame; timid
data: information
date: age; epoch; time
daunt: alarm; appall; awe; discourage; dismay; shake
dauntless: audacious; bold; brave; daring; game; heroic; stout
dauntlessness: courage
dawdle: dally; fool; linger; loiter
dawdler: laggard
dawdling: delay
dawn: break; light; morning; opening
dawning: dawn
day of rest: Sabbath
daybreak: dawn; light; morning
daydream: trance
daydreaming: absent-minded
daylight: light
daze: amaze; astonish; bewilder; dazzle; fog; stun; trance
dazed with drink: cockeyed
dazed: groggy
dazzle: glare; panache; radiate; splendor
dazzling: gorgeous; magnificent; splendid; strong
de facto: factual
deactivate: hold; slacken
dead body: remain
dead-end: blind
dead: cold; dull; extinct; flat; inanimate; lifeless; low
deaden: blunt; dull; paralyze
deadlock: stalemate
deadly: contagious; deleterious; destructive; fatal; malignant; mortal; noisome; noxious; pernicious; toxic; virulent
deafening: loud
deal or parcel out: portion
deal in: sell
deal lightly: sport
deal out: administer; allot; distribute; divide; parcel; part; partition; share
deal with: touch; treat; use
deal: agreement; allot; apportion; deliver; dispense; distribute; mete; pact; ration; trade
dealing: commerce; deal; trade
dean: principal

dear: close; costly; expensive; high; intimate; precious; rich; sweet; valuable
dearest: favorite
dearly beloved: favorite
dearth: lack; want
death: destruction; doom; fate
deathless: eternal; immortal; perennial; undying
deathly pale: cadaverous
deathly: cadaverous; ghastly
deathwatch: wake
debacle: cataclysm
debar: exclude; suspend
debase: abase; corrupt; decline; degrade; depress; disgrace; humble; humiliate; lower; pollute; profane; reduce; shame; stain
debased: base; corrupt; depraved
debasement: degradation; infamy
debasing: abject
debatable: moot; open; questionable
debate: agitate; agitation; argue; argument; contend; contention; contest; controversy; discuss; dispute; moot; vex
debauch: dissipate
debauchee: libertine; rou,
debauchment: violation
debilitate: exhaust; relax; weaken
debilitated: feeble; languid; weak
debility: ailment; delicacy
debit: debt; expense
debonair: affable; brave; civil; courteous; exquisite; jaunty
debt: answer; charge
decadence: decay; degradation
decamp: abscond; escape
decay: corruption; decadence; decline; decompose; die; disintegrate; dwindle; ebb; fade; failure; perish; rot; ruin; wane; waste; wither
decayed: bad; old; rotten; unsound; waste
decease: death; die; perish
deceased: dead
deceit: art; artifice; bluff; cheat; craft; cunning; duplicity; fraud; guile; trick; trickery; wile
deceitful: artificial; crafty; crooked; deceptive; designing; dishonest; false; hypocritical; insidious; Machiavellian; mendacious; perfidious; plausible; rotten; sharp; slippery; spurious; tortuous; treacherous; unfaithful; wily
deceitfulness: craft; cunning; duplicity
deceive: abuse; beguile; betray; bite; bluff; catch; cheat; delude; fool; humbug; mislead; mock; seduce; sham; swindle; take; trick; victimize
deceiver: humbug; hypocrite; impostor; swindler
deceiving: deceit; deceitful; deception; deceptive; false; hypocritical; plausible
decelerate: retard
decency: decorum; modesty; propriety
decent: chaste; decorous; ethical; honest; modest; proper; respectable; seemly; serviceable
deception: abuse; artifice; cheat; chicanery; craft; cunning; deceit; delusion; duplicity; fake; fraud; guile; humbug; illusion; show; stratagem; swindle; trick; trickery; wile
deceptive: ambiguous; deceitful; false; fast; fictitious; hypocritical; illusory; plausible; seductive; sophisticated; specious; treacherous
decide: determine; determine; judge; resolve; rule; settle; umpire; will
decided: actual; emphatic; positive
decimate: slaughter
decipher: interpret
decision: conclusion; constancy; doom; judgment; resolve; will
decisive: critical; final; positive; ultimate
deck out: apparel; beautify; decorate; dress; furnish; habit
deck: adorn; array; beautify; decorate; grace; hatch; trick; trim
declaim: harangue
declamation: elocution; oration; tirade
declamatory: grandiloquent; tumid
declaration: assertion; assurance; decree; expression; profession; remark; speech; statement; testimony; word

declare: acknowledge; affirm; allege; announce; assert; communicate; confess; deliver; express; maintain; manifest; mention; proclaim; protest; publish; say; state; swear; tell; urge
declination: descent
decline: abate; abatement; age; break; decadence; decay; decrease; degradation; descent; die; dip; droop; dwindle; ebb; fade; fail; failure; refuse; reject; repel; set; settle; subside; twilight; wane; waste; wither
declining: feeble
declivity: decline; descent
decoction: extract
decode: decipher; interpret
decompose: decay; rot
decomposed: rotten
decomposition: decay; rot
decontaminate: clean
decontrolled: free
decorate: adorn; appoint; array; beautify; beset; deck; dress; embellish; flourish; furnish; garnish; grace; hang; ornament; trim
decorated: fancy; garish; ornate
decoration: accolade; flourish; garnish; ornament; pattern; set; trim
decorative: cosmetic
decorous: becoming; decent; demure; proper; respectful; seemly; staid
decorticate: peel; strip
decorum: etiquette; propriety
decoy: blind; entice; lure; seduce; tempt
decrease: abate; abatement; curtail; diminish; dwindle; ebb; lessen; lower; reduce; remission; shrink; shrivel; slack; subside; wane
decree: act; appoint; doom; establish; judgment; mandate; ordain; prescribe; rule; will
decrepit: aged; senile; shabby; superannuated; weak
decry: traduce; vilify
decrypt: decipher
dedicate: apply; consecrate; devote; sanctify
dedicated: conscientious; holy; sacred; single-minded
dedication: devotion
deduce: draw; extract; gather
deduct: abate; allow; subtract; take
deduction: allowance; conclusion; conjecture
deed: achievement; act; action; exploit; feat; procedure; quality; work
deem: account; hold; judge; reckon; regard; repute; rule; suppose; think
deep within: intimate
deep-rooted: intimate
deep-seated: intimate
deep: abstract; abstruse; earnest; fast; hold; intimate; low; profound; recondite; rich; sound; unbroken
deepen: intensify
def: excellent
deface: blemish; blot; deform; disfigure; maim; mangle; mar
defamation: abuse; detraction; obloquy; scandal
defamatory: derogatory; injurious
defame: abuse; disgrace; malign; traduce; vilify
default: neglect
defeat: beat; cast; conquer; conquest; counteract; disappointment; frustrate; mock; overcome; overpower; overthrow; overwhelm; quell; reverse; ruin; smash; subdue; thrash; thwart; upset; vanquish
defeated: lost
defect: absence; ailment; blame; blemish; failing; fault; flaw; foible; taint; vice; weakness
defective: bad; faulty; imperfect; inadequate; rotten; unsound; vicious
defectiveness: failure; lack; want
defend: assert; champion; cover; guard; justify; maintain; preserve; protect; safeguard; screen; shelter; support; vindicate
defendable: tenable
defendant: suspect
defender: advocate; champion; friend; guard; guardian; patron
defense: answer; apology; assertion; cover; guard; protection; rampart; safeguard; screen

defenseless: naked; unguarded; vulnerable
defensible: tenable
defer to: respect
defer: adjourn; delay; postpone; procrastinate; slacken; suspend; waive
deference: attention; duty; homage; honor; obeisance; regard; respect
deferential: attentive; civil; dutiful; obedient; obsequious; respectful
deferment: delay
deferral: abeyance
deferring: delay
defiance: rebellion
defiant: bold; brazen; disobedient; froward; rebellious; unreconstructed
deficiency: absence; defect; failing; failure; lack; poverty; want
deficient: defective; lean; meager; poor; scanty; scarce; short; weak
deficit: lack
defile: contaminate; corrupt; debase; foul; gorge; pass; pollute; profane; stain; taint
defiled: dirty; filthy; nasty
defilement: abomination; corruption; taint; violation
define: ascertain; fix; interpret; limit
defined: definite; precise
definite: absolute; actual; certain; clear; decided; distinct; emphatic; explicit; express; positive; precise; tangible; unerring
definitely: absolutely; clearly; flat
definition: explanation
deflated: flat
deflect: bend; divert; turn
deflected: bent
defloration: violation
deform: deface; deform; disfigure; mar
deformed: crooked; misshapen
defraud: bite; bluff; cheat; deceive; delude; rob; rook; sham; swindle; take; trick; victimize; wrong
defrauding: wile
defray: cover
deft: clean; dexterous; facile; handy; skillful
deftness: delicacy
defunct: dead; inanimate; lifeless
defy: brave; dare; disobey; mock
degeneracy: degradation
degenerate: decay; decline; depraved; dwindle; rot
degeneration: decadence; decay; decline; degradation; ebb
degradation: affront; disgrace; humiliation
degrade oneself: condescend
degrade: abase; break; debase; depress; disgrace; humble; humiliate; lessen; lower; reduce
degraded: base; ignoble; low; sordid; squalid; vile
degrading: abject; base; ignominious
degree: deal; extent; mode; order; shade; wise
degrees: scale
dehisce: gape
dehydrate: evaporate
deification: worship
deify: worship
deign: accord; condescend; stoop; vouchsafe
deject: chill; depress; discourage; dull
dejected: blue; depressed; despondent; disconsolate; downhearted; gloomy; glum; heavy; low; melancholy; sad; sorrowful; wretched
dejection: damp; despondency; discouragement; gloom; melancholy
delay: adjourn; arrest; check; dally; defer; detain; extension; hesitate; hesitation; hinder; impede; linger; loiter; pause; postpone; procrastinate; remain; respite; retard; stay; stop; suspend; tarry; wait
delayed: late
delayer: laggard
delaying: delay; laggard
dele: cancel; delete; obliterate
delectable: dainty; delightful; luscious; palatable; scrumptious
delectation: delight; enjoyment; pleasure
delegated: vicarious
delete: cancel; obliterate; zap
deleterious: bad; destructive; harmful; injurious; noisome;

noxious; pernicious; toxic; unhealthy; unwholesome
deliberate: advise; agitate; calculate; cold; confer; conscious; consider; consult; contemplate; cool; debate; discuss; intentional; leisurely; moderate; muse; pause; ponder; premeditate; reflect; see; slow; studied; voluntary; wanton
deliberating: reflective
deliberation: calculation; consideration; counsel; debate; reflection
deliberative: thoughtful
delicacy: dainty; sensibility
delicate: clean; dainty; delicious; exquisite; female; fine; frail; luxurious; mellow; nice; precious; queasy; sensitive; slender; slight; soft; squeamish; tender; touchy; unhealthy; weak
delicious: dainty; luscious; palatable; scrumptious
delight in: admire
delight: admiration; charm; divert; ecstasy; enchant; enjoyment; enliven; entrance; feast; happiness; joy; pleasure; rapture; regale; take
delighted: glad; happy; joyful
delightful: amusing; felicitous; glorious; nice; pleasant; pleasing; sweet
delimitation: boundary,
delineate: depict; describe; design; draw; outline; picture; portray; rehearse; relate; represent; silhouette; sketch; trace
delineation: silhouette; sketch
delinquency: dereliction; fault; malfeasance
delinquent: criminal
delirious: ecstatic; insane; light
delirium: frenzy
deliver up: ransom
deliver: betray; free; give; issue; liberate; negotiate; pass; ransom; refer; release; render; rescue; salvage
deliverance: ransom; release; relief; rescue
deliverer: savior
delivery: issue; labor
delude: beguile; cheat; deceive; fool; humbug; mislead; mock; trick
deluge: cascade; cataclysm; flood; flood; inundate
delusion: aberration; hallucination; idol; illusion
delusional: illusory; mental
delusive: deceptive; empty
demand noisily: clamor
demand: appetite; ask; call; claim; command; exact; lust; necessity; need; request; require; requirement; rule; take; ultimatum
demanding: conscientious; crying; delicate; exact; meticulous; nice; precise; punctilious; religious; rigorous; scrupulous; severe; strict
demarcation: division
demean oneself: behave
demean: debase
demeaning: derogatory
demeanor: air; appearance; bearing; behavior; carriage; cast; conduct; manner; poise
demented: crazy; insane
dementedness: lunacy
dementia praecox: insanity
dementia: insanity; lunacy; mania
demise: death
demit: waive
demitted: abandoned
demobilize: disband
d,mod.: antique
demoded: antique
demoiselle: maid
demolish: batter; break; destroy; level; overthrow; ruin; sack; scrap; spoil
demolition: destruction; overthrow
demon : goblin,
demon: monster; spirit
demoniac: devilish
demonstrable: factual
demonstrate: bear; display; evidence; exhibit; manifest; produce; prove; register; render; show
demonstration: array; exhibit; exposition; proof; scene
demonstrative: effusive; outgoing
demoralize: corrupt
demoralized: abandoned
demote: abase; break; degrade

demotic: vernacular

demur: difficulty; hang; hesitate

demure: coy; modest; prudish; sedate

den: hole; study

denigrate: pan

denominate: call; name; style; title

denomination: breed; faction; title

denotation: meaning; sense

denote: argue; express; mean; note; represent; signify

denouement: issue

denounce: abuse

dense: close; compact; dim; fatuous; firm; gross; heavy; simple; slow; solid; stiff

density: body

dent: mark; pit

denude: bare; divest; strip

denuded: naked; nude

denunciate: curse; denounce

denunciation: abuse; ban; curse; invective; malediction; satire; tirade

denunciatory: invective

deny: contradict; decline; deprive; dispute; oppose; refuse; reject; renounce; traverse

depart from: leave; quit

depart secretly: abscond

depart suddenly: abscond

depart: deviate; die; part; pass; retire; retreat; start; swerve; withdraw

departed: dead

department: bailiwick; branch; manner; realm

departure: aberration; death; retreat

depend upon: trust

depend: attend; hang; lean

dependable: certain; faithful; reliable; safe; steadfast

dependence: confidence; connection; relation

dependency: addiction; bearing

dependent: precarious; subject; subject; subordinate

depict: describe; draw; picture; portray; represent; sketch

depiction: imagery

deplete: bankrupt; weaken

deplorable: grievous; horrible; miserable; piteous; pitiful; sad; shabby; sorry

deplore: lament; moan; mourn; regret

depopulate: desolate

deport or comport oneself: behave

deport: banish; conduct

deportment: air; bearing; behavior; carriage; conduct; course; decorum; motion

depose: affirm; degrade; displace; reduce; swear; unseat; upset

deposit: cast; ground; lay; lodge; place; put

deposition: assurance; deposit; evidence; overthrow; testimony

depository: depot

depot: station; stop

deprave: corrupt; degrade; pollute

depraved: abandoned; bad; corrupt; enormous; evil; immoral; libertine; lost; mean; nefarious; shameless; sinful; sinister; sordid; ungodly; vicious; vile; wicked

depravity: abomination; corruption; evil; ill; vice

deprecate: pan

deprecatory: derogatory; injurious; pejorative

depreciate: decry; lessen; slur; traduce; vilify

depreciation: detraction

depreciative: derogatory; pejorative

depreciatory: derogatory

depredation: pillage

deprehension: abduction

depress: bow; chill; debase; desolate; discourage; dull; grieve; lower; oppress; reduce

depressed: blue; dejected; despondent; downhearted; gloomy; glum; heavy; low; melancholy; sad; sore; sorrowful; sorry; world-weary; wretched

depressing: black; chill; cloudy; cold; dreary; dull; heavy; lugubrious; somber; sore

depression: affliction; chill; crash; damp; despondency; discouragement; gloom; melancholy; oppression; pit; woe

deprivation: disadvantage; distress; loss; need; privation

deprive: abridge; divest; rob; strip

---

depths: abyss

depute: delegate

deputed: vicarious

deputy: delegate; surrogate

derange: disorder; litter; perturb; ruffle; trouble; turn; upset

deranged: crazy; insane; mad

derangement: disease; disorder; disturbance; frenzy; insanity; mania

dereliction: failure; neglect

deride: banter; jeer; jest; mock; pillory; ridicule; sneer; twit

de rigueur: right

derision: banter; contempt; irony; jeer; mock; mockery; ridicule; sarcasm; scorn; shame; sneer; sport; taunt

derisive: cynical; sarcastic; scurrilous

derivation: descent; origin; pedigree

derive: draw; extract

dermatitis: rash

derogative: derogatory

derogatory: injurious; snide

derrick: hoist

descant: melody; warble

descend: condescend; decline; light; plunge; stoop; subside

descendant: scion

descendants: race

descending: descent

descent: ancestry; birth; origin; parentage; pedigree; stem; stock; stoop; strain; succession

describe: depict; narrate; picture; recite; recount; rehearse; relate; represent; tell

description: account; breed; explanation; narrative; picture; quality; recital; relation; sort; stamp; story; view

descriptive: particular

descry: detect; discern; discover; espy; perceive

desecrate: abuse; pollute; profane

desecration: abuse; sacrilege; violation

desert: abandon; arid; defect; desolate; fail; forsake; leave; merit; naked; relinquish; reward; solitude; vacate; waste; wild

deserted: abandoned; desolate; forlorn; lone; solitary; waste

desertion: dereliction

deserve: earn; merit

deserved: just

deserving: estimable; good; worth; worthy

desideratum: want

design: aim; blueprint; contemplate; contrive; counsel; device; devise; end; hatch; intend; intent; maneuver; mean; meaning; model; ornament; pattern; plan; project; proposal; propose; purport; purpose; reason; scheme; sketch; stamp; think; thought; view

designate: appoint; assign; call; entitle; express; mark; name; note; qualify; represent; style; title

designating: appointment

designation: appointment; name; title

designed: intentional; voluntary

designer: artist; artist

designing: crafty; deceitful; Machiavellian; wily

desirability: value

desirable: advisable; eligible; expedient

desire: appetite; aspire; covet; crave; device; greed; hope; long; longing; lust; mind; pant; passion; pleasure; rage; thirst; want; will; wish; yearning; zeal

desirous: ambitious; greedy; mad; solicitous

desist or refrain from: stop

desist from: leave

desist: cease; discontinue; halt; pause; quit; refrain; suspend

desolate: alone; black; desert; desperate; destroy; devastate; disconsolate; forlorn; gaunt; lonesome; stark; strip; waste

desolation: destruction; havoc; misery; ravage; sack; waste; wreck

despair: despondency; discouragement

despairing: desperate; hopeless

desperate: hopeless

desperation: despair; despondency

despicable: abject; abominable; base; contemptible; detestable; dirty; ignominious; mean; miser-

---

able; nauseous; odious; pitiful; scurvy; sorry; vile; wretched

despisable: despicable

despise: abhor; abominate; defy; detest; disdain; hate; pan; scorn; spurn

despite: notwithstanding

despoil: desolate; devastate; loot; pillage; plunder; ravage; sack; spoil; strip; waste

despoilment: ravage

despondency: despair; gloom; melancholy

despondent: blue; dejected; depressed; downhearted; gloomy; heavy; hopeless; melancholy; sad

desponding: despondent

despot: tyrant

despotic: absolute; arbitrary; imperious; lordly; tyrannical

despotism: oppression

destination: destiny; object; objective

destine: appoint; doom; fate; mark; mean; ordain

destined for: bound

destined: sure

destiny: doom; fate; necessity

destitute: bankrupt; bare; forlorn; impecunious; miserable; naked; penniless; poor; void

destitution: defect; distress; need; penury; poverty; privation; want

destroy: abolish; absorb; assassinate; batter; blast; blot; break; consume; cripple; curse; demolish; desolate; devastate; disable; dissolve; eradicate; exterminate; kill; level; mangle; murder; obliterate; overthrow; overturn; ravage; remove; ruin; sack; slay; smash; spoil; stifle; waste; wreck

destroyed: desolate; lost; waste

destruction: abolition; fate; havoc; loss; overthrow; perdition; ravage; ruin; sack; shambles; smash; waste; wreck

destructive: deleterious; evil; fatal; injurious; noisome; noxious; pernicious

desultory: uncertain

detach: part; sever

detached: separate; temperate; world-weary

detachment: isolation

detail: facet; narrate; ornament; particular; recite; regard; relate; respect; way

detailed: elaborate; graphic; intimate; minute; particular

detain: delay; hold; retain; stay

detect: appreciate; catch; discover; learn; observe; scent

detectable: apparent

detective: operative

detention: arrest; arrest

deter: arrest; bar; block; discourage; forbid

deterge: clean

deteriorate: corrode; dash; debase; decay; decline; degrade; impair

deteriorated: old

deterioration: decay; decline; ebb; failure

determinant: cause

determinate: actual; certain; definite; explicit

determination: conclusion; constancy; judgment; perseverance; pluck; purpose; resolve; stand; volition; will

determine: appoint; arrange; ascertain; assign; cause; condition; decide; discover; fix; judge; ordain; prove; resolve; see; set; sound; state; take; will

determined: aggressive; bent; certain; constant; decided; decisive; definite; earnest; firm; positive; resolute; set; single-minded; strenuous; sturdy; unyielding

determining: critical

deterrent: arrest; bar; check; discouragement; embarrassment; hindrance

detest: abhor; abominate; disgust; hate; loathe; nauseate; scorn

detestable: abhorrent; abominable; atrocious; disgusting; hateful; hideous; infamous; loathsome; nauseous; nefarious; odious; offensive

detestation: abhorrence; abomination; antipathy; aversion; disgust; hatred; horror; odium

detesting: abhorrent

detonate: discharge

detonation: discharge

detract: deduct; subtract

---

detracting: detraction

detraction: scandal

detriment: cost; damage; disadvantage; expense; harm; hurt; injury; loss; mischief

detrimental: bad; harmful; injurious; noisome; noxious; pernicious

de trop: superfluous; unnecessary; waste

deuteron: particle

devalue: depress

devastate: desolate; destroy; harry; plunder; ravage; sack; slaughter; strip; waste; wreck

devastated: desolate; waste

devastating: traumatic

devastation: destruction; havoc; pillage; ravage; ruin; sack; shambles; waste; wreck

develop: amplify; breed; elaborate; expand; mature; mellow; progress; ripen; spin; spring

developed: complete; ripe

developing: development

development: growth; outgrowth; progress; seasoning

deviant: circuitous; cockeyed; different

deviate: aberrant; bend; depart; digress; diverge; sheer; swerve; vary; wander; warp

deviating: aberrant; different

deviation: aberration; change; excursion; turn; variation

device: appliance; artifice; attachment; deceit; emblem; expedient; gadget; machination; ploy; recourse; stratagem; tool; trick; type; way; wile

devil-may-care: daredevil

devil: blackguard; monster

devilish: atrocious; black; dark; satanic

devious: aberrant; circuitous; crooked; irregular; mealy-mouthed; sinuous; slippery; wry

devise: agitate; arrange; bequeath; cast; conspire; construct; contrive; design; fabricate; feign; form; hatch; invent; leave; meditate; plan; plot; prepare; project; scheme; will

devised: worked

devoid or destitute of: vacant

devoid: void

devote: apply; consecrate; spend

devoted: affectionate; assiduous; close; conscientious; constant; devout; faithful; loyal

devotedness: devotion

devotee: adherent; enthusiast; fanatic

devotion: affection; attachment; attention; constancy; enthusiasm; fidelity; grace; homage; homage; love; loyalty; party; piety

devotional: solemn

devour: absorb; consume; gobble; gorge; swallow

devouring: gluttonous; ravenous

devout: godly; holy; pious; religious

devoutness: devotion; grace; piety

dexterity: ability; address; art; craft; delicacy; knack

dexterous: adroit; apt; expert; facile; good; handy; neat; skillful

dexterousness: knack

dextrous: clean; clever

diabolic: black; devilish

diabolical: atrocious; devilish; satanic

diagram: blueprint; map; plan; scheme; trace

diagrammatic: graphic

dialect: language; slang; speech; talk; terminology; vernacular

dialogue: talk

diaphanous: clear; sheer; transparent

diaphoresis: perspiration,

dicey: iffy; shaky

dictate: decree; prescribe

dictator: tyrant

dictatorial: absolute; arbitrary; authoritative; imperious; intolerant; lordly; magisterial; overbearing; peremptory; tyrannical

diction: expression; language; parlance; phraseology; wording

dictionary: thesaurus

dictum: command; decree; position

didactic: sententious

diddly-squat: zilch

diddly: zilch

dido: caper

die out: fade

---

die-hard: orthodox; unreconstructed

die: depart; dissolve; part; pass; perish; stamp

diet: assembly; food

differ: alter; dissent; diverge; quarrel; vary

difference: breach; contrast; discrepancy; disparity; dissent; distinction; division; feud; misunderstanding; opposition; quarrel; strife; variance; variation; variety

different: distinct; diverse; novel; odd; opposite; special; unlike; various

differentiate: contrast; discern; discriminate; distinguish

differentiation: contrast; distinction

differing: alien; different; opposite; various

difficult: abstract; abstruse; ambiguous; arduous; blunt; deep; froward; hard; heavy; incompatible; knotty; laborious; painful; rugged; stiff; touchy; troublesome; wrongheaded

difficulty: dilemma; knot; matter; mess; misunderstanding; quagmire; snarl; strait; three; trouble

diffident: bashful; coy; shy; timid

diffuse through: permeate

diffuse: broad; disperse; extend; garrulous; pervade; radiate; rarefied; spread

diffused: broad

diffusion: spread

dig into: pick

dig up: discover

dig: cut

digest: abbreviate; abbreviation; abridge; abridgment; abstract; abstract; condense; summary; synopsis

digit: number

dignified: grand; grave; great; honorable; lordly; magnificent; majestic; noble; peaceful; solemn; state; stately

dignify: advance; elevate; exalt; grace

dignity: decorum; elevation; etiquette; honor; rank; state; station

digress: deviate; wander

digression: excursion

dike: bank; bank; wall

dilapidated: old; ramshackle; seedy

dilapidation: decay; ruin

dilatation: extension

dilate: amplify; distend; enlarge; expand; extend; grow; heave; increase; inflate; spread; stretch; swell; wax

dilated: tumid

dilation: extension

dilatory: inactive; laggard; late; remiss; shiftless; slack; slow; tardy

dilemma: difficulty; emergency; fix; plight; predicament; quagmire; quandary; strait

dilettante: aesthete; amateur; dabbler

diligence: patience; zeal

diligent: active; assiduous; busy; industrious; laborious; notable; painstaking; patient; sedulous

dilly-dally: dawdle

dillydallier: laggard

dilute: cut; rarefied; thin; watery

diluted: rarefied; small; watery

dim-sighted: purblind

dim-witted: silly

dim: blind; blot; cloudy; dark; dark; dusky; faint; feeble; fog; gloomy; indefinite; murky; obscure; obscure; pale; recondite; shade; somber; vague

dimension: mass

dimensions: bulk; capacity; proportion; size

diminish: abate; abridge; alleviate; condense; curtail; cut; decline; decrease; dwindle; impair; lessen; lower; moderate; palliate; pare; qualify; reduce; relax; relieve; remit; shorten; shrink; slacken; subside; subtract; thin; wane; waste; weaken

diminution: abatement; decline; decrease; remission; twilight; wane; waste

diminutive: dwarf; little; minute; petty; small

dimming: fog

dimness: gloom; haze

dimple: ripple

dimwit: yahoo
dimwitted: blunt; fatuous
din: bedlam; hubbub; noise; racket; uproar
dinghy: tender
dingus: gadget
dingy: black; dirty
diocese: see
dip: immerse; plunge; submerge
diplomacy: delicacy
diplomatic: politic; tactful
dipsomaniac: drunkard; lush
dire: bitter; dread; frightful; grim; horrendous; horrible; sad; terrible
direct (speech or writing to): address
direct: administer; aim; appoint; appropriate; bend; bid; bluff; cast; command; conduct; control; crude; dead; decree; deliver; earthy; enjoin; express; frank; govern; guide; head; immediate; influence; instruct; kibitz; lead; level; main; manage; master; naked; officious; order; oversee; plain; plump; positive; prescribe; present; primary; refer; regulate; require; right; rule; speed; straight; straightforward; superintend; sway; turn; unequivocal; unqualified; will; wish
directed: pointed; steadfast
direction: aim; aspect; bearing; charge; command; conduct; control; course; disposition; influence; instruction; leading; management; order; oversight; reference; regulation; rule; set; tendency; trend; turn; way; will
directive: decree; requirement
directly: fair; immediately; plump; presently; right
directness: candor
director: guide; head; manager
dirge: lament; moan
dirt: earth; ground; smirch
dirtiness: mess
dirty: black; coarse; filthy; foul; nasty; naughty; pollute; radioactive; ribald; roil; smirch; sordid; squalid; stain; sully; unclean
dirtying: dirty
dis: slight
disability: ailment
disable: cripple; maim; sabotage
disabuse: clear
disaccord: friction
disadvantage: detriment; hurt; loss; mischief
disadvantageous: inconvenient; ugly; unfavorable
disaffect: estrange,
disaffected: disloyal
disaffection: breach; disloyalty; treason
disagree with: quarrel
disagree: brawl; clash; dissent; diverge; quarrel
disagreeable: bad; beastly; contrary; dirty; distasteful; forbidding; nasty; offensive; peevish; sour; ugly; unpleasant; unsightly; willful
disagreeing: diverse
disagreement: brawl; breach; clash; contention; controversy; difference; discrepancy; dissent; division; haggle; misunderstanding; quarrel; row; strife; tiff; variance
disallow: abate; deprive; overrule; prohibit
disannul: abrogate
disannulment: abrogation
disappear: die; disperse; dissipate; evaporate; fade; fail; pass; perish; vanish
disappoint: betray; fail; frustrate; let; mock
disappointing: unsatisfactory
disappointment: dissatisfaction
disapprobation: blame; censure; disgrace; displeasure; dissatisfaction; reproach
disapproval: blame; censure; disgrace; displeasure; dissatisfaction; protest; reproach
disapprove: blame; censure; condemn; disgrace; object; repudiate
disarm: confuse; unnerve
disarrange: confuse; disconcert; disorder; litter; ruffle; trouble
disarrangement: confusion; disorder
disarray: confuse; confusion; disorder
disarrayed: chaotic
disaster: accident; adversity; affliction; blow; calamity; cataclysm;

catastrophe; evil; misadventure; misfortune
disastrous: adverse; black; evil; sad; sinister; tragic
disavow: abdicate; deny; renounce; repudiate; withdraw
disavowal: abdication
disband: cast
disbeliever: atheist; iconoclast; skeptic
disbelieving: cynical
disburden: discharge; ease; lighten; relieve; unburden
disburse: discharge; expend; spend
discard: abandon; cast; dismiss; reject; repudiate; scrap
discarded: abandoned
discern: comprehend; discover; distinguish; know; notice; penetrate; perceive; see; sense; tell; understand
discernible: apparent; conspicuous; perceptible; sensible; tangible; visible; vivid
discerning: acute; astute; bright; careful; deep; intelligent; keen; nice; penetrating; perceptive; perspicacious; quick; sagacious; selective; sharp; shrewd; wise
discernment: capacity; intelligence; judgment; knowledge; perception; perspicacity; sense; taste; vision; wisdom
discharge (a responsibility: answer
discharge: absolve; blast; break; deliver; dismiss; emit; empty; exercise; exonerate; expel; flow; flow; fulfill; issue; liberate; meet; pay; perform; redeem; release; remission; satisfaction; settle; take; teem; void
discharged: quit
disciple: adherent; convert; follower; partisan; pupil; scholar
discipline: breed; chasten; correct; educate; exercise; form; harden; instruct; punish; subdue; teach
disclaim: abdicate; renounce; repudiate
disclaimer: abdication
disclose to: apprise
disclose: bare; break; communicate; declare; demonstrate; divulge; exhibit; expose; impart; manifest; mention; open; publish; reveal; show; speak; tell; unburden; uncover; ventilate
disclosure: development; exposure
discolor: smirch; stain; tarnish
discoloration: stain
discomfit: chagrin; embarrass; overcome; snub
discomfiture: chagrin
discomfort: embarrassment
discomforting: uncomfortable
discommode: molest; pain; plague; trouble
discommodious: inconvenient
discompose: abash; disconcert; disorder; embarrass; excite; ruffle
discomposed: excited
discomposure: chagrin; embarrassment
disconcert: abash; affront; chagrin; confuse; defeat; dismay; elude; embarrass; frustrate; nonplus; shame; surprise; unnerve; upset
disconcerted: blank; upset
disconcertion: chagrin
disconcertment: embarrassment
disconnect: part; separate; sever
disconnection: isolation
disconsolate: desolate; forlorn; heavy; hopeless; lachrymose; melancholy; miserable; sad; unhappy
disconsolateness: woe
discontent: dissatisfaction
discontented: discontent; malcontent; peevish; plaintive; querulous
discontentment: discontent
discontinue: cease; end; interrupt; quit; stop; suspend
discontinuity: break
discontinuous: abrupt; temporary
discord: conflict; contention; division; friction; misunderstanding; strife; variance
discordance: discrepancy
discordant: contrary; harsh; incompatible; incongruous; raucous; rough
discount: abate; allowance; sport
discountenance: abash; affront
discourage: chill; daunt; depress; deter; dismay; dull; forbid; inhib-

it; intimidate; perplex; repel; unnerve
discouraged: dejected; despondent; downhearted; sad
discouragement: damp; despair; despondency
discouraging: chill; dark; halfhearted
discourse: address; confer; converse; oration; parley; speech; talk
discourteous: abrupt; blunt; brusque; disrespectful; ill-mannered; impolite; rude; uncivil; uncouth
discover: ascertain; detect; discern; espy; hit; invent; learn; observe; originate; perceive; position; reveal; show; tell; trace
discredit: decry; degrade; disgrace; ignominy; infamy; obloquy; odium; reproach; reproach; scandal; taint
discreditable: abject; base; dishonorable; ignominious; shabby
discreet: careful; cautious; gingerly; judicious; politic; practical; prudent; rational; thoughtful; wary
discrepancy: difference; variance; variation; variety
discrepant: incongruous; inconsistent
discrete: characteristic; particular; separate
discretely: particularly
discretion: calculation; caution; judgment; mercy; policy; prudence; volition; wisdom
discretionary: arbitrary
discriminate against: persecute
discriminate: contrast; differentiate; discern; distinguish; know; notice
discriminating: critical; delicate; exquisite; judicial; nice; particular; practical; selective; sharp; shrewd
discrimination: contrast; difference; distinction; judgment; respect
discriminative: discriminate; sentient
discriminator: aesthete
discriminatory: discriminate; sentient; shabby; xenophobic
discursive: rambling
discuss: advise; agitate; argue; confer; converse; debate; dispute; moot; parley; talk; treat; ventilate; vex
discussed: vexed
discussion: agitation; argument; converse; debate; parley
disdain: arrogance; contempt; despise; pan; scorn; slight; sneer; snub; spurn
disdainful: contemptuous; derogatory; haughty; proud; supercilious; uppity
disease: affection; ailment; disorder; ill; malady; plague
diseased: ill; morbid; unhealthy; unsound
disembark: light
disencumber: clear; excuse
disenfranchise: ostracize
disengage: abstract; clear; free; liberate; release; separate
disentangle: absolve; clear; deliver; untangle
disenthrall: clear; free; liberate
disfavor: disgrace
disfigure: blot; deface; deform; mangle; mar; mutilate; spoil
disfigured: crooked; deformed
disfigurement: blemish
disgrace: abase; affront; blot; contempt; degradation; degrade; foul; humiliate; ignominy; infamy; lower; obloquy; reproach; sacrilege; scandal; shame; slur; smirch; stain; stigma; sully; taint
disgraceful: abject; base; dishonorable; flagrant; ignominious; infamous; low; opprobrious; shameful
disguise: conceal; cover; hide; mask; secrete; shape; whitewash
disgust: abhorrence; antipathy; aversion; dislike; distaste; gorge; loathing; nauseate; revolt; satiate; shock; surfeit
disgusting: abhorrent; abominable; distasteful; foul; hateful; loathsome; mean; nasty; nauseous; noisome; obscene; odious; offensive; rank; rotten; vile

dish: scale; scuttlebutt
disharmony: conflict; friction
dishearten: chill; daunt; depress; discourage; dismay; dull
disheartened: dejected; despondent; downhearted; gloomy
disheartening: abject; cold; dark
disheartenment: despair
disheveled: wild
dishonest: abject; bad; corrupt; crooked; perfidious; rascal; rotten; sharp; sinister; tortuous; unconscionable; unfaithful; unprincipled; wrong
dishonesty: art; chicanery; corruption; duplicity
dishonor: abase; blot; contempt; degradation; degrade; disgrace; foul; humiliate; ignominy; indignity; infamy; pollute; reproach; scandal; shame; stain; sully; taint; wrong
dishonorable: abject; base; crooked; foul; ignoble; ignominious; infamous; low; opprobrious; shabby; shameful; underhand
dishonoring: humiliation
disillusioned: blas,
disinclination: aversion; distaste
disinclined: averse; backward; indisposed; loath; reluctant
disinfect: heal
disingenuous: artificial; bad; deceitful; false; smarmy
disingenuousness: deceit
disintegrate: crush; decay; decompose; dissipate; dissolve; resolve
disintegration: ruin
disinterested: fair; impartial; magnanimous; unbiased
disinterestedness: generosity
disjoin: abstract; part; separate; sever
disjoined: separate
disjointed: cranky
disjointedly: piecemeal
disklike: round
dislike: antipathy; aversion; disgust; displeasure; dissatisfaction; distaste; hate; loathing; odium; repugnance
dislocate: displace
dislodge: remove
disloyal: faithless; false; fickle; perfidious; recreant; treacherous; unfaithful
disloyalty: perfidy; treachery; treason
dismal: black; blue; cloudy; dark; desolate; dreary; ghastly; gloomy; joyless; lugubrious; lurid; melancholy; somber; somber; sorrowful; sorry; sullen
dismantle: strip
dismay: alarm; appall; consternation; daunt; discourage; fear; fright; frighten; horror; intimidate; terror
dismayed: aghast
dismaying: forbidding
dismiss: banish; break; cast; disband; discharge; displace; dissolve; expel; rebuff; release
dismissal: rebuff
disobedience: rebellion
disobedient: froward; naughty; perverse; rebellious; recalcitrant; refractory; restive; unruly; wayward
disobey: break; disregard; infringe; transgress
disoblige: excuse
disorder: affection; ailment; brawl; commotion; confuse; confusion; disconcert; disease; disturbance; hubbub; jumble; litter; malady; perturb; riot; ruffle; shambles; stir; trouble; tumult; turmoil; uproar; upset
disordered: chaotic; untidy; upset
disorderliness: disorder; impropriety
disorderly: chaotic; irregular; raucous; rough; rowdy; slovenly; tumultuous; unruly; wild
disorganization: disorder
disorganize: disband; disorder
disown: abdicate; deny; renounce; repudiate
disparage: abuse; decry; lessen; malign; pan; slur; traduce; vilify
disparagement: abuse; detraction; disgrace
disparaging: derogatory; dim; pejorative
disparity: difference
dispassionate: cool; sober; temperate

dispatch: accomplish; assassinate; expedite; expedition; haste; hasten; hurry; precipitate; send; speed; transmit
dispel: banish; disperse; dissipate; dissolve; resolve; scatter
dispensable: accidental; mean; unessential
dispensation: disposition
dispense: administer; allot; apportion; deal; distribute
disperse: disband; dissipate; dissolve; distribute; radiate; resolve; scatter; spread; sprinkle
dispersion: overthrow
dispirit: break; daunt; depress; discourage; dull
dispirited: blue; dejected; despondent; downhearted; gloomy; low; melancholy
dispiritedness: damp
dispiriting: blue; cold
displace: misplace; remove; supersede; supplant; unseat; upset
displacement: overthrow
display: air; array; betray; demonstrate; exhibit; expose; exposition; exposure; flash; flourish; manifest; ostentation; pageant; scene; show; splendor; spread; state
displease: anger; disgust; offend; pain; pique
displeasing: distasteful; offensive; ugly
displeasure: anger; discontent; dissatisfaction; distaste; offense; umbrage
disport: play
disposal: command; management; mercy; regulation
dispose of: spend
dispose: arrange; array; bend; bias; direct; distribute; form; get; marshal; organize; place; range; rank; regulate; set; spread
disposed: apt; prone; ready
disposition: affection; array; attitude; bent; character; habit; humor; liking; make; mercy; method; mettle; mind; mood; order; penchant; position; predilection; prejudice; proclivity; propensity; regulation; sentiment; set; spirit; taste; temper; temperament; tendency; will
dispossess: abridge; deprive; divest; strip
dispossession: abridgment
dispraise: pan
disproportionate: excessive; misshapen
disprove: refute
disputable: moot; open; questionable
disputation: controversy; debate; dispute
disputatious: acrimonious; quarrelsome; scrappy
dispute: agitate; agitation; argue; argument; brawl; breach; compete; contend; contention; contest; contradict; controversy; debate; deny; haggle; moot; passage; quarrel; question; row; tiff; variance
disputed: moot; vexed
disqualification: disability; inability
disqualify: disable; unfit
disquiet: agitation; annoy; anxiety; concern; pain; perturb; trouble; turmoil; worry
disquieted: afraid
disquieting: uncomfortable
disquietude: anxiety
disquisition: tract
disregard: blink; disobey; ignore; neglect; neglect; overlook; pass; skip; slight; slur
disregardful: neglectful; oblivious
disregarding: regardless
disrelish: disgust; dislike; distaste
disreputable: base; dishonorable; ignominious; infamous; low; opprobrious; shabby; shameful
disrepute: ignominy; infamy; reproach; scandal; stigma
disrespect: affront; disregard; familiarity; indignity; slight
disrespectful: familiar; impolite; insolent; uncivil
disrobe: divest
disrupt: break; rupture
disruption: break; rupture
disruptive: obtrusive
dissatisfaction: discontent; disgust; displeasure; dissent; distaste
dissatisfied: discontent; malcontent; weary

dissect: scrutinize
dissection: scrutiny
dissemble: act; bluff; cheat; conceal; counterfeit
dissembler: hypocrite
dissembling: bluff; hypocritical; pretense
disseminate: disperse; spread
dissension: breach; contention; contention; division; friction; misunderstanding; quarrel; variance
dissertation: tract
disservice: disadvantage
dissever: part; rend; separate
dissidence: dissent
dissimilar: distinct; diverse; unlike
dissimilarity: difference; disparity
dissimilitude: difference; disparity
dissimulate: act
dissimulation: chicanery; duplicity
dissipate: consume; disperse; exhaust; lavish; scatter; spend; squander; waste
dissipated: fast; immoral; lost
dissipation: excess; racket; waste
dissociate: abstract; part; segregate; separate
dissolute: abandoned; corrupt; depraved; fast; immoral; libertine; loose; lost; sensual; shameless; wanton; wicked
dissolution: corruption
dissolve: break; cut; disband; discharge; fuse; melt; thaw
dissonant: harsh; raucous
dissuade: deter; discourage; intimidate
distance: reach; span; stretch; way
distant: abhorrent; antisocial; cool; remote; strange; ulterior
distaste: aversion; disgust; dislike; displeasure; repugnance
distasteful: bitter; disgusting; indecent; offensive; repugnant; sour; unsavory
distemper: disease
distend: billow; dilate; expand; inflate; stretch; swell
distended: tumid; turgid; wide
distention: swell
distill: abstract; decompose; extract; try
distillate: extract
distillation: abstract
distilled: refined
distillery: still
distinct from: besides
distinct: clear; express; fair; lively; lucid; manifest; obvious; only; particular; perspicuous; plain; separate; sharp; single; special; strong; various; vivid
distinction: accolade; account; brilliance; celebrity; consequence; difference; disparity; eminence; excellence; glory; honor; luster; mark; name; note; peculiarity; prestige; quality; rank; renown; reputation; repute; splendor
distinctive: characteristic; grand; particular; peculiar
distinctly: clearly
distinctness: diction; perspicuity
distingu.: distinguished
distinguish: contrast; differentiate; differentiate; discern; discriminate; divide; know; notice; perceive; see; stamp; tell
distinguishable: distinct
distinguished: acclaimed; bright; celebrated; conspicuous; distinct; eminent; famous; glorious; great; high; honorable; notable; noted; peculiar; preeminent; prominent; remarkable; shining; special; splendid
distinguishing: discriminate
distort: mar; skew; twist; warp
distorted: misshapen; perverse; perverted; wry
distortion: falsehood
distract: divert; turn
distracted: mad; wild
distraction: confusion
distress-signal: alarm
distress: adversity; affliction; agony; anguish; anxiety; calamity; chagrin; embarrass; embarrassment; grief; grieve; harass; misery; misfortune; need; pain; poverty; privation; rack; rankle; sorrow; strait; tear; throe; torment; trial; trouble; woe
distressed: miserable; poor; sore; unhappy; wretched
distressing: acute; bitter; cruel; grievous; harrowing; heavy;

painful; piteous; poignant; pungent; severe; sharp; sore; sorrowful; terrible; tragic; unkind
distribute: administer; allot; apportion; arrange; assign; deal; dispense; divide; issue; mete; parcel; part; portion; publish; ration; sort; spread; sprinkle
distribution: deal; division; partition; proportion
district: circuit; part; region; tract; vicinity; zone
distrust: apprehension; doubt; misgiving; suspect; suspicion
distrustful: cynical; quizzical; shy
disturb the peace: riot
disturb: agitate; annoy; bother; concern; confuse; disconcert; disorder; excite; harass; harry; interrupt; molest; perplex; perturb; pester; plague; roil; ruffle; shake; startle; stir; tease; trouble; turn; upset; worry
disturbance: ado; agitation; brawl; commotion; disorder; excitement; hubbub; racket; riot; ruckus; ruffle; shake; shock; storm; trouble; tumult; turmoil; uproar; upset
disturbed: rough; solicitous; tumultuous; unquiet; upset; vexed
disturbing: agitation; vexatious
disunion: division; rent
disunite: abstract; dissolve; divide; part; separate; sever
disunited: separate
disunity: conflict
dither: ado; waffle; yo-yo
divagate: skew
dive: dip; plunge; sound
diverge: bend; branch; depart; deviate; digress; skew; swerve
divergence: aberration; difference; variance; variation; variety
divergent: aberrant; different; diverse
diverging: aberrant
divers: different; manifold; many; miscellaneous; various
diverse: different; multifarious; unlike; various
diversified: miscellaneous; various
diversify: sprinkle; vary
diversion: fun; game; pastime; play; sport
diversity: difference; mixture; variation; variety
divert: abstract; amuse; beguile; entertain; regale; turn
diverting: amusing; droll; funny
divertissement: fun; game
divest: abridge; deprive; strip
divide: allot; apportion; branch; cut; distinguish; distribute; diverge; parcel; part; partition; portion; rend; separate; sever; share; sort; tear; wall
divided: separate
dividend: advantage; bonus; part; portion; profit; share
dividing line: boundary,
dividing wall: partition
dividing: division
dividual: distinct
divination: necromancy; prediction; sorcery
divine: celestial; extract; heavenly; holy; predict; prophesy; sacred
diviner: wizard
division: boundary; compartment; faction; movement; part; partition; portion; rank; region
divulge: break; communicate; demonstrate; disclose; give; impart; mention; open; publish; reveal; show; spread; tell; ventilate
divulgement: exposure
dizzy: giddy; light; stun
do away with: abolish; kill; obliterate; remove
do business: deal
do imitations or impersonations: act
do imitations: act
do in: zap
do wrong: sin
do: accomplish; achieve; act; answer; complete; consummate; effect; execute; finish; fulfill; make; perform; perpetrate; play; practice; render; serve; take; work
doable: practicable; viable
docent: guru
docile: dutiful; gentle; meek; obedient; pliant; submissive; tame; tame; tractable
dock: abbreviate; curtail

doctrinaire: magisterial
doctrine: belief; faith; lore; position; principle; tenet
document: form; roll
doddering: crazy; senile; shaky; spindly
doddery: senile
dodge: elude; evade; malinger; ploy; shirk; trick
dodger: cheat
dodging: evasion
dodgy: shaky; slippery
dog in the manger: killjoy
dog-cart: carriage
dogcart: wagon
dogged: headstrong; inflexible; intractable; obstinate; pertinacious; perverse; single-minded; stubborn
doggedness: perseverance
dogma: belief; doctrine; faith; tenet
dogmatic: authoritative; magisterial; opinionated; oracular; peremptory; positive; stiff
dole out: administer; allot; apportion
dole: deal; dispense; distribute; mete; portion; ration; share
doleful: black; blue; lugubrious; melancholy; miserable; piteous; somber; sorrowful
doll up: decorate
dolor: trouble
dolt: block; fool; oaf
domain: bailiwick; kingdom; realm; sphere; terrain
domestic: household; menial; servant
domesticate: subdue; tame
domesticated: familiar; tame
domicile: address; home; house; place; residence
domiciliary: household
dominance: machismo
dominant: predominant; preeminent; prevailing
dominate: command; control; manage; predominate; subject; sway; terrorize
dominating: magisterial; master
domination: command; control; obsession; rule
domineering: arbitrary; imperious; lordly; overbearing; tyrannical
dominion: empire; kingdom; power; reign; rule; sway
don: teacher
donate: confer; give; present
donation: gift; present
done with: finished
done: complete; consummate; finished; thorough
donnybrook: row
doodad: gadget
doohickey: gadget
doom: condemn; curse; destiny; fate
doomed: fatal; poor
doomsayer: killjoy
door prize: premium
door: entrance; hatch
doormat: weakling
doorway: access; entrance
dope out: decipher; deduce
dope: yahoo
dopey: groggy
dormancy: abeyance; sleep
dormant: inactive; silent; torpid
dorp: hamlet; town
dose: administer
dot: atom; portion
doting: smitten
double-cross: deceive
double-dealing: artifice; chicanery; duplicity; Machiavellian
double-talk: jargon
double: duplicate
doubt: contest; distrust; hazard; hesitation; misgiving; problem; quandary; question; scruple; stagger; stick; suspect; suspense; suspicion
doubter: atheist; iconoclast; skeptic
doubtful: ambiguous; dubious; equivocal; iffy; incredulous; indefinite; moot; obscure; precarious; questionable; shaky; skeptical; uncertain; uncertain
doubtfully: askance
doubting: faithless; quizzical
dough: money
doughty: bold; brave; daring; dauntless; unabashed
dour : glum
douse: immerse
dove-gray: pearly
dowdy: tacky
down-at-heel: seedy

doctrinaire: magisterial
down-in-the-mouth: melancholy
down-to-earth: earthy; vernacular
down: pile
downbeat: world-weary
downcast: blue; depressed; downhearted; gloomy; heavy; melancholy; sad; unhappy
downfall: defeat; perdition; ruin
downgrade: abase; degrade
downhearted: dejected; despondent; gloomy; heavy; melancholy; sad
downpour: cascade; deluge; torrent
downright: direct; flat; frank; plain; plump; sheer; stark; unqualified
dowry: gift; portion
doze: sleep
drab: lackluster; tacky
draft: drink; outline; outline; plan; sketch
drag one's feet: shamble
drag: draw; hale; killjoy; trail
dragging: slow
drain dry: bankrupt
drain: draw; empty; exhaust
drama: play
dramatic: grandiose; theatrical
drape: curtain; hang
drapery: curtain
draught: design; draw; swallow; wind
draw or pull out: draw
draw or shrink back: recoil
draw aside or away: divert
draw away: abstract
draw back : wince,
draw back or away: withdraw
draw back: give; retreat; shy
draw forth or out: extract
draw out: extract; lengthen; protract; spin; spin; spread; stretch
draw together: contract
draw up: array; draw
draw: attract; attract; bend; bring; depict; design; drag; hale; invite; lead; lure; outline; picture; purchase; sketch; steal; take; trace; trail
drawback: disadvantage
drawing together: gather
drawing: outline; picture; plan; sketch
drawings: design
drawn out: long
drawn: cadaverous; careworn; haggard; peaked; taut
dray: wagon
dread: apprehension; awe; consternation; fear; formidable; frightful; horror; phobia
dreadful: dread; formidable; frightful; ghastly; grievous; grim; hideous; horrendous; horrible; monstrous; nefarious; terrible; tragic; tremendous
dream up: pioneer
dream: daydream; muse
dreamed-up: fictitious
dreamer: visionary
dreaming: absent-minded
dreamy: pensive
drear: dreary; dull; stark
dreary: desolate; dry; dull; forlorn; gaunt; lonely; sorrowful; stark
dregs: ground; refuse; sediment
drench: saturate; soak; wet
drenched: wet
dress down;bawl out: reprimand
dress up: beautify; decorate
dress-up: finery
dress: apparel; array; clothes; deck; decorate; garb; gown; habit; raiment; tease; trick; trim; wardrobe
drift: burden; design; end; purport; spirit; tendency; trend; turn
drill: bore; discipline; educate; exercise; instruct; instruction; pierce; practice; rehearse; teach
drink: imbibe; sip; swallow
drinker: drunkard
drip: ooze
drive or force away: expel
drive or force out: expel
drive apart: estrange
drive away: scatter
drive together: compel
drive: argue; bear; carry; compel; force; impel; moment; push; run; spin; thrust; turn; urge
drivel: babble
driving: urgent
drizzle: mist; wet
drizzling: wet
droll: amusing; comical; facetious; funny; humorous; jocose; laughable; ludicrous; ridiculous; risible; waggish; witty; zany

drollery: wit
dronish: sluggish
drool: fool
droop: fade; pine; wither
drooping: faint; lax
droopy: lax
drop-dead: extraordinary; final
drop: abandon; deposit; dip; forsake; lower; ooze; plump; plump; plunge; rebuff
dropped: abandoned
dross: refuse
drove: flock; herd
drown: overwhelm
drowse: sleep
drub: beat; thrash
drudge: labor; moil; plod; slave; work
drudgery: labor; moil; slavery; task; toil; work
drudging: slavish
drug: medicine; opiate; sedative
drum: throb
drumbeat: ruffle
drunk: cockeyed; drunken; lush
drunkard: inebriate
dry up: sear
dry: arid; curt; dull; evaporate; stale; wither
dryad: nymph
du jour: current; fashionable
dub: call; entitle; name; style
dubious: ambiguous; ambivalent; doubtful; equivocal; incredulous; obscure; precarious; questionable; quizzical; shaky; skeptical; uncertain
dubiously: askance
dubitable: dubious; questionable
duck duty: malinger
duck: dip; immerse; shirk
duct: main
ductile: malleable; pliant
dud: failure; washout
dude: coxcomb
dudgeon: wrath
duds: raiment; wardrobe
due: appropriate; debt; just; merit; outstanding; right
duet: couple
duke: peer
dulcet: mellifluous; mellow; soft; sweet; tuneful
dull-witted: silly
dull: apathetic; arid; barren; blunt; callous; cold; dead; depress; dim; dirty; dreary; dry; faint; fat; fatuous; flat; foolish; heavy; innocuous; lackluster; languid; lifeless; monotonous; pallid; pedestrian; prosaic; sad; shackle; slack; slow; sluggish; sober; soften; somber; stereotyped; stupid; sullen; tame; tarnish; tasteless; tedious; thick-skinned; tiresome; torpid; vapid; wearisome
dullard: yahoo
dulled: dull
dullwitted: blunt
dumb luck: serendipity
dumb: mute; silent; speechless; speechless; stupid
dumbfounded: aghast
dumfound: amaze; shock; stagger
dumfounded: blank; speechless
dump: shack
dun: uniform
dunce: block; fool; oaf; yahoo
dunderhead: fool
dunderpate: fool
dungeon: hold; keep
duo: couple
dupe: bite; cheat; deceive; delude; fool; humbug; mock; swindle; trick; victimize
dupery: chicanery
duplicate: copy; imitate; reproduce
duplicated: identical
duplicitous: mealy-mouthed
duplicity: art; artifice; deceit; fraud; guile; trick
durable: permanent; standing; tough; well-built
duration: age; standing; time
dusk: evening; shade; twilight
dusky: black; dark; dim; gloomy; murky; obscure; somber; swarthy
dust storm: sirocco; storm
dust: clean; haze
dustup: tiff
dusty: robust
dutiful: obedient; responsible
duty: allegiance; business; charge; custom; debt; obligation; office; part; place; task; trust
dwarf: diminutive; pygmy
dwarfed: dwarf
dwarfish: diminutive

dwarflike: diminutive
dwell on: brood; meditate
dwell: abide; house; reside; sit; stay
dwellers: household
dwelling: address; home; house; place; residence
dwindle: decrease; diminish; fail; lessen; melt; pine; shrink; waste
dwindling: decrease
dye: stain; tint
dyed-in-the-wool: complete
dying: low
dynamism: energy
eager: active; ambitious; ardent; earnest; enterprising; enthusiastic; excited; fervent; forward; greedy; intent; keen; sharp; solicitous; strenuous; strong; swift; urgent; vehement; warm; wild; zealous
eagerness: anxiety; ardor; devotion; enthusiasm; fervor; lust; rage; thirst; vehemence; zeal
eagle-eyed: astute
eagre: bore; breaker
earl: peer
earlier: above; previous
earliest: pioneer; primary
early: antique; forward; high; antique
earn: acquire; gain; get; make; merit; obtain; win
earnest: active; close; devout; direct; fervent; forward; grave; keen; passionate; resolute; serious; sincere; solemn; strenuous; strong; urgent; vehement; zealous
earnestly: hard
earnestness: devotion; enthusiasm; fervor; goodwill; zeal
earnings: income; wage
earth: ground; nature
earthly: carnal; mundane; secular; terrestrial; worldly
earthquake: quake; tremor
earthy: earthly; secular
ease: aid; allay; alleviate; appease; comfort; contentment; favor; freedom; grace; help; lighten; loose; palliate; qualify; redress; relax; relief; relieve; satisfaction; soften
easeful: cozy
easily affected: sensitive
easily influenced: pliant
easily: leisurely; readily
easy chair: seat
easy victory: romp
easy: affable; convenient; easygoing; facile; familiar; free; informal; lenient; light; smooth
easygoing: easy; laid-back; offhand; sweet
eat away: bite; waste
eat up: consume
eat: corrode; feast; feed; swallow
eating away: fret
ebb: abate; abatement; decrease; diminish; subside
ebbing: decrease
ebon: black; dark
ebullition: boil
eccentric: aberrant; abnormal; bohemian; crackpot; cranky; fantastic; irregular; odd; offbeat; peculiar; queer; screwball; singular; strange; wacky
eccentricity: aberration; peculiarity
echelon: caste
echo: repeat; reply; sound; vibrate
éclat: celebrity; dash; luster; magnificence; splendor; style
eclectic: selective
eclipse: blot; excel
economical: frugal; prudent; spare; thrifty
economize: save
economy: parsimony; prudence
ecstasy: bliss; delight; joy; rapture; trance; transport; triumph
ecstatic: rapt
ecumenical: broad-minded; universal
eczema: rash
edacious: gluttonous
edda: saga
eddy: maelstrom
edge: bank; border; boundary; brim; list; margin; rim; verge
edgy: skittish; splenetic; testy
edict: act; decree; mandate
edifice: building; pile; structure
edify: enlighten
edifying: uplifting
edit out: zap
edit: abstract; cut
edition: issue; number

educable: receptive
educate: breed; discipline; edify; enlighten; form; instruct; manage; teach
education: instruction; schooling
educational: uplifting
educe: extract
eerie: weird
efface: blot; cancel; deface; deform; delete; erase; obliterate
effect: accomplish; achieve; achieve; affect; apply; attain; carry; cause; complete; consequence; consummate; contrive; do; execute; exercise; force; force; fulfill; induce; issue; make; operate; operation; perform; perpetrate; procure; produce; purpose; **raise; realize; result; work**
effected: consummate
effecting: accomplishment
effective: active; brave; effectual; efficacious; efficient; energetic; lively; neat; operative; powerful; prevailing; serviceable; smart; sovereign; standing; stringent; strong; trenchant; useful; utilitarian; valid; vigorous
effectiveness: force; strength; virtue
effects: good; paraphernalia; property
effectual: effective; energetic; operative; powerful; prevailing; sovereign; useful; valid
effectuate: accomplish; execute; perpetrate; realize
effervesce: sparkle
effervescence: life
effervescent: brisk; bubbly; irrepressible
effete: decrepit
efficacious: available; effective; energetic; operative; potent; powerful; prevailing; sovereign; strong; useful; valid
efficacy: effect; energy; force; might; operation; strength; virtue; weight
efficiency: force
efficient: active; capable; effective; good; operative; practical; strong; valid
efficiently: well
effigy: image
effloresce: bloom
efflorescence: bloom; rash
effluvium: exhaust
effort: action; attempt; diligence; drive; exertion; main; push; stand; strain; struggle; study; toil; trial; trouble
effortless: facile
effortlessness: ease
efforts: pain
effrontery: arrogance; assumption; assurance; chutzpah; gall; impudence
effulgence: brilliance; glory
effulgent: bright; radiant; shining
effusive: bubbly; outgoing
egghead: intellectual; savant
egoism: egotism
egoistic: selfish; smug
egomaniacal: egocentric
egotism: arrogance; conceit; egoism; vainglory; vanity
egotistic: arrogant; egocentric
egotistical: arrogant; conceited; egocentric; proud; vain
egregious: enormous; extraordinary; precious; shabby
egress: issue
ejaculate: cry
ejaculation: cry; exclamation
eject: cast; discharge; emit; exclude; expel
ejection: discharge
elaborate: labor; ornate; studied
elaborated: mature
elaboration: development
élan: dash; luster; panache; splendor; style; verve
elapse: fly
elastic: all-around; flexible; malleable; resilient; supple
elasticity: spring; temper
elate: exalt; exhilarate
elated: blithe; ecstatic; glad; high; joyful
elation: ecstasy,
elbow-room: play
elbow: bend
elderly: aged; old
elect: appoint; choose; clannish; ordain; prefer; take
election: choice; option
electrocute: kill
electron: particle

elegance: beauty; finish; grace; polish; style
elegant: beautiful; chaste; dainty; delicate; exquisite; facile; fancy; fine; finished; gentle; magnificent; ornate; polished; polite; refined; rich; sleek; smart; smooth; stately; superb; swell; urbane; wanton
elegy: lament; moan
element: base; component; essential; ingredient; material; member; milieu; part
elementary: bottom; essential; fundamental; primary; rudimentary; simple
elements: ABC's
elephantine: enormous; gigantic
elevate: advance; ameliorate; consecrate; dignify; edify; exalt; heave; hoist; lift; promote; raise; raise; rear; uphold
elevated: chaste; grand; great; high; lofty; magnanimous; noble; tall; towering
elevating: humane
elevation: altitude; eminence; height; hill; rise
elevator: hoist
elf: brownie; fairy; goblin; spirit
elicit: extract
elide: contract
eliminate: abate; abolish; bar; blot; deface; disable; exclude; exterminate; reject; remove; stamp; zap
elimination: abolition
elite: clannish
elixir: cure-all
Elmo's fire: ephemeral
elocute: declaim
elongate: lengthen; stretch
eloquent: articulate,
else: besides
elucidate: account; decipher; explain; interpret; rationalize; show
elucidation: account; comment; explanation; exposition; illustration
elude: avoid; dodge; escape; evade; parry; shirk; shun
elysian: celestial
emaciate: waste
emaciated: cadaverous; gaunt; haggard; lean; meager; peaked; poor; spare; thin
emaciation: waste
emanate: emerge; issue; originate; proceed; radiate; spring
emancipate: clear; deliver; free; liberate
emancipation: release
emancipator: savior
embank: bank
embankment: bank; wall
embargo: prohibition
embarrass: abash; chagrin; confuse; disconcert; discourage; encumber; entangle
embarrassed: ashamed; bashful; diffident
embarrassing: awkward
embarrassment: chagrin; confusion; trouble
embed: immerse
embellish: adorn; beautify; beset; deck; decorate; flourish; garnish; grace; ornament; trim
embellished: ornate
embellishment: flourish; ornament; trim
embezzle: steal
embezzlement: crime
embitter: rankle
emblem: character; device; standard
embody: comprehend; comprise; contain; cover; embrace; include
embolden: encourage; reassure
embossed: prominent
embrace: clasp; comprehend; comprise; contain; cover; espouse; hold; include; involve; strain; take
embroider: embellish
embryonic: rudimentary
emend: amend; better; correct; fix; improve; mend; patch; rectify; redress; reform
emendation: mend
emerge: appear; emanate; issue; spring
emergence: beginning
emergency: crisis; difficulty; need; strait
emigrate: migrate
eminence: brilliance; celebrity; distinction; elevation; excellence; fame; glory; height; hill; luster;

mark; name; note; pinnacle; rank; renown; splendor
eminent: celebrated; conspicuous; distinguished; famous; glorious; grand; great; high; notable; noted; outstanding; preeminent; prominent; shining; splendid
eminently: chiefly
emission: discharge; issue
emit: cast; deliver; discharge; give; issue; radiate; spread; stream; void
emollient: mild
emolument: pay; wage
emotion: feeling; passion; sentiment; stir
emotional: excitable; feeling; hotheaded; impulsive; passionate; pathetic; warm
emotionalism: schmaltz
emotionless: apathetic
empathy: emotion; feeling; rapport; sympathy,
emperor: sovereign
emphasis: assertion; stress
emphasize: assert; dwell; stress
emphasized: pointed
emphatic: decided; expressive; positive
empire: kingdom; monarchy
employ: apply; exercise; expend; hire; occupy; play; retain; spend; take; use
employable: serviceable
employed: busy
employee: servant
employer: master
employment: business; charge; employ; exercise; job; occupation; place; position; profession; station; trade; use; vocation; work
empower: authorize; entitle
empress: sovereign
emptied: clear
emptiness: blank; vanity; wind
empty suit: weakling
empty words: talk
empty-headed: giddy; vacuous
empty: arid; bare; black; blank; clear; deceitful; exhaust; hypocritical; lone; tame; teem; trifling; vacant; vacuous; void
empyreal: celestial
empyrean: celestial
emulate: compete; feign; play; rival
emulating: rival
emulative: slavish
emulator: rival; wannabe
emulous: ambitious
enable: empower; give
enablement: ability
enact: establish; impersonate; ordain; pass; play; present; transact
enacted: positive
enactment: act; passage
enamor: attract; captivate; charm; fascinate
enamored: amorous; smitten
enamour: attach
enceinte: big
enchant: bewitch; captivate; catch; charm; delight; enamor; entrance; fascinate; take
enchanted: rapt
enchanter: magician; wizard
enchanting: delightful; lovely
enchantment: charm; conquest; magic; necromancy; sorcery
encircle: belt; beset; bind; circle; confine; embrace; enclose; ring; wind; zone
encircling: about
enclose: beset; cabin; close; confine; embrace; encircle; envelop; incarcerate; shut; wall
enclosed: close
enclosing: about
enclosure: pale; pound
encomium: commendation; compliment; paean; panegyric
encompass: beset; circle; encircle; enclose; envelop
enconium: praise
encounter: action; affront; attack; brush; charge; combat; conflict; contest; experience; face; fight; meet; passage; shock; skirmish; stand; strike; struggle
encountering: experience
encourage: abet; animate; cheer; cherish; console; countenance; favor; foster; help; incite; nourish; nurse; promote; reassure; spirit
encouragement: cheer; comfort; consolation; countenance; incentive

encourager: friend
encouraging: bright; genial
encroach: infringe; intrude; trespass
encroachment: trespass
encumber: hamper; hinder; hobble; load; perplex
encumbrance: burden; charge; hindrance; impediment; load; shackle
encyclopedia: thesaurus
end: abatement; aim; back; break; catastrophe; cause; cease; close; complete; conclusion; consequence; death; design; destroy; die; disappear; dissolve; do; effect; extreme; extremity; finish; fulfill; intent; issue; mark; object; objective; outcome; pass; purpose; reason; result; sake; stop; terminate; twilight; vanish; view
endanger: dare; expose; hazard; peril; risk; threaten; venture
endear: attach; attract
endearment: affection
endeavor: attempt; effort; exertion; strive; struggle; study; trial; try; zeal
ended: complete; extinct; finished
ending: abatement; conclusion; twilight
endless: eternal; immortal; measureless; perpetual; unbounded
endmost: extreme
endorse: affirm; approve; back; espouse; support
endorsement: reference
endow: lavish; portion; present
endowed: able
endowment: disposition; foundation; gift
endue: endow
endurance: nerve; patience; resignation; tolerance
endure: abide; bear; brook; continue; experience; hold; last; permit; persist; remain; stand; support; sustain; take; undergo
enduring: durable; fast; immortal; perennial; permanent; perpetual; persistent; sound; stable
enemy: adversary; antagonist; foe; offense; opponent; opposition
energetic activity: action
energetic: active; aggressive; arduous; brisk; bubbly; emphatic; enterprising; fast; high; lissome; lively; mercurial; quick; smart; spirited; spry; strenuous; strong; tireless; vibrant; vigorous; vivid
energetically: fast; hard
energize: animate; invigorate
energy: action; ambition; animation; drive; enterprise; force; life; nerve; power; spirit; strength; violence
enervate: break; exhaust; relax; weaken
enervated: feeble; lackadaisical; nerveless; tired
enervation: decline
enfeeble: break; disable; relax; shake; waste; weaken
enfeebled: decrepit; impotent; unhealthy
enfeeblement: decline
enfold: encircle; envelop; roll
enforce: execute
enforcement: force
enfranchise: empower
enfranchisement: permission
engage in battle: attack
engage in: hold; wage
engage with: encounter
engage: arrest; attach; attract; bind; concern; employ; fight; hire; immerse; occupy; play; promise; retain; take
engaged: active; busy
engagement: action; appointment; battle; brush; combat; fight
engaging: interesting; pleasing; sweet; winning
engender: breed; get; raise
engineer: manage
engorge: swallow
engraving: stamp
engross: absorb; dilate; monopolize
engrossed: preoccupied; rapt
engulf: absorb; swallow
enhance: adorn; beautify; elevate; embellish; garnish; grace; raise
enhancement: appendix
enhancing: cosmetic
enigma: problem; puzzle; riddle
enigmatic: ambiguous; dark; doubtful; mysterious; ulterior
enigmatical: dark

enisled: alone; retired

enjoin: bid; caution; charge; command; decree; prescribe; require

enjoy: have; relish

enjoyable: delightful; felicitous; pleasant; sweet

enjoyment: delight; fun; happiness; pleasure; relish; satisfaction; zest

enlarge: amplify; augment; bulk; dilate; distend; expand; extend; grow; increase; magnify; piece; raise; rise; stretch; swell; wax

enlarged: tumid

enlargement: addition; extension; increase; rise

enlighten: edify; instruct; teach

enlightened: judicious; rational

enlightening: luminous; uplifting

enlightenment: education; knowledge; wisdom

enlist: list

enliven: amuse; animate; cheer; exhilarate; inform; invigorate; refresh

enlivening: bright; genial

enmesh: entangle

enmity: abhorrence; friction; grudge; hostility; malice; rancor

ennoble: dignify; exalt

ennuyant: dull

enormous: crying; exorbitant; giant; gigantic; great; huge; large; mighty; monster; monstrous; prodigious; vast

enough: adequate; sufficient

enrage: anger; exasperate; incense; infuriate; irritate; madden; provoke

enraged: angry; irate; mad; savage; wrathful

enrapture: bewitch; charm; delight; enchant; entrance; fascinate

enraptured: rapt

enrich: endow

enroll: list; record; register; schedule

enrollment: register

ensanguined: bloody

enshrine: sanctify

enshroud: bury; cover

ensign: standard

enslave: tame

ensnare: catch; cheat; deceive; entangle; trap

ensue: follow; issue; proceed; result

ensure: guarantee; secure

entail: involve

entangle: catch; encumber; foul; implicate; involve; perplex; snare; snarl

entangled: foul

entanglement: snarl

entente cordiale: peace

entente: compact; peace

enter upon or into: commence

enter upon: begin

enter: access; debut; penetrate; pierce; record; register; schedule

enterprise: ambition; attempt; business; spirit; work

enterprising: active; adventurous; aggressive; ambitious

entertain: accommodate; amuse; bear; beguile; cherish; divert; harbor; hold; regale; see; treat

entertaining: amusing; interesting

entertainment: feast; pastime; sport; treat

enthrall: captivate

enthralled: rapt; spellbound

enthrallment: slavery

enthusiasm: animation; ardor; fervor; flame; frenzy; mania; rage; spirit; vehemence; zeal

enthusiast: visionary

enthusiastic: ardent; eager; excited; fanatical; fervent; irrepressible; passionate; sanguine; warm; wild; zealous

entice: cajole; corrupt; flatter; invite; lead; lure; persuade; seduce; tempt

enticement: incentive; lure; stimulus

enticing: seductive; tempting

entire: absolute; absolute; blank; clean; complete; dead; gross; intact; mere; rank; round; solid; sound; stark; thorough; total; unbroken; universal; unreserved; utter; whole

entirely: absolutely; clean; clearly; sheer

entirety: entire; integrity; total; totality; whole

entitle: call; empower; name; style; title

entitled: apparent

entitlement: merit

entomb: bury; sepulcher

entr,e: access; admission

entrammel: hobble

entrance: access; admission; admittance; charm; fascinate

entrancing: charismatic

entrap: bag; catch; cheat; deceive; snare; trap

entrapping: insidious

entreat: appeal; apply; ask; beg; beseech; beseech; crave; implore; petition; plead; pray; request; solicit; supplicate; urge

entreaty: appeal; cry; petition; request

entree: entrance

entrench: authorize

entrust: commend; delegate; trust

entry: access; entrance; entrance; entrance; register

enumerate: number; recite; reckon; recount; rehearse; tell

enunciation: diction

envelop: cover; roll

envelope: case

envenom: poison

envious: jealous; malevolent

enviousness: envy

environ: encircle

environment: element; habitat; medium; milieu; sphere; state; vicinity

environs: environment; habitat; vicinity

envision: fancy

envoy: delegate

envy: begrudge; covet; emulation; grudge

enwrap: cover

ephemeral: brief; temporary

ephemeron: ephemeral

epic: heroic; myth; saga

epicurean: epicure; luxurious; sybarite; voluptuous

epidemic: affliction; pandemic; pest; plague

epigram: proverb

epigrammatic: pithy; pointed; sententious

epilogue: supplement

episode: event; excursion; scene

epithet: byword; name; title

epitome: abbreviation; abridgment; abstract; argument; brief; burden; digest; ideal; summary; synopsis

epitomize: abbreviate; abridge; abstract; brief; condense; contract

epoch: age; period; time

equability: composure

equable: even; level; smooth

equal: abreast; adequate; associate; compare; even; flat; identical; level; parallel; peer; rival; same; tantamount; tie

equality: balance; parity

equalize: balance; level

equalizer: balance

equanimity: calm; composure; temper

equate: average

equidistant: middle

equilibrate: balance; even; poise

equilibration: balance

equilibrium: balance; balance; poise; symmetry

equip: accomplish; apparel; appoint; array; endow; furnish; habit; qualify

equipage: paraphernalia

equipment: apparel; paraphernalia; trim

equipoise: balance; balance; poise

equipped: ready

equitable: even; fair; honorable; impartial; just; reasonable; right; righteous; straight; true; unbiased

equitableness: right

equitably: right

equity: honesty; right

equivalence: parity

equivalent: equal; level; reciprocal; tantamount

equivocal: ambiguous; ambivalent; doubtful; dubious; indefinite; Machiavellian; oracular

equivocate: dodge; evade; prevaricate; quibble; waffle; yo-yo

equivocation: evasion; quibble

era: age; epoch; period; time

eradicate: abolish; delete; destroy; exterminate; stamp

eradication: abolition; destruction

eradicative: destructive

erase: abolish; blot; cancel; deface; delete; obliterate; zap

erasure: blot

Erebus: hell

erect: construct; fabricate; fabricate; raise; rear; stand; straight; upright; vertical

erection: building; edifice

eremite: monk; solitary

eremitic: antisocial

eremitical: antisocial

erode: abrade; bite; corrode; fret; waste

eroded: weather-beaten

erosion: abrasion; fret

erotic: amorous; X-rated

err: deviate; mistake; offend; slip; transgress; trip; wander

errant: aberrant; circuitous

erratic: aberrant; abnormal; capricious; irregular

erratum: misprint; mistake; oversight; trip

erring: aberrant

erroneous: false; inaccurate; incorrect; mistaken; unsound; wrong

erroneousness: inaccuracy

error: blunder; delusion; fault; impropriety; inaccuracy; mistake; misunderstanding; oversight; slip; trespass; trip

ersatz: artificial; counterfeit; false

erudite: wise

erudition: knowledge; learning; lore; scholarship; wisdom

eruption: access; convulsion; paroxysm; rash

escapade: caper; romp

escape from: evade

escape: abscond; avoid; break; elude; evade; evasion; shirk

eschew: avoid; shun

escort: accompany; attend; attendant; conduct; convoy; guard; guide; lead; see; take

esne: serf; slave

esoteric: abstruse; mysterious; rarefied

especial: certain; particular; private; special

especially: chiefly; mostly; particularly; principally

espouse: defend; embrace; hold; reflect

espouser: advocate

esprit: verve

espy: discern; discover; perceive; see

essay: attempt; endeavor; piece; proof; strive; test; theme; tract; trial; try

essence: abbreviation; abstract; aroma; burden; flavor; fundamental; goodness; lean; matter; perfume; spirit; substance; substance; summary

essential: capital; chief; element; fundamental; indispensable; inherent; intrinsic; material; necessary; necessity; organic; radical; requisite; subjective; substantial; vital

essentials: ABC's; basics

establish: affirm; appoint; arrange; ascertain; authorize; base; confirm; determine; erect; fix; ground; place; prescribe; prove; ratify; resolve; rule; set; settle; start; station; sustain

established: firm; regular; solid; stable; standing; steadfast

establishment: concern; foundation; house

estate: caste; heritage; property; state

esteem: admiration; admire; adore; appreciate; approve; consideration; credit; deference; estimation; hold; honor; judge; laud; prize; reckon; regard; reputation; repute; respect; think; value

esteemed: dear; favorite

estimable: admirable; creditable; excellent; honorable; respectable; rich; valuable; worthy

estimate or rate highly: appreciate

estimate: account; balance; calculate; calculation; call; compute; esteem; forecast; guess; judge; judgment; make; reckon; regard; set; study; value

estimation: account; calculation; consideration; credit; esteem; estimate; fame; opinion; regard; reputation; repute; respect; sense; value; view

estivating: torpid

estoppage: death; hindrance; obstruction

estrange: divide

estrangement: division

etc.): answer

etching: style

eternal: continual; endless; everlasting; fast; immortal; incessant; perennial; perpetual; stable; undying

eternally: always; ever

ether: medium

ethereal: celestial; rarefied

ethic: ideology

ethical: moral

ethics: moral

ethnic group: nation

ethnocentric: clannish; xenophobic

ethos: ideology

etiolate: blanch; bleach; pale; whiten

etiolated: weather-beaten

etiquette: decorum; propriety

eulogize: commend; extol; praise

eulogy: commendation; compliment; panegyric; praise

euphonious: mellifluous

euphony: harmony

evacuate: abandon; empty; vacate; void

evacuation: discharge

evade: avoid; blink; dodge; elude; escape; parry; quibble; shirk; shun

evaluate: estimate; reckon; set

evaluation: value

evanesce: disperse; evaporate; fade; vanish

evanescent: ephemeral; temporary

evangel: harbinger

evangelist: harbinger

evaporated: dry

evasion: device; excuse; mask; parry; quibble

evasive: slippery; tortuous

eve: evening

even if: although

even though: although; if

even-tempered: easygoing; equable; even

even: clear; equable; equal; evening; flat; level; plain; regular; smooth; steady; uniform

evenhanded: just

evening gown or dress: gown

evening: twilight

event: consequence; episode; incident; issue; occasion; occurrence; phenomenon; result

eventful: lively

eventfulness: movement

eventide: evening; twilight

eventuate: result; terminate

ever: always

everlasting: chronic; continual; endless; eternal; immortal; incessant; perennial; permanent; perpetual; stable; undying

everlastingly: always

evermore: always

every place: about

every time: always

everyday: common; household; lackluster; usual; vernacular

everything: totality

everywhere: about; abroad; ubiquitous

evidence: argument; demonstrate; exhibit; manifest; proof; prove; show; testimony; trace; vestige; witness

evident: apparent; bare; bold; clear; direct; indisputable; lucid; manifest; naked; obvious; open; palpable; patent; plain; self-evident; tangible; undeniable; unequivocal; unmistakable; visible

evidential: factual

evidentiary: factual

evidently: clearly

evil-minded: malevolent

evil: abomination; bad; black; calamity; corrupt; corruption; curse; danger; dark; depraved; harm; ill; immoral; malign; mischief; nefarious; pernicious; perverse; plague; satanic; sinful; sinister; unclean; ungodly; unnatural; unprincipled; vile; wicked; wrong

evildoer: criminal; malefactor

evince: argue; betray; demonstrate; display; exhibit; manifest; prove; register

evoke: extract; raise

evolve: ripen; spin

exacerbate: exasperate; provoke

exact satisfaction for: avenge

exact: accurate; ask; careful; close; command; correct; critical; dead; definite; delicate; demand;

explicit: express; extort; extract; faithful; identical; intimate; just; meticulous; minute; nice; particular; perfect; precise; proper; punctilious; refined; rigorous; scrupulous; severe; strict; take; true; unerring

exacting: close; conscientious; delicate; exact; hard; intimate; nice; religious; scrupulous; severe; strict

exactly: particularly; right; true

exactness: fidelity; truth

exaggerate about: embellish

exaggerate: amplify; boast; caricature; magnify; stretch

exaggerated: romantic; sweeping; theatrical

exaggeration: caricature; romance

exalt: advance; dignify; elate; elevate; extol; lift; praise; promote; raise

exaltation: elevation

exalted: eminent; grand; great; high; lofty; magnanimous; noble

exam: test

examination: experiment; inquiry; inspection; investigation; look; proof; research; review; scrutiny; search; survey; test; trial; view

examine: check; discuss; experiment; inquire; peruse; ponder; probe; prove; question; research; scrutinize; search; sound; study; survey; test; try; view

example: archetype; case; ideal; illustration; instance; model; paradigm; pattern; piece; prototype; sample; sort; specimen; standard; type

exanthema: rash

exasperate: anger; enrage; gall; incense; irritate; madden; provoke; tire

exasperated: mad

exasperation: anger; indignation; wrath

excavate: cut

excavation: grave; hole; pit

exceed: better; break; excel; outdo; pass; surpass

exceeding: above; exorbitant

excel: beat; exceed; head; lead; outdo; pass; surpass; top

excellence: beauty; brilliance; good; goodness; luster; merit; quality; virtue; worth

excellent: admirable; capital; choice; consummate; elegant; estimable; exquisite; fine; good; magnificent; perfect; polished; preeminent; pretty; rare; select; shining; superb; top-notch; worthy

excellently: well

except: bar; besides; but; exclude; exonerate; save

excepting or except that: only

excepting: but; except

exception: exemption; reserve

exceptional: aberrant; extraordinary; good; memorable; noteworthy; particular; peculiar; rare; singular; special; strange; uncommon; unusual

exceptionally: particularly

excerpt: extract

excess: exuberance; profusion; remainder; surfeit; surplus

excessive: desperate; exorbitant; extravagant; extreme; flagrant; immoderate; lavish; mad; preposterous; radical; rank; superfluous; terrible; unconscionable; unreasonable

exchange: barter; change; commerce; passage; sell; swap; trade

excise: duty

excitable: hasty; hot; nervous; passionate; skittish

excite: agitate; animate; arouse; elate; engender; entice; heat; incense; inflame; move; pierce; pique; provoke; raise; rouse; solicit; spirit; stimulate; stir; warm

excited: hot; mad; passionate; spirited; tense; warm; wild

excitement: agitation; agony; frenzy; heat; hurly-burly; mania; passion; racket; sensation; tumult

exciting: interesting; sensational; vibrant

exclaim: cry; shout

exclamation: cry

exclude: banish; bar; debar; eliminate; except; leave; reject; shut

excluding: but; except; exclusive

exclusion: taboo

exclusionary: clannish; xenophobic

exclusive: clannish; fashionable; only; peculiar; select; xenophobic

exclusively: only

exclusory: clannish

excommunicate: curse; ostracize

excommunication: ban

excoriate: pan; scorch; skin

excrescence: growth; outgrowth

excruciate: rack; torment

excruciating: harrowing; painful; sharp; traumatic

exculpate: absolve; acquit; excuse; exonerate; justify; rationalize; whitewash

excursion: expedition; journey; junket; passage; pilgrimage; ramble; tour; trip

excursus: appendix

excusable: venial

excuse: absolve; account; acquit; apology; clear; forgive; justify; overlook; palliate; pardon; pardon; pretense; rationalize; reason; remit; whitewash

execrable: atrocious; cursed; detestable; hateful; loathsome; nefarious; odious; offensive

execrate: abhor; abominate; curse; detest; hate

execrating: abhorrent

execration: abhorrence; curse; malediction

execratory: abhorrent

execute: accomplish; achieve; administer; conduct; consummate; discharge; do; finish; fulfill; hang; kill; make; perform; perpetrate; play; take; work;

execution: accomplishment; conduct; discharge; effect

executive: manager

exegesis: exposition; gloss

exemplar: paradigm; pattern; prototype; sort; standard; type

exemplary: good; standard; worthy

exemplification: instance

exemplify: represent

exempt: absolve; exonerate; free

exemption: immunity; impunity

exercise: appliance; discipline; instruction; play; practice; use

exert energy or force: act

exert influence on: affect

exert oneself: strive

exert: do; exercise; strain; toil

exerting: operative

exertion: action; effort; endeavor; energy; exercise; labor; strain; struggle; toil; trouble; work

exhalation: fume

exhale: emit; heave

exhaust: bankrupt; consume; expend; spend; tire; use; weaken; weary

exhausted: bankrupt; jaded; languid; low; seedy; tired; weary

exhausting: arduous; hard; tedious

exhibit: array; bear; betray; demonstrate; display; evidence; expose; exposition; express; fair; manifest; present; produce; render; show

exhibition: array; display; exhibit; exposition; fair; scene; show; show

exhilarate: animate; cheer; divert; elate; enliven; inebriate

exhilarating: bright

exhilaration: animation

exhort: charge

exhortation: advice; charge

exigency: crisis; difficulty; emergency; need; strait; turn

exile: banish; expel; ostracize; transport

exist: reside

existence: life; standing

existing: alive; living; present

exonerate: absolve; acquit; clear; discharge; excuse; justify; vindicate

exoneration: remission

exorbitant: dear; excessive; extravagant; immoderate; unconscionable; unreasonable

exotic: curious; recherch.; strange

exoticism: glamour

expand: amplify; billow; bulk; dilate; distend; enlarge; extend; grow; heave; increase; inflate; open; spread; swell

expanded: open; wide

expanse: extent; spread; stretch

expansion: comment; development; extension; growth; increase; spread

expansive: effusive; gay; outgoing

expansively: abroad

expatriate: banish; expel; ostracize

expect: anticipate; anticipate; ask; await; hope; intend; look; think; trust; wait; watch

expectance: prospect

expectancy: expectation; hope

expectant: hopeful; optimistic

expectation: calculation; hope; prospect; thought; trust

expected: orthodox; usual

expediency: advantage; policy

expedient: advisable; appliance; artifice; device; judicious; makeshift; politic; recourse; trick

expedite: hasten; hurry; precipitate; speed

expedition: haste; hurry; journey; pilgrimage; speed; tour

expeditious: fleet; quick; swift

expel: banish; discharge; eliminate; emit; exclude

expend: consume; disburse; exhaust; lavish; spend; squander; use; waste

expendable: accidental

expenditure: charge; cost; expense; price; waste

expense: charge; cost; price

expensive: costly; dear; high; rich; valuable

experience: endure; have; practice; seasoning; see; standing; suffer; take; taste; undergo

experienced: expert; finished; old; proficient; versed

experiment: trial

experimental: tentative; underground

experimentation: experiment

expert: able; adroit; aesthete; apt; authority; clever; dexterous; dilettante; experienced; good; guru; magisterial; master; perfect; savant; skillful; smart

expertness: ability; craft; cunning; knack

expiation: satisfaction

expire: die; dissolve; pass; perish

expiring: low

explain away: rationalize; whitewash

explain: account; comment; decipher; demonstrate; elucidate; gloss; interpret; paraphrase; rationalize; resolve; show; tell

explaining: explanation

explanation: account; apology; comment; exposition; gloss; illustration; reason; theory

explicate: account; demonstrate; elucidate; explain; interpret; paraphrase; rationalize; resolve

explication: account; explanation; exposition; illustration

explicit: express; formal; perspicuous; pointed; positive; precise; unequivocal

explicitness: perspicuity

explode: blast; burst; shatter; spring

exploit: achievement; act; deed; feat

exploration: inquiry; investigation; search

explore: examine; probe; prospect; search

explosion: access; blast; burst; paroxysm

expos.: account; exposure

expose: air; bare; betray; betray; detect; disclose; exhibit; express; open; subject; uncover

exposed: bare; insecure; liable; naked; nude; obnoxious; open; raw; subject; vulnerable

exposing: exposure

exposition: account; comment; exhibit; explanation

expostulation: rebuke; reproach

exposure: danger; limelight; risk; satire

expound: demonstrate; explain

express gratitude for: acknowledge

express: definite; direct; exhibit; explicit; fleet; formal; manifest; mean; pass; positive; purport; put; represent; say; shape; signify; sound; state; tell; utter; ventilate; word

expressage: freight

expressed: positive

expressing: wording

expression: appearance; aspect; countenance; face; language; parlance; phraseology; word

expressive: articulate; meaning; significant; suggestive

expressiveness: significance

expulsion: discharge

expunge: blot; cancel; delete; erase; obliterate

exquisite: coxcomb; dainty; delicate; fine; lovely; magnificent; matchless; perfect; rare; recherch; refined; superb

extant: living; present

extemporaneous: ad-lib; improvised; offhand

extemporary: extemporaneous

extempore: ad-lib; extemporaneous

extemporization: ad-lib

extemporize: ad-lib

extemporized: ad-lib

extend over: span

extend: amplify; augment; continue; dilate; draw; enlarge; expand; grow; increase; lengthen; open; piece; project; prolong; protract; range; reach; run; spin; spread; stretch; trend; wander; wax

extended: extensive; fat; long; open; spacious

extension: increase; span; spread; stretch; supplement

extensive: ample; big; broad; comprehensive; gigantic; huge; immense; large; long; prevalent; spacious; sweeping; unlimited; vast; wide

extent: deal; extension; latitude; limit; proportion; range; reach; run; scope; size; span; spread; stretch; tract; way

extenuate: excuse; rationalize; whitewash

exterior: face; semblance; superficial

exterminate: eradicate

extermination: destruction; massacre

external: apparent; exterior; extraneous; formal; superficial

extinct: dead; lifeless

extinction: abolition; destruction

extinguish: abate; abolish; damp; destroy; kill; quell; slay

extinguished: dead; extinct

extirpate: abolish; destroy; eradicate; exterminate

extirpation: abolition

extirpative: destructive

extol: celebrate; commend; eulogize; exalt; laud; praise

extort: exact; extract

extortionate: rapacious

extra: appendix; spare; superfluous; waste

extract: draw; exact; extort; flavor; remove; sip; summary; try; wrest

extraction: birth; breed; descent; origin; parentage; strain

extraneous: exterior

extraordinary: curious; distinguished; exceptional; magnificent; marvelous; memorable; miraculous; notable; noteworthy; odd; particular; peculiar; preternatural; prodigious; quaint; queer; rare; remarkable; singular; special; strange; supernatural; uncommon; unusual; wonderful

extravagance: abundance; plenty; romance

extravagant: effusive; excessive; exorbitant; extreme; fancy; fast; immoderate; lavish; palatial; preposterous; prodigal; profuse; radical; rank; romantic; sweeping; unconscionable; unreasonable; wild

extravagantly: fast

extravaganza: pageant

extreme: deep; desperate; end; excessive; extremity; forward; high; immoderate; last; morbid; profound; rabid; radical; severe; sovereign; terrible; ultimate; wild-eyed

extremist: fanatic; rabid; radical

extremity: emergency; end; extreme; limb

extricate: clear; deliver; release; rescue

extrinsic: exterior; extraneous

extroverted: outgoing

exuberance: plenty

exuberancy: exuberance

exuberant: ample; irrepressible; lyrical; plentiful; rambunctious; rank

exude: emit; ooze

exult: glory; triumph; vaunt

exultant: ecstatic

exultation: ecstasy; glee; joy; rapture; triumph

eye: mark

eyes only: private

eyewitness: witness

fête: feast; treat

fable: figment; legend; myth; romance; story; tale; untruth

fabled: fabulous

fabricate: construct; fable; feign; invent; make; manufacture; spin; weave

fabricated: artificial; fabulous; fake

fabrication: fable; falsehood; fiction; figment; pretense; untruth

fabulous: romantic

face up to: withstand

face-covering: mask

face-to-face: adverse

face: affront; appearance; brave; chutzpah; countenance; encounter; exterior; gall; impudence; look; meet; stand; visage; withstand

facet: cut

facetious: funny; humorous; jocose; pleasant; sportive; witty

facetiousness: humor; wit

facile: easy; eloquent; glib; pliant; ready

facilitate: aid; ease; favor; help

facility: ability; delicacy; freedom; knack

facing: adverse; opposite

facsimile copy: duplicate

facsimile: copy; image; model

fact: argument; certainty; object; phenomenon; truth

faction: party

factitious: fictitious

factor: ground

facts: information

factual: correct; genuine; real; realistic; true

faculties: endowment

faculty: ability; aptitude; capacity; genius; gift; power; talent

fad: fashion; mania; novelty; rage

faddish: popular

faddist: crackpot

fade away: abate

fade out: abate; melt

fade-out: abatement

fade: abate; blanch; die; dim; disappear; droop; evaporate; fail; lessen; melt; pass; pine; vanish; wither

faded: faint; pallid; weather-beaten

fading: abatement

fail in: butcher

fail: decline; die; droop; give; let; slacken; wane

failing: abortive; decline; failure; fault; foible

failure: crash; disappointment; neglect; wane; washout

faint-hearted: cowardly; faint; recreant

faint: cold; die; dim; droop; feeble; languid; pale; remote; sickly; small; thin; weak

fainthearted: timid

fair-haired boy: idol

fair-haired one: favorite

fair-haired: favorite

fair-spoken: plausible

fair: beautiful; candid; clear; disinterested; even; good; honest; honorable; impartial; just; moderate; objective; open; pleasant; pretty; reasonable; respectable; right; righteous; round; serene; serviceable; sound; straight; straightforward; true; unbiased; unprejudiced

fairish: serviceable

fairly good: respectable

fairly: pretty; right; well

fairness: beauty; honesty; right

fairy tale: tale

fairy: brownie; spirit

faith: confidence; credit; devotion; hope; ideology; trust; virtue

faithful: close; confidential; conscientious; consistent; constant; earnest; exact; express; fast; loyal; near; real; religious; staunch; steadfast; true; trustworthy

faithfulness: allegiance; constancy; fidelity; homage; loyalty

faithless,changeable: fickle,

faithless: abject; false; perfidious; recreant; treacherous; unfaithful

faithlessness: disloyalty; perfidy; treachery

fake: act; affect; artificial; base; bluff; cheat; counterfeit; counterfeit; fabricate; fictitious; flash; mock; pretend; pseudo; simulate

faker: phony

fall apart: disintegrate

fall away: decay

fall back: retire

fall behind or back: lag

fall guy: scapegoat

fall in: assent

fall off: decrease; fail

fall out: quarrel

fall short: fail

fall: cascade; decadence; decay; descent; overthrow; plump; plump; ruin; settle

fallacious: deceitful; deceptive; false; unsound

fallacy: delusion

fallible: uncertain

falling out: breach; contention; tiff

falling-off: decrease

falling-out: feud

falling: crash; descent

falls: cascade

false face: mask

false god: idol

false: abject; absurd; artificial; bogus; corrupt; counterfeit; deceitful; deceptive; dishonest; dishonorable; disloyal; erroneous; faithless; fake; flash; hypocritical; incorrect; mealy-mouthed; mendacious; meretricious; mock; perfidious; phony; pseudo; recreant; sham; smarmy; specious; spurious; unfaithful; unsound; wrong

falsehood: fable; lie; romance; tale; untruth

falseness: deceit; humbug

falsification: counterfeit; lie

falsify: counterfeit; lie; pretend

falsity: fiction

falter: hesitate; recoil; stagger; stammer; totter

faltering: doubt; faint; hesitation; unsettled; unsteady

fame: brilliance; celebrity; distinction; eminence; glory; honor; limelight; name; note; renown; reputation; splendor

famed: acclaimed; celebrated; distinguished; famous; glorious; great; notable; noted; prominent; splendid

familial: innate

familiar: accustomed; common; confidential; conversant; free; habitual; household; intimate; intimate; near; old; social; usual

familiarity: acquaintance; freedom

familiarize: habituate; possess; use

family tie: relationship

family tree: pedigree

family: ancestry; birth; breed; brood; home; household; order; parentage; pedigree; people; race; sort; stem; stock; strain; type

famished: hungry; ravenous

famishing: hungry

famous: acclaimed; bright; celebrated; distinguished; glorious; great; household; notable; noted; prominent; splendid

fan: adherent; enthusiast

fanatic: crackpot; enthusiast; rabid; wild-eyed; zealot

fanatical: extreme; intolerant; rabid; radical; wild-eyed

fancied: fictitious; illusory; imaginary; subjective; visionary

fanciful: arbitrary; fancy; fictitious; ideal; illusory; imaginary; romantic; visionary; whimsical; wild

fancy dress: finery

fancy: conceit; delusion; desire; fine; guess; humor; idea; imagine; invent; notion; prefer; romance; vagary; whim

fantasize: daydream

fantastic: extravagant; ideal; odd; queer; romantic; romantic; singular; wild

fantasy: daydream; fancy; fiction; illusion

far apart: remote

far off: remote

far-out: offbeat; wild-eyed

far-reaching: extensive

far: abhorrent

faraway: rapt
farce: burlesque; caricature; play
farcical: amusing; funny; laughable; ludicrous; ridiculous; risible; zany
fare: do; food; journey
farmer: countryman
farrago: jumble; mess; mixture
farther: ulterior
farthest: extreme; ultimate
fascinate: bewitch; captivate; catch; charm; enamor; enchant; take
fascinated: rapt; spellbound
fascinating: charismatic
fascination: charm; glamour
Fascist: absolute
Fascistic: absolute; arbitrary
fascistic: intolerant
fashion: cut; form; garb; guise; hew; make; manner; method; mode; model; rage; shape; sort; stamp; style; technique; turn; vogue; way; wise; work
fashionable: current; exclusive; smart; swell
fashioned: artificial; worked,
fast: close; express; firm; fix; fleet; hasty; quick; rapid; secure; sound; stable; steadfast; swift; unbroken
fasten firmly: brace
fasten on: grasp
fasten to: attach
fasten: bind; couple; fix; hitch; join; link; pin; secure; stick; tie
fastened: fast; secure; shut
fastener: bond
fastening: attachment; bond; clasp; pin
fastidious: chary; critical; dainty; delicate; difficult; exclusive; nice; particular; queasy; select; selective; squeamish
fastness: fortification
fat: obese; plump; roly-poly; stout
fatal: capital; deadly; destructive; mortal; pernicious; tragic
fate: chance; destiny; doom; necessity; ordain
fateful: fatal
father: breed
fathom: penetrate; sound
fatigue: bore; exhaust; exhaustion; pall; tire; weary
fatigued: jaded; tired; weary
fatiguing: arduous; hard; laborious; tedious; tiresome; wearisome
fatten: plump
fatty: fat; unctuous
fatuity: lunacy
fatuous: foolish; idiotic; vacuous
fault-finding: querulous
fault: blame; blemish; defect; dereliction; error; failing; flaw; foible; misdemeanor; mistake; offense; oversight; pan; slip; taint; trespass; vice; weakness
faultfind: pan
faultfinder: critic; kvetch
faultfinding: critical; criticism
faultily: ill
faultless: blameless; correct; innocent; perfect; pure; whole
faulty: bad; coarse; defective; ill; imperfect; inaccurate; incorrect; poor; unsound; vicious
faux pas: blunder; impropriety; slip
favor: abet; back; countenance; countenance; encourage; esteem; foster; goodwill; grace; honor; indulge; kindness; liking; memento; oblige; partiality; prefer; proclivity; speed; vogue
favorable opportunity or state or circumstance or means or situation: advantage
favorable: beneficial; bright; congenial; convenient; fair; fortunate; friendly; good; gracious; lucky; opportune; prosperous; well
favorably: fair; kindly; right
favored: happy; lucky
favoring: predilection
favorite: idol; pet; popular
favoritism: partiality
fawn: flatter
fawner: sycophant; toady
fawning: obsequious; saccharine; servile; slavish; supple
fay: fairy
fealty: allegiance; constancy; fidelity; homage; loyalty; obeisance
fear: alarm; anxiety; apprehension; awe; consternation; dismay; dread; dread; fright; horror; passion; phobia; terror; worry

fearful: afraid; cowardly; eerie; faint; formidable; frightful; horrendous; nervous; terrible; timid; tremulous
fearless: audacious; bold; brave; daring; dauntless; gallant; game; heroic; stalwart; stout; strong; tame; unabashed; undaunted
fearlessness: bravery; courage
feasible: possible; practicable; specious; viable
feast: treat; treat
feat: achievement; act; deed; exploit; quality; stroke; work
featherbrained: giddy
feature: character; characteristic; emphasize; facet; particular; peculiarity; property; quality; respect
features: face
febrile: hectic
feckless: feeble
fecund: fertile; fruitful
federal: state
federation: alliance; combination; confederation; state
fee: consideration; pay
feeble: decrepit; faint; frail; ineffectual; inefficient; languid; little; low; nerveless; pale; senile; sickly; slender; slight; small; soft; spineless; tender; thin; tinny; unhealthy; watery; weak; weakly
feebleness: delicacy; weakness
feed: nurse; nurse
feeder: affluent; branch
feel for: pity
feel sorry about: regret
feel: aura; experience; see; suffer; take; taste; touch
feeling: affection; aura; compassion; delicacy; emotion; experience; hunch; passion; respect; sensation; sense; sensuous; sentient; stir
feign: act; affect; assume; counterfeit; fabricate; fake; pretend; sham; simulate
feigned: affected; artificial; counterfeit; mock; spurious
feigning: pretense
feint: ploy
feisty: scrappy
felicific: felicitous
felicitate: compliment
felicitous: appropriate; apt; happy; opportune
felicity: joy
fell: cruel; cut; fierce; hew; merciless; ruthless; sanguinary; savage
fellow citizen: countryman
fellow countryman: brother
fellow feeling: empathy; rapport; sympathy,
fellow man: brother
fellow: associate; companion; comrade; equal
fellowship: association; company; rapport; society
felon: criminal; malefactor
felonious: atrocious; criminal
felony: offense
felony: trespassing; crime
felt: conscious
female: woman; womanly,
feminine: female; womanly,
fen: quagmire; wash
fence-sitting: ambivalent
fence: barrier; evade; pale
feral: barbarian; savage; wild
ferine: wild
ferment: agitate; confusion; hurly-burly; maelstrom; tumult; turn
fermented: sour
ferocious: barbarian; bloody; brutal; cruel; fierce; grim; ruthless; savage; truculent; wild
ferret out: discover
ferry: run
fertile: fat; fruitful; plentiful; productive; prolific; rich
fertility: abundance
fervency: ardor; vehemence; zeal
fervent: active; ardent; earnest; enthusiastic; fiery; hot; passionate; rabid; strong; vehement; warm; zealous
fervid: ardent; earnest; enthusiastic; fervent; fiery; hot; keen; passionate; strong; vehement; warm; zealous
fervor: ardor; enthusiasm; flame; heat; passion; rage; vehemence; zeal
fester: rankle
festival: fair
festive: jolly
festivity: riot
fetch: bring
fetid: foul; noisome; rank; rotten

fetish: talisman
fetter: band; hobble; shackle; shackle
fetters: bond
fettle: fitness
feud: brawl; brawl; contention; division; quarrel
fever: heat
fevered: hectic
feverish: hectic
few: slender
fewness: paucity
fiasco: washout
fiat: decree; mandate
fib: fable; falsehood; lie; prevaricate; tale; untruth
fiber: mettle; rush
fickle: capricious; faithless; inconstant; mercurial; mutable; unfaithful; unsettled; unsteady; variable
fiction: fable; falsehood; figment; legend; myth; novel; romance; romance; tale; untruth
fictional: fabulous
fictitious: fabulous; romantic; spurious; unreal
fidelity: allegiance; constancy; homage; loyalty; truth
fidget: worry
fidgety: skittish; unquiet
field: bailiwick; circle; circuit; study; terrain; walk
fiend: monster
fiendish: black; devilish; satanic
fierce: acute; bitter; ferocious; fiery; grim; lurid; rude; savage; sharp; truculent
fierceness: fury
fiery: ardent; excitable; fervent; hasty; hot; hotheaded; lurid; passionate; torrid; vehement
fifty-fifty: doubtful
fight for: champion
fight shy of: avoid
fight: action; battle; brawl; brush; close; combat; conflict; contend; contest; disorder; quarrel; riot; row; skirmish; strife; strive; struggle; tussle
fighter: champion
fighting: hostility
figment: fiction; idol
figure out: decipher
figure: calculate; character; compute; device; emblem; fashion; form; image; number; pattern; represent; shape; type
figuring: calculation
filch: pilfer; steal
file: range
filibuster: pirate
fill out: billow; extend
fill-in: surrogate
fill: fulfill; gorge; imbue; pall; pervade; satisfy; stock; stuff; supply; surfeit
filled with desire: amorous
filled: big; populous
fillet: band
film: picture; skin
filter: strain; strain
filth: abomination; squalor
filthy: dirty; foul; indecent; nasty; obscene; ribald; sordid; squalid; unclean
filtrate: strain
finagle: wangle
final offer: ultimatum
final: decisive; extreme; last; mortal; total; ultimate
finale: catastrophe; conclusion; death; disposition; end
finances: wherewithal
financial: monetary; pecuniary
find fault with: censure; pick; reproach
find fault: blame; kvetch
find guilty: condemn
find out: ascertain; detect; discover; see; trace
find: detect; hit
fine: admirable; beautiful; brave; capital; choice; dainty; delicate; delicate; elegant; excellent; exquisite; fair; fancy; gallant; gay; grand; handsome; magnificent; nice; precious; pretty; rare; shining; slender; splendid; superb; swell; top-notch; well
finery: gaiety
finesse: cunning; delicacy; maneuver
finger-pointing: blame
finical: careful; dainty; meticulous; nice; particular; queasy; rigorous; squeamish
finicky: meticulous; nice; particular; queasy; selective; squeamish
finish off: zap

finish: accomplish; close; complete; consummate; do; end; execute; fulfill; perfect; polish; terminate; twilight; work; zap
finished: complete; consummate; fine; neat; perfect; polished; polite; proficient; ripe; thorough; total
fire: animate; ardor; arouse; blaze; discharge; dismiss; fervor; flame; ignite; incite; inflame; kindle; light; mettle; provoke; rouse; spirit; stimulate; vehemence; verve
fireside: home; household
firing: discharge
firm: absolute; association; business; close; compact; company; concern; constant; decisive; determined; earnest; fast; free; hard; house; inexorable; inflexible; obdurate; obstinate; proof; resolute; rigid; robust; solid; stable; stalwart; staunch; steadfast; steady; stern; stiff; stout; strong; sturdy; substantial; sure; tough; uncompromising; unyielding
firmly: fast; hard
firmness: assurance; constancy; nerve; stability; strength; valor
first cause: beginning
first-class: top-notch
first-rate: capital; excellent; swell; top-notch
first: above; capital; chief; dominant; fundamental; head; pioneer; primary; primitive; principal
firstly: principally
fiscal: financial
fissure: breach; break; cleft; crack; flaw; gorge; opening; rent; spring; tear
fit for: adequate
fit out: equip; furnish
fit up: furnish
fit: able; access; accommodate; accord; adapt; adjust; advisable; applicable; apt; available; becoming; befitting; calculate; competent; convenient; convulsion; correspond; decent; decorous; dress; eligible; equal; expedient; fashion; felicitous; good; hit; meet; opportune; paroxysm; pertinent; proper; qualify; ready; right; seasonable; start; temper; throe
fitful: uncertain
fitly: right
fitness: aptitude; harmony; propriety
fitted: able; capable; eligible; opportune; pertinent; ready
fitting: applicable; appropriate; apt; available; becoming; befitting; competent; decent; decorous; felicitous; happy; meet; opportune; pertinent; proper; relevant; seemly; well
fittingly: right
five-by-five: roly-poly
five-star: top-notch
fix or settle on: resolve
fix on: mount
fix upon: prefer
fix: adjust; appoint; arrest; ascertain; assign; confirm; determine; difficulty; establish; fasten; ground; mend; patch; pin; place; position; prepare; quagmire; repair; set; settle; stand; state; station; take
fixated: rapt
fixation: addiction
fixed on: bent
fixed: certain; close; constant; definite; fast; firm; formal; intent; motionless; precise; rapt; regular; resolute; secure; set; stable; steadfast; steady; stereotyped; stubborn; usual
fixedly: fast
fixedness: stability
fizzle: washout
flabbergast: dazzle
flabby: nerveless
flaccid: apathetic; nerveless
flag: droop; standard
flagellate: whip
flagitious: atrocious; black; criminal; dark; enormous; evil; grievous; heinous; nefarious; wicked
flagrant: atrocious; audacious; crying; enormous; grievous; gross; heinous
flair: panache
flake: scale
flamboyance: panache

flame: blaze; burn; flash; pan
flaming: bright; fiery
flap: fly
flare up: blaze; fume
flare: flash; glare
flash flood: flood
flash: flame; gaiety; glance; glare; gleam; instant; moment; radiate
flashiness: gaiety
flashing: ardent; bright
flashy: flash; garish; gaudy; loud; showy; tawdry
flat broke: bankrupt
flat-out: downright
flat: apartment; even; lackluster; level; pallid; plain; rough; smooth; stale; stupid; tame; tasteless; vapid
flatten: level; smooth
flatter: cajole; coax; compliment; flatter
flatterer: parasite; sycophant; toady; yes-man
flattering: obsequious; smarmy; unctuous
flattery: blarney; compliment
flatulence: wind
flaunt: display; flourish; vaunt
flaunting: display; flash
flavor: relish; savor; seasoning; taste
flavorful: racy; scrumptious
flavoring: flavor; seasoning
flavorless: tasteless; vapid
flavorsome: palatable; piquant; scrumptious
flaw: blemish; crack; defect; failing; fault; spot; taint; weakness
flawless: clean; polished
flay: peel; skin
flecked: dappled
flee: abscond; escape
fleece: plunder; rook
fleet-footed: fleet
fleet: fast; hasty; quick; rapid; swift
fleeting: brief; ephemeral; temporary; transient
fleetness: rapidity; speed
fleshly: animal; carnal
fleshy: fat; plump; stout
flex: bend
flexed: bent
flexibility: ease
flexible: all-around; informal; laid-back; limber; pliant; soft; supple
flexile: flexible; malleable; pliant
flexuous: crooked
flicker: blaze; blink
flickering: mutable
flight: escape; flock; voyage
flighty: giddy; light; mercurial; skittish; thoughtless
flimsy: frivolous; light; ramshackle; slender; slight; thin; tinny; weak
flinch: recoil; shrink; wince,
fling: cast; send; shy; sprinkle; throw;
flinty: hard; stony
flip: saucy
flippancy: impudence
flippant: forward; impudent; pert; saucy
flirt: philander
flit: fly
flitting: transient
float: wave
flock together: crowd; troop
flock: drove; herd; run; swarm; troop
flog: beat; punish; thrash; whip
flogging: scourge
flood: abundance; cataclysm; deluge; flow; gush; inundate; run
floor: story
floorplan: plan
flop: washout
florid: ornate; ruddy
flot: hang
flounder: wallow
flourish: advance; bloom; breed; dash; display; ostentation; prosper; shake; show; succeed; thrive
flourishing: prosperous; thrifty
flout: defy; jeer; mock; taunt
flow out: issue
flow over: cascade
flow: emanate; ensue; flood; glide; gush; issue; originate; result; run; spout; spring; spurt; stream; torrent
flower: bloom; blow; ripen
flowery: bombastic; ornate
flowing: abundant; facile; fluent; generous; mellifluous; smooth; soft; watery
flub: blunder
fluctuant: skittish

fluctuate: oscillate; sway; vacillate; waffle; wave; waver; yo-yo
fluctuating: dubious; unsteady; variable; weak
fluent: articulate; eloquent; facile; glib; smooth; voluble
fluff: blunder
fluid: liquid; thin; watery
fluke: serendipity
flukiness: serendipity
flummery: blarney
flunky: attendant; menial; parasite; yes-man
flurry: ado; agitation; haste; hurry; ruffle; scramble; tear
flush: bloom; heat; level
flushed: ardent; hectic; rosy; ruddy
fluster: agitate; unnerve; upset
flutter: blink; flit; fly; hurry; palpitate; scramble; throb; wave; waver
fluttery: skittish
fly back: spring
fly-blown: seedy
fly: abscond; dart; dash; escape; escape; flit; lure; soar; spring
flying: transient
foam: boil; head; seethe
foamy: bubbly
focus: concentrate
fodder: feed
foe: adversary; antagonist; enemy; offense; opponent; opposition
fog: cloud; damp; haze; mist; mist
fogbank: mist
foggle: mist
foggy: dim
fogyish: senile
foible: defect; eccentricity; failing; fault
foil: cross; defeat; elude; evade; frustrate
fold: clasp; gather
folder: case
folks: household; people
follish: simple
follow: course; ensue; imitate; observe; pattern; practice; result; seek; succeed; trace
follower: adherent; attendant; disciple; partisan
following: sequence; successive
folly: lunacy; nonsense; vanity
foment: encourage; kindle; nourish; nurse; stir
fond of: amorous
fond: affectionate
fondle: dally; pet
fondness: affection; attachment; bent; fancy; liking; love; partiality; passion; penchant; taste
food: bite; cheer; feed; maintenance; nutrition; provision; ration
foofaraw: ado; ruckus
fool: bite; block; cheat; deceive; humbug; mock; oaf; trick; victimize
foolhardiness: lunacy
foolhardy: adventurous; daredevil; desperate; foolish; hasty; rash
fooling around: raillery
foolish: absurd; cockeyed; comical; empty; extravagant; fatuous; frivolous; funny; giddy; idiotic; inept; insane; mad; preposterous; puerile; senseless; silly; stupid; unreasonable; unwise; vacuous; wacky; weak
foolishness: lunacy
foot-dragger: laggard
foot-dragging: laggard
foot: base; bottom
foothill: hill
footing: foundation
footman: attendant; menial; servant
footnote: note
footpad: robber
footpath: path; street; walk
footprint: trace
fop: coxcomb; swell
for the most part: mostly
for the reason that: because
for: because
forage: feed
foray: descent
forbear: help; leave; pause; spare
forbearance: abstinence; clemency; mercy; resignation; tolerance
forbearing: broad-minded; lenient; meek
forbid: ban; inhibit; prohibit
forbidden: taboo
forbidding: austere; black; difficult; grim; odious; stern
force: bear; compel; constrain; crowd; drive; effect; energy;

exact: impel; jam; main; make; might; moment; nerve; oblige; operation; power; rack; run; strain; strength; stress; thrust; urge; value; violence; virtue
forced: compulsory; unnatural
forceful: ardent; emphatic; lively; officious; powerful; strenuous; stringent; strong; vigorous
forcefulness: will
forceless: impotent
forcible: emphatic; energetic; powerful; stringent; strong; vigorous
forcing: urgent
forebode: threaten
foreboding: anxiety; hunch; omen; ominous; pessimistic; presage; sign
forecast: anticipate; calculation; cast; foresight; predict; prediction; presage
foregoing: above; previous
foreign: alien; curious; exterior; extraneous; recherch; remote; strange
foreigner: alien; stranger
foreknowledge: foresight; presage
foremost: head; leading; principal; top
forensic: judicial
foreordain: doom; fate; mean
foreordained: fatal; set
forepart: bow
forerun: harbinger; pioneer
forerunner: harbinger; pioneer
foresee: anticipate; forecast; predict
foreshadow: presage; threaten
foreshadowing: presage
foreshow: harbinger
foresight: calculation; forecast; precaution; prudence
forest: stand
forestall: anticipate; prevent
foretaste: anticipate
foretell: cast; forecast; harbinger; predict; prophesy
forethought: calculation; caution; counsel; forecast; foresight; precaution; prudence
foretoken: predict; prediction
forever: always
forevermore: always
forewarn: caution; warn
forewarning: caveat
foreword: introduction; preface
forfeited: lost
forge: beat; counterfeit; fabricate; feign
forged: counterfeit; fake; false; worked,
forgery: counterfeit; fable; untruth
forget: leave
forgetful: absent-minded; careless; senile; unmindful
forgivable: venial
forgive: absolve; acquit; excuse; overlook; pardon; remit
forgiveness: grace; mercy; pardon; remission
forgiving: magnanimous; merciful
forgo: abandon; forsake; relinquish; renounce; resign; surrender; waive; yield
fork: diverge
forlorn: desolate; desperate; disconsolate; hopeless; miserable; wretched
form a collection: aggregate
form an opinion: judge
form: appearance; archetype; blank; block; cast; construct; contrive; custom; draw; establish; fashion; guise; hew; image; make; manner; mode; model; organize; rite; semblance; shape; stamp; state; structure; style; turn; type; version
formal: academic; austere; cold; conventional; nominal; prim; proper; regular; ritual; solemn; stiff
formality: ceremony; custom; form
formed: worked,
former: late; old; previous
formidable: grandiose; horrible; stalwart
formula: canon; form; plan
formulate: draw
formulation: parlance
forsake: abandon; desert; desolate; fail; leave; relinquish; renounce; resign; vacate
forsaken: abandoned; desert; desolate; forlorn
forswear: abandon; forsake; relinquish; renounce
fort: fortification
forte: capacity; gift; talent

forth: forward
forthcoming: near
forthright: innocent
forthrightness: candor
forthwith: instantly; presently
forthwith: *esp:* immediately
fortification: rampart
fortify: animate; barricade; brace; defend; harden; invigorate; nerve
fortifying: fortification
fortitude: constancy; courage; grit; heroism; nerve; patience; strength; virtue
fortress: castle; fortification
fortuitous: accidental; casual; chance; incidental; lucky; random
fortuitousness: hazard; serendipity
fortuity: accident; chance; hazard; serendipity
fortunate: good; happy; lucky; opportune; prosperous; prosperous; well
fortunately: well
fortune: cast; chance; destiny; doom; fate; serendipity; wealth
forward: advance; aggressive; audacious; bold; brazen; foster; gain; hurry; obtrusive; officious; onward; pert; presumptuous; promote; remit; saucy; send; serve; speed; support; transmit; unabashed
forwardness: assumption
foster: cherish; encourage; harbor; help; indulge; nourish; nurse
foul-tempered: cantankerous; grouchy
foul: abominable; contagious; dark; debase; dirty; disgusting; filthy; mean; nasty; noisome; rank; roil; rotten; sordid; squalid; turbid; unclean; vile
foully: foul
foulness: corruption; squalor
found: base; cast; erect; establish; ground; start
foundation: base; basis; bottom; cosmetic; ground; origin
founder: overturn
founding: seminal
fountainhead: origin; spring
four hundred: fashion
four-flusher: phony
four-leaf clover: talisman
foxy: cagey; cunning; insidious; politic; sly; wily
fracas: brawl; tumult; uproar
fraction: part
fractionally: piecemeal
fractionate: abstract; decompose
fractious: irritable
fractious: cantankerous; cross; froward; grouchy; intractable
fracture: breach; break; cleft; flaw; rend; rent; rupture
fragile: brittle; delicate; delicate; frail; shaky; slender; slight; spindly; tender; unsound; weak
fragility: delicacy; weakness
fragment: bit; part; piece; portion; scrap
fragmentary: scrap
fragments: litter
fragrance: aroma, flavor; incense; odor; perfume; savor; scent
fragrant: odoriferous; rich; sweet
frail: brittle; delicate; feeble; sickly; slight; unhealthy; weak
frailty: delicacy; failing; fault; foible
frame of mind: mood; spirit
frame: case; construct; draw; fabricate; fashion; form; organize; plot; project; rack; set; shape
framework: carcass; case; rack; structure
franchise: frank; freedom; immunity; liberty; permission; permit; prerogative; privilege
frangible: brittle; delicate; frail; slender; tender; unsound
frank: aboveboard; artless; bluff; candid; direct; free; guileless; honest; ingenuous; open; outspoken; plain; raw; round; straight; transparent; unreserved
frankly: aboveboard
frankness: candor; freedom; honesty; sincerity; truth
frantic: desperate; hectic; mad; rabid; wild; wild-eyed
frantically: pell-mell
fraternal: friendly
fraternity: association; circle; club; coterie; order; society
fraternize: associate
fraud: artifice; bluff; cheat; chicanery; deceit; deception; duplic-

ity; fake; guile; humbug; phony; swindle; trick; trickery; wile
fraudulence: chicanery
fraudulent: abject; counterfeit; counterfeit; crooked; deceitful; deceitful; dishonest; dishonorable; fake; flash
fray: brawl; fight; riot
freak: eccentric
freakish: eccentric; queer; whimsical
freckled: dappled
freckly: dappled
free and easy: bohemian
free from blame: absolve
free from imperfection: absolute
free spirit: bohemian
free-and-easy: laid-back
free-flowing: affluent
free-living: bohemian
free-spirited: bohemian
free: absolve; ample; broad; candid; clear; deliver; discharge; dissolve; excuse; exonerate; familiar; frank; ingenuous; liberal; liberate; loose; open; outspoken; quit; redeem; release; spontaneous; vacant; voluntary
freebooter: pirate; robber
freedom: ease; exemption; familiarity; independence; latitude; leave; liberty; permission; play; prerogative; privilege; release; swing
freeway: way
freeze: chill
freezing: cold; cool; sharp
freight: cargo; charge; load; shipment
freightage: freight
freighter: transport
frenetic: hectic; rabid
frenzied: fanatical; hectic; mad; rabid; wild; wild-eyed
frenziedly: pell-mell
frenzy: convulsion; fury; hurly-burly; mania; rage
frequent: attend; common; familiar; ordinary; usual
frequentative: continual
frequenter: attendant
frequently: often
fresh: froward; impertinent; impudent; lively; lush; modern; new; original; presumptuous; recent; rude; saucy; stiff; sweet; virgin; warm
freshen: refresh; ventilate
freshet: flood
freshly: new
freshman: initiate
freshness: bloom; novelty
fret: annoy; chide; fume; haggle; harry; irritate; molest; offend; plague; rage; torment; trouble; vex; worry
fretful: cross; cynical; fractious; hasty; impatient; moody; peevish; petulant; splenetic; testy
fretfulness: petulance
fretwork: fret
friable: rotten; short; tender
friar: monk; religious
fricative: consonant
friction: abrasion
friend: acquaintance; advocate; ally; associate; comrade; familiar; intimate
friendliness: affection; goodwill; love
friendly: affable; amiable; bland; congenial; familiar; genial; good; gracious; kind; nice; obliging; outgoing; peaceable; pleasant; social; warm
friendship: affection; association; attachment; harmony
fright: alarm; consternation; fear; panic; scare; terror
frighten: alarm; appall; awe; daunt; discourage; dismay; intimidate; panic; scare; shake; startle
frightened: afraid; tremulous
frightening: harrowing
frightful: dread; formidable; ghastly; grim; hideous; horrendous; horrible; monstrous; terrible
frigid: cold; cool; dead
frigidity: chill
frill: ruffle
frillery: finery
frills: finery
frippery: finery
frisk: caper; play; romp
frisky: bubbly; playful; skittish; sportive
fritter away: exhaust; idle
frivolous: empty; futile; giddy; idle; light; silly; skittish; trifling; trivial

frock: dress; gown
frolic: caper; fun; gambol; play; romp; sport
frolicsome: gay; jolly; merry; playful; sportive
front matter: introduction,
front: bow; face; gloss; head; look; right
frontier: back; border; boundary; limit
frontiers: confine
fronting: opposite
frontward: forward
frosty: cold
froth: boil; head; seethe
frothy: bubbly
froward: headstrong; intractable; wrongheaded
frown: lower
frowning: dark
frowzy: tacky
frozen: cold
frugal: abstemious; chary; economical; parsimonious; plain; prudent; spare; thrifty
frugality: economy; parsimony; prudence
fruit: result; scion; work; yield
fruitful: fat; fertile; plentiful; productive; prolific; rich
fruition: work
fruitless: futile; idle; ineffectual; poor; sterile; unfruitful; useless
fruits: produce
frumpish: tacky
frumpy: dowdy; tacky
frustrate: counteract; cross; daunt; defeat; disconcert; elude; thwart; traverse
frustrated: pent-up
frustration: cross; defeat; disappointment
fugitive: transient
fugue: trance
fulfill: accomplish; acquit; answer; appease; complete; consummate; discharge; meet; observe; perform; redeem; satisfy; supply
fulfilled: complete; consummate
fulfilling: interesting
fulfillment: accomplishment; discharge; effect
fulgent: bright
fulgid: bright
full of hope: optimistic
full-flavored: mellow
full-grown: adult; mature
full: ample; broad; complete; copious; entire; good; perfect; plentiful; plump; rich; ripe; round; round; total; unreserved; whole; zaftig
fullness: abundance; plenty
fully developed: womanly
fully-developed: mature
fully: clean; even; well
fulminate: curse
fulmination: curse
fulsome: smarmy
fume: chide; fret; rage; storm
fumes: exhaust
fun: game; humor; jest; play; sport
function: act; act; business; capacity; duty; office; part; place; serve
functional: handy; utilitarian
functioning: alive
fundament: seat
fundamental part: base
fundamental: bottom; elementary; essential; organic; primary; radical; rudimentary; seminal
fundamentals: ABC's; basics
funds: money; treasure; wealth; wherewithal
funereal: black; somber
funny feeling: hunch
funny: amusing; comical; droll; facetious; humorous; jocose; laughable; ludicrous; ridiculous; risible; waggish; witty; zany
fur: pile; skin
furbish: decorate
furious: angry; fierce; hectic; hot; impetuous; irate; mad; rabid; savage; warm; wild; wrathful
furnish or supply on credit: advance
furnish room for: accommodate
furnish: accommodate; accomplish; administer; appoint; equip; give; hang; present; produce; provide; render; supply; sustain; yield
furnishings: wardrobe
furniture: good
furor: confusion; convulsion; fury; rampage; uproar
furore: rampage
furrowed: rugged

further: abet; advance; advance; also; assist; besides; but; foster; help; moreover; new; promote; speed; support; ulterior
furtherance: aid
furthermore: also; besides; moreover
furthest: extreme; ultimate
furtive: sly; stealthy
furuncle: boil
fury: anger; frenzy; fume; indignation; passion; rage; vehemence; violence; wrath
fuse: melt; run; unite
fusee: fuse
fuselage: body
fuss: ado; racket; ruckus
fussy: nice; selective
futile: fruitless; ineffectual; nugatory; useless; vain
futility: vanity
future: destiny; forward
fuze: fuse
gab: babble
gabber: gossip
gabble: babble; jabber; waffle
gadget: device
gaffe: blunder; impropriety
gag: quip
gaga: smitten
gaggle: flock; run
gaiety: cheer; fun; glee; merriment; mirth; racket
gain weight: plump
gain: achieve; acquire; advantage; attain; carry; conquer; earn; get; good; have; hit; improve; income; make; obtain; procure; profit; score; secure; steal; win
gainsay: contradict; deny; oppose
gait: motion; pace; walk
gal Friday: sidekick
gale: blast; blow; storm
gall: chutzpah; gall; harry; irritate; offend; pester; rankle; satiate; spite; venom
gallant: bold; brave; chivalrous; civil; daring; game; heroic; stalwart; stout
gallantry: bravery; courage; heroism
galled: angry
gallimaufry: jumble; mixture
galling: troublesome
gallingly: hard
gallop: pace
gambit: ploy
gambol: caper; play; romp; skip; sport
game plan: blueprint
game: contest; play; sport
gamy: rank
gang: band; knot; pack; ring
gangling: spindly
gangly: spindly
gangrene: mortify
gangster: criminal
gap: breach; break; cleft; opening; rent; void
gape: gaze; yawn
garb: apparel; clothes; dress; habit; wardrobe
garbage: refuse; waste
garble: scramble
garbled: promiscuous
garden-variety: household
gargantuan: giant
gargoyle: monster
garish: gaudy; showy; tacky
garland: trophy
garments: apparel; array; clothes; dress; garb; raiment; wardrobe
garner: gather; treasure
garnish: array; beset; deck; decorate; embellish; ornament; trim
garnishment: garnish
garniture: garnish
garrison: defend
garrote: kill; stifle; strangle
garrulous: loquacious; talkative
gas: fluid
gasconade: vaunt
gaseous: fluid; rarefied
gash: cut; cut; hack; slash
gasp: pant; pant
gastronome: epicure
gate: entrance
gather together: assemble
gather: aggregate; assemble; collect; convene; deduce; marshal; mass; meet; muster; pick; raise; troop
gathering: assembly; company; muster; party
gauche: awkward; maladroit
gaudiness: gaiety
gaudy: flash; garish; loud; meretricious; showy; tacky; tawdry
gauge: estimate; make; standard; time

gaunt: angular; cadaverous; haggard; lean; meager; poor; scanty; spare; spindly; thin
gawky: awkward
gay: blithe; brave; bright; cheerful; gallant; happy; jolly; jovial; joyful; light; light-hearted; lively; merry; pleasant; rich; sportive
gaze: gape; look; regard; stare
gear: equipment; raiment; trim; wardrobe
geared: ready
Gehenna: hell
gelid: cold
genealogy: ancestry; descent; pedigree
genera: sort
general: broad; common; current; inaccurate; loose; pandemic; popular; prevailing; prevalent; universal; usual; vernacular
generalization: platitude
generally: mostly; often
generalship: strategy; tactics
generate: breed; engender; engender; get; produce; reproduce
generation: race
generative: productive; seminal
generosity: abundance; bounty; goodness; kindness
generous-hearted: broad-minded
generous: ample; benevolent; big; charitable; cheerful; chivalrous; disinterested; free; handsome; kind; lavish; liberal; magnanimous; merciful; munificent; noble; open; unsparing
genetic: innate
genial: bright; congenial; friendly; good; kindly; mellow; social; soft
genie: genius
genius: aptitude; capacity; endowment; gift; spirit; talent
genocide: destruction; massacre; slaughter
genteel: elegant; polite; refined
gentile: atheist; heathen; pagan
gentle-hearted: gentle
gentle: bland; compassionate; easy; female; flexible; gracious; gradual; humane; kind; kindly; lenient; low; meek; mild; mild; pacific; peaceable; small; soft; sweet; tame; tender
gentleman: man
gentleness: clemency; mercy
genuflection: obeisance
genuine: actual; authentic; factual; good; honest; intrinsic; native; pure; real; right; sincere; solid; tangible; true; unaffected; unsophisticated
genuineness: sincerity; truth
genus: kind; order; type
geography: terrain
geriatric: senile
germane: applicable; appropriate; apt; felicitous; relevant
germfree: sanitary
germinal: seminal
germinate: grow
germinative: seminal
gestalt: silhouette
gesture: action; motion
get or come down: light
get or make ready: prepare
get again: recover
get at: ascertain
get back: regain
get better: improve
get one's goat: gall
get out of: malinger
get ready: get; provide
get rid of: discharge; eliminate
get to: gain; reach
get together: gather
get up on: mount
get up: arouse; rise; wake
get: access; achieve; acquire; attain; draw; earn; extract; gain; have; make; obtain; pick; procure; purchase; secure; take
getup: raiment
gewgaw: novelty
ghastly: cadaverous; frightful; grim; hideous; horrendous; horrible; lurid; macabre; pallid
ghost: apparition; phantasm; shade; specter; spirit; vision; waste
ghostlike: cadaverous
ghostly: cadaverous; unearthly; weird
giant: humongous
gibber: babble
gibberish: babble; jargon
gibe at: twit
gibe: jeer; jest; mock; quip; sarcasm; scoff; sneer; taunt

gibes: ridicule
giddy: light; skittish; thoughtless
gift: aptitude; bonus; bounty; donation; endowment; favor; genius; premium; present; talent
gifted: able; capable; clever; finished; ingenious
gig: tender
gigantic: big; enormous; giant; great; huge; large; mammoth; monstrous; prodigious; tremendous; vast
giggle: chuckle; laugh
gilt-edge: top-notch
gimcrack: novelty
gimmick: ploy
gird: belt; bind; encircle; zone
girder: beam
girdle: band; belt; zone
girl Friday: sidekick
girl: female; maid
girth: belt; zone
gist: abstract; meaning; purport; spirit; substance
give or deliver up: surrender
give a name to: call
give access: admit
give advice: advise
give an account of: tell
give an explanation for: account
give away: denounce; give
give back: remit; render; restore
give birth to: bear; breed
give counsel to: advise
give direction to: aim
give ear: listen
give forth: deliver; yield
give heed: attend
give help or assistance: aid
give in: acknowledge
give notice to: apprise; notify
give off: radiate
give out (with): give
give out: fail
give over: deliver; give
give reasons for: account
give rise to: cause; engender; make; occasion; produce; provoke; raise
give suck to: nurse
give up or in: accord
give up: abandon; abdicate; betray; cede; deliver; desert; devote; forsake; give; quit; relinquish; render; renounce; resign; surrender; waive; yield
give voice: warble
give way to: indulge
give way: bend; bow; yield
give-and-take: raillery
give: administer; allow; bear; communicate; confer; deal; distribute; endow; extend; grant; impart; offer; present; produce; provide; render; vouchsafe
given: certain
giving: chivalrous
gizmo: gadget
glad: blithe; gay; happy; jolly; jovial; joyful; light-hearted; merry
gladden: cheer; comfort; enliven; exhilarate; lighten; regale
gladdened: happy
gladdening: cheerful
gladness: bliss; cheer; happiness; joy; pleasure
glamorize: beautify
glamorous: charismatic
glance: blink; flash; look
glare: flash; radiate; shine
glaring: bare; flagrant; garish; gross; lurid; strong
glaze: gloss; size
glazed: glossy
gleam: beam; blaze; brilliance; flash; glance; glare; glisten; lighten; radiate; shimmer; shine; sparkle
gleaming: bright; shining
glean: deduce; gather
glee: cheer; gaiety; hilarity; mirth
gleeful: cheerful; gay; lively; merry
glib: facile; fluent; plausible; smooth; voluble
glide: fly; slide; slip; soar
glimmer: beam; gleam; glisten; iota; radiate; shimmer; shine
glimmering: gleam
glimpse: blink; glance
glint: flash
glisten: beam; glance; luster; shimmer; shine; sparkle
glistening: bright; shining
glister: brilliance; sparkle
glistering: bright
glitter: beam; brilliance; flash; gaiety; glance; glare; gleam; glisten; luster; sparkle

glittering: bright; gorgeous; radiant
glitzy: tacky
gloaming: evening; twilight
gloat: glare; vaunt
globe: ball; circle; earth; orb; sphere
globular: round
gloom: despair; despondency; melancholy; shade
gloominess: gloom; melancholy; shade
gloomy Gus: killjoy
gloomy: black; blue; cloudy; cross; dark; depressed; disconsolate; dreary; glum; heavy; joyless; lugubrious; lurid; melancholy; moody; morbid; morose; murky; obscure; pessimistic; sad; somber; sullen
glorified: heavenly
glorify: celebrate; dignify; exalt; extol; praise; worship
glorious: bright; grand; splendid
glory: fame; honor; luster; renown; splendor; state; triumph
gloss over: palliate; rationalize; smooth; whitewash
gloss: luster; polish; shine
glossy: bright; polished; sleek; smooth
glow: ardor; blaze; bloom; burn; flame; radiate; shine; sparkle; swell
glower: glare; glare; lower
glowering: cross
glowing: ardent; ardent; bright; fervent; fiery; lively; passionate; ruddy; warm
glue: bond; size; stick
glum: blue; gloomy; melancholy
glut or stuff or gorge oneself: feast
glut: cram; gorge; inundate; pall; satiate
glutinous: tenacious; viscous
glutted: jaded
glutton: epicure
gluttonous: greedy; ravenous
gnaw: bite; corrode; fret
gnawing: fret
gnome: goblin; sylph
gnomon: style
go or come forth: proceed
go or get up: ascend
go after: seek
go along: accompany
go astray: wander
go away: depart; pass; retire
go backward: back
go before: lead
go counter to: traverse
go down: set
go into: access
go on all fours: scramble
go on: abide; last; pass; proceed
go onward or forward: continue
go swimmingly: succeed
go through: support
go up: mount
go well: succeed
go with: attach; attend
go-ahead: start
go: depart; drive; journey; pace; part; pass; quit; range; roam; run
goad: fret; incense; incentive; incite; pique; prod; spur; stimulate; stir; urge
goal: aim; base; object
goat: scapegoat
goatish: lascivious
gob: tar
gobble up: monopolize
gobble: gorge
goblin: brownie; gnome; spirit
God: spirit
godless: profane; wicked
godliness: devotion; piety
godly: holy; pious; religious
going before: advance
going: bound
goings-on: procedure
gold-bearing: pay
goldbrick: malinger; shirk
goldbricking: shiftless
golden-tongued: mellifluous
golden: bright; prosperous
Goliath: giant
gone: extinct; lost
good behavior: propriety
good deed: favor
good fortune: happiness
good purchase: bargain
good turn: kindness
good will: favor; grace
good-for-nothing: shiftless; vagabond
good-humored: gay; mellow
good-looking: handsome
good-luck charm: talisman

good-natured: kind; kindly; mellow
good: estimable; excellent; godly; goodness; just; kind; moral; nice; profit; right; righteous; solid; sound; undeniable; upright; use; valid; virtuous; well; wholesome
goodness: excellence; integrity; principle; right; virtue
goods: property; stock; wealth
goodwill: rapport
goody-goody: sanctimonious
goody-two-shoes: sanctimonious
goody: delicacy
goof off: shirk
goof up: blunder
goof: blunder
goofy: giddy; screwball; wacky
goose egg: zilch
gore: stab; stick
gorge: cram; pall; pass; satiate; surfeit; swallow
gorgeous: magnificent; splendid; superb
gormandize: gorge
gory: bloody
gossamer: light
gossip: babble; rumor; scandal; scuttlebutt; talk
gourmand: epicure
gourmandize: feast
gourmet: epicure
govern: administer; bridle; command; control; direct; guide; head; manage; master; reign; rule; sway
governable: tractable
governess: companion
governing: dominant; leading
government: control; discipline; empire; rule; sovereign; state; sway
governor: bridle; manager; stop
gown: dress
grab: capture; grasp; monopolize; seize
grabby: avaricious,
grace: beauty; delicacy; dignify; garnish; ornament; piety; polish
graceful: beautiful; becoming; clean; delicate; elegant; facile; lyrical
gracefulness: beauty; grace
graceless: abandoned; obdurate; stiff
gracious: affable; amiable; chivalrous; civil; compassionate; courteous; fair; good; handsome; kind; merciful; peaceful; polite; sweet
gradate: scale
gradation: scale
grade: caste; descent; order; quality; standard
gradual: gentle; slow
gradually: piecemeal
graduation: mode
grain: bit; iota; particle
grammar: ABC's; basics; diction; parlance
grand total: totality
grand: chief; giant; gorgeous; great; kingly; large; lordly; magnificent; majestic; noble; palatial; solemn; splendid; stately; superb; swell
grandeur: elevation; glory; magnificence; splendor; state
grandiloquent: tumid
grandiose: kingly; palatial; tumid
grandness: grandeur
grandstand: stand; vaunt
grant or afford entrance to: admit
grant permission: admit
grant: accord; acknowledge; agree; allow; cede; confer; confess; deliver; donation; endowment; extend; gift; give; impart; let; present; show; subsidy; vouchsafe
granted: provided
granting: if
granulate: crush
graph: map
graphic: picturesque
grapple: close
grasp: catch; clasp; comprehend; get; hold; reach; realize; seize; take; understand
grasping: avaricious; gluttonous; greedy; mercenary; parsimonious; rapacious
grate: grind
grateful: thankful
gratification: enjoyment; happiness; pleasure; satisfaction
gratified: glad
gratify: content; divert; feast; feed; humor; indulge; meet; pamper; satisfy

gratifying: grateful; interesting; pleasant
grating: hoarse; raucous; rough; rugged; screen
gratuitous: spontaneous
gratuity: donation; gift; present
grave: austere; deep; desperate; heavy; heinous; high; sedate; sepulcher; serious; severe; sober; solemn; staid; weighty
gravel: grit
graver: style
gravity: moment
greased: slippery
greasepaint: cosmetic
greasy: fat; unctuous
Great Plague: plague
great: acclaimed; ample; big; bulky; chief; crying; deep; desperate; giant; good; grand; gross; honorable; immense; large; magnificent; massive; monstrous; noble; notable; noteworthy; solid; stiff; towering
greaten: amplify; enlarge; grow; increase
greater part: bulk
greater than: above
greater: better; major
greatest: extreme; sovereign; top
greathearted: chivalrous
greediness: greed
greedy: avaricious; gluttonous; rapacious; ravenous; voracious
green around the gills: sallow
green: fresh; inexperienced; raw
greenhorn: amateur; dabbler; neophyte; pupil; tyro
greenish: sallow
greet: bid
gregarious: outgoing
gremlin: gnome; goblin,
grief-stricken: lachrymose
grief: affliction; distress; misery; passion; regret; sorrow; tear; trial; trouble; woe; wound
grievance: burden; hardship
grieve at: regret
grieve: cry; deplore; distress; hurt; lament; moan; mourn; pain; sorrow
grieved: sore; sorrowful; sorry
grieving: plaint
grievous: atrocious; bitter; deep; gross; heavy; sad; sore; sorrowful; sorry
griffin: monster
grim: forbidding; gaunt; hideous; horrible; macabre; stark
grimy: dirty
grin: beam; laugh
grinch: killjoy
grinding: hard
grip: catch; clasp; grasp; hold; take
gripe: kvetch; roil
gripped: rapt; spellbound
grisly: ghastly; grim; hideous
gritty: stony
groan: moan
groggy: giddy
groomed: sleek
gross: aggregate; broad; brutal; carnal; coarse; earthy; flagrant; foul; grievous; indecent; nasty; obese; obscene; precious; rank; rank; ribald; scurrilous; sensual; total; unrefined
grotesque: fantastic; wild
grouch: killjoy
ground plan: blueprint
ground: argument; base; cause; earth; evidence; foundation; matter; motive; occasion; place; reason; score; subject
groundless: idle; precarious; wanton
groundling: yahoo
grounds: cause; evidence; sediment
groundwork: base; bottom
group: arrange; band; body; bunch; company; faction; flock; form; gang; knot; pack; parcel; party; run; set; sort; troop; troop; type; variety
grouping: disposition
grouse: kvetch; murmur
grove: forest; stand
groveling: abject; dirty; low; servile; slavish; supple
grow old: age
grow up: ripen
grow: advance; breed; bulk; flourish; gather; get; increase; progress; raise; ripen; rise; spring; swell; wax
growing: thrifty
growl: complain; snarl
grown up: adult
grown-up: adult

grown: mature; ripe
growth: cover; development; increase; progress; stand; swell
grudge: begrudge; envy; malevolence; malice; spite; umbrage
gruesome: frightful; grim; macabre; terrible
gruff: blunt; brusque; coarse; hoarse
grumble: complain; growl; murmur; snarl; whine
grumpy: cantankerous; grouchy
guarantee: secure; warrant
guaranty: assurance; charter; guarantee
guard: conduct; convoy; cover; defend; escort; guardian; keeper; preserve; protect; protection; rampart; safeguard; screen; secure; shelter; warden; watch
guarded: careful; cautious; gingerly; safe
guardian angel: genius
guardian: caregiver; guard; keeper; warden
guardianship: custody; keeping
gudgeon: cheat; fool
guess: assumption; cast; conjecture; deduce; forecast; imagine; surmise; suspect; suspicion; theory
guest house: hotel
guest: visitor
guffaw: laugh
guidance: advice; conduct; escort; leading; management
guide: bear; bring; conduct; direct; escort; govern; guru; lead; manage; paradigm; pattern; pioneer; regulate; rule; show; speed; standard
guidelines: basics
guiding: standard
guild: association
guile: art; artifice; craft; cunning; deceit; duplicity; fraud
guileful: insidious
guileless: aboveboard; artless; candid; childish; ingenuous; innocent; naive; open; plain; pure; simple; sincere; unaffected; unreserved; unsophisticated
guilelessly: aboveboard
guilelessness: sincerity
guillotine: kill
guilt: blame
guiltiness: guilt
guiltless: blameless; innocent; pure
guise: apparel; appearance; manner; shape
gulch: pass
gulf: abyss
gull: bite; cheat; deceive; delude; fool; swindle
gullible: credulous
gulling: deception
gulp: gobble; gorge; swallow
gush: flow; spurt
gushing: effusive
gussy up: decorate
gust: blast; blow; burst; wind
gustatory: palatable
gusto: appetite; relish; verve; zest
gut sense: hunch
gut: abdomen
gutless wonder: weakling
guts: abdomen
gutsy: daredevil
guttural: hoarse
guy line: stay
guy: stay
gypsy: vagabond
gyrate: move; roll; spin; whirl
gyration: turn; whirl
gyve: shackle
haberdashery: wardrobe
habiliment: dress; habit; raiment; wardrobe
habiliments: apparel; clothes; garb
habit: addiction; clothes; custom; dress; garb; idiosyncrasy; knack; manner; practice; raiment; use; way; wont
habitancy: residence
habitat: element
habitation: address; home; lodge; residence
habitual: accustomed; chronic; common; continual; conventional; customary; ordinary; regular; set; steady; usual
habituate: harden; reside; use
habituated: wont
hack: cut; haggle; hew
hackney: hack
hackneyed: common; commonplace; hack; stale; stereotyped; trite

Hades: hell
haft: stock
hag: fury
haggard: cadaverous; careworn; gaunt; peaked
haggling: haggle
hail: deposit; greet; storm
hailstorm: storm
hair: pile; shade
hairless: smooth
hairy: harrowing; rough
hale: hardy; healthy; robust; sound; strong; vigorous; well
half round: about
half-breed: hybrid; mongrel
half-hearted: faint
half-witted: idiotic; stupid
halfhearted: lukewarm
halfway: middle
hallelujah: paean
hallmark: idiosyncrasy
hallow: consecrate; honor; sanctify
hallowed: holy; sacred; sacrosanct
hallucination: aberration; delusion; fancy; illusion
hallucinatory: phantom
halt: arrest; check; hang; hitch; hobble; pause; stand; stay; stop; wait
halting: hesitation
hamadryad: nymph
hamlet: community; town; village
hammer: beat
hamper: embarrass; encumber; hinder; hobble; impede; perplex; prevent
hand down: bequeath; prescribe
hand over: deliver; give
hand-clapping: applause
hand: knot; operative
handbag: bag
handbill: bill
handcuff: shackle
handicap: ailment; hobble
handicraft: craft
handicraftsman: craftsman
handle: manage; maneuver; rule; stock; touch; treat; work
handler: guru
handling: management; policy; use
handsome: beautiful; fair
handy: apt; available; clever; convenient; dexterous; serviceable; utilitarian
handyman: help
hang down: droop
hang: execute; kill; suspend; swing
hanger-on: parasite
hanging: curtain; pendulous
hanker for or after: long
hanker: yearn,
hankering: longing; thirst
hanky-panky: chicanery
hansom: carriage
hap: hazard
haphazard: random; slapdash
hapless: poor; unfortunate; unhappy; unlucky
happen upon: hit
happen: chance; occur; pass; rise
happening: episode; event; incident
happenstance: serendipity
happily: well
happiness: bliss; contentment; ease; ecstasy; enjoyment; joy; pleasure; transport; welfare
happy as a lark: ecstatic
happy: blithe; bright; cheerful; felicitous; fortunate; gay; glad; high; jolly; jovial; joyful; light; light-hearted; lucky; merry; well
harangue: declaim; oration; speech; tirade
harass: annoy; bedevil; beset; bother; embarrass; fret; grind; haggle; harry; molest; nag; perplex; persecute; pester; plague; ruffle; tease; torment; trouble; vex; weary; worry
harassing: troublesome
harassment: embarrassment; fret; trouble
harbor: bear; cherish; entertain; house; lodge; port; protect; refuge; shelter
hard up: poor
hard-featured: ugly
hard-headed: hard
hard-hearted: hard; merciless; obdurate; pitiless; ruthless; unfeeling; unnatural
hard-working: industrious; laborious
hard: arduous; astringent; austere; brave; callous; cruel; difficult; firm; grim; harsh; knotty; merciless; obdurate; relentless; rigid; rigorous; rugged; ruthless;

severe; shameless; solid; stale; stern; stony; stubborn; tough; troublesome; unfeeling; unrelenting
harden: habituate; sear; set
hardened: callous; chronic; lost; obdurate; shameless; stale; tough
hardening: seasoning
hardheaded: realistic
hardihood: chutzpah; courage
hardly: scarcely
hardness: temper
hardship: calamity; distress; misfortune; oppression; privation; trial
hardworking: busy; sedulous
hardy: bold; fresh; resolute; robust; sound; stout; strong; sturdy; tough
harebrained: wild-eyed
harem: seraglio
hark: listen
harlequin: fool
harlot: prostitute
harm: abuse; break; damage; deface; detriment; disadvantage; evil; expense; hurt; ill; injure; injury; lacerate; mischief; pain; spite; spoil; wound; wrong
harmful: bad; deleterious; evil; inimical; injurious; mad; malignant; noisome; noxious; pernicious; toxic; traumatic; unhealthful
harmless: innocuous
harmonic: parallel
harmonious: consistent; consonant; rich; sweet; tuneful
harmoniousness: coherence
harmonize: accommodate; accord; agree; concur; conform; correspond; heal; organize; proportion; reconcile
harmony: symmetry,
harmony: agreement; coherence; keeping; order; peace; proportion; rapport; unanimity; unity
harness: hitch
harrow: harry
harrowing: horrible
harry: annoy; bedevil; bother; harass; molest; nag; persecute; pester; plague; ruffle; tease; torment; trouble; vex; weary; worry
harsh-sounding: barbarian
harsh: acrimonious; astringent; austere; barbarian; bitter; blunt; brutal; grim; hard; harrowing; heavy; hoarse; raucous; rigid; rigorous; rough; rude; rugged; ruthless; severe; sharp; sour; stark; stern; stiff; strict; truculent; tyrannical; unkind; unrefined; unrelenting; unsparing
harshly: hard; hardly
harshness: austerity; cruelty
harvest: crop; cut; gather; yield
hasp: clasp
hassle: bedevil
haste: expedition; hurry; rapidity; rush; speed
hasten: advance; expedite; hurry; plunge; precipitate; race; run; rush; scramble; urge
hasty: abrupt; excitable; fleet; headlong; impatient; impetuous; impulsive; passionate; precipitate; quick; rash; sketchy; slapdash; sweeping; unwary
hatch: brood; contrive; flock; plan; plot
hatchway: hatch
hate: abhor; abhorrence; abominate; antipathy; aversion; detest; hatred; loathe; loathing; malevolence; malice; spite; venom
hateful: abhorrent; abject; abominable; cursed; detestable; disgusting; heinous; loathsome; malevolent; obnoxious; odious; offensive; opprobrious; spiteful
hating: abhorrent
hatred: abhorrence; abomination; antipathy; aversion; disgust; grudge; hate; horror; hostility; loathing; malevolence; malice; odium; phobia; rancor; repugnance; spite
haughtiness: air; arrogance; assumption; disdain; pride
haughty: arrogant; big; contemptuous; disdainful; grandiloquent; high; lofty; lordly; overbearing; proud; supercilious; uppity
haul: drag; draw; hale; purchase
haunt: habitat
haunting: memorable
haut monde: fashion

hauteur: arrogance; assumption; disdain; pride
have a bearing: apply
have affection for: love
have an appearance: appear
have an aversion or be averse to: dislike
have concern or regard: care
have confidence in: trust
have control: govern
have faith in: credit
have force or effect: tell
have in mind: intend
have the ability or power or right or qualifications or means to: can
have the appearance: appear
have: hold; keep; own; possess
haven: asylum; harbor; port; refuge; shelter
haver: waffle; yo-yo
having in one's possession: about
havoc: ravage; ruin
hawhaw: laugh
hayseed: yahoo
hazard: chance; danger; dare; guess; jeopardy; peril; risk; stake; venture; wager
hazardous: awkward; critical; precarious; slippery
haze: cloud; fog; mist
hazy: dim; murky; nebulous
head: chief; high; lead; master; master; member; principal; spring
headland: bluff; head
headlong: blind; desperate; hasty; pell-mell; precipitate; rash; unwary
headmaster: principal
headstart: start
headstrong: contrary; hotheaded; inflexible; intractable; obstinate; perverse; refractory; stubborn; unyielding; wayward; willful
headwaters: head
heal: cure; help; mend; recover; remedy
healing: therapeutic
health-giving: salutary
health: fitness; stamina; strength
healthful: healthy; well; wholesome
healthfulness: fitness
healthy: fresh; hale; hardy; lusty; right; robust; rosy; salutary; sanitary; sound; strong; vigorous; well; wholesome
heap or pile up: mass
heap up: pile
heap: bank; collection; mass; pile
hear of: detect
hear: detect; learn; listen; understand
hearken: listen
hearsay: gossip; rumor; scuttlebutt
heart-broken: disconsolate
heart: abbreviation; abstract; affection; bosom; compassion; midst; nucleus
heartache: grief
heartbreak: affliction
heartbroken: miserable
hearten: animate; encourage; reassure
heartfelt: deep; poignant
hearth and home: household
hearth: home; household
heartily: kindly
heartiness: goodwill; zest
heartless: cold; unnatural
hearty: bluff; cheerful; devout; fresh; genial; hale; hardy; healthy; lusty; sound; strong; warm; well
heat up: warm
heat: animate; ardor; fervor; flame; warm
heated: fervent; fiery; hectic; hot; warm
heathen: atheist; faithless; pagan; profane; skeptic
heathenish: heathen; pagan
heave: hoist; pant; raise; swell
heavenly: celestial
heavy drinker: lush
heavy-handed: clumsy
heavy-hearted: heavy
heavy: close; clumsy; gross; massive; ponderous; solid; stout; stupid; unwieldy; weighty
hector: annoy; molest; nag; pester; plague; tease; torment; trouble; vex; worry
hedge: palliate
heed: attend; attention; care; caution; follow; hear; mark; mind; note; notice; remark; respect

heedful: alert; attentive; careful; cautious; discreet; gingerly; good; observant; shy; thoughtful; watchful
heedfully: gingerly
heedfulness: caution; heed
heedless: blind; careless; daredevil; improvident; inadvertent; lax; loose; mindless; neglectful; oblivious; perfunctory; rash; reckless; regardless; remiss; thoughtless; unmindful; unwary; wanton
heedlessness: listlessness; neglect
heel over: careen
height: altitude; elevation
heighten: aggravate; elevate; raise; raise
heinous: atrocious; black; flagrant; grievous; gross; infamous; nefarious; ugly; wicked
heir: scion
heiress: scion
held: rapt; spellbound
helix: twist
hell: perdition
hellish: atrocious; dark; devilish; satanic
helmsman: guide
help: abet; accommodate; advantage; aid; assist; concur; encourage; favor; nourish; nurse; promote; recourse; relief; relieve; serve; succor; support; sustain; use
helper: aid; auxiliary; help
helpful: auxiliary; beneficial; chivalrous; convenient; friendly; obliging; serviceable; therapeutic; useful; utilitarian; wholesome
helping: auxiliary
helpless: forlorn; impotent; vulnerable
hem and haw: waffle; yo-yo
hence: accordingly; therefore
henchman: sidekick
herald: harbinger
herb: seasoning
herculean: arduous; gigantic
Herculean: strong
herd: compel; crowd; drove; flock; run; throng; troop
here and now: actual
here and there: about; sparse
here: present
hereditary: ancestral; innate,
heresy: sacrilege
heretic: iconoclast
heritage: inheritance; origin; pedigree
hermetic: abstruse
hermit: solitary
hermitlike: antisocial
hernia: rupture
hero: champion
heroic: bold; brave; daring; dauntless; desperate; fearless; game
heroism: bravery; courage; daring
hesitancy: doubt; hesitation; suspense
hesitant: ambivalent; backward; doubtful; pendulous; reluctant; scrupulous; skittish
hesitate: doubt; falter; halt; hang; pause; scruple; stagger; stammer; stick; vacillate; waffle; waver; yo-yo
hesitating: doubtful
hesitation: demur; doubt; misgiving; pause; scruple; suspense
heterogeneous: miscellaneous; unlike
hew: cut; hack
hiatus: abeyance; break; pause; remission; respite; stay
hibernating: torpid
hick: yahoo
hidden: blind; clandestine; dark; inscrutable; latent; mysterious; occult; recondite; secret; ulterior; underground
hide: blot; bury; conceal; cover; envelop; harbor; mask; pelt; screen; secrete; shade; shelter; shroud; skin; skulk; whitewash
hidebound: bigoted; orthodox; straitlaced
hideous: frightful; ghastly; grim; horrible; monstrous; terrible; unsightly
hiding place: blind; refuge
hie: race; run
higgle: haggle
higgledy-piggledy: chaotic; pell-mell
high seas: main
high-born: noble
high-brow: intellectual
high-colored: ruddy

high-flown: grandiloquent
high-grade: fine
high-hat: rebuff
high-minded: generous; magnanimous; noble
high-pitched: high
high-priced: costly; dear; expensive; high; rich
high-principled: ethical
high-spirited: bubbly; gallant; irrepressible; rambunctious
high-strung: skittish; taut
high: acute; arduous; dear; eminent; giddy; lofty; sharp; stiff; tall; towering
highborn: gentle
higher than: above
higher: above
highest: extreme; primary; principal; top; uppermost
highfalutin: grandiloquent; grandiose; pretentious
highlight: emphasize
highminded: honorable
highroad: way
highway: street; way
highwayman: outlaw; robber
hijack: abstract
hike: walk
hilarious: gay; high; merry; risible; zany
hilariousness: hilarity
hilarity: gaiety; glee; merriment; mirth
hill: bank; bluff; decline; elevation; eminence; height; mount
hillock: bank; hill
hilly: rugged
hind: back; reverse
hinder: arrest; bar; block; check; control; counteract; debar; delay; deter; discourage; embarrass; hamper; hobble; hold; impede; inhibit; interrupt; limit; obstruct; oppose; prevent; prohibit; restrain; retard; slow; stay; stem; stop; thwart
hindmost: last
hindrance: arrest; bar; barrier; block; check; disadvantage; embarrassment; hitch; impediment; limit; obstacle; obstruction; stop
hint at: refer
hint: aroma; beam; cast; dash; ghost; insinuate; intimate; proffer; shade; sign; strain; suggest; suspicion; touch; trace; vestige; wind
hinterland: backwater
hip: cagey; fashionable
hippogriff: monster
hire: buy; charter; employ; hack; let; place; rent; retain; wage
hired: hack
hireling: menial
hirsute: rough
history: account; narrative; recital; record; relation; saga; story
histrionic: theatrical
hit up: mooch
hit-and-miss: slapdash
hit-or-miss: slapdash
hit: beat; catch; strike; touch
hitch: hindrance
hither and thither: about
hither and yon: about
hitting: stroke
hoard: collection; deposit; gather; save; stock; supply; treasure
hoax: cheat; deception; fake; fool; fraud; humbug; trick
hobble: check; hindrance; shackle; shackle
hobgoblin: spirit
hobo: vagabond
hodgepodge: jumble; mess; mixture; promiscuous
hog: monopolize
hoggish: gluttonous
hoist: heave; raise
hold or bear up: sustain
hold back: hamper; stay; withhold
hold closely or firmly to: adhere
hold dear: cherish
hold fast: hang
hold forth: declaim; extend
hold off: suspend
hold on: persevere
hold oneself back: refrain
hold out against: endure; withstand
hold out: stretch
hold sway: govern; reign
hold true or good: apply
hold up under: bear
hold up: bear; hold; lift; rear; support; suspend
hold: accommodate; account; adhere; argue; arrest; bear; con-

tain; debate; deem; entertain; grasp; guard; halt; have; keep; maintain; own; possess; regard; repute; reserve; restrain; retain; say; stay; stick; take
holding: custody
holdup man: outlaw
hole: bore; cavity; opening; pit
holier-than-thou: sanctimonious
holiness: grace; piety
hollow out: cut
hollow-eyed: cadaverous; careworn; haggard; peaked
hollow: abyss; cavity; deceitful; empty; hole; hypocritical; pit; pit; tinny; vacuous; vain
hollowness: vanity
holocaust: blaze; destruction; flame; shambles
holy: devout; godly; hallowed; heavenly; pious; religious; sacred; sacrosanct
homage: allegiance; attention; deference; duty; honor; obeisance; paean; respect; reverence; worship
home ground: habitat
home quarters: address
home: habitat; house; household; place; residence
homeless: vagabond
homelike: cozy
homely: ordinary; plain; rugged; simple; ugly
homespun: cozy; household
homestead: household
homework: project
homey: cozy; plain
homicidal: bloody; fierce
homicide: murder; slaughter
homily: tract
homogeneous: pure
homogenize: fuse; mix
homograph : homonym,
homophone: homonym,
homosexual: gay
homunculus: dwarf
honed: keen
honest-to-God: genuine
honest: aboveboard; artless; bluff; candid; chaste; confidential; conscientious; devout; ethical; fair; good; guileless; honorable; innocent; just; moral; open; plain; pure; respectable; responsible; right; righteous; round; sincere; single; solid; sound; straight; straightforward; sure; true; trustworthy; unaffected; upright; worthy
honestly: aboveboard
honesty: candor; goodness; honor; integrity; principle; probity; sincerity; truth
honey: blarney; flatter
honeyed: luscious; mellifluous; sweet
honor: accolade; adore; celebrate; celebrate; compliment; consider; consideration; credit; deference; dignify; discharge; distinction; esteem; estimation; fame; glory; grace; homage; honesty; integrity; laud; luster; name; obeisance; praise; principle; regard; renown; reputation; repute; respect; reverence; worship
honorable: candid; clean; confidential; creditable; ethical; gentle; good; honest; just; liberal; magnanimous; manly; moral; noble; proud; respectable; solid; sound; straight; straight-forward; true; trustworthy; upright
honorarium: bonus
honored: acclaimed; famous; hallowed
hood: rowdy
hoodlum: criminal; rowdy
hoodwink: cheat; deceive; fool; victimize
hook: clasp; fasten; hitch
hooked: bent
hooligan: rowdy
hoop: ring
hooplike: round
hoot: cry; shout
hop: jump; leap; skip; spring; trip
hope for: expect
hope: expectation; passion; recourse; trust; virtue
hopeful: fair; optimistic; sanguine; wannabe
hopeless: black; desperate; despondent; useless
hopelessness: despair; discouragement
horde: band; cloud; crowd; gang; number; swarm; throng

horizontal: flat; level
horizontally: flat
horny: lascivious
horrendous: horrible; monstrous; nefarious; terrible; tremendous
horrible: abhorrent; abominable; black; dread; formidable; frightful; ghastly; grim; hideous; macabre; monstrous; nefarious; terrible
horrid: frightful; grim; horrible; terrible; tremendous
horrific: horrendous
horrified: aghast
horrify: appall; dismay; shock
horrifying: abhorrent; abominable; horrible; terrible; tremendous
horror-struck: aghast
horror: abhorrence; antipathy; consternation; dismay; fear; hatred; terror
horse: mount; nag
horses: stock
hosanna: paean
hospitable: broad; receptive
hospital: asylum
hostel: hotel; inn
hostelry: hotel; inn; tavern
hostile condemnation: abuse
hostile: acrimonious; adverse; alien; cold; contrary; ill; inimical; malevolent; opposite; repugnant; unfriendly; virulent; warlike
hostility: feud; loathing; opposition; repugnance
hot-tempered: excitable; hotheaded; irascible; petulant; scrappy; sour; temperamental
hot: ardent; fervent; fiery; hectic; impatient; impetuous; peppery; pungent; radioactive; sharp; strong; torrid
hotchpotch: jumble; mess; mixture; promiscuous
hotdog: vaunt
hotel: inn; tavern
hothead,freak: fanatic,
hotheaded: passionate; peppery; petulant; scrappy
hotness: heat
hottempered: peppery
house: address; ancestry; company; concern; firm; home; hotel; lodge; place; protect; residence; shanty; shelter; stock
housebreaker: thief
household word: catchword
household: home; house; vernacular
housing project: development
hovel: cabin; hole; hut; shack; shanty
hover: fly; hang
however: but; notwithstanding; only
howler: blunder
hub: center
hubbub: ado; bedlam; maelstrom; noise; racket; ruckus; tumult; uproar
hue: cast; tint
hug: clasp; clasp; embrace; strain
huge: big; bulky; enormous; giant; gigantic; great; humongous; immense; large; mammoth; massive; mighty; monster; monstrous; prodigious; spacious; tremendous; vast
hull: body; skin
hullabaloo: bedlam; clamor
human: man
human being: man; mortal; person
human beings: people
human: carnal; humane; mortal; person
humane: benevolent; gentle; good; kind; merciful
humanities: literature
humanity: goodness; kindness; man
humanizing: humane
humankind: man
humans: people
humble: abase; base; chasten; depress; humiliate; ignoble; low; lower; mean; meek; modest; mortify; poor; shame; simple; small; snub; submissive; unassuming
humbleness: humility
humbling: humiliation
humbug: blarney; fraud; phony
humdrum: monotonous; prosaic; slow; stupid; tiresome; wearisome
humid: damp; moist; wet
humidify: damp

humidity: damp; wet
humiliate: abase; abash; chagrin; degrade; depress; disgrace; humble; lower; mortify; shame; snub
humiliated: ashamed
humiliating: abject; ignominious; shameful
humiliation: chagrin; degradation; indignity; shame; stoop
humor: cherish; disposition; fancy; gratify; indulge; mood; pamper; spirit; temper; whim; wit
humorous: comical; dry; facetious; funny; jocose; laughable; light; pleasant; risible; waggish; witty
hunger for: lust
hunger: appetite; desire; pant; pine; thirst; yearn
hungry: poor; ravenous; sharp; voracious
hunky: muscular; well-built
hunt down: trail
hunt: course; run
hunting: hunt
hurl or fling down: precipitate
hurl: cast; send; shy; throw
hurly-burly: ado
hurricane: storm
hurried: hasty; headlong; quick
hurriedly: pell-mell
hurry-scurry: hurly-burly
hurry: expedite; haste; hasten; hurly-burly; precipitate; race; run; rush; scramble; speed
hurt: abuse; ache; break; cut; damage; detriment; disadvantage; harm; ill; injure; lacerate; mischief; pain; sabotage; smart; sore; spite; wound
hurtful: bad; deleterious; harmful; injurious; malignant; noisome; noxious; pernicious; tasteless
hurtle over: plunge
husband: partner; reserve; save; treasure
husbandman: countryman
hush: appease; quell; quiet; still
hushed: still
husk: skin; skin
husky: hoarse; muscular
hussy: shrew
hustle: hurry; scramble
hut: cabin; cottage; lodge; shack; shanty
hutch: shack
hybrid: mongrel
hydrated: watery
hydrous: watery
hygienic: healthy; sanitary
hymn: paean
hyper: hectic
hypercritical: squeamish
hypersensitive: temperamental; touchy
hypnotic: sedative
hypnotize: bewitch; captivate
hypnotized: spellbound
hypochondria: melancholy
hypocrisy: deceit; duplicity; humbug
hypocrite: impostor
hypocritical: false; mealymouthed; plausible; sanctimonious; smarmy
hypothecate: plight
hypothesis: assumption; conjecture; speculation; theory
hypothesize: conjecture; imagine
hysterical: hectic; risible
hysterics: hilarity
icky: saccharine
icon: idol; image
iconography: imagery
icy: cold
idea: abstract; apprehension; conceit; fancy; image; main; meaning; notion; opinion; sense; surmise; suspicion; thought; view; vision
ideal: absolute; archetype; model; nonesuch; paradigm; paragon; visionary
idealist: visionary
ideas: theme
ideate: conceive
identical: same
identifiable: sensible
identification: empathy
identify: adhere; band; mark; name; place; tell
identity: community; sameness
idiom: dialect; expression; jargon; parlance
idiosyncrasy: abnormality; eccentricity; peculiarity
idiosyncratic: abnormal
idiot: block; fool; oaf

idiotic: fatuous; senseless; silly; unreasonable

idle away: idle

idle talk: gossip

idle: dawdle; fool; frivolous; fruitless; futile; inactive; indolent; lazy; loiter; puerile; slack; slothful; standing; unemployed; vain

idler: vagabond

idol: icon; image

idolater: pagan

idolatrous: pagan

idolatry: worship

idolize: adore; adore; worship

idolizing: worship

if: provided; provision

iffy: shaky

ignite: kindle; light

ignoble: base; dishonorable; low; mean; slavish; sordid; vulgar

ignominious: abject; dishonorable; ignoble; infamous; opprobrious; shabby; shameful; vile

ignominy: disgrace; infamy; reproach; scandal; shame

ignoramus: fool; yahoo

ignorant: backward; barbarian; blind; dark; raw; rude; simple; uneducated; unwitting

ignore: blink; disregard; eliminate; neglect; overlook; pass; slight; slur

ignoring: regardless

ill at ease: restive; uncomfortable

ill fortune: calamity; misadventure; misfortune

ill luck: misadventure; misfortune

ill will: grudge; hostility; malevolence; malice; rancor; spite

ill-advised: mad; unwise

ill-behaved: naughty

ill-bred: common; ill-mannered; loutish; unrefined

ill-chosen: tasteless

ill-considered: foolish

ill-defined: dim; faint; general; loose

ill-dressed: dowdy

ill-famed: infamous

ill-fated: unlucky

ill-favored: ugly

ill-formed: misshapen

ill-humored: moody; morose; sulky; sullen

ill-mannered: impolite; rude; uncivil; uncouth

ill-natured: acid; cross; cynical; harsh; malevolent; morose; peevish; ugly

ill-omened: unlucky

ill-qualified: bad

ill-smelling: rotten

ill-starred: miserable; unfortunate

ill-tempered: acid; cranky; cross; cynical; fretful; peevish; sour; vicious

ill-timed: unseasonable

ill-treat: maltreat

ill-use: abuse

ill: ailing; ailment; bad; indisposed; nauseous; seedy; sick; unhealthful; unhealthy; unsound

illegal: criminal; crooked; unlawful

illegality: malfeasance

illegitimate: illegal; spurious; unlawful

illiberal: bigoted; exclusive; intolerant; little; mean; narrow-minded; niggardly; parsimonious; selfish; small; small-minded; strict

illiberality: parsimony

illicit: illegal; unlawful

illimitable: endless; unbounded

illiterate: ignorant; uneducated

illness: affection; disease; disorder; ill; malady

illogical: incongruous; weak

illume: lighten

illuminate: edify; lighten; rationalize

illuminated: luminous

illumination: light

illumine: enlighten

illusion: aberration; apparition; delusion; hallucination; idol; phantasm; show; vision

illusive: phantom; unreal

illusory: deceitful; fictitious; ideal; imaginary; phantom; subjective; unreal; visionary

illustrate: demonstrate; impersonate

illustration: case; example; imagery; instance; pattern; sample

illustrious: bright; celebrated; conspicuous; distinguished; eminent; famous; glorious; grand; great; honorable; noted; splendid

illustriousness: brilliance; celebrity

illy: ill

image: emblem; fancy; icon; idol; imagine; model; picture; reflection; represent; resemblance; type; vision

imaginable: earthly

imaginary: fabulous; fictitious; ideal; illusory; phantom; quixotic; romantic; subjective; unreal; visionary; wild

imagination: conceit; fancy; suspicion

imaginative: romantic

imagine: comprehend; conceive; daydream; fancy; feign; guess; image; invent; picture; realize; surmise; suspect; think

imagined: imaginary; subjective

imagining: daydream

imbalance: difference

imbecile: block; fool; oaf

imbecilic: idiotic

imbibe: drink; swallow

imbue: saturate

imitate: act; affect; ape; copy; counterfeit; duplicate; feign; mock; pattern; play; present; reproduce; sham; simulate

imitation: artificial; burlesque; copy; counterfeit; mockery; model; parody; sham

imitative: slavish

imitator: wannabe

immaculate: clean; clear; good; guiltless; innocent; pure

immaterial: simple; trifling; trivial; unessential

immature: abortive; adolescent; crude; imperfect; infantile; puerile; tender; young

immaturity: youth

immeasurable: endless; measureless; unbounded

immediate: close; direct; primary; quick; urgent

immediately: instantly; presently; right

immense: big; enormous; giant; gigantic; great; huge; large; mammoth; massive; measureless; mighty; monstrous; prodigious; unbounded; unmeasured; vast

immerge: immerse

immerse: dip; plunge; submerge

immigrant: alien

immigrate: migrate

imminent: near

immobile: inactive; inert

immoderate: excessive; extravagant; extreme; radical; unbounded; unreasonable

immoderation: excess

immodest: bold; brazen; indecent; obscene; shameless; unabashed

immolate: offer

immoral: abandoned; bad; blue; coarse; depraved; dirty; evil; free; libertine; licentious; loose; mean; noxious; obscene; rotten; sinful; vicious; wicked; wrong

immorality: abomination; corruption; wrong

immortal: eternal; perennial; undying

immovability: stability

immovable: fast; firm; inflexible; persistent; rigid; set; stable

immune: free; sacred

immunity: charter; exemption; freedom; liberty; prerogative; privilege

immure: confine; wall

immutability: constancy

immutable: constant; invariable; permanent

imp: brownie; scamp

impact: shock

impair: blemish; break; corrode; cripple; damage; debase; hurt; injure; maim; mar; spoil; strain; weaken

impaired: crazy; sick; unsound

impairment: damage; decay; detriment; injury; waste

impale: stick

impart: cast; communicate; convey; deliver; divulge; extend; give; mention; possess; publish; reveal; tell; yield

impartial: candid; disinterested; even; fair; general; just; objective; unbiased; unprejudiced

impartiality: tolerance

impasse: stalemate

impassionate: cold; hard

impassioned: amorous; ardent; enthusiastic; excited; feeling; fervent; fiery; passionate; vehement

impassive: apathetic; stoical; world-weary

impassiveness: phlegm

impassivity: phlegm

impatient: cross; eager; quick; restive; testy; weary

impeach: accuse; charge

impeachment: recall

impeccable: innocent

impecunious: bankrupt; poor

impede: bar; block; delay; embarrass; encumber; hamper; hinder; obstruct; prevent; retard; shackle; slow; stop

impediment: bar; barrier; block; burden; check; discouragement; hindrance; hitch; obstacle; obstruction; shackle; stop

impeding: hindrance

impel: carry; compel; determine; drive; force; induce; influence; move; persuade; push; send; solicit; urge

impend: hang; threaten

impending: imminent; near

impenetrable: hard; inscrutable; invincible; mysterious; proof; strong

impenitent: abandoned; unreconstructed

imperative: imperious; peremptory; urgent

imperfect: bad; defective; faulty; inadequate; obscure; partial; rough; rudimentary; sketchy

imperfection: defect; failing; fault; flaw; foible; stain; vice

imperial: kingly; majestic; royal; sovereign

imperil: expose; hazard; peril; risk; stake; venture

imperious: absolute; arbitrary; arrogant; authoritative; lordly; magisterial; overbearing; peremptory; proud; tyrannical

imperishable: eternal; immortal; perennial

impermanent: temporary

impersonal: objective

impersonate: act; imitate; play; present

impertinence: affront; assurance; chutzpah; impudence

impertinent: audacious; disrespectful; forward; impudent; insolent; obtrusive; offensive; pert; presumptuous; rude; saucy

imperturbable: cold; composed; easygoing; sedate; serene; stoical; unruffled

impervious: proof

impetuosity: fury; heat; vehemence; violence

impetuous: boisterous; brave; fierce; fiery; headlong; hot; hotheaded; impatient; impulsive; passionate; rash; tempestuous; vehement; wild

impetuousness: fury

impetus: force; moment

impiety: sacrilege

impinge: apply

impious: profane; ungodly; wicked

impiousness: blasphemy

impish: playful

implacable: cruel; deadly; inexorable; inflexible; pitiless; relentless; remorseless; revengeful; unrelenting

implant: fix

implement: gadget; instrument; tool

implicate: involve

implication: hint; purport

implicit: tacit

implied: tacit

implore: ask; beg; beseech; crave; entreat; pray; solicit; supplicate; urge

imply: argue; betray; hint; involve; mean; purport; signify

impolite: blunt; brusque; brutal; coarse; disrespectful; earthy; ill-mannered; rough; rude; uncivil

import: effect; importance; matter; meaning; moment; purport; sense; significance; substance; value; weight

importance: account; consequence; consideration; distinction; mark; matter; moment; prestige; significance; stress; value; weight; worth

important: big; broad; capital; critical; crying; dominant; essential; grand; grave; great; heavy; high; material; momentous; notable;
ponderous; prominent; salient; serious; significant; substantial; valuable; vital; weighty

importunate: urgent

importune: beg; beseech; clamor; entreat; nag; persecute; pray; solicit; supplicate; urge

impose or insist on: appoint

impose on: fool

impose upon: humbug

impose: administer; lay; put; sham

imposing: grand; magnificent; majestic; massive; noble; palatial; proud; solemn; splendid; state; stately

imposition: cheat; humbug; wile

impost: custom; duty

imposter: cheat

impostor: humbug; phony; swindler

imposture: cheat; deception; fake; humbug; phony; wile

impotence: disability; inability

impotent: incapable; ineffectual; weak

impound: pound

impoverish: bankrupt

impoverished: bankrupt; destitute; poor

impracticable: quixotic; visionary; wild

impractical: academic; crackpot; ideal; mad; unpractical; unreal; visionary

imprecate: curse; swear

imprecation: curse; malediction; oath

imprecise: general; loose; unfaithful; vague

impregnable: fast; invincible; strong

impregnate: saturate

impress: affect; influence; mark; stamp; strike; strike; touch

impressibility: sensibility; susceptibility

impressible: soft

impression: air; fancy; feeling; hunch; idea; mark; notion; opinion; presence; proof; stamp; view

impressionable: receptive; sensitive; sentient; soft

impressive: affecting; authoritative; magnificent; memorable; noble; noteworthy; picturesque; solemn; splendid; strong

impressiveness: magnificence

imprimatur: allowance

imprint: mark; stamp

imprison: capture; confine; incarcerate; pound; shut

imprisonment: arrest; bond; bondage; captivity; custody

improbable: marvelous; romantic

impromptu: ad-lib; extemporaneous; improvised; offhand

improper: false; inaccurate; incorrect; indecent; naughty; tasteless; unbecoming; uncalled-for; unseemly; vicious; wrong

improperly: ill

impropriety: blunder

improve upon: better

improve: advance; ameliorate; better; edify; elaborate; elevate; gain; grow; help; mellow; mend; profit; progress; rectify; reform; touch

improved: mellow; onward

improvement: advance; mend; profit; progress; reform; reformation

improvident: lavish; profuse; reckless; shiftless

improving: cosmetic; uplifting

improvisation: ad-lib; makeshift

improvisatory: offhand

improvise: ad-lib

improvised: ad-lib; extemporaneous; makeshift

imprudent: extravagant; foolish; improvident; mad; reckless; short-sighted; unguarded; unwary; unwise

impudence: assurance; chutzpah; gall

impudent: audacious; bold; brazen; cool; disrespectful; forward; froward; impertinent; pert; rude; saucy; shameless; uncivil

impugn: assail; attack; contradict; dispute; resist

impulse: incentive; passion; spur; start; stir; urge

impulsive: capricious; headlong; impetuous; offhand; passionate; rash; voluntary

impunity: exemption

impure: base; carnal; coarse; corrupt; foul; licentious; nasty; obscene; profane; unclean

impurity: abomination

imputation: charge; reflection

impute to: account

impute: ascribe; attribute; charge; lay; refer

in a brown study: absent-minded; preoccupied

in a flash or trice or jiffy: instantly

in a higher place than: above

in abeyance: dormant

in addition to: besides

in addition: also; besides

in advance: forward

in agreement: consonant

in alignment: abreast

in all directions: abroad

in all respects: clean

in attendance: attendant

in business contexts *ASAP*: immediately

in case: if; provided

in circulation: abroad

in connection with: about

in detail: particularly

in due course: accordingly

in effect: standing

in equilibrium: even

in every direction: about

in evidence: tangible

in fashion: fashionable

in force: effective; standing

in general: generally

in heaven: above

in love: amorous

in open sight: aboveboard

in place: still

in poor taste: grandiose,

in receivership: bankrupt

in regard to: about

in rotation: about

in seventh heaven: ecstatic

in sight: apparent

in spite of: despite; notwithstanding

in style: fashionable

in succession: about

in sway: predominant

in the altogether: nude

in the dark: dark

in the habit of: accustomed

in the main: mostly

in tune: sweet

in turn: alternate

in vogue: current; fashionable; popular

in-your-face: defiant

in: about; inside

inability: disability

inaccuracy: mistake

inaccurate: careless; erroneous; incorrect; mistaken; unfaithful; wrong

inactive: dead; dormant; dull; idle; indolent; inert; languid; lazy; lifeless; passive; silent; slack; slothful; sluggish; torpid

inactivity: abeyance; sleep

inadequacy: want

inadequate: bad; defective; incompetent; lean; poor; scanty; short; slender; unsatisfactory; unworthy; weak

inadvertent: unwitting

inane: absurd; foolish; impertinent; inept; mindless; preposterous; senseless; silly; stereotyped; stupid; vacant; vacuous

inanimate: dead; dull; lifeless

inanity: stuff

inapplicable: impertinent; improper; unapt

inappropriate: extraneous; impertinent; improper; incongruous; inconsistent; inept; tasteless; unapt; unbecoming; unfit; unhappy; unseasonable; unseemly; unsuitable; untimely; wrong

inapt: inadequate; inept; tasteless; unapt; unfit; unhappy; unskillful

inartistic: harsh; rude

inasmuch as: because; since

inattention: disregard; indifference; listlessness; neglect; oversight; slight

inattentive: absent-minded; careless; inadvertent; neglectful; preoccupied; reckless; regardless; remiss; thoughtless; unmindful

inattentiveness: disregard; listlessness

inaudible: noiseless

inaugurate: begin; commence; initiate

inauguration: beginning; debut

inauspicious: ominous; sinister; unhappy

inauthentic: artificial; bogus; phony

inborn: inherent; innate; intrinsic; native

inbred: inborn; inherent; innate; intrinsic; native

incalculable: iffy

incandesce: radiate

incapability: disability; inability

incapable: incompetent; inefficient; unfit

incapacious: incapable

incapacitate: disable; sabotage

incapacity: disability; inability

incarcerate: capture; confine

incarceration: captivity

incautious: careless; hotheaded; improvident; rash; reckless; unguarded; unwary

incense: anger; enrage; exasperate; infuriate; irritate; perfume; provoke; rankle

incensed: angry; mad; wrathful

incentive: inducement; motive; spur; stimulus

inception: beginning

incertitude: suspense

incessant: continual; endless; perennial; perpetual

incessantly: hard

inch: edge

inchmeal: piecemeal

inchwise: piecemeal

incident: episode; event; occasion; occurrence; phenomenon; scene; story

incidental: accidental; fortuitous

incise: cut

incision: cut

incisive: caustic; cutting; sharp; trenchant

incite: animate; arouse; encourage; engender; excite; impel; induce; inflame; influence; kindle; move; pique; prod; provoke; rouse; solicit; spur; stimulate; stir; summon; urge

incitement: cause; incentive; inducement; motive; spur; stimulus

inclement: beastly; hard; nasty; rigorous; rough

inclination: affection; aptitude; bent; bias; cast; descent; device; disposition; fancy; liking; love; mind; partiality; penchant; pleasure; predilection; proclivity; propensity; relish; respect; set; slant; tendency; trend; turn; weakness; will; wish

incline or bend downward: decline

incline: bend; bias; decline; determine; dip; lean; list; slant; slope; sway; trend; verge

inclined: apt; prone; ready

inclining: inclination

inclosing: about

include: circle; comprehend; comprise; concern; contain; cover; embrace; involve; number

inclusive: comprehensive; extensive; grand

incognito: nameless

incoherent: incongruous; inconsistent

income: mean; pay

incommensurate: inadequate

incommode: pain; plague; trouble

incommodious: inconvenient

incommunicative: close

incomparable: matchless; rare; unequaled

incompatibility: friction; opposition; repugnance

incompatible: exclusive; incongruous; inconsistent; opposite

incompetence: disability; inability

incompetent: bad; inadequate; incapable; unapt; unfit; unqualified

incomplete: crude; defective; faulty; imperfect; inadequate; partial; poor; rough

incomprehensible: dark; inscrutable; mysterious; unaccountable

inconceivable: unthinkable

inconclusive: weak

incongruity: discrepancy

incongruous: absurd; funny; impertinent; incompatible; inconsistent

inconsequent: mean

inconsequential: simple; small

inconsiderable: light; little; minor; paltry; petty; remote; slight; slim; weak

inconsiderate: abrupt; blind; careless; short-sighted; tasteless; thoughtless; wanton

inconsistency: conflict; difference; discrepancy; opposition; repugnance

inconsistent: contradictory; fickle; incompatible; incongruous; inconstant; opposite

inconsolable: desolate; disconsolate; melancholy; unhappy

inconsonant: incongruous

inconspicuous: obscure; quiet

inconstant: capricious; faithless; false; fast; fickle; mercurial; mutable; unfaithful; unstable; variable; wayward

incontestable: certain; incontrovertible; indisputable; undeniable; unequivocal; unquestionable

incontinent: wanton

incontrovertible: certain; decided; decisive; hard; indisputable; positive; undeniable; unquestionable

inconvenience: disadvantage; molest; pain; trouble

inconvenient: rough

incorporate: combine; unite

incorrect: bad; erroneous; false; inaccurate; mistaken; wrong

incorrectness: inaccuracy

incorrigible: abandoned; shameless; tough

incorruptibility: principle

incorruptible: conscientious; honest

increase: add; addition; advance; aggravate; augment; development; elevate; enlarge; expand; extension; flourish; gain; gather; grow; growth; lengthen; magnify; progress; raise; rise; spring; swell; thrive; wax

incredible: fabulous; marvelous; miraculous

incredulous: doubtful; quizzical; skeptical

increment: addition

incriminate: accuse; charge

incrimination: charge

incrustation: scale

incubate: brood; hatch

incubus: load

inculcate: insinuate

inculpable: blameless

inculpate: accuse; charge

incurable: hopeless

incursion: descent; raid

indebted: grateful; thankful

indecency: impropriety

indecent: blue; broad; coarse; dirty; gross; improper; incorrect; nasty; obscene; rank; ribald; scurrilous; shameless; unbecoming; unseemly

indecision: doubt; hesitation; poise; suspense

indecisive: doubtful; pendulous

indecorous: improper; indecent; unseemly

indecorousness: impropriety

indecorum: blunder; impropriety

indeed: even

indefatigability: patience; perseverance

indefatigable: diligent; patient; persistent; tireless

indefatigableness: patience

indefinite: dim; general; loose; tentative; uncertain; vague

indelible: memorable

indelicate: broad; coarse; gross; indecent; nasty; obscene; rough; shameless; tasteless

indemnification: compensation; recompense; redress; reparation; restitution; satisfaction

indemnify: pay; repay

indemnity: compensation; redress

indeniable: decided

indent: pick

indentation: pit

indenture: bind; bondage

independence: freedom; liberty

independent: free; self-governed; separate

indescribable: nameless; nondescript; unspeakable

indestructible: eternal; immortal

indeterminate: ambiguous; doubtful; dubious; equivocal; loose; uncertain; unsettled; vague

indetermination: suspense

indicate: argue; betray; exhibit; express; mark; mean; name; note; show; sign; signify; suggest; threaten

indication: evidence; guide; mark; portent; presage; show; sign; trace

indicative or suggestive of: significant

indicative: expressive

indict: accuse; charge; impeach

indictment: charge

indifference: disregard; insensibility; listlessness; phlegm; slight; unconcern

indifferent: apathetic; blas; callous; cold; cool; dead; grudging; half-hearted; hard; lackadaisical; languid; lukewarm; mediocre; neglectful; nonchalant; ordinary; perfunctory; reckless; regardless; stoical; uninterested; world-weary

indigence: distress; necessity; need; penury; poverty; want

indigenous: native

indigent: bankrupt; destitute; penniless; poor

indignant: angry; wrathful

indignation: anger; displeasure; offense; passion; wrath

indignity: affront; insult; outrage; reproach; stoop

indisposed: ill

indirect reference: mention

indirect: circuitous; sinuous; tortuous

indiscreet: careless; hasty; precipitate; rash; short-sighted; unwary; unwise

indiscretion: blunder; fault; impropriety; slip

indiscriminate: blind; miscellaneous; promiscuous

indispensability: necessity

indispensable: essential; fundamental; necessary; requisite; vital

indispensableness: necessity

indisposed: reluctant; sick; unapt

indisposition: disease; disorder; malady

indisputable: certain; clear; decided; incontrovertible; positive; sure; undeniable; unquestionable

indistinct: ambiguous; cloudy; dim; faint; indefinite; loose; nebulous; obscure; uncertain; vague

indistinguishable: identical

individual: appropriate; distinct; particular; peculiar; person; private; proper; separate; single; singular; sole; special; subjective

individuality: character; unity

individually: particularly

indivisible particle: atom

indoctrinate: educate; initiate; instruct; teach

indoctrination: instruction

indolence: slack

indolent: idle; inactive; lackadaisical; laggard; lazy; shiftless; slack; slothful; slow; sluggish; torpid

indomitable: dauntless; invincible; stalwart; stout; sturdy; unyielding

indorse: acknowledge

indubitable: absolute; certain; decided; indisputable; positive; sure; undeniable; unquestionable

indubitably: absolutely

induce: bring; determine; get; guide; incite; influence; lead; make; move; persuade; provoke; spur; tempt; urge

inducement: cause; incentive; motive; occasion; spur

induct: place

induction: debut

indulge: cherish; gratify; harbor; humor; pamper; pet

indulgence: latitude; mercy; pardon; remission

indulgent: gracious; mild

indurate: harden

indurated: callous

industrious: active; assiduous; busy; diligent; laborious; notable; sedulous

industry: application; diligence; work

inearth: bury

inebriate: drunkard

inebriated: cockeyed; drunken

ineffable: nameless; unspeakable

ineffective: barren; empty; feeble; idle; impotent; ineffectual; inefficient; void; weak

ineffectual: barren; empty; feeble; fruitless; futile; idle; impotent; nugatory; useless; void; weak

inefficacious: weak

inefficient: incapable; shiftless; vain; weak

inelastic: firm; rigid; taut

inelegant: homely; rude; stiff; vulgar

ineluctable: compulsory; tangible

inept: awkward; clumsy; maladroit; unapt

inequality: difference; disparity

inequitable: injurious; shabby; unfair; unjust

inert: dead; dormant; dull; inactive; inanimate; indolent; languid; lazy; lifeless; passive; senseless; slothful; sluggish; still; torpid

inescapable: compulsory; fast

inestimable: invaluable

inevitability: certainty; necessity

inevitable: certain; fatal; sure

inevitableness: necessity

inexact: careless; general; inaccurate; incorrect; loose; rough; unfaithful

inexactitude: inaccuracy

inexactness: inaccuracy

in excelsis: above

inexhaustible: ample

inexpensive: cheap

inexpensively: low

inexperienced: fresh; raw

inexpert: awkward; clumsy; unskillful

inexplicable: inscrutable; mysterious; strange; unaccountable

inexpressible: nameless; unspeakable

inextravagant: modest

inextricable: fast

infallible: certain; reliable; sure; sure; unerring

infamous: base; black; dark; dishonorable; foul; heinous; ignominious; nefarious; opprobrious; shameful

infamy: disgrace; ignominy; reproach; sacrilege; shame; stigma

infantile: childish

infatuate: fascinate; turn

infatuated: mad; smitten

infect: contaminate; corrupt; poison; taint

infected: corrupt

infection: sore; taint

infectious: contagious

infecund: barren; fruitless; sterile

infelicitous: tasteless; unhappy

infer: argue; assume; deduce; draw; gather; reason; suppose; surmise

inference: conclusion; conjecture

inferior: bad; base; cheap; coarse; common; ignoble; mean; minor; ordinary; poor; short; subject; subordinate; tacky; tinny

inferiority: indifference

infernal: atrocious; black; dark; devilish; satanic

inferno: blaze; flame; hell

inferred: tacit

infertile: arid; barren; dead

infidel: atheist; faithless; skeptic

infinite: endless; eternal; gigantic; innumerable; measureless; numberless; perpetual; unbounded; unlimited; unmeasured

infinitesimal: little; minute

infirm: crazy; decrepit; feeble; peaked; sick; sickly; unsettled; unsound; unstable; unsteady; weak

infirmity: ailment; disease; foible

infix: lodge

inflame: enamor; enrage; exasperate; excite; flame; incense; kindle; madden; provoke; rankle; rouse; stimulate

inflamed: angry; fervent; fiery

inflate: billow; expand; swell

inflated: big; grandiloquent; grandiose; tumid; vain

inflation: swell

inflect: bow

inflexibility: austerity; constancy

inflexible: austere; determined; hard; implacable; inexorable; intractable; obdurate; obstinate; relentless; resolute; rigid; rigorous; stern; stony; strict; stubborn; tough; uncompromising; unyielding; willful

inflict: put

influence: affect; authority; bend; bias; credit; determine; get; govern; guide; hold; induce; lead; manage; motive; move; occasion; operation; overrule; persuade; power; prejudice; prestige; reach; reason; reign; solicit; subject; sway; urge; weight; work

influenceable: receptive

influenced: partial

influences: medium

influencing: operative

influential: operative; potent; powerful; prevailing; strong; substantial

inform against: charge; denounce

inform: admonish; advise; apprise; enlighten; imbue; instruct; notify; possess; teach; tell; warn

informal: colloquial; easy; familiar; free; offhand; vernacular

informality: ease; familiarity

information: advice; evidence; intelligence; knowledge; notice; observation; wisdom; word

informational: uplifting

informative: uplifting

informed: aware

infra dig: low

infract: break

infraction: breach; crime

infrequent: rare; scarce; uncommon

infrequently: seldom

infringe: break; disobey; encroach; intrude; transgress; trespass

infringement: breach; trespass; violation

infuriate: anger; enrage; exasperate; irritate; madden; provoke; turn

infuriated: angry; savage

infuse: imbue; insinuate

ingenious: able; acute; adroit; apt; astute; bright; cagey; capable; clever; cunning; sharp; shrewd; skillful

ingenue: virgin

ingenuity: ability; address; art; craft

ingenuous: artless; candid; childish; direct; frank; guileless; honest; innocent; naive; open; plain; simple; unreserved; unsophisticated

ingenuousness: freedom; sincerity; truth

inglorious: abject

ingrained: radical

ingratiating: saccharine; smarmy; soft; unctuous

ingredient: base; component; element; part

ingress: access; entrance

ingurgitate: absorb

inhabit: abide; dwell; reside

inhabitancy: residence

inhabitant: countryman; native

inhale: draw

inharmonious: incompatible; incongruous; inconsistent; rough; rugged

inhere: reside

inherent: essential; inborn; native; organic; subjective

inheritance: gift; heritage

inherited: ancestral; inborn; inherent; native

inhibit: damp; forbid

inhuman: barbarian; beastly; black; bloody; brutal; cruel; ruthless; savage; tyrannical; unnatural

inhumanity: cruelty

inhume: bury

inimate: warm

inimical: adverse; cold; hostile; opposite; repugnant; unfavorable; unfriendly; warlike

inimitable: matchless; rare; unequaled

iniquitous: criminal; depraved; evil; grievous; ill; injurious; nefarious; sinful; vicious; vile; wicked; wrong

iniquity: error; evil; vice; wrong

initial: pioneer; rudimentary

initiate: begin; open; originate; pioneer; start

initiated: initiate

initiation: beginning; debut; opening; start

inject: insinuate

injudicious: unwise

injunction: caution; charge; command; decree; mandate; order; requirement

injure: abuse; blemish; break; damage; deface; disfigure; harm; hurt; impair; insult; lacerate; maim; maltreat; mar; mutilate;

outrage; pain; spite; sprain; strain; tear; wound; wrong
injurious: bad; deleterious; evil; harmful; malign; noisome; noxious; pernicious; toxic; traumatic
injury: affront; damage; danger; detriment; disadvantage; expense; harm; hurt; ill; indignity; loss; mischief; sabotage; strain; violence; wound
injustice: injury; oppression; partiality; violence
inkling: hint
inkstain: blot
inky: black
inlet: entrance
inmost: intimate
inn: hotel; tavern
innards: inside
innate: inborn; inherent; intrinsic; native; radical
inner strength: patience
inner: intimate
innervate: nerve
innerve: invigorate
innocent: blameless; clean; clear; guiltless; ingenuous; innocuous; pure; simple
innovation: change; novelty
innuendo: hint; slur
innumerable: many; numberless
inoffensive: innocuous
inoperative: dead; dormant; inactive; nugatory
inopportune: inconvenient; unseasonable
inordinate: excessive; exorbitant; extraordinary; extravagant; immoderate
inorganic: inanimate; lifeless
inpecunious: penniless
inquietude: discontent
inquire after: seek
inquire of: ask
inquire: ask; demand; question; research
inquiring: curious; inquiry; inquisitive; quizzical
inquiry: demand; examination; investigation; question; research; scrutiny; search; study
inquisition: examination; scrutiny; search
inquisitive: curious; prying; quizzical
inroad: raid
insalubrious: unhealthful; unhealthy; unwholesome
insane: crazy; mad; mental; wild
insanity: frenzy; lunacy; mania
insatiable: gluttonous; greedy; ravenous
inscription: mark
inscrutable: mysterious; unaccountable
insecure: precarious; treacherous; uncertain
insensate: dull; senseless; unfeeling
insensibility: indifference
insensible: apathetic; callous; dead; dull; hard; senseless; unfeeling
insensitive: hard; thick-skinned
insensitiveness: indifference
insert: weave
inside of: inside
inside: fashionable; rarefied
insidious: crafty; crooked; Machiavellian; sly; treacherous
insight: perspicacity; wisdom
insightful: perceptive
insignificance: indifference
insignificant: idle; ignoble; little; meager; mean; negligible; paltry; petty; simple; slender; slight; slim; small; tenuous; trifling; trivial; unimportant
insincere: artificial; deceitful; false; fast; hypocritical; mealy-mouthed; smarmy
insincerity: affectation; deceit
insinuate: hint; intimate; suggest
insinuating: saccharine; smarmy; snide; unctuous
insinuation: hint
insipid: flat; innocuous; pallid; stale; stereotyped; stupid; tame; tasteless; unsavory; vacuous; vapid
insist upon: urge
insist: persist
insistence: ultimatum
insistent: urgent
insolence: arrogance; assumption; chutzpah; gall; impudence; pride
insolent: arrogant; audacious; bold; brazen; contemptuous; defiant; impertinent; impolite; impudent; lordly; offensive;

opprobrious; presumptuous; scurrilous; shameless
insolvency: failure
insolvent: bankrupt
insomnious: wakeful
insouciance: unconcern
insouciant: easygoing
inspect: examine; peruse; review; search; sound; survey; view
inspection: examination; investigation; review; scrutiny; search; survey; view; watch
inspiration: vagary
inspirational: oracular
inspire: animate; arouse; empower; enliven; exhilarate; inform
inspired: oracular
inspiring: bright; cheerful
inspirit: animate; arouse; cheer; elate; encourage; enliven; exhilarate; inform; provoke; raise; reassure; spirit
inspiriting: bright
install: establish
installation: appointment; debut
instance: case; piece
instant: flash; immediate; minute; moment
instantaneous: immediate; quick
instantaneously: immediately; instantly
instanter: immediately; instantly
instantly: immediately
instigate: arouse; incite; induce; influence; move; provoke; spur; stimulate; stir; urge
instigation: spur
instill: insinuate; spirit
instinct: hunch
instinctive: inborn; involuntary
institute: asylum; begin; erect; establish; prescribe; start
institution: home
instruct: breed; command; decree; direct; discipline; educate; enlighten; form; ground; guide; initiate; order; teach
instruction: charge; command; counsel; decree; discipline; education; order; schooling
instructive: uplifting
instructor: guru; teacher
instrument: appliance; gadget; medium; tool
instrumentality: mean; medium
insubordinate: defiant; disobedient; mutinous; rebel; rebellious; unruly
insubordination: rebellion
insubstantial: light; rarefied; tinny
insufferable: intolerable; unbearable
insufficiency: failure; lack; want
insufficient: defective; inadequate; incompetent; poor; scanty; scarce; short; slender; unsatisfactory; weak
insular: small-minded; xenophobic
insult: affront; cut; disregard; indignity; offend; outrage; reproach; slight; slur; smart; snub; taunt; wound
insulted: miffed
insulting: derogatory; impertinent; impudent; injurious; insolent; offensive; opprobrious; scurrilous
insuperable: invincible
insupportable: intolerable; unbearable
insurance: safeguard
insure: guarantee
insurgency: insurrection
insurgent: mutinous; rebel; rebellious
insurmountable: invincible
insurrection: commotion; mutiny; rebellion; revolt; sedition; uprising
insurrectionary: mutinous
insurrectionist: rebel
insusceptibility: immunity; insensibility
intact: complete; entire; unbroken; whole
integral: whole
integrity: goodness; honesty; honor; moral; principle; probity; right; truth; virtue
integument: cover; skin
intellect: brains; mind; reason; wit
intellective: mental
intellectual: intelligent; mental; savant
intelligence: advice; apprehension; aptitude; brains; information; judgment; mind; notice; reason; wit; word
intelligent: acute; apt; astute; bright; capable; clever; con-

scious; deep; intellectual; luminous; old; penetrating; quick; rational; reasonable; sagacious; sensible; sharp; shrewd; skillful; smart; wise
intelligibility: perspicuity
intelligible: clear; lucid; luminous; perspicuous; plain; simple
intemperance: excess
intemperate: cross; immoderate; unmeasured
intend: contemplate; design; mean; propose; purport; purpose; think
intended: intentional; voluntary
intense: acute; ardent; bitter; close; deep; exquisite; heavy; high; hot; lurid; picturesque; poignant; profound; severe; sharp; strong; vivid; zealous
intenseness: zeal
intensified: high
intensify: aggravate; concentrate; elevate; exalt; raise; raise
intensity: energy; fervor; force; heat; strength; violence; zeal
intent: aim; close; design; earnest; effect; end; intention; meaning; mind; object; purpose; spirit; thought; view
intention: aim; design; end; idea; ideal; intent; meaning; mind; object; purport; purpose; resolve; spirit; thought; view
intentional: conscious; deliberate; voluntary; willful
intently: hard
inter: bury; sepulcher
interacting: symbiotic
interactive: symbiotic
interbreed: cross
intercede: mediate
intercept: prevent; stop
intercessor: advocate
interchange successively: alternate
interchange: change; commerce; exchange; exchange; permutation; trade
interchangeable: exchangeable; mutual; reciprocal; same
intercourse: commerce
interdependence: connection
interdict: ban; debar; enjoin; forbid; inhibit; prohibit
interdicted: taboo
interdiction: ban; prohibition; taboo
interest-bearing: active; pay
interest: concern; consequence; consideration; enthusiasm; faction; income; part; pique; regard; sake; take; zest
interested: curious
interesting: picturesque; piquant; pleasing
interfere with: attack; damp; interrupt
interfere: clash; conflict; kibitz; oppose; tamper
interference: check; clash; conflict; obstacle
interfering: meddlesome; obtrusive; officious
interior: inside
interjection: exclamation
interlace: weave
intermarriage: alliance
intermediate: average; mean; middle
interminable: endless; eternal; perpetual; unbounded
intermingle: blend; confuse; fuse; mingle; weave
intermingled: promiscuous
intermission: abeyance; pause; suspense
intermit: interrupt; stop; suspend
intermix: fuse; mingle; scramble; weave
intermixed: promiscuous
interpose: mediate
interpret: accept; decipher; explain; gloss; paraphrase; render; show; understand
interpretation: explanation; exposition; gloss; meaning; sense; translation; version
interregnum: abeyance
interrelating: symbiotic
interrelationship: rapport
interrogate: ask; question
interrogation: demand; inquiry; question
interrogatory: quizzical
interrruption: stick
interrupt: adjourn; arrest; break; discontinue; hinder; impede; obstruct; pause; prevent; stop; stop; suspend

interruption: arrest; break; pause; remission; stay; suspense
interruptive: obtrusive
intersect: cross; cut; meet
intersperse: sprinkle
interstice: crack
intertwine: twist; weave
interval: period; respite; run; time; way
intervening: middle
interview: conference
intimacy: association; commerce; familiarity
intimate: bosom; close; comrade; cozy; familiar; friend; hint; insinuate; near; suggest
intimately: nearly; well
intimation: hint; hunch; notice; wind
intimidate: awe; daunt; discourage; dismay; frighten; menace; scare; shake; terrorize
intolerable: unbearable
intolerant: bigoted; narrow-minded; small-minded; xenophobic
intonation: expression
intone: warble
intoxicate: inebriate
intoxicated: cockeyed; drunken
intoxicating: hard; strong
intractable: contrary; headstrong; inflexible; moody; obstinate; perverse; refractory; stubborn; unyielding; wayward; willful
intransigent: willful
intrepid: audacious; bold; brave; confident; daring; dauntless; fearless; gallant; game; heroic; manly; stalwart; stout; strong; undaunted; valiant
intrepidity: assurance; bravery; confidence; courage; daring; heroism; nerve; valor
intricacy: meander; snarl
intricate: complex; difficult; elaborate; hard; knotty
intrigue: conspiracy; conspire; cunning; machination; maneuver; plot; practice; scheme; stratagem; wangle
intrigued: spellbound
intriguing: insidious; Machiavellian; politic; practice; wily
intrinsic: essential; intimate
introduce: initiate; insinuate; pioneer; present; weave
introduction: admission; admittance; debut; debut; overture; preface; preliminary
introductory: preliminary
introspective: subjective
introversive: subjective
intrude: encroach; trespass
intruder: impostor
intrusion: trespass
intrusive: impertinent; meddlesome; obtrusive
inundate: flood; overwhelm
inundation: cataclysm; deluge; flood
inure: habituate; harden; use
inured: callous
inutile: fruitless; useless
invade: assault; encroach; trespass
invading: offensive
invalid: bad; patient; unsound; weak
invalidate: abolish; abrogate; destroy; nullify; void; weaken
invalidation: abolition; abrogation
invaluable: precious
invariable: constant; permanent; stable; steady; uniform
invariant: equal; invariable; permanent; regular
invasion: assault; occupation; raid; trespass
invasive: obtrusive
invective: abuse
inveigh against: abuse
inveigle: bite; cajole; cheat; coax; entice; flatter; seduce; tempt
invent: ad-lib; contrive; create; devise; discover; fable; fabricate; feign; form; originate; pioneer; plan
invented: fabulous; fictitious
invention: ad-lib; device; fable; figment; gadget; patent; untruth
inventive: ingenious; original
inventiveness: novelty
inventory: account; catalogue; list; roll; schedule; stock; supply
invert: reverse
invertebrate: weakling
invest: cover; endow
investigate: check; examine; inquire; probe; research; scrutinize; search; sound; study; try

investigation: examination; experiment; inquiry; inspection; research; review; scrutiny; search; study
investigator: operative
investment: capital
inveterate: chronic; habitual
invidious: abhorrent; hateful; odious
invigorate: animate; enliven; nerve; raise; stimulate
invigorating: fresh; healthy; wholesome
invincible: impregnable; indomitable
inviolable: sacred; sacrosanct
inviolate: sacred; sacrosanct
invitation: call
invite: ask; attract; call; summon; tempt
inviting: tempting
invocation: appeal
invoice: bill
invoke: address; pray
involuntary: automatic; necessary
involve: accuse; charge; combine; concern; encumber; entangle; immerse; implicate; perplex; snarl
involved: abstruse; complex; deep; knotty
involvement: empathy; snarl
invulnerable: impregnable; proof
iota: atom; bit; particle
IOU: note
irascible: cantankerous; cross; excitable; grouchy; hasty; hot; irritable; moody; passionate; peppery; petulant; quick; splenetic; testy; touchy; waspish
irate: angry; mad; savage; warm; wrathful
ire: anger; displeasure; fury; indignation; irritate; offense; passion; provoke; rage; rouse; wrath
ireful: wrathful
iridescent: opalescent; pearly
irk: annoy; gall; provoke; roil; tire; trouble; vex; weary
irksome: tedious; wearisome; weary
iron: smooth
ironic: acerbic; caustic
ironical: sarcastic; sardonic; satirical
irony: ridicule; sarcasm; satire
irradiant: bright
irrational: absurd; blind; brutal; brute; foolish; mental; preposterous; puerile; rabid; unreasonable; wacky
irreclaimable: abandoned; lost; obdurate
irreconcilable: contradictory; contrary; incompatible; inconsistent; opposite
irreconcilableness: repugnance
irredeemable: lost
irrefutable: certain; hard; peremptory; undeniable; unquestionable
irregular: aberrant; abnormal; casual; exceptional; fancy; improper; informal; misshapen; preternatural; rambling; rough; rugged; strange; tumultuous; uncertain; unnatural; unsteady; wayward
irregularity: aberration; abnormality; disorder
irrelevant: impertinent; unapt
irreligious: heathen; pagan; profane; ungodly
irremediable: hopeless
irrepressible: invincible; rambunctious; saucy
irreproachable: blameless; clear; unimpeachable
irresistibility: necessity
irresolute: ambivalent; doubtful; faint; fickle; pendulous; soft; spineless; unsettled; weak
irresolution: doubt; hesitation; suspense
irresponsible: unaccountable
irreverence: sacrilege
irreverent: blue; disrespectful; profane; ribald
irrevocable: stark
irritability: petulance
irritable: cantankerous; cross; excitable; fractious; fretful; grouchy; hasty; impatient; irascible; moody; peevish; peppery; petulant; quick; splenetic; temperamental; testy; touchy
irritate: anger; annoy; exasperate; excite; fret; gall; incense; madden; molest; nag; offend; pain; pester; pique; plague; provoke; rankle; roil; ruffle; tantalize;

tease; torment; trouble; vex; worry
irritated: angry; irate; miffed; sore; upset; warm
irritating: offensive; vexatious
irritation: fret; temper; wrath
irruption: convulsion; paroxysm
Ishmael: pariah
isolate: abstract; segregate
isolated: abstract; alone; lone; lonesome; retired; secluded; separate; single; solitary; sporadic
isolation: solitude
issue: brood; conclusion; consequence; effect; emanate; emerge; emit; end; ensue; event; give; number; outcome; proceed; publish; result; rise; spring; spurt; start; stream; terminate
italicize: emphasize
itch: addiction; pine
item: particular; scuttlebutt
iterate: repeat; say
iteration: repeat
itinerating: itinerant
jab: prod
jabber: babble
jackanapes: coxcomb
jade: hack; pall; tire; weary
jaded: blas,; world-weary
jagged: rough
jail: incarcerate; pound; shut
jailer: keeper
jam-packed: populous
jam: block; quagmire; spread
jammed: foul
jangle: ring
jape: jest; joke; quip
jar: agitate; quarrel
jargon: dialect; language; language; slang; terminology; vernacular
jarred: aghast
jarring: agitation; harsh; raucous; rough
jaundiced: sallow
jaunt: excursion; journey; trip
jaunty: perky
jaw: babble
jazz: swing
jealousy: envy
jeer or scoff at: ridicule
jeer: banter; jest; mock; sarcasm; scoff; sneer; taunt; taunt
jeers: ridicule
jejune: arid; bankrupt; dry; dull; lean; tame
jejuneness: poverty
jelly: spread
jellyfish: weakling
jeopardize: expose; risk; stake; venture
jeopardy: chance; danger; hazard; peril; risk; stake; venture
jerk: pluck; start; whip
jerry-built: makeshift; poor
jest: droll; fool; joke; play; quip
jester: droll; fool
jesting: banter; fun; jocose; sport; sportive
jet: flow; spurt
jettison: reject
jewelry: charm
jewels: charm
jiffy: instant; minute; moment
jingle: ring
jingoistic: xenophobic
jinn: genius
jittery: shaky
job: administer; place; position; situation; task
jobless: unemployed
jocose: humorous; jocular; jovial; pleasant; sportive; waggish; witty
jocular: facetious; humorous; jocose; jovial; pleasant; scurrilous; sportive; waggish; witty
jocularity: hilarity; merriment
jocund: jolly; jovial; joyful; light-hearted
jog: pace
Johnny-come-lately: parvenu
joie de vivre: verve
join: accompany; add; ally; associate; attach; close; combine; conjoin; connect; couple; link; meet; mingle; mix; pair; sort; tie; unite
joined: mixed
joining: addition; close; connection; junction
joint: common; community; junction
joke: droll; fool; game; jest; quip; trick
joker: zany
jokester: zany
joking: banter; fun; jocose; sportive

jollity: gaiety; glee; hilarity; merriment; mirth
jolly: cheerful; gay; jovial; joyful; merry
jolted: aghast
josh: quip
joshing: raillery
jostle: scramble; shove; throng
jot down: note
jot: atom; bit; iota; particle
journal: account
journey: circuit; excursion; expedition; passage; pilgrimage; tour; trip
journeying: itinerant
jovial: gay; jocose; jolly; joyful; light-hearted; mellow; merry
joviality: gaiety; glee; merriment; mirth
joy: bliss; cheer; delight; ecstasy; glee; happiness; hilarity; mirth; passion; pleasure; rapture; transport; triumph
joyful: blithe; cheerful; ecstatic; gay; glad; happy; jovial; light-hearted; merry
joyous: blithe; cheerful; gay; glad; happy; jolly; jovial; joyful; light-hearted; merry
joyousness: gaiety; mirth
jubilant: ecstatic; joyful
jubilation: ecstasy; triumph
judge: account; authority; critic; deduce; deem; discern; estimate; hold; make; reckon; referee; referee; regard; rule; suppose; think; umpire; umpire
judgment-seat: bar
judgment: account; act; conclusion; doom; estimate; estimation; fancy; guess; idea; knowledge; mind; notion; opinion; prudence; reason; review; sense; sentiment; taste; thought; view; wisdom
judicial: critical; sententious
judicious: advisable; discreet; judicial; moderate; perceptive; politic; practical; prudent; rational; reasonable; sagacious; sane; sensible; sound; wise
judiciously: well
jugglery: trick
juicy: dainty; luscious; lush
juju: talisman
jumble: confuse; confusion; disorder; mess; mix; mixture; scramble; scramble; shambles
jumbled: heterogeneous; promiscuous
jumbo: giant; humongous
jump: bound; leap; skip; spring; start; vault
jumpy: shaky; skittish
junction: attachment; close; connection; union
juncture: crisis; junction; pass
junket: excursion; expedition; trip
junky: tacky
juridical: judicial
jurisdiction: bailiwick
just deserts: pay
just: bare; but; candid; conscientious; ethical; even; fair; felicitous; honest; honorable; impartial; little; moderate; moral; only; proper; right; sound; straight; straightforward; true; upright; valid
justice: honesty; judge; right; virtue
justifiable: righteous
justification: apology; authority; excuse; explanation; reason; warrant
justify: authorize; clear; defend; excuse; exonerate; explain; legitimate; maintain; prove; rationalize; reason; sustain; vindicate; warrant; whitewash
justifying: worth
justly: right
justness: propriety
jut out: project
jutting out: prominent
juvenile: puerile; young; youth
juxtaposed: adjacent
karma: destiny; fate; necessity
keen-eyed: keen
keen-sighted: keen
keen: acute; astute; bright; caustic; cutting; dry; exquisite; fine; incisive; lively; penetrating; perceptive; perspicacious; poignant; pointed; pungent; quick; ready; sagacious; satirical; severe; sharp; shrewd; smart; trenchant
keening: plaint
keenness: sensibility
keep (up): hold
keep or bear in mind: remember

keep apart: separate
keep away from or clear of: avoid
keep away: absent
keep back: detain; hold; reserve; stifle; withhold
keep company: associate; herd
keep down: appease; restrain
keep from: spare
keep on: abide; continue; persevere
keep out: exclude
keep safe: guard
keep secret: conceal
keep up: bear; maintain; maintain; preserve; support
keep: defend; detain; hold; maintain; observe; occupy; preserve; preserve; reserve; restrain; retain; save; support
keeper: guardian; warden
keeping: custody
keepsake: memento; remembrance; trophy
kermis: fair
kernel: nucleus
key: admission; explanation; guide
kick up one's heels: romp
kidding around: raillery
kidding: raillery
kidnap: abduct
kidnapper: abductor
kidnapping: abduction
kill: assassinate; bag; blast; butcher; destroy; execute; massacre; murder; remove; slaughter; slay
killer: butcher
killing: massacre; murder; slaughter; slaughter
kin: connection; race
kind-hearted: amiable; friendly; gentle
kind: affectionate; amiable; benevolent; breed; brood; cast; charitable; compassionate; considerate; cut; fashion; fatherly; form; friendly; gentle; good; gracious; humane; kindhearted; mild; manner; merciful; mild; nature; nice; order; pattern; quality; range; sort; stamp; style; sweet; sympathetic; tender; touch; type; variety
kindhearted: benevolent; chivalrous; humane; kind; merciful
kindle: animate; arouse; excite; ignite; inflame; light; rouse; wake
kindliness: clemency; compassion; consideration; goodness; grace
kindly: benevolent; big; bland; charitable; chivalrous; compassionate; friendly; genial; gentle; good; gracious; humane; kind
kindness: clemency; compassion; consideration; favor; good; goodness; goodwill; grace; love; mercy
kindred: congenial; race
king-size: giant; humongous
king: sovereign
kingdom: monarchy; nation; realm
kinglike: kingly
kingly: grand; lordly; majestic; regal; royal; sovereign
kink: vagary
kinship: rapport; relationship
kinsman: brother; connection
kismet: destiny; fate; necessity
kiss off: rebuff
kiss-off: rebuff
kit and caboodle: totality
kith: connection
kittenish: playful
kleptomaniac: robber
knack: ability; aptitude; art; faculty
knapsack: pack
knave: cheat; impostor; rascal; rogue; scoundrel; swindler; vagabond; villain
knavery: chicanery; swindle; trickery
knavish: crooked; dishonest; rascal
knead: temper
kneel: bend
knickknack: novelty
knit: tie
knob: bunch; knot
knock down: overthrow
knock out: stun; zap
knock-down-drag-out: row
knock: beat; blow; pan; strike; stroke
knockabout: rambunctious; wacky
knocked out: senseless
knoll: bank; hill

knot: entangle; snarl; tie
knotted: fast
knotty: abstruse
know how to: can
know-nothing: bigoted; yahoo
know: comprehend; distinguish; experience; see; understand
knowing: acute; blas; conscious; meaning
knowledge: education; experience; familiarity; information; intelligence; learning; scholarship; wisdom
knowledgeable: skillful
known: old
kook: screwball; zany
kooky: screwball
kosher: orthodox
kowledge: lore
kowtow: flatter; obeisance
kudos: accolade; praise
la-di-da: pretentious
label: call; denounce; mark; name; qualify; stamp
labor: drudgery; endeavor; exercise; moil; pain; plod; slavery; struggle; task; toil; work
labored: elaborate; tedious
laborer: operative
laborious: arduous; hard; painful; stiff; troublesome
labyrinth: meander
lacerate: break; maim; mangle; rend; tear; wound
laceration: rent; rip; wound
lack: absence; defect; need; poverty; privation; want; wish
lackey: attendant; menial; yes-man
lacking: absent; poor; short; vacant; weak
laconic: brief; compact; concise; curt; pithy; sententious; short; summary
laconicism: conciseness
lacuna: break; pause; stay
lad: youngster; youth
lade: charge; freight; load; pack
lading: cargo; shipment
lady: noble; woman
lag: dawdle; loiter
lagging: laggard
laic: lay
laical: lay
laid waste: desolate; waste
laid-back: easygoing; offhand
lair: hole
Lally column: pillar; upright
lallygag: dawdle
lambent: bright; bright
lambrequin: curtain
lame: weak
lament: complain; cry; deplore; grieve; moan; mourn; plaint; regret; sorrow; weep
lamentable: grievous; miserable; piteous; sorrowful
lamentation: cry; lament; moan; plaint; regret
lamina: scale
lampoon: abuse; burlesque; caricature; ridicule; satire; travesty
lance: cut
land: ground; light; parcel; property; terrain
landing: platform
landscape: scene
lane: alley; passage; path; walk
language: dialect; diction; expression; jargon; parlance; phraseology; speech; talk; terminology; vernacular
languid: faint; faint; lackadaisical; remiss
languish: decline; droop; fade; pine; wither
languorous: lackadaisical
lank: gaunt; lean; meager; poor; spare; thin
lanky: spindly
Laodicean: lukewarm
lap-dog: pet
lapse: blunder; oversight; trip
lapsus mentis: aberration
lardaceous: unctuous
large-heartedness: abundance
large-minded: broad-minded
large-size: capital
large: ample; big; broad; broad; bulky; capacious; comprehensive; copious; extensive; generous; good; grand; great; gross; handsome; huge; magnanimous; massive; merciful; monstrous; noble; respectable; spacious; wide
larger: better; major
largess: donation; endowment; gift; present

lark about: romp
lark: caper
larky: playful
lascivious: blue; carnal; coarse; depraved; dirty; filthy; indecent; libertine; licentious; nasty; salacious; sensual; wanton
lasciviousness: lust
lash: beat; punish; scourge; scourge; slash; whip
lass: maid
lassie: maid
lassitude: exhaustion
last resort: recourse
last: abide; continue; endure; extreme; extreme; final; hold; persevere; persist; remain; ultimate
lasting: durable; fast; late; perennial; permanent; stable; standing
late: backward; modern; new; recent; slack; slow; tardy
lately: new
latent: dormant; potential; secret; ulterior
latest: final; last
latitude: range; scope
lattice: traverse
laud: celebrate; commend; eulogize; extol; paean; praise
laudation: paean; praise
laugh-provoking: comical; risible
laugh: chuckle; roar
laughable: amusing; comical; funny; humorous; ludicrous; ridiculous; risible
laughingstock: sport
laughter: laugh; merriment; mirth
launch: debut; throw
launching: debut
launder: wash
laurel: applause; trophy
laurels: accolade; trophy
lave: clean; wash
lavish: ample; charitable; extravagant; free; liberal; magnificent; prodigal; profuse; spend; squander; unmeasured; unsparing; wanton
lavishness: exuberance
law: act; authority; canon; order; principle; regulation; rule
lawful: just; legitimate; right
lawfully: right
lawfulness: right
lawless: irregular; licentious; unruly; wanton; wild
lawsuit: action; case
lawyer: advocate; counsel
lawyers: bar
lax: free; general; laid-back; loose; remiss; remiss; vague
laxity: freedom
lay a wager: wager
lay aside: cast
lay away or aside: spare
lay away: treasure
lay bare: open; uncover
lay by: save
lay down: deposit; prescribe
lay hold of: catch; grasp
lay on: apply
lay open: bare; disclose; expose; subject; ventilate
lay out: disburse; expend
lay waste: demolish; desolate; destroy; devastate; plunder; ravage; sack; strip; waste
lay: deposit; lie; lodge; place; put; secular
layer: course
laze: dawdle
laziness: slack
lazy: idle; inactive; indolent; lackadaisical; shiftless; slack; slothful; slow; sluggish
lead astray: corrupt; mislead; seduce; tamper; tempt
lead on: lead
lead: bring; carry; command; conduct; convey; determine; direct; draw; guide; head; introduce; leading; pioneer; rule; show; start; take
leaden: lackluster
leader: chief; head; principal; tycoon
leadership: conduct
leading: capital; chief; great; head; main; master; principal; prominent
leaf: cutting
league: alliance; ally; combination; confederation; link; pact; party; ring; union
leak: run
lean on: stay
lean-to: shack

lean: careen; gaunt; list; meager; poor; scanty; slant; spare; spindly; stoop; sway; thin; verge

leaning forward: imminent

leaning: bent; bias; capacity; inclination; inclination; liking; list; mind; partiality; penchant; predilection; proclivity; propensity; slant; tendency

leap: bound; jump; plunge; skip; spring; vault

learn of: discover

learn: ascertain; detect; gather; get; see; understand

learned: conversant; skillful; wise

learner: initiate; pupil; scholar; tyro

learning: education; knowledge; lore; scholarship; schooling; wisdom

lease: charter; hack; hire; let; rent

leash: whip

leave behind: desert

leave off: stop

leave out: except

leave: abandon; allowance; bequeath; depart; desert; forsake; liberty; part; pass; permission; privilege; quit; relinquish; renounce; resign; retire; retreat; vacate; will

leavings: remain

lecher: libertine

lecherous: carnal; dirty; lascivious; licentious; salacious; wanton

lechery: lust

lecture: address; declaim; oration; reprove

lecturer: teacher

ledger: account; register

leech: parasite

lees: ground; refuse; sediment

left: abandoned

leg: limb; member

legacy: gift

legal: just; lawful; legitimate; valid

legalize: authorize; legitimate

legate: bequeath; delegate

legend: device; fable; myth; saga; story

legerdemain: magic; trick

legible: clean; fair

legion: multifarious

legislature: assembly

legitimate: just; lawful; right; true

leisure: vacant

leisurely: deliberate; slow

lend an ear: listen

lend: advance

length: extent; scope; span; stretch

lengthen: draw; extend; prolong; protract; spin; stretch; wax

lengthening: extension

lengthy: long

lenience: clemency

leniency: clemency; grace; mercy

lenient: broad-minded; charitable; easy; gentle; gracious; merciful; soft; tender

lenity: grace; mercy

leprechaun: brownie; fairy

lesbian: gay

lese majesty: treason

lesion: wound

lessen: abate; abridge; allay; alleviate; appease; contract; curtail; cut; decrease; diminish; dwindle; ease; impair; lower; moderate; palliate; pare; reduce; relax; relieve; shorten; shrink; slacken; subside; subtract; weaken

lessening: abatement; decline; decrease; remission

lesser: minor; petty

lesson: lore; project

let alone: leave

let down: lower

let fly: throw

let go: clear; dismiss; quit; relinquish

let in: admit

let out: liberate

let-up: abatement

let: agree; allow; authorize; charter; consent; hack; hire; permit; rent

lethal: deadly; deleterious; destructive; fatal; malignant; mortal; noisome; pernicious; toxic

lethargic: lackadaisical; torpid

letter: character

lettered: academic

letters of alphabet: ABC's

letters: literature

lettuce: money

level: demolish; destroy; even; flat; overthrow; plain; present; rank; smooth; standard; story

levelly: flat

lever: purchase

levity: hilarity

levy: duty; put

lewd: blue; carnal; coarse; depraved; dirty; free; gross; indecent; lascivious; libertine; licentious; nasty; obscene; salacious; sensual; wanton; X-rated

lexicon: terminology; vernacular

liability: charge; danger; debt

liable: apt; likely; obnoxious; open; prone; responsible; subject; vulnerable

libel: crime; malign

libelous: injurious; snide

liberal: ample; benevolent; broad; broad-minded; charitable; charitable; disinterested; free; generous; handsome; large; magnanimous; munificent; open; unsparing

liberality: bounty; generosity; tolerance

liberate: absolve; acquit; clear; deliver; discharge; excuse; free; loose; redeem; release; rescue

liberated: quit

liberation: liberty; ransom; release; rescue

liberator: savior

libertine: free; licentious; loose

libertinism: lust

liberty: authority; familiarity; freedom; immunity; independence; latitude; leave; permission; permission; play; prerogative; privilege; scope

libidinous: amorous; carnal; lascivious; licentious; salacious; wanton

library: study

license: allowance; empower; familiarity; freedom; immunity; impunity; leave; liberty; lust; pass; permission; permit; prerogative; privilege; warrant

licentious: abandoned; blue; depraved; dirty; filthy; free; immoral; indecent; libertine; loose; lost; nasty; sensual; wanton

licentiousness: lust

licit: lawful; legitimate

lick-and-a-promise: slapdash

lickerish: lascivious

lid: cover

lie down: stretch

lie hidden or concealed: lurk

lie in ambush: lurk

lie in wait: lurk; skulk

lie: bluff; fable; falsehood; lay; pretend; prevaricate; range; reside; romance; sit; tale; untruth

lien: charge; place

life: age; animation; energy; gaiety; glee; spirit

lifeboat: tender

lifeless: apathetic; arid; dead; dull; dull; flat; heavy; inanimate; inanimate; inert; lackluster; pallid; stereotyped; vapid

lifelike: graphic; vivid

lifesaver: savior

lift up: elevate; raise; rear

lift: edify; elate; heave; hoist; hoist; pilfer; raise; rear

ligament: bond

ligature: bond; tie

light-headed: giddy; light; thoughtless

light-hearted: light

light: agile; bright; clean; clear; easy; facet; fair; gentle; giddy; glad; kindle; nimble; pearly; shine; splendor; trifling

lighted: luminous

lighten: allay; alleviate; ease; relieve

lighthearted: blithe; bright; gay; giddy; jaunty; lyrical

lightness: ease

lightsome: light; light-hearted; lyrical

lightweight: impotent

like better: prefer

like-mindedness: rapport

like: admire; care; equal; fancy; love; parallel; relish; same; similar; worship

liked: popular

likelihood: surmise

likely: apt; fair; feasible; liable; possible

liken: compare

likeness: community; image; parallel; parity; picture; resemblance; semblance; similarity

likewise: also; moreover

liking: admiration; affection; appetite; attachment; bent; fancy; inclination; love; mind; partiality; penchant; regard; relish; taste; weakness

Lilliputian: dwarf; pygmy

lilt: warble

lilting: lyrical

lily-livered: cowardly

limb: bough; branch; cutting; member

limber: flexible; lissome; pliant; supple

limbo: hell

limit: barrier; border; bound; condition; confine; end; extension; extreme; extremity; fix; margin; mete; modify; qualify; restrict; shorten; stint; terminate; tie; verge

limitation: abridgment; stint

limited: partial; small-minded; vernacular

limitless: clear; endless; measureless; unbounded; unlimited

limits: confine; pale; range

limn: depict; describe; portray; silhouette

limp: hobble; lackadaisical; spineless

limpid: bright; clear; lucid; pellucid; transparent

line of demarcation: boundary

line up: rank

line: ancestry; birth; blank; boundary; breed; brood; hatch; mark; passage; pedigree; race; range; rank; score; series; stock

lineage: ancestry; birth; breed; brood; descent; origin; parentage; pedigree; race; stem; stock; strain; succession

lineaments: silhouette

lineation: silhouette

linger: dawdle; delay; drag; dwell; hang; lag; loiter; stay; tarry; wait

lingerer: laggard

lingering: laggard; slack; wait

linging: desire

lingo: jargon; language; parlance; speech; talk; terminology; vernacular

lingua franca: language

link: associate; bond; connect; connection; couple; fasten; join; tie; unite

linking: junction

lip: border; brim; edge; impudence; rim; verge

liquefy: dissolve; fuse; melt; run; run; thaw

liquid refreshment: drink

liquid: fluid; fluid; watery

liquidate: discharge; pay; settle

liquidy: watery

liquor: liquid

lissome: supple

list: catalogue; inventory; register; roll; schedule

listen to: attend

listen: attend; hear

listing: inventory

listless: dull; indolent; lackadaisical; languid; world-weary

listlessness: indifference

lit: luminous

literal: exact; near

literary: academic

lithe: limber; lissome; pliant; supple

lithesome: lissome

litigant: adversary

litigate: contest

litter: brood; disorder; flock; mess

little by little: gradual

little devil: scamp

little: diminutive; dwarf; fine; mean; minute; petty; small

littoral: beach; coast

live through: experience; see

live-and-let-live: broad-minded

live: abide; dwell; living; reside; survive

livelihood: living; maintenance; support; trade

liveliness: animation; gaiety; glee; sparkle; spirit

lively: active; agile; alert; alive; amusing; animate; blithe; bright; brisk; bubbly; cheerful; expressive; gay; genial; living; mercurial; nimble; picturesque; pleasant; quick; racy; sanguine; skittish; smart; spirited; spry; vivacious; vivid; warm

livery: uniform

livestock: stock

livid: cadaverous

living: alive; animal; kind; livelihood; maintenance; support; trade

load: burden; cargo; charge; encumber; freight; onus; oppress; pack

loaded: cockeyed

loaf: loiter

loafer: vagabond

loam: ground

loan: advance

loath: averse; indisposed; reluctant

loathe: abhor; abominate; detest; hate; nauseate

loathing: abhorrence; abhorrent; abomination; antipathy; aversion; disgust; dislike; hatred; horror; revolt

loathsome: abhorrent; abominable; detestable; disgusting; distasteful; foul; hateful; nasty; nauseous; odious; offensive

loathsomeness: abomination

local: vernacular

locale: habitat; place; position; region; seat; situation; spot

localism: dialect

locality: habitat; locale; place; position; seat; situation; spot

localized: vernacular

locate in: settle

locate: lay; place; position; set; station

location: address; disposition; lie; locale; place; position; seat; situation; station

lock: tie

locum tenens: surrogate

locus classicus: paradigm

locution: parlance

lode: deposit

lodge: association; cottage; harbor; house; reside; stay; tarry

lodging: address

loft: raise; rear

loftiness: elevation; grandeur

lofty: eminent; grand; grandiloquent; great; high; lordly; lordly; magnanimous; majestic; noble; tall; towering

logical: legitimate; reasonable; valid

logotype: device

loiter: dally; dawdle; delay; drag; fool; hang; idle; lag; linger; tarry

loitering: delay

loll: dawdle

lone: alone; desolate; lonely; only; solitary

loneliness: isolation; solitude

lonely: alone; desolate; lone; lonesome; solitary

lonesome: alone; desolate; lonely

long for: covet; crave; wish

long green: money

long-drawn: talkative

long-suffering: lenient; patient; submissive

long-winded: long

long: aspire; pant; pine; tedious; yearn,

longhair: intellectual

longing: ambition; appetite; hope; yearning

look after: mind

look at: contemplate; note; regard; see; view; witness

look for: await; search; seek

look forward to: expect

look upon: account; regard; think; treat; watch

look: air; appear; appearance; aspect; countenance; expression; face; glance; manner; regard; seem; show; watch

lookout: watch

loony: cockeyed

loop: ring

loopy: zany

loose: absolve; absolve; clear; cranky; crazy; dissolve; free; free; inaccurate; laid-back; lax; liberate; licentious; release; release; ribald; slack; slovenly; untie; vague; wanton

loosen: dissolve; loose; relax; slacken

looseness: freedom

loosening: slack

loot: plunder; sack; spoil

looting: sack

lop off: cut

lop: crop; top; trim

loquacious: garrulous; talkative; voluble

Lord's day: Sabbath

lord: noble; peer; sovereign

lordliness: assumption

lordly: haughty; high; magisterial; noble

lore: knowledge; learning

lorry: wagon

lose: cast; misplace

loser: washout

loss: affliction; cost; damage; decline; detriment; disadvantage; expense; failure; privation; washout; waste

lost: desolate; forlorn; obdurate; shameless

lot: bunch; cast; destiny; doom; fate; parcel; part; portion; share

loud: boisterous; bombastic; garish; gaudy; noisy; sharp; showy; strong; tacky; vociferous

loudness: strength; volume

louse up: blunder

lout: yahoo

lovable: sweet

love affair: romance

love: adore; affection; attachment; devotion; grace; passion; passion; regard; respect; worship

loved: dear; favorite

loveliness: beauty

lovely: beautiful; fair

lover: gallant

lovestruck: smitten

loving: affectionate; amorous; tender

low (morally): base

low-class: tacky

low-grade: tinny

low-priced: cheap; inexpensive

low-rent: tacky

low-spirited: dejected; despondent; melancholy

low: abject; cheap; common; contemptible; despicable; dirty; flat; foul; gross; humble; ignoble; mean; menial; miserable; pitiful; profane; rascal; ribald; scurvy; servile; shameful; short; slavish; small; soft; sordid; sorry; vile

lowborn: low

lower house: assembly

lower oneself: decline; stoop

lower: abase; abate; cut; debase; degrade; depress; humble; lessen; reduce; subordinate; subside; subtract; weaken

lowering: cloudy; gloomy; heavy; lurid; murky

lowest: bottom

lowliness: humility

lowly: base; cheap; humble; ignoble; low; simple

loyal: constant; faithful; fast; sound; staunch; steadfast; true; trustworthy

loyalty: allegiance; constancy; fidelity; homage

lubberly: clumsy

lubricated: slippery

lubricious: carnal; lascivious; obscene; slippery

lubricity: lust

lubricous: carnal

lucent: bright; candid; clear; lucid; luminous

lucid: bright; candid; clear; limpid; luminous; perspicuous; plain; rational; sane; simple; transparent; vivid

lucidity: perspicuity

luck: chance; fate; hazard; serendipity

luckless: miserable; poor; unfortunate

lucky-piece: talisman

lucky: fortunate; happy; opportune; prosperous

lucrative: fat

luculent: lucid

ludic: comical

ludicrous: amusing; comical; funny; humorous; laughable; ridiculous; risible; zany

lugubrious: melancholy; somber; sorrowful

lukewarm: cool; dead; grudging; warm

lull: appease; quell; quiet; soothe

lumber: shamble

lumbering: clumsy

luminary: celebrity

luminesce: radiate

luminosity: luster

luminous: bright; clear; lucid

lump: bunch; knot

lunacy: frenzy; insanity; mania

lunatic: crackpot; crazy; insane; mad; zany

lunge: pass; thrust

lurch: careen

lure: corrupt; entice; invite; lead; seduce; steal; tempt

lurid: obscure

lurk: prowl; skulk; sneak

lurker: sneak

luscious: dainty; delicious; palatable; scrumptious
lust: addiction; desire
luster: brilliance; glare; gloss; polish; shine; sparkle; splendor
lustful: amorous; carnal; lascivious; licentious; wanton
lustrous: bright; glossy; polished; shining
lustry: salacious
lusty: able-bodied
luxuriance: exuberance; plenty
luxuriant: lush; plentiful; rank; rich
luxuriate: flourish; thrive
luxurious: elegant; magnificent; opulent; palatial; sensual; splendid; superb; voluptuous; wanton
luxuriousness: magnificence
luxury: magnificence; pleasure
lying: false; mendacious
lynch: hang
lyric: lay
lyrical: mellifluous
m,lange: mess
m,nage: household
m,tier: vocation
macabre: hideous
mace: verge
Machiavellian: designing; politic
machinate: wangle
machination: artifice; conspiracy; plot; scheme; stratagem
machinist: mechanic
maculate: dappled
mad: angry; crazy; insane; rabid; wild; wild-eyed
madcap: screwball; wacky; zany
madden: anger; enrage
made up: ad-lib; fabulous
made-up: fictitious
madness: frenzy; insanity; lunacy; mania; rage
maenad: fury; nag; scold; shrew; termagant
magic: charm; necromancy; sorcery
magician: wizard
magisterial: sententious
magistrate: judge
magnanimity: generosity; tolerance
magnanimous: chivalrous; generous; handsome; liberal; noble; open
magnate: tycoon
magnetic: charismatic
magnetism: glamour
magnetize: attract; draw
magnificence: glory; grandeur; splendor; state
magnificent: gallant; gorgeous; grand; kingly; lordly; majestic; noble; palatial; proud; splendid; stately; superb; wanton
magnify: amplify; dignify; enlarge; praise
magnitude: bulk; capacity; extent; grandeur; mass; size; volume
maid: menial; servant; virgin
maiden: maid; pioneer; virgin
maidservant: maid; menial; servant
maim: cripple; lacerate; mangle; mar; mutilate
main body: mass
main part: body
main: broad; fundamental; grand; great; head; high; master; might; primary; principal; prominent
mainly: chiefly; principally
maintain: affirm; argue; assert; assert; bear; champion; claim; contend; continue; defend; have; hold; keep; preserve; say; support; support; sustain; uphold; vindicate
maintainer: advocate
maintenance: assertion; livelihood; living; support
majestic: grand; great; kingly; lordly; magnificent; palatial; proud; royal; solemn; sovereign; stately; superb
majesty: grandeur; magnificence
major: acclaimed; capital; noteworthy
majority: bulk; mass
make or write a contract or bargain: agree
make a debut: debut
make a fool of: bite
make a hit: succeed
make a note of: note
make a plea: plead
make amends for: answer; repair; retrieve
make amends: appease; compensate; pay
make an addition to: add

make an effort: attempt; endeavor
make aware: admonish
make bankrupt: break
make believe: feign; pretend
make better: mend
make bold: venture
make certain or sure: confirm
make certain: secure
make cheerful or merry: exhilarate
make clear or known: show
make clear: demonstrate; evidence
make compatible or consistent: reconcile
make compensation: pay
make conformable or suitable: adapt
make correspondent or conformable to: adjust
make different: change
make difficult: embarrass
make do: give
make drunk: inebriate
make elegant: polish
make excuse for: account
make excuse: plead
make fast: bind; fasten; hitch
make favorable: appease
make felt: assert
make firm: confirm; secure
make fun of: banter; ridicule; taunt
make fun: sport
make good on: discharge
make good: repair; replace; retrieve
make happen: effect
make headway against: stem
make hostile: estrange,
make inquiry: ask
make insensible: blunt
make known to: notify
make known: communicate; declare; disclose; divulge; expose; impart; inform; manifest; mention; possess; reveal; signify; tell; ventilate
make liable: subject
make miserable or unhappy: distress
make obedient: break
make oneself suitable or suited for: adjust
make out: deduce; espy; tell
make over: cede
make plain or clear: elucidate
make plain or manifest: explain
make plain: demonstrate; tell
make preparations or plans: arrange
make progress: advance; move
make prominent or conspicuous or eminent: distinguish
make proud: exalt
make provision for: provide
make public: ventilate
make ready: mount; ready
make reply or response: answer
make serious or grave: aggravate
make severe: aggravate
make sport of: mock
make suitable: accommodate
make tense: brace
make tractable: tame
make uncomfortable: embarrass
make uneasy: exercise
make unfriendly: estrange,
make up for: balance; compensate; repair; supply
make up: ad-lib; form; reconcile; supply
make use of: employ; take; use
make used (to): habituate
make valid or binding: confirm
make visible: display
make warm: warm
make well or whole: cure
make-believe: pretense
make-do: makeshift
make-up: temper; temperament
make: cause; construct; contrive; create; cut; fabricate; fashion; fashion; fix; form; hew; manufacture; organize; prepare; produce; render; stamp; work
makeshift: apology; excuse; raw
makeup: cosmetic
maladroit: awkward; clumsy; unskillful
malady: affection; ailment; disease; disorder
male: man; manly; virile
maledict: curse
malediction: ban; curse; oath
malefactor: criminal
malevolence: grudge; malice; malignity; rancor; spite; venom
malevolent: evil; malicious; malign; malignant; pernicious;

revengeful; spiteful; truculent; vicious
malformation: abnormality
malformed: deformed; misshapen
malice: grudge; malevolence; mischief; rancor; spite; venom
malicious: mischief
malicious: derogatory; evil; malevolent; malignant; pernicious; revengeful; sardonic; satanic; spiteful; vicious; wanton
maliciousness: malevolence; spite; venom
malign: abuse; assail; traduce; vilify
malignant: evil; malevolent; revengeful; sardonic; toxic; vicious; virulent
maligning: derogatory
malignity: malevolence; spite; venom
malignment: abuse
malinger: shirk; skulk; slack
malleable: soft; tractable
malpractice: malfeasance
maltreat: abuse; assail; harm; injure; oppress; outrage; wrong
mama's boy: weakling
mammoth: enormous; giant; gigantic; huge
man Friday: sidekick
man: adult; mortal; people; person; race
manacle: band; shackle
manage: administer; command; conduct; contrive; control; direct; do; govern; guide; master; operate; order; oversee; regulate; rule; run; superintend; transact; work
manageable: gentle; pliant; sweet; tractable; viable
management: charge; command; conduct; control; disposition; economy; oversight; policy; procedure; regulation; surveillance
mandate: charge; command; decree; instruction; order; requirement
mandible: bill
maneuver: device; machination; operation; ploy; practice; procedure; stratagem; trick; wangle; wile
maneuvering: tactics
maneuvers: tactics
manful: manly
mangle: hack; haggle; lacerate; maim; mutilate; tear
mania: frenzy; insanity; lunacy
maniac: fanatic; zealot
maniacal: insane; mad; rabid; wild-eyed
manic: wild-eyed
manifest: apparent; betray; clear; conspicuous; declare; demonstrate; display; evidence; evident; exhibit; express; naked; obvious; overt; palpable; plain; plain; prominent; prove; reflect; transparent; visible
manifestation: apparition; display; exhibit; expression; object; shape
manifold: different; diverse; many; multifarious
manikin: dwarf
manipulate: manage; maneuver; wangle; work
manipulation: machination; operation
mankind: man; race
manliness: machismo
manly: bold; brave; male; manful; mannish; virile
manmade: artificial
manner: address; air; appearance; attitude; bearing; carriage; decorum; fashion; form; guise; habit; look; method; mode; sort; style; taste; technique; turn; way; wise
mannered: pretentious; theatrical
mannerism: idiosyncrasy
mannerisms: affectation
manners: behavior; conduct; decorum
mannish: manly
manse: residence
mansion: castle; residence
manslaughter: crime; murder
manufactory: factory
manufacture: assemble; fabricate; make; prepare; produce
manumit: free
manuscript: copy; volume
many times: frequently
many-sided: all-around
many-talented: all-around
many: innumerable; manifold; multifarious; number; numerous; various

revengeful; spiteful; truculent;
map: chart; plan
mar: blemish; damage; deface; defect; deform; disfigure; hurt; injure; maim; mangle; murder; mutilate; ravage; spoil
marauder: robber
marc: refuse
march: advance; demonstrate; walk; walk
marge: margin
margin: beach; border; edge; rim; scope; shore; swing; verge
marginal: negligible
mariner: sailor; tar
mark down: mark; note
mark up: mark
mark: attribute; band; character; characteristic; daub; distinguish; division; emblem; emphasize; feature; frank; guide; heed; idiosyncrasy; intent; mind; notice; observe; regard; score; sign; slur; smirch; spot; stain; stamp; stigma; style; trace; vestige; watch; witness
marked: conspicuous; distinguished; emphatic; memorable; particular; pointed; sharp; strong
markedly: especially
market: exchange
marmalade: jam
marquis: peer
marriage: alliance; union
marry: ally; pair; unite
marsh: quagmire; wash
marshal: array; gather; mass; muster
martial: warlike
marvel: phenomenon; wonder
marvelous: miraculous; prodigious; wonderful
mascot: talisman
masculine: male; manly; virile
mash: crush
mask: cover; hide; pretense; screen; whitewash
masque: pageant
masquerade: mask
mass: aggregate; block; bulk; collection; gross; heap; multitude; pile; size; swarm; volume
massacre: butcher; destruction; kill; slaughter; slay
massage: stroke
masses: crowd
massive: big; bulky; giant; gross; heavy; large; ponderous
massiveness: mass
massy: massive
master plan: blueprint
master: chief; conquer; expert; guru; head; overthrow; principal
masterful: magisterial
masterly: magisterial
masterpiece: paragon
mastery: command; conquest; control; custody; grasp; rule; sway
mat: entangle; snarl
match: agree; contest; correspond; equal; fuse; meet; pair; parallel; peer; rival
matchless: exquisite; peerless; topnotch; unequaled; unparalleled
mate: associate; companion; comrade; equal; pair
material: corporal; matter; palpable; physical; secular; stuff; substance; substantial; tangible
maternal: female
matrimony: marriage; union
matter-of-fact: earthy; prosaic
matter: argument; body; business; concern; material; nature; regard; respect; stuff; substance
maturate: ripen
maturated: mature
maturation: development; seasoning
mature: adult; age; mellow; ripe; ripen; womanly,
maturing: development
maturity: age
maudlin: saccharine
maul: beat; thrash
maven: dilettante; savant
maverick: bohemian
mawkish: saccharine; sickly
mawkishness: schmaltz
maxim: byword; catchword; principle; proverb
maze: meander; puzzle
mazuma: money
meager: bare; gaunt; haggard; lean; poor; scanty; slender; spare; sparse; thin
meagerness: poverty; want
mealymouthed: smarmy
mean average: medium

mean proportion: average; medium
mean-spirited: base; bigoted; grudging; shabby; small
mean-tempered: cantankerous; grouchy
mean: abject; average; bad; bare; base; beastly; bitter; cheap; close; common; contemplate; contemptible; cross; design; despicable; dirty; ignoble; intend; little; low; meager; mediocre; medium; menial; mercenary; miserable; miserly; niggardly; obsequious; ordinary; paltry; parsimonious; penurious; petty; pitiful; pitiless; poor; profane; propose; purport; purpose; ragged; rascal; ribald; scurvy; selfish; servile; shabby; sign; signify; slavish; small; small-minded; sordid; sorry; spiteful; stingy; think; vile; vulgar; wretched
meander: stroll; wander; wind
meandering: circuitous
meaning: design; effect; explanation; expressive; intent; purport; sense; significance; spirit; substance
meaningful: compact; expressive; meaning; significant
meaningfulness: significance
meaningless: empty; senseless
meanness: parsimony
means: appliance; expedient; medium; method; recourse; sort; way; wherewithal
measure out: allot
measure: apportion; assign; check; criterion; extent; mete; size; span; standard; time; volume
measureless: unmeasured; vast
meat dealer: butcher
meat dresser: butcher
meat: food; lean
mechanic: craftsman
mechanical: automatic; inanimate; perfunctory
mechanism: action; gadget; technique
medal: commendation
meddle: kibitz; tamper
meddlesome: busy; curious; obtrusive; officious
medial: average; middle
median: average; mean
mediate: think; wonder
medicament: medicine; remedy
medication: medicine; remedy
medicine: remedy
mediocre: average; common; lackluster; medium; moderate; ordinary
mediocrity: average; indifference
meditate morbidly: brood
meditate on: brood; contemplate
meditate: consider; deliberate; intend; muse; ponder; reflect; ruminate; think
meditating: preoccupied
meditation: consideration; reflection; study; thought
meditative: contemplative; pensive; preoccupied; reflective; thoughtful
medium: element; environment; mean; mediocre; milieu; moderate
medley: jumble; mess; mixture
meek: gentle; humble; low; tame
meekness: humility; resignation
meet face to face: face
meet the eye: occur
meet with: experience; face; hit; see; strike; suffer
meet: affront; appropriate; apt; assemble; assembly; becoming; convene; encounter; face; felicitous; fulfill; proper; satisfy; seemly; shock; sit; stand; strike
meeting: action; assembly; brush; conference; congress; convention; encounter; gathering; meet; tryst
megastar: celebrity
megrim: vagary
mein: bearing
melancholy: blue; depressed; despondency; despondent; disconsolate; gloom; gloomy; grief; heavy; lugubrious; plaintive; sad; somber; sorrowful; sorry; tragic; woe
melange: mixture
melee: brawl; fight; riot; tumult; uproar
meliorate: better; cushion; mend; moderate; pacify; qualify
mellifluous: mellow; soft; sweet

mellow: peaceful; rich; ripe; ripen; sweet
mellowing: seasoning
melodious: harmonious; mellifluous; mellow; soft; sweet; tuneful
melodiousness: harmony
melodrama: play
melodramatic: theatrical
melody: harmony
melt: dissolve; fuse; run; soften; thaw; touch; try
meltdown: cataclysm
member: branch; limb; part
membership: rank; standing
membrane: skin
memento mori: memento
memento: remembrance; trophy
memoir: life
memorable: notable
memorandum: hint; minute; note; observation; record
memorial: memento; remembrance; trophy
memorize: learn; remember
memory: mind; recall; remembrance
men: people
menace: threaten
menacing: forbidding; formidable
mend: cure; fix; improve; patch; piece; recover; rectify; redress; reform; renew; repair; restore
mendacious: false
mendacity: lie
menial: attendant; base; low; servant; servile; slavish; vile
mental balance: mind
mental giant: intellectual
mental picture: image
mental: intellectual; moonstruck; subjective
mention: hint; name; note; notice; observe; reference; speech; talk; tell
mentioned previously: above
menu: food
Mephistophelian: devilish
mephitic: noisome; noxious; rank; toxic
mercantile: commercial
mercenary: avaricious; hack; mean; niggardly; penurious; sordid; venal
merchandise: good
merciful: compassionate; gentle; gracious; humane; lenient; tender
mercifulness: clemency
merciless: bitter; cruel; grim; implacable; inexorable; pitiless; relentless; remorseless; ruthless; sanguinary; savage; sharp; stony; unmerciful; unrelenting; unsparing
mercurial: capricious; inconstant
mercy: clemency; compassion; grace; pity
mere: bare; blank; naked; sheer; simple; stark
merely: only
meretricious: spurious; tawdry
merge: fuse
merit: credit; earn; excellence; good; luster; reward; value; virtue; worth
merited: just
meriting: worth
meritorious: creditable; estimable; good; worthy
meritoriously: well
mermaid: siren
merriment: cheer; fun; gaiety; glee; hilarity; mirth
merry-andrew: droll; fool; zany
merry: blithe; bright; gay; giddy; glad; happy; high; jocose; jolly; jovial; joyful; light-hearted; pleasant; sportive; waggish
mesa: plain
mesmerized: spellbound
meson: particle
mess up: blunder; disorder; litter
mess: confusion; disorder; jumble; shambles; upset
messenger: harbinger
messy: upset
metamorphose: transform; turn; vary
metamorphosis: permutation
metaphysical: occult
mete out: allot; parcel; part; partition; share
mete: apportion; deal; distribute; ration
meter: poetry; verse
method: course; economy; fashion; form; manner; mean; mode; order; plan; sort; style; technique; way; way

methodical: deliberate; exact; formal; orderly; regular; severe
meticulous: careful; sedulous
metier: business; craft; occupation; station; trade; work
metropolis: capital; town
mettle: bravery; courage; pluck; spirit
mettlesome: bold; brave; scrappy; spirited
mewl: cry
mews: stable
miasmal: noisome
miasmatic: noisome; noxious; rank; rotten
miasmic: noisome
micrify: lessen
microscopic: diminutive
middle of nowhere: backwater
middle-of-the-road: moderate
middle-of-the-roader: moderate
middle: average; center; mean; mean; midst
middling: average; fair; mediocre; medium; respectable; serviceable
midget: dwarf; pygmy
midpoint: mean; middle
midst: center; middle
mien: air; appearance; aspect; attitude; behavior; carriage; cast; character; conduct; countenance; expression; exterior; face; gloss; look; manner; poise; presence; semblance; set
might: energy; force; main; nerve; power; strength
mighty: muscular; potent; powerful; strong
mild-mannered: bland
mild: abortive; affable; bland; bland; calm; charitable; genial; gentle; gracious; kind; kindly; lenient; meek; moderate; open; peaceable; soft; tame; tender
mildness: clemency; mercy
milieu: element; environment; habitat; vicinity
militant: aggressive
military engagement or encounter: battle
military: warlike
milksop: coward; weakling
mill: factory
Milquetoast: weakling
mime: impersonate
mimic: affect; ape; feign; imitate; impersonate; mock; play; simulate
mimicry: mockery
minaciousness: menace
minacity: menace
minatory: forbidding
mince: chop
mind: brains; intellect; intelligence; pleasure; reason; spirit; wit
mindful: attentive; aware; gingerly; observant; thoughtful
mindfulness: attention
mineral: inanimate; lifeless
mingle: blend; confuse; dash; mix; mix; scramble
mingled: complex; miscellaneous; mixed; promiscuous
minimize: weaken
minion: menial; subject; yes-man
minister to: accommodate; attend; feed
minister: attend
minnow: lure
minor: adolescent; futile; paltry; small
minority: youth
minuscule: minute; negligible
minute: close; diminutive; fine; instant; little; moment; nice; note; particular; refined; scrupulous; strict; tenuous
minutely: particularly
miracle: phenomenon
miraculous: marvelous; prodigious; supernatural; wonderful
mire: ooze; quagmire
mirror: reflect
mirth-provoking: amusing
mirth: cheer; gaiety; glee; hilarity; merriment
mirthful: blithe; cheerful; jolly; jovial; merry
mirthless: solemn
misadventure: accident; disaster; reverse
misanthropic: antisocial
misapplication: abuse
misapplied: perverted
misapply: abuse; misplace; prostitute
misapprehend: misconstrue; mistake

misapprehension: mistake; misunderstanding
misappropriate: abuse
misappropriation: abuse
misbehaved: naughty
misbehavior: impropriety; malfeasance; misdemeanor
misbestow: misplace
miscarriage: failure
miscarrying: abortive
miscellaneous: different; general; heterogeneous; indiscriminate; promiscuous
miscellany: mess; mixture
mischance: accident; calamity; catastrophe; disaster; misadventure; misfortune
mischief-maker: rogue; rowdy; scamp
mischief: damage; evil; harm; injury
mischievous: bad; destructive; evil; harmful; injurious; malevolent; sinful; sly; waggish
misconceive: mistake
misconceived: mistaken
misconception: mistake; misunderstanding
misconduct: impropriety; malfeasance; misdemeanor; mislead
miscreant: monster; rascal; rascal; scoundrel; villain
miscue: blunder
misdeed: blame; error; fault; malfeasance; misdemeanor; trespass; wrong
misdemeanor: crime; fault; malfeasance; offense; trespass
misdirect: mislead
misdirected: wry
misdoing: blame; blunder; wrong
misemploy: abuse
misemployment: abuse
miserable: beastly; contemptible; dejected; depressed; desolate; disconsolate; evil; forlorn; joyless; low; melancholy; piteous; poor; sorry; squalid; uncomfortable; unhappy; wretched; wretched
miserliness: parsimony
miserly: close; mean; mercenary; near; niggardly; parsimonious; penurious; petty; sordid; stingy
misery: adversity; affliction; calamity; cross; distress; evil; grief; ill; oppression; oppression; pain; sorrow; squalor; tear; torment; trial; trouble; woe
misfortune: accident; adversity; affliction; blow; calamity; catastrophe; cross; curse; disaster; evil; hardship; ill; misadventure; mischief; reverse; sorrow; trouble
misgiving: apprehension; distrust; doubt; qualm; suspense; suspicion; worry
misguide: mislead
misguided: perverted
mishap: accident; affliction; calamity; catastrophe; disaster; misadventure; misfortune; reverse
mishmash: scramble
misinterpret: misconstrue
misjudge: misconstrue; mistake
misjudgment: blunder
mislay: misplace
mislead: beguile; bite; bluff; cheat; deceive; delude; mock
misleading: deceitful; deceptive; false; hypocritical; illusory; illusory; sophisticated; specious
misplace: displace
misprint: mistake
misproportioned: misshapen
misread: misconstrue
miss: overlook; trip; trip
missed: lost
misshape: deform
misshapen: crooked; deformed
missile: ball
missing: absent; lost
misspend: waste
misspent: lost
misstep: blunder; trip
mist: cloud; fog; haze
mistake: blunder; delusion; error; fault; inaccuracy; misconstrue; misunderstanding; oversight; slip; slip; trip
mistaken: erroneous; false; wrong
mistreat: abuse; injure; maltreat
mistreatment: abuse
mistrust: apprehension; distrust; distrust; doubt; doubt; misgiving; suspect; suspicion
mistrustfully: askance
misty: murky; wet

misunderstand: misconstrue; mistake
misunderstanding: breach; mistake; quarrel
misuse: abuse; abuse; profane; prostitute; squander; tamper
mite: bit; iota; particle
mitigate: allay; alleviate; appease; ease; lighten; moderate; palliate; qualify; relax; relieve; slack; slacken; soften; solace; soothe; temper
mitigation: abatement; relief; remission
mix up: confuse; jumble; mess; scramble; scramble
mix: blend; combine; confuse; dash; jumble; mess; mingle; scramble; temper
mixed: complex; heterogeneous; indiscriminate; miscellaneous; promiscuous
mixture: blend; combination; jumble; mess; mix
moan: complain; lament; whine
moaning: lament
mob: assembly; crowd; ring; wash
mock: artificial; banter; bogus; counterfeit; fictitious; imitate; jeer; phony; pillory; ridicule; scoff; sham; spurious; taunt
mockery: banter; irony; mock; ridicule; scorn; sport
mocking: ribald
mode: course; cut; fashion; form; garb; guise; manner; mean; method; mood; rage; style; technique; vogue; way
model: archetype; blueprint; copy; example; fashion; form; ideal; nonesuch; original; paradigm; paragon; pattern; pose; prototype; sample; shape; specimen; standard; type
moderate: allay; cool; damp; easy; gentle; gradual; mean; modest; modify; open; pacify; palliate; qualify; reasonable; respectable; slack; slow; sober; soften; temper; temperate
moderately warm: lukewarm
moderately: pretty
moderation: abstinence; modesty; remission; temper
modern: late; new; recent
modest: bashful; chaste; coy; decent; demure; diffident; humble; meek; prudish; pure; small; squeamish; unassuming; unpretentious
modesty: propriety
modification: change; mode; permutation; variation
modify: adapt; affect; alter; change; influence; palliate; qualify; soften; temper; touch; trim; vary
modus operandi: technique
mogul: tycoon
moil: plod; slavery; toil; work
moist: damp; humid; wet
moisten: damp; temper; wash
moistened: wet
moisture: damp; wet
moistureless: arid
mold: bend; block; cast; fashion; form; ground; make; model; rot; shape; stamp; turn
moldable: malleable; soft
molder: perish; rot
molecule: particle
molest: annoy; attack; bother; harass; harm; harry; persecute; pester; plague; ruffle; tease; trouble; worry
molestation: trouble
mollify: allay; alleviate; appease; calm; melt; moderate; pacify; qualify; smooth; soften; soothe; subdue; temper
mollifying: mild; soft
mollycoddle: weakling
moment: consequence; consideration; flash; importance; instant; matter; minute; significance; weight
momentary: ephemeral
momentous: critical; grave; great; heavy; material; ponderous; serious; significant; weighty
momentousness: importance
momentum: moment
monarch: sovereign
monarchical: sovereign
monarchy: kingdom
monastery: cloister
Monday-morning quarterback: kibitz
monetary: financial; pecuniary
money: wherewithal

moneybag: bag
moneyed: opulent; rich; wealthy
mongrel: hybrid
mongrelize: cross
monition: caveat
monk: religious
monkey: addiction
monody: lament; moan
monopoly: combination
monotonous: dreary; tedious; wearisome
monotony: sameness
monster: animal; giant; monstrous
monstrosity: abnormality; monster
monstrous: atrocious; black; enormous; flagrant; giant; gigantic; hideous; monster; prodigious; prodigious; terrible; ugly
monticule: hill
monument: memento
moo: low
mood: aura; humor; spirit; temper
moodiness: pet
moody: cross; glum; inconstant; melancholy; morose; sulky; sullen; temperamental
mooncalf: monster
moonshine: nonsense
moonstruck: smitten
moony: moonstruck
mop: clean
moral: blue; chaste; clean; clear; ethical; good; honest; righteous; squeamish; virtuous
moralistic: straitlaced
morality: goodness; moral; virtue
morass: quagmire; wash
morbid: dark; depressed; heavy; macabre
morbidity: disease
mordacious: caustic; cutting; satirical; severe; sharp
mordant: acerbic; caustic; cutting; poignant; pointed; pungent; sarcastic; satirical; severe
mordent: tart
more applicable: better
more appropriate: better
more fit: better
more good: better
more suitable: better
more than: above
more useful: better
more valuable: better
more: above
moreover: also; besides; but
morn: morning
moron: fool; oaf
morose: blue; cross; dark; depressed; glum; harsh; heavy; moody; piteous; sour; sulky; sullen
moroseness: grief
morsel: bite; delicacy; portion; scrap; taste
mortal: deadly; fatal; physical
mortgage: bond
mortification: chagrin; confusion; disappointment; embarrassment; humiliation; shame
mortified: ashamed; small
mortify: abash; chagrin; confuse; humble; humiliate; offend; shame; snub
mortifying: shameful
most important: chief; leading
most influential: dominant
most: bulk
mostly: chiefly
mot: jest
mote: atom; particle; thought
motel: hotel
moth-eaten: hackneyed; seedy; shabby
mother-of-pearl: pearly
mother: breed
motherly: womanly,
motif: theme
motion picture: picture
motion: move; movement; play; run
motionless: calm; dead; inert; quiet; standing; still; stony; torpid
motivate: compel; occasion; wake
motivation: motive
motive: account; cause; ground; incentive; inducement; object; occasion; reason; score; stimulus; subject
motley: dappled; heterogeneous
motorboat: tender
mottled: dappled
motto: byword; catchword; device; watchword
mould: decompose
mound: hill
mount: ascend; bank; climb; rise; scale; set; soar
mountain: height; mount

mountebank: cheat; impostor; phony; rogue; scoundrel; swindler

mounting: rise

mourn or sorrow over or for: lament

mourn for: regret

mourn: deplore; grieve; moan; sorrow

mournful: black; heavy; lachrymose; lugubrious; piteous; plaintive; sad; somber; sorrowful; sorry; sullen; tragic

mouth off: declaim

mouth-watering: scrumptious

mouth: spring; tell

mouthed: oral

mouthful: bite; swallow

move or go forward: advance

move or push backward: back

move or set or push or bring forward: advance

move on: advance; move; proceed

move swiftly or quickly: hurry

move to and fro: agitate

move upward: rise

move: affect; cut; displace; induce; influence; maneuver; migrate; motion; movement; occasion; offer; pace; pass; persuade; pierce; push; run; shake; stir; stir; touch; urge; vacate; wander; work

movement: action; motion; move; passage; play; stir; tendency

movie: picture

moving forward: advance

moving: action; active; affecting; lively; pathetic; piteous

mow: crop; cut

muckrake: disclose; expose

mucky: turbid

mucus: phlegm

mud: deposit; ooze

muddle: bewilder; fog; jumble; mess; obfuscate; perturb; scramble

muddled: cloudy; groggy

muddy: cloudy; roil; turbid

muff: blunder

muffle: mumble; still

mugger: thief

muggy: close

mugwump: moderate

mulish: obstinate; refractory; restive; wrongheaded

multicolored: dappled

multifaceted: manifold

multifarious: heterogeneous; manifold; many

multifold: multifarious

multiform: diverse

multihued: dappled

multiplicity: variety

multiply: increase

multitude: cloud; crowd; number; swarm; throng

multitudinous: large; manifold; multifarious; rife

multivarious: multifarious

mumble: growl; murmur

mumbo jumbo: babble

mumbo-jumbo: jargon

mummery: mask

mundane: carnal; earthly; secular; sophisticated; suave; terrestrial; worldly; worldly

municipality: village

munificence: bounty; generosity

munificent: free; generous; liberal; open

murder: assassinate; butcher; crime; destruction; kill; massacre; remove; slaughter; slay

murderer: butcher

murderous: bloody; deadly; fierce; sanguinary

murky: cloudy; dark; dusky; lurid; obscure; somber; turbid

murmur: complain; mumble; mutter; snarl

muscular: robust; stalwart; strong; sturdy; well-built

muse: daydream; meditate; ponder; reflect; ruminate; think

mush: schmaltz

mushiness: schmaltz

mushroom: billow

mushy: moonstruck; saccharine

musical poem: lay

musical: mellifluous; sweet; tuneful

musing: absent-minded; contemplative; preoccupied; reflection; thought

muster: call; gather; gathering; meet

mutable: ambivalent; inconstant; slippery

mutation: change; metamorphosis; permutation; variation

mute: dumb; silent; speechless; speechless; still; still

mutilate: maim; mangle

mutineer: rebel

mutinous: rebel; rebellious

mutiny: insurrection; rebellion; revolt; revolt; revolution; sedition; tumult

mutt: hybrid; mongrel

mutter: mumble; murmur

mutual: common; reciprocal; symbiotic

mutually exclusive (choice between two things): alternative

muzzy: groggy

myopic: purblind; short-sighted

myriad: many; multifarious; numberless

myrmidon: yes-man

mysterious: dark; deep; inscrutable; obscure; occult; recherch,; recondite; secret; secret; strange; weird

mystery: secret

mystic: dark

mystical: dark; mysterious; occult

mystify: bewilder; confuse; embarrass; perplex; puzzle

mystifying: strange

myth: fable; legend

mythical: fictitious

nab: capture

nabob: celebrity; tycoon

nacreous: opalescent; pearly

nada: zilch

nag: bedevil; fury; hack; scold; shrew; termagant

naiad: nymph

naive: artless; candid; direct; guileless; inexperienced; ingenuous; innocent; simple; unaffected; unreserved; unsophisticated

naked: bare; nude; unguarded

name: appoint; call; celebrity; character; credit; distinction; entitle; enumerate; face; mention; note; propose; qualify; renown; reputation; repute; style; title

nap: pile; sleep

narcissistic: egocentric

narcotic: opiate; sedative; sedative

nard: ointment; remedy

narrate: describe; recite; recount; rehearse; relate; spin; tell

narration: account; relation; story

narrative: account; history; recital; relation; story; tale

narrow-minded: bigoted; exclusive; petty; small-minded

narrow: bigoted; contract; exclusive; exclusive; intolerant; little; mean; near; petty; qualify; restrain; slender; small; small; small-minded; strict; stringent

nasty: dirty; nauseous; peevish; snide; squalid; unclean

nation: people; race

national leader: politician,

national: state

native: countryman; inborn; inherent; innate; intrinsic

nativity: birth

natter: babble; jabber

natty: jaunty

natural: artless; carnal; inborn; informal; inherent; intrinsic; naive; native; physical; simple; spontaneous; unaffected; unlawful; voluntary

naturalness: ease

nature: breed; character; disposition; kind; make; manner; quality; sort; spirit; temper; temperament

naught: zilch

naughtiness: impropriety

naughty: ill

nausea: disgust; surfeit

nauseate: disgust; revolt; shock

nauseated: queasy; sick

nauseating: abhorrent; abominable; disgusting; distasteful; hateful; loathsome; nasty; nauseous; offensive; vile

nauseous: disgusting; nasty; offensive; queasy; sick; vile

Nazi: absolute

Neanderthal: yahoo

near or close or next to: adjoining

near-at-hand: handy

near-sighted: short-sighted

near: about; adjacent; close; gain; handy; immediate; imminent; present

nearby: about; adjacent; close; handy; near; present

nearly: about; almost; hardly

nearness: presence; vicinity

nearsighted: purblind

neat: becoming; chaste; clean; clean; nice; orderly; simple; smart; smug; terse; tidy; trim

neatly: clean

neb: bill

nebbish: weakling

nebbishy: impotent

nebular: nebulous

nebulous: dim

necessary: compulsory; essential; fundamental; imperious; indispensable; necessity; requisite; vital

necessitate: compel; force; oblige; require

necessitous: penniless; poor

necessitousness: necessity; poverty

necessity: distress; emergency; essential; necessary; need; poverty; privation; requisite; turn; want

necktie: tie

necromancer: magician; wizard

necromancy: magic; sorcery

necrose: mortify

need: absence; call; crave; desire; distress; hardship; haste; lack; lust; necessity; penury; poverty; privation; require; requirement; strait; take; turn; use; want; wish

needed: indispensable; necessary; requisite

needful: necessary; requisite

needfulness: necessity

neediness: necessity; need; poverty

needle: exasperate; fret; torment

needless: superfluous; unnecessary

needy: destitute; miserable; penniless; poor

nefarious: black; criminal; dark; evil; heinous; infamous; wicked

negate: break; nullify

neglect: dereliction; disregard; failure; ignore; negligence; overlook; oversight; slack; slacken; slight

neglected: shabby

neglectful: careless; improvident; lax; negligent; oblivious; regardless; remiss; thoughtless; unmindful

negligence: dereliction; neglect; slack

negligent: careless; casual; inadvertent; lax; loose; neglectful; oblivious; perfunctory; reckless; regardless; remiss; slack; thoughtless; unmindful

negligible: petty; trifling

negotiate: haggle; transact; treat

neighborhood: habitat; presence; vicinity

neighboring: adjacent; close

neophyte: amateur; convert; dabbler; pupil; tyro

neoteric: modern; new

nereid: nymph

nerve: assurance; bravery; chutzpah; gall; harden; impudence; mettle; pluck

nervous: restive; skittish; tense; tumultuous; unquiet

nervousness: upset

nervy: daredevil

nescient: ignorant

ness: head

net: bag; clear; complex; snare

nettle: anger; exasperate; fret; gall; irritate; offend; pester; pique; provoke; rankle; torment; vex

nettled: angry; miffed

network: complex

neurotic: mental; tense

neutral: innocuous; sober; unbiased

neutralize: balance; counteract; supersede

neutrino: particle

neutron: particle

never-ending: chronic; eternal; immortal; incessant

nevertheless: but; notwithstanding; still

new member: initiate

new: fresh; modern; novel; original; recent; sweet; unaccustomed; virgin

newly: new

newness: novelty

news: advice; information; intelligence; notice; rumor; word

newsmongering: gossip

newsworthy: memorable; noteworthy

next: immediate

Niagara: cascade

nib: bill

nice: close; critical; delicate; elegant; exact; neat; particular; punctilious; squeamish

nicety: truth

nick: pilfer

nictitate: blink; wink

niggard: miser; niggardly

niggardliness: parsimony

niggardly: close; little; mean; mercenary; miserly; near; parsimonious; penurious; small; sordid; stingy

niggling: vile

nigh: near

nightclub: bar

nightfall: evening; twilight

nil: zilch

nimble-footed: fleet

nimble-witted: cagey

nimble: active; agile; alert; brisk; busy; clever; dexterous; light; lively; mercurial; quick; ready; smart; spry

nimiety: excess

nincompoop: fool; oaf

nine inches: span

ninny: fool; oaf

nip: bite

nipping: bitter; cold; sharp

nisus: effort

nitpicker: kvetch

nix: brownie; fairy; zilch

nixie: brownie; fairy

no more than: but; only

no-brain: mindless

nobble: wangle

nobility: elevation; grandeur

noble: chivalrous; gallant; generous; gentle; grand; great; honorable; lordly; magnanimous; magnificent; majestic; palatial; proud; splendid

nobleman: noble; peer

nobleness: elevation; generosity; honor

nobody home: vacuous

nocuous: noisome; noxious

noise: bedlam; clamor; hubbub; racket; sound; uproar

noiseless: silent; still

noisome: foul; noxious; unpleasant; unwholesome

noisy: boisterous; loud; obstreperous; raucous; rough; rowdy; tumultuous; vociferous

nomadic: itinerant; vagabond

nomenclature: terminology; vernacular

nominate: appoint; call; name; ordain; propose

non-appearance: absence

non-native: foreigner

nonbeliever: atheist

nonchalance: unconcern

nonchalant: blas,; easygoing; lackadaisical; laid-back; offhand

nonclerical: secular

non compos mentis: insane

nonconformant: abnormal

nonconforming: aberrant; abnormal

nonconformist: bohemian; iconoclast; irregular

nonconformity: dissent

nonessential: accidental; extraneous; mean; simple; unessential

nonesuch: nonpareil; paragon

nonexclusive: general

nonindulgence: abstinence

nonirritating: bland

nonliterary: vernacular

nonpareil: nonesuch

nonperformance: failure

nonplus: bewilder; confuse; stagger

nonplussed: blank

nonprofessional: amateur; dabbler; dilettante

nonrepresentational: abstract

nonrestrictive: frank

nonselective: promiscuous

nonsense: babble; blarney; jargon; stuff

nonsensical: foolish; ridiculous; senseless; silly; unreasonable

nonspecific: general

nonstarter: washout

nonstop: express

noose: snare

normal: average; just; legitimate; ordinary; regular; right; sane

northeaster: storm

northerly: high

nose: spout

nostrum: cure-all; panacea

nosy Parker: gossip

nosy: obtrusive; prying

not far from: about

not far: about

not germane: extraneous

not guilty: blameless; clear

not in: absent

not often: seldom

not pertinent: extraneous

not present: absent

not quite: scarcely

not radioactive: clean

not sharp: blunt

not valid: incorrect

notable: acclaimed; celebrity; eminent; famous; great; memorable; noted; noteworthy; particular; remarkable

notch: gorge; hack; pass; score

note: comment; distinction; eminence; gloss; mark; mind; minute; name; notice; observe; perceive; record; regard; remark; renown; witness

noted: conspicuous; distinguished; eminent; glorious; great; notable

noteworthy: conspicuous; eminent; great; memorable; notable; particular; remarkable

nothing: zilch

notice: advice; attention; bill; caveat; discern; discover; heed; mark; mind; note; observation; observe; perceive; regard; remark; respect; see; ultimatum; witness

noticeable: conspicuous; notable; obtrusive; prominent

noticing: observation

notification: advice; caveat; notice

notify: admonish; advise; apprise; inform; warn

notion: conceit; fancy; guess; idea; image; opinion; sense; suspicion; tenet; thought; vagary; view; whim

notional: whimsical

notoriety: celebrity; credit; disgrace; fame; infamy; limelight

notorious: base; common; crying; dishonorable; household; infamous; notable

notwithstanding: although; despite

nourish: cherish; feed; foster; nurse; support; sustain

nourishing: healthy; wholesome

nourishment: nutrition

novel: curious; fiction; fresh; modern; new; original; recent; recherch,; romance

novella: piece

novelty: change

novice: amateur; dabbler; neophyte; pupil; tyro

novitiate: neophyte

now existing: actual

now: present

noxious: abominable; contagious; deleterious; inimical; noisome; pernicious; rank; rotten; unhealthful; unhealthy; unpleasant; unwholesome

nozzle: spout

nude: bare; naked

nugatory: futile; ineffectual; petty; puerile; slight; slim; small; tenuous; trifling; trivial; unimportant; vain; vile; void

nuisance: pest; plague; scourge

nuke: zap

nullification: abolition; abrogation; recall

nullifidian: skeptic

nullify: abate; abolish; abrogate; destroy; frustrate; overrule; recall; void

numb: blunt; dead; lackadaisical; unfeeling

number: issue; recite; tell

numberless: innumerable; numerous

numbers: poetry; verse

numeral: number

numerate: number

numerous: great; innumerable; manifold; many; multifarious; numberless; rife

nummary: monetary

nummular: monetary; pecuniary

numskull: fool

nun: religious

nuncupative: verbal

nunnery: cloister

nuptials: marriage

nurse: caregiver; cherish; companion; foster; nourish; nurture; rear

nurture: breed; cherish; nourish; nurse; rear; support; sustain

nurturing: female

nut: fanatic; screwball; zany

nutcase: crackpot; screwball

nutriment: food; nutrition

nutrition: food

nutritious: healthy; wholesome

nutty: screwball

nymph: sylph

oath: assurance; curse

obdurate: hard; inflexible; intractable; obstinate; relentless; shameless; stony; stubborn; unreconstructed; willful

obedient: dutiful; good; observant; subject; submissive

obeisance: deference; homage; reverence

obese: fat; plump

obey: comply; follow; fulfill; heed; mind; observe; submit

obfuscate: fog; shade

obfuscation: fog

object: aim; cause; demonstrate; demur; design; end; idea; ideal; intent; mark; meaning; mind; objective; protest; purpose; reason; subject; view

objecting: repugnant

objection: aversion; demur; difficulty; protest; repugnance

objectionable: ill; nasty; obnoxious; repugnant; tasteless; ugly; vile

objective: end; idea; ideal; mark; object; reason

objet d'art: antique

objurgate: vituperate

obligate: bind; oblige; require; tie

obligation: allegiance; bond; debt; duty; trust

obligatory: compulsory

oblige: accommodate; bind; compel; constrain; force

obliged: grateful; liable; thankful

obliging: affable; benevolent; civil; courteous; good

oblique: circuitous; cockeyed

obliquely: askance

obliqueness: slant

obliquity: slant

obliterate: abolish; blot; cancel; deface; eradicate; erase

obliteration: abolition; blot

oblivious: absent-minded; senile

obloquy: disgrace; ignominy; indignity; infamy; odium; reproach; scandal; shame

obnoxious: abominable; hateful; odious; offensive; unpleasant; vile

obscene: blue; dirty; earthy; filthy; foul; indecent; lascivious; nasty; ribald; salacious; scurrilous; vile; X-rated

obscure: ambiguous; blind; blot; cloud; cloudy; dark; deep; difficult; dim; dubious; dusky; gloomy; ignoble; indefinite; murky; mysterious; nameless; obfuscate; oracular; pale; recondite; secret; shade; shroud; ulterior; vague

obscurity: gloom; haze; mist; shade

obsecrate: beseech; entreat

obsequious: saccharine; servile; slavish; smarmy; supple; unctuous

observable: visible

observance: ceremony; custom; discharge; exercise; observation; rite

observant: alert; attentive; sensible; sharp; wakeful; watchful

observation: attention; comment; examination; heed; note; notice; remark; speech; watch

observe: celebrate; contemplate; discharge; experience; follow; fulfill; heed; hold; mark; note; notice; perceive; practice; regard; remark; see; survey; watch; witness

observer: student

obsession: addiction

obsolescent: antique

obsolete: antique; extinct; oldfashioned; superannuated

obstacle: bar; barrier; block; check; difficulty; discouragement; hindrance; impediment; obstruction; shackle; stop; traverse

obstinacy: difficulty; tenacity

obstinate: contrary; disobedient; froward; headstrong; inflexible; intractable; obdurate; opinionated; perverse; positive; refractory; restive; set; single-minded; stiff; stout; stubborn; tenacious;

uncompromising; unyielding; wayward; willful; wrongheaded

obstreperous: boisterous; noisy; raucous; rowdy; tumultuous; vociferous

obstruct: arrest; bar; barricade; block; check; close; discourage; encumber; hamper; hinder; impede; inhibit; oppose; prevent; prohibit; retard; slow; stay; stem; stop; stuff; thwart; traverse

obstruction: arrest; bar; barricade; barrier; block; check; discouragement; hindrance; hitch; impediment; obstacle; shackle; stop; traverse; wall

obtain: achieve; acquire; attach; attain; earn; gain; get; have; make; procure; purchase; refer; secure; take; win

obtest: beseech; entreat

obtrude: intrude; project

obtrusive: loud; officious

obtund: blunt; dull

obtuse: apathetic; blunt; callous; dead; dull; stupid; thick-skinned

obverse: right

obviate: anticipate; forbid; parry; prevent; stifle

obvious: apparent; bare; bold; broad; certain; clear; conspicuous; direct; evident; express; gaudy; indisputable; loud; lucid; manifest; open; palpable; patent; plain; self-evident; tangible; transparent; undeniable; unequivocal; unmistakable; visible

obviously: clearly

occasion: breed; call; cause; chance; create; engender; make; motive; operate; opportunity; place; produce; use

occasional: casual; odd; sporadic

occlude: obstruct

occlusion: obstruction

occult: dark; mysterious; recondite; secret

occupancy: occupation

occupants: household

occupation: business; possession; profession; station; trade; vocation; work

occupied: active; busy; diligent; rapt

occupy: absorb; arrest; employ; have; hold; possess; range; supply; take

occur: chance; happen; pass; rise

occurrence: case; episode; event; incident; occasion; phenomenon

ocean: deep; main

oceanid: nymph

odd characteristic: eccentricity

odd duck: crackpot; eccentric

odd trait: peculiarity

odd: aberrant; abnormal; cranky; droll; eccentric; fantastic; nondescript; particular; peculiar; preternatural; quaint; queer; singular; strange; uncanny; uncommon; uncouth; unique; unusual; whimsical; wonderful

oddball: crackpot; eccentric; screwball; wacky

oddity: aberration; crackpot; eccentric; peculiarity; screwball; vagary

oddments: odd

oddness: aberration

ode: lay; piece

odious: abhorrent; abominable; detestable; disgusting; hateful; heinous; hideous; horrible; infamous; loathsome; obnoxious

odiousness: abomination

odium: abhorrence; abomination; disgrace; hatred; ignominy; infamy; obloquy; reproach; scandal; shame

odor: aroma; flavor; perfume; savor; scent

odoriferous: fragrant; strong

odorous: fragrant; odoriferous

of age: adult

of the age of: aged

of unsound mind: insane

of use or service: available

of yore: ancient

of: about

off the cuff: extemporaneous

off-balance: eccentric

off-center: eccentric; screwball

off-color: naughty

off-hand: ad-lib; laid-back

off-putting: forbidding

off-the-cuff: ad-lib; offhand

off-the-wall: eccentric; wild-eyed; zany

off: absent; negligible

offbeat: bohemian; eccentric

offend: affront; disgust; insult; outrage; pique; shock; sin; transgress; trespass

offended: miffed

offender: criminal; malefactor

offending: disgusting

offense: abuse; affront; attack; crime; displeasure; error; fault; insult; misdemeanor; outrage; reproach; sacrilege; scandal; sin; trespass; umbrage

offensive: aggressive; bad; disgusting; distasteful; foul; hateful; indecent; injurious; loathsome; nasty; nauseous; noisome; obnoxious; obscene; odious; opprobrious; rank; repugnant; ribald; rotten; scurrilous; tasteless; ugly; unpleasant; unsavory; vile

offer counsel: advise

offer: administer; advance; assign; bid; exhibit; extend; give; hazard; occur; overture; prefer; present; proffer; proposal; propose; tender

offering: advance; donation; exhibit; gift; scapegoat; tender

offhand: casual; extemporaneous

office: appointment; business; capacity; charge; duty; part; place; post; station; station; trust

official: authoritative; formal

officious: busy; impertinent; meddlesome; obtrusive

offset: balance; compensate; counteract; cover; oppose; opposition

offshoot: branch; limb; outgrowth

offspring: brood; issue; race; scion; young

often: frequently; generally

ogre: goblin

oiler: transport

oily: fat; slippery; smarmy; smooth; unctuous

ointment: remedy

okay: pass

old age: age

old hat: hack; stale

old saw: platitude

old-fashioned: antique; archaic; dowdy; obsolete; old; quaint; tacky

old-fogyish: senile

old-hat: hackneyed

old-maid: single

old-maidish: dowdy

old: aged; ancient; antique; archaic; hack; obsolete; old-fashioned; stale; superannuated; weak

olden: old

oleaginous: unctuous

olent: strong

olio: mixture

omen: portent; presage; sign; warning

ominous: sinister; ugly

omission: failure; neglect; oversight

omit: abate; eliminate; except; exclude; leave; neglect; spare

omnipresent: ubiquitous

on a par: level

on cloud nine: ecstatic

on every side: about

on foot: pedestrian

on high: above

on one's person: about

on the condition or supposition that: provided

on the lookout: alert

on the point of: about

on the qui vive: alert; attentive; brisk; nimble; sharp; wakeful

on top of: above

on-dit: scuttlebutt

on: about

once-over-lightly: slapdash

one after another: alternate

one and the same: identical

180° turn: about-face

one-sided: partial

one-sidedness: partiality

one: complete; particular; person; single; some

oneness: rapport; unity

onerous: arduous; hard; heavy; laborious; weighty

only: but; exclusive; single; sole; unique

onset: assault; attack; beginning; charge; offense; push; raid; start

onslaught: assault; attack; charge

onus: load

onward: forward

oomph: verve

ooze: seep; strain

opalescent: pearly

opaline: pearly

opaque: cloudy; turbid

open out: display

open to suggestion or advice: advisable

open-handed: charitable; free; generous; open

open-hearted: ingenuous; plain

open-minded: broad; broad-minded; receptive

open-mindedness: tolerance

open: aboveboard; apparent; artless; bare; bluff; break; broad; broad-minded; candid; capable; clear; commence; conspicuous; dawn; direct; explicit; fair; frank; free; gape; guileless; honest; ingenuous; initiate; liable; manifest; moral; naive; naked; obvious; outgoing; outspoken; overt; patent; plain; receptive; round; sincere; spread; straight; subject; tangible; transparent; uncover; unguarded; unreserved; visible; vulnerable

openhanded: lavish; liberal

opening: breach; chance; development; hole; occasion; overture; primary; rent; void; yawn

openly: aboveboard

openness: candor; freedom; truth

operable: viable

operate: act; bear; move; order; run; tell; work

operatic: theatrical

operating: operative

operation: action; effect; energy; exercise; force; play; practice; procedure; process

operative: active; alive; effective; standing

operose: industrious

opiate: sedative

opinion: advice; apprehension; belief; conjecture; counsel; estimate; estimation; fame; feeling; idea; judgment; mind; notion; principle; sense; sentiment; tenet; thought; view

opinionated: resolute; stubborn; tenacious

oppilate: obstruct

opponent: adversary; antagonist; competitor; enemy; foe; rival

opportune moment: opportunity

opportune: appropriate; happy; seasonable; timely

opportunity: chance; occasion; opening; place; scope; start

oppose: combat; compete; conflict; contest; contrast; counteract; cross; deny; dispute; face; meet; repel; resist; rise; rival; stand; stem; struggle; thwart; withstand

opposed: adverse; alien; averse; contradictory; contrary; hostile; incompatible; opposite; repugnant; rival

opposing: contradictory; contrary; cross; opposition; recalcitrant; repugnant; rival

opposite direction: about

opposite: adverse; contradictory; contrary; converse; reverse

opposition: antipathy; clash; conflict; contention; contrast; cross; dissent; hostility; strife

oppress: burden; crush; depress; encumber; grind; load; persecute; wrong

oppression: hardship

oppressive: close; hard; heavy; tyrannical

oppressor: tyrant

opprobrious: ignominious; offensive; pejorative; scurrilous

opprobrium: abuse; disgrace; ignominy; indignity; infamy; odium; reproach; scandal; shame

oppugn: attack; oppose

oppugnant: contrary; hostile

optimistic: hopeful; rosy

option: alternative; choice; volition

opulence: wealth

opulent: affluent; luxurious; rich; wealthy

oral: verbal

orate: declaim

oration: address; speech

oratorical: grandiloquent

oratory: elocution

orb: ball; circle; sphere

orbed: round

orbit: circle; circuit; revolve; sphere

ordain: appoint; decree; doom; establish; order; prescribe; set

order: appoint; arrange; array; bid; breed; brood; charge; command; course; decree; devise; direct;

discipline; disposition; enjoin; faction; fitness; form; instruct; instruction; mandate; marshal; method; ordain; organize; peace; place; prepare; range; rank; regulate; regulation; require; requirement; rule; sequence; series; set; shape; shape; sort; succession; symmetry; system; tell; trim; warrant; will; wish; word

ordered: neat; successive; trim

ordering: regulation

orderly: exact; neat; regular; tidy

ordinance: act

ordinarily: generally

ordinary: average; common; commonplace; general; habitual; household; lackluster; mediocre; plain; run; simple; stereotyped; stock; trite; usual; vernacular

ordinate: primary

oread: nymph

organ: part

organization: association; club; office; society; structure

organize: arrange; establish; form

organized: orderly; organic

organs: inside

orgy: rampage

Oriental Plague: plague

orientation: exposure

orifice: opening

origin: beginning; birth; head; parentage; rise; spring

original: copy; eccentric; fundamental; model; native; pattern; pioneer; primary; primeval; primitive; prototype; radical; seminal; type; witty

originality: novelty

originate: begin; breed; cause; commence; create; discover; emanate; form; grow; initiate; invent; issue; occasion; proceed; produce; raise; result; rise; spring; stem; work

ornament: adorn; apparel; array; beautify; beset; decorate; dress; embellish; flourish; fret; garnish; grace; trim

ornamental: fancy

ornamentation: garnish; ornament

ornamented: fine; garish

ornate: elaborate; fancy; fine; garish; labored; luxurious; meretricious

ornery: cantankerous; grouchy; wrongheaded

orotund: clear

orphic: abstruse

orphrey: border; brim

orthodox: sound

orts: remain

oscillate: fluctuate; shake; swing; totter; tremble; vibrate; wave

oscillating: vibrant

oscillation: swing; tremor

osmose: permeate; seep; soak

ossify: harden

ossuary: sepulcher

ostensible: apparent; specious

ostensive: ostensible

ostentation: display; flash; flourish; show; vainglory

ostentatious: ambitious; flash; grandiose; magnificent; pretentious; showy; tawdry; theatrical

ostracism: taboo

ostracize: banish

other than: besides

other: alternative

otherwise: besides

otherworldly: celestial

oust: displace; expel

out and out: clean

out of character: unnatural

out of keeping: incongruous; inconsistent

out of kilter: cockeyed

out of order: cranky; sick; wrong

out of place: inept

out of the house: abroad

out of use: standing

out to lunch: vacuous

out-and-out: downright; regular; unqualified

out-at-the-elbows: shabby

out-of-date: ancient; antique; archaic

out-of-doors: abroad

out-of-the-ordinary: offbeat

out-of-the-way: odd; offbeat

out: absent; dead; extinct; forward

outback: backwater

outbreak: blast; convulsion; riot; storm; tumult

outbuilding: shack

outburst: access; blast; blaze; convulsion; flash; paroxysm; rampage; spurt; storm; tear; tirade
outcast: pariah; vagabond
outcome: conclusion; consequence; disposition; effect; end; event; issue; result; sequence
outcry: call; clamor; cry; exclamation; noise; racket; scream
outdistance: outdo
outdo: beat; break; exceed; excel; head; surpass; top
outer: exterior
outermost: extreme
outfit: apparel; appoint; array; equip; furnish; set
outgoing: obliging
outgrowth: growth
outhouse: shack
outing: excursion
outlander: foreigner
outlandish: fantastic; strange
outlast: outlive; stand
outlaw: ban; banish; debar; malefactor
outlay: charge; cost; expense; price
outlet: issue
outline: abridgment; abstract; argument; blueprint; brief; design; form; map; shape; silhouette; sketch; summary; synopsis; trace
outlive: survive
outlook: aspect; ideology; prospect
outlying: exterior
outmoded: old-fashioned; tacky
outpouring: burst; flow
output: make
outrage: affront; indignity; insult; shock; violence
outrageous: atrocious; black; enormous; excessive; flagrant; grievous; gross; indecent; infamous; shameful; wild
outré: fantastic; extreme
outrider: harbinger
outright: downright; flat; frank
outset: beginning; start
outside: abroad; exterior; negligible; periphery; skin
outsider: foreigner; stranger
outsize: giant
outspoken: candid; direct; explicit; frank; naked; plain; round
outspokenness: candor
outstanding: acclaimed; conspicuous; dominant; eminent; humongous; memorable; noteworthy; prominent; shining
outstrip: exceed; excel; lead; outdo; surpass
outward: exterior; superficial
outweigh: predominate
outwit: bite; cheat; deceive
over and above: besides
over-abundant: rank
over-confident: positive
over-indulgence: excess
over-refined: recherché
over-the-top: rabid
over: above; extinct; finished; preeminent
overactive: hectic
overawe: daunt; discourage; intimidate
overbearing: arbitrary; arrogant; imperious; insolent; lordly; positive; proud; truculent
overblown: grandiose
overbrim: cascade
overburden: drive; overwhelm
overcast: cloudy; heavy; murky; sullen
overcautious: afraid
overcome: affect; beat; break; conquer; crush; defeat; force; master; overpower; overthrow; overwhelm; quell; reduce; rush; stun; subdue; vanquish
overconfident: bold; proud
overcrowd: cram
overcrowded: populous
overdo: labor
overdone: flagrant; hack; labored
overexert: strain
overfastidious: queasy
overfeed: surfeit
overflow: abundance; cascade; deluge; exuberance; flood; flow; inundate; plenty; run
overflowing: abundant; ample; big; copious; flow; generous
overfullness: plenty
overhanging: imminent; pendulous
overhead: above
overjoyed: ecstatic
overlap: stagger
overlay: cover; spread

overload: burden; encumber; overwhelm
overlong: long
overlook: blink; command; disregard; excuse; ignore; neglect; oversee; pardon; remit; slight; slur; trip
overmaster: overpower
overmodest: demure
overnice: dainty
overpower: beat; compel; conquer; crush; force; master; oppress; overcome; overthrow; overwhelm; quell; reduce; subdue; vanquish
overrule: predominate; supersede
overseas: abroad
oversee: administer; command; master; overlook; superintend
overseer: manager
oversentimental: saccharine
overshadow: blot; cloud
oversight: disregard; error; management; mistake; slip; trip
oversize: giant
overspread: cover; inundate; strew
overstate: amplify; magnify
overstated: sweeping
overstep: exceed
overstrain: sprain
overstuff: pall
oversupply: abundance
oversweet: saccharine
overt: aboveboard
overtask: drive
overtax: drive
overthrow: conquer; defeat; overturn; reduce; reverse; revolt; revolution; ruin; smash; upset
overtly: aboveboard
overtone: aura
overture: advance; offer; proposal
overturn: capsize; overthrow; upset
overturned: upset
overused: hackneyed; stereotyped
overweening: arrogant; proud; vain
overwhelm: astonish; cast; conquer; crush; dazzle; defeat; inundate; oppress; overcome; overpower; overthrow; strike; stun
overwhelmed: aghast
overwhelming: horrendous
overwork: drive
overworked: labored
overwrought: labored; rabid
overzealous: rabid
owing: outstanding
own: acknowledge; admit; allow; confess; have; hold; possess; tell
ownership: custody; possession; property; right
pace: plod; trudge; walk
pachydermatous: thick-skinned
pacific: composed; gentle; meek; mild; peaceable; peaceful; quiet; restful; smooth; still
pacifier: sedative
pacify: appease; calm; comfort; conciliate; moderate; propitiate; quell; quiet; reconcile; satisfy; settle; still; temper
pack: bundle; cram; crowd; flock; jam; package; parcel; run; stuff
package: bundle; pack; parcel
packed: populous
packet: bundle; pack; package; parcel
pact: agreement; alliance; compact; contract; convention; deal; peace
pad: compress; cushion; pillow
pagan deity: idol
pagan: atheist; heathen; profane
pageantry: ostentation; show
pain: ache; affliction; agony; anguish; anxiety; cost; distress; evil; exercise; grieve; hurt; ill; pang; rack; smart; throe; torment; trouble; wound
pained: sore
painful: bad; bitter; grievous; harrowing; pungent; sharp; smart; sore; sorry; tender; traumatic
pains: care; struggle; toil; trouble
painstaking: careful; conscientious; delicate; diligent; elaborate; laborious; sedulous
paint: cosmetic; depict; picture; portray
painter: artist
painting: picture
pair: brace; couple; span
pal: comrade
palace: castle
palatable: dainty; delicious; luscious; scrumptious
palatial: grand
palaver: babble; gossip; jabber

pale: blanch; bleach; decline; fade; fair; ghastly; light; lurid; pallid; peaked; pearly; sick; stake; wan
palfrey: mount
paling: pale
palisade: barrier
palladium: safeguard
palliate: excuse; smooth
palliative: sedative; therapeutic
pallid: cadaverous; lurid; pale; sallow; wan
palmer: pilgrim
palpable: actual; bare; clear; evident; manifest; obvious; patent; tangible; unmistakable; visible
palpitate: pant; pulsate; throb
palter: haggle; rationalize; whitewash
paltry: cheap; frivolous; little; mean; petty; poor; rascal; scanty; slight; slim; small; sorry; trifling; trivial; unimportant; vile
pampas: plain
pamper: indulge
pamphlet: tract
pan: scale
panacea: cure-all
panache: verve
pancake: cosmetic
pandemic: pest
pandemonium: bedlam; hell
pander: procure
panegyric: commendation; compliment; praise
panegyrize: eulogize; extol; praise
pang: agony; anguish; pain; throe
Panglossian: optimistic
panhandle: mooch
panic: alarm; consternation; dismay; fear; fright; horror; scare; terror
panjandrum: tycoon
panoply: array; dress
pant: blow; gasp; heave
pantywaist: weakling
paper over: whitewash
paper: form; piece; theme
papyrus: volume
parable: fable
parade: display; flourish; pageant; strut; swagger; vaunt
paradigm: blueprint
paradisaic: celestial
paradisial: celestial
paradoxical: contradictory
paragon: archetype; model; nonesuch; pattern
paragraph: passage
parallel: even
parallelism: parity; similarity
paralysis: stroke
paralyze: blunt; disable; dismay; dull; shock
parameter: criterion; principle
paramount: chief; dominant; main; preeminent; principal; sovereign
paramour: gallant
paranoia: insanity
paranoiac: insane
paraphernalia: equipment
paraphrase: translation
parasite: sycophant
parcel out: allot; apportion; mete; part; partition; ration; share
parcel: bundle; pack; package
parch: scorch
parched: arid; dry
parching: torrid
pardon: absolve; acquit; excuse; forgive; grace; overlook; remission; remit
pardonable: venial
pare down: abbreviate
pare: cut; peel; skin; trim
parentage: birth; descent; origin; stock
parlance: speech
parley: confer; conference; speech; talk
parliament: assembly
parochial: bigoted; small-minded; vernacular
parody: burlesque; caricature; caricature; travesty
paroxysm: agony; convulsion; frenzy; throe
parrot: impersonate; simulate
parry: repel
parsimonious: close; frugal; mean; mercenary; miserly; near; niggardly; penurious; selfish; small; sordid; spare; stingy
parsimoniously: nearly
part with: cast
part: branch; component; deviate; divide; division; element; limb; member; movement; partition; person; piece; portion; propor-

tion; region; separate; sever; share; way
partake: participate; share
partaker: partner
partial: narrow-minded; partisan; unfair; unjust
partiality: affection; bent; bias; favor; liking; penchant; predilection; prejudice; relish; respect; taste
participant: partner
participate: mingle; partake; share
participation: part
particle: bit; iota
particular: certain; chary; conscientious; dainty; definite; difficult; express; facet; nice; peculiar; precise; private; queasy; regard; respect; selective; separate; single; solicitous; some; special; squeamish; strict; way
particularity: particular
particularly: chiefly; especially; mostly; principally
partisan: adherent; follower
partisanship: party
partition: apportion; divide; division; screen
partner: accomplice; ally; associate; companion; comrade; helper; sidekick
partnership: alliance; association; business; company; concern; firm; house; society
parturition: birth; labor
party pooper: killjoy
party: band; body; company; faction; gang; troop
pasquinade: satire
pass or die away: fail
pass or go across: traverse
pass along: bequeath
pass away or on: die
pass away: disappear; fade; perish
pass judgment: judge
pass on or away: depart; part
pass on: bequeath; perish; proceed
pass out: faint
pass over: pass; slur; span
pass sentence upon: judge
pass through: permeate; pervade
pass,: antique; antique; old; old-fashioned; superannuated
passé: admission; answer; fly; gorge; melt; passage; protection; state; wander
passable: average; fair; mediocre; respectable; serviceable
passage: access; course; cut; entrance; lane; path; run; walk; way
passing: cosmetic; death; passage; temporary; transient
passion: addiction; ardor; enthusiasm; feeling; fervor; flame; fury; love; lust; rage; tear; temper; vehemence; wrath; zeal
passionate: amorous; angry; ardent; enthusiastic; excitable; feeling; fervent; fierce; fiery; hot; hotheaded; lurid; torrid; vehement; zealous
passionless: apathetic; cold
passive: inactive; inert; lifeless; patient; submissive
passport: pass; protection
passus: passage
password: watchword; word
past: old
paste: stick
pastel: tint
pastime: game; play; sport
pasty-faced: sallow
pasty: pallid; sallow
pat: stroke; touch
patch: mend; piece; repair
patent: apparent; certain; clear; evident; manifest; obvious; plain; unmistakable; visible
patented: patent
paternal: fatherly; male
path: course; lane; orbit; passage; street; trail; wake; walk; way
pathetic: affecting; piteous; pitiful; tragic
pathetical: pathetic
pathfinder: pioneer
pathway: path
patience: consideration; resignation; tolerance
patient: case; considerate; meek; passive; submissive
patois: dialect; jargon; slang; speech
patrimonial: ancestral
patrimony: heritage; inheritance; pedigree
patriotic: loyal
patriotism: loyalty
patron: advocate; caregiver; friend

patronage: countenance; custom; favor; protection
patronize: assist; countenance; favor; foster; support
patronizing: gracious
patrons: custom
patsy: scapegoat
patter: jargon
pattern: archetype; copy; example; fashion; form; model; nonesuch; original; paradigm; paragon; prototype; sample; scheme; shape; sort; specimen; stamp; standard; type
patulous: open
paucity: lack; want
paunch: abdomen
pauperize: bankrupt
pauperized: bankrupt
pause: break; check; hesitate; remission; stammer; stand; stay; stop; suspense; wait
pay or give attention to: heed
pay attention to: attend; mark; notice
pay attention: attend; mind
pay no attention or heed or regard to: disregard
pay out: spend
pay respect: attend
pay: acquit; compensate; consideration; disburse; discharge; expend; hire; income; payment; requite; reward; settle; wage
payback: repay
payment: compensation; consideration; pay; recompense; rent; satisfaction
peace: ease; harmony; order; quiet; serenity
peaceable: gentle; pacific; quiet; smooth; still
peaceful: calm; composed; even; gentle; meek; mild; moderate; pacific; peaceable; placid; quiet; restful; serene; smooth; sober; still; unruffled
peacefulness: calm; composure; peace; serenity
peak: height; pinnacle; summit; top
peaked: cadaverous; sharp
peal: blast; ring; roar
peanut butter: spread
pear-shaped: rich
pearl-gray: pearly
peart: brisk; lively
peasant: countryman; ignoble
pebbly: stony
peck: pick
Pecksniffian: hypocritical; sanctimonious; unctuous
peculate: steal
peculiar: aberrant; abnormal; characteristic; cranky; eccentric; exceptional; nondescript; odd; particular; preternatural; private; proper; queer; singular; special; strange; uncommon; unique; whimsical; wonderful
peculiarity: aberration; abnormality; attribute; characteristic; eccentricity; feature; idiosyncrasy; vagary
pecuniary: financial; monetary
pedagogue: instructor
pedant: blue
pedantic: orthodox
pedestal: base
pedestrian: hackneyed; lackluster
pedicel: stem
pedigree: ancestry; breed; parentage; stem; stock; strain
pedigreed: pure
peduncle: stem
peeking: prying
peel: pare; scale; skin; strip
peep: blink; peek
peeping: curious; prying
peer: associate; equal; noble; peek
peering: prying
peerless: matchless; nonpareil; preeminent; recherché; topnotch; unequaled; unique; unparalleled
peeve: gall; roil
peeved: miffed
peevish: cantankerous; cross; fractious; fretful; grouchy; hasty; moody; petulant; querulous; sour; splenetic; testy
peevishness: pet; petulance
peg: pin
pejorative: derogatory
pelage: pile
pelf: wealth
pellucid: bright; candid; clear; limpid; lucid; transparent
pelt: batter; hide; skin
peltry: pelt

pen: pound
penalize: lay; punish
penalty: cost
penchant: bent; inclination
pencil: beam
pendent: pendulous
penetrable: vulnerable
penetrate: cut; guess; permeate; pervade; pierce; search; see; soak; stab; stick; thrust
penetrating: acute; astute; deep; incisive; keen; perspicacious; pointed; profound; pungent; sharp; shrewd; smart; wise
penetration: intelligence; judgment; perspicacity
penitence: regret; remorse; repentance
penitent: obdurate; remorseful
pennant: standard
penniless: destitute; impecunious; miserable; poor
pennon: standard
penny-pinching: miserly
pensive: meditative; melancholy; reflective; thoughtful
pensiveness: melancholy
penumbral: dark; dusky
penurious: close; economical; frugal; mean; mercenary; miserly; niggardly; parsimonious; sordid; stingy
penuriously: nearly
penury: need; poverty; want
people: crowd; household; nation; race; settle
peppery: hot; irascible; petulant; pungent; quick
peppy: bubbly
perambulate: walk
perceivable: perceptible
perceive: comprehend; discern; distinguish; espy; hear; know; note; notice; observe; remark; scent; see; sense; take; understand; witness
perceiving: observation; perception
percept: perception
perceptible: apparent; clear; conspicuous; obvious; sensible; tangible; visible; vivid
perception: knowledge; notice; perspicacity; sensation; sense; taste; vision
perceptive: acute; observant; perspicacious; sentient; shrewd; tactful
perceptiveness: empathy; sensibility
perceptivity: empathy
perch: sit
percipient: conscious
percolate: ooze; strain
perdition: ruin
perdurable: immortal; perennial; permanent; stable
peregrinate: journey; roam
peremptory: arbitrary; authoritative; flat; positive; severe; summary
perfect: absolute; accomplish; blank; clean; complete; consummate; correct; downright; entire; exquisite; fine; finish; finished; fulfill; ideal; mature; mellow; polished; pure; regular; ripe; strict; thorough; whole
perfected: elaborate; finished; mature
perfectly: clean
perfervid: hectic; rabid
perfidious: abject; dishonest; disloyal; faithless; false; treacherous; unfaithful
perfidy: deceit; disloyalty; duplicity; treachery
perforate: bore; pierce; riddle
perforated: open
perforation: opening
perform: accomplish; achieve; act; discharge; do; effect; execute; exercise; finish; fulfill; give; make; operate; perpetrate; play; practice; realize; redeem; render; take; touch; transact; work
performable: practicable
performance: act; action; deed; discharge; exercise; operation; practice; work
performing: action
perfume: aroma; flavor; incense; odor; scent
perfumed: fragrant; odoriferous; sweet
perfunctory: formal; grudging; half-hearted
perfuse: imbue
periapt: talisman

peril: chance; danger; hazard; jeopardy; risk; venture
perilous: critical; mad; malignant; precarious; uncertain
perimeter: boundary; circuit; confine; periphery
period: age; circle; epoch; round; run; span; time; tract
periodic: regular
periphery: border; brim; circle; circuit; confine
perish: decay; die; dissolve; waste
perky: bubbly; jaunty
permanence: constancy; stability
permanent: constant; continual; durable; eternal; fast; immortal; perennial; perpetual; stable; standing; stock; undying
permeate: imbue; penetrate; pervade; soak
permissible: competent
permission: allowance; authority; consent; impunity; leave; liberty; pass; permit; privilege; sanction
permissive: capable
permit entrance: admit
permit: admit; agree; allow; allowance; authority; authorize; bear; consent; endure; have; indulge; let; permission; protection; suffer; vouchsafe; warrant
permitting: capable
permute: alter
pernicious: bad; deleterious; destructive; evil; fatal; harmful; injurious; malign; malignant; noisome; noxious; unwholesome
perorate: declaim
peroration: end
perpendicular: precipitous; sheer; upright; vertical
perpetual: chronic; constant; continual; endless; eternal; immortal; incessant; perennial; permanent; stable
perpetually: always; ever
perpetuate: continue; dwell; last
perplex: amaze; bewilder; confuse; disconcert; embarrass; entangle; nonplus; obfuscate; puzzle
perplexed: lost
perplexing: complex; difficult; hard; knotty; troublesome
perplexity: confusion; embarrassment; knot; mist
perquisite: bonus
persecute: bedevil; grind; oppress; vex; worry
persecution: affliction; oppression
perseverance: application; diligence; patience; tenacity
persevere: abide; continue; persist
persevering: constant; diligent; industrious; inflexible; patient; persistent; pertinacious; sedulous; stubborn; sturdy; true
persiflage: banter; raillery
persist in: continue
persist: abide; continue; endure; hold; persevere; stand; stick; survive
persistence: agitation; application; diligence; patience; perseverance
persistency: tenacity
persistent effort: application
persistent: assiduous; constant; diligent; industrious; invincible; obstinate; patient; pertinacious; perverse; single-minded; stubborn; tenacious; willful
persisting: assiduous; persistent
persona non grata: pariah
personable: pleasant
personage: celebrity; person; tycoon
personal identity: personality
personal knowledge: acquaintance
personal: direct; intimate; particular; pointed; private; subjective
personality: character; presence
personally: well
personate: impersonate; play; present; represent
personify: impersonate
persons: people
perspective: prospect
perspicacious: acute; astute; luminous; perceptive; sagacious; sharp; shrewd; wise
perspicacity: judgment
perspicuous: clear; luminous; plain; shrewd
perspiration: sweat
perspire: sweat
persuadable: receptive
persuade: argue; bend; coax; convince; entice; get; induce; influence; lead; plead; push; reason;

reconcile; satisfy; tempt; urge; win; work
persuasion: advice; belief; faith; opinion
persuasive: eloquent; stringent; strong
pert: bubbly; forward; impertinent; impudent; perky; rude; saucy
pertain or relate to: touch
pertain: attach; refer
pertaining: pertinent
pertinacious: obstinate; persistent; resolute; stiff; tenacious; unyielding
pertinacity: perseverance; tenacity
pertinence: application
pertinent: applicable; appropriate; apt; happy; relevant
pertness: impudence
perturb: agitate; disconcert; trouble; upset
perturbate: roil
perturbation: agitation; commotion; disturbance; excitement; hurry; ruffle; sensation; tumult; upset
perturbed: excited; unquiet; upset
pervade: imbue; permeate
perverse: contrary; cranky; evil; froward; intractable; moody; morose; obstinate; refractory; sinister; stubborn; unyielding; wayward; willful; wrongheaded
perversion: corruption
perversity: degradation
pervert: corrupt; twist; warp
perverted: corrupt; depraved; libertine; perverse; wry
pessimist: killjoy
pessimistic: cynical; world-weary
pest: nag; scourge
pester: annoy; bedevil; bother; fuss; harass; harry; molest; nag; persecute; plague; torment; trouble; vex; worry
pestilence: pest; plague
pestilential: contagious; noisome; noxious
pet: favorite; favorite; idol
peter out: shrink
petiole: stem
petition: appeal; application; apply; ask; beg; beseech; entreat; entreaty; pray; request; solicit; supplicate
petrify: appall; harden
pettish: fractious; fretful; hasty; moody; petulant
pettishness: petulance
petty sin or offense: peccadillo
petty: frivolous; little; mean; minor; paltry; small; small-minded; trifling; trivial; unimportant
petulancy: petulance
petulant: cantankerous; cross; cynical; fractious; fretful; hasty; irascible; irritable; peevish; peppery; querulous; quick; short; sour; splenetic; testy; waspish
phantasm: apparition; ghost; hallucination; phantom; vision
phantasmal: phantom
phantom: apparition; ghost; phantasm; shade; shape; specter; spirit; vision
pharisaical: hypocritical; sanctimonious
pharisee: hypocrite
phase: facet; state
phat: wonderful
phenomenal: extraordinary; wonderful
phenomenon: apparition; object
philanthropic: benevolent
philanthropy: kindness
philistine: barbarian
philosopher: sage
philosophy: ideology
phlegmatic: apathetic; cold; sluggish
phony: bogus; cheat; fake; false; mountebank; phony; spurious
photograph: picture
photoplay: picture
phrase: expression; word
phraseology: diction; expression; jargon; language; parlance
phrasing: expression; parlance; wording
phylactery: talisman
phylum: sort; type
physic: medicine
physical condition: fitness
physical: animal; corporal; material
physiognomy: countenance; visage
piacular: perverse; profane; shameless; sinful; sinister; ungodly; wicked; wrong

picaroon: pirate; robber
pick out: elect; prefer; select
pick: choose; prefer; preference; select; single; take
pickax: pick
picked: select
picket: demonstrate; pale; stake
pickle: mess; quagmire
pickpocket: thief
picky: queasy; selective
pictorialization: imagery
picture: fancy; icon; imagery; imagine; portray; scene; think
pictures: imagery
picturesque: graphic; quaint; romantic; vivid
piddling: trifling
piece: part; partition; play; portion; proportion; scrap; span
piecemeal: scrap
pied: dappled
pier: pile; pillar; upright
pierce: bite; bore; cut; penetrate; pick; riddle; run; search; stab; stick; thrust
piercing: acute; bitter; cutting; keen; penetrating; pointed; pungent; raucous; sharp
pietistic: sanctimonious
piety: devotion; grace
pig-headed: contrary
piggish: gluttonous
piggy: gluttonous
pigheaded: headstrong; inflexible; intractable; obdurate; persistent; perverse; refractory; restive; stubborn; willful
pike: stake
pilaster: column
pile or heap up: heap
pile: bank; collection; edifice; heap; mass; upright
pilfer: abstract; pick; rob; steal
pilferer: robber
pilgrimage: journey; trip
pillage: devastate; harry; loot; maraud; plunder; prowl; ravage; rob; sack; spoil; strip; waste
pillaging: predatory; sack
pillar: column; mainstay; post
pillory: stock
pillow: cushion
pilot: guide
pimp: procure
pimple: gathering
pin: clasp; fasten; fix; link; stab; stick
pinch hitter: surrogate
pinch: crisis; dash; emergency; pilfer; rob; stint; strait
pinchbeck: bogus; fake; phony
pinched: careworn; peaked
pinchpenny: miser
pine away: pine
pine for: long
pine: yearn,
pinguid: fat
pink: rosy
pinnace: tender
pinnacle: apex; height; peak; summit; top
pinpoint: ascertain; assign
pious: devout; godly; good; holy; religious; sanctimonious
pip: pit
pipe-dream: daydream
pipe: main; spout; warble
piquancy: sparkle; zest
piquant: hot; lively; poignant; pointed; pungent; racy; sharp; strong; tart; trenchant
pique: irritate; spite; umbrage
piqued: angry; irate
pirate: robber
pirouette: whirl
pis aller: recourse
pit: abyss; grave; hole
pitch: cast; shy; slant; tar; throw
pitchman: mountebank
pitchy: dark
piteous: affecting; pitiful; poor; sorrowful
pitfall: cheat; pit; trap
pith: substance
pithiness: brevity; conciseness
pithy: brief; compact; heavy; laconic; sententious; summary; terse
pitiable: forlorn; miserable; pathetic; piteous; pitiful; poor; sorry; wretched
pitiful: despicable; forlorn; piteous; sorry; tender; tragic; wretched
pitiless: beastly; brutal; cruel; inexorable; merciless; relentless; remorseless; ruthless; sanguinary; savage; stony; unmerciful; unrelenting; unsparing

pity: compassion; feeling; mercy; sympathy,
pitying: compassionate; sorry
pivot: center
pixie: brownie
pixilated: giddy
pixy: fairy
placard: bill; notice
placate: appease; conciliate; reconcile
place of interment: grave
place on or upon: apply
place: appointment; arrange; array; caste; deposit; lay; lie; locale; lodge; position; post; put; set; situation; sphere; spot; stand; station; true
placement: disposition; position
placid: composed; cool; easygoing; even; mild; peaceful; sedate; serene; still
plague: affliction; bedevil; bother; curse; destruction; grind; harass; harry; molest; pest; pester; rankle; ruffle; scourge; tease; torment; trouble; vex; worry
plain speaking: candor
plain-Jane: household
plain-spoken: broad
plain: apparent; artless; austere; bare; broad; candid; certain; clear; conspicuous; direct; distinct; dry; earthy; evident; express; fair; homely; household; humble; lackluster; level; low; lucid; luminous; manifest; naive; naked; obvious; open; ordinary; overt; palpable; patent; perspicuous; rough; round; rugged; severe; simple; sincere; smooth; special; tangible; unaffected; unequivocal; uniform; unmistakable; unvarnished
plainly: clearly
plainness: perspicuity
plainspoken: naked
plaint: murmur
plaintive: pathetic; sorrowful
plait: gather; twist; weave
plan for: prepare
plan out: cast
plan: agitate; arrange; blueprint; cast; chart; contemplate; contrive; counsel; design; device; devise; enterprise; forecast; game; hatch; idea; intent; maneuver; map; meditate; model; outline; plot; premeditate; prepare; project; proposal; propose; purpose; scheme; stratagem; system; theory; way
plane: craft; even; flat; plain; smooth
planet: sphere
planned: intentional; voluntary
planning: calculation
plant: factory; fix; lodge; set
plastered: cockeyed
plastic: flexible; malleable; soft
plate: scale
plateau: plain
platform: pace; stand
platitudinous: hackneyed
plaudit: applause; praise
plausible: glossy; ostensible; specious; tenable
play at ducks and drakes: scale
play parts: act
play the part of: act
play up: emphasize
play-act: simulate
play: act; caper; dally; fool; game; piece; romp; sketch; sport; swing; touch
playboy: prodigal
playful: comical; giddy; jocose; jolly; pleasant; sportive
playfulness: fun
plaything: sport
plea: answer; apology; entreaty; excuse
plead in favor of: advocate
plead: allege; argue; defend; show
pleasant-sounding: mellifluous
pleasant: affable; bright; cheerful; congenial; delightful; felicitous; genial; good; grateful; kindly; mild; nice; pleasing; pretty; smooth; soft; sweet
pleasantry: banter; humor; jest
please: amuse; charm; delight; entertain; exalt; feed; gratify; oblige; regale; satisfy
pleased: glad; happy
pleasing: amusing; congenial; delicious; delightful; fair; felicitous; grateful; interesting; nice; pleasant; pretty; soft; sweet

pleasingly plump: zaftig

pleasurable: delightful; felicitous; pleasant; pleasing; sweet

pleasure: admiration; delight; enjoyment; fun; happiness; joy; satisfaction; will

pleat: gather

plebeian: base; ignoble; low; mean; vulgar

plebeians: mass

plebians: crowd

plectrum: pick

pledge: assurance; guarantee; initiate; oath; plight; promise; promise; vow; wager; warrant; word

plenteous: abundant; ample; copious; plentiful; prodigal; rich; rife

plenteousness: abundance; plenty

plentiful: abundant; ample; copious; fat; fruitful; generous; large; liberal; opulent; prodigal; rich; rife

plentifulness: plenty

plenty: abundance; profusion

pleonastic: wordy,

plethora: plenty

pliable: flexible; limber; malleable; pliant; soft; supple

pliant: flexible; limber; malleable; submissive; supple

plight: case; fix; mess; predicament; situation; state; strait; trim

plod: pace; shamble; trudge

plodder: laggard

plot: conspiracy; conspire; contrive; game; hatch; intent; machination; maneuver; meditate; parcel; place; plan; practice; project; scheme; story; wangle

plotting: crafty; practice

ploy: machination

pluck: bravery; chutzpah; courage; gather; grit; mettle; pick

plucky: game

plug: shamble; stem; stop; stuff

plumb: lead; sound; upright; vertical

plummet: cascade

plump: fat; obese; roly-poly; stout; zaftig

plunder: devastate; harry; loot; maraud; pillage; prowl; ravage; ravage; rob; sack; spoil; strip; waste

plunderer: pirate

plundering: plunder; predatory; sack

plunge: dip; immerse; precipitate; sound; stab; submerge

pneumatic: zaftig

poach: infringe

pocket: pilfer

poem: lay; piece; stanza

poesy: poetry; verse

poetry: verse

poignant: acute; bitter; exquisite; keen; meaning; pungent; sharp; smart

point or needle: style

point man: pioneer

point of departure: base

point of view: aspect; light

point out: appoint; mark; show

point person: pioneer

point to: accuse

point woman: pioneer

point: aim; apex; burden; center; direct; issue; level; main; particular; peak; present; regard; respect; subject; theme

pointed: acute; applicable; compact; dry; meaning; poignant; sharp; trenchant

pointless: flat; ineffectual; inept; mindless; stereotyped; stupid

poise: balance; polish

poised: polished; polite

poison: contaminate; foul; taint; toxin; venom; virus

poisonous: contagious; deleterious; noisome; noxious; toxic; unhealthful; unhealthy; unwholesome; virulent

poke along: dawdle

poke: prod

poky: laggard

polar: cold; high

pole: bar; post; upright

polish: finish; gloss; grace; shine; smooth

polished: elegant; exquisite; finished; gentle; polite; refined; sleek; smooth; urbane

polite: affable; attentive; civil; cold; courteous; fair; gallant; gentle; gracious; humane; humble; nice; pleasant; polished; proper; refined; respectful; smooth; suave; urbane

politely: kindly

politeness: attention; decorum

politesse: decorum

politic: advisable; diplomatic; gingerly; judicious

political leader: politician

political: politic

politico: politician

polka-dot: dappled

poll: survey

pollute: contaminate; corrupt; debase; foul; poison; profane; roil; stain; sully; taint

polluted: foul; nasty; profane; turbid; unclean; ungodly

pollution: abomination; corruption

Pollyanna: optimistic

Pollyannaish: optimistic

poltroon: coward; cowardly; scoundrel; weakling

poltroonery: cowardice

polychromatic: opalescent

polymath: savant

pommel: beat

pomp: glory; magnificence; ostentation; show; splendor; state; vainglory

pompous: big; bombastic; grandiloquent; grandiose; large; majestic; state; tumid; turgid

pompousness: ostentation

ponder over: deliberate

ponder: brood; cast; consider; contemplate; digest; meditate; muse; reflect; revolve; ruminate; study; think; weigh; wonder

pondering: preoccupied; reflective

ponderous: bulky; clumsy; heavy; massive; unwieldy; weighty

pony: nag

poor substitute: apology

poor: bad; bare; barren; base; cheap; destitute; humble; ill; impecunious; low; mean; miserable; niggardly; penniless; ragged; scanty; short; slim; soft; sorry; thin; vile; weak; wretched

poorly: ill

popinjay: coxcomb; swell

populace: crowd; people

popular: common; current; favorite; general; vernacular

populate: people

population: nation

pore over: peruse

pornographic: filthy; indecent; nasty; obscene; salacious; X-rated

porous: open; rarefied

port: harbor

portal: entrance

portend: predict; presage; signify; threaten

portending: sinister

portent: omen; prediction; presage; sign; warning

portentous: bombastic; ominous; oracular; sinister

portière: curtain

portion: branch; divide; member; parcel; part; partition; piece; proportion; ration; region; scrap; share; stint

portly: fat; obese; plump; stout

portray: depict; describe; impersonate; rehearse; represent; sketch

portrayal: imagery

pose: affectation; attitude; position; posture; propose; set

posed: easygoing

poser: puzzle; riddle

posh: palatial

posit: propose

position: appointment; attitude; business; capacity; caste; credit; eminence; environment; facet; job; lay; lie; office; place; pose; post; posture; predicament; rank; reputation; set; situation; stand; standing; state; station; status; tenet

positive: absolute; actual; authoritative; certain; clear; confident; downright; emphatic; express; flat; peremptory; round; stiff; sure; tangible; tenacious

positively: absolutely; flat

positron: particle

possess: have; hold; monopolize; occupy; own

possession: custody; grasp; occupation; property

possessions: property; wealth

possibility: chance; potential; surmise

possible: earthly; feasible; likely; potential; practicable

post office: address

post: appointment; capacity; job; office; pile; place; position; set; shore; situation; stake; stand; station

poster: bill; notice

posterior: back; back

postpone: adjourn; continue; defer; delay; procrastinate; remit; respite; suspend

postponement: delay; respite

postscript: supplement

postulant: wannabe

postulate: assumption; principle

posture: attitude; bearing; facet; pose; position; set

posy: pretentious

pot: abdomen

potbelly: abdomen

potency: energy; force; machismo; strength; virtue

potent: energetic; mighty; powerful; sovereign; strong

potentate: sovereign

potential: dormant; force; latent; possible

potentiality: potential

pother: ado; commotion; fuss

potion: drink

potpourri: jumble; mixture

pouch: bag; sack

pound avoirdupois: pound

pound Scots: pound

pound sterling: pound

pound troy: pound

pound: batter; beat; grind; stamp; strike; throb

pour down: cascade

pour out: empty; teem

pour: abound; cascade; flow; gush; run; spout; stream

poverty-stricken: destitute; impecunious; miserable; penniless; poor

poverty: distress; necessity; need; paucity; penury; want

powder: crush; grind; pound

powdered: fine

power: ability; authority; capacity; command; credit; effect; empire; endowment; energy; force; gift; influence; main; might; moment; nerve; reign; stamina; strength; sway; virtue; weight

powerful: able-bodied; eloquent; energetic; mighty; muscular; potent; robust; stringent; strong; sturdy; vibrant; vigorous

powerless: impotent; ineffectual

précis: abridgment; abstract; argument; brief; summary; synopsis

practicable: feasible; possible; useful; viable

practical joke: trick

practical: active; earthy; feasible; handy; judicious; positive; realistic; useful; utilitarian

practice: appliance; application; custom; discipline; exercise; form; habit; knack; make; rehearse; rite; seasoning; study; technique; use; vogue; way; wont

practiced: conversant; experienced; finished; old; proficient; skillful; versed

pragmatic: earthy; practical; realistic

pragmatical: utilitarian

prairie: plain

praise: accolade; approve; celebrate; commend; commendation; compliment; eulogize; exalt; extol; glory; laud; name; paean; panegyric

praiseworthy: admirable; creditable

praising: praise

prank: caper; joke; trick

prankish: playful; sportive; zany

prankster: zany

prate: babble; gossip; jabber; talk; waffle

prating: garrulous

prattle: babble; gossip; jabber; talk; waffle

prattling: garrulous

pray: ask; beg; beseech; entreat; petition; solicit; supplicate

prayer: appeal; petition; request

preach: declaim

preamble: introduction; preface

prearrange: forecast; premeditate

precarious: critical; delicate; shaky; slippery; touchy; uncertain; unstable

precaution: foresight; safeguard

precede: head; lead; pioneer

precedence: lead; prerogative

precedent: advance; convention

preceding: above; advance; preliminary; previous

precept: charge; doctrine; mandate; proverb; regulation; requirement; rule

preceptor: guru; instructor

precinct: bailiwick

precincts: habitat; vicinity

precious: choice; costly; dear; exquisite; exquisite; favorite; good; invaluable; pay; pretentious; recherché; rich; sweet; valuable

precipitancy: haste

precipitate: anticipate; deposit; expedite; hasten; hasty; headlong; impatient; impetuous; quick; rash; sediment; subside

precipitation: haste; hurry

precipitous: abrupt; bluff; bold; headlong; sheer; unwary

precise: accurate; close; correct; critical; dead; definite; delicate; exact; explicit; express; faithful; formal; intimate; meticulous; minute; nice; particular; positive; prim; proper; punctilious; refined; scrupulous; strict; sure; true; unerring

precisely: particularly; right; true

precision: fidelity; truth

preclude: anticipate; enjoin; exclude; forbid; obviate; parry; prevent; prohibit; shut; stifle; stop

preconception: bias; prejudice

precontrive: premeditate

precursive: preliminary

precursor: harbinger; pioneer

predacious: predatory; rapacious; ravenous

predatory: avaricious; rapacious; ravenous

predesign: premeditate

predestinate: mean

predestine: doom; fate; ordain

predestined: fatal

predetermine: fate; ordain; premeditate; prescribe; set

predetermined: set; studied

predicament: case; difficulty; dilemma; fix; mess; plight; quagmire; quandary; situation; state; strait

predication: assertion; position

predict: forecast; presage; prophesy

predictable: usual

prediction: forecast; presage

predilection: aptitude; attachment; bent; bias; inclination; liking; love; partiality; penchant; pleasure; preference; prejudice; relish; taste

predispose: bias

predisposition: affection; bias; disposition; inclination; liking; penchant; predilection; prejudice; proclivity; taste; tendency

predominance: influence; sway

predominant: dominant; master; preeminent; prevailing; prevalent; sovereign; uppermost

predominate: prevail; reign

predominating: prevalent

preeminence: advantage; brilliance; excellence

preeminent: acclaimed; dominant; high; paramount; principal

preempt: monopolize

preface: introduction; preliminary

prefatory: preliminary

prefer: affect; choose; elect; favor; relish; select

preference: choice; fancy; favorite; inclination; liking; option; partiality; penchant; pleasure; predilection; relish; respect; taste; volition

preferred: favorite; select

prefixed: set

pregnant: big

prehistoric: ancient; high; primitive

preindicate: harbinger

prejudgment: prejudice

prejudice: bias; detriment; favor; inclination; partiality; penchant; predilection; proclivity; respect; slant; tendency

prejudiced: bigoted; intolerant; narrow-minded; opinionated; partial; unfair; unjust

prejudicial: injurious

preliminary: forward; preface

prelude: overture; preface; preliminary

premature: abortive; forward

premeditated: deliberate; intentional; leisurely; studied

premiere: acclaimed; debut

premise: ground

premium: bonus; bounty; prize; reward

premonition: hunch; notice; presage

preoccupation: obsession

preoccupied: absent-minded; rapt

preordain: fate

preparation: preliminary

preparatory: preliminary

prepare for action: alert

prepare: adapt; arrange; devise; draw; dress; get; mount; provide; qualify; ready; trim

prepared: about; mature; ready; ripe; trim

preponderant: prevailing

preponderate: predominate; prevail

preponderating: prevailing

prepossessing: charismatic

prepossession: bias; predilection

preposterous: absurd; foolish; ridiculous; silly; unreasonable

prepotency: ability; machismo

prepublication: advance

prerequisite: condition; mandate; necessary; requirement

prerogative: advantage; immunity; power; privilege

presage: harbinger; portent; predict; prediction; sign; threaten; warning

prescience: forecast; foresight

prescribe: apply; appoint; decree; enjoin; instruct; ordain; set

prescribed: certain; set

prescript: decree

prescription: decree; order

presence: appearance; face

present: actual; attendant; bounty; current; demonstrate; donation; endowment; exhibit; favor; gift; give; immediate; introduce; modern; offer; omnipresent; prefer; propose; render; represent; tender; ubiquitous

presentation: exposure; expression

presentiment: hunch; presage

presently: immediately

preservation: custody; protection

preserve: asylum; defend; guard; jam; keep; maintain; rescue; retain; safeguard; save; spread

preserver: savior

preserving: custody

preside over: command; hold

preside: moderate

press or squeeze out: express

press on: impel

press: assert; bear; compress; cram; crowd; crush; hasten; push; smooth; strain; stuff; throng; urge

pressing: urgent

pressure: drive; load; strain

prestidigitation: trick

prestige: face

presume: conjecture; consider; deduce; suppose; take; venture

presuming: familiar

presumption: assumption; assurance; chutzpah; impudence; pride

presumptive: familiar; impudent

presumptiveness: impudence

presumptuous: arrogant; audacious; bold; forward; impertinent; impudent; obtrusive; pert; proud; uppity

presumptuousness: chutzpah

presuppose: assume; presume; suppose

presupposition: assumption

pretence: gloss

pretend: act; affect; artificial; assume; counterfeit; fake; feign; seem; sham; simulate

pretended: affected; counterfeit; mock; ostensible; pseudo; sham; spurious

pretender: humbug; hypocrite; impostor; mountebank; phony

pretending: hypocritical; pretense

pretense: affectation; appearance; blind; bravado; excuse; face; humbug; mask; mockery; ostentation; phony; sham; show

pretension: affectation; claim; ostentation; pretense

pretentious: ambitious; artificial; bombastic; flash; grand; grandiloquent; grandiose; smart

pretentiousness: ostentation

preternatural: miraculous; supernatural; uncanny; unearthly; weird

pretext: appearance; blind; excuse; face; gloss; mask; mockery; ostentation; pretense; show
prettify: beautify; decorate; palliate
pretty up: decorate
pretty: beautiful; becoming; fair; precious
prevail on or upon: get
prevail on: persuade
prevail over: overrule
prevail upon: bring; induce
prevail: abound; predominate; reign; succeed; sway; triumph
prevailing: current; dominant; general; popular; predominant; prevalent; rife; usual
prevalent: common; current; dominant; general; pandemic; popular; predominant; prevailing; rife; usual
prevaricate: evade; lie; quibble
prevarication: evasion; lie; quibble
prevent: anticipate; bar; debar; defer; deter; discourage; exclude; forbid; hamper; hinder; impede; inhibit; obstruct; obviate; oppose; parry; prohibit; stay; stifle; stop; thwart
preventing: hindrance
prevention: parry; prohibition
previous: above
prevision: forecast; foresight; foresight
prey: game; prowl
preying: rapacious
price rise: advance
price: charge; cost; expense; set; value
priceless: exquisite; invaluable; precious; risible
prick: pang; pique; spur; stimulate
pride: arrogance; assumption; flock; run; vanity
prideful: lofty
prig: stiff
priggish: demure; prim; stiff; straitlaced
prim: demure; formal; stiff; straitlaced
primacy: machismo
primal: primitive; seminal
primarily: principally
primary: capital; elementary; fundamental; main; master; original; primeval; primitive; rudimentary; seminal
prime: bloom; capital; chief; excellent; main; master; primeval; primitive; principal; shining
primeval: high; old; original; primary; primitive
primigenial: primeval
priming: trim
primitive: abortive; ancient; barbarian; beastly; old; original; primary; primeval; rude
primordial: original; primeval; primitive
prince: sovereign
princely: grand; kingly; magnificent; majestic; regal; royal; sovereign
principal: capital; chief; dominant; fundamental; grand; great; head; high; leading; main; master; paramount; primary; prominent; right; sovereign; top
principally: chiefly; especially
principle: base; canon; criterion; doctrine; element; fundamental; honor; integrity; position; rule; tenet
principled: ethical; staunch
principles: ABC's; basics; platform
print: mark; stamp
printing: issue
prior: above; preliminary; previous
priory: cloister
prison: bond; hold
prissy: straitlaced
pristine: primeval; primitive
privacy: retreat; solitude
private eye: operative
private: clandestine; confidential; intimate; secluded; secret
privation: distress; hardship; loss; need; poverty; want
privilege: advantage; charter; claim; exemption; freedom; honor; immunity; liberty; prerogative
privileged: rarefied
privy: intimate; secret
prize: appreciate; approve; esteem; premium; reward; set; stake; treasure; trophy; value
prized: favorite
probability: chance

probable: feasible; likely
probation: trial
probationary: tentative
probe: examine; penetrate; search; sound
probity: goodness; honesty; honor; integrity; principle; sincerity; truth; virtue
problem: difficulty; dilemma; enigma; issue; puzzle; riddle
problematic: ambiguous; doubtful; iffy; shaky
problematical: uncertain
procedure: advance; course; custom; exercise; experiment; form; maneuver; method; operation; plan; policy; process; rite; system; tactics; technique
proceed: advance; do; emanate; flow; follow; issue; journey; move; originate; pass; progress; result; rise; run; spring
proceeding: action; occurrence; operation; procedure; process; progress
proceedings: minute
proceeds: profit
process: action; case; course; method; operation; practice; procedure
procession: advance; pageant
proclaim: announce; call; celebrate; declare; deliver; publish; release; reveal; ring; show; tell; utter
proclamation: cry; decree; statement
proclivity: affection; aptitude; bent; bias; disposition; inclination; liking; mind; penchant; tendency; turn; twist
procrastinate: dawdle; defer; delay; postpone
procrastinating: laggard
procrastination: delay
procrastinator: laggard
procreate: breed; engender; get
procure: achieve; acquire; attain; earn; gain; get; have; make; obtain; provide; purchase; secure; take; win
prod: incentive; incite; stimulate
prodigal: extravagant; fast; improvident; lavish; profuse
prodigality: abundance; plenty; profusion
prodigally: fast
prodigious: desperate; enormous; gigantic; monstrous; vast; wonderful
prodigy: phenomenon
produce an effect: act
produce: bear; breed; cause; create; crop; draw; elaborate; engender; form; give; grow; growth; induce; invent; make; mount; occasion; operate; provide; raise; spin; work; yield
product: growth; issue; make; outgrowth; produce; result
production: growth; make; produce
productive: active; big; fat; fertile; fruitful; plentiful; prolific; rich
proem: preface
profanation: abuse; sacrilege
profane: abuse; curse; foul; naughty; pollute; secular; ungodly; wicked
profanity: blasphemy; oath; sacrilege
profess: affect; pretend; purport
professed: ostensible
professing: profession
profession: business; occupation; trade; vocation; work
professor: intellectual; teacher
proffer: administer; advance; bid; bid; offer; prefer; present; propose; tender
proficiency: ability; accomplishment
proficient: able; competent; conversant; expert; finished; good; handy; skillful
profile: silhouette
profit: account; advantage; gain; good; use; welfare
profitable: active; available; beneficial; expedient; fat; fruitful; good; helpful; pay; useful
profitless: fruitless; futile; useless
profits: gain; income
profligacy: abomination; corruption; profusion
profligate: abandoned; corrupt; depraved; fast; immoral; libertine; lost; prodigal; profuse; roué; shameless; vicious; wicked

profound: abstruse; deep; fast; low; recondite; sound; unbroken; wise
profuse: abundant; copious; effusive; lavish; prodigal; unsparing
profusion: abundance; exuberance; plenty; wealth
progenitive: seminal
progeny: breed; brood; issue; race
prognostic: presage
prognosticate: predict; prophesy; threaten
prognostication: prediction
program: blueprint; scheme
progress against: stem
progress: advance; course; current; development; gain; move; movement; passage; proceed; run; scale; way
progression: current; progress; scale
progressive: broad-minded; forward; liberal
prohibit: ban; bar; debar; enjoin; exclude; forbid; inhibit; outlaw; shut
prohibited: taboo
prohibition: ban; taboo
prohibitionary: xenophobic
project: design; development; device; devise; enterprise; forecast; hatch; intend; plan; scheme; send; throw; work
projectile: ball
projecting: eminent; prominent
prolegomena: preface; preliminary
proletariat: crowd; mass
prolific: fertile; fruitful; productive; rich
prolix: garrulous; long; talkative; tedious; wordy
prologue: overture; preface
prolong: continue; extend; increase; lengthen; procrastinate; protract; spin
prolongation: extension
prolonged: long
promenade: stroll; walk
prominence: brilliance; eminence; eminence; height; hill
prominent: acclaimed; bold; conspicuous; eminent; great; high; notable; obtrusive; outstanding; remarkable; salient
prominently: especially
promiscuous: indiscriminate; miscellaneous
promise: bond; confer; guarantee; oath; swear; vow; warrant; word
promising: bright; fair; rosy
promissory note: bond
promontory: head
promote: abet; advance; aid; ameliorate; assist; better; dignify; elevate; encourage; exalt; foster; help; nourish; nurse; prefer; raise; serve; speed
promoter: advocate
promotion: advance; rise
prompt: animate; forward; induce; make; move; quick; ready; smart; spry; stir; suggest; swift; timely
promptitude: haste; hurry
promptly: readily
promptness: expedition
promulgate: announce; deliver; nourish; proclaim; publish; spread; utter
promulgation: issue
prone: apt; flat; low; passive; subject; vulnerable
proneness: bent; bias; disposition; inclination; liking; proclivity; tendency
pronounce: affirm; assert; declare; decree; deliver; give; pass; say; sound; speak; utter
pronounced: decided; emphatic; obtrusive
pronunciamento: decree
pronunciation: diction
proof: argument; criterion; evidence; experiment; ordeal; test; trial
prop: brace; mainstay; pillar; shore; stay; strength; strut; support; upright
propagate: breed; radiate; raise; reproduce; spread
propel: cast; drive; force; move; send; shove; throw
propensity: appetite; aptitude; bent; bias; capacity; inclination; liking; penchant; proclivity; turn; twist
proper: advisable; applicable; appropriate; becoming; befitting; congenial; correct; decent; decorous; expedient; felicitous; honorable; just; legitimate; meet; modest; nice; peculiar; pertinent; prim; prudish; relevant; respectable; right; seemly; sound; staid; true; well
properly: right; well
property: attribute; characteristic; feature; good; idiosyncrasy; mean; money; quality; wealth
prophecy: prediction
prophesy: predict
prophetic: oracular
propinquity: vicinity
propitiate: appease; conciliate; favor; reconcile
propitious: bright; fortunate; friendly; good; happy; lucky; opportune; prosperous
proportion: average; balance; share; symmetry
proportionate: equal
proportions: size
proposal: advance; bid; design; offer; overture; project; tender; theory
propose: advance; bid; design; intend; move; offer; plight; proffer; project; purpose; suggest
proposition: advance; design; offer; overture; position; principle; proposal
propound: advance; pose; propose
propriety: decorum; etiquette; fitness; modesty
prorogue: adjourn
prosaic: flat; household; lackluster; pedestrian; stupid; tame; vapid; wearisome
prosaicism: platitude
proscribe: ban; enjoin; exclude; outlaw
proscription: ban
proscriptive: intolerant
proselyte: convert; neophyte
proselytize: convert
prospect: aspect; calculation; expectation; foresight; scene; view
prosper: flourish; succeed; thrive
prosperity: welfare
prosperous: fortunate; happy; lucky; thrifty; wealthy
prostitute: abuse
prostitution: abuse
prostrate: exhaust; flat; low; prone
prostration: obeisance
prosy: prosaic; wearisome
protect: cover; defend; guard; harbor; preserve; safeguard; screen; secure; shade; shelter; wall; watch
protected: sacred; safe; secure
protecting: fatherly
protection: convoy; cover; custody; escort; guard; harbor; keeping; refuge; safeguard; screen; shelter
protective: fatherly
protector: caregiver; champion; guard; guardian; patron
protest: declare; demonstrate; exclamation; object; plaint
protestation: protest
protesting: repugnant
protocol: propriety
prototype: archetype; model; original; pattern; type
protract: extend; lengthen; prolong; spin
protracted: late; long
protraction: extension
protrude: project; swell
protruding: eminent; obtrusive
protuberance: bunch; swell
protuberant: eminent; prominent
proud: arrogant; big; conceited; haughty; high; lofty; vain
provable: factual; genuine
prove: argue; bear; control; establish; experiment; probe; show; tempt; terminate; test; try
provender: feed; provision
proverb: byword; maxim
provide aid: administer
provide for: cover; maintain; provide; support
provide: accommodate; accomplish; equip; furnish; give; prepare; serve; supply
provided: if
providence: caution; precaution; prudence
provident: cautious; economical; frugal; politic; prudent; thrifty
providing: if
province: bailiwick; capacity; circle; circuit; realm; sphere; terrain
provincial: small-minded; vernacular
provincialism: dialect

provision: condition; stock
provisional: makeshift
provisions: cheer; food; maintenance
proviso: condition; provision
provocation: spur; stimulus
provoke: animate; arouse; enrage; exasperate; excite; gall; incense; incite; irritate; kindle; madden; offend; pester; roil; rouse; spur; stimulate; stir; tantalize; taunt; tease; tempt; torment; vex; wake
provoked: angry; irate; mad
prow: bow
prowess: bravery; heroism
prowl: lurk; roam
proximate: immediate
proximity: presence; vicinity
proxy: surrogate
prude: blue; stiff
prudence: calculation; caution; foresight; judgment; policy; precaution; virtue; wisdom
prudent: advisable; careful; cautious; discreet; gingerly; judicious; politic; sage; sane; thoughtful; wise
prudential: politic
prudery: modesty
prudish: blue; demure; modest; squeamish; straitlaced
prudishness: modesty
prune: abbreviate; cut; top; trim
prunes and prisms: prim
prurient: lascivious; salacious; wanton
pry: kibitz; peek
prying: busy; curious; inquisitive; meddlesome; obtrusive
pseudo: bogus; phony
psychic: mental
psychological: mental
psychosis: lunacy
psychotic: mental
pub: bar; tavern
public eye: limelight
public house: tavern
public notice: limelight
public: common; community; household; open; overt; people; state
publication: air
publicity: air; limelight
publicize: announce; post; publish; tell
publicness: limelight
publish: announce; declare; deliver; emit; give; issue; proclaim; release; reveal; show; spread; tell; utter
pucker: gather
puckish: playful
pudgy: fat; obese; roly-poly
puerile: childish; frivolous; infantile
puff up or out: inflate
puff up: billow; rise
puff: blow; gasp; pant
pugnacious: aggressive; quarrelsome; scrappy
puissance: ability; might; power
puissant: mighty; potent; strong
puke: cast
puky: queasy
pulchritude: beauty
pulchritudinous: beautiful
pule: cry
pull or pry out: extract
pull apart: tear
pull off: perpetrate
pull: drag; draw; hale; pluck; whip
pulley: block
pulpit: platform
pulsate: beat; palpitate; pant; throb
pulsating: vibrant
pulsation: beat; stroke
pulse: pulsate; throb
pulverize: crush; grind; pound
pulverized: fine
punch: beat; droll
punchy: groggy
punctilious: exact; formal; religious; scrupulous; stiff
punctual: timely
punctuate: emphasize
puncture: pierce; riddle; stick; thrust
pundit: savant
pungency: strength
pungent: hot; peppery; piquant; poignant; racy; rank; sharp; strong
punish: chasten; correct; discipline; pay; persecute; requite; scourge; thrash; whip
punishment: discipline; pay; scourge
puny: sickly

pupil: disciple; follower; neophyte; scholar; student

puppyish: playful

purblind: blind

purchasable: venal

purchase: buy; trade

pure: absolute; authentic; blank; candid; chaste; clean; clear; fair; fresh; good; guiltless; holy; honest; innocent; just; main; mere; modest; neat; perfect; prudish; sheer; single; stark; sweet; unmixed; unsophisticated; upright; virgin; virtuous

purebred: pure

purge: heal

purified: clean; refined

purify: clean; clear; concentrate; heal; purge; sanctify; strain

puritanical: blue; precise; prim; straitlaced

purity: excellence; honor; modesty; virtue

purl: ripple

purlieus: vicinity

purloin: abstract; pilfer; steal

purport: design; effect; meaning; significance; signify; spirit

purpose: account; aim; cause; contemplate; counsel; decide; design; end; intend; intent; mark; mean; meaning; mind; motive; object; pleasure; propose; reason; resolve; sake; score; think; thought; view; will

purposeful: conscious; deliberate; earnest; intentional; resolute; single-minded; steadfast; voluntary

purposeless: ineffectual; mindless

purposive: deliberate; stiff

purse: bag; stake; wherewithal

pursue: course; follow; hold; hunt; run; seek

pursuit: business; hunt; occupation; search; trade; vocation

purvey: feed; furnish; serve; sustain

purveying: provision

purview: bailiwick

push: bear; crowd; drive; energy; expedite; incite; shove; thrust; urge

pushing: aggressive; bold

pushover: romp

pushy: obtrusive

pusillanimity: cowardice

pusillanimous: afraid; cowardly; faint; nerveless; recreant; tame; timid

pustule: boil; gathering; sore

put or cut apart: sever

put or set right: remedy

put a question to: ask

put aground: beach

put an end to: abolish; demolish; discontinue; murder; quell

put apart: separate

put aside: renounce

put away: conceal

put down: crush; pan; quell; repress; stifle

put forth effort: try

put forth: do; give

put forward: offer; prefer

put into position: mount

put off or aside: waive

put off: adjourn; cast; dawdle; defer; delay; postpone; procrastinate; remit; respite

put on rations: ration

put on: assume; pretend; simulate

put out: abolish; dismay; extinct; issue; trouble

put right: rectify

put to death: execute

put to use: apply; use

put together: assemble; fabricate

put up with: abide; allow; bear; brook; support

put up: rear

put-on: artificial; recherché

put-out: miffed

put: cast; deposit; lay; lodge; place; position; set; stand

putrefaction: corruption; decay; rot

putrefied: rotten

putrefy: corrupt; decay; decompose; rot

putrescence: corruption

putrescent: corrupt; rotten

putrid: corrupt; foul; noisome; rank; rotten

putterer: dabbler; dilettante

puzzle out: decipher

puzzle: bewilder; enigma; knot; nonplus; perplex; problem; riddle

puzzled: doubtful; lost

puzzlement: wonder

puzzling: ambiguous; dark; hard; mysterious

pygmy: dwarf

pyre: pile

quack: humbug; mountebank; rogue

quadruped: brute

quaff: drink

quail: recoil; wince

quaint: odd; primitive; recherché; whimsical

quake: quiver; shiver; throb; tremble; tremor

quaking: tremor

qualification: nature; reserve

qualified: able; capable; competent; eligible; experienced; finished; good; proficient; skillful

qualify: adapt; entitle; moderate; modify; palliate; soften; temper

qualities: stuff

quality: attribute; aura; character; characteristic; endowment; flavor; goodness; nature; property; sort; touch; virtue

qualm: pang; scruple

qualmish: queasy

quandary: difficulty; dilemma; emergency; predicament

quantity made: make

quantity: deal; mass; number; parcel; piece; volume

quarrel: brawl; breach; contention; contest; controversy; disorder; dispute; feud; misunderstanding; row; strife; tiff; variance

quarrelsome: cantankerous; ugly

quarry: game

quarter: lodge; part; region; sphere

quash: crush; nullify; quell; repress; stamp

quasi: apparent

quatrain: stanza

quaver: quake; tremble

quean: prostitute

queen: sovereign

queer fish: crackpot

queer: aberrant; abnormal; cranky; curious; droll; fantastic; odd; peculiar; queasy; singular; strange; uncommon; unusual; whimsical; wild

queerish: queasy

quell: alleviate; appease; crush; repress; soften; stay; vanquish

quenched: extinct

querulous: fretful; peevish

query: inquire; inquiry; question; question

quest: search

question: ask; contest; demand; dilemma; doubt; enigma; inquire; inquiry; issue; matter; probe; problem; puzzle; riddle; wonder

questionable: dubious; equivocal; uncertain

questioner: iconoclast

questioning: inquiry; inquisitive; quizzical

quibble: dodge; evade; prevaricate

quibbling: evasion

quick-and-dirty: slapdash

quick-tempered: excitable; hasty; irascible; passionate

quick-thinking: cagey

quick-witted: bright; cagey; clever

quick: active; adroit; agile; alert; alive; astute; brisk; clever; dexterous; expert; fast; fleet; hasty; impulsive; intelligent; keen; lively; living; nimble; observant; rapid; ready; round; sharp; shrewd; smart; spry; sudden; swift

quicken: advance; animate; enliven; expedite; hasten; hurry; inform; intensify; invigorate; precipitate; revive

quickening: living

quickly: fast; readily

quickness: expedition; haste; hurry; rapidity; sensibility; speed; velocity

quiescence: abeyance; suspense

quiescent: dormant; motionless; passive; silent; still

quiet down: lower

quiet: allay; appease; calm; composed; composure; cool; ease; easy; gentle; lay; low; noiseless; pacific; pacify; patient; peace; peaceable; placid; quell; reticent; sedate; settle; silent; slack; sober; soften; staid; still; subside; taciturn

quietener: sedative

quieter: sedative

quietude: ease; quiet

quintessence: spirit

quip: jest; joke

quirk: attribute; eccentricity; fancy; idiosyncrasy; vagary; whim

quirkiness: eccentricity,

quit: abandon; abdicate; depart; desert; discontinue; forsake; leave; part; relinquish; renounce; resign; stop; vacate

quite: even; pretty; right; sheer; stark; well

quittance: abdication

quitter: weakling

quiver: pulsate; quake; shake; shudder; totter; tremble; vibrate; waver; waver

quivering: shaky; tremble; tremor; tremulous

quivery: shaky; skittish

quixotic: romantic; wild-eyed

quiz: test

quota: portion; share

quotation: extract

réclame: limelight

rabbit's foot: talisman

rabble: crowd

rabid: fanatical; mad; wild-eyed

race: ancestry; birth; breed; course; course; kind; nation; pedigree; people; run; sort; stem; stock; strain; succession

racist: xenophobic

rack: agony; anguish; pace; torment

racket: bedlam; hubbub; noise; ruckus

rackety: raucous; rowdy

racy: piquant; strong

radiance: brilliance; light; luster; shine

radiant: bright; lucid; luminous; magnificent; shining

radiate: beam; shine; spread

radiating: bright

radical: extreme; forward; organic; rabid; underground

radioactive: dirty

rage: anger; boil; fashion; frenzy; fret; fume; fury; indignation; novelty; passion; rampage; storm; tear; wrath

ragged: seedy; shabby

ragging: raillery

raging: mad; rabid; wrathful

ragout: stew

ragtime: swing

raid: descent; harass; maraud

rail at: abuse; ridicule; scold; tease

railing: barrier; invective; traverse

raillery: jest; joke; ridicule

raiment: apparel; array; clothes; dress; garb; wardrobe

rain: deposit; sprinkle; storm; wet

rainstorm: storm

rainy: dirty; foul; wet

raise or make objection: demur

raise a nap: tease

raise the pride of: advance

raise the value of: appreciate

raise: advance; ameliorate; breed; construct; dignify; edify; elevate; erect; exalt; grow; heave; hoist; lift; mount; nurse; promote; purchase; rear; uphold

raison d'être: reason

rake: blackguard; libertine; roué

rakish: salacious

rally: demonstrate; recover; ridicule

rallying cry: catchword

ram: jam

ramble: roam; rove; saunter; stroll; stroll; wander

rambling: aberrant; aberration

rambunctious: robust; rowdy

ramification: branch

ramify: branch

rampart: wall

ramshackle: seedy; shabby; tacky

rancid: rank

rancor: grudge; malevolence; malice; spite

rancorous: acrimonious; implacable; malevolent; malignant; spiteful; vindictive

random: casual

randomness: serendipity

randy: lascivious

range: array; circuit; course; extent; habitat; latitude; place; ramble; rank; reach; roam; rove; scope; size; stretch; swing; wander

rank and file: rank

rank: arrange; array; breed; caste; credit; eminence; marshal; order; place; position; quality; range; rotten; sort; sphere;

standing; state; station; status; strong

ransack: loot; maraud

ransom: redeem; rescue; salvage

rant: declaim; rampage; storm

rap: blow; pan; stroke

rapacious: avaricious; ferocious; gluttonous; greedy; predatory; ravenous; voracious

rapacity: greed

rape: abduct; abduction; arrest; crime; force; loot; outrage; pillage; plunder; sack; spoil; violation

rapid: express; fast; fleet; hasty; quick; swift

rapidity: haste; speed; velocity

rapidly: fast

rapine: pillage; plunder; sack

rapist: abductor

rapport: sensibility

rapscallion: blackguard; rascal; rogue; scamp; scoundrel; villain

rapt: spellbound

raptorial: rapacious; ravenous

rapture: bliss; delight; ecstasy; joy; passion; trance; transport

rapturous: delightful; ecstatic; rapt

rare treat: delicacy

rare: admirable; choice; close; curious; exceptional; exquisite; exquisite; extraordinary; odd; offbeat; recherché; remarkable; scarce; singular; strange; tenuous; thin; uncommon; unique; unusual; valuable

rarefied: tenuous; thin

rarefy: thin

rarely: seldom

rarest: extreme

raring to go: eager

rarity: antique; peculiarity

rascal: blackguard; knave; rogue; scamp; scoundrel; swindler; vagabond; villain

rascality: chicanery

rascally: bad; rascal

rash: adventurous; blind; daredevil; desperate; hasty; hotheaded; impetuous; impulsive; precipitate; reckless; unwary; wild

ratchet: catch

rate: abuse; account; calculate; pace; scold; set; stint; value

rather: well

ratification: sanction

ratify: affirm; approve; confirm; espouse; sanction; sustain

ratiocinate: reason

ratiocination: reason

rational: conscious; judicious; lucid; mental; reasonable; sagacious; sane; sensible; sober; sound; wise

rationale: reason; subject; theory

rationality: coherence

rationalization: reason

rationalize: reason

rations: food

rattle: noise

ratty: seedy

raucous: barbarian; hoarse; rough; rowdy

ravage: desolate; destroy; devastate; harry; maraud; plunder; sack; spoil; waste

ravaged: careworn; desolate; waste

ravaging: predatory

rave: declaim; fume; rage; rampage; wander

ravel: snarl

raven: rook

ravening: gluttonous; ravenous

ravenous: ferocious; gluttonous; greedy; hungry; rapacious; savage; voracious

ravenousness: greed

ravine: gorge; pass

raving: frenzy; mad; rage; wild-eyed

ravish: abduct; charm; delight; force; outrage

ravisher: abductor

ravishment: abduction; violation

raw recruit: dabbler

raw-boned: gaunt; spare

raw: cold; crude; fresh; inexperienced; rude

rawhide: hide

ray: beam; gleam

raze: demolish; destroy; level; overthrow

razor-sharp: keen

re-create: renew

reach a point: arrive

reach forth: stretch

reach: access; achieve; attain; extent; gain; get; grasp; hit; range; run; span; spread; stretch; touch; win

reachable: receptive

reaching: arrival

react: recoil

reactionary: orthodox

reactivate: revive

reactive: sentient

read: peruse; study

readable: clean

readiness: aptitude; capacity; enterprise; generosity

reading: study

ready: about; adroit; agile; available; dexterous; enterprising; forward; glib; good; mature; mount; nimble; ripe; sharp; skillful; spry; swift

reagent: stain

real estate: property

real: actual; authentic; factual; genuine; intrinsic; native; palpable; physical; sincere; solid; substantial; tangible; true; unaffected

realistic: vivid

reality: nature; object; truth

realization: achievement; sense

realize: accomplish; achieve; acknowledge; effect; fulfill; imagine; understand

really: absolutely

realm: bailiwick; kingdom; monarchy; nation; sphere

reanimate: refresh; revive

reap: cut; gather; pick

rear: back; breed; foster; nurse; raise; reverse

rearrange: ruffle; stagger

rearrangement: permutation

rearward: backward

reason upon: argue

reason: account; aim; apprehension; argue; argument; brains; cause; deduce; discuss; ground; intellect; intelligence; matter; mind; motive; object; occasion; place; plead; sake; score; subject; view

reasonable: fair; judicious; legitimate; lucid; moderate; rational; sane; sensible; sober; sound; tenable; wise

reasonably: well

reasoned: practical

reasoning: argument; conscious; mental; reflective; sane; sharp

reassure: encourage

reawake: revive

rebarbative: forbidding

rebate: abate; allowance

rebel: defect; mutiny; rebellious; revolt; rise

rebellion: insurrection; mutiny; revolt; revolution; sedition; uprising

rebellious: defiant; disobedient; mutinous; rebel; recalcitrant

rebound: bound; recoil; reflect; skip; spring

rebounding: resilient

rebuff: check; refuse; reject; repel; resist

rebuild: restore

rebuke: admonish; censure; chide; correct; reprimand; reproach; reprove; scold; snub

rebus: knot

rebut: refute

recalcitrant: defiant; refractory; restive

recall to duty: admonish

recall: mind; open; overrule; recollect; remember; retain; revive; think; withdraw

recant: forsake; recall; renounce; withdraw

recantation: recall

recapitulate: enumerate; recite; rehearse; repeat

recapture: regain

recede: ebb; give; retire; retreat

receipt: check; warrant

receipts: income

receive: accept; acknowledge; admit; entertain; have; imbibe; see; swallow; take

received: orthodox; popular

receiving: passive

recent: fresh; late; modern; new

recently deceased: late

recently: new

receptacle: bag; case

reception: admittance

receptive: advisable; passive; sentient

recess: abeyance; respite

reciprocal: alternate; mutual; symbiotic

reciprocate: alternate; exchange

reciprocity: exchange

recital: account; narrative; relation; relation; story
recitation: relation
recite: narrate; recount; rehearse; relate; repeat; say
rectitude: right
reckless: audacious; careless; daredevil; desperate; fast; hasty; headlong; hotheaded; mad; perfunctory; precipitate; prodigal; rash; thoughtless; wanton; wild
recklessly: fast; pell-mell
reckon: account; calculate; call; cast; compute; deduce; estimate; judge; make; number; repute; score; tell
reckoning: bill; calculation; score
reclaim: recover
recline: lie; stretch
recluse: solitary
reclusive: antisocial
recognition: celebrity; perception; sense
recognize: acknowledge; discern; distinguish; know; notice; own; sense
recognized: orthodox
recoil: shrink; shy; spring; wince,
recoiling: resilient
recollect: recall; remember; think
recollection: mind; recall; remembrance
recommend to: advise
recommend: advise; advocate; approve; commend; move; propose; suggest; urge
recommendation: advice; caveat; commendation; counsel; proposal
recompense: compensate; compensation; consideration; pay; premium; requite; restitution; retribution; reward; satisfaction; wage
reconcile: accommodate; accord; adapt; adjust; conciliate; mediate
recondite: abstruse; dark; deep; mysterious; occult; rarefied; secret
recondition: remedy
reconsideration: review
reconstruct: restore
record: account; act; catalogue; history; inventory; minute; note; observation; register; score; story; trace
recount: describe; enumerate; narrate; recite; rehearse; relate; tell
recoup: salvage
recourses: wherewithal
recover: mend; reclaim; redeem; regain; rescue; retrieve; revive; salvage
recovery: rescue
recreant: cowardly; false; treacherous; unfaithful; weakling
recreation: pastime; play; sport
rectification: mend
rectify: adjust; better; correct; improve; mend; redress; reform
rectitude: honesty; integrity; principle; probity; virtue
recumbent: prone
recuperate: recover
recurrent: constant; continual; regular
recurring: continual
recusant: bohemian; obstinate
recycle: salvage
red-blooded: able-bodied
red: lurid; rosy; ruddy
reddish: rosy; ruddy
redecorate: refurbish
redeem: deliver; ransom; rescue; salvage
redeemer: savior
redemption: ransom; rescue
redistribute: proportion
redneck: yahoo
redo: repeat
redolence: aroma; odor; perfume; scent
redolent: fragrant; odoriferous; sweet
redoubtable: stalwart
redress: relief; remedy; repair; reprisal; restitution
reduce to a mean: average
reduce to particles or fragments: disintegrate
reduce to ruin: ruin
reduce: abase; abate; abbreviate; abridge; condense; conquer; contract; cut; debase; depress; diminish; ease; humble; lessen; lower; moderate; modify; palliate; pare; qualify; relax; repress; resolve; shorten; slack; slash; subdue; subordinate; thin; trim; waste; weaken

reduced: poor
reduction: abbreviation; abridgment; decrease; trim
redundancy: excess; exuberance
redundant: superfluous; wordy,
reduplicated: identical
reecho: repeat; ring
reeds: rush
reedy: tinny
reef: bar
reel: careen; stagger; totter; vacillate
reeling: giddy
reestablish: renew; restore
reexamination: review
refer to: mention; note; regard; respect
refer: apply; ascribe; assign; bear; fix; impute
referee: judge; moderate; umpire; umpire
reference: bearing; mention; regard; relation; respect
referral: reference
refine: clear; elaborate; elevate; polish; smooth; test; try
refined: chaste; civil; distinguished; elegant; exquisite; fine; finished; gentle; nice; polished; polite; rarefied; urbane
refinement: delicacy; elevation; finish; grace; polish
refining: humane
reflect on: meditate
reflect upon: contemplate; digest; revolve
reflect: consider; deliberate; glance; meditate; muse; ponder; ruminate; study; think
reflecting: meditative; reflective
reflection: consideration; criticism; image; study; thought
reflective: contemplative; pensive; thoughtful
reflex: involuntary; urge
reflux: ebb
reform: better; correct; liberal; modify; reformation
reformation: reform
refractory: contrary; defiant; disobedient; fractious; froward; inflexible; intractable; mutinous; obstinate; opposite; rebellious; recalcitrant; restive; stubborn; unruly; vicious; wayward; willful
refrain or abstain from: resist
refrain from: help; spare
refrain: burden
refresh: animate; comfort; regale; revive; soothe; ventilate
refreshing: fresh; grateful
refuge: asylum; cover; harbor; home; port; protection; recourse; retreat; shelter
refulgence: brilliance; splendor
refulgent: bright
refund: repay; replace
refurnish: refurbish
refusal: demur
refuse: decline; demur; deny; object; oppose; reject; remain; repel; spurn; waste
regain: reclaim; recover; retrieve; salvage
regal: grand; kingly; lordly; majestic; royal; sovereign
regale: treat
regalia: dress; finery
regard with aversion: abominate
regard with repugnance: abhor; abominate
regard: account; admiration; attachment; attention; care; compliment; consider; consideration; contemplate; credit; deem; esteem; estimation; hear; heed; hold; judge; love; mark; mind; note; notice; observe; piety; reckon; reference; relation; remark; reputation; repute; respect; sake; see; take; think; thought; touch; treat; value; view; watch; worship
regardful: attentive; thoughtful
regarding: observation
regardless: reckless; unmindful
regenerate: renew
regimen: food
region: circle; circuit; part; place; range; terrain; tract; zone
regional: vernacular
register: account; catalogue; inventory; list; note; record; record; roll; schedule
registration: register
registry: register
regress: ebb
regression: ebb
regret: deplore; grief; remorse; repent; repentance; sorrow; tear

regretful: bad; remorseful; sorry
regrettable: grievous
regular: clear; consecutive; conventional; customary; equable; equal; even; exact; formal; general; habitual; just; legitimate; orderly; ordinary; orthodox; run; smooth; steadfast; steady; uniform; usual
regularity: constancy; course; order; symmetry,
regulate: adjust; conduct; direct; guide; manage; moderate; order; proportion; rectify; set; shape; time
regulation: control; discipline; disposition; management; rule
regulations: discipline
rehearsal: relation; story
rehearse: enumerate; relate; repeat; say
reign over: control
reign: control; govern; sway
reimburse: compensate; pay; repay; requite
rein: bit; curb
reinforcement: supplement
reinspirit: revive
reinstate: renew; restore
reinvigorate: refresh; revive
reiterate: recapitulate; repeat; say
reject: cast; decline; deny; dismiss; eliminate; except; exclude; nauseate; pan; rebuff; refuse; renounce; repel; repudiate; spurn
rejected: abandoned; waste
rejection: rebuff
rejoice: glory; triumph
rejoicing: mirth
rejoin: answer; reply; retort
rejoinder: answer; reply; response; retort
rejuvenate: renew
relate to: concern; regard; respect
relate: ally; bear; describe; impart; narrate; recite; recount; refer; rehearse; repeat; spin; tell; ventilate
related: near
relating or relative to: about
relating: pertinent; relation
relation: alliance; bearing; capacity; concern; connection; history; proportion; recital; reference; regard; relationship; respect; story
relationship: alliance; connection; kinship; rapport; relation
relative: connection
relax: give; loose; melt; remit; slack; slacken; yield
relaxation: ease; remission; slack
relaxed: easygoing; laid-back; lax; offhand; slack
release or discharge: acquit
release: absolve; deliver; discharge; dismiss; escape; excuse; exonerate; free; liberate; loose; pardon; quit; ransom; relief; remission; remit; rescue
released: loose; quit
relent: relax
relentless: austere; bitter; close; cruel; hard; implacable; incessant; inexorable; inflexible; merciless; pitiless; remorseless; ruthless; severe; single-minded; unmerciful; unrelenting; unsparing
relevance: application
relevant: applicable; apt; felicitous; pertinent
reliable: authentic; certain; faithful; firm; good; infallible; responsible; safe; solid; sound; stable; steadfast; sure; true; trustworthy
reliance: belief; confidence; credit; faith; hope; trust
relic: memento
relics: remain
relief: aid; comfort; consolation; cure-all; help; panacea; redress; remedy; remission; respite; solace; succor; support; surrogate; suspense
relieve: aid; allay; alleviate; assist; comfort; console; discharge; ease; exonerate; free; help; palliate; redress; respite; slacken; solace; soothe; succor; support; unburden
religion: devotion; faith; ideology
religious: devout; godly; good; pious; solemn
religiousness: devotion
relinquish: abandon; abdicate; allow; cede; deliver; desert; forsake; give; leave; quit; renounce; resign; surrender; vacate; waive; yield

relinquished: abandoned
relinquishment: remission; resignation; surrender
relish: appetite; savor; taste; zest
reluctance: aversion; difficulty; repugnance; scruple
reluctant: averse; backward; grudging; indisposed; involuntary; loath; scrupulous; shy; tardy; tender
rely or depend on: stay
rely on: expect; trust
rely upon: credit
rely: attend; hang; lean
remain firm: bear
remain steadfast or faithful or constant: abide
remain: abide; continue; continue; endure; hold; last; linger; persist; reside; sit; stand; stay; stick; survive; tarry; wait
remainder: excess; remain; remnant; residue; surplus
remaining: permanent
remains: corpse; remnant; residue
remark: comment; note; notice; observation; observe; regard; say; see; speech
remarkable: extraordinary; great; humongous; memorable; notable; noteworthy; salient; singular; splendid; uncommon; unusual; wonderful
remedial: therapeutic
remediless: hopeless
remedy: correct; cure; cure-all; heal; help; medicine; panacea; rectify; redress; relief; relieve; repair
remember: recall; recollect; retain; think
remembrance: memento; mind; trophy
remembrancer: remembrance
remind: admonish
reminder: hint; memento
reminiscence: remembrance
remiss: careless; lax; neglectful; reckless; slack; thoughtless
remission: pardon; suspense
remissness: neglect; slack
remit: abate; allow; pardon; relax; slacken; transmit; waive
remnant: remain; remainder
remnants: odd
remodel: repair
remonstrance: reproach
remonstrate or expostulate with: reprove
remonstrate with: rebuke
remonstrate: protest
remonstration: rebuke
remorse: qualm; regret; repentance
remorseful: penitent
remorseless: relentless; unrelenting
remote: abhorrent; back; blind; high; lonely; negligible; obscure; solitary
remoteness: solitude
remoter: ulterior
remotest: extreme; ultimate
removal: discharge
remove: abate; abstract; deduct; delete; discharge; displace; eliminate; eradicate; move; remedy; strip; supersede; supplant; withdraw
removed: abhorrent; remote; retired
remunerate: compensate; pay; recompense; requite; reward
remuneration: compensation; consideration; hire; pay; recompense; restitution; reward; satisfaction; wage
remunerative: fat
rend: bite; burst; lacerate; rip; tear
render: bear; give; make; paraphrase; put; try; yield
rendering: imagery; paraphrase; translation; version
rendezvous: appointment; tryst
rendition: imagery; version
renegade: recreant
renew: mend; refresh; repair; restore; revive
renewal: mend; reparation
renounce: abandon; abdicate; deny; desert; forsake; leave; reject; relinquish; repudiate; resign; surrender; waive
renovate: refresh; refurbish; renew; repair; restore
renovation: reparation
renown: brilliance; celebrity; distinction; eminence; fame; glory; luster; name; note; reputation; splendor

renowned: acclaimed; celebrated; distinguished; eminent; famous; glorious; great; noted; splendid
rent: breach; break; charter; hack; hire; let; opening; ragged; rip; tear
rental: hire; rent
renunciation: abdication; dereliction
reorder: stagger
repair: adjust; cure; fitness; fix; mend; patch; redress; reform; refresh; remedy; renew; reparation; restore; retrieve
repairman: mechanic
reparation: apology; compensation; redress; restitution; satisfaction
repartee: retort; wit
repast: cheer; feast
repay: pay; recompense; replace; requite; retaliate; settle
repayment: recompense; restitution; retribution; satisfaction
repeal: abolish; abolition; abrogate; abrogation; overrule; recall; recall; reverse; revoke
repeat: duplicate; recapitulate; recite; rehearse; relate; reproduce; say
repeated: continual; persistent
repeatedly: frequently; often
repel: disgust; rebuff; reject; revolt
repellent: cool; foul; grim; hideous; horrible; loathsome; mean; nasty; nauseous; odious; offensive; rank; unpleasant; vile
repent: regret
repentance: regret
repentant: penitent; remorseful
repetition: repeat
repetitious: continual
repetitive: continual
replace: change; displace; remit; remove; restore; succeed; supersede; supplant
replaceable: exchangeable
replacement: permutation; relief; surrogate
replenish: renew; replace; supply
replete: abundant
replica: duplicate
replicate: duplicate
replication: rejoinder; reply; response; retort
reply to: acknowledge; answer
reply: account; answer; rejoinder; response; retort
report: account; advice; announce; crack; relate; relation; rumor; say; scuttlebutt; statement; story; talk; tell; word
repose: calm; ease; lean; quiet; sit; sleep; stay
repository: safe; thesaurus
repossess: regain
reprehend: blame; censure; chide; rebuke; reproach; reprove
reprehensible: faulty; heinous; vicious; wrong
reprehension: blame; censure; rebuke; reproach
represent: act; depict; describe; express; impersonate; picture; play; portray; present; reproduce; signify; sketch
representation: icon; image; imagery; model; picture; plan; reflection; resemblance
representative: delegate; example; type
repress: abate; check; curb; inhibit; restrain; slacken; stifle; stop; subdue; tame; withhold
repressed: quiet
repression: check
reprieve: respite
reprimand: censure; chide; rebuke; reproach; reprove; scold; snub
reprisal: revenge
reproach: abuse; blame; blot; censure; disgrace; impeach; indignity; invective; obloquy; odium; plaint; rebuke; reflection; reprove; scold; shame; stigma; taunt; twit; upbraid; vituperate
reproachful: opprobrious; scurrilous
reprobate: abandoned; corrupt; depraved; lost; obdurate; shameless; villain
reproduce: depict; duplicate; imitate; reflect; repeat; restore
reproduction: copy; duplicate
reproof: blame; censure; rebuke; reproach
reprove: admonish; blame; censure; chide; punish; rebuke; reproach; scold; snub; upbraid

repudiate: abandon; abdicate; deny; overrule; refuse; reject; renounce

repudiation: abdication

repugnance: abhorrence; antipathy; aversion; disgust; dislike; distaste; hatred; horror

repugnant: abhorrent; abominable; disgusting; distasteful; hateful; hostile; offensive

repulse: check; disgust; rebuff; repel

repulsion: gorge; rebuff

repulsive: abhorrent; disgusting; distasteful; foul; hateful; hideous; horrible; loathsome; mean; monstrous; nasty; odious; offensive; rank; squalid; ugly; unpleasant; vile

repurchase: redeem

reputable: creditable; eminent; estimable; honorable; respectable

reputation: account; celebrity; character; credit; face; fame; honor; name; note; prestige; renown; repute; standing

repute: account; celebrity; character; credit; distinction; eminence; fame; honor; luster; name; note; renown; reputation

request: appeal; application; ask; beg; claim; desire; invite; petition; require; seek; solicit

require: appoint; ask; bid; charge; claim; command; crave; decree; demand; enjoin; exact; need; oblige; order; request; take; want

required: necessary; requisite

requirement: claim; command; condition; demand; mandate; necessary; necessity; need; obligation; requisite; turn; want

requiring: urgent

requisite: condition; indispensable; mandate; necessary; necessity; requirement

requisition: call; claim; command; demand; requirement

requital: compensation; pay; recompense; restitution; retribution; revenge; reward; satisfaction; vengeance

requite: pay; recompense; retaliate; revenge; reward

rereading: review

rescind: abolish; abrogate; cancel; overrule; recall; reverse; revoke; supersede; withdraw

rescission: abrogation

rescue: deliver; redeem; retrieve; salvage; save

rescuer: savior

research: experiment; inquiry; investigation; study

resemblance: parallel; semblance; similarity

resemble: agree; compare; counterfeit; parallel

resembling: parallel; similar

resent: envy

resentful: angry; cross; jealous; malevolent; miffed; revengeful; sulky; waspish; wrathful

resentment: anger; grudge; indignation; malevolence; offense; passion; rancor; temper; umbrage; wrath

reservation: reserve

reserve: asylum; keep; makeshift; retain; save; spare; stock; supply

reserved: close; cold; difficult; prudish; reticent; spare; strange; sullen; taciturn; uncommunicative

resettle: migrate

reside: abide; dwell; house; stay

residence: address; home; house; place; standing

residential: household

residue: remain; remainder; remnant; surplus

residuum: remainder; remnant; residue

resign or reconcile oneself: acquiesce

resign oneself to: accept

resign: abandon; abdicate; cede; deliver; quit; relinquish; renounce; secede; submit; surrender; waive; yield

resignation: abdication; patience; surrender

resigned: content; patient; submissive

resiliency: spring

resist: combat; counteract; defy; oppose; repel; rise; stand; withstand

resistance: opposition; rebellion; stamina

resistant: defiant; fast; hard; recalcitrant; strong

resisting: hard; opposition

resistive: recalcitrant; strong

resolute: bold; constant; decided; decisive; determined; earnest; firm; game; inflexible; intent; obstinate; single-minded; stalwart; staunch; steadfast; stout; strenuous; strong; stubborn; sturdy; substantial; unyielding

resoluteness: nerve; will

resolution: constancy; grit; nerve; perseverance; pluck; resolve; strength; will

resolve: act; decide; decipher; determine; result

resolved: bent; decided; resolute; set; single-minded; stiff

resonant: vibrant

resonate: ring; throb

resort: appeal; expedient; makeshift; recourse

resorts: wherewithal

resound: ring; roar; sound; vibrate

resounding: loud

resource: appliance; expedient; recourse

resourceful: adroit; enterprising; ingenious; strong

resourcefulness: spirit

resources: capital; mean; wherewithal

respect: adore; attend; attention; awe; compliment; consider; deference; duty; esteem; estimation; homage; honor; honor; obeisance; piety; refer; reference; regard; relation; reverence; sake; veneration; way; wise; worship

respectable: creditable; estimable; gentle; proper; serviceable

respected: respectable

respectful: attentive; civil; courteous; dutiful; humble; obedient

respecting: about

respite: delay; remission; suspense

resplendence: glory; grandeur; luster

resplendent: bright; gorgeous; lucid; luminous; radiant; shining

respond to: answer

respond: answer; reply; retort

response: answer; rejoinder; reply; retort

responsibility: capacity; care; charge; concern; duty; obligation; office; onus; part; place; trust; work

responsible: liable; substantial

responsive: exquisite; perceptive; receptive; sentient

responsiveness: empathy; sensibility

rest: acquiesce; base; brood; continue; ease; hang; lean; pause; quiet; remain; remainder; remnant; residue; respite; settle; sit; sleep; stand; stay; suspense; tarry; wait

restate: paraphrase

restitution: redress; reparation; satisfaction

restive: solicitous; tumultuous; unquiet

restless: impatient; restive; solicitous; tumultuous; unquiet; wakeful

restlessness: discontent

restock: renew

restoration: mend; redress; reparation; restitution

restorative: cure; remedy; therapeutic

restore: cure; heal; help; mend; patch; ransom; reclaim; recover; reform; refresh; remedy; remit; render; renew; repair; replace; retrieve

restrain: arrest; bar; bind; bridle; chasten; check; constrain; control; curb; damp; detain; deter; exclude; govern; hamper; hobble; hold; impede; inhibit; limit; mortify; qualify; refrain; repress; restrict; shackle; slacken; stay; stint; stop; temper; withhold

restrained: ashamed; pent-up; severe

restrainer: bit

restraint: arrest; barrier; bridle; check; curb; hindrance; limit; reserve; scruple; stint

restrict to rations: ration

restrict: bind; cabin; condition; confine; incarcerate; limit; modify; qualify; restrain; shackle; shackle; shorten; stint; tie

restricted: clannish; confidential; spare; sparse; xenophobic

restriction: bond; check; limit; prohibition; stint

restrictive: austere; clannish; exclusive; stringent; xenophobic

result: achieve; conclusion; consequence; disposition; effect; end; ensue; event; follow; growth; issue; outcome; outgrowth; proceed; purpose; sequence; terminate

resuscitate: revive

ret: drench; saturate; seethe; wet

retail: narrate

retain: continue; detain; employ; hold; keep; maintain; preserve; remember; reserve

retainer: follower; servant

retaliate: pay; requite; retort; revenge

retaliation: reprisal; retribution; revenge; vengeance

retard: damp; delay; detain; encumber; hinder; impede; obstruct; slow

retardation: lag

retarded: backward

retch: heave

retention: reserve

retentive: tenacious

reticence: reserve

reticent: close; dark; secret; taciturn; uncommunicative

reticulated: open

reticule: bag

retire from: leave

retire: abandon; abdicate; back; depart; ebb; give; retreat; secede; shrink; withdraw

retired: backward; obscure; odd; private; secluded; secret; solitary

retirement: abdication; retreat; solitude

retiring: coy; modest; shy; timid; unpretentious

retort: answer

retouch: mend; refresh

retract: recall; retire; revoke; withdraw

retraction: recall

retreat: asylum; back; harbor; hole; home; hospital; refuge; retire; shelter; shrink; withdraw

retrench: reduce

retrenchment: abridgment

retribution: recompense; revenge; vengeance

retrieve: recover; regain; repair; salvage

retrocede: retire; retreat

retrograde: retire; retreat

retrogress: decay

retrogression: decadence; decline; ebb

retrogressively: backward

return: advantage; income; profit; remit; render; rent; repay; replace; restore; retaliate; retort; wage

returnable: exchangeable

returning: backward

returns: income; profit

reveal: betray; communicate; declare; disclose; display; divulge; exhibit; expose; express; impart; manifest; open; publish; show; speak; stamp; tell; unburden; uncover; ventilate

revel: mask; play; riot; romp

revelation: exposure

revelry: riot

revenant: ghost

revenge: avenge; pay; reprisal; requite; retaliate; retribution; vengeance

revengeful: spiteful; vindictive

revengefulness: revenge

revenue: income; mean; profit

reverberate: recoil; ring

revere: admire; adore; esteem; fear; honor; regard; respect; reverence; worship

revered: hallowed; sacred

reverence: adore; awe; deference; dread; duty; esteem; estimation; fear; homage; honor; obeisance; piety; regard; respect; veneration; worship

reverent: pious; religious

reverential: dutiful; solemn

reverie: daydream; study; trance

reversal: about-face; turn

reverse: about-face; back; blow; calamity; converse; disaster; invert; misfortune; opposite; revoke; turn

reversed: about; backward

reversion: about-face

review: criticism; notice; peruse; recapitulate

reviewer: critic

revile: abuse; malign; pillory; taunt; traduce; vilify; vituperate

revilement: obloquy

revise: amend,

revitalize: revive

revive: refresh; renew

revivify: revive

revocation: abolition; abrogation; recall

revoke: abolish; abrogate; cancel; open; overrule; recall; reverse; supersede; withdraw

revolt: defect; disgust; insurrection; mutiny; nauseate; rebel; rebellion; revolution; rise; sedition; shock; tumult; uprising

revolting: abhorrent; abominable; disgusting; hateful; hideous; horrible; loathsome; monstrous; nauseous; offensive; ugly; vile

revolution: circuit; commotion; mutiny; rebellion; revolt; round; sedition; tumult; turn; uprising; whirl

revolutionary: mutinous; underground

revolve or turn over in the mind: agitate

revolve: circle; consider; contemplate; move; roll; rotate; turn; twist; whirl

revulsion: abhorrence; abomination; gorge

reward: bonus; bounty; compensate; compensation; hire; pay; pay; premium; prize; recompense; retribution; trophy; wage

rhapsodic: lyrical

rhetoric: elocution

rhetorical: grandiloquent; tumid

rhythm: beat; movement; number; poetry; stroke; time

rib: bend

ribald: blue; coarse; free; nasty; naughty; obscene; scurrilous; vulgar; X-rated

ribbing: raillery

ribbon: strip

rich: abundant; affluent; ample; copious; costly; fat; fertile; fruitful; gorgeous; luxurious; magnificent; mellow; opulent; plentiful; prosperous; risible; solid; strong; superb; wealthy

riches: money; treasure; wealth

rickety: crazy; ramshackle; senile; shaky; spindly

ricochet: bound; skip

rid: absolve; clear; free; quit

riddle: enigma; problem; puzzle; screen

ride: drive; spin

ridge: bank; bar; wave

ridicule: banter; jeer; mock; mockery; pan; pillory; sarcasm; satire; scoff; sneer; sport; taunt

ridiculing: cynical

ridiculous: absurd; amusing; comical; foolish; funny; impertinent; inept; laughable; ludicrous; preposterous; puerile; risible; silly

rife: current

rifle: loot; pilfer; rob

rift: breach; break; cleft; division; flaw; opening; rent

rig: apparel; appoint; array; dress; equip; furnish; habit; paraphernalia

right away: presently

right hand: sidekick

right of entry: access

right-minded: ethical

right-thinking: ethical

right: becoming; claim; correct; honorable; immunity; improve; integrity; just; prerogative; privilege; proper; property; reasonable; redress; remedy; righteous; seemly; sound; straight; title; true; unerring; virtuous

righteous: blue; ethical; godly; good; just; moral; upright; virtuous; worthy

righteously: right

righteousness: good; goodness; integrity; principle

rightful place: home

rightful: just; right; true

rightfully: right

rightly: right

rightness: propriety

rigid: blue; determined; difficult; exact; faithful; firm; formal; hard; inflexible; precise; prim; relentless; religious; rigorous; set; severe; stable; stark; stern; stiff; stony; straitlaced; strict;

stubborn; taut; tense; tough; uncompromising

rigidity: austerity

rigor: austerity

rigorous: astringent; austere; blue; determined; exact; formal; formal; inflexible; nice; rigid; scrupulous; severe; stern; stiff; strict

rigorously: hardly

rigorousness: austerity

rile: rankle; roil

rill: brook; burn; flow; run; stream

rim: bank; beach; brim; edge; margin; verge

rind: peel; skin

ring up: call

ring-shaped: round

ring: circle; party; round

rink: ring

rinse: clean; tint

riot: brawl; commotion; disorder; disturbance; fight; hubbub; rampage; sedition; tumult; uproar

riotous: mutinous; noisy; obstreperous; raucous; rough; rowdy; tumultuous; unruly; wild

rip off: pilfer

rip-roaring: rowdy

rip: bite; break; pluck; rend; rent; tear

ripe : womanly,

ripe: adult; mature; mellow

ripen: age; mature; mellow

riposte: rejoinder; reply; retort

ripple: wave

riptide: undertow

rise or increase in value: appreciate

rise up: mutiny

rise: advance; ascend; beginning; birth; breed; climb; head; heave; origin; originate; raise; rear; result; revolt; soar; spring; stem; wake

risible: amusing; comical; laughable

rising: rise

risk-taking: adventurous; daredevil

risk: chance; danger; dare; hazard; hazard; jeopardy; lay; peril; stake; venture; wager

risky: critical; insecure; precarious; shaky; slippery

risqué: blue; naughty; racy

rite: ceremony; ritual

ritual: ceremony; exercise; form; formal; solemn

ritualize: celebrate

ritzy: palatial

rival: antagonist; compete; competitor; contend; contest; opponent; vie

rivalry: contention; contest; emulation

rive: rend

river: current; flow; stream

riverbank: shore

rivet: arrest; fasten

riveted: rapt

riveting: charismatic

rivulet: brook; burn; flow; run; stream

road: course; passage; path; street; way

roadway: street

roam: journey; prowl; ramble; range; rove; stroll; wander

roaming: itinerant

roar: cry; laugh

roaring: boisterous

rob: abstract; harry; loot; pick; pilfer; pillage; plunder; rook; sack; spoil; strip

robber: outlaw; thief

robbery: crime; plunder

robe: dress; gown; throw

robes: apparel

robust: able-bodied; cheerful; fresh; hale; hardy; healthy; lusty; mighty; rude; sound; stalwart; strong; sturdy; vigorous

robustness: stamina

rock: careen; roll; swing; totter; wave

rocket scientist: savant

rocky: rugged; stony

rod: bar; standard; stick; verge

rodomontade: boast; brag

roentgenize: x-ray

roentgenogram: x-ray

rogue: blackguard; cheat; knave; rascal; scamp; scoundrel; swindler; villain

roguery: chicanery

roguish: rascal; sly; waggish

roiled: turbid

roily: turbid

roister: romp

roistering: boisterous; rowdy
roisterous: rambunctious
role: part; person
roll on: flow
roll: careen; catalogue; inventory; list; register; revolve; schedule; smooth; twist; wallow
roller: breaker; roll
rollick: caper; romp
rollicking: rambunctious
roman: romance
romance: novel; story
romantic: moonstruck; quixotic; visionary
romp: caper; gambol; play; sport
roof: vault
rook: castle; rob
room-temperature: lukewarm
room: scope; verge
roomette: compartment
roomy: ample; capacious; spacious
roost: sit
root: cutting; origin
rooted: firm
rope: bond; stay; tie
ropy: viscous
rose-colored: ruddy
roseate: rosy
roster: catalogue; inventory; register; roll
rostrum: platform
rosy-cheeked: ruddy
rosy: optimistic; ruddy
rot: corruption; decay; decompose; disintegrate; perish
rotate: move; revolve; roll; spin; turn; twist; whirl
rotating: twist
rotation: revolution; turn; twist; whirl
rotten: bad; corrupt; noisome; unsound
rotting: decay
rotund: roly-poly; round
roué: blackguard; libertine
rouge: cosmetic
rough out: sketch
rough-and-tumble: rowdy
rough: abrupt; austere; awkward; barbarian; bluff; blunt; boisterous; broad; brusque; brutal; coarse; crude; hard; harsh; hoarse; ill-mannered; impolite; loutish; outline; raw; robust; rude; rugged; rural; savage; sour; stern; ugly
roughened: weather-beaten
roughly: hardly
round out: complement
round: about; circle; plump; post; revolution
roundabout: circuitous; sinuous; tortuous
rounded: blunt; zaftig
rouse: agitate; arouse; call; excite; heat; inflame; influence; kindle; move; pierce; prod; provoke; raise; revive; stimulate; stir; summon; wake; warm
rout: conquer; conquest; defeat; overcome; overpower; overthrow; vanquish
route: access; course; passage; path; way
routine: act; lackluster; sketch; technique
rove: journey; prowl; ramble; range; roam; stroll; wander
roving: itinerant
row: bank; brawl; course; fight; range; rank; ruckus
rowboat: tender
rowdy: rambunctious; raucous
rowel: spur
royal: grand; kingly; lordly; majestic; regal; sovereign
rub gently: stroke
rub off: abrade
rub out: blot; cancel; obliterate
rub: grind; wash
rubber stamp: yes-man
rubbing off: abrasion
rubbing: abrasion
rubbish: blarney; litter; refuse; stuff; waste
rube: yahoo
Rubenesque: zaftig
rubicund: rosy; ruddy
ruckus: ado; bedlam
ruction: ruckus
ruddy: ripe; rosy
rude: abrupt; artless; awkward; barbarian; blunt; brusque; brutal; coarse; crude; curt; disrespectful; earthy; ill-mannered; impertinent; impolite; impudent; indecent; insolent; low; low; mean; offensive; presumptuous; raw; robust; rough; rugged; savage; short; sour; uncivil;

uncouth; unrefined; vulgar
rudeness: assurance; impudence
rudimental: elementary; rudimentary
rudimentary: abortive; elementary; essential; imperfect
rudiments: ABC's; basics; element
rue: regret
ruff: ruffle
ruffian: barbarian; rowdy; yahoo
ruffianly: rowdy
ruffle: agitate; bridle; disconcert; irritate; ripple
ruffled: excited
ruffling: ripple
rufous: ruddy
rugged: rough; rude; rural; savage; well-built
ruin: bankrupt; batter; blast; break; crash; cripple; deform; demolish; desolate; destroy; destruction; disfigure; dissolve; doom; fate; havoc; injure; injury; mangle; mar; murder; overthrow; perdition; poison; ravage; ravage; sack; shambles; slay; smash; spoil; waste; wreck
ruination: ruin; sack; shambles
ruined: bankrupt; black; lost; waste
ruinous: destructive; fatal; injurious; pernicious
rule: administer; authority; canon; command; control; criterion; custom; decree; direct; empire; form; fundamental; govern; guide; head; influence; manage; master; method; order; policy; power; principle; regulate; regulation; reign; standard; sway
ruler: chief; sovereign
rules: basics; discipline
ruling: authority; decree; dominant; leading; mandate; rule
ruminate over: brood; digest
ruminate upon: revolve
ruminate: consider; deliberate; meditate; muse; ponder; reflect; think
rumination: consideration; reflection
rumor: noise; scuttlebutt; talk
rumple: crush; ruffle
rumpus: bedlam; brawl; ruckus
run ashore: beach
run away or off with: abduct
run away: abscond; escape
run off: abscond
run on: jabber
run through or into: pierce
run-down: seedy; shabby; tacky; weather-beaten
run-in: tiff
run: brook; burn; course; flow; operate; order; pace; race; range; range; rush; spin; stream; superintend; trend
runaway: romp
rung: round
runlet: brook; burn
runnel: brook; burn; run; stream
runny: watery
runt: dwarf; pygmy
rupture: breach; break; contention; division; quarrel; rend; rent
rural: rustic
ruse: artifice; blind; deception; device; fraud; maneuver; mask; ploy; practice; stratagem; trick; wile
rush: dart; dash; hurry; plunge; precipitate; scramble; storm; stream
rushed: headlong; hectic
rust: corrode; fret
rustic: countryman; rude; rural
ruth: compassion
ruthless: bitter; bloody; brutal; cruel; grim; pitiless; relentless; remorseless; sanguinary; savage; unrelenting; unsparing
ruthlessness: cruelty
ryot: serf; slave

sable: black
saccharine: luscious; sweet
sack: bag; desolate; devastate; loot; pillage; plunder; ravage; rob; strip; waste
sacked: waste
sacramental: ritual
sacred: hallowed; holy; pious; sacrosanct; solemn; taboo
sacrifice: cost; offer; scapegoat
sacrilege: blasphemy
sacrilegious: profane
sacrosanct: sacred

sad: black; blue; dark; dejected; depressed; desolate; despondent; disconsolate; downhearted; gloomy; glum; grievous; heavy; joyless; low; melancholy; piteous; plaintive; sorrowful; sorry; unhappy
sadden: depress; desolate; dull; grieve
saddened: depressed
sadness: despondency; gloom; grief; melancholy; oppression; sorrow
safari: expedition
safe deposit box: safe
safe-conduct: protection
safe: cozy; good; secure; solid; sure; vault
safecracker: thief
safeguard: defend; escort; preserve; save; secure; shelter
safekeeper: caregiver; savior
safekeeping: custody
safety deposit box: vault
safety: guard; protection; refuge
sagacious: acute; astute; capable; deep; judicious; keen; penetrating; perceptive; politic; profound; prudent; rational; sage; sane; sapient; sensible; shrewd; wise
sagacity: experience; judgment; policy; wisdom; wit
sage: acute; sagacious; sane; sapient; savant; scholar; sensible; wise
said: above; oral
sailing: voyage
sailor: mariner; tar
sainted: heavenly; sacred
saintliness: devotion
saintly: devout; godly; heavenly; holy
salaam: obeisance
salacious: carnal; lascivious; wanton; X-rated
salaciousness: lust
salamander: sylph
salary: hire; income; pay; wage
sale: trade
salient: conspicuous
sallow: pallid
sally: joke; quip
salmagundi: mess; mixture
saloon: bar
salt: sailor
salubrious: healthy; salutary; wholesome
salubriousness: fitness
salubrity: fitness
salutary: beneficial; healthy; sanitary; therapeutic; useful; wholesome; wholesome
salute: cheer; greet
salvage: save
salve: ointment
same-old same-old: identical
same: identical
sameness: constancy; parity
sample: example; pattern; sort; specimen; standard; type
sanatorium: hospital
sanctified: sacrosanct
sanctify: consecrate
sanctimonious : smarmy; hypocritical
sanction: abet; allowance; approve; authority; authorize; confirm; countenance; countenance; empower; pass; ratify; warrant; warrant
sanctioned: lawful; legitimate; orthodox
sanctity: devotion; grace; piety
sanctuary: asylum; harbor; refuge; shelter
sanctum: sanctuary
sand-bar: bar
sand-bunk: bar
sand: deposit; grit
sands: beach
sane: lucid; rational; reasonable; right; sober; sound
sang-froid: assurance
sanguinary: bloody; cruel; deadly; savage
sanguine: ardent; content; hopeful; optimistic
sanitarium: asylum; hospital
sanity: mind; reason
sap: fool; weaken
sapid: palatable; scrumptious
sapience: wisdom
sapient: acute; sane
sapor: sip
sapphire: blue
sappy: saccharine
sarcasm: irony; ridicule; satire; taunt

sarcastic: acerbic; acid; bitter; caustic; cutting; cynical; dry; incisive; pointed; pungent; sardonic; satirical; sharp; tart; trenchant
sardonic: acerbic; acid; bitter; caustic; cutting; dry; incisive; pungent; sarcastic; satirical; sharp; trenchant
sassy: saucy
Satan: adversary
satanic: dark; devilish
sate: pall; satiate; satisfy
sated: jaded
satiate: pall; satisfy; surfeit
satiated: jaded
satiety: surfeit
satire: burlesque; caricature; irony; mockery; ridicule
satiric: acerbic; caustic
satirical: cynical; incisive; sarcastic; severe
satirize: abuse; caricature; mock; ridicule
satisfaction: compensation; contentment; happiness; joy; pleasure; recompense; redress; reparation; restitution
satisfactorily: well
satisfactory: adequate; average; good; grateful; serviceable; sufficient; well
satisfied: certain; content; easy; happy; self-satisfied; smug
satisfy: answer; appease; content; convince; delight; feed; fulfill; gratify; indulge; meet; pay; persuade; placate; requite; serve; stay; supply
satisfying: grateful
saturate: drench; permeate; seethe; soak; wet
sauciness: impudence
saucy: bold; impertinent; impudent; pert; rude
saunter: ramble; stroll; stroll; walk; wander
savage: barbarian; bitter; bloody; brutal; brute; cruel; ferocious; fierce; grim; impolite; remorseless; ruthless; sanguinary; truculent; wild
savanna: plain
savant: scholar
save: besides; but; deliver; deposit; except; guard; help; preserve; protect; redeem; rescue; reserve; retrieve; salvage; spare; treasure
saver: savior
saving: economical; economy; frugal; niggardly; prudent; thrifty
savoir-faire: poise
savor: flavor; relish; scent; sip; taste
savorless: tasteless
savory: dainty; delicious; luscious; palatable; scrumptious
savvy: cagey
saw: byword; cut; proverb
say: affirm; assert; bid; observe; remark; speak; state; tell; utter
saying: byword; maxim; proverb
scabrous: rough; rugged
scalawag: scamp
scale down: abridge
scale: ascend; climb; mount
scales: balance
scaling: climb
scamp: blackguard; knave; rascal; rogue; scoundrel; vagabond; villain
scamper: run; scramble
scan: survey
scandal: disgrace; gossip; ignominy; infamy; reproach; sacrilege; shame
scandalize: shame
scandalous: base; dishonorable; enormous; flagrant; foul; ignominious; infamous; opprobrious; shameful
scanning: examination
scant: mere
scantiness: lack; poverty; want
scantly: scarcely
scanty: little; meager; niggardly; poor; short; slim; spare; sparse; thin
scapegrace: knave; rascal; rogue; scamp; villain
scar: defect
scarce: close; rare; uncommon
scarcely: hardly
scarceness: want
scarcity: lack; paucity; want
scare: alarm; dismay; frighten; startle
scared: afraid; cowardly
scarf: throw
scathing: acerbic; caustic; vitriolic

scatological: earthy
scatter-brained: thoughtless
scatter: disband; disperse; dissipate; distribute; litter; radiate; resolve; spread; sprinkle; strew
scattered: chaotic; sparse; sporadic
scene: prospect; set; view
scenic: picturesque
scent: aroma; incense; odor; perfume; savor; taste; trail
scented: sweet
schedule: list; register
schema: blueprint; scheme
scheme: aim; blueprint; cast; conspiracy; contrive; counsel; design; device; devise; game; hatch; machination; maneuver; meditate; plan; plot; ploy; project; proposal; stratagem; system; theory; wangle; way
scheming: crafty; designing; politic
schism: breach; break; rent
schizophrenia: insanity
schizophrenic: insane
schlep: shamble
schmooze: babble
scholar: disciple; pupil; savant; student
scholarship: knowledge; learning
scholastic: academic
school: breed; educate; exercise; faction; flock; ideology; instruct; run; teach
schooled: wise
schooling: education; exercise; instruction
schoolmaster: instructor
schwarmerei: schmaltz
science: knowledge
scintilla: atom; bit; iota
scintillate: flash; glance; sparkle
scintillating: bright
scintillation: sparkle
sciolist: dabbler
scion: slip
scoff at: taunt
scoff: jeer; jest; mock; scorn; sneer; taunt
scold: abuse; chide; punish; rebuke; reprimand; reproach; shrew; vituperate
scolding: rebuke
sconce: luster
scope: extent; grandeur; grasp; latitude; play; range; reach; swing; verge
scorch: burn; sear; singe
scorched: desolate
scorching: torrid
score: account; bill; sake
scoria: refuse
scorn: abuse; affront; arrogance; contempt; defy; despise; disdain; indignity; insult; invective; mockery; obloquy; pillory; reproach; scoff; slight; sneer; spurn; taunt
scornful: acid; arrogant; bitter; contemptuous; cynical; derogatory; disdainful; injurious; supercilious; uppity
scotch: mean
scoundrel: blackguard; knave; rascal; rogue; villain
scour: clean; hunt
scourge: affliction; curse; pest; punish; whip
scowl: glare; lower
scrabble: scramble
scrambled: heterogeneous
scrap: iota; particle; piece; portion; remain; row; tiff
scrape off: abrade
scrape together: collect
scrape: abrasion; smooth
scraps: odd
scratch: abrasion; score
scrawny: cadaverous; gaunt; spindly; thin
screak: scream
scream: cry; shriek
screech: cry; scream; shriek
screechy: raucous
screen play: picture
screen: blind; conceal; cover; defend; hide; mask; partition; protect; protection; shade; shelter; traverse
screw up: blunder
screwball: crackpot; wacky
scrimmage: fight
scroll: roll; volume
scrounge: mooch
scrub: brush; clean; wash; zap
scruffy: seedy; shabby
scruple: pang; qualm; stick; suspense
scrupulous: careful; close; conscientious; dainty; delicate; ethical;

exact; nice; particular; punctilious; religious; selective; squeamish; strict; wary

scrupulousness: pang

scrutinize: examine; peruse; probe; research; search; study; survey

scrutinizing: inquisitive

scrutiny: examination; inquiry; inspection; investigation; research; search

scud: run

scuff: shamble

scuffle: fight; shamble; tussle; tussle

sculptor: artist

scum: refuse

scurrilous: blue; foul; opprobrious; ribald

scurry: scramble

scurvy: abject; abominable; bad; dirty; shabby

scuttle: scramble

sea puss: maelstrom

sea: deep; main; swell; wave

seacoast: coast

seafarer: mariner; sailor; tar

seafaring man: mariner; sailor; tar

seal off: stop

seal: device; execute; frank; stamp

seam: junction

seaman: mariner; sailor; tar

sear: burn

search for: hunt; look; seek

search: examine; hunt; look; probe; prospect; scrutiny

searching: close; search

seashore: beach; coast; shore

seasick: queasy

seaside: coast

season: harden; palliate; savor; time

seasonable: opportune; timely

seasoner: seasoning

seasoning: flavor

seat: bottom; capital; place; thwart

secede: withdraw

scenery: set

secluded: lone; lonesome; obscure; odd; private; retired; secret; solitary

seclusion: retreat; solitude

second-guess: kibitz

second-hand: tacky

second-rate: ordinary

second-story man: robber; thief

second: abet; abide; aid; assist; back; encourage; help; instant; minute; moment; reject; support

secondary: accidental; auxiliary; minor; small; subordinate; subsidiary; unimportant

secret plan: conspiracy

secret: abstruse; clandestine; confidential; dark; intimate; mysterious; occult; private; rarefied; recondite; sly; stealthy; surreptitious; ulterior; underground; underhand

secrete: bury; conceal; cover; harbor; hide

secretive: close; secret

sect: faction; set

section: branch; compartment; division; movement; part; partition; passage; piece; place; portion; region; verse; zone

sector: place

secular: mundane; profane; worldly

secure: achieve; acquire; arrest; attain; bind; carry; command; cozy; defend; deposit; earn; fast; fasten; firm; fix; gain; get; guarantee; have; make; obtain; procure; protect; sacred; safe; safeguard; sound; stable; strong; sure; take; warrant; win

securely: fast

security: bond; guarantee; guard; peace; protection; rampart; refuge; safeguard; trust; warrant

sedate: calm; composed; cool; decorous; demure; grave; old; serene; serious; sober; staid; steady

sedation: opiate

sedative: opiate

sediment: deposit; ground; refuse

sedition: commotion; mutiny; rebellion; revolt; treason

seditious: mutinous; rebellious; wily

seduce: abuse; entice; lead; lure; tamper; tempt

seduction: abuse; conquest

seductive: tempting

seductiveness: glamour

seductress: siren

sedulous: assiduous; busy; diligent; industrious; laborious; notable; painstaking; patient

sedulousness: patience; study

see eye to eye: meet

see the light: appear

see: account; comprehend; discern; discover; note; notice; observe; perceive; regard; understand; view; watch; witness

seed: pit

seedy: poor; shabby; tacky

seeing double: giddy

seek information: ask

seek: ask; attempt; endeavor; hunt; look; search; solicit

seeker: wannabe

seem: appear; look; show

seeming: apparent; appearance

seemliness: beauty; propriety

seemly: appropriate; beautiful; becoming; befitting; decent; decorous; right

seep through: strain

seep: ooze; strain

seer: wizard

seesaw: waffle; yo-yo

seethe: boil; simmer; stew

segment: division; partition; piece; portion

segregation: isolation

segregationist: xenophobic

seine: snare

seize upon: get; grasp

seize: abduct; arrest; capture; catch; embrace; grasp; occupy; reach; take; whip

seizer: abductor

seizure: abduction; access; agony; apprehension; arrest; capture; catch; convulsion; occupation; paroxysm; raid; throe

select: affect; appoint; choice; choose; clannish; elect; exclusive; exquisite; fine; gather; ordain; peculiar; pick; precious; prefer; recherché; shining; single; take

selected: select

selection: alternative; choice; extract; option; pick; preference

selective: clannish; select; xenophobic

self-absorbed: egocentric

self-acting: automatic

self-actualize: empower

self-admiration: vanity

self-assertiveness: chutzpah

self-assured: confident; positive

self-centered: egocentric

self-centeredness: egotism

self-complacency: vanity

self-complacent: self-satisfied; smug; vain

self-conceit: egoism

self-confidence: arrogance; assurance; chutzpah; confidence

self-confident: positive; smug

self-conscious: diffident

self-contradictory: absurd

self-control: balance; poise

self-denial: abstinence

self-denying: abstemious

self-effacing: bashful; chary; coy; diffident; unpretentious

self-esteem: conceit; pride; vanity

self-explanatory: self-evident

self-governing: self-governed

self-importance: arrogance; pride

self-important: big; conceited; proud; smug

self-indulgent: immoral; luxurious

self-interested: selfish

self-love: egoism

self-loving: egocentric

self-moving: automatic

self-opinionated: smug

self-possessed: calm; composed; cool; easygoing; patient

self-possession: balance; calm; composure; patience; phlegm; poise

self-referencing: egocentric

self-reliance: assurance; confidence

self-reliant: smug

self-restrained: temperate

self-restraint: abstinence; reserve

self-righteous: blue; sanctimonious

self-satisfied: bland; conceited; proud; smug

self-seeking: selfish; sordid

self-sufficient: big; conceited; smug

self-willed: contrary; headstrong; wild; willful

selfish: base; egocentric; exclusive; greedy; little; mean; mercenary; small; sordid

selfishness: egoism

selfsame: identical

sell: bargain; barter; negotiate

selvage: list

semblance: appearance; guise; image; ostentation; picture; pretense; resemblance; trick

semitransparent: translucent

senate: sovereign

send or drive or put away: banish

send down: discharge; expel

send for: call

send forth: cast; discharge

send out: issue

send: drive; pass; remit; throw; transmit; turn

sending: issue

sendup: burlesque

senescent: senile

senile: superannuated; weak

sensate: sensitive; sentient

sensation: sense; stir; taste

sensational: lurid; theatrical

sense: aura; brains; intellect; meaning; mind; sensation; significance; spirit; taste; wisdom; wit

senseless: foolish; idiotic; insane; mad; preposterous; silly; stupid; unreasonable; weak

senselessness: nonsense

sensibility: delicacy; feeling; sensitivity; sentiment; susceptibility

sensible: advisable; conscious; judicious; legitimate; old; physical; practical; prudent; rational; reasonable; sane; sensuous; sentient; solid; sound; wise

sensitive: acute; conscious; delicate; exquisite; feeling; morbid; perceptive; quick; sentient; sharp; skittish; sore; tactful; temperamental; tender; touchy

sensitiveness: fancy; sensibility; sentiment; susceptibility

sensitivity: delicacy; empathy; fancy; feeling; sensibility; susceptibility

sensual: brute; carnal; gross; libertine; licentious; luxurious; voluptuous

sensualist: epicure; libertine; sybarite

sensuality: pleasure

sensuous: sensual

sent down: abandoned

sentence: condemn; doom

sententious: compact; laconic; oracular; short; terse

sententiousness: conciseness

sentient: animal; conscious; feeling; sensuous

sentiment: apprehension; feeling; idea; notion; opinion; sense; sentimentality

sentimental: moonstruck; sickly; soft; tender

sentimentalism: schmaltz

sentimentality: feeling; schmaltz; sentiment

sentiments: mind

sentinel: guard; watch

sentry: guard; watch

separate: abstract; alien; break; decompose; differentiate; disband; disintegrate; disperse; distinct; distinguish; distribute; diverge; diverse; divide; gape; lone; part; particular; partition; remove; resolve; rupture; scatter; secede; segregate; sever; single; singular; sort; sporadic; tease

separated: lone; remote; separate

separately: particularly; piecemeal

separation: breach; break; dissent; division; isolation; partition; rent

separatist: xenophobic

sepulchre: grave

sequel: consequence; sequence

sequence: course; order; series; succession

sequential: successive

sequestered: lonely; private; retired; secluded; separate

seraphic: heavenly

serene: calm; clear; composed; easygoing; patient; peaceable; peaceful; placid; quiet; restful; sedate; sober; staid; still; unruffled

sereneness: serenity

serenity: calm; composure; ease; order; quiet

serf: menial; slave

serfdom: bondage; captivity; servitude

series: circle; course; list; range; rank; round; run; scale; sequence; set; succession

serious: austere; bad; capital; deep; demure; desperate; devout; earnest; grave; great; heavy; high; melancholy; momentous; pensive; poignant; sedate; severe; sober; solemn; staid; weighty

seriousness: melancholy

sermon: tract

sermonize: declaim

serous: watery

serpentine: circuitous; crooked; sinuous; tortuous

servant-girl: servant

servant: aid; attendant; employee; follower; menial

serve for: form

serve: accommodate; advantage; aid; answer; assist; attend; do; oblige

service: advantage; aid; duty; employ; exercise; kindness; office; use

serviceable: available; beneficial; convenient; good; handy; operative; useful; utilitarian; valuable

servile: base; low; menial; obsequious; slavish; supple

serving: portion

servitor: servant

servitude: bondage; captivity; slavery

set or fall upon: assail

set or put aside: dismiss

set about: begin

set afire: light

set apart: allot; allow; appoint; appropriate; discriminate; reserve; save; segregate

set aside or apart: spare

set aside: cast; overrule; reserve

set at liberty: release

set down: record

set fire to: ignite; kindle; light

set forth: announce; give; represent; spread; state

set free: absolve; acquit; clear; deliver; discharge; free; liberate; loose; release; rescue

set going: initiate

set loose: liberate

set off: contrast; differentiate; discharge; garnish

set on fire: ignite

set on: bent; charge

set out or forth: start

set out: depart

set right: correct; mend; rectify

set up: assemble; erect; establish; raise; start

set upon: attack

set-to: row

set: adjust; association; band; beset; body; brood; circle; club; collection; company; connection; coterie; fix; formal; gang; ground; hackneyed; inclination; intent; kind; lay; lodge; pack; party; place; post; put; ready; regulate; resolute; ring; ripe; run; series; settle; sphere; stand; station; stubborn

setting: environment; set

settle: acquit; adjust; appoint; arrange; ascertain; confirm; decide; determine; discharge; establish; fix; ground; heal; lodge; mediate; meet; negotiate; patch; pay; reconcile; rule; set; sit; state; subside; transact; treat; umpire

settled: certain; firm; sedate; staid; standing; steady; stereotyped; usual

settlement: agreement; conclusion; disposition; foundation

sever: cut; dissolve; divide; hew; part; rend; separate; tear

several: various

severance: breach; break

severe: acute; arduous; astringent; austere; bad; beastly; bitter; blue; critical; cruel; cutting; exact; grim; hard; harsh; heavy; incisive; inexorable; keen; merciless; painful; poignant; pointed; pungent; relentless; rigid; rigorous; rough; rugged; ruthless; satirical; sharp; smart; sore; sour; stern; stiff; strict; terrible; tough; tyrannical; unsparing

severed: separate

severely: hard; hardly

severity: austerity; oppression; violence

sexual: X-rated

sexy: X-rated

shabby: bad; base; dirty; dowdy; mean; poor; ragged; seedy; sorry; tacky

shack: cabin; cottage; shanty

shackle: band; hobble

shade: apparition; blind; cast; cloud; curtain; ghost; gloom; hatch; specter; spirit

shaded: gloomy

shadow: cloud; ghost; gloom; iota; shade; silhouette; specter; spirit

shadowed: dappled

shadowy: cloudy; dappled; dark; dim; dusky; gloomy; imaginary; obscure; somber

shady: dark; dusky; shabby; sharp; unconscionable

shaft: abyss; column; pillar

shaggy: rough

shake or move briskly: agitate

shake: move; quake; quiver; shiver; shudder; stir; totter; tremble; unnerve; vibrate; waver

shaken up: aghast

shaking: agitation; tremble; tremor; tremulous; vibrant

shaky: cranky; crazy; ramshackle; spindly; unsettled

shallow: bar; cosmetic; facile; light; simple; slight; superficial; trifling

sham: act; artificial; bogus; counterfeit; deception; fake; false; flash; humbug; meretricious; mock; mockery; phony; pretend; pseudo; simulate; spurious; unreal; vanity

shame: abash; affront; chagrin; confuse; confusion; contempt; disgrace; foul; humble; humiliate; humiliation; ignominy; infamy; mortify; reproach; reproach; scandal

shamefaced: ashamed; bashful

shamefacedness: confusion

shameful: abandoned; base; dishonorable; foul; grievous; gross; ignominious; infamous; opprobrious; shabby

shameless: abandoned; audacious; bold; brazen; cool; dishonorable; flagrant; lost; obdurate; unabashed

shamming: pretense

shanty: cabin; cottage; shack

shapable: malleable

shape: block; cast; fashion; fitness; form; guise; hew; make; model; modify; organize; silhouette; structure; true; turn

shapeless: rude

shapely: clean

share: deal; divide; part; partake; participate; partition; portion; proportion; stint

sharer: partner

sharing: division; empathy

sharp practice: fraud

sharp-witted: acute; cagey; keen; penetrating; perspicacious; sagacious

sharp: acrimonious; acute; astringent; astute; bright; brisk; cagey; caustic; cutting; dry; fine; high; hot; incisive; keen; penetrating; peppery; perceptive; piquant; piquant; poignant; pointed; pungent; quick; ready; rigorous; rough; sagacious; satirical; severe; short; shrewd; smart; sore; strong; tart; trenchant

sharpen: grind

sharpened: acute

sharper: cheat; rogue; rook; scoundrel; swindler

sharpness: perspicacity

shatter: batter; break; crash; crush; smash; tear; wreck

shattering: smash

shave: pare; trim

shay: carriage

shear: cut; divide; trim

sheath: case

sheave: block

shed or cast light on: interpret

shed tears: cry; weep

shed: cabin; cast; hut; shack; spread

sheen: gloss; luster; polish

sheeny: bright

sheep: stock

sheepish: bashful; diffident

sheer: absolute; bare; main; mere; naked; plain; precipitous; pure; rank; skew; stark

shell game: swindle

shell: skin; sphere

shelter: asylum; cover; defend; guard; harbor; house; lodge; pre-

serve; protect; protection; refuge; retreat; screen; shade
shibboleth: admission; password; watchword; word
shield: cover; defend; guard; preserve; protect; protection; safeguard; screen; shelter; shroud
shift: change; device; expedient; gang; move; prevaricate; quibble; trick; yo-yo
shifting: fickle; slippery
shiftless: improvident
shifty: slippery
shimmer: glisten; shine
shimmering: bright
shine: beam; blaze; flame; glance; glare; gleam; glisten; gloss; lighten; polish; radiate; shimmer; sparkle
shined: polished
shining: bright; clear; glossy; lucid; luminous; lurid; polished; radiant
shiny: bright; glossy; polished
ship: craft
shipment: freight
shipwreck: destruction; wreck
shirk: malinger; skulk; slack
shiver: batter; break; crash; quake; quiver; shake; shatter; shudder; tremble; vibrate; waver
shivering: chill; tremor; tremulous
shivers: cold
shivery: shaky
shoal: bank; bar; flock; swarm
shock-absorber: cushion
shock: alarm; appall; astonish; blow; confuse; confusion; frighten; outrage; paralyze; revolt; scare; shake; stagger; startle; stroke; stun
shocked: afraid; aghast; speechless
shocking: abhorrent; flagrant; frightful; ghastly; hideous; horrible; infamous; monstrous; offensive; traumatic
shoddy: seedy; shabby; tacky
shook-up: aghast
shoot: bough; branch; cutting; dart; discharge; spring; stick
shooting: discharge
shoplift: abstract; pilfer; rob
shoplifter: robber
shopworn: seedy; shabby
shore: bank; beach; coast
short and sweet: pithy
short story: piece
short-lived: brief; ephemeral; temporary
short-sighted: purblind
short-tempered: fretful; irascible; moody; passionate; peevish; peppery; petulant; short; sour; temperamental; testy
short: abortive; abrupt; blunt; brief; compact; concise; curt; little; pithy; quick; severe; shy; summary; weak
shortcoming: blame; defect; failing; fault; lack; peccadillo
shorten: abbreviate; condense; contract; curtail; cut; reduce
shortened: curt
shortening: abbreviation; abridgment
shortly: presently
shortness: brevity
shot: ball
shoulder: push
shout: call; cheer; clamor; cry; declaim; exclamation; roar
shouting: applause; clamor
shove: crowd; push; thrust
show or point the way: guide
show or produce a mean: average
show and tell: demonstrate
show off: display; flourish; vaunt
show: appear; appearance; argue; array; assign; bear; betray; demonstrate; disclose; display; evidence; exhibit; exposition; express; face; flourish; give; manifest; mockery; ostentation; pageant; play; present; pretense; produce; prove; reflect; register; render; scene; semblance; splendor; vainglory
shower: abound; cascade
showiness: gaiety; glare; ostentation; panache
showing: array; exhibit; overt; show
showmanship: panache
showy: ambitious; brave; flash; gallant; garish; gaudy; gay; loud; magnificent; meretricious; ornate; pretentious; smart; tawdry

shred: piece; tease
shredded: ragged
shreds: litter
shrew: fury; nag; scold; termagant
shrewd: acute; astute; cagey; crafty; deep; hard; intelligent; keen; Machiavellian; penetrating; politic; practical; quick; sagacious; sharp; sly; smart; unprincipled
shrewdness: craft; cunning; perspicacity; policy
shriek: cry; scream
shrieky: raucous
shrill: high; raucous; sharp
shrine: sanctuary
shrink from: abhor; abominate
shrink: constrict; contract; decrease; diminish; dwindle; lessen; shrivel; shy; wince; wither
shrinking: coy; decrease; timid
shrivel up: diminish
shrivel: blast; contract; perish; scorch; shrink; wither
shriveled: cadaverous
shroud: bury; cover; hide; mask; pall; screen; secrete; shelter
shrouded: occult
shrubbery: cover
shrubs: brush
shrunk: poor
shudder at: abhor; abominate
shudder: quake; quiver; shake; shiver; tremble
shuffle: quibble; shamble
shun: avoid; elude; escape; evade; shirk
shut in: barricade; close
shut off: wall
shut out: bar; debar; exclude
shut up: pound
shut: blind; close
shutter: curtain
shutters: curtain
shy: afraid; bashful; cast; chary; coy; diffident; skittish; timid; unpretentious
sibling: brother
sick to one's stomach: nauseous
sick: ailing; bad; ill; indisposed; morbid; seedy; sickly; unhealthful; unsound
sicken: disgust; nauseate; revolt; shock
sickening: abhorrent; abominable; disgusting; distasteful; loathsome; nasty; nauseous; offensive
sickish: queasy; seedy
sickly-sweet: saccharine
sickly: ailing; feeble; morbid; peaked; sallow; sick; unhealthy; unsound; wan; weak; weakly
sickness: affliction; ailment; disease; disorder; malady
side by side: abreast
side with: back
side: border; facet; faction
sidekick: comrade
sideslip: skew
sidestep: evade; shirk
sidewalk: walk
sideways: askance
sidewise: askance
sidle: edge
siege: conflict; storm
sieve: riddle; screen; strain
sift: discuss; probe; screen; scrutinize; strain
sigh: pine
sight: blink; face; show; view; vision
sighting: aim
sightless: blind; purblind
sign: character; emblem; evidence; execute; expression; frank; guide; icon; mark; notice; omen; portent; presage; trace; type; warning
signal: call; eminent; evidence; express; extraordinary; guide; memorable; notable; noteworthy; presage; ring; sign; signify; start; word
signally: especially
signature: frank
significance: consequence; consideration; effect; importance; matter; meaning; moment; purport; sense; spirit; stress; substance; value; weight
significant: emphatic; expressive; meaning; memorable; noteworthy; ominous; weighty
significantly: especially
significate: speak
signification: effect; meaning; purport; sense
signify: express; matter; mean; purport; qualify; sign

signifying: significant
silence: quiet; reserve; still
silent: close; dark; dumb; mute; noiseless; quiet; reticent; speechless; still; sullen; tacit; taciturn
silhouette: outline; shape
silken: saccharine
silky: saccharine
silliness: lunacy
silly: childish; cockeyed; comical; fatuous; foolish; frivolous; giddy; impertinent; mindless; puerile; senseless; simple; unreasonable; vacuous; wacky; weak
silt: deposit; ground
silver-tongued: eloquent
silver: bright
silvery: mellifluous
similar: congenial; parallel; same; uniform
similarity: community; parallel; parity; resemblance; semblance
similitude: picture; resemblance; similarity
simmer: boil; stew
simon-pure: sanctimonious
simoom: sirocco; storm
simple-minded: guileless; senile
simple: artless; austere; bare; blank; chaste; childish; direct; earthy; homely; foolish; homely; household; innocent; mere; mindless; naive; naked; plain; primitive; pure; rude; senseless; severe; sheer; sincere; single; stark; stupid; unaffected; unequivocal; unsophisticated; weak
simpleton: block; fool; oaf
simplex: simple
simplicity: modesty
simplify: aid
simulate: assume; counterfeit; fake; feign; imitate; pretend
simulated: artificial; counterfeit
simulation: show
sin: abomination; blame; crime; error; evil; fault; offend; offense; sacrilege; transgress; trespass; vice; wrong
since: because
sincere: aboveboard; artless; candid; devout; direct; earnest; forward; frank; guileless; honest; ingenuous; open; plain; poignant; real; resolute; simple; single; true; unaffected; unreserved
sincerely: aboveboard
sincerity: candor; enthusiasm; honesty; truth
sine qua non: condition; mainstay; necessary; necessity
sinecure: appointment
sinewy: muscular; robust; stalwart; stout; strong; sturdy
sinful: abandoned; bad; black; corrupt; criminal; dark; depraved; evil; foul; immoral; perverse; shameless; sinister; unclean; ungodly; vicious; wicked; wrong
sinfulness: corruption; harm
sing: warble
singe: burn; scorch; sear
singer: artist
single out: emphasize; mark; prefer; single
single-minded: rapt
single: alone; exclusive; only; particular; singular; sole; special; unique
singlefoot: pace
singleness: unity
singleton: single
singly: only; particularly
singular: aberrant; abnormal; characteristic; curious; express; extraordinary; fantastic; odd; particular; peculiar; private; queer; rare; remarkable; special; strange; uncommon; unique; unusual; whimsical
singularity: abnormality; brilliance; consequence; idiosyncrasy; peculiarity; unity
sinister: grim
sink down: settle
sink in: penetrate; permeate
sink: abate; bury; die; dip; droop; dwindle; ebb; fail; give; immerse; lower; overwhelm; plump; set; settle; submerge; subside; wane
sinking: abatement; descent; low
sinless: innocent
sinner: criminal
sinuate: sinuous; tortuous
sinuous: crooked; tortuous
sip: drink; soupçon; taste
siren: alarm

sirocco: storm
sissy: weakling
sit: brood; pose
site: environment; habitat; lay; lie; locale; place; position; region; seat; situation; spot
situate: place; position; set
situation: aspect; case; condition; environment; information; job; office; pass; place; plight; position; predicament; scene; seat; shape; spot; state; station; trim
sizable: mighty; substantial
size: bulk; extent; mass; proportion; volume
sizeable: large
skeletal: cadaverous; spindly
skeleton: carcass
skeptic: atheist; skeptical
skeptical: doubtful; incredulous; quizzical; skeptic
skeptically: askance
sketch: depict; design; draw; outline; plan; portray
sketcher: artist
skewed: cockeyed
skewer: pillory
skiff: tender
skill: ability; address; art; capacity; craft; cunning; delicacy; knack; policy
skilled: able; conversant; experienced; expert; fine; finished; handy; master; nice; old; perfect; proficient; skillful; versed
skillful management: address; strategy
skillful: able; adroit; apt; artifice; capable; clever; crafty; cunning; dexterous; expert; good; handy; ingenious; master; proficient; ready; skilled; tactful
skillfully: well
skillfulness: ability; capacity; cunning; knack
skim along: flit
skim over: pass; skip
skim: pass
skin-deep: cosmetic
skin: hide; peel; pelt
skinflint: miser
skinny: angular; gaunt; lean; meager; poor; spare; spindly; thin
skip over: skip
skip: jump; play; scale; sport; trip
skirmish: action; battle; brush; combat; fight; passage; struggle
skirt: rim
skit: sketch
skittery: skittish
skittish: shaky
skulk: lurk; slack; sneak
sky-blue: blue
skyscraping: high
slack off: abate; malinger; shirk
slack: abatement; lax; loose; malinger; shiftless; slacken; slothful; slow; tardy
slacken: abate; loose; relax; remit; slack
slackening: abatement
slag: refuse
slam: shut
slander: abuse; crime; detraction; insult; malediction; malign; scandal; slur; traduce; vilify
slanderous: injurious; snide
slang: jargon
slant: facet; inclination; skew; slope
slap-dash: cosmetic
slap-happy: groggy
slap: blow; strike
slash: cut; mangle; rip
slashing: caustic
slaughter: butcher; destruction; kill; massacre; shambles; slay
slaughterer: butcher
slave: attendant; menial; serf
slavery: bondage; captivity; servitude
slavish: base; obsequious; servile; supple
slay: assassinate; destroy; kill; massacre; murder; slaughter
slayer: butcher
slaying: slaughter
sleazy: tacky
sleek: glossy; smarmy; smooth; smug
sleep-inducing: sedative
sleep: slumber
sleepless: vigilant; wakeful
sleet: deposit
sleight of hand: magic
sleight-of-hand: trick
slender: delicate; gaunt; negligible; slight; slim; small; spare; tenuous; thin; weak
slew: skew

slice: slash
slick: cagey; facile; sleek; slippery
slide: glide; push; slip
slight crime: peccadillo
slight: affront; cut; delicate; delicate; disregard; disregard; facile; ignore; indignity; light; little; neglect; negligible; overlook; paltry; petty; rebuff; remote; sketchy; slender; slim; slur; small; snub; spare; superficial; thin; trifling; trivial; unimportant; weak
slighting: derogatory
slightly: little
slim: negligible; slender; slight; thin; weak
slime: deposit; ooze
sling: cast
slink: lurk; skulk; sneak
slip away from: elude
slip: blunder; error; fault; fly; glide; inaccuracy; mistake; oversight; slide; trip
slippery: glib; touchy
slipshod: lax; slapdash; slovenly
slipup: blunder
slit: cut; opening; rent; rip; slash
slither: slide; slip
slithery: slippery
slob: yahoo
slog: shamble
slogan: byword; catchword; device; watchword
slope backward: retreat
slope downward: dip
slope: bank; decline; descent; inclination; lean; slant
sloppy: dirty; slapdash; untidy; upset
slot: opening
slothful: idle; inactive; indolent; laggard; lazy; remiss; shiftless; slow; sluggish
slough: cast; quagmire; wash
slovenly: lax; perfunctory; untidy
slow-moving: lazy
slow: abate; backward; blunt; callous; cushion; damp; delay; deliberate; detain; dim; drag; dull; foolish; gradual; heavy; impede; indolent; laggard; late; leisurely; obstruct; remiss; retard; shackle; slack; sluggish; sullen; tardy; tardy; torpid; unapt
slowdown: lag
slowing: lag; slack
slowpoke: laggard
slue: skew
sluggardly: slothful; slow
sluggish: apathetic; callous; cold; dull; fat; idle; inactive; inanimate; indolent; lackadaisical; languid; lazy; lifeless; remiss; slack; slothful; slow; sullen; tardy; torpid
sluggishness: phlegm
slumber: sleep
slummy: shabby
slur: pillory; vilify
sly: astute; clandestine; crafty; designing; dry; insidious; Machiavellian; politic; stealthy; underhand; wily
slyness: cunning; deceit
smack: dash; taste
small talk: gossip
small-minded: bigoted; mean
small: diminutive; dwarf; fine; little; minor; minute; negligible; niggardly; petty; scanty; slender; slight; slim; small-minded; tenuous; trivial
smaller: minor
smallness: paucity
smarmy: mealy-mouthed; unctuous
smart: active; acute; agile; cagey; clever; fashionable; intelligent; jaunty; luminous; neat; notable; piquant; round; sharp; spry; trim
smarten: decorate
smartness: style
smash: batter; break; crash; crush; destroy
smashing: smash
smear: daub; pillory; smirch; smirch; smirch
smell: flavor; odor; perfume; scent
smelly: strong
smelt: fuse; run
smile: beam; laugh
smirch: daub
smite: batter; strike
smog: fog; haze; mist
smoke: exhaust; fume
smoky: turbid

smooth: calm; clear; easy; even; facile; flat; fluent; glib; glossy; grind; level; mellifluous; mellow; pacify; patch; plain; polish; polished; sleek; slippery; smug; soft; still; suave; unruffled; urbane

smoothness: calm; polish

smother: stifle; still; strangle

smudge: daub; smirch; smirch

smug: conceited; sanctimonious; self-satisfied; smarmy

smut: foul; smirch

smutch: smirch

smutty: foul; nasty; obscene

snack: bite

snap: crack; rend

snappish: cantankerous; cross; curt; fractious; fretful; irascible; irritable; moody; peevish; peppery; petulant; querulous; quick; sour; splenetic; testy; waspish

snappy: fleet

snare: capture; cheat; trap

snarl: growl; perplex

snarling: peppery; petulant

snatch: catch; pluck; whip

sneak off or out: abscond

sneak: lurk; skulk

sneaker: sneak

sneaking: slavish

sneer at: jeer; pillory; ridicule; taunt

sneer: jeer; mock; ridicule; scoff; scorn

sneering: bitter; contemptuous; cynical; sardonic

snicker: laugh

snigger: laugh

snob: parvenu

snobbish: clannish; exclusive; haughty; high; uppity

snobbishness: pride

snobby: clannish; uppity

snoop: kibitz

snooty: proud; uppity

snow: deposit; storm

snowstorm: storm

snowy: pearly

snub: rebuff

snug: cozy

so-called: nominal

so-so: lackluster; lukewarm; serviceable

so: accordingly; therefore

soak: drench; saturate; seethe; wet

soaked: wet

soar: ascend; fly

sob: cry; weep

sobbing: lachrymose

sober-minded: solid

sober: abstemious; austere; demure; grave; judicious; lucid; melancholy; moderate; pensive; rational; realistic; reasonable; sedate; sensible; serious; solemn; solid; staid; steady; temperate

soberness: abstinence

sobriety: abstinence; melancholy

sobriquet: nickname

sociable: outgoing; social

social level: caste

social stratum: caste

social: affable; sociable

society: association; band; body; circle; club; combination; community; company; coterie; faction; fashion; lodge; order; union

sociopathic: antisocial

sod: earth

sodality: band; society

soft soap: blarney

soft spot: penchant

soft-hearted: kind; merciful; tender

soft-soap: cajole; flatter

soft-spoken: smooth

soft: bland; cozy; female; gentle; low; meek; mellow; mild; rotten; small; tender; tender

soften: allay; calm; lower; mellow; melt; moderate; pacify; palliate; qualify; relax; smooth; solace; soothe; subdue; tame; temper; touch

softened: mellow

softness: volume

soigné: fashionable

soigné: fashionable

soil: contaminate; daub; deface; earth; foul; ground; pollute; shame; smirch; spot; stain; sully; tarnish

soiled: black; dirty; foul; sordid; unclean

soiling: dirty

sojourn: abide; reside; residence; stay; stop; tarry

sojourner: pilgrim

solace: beguile; cheer; comfort; comfort; consolation; console

sole: bare; exclusive; lone; only; single; unique

solecism: blunder; impropriety

solely: only

solemn: grave; serious; sober; staid

solemnification: sanction

solemnize: awe; celebrate; observe

solicit: apply; ask; beg; beseech; crave; desire; entreat; implore; invite; petition; request; seek; supplicate; urge

solicitant: wannabe

solicitation: appeal; application; entreaty; petition; request

solicitor: advocate; counsel

solicitous desire: anxiety

solicitous: assiduous; jealous; meticulous; obliging

solicitousness: delicacy

solicitude: care; concern; delicacy; fear; worry

solid: close; compact; firm; hard; inexorable; inflexible; massive; solid; stable; stiff; strong; substantial; sure; uniform; well-built

solidify: compact; harden; set

solidly: hard

solitary: alone; antisocial; desolate; forlorn; lone; lonely; only; private; retired; single; sole

solitude: isolation; retreat

solo: alone

solution: answer; explanation; extract

solve: decipher; guess; resolve

solvent: responsible; solid; sound

somber: black; obscure; sad; sober; sullen

somebody: celebrity; person

somewhat: almost; pretty

somniferous: sedative

song: lay; melody

songful: lyrical

sonnet: piece

sonorant: consonant

sonorous: mellifluous; round

soon: presently

sooner: above

soothe: allay; appease; calm; comfort; conciliate; console; ease; heal; pacify; qualify; quiet; relieve; smooth; soften; solace; solace; still; temper

soother: sedative

soothing: bland; gentle; lenient; mild; sedative; soft

soothsayer: wizard

soothsaying: prediction

sooty: black

sop: soak

sophism: quibble

sophisticated: blasé; suave

sophistry: evasion

soporific: opiate; sedative; sedative

soppy: saccharine

sorcerer: magician; wizard

sorcery: charm; magic; necromancy

sordid: base; low; mean; mercenary; shabby; venal

sore: abrasion; bitter; gathering; sharp; tender

sorority: association; club

sorrow for: mourn

sorrow: compassion; cry; distress; evil; grief; grieve; misery; regret; repentance; tear; trial; trouble; woe

sorrowful: bitter; disconsolate; downhearted; grievous; heavy; lachrymose; lugubrious; melancholy; piteous; plaintive; sad; sore; sorry; tragic; unhappy

sorrowing: sorry

sorry: bad; penitent; sorrowful; wretched

sort out: gather

sort: arrange; breed; brood; cast; cut; distribute; divide; fashion; form; gather; kind; manner; nature; order; pattern; quality; range; rank; size; stamp; style; type; variety

sorts: spirit

sot: drunkard

sotted: drunken

soul: abbreviation; flavor; spirit

soulless: apathetic

sound: fast; good; hale; hardy; healthy; intact; judicious; lucid; perfect; practical; rational; reasonable; right; robust; safe; sane; sensible; sober; solid; staunch; substantial; unbroken; valid; vigorous; well; whole

soundless: noiseless; silent; still

soundly: well

soundness: strength

soupçon: dash; trace

soup: mist

sour: acerbic; acid; austere; cross; glum; morose; sharp; stale; sullen; tart; turn

source: beginning; growth; head; origin; rise; spring

sourish: tart

sourpuss: killjoy

southerly: high

souvenir: memento; remembrance; trophy

sovereign government: state

sovereign remedy: cure-all

sovereign: authority; kingly; predominant

sovereignty: control; empire; kingdom; power; realm; reign; sway

sow: disperse

space: blank; circuit; extent; leading; place; region; scope; time; tract; void; way; yawn

spacey: giddy

spacing: leading

spacious: ample; broad; capacious; extensive; large; wide

span: couple; pair; time

spar: dispute; quarrel

spare: gaunt; give; haggard; makeshift; meager; scanty; slender; sparse; spindly

sparing: abstemious; chary; economical; frugal; niggardly; parsimonious; prudent; spare; thrifty

sparingness: parsimony; poverty

spark: iota; sparkle

sparkle: brilliance; glare; gleam; glisten; life; radiate; shine; wink

sparkling: bright; bubbly; lively; piquant; radiant; witty

sparky: bubbly

sparse: lean; meager; rare; scanty; thin

sparseness: paucity

spasm: access; agony; convulsion; paroxysm; start; throe

spasmodic: abrupt

spasmodically: piecemeal

spat: brawl; dispute; quarrel; tiff

spay: alter

speak for: advocate

speak of: mention

speak to: address

speak: converse; express; parley; say; talk; tell; utter

spear: stab; stick

special messenger: express

special: abstract; certain; characteristic; exclusive; express; extraordinary; offbeat; particular; peculiar; private; proper; rarefied; recherché; select; some; specific

specialist: dilettante; expert

specially: especially; particularly; particularly

specialty: terrain

specie: money

species: breed; brood; kind; nature; sort; variety

specific: cure; definite; particular; peculiar; proper; remedy; some; special; tangible

specifically: particularly

specify: assign; mention; name; state

specimen: example; pattern; piece; sample; type

specious: apparent; deceptive; glossy; ostensible; plausible

speck: bit; blemish; particle; spot

speckle: spot

spectacle: pageant; scene; show; show

spectator: witness

specter: apparition; ghost; phantasm; shade; shape; spirit; vision

spectral: cadaverous; phantom; unearthly

speculate: deduce; wonder

speculation: thought; venture

speculative: iffy; unpractical; visionary

speech: address; dialect; harangue; language; oration; talk; terminology; vernacular

speechify: declaim

speechless: dumb; mute; silent

speed up: advance; expedite; precipitate

speed: assist; expedite; expedition; haste; hasten; hurry; precipitate; race; rapidity; run; velocity

speedily: fast

speedy: fleet; hasty; quick; rapid; swift

spell out: demonstrate

spell: aid; assist; charm; run; sorcery; span; throe; time

spellbinding: charismatic

spend: consume; disburse; exhaust; expend; pass; squander; waste

spendthrift: extravagant; prodigal

splenetic: moody

spent: bankrupt; jaded; weary

spew forth: cast

sphere: bailiwick; ball; capacity; circle; circuit; milieu; orb; reach; realm; region; terrain; walk

spherical: round

sphinx: monster

spice: savor; seasoning; zest

spicy: hot; peppery; piquant; sharp; strong

spill over: cascade

spill: cascade

spin: move; revolve; roll; rotate; turn; twist; whirl; whirl

spindle: roll

spindly: shaky

spine: mainstay

spinsterish: single

spiral: twist

spirit: animation; apparition; aroma; aura; bravery; courage; dash; energy; enterprise; flavor; gaiety; genius; ghost; grit; life; mettle; pluck; purport; shade; sparkle; specter; valor; verve; zeal

spirited: active; alert; audacious; bold; brisk; cheerful; enterprising; fiery; jolly; lively; mercurial; racy; sanguine; scrappy; strenuous; vivacious; vivid; zealous

spiritedness: verve

spiritless: cold; dull; flat; inanimate; languid; lifeless; meek; nerveless; tame; tame; vapid

spiritual: holy; humane

spirituous: hard

spite: grudge; malevolence; malice; rancor; venom

spiteful: cross; derogatory; malevolent; malignant; moody; nasty; revengeful; splenetic; ugly; vicious; vindictive; virulent

spitefulness: malevolence; malice; venom

splash: dash

splatter: dash

spleen: anger; spite; venom

spleenish: splenetic

spleeny: moody; splenetic

splendid: bright; capital; costly; gallant; gorgeous; grand; luxurious; magnificent; majestic; noble; ornate; palatial; pretty; proud; radiant; regal; shining; superb; top-notch

splendiferous: palatial

splendor: brilliance; glory; grandeur; magnificence

splenetic: fractious; fretful; morose; peevish; sulky; sullen; testy

splinter: break; crash

split second: flash

split: blast; breach; break; burst; cleft; crack; gape; rend; rent; rupture; separate; shatter; spring; tear

spoil: corrupt; deface; deform; destroy; devastate; disfigure; injure; mangle; mar; murder; pamper; pillage; rot; ruin; sack; strip; waste; wreck

spoiled: corrupt; egocentric; jaded

spoils: loot; pillage; plunder

spoilsport: killjoy

spoken: oral; verbal; vernacular

spoliation: pillage; plunder; ruin; sack; waste

sponsorship: protection

spontaneous: ad-lib; impetuous; improvised; offhand; voluntary

spoof: burlesque

spook: ghost

spoor: scent; trace; trail

sport: dally; fun; game; jest; mock; pastime; play

sportive: gay; humorous; jocose; jolly; playful; pleasant; vivacious; waggish

sportiveness: gaiety

spot: blemish; blot; daub; fix; flaw; locale; mark; note; place; position; situation; stain; stand; stigma; taint

spotless: blameless; clean; clear; fair; guiltless; innocent; perfect; pure

spotlight: emphasize

spotted: dappled

spouse: partner

spout: flow; gush; spurt; spurt

sprain: strain

spread or stretch out: expand

spread out: dilate; display; extend; open

spread: bear; disperse; distribute; emerge; noise; radiate; run; sprinkle; stretch

spree: rampage

sprightliness: animation; life

sprightly: active; agile; alert; blithe; bright; bubbly; cheerful; gay; jaunty; lively; mercurial; playful; pleasant; racy; sportive; vivacious

spring or fly back: recoil

spring up: rise

spring: bound; dart; emanate; gambol; issue; jump; leap; originate; proceed; result; skip; spurt; start; trap; vault; warp

springe: trap

springiness: spring

springtime: spring

sprinkle: dash; scatter; strew

sprinkling: dash

sprite: apparition; brownie; fairy; spirit

sprout: grow

spruce up: decorate

spruce: jaunty; neat; smart; smug

spry: agile; brisk; busy; lively; nimble

spumescent: bubbly

spunk: bravery

spunky: scrappy

spur-of-the-moment: ad-lib; offhand

spur: incentive; incite; induce; inducement; motive; pique; stimulate; stir; urge

spurious: artificial; base; bogus; counterfeit; fake; false; meretricious; mock; phony; pseudo; sham; unlawful; unreal

spurn: despise; disdain; rebuff; refuse

spurt: burst; flow; gush; spout

spy: see

spying: curious

squabble: brawl; contention; dispute; quarrel; row

squad: gang; knot; pack; troop

squalid: dirty; filthy; foul; mean; shabby; sordid

squalidness: squalor

squall: blast; cry; storm

squally: dirty

squander: consume; dissipate; exhaust; lavish; spend; wanton; waste

squandered: lost

squanderer: prodigal

square: balance; conform; even

squash: stamp

squat: zilch

squawky: raucous

squeamish: dainty; nice; queasy

squeeze: compress; constrict; cram; crowd; crush; jam

squirm: twist

squirt: spout

stab: pang; pierce; run; stick; thrust; wound

stability: constancy; patience; poise

stabilize: compact; fix; settle; steady

stabilizer: balance

stable: constant; durable; earnest; faithful; firm; motionless; permanent; secure; solid; staunch; steadfast; steady; substantial; sure

stack: heap

stacked: well-built

staff: office; stanza; verge

stage: pass; platform; scene; set; state

stagger: amaze; astonish; bewilder; hobble; shock; totter; vacillate

stagnant: standing; sullen

stagy: recherché; theatrical

staid: grave; sedate; serene; serious; sober; steady

stain: blemish; blot; contaminate; daub; disgrace; foul; mark; pollute; shame; slur; smirch; spot; spot; stigma; sully; taint; tarnish; tint

stained: black; foul

stake: lay; pale; play; wager

stale: common; flat; hack; hackneyed; stereotyped; tacky; trite

stalk: stem

stall: stand

stalwart: robust; stout; strong; sturdy

stammer: falter

stammering: hesitation

submicroscopic: diminutive
submission: deference; obeisance; patience; resignation
submissive: dutiful; easy; gentle; humble; meek; obedient; obsequious; passive; patient; servile; slavish; soft; subject; supple; tame
submissiveness: deference; humility; patience
submit to: bear; brook; grudge; stand; support; take
submit: acquiesce; bend; bow; endure; resign; surrender; yield
submitting: passive
subordinate: adjunct; auxiliary; minor; postpone; sidekick; subject; subject; subsidiary
suborn: tamper
subrepitious: surreptitious
subsequently: since
subservient: obedient; subject; subordinate
subside: abate; decrease; die; diminish; ebb; settle
subsidence: abatement; decrease; remission
subsidiary: accidental; auxiliary
subsidize: abet
subsidy: bonus; gift; subvention
subsist: feed; sustain
subsistence: keep; livelihood; living; maintenance; nutrition; support
substance: abstract; body; burden; material; matter; mean; stuff
substandard: poor; short
substantial: actual; massive; positive; solid; sound; staunch; strong; subjective; tangible; valid
substantiate: confirm; establish; prove; ratify
substitute for: act; supply
substitute: alternate; change; false; makeshift; replace; surrogate
substituted: vicarious
substitution: change
substructure: base
subsurface: underground
subterfuge: artifice; chicanery; deception; evasion; excuse; mask; pretense; quibble
subterranean: underground
subterrestrial: underground
subtle quality: aroma
subtle: delicate; insidious; Machiavellian; nice; penetrating; politic; refined; sly
subtlety: craft
subtract: abate; deduct; take; withdraw
subvention: subsidy
subversion: abuse; disloyalty; ruin; sabotage
subversive: disloyal; underground
subversiveness: sabotage
subvert: abuse; overthrow; sabotage
succeed in: accomplish
succeed: bear; ensue; flourish; follow; follow; manage; prevail; prosper; replace; rise; supersede; supplant; survive; thrive; triumph; win
success: accomplishment; hit; triumph; victory; welfare
successful: fortunate; happy; prevailing; prosperous; solid; thrifty; well
succession: course; order; round; sequence; series; stream
successive: alternate; consecutive; continual
succinct: brief; compact; concise; laconic; sententious; short; summary; terse
succinctness: brevity
succint: pithy
succor: abet; aid; assist; help; nourish; nurse; relief; relieve; serve; support
succulent: lush; scrumptious
suck up to: flatter
suck: draw
suckle: nurse
sudden: abrupt; acute; headlong; impatient; precipitate; sharp; unexpected
suddenly: plump; short
sue for: beg
sue: apply; ask; beg; entreat; petition; pray; request; solicit; supplicate
suffer pain: ache
suffer: abide; ache; allow; bear; brook; carry; endure; experience; grieve; grudge; have; indulge; labor; let; pay; permit; see; stand; support; sustain; take; undergo

sufferance: allowance; patience; resignation; tolerance
suffering: affliction; agony; anguish; cost; distress; evil; grief; hardship; misery; oppression; pain; passive; sorrow; trial; trouble
suffice for: do
suffice: answer; cover; satisfy; serve
sufficient: adequate; competent; equal; good
sufficiently: well
suffocate: damp; stifle; strangle
suffuse: imbue
sugarcoat: palliate
sugary: saccharine; sweet
suggest: advise; hint; insinuate; intimate; move; proffer; propose
suggestible: receptive
suggestion: advice; aroma; beam; cast; caveat; counsel; dash; ghost; hint; proposal; purport; shade; sign; soupçon; strain; suspicion; touch; trace; vestige; wind
suggestive: blue; expressive; racy
sui generis: appropriate
suit: accommodate; accord; action; adapt; adjust; agree; answer; appeal; attention; calculate; case; correspond; dress; entreaty; fashion; hit; petition; qualify; request; temper
suitability: application; aptitude; fitness; harmony; propriety
suitable: adequate; advisable; applicable; appropriate; available; becoming; befitting; competent; congenial; consistent; consonant; convenient; decent; decorous; eligible; equal; expedient; feasible; felicitous; good; just; likely; meet; nice; opportune; pertinent; proper; relevant; right; seasonable; seemly; well
suitableness: propriety
suitably: right; well
suite or set of rooms: apartment
suite: flat
suited: applicable; appropriate; apt; capable; congenial; convenient; decent; feasible; good; just; meet; opportune; pertinent; proper; relevant; seemly
suitor: gallant
sulk: pet
sulky: carriage; cross; glum; moody; morose; sullen
sullen: black; cloudy; cross; dark; glum; moody; morose; sulky
sullied: dirty; foul
sully: blemish; blot; contaminate; disgrace; foul; shame; smirch; spot; stain; taint; tarnish
sultry: hot
sum total: totality; whole
sum: add; aggregate; number; total; whole
summarize: abstract; brief; recapitulate
summary: abridgment; abstract; argument; brief; conciseness; digest; pithy; synopsis
summation: conclusion
summing up: addition; conclusion
summit: apex; head; height; peak; pinnacle; top
summon: assemble; bid; call; convene; invite; muster; ring
summons: call
sumptuous repast: feast
sumptuous: costly; gorgeous; luxurious; magnificent; opulent; ornate; palatial; rich; splendid; state; superb
sumptuousness: magnificence
Sunday best: finery
Sunday painter: dabbler
Sunday: Sabbath
sunder: cut; divide; part; rend; separate; sever; tear
sundown: evening; twilight
sundry: different; many; multifarious; various
sunless: dark; somber
sunny: bright; cheerful; clear; fair; lyrical; optimistic; pleasant
sunrise: dawn; light; morning
sunset: twilight
superabundance: excess; exuberance; plenty; surfeit; surplus
superabundant: superfluous
superannuated: decrepit
superb: gorgeous; grand; magnificent; splendid
supercilious: arrogant; contemptuous; disdainful; haughty; high; overbearing; proud; strange; uppity

superciliousness: arrogance; assumption; disdain; pride
superficial: apparent; cosmetic; empty; exterior; facile; flash; perfunctory; sketchy; slapdash; slight
superfluity: excess; exuberance; surfeit
superfluous: extraneous; unnecessary; waste; wordy
superhuman: supernatural
superintend: administer; govern; manage; master; overlook; oversee
superintendence: charge; command; control; management; oversight; surveillance
superintendent: manager; warden
superior condition: advantage
superior to: above
superior: above; choice; cool; elegant; excellent; fine; magnificent; noble; paramount; preeminent; prevailing; recherché; strange; top-notch
superiority: advantage; distinction; excellence; quality
superlative: extreme; peerless; recherché; top-notch
supermanliness: machismo
supernal: celestial
supernatural being: ghost
supernatural: miraculous; occult; preternatural; uncanny; unearthly; weird
supersede: replace; supplant
superstar: celebrity
superstardom: celebrity
supervise: administer; conduct; govern; manage; overlook; oversee; superintend
supervision: oversight; surveillance
supervisor: manager
supine: flat; low; slothful
supplant: replace; supersede
supple: active; flexible; limber; lissome; malleable; pliant
supplement: add; addition; adjunct; appendix; complement; complement
supplementary: false; subsidiary
supplicate: appeal; ask; beg; beseech; crave; entreat; implore; petition; plead; pray; request; solicit
supplication: appeal; entreaty; petition; request
supplies: provision; stock
supply: accommodate; accomplish; administer; appoint; furnish; give; produce; provide; render; reserve; stock; surfeit; sustain; yield
supplying: provision
support: abet; abide; advocate; aid; approve; argue; assert; assertion; assist; authorize; back; bear; brace; carry; champion; cherish; countenance; encourage; endure; favor; foster; help; hold; livelihood; living; mainstay; maintain; maintenance; mean; nourish; pillar; post; promote; relieve; sanction; sanction; shore; standard; stay; strength; strut; subsidy; succor; sustain; sustain; sympathy; uphold; upright; vindicate
supportable: tenable; viable
supporter: adherent; advocate; aid; disciple; follower; friend; helper; mainstay; partisan; patron
supporting: auxiliary
suppose: assume; conjecture; consider; deduce; deem; give; guess; imagine; presume; regard; surmise; suspect; take; think; think
supposing: if
supposition: assumption; conjecture; guess; idea; if; speculation; suspicion
suppress: abate; abolish; defeat; hide; lay; oppress; quell; reduce; repress; restrain; stay; stifle; stop; subdue; vanquish; withhold
suppressed: tame
suppression: abatement
supra: above
supremacy: authority; empire
supreme: chief; consummate; preeminent; sovereign; uppermost
surcease: death; suspense
sure: absolute; actual; certain; clear; confident; dead; decided; definite; indisputable; infallible; positive; safe; secure; steadfast; tenacious; true; unabashed; undeniable; unerring

surely: clearly
surety: assurance; guarantee; warrant
surf: wave
surface: cosmetic; facile; periphery
surfeit: pall; satiate; satisfy; surplus
surge: breaker; seethe
surly: cantankerous; cynical; grouchy; morose; sulky; ugly
surmise: conjecture; conjecture; deduce; guess; speculation; suspect
surmount: climb; conquer; overcome
surpass: beat; better; break; exceed; excel; head; lead; outdo; pass; predominate; top
surpassing: above; preeminent
surplus: excess; remainder; residue
surprise: amaze; astonish; catch; confuse; confusion; shock; stagger; startle; wonder
surprising: marvelous; unexpected
surrejoinder: rejoinder; reply; retort
surrender: abandon; abdicate; abdication; cede; deliver; quit; relinquish; render; resign; resignation; submit; waive; yield
surreptitious: sly; stealthy; underground; underhand
surrey: carriage
surround: belt; beset; circle; embrace; encircle; enclose; envelop; ring
surrounded by: amid; among
surrounding: about
surroundings: environment; habitat; milieu; state; vicinity
surveillance: management; oversight
survey: contemplate; oversee; peruse; prospect; review; view
survive: outlive
surviving: living
susceptibility: feeling; sensibility
susceptible: capable; patient; receptive; sensitive; sentient; vulnerable
susceptibleness: susceptibility
susceptive: sentient
susceptiveness: susceptibility
suspect: conjecture; distrust; doubt; surmise
suspected: suspect
suspend (for a day): adjourn
suspend: abate; break; hang; interrupt; respite; stay; swing
suspended: dormant; pendulous
suspense: abeyance; agony; doubt; poise; remission
suspenseful: critical
suspension: abeyance; break; pause; remission; respite; suspense
suspicion: apprehension; distrust; doubt; hunch; misgiving; soupçon
suspicious: careful; jealous; quizzical; shy; suspect
suspiciously: askance
sustain: abet; approve; assist; back; bear; carry; cherish; endure; feed; foster; hold; maintain; nourish; preserve; relieve; stand; stay; suffer; support; undergo; uphold
sustainer: mainstay
sustenance: food; livelihood; living; nutrition; support
susurration: murmur
susurrus: murmur
suzerainty: power; reign
svelte: sleek
swab: wash
swabby: tar
swagger: boast; strut; swell
swaggering: boast; bravado
swallow: absorb; drink; gobble; imbibe; swift
swamp: quagmire; wash
swank: fashionable; palatial
swap: exchange; trade
swarm: abound; cloud; crowd; flock; multitude; teem; throng; troop
swarming: alive; populous
swart: black; swarthy
swarthy: black; dark; dusky
sway: affect; authority; careen; command; empire; govern; influence; power; reign; roll; rule; shake; stagger; swing; totter; vacillate; wave; waver
swayable: receptive
swear: curse
swearing: blasphemy

sweat: perspiration; plod
sweep: clean; grandeur; range; swing
sweeping: comprehensive
sweet talk: blarney
sweet-scented: fragrant
sweet-smelling: fragrant
sweet-sounding: mellifluous
sweet-talk: cajole; flatter
sweet: fresh; luscious; mellifluous; mellow; rich; soft; tuneful
sweetmeat: dainty
swell out: inflate
swell: augment; billow; bulk; dilate; distend; expand; grow; grow; heave; inflate; rise; wave
swelling: big; gathering; rise; swell
swerve: bend; deviate; sheer; wander; warp
swift: express; fast; fleet; free; hasty; nimble; quick; rapid
swiftly: fast
swiftness: haste; rapidity; speed; velocity
swimmy: giddy
swindle: cheat; humbug; rook; steal; trick; victimize
swindler: cheat; humbug; knave; rogue; rook
swing: careen; oscillate; roll; sway
swinging: pendulous
swipe: pilfer
switch: stick; whip
swollen: big; tumid; turgid
swoon: faint; trance
swooning: faint
sycophant: parasite; toady; yesman
sycophantic: obsequious; saccharine; servile; slavish; smarmy; supple; unctuous
syllabus: abridgment; abstract; brief; synopsis
sylph: gnome; nymph
sylvan: savage
symbol: character; device; emblem; icon; idol; mark; sign; standard; type
symbolize: represent
symmetrical: harmonious; regular
symmetricalness: symmetry
symmetry: balance; grace; order; proportion
sympathetic: affectionate; compassionate; congenial; feeling; genial; harmonious; humane; kind; kindly; merciful; receptive; soft; sorry; tender
sympathize with: pity
sympathizing: sympathetic
sympathy: compassion; consideration; emotion; empathy; feeling; kindness; pity; rapport
syndicate: company; ring
synergistic: symbiotic
synod: assembly
synopsis: abridgment; abstract; brief; digest; summary
synthetic: fictitious
syrupy: sweet
system: economy; form; method; plan; scheme; structure; style; technique; theory
systematic: orderly; organic; regular; severe
systematize: digest; form; order; organize; regulate
systematized: organic
table: schedule; stand
tablecloth: spread
taboo: ban; forbid; sacrosanct
tabu: sacrosanct
tabulate: schedule; score
tacit: silent
taciturn: close; reticent; silent; uncommunicative
taciturnity: reserve
tack on: add; attach
tackle: block; purchase
tacky: tasteless
tact: address; delicacy
tactful: careful; diplomatic; nice; politic; prudent
tactic: machination; ploy; policy
tactics: strategy
tactless: maladroit; short-sighted
tag line: catchword
tag: band; check; mark; name
taint: blemish; blot; contaminate; corrupt; disgrace; foul; poison; pollute; shame; smirch; spot; stain; stigma; sully; tarnish
tainted: corrupt; foul; morbid; rotten
take a chance: risk
take a fancy to: fancy
take aback: chagrin
take action: move
take advantage of: exploit

take along: bring
take as one's own: appropriate
take away: abstract; subtract
take back: revoke; withdraw
take care or charge: attend
take care of: mind; nurse
take charge of: attend
take counsel: advise
take down: abase; lower
take effect: bear
take exception: demur
take for granted: assume; presume; suppose
take hold of: occupy
take in: comprehend; cover; imbibe; shorten
take into custody: arrest; seize
take no notice of: disregard
take off: caricature
take on: assume
take one's time: dawdle
take out: zap
take over: acquire; monopolize
take place: chance; happen; occur; pass
take possession of: acquire
take prisoner: arrest; capture
take unawares: catch; surprise
take up: espouse; occupy
take upon oneself: assume
take vengeance: avenge
take wing: fly
take-no-prisoners: aggressive
take-off: caricature; travesty
take: accept; arrest; bear; carry; catch; have; pilfer; remove; seize; steal; wrest
takeoff: burlesque
taking for granted: assumption
taking: winning
tale: account; fable; narrative; novel; relation; romance; saga; story; untruth
talent: ability; aptitude; capacity; craft; endowment; faculty; genius; gift; turn
talented: able; clever; finished
talk into: wangle
talk of the town: scuttlebutt
talk over: discuss
talk: babble; confer; converse; parley; rumor; scuttlebutt; speak; speech
talkative: effusive; garrulous; glib; loquacious; outgoing; voluble
talking: talk
tall tale: untruth
tall: high; lofty; rank; towering
tallness: height
tally: agree; conform; correspond
tame: break; familiar; gentle; meek; subdue; submissive
tamp: stem
tan: burn
tang: zest
tangible: actual; palpable; physical
tangle: complex; entangle; foul; perplex; snarl
tangled: complex; foul
tanker: transport
tanned: weather-beaten
tantalize: mock; torment
tantamount: equal
tap: stroke; touch
tar: mariner; sailor
tardy: backward; late; remiss; slack; slow
target: aim; mark; object; objective; scapegoat
tarnish: blemish; contaminate; disgrace; pillory; pollute; shame; smirch; spot; stain; stigma; sully; taint
tarnished: dim; foul
tarry: abide; continue; dawdle; delay; fool; linger; loiter; pause; remain; stay; wait
tarrying: delay; wait
tart: acerbic; acid; piquant; sour
Tartarus: hell
Tartuffian: sanctimonious
task: office; work
taste: fancy; flavor; judgment; penchant; relish; savor; sip; soupçon; trace
tasteful: critical; decent; elegant
tasteless: atrocious; flat; stale; tacky; unsavory; watery
tasty: palatable; scrumptious
tattered: ragged; shabby
tattle: gossip
tattoo: beat
tatty: seedy; shabby; tacky
taunt: fret; jeer; mock; ridicule; sarcasm; scoff; twit
taunting: satirical
taunts: ridicule
taut: stiff; tense
tauten: brace; strain; stretch
tavern: hotel; inn

tawdry: base; flash; garish; gaudy; meretricious; tacky
tawny: swarthy
tax: charge; custom; duty
taxonomy: system
tchotchke: novelty
teach: breed; discipline; educate; enlighten; form; initiate; instruct; tell
teachable: receptive
teacher: guru; instructor
teaching: instruction; lore
teachings: doctrine
team up with: associate
team: gang; pair; span
tear apart: rend; rip
tear around: rampage
tear: bite; break; burst; lacerate; pluck; rampage; rend; rent; rip; strain
tearful: lachrymose
tears: cry
teary: lachrymose; watery
tease: annoy; banter; bother; fret; haggle; mock; molest; pain; persecute; pester; plague; tantalize; torment; twit; worry
teasel: tease
teasing: raillery
technique: address; method
ted: spread
teddy boy: rowdy
tedious: dreary; dry; dull; flat; heavy; long; monotonous; prosaic; slow; stupid; tame; tiresome; vapid; wearisome; weary; wordy
teed off: miffed
teem: abound; flow; swarm
teeming: abundant; affluent; big; fertile; populous; prolific
teen-ager: adolescent; youth
teens: youth
teetering: shaky; spindly
teetery: shaky; spindly
teetotalism: abstinence
tegument: cover
telephone: call
tell: apprise; describe; disclose; distinguish; divulge; impart; inform; mention; narrate; number; recount; relate; reveal; say; spin; ventilate
telling: graphic; lively; relation
temblor: quake; tremor
temerarious: daredevil
temerariousness: chutzpah
temerity: chutzpah
temper: allay; appease; cool; disposition; medium; mettle; mind; moderate; modify; mood; palliate; qualify; soften; spirit; temperament
temperament: disposition; humor; temper
temperamental: capricious; irascible; touchy
temperance: abstinence; virtue
temperate: abstemious; equable; even; gentle; mild; moderate; sober; spare
tempered: gentle
tempering: seasoning
tempest: storm
tempestuous: boisterous; foul; hard; rough; rude; rugged; ugly; wild
temple: sanctuary
tempo: movement; time
temporal: carnal; mundane; profane; secular; worldly
temporary: brief; ephemeral; makeshift; transient
temporize: dawdle
tempt: entice; invite; lure; seduce
temptation: lure
tempting: seductive
temptress: siren
tenable: viable
tenacious: persistent; pertinacious; single-minded; stiff; strong
tenaciously: fast
tenacity: constancy; perseverance
tenant: abide
tend toward: lean
tend: attend; bear; mind; nourish; nurse; sway; trend; verge; watch
tendency: aptitude; bent; bias; cast; disposition; habit; humor; inclination; liking; partiality; proclivity; propensity; strain; trend; turn
tender-hearted: benevolent; compassionate; kind; merciful; tender
tender-heartedness: compassion
tender: administer; advance; affectionate; amorous; benevolent; bid; childish; compassionate; dainty; delicate; fatherly; feeling;

gentle; gracious; humane; kind; lenient; lush; merciful; offer; pathetic; prefer; proffer; propose; soft; sore; sympathetic
tenderfoot: dabbler
tenderize: soften
tenderness: affection; clemency; compassion; delicacy; feeling; kindness; love; mercy; sentiment; weakness
tending: bound; inclination; prone
tenement: apartment
tenet: belief; doctrine; faith; principle; thought
tenets: platform
tenor: burden; effect; feeling; meaning; purport; spirit; theme
tense: stiff; taut
tentative: pendulous
tenuous: rarefied; thin
tenure: occupation; possession
tepid: grudging; lukewarm; warm
tergiversate: waffle; yo-yo
term: call; expression; mete; period; shape; style; time; title
termagant: fury; nag; scold; shrew
terminal: depot; extremity; last; station; stop
terminate: cease; close; complete; dissolve; do; end; finish; fulfill; pass; result; stop; zap
terminated: extinct
termination: abatement; catastrophe; close; conclusion; end; extremity; finish; limit; objective; result; stop
terminology: language; vernacular
terminus: end
terra firma: earth
terrain: bailiwick
terraqueous: mundane
terrene: terrestrial
terrestrial: earthly; mundane; worldly
terrible: dread; formidable; frightful; ghastly; hideous; horrendous; horrible; lurid; monstrous; tremendous; ugly
terrific: frightful; terrible; tremendous
terrified: afraid
terrify: alarm; appall; dismay; frighten; scare
terrifying: hideous; horrendous; terrible; tremendous
territory: bailiwick; habitat; region; state; terrain; tract
terror: alarm; awe; consternation; dismay; dread; fear; fright; horror; panic; scare
terrorize: panic
terse: brief; compact; concise; curt; laconic; pithy; sententious; short; summary
terseness: brevity; conciseness
test: check; control; criterion; examination; examine; experiment; ordeal; principle; probe; proof; prove; standard; tempt; trial; try
testify: affirm; have; protest; swear; witness
testimonial: memento; reference
testimony: authority; evidence; exhibit; proof; witness
testiness: petulance
testing: trial
testy: cantankerous; cross; cynical; fractious; fretful; grouchy; hasty; impatient; irascible; irritable; moody; passionate; peevish; peppery; petulant; querulous; quick; short; sour; splenetic; temperamental; touchy; waspish
tetchy: testy; touchy
tether: fasten; hitch
text: passage; theme
thankful: grateful
thaw: melt
The Comforter: spirit
The Devil: adversary
the Evil One: adversary
The Holy Ghost: spirit
The Holy Spirit: spirit
the legal fraternity: bar
the lot: totality
the Prince of Darkness: adversary
the real McCoy: genuine
The Spirit of God: spirit
the Tempter: adversary
the works: totality
theater: scene
theatrical: recherché.
theft: crime; plunder
theme: argument; melody; piece; plot; refrain; story; subject; substance; topic
then: therefore

theorem: principle
theoretical: abstract; academic; unpractical; unreal
theorist: visionary
theorize: conjecture
theory: assumption; conjecture; doctrine; speculation; view
therefore: accordingly
theriac: cure-all; panacea
theriacal: therapeutic
thesis: argument; position; subject; theme; topic
thespian: artist
thewless: spineless
thick-set: stout
thick: abundant; blunt; close; fat; gross; heavy; midst; solid; stout; turbid; viscous
thicken: gather
thicker: waver
thicket: brush; cover
thickness: body
thickset: well-built
thief: outlaw; robber
thieve: pilfer
thievish: dishonest
thimblerig: swindle
thin-skinned: touchy
thin: cut; gaunt; lean; meager; poor; rarefied; scanty; sheer; slender; slim; small; spare; sparse; spindly; tenuous; tinny; watery
thing: matter; object; piece
thingamabob: gadget
thingamajig: gadget
things: raiment
think about: consider; contemplate; revolve
think of or about: muse
think of: regard
think out: devise
think over: digest; meditate
think: conceive; consider; deduce; deem; deliberate; guess; hold; imagine; meditate; muse; ponder; reflect; ruminate; see; study; suppose; surmise; wonder
thinking: pensive; reflection; thought
thirst: appetite; desire; pant; pine
thirsty: dry
thither: ulterior
thong: scourge
thorn: curse
thorny: knotty
thorough: careful; complete; entire; extensive; faithful; perfect; radical; regular; solid; sound; unqualified
thoroughbred: pure
thoroughfare: passage
thoroughgoing: downright; radical; sedulous; strong; thorough; trenchant
thoroughly: clean; well
thorp: town
though: although; if; notwithstanding
thought: conceit; fancy; idea; regard; sentiment; study; surmise
thoughtful: attentive; careful; chivalrous; considerate; contemplative; deliberate; grave; meditative; melancholy; obliging; old; pensive; rapt; reflective; sedate; serious
thoughtfulness: consideration; delicacy; melancholy
thoughtless: blind; careless; foolish; hasty; improvident; inadvertent; insane; mindless; neglectful; perfunctory; rash; reckless; remiss; short-sighted; tasteless; unguarded; vacant
thoughtlessness: listlessness
thraldom: bondage
thrall: serf; slave
thralldom: captivity; servitude; slavery
thrash: beat; pound; whip
thread: plot; theme
threadbare: hackneyed; shabby; tacky
threads: raiment; wardrobe
threat: assault; menace; ultimatum
threaten: assault; attack; lower; menace
threatening: forbidding; formidable; imminent; menace; ominous; sinister; truculent; ugly
three-dimensional: solid
threnody: lament; moan
thrift: economy
thriftiness: economy
thriftless: improvident
thrifty: economical; frugal; notable; prudent
thrill: pierce; swell

thrilling: sensational; vibrant
thrive: advance; flourish; prosper; spring; succeed
thriving: prosperous; thrifty
throaty: hoarse
throb: beat; palpitate; pant; pulsate; stroke
throe: access; agony; pain; pang; paroxysm
throne: seat
throng: assembly; cloud; crowd; crowd; gathering; multitude; swarm; troop
thronged: alive
throttle: strangle
through-and-through: complete
throughway: way
throw a spell over: bewitch
throw aside: cast
throw away: ad-lib; reject; scrap; squander
throw down: cast; deposit
throw light on: explain
throw off: cast; radiate
throw out: cast; spend; waste
throw: cast; dash; project; send; shy; toss; unseat
throwaway: ad-lib; bill
thrum: throb
thrust: bear; dash; pass; push; run; stab; stick; strike
thug: butcher; rowdy
thump: beat; blow; stroke; throb
thunder and lightning: storm
thunder: declaim; roar
thunderstorm: storm
thunderstruck: aghast
thus: accordingly
thwack: beat; blow
thwart: counteract; cross; daunt; defeat; elude; frustrate; hinder; impede; oppose; prevent; spite; stop; traverse
thwarting: cross
tic: idiosyncrasy
ticket: admission; check; pass
tickle: regale
ticklish: critical; shaky; slippery; tender; touchy
tidal wave: bore
tidbit: dainty; delicacy
tiddly: giddy
tide: current; stream
tidings: advice; intelligence; word
tidy: neat; trim
tie: attachment; bind; bond; connection; fasten; fix; hitch; involve; link
tied: fast
tier: bank; range; rank
tiff: dispute; quarrel
tight spot: quagmire
tight-fisted: parsimonious
tight-fistedness: parsimony
tight: close; economical; fast; mean; mercenary; near; niggardly; parsimonious; penurious; small; sordid; stiff; stingy; taut; tense
tighten: brace; constrict; stem; strain; stretch
tightfisted: miserly; near; niggardly; penurious
tightly packed: compact
tightly: fast
tightwad: miser
tilt: list; roll; thrust; trip
tilting: list
timber: standard
time-wasting: shiftless
time: age; movement; occasion; opportunity; period
timeless: eternal
timely: opportune; seasonable
timepiece: watch
timetable: schedule
timeworn: hackneyed
timid: afraid; backward; bashful; coward; cowardly; coy; diffident; faint; nervous; shy; skittish; tremulous
timidity: cowardice
timorous: afraid; bashful; cowardly; faint; nervous; skittish; timid; tremulous
tin: can
tincture: tint
tinge: cast; dash; stain; tint
tingle: burn
tinkle: ring
tinny: tacky
tint: cast; stain
tiny: diminutive; dwarf; little; minute; small
tip-off: caveat
tip: apex; caveat; end; gift; present; trip
tipple: drink
tippler: drunkard; lush
tipsy: drunken; giddy

tire or wear out: weary
tire: bore; exhaust; pall; weary
tired: hackneyed; jaded; weary
tireless: assiduous; diligent; sedulous
tiresome: dreary; dry; dull; heavy; laborious; monotonous; prosaic; stupid; tedious; vapid; wearisome; weary
tiring: tedious; wearisome
titan: giant
titanic: gigantic
titillate: regale
titivate: beautify; decorate
title: claim; entitle; name; right; style
titter: chuckle; laugh
tittle-tattle: jabber
tittle: atom; bit; iota; particle
titular: nominal
to and fro: about
to die for: beautiful; gorgeous
to do: excitement
to some extent: pretty
to the point: appropriate; concise; pithy
to-do: agitation; fuss; ruckus
toady: flatterer; parasite; sycophant; yes-man
toast: burn
tocsin: alarm
toffee-nosed: uppity
toggery: finery; raiment
togs: raiment; wardrobe
toil: exercise; labor; moil; plod; slavery; strive; task; work
toilet water: perfume
toilsome: arduous; hard; laborious
token: emblem; idiosyncrasy; mark; memento; presage; remembrance; sign; trophy; vestige
tolerable: average; fair; respectable; serviceable
tolerance: allowance
tolerant: broad; broad-minded; liberal; unbiased
tolerate: abide; allow; bear; brook; endure; permit; stand; suffer; support; take; undergo
toleration: tolerance
toll: custom; duty
tomb: grave; sepulcher; vault
tome: volume
tone down: subdue; tame; temper
tone: expression; fitness; sound
toned down: mellow
tongue: dialect; language; parlance; speech; vernacular
tonic: parallel
tony: fashionable
too: also; besides; moreover
tool: appliance; gadget; instrument
toot: blast
toothsome: dainty; scrumptious
top executive: tycoon
top secret: private
top-drawer: top-notch
top-shelf: top-notch
top: apex; cover; exceed; excel; head; height; peak; summit
tope: drink
toper: drunkard; lush
topic: argument; matter; subject; theme
topmost: head; uppermost
topography: terrain
topsy-turvy: cockeyed
torment oneself: worry
torment: agony; anguish; bedevil; curse; fret; grind; harass; harry; haze; misery; molest; nag; persecute; pester; plague; rack; ruffle; scourge; tantalize; torture; trouble; vex; worry
tormenting: painful
torn: ragged
tornado: storm
torpid: apathetic; callous; cold; dormant; dull; inactive; indolent; languid; lazy; lifeless; slothful
torque: twist
torrent: cascade; stream
torrid: hot
torsion: twist
torso: body
tort: crime
tortuous: circuitous
torture: agony; anguish; harass; haze; misery; molest; pain; persecute; pester; plague; rack; tantalize; torment; trouble; vex
torturous: harrowing; painful
toss: agitate; cast; project; send; shy; throw
tot: add
total: absolute; add; aggregate; dead; gross; number; thorough; totality; universal; utter; whole

totalitarian: arbitrary; intolerant
totality: total; whole
totally: clearly; sheer
totter: hobble; shake; stagger; tremble
tottering: crazy; shaky; spindly
tottery: shaky; spindly
touch: affect; cast; concern; cut; dash; hit; join; move; penetrate; pierce; reach; style; trace
touchable: tangible
touched: moonstruck
touching: acute; adjacent; adjoining; affecting; near; pathetic
touchstone: criterion; trial
touchy: cantankerous; cross; cynical; fractious; fretful; grouchy; hasty; irascible; irritable; passionate; peppery; petulant; quick; sour; splenetic; temperamental; testy
tough-minded: realistic
tough: hard; knotty; rowdy; strong; stubborn; tenacious
toughen: harden
toughened: weather-beaten
toughening: seasoning
tour: circuit; excursion; journey; passage; pilgrimage; ramble; trip
tournament: contest
tourney: contest
tow: draw
toward: almost
towards: almost
tower: ascend; hold; keep; pinnacle; soar
towering: high; lofty; tall
town: community; hamlet; village
toxin: poison; virus
toy: dally; fool; play; sport
trace: cast; draw; follow; iota; mark; range; remnant; shade; show; sign; soupçon; strain; suspicion; touch; trail; vestige
track: course; follow; hunt; lane; path; run; scent; trace; trail; wake; way
trackless: spacious
tract: parcel; region; scope; stretch; zone
tractable: flexible; gentle; obedient; pliant; submissive; sweet; tame
trade name: art; bargain
trade: art; bargain; barter; business; change; commerce; craft; deal; exchange; occupation; sell; station; swap; traffic; vocation; work
trademark: device; idiosyncrasy
trademarked: patent
tradition: myth; saga
traditional: orthodox
traduce: abuse; vilify
traffic or deal in: trade
traffic: barter; business; commerce; deal; exchange; trade
trafficking: commercial
tragedy: play
trail-blazing: pioneer
trail: drag; follow; path; run; scent; trace; wake
trailblazer: pioneer
train: breed; discipline; educate; exercise; form; ground; habituate; harden; initiate; instruct; manage; rehearse; teach
trained: expert; finished; gentle; proficient
trainer: guru
training: discipline; education; exercise; instruction; schooling
trait: character; characteristic; feature; idiosyncrasy; mark; quality; strain; touch
traitor: rebel; recreant
traitorous: black; disloyal; false; perfidious; treacherous; unfaithful
traitorousness: perfidy
trammel: hinder; hobble; shackle
tramp: shamble; trudge; vagabond; walk
trample: stamp
tranquil: calm; composed; easy; easygoing; equable; even; mild; pacific; peaceable; peaceful; placid; quiet; restful; sedate; serene; smooth; sober; still; unruffled
tranquilize: appease; calm; ease; pacify; quiet; settle; smooth; soothe; still; temper
tranquilizer: sedative
tranquilizing: sedative
tranquillity: calm; composure; ease; peace; quiet; serenity; temper
transact: bargain; perform

transaction: act; bargain; business; occurrence; operation; procedure
transcend: exceed; excel; pass; surpass
transcendence: excellence
transcendental: celestial
transcribe: copy
transcript: copy; duplicate
transect: cut
transfer: adjourn; bargain; carry; cede; deliver; grant; move; negotiate; pass; remove; take; transmit; turn
transference: passage
transfigure: transform
transfigured: rapt
transfix: stab; stick
transfixed: motionless; spellbound
transform: affect; change; convert; deform; edify; make; resolve; turn; vary
transformation: change; converse; metamorphosis; permutation
transgress: break; disobey; infringe; offend; sin; trespass
transgression: error; fault; misdemeanor; offense; sin; trespass; violation
transgressor: criminal
transient: brief; temporary; transitory
transit: passage
transition: change; passage
transitory: brief; ephemeral; temporary; transient
translate: decipher; interpret; paraphrase; put; render
translation: paraphrase; version
translucent: bright; pellucid; transparent
translucid: translucent
transmission: passage; succession
transmit: bear; bequeath; carry; communicate; convey; grant; leave; pass; remit; send
transmogrification: permutation
transmutation: change; metamorphosis; permutation
transmute: change; convert; transform; turn; vary
transparency: perspicuity
transparent: bright; candid; clear; limpid; lucid; pellucid; perspicuous; plain; sheer; thin; translucent
transpicuous: transparent
transport: bear; bewitch; bliss; bring; carry; charm; convey; delight; delight; ecstasy; enchant; entrance; joy; passion; rapture; remove; run; transmit
transportation: freight; transport
transported: ecstatic; rapt
transpose: reverse
transposition: permutation
transverse: thwart; traverse
trap: arrest; bag; cheat; pit; pound; snare
trappings: apparel; finery; paraphernalia; trim
trash: nonsense; refuse; stuff; waste
trashy: paltry
travail: labor; toil
travel: drive; journey; roam; tour; trip
traveler: pilgrim
traveling: itinerant
traverse: cross; do
travesty: burlesque; caricature; caricature; mockery; parody
treacherous: abject; black; crooked; designing; dishonest; disloyal; faithless; false; insidious; perfidious; recreant; rotten; unfaithful; wicked; wily
treachery: deceit; deception; disloyalty; duplicity; fraud; guile; perfidy; treason
treacly: saccharine
tread: walk
treason: conspiracy; crime; disloyalty; perfidy; sedition; treachery
treasonable: disloyal; treacherous
treasonous: treacherous
treasure: cherish; wealth
treasured: favorite
treasury: thesaurus
treat: delicacy; touch; use
treatise: exposition; tract
treatment: management; remedy; translation; use
treaty: agreement; alliance; bargain; compact; contract; convention; pact; peace; protection
tremble: falter; quake; quiver; shake; shiver; shudder; totter; vibrate; waver

trembling: quiver; tremble; tremor; tremulous
trembly: shaky
tremendous: big; gigantic; huge; massive; mighty; monstrous; prodigious; spacious
tremor: quiver; shake
tremulant: shaky
tremulous: shaky; timid
trenchant: caustic; cutting; incisive; pungent; severe; sharp
trend: cast; meaning; tendency; theme; turn
trendy: fashionable
trepidation: fear
trespass: encroach; error; fault; infringe; intrude; misdemeanor; offense; sin; transgress
tret: allowance
trial: affliction; attempt; burden; calamity; case; distress; endeavor; examination; exertion; experiment; hardship; misery; ordeal; proof; tentative; test; trouble; woe
tribe: nation; order; people; race; stock
tribulation: affliction; distress; misery; trial; trouble; woe
tribunal: bar
tributary: affluent; branch; subsidiary
tribute: accolade; compliment; custom; homage; paean; panegyric; subsidy
trice: instant; moment
trick out: trim
trick: artifice; bite; cheat; deceit; deceive; deception; delude; delusion; device; fool; fraud; haze; humbug; idiosyncrasy; joke; machination; maneuver; mask; ploy; stratagem; swindle; take; trickery; victimize; wile
trickery: artifice; chicanery; cunning; deceit; fraud; guile; practice; swindle; trick; wile
trickster: artist; cheat; impostor; rogue; scoundrel; swindler
tricky: crafty; crooked; cunning; deceitful; designing; insidious; Machiavellian; politic; slippery; touchy; unprincipled; waggish; wily
trifle: dally; fool; jest; novelty; philander; play; quibble; sport
trifler: dabbler
trifling fault: peccadillo
trifling: frivolous; futile; idle; light; nugatory; paltry; petty; play; simple; slender; slim; small; tenuous; trivial; unimportant; vain; vile; weak
trill: warble
trim: adorn; array; clean; deck; decorate; dress; fitness; garnish; neat; nice; orderly; ornament; sleek; smart; smug; tidy
trimming: ruffle; trim
trimmings: trim
trinket: charm; novelty
trip: excursion; expedition; journey; passage; pilgrimage; tour; voyage
trite: common; commonplace; hack; hackneyed; stale; stereotyped
triturate: grind; pound
triumph over: accomplish
triumph: conquest; glory; romp; victory
trivial: frivolous; futile; idle; impertinent; light; little; nugatory; paltry; petty; puerile; simple; slender; slight; slim; small; tenuous; trifling; unimportant; vain; vile; weak
triviality: indifference; vanity
troll: gnome; goblin
trollop: prostitute
troop: band; company; troupe
troopship: transport
trophy: memento; remembrance
tropical: torrid
trot: pace
trouble: adversity; affliction; annoy; anxiety; bedevil; bother; calamity; care; concern; cross; curse; difficulty; distress; embarrass; embarrassment; exercise; grind; harass; hardship; harry; ill; matter; mischief; misfortune; moil; molest; pain; perplex; perturb; pester; plague; ruffle; sorrow; tease; torment; trial; turmoil; woe; worry
troubled: solicitous; vexed
troublesome: inconvenient; tough; ugly; vexatious

troupe: troop
truce: peace
truck: wagon
truckle: flatter
truculent: brutal; cruel; fierce; quarrelsome; ruthless; sanguinary; savage
trudge: pace; plod; shamble
true believer: crackpot
true: accurate; actual; artless; authentic; constant; correct; earnest; express; factual; faithful; genuine; honorable; intrinsic; just; loyal; pure; real; right; sincere; sound; staunch; trustworthy; upright
truism: platitude
truly: right; true
trumpet: declaim; vaunt
truncate: abbreviate
truncation: abbreviation
trunk: body; stem; stock
trust: assurance; belief; charge; confidence; credit; expectation; faith; hope; keeping; lean; office
trusted: confidential
trustee: guardian
trustful: artless; credulous
trusting: artless; childish; credulous
trustworthiness: credit; principle
trustworthy: authentic; careful; certain; confidential; faithful; faithful; good; honest; honorable; infallible; reliable; responsible; safe; solid; sound; sure; true
trusty: certain; confidential; constant; faithful; honest; honorable; reliable; responsible; sure; true
truth: certainty; honesty; proverb
truthful: artless; correct; frank; guileless; honest; sound; straightforward; true
truthfully: true
truthfulness: candor; honesty
try: aim; attempt; bedevil; endeavor; exercise; experiment; judge; prove; strive; taste; tempt; test
trying: awkward; harrowing; heavy; rugged; wearisome
tryst: appointment
tub-thump: declaim
tube: spout
tuck: gather
tug: drag; draw; hale; pluck
tuition: education; schooling
tumid: big; turgid
tumor: gathering; growth
tumult: agitation; bedlam; brawl; commotion; confusion; convulsion; disorder; disturbance; hubbub; hurly-burly; noise; quarrel; racket; riot; ruffle; stir; turmoil; uproar
tumultuous: boisterous; chaotic; loud; noisy; obstreperous; rude; tempestuous; unquiet; unruly
tumultuousness: rage
tumulus: bank
tune: melody
tuneful: harmonious; mellow; sweet; sweet
turbid: cloudy
turbulence: commotion; disorder; fury; maelstrom; rage; tumult; turmoil; uproar
turbulent: boisterous; chaotic; fierce; mutinous; rough; rude; tempestuous; tumultuous; unquiet; unruly; wild
turf: earth; habitat
turgid: bombastic; grandiloquent; tumid
turkey: washout
turmoil: ado; agitation; commotion; confusion; hurly-burly; maelstrom; moil; ruckus; shambles
turn around or upside down: invert
turn aside: depart; deviate; divert; sheer
turn down: lower; refuse
turn one's stomach: disgust
turn out: terminate
turn over: give; study
turn up: appear
turn: act; bend; cast; change; course; faculty; make; meander; move; revolution; revolve; roll; rotate; skew; spin; throe; twist; vagary; warp; wind
turnabout: about-face
turning-point: emergency
turning: bend; turn; twist
tussle: fight
tutelage: schooling
tutor: guru; instruct; instructor; teach; teacher

tutoring: instruction
twaddle: babble; nonsense; stuff
twenty: score
twilight: evening
twin: identical
twine: wind
twinge: pain; pang; qualm
twinkle: blink; radiate; sparkle; wink
twinkling: bright; flash; instant; moment; sparkle
twirl: spin; whirl
twist: cast; prejudice; skew; spin; sprain; strain; turn; vagary; warp; wind
twisted: cranky; crooked; misshapen; tortuous; wry
twisting: circuitous; tortuous; wind
twit: banter; ridicule; taunt
twitch: start
twitting: raillery
two-faced: deceitful; false; mealy-mouthed; oracular
two: couple; pair
twofold: duplicate
type: archetype; form; nature; pattern; sort; specimen; stamp; style
typical: characteristic; perfect; standard
typo: misprint; mistake
typographical error: misprint
tyrannical: absolute; arbitrary; imperious; lordly
tyrannous: absolute
tyranny: oppression
tyro: amateur; dabbler; dilettante; initiate; neophyte; pupil
ubiquitous: omnipresent
ubiquitously: abroad
ugly: hideous; homely; nasty; plain; rugged; unsightly
ukase: decree; mandate; order; requirement; rule
ulcer: sore
ultimate: extreme; final; last
ultramundane: unearthly; weird
umbrage: offense; shade
umbrageous: dark
umpire: judge; moderate; referee; referee
unabashed: audacious; explicit; shameless
unabated: blank; clean; complete
unabating: unrelenting
unable: incapable; incompetent
unacceptable: short
unaccommodating: difficult
unaccompanied: alone; lone
unaccountable: singular
unaccustomed: new; strange
unacknowledged: ulterior
unacquainted: strange
unadorned: bare; blank; dry; earthy; naked; native; plain; rude; severe; simple
unadulterated: absolute; authentic; blank; candid; clean; clear; fresh; honest; neat; perfect; pure; sheer; single; unmixed; unsophisticated; virgin
unaesthetic: harsh
unaffected: artless; chaste; cold; naive; simple; sincere
unaffectedness: ease
unaffecting: cold
unagitated: peaceful
unallied: alien
unalloyed: pure; unmixed; virgin
unalterable: firm; inexorable; invariable
unaltered: intact; permanent; straight
unambiguous: clear; decided; direct; explicit; express; plain; special; unequivocal
unambitious: shiftless
unanimated: flat; tame; vapid
unanimity: agreement; unity
unanimous: solid
unanimousness: unanimity
unanswerable: unaccountable
unanticipated: sudden; unexpected
unapologetic: unreconstructed
unappealing: forbidding
unappeasable: implacable; relentless
unappeased: implacable
unappetizing: unpleasant
unappreciative: senseless
unapproachable: antisocial
unapt: unbecoming; unfit; unhappy
unarmed: naked
unashamed: audacious; explicit; shameless
unassailable: impregnable; undeniable; unimpeachable
unassuming: humble; meek; modest; simple; unpretentious

unassured: uncertain
unattached: free; loose; separate
unattended: sole; solitary
unattractive: homely; plain; unsightly
unauthentic: spurious
unauthorized: illegal; surreptitious
unavailing: fruitless; futile; idle; ineffectual; useless; vain
unavoidability: necessity
unavoidable: compulsory; necessary; sure
unavoidableness: necessity
unavowed: ulterior
unaware: unwitting
unbalance: skew
unbalanced: eccentric; moonstruck; shaky
unbearable: intolerable
unbeatable: sturdy
unbecoming: improper; incongruous; indecent; low; unseemly; unsuitable
unbefitting: unseemly; unsuitable
unbelievable: fabulous; fantastic; marvelous
unbeliever: iconoclast
unbelieving: cynical; faithless; incredulous; quizzical; skeptical
unbend: relax
unbendable: stiff
unbending: angular; blue; exact; implacable; inexorable; inflexible; intractable; obdurate; obstinate; relentless; rigid; stiff; stony; strict; stubborn
unbiased: candid; disinterested; fair; impartial; objective; single; unprejudiced
unbigoted: broad-minded; liberal
unbind: loose; untie
unblemished: blameless; clean; clear; fair; good; perfect
unblushing: shameless; unabashed
unbound: absolute; loose
unbounded: absolute; unlimited
unbridled: unbounded; wanton; wild
unbroken: complete; continual; direct; entire; intact; round; solid; sound; whole; wild
unburden: discharge; empty; lighten; relieve
uncalled-for: wanton
uncanny: eerie; weird
uncaring: world-weary
unceasing: continual; endless; eternal; incessant; perennial; perpetual; standing
unceasingly: always
uncentered: eccentric
unceremonious: abrupt; brusque; familiar; free; informal; offhand; quick
uncertain: ambiguous; ambivalent; arbitrary; doubtful; dubious; equivocal; iffy; inconstant; indefinite; insecure; obscure; pendulous; precarious; questionable; shaky; skittish; slippery; vague
uncertainty: doubt; hazard; hesitation; problem; quandary; suspense
unchain: clear
unchained: unbounded
unchangeable: invariable; stable; steady
unchanged: permanent; straight; uniform
unchanging: constant; invariable; permanent; same; stable; standing; steady; uniform
uncharitable: exclusive
unchaste: licentious; loose; obscene; sensual; unclean
uncivil: beastly; blunt; brusque; brutal; coarse; disrespectful; ill-mannered; impolite; rough; rude; short; sour; uncouth
uncivilized: barbarian; brutal; primitive; rude; savage; uncivil; wild
unclassifiable: ambiguous; nondescript
unclean: dirty; filthy; foul; mean; nasty; sordid; squalid; taboo
unclear: ambiguous; cloudy; dim; dubious; obscure; vague
unclerical: lay
unclose: open
unclosed: open
unclothe: divest
unclothed: bare; naked; nude
unclouded: bright; clear; serene
uncolored: naked
uncombined: loose
uncomely: homely

uncomfortable: close; miserable; rough; severe
uncommon behavior: eccentricity
uncommon: choice; extraordinary; notable; odd; offbeat; particular; peculiar; prodigious; quaint; queer; rare; recherché; remarkable; scarce; singular; special; unique; unusual
uncommunicative: close; reticent; taciturn
uncompared: absolute
uncompassionate: merciless; remorseless; ruthless; unrelenting
uncomplaisant: abrupt
uncompliant: disobedient; recalcitrant
uncomplicated: earthy; elementary; simple
uncomplimentary: derogatory; dim
uncompounded: elementary; single
uncomprising: stern
uncompromising: austere; extreme; grim; single-minded; stalwart; stiff; strict; unsparing
unconcealed: bare; open; patent
unconcern: indifference
unconcerned: apathetic; blasé; careless; casual; cold; cool; lackadaisical; nonchalant; reckless; regardless; sober; uninterested
unconditional: absolute; positive; utter
unconditionally: absolutely
unconditioned: unconditional
unconfined: broad; indefinite; loose; unbounded
unconforming: aberrant; irregular
unconformity: abnormality
unconfused: distinct
unconnected: alien; remote; sporadic
unconquerable: dauntless; indomitable; invincible; sturdy
unconscionable: exorbitant; unmerciful
unconscious: senseless; unwitting
unconsciousness: faint; insensibility
unconsecrated: profane
unconsidered: careless
unconstrained: bohemian; easy; familiar; free; irrepressible; spontaneous; unlimited; unmeasured; voluntary
unconstraint: familiarity
uncontaminated: clean; pure; sterile
uncontrollable: automatic; obstinate; unruly
uncontrolled: arbitrary; free; involuntary; obstreperous; unbounded; wild
unconventional: bluff; bohemian; eccentric; forward; informal; offbeat; queer; strange
unconvincing: weak
uncooked: raw
uncooperative: froward
uncorrected: rough
uncorrupt: just
uncorrupted: authentic; pure; sterile
uncounted: numberless
uncourteous: blunt
uncourtly: blunt; ill-mannered
uncouth: crude; ill-mannered; loutish; rude; uncivil; ungainly
uncover: ascertain; betray; disclose; display; expose; open; reveal; strip
uncovered: bare; naked; nude; open
uncritical: blind
unctuous: fat; sanctimonious; smarmy; smooth
uncultivated: barbarian; fresh; rugged; savage; uneducated; wild
uncultured: primitive; rough; rude; unrefined
uncut: rough
undamaged: whole
undaunted: audacious; bold; daring; dauntless; manly; resolute; unabashed
undeceived: realistic
undecided: ambivalent; doubtful; dubious; mercurial; open; soft; uncertain; unstable; weak
undecidedness: doubt
undecorated: bare; rude
undefended: open; unguarded
undefiled: blameless; chaste; clean; clear; pure; virgin
undefined: indefinite
undemanding: laid-back; mindless

undemocratic: arbitrary
undeniable: certain; clear; decided; hard; incontrovertible; indisputable; peremptory; unquestionable
undependable: precarious; uncertain; unsettled
under the weather: seedy
underbred: vulgar
underbrush: cover
undercover: underground
undercurrent: undertow
underdeveloped: abortive; backward; imperfect
underdone: rare
underearth: underground
underfed: poor
undergo: bear; endure; experience; have; see; stand; suffer; support; sustain; take; taste
undergoing: experience
underhand: clandestine
underhanded: foul; politic; sly
underhandedness: chicanery
underline: emphasize
underling: menial
underlying: fundamental
undermine: sabotage; weaken
undermining: sabotage
undermost: bottom
underscore: emphasize
underset: undertow
underside: bottom
undersized: dwarf
understand: accept; comprehend; conceive; deduce; digest; draw; extract; gather; grasp; interpret; know; notice; penetrate; perceive; realize; see; take
understandable: lucid; luminous; perceptible; plain; simple; visible
understandably: clearly
understanding: agreement; apprehension; aptitude; brains; empathy; familiarity; intellect; intelligence; intelligent; judgment; knowledge; mind; perception; perceptive; rapport; reason; sense; sensibility; sensible; sharp; sympathy; wisdom; wit
understood: clear; tacit
understructure: base
understudy: surrogate
undertake: assume; attempt; presume; wage
undertaking: attempt; enterprise; game; work
undertone: aura
undeserved: unjust
undeserving: unworthy
undesigned: accidental
undesigning: unreserved
undesirable: pariah
undetermined: doubtful; indefinite; open; spineless; uncertain; unsettled; vague
undeveloped: abortive; backward; crude; imperfect; rudimentary
undeviating: direct; inflexible; steady; straightforward
undifferentiated: identical
undignified: low; mean
undiluted: neat
undiminished: complete; entire; intact; whole
undine: sylph
undiscerning: blind; senseless
undisciplined: raw; wild
undisclosed: occult
undiscouraged: undaunted
undiscoverable: inscrutable
undiscriminating: indiscriminate
undisguised: bare; crude; frank; naked; open
undismayed: dauntless; undaunted
undistinguishable: indiscriminate; obscure
undistinguished: blank; common; nameless; obscure
undistinguishing: indiscriminate
undisturbed: calm; composed; cool; placid; restful; sedate; serene; smooth; sound; unbroken; unruffled
undiversified: uniform
undivided: complete; entire; solid; whole
undo: loose; nullify; untie; zap
undoing: ruin
undomesticated: wild
undone: aghast
undoubted: factual; sure
undraped: nude
undress: divest
undressed: bare; naked; nude; rough
undulate: fluctuate; ripple; roll; wave
undulation: ripple; wave

undying: eternal; immortal; perennial
unearth: discover
unearthly: celestial; weird
uneasiness: anxiety; apprehension; discontent; dissatisfaction; qualm; worry
uneasy: anxious; impatient; miserable; nervous; restive; solicitous; tumultuous; uncomfortable; unquiet
uneducated: dark; ignorant; rude; simple
unembarrassed: easy
unembellished: dry; simple; unvarnished
unemotional: cold
unemployed: dead; idle; vacant
unenclosed: open
unencumbered: clear; fair; free; vacant
unending: chronic; continual; endless; eternal; immortal; incessant; measureless; perpetual; undying
unendurable: arduous; intolerable; unbearable
unenlightened: blind; dark; heathen; ignorant; uneducated
unentangled: clear
unenthusiastic: cold; grudging; half-hearted; lukewarm
unequaled: matchless; nonpareil; peerless; unique; unparalleled
unequalled: preeminent
unequivocal: aboveboard; absolute; clear; decided; direct; emphatic; explicit; perspicuous; plain; positive
unequivocally: aboveboard; absolutely
unequivocating: aboveboard; absolute
unequivocatingly: aboveboard
unerring: accurate; dead; sure
unessential: mean
unethical: unscrupulous
uneven: abrupt; irregular; rough; rugged
unexaggerated: naked; unvarnished
unexceptionable: undeniable; unimpeachable; unquestionable
unexceptional: lackluster; serviceable
unexcited: cool; nonchalant; patient; peaceful; sedate; sober
unexciting: pallid
unexpected: casual; offbeat; sudden
unexperienced: strange
unexplainable: inscrutable; mysterious; unaccountable
unexplained: strange
unexpressed: tacit; ulterior
unextinguished: alive
unfailing: certain; constant; infallible; reliable; sure; true; unerring
unfair: foul; partial; shabby; unjust; unreasonable
unfairly: foul
unfairness: partiality
unfaithful: disloyal; false; perfidious; recreant; treacherous
unfaithfulness: disloyalty
unfaltering: determined; single-minded; strong; true
unfamiliar: recherché; strange; strange; strange; unaccustomed; uncouth
unfashionable: tacky
unfasten: loose; release; untie
unfastened: loose
unfathomable: deep; inscrutable; mysterious
unfavorable: adverse; bad; contrary; foul; ill; inimical; malign; repugnant; sinister; thwart; unhappy
unfavorably: ill
unfeeling: apathetic; brutal; callous; cold; cruel; dead; dull; hard; harsh; merciless; senseless; stern; stony; tasteless; unkind
unfeigned: real; sincere; unaffected
unfertile: poor
unfetter: clear; free; liberate
unfettered: free; loose; unbounded; unlimited
unfilled: open; void
unfinished: crude; partial; raw; rough
unfit: improper; incompetent; unapt; unbecoming; unqualified; wrong
unfitted: inept; unapt; unbecoming; unfit
unfitting: improper; incongruous; inept; unseemly; unsuitable

unfixed: uncertain; unsettled; unsteady; vague

unflexible: stiff

unflinching: determined; resolute

unfold: break; display; expand; spread

unfolding: development

unforced: voluntary

unforeseeable: iffy

unforeseen: casual; sudden; unexpected

unforgettable: memorable

unforgiving: relentless; unsparing; vindictive

unfortunate: adverse; bad; evil; miserable; poor; sinister; unhappy; unlucky

unfortunately: ill

unfounded: precarious; unsound

unfrequented: solitary

unfriendliness: hostility

unfriendly: adverse; alien; antisocial; chill; cold; contrary; hard; hostile; inimical; warlike

unfruitful: barren; fruitless; lean; vain

unfruitfulness: poverty

unfulfilled: malcontent

unfulfillment: disappointment

unfurnished: bare; naked

ungainly: awkward; clumsy

ungenerous: grudging; petty; small

ungentle: harsh; rude

ungentlemanly: brutal

ungenuine: fictitious

ungodly: profane; wicked

ungovernable: refractory; unruly

ungoverned: wild

ungraceful: awkward; clumsy; ungainly

ungracious: brusque; brutal

ungrudging: cheerful

unguarded: naked; unwary; vulnerable

unguent: ointment; unctuous

ungullible: realistic

unhallowed: profane

unhampered: clear

unhandy: clumsy

unhappiness: misery

unhappy: bad; blue; dejected; depressed; desolate; disconsolate; downhearted; forlorn; joyless; low; melancholy; miserable; poor; sad; sorrowful; sorry; uncomfortable; unfortunate; wretched

unharmed: sound

unharmonious: harsh

unhealthful: unhealthy; unwholesome

unhealthiness: delicacy

unhealthy: ill; morbid; noisome; noxious; peaked; sickly; unhealthful; unsound; unwholesome; weak

unheard-of: extraordinary; recherché

unhesitating: decided

unhindered: clear

unholy: profane

unhurried: deliberate; leisurely; slow

unhurtful: innocuous

unhygienic: unhealthy

uniform: constant; equable; equal; even; invariable; level; monotonous; regular; solid; steady

uniformity: agreement; constancy; sameness; unity

unify: ally

unilluminated: dark; obscure

unimaginative: dull; prosaic

unimpaired: clean; complete; entire; intact; sound; unbroken; whole

unimpassioned: cool; dull; lukewarm; sober

unimpeachable: blameless; undeniable

unimpeached: good

unimpeded: clear; free

unimportance: indifference

unimportant: frivolous; futile; idle; little; mean; minor; paltry; petty; simple; slight; slim; small; subordinate; tenuous; trifling; trivial; unessential; vain

unimposing: mean

unimpressed: cold; unaffected

unimpressible: callous; cold; hard

uninfluential: impotent

uninformed: inexperienced; uneducated

uninhabited: desert; desolate; empty; lone; waste; wild

uninhibited: frank; irrepressible; rambunctious

uninitiated: inexperienced

uninjured: intact; sound; whole

uninspiring: cold

uninstructed: ignorant; uneducated

uninstructive: barren

unintelligent: dull; weak

unintelligible: dark; mysterious; unaccountable

unintentional: casual; inadvertent; involuntary; unwitting

uninterested: apathetic; blasé; half-hearted; perfunctory; senseless

uninteresting: arid; barren; commonplace; dreary; dry; dull; flat; prosaic; stale; stereotyped; stupid; tame; tasteless; vapid

uninterrupted: consecutive; constant; continual; incessant; perennial; perpetual; steady; unbroken

uninterruptedly: always

unintoxicated: sober

uninvolved: lackadaisical; mindless

uninvolving: mindless

union: alliance; association; bond; close; coherence; combination; confederation; connection; junction; league; marriage; pact; unity

unionize: organize

unique: appropriate; curious; lone; odd; offbeat; only; peculiar; peerless; quaint; singular; sole; wonderful

uniquely: only; particularly

uniqueness: novelty

unison: harmony; unanimity; unity

unit: company; element; troop

unite: add; agree; ally; associate; band; blend; close; combine; compel; conjoin; connect; couple; hitch; join; league; link; meet; mingle; mix; organize; sort; tie

united: common; solid

uniting: addition

unity: agreement; coherence; harmony; rapport; unanimity; union

universal remedy: cure-all

universal: common; general; pandemic

universe: nature; system

university: academic

unjust: injurious; partial; shabby; tyrannical; unfair; unreasonable; wrong

unjustifiable: unjust; wanton

unjustified: unjust

unkempt: wild

unkind: beastly; cross; hard; harsh; ill; unfriendly

unkindly: hardly; ill; unfriendly

unknot: untie

unknowing: unwitting

unknowledgeable: inexperienced

unknown: base; nameless; obscure; occult; secret; strange; uncouth; vague

unlawful: criminal; crooked; illegal; sharp; unconscionable; unfaithful

unlearned: ignorant; rude; simple

unleavened: heavy

unlettered: barbarian; dark; ignorant; uneducated

unlicensed: illegal

unlighted: somber

unlike: different; diverse; opposite

unlikely: unapt

unlikeness: difference

unlimited: absolute; arbitrary; clear; endless; indefinite; unbounded; unmeasured; unreserved; vast

unlit: dark

unload: discharge; empty; unburden

unlock: loose

unlooked for: sudden

unloose: loose; release

unlovely: ugly

unlucky: adverse; bad; miserable; poor; sinister; unfortunate; unhappy

unmade: raw

unmanageable: awkward; froward; intractable; refractory; unruly; unwieldy

unmannerly: brutal; rude; uncivil; uncouth

unmarked: blank

unmarried: single

unmask: expose

unmasking: exposure

unmatched: matchless; peerless; unequaled; unparalleled

unmediated: immediate

unmerciful: cruel; hard; pitiless; relentless; remorseless; ruthless; sanguinary; savage; sharp; unkind; unrelenting; unsparing

unmerited: unjust

unmethodical: irregular

unmindful: careless; mindless; regardless; thoughtless

unmingled: unmixed

unmistakable: apparent; clear; decided; distinct; evident; household; lucid; manifest; obvious; palpable; patent; plain; positive; simple; stark; unequivocal; visible

unmitigated: blank; downright; entire; unqualified

unmixed: absolute; blank; clean; mere; neat; perfect; pure; sheer; single; virgin

unmodified: pure; round; straight

unmoral: fast

unmoved: cool; cruel; lukewarm; quiet; unaffected

unmoving: inactive; inert; motionless; quiet; rigid; standing; still

unnamable: nameless

unnamed: nameless

unnatural: abnormal; exceptional; fantastic; labored; preternatural; recherché; supernatural; unearthly; weird

unnaturalness: affectation

unnecessary: simple; superfluous; uncalled-for; unessential

unnerve: defeat; paralyze; upset

unnoted: obscure

unnoticeable: obscure

unnoticed: obscure

unobservant: thoughtless; unmindful

unobstructed: clear; fair; free

unobtrusive: modest; quiet; unpretentious

unobtrusiveness: modesty

unoccupied: empty; idle; lone; open; unemployed; vacant; void

unoriginal: hackneyed

unornamented: severe

unorthodox: bohemian

unostentatious: modest; plain; unassuming

unpacified: implacable

unpaid: outstanding

unpalatable: distasteful; offensive; unpleasant

unparalleled: matchless; nonpareil; singular; unequaled

unparochial: broad-minded

unparticular: general

unpatriotic: disloyal

unpenetrable: inscrutable

unperceiving: senseless

unperturbed: cold; composed; sedate; serene; unruffled

unphotographic: abstract

unpitying: hard; relentless; ruthless; unmerciful; unrelenting

unplanned: accidental

unpleasant: cross; distasteful; hard; harsh; horrible; nasty; offensive; peevish; severe; sour; ugly; unsavory; unsightly

unpleasantness: mess; offense

unpleasing: unpleasant

unpolished: awkward; coarse; crude; ill-mannered; impolite; rough; rude; rugged; savage; unrefined

unpolluted: guiltless; pure; sanitary; sterile; virgin

unpopulated: back; lone

unpractical: abstract; academic; ideal; romantic; unreal; visionary

unpracticed: inexperienced; raw

unprecedented: singular

unpredictable: capricious; fickle; iffy; skittish; uncertain

unprejudiced: candid; disinterested; fair; impartial; liberal; objective; unbiased

unpremeditated: ad-lib; casual; extemporaneous; improvised; impulsive; offhand; spontaneous

unprepared: crude; raw; rough

unpretending: humble; unassuming; unpretentious

unpretentious: earthy; homely; humble; modest; plain; poor; simple; small; unassuming

unprincipled: abandoned; bad; dishonorable; immoral; shameless; unscrupulous; wicked

unproductive: barren; fruitless; futile; poor; sterile; unfruitful

unprofessional: academic; lay

unprofitable: fruitless; futile

unprolific: barren; fruitless

unpropitious: ominous; unfavorable; unhappy; untimely

unprotected: bare; insecure; naked; open; unguarded; vulnerable

unpurified: unrefined

unpurposeful: mindless

unqualified: absolute; blank; clear; downright; entire; flat; incapable; incompetent; perfect; plump; pure; radical; round; sheer; sweeping; thorough; total; unapt; unconditional; unfit; unmitigated; utter

unqualifiedly: absolutely

unquestionable: absolute; apparent; certain; clear; decided; incontrovertible; indisputable; undeniable

unquestionableness: certainty

unquestionably: absolutely

unquestioned: authoritative; certain; factual

unquestioning: positive

unquiet: impatient; restive; tumultuous

unravel: decipher; untangle

unreal: apparent; artificial; counterfeit; fabulous; fake; fictitious; ideal; illusory; imaginary; phantom; romantic; subjective; visionary

unrealistic: abstract; fabulous; romantic; wild-eyed

unreality: fiction; vanity

unreasonable: absurd; arbitrary; excessive; exorbitant; extravagant; extreme; foolish; immoderate; preposterous; unconscionable; wrongheaded

unreasoning: blind; brutal; brute

unredeemable: profane

unredeemed: profane

unrefined: awkward; base; broad; crude; earthy; impolite; indecent; loutish; raw; rough; rude; rugged; vulgar

unregenerate: carnal; obdurate; regular

unregulated: free

unrehearsed: ad-lib; improvised

unrelated: abstract; remote

unrelaxed: taut

unrelenting: astringent; close; cruel; grim; hard; incessant; inexorable; inflexible; merciless; relentless; remorseless; ruthless; severe; stern; stiff; unsparing; vindictive

unreliable: faithless; fast; precarious; treacherous; uncertain; unsound; unsteady

unremarked: nameless

unremitting: assiduous; close; constant; continual; diligent; incessant; inflexible; steady; stiff; unrelenting

unrepenting: unreconstructed

unrepining: patient

unrepressed: effusive

unreserved: bare; familiar; frank; honest; ingenuous; open; outspoken; plain; plump; unconditional

unresisting: passive; submissive

unresolved: ambivalent

unresonant: tinny

unresourceful: shiftless

unresponsive: cold

unrest: agitation; disorder

unrestrained: abandoned; arbitrary; boisterous; broad; easy; effusive; frank; free; indefinite; ingenuous; irrepressible; loose; lurid; rambunctious; unbounded; unlimited; unmeasured; unscrupulous; wild

unrestricted: absolute; ample; entire; frank; free; general; loose; open; unconditional; unlimited; unqualified; unscrupulous

unreticent: effusive

unrevealed: occult; secret

unriddle: decipher

unrighteous: wicked

unrighteousness: evil

unrigorous: lax

unripe: crude

unrivaled: matchless; unequaled; unparalleled

unroll: spread

unromantic: realistic

unruffled: calm; composed; cool; easygoing; pacific; patient; peaceful; placid; sedate; serene; smooth; sober

unruly: chaotic; disobedient; fractious; mutinous; obstreperous; raucous; refractory; rowdy; wanton; wayward; wild; willful

unsafe: insecure; mad; slippery; uncertain

unsaid: tacit

unsanitary: unhealthy

unsatisfactorily: ill

unsatisfactory: empty; ill; poor; weak

unsatisfied: malcontent

unsatisfying: empty

unsavory: distasteful; flat

unschooled: inexperienced; uneducated

unscientific: academic

unscrupulous: crooked; designing; dishonest; dishonorable; Machiavellian; mean; politic; unconscionable; unprincipled; venal

unseasonable: untimely

unseemliness: impropriety

unseemly: improper; indecent; tasteless; unbecoming

unselfish: benevolent; chivalrous; disinterested; generous; magnanimous; spontaneous

unsentimental: hard; realistic

unserviceable: useless

unset: rough

unsettle: disorder; shake

unsettled: doubtful; iffy; inconstant; indefinite; itinerant; moot; mutable; open; outstanding; uncertain; unstable; unsteady; vague

unshakable: constant; firm; intent

unshaken: resolute

unshaking: constant

unshapely: misshapen

unsheathed: naked

unsheltered: bare

unshielded: bare

unsightly: ugly

unskilled: fresh; inexperienced; raw

unskillful: artless; awkward; clumsy; maladroit; unapt

unsmiling: solemn

unsnarl: untangle

unsociable: antisocial

unsoiled: clean

unsophisticated: artless; earthy; guileless; innocent; naive; primitive; rural; simple

unsound: bad; mad; rotten; sick

unsoundness: aberration

unsparing: hard; unmerciful

unspeakable: nameless

unspecialized: general

unspecific: inaccurate; indefinite; vague

unspecified: nameless; some

unspiritual: animal; carnal; secular

unspoken: tacit

unsporting: shabby

unsportsmanlike: shabby

unspotted: blameless; clear; fair

unstable: capricious; fickle; inconstant; mutable; precarious; shaky; skittish; slippery; treacherous; uncertain; unsettled; unsteady; weak

unstained: clean; fair; pure

unsteadfast: unstable

unsteady: cranky; mutable; precarious; shaky; spindly; uncertain; unsettled; unstable; variable; wayward; weak

unstinted: free; lavish

unstinting: generous; liberal; unmeasured

unstirred: unaffected

unstrained: quiet

unstudied: offhand

unstylish: tacky

unsubmissive: disobedient

unsubstantial: light; slight; slim; tenuous; thin; unsound

unsubtle: express; gaudy

unsuccessful: abortive; futile; unfortunate; unlucky

unsuccessfulness: failure

unsuggestive: barren

unsuitable: improper; incompatible; inconsistent; inept; tasteless; unapt; unbecoming; unfit; wrong

unsuitableness: repugnance

unsuited: improper; incompatible; inept; unapt; unbecoming; unfit

unsullied: blameless; chaste; clean; clear; fair; good; guiltless; pure; virgin

unsure: doubtful; iffy; insecure; precarious; shaky; uncertain; unsettled; vague

unsureness: suspense

unsurpassed: peerless

unsurprised: blasé

unsusceptible: callous; cold

unsuspecting: artless; credulous; naive

unsuspicious: artless

unswerving: constant; single-minded; straightforward

unsymmetrical: irregular

unsympathetic: cold; dead; hard; hard; lukewarm; merciless; stern; unfeeling; unsparing

unsystematic: irregular

untainted: innocent; pure

untamed: fierce; rambunctious; savage; wild

untarnished: fair; guiltless; pure

untaught: dark; ignorant; rude; uneducated

untenable: unsound

untenanted: vacant

unthinking: brutal; hasty; mindless; short-sighted; tasteless; thoughtless; vacant

unthoughtful: careless

unthreatening: innocuous

untidiness: litter; mess

untidy: slovenly

untie: loose

untied: loose

untimely: inconvenient; unseasonable

untiring: assiduous; diligent; patient; tireless

untitled: nameless

untold: numberless

untouchable: pariah; sacrosanct

untouched: unaffected; virgin

untoward: contrary

untrained: fresh; inexperienced; raw; rude; unskillful

untrammeled: wild

untried: raw; virgin

untroubled: clear; easy

untrue: abroad; disloyal; erroneous; fabulous; faithless; false; incorrect; mendacious; recreant; unfaithful; wrong

untrusting: faithless

untrustworthy: corrupt; faithless; perfidious; slippery; treacherous; unfaithful

untruth: fable; falsehood; lie

untruthful: false; mendacious

untutored: barbarian; dark; ignorant; inexperienced; rude; simple; uneducated

unusable: useless

unused: new; standing; strange; unaccustomed; virgin; waste

unusual: aberrant; abnormal; curious; eccentric; exceptional; extraordinary; great; informal; irregular; notable; odd; offbeat; particular; peculiar; preternatural; prodigious; quaint; rare; recherché; remarkable; singular; singular; special; strange; unaccustomed; uncommon; uncouth; unique; unnatural

unusually: especially; particularly

unutterable: nameless; unspeakable

unvanquishable: invincible

unvaried: monotonous; uniform

unvariegated: uniform

unvarnished: naked

unvarying: constant; equal; invariable; monotonous; regular; stable; steady; uniform

unveil: disclose; expose; reveal

unveiling: debut

unventilated: close

unvirtuous: unclean

unwarranted: uncalled-for

unwary: careless; improvident; rash

unwatchful: thoughtless

unwavering: consistent; constant; decided; determined; firm; resolute; stable; steadfast; steady; straightforward; strong; true; uniform

unwed: single

unwell: ailing; ill; indisposed; seedy; sick; sickly; weak

unwholesome: morbid; noisome; noxious; rotten; unhealthful; unhealthy; unsound

unwieldy: awkward; bulky

unwilled: involuntary

unwilling: ashamed; averse; grudging; indisposed; loath; reluctant

unwillingness: aversion; difficulty

unwise: absurd; foolish

unwrought: rough; rude

unyielding: grim; hard; indomitable; inexorable; inflexible; intractable; invincible; obdurate; obstinate; perverse; relentless;

rigid; rigorous; set; stiff; strict; stubborn; uncompromising

up ahead: forward

up front: forward

up to date: new

up-country: backwater

up-to-date: modern; recent

upbeat: jaunty; optimistic

upbraid: abuse; chide; rebuke; reprimand; reproach; reprove; taunt; twit; vituperate

upbraiding: reproach

update: advance

upheaval: ado; convulsion

uphold: abet; approve; assert; bear; claim; defend; help; maintain; preserve; stay; support; sustain; vindicate

upholder: advocate; mainstay

uplift: dignify; edify; elate; lift

upper case: capital

upper: right; top

uppermost: top

upraise: erect

upright: clean; conscientious; erect; ethical; good; honest; honorable; innocent; just; moral; perpendicular; post; pure; right; righteous; round; sound; standard; straight; vertical; virtuous; worthy

uprightly: right

uprightness: excellence; goodness; honesty; honor; integrity; principle; probity; right; truth; virtue

uprising: commotion; insurrection; mutiny; revolt; sedition; tumult

uproar: ado; bedlam; clamor; disorder; disturbance; hubbub; hurly-burly; noise; racket; riot; ruckus; stir; tumult; turmoil

uproarious: boisterous; noisy; obstreperous; rambunctious; tumultuous; vociferous

uproot: destroy; eradicate

upset: ado; bad; capsize; chaotic; disorder; overthrow; overturn; overturn; ruffle; skew; trouble; unnerve; unquiet

upsetting: traumatic

upshot: catastrophe; consequence; issue

upstanding: ethical

upstart: parvenu

urbane: affable; bland; civil; courteous; polite; suave; worldly

urge on: incite

urge: advocate; animate; carry; charge; drive; encourage; hasten; hurry; impel; induce; persuade; push; solicit; spur; stimulate; stir; tell

urgency: emergency; need

urgent: crying; imperious; stringent

urging: advice; agitation

usability: application

usable: available; feasible

usage: custom; diction; habit; order; parlance; rite; use; vogue; way

use up: consume; exhaust; expend; finish; spend; take; use

use: advantage; affect; appliance; application; apply; consume; employ; exercise; expend; exploit; occupation; occupy; operate; play; spend; take; utilize; wont; work

used to: accustomed

used: hack; prevalent; wont

useful: beneficial; convenient; good; handy; helpful; serviceable; utilitarian; valuable

usefulness: advantage; good; use; value; worth

useless: dead; fruitless; futile; idle; ineffectual; nugatory; vain; void; waste

usher in or out: ring

usher: escort; show

usual: accustomed; common; conventional; customary; general; habitual; moderate; ordinary; regular; set; simple; stock

usually: generally; often

usurp: assume; monopolize

utensil: gadget; instrument; tool

utile: serviceable; utilitarian

utilitarian: serviceable

utility: advantage; application; good; use; value

utilization: application; use

utilize: apply; exploit; use

utmost: extreme; extremity; last; main; sovereign

utter: absolute; bear; blank; dead; declare; deliver; downright; express; give; observe; pass; pure; put; rank; say; sheer;

sound; speak; stark; talk; tell; total

utterance: expression; observation; remark; speech; word

uttered: oral

utterly: stark

uttermost: extreme

vacancy: blank; opening

vacant: empty; foolish; vacuous; void

vacate: abandon; leave; void

vacated: void

vacillate: falter; fluctuate; hesitate; oscillate; stagger; sway; waffle; waver; yo-yo

vacillating: ambivalent; doubtful; inconstant; mutable; pendulous; unsettled; unstable; unsteady; variable; weak

vacillation: doubt; hesitation; suspense

vacuous: tame; vacant

vacuum: void

vagabond: vagrant

vagary: conceit; fancy; humor; whim

vagrant: circuitous; vagabond

vague: ambiguous; dim; general; indefinite; loose; nebulous; rough; uncertain; unreal; weak

vagueness: haze

vain: conceited; egocentric; empty; fruitless; futile; idle; nugatory; pretentious; proud; useless; void

vainglorious: egocentric; pretentious; vain

vainglory: pride

valance: curtain

valet: attendant; menial

valetudinarianism: delicacy

valiant: audacious; bold; brave; daring; dauntless; gallant; manly; stalwart; stout; strong

valid: available; factual; good; lawful; legitimate

validate: approve; confirm; ratify

validity: effect; force; strength

valor: bravery; courage; heroism; mettle

valorous: bold; daring; dauntless; gallant; game; heroic; stalwart; strong

valuable: choice; costly; exquisite; good; invaluable; pay; precious; rich; select; serviceable; substantial; utilitarian

valuables: treasure

valuation: esteem; estimate; value; view

value: account; advantage; appreciate; approve; esteem; estimate; goodness; merit; prize; regard; set; worth

valued: rich

valueless: futile; poor; useless; vile

vamp: siren

vampire: siren

van: wagon

vandalism: mischief

vanguard: lead; pioneer

vanish: die; disappear; disperse; dissipate; evaporate; fade; pass; perish

vanished: extinct

vanity: conceit; pride; vainglory; wind

vanquish: beat; conquer; defeat; overcome; overpower; overthrow; overturn; overwhelm; quell; reduce; subdue

vanquished: lost

vanquishment: conquest; defeat

vantage point: advantage

vantage: advantage

vapid: dry; dull; flat; foolish; prosaic; stale; stupid; tame; tasteless; vacuous; vain

vapor: cloud; damp; exhaust; fluid; fume; haze

vaporize: evaporate; fume

vaporous: rarefied

variable: inconstant; mutable; mutable; uncertain

variance: breach; conflict; discrepancy; division; strife

variant: dialect; different; diverse; unlike; version

variation: change; difference; discrepancy; permutation; shade; tolerance; turn

varicolored: dappled

varied: distinct; diverse; heterogeneous; manifold; many; miscellaneous; various

variegated: various

variety: change; mixture; mode; sort

various and sundry: multifarious

various: different; distinct; diverse; manifold; many; miscellaneous; multifarious

varnish: gloss; palliate

vary with: conflict

vary: alter; change; depart; diverge; fluctuate; modify; oscillate; range; yo-yo

varying: mutable

vassal: slave

vast: ample; broad; bulky; endless; enormous; extensive; giant; gigantic; great; huge; immense; large; measureless; mighty; monstrous; spacious; sweeping; unbounded; unlimited; unmeasured; wide

vault: jump; leap; spring; spring

vaunt: boast; flourish

veer: deviate; skew; wander

vegetable: inanimate

vehemence: fervor; fury; heat; passion; rage; violence

vehement: ardent; enthusiastic; fervent; fierce; fiery; hot; impatient; passionate; strong; warm

vehicle: carriage

veil: cover; hide; mask; pall; pretense; screen; shade; shroud

veiled: latent; obscure; occult

vein: deposit; mood

velocity: rapidity; speed

venal: base; corrupt; mercenary; perfidious

vend: sell

vendetta: reprisal

veneer: face

venerable: sacred; sacrosanct; solemn

venerate: admire; adore; consecrate; fear; honor; respect; reverence; worship

veneration: awe; deference; dread; esteem; estimation; fear; honor; respect; reverence

vengeance: reprisal; retribution; revenge

vengeful: vindictive

vengefulness: revenge

venom: malevolence; malice; poison; rancor; spite; toxin; virus

venomous: malevolent; spiteful; toxic; virulent

vent: emit; issue; ventilate

ventilate: air

venture upon: risk

venture: dare; enterprise; game; hazard; presume; risk; stake; throw; wager

venturesome: adventurous; audacious; daredevil; daring; enterprising

venturous: adventurous

veracious: true

veracity: honesty; truth

verbal: oral

verbiage: terminology; vernacular

verbose: bombastic; garrulous; loquacious; talkative; wordy

verbum sapienti or verbum sap or verbum sat or verb: caveat

verdict: judgment

verge: border; bound; edge; extremity; margin; rim

verging: inclination

verifiable: factual; genuine

verify: ascertain; check; confirm; control; determine; establish; prove

veritable: actual; authentic; true

verity: truth

vernacular: jargon; language; terminology; vulgar

vernal: spring

versatile: all-around

verse: passage; poetry; refrain

versed: able; conversant; experienced

versification: verse

version: paraphrase; translation

vertex: apex; summit; top

vertical: erect; perpendicular; upright

vertiginous: giddy

verve: glee; life; panache; vehemence

very: pretty

vessel: craft

vestige: remnant; sign; trace

vestigial: rudimentary

vestments: apparel; clothes; dress

vesture: apparel; clothes; dress; garb

vet: peruse

veteran: experienced

veto: reverse

vex: anger; bedevil; bother; curse; embarrass; exasperate; fret; gall; haggle; harass; harry; incense;

irritate; madden; molest; nag; offend; pain; perplex; persecute; pester; pique; plague; provoke; rankle; roil; ruffle; tantalize; tease; torment; **trouble; worry**

vexation: curse; displeasure; embarrassment; fret; plague; ruffle

vexatious: inconvenient; offensive; peevish; petulant; splenetic; sullen; testy; tiresome; troublesome; wearisome

vexed: miffed; peevish; sore; warm

vexing: offensive; vexatious

viable: tenable

viands: cheer; food

vibrate: oscillate; pulsate; quiver; ring; shake; swing; throb; tremble

vibrating: tremulous; vibrant

vibration: swing; tremor

vibratory: tremulous

vice-ridden: abandoned

vice: abomination; fault; wrong

vicinage: presence; region; vicinity

vicinity: habitat; presence; region

vicious: abandoned; evil; immoral; malevolent; nasty; shameless; snide; ugly; vile; virulent; wicked

viciousness: abomination

vicissitude: change; permutation; turn; variation

victim: scapegoat

victimize: cheat; swindle

victor: champion

victoria: carriage

Victorian: straitlaced

victory: conquest; triumph

victuals: cheer; food; maintenance

vie: compare; compete; contend; contest; scramble

view with horror: abhor; abominate

view: account; apprehension; aspect; belief; contemplate; facet; idea; ideology; notion; observe; opinion; prospect; purpose; regard; scene; see; speculation; survey; theory; vision; vista; watch

viewpoint: aspect; facet; light

vigil: wake; watch

vigilance: alert; care; caution; heed

vigilant: alert; careful; cautious; jealous; sharp; wakeful; wary; watchful

vigor: animation; bloom; dash; drive; energy; force; life; mettle; nerve; spirit; spring; stamina; strength

vigorous: able-bodied; active; aggressive; animate; energetic; fresh; hale; hard; hardy; healthy; lively; living; lusty; mighty; quick; racy; rank; robust; round; rude; sharp; smart; solid; sound; spirited; stalwart; stout; strenuous; strong; sturdy; thrifty; tough; trenchant; vibrant; virile; vivid; warm

vigorously: hard

vile: abject; bad; base; contemptible; despicable; detestable; dirty; evil; filthy; foul; hateful; infamous; low; mean; nefarious; pitiful; ribald; scurvy; shameful; sorry; ugly; unclean; ungodly; wicked; wretched

vilification: abuse; detraction; reproach

vilify: abuse; malign; pillory; traduce; vituperate

village: community; hamlet; town

villain: blackguard; knave; monster; rascal; rogue; scoundrel

villainous: bad; black; cursed; heinous; infamous; nefarious; wicked

villainy: chicanery

villein: serf; slave

vincible: vulnerable

vinculum: link

vindicate: assert; avenge; clear; defend; excuse; exonerate; justify; maintain; revenge; whitewash

vindication: apology; assertion

vindicator: advocate; champion

vindictive: revengeful; spiteful

vindictiveness: revenge

vinegarish: acerbic; cantankerous

vinegary: acerbic; acid; cantankerous; grouchy

vintage: exquisite

violate: break; disobey; force; infringe; intrude; pollute; profane; transgress

violation: breach; crime; outrage; sacrilege; sin

violence: commotion; force; fury; heat; outrage; rage; storm; vehemence

violent: acute; boisterous; ferocious; fierce; hard; hot; impatient; impetuous; mad; passionate; precipitate; radical; rough; rude; severe; sharp; stiff; tempestuous; tough; tumultuous; vehement; wild

violently: hard

VIP: celebrity; tycoon

virago: fury; nag; scold; shrew; termagant

virgin: maid

virginal: honest; innocent

virginity: honor; virtue

virile: male; manly

virility: machismo

virtue: excellence; good; goodness; integrity; operation; principle; right; truth

virtuosity: panache

virtuoso: aesthete

virtuous: chaste; clear; ethical; good; honest; honorable; innocent; just; modest; moral; pure; righteous; sound; straight; upright

virulent: bitter; malignant; toxic

virus: poison; toxin; venom

vis-à-vis: adverse

visa: pass; protection

visage: aspect; countenance; face

viscera: abdomen

visceral cavity: abdomen

viscount: peer

viscous: tenacious

vise: brace

visible: apparent; conspicuous; manifest

vision: apparition; hallucination; phantasm; view

visionary: crackpot; fanatical; fictitious; ideal; illusory; imaginary; quixotic; unpractical; unreal; wild; wild-eyed

visit with: see

visit: call; see; tour

visitant: visitor

visitor: guest

vista: prospect; view

visualization: imagery

vital: able-bodied; capital; chief; essential; great; material; momentous; necessary; organic; significant

vitality: life; spirit

vitalize: animate; invigorate; spirit

vitiate: contaminate; corrupt; debase; degrade; nullify; poison; pollute; spoil

vitiated: morbid

vitriolic: acrimonious

vituperate: abuse

vituperation: abuse; invective

vituperative: invective; opprobrious; scurrilous

vivacious: blithe; bright; brisk; bubbly; gay; irrepressible; lively; lively; pleasant; spirited; vivid

vivacity: animation; gaiety; life; sparkle; spirit; verve

vivid: bright; expressive; graphic; lively; lurid; picturesque; rich; strong

vividness: strength

vivify: animate; enliven

vixen: fury; termagant

vocabulary: jargon; terminology; vernacular

vocal: oral

vocalize: warble

vocation: business; craft; occupation; profession; trade; work

vociferate: clamor; cry; roar; shout

vociferation: clamor; exclamation

vociferous: boisterous; noisy

vogue: fashion; rage

voguish: fashionable; smart

voice: call; speak; utter

voiceless: dumb

void: abolish; abrogate; blank; cancel; cavity; empty; exhaust; supersede; vacant; vacuous

voiding: discharge

voile: sheer

volatile: capricious; fickle; inconstant; light; mercurial; touchy

volition: will

volitional: willful

volte-face: about-face

voluble: fluent; glib; loquacious; smooth

volume: bulk; capacity; extent; size

voluntary: deliberate; spontaneous; willful

volunteer: offer; proffer

voluptuary: epicure; sybarite

voluptuous: luxurious; sensual; zaftig

voluptuousness: pleasure

vomit: cast; heave

vomiting: sick

voracious: gluttonous; greedy; predatory; rapacious; ravenous

voracity: greed

vortex: maelstrom

vouch for: warrant

voucher: warrant

vouchsafe: accord; confer; give

vow: oath; swear

voyage: expedition; passage; passage; trip

vulgar: base; broad; coarse; common; dirty; earthy; foul; gaudy; gross; ignoble; indecent; loud; low; mean; profane; ribald; rude; scurrilous; tacky; tasteless; unrefined; vernacular; vile

vulgarian: yahoo

vulgarism: impropriety

vulgarity: impropriety

vulgate: vernacular

wacky: cockeyed; giddy; screwball

waffle: yo-yo

waffling: pendulous

waft: bear

wag: droll

wage earner: employee

wager: lay; play; stake

wages: hire; income; pay

waggish: droll; humorous; jocose; zany

wagon: carriage

wail: cry; lament; moan; plaint

wailing: crying; lament

wain: wagon

wait for: abide; anticipate; await; expect; look; watch

wait on: accompany; attend; attend; serve

wait out: stay

wait: abide; await; hesitate; pause; pause; remain; stay; tarry

waiter: attendant; menial

waiting: wait

waive: abandon; abdicate; relinquish; surrender; yield

waiver: abdication

wake up: call

wake: waken

wakeful: careful; watchful

wakefulness: care

waken: animate; call; wake; warm

walk heavily: plod

walk of life: sphere

walk: pace; pace; path; ramble; ramble; roam; saunter; stroll; trudge

walkaway: romp

walker: pedestrian

walking: pedestrian

walkover: romp

wall: barrier; partition

wallet: bag

wallop: thrash

wan: ghastly; lurid; pale; pallid; peaked; sallow; sick

wand: stick; verge

wander: deviate; digress; meander; prowl; ramble; range; roam; rove; stroll

wanderer: pilgrim

wandering: aberrant; aberration; absent-minded; circuitous; itinerant; rambling; vagabond

wane: abate; decrease; dwindle; ebb; fail; set; shrink; subside; waste

want: absence; crave; defect; desire; distress; lack; lust; necessity; need; penury; poverty; privation; require; wish

wanter: wannabe

wanting: short; vacant; weak

wanton: carnal; licentious; light; loose; ribald; salacious

wantonness: lust

war paint : cosmetic

war: battle; combat; fight; hostility

ward off: parry; repel

ward: bond; charge

warden: caregiver; guardian; keeper

warder: warden

warehouse: depot

wares: good

warfare: battle; hostility

wariness: alert; calculation; caution; precaution

warlike: hostile

warm up: warm

warm: affectionate; arouse; cozy; fervent; flame; genial; heat; passionate; swell; thaw; zealous

warmed-over: hackneyed

warmish: lukewarm

warmth: ardor; enthusiasm; flame; heat; love; passion; zeal

warn: admonish; advise; alert; caution; correct

warning: advice; caution; caveat; counsel; notice; portent; presage; ultimatum

warp: bias; cast; prejudice; spring; spring

warped: misshapen

warrant: authority; authorize; empower; guarantee; justify; word

warranted: legitimate

warranty: assurance; charter; warrant

warrior: champion

wary: alert; attentive; careful; cautious; chary; deliberate; discreet; politic; prudent; quizzical; safe; scrupulous; shy; skittish; thoughtful; vigilant; wakeful; watchful

wash: clean

washed-out: pallid; sallow; weather-beaten

washing: wash

waspish: cantankerous; cross; cynical; fractious; fretful; hasty; irascible; moody; peevish; peppery; petulant; pungent; querulous; quick; sour; splenetic; testy

waspishness: petulance

waste or fade away: ebb

waste away: dwindle; wither

waste time: dally

waste: consume; desert; destroy; dissipate; exhaust; havoc; idle; lavish; profusion; ravage; refuse; sack; scrap; solitude; spend; spoil; squander; stuff; use; wanton; wild; wither; zap

wasted: bankrupt; cadaverous; haggard; lost; peaked

wasteful: extravagant; idle; improvident; lavish; prodigal; profuse

waster: prodigal

wastrel: blackguard; prodigal

watch over: defend; guard

watch: custody; guard; look; mind; observe; oversee; see; surveillance; survey; witness

watchful: alert; attentive; careful; cautious; jealous; notable; observant; vigilant; wakeful; wary

watchfulness: attention; care; caution; heed; watch

watching: observation

watchman: guard; watch

watchword: catchword; password; word

water: cut; perspiration

water down: cut

watered-down: rarefied; watery

watered: watery

waterfall: cascade

watery: tasteless

wave: breaker; flourish; fluctuate; ripple; roll; sway; swell; swing

wavelet: ripple

waver: careen; doubt; falter; fluctuate; halt; hang; hesitate; pause; scruple; shake; stagger; stick; totter; vacillate; vacillate; waffle; yo-yo

wavering: backward; doubtful; dubious; inconstant; mutable; pendulous; suspense; unsettled; unstable; unsteady; variable; weak

wax: grow; spring

waxen: sallow

way in: access

way-out: offbeat

way-station: station

way: abatement; access; advance; appliance; course; fashion; habit; lane; manner; mean; method; mode; passage; path; run; sort; street; technique

wayfarer: pilgrim

wayward: capricious; froward; perverse; wild; willful; wrong-headed

weak sister: weakling

weak-kneed: weak

weak-minded: senseless

weak: childish; cold; crazy; decrepit; delicate; faint; feeble; frail; impotent; ineffectual; inefficient; infantile; languid; little; low; nerveless; rarefied; sickly; slack; slender; slight; slim; small; soft; spineless; tender; thin; tinny; unhealthy; watery; weakly

weaken: break; cripple; decline; depress; die; disable; droop;

weakening: decline; sabotage

weakly: sickly; weak

weakness: defect; delicacy; exhaustion; failing; fault; foible; peccadillo; slack

weal: welfare

wealth: abundance; capital; mean; money; treasure

wealthy: affluent; opulent; prosperous; rich; solid; substantial

wear away: abrade; corrode; fret; waste

wear down: abrade; waste

wear off: abrade

wear on: pall

wear out: exhaust

wear: wardrobe

wearied: tired; weary

weariness: exhaustion

wearing down: abrasion

wearing: tedious

wearisome: arduous; dreary; dull; hard; heavy; laborious; prosaic; tedious; tiresome; troublesome; weary

weary: bore; jaded; languid; pall; satiate; tire; tired

wearying: hard

weather-scarred: weather-beaten

weather: stand

weathered: weather-beaten

weave: careen

web: complex

wed: ally; unite

wedding: marriage

wedge: jam

wedlock: marriage; union

wee: little

weep: cry; grieve; lament

weeping: cry; crying; lachrymose

weepy: lachrymose

Wiedergutmachung: redress; reparation; restitution; satisfaction

weigh down: load; oppress

weigh: balance; calculate; consider; deliberate; ponder; scale; study

weighed: deliberate

weight: burden; consequence; consideration; effect; importance; lead; load; moment; prestige; significance; stress

weightiness: importance

weighty: grave; great; heavy; heavy; momentous; ponderous; ponderous; serious; significant

weird: aberrant; abnormal; eccentric; eerie; fantastic; macabre; odd; queer; uncanny; unearthly

weirdo: zany

welcome: embrace; grateful; greet; pleasant

welcoming: receptive

weld: unite

welfare: profit

well up: swell

well-acquainted: familiar

well-advanced: forward

well-advised: judicious

well-appointed: luxurious

well-balanced: even

well-behaved: good; orderly

well-being: ease; pleasure; welfare

well-bred: civil; courteous; gentle; polite; refined; respectful

well-built: muscular; sturdy

well-constructed: well-built

well-defined: distinct

well-delineated: graphic

well-developed: stalwart

well-disciplined: orderly

well-disposed: benevolent; considerate; friendly; genial; good; gracious

well-equipped: trim

well-established: solid; sound

well-finished: well-built

well-founded: valid

well-informed: conversant

well-knit: able-bodied; muscular; well-built

well-known: celebrated; familiar; famous; household; notable; noted; prominent

well-made: well-built

well-mannered: civil; courteous; nice; polite; proper; respectful

well-matured: mellow

well-meaning: innocuous

well-muscled: muscular; well-built

well-nigh: about; almost; nearly

well-off: prosperous; well

well-ordered: trim

well-organized: orderly

well-planned: neat

well-proportioned: well-built

well-regulated: orderly

well-rounded: all-around

well-spoken: nice

well-suited: congenial; convenient; seemly

well-supplied: strong

well-timed: opportune; timely

well-to-do: prosperous; rich; wealthy

well-trained: orderly

well-versed: familiar

well-wisher: friend

well-worn: hackneyed

well: abyss; fresh; healthy; pit; right; spurt

wellborn: gentle

welt: junction

weltanshauung: ideology

welter: wallow

wet blanket: discouragement; killjoy

wet: damp; drench; humid; moist; raw; saturate; soak; wash; watery

wetness: damp; wet

whack: beat

whatchamacallit: gadget

whatnot: novelty

wheedle: cajole; coax; entice; flatter

wheel: roll; rotate; tycoon; whirl

wheeze: blow

whence: therefore

wherefore: accordingly; therefore

wherewithal: mean

whether or not: if

whether: if

whey-faced: pallid; sallow

whim: conceit; fancy; humor; notion; vagary

whimper: cry; murmur

whimsical: arbitrary; capricious; cockeyed; fancy; giddy; odd; playful; screwball; skittish; wacky; zany

whimsied: capricious

whimsy: vagary; whim

whine: complain; kvetch

whiner: kvetch

whip up: roil

whip: beat; punish; roil; scourge; spur

whipping boy: scapegoat

whirl: hurly-burly; maelstrom; roll; rotate; spin

whirlpool: maelstrom

whirlwind: storm

whisk: whip

whisper: murmur; scuttlebutt

whistle-stop: station

whit: atom; bit; iota; particle

white-livered: cowardly

white: candid; fair; ghastly; pale; pallid; sick

whitecap: breaker

whiten: blanch; bleach; pale

whitener: bleach

whitewash: palliate; rationalize

whitish: light; pallid; pearly

whole ball of wax: totality

whole bit: totality

whole nine yards: totality

whole schmear: totality

whole shebang: totality

whole shooting match: totality

whole-hearted: single

whole: absolute; clean; complete; entire; gross; intact; round; solid; sound; total; unbroken; universal

wholeness: integrity

wholesale: sweeping

wholesome: beneficial; healthy; salutary; sound

wholly: absolutely; clean

whoop: cry

whore: prostitute

wicked: abandoned; atrocious; bad; black; corrupt; criminal; dark; depraved; enormous; evil; foul; heinous; ill; immoral; infamous; nefarious; pernicious; perverse; perverted; profane; satanic; sinful; sinister; ungodly; unprincipled; wrong

wickedly: ill

wickedness: abomination; corruption; evil; harm; ill; malfeasance; sin; vice; wrong

wide of the truth: abroad

wide: ample; broad; capacious; comprehensive; extensive; fat; spacious; sweeping

widely: abroad

widen: amplify; dilate; extend; stretch

widespread: common; current; general; prevalent; rife

widget: gadget

widsom: policy

wield: manage

wife: partner

wild about: mad
wild-eyed: rabid
wild-looking: haggard
wild: barbarian; boisterous; daredevil; desert; desolate; extravagant; fast; ferocious; fierce; mad; obstinate; quixotic; rabid; rambunctious; robust; romantic; rough; savage; wanton; waste; wilderness; wild-eyed
wilderness: desert; solitude; waste; wild
wildly: fast; pell-mell
wile: artifice; cheat; deceit; deception; device; fraud; machination; ploy; stratagem; trick
wiliness: art; cunning
will o' the wisp: ephemeral
will-power: volition
will: bequeath; device; leave; mind; pleasure; volition; wish
willed: willful
willful: arbitrary; deliberate; froward; headstrong; inflexible; intractable; obstinate; perverse; studied; unyielding; voluntary; wanton; wayward
willing: content; forward; ready; tractable
willingly: readily
willingness: disposition
wilt: droop; pine; wither
wily: astute; cagey; crafty; cunning; deceitful; designing; insidious; Machiavellian; politic; slippery; sly
wimp: weakling
wimpish: impotent
wimpy: impotent
win out: win
win over: accomplish; appease; conciliate; excel; persuade; reconcile; win
win: achieve; acquire; attain; attract; beat; captivate; carry; catch; conquer; earn; gain; get; hit; make; obtain; prevail; procure; score; steal; triumph
winch: purchase
wind up: end
wind-up: conclusion
wind: air; blast; blow; breeze; meander; spin; storm; twist
inding: crooked; sinuous; tortuous; wind
windstorm: sirocco
windup: catastrophe
windy: raw
wing it: ad-lib
wing: faction; fly; limb; member
wink: blink; flash
winner: champion
winning: lovely; sweet
winnings: gain; stake
winsome: cheerful; sweet; winning
wintry: cold
wipe out: slaughter
wipe: clean
wiped or drained away: dry
wisdom: experience; judgment; knowledge; lore; prudence; scholarship; wit

wise man: sage; scholar
wise: acute; cagey; deep; discreet; judicious; old; penetrating; politic; prudent; rational; reasonable; sagacious; sane; sapient; sensible
wisecrack: quip
wish or long for: desire
wish: bid; desire; mind; pleasure; want; will
wisher: wannabe
wishy-washy: lackluster; soft; tasteless; watery
wistful: pensive; plaintive
wit: capacity; humor; ridicule
witch doctor: magician
witchcraft: magic; sorcery
witchery: charm; sorcery
with angles or corners: angular
with child: big
with difficulty: hard
with regard or respect or reference to: about
with-it: fashionable
withdraw or escape from: leave
withdraw or retire from: quit
withdraw from: vacate
withdraw: abandon; back; deduct; depart; extract; recall; remove; resign; retire; retreat; revoke; secede; separate; shrink; subtract
withdrawal: recall; retreat
withdrawn: absent-minded; antisocial; close; retired; secluded; separate
wither: blast; decay; die; droop; fade; perish; sear; shrink; shrivel
withered: cadaverous
withhold: arrest; detain; exclude; hide; keep; refrain; retain; spare; stop; strip; suspend
within: inside; near
without or lacking foresight: improvident
without delay: immediate; immediately; presently
without disguise: aboveboard
without doubt: absolutely
without intervention: immediately
without notice or warning: short
without ornament: austere
without symptoms: abortive
without tricks: aboveboard
withstand: combat; oppose; repel; resist; stem
witless: foolish; giddy; senseless; silly; stupid
witness: authority; observe; reference; view
witticism: jest; joke; quip
witting: sentient
witty: droll; facetious; funny; humorous; jocose; pleasant
wizened: cadaverous
wobble: careen
wobbly: shaky; spindly
woe: affliction; evil; grief; misery; sorrow; trial; trouble
woebegone: careworn; desolate; forlorn; wretched
woeful: desolate; lachrymose; piteous; wretched

woman: adult; female
womanish: womanly
womanlike: womanly
womanly: female
wonder: admiration; gape; gaze; phenomenon; surprise
wonderful: marvelous; miraculous; prodigious; remarkable
ondrous: marvelous; miraculous; prodigious; wonderful
wonk: savant
wonky: cockeyed
wont: accustomed; habit; mind; practice; way
wonted: customary; wont
wood: forest; stand
wooden: awkward
woodland: forest
woods: cover; forest
wooer: gallant
wooing: attention
wool: pile
woolgather: daydream
woolgathering: daydream
woozy: groggy
word to the wise: caveat
word: advice; agreement; express; promise; say; shape; tell
wordage: parlance
worded: verbal
wording: diction; expression; parlance
words: parlance; speech; talk
wordy: garrulous; long; loquacious; talkative
work hard: moil
work out: decipher; elaborate
work: act; action; bear; drudgery; exercise; labor; office; operate; task; temper; toil
workable: feasible; practicable; useful; viable
workaday: utilitarian
worker: employee; operative
working class: labor; mass
working: action; active; busy
workingmen: labor
workman: artist; craftsman; mechanic; operative
workshop: factory
world-class: acclaimed; top-notch
world-famous: acclaimed
world-renowned: acclaimed
world-weary: blasé; jaded
world: earth; nature; system
worldly-wise: blasé
worldly: blasé; carnal; earthly; mundane; secular; sophisticated; suave; terrestrial
worn out: bankrupt; hack
worn-down: careworn; weatherbeaten
worn-out: hackneyed; jaded
worn: careworn; haggard; old; shabby; stereotyped; weatherbeaten
worried: anxious; solicitous; upset
worry: annoy; anxiety; apprehension; bedevil; bother; care; concern; distress; exercise; fret; haggle; harass; harry; molest; pain;

pester; plague; ruffle; tease; torment; trouble; vex
worrywart: killjoy
worsen: aggravate; impair
worship: adore; homage; honor; love; praise; reverence
worshipful: devout; sacred
worth: account; capital; good; goodness; merit; value
worthiness: worth
worthless: bad; base; despicable; futile; idle; miserable; nugatory; paltry; poor; scurvy; sorry; trifling; unworthy; useless; vagabond; vain; wretched
worthwhile: worthy
worthy: choice; eligible; estimable; excellent; good; noble; respectable; substantial; tycoon; valuable
wound: batter; break; cut; hurt; injury; lacerate; maim; pique; slash; smart; sore; stab; tear
woundable: vulnerable
wounding: cutting
wraith: apparition; ghost
wrangle: brawl; contend; contention; controversy; dispute; haggle; quarrel
wrap: envelop; roll
wrath: anger; displeasure; fury; indignation; offense; passion; rage
wrathful: angry; mad
wreathe: wind
wreck: ruin; sabotage; spoil
wreckage: shambles
wrench: sprain; strain
renching: traumatic
wrest: exact; extort; extract; rack
wrestle: tussle
wretch: monster; scoundrel
wretched: bad; desolate; desperate; forlorn; mean; miserable; piteous; shabby; sorry; squalid; unhappy; vile; vile
wretchedness: adversity; affliction; misery; sorrow; woe
wriggle: twist
wring: exact; extort; extract
wrinkle: crush; novelty; ruffle; shrivel; wither
wrinkled: rugged
writ: warrant
write: draw
writhe: twist
writings: literature
written: above
wrong: blame; crime; criminal; erroneous; evil; false; fault; harm; ill; immoral; inaccurate; incorrect; injure; injury; mistaken; offense; oppress; sin; trespass; vicious; violence
wrongdoing: error; malfeasance
wrongful: injurious
wroth: angry
wrought: worked
wry: acerbic
wuss: weakling
Xantippe: termagant
yank: pluck
yawn: gape

yearn or hunger for: crave
yearn for: long
yearn: aspire; pant; pine
yearning: ambition; desire; longing; thirst
years of discretion: age
yelding: easy
yell: cry; roar; shriek
yellow: cowardly; recreant
yellowish: sallow
yelp: cry
yen: yearn
yes-man: parasite; sycophant; toady; weakling
yet: besides; but; even; notwithstanding
yield profit or gain to: advantage
yield to: indulge
yield: abandon; accept; accord; acquiesce; agree; allow; assent; bear; bend; bow; cede; comply; conform; consent; crop; deliver; extend; give; grant; grudge; pay; present; produce; produce; provide; relinquish; render; resign; submit; surrender
yielding: flexible; meek; obedient; pliant; rotten; soft; submissive; supple
yo-yo: waffle
yob: rowdy
yobbo: rowdy
yoke: connection; couple; hitch; pair; span; tie; unite
yokefellow: comrade
yokel: yahoo
yon: ulterior
yonder: ulterior
young man: youth
young: adolescent; brood; childish; tender; youthful
youngness: youth
youngster: youth
youth: adolescent; youngster
youthful: adolescent; fresh; puerile; tender; young
yowl: cry
yummy: scrumptious
zany: droll; fool; screwball; screwball; wacky
zeal: appetite; ardor; devotion; energy; enthusiasm; flame; goodwill; heat; passion; spirit; vehemence
zealot: crackpot; enthusiast; fanatic
zealous: ardent; assiduous; eager; earnest; enterprising; enthusiastic; fanatical; fervent; forward; keen; passionate; sedulous; strenuous; strong; swift; vehement; warm
zealousness: spirit; study
zenith: apex; height; pinnacle; summit; top
zenithal: vertical
zephyr: air; breeze; wind
zero: zilch
zest: appetite; relish; verve
zigzag: stagger
zing: verve
zip: zilch
zone: belt; belt

AVOIDING INSENSITIVE AND OFFENSIVE LANGUAGE

This essay is intended as a general guide to language that can, intentionally or not, cause offense or perpetuate discriminatory values and practices by emphasizing the differences between people or implying that one group is superior to another.

Several factors complicate the issue. A group may disagree within itself as to what is acceptable and what is not. Many seemingly inoffensive terms develop negative connotations over time and become dated or go out of style as awareness changes. A "within the group" rule often applies, which allows a member of a group to use terms freely that would be considered offensive if used by an outsider.

While it is true that some of the more extreme attempts to avoid offending language have resulted in ludicrous obfuscation, it is also true that heightened sensitivity in language indicates a precision of thought and is a positive move toward rectifying the unequal social status between one group and another.

Suggestions for avoiding insensitive or offensive language are given in the following pages. **The recommended terms are given on the right.** While these suggestions can reflect trends, they cannot dictate or predict the preferences of each individual.

Sexism

Sexism is the most difficult bias to avoid, in part because of the convention of using *man* or *men* and *he* or *his* to refer to people of either sex. Other, more disrespectful conventions include giving descriptions of women in terms of age and appearance while describing men in terms of accomplishment.

Replacing *man* or *men*

Man traditionally referred to a male or to a human in general. Using *man* to refer to a human is often thought to be slighting of women.

Avoid This	Use This Instead
mankind, man →	human beings, humans, humankind, humanity, people, society, men and women
man-made →	synthetic, artificial
man in the street →	average person, ordinary person

Using gender-neutral terms for occupations, positions, roles, etc.

Terms that specify a particular sex can unnecessarily perpetuate certain stereotypes when used generically.

Avoid This	Use This Instead
anchorman →	anchor
bellman, bellboy →	bellhop
businessman →	businessperson, executive, manager, business owner, retailer, etc.
chairman →	chair, chairperson
cleaning lady, girl, maid →	housecleaner, housekeeper, cleaning person, office cleaner
clergyman →	member of the clergy, rabbi, priest, etc.
clergymen →	the clergy
congressman →	representative, member of Congress, legislator
fireman →	firefighter
forefather →	ancestor
girl/gal Friday →	assistant
housewife →	homemaker
insurance man →	insurance agent
layman →	layperson, nonspecialist, nonprofessional
mailman, postman →	mail or letter carrier
policeman →	police officer or law enforcement officer
salesman, saleswoman, saleslady, salesgirl →	salesperson, sales representative, sales associate, clerk
spokesman →	spokesperson, representative
stewardess, steward →	flight attendant
weatherman →	weather reporter, weathercaster, meteorologist
workman →	worker
actress →	actor

Replacing the pronoun *he*

Like *man*, the generic use of *he* can be seen to exclude women.

Avoid This	Use This Instead
When a driver approaches a red light, he must prepare to stop. →	When drivers approach a red light, they must prepare to stop.
When a driver approaches a red light, he or she must prepare to stop. →	When approaching a red light, a driver must prepare to stop.

Referring to members of both sexes with parallel names, titles, or descriptions

Don't be inconsistent unless you are trying to make a specific point.

Avoid This	Use This Instead
men and ladies →	men and women, ladies and gentlemen
Betty Schmidt, an attractive 49-year-old physician, and her husband, Alan Schmidt, a noted editor →	Betty Schmidt, a physician, and her husband, Alan Schmidt, an editor
Mr. David Kim and Mrs. Betty Harrow →	Mr. David Kim and Ms. Betty Harrow (unless *Mrs.* is her known preference)
man and wife →	husband and wife
Dear Sir: →	Dear Sir/Madam: Dear Madam or Sir: To whom it may concern:
Mrs. Smith and President Jones →	Governor Smith and President Jones

Race, Ethnicity, and National Origin

Some words and phrases that refer to racial and ethnic groups are clearly offensive. Other words (e.g., *Oriental, colored*) are outdated or inaccurate. *Hispanic* is generally accepted as a broad term for Spanish-speaking people of the Western Hemisphere, but more specific terms (*Latino, Mexican American*) are also acceptable and in some cases preferred.

Avoid This	Use This Instead
Negro, colored, → Afro-American	black, African-American (generally preferred to Afro-American)
Oriental, → Asiatic	Asian, or more specific designation such as Pacific Islander, Chinese American, Korean
Indian →	*Indian* properly refers to people who live in or come from India.
	American Indian, Native American, and more specific designations (*Chinook, Hopi*) are usually preferred when referring to the native peoples of the Western hemisphere.
Eskimo →	Inuit, Alaska Natives
native (n.) →	native peoples, early inhabitants, aboriginal peoples (but not *aborigines*)

Age

The concept of aging is changing as people are living longer and more active lives. Be aware of word choices that reinforce stereotypes (*decrepit, senile*) and avoid mentioning age unless it is relevant.

Avoid This	Use This Instead
elderly, aged, → old, geriatric, the elderly, the aged	older person, senior citizen(s), older people, seniors

Sexual Orientation

The term *homosexual* to describe a man or woman is increasingly replaced by the terms *gay* for men and *lesbian* for women. *Homosexual* as a noun is sometimes used only in reference to a male. Among homosexuals, certain terms (such as *queer* and *dyke*) that are usually considered offensive have been gaining currency in recent years. However, it is still prudent to avoid these terms in standard contexts.

Avoiding Depersonalization of Persons with Disabilities or Illnesses

Terminology that emphasizes the person rather than the disability is generally preferred. *Handicap* is used to refer to the environmental barrier that affects the person. (Stairs handicap a person who uses a wheelchair.) While words such as *crazy, demented*, and *insane* are used in facetious or informal contexts, these terms are not used to describe people with clinical diagnoses of mental illness. The euphemisms *challenged, differently abled*, and *special* are preferred by some people, but are often ridiculed and are best avoided.

Avoid This	Use This Instead
Mongoloid →	person with Down syndrome
wheelchair-bound →	person who uses a wheelchair
AIDS sufferer, → person afflicted with AIDS, AIDS victim	person living with AIDS, P.W.A., HIV +, (one who tests positive for HIV but does not show symptoms of AIDS)
polio victim →	has/had polio
the handicapped, → the disabled, cripple	persons with disabilities or person who uses crutches *or* more specific description
deaf-mute, → deaf and dumb	deaf person

Avoiding Patronizing or Demeaning Expressions

Avoid This	Use This Instead
girls (when referring → to adult women), the fair sex	women
sweetie, dear, → dearie, honey	(usually not appropriate with strangers or in public situations)
old maid, → bachelorette, spinster	single woman, woman, divorced woman (but only if one would specify "divorced man" in the same context)
the little woman, → old lady, ball and chain	wife
boy (when referring → to or addressing an adult man)	man, sir

Avoiding Language That Excludes or Unnecessarily Emphasizes Differences

References to age, sex, religion, race, and the like should be included only if they are relevant.

Avoid This	Use This Instead
lawyers and → their wives	lawyers and their spouses
a secretary and → her boss	a secretary and boss, a secretary and his or her boss
the male nurse →	the nurse
Arab man denies → assault charge	Man denies assault charge
the articulate → black student	the articulate student
Marie Curie was a → great woman scientist	Marie Curie was a great scientist (unless the intent is to compare her only with other women in the sciences)
Christian name →	given name, personal name, first name
Mr. Johnson, the → black representative, met with the President today to discuss civil-rights legislation.	Mr. Johnson, a member of the Congressional Black Caucus, met with the President today to discuss civil-rights legislation.

Punctuation

There is a considerable amount of variation in punctuation practices. At one extreme are writers who use as little punctuation as possible. At the other extreme are writers who use too much punctuation in an effort to make their meaning clear. The principles presented here represent a middle road. As in all writing, consistency of style is essential.

The punctuation system is presented in six charts. Since punctuation marks are frequently used in more than one way, some marks appear on more than one chart. Readers who are interested in the various uses of a particular mark can scan the left column of each chart to locate relevant sections.

1. Sentence-Level Punctuation

	Guidelines	Examples
•	Ordinarily an independent clause is made into a sentence by beginning it with a capital letter and ending it with a period.	Some of us still support the mayor. Others think he should retire. There's only one solution. We must reduce next year's budget.
,	Independent clauses may be combined into one sentence by using the words *and, but, yet, or, not, for,* and *so.* The first clause is usually, but not always, followed by a comma.	The forecast promised beautiful weather, but it rained every day. Take six cooking apples and put them into a flameproof dish.
;	The writer can indicate that independent clauses are closely connected by joining them with a semicolon.	Some of us still support the mayor; others think he should retire. There was silence in the room; even the children were still.
:	When one independent clause is followed by another that explains or exemplifies it, they can be separated by a colon. The second clause may or may not begin with a capital letter.	There's only one solution: we must reduce next year's budget. The conference addresses a basic question: How can we take the steps needed to protect the environment?
?	Sentences that ask a question should be followed by a question mark.	Are they still planning to move to Houston? What is the population of Norway?
!	Sentences that express strong feeling may be followed by an exclamation mark.	Watch out! That's a stupid thing to say!
• ? ! .	End-of-sentence punctuation is sometimes used after groups of words that are not independent clauses. This is especially common in advertising and other writing that seeks to reflect the rhythms of speech.	Somerset Estates has all the features you've been looking for. Like state-of-the-art facilities. A friendly atmosphere. And a very reasonable price. Sound interesting? Phone today!

2. Separating Elements in Clauses

When one of the elements in a clause is compounded—that is, when there are two or more subjects, predicates, objects, and so forth—punctuation is necessary.

	Guidelines	Examples
	When two elements are compounded, they are usually joined together with a word such as *and* or *or* without any punctuation. Occasionally more than two elements are joined in this way.	Haiti and the Dominican Republic share the island of Hispaniola. Tuition may be paid by check or charged to a major credit card. I'm taking history and English and biology this semester.
,	Compounds that contain more than two elements are called series. Commas are used to separate items in a series, with a word such as *and* or *or* usually occurring between the last two items.	England, Scotland, and Wales share the island of Great Britain. Environmentally conscious businesses use recycled paper, photocopy on both sides of a sheet, and use ceramic cups. We frequently hear references to government of the people, by the people, for the people.
; ,	When the items in a series are very long or have internal punctuation, separation by commas can be confusing, and semicolons may be used instead.	Next year, they plan to open stores in Pittsburgh, Pennsylvania; Cincinnati, Ohio; and Baltimore, Maryland. Students were selected on the basis of grades; tests of vocabulary, memory, and reading; and teacher recommendations.

Note: Some writers omit the final comma when punctuating a series, and newspapers and magazines often follow this practice. Book publishers and educators, however, usually follow the practice recommended above.

3. Quotations

Quotations are used for making clear to a reader which words are the writer's and which have been borrowed from someone else.

Guidelines	Examples
" " When writers use the exact words of someone else, they must use quotation marks to set them off from the rest of the text.	In 1841, Ralph Waldo Emerson wrote, "I hate quotations. Tell me what you know."
Indirect quotations—in which writers report what someone else said without using the exact words—should not be set off by quotation marks.	Emerson said that he hated quotations and that writers should instead tell the reader what they themselves know.

When quotations are longer than two or three lines, they are often placed on separate lines. Sometimes shorter line length and/or smaller type is also used. When this is done, quotation marks are not used.	In his essay "Notes on Punctuation," Lewis Thomas* gives the following advice to writers using quotations:
	
	   If something is to be quoted, the exact
	   words must be used.
	
	If part of it must be left out because of space limitations, it is good manners to insert three dots to indicate the omission, but it is unethical to do this if it means connecting two thoughts which the original author did not intend to have tied together.

• • •   If part of a quotation is omitted, the omission must be marked with points of ellipsis. When the omission comes in the middle of a sentence, three points are used. When the omission includes the end of one or more sentences, four points are used.
 	
• • • •
	Lewis Thomas offers this advice:
	
	   If something is to be quoted, the exact
	   words must be used.
	
	If part of it must be left out…insert three dots to indicate the omission, but it is unethical to do this if it means connecting two thoughts which the original author did not intend to have tied together.

When writers insert something within a quoted passage, the insertion should be set off with brackets. Insertions are sometimes used to supply words that make a quotation easier to understand.	Lewis Thomas warns that "it is unethical to [omit words in a quotation]…if it means connecting two thoughts which the original author did not intend to have tied together."
[ ] Writers can make clear that a mistake in the quotation has been carried over from the original by using the word *sic*, meaning "thus."	As Senator Claghorne wrote to his constituents, "My fundamental political principals [*sic*] make it impossible for me to support the bill in its present form."
, Text that reports the source of quoted material is usually separated from it by a comma.	Mark said, "I've decided not to apply to law school until next year." "I think we should encourage people to vote," said the mayor.
When quoted words are woven into a text so that they perform a basic grammatical function in the sentence, no introductory punctuation is used.	According to Thoreau, most of us "lead lives of quiet desperation."
' ' Quotations that are included within other quotations are set off by single quotation marks.	The witness made the same damaging statement under cross-examination: "As I entered the room, I heard him say, 'I'm determined to get even.'"
Final quotation marks follow other punctuation marks, except for semicolons and colons.	Ed began reading Williams's "The Glass Menagerie"; then he turned to "A Streetcar Named Desire."
" " Question marks and exclamation marks precede final quotation marks when they refer to the quoted words. They follow when they refer to the sentence as a whole.	Once more she asked, "What do you think we should do about this?" What did Carol mean when she said, "I'm going to do something about this"? "Get out of here!" he yelled.

* *New England Journal of Medicine,* Vol. 296, pp. 1103–05 (May 12, 1977). **Quoted** by permission.

4. Word-Level Punctuation

The punctuation covered so far is used to clarify the structure of sentences. There are also punctuation marks that are used with words.

Guidelines	Examples
, The apostrophe is used with nouns to show possession:	The company's management resisted the union's demands. She found it impossible to decipher the students' handwriting.
(1) An apostrophe plus *s* is added to all words—singular or plural—that do not end in *-s*.	the boy's hat children's literature a week's vacation
(2) Just an apostrophe is added at the end of plural words that end in *-s*.	the boys' hats two weeks' vacation
(3) An apostrophe plus *s* is usually added at the end of singular words that end in *-s*. Just an apostrophe is added to names of classical or biblical derivation that end in *-s*.	the countess's daughter Dickens's novels Achilles' heel Moses' brother
An apostrophe is used in contractions to show where letters or numerals have been omitted.	he's didn't let's ma'am four o'clock readin', writin', and 'rithmetic the class of '55
An apostrophe is sometimes used when making letters or numbers plural.	45's ABC's
• A period is used to mark shortened forms like abbreviations and initials.	Prof. M. L. Smith 14 ft. 4:00 p.m. U.S.A. or USA etc.
— A hyphen is used to end a line of text when part of a word must be carried over to the next line.	... insta- bility
Hyphens are sometimes used to form compound words.	twenty-five self-confidence
In certain situations, hyphens are used between prefixes or suffixes and root words.	catlike *but* bull-like preschool *but* pre-Christian recover *vs.* re-cover
Hyphens are often used to indicate that a group of words is to be understood as a unit.	a scholar-athlete hand-to-hand combat
When two modifiers containing hyphens are joined together, common elements are often not repeated.	The study included fourth- and twelfth-grade students.

Note: It is important not to confuse the hyphen (-) with the dash (—), which is more than twice as long. The hyphen is used to group words and parts of words together, while the dash is used to clarify sentence structure. With a typewriter, a dash is formed by typing two successive hyphens(--). Many word-processing programs will create a dash automatically.

WRITING A TERM PAPER

A term paper, or any research paper, calls upon the writer to focus on an assigned or chosen topic, gather and interpret source materials, marshal arguments, and organize, document, and express ideas forcefully.

A term paper may be a factual inquiry, an analysis of causes and effects, or an account or interpretation of events, ideas, or themes. It may explain or analyze a phenomenon or describe an experience. But whether it is basically informative, argumentative, or narrative, it should always be (1) clear in purpose, (2) unslanted (not omitting contrary evidence), (3) concise and to the point, and (4) well documented, with sources acknowledged in footnotes and/or a bibliography.

Begin the assignment as early as possible, to allow time for proper research, for rethinking the subject or approach, and for reorganizing and revising the paper.

The Subject

The subject and scope of the term paper should be neither too ambitious nor too narrow or technical in scope. Do not pose a question whose answer is obvious or address an issue whose solution is self-evident. First make sure that adequate information on the topic is conveniently available. If there is a choice of topics, make a preliminary visit to the library for exploratory reading and research before making the final choice.

Remember that the term paper has not only a subject but a thesis. Your thoughts and conclusions, not those of other writers, are the essence of the paper. These personal thoughts and conclusions, however, must be well organized and supported by the research.

Research

The student who knows how to use the library and all its resources will avoid many problems in researching. Although primary sources and direct information (as from interviews) are valuable for certain topics, it is usually the books, journals, microfilm, etc., available in the reference room of the library that form the backbone of the term paper.

Particularly useful sources, in addition to books on the subject, are (1) encyclopedias; (2) the *Reader's Guide to Periodical Literature* (for leads to pertinent magazine and journal articles); (3) book bibliographies and cross-references that lead to other usable sources; and, with some subjects, (4) government agencies and private organizations and their publications. Make a preliminary list of sources that promise to be helpful; the paper's final bibliography will come from this list. Many librarians will do on-line research for you (often for a fee), giving you access to material in electronic databases.

While reading, take systematic notes, organizing and explaining various aspects of the topic. Taking notes on index cards will facilitate the sorting and rearranging of information. If you prefer using a notebook, write on only one side of each page so that the pages can be pulled out and rearranged later. Some students enter their notes into a computer, so that they may take advantage of electronic or word-processing programs to organize their data.

While taking notes, record not only factual information but also relevant quotations, questions that come to mind, and personal observations and ideas. It is also helpful to summarize various points as you go along—in your own words, not those of the authors consulted. This will make the actual writing of the paper easier and lessen the risk of inadvertent plagiarism. Research sources (with title, author, page number, and all necessary bibliographic information) for both quotations and paraphrases should be written down carefully on first reading, to avoid having to recheck later.

Outline

An outline helps the writer not only to plan the overall paper but also to organize and develop individual sections and ideas. Based on the research notes and sequentially arranged, the outline helps to crystallize the major and supporting points to be made and the step-by-step presentation required. Preparing the outline will also help you decide how best to organize the material: chronologically, by category, or in some other logical way.

Many students make a sketchy outline early in their research stage, then revise and expand it as the research continues. A topic outline, indicating the sequence of ideas and subtopics, may later be expanded into a paragraph outline, which expresses these points as complete, final units and which may grow into the final term paper.

Writing

Before beginning the actual writing, have a clear idea of the intended approach of the paper. How formal is it to be? Should it be completely objective and factual, somewhat argumentative, or strong and impassioned?

Beginning the actual writing often seems the hardest part of the term paper. Begin at all costs, even if not satisfied with the opening sentence or paragraph; this can be improved later. (Some find it easier to start in the middle of the paper or even with the conclusion, and to write the beginning later.)

There are four standard openings with which to begin a term paper: a summary sentence, a defining statement, a quotation, or a posed question. As you write, remember: (1) The thesis should be made clear to the reader at the very beginning of the paper. What are you setting out to discuss or prove? (2) The purport of each paragraph should be made clear by a topic, or key, sentence, usually the first sentence of the paragraph. (3) Depending on the nature of the paper, first-person references—such as "I" and "me"—should be avoided or minimized.

Do not expect to write a good term paper in just one draft. A second and third draft will almost always be necessary. In the first draft concentrate on substance and organization. Grammar, sentence construction, and spelling can be corrected later. Leave nothing of substance out of the first draft; it will be easier to shorten the paper later than to add to it. If you are typing rather than using a word processor or computer, triple-space your early drafts and use wide margins to allow for corrections and additions.

After the first draft has been read and reread, it should be rewritten and reorganized as much as necessary. Use of scissors and tape or glue can be helpful in reordering or inserting material; a word processor or computer can ease this part of the process.

The final manuscript should be as perfect as you can make it in all ways: in organization, clarity, and style; in grammar, punctuation, and spelling; and in exactness of quotations, footnotes, and bibliography. It should be clear and to the point, and free of pretentious words, of overly long sentences, and of digressions. Footnotes or parenthetical acknowledgments should be scrupulously incorporated wherever there is a debt to another source for a specific idea or quotation, or to another writer's statement of "fact" that is clearly debatable or controversial. On the other hand, do not quote or footnote excessively: a term paper is meant to be a documented presentation of your themes or ideas, not a dense, pedantic recitation of material from other sources. It is the use of research material, the process of reasoning, personal insights, and writing skills that are the essence of the term paper.